KU-202-543

NEW MUSICAL EXPRESS
NME
THE ROCK 'N' ROLL YEARS

BCA
LONDON · NEW YORK · SYDNEY · TORONTO

Consultant Editor: John Tobler

Contributors: Pete Frame, Roy Carr, Barry Lazell, Fred Dellar, Hugh Fielder, Michael Heatley, Dave McAleer, David Sandison

Editor: David Heslam

Assistant Editor: Mike Evans

Art Editor: Leigh Jones

Designed by Christopher Matthews

Picture Researchers: Emily Hedges, Christina Rista

Production Controllers: Garry Lewis, Alison Myer

The publishers wish to thank the New Musical Express (NME) for their kind assistance and access to archive material without which this project would not have been possible. All American chart information is © 1955-1992 BPI Communications, Inc. and appears courtesy of Billboard magazine.

This edition published 1992 by BCA
by arrangement with Octopus Illustrated Publishing,
part of Reed International Books
Michelin House, 81 Fulham Road
London SW3 6RB

Revised and updated reprint 1992

CN 5585

Printed in Slovenia

Jacket Photography
Top right front cover, Rex Features Ltd. London
All other photographs London Features International

Half-title
Reelin' and rockin', Chuck Berry. His low-slung guitar licks, on-stage duck walk, and lyrics that made poetry out of teenage life in Fifties America, sum up the essential spirit of rock 'n' roll

Title page
The Boss, Bruce Springsteen. Born, like the music, in the USA, he has been acclaimed as the latter-day successor to the mantle of Chuck, Elvis, even Dylan – with that streetwise, no nonsense self-confident assertiveness that has made rock the ultimate soundtrack of our times

CONTENTS

INTRODUCTION

Popular culture, by definition, is instant, accessible and of its time. No more so than rock'n'roll, which is at one and the same time locked into a particular moment of history – we all remember when we first heard certain records – and therefore almost immediately nostalgic.

'The NME Rock'n'Roll Years', presenting the story of rock'n'roll in the form of news articles of the period, captures for the first time this immediacy of pop, the vital spark which has often been lost in previous works of reference.

'The Rock'n'Roll Years' has been compiled from the archives of the New Musical Express, which itself holds a unique place in pop music journalism.

Launched in 1952, just a couple of years before the rock'n'roll revolution, while other music papers condemned the new teen-oriented sounds in favour of the established dance bands and crooners, the NME became the bible of rock'n'roll fans in Britain.

It even introduced the first British charts in 1953, which very soon became the commercial slide-rule of the music business.

Over the years it lost none of its vitality. After the initial impact of rock in the fabulous Fifties, the NME went on to chronicle the astonishing assault of the British Beat invasion on America and the rest of the world.

No sooner had that phenomenon passed when another rock inspired revolution emerged. Against the background of the Vietnam war, the peace and love of the hippy era also had its basis in rock. There would have been no Flower Power without Monterey and the West Coast sound, no psychedelic magic without the music.

Through the supergroups of the Seventies and the protest of punk that followed in their wake, rock'n'roll has continued to mirror a youthful view of the world; a world that towards the close of the Eighties reverberated, in Band Aid and Live Aid, to a global concern reflected in rock music.

Like the music itself, through the beat boom to psychedelia, punk to the present, the NME has continued to be critical, controversial and never afraid of change.

Open 'The NME Rock'n'Roll Years' on any page and you will immediately be plunged into the roller-coaster history of rock as it happened, a month-by-month, blow-by-blow account of the famous and the forgotten, the ups and downs, the sights and sounds of pop music.

Whether you were there 'first time round' or are experiencing the dynamic of these events in their immediate context for the first time, this musical time machine is a must for anyone who has been touched, and who hasn't, by the impact of the past four decades of Rock'n'Roll Years.

The Rolling Stones: with their musical roots in black American rhythm and blues, they spearheaded – along with the Beatles – the beat boom of the Sixties. Through the Seventies and Eighties they took on disco, soul and good old rock'n'roll to become the biggest of the stadium Superstars. Their history has virtually spanned the three and a half decades of the Rock'n'Roll Years

THE 1950's

After the devastation of The Second World War it was to the USA that British and European kids looked for inspiration.

This was the austere Britain that the War Babies grew up in. They were the children born in the early 'Forties, who became the first teenagers – the word hadn't existed previously – in the explosive years of the 'Fifties.

The sudden identification of adolescents in this way, first of all in America, was society's recognition that they were a separate economic group, young people with money in their pockets for the first time, the offspring of an affluence that was to be felt in Europe as the decade progressed.

The inspiration for this new generation came in films initially (it was before the mass-popularity of television) when new heroes led by Marlon Brando and James Dean provided icons for the emergent 'teenager'.

Among the movies the most influential were undoubtedly *Rebel Without A Cause* and *Blackboard Jungle*, the latter because it used Bill Haley's *Rock Around the Clock* under the opening credits. Its effect was without precedent. Cinema riots ensued across America, while in England similar mayhem was spearheaded by the first teenage subculture, the Teddy Boys. These were kids ripe for rock'n'roll.

Rock'n'roll didn't happen overnight of course – its roots in Rhythm and Blues and country music had been slowly fusing until the time was right. Record stars like Louis Jordan, Earl Bostic and, most spectacularly, Johnnie Ray were hinting at what was to come, but it took the already balding Bill Haley to light the fuse with a series of classics that made him absolute King for a few months in 1955.

Haley was the first rock'n'roll star, but he didn't look like a rebel and certainly not a sex symbol, and a moody looking kid with the curious name of Elvis Presley effortlessly took his crown with the devastating impact of 'Heartbreak Hotel'.

Presley's success heralded the musical revolution that made legends out of Fats Domino, Jerry Lee Lewis, Little Richard, Buddy Holly and Chuck Berry.

In England, the teenage parallel to the American soda fountain was the coffee bar, and out of this emerged home-grown talents. Many of the stars – Tommy Steele was the first – were pale imitations of the transatlantic 'real thing', but genuinely original styles began to pop up on the all-teenage TV shows *Six Five Special* and *Oh Boy*, singers like Cliff Richard and Billy Fury avoiding mere Elvis-mimicry.

But most important was the skiffle craze led by Lonnie Donegan, which put guitars into the hands of thousands of youngsters for the first time.

By the end of the decade, however, the music being put out by the record industry was a watered-down parody of rock'n-'roll, with clean-cut All-American boys such as Fabian and Bobby Vee dominating the charts. In Britain, similarly, the polite dance-on sound of the Shadows summed things up as the decade came to a close.

But the influence of the Fifties rock'n'roll revolution was not extinguished. A generation of British 'war baby' musicians were waiting in the wings, kids who had been mesmerized by rock'n'roll as mid-Fifties teenagers and came out of the skiffle boom as self-taught rock players. They would be the new disciples of the rock'n'roll religion which had its roots in that most dynamic decade of change, the 'Fifties.

1 Buddy Holly
2 Elvis Presley
3 Chuck Berry
4 Cliff Richard and the Shadows

1

2

3

4

BILL HALEY CHAMPIONS ROCK'N'ROLL CRAZE

Bill Haley & His Comets

Generating excitement on both sides of the Atlantic is the frantic new pop style known as rock'n-'roll.

Its most successful practitioner is 29-year-old Bill Haley, a former hillbilly singer from Chester, Pennsylvania, who has been cutting discs in the teenage idiom since 'Rock The Joint' in 1952. He and his group, The Comets, have drawn inspiration from country and western star Hank Williams and rhythm and blues bandleader Louis Jordan to create the unique driving sound which has put both 'Rock Around the Clock' and 'Shake Rattle And Roll' into the best sellers list.

The latter, originally recorded by coloured blues singer Joe Turner, is also in the American charts, together with another Haley side, 'Dim Dim The Lights' – as yet unreleased here.

The emotional Johnnie Ray

THAT 'CRY GUY' IMAGE IS NO JOKE

The half a million dollars which he is expected to earn this year apparently provide little comfort to Johnnie Ray. According to a New York newspaper report, the 'Nabob of Sob' often slips into a frustrated slough of despair, feeling that his work is futile and that his contribution to the world is insignificant compared with that of 'the wonderful evangelist Billy Graham'.

Remarkable evidence that living the life of a star isn't always as satisfying and joyous as it may appear to his fans.

EMI BUYS CAPITOL

The British recording company EMI has entered a contract to purchase a majority shareholding in the Hollywood-based Capitol label – started in 1942 by songwriters Johnny Mercer and Buddy de Sylva.

Capitol's illustrious roster includes Peggy Lee, Nat King Cole, Dean Martin and Tennessee Ernie Ford.

CHARTS

US45	Mr. Sandman – *Chordettes*
USLP	The Student Prince – *Mario Lanza*
UK45	The Finger Of Suspicion – *Dickie Valentine*
WEEK 2	
US45	Let Me Go Lover – *Joan Weber*
USLP	The Student Prince – *Mario Lanza*
UK45	Mambo Italiano – *Rosemary Clooney*
WEEK 3	
US45	Let Me Go Lover – *Joan Weber*
USLP	The Student Prince – *Mario Lanza*
UK45	The Finger Of Suspicion – *Dickie Valentine*
WEEK 4	
US45	Hearts Of Stone – *Fontane Sisters*
USLP	The Student Prince – *Mario Lanza*
UK45	The Finger Of Suspicion – *Dickie Valentine*

THE GRAPEVINE

- **British heart-throb David Hughes, on tour Down Under, has described Australia as 'a singer's paradise, a land of popportunity!'**
- **Tributes have flooded in for R & B balladeer Johhny Ace, who died on Christmas Day, aged 25. Reportedly, Ace was fatally wounded playing Russian roulette.**
- **The NME is now the world's biggest-selling music paper with sales in excess of 100,000.**

78 RPM DISCS ON THE WAY OUT?

Hoping to persuade record buyers to invest in 45 rpm singles, three major American companies – RCA Victor, Columbia and MGM – have announced startling retail price changes. In future, ten inch 78 rpm records will cost ten cents more than their seven inch 45 rpm counterparts – indicating that the old-style breakable discs may soon be phased out of production.

In Britain, where a 78 is now cheaper than its American equivalent, there are no plans for a price incentive to develop interest in the slower speed items.

CONTROVERSY AS R&B SWEEPS AMERICA

Seven of America's current Top 15 pop best sellers have their roots in the rhythm and blues field. Produced primarily for the black market, the songs have hit a responsive chord with white teenagers – but they are rushing to buy not the original versions but duplications by white acts who benefit from airplay on US radio stations, most of which are racially segregated.

This means that while the McGuire Sisters reign at number one with 'Sincerely', the original recording by The Moonglows is nowhere to be seen. Similarly, The Charms' R&B climber, 'Hearts Of Stone', stands at No. 2 in a version by the Fontane Sisters, while both Perry Como and The Crew Cuts are riding high with 'Ko Ko Mo', originally cut by Gene & Eunice.

The exception to the trend is 'Earth Angel', where the original disc by the Penguins is outselling a replica by The Crew Cuts.

Suffering from what they see as unfair competition are not only the black artists, but also their record companies – mostly small independent operations without the power and influence of the majors.

Atlantic, the top selling R&B label for the past three years, is particularly angry about the proliferation of white copies, or 'cover versions' as they are known.

'Radio stations are falling over themselves to play the Georgia Gibbs version of 'Tweedle Dee', while listeners aren't given a chance to hear the original by LaVern Baker. Consequently, Georgia Gibbs has the hit,' says Atlantic executive Jerry Wexler, who also saw The Crew Cuts 'obliterate' The Chords' novel waxing 'Sh-Boom'.

Saucy songstress LaVern Baker – smiling despite her tribulations

THE JUKE BOX ERA HITS BRITAIN

Britain is set to enter the juke box age. Recently freed from restrictive controls, the industry manufacturing these public record players is poised to emulate its success in America, where the number of boxes in operation is said to number half a million - one for every 300 of the population!

On a visit to Britain, John Haddock, owner of the leading US manufacturer AMI, said an ideal location for juke boxes would be the coffee houses which have become a London institution and are rapidly spreading to the provinces. 'In the States', he points out, 'music is usually associated with refreshment'.

So the British should look out for records with their coffee. If the juke box makers have a say in the matter, silent refreshment is on its way out!

Soon to become a feature of every coffee bar?

CHARTS

US45	Sincerely	*McGuire Sisters*
USLP	The Student Prince	*Mario Lanza*
UK45	Mambo Italiano	*Rosemary Clooney*
	WEEK 2	
US45	Sincerely	*McGuire Sisters*
USLP	The Student Prince	*Mario Lanza*
UK45	Mambo Italiano	*Rosemary Clooney*
	WEEK 3	
US45	Sincerely	*McGuire Sisters*
USLP	The Student Prince	*Mario Lanza*
UK45	Softly, Softly	*Ruby Murray*
	WEEK 4	
US45	Sincerely	*McGuire Sisters*
USLP	Music, Martinis & Memories	*Jackie Gleason*
UK45	Softly, Softly	*Ruby Murray*

THE GRAPEVINE

- **Weighing in with his version of 'You'll Never Walk Alone', former boxer Roy Hamilton is tipped as a new contender for the heavyweight ballad crown.**
- **Orchestra leader Ray Anthony is engaged to sultry film actress Mamie Van Doren.**
- **On tour in Australia, Winifred Atwell is fêted wherever she goes. Said one reporter: 'England may have won the Ashes, but we'll be more than happy to keep Winifred Atwell'.**

NO LET-UP IN LATIN TREND

Latin American rhythms continue to influence the pop music mainstream.

In the wake of Rosemary Clooney's chart topping 'Mambo Italiano' have come 'Papa Loves Mambo', 'I Can't Tell A Waltz From A Tango', 'Who Stole The Beans From His Maracas?', 'Elephant Tango' and a host of others. Even Bill Haley is joining the bandwagon with his new release, 'Mambo Rock'.

It is therefore gratifying to welcome to the best sellers the man who started it all, bandleader Perez Prado.

A Cuban who has been living in Mexico for the last seven years, Prado began experimenting with the mambo as long ago as 1942 – yet he remained largely undiscovered until Hollywood stepped in. Boosted by its use as the theme music of the Jane Russell romp *Underwater*, his recording of 'Cherry Pink And Apple Blossom White' seems set to propel him to international prominence.

DANKWORTH SAYS NO TO SOUTH AFRICA

British Orchestra leader Johnny Dankworth has turned down an offer of £10,000 to tour South Africa because of the colour-bar policy operated there.

'I don't want to appear as a hero in any respect, but I feel it is time to make a stand on this colour prejudice,' said Dankworth, who also backed a plea by Father Trevor Huddleston for a cultural boycott of South Africa by entertainers who believe racialism is wrong.

CHARTS

US45 Sincerely — *McGuire Sisters*
USLP The Student Prince — *Mario Lanza*
UK45 Softly, Softly — *Ruby Murray*

WEEK 2

US45 Sincerely — *McGuire Sisters*
USLP The Student Prince — *Mario Lanza*
UK45 Give Me Your Word — *Tennessee Ernie Ford*

WEEK 3

US45 Ballad Of Davy Crockett — *Bill Hayes*
USLP The Student Prince — *Mario Lanza*
UK45 Give Me Your Word — *Tennessee Ernie Ford*

WEEK 4

US45 Ballad Of Davy Crockett — *Bill Hayes*
USLP The Student Prince — *Mario Lanza*
UK45 Give Me Your Word — *Tennessee Ernie Ford*

WEEK 5

US45 Ballad Of Davy Crockett — *Bill Hayes*
USLP The Student Prince — *Mario Lanza*
UK45 Give Me Your Word — *Tennessee Ernie Ford*

THE GRAPEVINE

- Marlon Brando is taking singing lessons for his forthcoming role in *Guys And Dolls*. Says his coach: 'With more tuition he could sing at the Metropolitan Opera House!'
- Bill Haley & His Comets are soon off to Hollywood to begin work on a feature film.
- Vocalist Ross McManus has joined the Joe Loss Orchestra.
- Singer Dick James is starting his own music publishing firm.

'Sure I can sing!' says Brando

TENNESSEE ERNIE RIDES AGAIN!

His friends say that Tennessee Ernie Ford just can't stop chuckling! Originally recorded as the throwaway B-side of 'River Of No Return', 'Give Me Your Word' lay dormant for months – until an AFN disc-jockey programmed the side as a novelty.

English language station Radio Luxemburg got in on the act and a bemused Ford watched his record climb to the top of the British best sellers.

A former radio announcer and air force navigator, Ford found fame as a country and western singer after the war – and starred at the London Palladium in April 1953. He now plans to return to Britain to reap the rewards of his unexpected hit!

JAZZ GIANT CHARLIE PARKER DEAD AT 34

The jazz world has been stunned by the sudden death of alto saxophonist Charlie Parker – the greatest solo genius in American jazz, according to his fellow musicians.

He passed away in the New York apartment of his friend the Baroness Nica Rothschild de Koenigswarter on March 12, stricken with what seemed to be a heart attack, although the cause of death has since been diagnosed as pneumonia.

FROM CALL-BOY TO STAR

Adoring fans are seldom far from chart-topping heart-throb Dickie Valentine

Winner of the male vocalist category in the recent NME poll, Dickie Valentine tops the bill at the London Palladium for two weeks this month. The last British male singer to headline at this world-famous showplace was Donald Peers, in 1950.

Dickie's rise has been meteoric. He left the Ted Heath Orchestra to launch a solo career less than a year ago, since when he has flown to New York to appear on Ed Sullivan's coast-to-coast television show, has taken part in a Royal Variety Performance, and has reached the top of the best sellers chart with 'Finger of Suspicion'.

His Palladium fortnight comes between the appearances of two major American stars, Eddie Fisher and Johnnie Ray. It is indeed an honour, reflecting favourably on the entire British entertainment profession, that a London born singing celebrity should now find himself in such exalted company.

Only ten years ago, Dickie was a call-boy at the Palladium – and now he returns as a top-liner.

WELCOME, JOHNNIE RAY!

Possibly more than any other entertainer, Johnnie Ray, the fantastic 'Cry Guy', has completely captured the imagination of Britain's teenage fans – and many older people too. He flies in this month for a series of sold-out shows.

His supporters are countless and unashamedly vocal. So are his detractors. Here, in fact, is one case where an ancient adage fits like the proverbial glove: you may like Johnnie Ray, you may detest him, but you surely cannot ignore him!

Enjoying a rare quiet moment!

Whatever his qualities as a vocalist, Johnnie has the knack of rousing a theatre crowd to a frenzy of shouting, screaming, whistling, clapping and stamping appreciation – and it is rare that he can escape from a stage door without having at least one item of clothing torn off!

But Johnnie has nothing but praise for his legion of fans – never once have they touched his deaf-aid.

CHARTS

US45 Ballad Of Davy Crockett *Bill Hayes*
USLP The Student Prince *Mario Lanza*
UK45 Give Me Your Word *Tennessee Ernie Ford*

WEEK 2

US45 Ballad Of Davy Crockett *Bill Hayes*
USLP The Student Prince *Mario Lanza*
UK45 Give Me Your Word *Tennessee Ernie Ford*

WEEK 3

US45 Cherry Pink & Apple Blossom White *Perez Prado*
USLP The Student Prince *Mario Lanza*
UK45 Give Me Your Word *Tennessee Ernie Ford*

WEEK 4

US45 Cherry Pink & Apple Blossom White *Perez Prado*
USLP The Student Prince *Mario Lanza*
UK45 Cherry Pink & Apple Blossom White *Perez Prado*

STEREOSONIC DISCS ARE HERE

Hailed as the most important development since the advent of long-playing records, a new type of sound reproducing equipment is on show at EMI Studios.

Known as stereosonic, the new system brings a three dimensional aural effect into one's own home. Listening to a stereosonic record is like being in the middle of an orchestra or a group of singers – yet this uncanny realism is accomplished with the use of only two loudspeakers!

Manufacturers hope to market the first record players and discs towards the end of the year.

George Martin takes over

THE GRAPEVINE

- **After a distinguished career of more than 50 years in the UK recording industry, Parlophone manager Oscar Preuss is retiring. Succeeding him is George Martin, his assistant for the past five years.**
- **Former Duke Ellington vocalist Al Hibbler is on the way to his first big international record hit – with the film song, 'Unchained Melody'.**

MAY

ROCKING ROLLING FREED DISMISSES CRITICS

Alan Freed: Oblivious to criticism, he spins the discs that American teenagers want to hear

American disc jockey Alan Freed, who three years ago realized that white teenagers were responding to the rhythm and blues records he was spinning on his Cleveland, Ohio radio show, is being hailed as the 'King of Rock'n'roll'.

Since moving to New York station WINS last August, Freed has not only established himself as the leading authority on the new music, but has also branched out into concert promotion. Last month, at the Brooklyn Paramount Theatre, he grossed 107,000 dollars with a week's bill of well known R&B artists. This month he's touring the New England area with another package headed by Dinah Washington.

As rhythm and blues continues to grow in popularity, critics are rushing to condemn what they describe as either 'musically infantile, lyrically ignorant', 'vulgar and ungrammatical', 'off-key trash' or 'sheer garbage'.

According to Los Angeles disc jockey Peter Potter: 'all rhythm and blues records are dirty and as bad for the kids as dope.'

Freed disagrees. 'As in the past, the shrill outraged cries of critics will be lost beneath the excitement of a new generation seeking to let off steam. There's nothing they can do to stop this new solid beat of American music from sweeping across the land in a gigantic tidal wave of happiness,' he says.

BBC-TV ACKNOWLEDGES RECORD BOOM

Disc jockey and former bandleader Jack Payne has been selected as frontman for *Off The Record*, the first British television show to highlight the recording industry. Featured guests on the opening show include Max Bygraves, Alma Cogan, George Shearing and the Four Aces.

CHARTS

US45	Cherry Pink & Apple Blossom White — *Perez Prado*
USLP	The Student Prince — *Mario Lanza*
UK45	Cherry Pink & Apple Blossom White — *Perez Prado*
WEEK 2	
US45	Cherry Pink & Apple Blossom White — *Perez Prado*
USLP	The Student Prince — *Mario Lanza*
UK45	Stranger In Paradise — *Tony Bennett*
WEEK 3	
US45	Cherry Pink & Apple Blossom White — *Perez Prado*
USLP	Crazy Otto — *Crazy Otto*
UK45	Stranger In Paradise — *Tony Bennett*
WEEK 4	
US45	Unchained Melody — *Les Baxter*
USLP	Crazy Otto — *Crazy Otto*
UK45	Cherry Pink & Apple Blossom White — *Eddie Calvert*

THE GRAPEVINE

- **Earl Bostic has been presented with a gold disc to mark million-plus sales of 'Flamingo' – the instrumental he recorded in 1952.**
- **Frank Sinatra is set to play a drug addict in the movie of Nelson Algren's novel *The Man With The Golden Arm*.**
- **Decca UK have acquired European rights to the American labels Cadence and Dot. Both will be distributed under the London American banner.**

A dramatic role for Frank

CRAZY OVER CROCKETT!

It seems the whole of America has fallen under the spell of Davy Crockett, the buckskin-clad hero of a Walt Disney television series.

Astonished merchandisers are struggling to meet the demand for replicas of his 'coonskin' hat, and some 17 recordings of the series theme-song have already sold in excess of four million copies.

Leading the pack is Bill Hayes, whose Cadence Records waxing topped the best sellers for the whole of last month, although versions by Fess Parker (who plays Crockett in the series) and Tennessee Ernie Ford also reached the Top 10.

A full length feature film is now in production at the Disney studios in Hollywood, but British cinemagoers will have to wait until January to discover the appeal of this 'King of the Wild Frontier'!

JUNE

DELINQUENCY MOVIE BOOSTS ROCK'N'ROLL

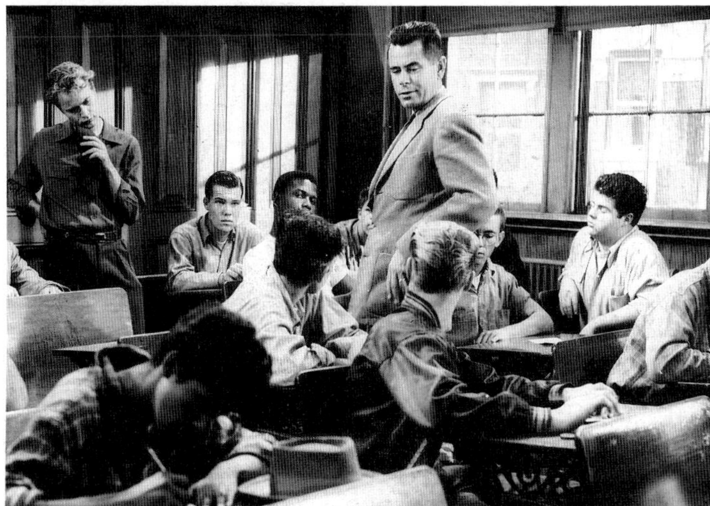

Glenn Ford confronts his pupils

Playing over the credits of the movie, *Blackboard Jungle*, has rocketed Bill Haley's 'Rock Around The Clock' high into the American best sellers.

Considered dead and buried months ago, the disc was reactivated as an appropriate soundtrack to the Glenn Ford flick, which explores juvenile delinquency in a New York high school.

Haley himself is clearly pleased and flattered by the unexpected attention, but the connection between rock'n'roll and delinquent behaviour has only helped to reinforce public prejudice. Influential disc jockey Bill Randle sees a tie-up, but doesn't believe the new beat actually causes juvenile delinquency - 'it just reflects it', he says.

Though doing brisk box-office business Stateside, the film is not scheduled for British release until November.

LET ME GO JERRY!

An end to the laughter?

It looks as if the five million dollars a year comedy partnership of Dean Martin and Jerry Lewis is on the point of collapse.

Martin, who has recently enjoyed such hits as 'Naughty Lady of Shady Lane', 'Let Me Go Lover' and 'Under The Bridges of Paris', would like to concentrate on his vocal career. He doesn't want to travel as much as the duo has in the last few months, and he wants his own television show.

It is also reported that personal feelings between the two are not of the warmest!

CHARTS

US45	Unchained Melody *Les Baxter*
USLP	Starring Sammy Davis Jr. *Sammy Davis Jr.*
UK45	Cherry Pink & Apple Blossom White *Eddie Calvert*
WEEK 2	
US45	Unchained Melody *Les Baxter*
USLP	Starring Sammy Davis Jr. *Sammy Davis Jr.*
UK45	Cherry Pink & Apple Blossom White *Eddie Calvert*
WEEK 3	
US45	Unchained Melody *Les Baxter*
USLP	Starring Sammy Davis Jr. *Sammy Davis Jr.*
UK45	Cherry Pink & Apple Blossom White *Eddie Calvert*
WEEK 4	
US45	Unchained Melody *Les Baxter*
USLP	Starring Sammy Davis Jr. *Sammy Davis Jr.*
UK45	Unchained Melody *Jimmy Young*
WEEK 5	
US45	Rock Around The Clock *Bill Haley & The Comets*
USLP	Starring Sammy Davis Jr. *Sammy Davis Jr.*
UK45	Unchained Melody *Jimmy Young*

STAR

JOHNNIE RAY

'The mambo craze is passing and rhythm and blues will pass away too – the sooner the better as far as I'm concerned!'

THE GRAPEVINE

- **Doris Day re-signed with Columbia when her contract expired this month, even though she and husband Marty Melcher has just launched their own record label, Arwin.**
- **Set for June 17, the long awaited marriage of 26 year-old singing star Eddie Fisher and Hollywood's most publicised up-and-coming actress, Debbie Reynolds, has been postponed.**

INTRODUCING THE FABULOUS LIBERACE

New to the charts, with his instrumental version of 'Unchained Melody', is a man who wears gold *lamé* suits designed by Christian Dior, has a piano-shaped swimming pool, who can fill an 18,000 seat hall in New York and command a fee of £20,000 for one week's work in Las Vegas, but is almost unknown in Britain. His name . . . Liberace.

He is an idol to his worshipful fans, a godsend to entertainment columnists, and a frightful bore to music critics – most of whom agree that he is a thoroughly mediocre piano player! This, however, does not prevent him from tackling anything from 'The Beer Barrel Polka' to Grieg's Piano Concerto, 'Ave Maria' to 'Maiden's Wish Samba'.

As one journalist commented: 'Let's get one thing straight . . . Liberace is a skilled artist – but his art is comedy, not music!'

Controversial pianist Liberace

JULY

'I JUST WON'T ROCK'N'ROLL' DECLARES CLOONEY

American songstress Rosemary Clooney visited Britain this month for TV, radio and concert dates – including a bill-topping spot at the Palladium.

Miss Clooney delighted her fans with such hits as 'This Ole House', 'Mambo Italiano' and 'Where Will the Dimple Be'. No mass hysteria or false emotions, no attempt to palpitate the pulse, but a clever Clooney showing an audience how they can be nursed, coaxed, humoured and sent home content.

Later, a somewhat cycnical Rosemary offered her opinion on America's latest craze. 'I won't record rock'n'roll', she stated. 'Where's the story value in those songs? I feel that every good song should tell a story.'

The new style obviously offends her ingrained musical beliefs . . . 'those sax players, for instance, they don't tune up from year to year, let alone from day to day, and the singers just have no respect for the basic do-re-mi'.

Quite so, Rosemary!

Houses mean a lot to Rosemary Clooney! She first rocketed to fame with Come-On-A My House in 1951, and this year she topped the charts with This Ole House

CHARTS

US45	Rock Around The Clock *Bill Haley & The Comets*
USLP	Starring Sammy Davis Jr. *Sammy Davis Jr.*
UK45	Unchained Melody *Jimmy Young*
WEEK 2	
US45	Rock Around The Clock *Bill Haley & The Comets*
USLP	Lonesome Echo *Jackie Gleason*
UK45	Dreamboat *Alma Cogan*
WEEK 3	
US45	Rock Around The Clock *Bill Haley & The Comets*
USLP	Lonesome Echo *Jackie Gleason*
UK45	Dreamboat *Alma Cogan*
WEEK 4	
US45	Rock Around The Clock *Bill Haley & The Comets*
USLP	Love Me Or Leave Me *Doris Day*
UK45	Rose Marie *Slim Whitman*

GUY'S IDEAL GIRL

Though absent from the best sellers for over a year, Guy Mitchell is confident of a speedy return. 'These days, my basic goal is to work as hard as I can and centralize all my efforts on building my career further,' he said.

'I'm really working at it, and I'm no longer interested in being a good-time Charlie. I'm also most interested in realizing my other major ambition – to settle down, find myself a wife, and buy myself a ranch,' he added.

'I'm looking for a girl who likes to dance and laugh, and who loves children – because I want as many kids as possible!'

LEONARD PLOTS CHESS MOVES

Regarded by many as home of the blues, Chicago could soon become a centre for rock'n'roll – according to Leonard Chess, the owner of the locally based Chess and Checker labels.

Chess has already enjoyed regional success with Muddy Waters, Howling Wolf, Little Walter and The Moonglows – who cut the original version of the McGuire Sisters' million seller, 'Sincerely' – but he is convinced that his two latest discoveries 'will change the face of rock'n'roll'!

Both are vocalists who are equally adept as guitarists and songwriters. Bo Diddley (26), hails from Mississippi, but has been playing around the clubs of Chicago for several years, while Chuck Berry, (two years older), is from St Louis.

Both their debut discs are rising up the US R&B chart: Berry is clicking with 'Maybellene', while Diddley's tune is actually called 'Bo Diddley'!

THE GRAPEVINE

■ **Released this month is Bill Haley's latest single, 'Razzle Dazzle'/'Two Hound Dogs'. Meanwhile, London Records are cashing in by issuing 'Green Tree Boogie' – recorded way back in 1951!**

■ **Ken Colyer's Skiffle Group, comprising members of his jazz band, are currently recording eight titles for Decca. Colyer expects 'skiffle' – a mixture of American folk and blues styles – to catch on with UK fans.**

A NEW BARBER SHOP QUARTET?

Top Canadian vocal group The Crew Cuts have a professional slickness which their rivals might well envy. Last summer, their note-for-note copy of 'Sh-Boom', originally recorded by The Chords, outsold all competition and was voted 'Rhythm and Blues Record of the Year' by a critics' panel in Down Beat magazine.

Realizing that the R&B boom was infiltrating the pop market, the boys collected more items from that field. One was 'Ko Ko Mo', another 'Earth Angel' – which has been around the British best sellers since April.

The folks who prophesied a short commercial life for rhythm and blues had better think again.

Incidentally, the lads have taken out insurance with Lloyds of London – against losing their hair and consequently their tonsorial trademark!

The Crew Cuts

LAINE SEEKS WATER, FINDS GOLD!

Some people might find it faintly comical that a 42 year-old Jewish cabaret singer from Chicago should pose as a hapless cowpoke lost in an endless desert – as he does in 'Cool Water' – but not the countless fans who have returned Frankie Laine to the higher reaches of the charts yet again.

Of course, Laine is no stranger to western ballads. His past hits include 'Mule Train', 'Cry of the Wild Goose' and 'High Noon'.

Says Frankie: 'There is something fascinating about the lone adventurer, out in the wide open spaces, facing up to adversity.' And he should know. Back in 1932, as a contestant in a marathon dance competition held in Atlantic City, he set a world record of 3,501 hours non-stop dancing!

WHITFIELD GOES GOLD

Decca UK singing star David Whitfield is the third British artist in recent years to win a coveted 'Golden Record'. Thanks to a spell in the American charts, the sales of his 'Cara Mia' have now exceeded one million copies. Only three years ago, Whitfield was working as a building labourer in Hull, Yorkshire.

The only other British artists to have been awarded a Golden Record are Vera Lynn (for 'Auf Weidersehn') and trumpeter Eddie Calvert (for 'Oh Mein Papa').

Thanks a million, David!

Harry Belafonte

WATCH OUT FOR BELAFONTE

Fast-rising New York folk and calypso singer Harry Belafonte has become one of the most in-demand entertainers in the country. This month, he begins a six week residency at the Waldorf Astoria's plush Empire Room at the highest salary ever paid to a performer.

Another project involves Belafonte and Cary Grant starring in a movie as two jazz pianists who start out broke, but go to the top as a team.

THE GRAPEVINE

■ The most consistently successful R&B label, Atlantic, has recently begun an extensive jazz album programme. The company has also started a new subsidiary, Atco.

■ Despite victory in this year's Down Beat poll, jazz trumpeter Miles Davis is, according to his English label boss, 'one of our worst sellers'!

■ Modelled on Bill Haley's Comets, Boyd Bennett & The Rockets have a US hit with 'Seventeen'.

CHARTS

WEEK 1	US45	Rock Around The Clock	*Bill Haley & The Comets*
	USLP	Love Me Or Leave Me	*Doris Day*
	UK45	Rose Marie	*Slim Whitman*
WEEK 2	US45	Rock Around The Clock	*Bill Haley & The Comets*
	USLP	Love Me or Leave Me	*Doris Day*
	UK45	Rose Marie	*Slim Whitman*
WEEK 3	US45	Rock Around The Clock	*Bill Haley & The Comets*
	USLP	Love Me Or Leave Me	*Doris Day*
	UK45	Rose Marie	*Slim Whitman*
WEEK 4	US45	Yellow Rose Of Texas	*Mitch Miller*
	USLP	Love Me Or Leave Me	*Doris Day*
	UK45	Rose Marie	*Slim Whitman*
WEEK 5	US45	Yellow Rose Of Texas	*Mitch Miller*
	USLP	Love Me Or Leave Me	*Doris Day*
	UK45	Rose Marie	*Slim Whitman*

EVERYTHING'S COMING UP ROSES FOR SLIM!

In recent months, American C&W singer Slim Whitman has astounded the music world with his British record sales.

His 'Rose Marie' disc has been No. 1 since July and is almost certain to become the biggest seller of any record ever released in Britain.

Slim – aged 31 – worked as a shipfitter and boilermaker in his home town of Tampa, Florida before taking up guitar while serving in the US Navy. Since his demobilization in 1945, he's never looked back.

A well known name on the American country circuit, Slim was virtually unknown in Britain three months ago, yet today his records outsell all competition. In addition to his fantastic success with 'Rose Marie', an earlier recording of 'Indian Love Call' has occupied a high place in the best sellers for several weeks, and now a third disc, 'China Doll', has joined them in the chart.

Two more titles, 'Roll On Silvery Moon' and 'Cattle Call', are also enjoying brisk sales in every corner of Britain.

Coincidentally, another Rose is topping the US best sellers – Mitch Miller's 'Yellow Rose of Texas'.

CHARTS

US45	Yellow Rose Of Texas *Mitch Miller*
USLP	Love Me Or Leave Me *Doris Day*
UK45	Rose Marie *Slim Whitman*
WEEK 2	
US45	Yellow Rose Of Texas *Mitch Miller*
USLP	Love Me Or Leave Me *Doris Day*
UK45	Rose Marie *Slim Whitman*
WEEK 3	
US45	Yellow Rose Of Texas *Mitch Miller*
USLP	Love Me Or Leave Me *Doris Day*
UK45	Rose Marie *Slim Whitman*
WEEK 4	
US45	Love Is A Many Splendored Thing *Four Aces*
USLP	Love Me Or Leave Me *Doris Day*
UK45	Rose Marie *Slim Whitman*

WHAT'S IN A NAME?

The rise of R&B in America has seen a proliferation of black vocal groups, usually quartets or quintets, patterned after such pioneering teams as The Ravens, The Orioles and The Dominoes. The number of groups is as incredible as some of their fanciful names.

The Crows, The Charms and The Penguins have all had fleeting pop success, but what of The Drifters, The Dreamers, The Roamers, The Leaders, The Flamingos, Robins, Larks, Blues Jays, Cardinals, Wrens, Hawkettes, Meadowlarks, Swallows and Spaniels? Or The Spiders, Crickets, Turks, Turbans, Sultans, Squires, Regals, Barons, Counts, Coronets, Crowns and Queens? Not to forget The Royals, The Orchids, Clovers, Marigolds, Nutmegs, Willows, Evergreens, Rivileers, Vocaleers, Danderliers, Buccaneers, Blue Flames, Blazes, Embers, The Diablos or The Angels . . . and countless others.

THE GRAPEVINE

■ Commercial TV has begun transmission in Britain, creating an alternative channel to the BBC.

■ Bill Haley & His Comets have turned down a tour of Australia because some of the combo refuse to travel by air!

■ Eddie Fisher and Debbie Reynolds finally wed, ditto Ray Anthony and Mamie Van Doren. But screen goddess Rita Hayworth and Singer Dick Haymes (her fourth husband) have parted company.

PEGGY'S FELINE BLUE

Peggy Lee is winning rave reviews for her screen role in *Pete Kelly's Blues*, the story of a jazz band's bloody skirmishes with protection racketeers in Kansas City during the twenties. Star and producer is Jack Webb, whose crime series, *Dragnet*, begins on British television this month.

Miss Lee also embellishes the latest Disney release, *The Lady And The Tramp*. She co-wrote the score and also does the voice characterizations of the Siamese cats!

The versatile Peggy Lee

HIT RECORD PARALLELS TRAGIC DEATH OF ACTOR

This month's most unusual US chart entry is 'Black Denim Trousers And Motor Cycle Boots', recorded by Capitol Records group The Cheers. The idea came from Marlon Brando's *The Wild One* – banned in Britain after the censors described it as 'a screen essay in violence and brutality'.

Since it was recorded, the song's youthful authors, Jerry Leiber and Mike Stoller, have signed a pact with the Atlantic label to become independent record producers. Their first offering will be 'Smokey Joe's Cafe' by Los Angeles vocal group, The Robins.

Meanwhile, we learn of the death of James Dean, who had been widely tipped as 'the new Brando'. Dean (24) whose first major film *East Of Eden* opens in London this month, died at the wheel of his Porsche sports car on September 30.

It is a gruesome coincidence that, like the motorcycle hero of The Cheers' record (cut weeks earlier), he was killed on Highway 101 in California. Two more Dean movies are in the can, awaiting release: *Rebel Without A Cause* and *Giant*.

The role of Rocky Grazziano in *Somebody Up There Likes Me*, which Dean was to play, has now been assigned to screen newcomer Paul Newman.

Screen star James Dean

CHARTS

	US45	Yellow Rose Of Texas	*Mitch Miller*
	USLP	Love Me Or Leave Me	*Doris Day*
	UK45	Rose Marie	*Slim Whitman*
WEEK 2	US45	Love Is A Many Splendored Thing	*Four Aces*
	USLP	Love Me Or Leave me	*Doris Day*
	UK45	The Man From Laramie	*Jimmy Young*
WEEK 3	US45	Autumn Leaves	*Roger Williams*
	USLP	Love me Or Leave Me	*Doris Day*
	UK45	The Man From Laramie	*Jimmy Young*
WEEK 4	US45	Autumn Leaves	*Roger Williams*
	USLP	Love Me Or Leave Me	*Doris Day*
	UK45	The Man From Laramie	*Jimmy Young*

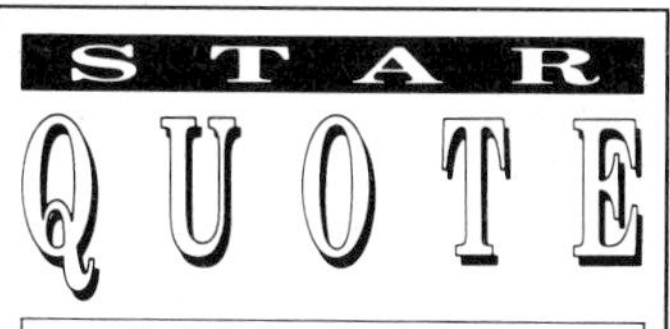

BILL HALEY

'Frankly, our market is the teenagers. They are the ones we constantly try to please. We keep very close to them, listening for their new expressions and asking what they want in the way of music.'

THE GRAPEVINE

- ***Blackboard Jungle*** **has opened in London. One leading film critic said the movie was: 'one for those with strong stomachs'!**
- **EMI are introducing new colours for their labels. HMV will now be blue, Columbia green and Parlophone red. Printing will be in silver.**
- **American Dick Lester is new producer of the commercial television jazz programme *Downbeat*.**

Tipped for stardom: Paul Newman

AFM LIFTS 20 YEAR BAN ON ANGLO-US EXCHANGES

James Petrillo, President of the American Federation of Musicians, has authorized the first transatlantic exchange of musicians. The ban on American bands playing in this country, and on British bands playing in the States, has existed since 1935 – since when only vocalists have been allowed exchange facilities.

The first parties to take advantage of this new freedom will be the orchestras of Ted Heath (UK) and Stan Kenton (US).

A BOONE TO THE CHARTS

Though rock'n'roll has made little impact in the British best sellers, Bill Haley, Boyd Bennett, The Crew Cuts, The Fontane Sisters and Chuck Berry have all made chart inroads in America. So too has Pat Boone, who scored a million seller with 'Ain't That A Shame'.

For eleven weeks this summer, the original version by Fats Domino, a singing piano-thumper from New Orleans, was number one on the R&B chart – but it was Boone's cover which garnered most pop sales. A college graduate from Nashville, Tennessee 21 year old Pat is a descendant of the legendary frontiersman Daniel Boone.

Pat Boone has a degree in English . . . ain't that a surprise!

NOVEMBER

DJs PICK FRANK AND DORIS – BOX OPS OPT FOR PERRY AND JAYE

The American trade magazine 'Billboard' has announced the results of its annual disc jockey poll. Doris Day and Frank Sinatra were favourite vocalists, Pat Boone was the most promising newcomer, and The Four Aces won the vocal group section.

The year's most played records were 'Sincerely' by the McGuire Sisters, 'Rock Around The Clock' by Bill Haley & His Comets, and 'Learnin' The Blues' by Frank Sinatra.

Also announced were the 'Cash Box' poll winners, voted by the nation's juke box operators. Perry Como and Jaye P. Morgan were their preferred vocalists, The Four Aces consolidated their success as top vocal group and Pat Boone was their most promising newcomer too.

In the NME readers' poll, Dickie Valentine, Ruby Murray and The Stargazers won their respective categories.

SCREEN STARS WAX LYRICAL

Having hit the top with the theme from the film *Unchained*, British singer Jimmy Young has again been reclining at No. 1 with the title song from James Stewart's wild-west epic, *The Man From Laramie*.

It seems that records boosted by movies just can't fail – as Bill Haley will confirm – but film stars are now rushing to make discs themselves. Among those to have done so recently are Jeff Chandler, Marilyn Monroe, Jane Russell, José Ferrer, Errol Flynn, Kirk Douglas, Van Johnson, Marlon Brando, Rhonda Fleming, Diana Dors, Diane Cilento, Brigitte Bardot and Tony Curtis – the man who came out top in the recent *Picturegoer* magazine poll.

Chart-topping Jimmy Young

CHARTS

US45	Autumn Leaves – *Roger Williams*
USLP	Love Me Or Leave Me – *Doris Day*
UK45	The Man From Laramie – *Jimmy Young*
WEEK 2	
US45	Love Is A Many Splendored Thing – *Four Aces*
USLP	Love Me Or Leave Me – *Doris Day*
UK45	Hernando's Hideaway – *Johnston Brothers*
WEEK 3	
US45	Love Is A Many Splendored Thing – *Four Aces*
USLP	Love Me Or Leave Me – *Doris Day*
UK45	Hernando's Hideaway – *Johnston Brothers*
WEEK 4	
US45	Sixteen Tons – *Tennessee Ernie Ford*
USLP	Love Me Or Leave Me – *Doris Day*
UK45	Rock Around The Clock – *Bill Haley & The Comets*
WEEK 5	
US45	Sixteen Tons – *Tennessee Ernie Ford*
USLP	Love Me Or Leave Me – *Doris Day*
UK45	Rock Around The Clock – *Bill Haley & The Comets*

DECCA BACK SKIFFLE HUNCH

If growing attendances at the London Skiffle and Blues Club – which opened at The Roundhouse, Wardour Street in September – are anything to go by, 'skiffle' could well catch on nationally next year.

Sharing this belief, Decca have issued two singles in the style: 'Take This Hammer' by Ken Colyer and 'Rock Island Line' by Lonnie Donegan. The latter is culled from a long-player by Chris Barber's jazz band, of which Donegan is a member.

RCA SIGNS HILLBILLY CAT!

Rising to meet the challenge of Bill Haley and Pat Boone, RCA Victor have signed former truck driver-cum-rock'n'roller Elvis Presley – known around his hometown of Memphis, Tennessee, as 'The Hillbilly Cat'.

Though virtually unknown outside the southern states, 'the girls down there are tearing off his clothes', according to his manager, Colonel Tom Parker. The transfer fee from his previous label, Sun, is understood to be in the region of 40,000 dollars.

Twenty year old Presley will make enough from the deal to realize his big ambition – to buy a Cadillac!

R&B best sellers, The Platters

THE GRAPEVINE

- **The top selling US R&B single is 'Only You' by The Platters, deposing Chuck Berry's million-selling debut, 'Maybellene'.**
- **Johnnie Ray and Ruby Murray were among those appearing before the Queen and Prince Philip at the British Royal Command Performance.**
- **An increase in U.K. purchase tax, plus a general rise in costs, has raised the price of EMI and Decca singles from five shillings (48 cents) to 5s/7d (53 cents).**

DOT CAPTURES BIG SLICE OF ROCK'N'ROLL MARKET

Last year, Randy Wood, the owner of a mail-order record business in the small Tennessee town of Gallatin, noticed that his white teenage customers were increasingly interested in rhythm and blues. Consequently, he set about modernizing his small sideline record label, Dot, which had previously specialized in country music.

Adopting a policy of signing white artists to cover rising R&B hits, he has put the American disc industry into a flat spin! In just twelve months, Dot has cornered an astonishing 15 per cent of the pop singles market.

The label's biggest star is Pat Boone, who has scored five hits, including 'Ain't That A Shame' (originally cut by Fats Domino) and 'At My Front Door' (an R&B climber for The El Dorados). Close behind are The Fontane Sisters, with covers of 'Hearts of Stone' (The Charms), 'Rock Love' (Lula Reed), 'Rollin' Stone' (The Marigolds), 'Seventeen' (Boyd Bennett) and 'Daddy-O' (Bonnie Lou).

Currently on the chart are Gale Storm's 'I Hear You Knocking' (Smiley Lewis), The Hilltoppers' 'Only You' (The Platters), and Billy Vaughan's mysterious monologue 'The Shifting Whispering Sands'.

Ruby Murray – the year's most consistent hit parade star

THE GRAPEVINE

- **Ruby Murray has moved into a luxury flat overlooking London's Regents Park – at a weekly rental of more than £15 ($45).**
- **That man of the moment, Bill Haley, has two new releases this month. While American fans are clamouring for 'See You Later Alligator', his British label are only just getting round to issuing his last US hit, 'Rock A-Beating Boogie'/'Burn That Candle.'**

CHARTS

US45	Sixteen Tons — *Tennessee Ernie Ford*
USLP	Love Me Or Leave Me — *Doris Day*
UK45	Rock Around The Clock — *Bill Haley & The Comets*
WEEK 2	
US45	Sixteen Tons — *Tennessee Ernie Ford*
USLP	Love Me Or Leave Me — *Doris Day*
UK45	Christmas Alphabet — *Dickie Valentine*
WEEK 3	
US45	Sixteen Tons — *Tennessee Ernie Ford*
USLP	Oklahoma — *Soundtrack*
UK45	Christmas Alphabet — *Dickie Valentine*
WEEK 4	
US45	Sixteen Tons — *Tennessee Ernie Ford*
USLP	Oklahoma — *Soundtrack*
UK45	Christmas Alphabet — *Dickie Valentine*

JOHNNIE BRINGS JO'BURG TO STANDSTILL

Thousands of screaming, swooning bobbysoxers greeted Johnnie Ray as he landed in South Africa for a Christmas/New Year season - and fans lined the 15 mile route from Johannesburg airport as an escort of motorcycle police, with sirens howling, led his open Cadillac into the city.

Johnnie was twice mobbed at traffic lights and, on arrival at his hotel, was literally forced to sing 'Hey There' to the thronging admirers who paralysed the city centre.

The singer is being paid £26,000 for his five week engagement.

YOU LOAD 16 TONS AND WHAT DO YOU GET? A HIT!

In only nine days, Tennessee Ernie Ford sold more than 600,000 copies of his US chart topper 'Sixteen Tons' – making it a contender for the fastest million seller in pop history and giving the country star his biggest American hit since 'Shotgun Boogie', five years ago.

The background to this novel ditty is intriguing. It was written by C&W guitarist Merle Travis, who based it on his father's experiences as a coal-miner in Kentucky.

Living a hand-to-mouth existence he, along with the whole community, fell into debt and was forced to pay the inflated prices charged at the only local store, belonging to the mine owners. Hence the weary chorus line: 'I owe my soul to the company store'.

Johnny Ray – a happy man!

SPINNING TO THE FORE . . . THE PLATTERS

In the States, two discs by black R&B vocal group The Platters have reached the Top 10 of the pop best sellers – 'Only You' and 'The Great Pretender'. Since record buyers have gone for their original waxings rather than copies by white singers, it seems as if the popularity of 'cover versions' may be on the wane.

Both songs were penned, and produced, by the group's manager, Buck Ram – but the unearthly voice – which has captured the hearts of so many fans is that of lead tenor Tony Williams.

The Platters are currently in Hollywood, shooting scenes for the forthcoming movie *Rock Around The Clock* – also starring disc jockey Alan Freed and, as you might expect, Bill Haley & His Comets.

RECORD BIZ ANTICIPATES CROCKETT CORNUCOPIA

Fess Parker as Davy Crockett

Hoping to see a repeat of the sales bonanza which swept the States, virtually every record label in Britain has found someone to cut the theme song from the *Davy Crockett* movie, which goes on release this month.

Held back for almost a year, the hit versions by Fess Parker, who portrays the 'buckskin buccaneer' in the film, and Bill Hayes, who topped the US chart, can finally be heard by British fans.

Vying for attention are several other American recordings – by Burl Ives, Tennessee Ernie Ford, Steve Allen, and Fred Waring's Pennsylvanians, to name but a few – while homegrown frontrunners include Gary Miller, Ronnie Ronalde, Dick James, Max Bygraves and Billy Cotton.

THE GRAPEVINE

■ British singer Dick James has a rising hit with *Robin Hood* – familiar after several episodes of the ATV series it introduces every Sunday. However, Gary Miller's cover has found a higher placing!

■ Former members of Bill Haley's Comets, The Jodimars, are seeking to break through with 'Well Now Dig This'.

■ Capitol Records have re-signed Tennessee Ernie Ford for a further five years at maximum royalty.

CHARTS

US45	Memories Are Made Of This – *Dean Martin*
USLP	Oklahoma – *Soundtrack*
UK45	Rock Around The Clock – *Bill Haley & The Comets*
WEEK 2	
US45	Memories Are Made Of This – *Dean Martin*
USLP	Oklahoma – *Soundtrack*
UK45	Rock Around The Clock – *Bill Haley & The Comets*
WEEK 3	
US45	Memories Are Made Of This – *Dean Martin*
USLP	Oklahoma – *Soundtrack*
UK45	Sixteen Tons – *Tennessee Ernie Ford*
WEEK 4	
US45	Memories Are Made Of This – *Dean Martin*
USLP	Oklahoma – *Soundtrack*
UK45	Sixteen Tons – *Tennessee Ernie Ford*

NEW UK STARS FOR '56?

Tipped for the top is Cherry Wainer, the young Hammond organist who is being dubbed 'the female Liberace'. She has given her organ the 'Dior treatment' in that it's covered in quilted white leather with diamante studs to match. The 22 year old also has a complete wardrobe to tone in with her glamourized instrument.

Also thought to be going places fast this year are recent UK discoveries Ronnie Carroll, Edna Savage, Shirley Bassey, and former dance-band trombonist Don Lang, who could soon establish himself as top British rhythm singer.

IF YOU CAN'T BEAT 'EM . . .

The latest showbiz celebrity to climb aboard the rock'n'roll bandwagon is Kay Starr, whose 'Rock And Roll Waltz' has taken her high into the US best sellers.

Born on an Indian reservation in Oklahoma in 1922, Miss Starr sang with bands led by Joe Venuti, Bob Crosby, Glenn Miller and Charlie Barnet before hitting the jackpot with her 1952 million seller, 'Wheel of Fortune'.

BBC BANS FILM THEME

Having recently banned Gale Storm's recording of 'Teenage Prayer', because the title has 'religious connotations', the BBC has now banned the theme from Frank Sinatra's much acclaimed movie *The Man With The Golden Arm* – recorded by 'The Man With The Golden Trumpet', Eddie Calvert.

Despite the fact that this is an instrumental disc, a BBC spokesman says: 'The ban is due to its connection with a film about drugs.' Paradoxically, Billy May's version of the very same tune, cleverly retitled 'Main Theme', has been approved for transmission!

As readers may recall, Johnnie Ray's 1954 hit, 'Such A Night', was not allowed to be broadcast because of his grunts in the chorus, while Annie Ross was deemed unacceptable on 'I Want You To Be My Baby' because of the line 'come upstairs and have some loving'.

Whatever next? Will they be banning 'Who Killed Cock Robin', on the grounds that it deals with cold blooded murder? All we can say is 'Come on, auntie . . . get with it!'

FEBRUARY 1956

Masking his disbelief and fury with his customary polish and professionalism is trumpet star Eddie Calvert – banned by the BBC!

DONEGAN HANDS IN HIS BANJO, GOES SOLO

Lonnie – going it alone

The success of Lonnie Donegan's skiffle disc, 'Rock Island Line', has taken everybody by surprise – not least Lonnie himself!

Until this month, he was the banjo player in Chris Barber's trad-jazz band, and only picked up the guitar to sing a few blues songs during the skiffle intermission they incorporated into their set. But now Glasgow-born Lonnie has decided to strike out on his own, and form a permanent skiffle group for personal appearances and recording.

Within days of his disc entering the chart, the Nixa label offered the 24 year-old a solo contract, which he accepted. He cuts his first single for them shortly.

Meanwhile, 'Rock Island Line' – which Lonnie learned from a recording by the veteran blues singer Huddie 'Leadbelly' Ledbetter – is stirring up considerable interest in the States.

STAR QUOTE

ALAN FREED

'Rock'n'roll is really swing with a modern name. It began on the levees and plantations, took in folk songs, and features blues and rhythm. It's the rhythm that gets the kids – they're starved of music they can dance to, after all those years of crooners.'

Disc jockey Alan Freed

THE GRAPEVINE

■ Bounding up the charts with torrid instrumental, 'Zambesi', is Lou Busch – aka US pianist Joe 'Fingers' Carr.

■ Billy Cotton and Ronnie Ronalde have released versions of 'Happy Trails', the theme of ATV's weekly *Roy Rogers* series.

■ Without a British outlet, The Platters must watch cover versions of their songs climb the British chart: 'Only You' by The Hilltoppers, and 'The Great Pretender' by Jimmy Parkinson.

MARTIN STAKES HIS CLAIM!

In less than a year as manager of EMI's Parlophone label, George Martin has achieved quite a feat in steering three discs into the British Top 20 frame at the same time.

Dick James has hit the mark with 'Robin Hood', Eve Boswell has broken through with 'Pickin' A Chicken', and TV's *What's My Line?* anchorman Eamonn Andrews has scored a hit with his cover of 'The Shifting Whispering Sands'.

CHARTS

Chart	Title	Artist
UK45	Memories Are Made Of This	*Dean Martin*
USLP	Oklahoma	*Soundtrack*
US45	Sixteen Tons	*Tennessee Ernie Ford*
WEEK 2		
UK45	Memories Are Made Of This	*Dean Martin*
USLP	Oklahoma	*Soundtrack*
US45	Sixteen Tons	*Tennessee Ernie Ford*
WEEK 3		
US45	Rock And Roll Waltz	*Kay Starr*
USLP	Oklahoma	*Soundtrack*
UK45	Memories Are Made Of This	*Dean Martin*
WEEK 4		
US45	Rock And Roll Waltz	*Kay Starr*
USLP	Oklahoma	*Soundtrack*
UK45	Memories Are Made Of This	*Dean Martin*
WEEK 5		
US45	Rock And Roll Waltz	*Kay Starr*
USLP	Oklahoma	*Soundtrack*
UK45	Memories Are Made Of This	*Dean Martin*

PRESLEY AND PERKINS SET AMERICA ROCKING!

Almost fixtures in the US Top 20, Pat Boone (who is currently hot with 'Tutti Frutti') and Bill Haley (ditto with 'See You Later Alligator') have been joined by two new names.

The first is Elvis Presley, in whom RCA have invested heavily. Described as 'a wild and turbulent rock'n'roller', Presley has crashed the charts with his very first single for the label, 'Heartbreak Hotel'. Reactions to his brash new style have been mixed, but one thing's for sure: he's a solid hit with the American teenagers, especially those of the female persuasion.

He hails from Memphis, Tennessee and has been described as slinky and dark, rather like a junior Rock Hudson. He shakes, rattles and rolls a lot in his act, like a dry-eyed Johnnie Ray, but with twice the locomotion!

Before signing with RCA, Presley released five discs on Sun – the label which presents the second chart entrant, Carl Perkins. In the same mould as his former stablemate, 23 year-old Perkins is also from Tennessee. His hit is 'Blue Suede Shoes' – a number he wrote himself.

Whether they can repeat their success in Britain remains to be seen, but if the NME singles reviewer has any say in the matter, they won't! 'If this is singing, then I give up', he wrote when the Presley disc was released here last month. 'If this is the stuff American fans are demanding, I'm glad I'm on this side of the Atlantic!'

Above: Presley – slinky and dark, like a junior Rock Hudson

Sun star Carl Perkins

WEAVERS' HIT RECORD IS NO DREAM

Overnight success stories are rare in the music business, but if you want to hear about a fairy tale rise to fame, take the case of The Dream Weavers and their million selling debut, 'It's Almost Tomorrow'.

Two talented young Florida University students get together and write a couple of songs. They team up with five others and make a private recording in Jacksonville. A local disc jockey plays it for a record company pal, who arranges for it to be released, and . . . snap! The record takes off and becomes a hit – not only in the States, but in Britain too, where it has now climbed all the way to the top of the charts!

THE GRAPEVINE

- **The Crew Cuts have been signed by American brewers Annhauser Busch, to appear in TV commercials for their products.**
- **Stan Kenton and his Orchestra have arrived in England for a full tour – the first US band to do so since the thirties.**
- **The *Rock Around The Clock* movie had its world premiere in Washington, DC on March 17.**

OKLAHOMA SURRENDERS TO HARRY

After twelve weeks, the *Oklahoma* movie soundtrack album has finally been ousted from the top spot on the US best sellers list. That position is now occupied by 'Belafonte', the long-player by Harlem-born folk balladeer, Harry Belafonte.

CHARTS

US45	The Poor People Of Paris *Les Baxter*
USLP	Oklahoma *Soundtrack*
UK45	Memories Are Made Of This *Dean Martin*
WEEK 2	
US45	Rock And Roll Waltz *Kay Starr*
USLP	Belafonte *Harry Belafonte*
UK45	It's Almost Tomorrow *Dream Weavers*
WEEK 3	
US45	The Poor People Of Paris *Les Baxter*
USLP	Belafonte *Harry Belafonte*
UK45	It's Almost Tomorrow *Dream Weavers*
WEEK 4	
US45	The Poor People Of Paris *Les Baxter*
USLP	Belafonte *Harry Belafonte*
UK45	Rock And Roll Waltz *Kay Starr*

NAT 'KING' COLE ATTACKED AT ALABAMA CONCERT

In America's Deep South, where racial segregation is still strictly enforced, the shared billing by black singer Nat 'King' Cole and Britain's all-white Ted Heath Orchestra has resulted in a vicious attack on the American artist.

During a concert in Birmingham, Alabama, six men stormed the stage and attacked Cole during his second number. The singer was knocked down and dragged into the auditorium, but serious injury was prevented by police, who rushed to his rescue.

Cole's assailants were arrested, but showed no remorse. At least one was connected with the White Citizens Council, a group which has been endeavouring to boycott what they call 'bop and negro music'. The audience – numbering over 3,000 – was all white.

Said Cole: 'I was a guinea-pig for some hoodlums who thought they could frighten me, and in that way keep other Negro entertainers from the South . . . but I think the attack will do a lot for the cause of integration.'

A WORLDWIDE HIT, BUT RAIL LINE FAILS TO MAKE PROFIT

As his 'Rock Island Line' leads him directly into the American Top 10, Lonnie Donegan has been counting the money he could have made. Normally, a recording artist would earn a royalty based on sales – which from a universal hit like this could amount to several thousand pounds.

But Lonnie was a member of Chris Barber's band when he recorded the song, and received a flat session fee of less than ten pounds!

Nevertheless, the disc has made him an overnight star on both sides of the Atlantic, and should be the foundation for a solid solo career. Under his new contract with Nixa, he will be receiving a royalty – which is good news, as his latest release, 'Lost John', is currently zipping up the British chart!

FREED FOR 208 SERIES

Noted American disc jockey Alan Freed – the man who coined the term 'rock'n'roll' – is to be featured in a new Radio Luxembourg series. Called *Jamboree*, the show will be transmitted for two hours every Saturday from Europe to the U.K.

If the series meets with a big response, Freed plans to bring a complete rock'n'roll package show to Britain this Autumn.

Chart-topping Winifred Atwell

CHARTS

US45	The Poor People Of Paris – *Les Baxter*
USLP	Belafonte – *Harry Belafonte*
UK45	It's Almost Tomorrow – *Dream Weavers*
WEEK 2	
US45	The Poor People Of Paris – *Les Baxter*
USLP	Belafonte – *Harry Belafonte*
UK45	The Poor People Of Paris – *Winifred Atwell*
WEEK 3	
US45	The Poor People Of Paris – *Lex Baxter*
USLP	Belafonte – *Harry Belafonte*
UK45	The Poor People Of Paris – *Winifred Atwell*
WEEK 4	
US45	Heartbreak Hotel – *Elvis Presley*
USLP	Elvis Presley – *Elvis Presley*
UK45	The Poor People Of Paris – *Winifred Atwell*

Hollywood dreams for Elvis

THE GRAPEVINE

- **Elvis Presley, the hottest new property in the music business, has signed a film contract with Paramount. Currently, sales of his records are accounting for 50% of RCA's total pop business!**
- **Top record on America's R&B chart is 'Long Tall Sally' by Little Richard, whose last disc, 'Tutti Frutti', was turned into a big pop hit by Pat Boone. Will Boone try again?**

At full cry . . . Little Richard

LAWSUIT HALTS WALTZ

She may have a million seller, but Kay Starr is one of the defendants in a lawsuit alleging that 'Rock And Roll Waltz' has violated the copyright of a 1920 number, 'Sweet Man O' Mine'.

The latter's composer claims that his music was lifted by the writers of Miss Starr's hit.

MAY

ARCHBISHOP OF CANTERBURY DECLINES TO INTERCEDE

American singing star Don Cornell has appealed to the Archbishop of Canterbury to give official approval to the current religious trend in popular songs. In a letter, Cornell explained that his recordings of 'Hold My Hand' and 'The Bible Tells Me So' had both been banned by the BBC, whereas religious bodies in America had wholeheartedly approved of such music

In his reply, the Archbishop wrote: 'Let me say that I do not in any way doubt your sincerity. However, I do not for a moment suppose that the BBC ban has been imposed on any religious ground, but rather on general grounds of taste. In this respect, we differ in many ways from the United States, and there is a general unwillingness to have religious subjects loudspeakered into restaurants and milk bars.

'I have not played your records, but I must say that the words of this song ('The Bible Tells Me So'), in my judgement, would hardly accord with taste in this country.'

Comedian Stan Freberg got his start adding voices to Walt Disney cartoons. Now he's building a reputation for mocking rock 'n' roll hits

CHARTS

US45	Heartbreak Hotel *Elvis Presley*
USLP	Elvis Presley *Elvis Presley*
UK45	No Other Love *Ronnie Hilton*
WEEK 2	
US45	Hot Diggity *Perry Como*
USLP	Elvis Presley *Elvis Presley*
UK45	No Other Love *Ronnie Hilton*
WEEK 3	
US45	Heartbreak Hotel *Elvis Presley*
USLP	Elvis Presley *Elvis Presley*
UK45	No Other Love *Ronnie Hilton*
WEEK 4	
US45	Heartbreak Hotel *Elvis Presley*
USLP	Elvis Presley *Elvis Presley*
UK45	No Other Love *Ronnie Hilton*
WEEK 5	
US45	Heartbreak Hotel *Elvis Presley*
USLP	Elvis Presley *Elvis Presley*
UK45	No Other Love *Ronnie Hilton*

THE GRAPEVINE

- **Stan Freberg, who parodied 'Sh-'Boom' last year, is now having a go at 'The Great Pretender'. Meanwhile, English comic Max Bygraves has issued a disc called 'Seventeen Tons'!**
- **The Fosters Agency is negotiating for Elvis Presley to visit Britain for TV and concert dates.**
- **Lonnie Donegan has flown to New York for an appearance on Perry Como's TV show.**

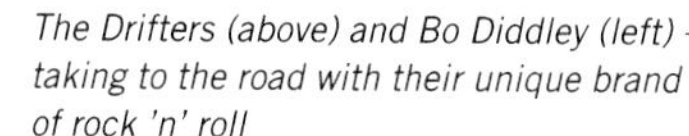

The Drifters (above) and Bo Diddley (left) – taking to the road with their unique brand of rock 'n' roll

ROCK'N'ROLL EXTRAVAGANZA HITS THE ROAD

Rock'n'roll is certainly going places in the States! Currently on a 45-date tour is 'The Biggest Rock'n'Roll Show of 1956' – and it sounds like quite a show!

Headlined by Bill Haley & His Comets, the package also includes Clyde McPhatter, LaVern Baker, Bo Diddley, Big Joe Turner, The Teenagers, The Teen Queens, The Drifters and Red Prysock's Orchestra.

Questioned about the recent attack on Nat 'King' Cole, Haley – whose band is the only white act on the bill – told reporters that he would not appear before segregated audiences.

THE WORLD'S FIRST CIRCULAR OFFICE BLOCK!

EMI executives have flown to Los Angeles for the opening of their Capitol Records building, a 13-storey edifice designed to represent a stack of records.

Capitol are hoping to break into the rock'n'roll market with their latest signing, Gene Vincent. Not long out of the US Navy, the 21-year-old has recently cut his first sides in Nashville – some 2500 miles from the label's head office!

IT'S ONE FOR THE MONEY; TWO FOR THE SHOW . . .

An interesting story lies behind 'Blue Suede Shoes' – currently in the charts, courtesy of Elvis Presley and composer Carl Perkins.

One night, Carl was playing at a dance when he heard a young fellow make a remark to his dancing partner as they shuffled past the rostrum. 'Don't step on my blue suede shoes!' he exclaimed. Carl made a mental note of the phrase, thinking it might come in handy one day!

MR. DYNAMITE! THAT'S ELVIS THE PELVIS

'In a pivoting stance, his hips swing sensuously from side to side and his entire body takes on a frantic quiver, as if he had swallowed a jackhammer. His movements suggest, in a word, sex.'

The American press continues to wage war on Elvis Presley because of his suggestive gyrations while singing. They even criticized his appearance on the Milton Berle TV show – although his guest spot resulted in the show's highest audience rating this year.

Said an Oakland, California cop about Presley's recent stage antics in that city: 'If he did it in the street, we'd arrest him!'

His album, entitled 'Elvis Presley', has sold more than 300,000 copies – about three times the total of RCA's previous top LPs by Mario Lanza and Glenn Miller. Meanwhile an old song, 'I Forgot To Remember To Forget', cut for Memphis-based Sun label last year, has figured on Billboard's country-and-western chart for the tremendous total of 39 consecutive weeks!

Both titles on his new double-sided hit single, 'I Want You, I Need You, I Love You'/'My Baby Left Me', are controlled by his own, newly opened publishing company – so the lad obviously has a head for business too.

Though a resident of Tennessee, the 21 year old was born in Tupelo, Mississippi. And, yes – Elvis Presley is his real name!

The Teenagers vocal group, featuring the sensational Frankie Lymon (centre)

BILL HALEY TO TOUR BRITAIN IN '57

In deep water in the deep South, Bill Haley should fare better in Britain

As his recording of 'The Saints Rock'n'Roll' bounces around the UK Top 10, Bill Haley has confirmed that he and his Comets will be touring Britain early next year. Meanwhile, the band has a new US release: 'Hot Dog Buddy Buddy'/'Rockin' Through The Rye'.

Lately, it hasn't all been smooth sailing for the boys. Outside a concert in Alabama, pickets held up placards reading 'Christians Will Not Attend This Show' and 'Ask Your Preacher About Jungle Music'.

Speaking for The Alabama White Citizens Council, Asa Carter is quoted as saying: 'Rock'n'roll is a means of pulling down the white man to the level of the negro. It is part of a plot to undermine the morals of the youth of our nation.'

Haley encountered more opposition in Florida, where the Miami Board of Review condemned his music after it inspired fans to leave their seats and dance in the aisles.

CHARTS

US45	Heartbreak Hotel *Elvis Presley*
USLP	Elvis Presley *Elvis Presley*
UK45	No Other Love *Ronnie Hilton*
WEEK 2	
US45	Wayward Wind *Gogi Grant*
USLP	Elvis Presley *Elvis Presley*
UK45	I'll Be Home *Pat Boone*
WEEK 3	
US45	Wayward Wind *Gogi Grant*
USLP	Elvis Presley *Elvis Presley*
UK45	I'll Be Home *Pat Boone*
WEEK 4	
US45	Wayward Wind *Gogi Grant*
USLP	Elvis Presley *Elvis Presley*
UK45	I'll Be Home *Pat Boone*

THE GRAPEVINE

- **Last year, Ruby Murray had seven UK top ten hits. So far this year, she hasn't managed one!**
- **It's been reported from Las Vegas that in one night, Johnnie Ray lost his entire four weeks salary at the gambling tables.**
- **Is 13 year-old Teenager, Frankie Lymon, lead singer on 'Why Do Fools Fall In Love', the first 'war baby' to reach the best sellers?**

LONNIE DONEGAN

I'm trying to sing acceptable folk music. I want to widen the audience beyond the artsy-craftsy crowd and the pseudo intellectuals – but without distorting the music itself.

Lonnie Donegan with Beryl Bryden

TEENAGER'S POEM BECOMES A MILLION SELLER!

One day last year, an English teacher at a New York High School set his class the task of writing a poem. Among those handed in was one entitled 'Why Do Fools Fall In Love?' – the work of 13 year-old black pupil Frankie Lymon.

The teacher, none too pleased at the boy's apparent precocity, marked the poem and handed it back. He thought he'd heard the last of it . . . but within a few months, all America was familiar with it!

Lymon had just joined four neighbourhood friends in forming a vocal group – called, logically, The Teenagers – and they were experimenting with a musical version of the poem when George Goldner, the head of Gee Records, happened to hear them. He couldn't get them into the studio fast enough, and 'Why Do Fools Fall In Love' became their first disc.

Within weeks of its release in January, it became a hot seller in the States and now it has steadily climbed to the top of the best sellers in Britain.

Frankie and his pals plan to fly in and meet their British fans – just as soon as they can get time off from school!

CHARTS

US45	Wayward Wind *Gogi Grant*
USLP	My Fair Lady *Original Cast*
UK45	I'll Be Home *Pat Boone*
WEEK 2	
US45	Wayward Wind *Gogi Grant*
USLP	My Fair Lady *Original Cast*
UK45	I'll Be Home *Pat Boone*
WEEK 3	
US45	I Want You, I Need You, I Love You *Elvis Presley*
USLP	My Fair Lady *Original Cast*
UK45	Why Do Fools Fall In Love? *Teenagers*
WEEK 4	
US45	My Prayer *Platters*
USLP	My Fair Lady *Original Cast*
UK45	Why Do Fools Fall In Love? *Teenagers*

LOOK OUT ELVIS, HERE COMES GENE!

With his debut disc, 'Be Bop-A-Lula', zooming towards the Top 10, latest Stateside sensation Gene Vincent – tagged as 'the Screaming End' – has been hailed as Elvis Presley's most serious rival. However, the NME singles reviewer does not concur! He has branded it a 'junior idiot chant . . . strictly from the booby hatch'.

If nothing else, rock'n'roll is certainly creating a huge rift between those who like it and those who don't!

THE GRAPEVINE

- After breaking all box-office records during its first European run in Dublin, the *Rock Around The Clock* movie premiered in London on July 20.
- No matter where he's appearing in America, Elvis Presley telephones his mother in Memphis every afternoon at 3 pm.
- Is Britain heading for a jazz boom? Currently in the best sellers: 'Experiments With Mice' (Johnny Dankworth) and 'Bad Penny Blues' (Humphrey Lyttelton).

CROSBY OPTIMISTIC ABOUT ROCK'N'ROLL'S DEMISE

In a recent column, John Crosby, the most influential of America's TV and radio journalists, echoed the anxiety of many in the popular music mainstream.

Referring to Elvis Presley as an 'unspeakably untalented and vulgar young entertainer', Crosby hoped that this aberration might herald 'the end of rock'n'roll and a return to musical sanity.

'I mean,' he continued, 'where do you go from Elvis Presley, short of open obscenity, which is against the law?'

'Popular music has been in a tailspin for years now, and I have hopes that with Presley it has touched bottom and will just have to start getting better.'

Earlier, in the month Elvis appeared on the Steve Allen Show on which he was instructed by his host *not* to dance while singing 'Hound Dog'.

Since forming his band in 1948, Old Etonian and former Guards officer Humphrey Lyttelton has been popularising the traditional jazz of New Orleans in specialist clubs around London – including his own at 100 Oxford Street.

ELVIS CONTROVERSY RAGES ON

In America, where his latest disc, 'Hound Dog', sold over a million copies within days of release, Elvis Presley has been scheduled to star in his first movie. Called *Love Me Tender*, it's a western musical based on Margaret Thompson's book, *The Lonesome Cowboy*.

Presley has also signed a unique merchandising deal, where he will endorse products designed for the teenage market – such as jeans, T-shirts and charm bracelets.

Meanwhile, in Britain, journalists seem anxious to duplicate the over-emotional rantings of their transatlantic counterparts.

'I know that this man is dangerous, and I don't want to see British youngsters hacking out his name on their arms with clasp-knives, or see sex treated as an appalling commercial freak-show,' raved one.

'Neither Sinatra nor Crosby have to rely on a tom-cat's caterwauling to achieve their vocal effects,' proclaimed another, 'and their fans are not unhealthily stimulated to morbid hysteria.'

The debate continues!

FLYING SAUCER IS LATEST GIMMICK HIT

The biggest record industry furore in a long time has been caused by the fantastically selling disc 'Flying Saucer', an independent production by Bill Buchanan and Dick Goodman on the Luniverse label. Currently in the American Top 5, this hilarious record contains exerpts of some 15 recent hits.

Luniverse have paid no royalties to the song publishers or record companies whose products they have 'borrowed'. All kinds of legal actions are being threatened, but meanwhile, Buchanan and Goodman are laughing all the way to the bank!

CHARTS

US45	My Prayer	*Platters*
USLP	My Fair Lady	*Original Cast*
UK45	Why Do Fools Fall In Love?	*Teenagers*
WEEK 2		
US45	Hound Dog/Don't Be Cruel	*Elvis Presley*
USLP	My Fair Lady	*Original Cast*
UK45	Whatever Will Be, Will Be	*Doris Day*
WEEK 3		
US45	Hound Dog/Don't Be Cruel	*Elvis Presley*
USLP	My Fair Lady	*Original Cast*
UK45	Whatever Will Be, Will Be	*Doris Day*
WEEK 4		
US45	Hound Dog/Don't Be Cruel	*Elvis Presley*
USLP	My Fair Lady	*Original Cast*
UK45	Whatever Will Be, Will Be	*Doris Day*
WEEK 5		
US45	Hound Dog/Don't Be Cruel	*Elvis Presley*
USLP	Calypso	*Harry Belafonte*
UK45	Whatever Will Be, Will Be	*Doris Day*

THE GRAPEVINE

- **After a successful 10 weeks in America, Lonnie Donegan has bought a Daimler and formed a new group.**
- **It's reported that Pat Boone has more fan clubs in America than any other singing star.**
- **Bill Haley's first LP record has been released in Britain. Even Billy Eckstine's got in on the act: his latest waxing is 'Condemned For Life With A Rock And Roll Wife'!**

Buchanan and Goodman: splicing snippets of others' hits

Pat Boone: fan club inspiration

ROCK'N'ROLL IN BRITAIN GATHERS MOMENTUM

To the horror of London's jazz community, former Ronnie Scott drummer Tony Crombie has forsaken be-bop to launch a rock'n-'roll band. Called Tony Crombie's Rockets, they start a nationwide tour of one night stands at the end of the month.

Tony plans a spectacular visual presentation to supplement the unit's musical stylings – including a team to demonstrate dance steps.

Crombie has also become the first British rocker to win a recording contract – EMI Columbia's Norrie Paramor snapped him up – but he's not alone in his conversion. Several other London-based rock'n'roll groups have sprung up over the last few months, including Rory Blackwell's Rock'n'Rollers, who will play at Studio 51's twice-weekly rock'n'roll nights, commencing September 6.

THE CLUB'S GOING TRAD, DAD!

London's oldest established modern jazz centre, the Studio 51 Club in Great Newport Street, is closing its doors to faithful supporters this month.

A change of policy will be reflected when, after a three week period of refurbishing, it reopens as a venue for traditional jazz and rock'n'roll.

Taking time out from rehearsals – Lonnie Donegan

CHARTS CHOCK-A-BLOCK WITH ROCK

During the past year, rock'n'roll and teen-slanted music has penetrated deep into the popular music mainstream.

This month, Britain's Top 30 listing contains records by The Platters, The Teenagers, Freddie Bell & The Bellboys, Fats Domino, Gene Vincent, Lonnie Donegan (one each), two by Pat Boone, three by Elvis Presley and a remarkable five by Bill Haley & His Comets. All Haley's discs are in the top twenty – equalling British singer Ruby Murray's achievement last year.

When he visits Britain next February, Haley will have to answer potentially embarrassing questions about the film *Rock Around The Clock*, which has been at the centre of highly publicised youth riots and cinema smashing in the UK.

The film has been banned in some cities and heavily criticized by senior police officers and councillors in others.

Bill Haley with sax-man Rudy Pompilli

SHIPWRECKED SONGWRITER COUNTS HIS LUCKY STARS

Elvis Presley's 'Hound Dog' is no new breed. Its pedigree stretches back to 1953, when it became a R&B chart topper in the hands of Alabama blues singer, Big Mama Thornton.

That record was the first major success for the young songwriting/producing team of Leiber and Stoller – although Elvis picked up the song when he played Las Vegas, earlier this year. Freddie Bell & The Bellboys, currently on view in *Rock Around The Clock*, were featuring it in their night club act, and Elvis took a fancy to it.

He performed it on Steve Allen's TV show in early July and went straight into RCA's New York studio to record it the next day. Only after the 28th take was everybody happy!

Willie Mae "Big Mama" Thornton

Freddie Bell & the Bellboys

Mike Stoller was fortunate to hear the results at all. He was returning from Europe on the 'Andrea Doria' when the liner collided with another vessel. Fifty people were lost, but Stoller escaped by lifeboat and eventually reached New York – where Jerry Leiber greeted him with the news that Presley's next single was going to be their song!

BELAFONTE INTRODUCES CALYPSO STYLE

Harry Belafonte has reached the top of the US album charts for the second time this year. On 'Calypso', New York-born Belafonte has chosen to record a selection of Caribbean songs, including 'Jamaica Farewell' and 'The Banana Boat Song'.

Pundits are speculating that calypso music could well become the next trend when the rock'n'roll craze fades.

- **Now the Mercury label has a UK outlet, The Platters have finally found their way into the British best sellers – with a coupling of 'Only You'/'The Great Pretender'.**
- **Tremendous British interest has developed in the weekly rock'n'roll programme, *Jamboree*, presented on Radio Luxembourg by American disc-jockey Alan Freed.**
- **Decca UK are bubbling with enthusiasm about their first rock'n'roll signing, Tommy Steele.**

CHARTS

US45	Don't Be Cruel – *Elvis Presley*
USLP	Calypso – *Harry Belafonte*
UK45	Whatever Will Be, Will Be – *Doris Day*
WEEK 2	
US45	Don't Be Cruel – *Elvis Presley*
USLP	Calypso – *Harry Belafonte*
UK45	Whatever Will Be, Will Be – *Doris Day*
WEEK 3	
US45	Don't Be Cruel – *Elvis Presley*
USLP	Calypso – *Harry Belafonte*
UK45	Lay Down Your Arms – *Anne Shelton*
WEEK 4	
US45	Don't Be Cruel – *Elvis Presley*
USLP	The King & I – *Original Cast*
UK45	Lay Down Your Arms – *Anne Shelton*

ELVIS PRESLEY

'I'm afraid to wake up each morning. Everything is going so fine for me that I can't believe it's not a dream. I just hope it lasts.'

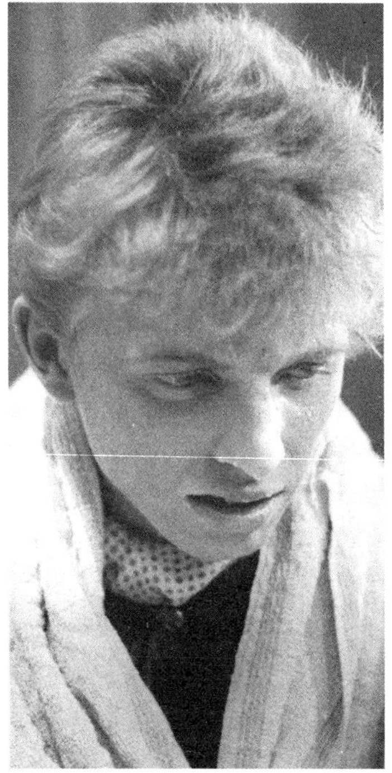

Tommy Steele

MUSIC HALL'S GOLDEN CROCK

Britain's current obsession with rock'n'roll has led to a spate of new bands performing in that style. Among those now attracting attention are Dave Shand & His Rockin' Rhythm, Bobby Breen & His Rockin' Rock'n' Rollers, and Art Baxter & His Rocking Sinners.

Journalist Benny Green was dispatched to witness a show by Baxter, with whom he formerly shared the spotlight in Ronnie Scott's jazz band. 'After years of tawdry revues, music hall has stumbled on a crock of gold,' he writes. 'A small crock admittedly, for in a year or two rock'n-'roll will be as *passé* as Clara Bow'.

'To ask a grown-up musician to discuss such music is like asking an epicure to compose a sonnet about bread and water. The new musical rash is so devoid of aesthetic content that there is nothing left to say except that it is a silly noise, and leave it at that.'

However, Green was moved to admit that he was in a distinct minority: 'If audience reaction is the criterion, then Baxter is one of variety's all time greats!'

ROCK'N'ROLL GETS MEDICAL BACKING

Interviewed on Radio WNEW in New York, psychologist Dr Ben Walstein expressed the view that 'there is nothing particularly harmful about rock'n'roll'. He went on to explain that 'in every generation, adolescents find a style of music that expresses some of the yearning, the frustrations, and the frantic searching quality that young people have – and I don't see why we should try to ban it or interefere with their enjoyment of it.'

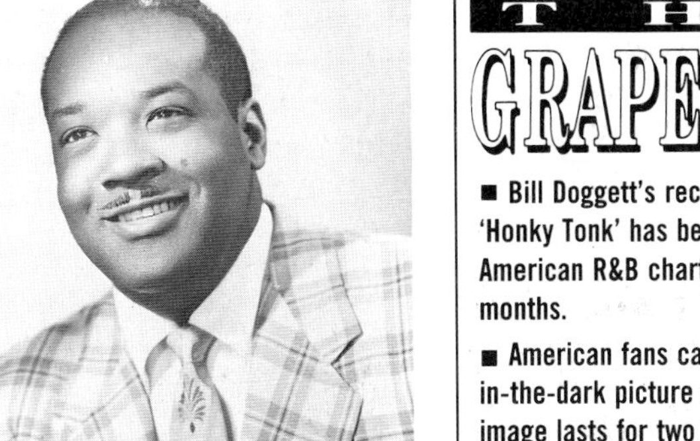

Philadelphia organist Bill Doggett scores with a double-sided instrumental hit

MORE CELLULOID ROCK . . . DON'T KNOCK IT!

The cinematic launching pad for the current rock'n'roll craze, 'Rock Around the Clock' with Bill Haley and His Comets has been causing movie theatre mayhem worldwide, with a line-up of musical cameos that also includes The Platters, and Freddy Bell and the Bellboys.

In relation to its cost – 450,000 dollars – the sensational film *Rock Around The Clock* is certain to become one of Columbia's biggest money-makers.

The studio are so happy with the outcome that producer Sam Katzman has already begun lining up talent for a follow-up – probably titled *Don't Knock The Rock*.

On a budget of 600,000 dollars, the film will be shot in fourteen days and rushed into general release.

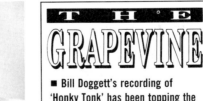

THE GRAPEVINE

- **Bill Doggett's recording of 'Honky Tonk' has been topping the American R&B chart for over two months.**
- **American fans can buy a glow-in-the-dark picture of Elvis, whose image lasts for two hours after the lights have been turned off!**
- **Johnnie Ray's latest hit, 'Just Walkin' In The Rain', was written by a convict and originally recorded by The Prisonaires!**

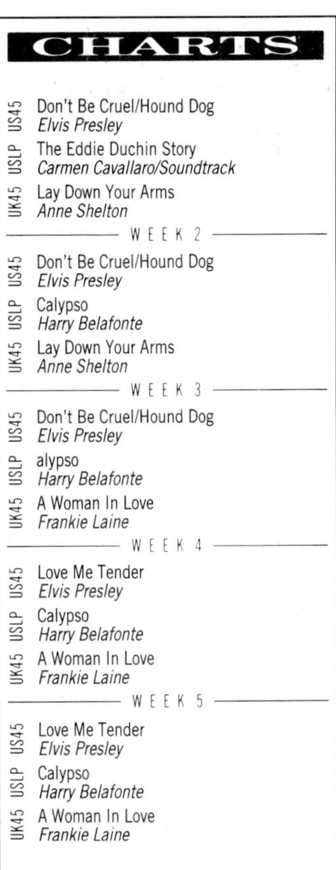

CHARTS

US45 Don't Be Cruel/Hound Dog – *Elvis Presley*
USLP The Eddie Duchin Story – *Carmen Cavallaro/Soundtrack*
UK45 Lay Down Your Arms – *Anne Shelton*

WEEK 2

US45 Don't Be Cruel/Hound Dog – *Elvis Presley*
USLP Calypso – *Harry Belafonte*
UK45 Lay Down Your Arms – *Anne Shelton*

WEEK 3

US45 Don't Be Cruel/Hound Dog – *Elvis Presley*
USLP alypso – *Harry Belafonte*
UK45 A Woman In Love – *Frankie Laine*

WEEK 4

US45 Love Me Tender – *Elvis Presley*
USLP Calypso – *Harry Belafonte*
UK45 A Woman In Love – *Frankie Laine*

WEEK 5

US45 Love Me Tender – *Elvis Presley*
USLP Calypso – *Harry Belafonte*
UK45 A Woman In Love – *Frankie Laine*

ONE MILLION DISCS ORDERED PRIOR TO RELEASE!

Elvis Presley has made recording history. When he appeared on Ed Sullivan's television show, he introduced the title song from his forthcoming film, *Love Me Tender*.

At the time, this composition had not been recorded, but from every part of America, RCA were besieged with fantastic orders which reached the phenomenal figure of one million!

Accordingly, for the first time ever, an artist has attained a Golden Record before the disc is on sale.

LITTLE RICHARD WITH THE BIG HAIR-DO

British fans will finally be able to hear one of America's most explosive young rock'n'rollers, Little Richard – recently described as 'a man with a hair-do as high as the rest of his body'!

His US label, Specialty, has entered a deal with Decca's London subsidiary to issue his records here – beginning with 'Rip It Up', which topped the R&B chart this summer. Previous Richard discs, 'Tutti Frutti' and 'Long Tall Sally', were covered by Pat Boone, who stole much of the black singer's thunder – and it looks as if Bill Haley's version of 'Rip It Up' may also outsell the original in Britain.

However, Little Richard's dynamic, exciting act will soon be on view in two new films, *Don't Knock The Rock* and *The Girl Can't Help It* – and pundits predict that these will be his keys to world stardom.

Prince of the pompadour Little Richard

TOMMY – BRITAIN'S FIRST ROCK'N'ROLL STAR

Since his debut in October, 19-year-old South London rock'n'roll specialist Tommy Steele has been releasing singles at a rate of one every three weeks! First came 'Rock With The Caveman', then 'Doomsday Rock', and now he's taking on Guy Mitchell by covering his US top tenner, 'Singing The Blues'.

Steele has taken off like a rocket, making his mark on the television shows of both Jack Payne and Jack Jackson before embarking on a nationwide variety tour.

Squeals, whoops, yells and moans of ecstasy greeted his opening night at the Sunderland Empire. The mere announcement 'and here he is – Tommy Steele' brought a crescendo of screams from the girls of the city's shops and factories.

Wearing drain-pipe trousers and checked shirt, the tousle-haired teenager hip-swivelled around the microphone, strumming his electric guitar to the accompaniment of a rock'n'roll quartet billed as The Steelmen.

An unusually subdued audience for rock'n'roll star Tommy Steele

THE GRAPEVINE

- At the premiere of *Love Me Tender*, a 40-ft likeness of Elvis towered above the Paramount Theatre in Times Square.
- After five British acts rushed to cover Jim Lowe's 'Green Door', a similar stampede is expected for Joe Valino's US chart entry, 'Garden Of Eden'.
- A British skiffle boom is gathering momentum; latest acts to sign recording contracts – The Chas McDevitt Group and The Vipers.

CHARTS

US45	Love Me Tender *Elvis Presley*
USLP	Calypso *Harry Belafonte*
UK45	A Woman In Love *Frankie Laine*
WEEK 2	
US45	Love Me Tender *Elvis Presley*
USLP	Calypso *Harry Belafonte*
UK45	Just Walkin' In The Rain *Johnnie Ray*
WEEK 3	
US45	Love Me Tender *Elvis Presley*
USLP	Calypso *Harry Belafonte*
UK45	Just Walkin' In The Rain *Johnnie Ray*
WEEK 4	
US45	Singing The Blues *Guy Mitchell*
USLP	Elvis *Elvis Presley*
UK45	Just Walkin' In The Rain *Johnnie Ray*

OLDIES TURN GOLDEN

Recorded as an album track, 'My Prayer' proved so popular that The Platters issued it as a single – which is now in the UK Top Five after selling two million copies in America. However, the song is no recent concoction: Britain's Jimmy Kennedy wrote the lyric and adapted the melody from a Continental hit, *Avant de Mourir*, as long ago as 1939.

But even 'My Prayer' is not the oldest song in the best-sellers. 'Tonight You Belong To Me', the debut hit by the youthful Patience And Prudence – 11 and 14-years old respectively – predates it by 13 years!

The Platters – a US & UK hit

HALEY AND PRESLEY TOP MUSIC POLLS

In the annual NME readers' poll, Bill Haley has been voted The World's Outstanding Musical Personality, drawing almost twice as many votes as his nearest rival, Elvis Presley. Dickie Valentine came third, but topped both the Outstanding British Musical Personality and Outstanding British Male Singer categories. Heading the Outstanding British Female Singer list was Alma Cogan.

Meanwhile, Elvis Presley was a clear winner in the eleventh annual *Cash Box* American juke box operators' poll. As well as beating Perry Como and Pat Boone in the Best Vocalist section, his waxing of 'Don't Be Cruel' – a B-side! – was voted the year's Best Record. Doris Day was the most popular Female Vocalist and Bill Haley won the Small Instrumental Group honours. Top C&W Record was 'Crazy Arms' by Ray Price, and top R&B Record was 'Fever' by Little Willie John.

Cash Box pollwinners: Little Willie John (far left) and Ray Price

MITCH GIVES ROCK'N'ROLL A LATIN TWIST

The British teenagers who save their threepenny pieces for coffee bar juke boxes were pretty keen on a disc called 'Caribbean' about four months ago – and, although it narrowly missed entering the hit parade, it at least built up quite a fan following for composer-singer Mitchell Torok.

An eager public awaited the release of his next disc, and as soon as 'When Mexico Gave Up The Rumba' was issued, it bounced quickly into the Top 10. As a result, the rocking Mr Torok has been lined up for a lengthy British tour early next year.

In Britain, the 27-year-old from Texas has been hailed as one of the year's stars – but, strangely, he has yet to score a hit in his own country!

BASKETBALL HEROES COURT LONNIE!

Rarely does a long player penetrate the UK Top 30 best sellers list, but 'Lonnie Donegan's Showcase' has done just that. Although Frank Sinatra and Bill Haley have recently charted with albums, Donegan has attained the unique distinction of being the first Briton to do so.

Hard-working Lonnie expects to return to the States for another stint very soon, this time accompanied by his Skiffle Group – the reciprocal unit for British appearances being Bill Haley & His Comets.

Among plans under discussion is a tour where Lonnie would become an added attraction on a coast-to-coast tour by the legendary Harlem Globetrotters basketball team!

STAR QUOTE

PAT BOONE

'I have no special or extraordinary talent; it's just that I've had the right breaks at the right time.'

Modest self-analysis from Pat Boone

THE GRAPEVINE

■ Currently making yet another deep impression with his latest release, 'Friendly Persuasion', Pat Boone flew into Britain for a seven-date lightning tour.

■ Opening in London this month are *Love Me Tender*, starring you-know-who!, and *Shake Rattle And Rock*, starring Fats Domino and Joe Turner.

■ Visiting Britain, jazz trumpeter Louis Armstrong described rock'n'roll as 'cold soup warmed up'!

CHARTS

US45	Singing The Blues *Guy Mitchell*
USLP	Elvis *Elvis Presley*
UK45	Just Walkin' In The Rain *Jonnie Ray*
WEEK 2	
US45	Singing The Blues *Guy Mitchell*
USLP	Elvis *Elvis Presley*
UK45	Just Walkin' In The Rain *Johnnie Ray*
WEEK 3	
US45	Singing The Blues *Guy Mitchell*
USLP	Elvis *Elvis Presley*
UK45	Just Walkin' In The Rain *Johnnie Ray*
WEEK 4	
US45	Singing The Blues *Guy Mitchell*
USLP	Elvis *Elvis Presley*
UK45	Just Walkin' In The Rain *Johnnie Ray*

The first – 'Rock Around The Clock'

Début for Elvis – 'Love Me Tender'

ROCK AT THE MOVIES

It is difficult to know whether the fact that there have now been hundreds of movies based – often almost invisibly – on popular music is a good thing. Almost immediately after 'Rock Around The Clock' was a big hit in 1955, Bill Haley starred in an identically titled movie, which also featured The Platters, Freddie Bell & The Bellboys and the original rock DJ, Alan Freed. It featured loads of music, the vast majority of which was accompanied by pictures of an act performing (often in a night club), but while its plot might be said to have been original, it became the blueprint for innumerable subsequent exploitation movies (as they are known, since they are capitalising on an act's often shortlived popularity). This is how it goes: happy family is split asunder by new pop music craze, which kids like, parents hate and the church calls devilish. Kids disobey parents in pursuit of this new craze, parents call new craze worthless. Visiting rock star prevents church burning down by raising the alarm, parents impressed that rock star – and thus rock'n'roll – is really OK. Roll the credits!

The other stereotype was the Elvis Presley movie. Over 30 of them, mostly in the 1960s, about 10% watchable – at the end, they didn't even have much good music. Most of the time, Elvis got the girl after the scriptwriter tried unsuccessfully to make the ending a surprise, although the early Elvis films like *Love Me Tender, Loving You* and *Jailhouse Rock* had some great songs. Eventually, even Presley is said to have got bored with making them, despite the King's ransom he was paid every time.

Still, in the opinion of many, the best rock'n'roll movie ever, *The Girl Can't Help It* broke the predictable mould. Starring real actors like Tom Ewell and Edmond O'Brien plus the latest pneumatic blonde sensation, Jayne Mansfield, with at least the

The classic 'The Girl Can't Help It'

'Mrs. Brown You've Got a Lovely Daughter' with Herman's Hermits

'Jailhouse Rock'

More Elvis – 'Loving You'

semblance of a plot, and featuring Little Richard, Fats Domino, The Platters, Eddie Cochran, Gene Vincent plus others (and Julie London's 'Cry Me A River' for a touch of class), it wouldn't be too bad a film even without the music.

Nothing too significant would subsequently arise from of the unsteady alliance between rock and the movies until The Beatles made a couple of great movies before they lost interest. Because although *A Hard Day's Night* and *Help!* were very worthwhile vehicles, the reasons for their existence were still the same as with the early rock movies – cashing in on a hit while the act's still popular.

During the second half of the 1950s, literally dozens of American rock'n'roll stars (and pretenders) appeared in some of the most uninspired and least memorable feature films ever made. Thirty years on, the sole value in these low budget, swiftly made apologies for movies (with one notable exception) lies in the often punctuated performance of, for example, 'Only You' by The Platters, or 'High School Confidential' by Jerry Lee Lewis on the back of a flatbed truck. These cameo appearances are often the only surviving film of an act performing their hit(s)! Chuck Berry first appeared in a movie made at the Newport Jazz Festival in 1958, *Jazz On A Summer's Day,* in which he was the only non-jazzer on the bill and played 'Sweet Little Sixteen' backed by a jazz band with a clarinet player who takes a solo! No-one who has seen that could forget it, and that was the first occasion many young British rock'n'roll fans saw Chuck Berry performing . . .

The first five years of rock on film were really only memorable for the early Presley movies (made before he became a G.I.) and *The Girl Can't Help It.* Apart from their historical usefulness as a document of how people looked, there is nevertheless immense nostalgia value in a genre which, to be honest, deserves to be forgotten. Splice together all the performances and throw away all the plot-free remainder and you've got a great movie. Somebody should make it soon . . . .

The Beatles in 'A Hard Days Night'

'Jazz On A Summer's Day' with Louis Armstrong

MITCH MILLER SLAMS ROCK'N'ROLL

Mitch Miller, the Columbia Records A&R manager who has produced chart-topping hits for Johnnie Ray, Guy Mitchell, Doris Day, Frankie Laine and a host of others, is no fan of rock'n-'roll.

'Rock'n'roll's appeal to youngsters is the equivalent of those "confidential" magazines to adults,' he said in a recent interview. 'This is the first time in the history of our business that records have capitalized on illiteracy and bad recording.'

Columbia expect to ride out the current fad without acquiring any rock-orientated acts.

Bill Haley arrives in Britain

HALEY HYSTERIA FIRES BOX-OFFICE BONANZA

Never in the history of British entertainment has there been such colossal interest and fantastic ticket demand as that which followed the announcement of Bill Haley's concert tour, which starts at London's Dominion cinema next month.

Extra dates have already been added and impressario Leslie Grade is thanking his lucky stars that he had the foresight to book only super-size Rank cinemas for the tour – a bold move which could see more rock'n'roll acts forsaking the traditional variety theatres.

Meanwhile, as weekly sales of 'Rock Around The Clock' have accrued over the last two years, Haley has become the first artist to win a British gold disc. Said a Decca Records spokesman: 'We have made exhaustive enquiries and to the best of our knowledge, no other record has achieved the astronomical total of one million in the United Kingdom alone'.

STAR

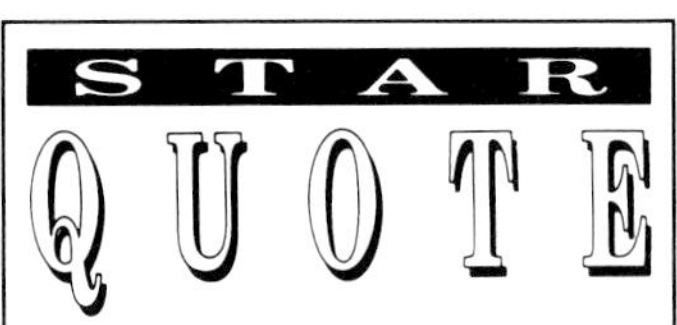

BILL HALEY

'There has to be a Cadillac music and a Ford music. Tchaikovsky and Bach is Cadillac music, while we play more down-to-earth Ford music. It's got a good solid beat that can't be missed . . . definitely designed for teenage kids to dance to.'

THE GRAPEVINE

■ Because the chocolate bar is unknown there, George Hamilton IV's huge American hit, 'A Rose And A Baby Ruth' has been re-recorded as 'A Rose And A Candy Bar' for British consumption.

■ At President Eisenhower's request, Pat Boone had the honour of singing at the Inaugural Ball in Washington, DC.

■ Paramount Pictures have purchased the Tennessee-based label Dot for a reputed two million dollars.

Tommy Steele in cabaret

CABARET AND MOVIES FOR TOMMY STEELE

Tommy Steele has made a sensational start to 1957. Within days of topping the U.K. best sellers with 'Singing The Blues', he was signed for an engagement at the exclusive *Café de Paris* in London's West End.

He will soon take time out from his hectic variety tour schedule to appear in a full-length feature film, *Kill Me Tomorrow* – starring Pat O'Brien – and plans have also been solidified for a biographical movie called *The Tommy Steele Story*, depicting his meteoric rise from cabin-boy to star!

Having secured his last hit from Guy Mitchell, Steele is repeating the formula by waxing Mitchell's latest as his own follow-up: no longer 'Singing The Blues', he is now 'Knee Deep In The Blues'!

CHARTS

US45	Singing The Blues *Guy Mitchell*
USLP	Calypso *Harry Belafonte*
UK45	Singing The Blues *Guy Mitchell*
WEEK 2	
US45	Singing The Blues *Guy Mitchell*
USLP	Calypso *Harry Belafonte*
UK45	Singing The Blues *Tommy Steele*
WEEK 3	
US45	Singing The Blues *Guy Mitchell*
USLP	Calypso *Harry Belafonte*
UK45	Singing The Blues *Guy Mitchell*
WEEK 4	
US45	Young Love *Sonny James*
USLP	Calypso *Harry Belafonte*
UK45	Garden Of Eden *Frankie Vaughan*
WEEK 5	
US45	Young Love *Sonny James*
USLP	Calypso *Harry Belafonte*
UK45	Garden Of Eden *Frankie Vaughan*

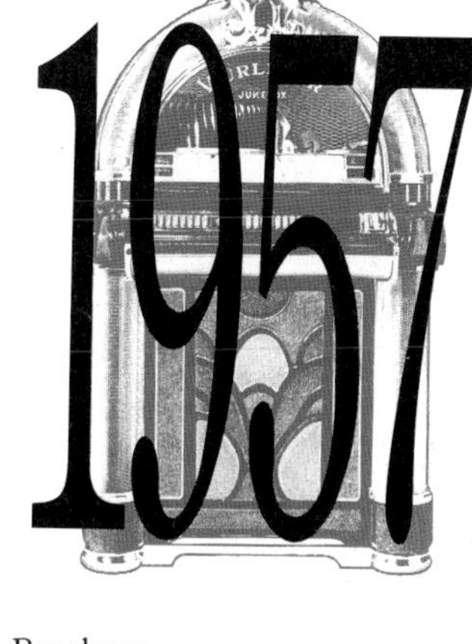

ALL HAIL TO BILL HALEY!

It seemed that half the population turned out to welcome Bill Haley to Britain. As soon as he and his Comets had disembarked from the liner Queen Mary, a chartered train – 'The Bill Haley Rock'n'Roll Special' – whisked them from Southampton to London. All along the route, people waved from windows, stood in gardens and on railway embankments, and hung precariously over bridges.

On arrival at Waterloo, the whole forecourt was crammed with over 4000 Haley worshippers, making a noise which rapidly reduced Glasgow's famous Hampden Roar to a whisper. Nobody could do much with that crowd, least of all the police. Once in the middle, Haley's chauffeur driven car was powerless – he was hemmed in for a full 20 minutes while fans clamoured and cheered.

But that was nothing compared with the band's opening concert at the Dominion Cinema. You've seen them in their films and heard them on your record players – but how can one possibly describe or explain it, that deafening, devastating EXTRA roar of enthusiasm which greeted and sustained Haley and his Comets that night? The Comets' overwhelming triumph became an undeniable, exultant fact from the opening bars of their very first number, a short but ferociously emphatic version of the familiar 'Razzle Dazzle'.

In his down-to-earth announcements, unpretentious vocals and friendly demeanour, Bill looks and sounds like the homespun fellow whom his fans have pictured in their minds – and one can legitimately add that every member of The Comets represents a denial of the so-called 'delinquency' label attached by some killjoys to rock'n'roll, in that their total performance, measured by the yardstick of family entertainment, is as wholesome and forthright as a Billy Cotton Band Show.

BBC WOOING TEENAGERS WITH EXTRA-HOUR TV SHOW

The BBC are making an all-out drive to capture U.K. teenagers when the 'extra hour' television begins on February 16.

Rock'n'roll and traditional jazz will be two staple ingredients of a new Saturday night show, *Six-Five Special*, which is being specifically aimed at the 16-25 age group. A number of artists have already been booked for the first programmes, including Tommy Steele & His Steelmen (for the first four), Lonnie Donegan, Humphrey Lyttelton, Kenny Baker and the King Brothers.

Star comedians and sportsmen will also appear on the shows, which will be hosted by Pete Murray and Josephine Douglas.

Commercial television are also hoping to impress the teenage audience with their new series, *Cool For Cats*.

THE GRAPEVINE

- Critics agree that *The Girl Can't Help It*, released this month, is the best rock'n'roll film so far.
- Elvis Presley is rehearsing his second Hollywood film, *Loving You*.
- Capitol Records have been deluged by an unexpected half a million advance orders for Tommy Sands' debut disc, 'Teenage Crush'.
- It has been announced that leading folk-blues singer, Big Bill Broonzy to visit Great Britain next month.

Tommy Steele rocks with The Steelmen

British jazz star Humphrey Lyttleton

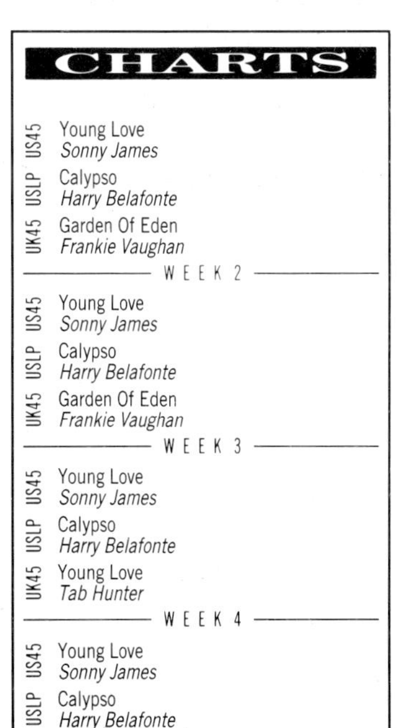

CHARTS

	US45	Young Love	*Sonny James*
	USLP	Calypso	*Harry Belafonte*
	UK45	Garden Of Eden	*Frankie Vaughan*
WEEK 2	US45	Young Love	*Sonny James*
	USLP	Calypso	*Harry Belafonte*
	UK45	Garden Of Eden	*Frankie Vaughan*
WEEK 3	US45	Young Love	*Sonny James*
	USLP	Calypso	*Harry Belafonte*
	UK45	Young Love	*Tab Hunter*
WEEK 4	US45	Young Love	*Sonny James*
	USLP	Calypso	*Harry Belafonte*
	UK45	Young Love	*Tab Hunter*

Six-Five Special Host Pete Murray

Legendary folk/blues performer Big Bill Broonzy

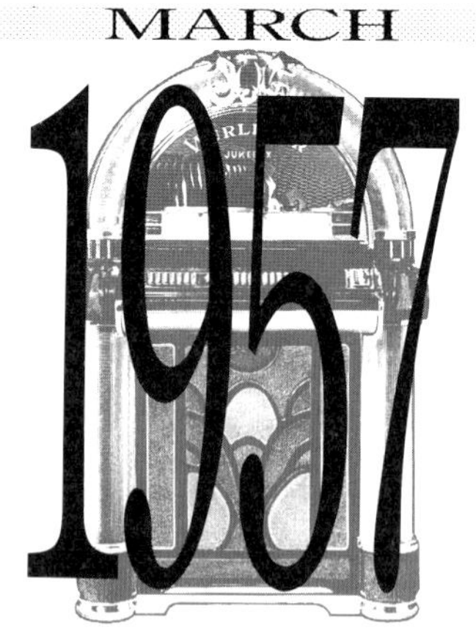

ROCK'N'ROLL STAMPEDE FOR FREED NEW YORK SHOW

Anxious to attend the opening of Alan Freed's Rock'n'Roll Show at New York's Paramount Theatre, teenage fans stormed into the Times Square area before dawn and thronged throughout the day, holding up traffic and requiring the attention of 175 policemen.

The stage show, which is running for a week, lasts one hour 20 minutes and is presented five times a day. On the first day, 15,200 patrons crammed the theatre from floor to ceiling, creating an all-time record for the 31-year-old venue, but causing great alarm to building inspectors who feared the balcony might collapse as a result of over-enthusiastic foot stamping.

In addition to being treated to such performers as The Teenagers, The Platters, Ruth Brown, Buddy Knox and The Rhythm Orchids, fans watched Freed's latest movie, *Don't Knock The Rock*. The only parts of the show that were not rock'n'roll were the neswreel and the advertisements – and these were heartily and lustily booed!

CHARTS

US45	Young Love *Sonny James*
USLP	Calypso *Harry Belafonte*
UK45	Young Love *Tab Hunter*
WEEK 2	
US45	Young Love *Sonny James*
USLP	Calypso *Harry Belafonte*
UK45	Young Love *Tab Hunter*
WEEK 3	
US45	Party Doll *Buddy Knox*
USLP	Calypso *Harry Belafonte*
UK45	Young Love *Tab Hunter*
WEEK 4	
US45	Butterfly *Charlie Gracie*
USLP	Calypso *Harry Belafonte*
UK45	Young Love *Tab Hunter*

YOUNG LOVE IN SEASON – THANKS TO TAB

Some of you may have seen his movies – fairly modest affairs with titles like *The Sea Chase, Return To Treasure Island and The Girl He Left Behind*.

The guy we call Tab Hunter (real name: Arthur Gelien) has also been a skating champion, coast guard, sheet metal worker, counter hand and garage mechanic in his 25 years . . . but one record has given Tab his biggest boost to date in a way he never expected – as the new singing heart-throb of America and Britain!

Originally recorded by country singer Sonny James, Tab's version of 'Young Love' has sprung to the top of both nation's hit parades, selling well over a million copies in the process.

A fine, fresh performer in the 1957 idiom, Tab shrugs off cynical critics who maintain that the disc is a triumph of image, personality and screen exposure over vocal ability.

THE

- **Elvis Presley has signed a contract to make a third film with a working title of *Jailhouse Rock*.**
- **För his film, *The Tommy Steele Story*, Steele and his collaborators – Lionel Bart and Mike Pratt – wrote 12 songs in only seven days!**
- **Robert Mitchum has cut his first disc for Capitol: 'What Is This Generation Coming To!'**

CALYPSO BRINGS CARIBBEAN FLAVOUR TO CHARTS

In the States, where long playing records have a separate best sellers list, Harry Belafonte's 'Calypso' has been at number one since early last October – except for five weeks when Elvis Presley temporarily deposed him.

Now Belafonte is making his presence felt in the singles chart, with 'Jamaica Farewell' and 'Banana Boat Song' – the latter a hit in Britain too – for not only himself, but also for The Tarriers and Shirley Bassey. Also in the US Top 20 are two versions of another calypso, 'Marianne'.

Screen actor turned singer Tab Hunter, whose observations on Young Love brought teenage adulation!

Robert Mitchum: hoping to follow Tab?

FATS WALKIN' UP THE CHARTS AGAIN

Ever since Bill Doggett's 'Honky Tonk' vacated the position in November, the No. 1 slot on America's R&B chart has been occupied by piano thumping Fats Domino – seen recently in *The Girl Can't Help It*.

From New Orleans, 29-year old Fats has been cutting locally popular records since 'The Fat Man' in 1949, but now his rocking style has found a groove in the international teenage market and titles like 'Ain't That A Shame', 'I'm In Love Again', 'Blueberry Hill' and 'Blue Monday' have all become million sellers.

His latest R&B chart-topper is another of his own compositions, 'I'm Walkin'' – but he could now face stiff competition from the newly released version by Ricky Nelson, teenage star of the long-running American TV series, *The Adventures of Ozzie And Harriet*.

One of nine children, Antoine Domino celebrated his stage name on his very first hit . . . "They call me The Fat Man!"

CHARTS

US45	Butterfly	*Andy Williams*
USLP	Calypso	*Harry Belafonte*
UK45	Young Love	*Tab Hunter*
WEEK 2		
US45	Butterfly	*Andy Williams*
USLP	Calypso	*Harry Belafonte*
UK45	Cumberland Gap	*Lonnie Donegan*
WEEK 3		
US45	All Shook Up	*Elvis Presley*
USLP	Calypso	*Harry Belafonte*
UK45	Cumberland Gap	*Lonnie Donegan*
WEEK 4		
US45	All Shook Up	*Elvis Presley*
USLP	Calypso	*Harry Belafonte*
UK45	Cumberland Gap	*Lonnie Donegan*

CALYPSO: HERE TODAY, GONE TOMORROW?

Hollywood producer Sam Katzman, whose *Rock Around The Clock* has already grossed four million dollars, is now on a calypso kick and has just completed *Calypso Heat Wave*.

Said the sage Katzman: 'I want to get the picture out in a hurry because this calypso craze won't last long. The kids like it now, but it will blow over. They like something with a beat, something they can dance to – and calypso is not it!'

DENE PICKED AS LATEST COFFEE BAR SENSATION

The unprepossessing 2-Is coffee bar in the heart of London's Soho district is rapidly becoming mecca to Britain's would-be recording stars. It was here, last autumn, that Tommy Steele was first noticed, strumming his guitar, and here also that The Vipers took their first steps – steps which have subsequently taken them into the charts with 'Don't You Rock Me Daddy-O' and 'Cumberland Gap'.

The latest discovery to take the eye of owner Paul Lincoln – once the wrestling champion of New South Wales! – is 18-year old Terry Dene, from South London. Formerly a packer at HMV's Oxford Street record shop, Dene has already signed a recording contract with Decca and is lined up to appear on *Six-Five Special*. Lincoln rates his chances high enough to become 'the next Tommy Steele'.

Latest Soho discovery, Terry Dene

THE GRAPEVINE

- **The latest film actress to take lessons in pop singing is Joan Collins.**
- **The 1933 Young Persons Act, prohibiting any person under 15-years of age from broadcasting, prevented Frankie Lymon from appearing on the ATV show, *Sunday Night At The London Palladium.***
- **In Chicago, Elvis Presley sang to 12,000 shrieking teenagers in a 2,500 dollar gold leaf suit and 100 dollar golden slippers!**

STAR QUOTE

ELVIS PRESLEY

'The majority are nice, decent folks, but a few want to go around saying they beat up Elvis Presley. I'm just like they are, with skin on my bones and blood in my veins – so what would be so big about beating me up?'

Joan Collins – if Tab can do it . . .

SKIFFLE – THE DO-IT-YOURSELF BOOM

Because the instruments are relatively cheap, and the music is not difficult to master, thousands of fans in Britain are forming their own skiffle groups in the wake of the do-it-yourself boom created by Lonnie Donegan, The Vipers, Johnny Duncan & The Bluegrass Boys, and The Chas McDevitt Skiffle Group.

Equipped with guitars, washboards, kazoos and tea-chest basses, groups have sprung up in every school, college and youth club – in what was described in one newspaper as a 'snowballing skiffle epidemic'!

Some groups try to incorporate rock'n'roll numbers, but most stick to the Donegan/Vipers songbag – plus current skiffle hits, like 'Freight Train', the debut by the McDevitt Group and their sweet-voiced singer Nancy Whiskey.

The disc seems certain to give McDevitt a million seller first time out. As well as reaching the UK Top 10, it has captured the imagination of transatlantic fans and is now emulating Lonnie Donegan's debut by rocketing up the American charts. The Americans gave Britain rock'n-'roll, and the British are returning the favour with skiffle!

THE GRAPEVINE

- If company executives take a favourable view of Alan Freed's two ABC-TV rock'n'roll shows, transmitted this month, he'll probably be given a series.
- Alarmingly, after nine Top 10 entries, Bill Haley's flow of hit records appears to have dried up!
- Freddie Bell & The Bellboys have arrived in Britain for a tour on which they share top billing with Tommy Steele & The Steelmen.

STAR QUOTE

HARRY BELAFONTE

'The sham engineers of the music industry, who steer the wheel of public opinion, are driving the good features of calypso into the ground. I shudder to think what these greedy men will eventually do to this true art form.'

CHARTS

US45	All Shook Up *Elvis Presley*
USLP	Calypso *Harry Belafonte*
UK45	Cumberland Gap *Lonnie Donegan*
	WEEK 2
US45	All Shook Up *Elvis Presley*
USLP	Calypso *Harry Belafonte*
UK45	Cumberland Gap *Lonnie Donegan*
	WEEK 3
US45	All Shook Up *Elvis Presley*
USLP	Love Is The Thing *Nat 'King' Cole*
UK45	Rock-A-Billy *Guy Mitchell*
	WEEK 4
US45	Love Letters In The Sand *Pat Boone*
USLP	Love Is The Thing *Nat 'King' Cole*
UK45	Yes Tonight Josephine *Johnnie Ray*
	WEEK 5
US45	Love Letters In The Sand *Pat Boone*
USLP	Love Is The Thing *Nat 'King' Cole*
UK45	Yes Tonight Josephine *Johnnie Ray*

WILLIAMS NETS BUTTERFLY HIT

Philadelphian guitar-plucker Charlie Gracie recorded it first, but the man who has outsold him and fluttered 'Butterfly' to the top of the best sellers is Andy Williams.

Born in Iowa, Williams sang in the local church choir before heading to California, where he soon established himself as resident singer on Steve Allen's popular TV show, *Tonight*.

'Butterfly' is his British chart debut, but he made his initial Top 10 impact in the States last year – with 'Canadian Sunset' – and he looks set to return there with his latest climber, 'I Like Your Kind Of Love'.

Meanwhile, Gracie can console himself on two counts. He can expect a large royalty cheque from Tab Hunter's hit, 'Ninety Nine Ways' – which he wrote – while his new disc, 'Fabulous', is fast becoming a sizeable hit on both sides of the Atlantic.

Butterflies for Charlie Gracie (right) and Andy Williams (far right)

LEIBER AND STOLLER FOR ELVIS MOVIE

Jerry Leiber and Mike Stoller, the composers of Elvis Presley's four million seller 'Hound Dog', have been commissioned to write songs for his next picture, *Jailhouse Rock*.

Meanwhile, two more Leiber-Stoller penned songs, 'Searchin''/'Young Blood', are heading towards the US Top 10 care of the versatile Coasters.

Mike Stoller, Elvis Presley and Jerry Leiber get down to work at MGM Studios in Culver City, California

BOOM-TIME FOR COUNTRY & WESTERN?

Left to right: Marty Robbins, Ferlin Huskey and Rusty Draper – spreading the word on Country & Western

Traditionally, country music, most of which is produced in Nashville, Tenessee, has a fairly localised appeal – but a bunch of country stars are currently making a considerable impact on America's national pop chart.

Marty Robbins, who cut the original version of 'Singing The Blues', is hitting the high spots with 'A White Sport Coat'; Ferlin Husky has sold over a million copies of 'Gone'; deep-voiced balladeer Jim Reeves has made 'Four Walls' a nationwide favourite; Rusty Draper is chugging up the list with his version of 'Freight Train'; and a guitar-strumming vocal duo, the Everly Brothers, are rapidly moving towards the Top Three with 'Bye Bye Love'.

Additionally, newcomers like Johnny Cash, Patsy Cline and Sonny James have also dented the chart in recent weeks. All in all, activity is so intense that some columnists are tipping country & western to eclipse calypso as the new trend.

CHARTS

US45 Love Letters In The Sand
Pat Boone

USLP Love Is The Thing
Nat 'King' Cole

UK45 Puttin' On the Style
Lonnie Donegan

WEEK 2

US45 Love Letters In The Sand
Pat Boone

USLP Love Is The Thing
Nat 'King'Cole

UK45 Yes Tonight Josephine
Johnnie Ray

WEEK 3

US45 Love Letters In The Sand
Pat Boone

USLP Love Is The Thing
Nat 'King' Cole

UK45 Puttin' On the Style
Lonnie Donegan

WEEK 4

US45 Teddy Bear/Loving You
Elvis Presley

USLP Love Is The Thing
Nat 'King' Cole

UK45 All Shook Up
Elvis Presley

Latest Canadian vocal group to reach the charts – The Diamonds . . . currently scoring with Little Darlin'

LITTLE DARLIN' BRINGS GOLD FOR DIAMONDS

Following in the footsteps of the Four Lads and The Crew Cuts come another foursome from Toronto, The Diamonds, who are riding high in the charts with 'Little Darlin''. One of the most imaginative vocal group novelties for years, it has truly vindicated their decision to turn professional after harmonising for their own amusement.

Other vocal outfits scoring in the States include The Dell Vikings, with 'Come Go With Me', and The Coasters with 'Searchin'' – currently the hottest seller on the R&B chart.

TOMMY STEELE TRIUMPHS ON THE SCREEN

Although British film studios were rather late climbing on the rock'n'roll bandwagon, they have produced something far better than any of those Hollywood epics. Make no mistake about it, *The Tommy Steele Story* is a film you must not miss.

Though hardly in the James Dean class that had been predicted for him, Tommy emerges as a sincere actor and a fine all-round performer, and the cynics who said he would fade out with the end of rock'n'roll can get ready to eat their hats!

THE GRAPEVINE

- **Currently in the US Top Five with 'School Day', Chuck Berry is enjoying his biggest success since 'Maybellene', two years ago.**
- **UK Decca's new discovery, Terry Dene, has covered 'Start Movin'' – an American hit for Sal Mineo.**
- **Pat Boone isn't the first to score with 'Love Letters In The Sand'. Written in 1931, it was a winner for Rudy Valee and Bing Crosby, among others.**

BANDLEADER JIMMY DORSEY DIES

Well loved altoist-bandleader Jimmy Dorsey has died in New York, aged 53 – a victim of cancer. His death closely follows the untimely passing of his trombonist brother Tommy, last November.

By a bizarre twist of fate, Jimmy's last recording, 'So Rare' – now in the American Top Five – has been his biggest disc hit for many years.

FRANKIE LYMON QUITS TEENAGERS

Frankie Lymon, one of America's youngest and most successful new recording stars, has split away from The Teenagers vocal team. Tension began to develop in London, when Lymon recorded an album without the other members of the group.

Said 14-year old Frankie: 'The headline notices I received in Britain caused the others to become jealous. Since our return to New York, the quartet and I have hardly spoken to each other.'

Both factions intend to pursue separate careers, although The Teenagers will undoubtedly encounter difficulty finding another vocalist as dynamic as Lymon.

Young Frankie Lymon (centre) has handed in his pullover

CHARTS

US45 Teddy Bear/Loving You *Elvis Presley*
USLP Love Is The Thing *Nat 'King' Cole*
UK45 All Shook Up *Elvis Presley*

WEEK 2

US45 Teddy Bear/Loving You *Elvis Presley*
USLP Around The World In 80 Days *Soundtrack*
UK45 All Shook Up *Elvis Presley*

WEEK 3

US45 Teddy Bear/Loving You *Elvis Presley*
USLP Loving You *Elvis Presley*
UK45 All Shook Up *Elvis Presley*

WEEK 4

US45 Teddy Bear/Loving You *Elvis Presley*
USLP Loving You *Elvis Presley*
UK45 All Shook Up *Elvis Presley*

THE BUTLIN REDCOAT WITH THE DOUBLE-SIDED HIT

A new name to the charts is Russ Hamilton, a 24-year old who sings, plays a guitar and writes his own songs. Born in Liverpool, the freckled, tousle-haired youngster was working as a factory cost clerk until last year, when he became a Redcoat with the Butlin's leisure organisation – so that he could get some show business experience. He was Uncle Russ to the kiddy-winkies at the holiday camp in Blackpool.

Early this year, he signed a contract with the Oriole label, and, in storybook fashion, his first disc romped to No. 2. But the story doesn't end there: American record-buyers took a liking to Russ too . . . but they preferred the flip side of his record! So the chirpy newcomer has two Top 10 hits – 'We Will Make Love' in Britain, and 'Rainbow' in the States!

This summer, he's back on duty at Butlin's – singing to some 10,000 holidaymakers a week at their Clacton camp.

PAT BOONE SPEAKS OUT

Pat Boone refuses to compromise his religious views, which prohibit physical contact with any woman other than his wife. 20th Century Fox are respecting his feelings to the extent of writing out all his love scenes with Shirley Jones when they begin filming *April Love*.

Pat also has some pertinent comments about today's rock'n-'roll scene. 'I think some of its exponents are giving it a black eye', he explained recently. 'They are way off base with their stage contortions. I don't think anything excuses the suggestive gyrations that some go in for.

'Why do musicians find it necessary to get down on the floor, or quiver like a slab of aspic? I belong to the finger-snapping school myself – that, and a little tapping of the feet is enough to satisfy my soul . . . and it seems to satisfy my audiences too'.

Pat Boone: outspoken critic of rock'n'roll's unsavoury side

THE GRAPEVINE

- **Songwriters Kal Mann and Bernie Lowe, who penned the chart-topping 'Butterfly', are also responsible for Elvis Presley's new waxing, 'Teddy Bear'.**
- **A report in Jet magazine, that Little Richard is retiring to become an evangelist, has been denied by his agent.**
- **George Treadwell, manager of The Drifters vocal group and several other R&B acts, is divorcing his wife, Sarah Vaughan, in Mexico.**

INFLUENCE OF R&B STRONGER THAN EVER

Rhythm & blues acts are increasing their intensive invasion of the American pop parade.

Recent Top 20 entrants include The Coasters with 'Searchin'', Fats Domino with 'Valley Of Tears', Larry Williams with 'Short Fat Fannie', Chuck Willis with 'CC Rider', The Del-Vikings with 'Whispering Belles', Little Richard with 'Jenny Jenny', Johnnie & Joe with 'Over The Mountain', and Billy Ward with 'Stardust'.

And to think that two years ago R&B was viewed as a passing fad!

ANKA'S AWAY WITH DIANA!

The fastest selling disc in Britain this month is 'Diana', written and recorded by Canadian Paul Anka. Now 16 years old, Anka made his first night club appearance when he was 12 – doing impersonations of Johnnie Ray and other famous singers – and then struck out leading a vocal trio, The Bobbysoxers.

After leaving them, he journeyed from his home in Ottawa to Hollywood, but failed to make any headway. His next trip took him to New York, where A&R manager Don Costa was impressed enough to sign him to ABC Paramount.

Waxed when he was only 15, 'Diana' is dedicated to an older girl – Diana Ayoub – with whom Paul sang in Ottawa's Syrian Church Choir. Missing her in New York, he poured his sorrow into a poem, which he promptly set to music.

Apparently, Miss Ayoub is overjoyed about all the attention her name is attracting!

Screenland's latest rocker, Sal Mineo

EQUALLY AT HOME ON STAGE, SCREEN OR DISC – THAT'S SAL!

Emulating its success in America, film actor Sal Mineo's debut single, 'Start Movin'', has jumped into the British Top 20. Born in New York's toughest neighbourhood, The Bronx, Sal first established himself on Broadway, in the role of the Crown Prince in *The King And I* – with Yul Brynner as his father.

Hollywood roles in *Rebel Without A Cause* and *Giant* followed, and he recently won acclaim as the drum-crazy college undergraduate in *Rock Pretty Baby*.

THE GRAPEVINE

■ British fans have been dazzled by the guitar virtuosity of American Charlie Gracie, currently on a two month UK tour.

■ Top selling album in America is the soundtrack from Elvis Presley's new film, *Loving You*.

■ Tommy Steele has purchased a four-bedroomed house in South London for his parents.

■ Dick Clark's TV show, *American Bandstand*, has grown so popular that it is now being transmitted coast to coast.

Dick Clark – taking America by storm

CHARTS

	US45	Teddy Bear/Loving You – *Elvis Presley*
	USLP	Loving You – *Elvis Presley*
	UK45	All Shook Up – *Elvis Presley*
WEEK 2	US45	Teddy Bear/Loving You – *Elvis Presley*
	USLP	Loving You – *Elvis Presley*
	UK45	All Shook Up – *Elvis Presley*
WEEK 3	US45	Tammy – *Debbie Reynolds*
	USLP	Loving You – *Elvis Presley*
	UK45	All Shook Up – *Elvis Presley*
WEEK 4	US45	Tammy – *Debbie Reynolds*
	USLP	Loving You – *Elvis Presley*
	UK45	All Shook Up – *Elvis Presley*
WEEK 5	US45	Diana – *Paul Anka*
	USLP	Loving You – *Elvis Presley*
	UK45	Diana – *Paul Anka*

SEPTEMBER

Jim Dale, now a firm favourite of Saturday tea-time viewers

EVERYBODY'S HAPPY ON THE SIX-FIVE SPECIAL

After 29 shows, BBC-TV's *Six-Five Special* has become something of an institution, enhancing the reputations of established stars, and launching new ones – like Jim Dale and Terry Dene. Always on the look-out for impressive talent, producer Jack Good is optimistic about the John Barry Seven, from York, and Larry Parnes' recent discovery, Marty Wilde.

Shooting will soon begin on a full-length feature film, entitled *Six-Five Special* and featuring many of the stars of the series.

Meanwhile, Tommy Steele is currently hard at work on his latest film, *The Duke Wore Jeans*, and Terry Dene is following in his footsteps by playing to the cameras in *The Golden Disc*.

INTRODUCING THE SENSATIONAL EVERLY BROTHERS

Riding high in the charts on both sides of the Atlantic with their debut disc, 'Bye Bye Love', are Kentucky's favourite sons, the Everly Brothers – Don (aged 20) and Phil (18).

Their unique blend of country-style rock was developed over many years in a family hillbilly act: the lads have been singing on radio shows with their parents, Ike and Margaret, ever since they could stand in front of a microphone!

Last year, Ike persuaded his friend Chet Atkins, an influential guitarist and producer in Nashville, to take an interest in the duo and with his encouragement and guidance they soon landed a contract with Cadence – the label which carried The Chordettes and Andy Williams to the top.

Their solid unison strumming and distinctive vocal harmonies can be heard to even better effect on their rocking follow-up, 'Wake Up Little Susie', which has just entered the American best sellers and is due for release here next month.

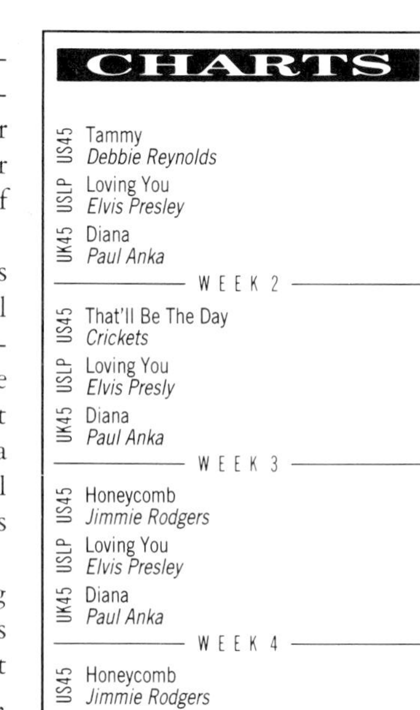

CHARTS

	US45	USLP	UK45
	Tammy – *Debbie Reynolds*	Loving You – *Elvis Presley*	Diana – *Paul Anka*
WEEK 2	That'll Be The Day – *Crickets*	Loving You – *Elvis Presly*	Diana – *Paul Anka*
WEEK 3	Honeycomb – *Jimmie Rodgers*	Loving You – *Elvis Presley*	Diana – *Paul Anka*
WEEK 4	Honeycomb – *Jimmie Rodgers*	Loving You – *Elvis Presley*	Diana – *Paul Anka*

THE GRAPEVINE

- **Dot Records have signed Pat Boone's brother – who will be known as Nick Todd.**
- **Vocalist Nancy Whiskey has left the Chas McDevitt Skiffle Group to go solo. Her replacement is Shirley Douglas.**
- **13-year old Laurie London, who attracted attention at *The Radio Show* in London by walking onto the BBC stand and breaking into song, has signed a contract with EMI.**

TOMMY STEELE

'I owe it all to Dick Campion, a waiter on the 'Mauretania'. He taught me to play the guitar when we were at sea together.'

A DATE WITH ELVIS

If fans are wondering what a date with Elvis Presley would be like, listen to Anita Wood, a 19-year-old who has been dating him for a month and a half.

'When we go to a picture show, we have to call the manager – Elvis has telephones in two of his cars – and ask him to let us in a side door', she reports.

'We usually go to the late show and sit in the balcony. Then we'll go to his house, play records, play the piano and sing a few songs.'

SUN SHINES FOR ROCKIN' JERRY LEE

Above: Piano sensation Jerry Lee

Below: Roy Orbison

Within the short space of six weeks, Jerry Lee Lewis, a fair-haired, blue-eyed youngster from Ferriday, Louisiana, has developed into the latest rock sensation in the States – largely on the strength of one record.

Now booming out of loudspeakers in America and Britain, 'Whole Lotta Shakin' Goin' On' is acknowledged to be one of the hottest rock'n'roll records ever heard on the airwaves.

Not only a wild vocalist, Jerry Lee plays piano too – using the instrument in much the same thumping, pounding way that Presley uses his guitar. And, speaking of Presley, Jerry Lee was discovered by the same man – Sam Phillips, owner of the Memphis-based Sun label.

As if Jerry Lee isn't enough, Phillips is also expecting big things for 21-year old Texan singer-guitarist Roy Orbison, whose first two Sun singles have just been issued in the UK on the EP, 'Hillbilly Rock'.

THE GRAPEVINE

■ The BBC has banned Jimmie Rodgers' US chart-topper, 'Honeycomb', because of references to God – but Marty Wilde's modified cover version has been sanctioned.

■ Looks like Pat Boone is one young performer who won't be playing Las Vegas: he refuses to sing anywhere hard liquor is sold.

■ Next craze may be for Rock-a-Hula! First US chart entry in this idiom is 'Hula Love' by Buddy Knox.

THUMBS DOWN FOR FREED AND PAGE

Alan Freed may be doing well with his new film, *Mister Rock'n-'Roll*, but his ABC-TV show has been axed because, it has been suggested, no sponsor was willing to take a chance on a programme featuring so many black artists.

Meanwhile, Patti Page's new CBS-TV series, *The Big Record*, has been panned by the New York Times critic, who felt that the show 'helps to illustrate how sterile so much of today's popular recorded music really is'.

The "Singing Rage", Miss Patti Page

PAT BOONE SCORES GREAT DOUBLE TRIUMPH

In the annual NME readers poll, Pat Boone has been voted The World's Outstanding Popular Singer and Favourite US Male Singer – beating Elvis Presley and Frank Sinatra to second and third positions in both categories. Doris Day was top American Female Singer, while Dickie Valentine and Alma Cogan headed the British Singer sections.

Tommy Steele was elected the year's British Musical Personality and Lonnie Donegan outdistanced all competition in the Skiffle Group list.

CHARTS

US45	Wake Up Little Susie *Everly Brothers*
USLP	Around The World In 80 Days *Soundtrack*
UK45	Diana *Paul Anka*
WEEK 2	
US45	Jailhouse Rock/Treat Me Nice *Elvis Presley*
USLP	Around The World In 80 Days *Soundtrack*
UK45	Diana *Paul Anka*
WEEK 3	
US45	Jailhouse Rock/Treat Me Nice *Elvis Presley*
USLP	Around The World In 80 Days *Soundtrack*
UK45	Diana *Paul Anka*
WEEK 4	
US45	Jailhouse Rock/Treat Me Nice *Elvis Presley*
USLP	Around The World In 80 Days *Soundtrack*
UK45	Diana *Paul Anka*

ELVIS STARTS FOURTH FILM BEFORE ARMY BECKONS!

The new Elvis film, *Jailhouse Rock*, has had its world premiere at Loew's State Cinema in Memphis – where the singer once worked as an usher.

Wasting no time, Presley is about to start work on another movie. Paramount's Hal Wallis will produce him in an adaptation of the Harold Robbins novel, *A Stone For Danny Fisher* – the vigorous tale of an ambitious boy from the slums. In between times, he managed to squeeze in a five date tour of the American North-West, netting 200,000 dollars.

One reason for this non-stop activity is that Elvis is expected to be drafted into the military very soon.

THE CRICKETS MAKE THEIR DAY

A fabulous four-piece from Texas, The Crickets, have shot from obscurity to top position in the charts in record time with their very first release, 'That'll Be The Day'.

The boys hail from the town of Lubbock but got their big break when they drove across the state border to Clovis, New Mexico, where producer Norman Petty has a recording studio. He was impressed enough to record them, there and then, and the resulting tapes were issued by the New York label, Coral.

When 'That'll Be The Day' began to climb the US charts, The Crickets were invited to appear on Alan Freed's famous Brooklyn Paramount Show – and they are now on tour with The Biggest Show Of Stars For 1957, alongside Chuck Berry, Fats Domino, The Everly Brothers and other top acts.

Very excited about their phenomenal success in Britain, the quartet plan to visit these shores early next year.

LITTLE RICHARD QUITS SHOWBIZ FOR CHURCH

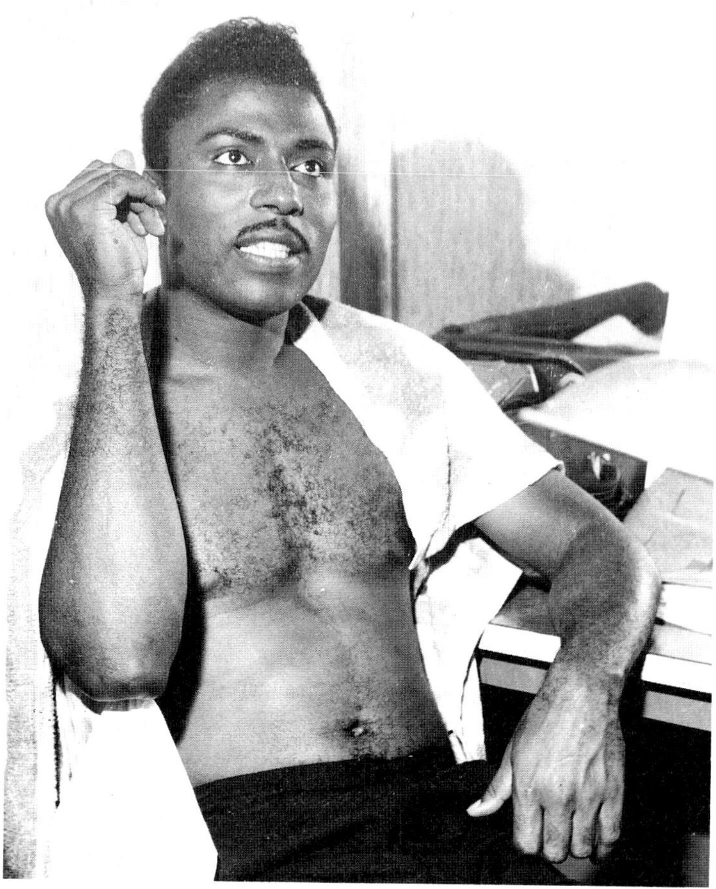

Though only 21, Little Richard is giving up a spectacular and lucrative career to devote his life to evangelism. In future he will make only spiritual records; he is finished with rock'n'roll.

The astonishing decision was made on his return from Australia, where he is said to have thrown four diamond rings into Sydney harbour to prove his faith to God.

His latest American Top Tenner, 'Keep A-Knockin'', is released here later this month – but his eagerly awaited UK tour, scheduled for next February, is now obviously off.

He plans to enrol at a theological college in Atlanta, Georgia.

THE GRAPEVINE

- **After an absence of over a year, Gene Vincent is back in the US Top Twenty with 'Lotta Lovin''.**
- **At the UK Royal Variety Show, The Queen was entertained not only by Mario Lanza and Judy Garland, but also Tommy Steele; she clapped along to 'Singing The Blues'!**
- **Frank Sinatra's 17-year old daughter, Nancy, has made her singing debut – on her father's US television show!**

Nancy: pop's on TV

STEELE'S BROTHER LEADS NEW ROCK'N'ROLL BRIGADE

Tommy Steel's manager, Larry Parnes, has signed up the former's younger brother, Colin Hicks, who takes to the road for the first time this month. Sharing the bill on the ten week variety tour will be another Parnes hopeful, Marty Wilde.

Britain seems to be experiencing a proliferation of would-be rock'n'roll stars. Recent weeks have seen the launch of 16-year old Terry Wayne, Larry Page (billed as 'The Teenage Rage'), former tumbler-comedian Jim Dale, The Most Brothers, and another 2-Is coffee bar discovery, Wee Willie Harris.

So legendary has the 2-Is now become that BBC TV took the place over for a live broadcast of *Six-Five Special* on November 16 . . . and the man who started it all, Tommy Steele, has now become the latest wax-attraction at Madame Tussaud's!

CHARTS

US45	Jailhouse Rock/Treat Me Nice	*Elvis Presley*
USLP	Around The World In 80 Days	*Soundtrack*
UK45	That'll Be The Day	*Crickets*
WEEK 2		
US45	Jailhouse Rock/Treat Me Nice	*Elvis Presley*
USLP	My Fair Lady	*Original Broadway Cast*
UK45	That'll Be That Day	*Crickets*
WEEK 3		
US45	Jailhouse Rock/Treat Me Nice	*Elvis Presley*
USLP	Around The World In 80 Days	*Soundtrack*
UK45	That'll B. The Day	*Crickets*
WEEK 4		
US45	You Send Me	*Sam Cooke*
USLP	Around The World In 80 Days	*Soundtrack*
UK45	Mary's Boy Child	*Harry Belafonte*
WEEK 5		
US45	You Send Me	*Sam Cooke*
USLP	Around The World In 80 Days	*Soundtrack*
UK45	Mary's Boy Child	*Harry Belafonte*

BUDDY DOUBLES CRICKETS' POTENTIAL

Currently zipping up the charts on both sides of the Atlantic is 'Peggy Sue', a pulsating rocker by one Buddy Holly – and if his voice sounds familiar, it should!

21 year old Buddy is lead singer with The Crickets, but so prolific is his songwriting ability that his record company have decided to launch him as a solo artist too. That way, Holly will be able to issue twice as many discs . . . the newest in the States being 'Oh Boy' – by The Crickets!

UK FANS GO WILD FOR JACKIE'S US FLOP!

Reviewer Keith Fordyce was certainly on the ball when he predicted a hit for 'a gimmick-laden disc which combines pep, beat and originality with an irresistible go' . . . for that's how he described Jackie Wilson's 'Reet Petite'.

Colleague Derek Johnson was not so sure, however. He thought 'the strange collection of noises, ranging from gargling to an outboard motor, was obviously Stan Freberg indulging in one of his satires'!

Well, like it or loathe it, 'Reet Petite' is now a smash hit, firmly lodged in the NME Top 10 – even though it stalled at No. 62 on the US 'Hot 100' chart.

Wilson was born in Detroit, but in 1953 moved to New York to make his name in R&B vocal outfit, The Dominoes. Wherever the group went, audiences were thrilled by his distinctive vocal stylings – and it is even said that Elvis derived some of his presentation from studying Jackie's dynamic stage act. It was only a matter of time before he broke away to go solo.

Jackie Wilson: "an irresistible go!"

Co-writer Berry Gordy

'Reet Petite' was co-written by his friend Berry Gordy. Maybe he can explain what the words are all about!

THE GRAPEVINE

- **With 'I Love You Baby', a chart's hit, Paul Anka has arrived in Britain for a 16-date tour; backing him will be The John Barry Seven.**
- **Following Little Richard's retirement, Specialty Records are pinning their hopes on the equally wild Larry Williams – currently scoring with 'Bony Moronie'.**
- **Currently at No. 2 in the US is 'Raunchy' by Bill Justis – yet another Sam Phillips discovery!**

CHARTS

US45	Jailhouse Rock *Elvis Presley*
USLP	Elvis' Christmas Album *Elvis Presley*
UK45	Mary's Boy Child *Harry Belafonte*
WEEK 2	
US45	April Love *Pat Boone*
USLP	Elvis' Christmas Album *Elvis Presley*
UK45	Mary's Boy Child *Harry Belafonte*
WEEK 3	
US45	April Love *Pat Boone*
USLP	Elvis' Christmas Album *Elvis Presley*
UK45	Mary's Boy Child *Harry Belafonte*
WEEK 4	
US45	At The Hop *Danny & The Juniors*
USLP	Elvis' Christmas Album *Elvis Presley*
UK45	Mary's Boy Child *Harry Belafonte*

MEET JOHNNY OTIS, MAN BEHIND THE STARS

Latest addition to the growing list of revivals which are being dusted off and presented in new dress, is the bouncy wartime song, 'Ma He's Makin' Eyes At Me' – and the man who has added the forceful beat which has driven it into the Top Five is bandleader Johnny Otis.

He may be a new name here, but 36-year old Johnny is a well-known R&B hitmaker in the States. Among artists he has discovered and helped are Johnny Ace, Little Willie John, and current chart star Jackie Wilson.

No doubt the success of 'Ma' can be attributed in part to the gimmick effect of teenagers screaming throughout the record – but its principal appeal lies in the robust, belting vocals of Johnny's latest *protégées*, Marie Adams and the aptly named Three Tons of Joy.

Pillar of West Coast R&B, Johnny Otis

1958

CHARTS

US45	At The Hop *Danny & The Juniors*
USLP	Elvis' Christmas Album *Elvis Presley*
UK45	Mary's Boy Child *Harry Belafonte*
WEEK 2	
US45	At The Hop *Danny & The Juniors*
USLP	Elvis' Christmas Album *Elvis Presley*
UK45	Great Balls Of Fire *Jerry Lee Lewis*
WEEK 3	
US45	At The Hop *Danny & The Juniors*
USLP	Ricky *Ricky Nelson*
UK45	Great Balls Of Fire *Jerry Lee Lewis*
WEEK 4	
US45	At The Hop *Danny & The Juniors*
USLP	My Fair Lady *Original Cast*
UK45	Jailhouse Rock *Elvis Presley*

FREED PACKAGE BREAKS RECORDS

Oh for another show with a bill like the one presented by Alan Freed at New York's Paramount Theatre over Christmas!

The star-studded line-up comprised Fats Domino, The Everly Brothers, The Rays, Buddy Holly & The Crickets, Paul Anka, Jerry Lee Lewis, Lee Andrews & The Hearts, Danny & The Juniors, The Teenagers, The Dubs, Thurston Harris and at least five more acts . . . all on the same show!

No wonder it broke the previous box-office record – held by erstwhile comedy duo, Dean Martin and Jerry Lewis. Headliner Fats Domino went home with 28,350 dollars – not bad for a week's work!

GALAXY OF NEW US STARS ON VIEW

'Sugartime' songstress Alma Cogan raves about "Great Balls" man Jerry Lee Lewis

Jerry Lee Lewis, Carl Perkins, Lewis Lymon (Frankie's younger brother), Jodie Sands, Buddy Knox, Fats Domino and Frankie Avalon are some of the American stars British audiences will be able to see for the first time in the new Warner Brothers film, *Disc Jockey Jamboree*, which opens in the UK this month.

Jerry Lee – whose torrid performance of his current hit, 'Great Balls Of Fire', is one of the most exciting segments of the movie – has been booked for a UK tour this Spring.

British singer Alma Cogan, who saw the star onstage in New York recently, reports: 'He's tall, he wears thick-soled white shoes and he hits the piano keys so hard you can't understand why the piano doesn't collapse! All the time, he's yelling "go, go, go" and whips the fans up to such a pitch that it takes a bunch of police to stop them tearing the place apart!'

SAM COOKE – THE SOLO SOUL STIRRER

Is rock'n'roll a pernicious influence? Little Richard, about to enter Oakwood College, a Seventh Day Adventist school in Huntsville, Alabama, thinks it is. 'I'd like to tell my fans that rock'n'roll glorifies Satan,' he said recently.

Sam Cooke, however, disagrees: he left a gospel group to find success in the rock field.

Born in Chicago, the son of a Baptist minister, 26-year old old Cooke won acclaim singing hymns with The Soul Stirrers – who, coincidentally, recorded for the same label as Little Richard – but A&R man 'Bumps' Blackwell convinced him to go out on his own.

The move paid handsome dividends: Cooke's wistful self-penned ballad, 'You Send Me', became America's top selling pop single . . . and now it's making headway in Britain too.

Sam Cooke: moving from gospel to pop

THE GRAPEVINE

- **BBC-TV have begun weekly transmissions of Perry Como's US television series.**
- **Elvis Presley's 'Jailhouse Rock' is the first record ever to have entered the NME chart at No. 1.**
- **In America, a new dance craze is The Stroll – presumably more energetic than the Hand Jive now sweeping Britain!**
- **HMV have signed Adam Faith – former leader of 2-Is resident skiffle group, The Worried Men.**

STAR QUOTE

MITCH MILLER

'Rock'n'roll is musical baby food: it is the worship of mediocrity, brought about by a passion for conformity.'

Coffee-bar discovery Adam Faith

'ROCK IS HERE TO STAY' INSISTS DANNY

The Juniors provide backing vocals while leader Danny Rapp extols the virtues of rock'n'roll

Having reached No. 1 with 'At The Hop', Philadelphian foursome Danny & The Juniors are now streaking up the American best sellers with their follow-up, 'Rock'n'Roll Is Here To Stay'.

The song was written in response to incessant criticism of teenage music – not least by radio station KWK in St Louis. Last month, they instituted a policy of playing every rock'n'roll record once – and then smashing it!

The station feels that rock 'has dominated the music field long enough. The majority of listeners will be surprised and pleased at how pleasant radio listening can be without rock'n'roll.'

Danny & The Juniors became popular nationally after appearing on the Dick Clark TV show, *American Bandstand*, which is broadcast from their home town.

THE GRAPEVINE

- Latest US teen movie is *The Big Beat* – with The Diamonds, The Del-Vikings and Fats Domino.
- The Crickets, visiting Britain next month, are currently touring Australia – along with Paul Anka, Jerry Lee Lewis, Jodie Sands and homegrown rocker Johnny O'Keefe.
- British TV's popular disc programme, *Cool For Cats*, is now presented by Kent Walton; meanwhile, *Six-Five Special* producer Jack Good has left the BBC.

New Cool For Cats compere is Radio Luxembourg DJ Kent Walton

DOT EXCEL YET AGAIN

Statistics reveal that of the Top Six best selling records in America last year, three were on the remarkably successful Dot label . . . 'Love Letters In the Sand' by Pat Boone (2), 'Young Love' by Tab Hunter (4), and 'Don't Forbid Me' by Pat Boone (6).

No. 1 was 'Tammy' by Debbie Reynolds, while third and fifth were both taken by Johnny Mathis – with 'It's Not For Me To Say' and 'Chances Are'.

THUMBS DOWN FOR TOP VOCAL GROUP

The best selling R&B hit in America is 'Get A Job' by The Silhouettes – but according to reviewer, Keith Fordyce, its chances of scoring over here look slim.

'This is one of the worst rock'n'roll discs I have ever heard,' says Keith. 'I'm no square, but I do ask that pop music should be entertaining. This opens with a fair imitation of hens clucking, but is monotonous, meaningless, miserable mumble jumble.'

You didn't like it then, Keith?

Top vocal team, the Silhouettes

WEE WILLIE'S IN THE PINK!

The latest British musical personality to fill theatres is Decca recording artist Wee Willie Harris – the man with the famous pink hair! Whether it is this, his voice, or his flamboyant stage behaviour, we don't know – but he has certainly captured the imagination of the teenage public.

'My gimmick goes everywhere with me, even to bed', he says. 'As long as I keep my thatch nice and rosy, my future will be the same!'.

Formerly a pudding mixer at Peak Frean's London bakery, 24-year-old Harris turned professional after realizing he could make more money singing.

'People say I sound like Little Richard,' he says, 'but one thing's for certain – I won't be giving up show business to become an evangelist!'

CHARTS

US45	At The Hop – *Danny & The Juniors*
USLP	Come Fly With Me – *Frank Sinatra*
UK45	Jailhouse Rock – *Elvis Presley*
WEEK 2	
US45	At The Hop – *Danny & The Juniors*
USLP	Come Fly With Me – *Frank Sinatra*
UK45	Jailhouse Rock – *Elvis Presley*
WEEK 3	
US45	Sugartime – *McGuire Sisters*
USLP	Come Fly With Me – *Frank Sinatra*
UK45	The Story Of My Life – *Michael Holliday*
WEEK 4	
US45	Sugartime – *McGuire Sisters*
USLP	Come Fly With Me – *Frank Sinatra*
UK45	The Story Of My Life – *Michael Holliday*

ELVIS JOINS THE US ARMY

By the end of 1957, Elvis Presley was the unchallenged King of Rock'n'Roll. With nine US chart-topping hits behind him achieved in less than two years, he was the hottest item on any menu, but that very fact may have strongly influenced the US Government in their insistence that Presley should be drafted for national service in the US Army.

Inevitably, there was considerable wailing and gnashing of teeth among the multitude of heartbroken female fans, although the media was correctly suspicious about whether Presley would be forced to serve his time like any other John Doe. The cynics felt that their case was proven when an Army spokesman suggested that the most likely posting for Elvis might be to the Army's Special Services Division, as an entertainer performing for his fellow servicemen, as a result of which he might not have to submit to a regular army haircut, and might be allowed to retain his pompadour and long sideburns. At which point a Republican Senator vociferously enquired why Presley should be treated differently from other conscripts, and it became clear that the publicity scam would fail disastrously unless Elvis was treated like every other recruit and given no special privileges. And yes, his luxuriant crowning glory would be cropped.

Of course, his manager Colonel Tom Parker wasn't about to miss any publicity opportunities – having already arranged for a brief deferment to allow Elvis to complete filming on *'King Creole'*, he also wanted to ensure that enough recorded material was 'in the can' to cover at least the major part of his star's unavoidable absence. On the fateful day – Monday March 24th, 1958 – Elvis arrived at the Draft Board office in Memphis to find not only a number of fans awaiting his arrival but also a crowd of media representatives primed to document the occasion when The King was transformed into Army Private US53310761, and heard that his pay was to be reduced from $1000 per week to $83.20 per month. His initial posting was to Fort Chaffee, Arkansas.

On the next day, it was time for the haircut and Parker made a meal out of ensuring that there was no chance for anyone to collect a lock of Elvis's hair from the floor. When Presley went to collect his uniform, Parker made a point of trying to slip a bootlace tie in his charge's kitbag,

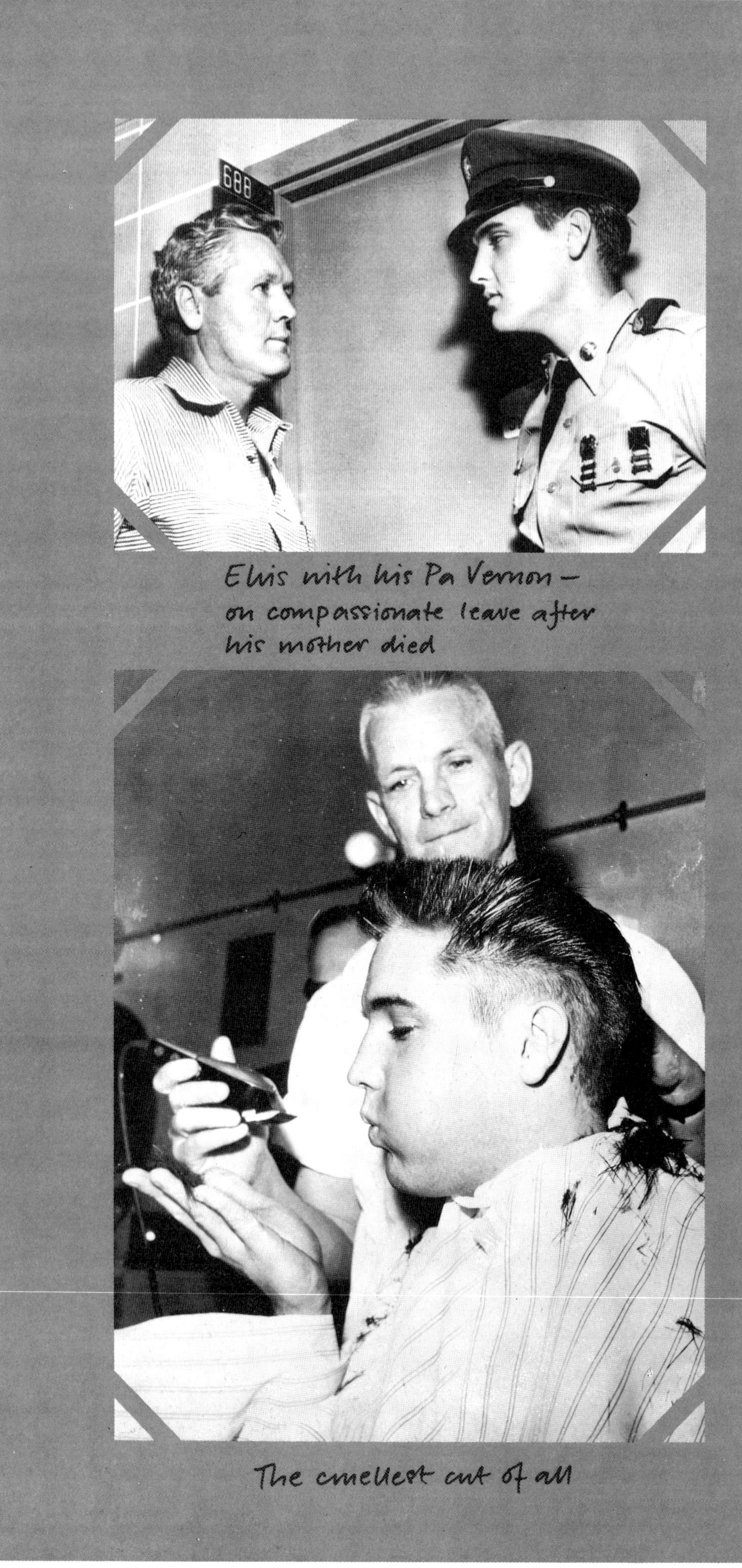

Elvis with his Pa Vernon – on compassionate leave after his mother died

The cruellest cut of all

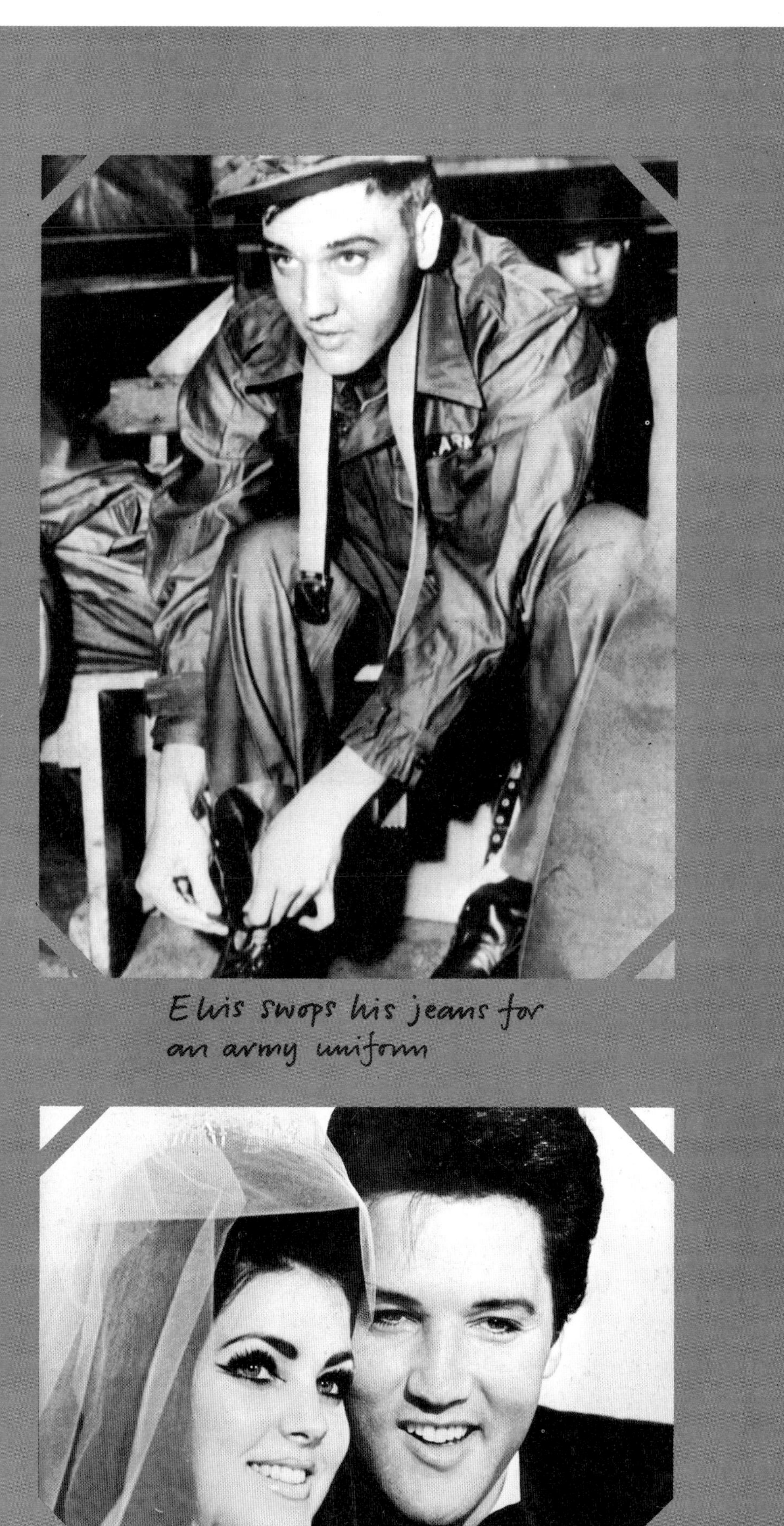

Elvis swops his jeans for an army uniform

Elvis marries Priscilla Beaulieu – his girlfriend from army days

but Elvis seemed to think that was taking the circus concept too far. The Army felt much the same, and it was announced – at a press conference – that he would receive his basic combat training at Fort Hood, Texas, with the 2nd Armoured Division.

During the two week leave which followed basic training, Presley undertook his only recording sessions during his two years as a GI, and also attended the Memphis premiere of *King Creole.* It was also arranged that Vernon & Gladys Presley, his parents, would live close to Fort Hood so that Elvis could visit them, as he was particularly concerned about his mother's poor health. His concern was justified – on August 14th, 1958, Gladys died of a heart attack at the age of 46. Soon after his mother was cremated, the 2nd Armoured Division was posted to West Germany, and this was the only time during his life that Elvis set foot in Europe. Perhaps in view of his recent bereavement, Vernon Presley and Elvis's grandmother, Minnie Mae Presley, were permitted to rent a house near the Army base so that Elvis could spend his off-duty time in the bosom of his family.

Much of the rest of his period as a GI was spent in being a soldier, but it subsequently became clear that Elvis had also found himself a girlfriend in the glamorous shape of Priscilla Beaulieu, the daughter of an Air Force major also stationed in Germany. Priscilla was only 14 and although rumours of a romance were denied at the time, some years later she married Presley and bore his only legitimate child, Lisa Marie.

Two months before the end of his tour of duty in Germany, Elvis was promoted to sergeant, and when he was honourably discharged in early March, 1960, it became clear that if anything, his absence had made the hearts of his fans grow fonder: *King Creole* had been a great success, both as a film and also as a soundtrack album, while the two years had seen eight more US Top 10 hits, including two chart-toppers, 'Hard Headed Woman' and 'A Big Hunk O' Love'.

The problem becomes clear in retrospect – Parker had always wanted Elvis to be a so-called family entertainer à la Dean Martin rather than a rock'n'roller, and the enforced hiatus was used to transform the Hillbilly Cat into a Frank Sinatra figure. For Elvis, the change of style made little impact on his success, but 30 years later, it's all too clear that the original primeval rocker had his teeth removed in the late 1950s. Had he continued in the vein in which he started, maybe The Beatles wouldn't have been so necessary a couple of years later. . . .

1958

LITTLE RICHARD IS BACK – ON DISC ONLY

Little Richard may be immersed in religious studies, but after searching the vaults, his Hollywood record label, Specialty, have come up with another rip-roaring hit, 'Good Golly Miss Molly'.

It couldn't be more contemporary; the latest fashion seems to require a girl's name in the title. Also in the US charts are 'Dede Dinah' by Frankie Avalon, 'Jo Ann' by The Playmates, and 'Oh Julie' by The Crescendos.

These follow hot on the heels of Little Richard's previous girlfriends – 'Long Tall Sally', 'Lucille', 'Jenny Jenny' and 'Miss Ann' – and 'Peggy Sue' (Buddy Holly), 'Wake Up Little Susie' (The Everly Brothers), 'Diana' (Paul Anka), 'Yes Tonight Josephine' (Johnnie Ray), 'Betty And Dupree' (Chuck Willis), 'Cindy Oh Cindy' (Eddie Fisher), 'Marianne' (The Hilltoppers), 'Bernardine' (Pat Boone), and 'Short Fat Fannie' (Larry Williams).

And wouldn't you just know it . . . Larry's latest release is called 'Dizzy Miss Lizzy'!

'WE HAD A REAL BALL!' SAYS BUDDY

Never have British rock'n'roll audiences been as thrilled as they were with The Crickets, who managed to squeeze 25 concerts into as many days, with a couple of TV spots thrown in for good measure.

With four hits in the UK Top 30 – two by the group ('Oh Boy' and 'Maybe Baby',) and two by leader Buddy Holly, ('Peggy Sue' and 'Listen To Me') – the trio have won the hearts of rock'n'roll fans throughout the land . . . and the feeling is mutual.

'We had a real ball, it was just great,' said Buddy, as the group prepared to return to New York, where they will join Alan Freed's latest tour. 'We've hardly had a day off since we started,' he joked.

Holly and his companions – drummer Jerry Allison and bassist Joe Mauldin – have all become obsessed with British sports cars and motorcycles. Their fans, meanwhile, have become hooked on Buddy's guitar – a Fender Stratocaster model which is unavailable here.

His horn-rimmed glasses caused a stir too . . . expect a spate of guitarists with specs!

DENE IN THE DUMPS

'Terry Dene is seeing a psychiatrist this week,' reports his manager, Paul Lincoln. 'He will then receive treatment and will not resume work until both he and the doctors are satisfied he is better.'

This follows an incident in Gloucester, England, where Dene was charged with being drunk and disorderly and causing wilful damage. Local magistrates fined him £155.

Marty Wilde and Colin Hicks have been fulfilling his contracted dates.

Currently debilitated by the demands of stardom, Terry Dene hopes to resume his touring schedule as soon as possible.

CHARTS

US45	Sugartime – *McGuire Sisters*
USLP	Come Fly With Me – *Frank Sinatra*
UK45	Magic Moments – *Perry Como*
WEEK 2	
US45	Catch A Falling Star – *Perry Como*
USLP	The Music Man – *Original Cast*
UK45	Magic Moments – *Perry Como*
WEEK 3	
US45	Tequila – *Champs*
USLP	The Music Man – *Original Cast*
UK45	Magic Moments – *Perry Como*
WEEK 4	
US45	Tequila – *Champs*
USLP	The Music Man – *Original Cast*
UK45	Magic Moments – *Perry Como*
WEEK 5	
US45	Tequila – *Champs*
USLP	My Fair Lady – *Original Cast*
UK45	Magic Moments – *Perry Como*

Burt Bacharach . . . and Hal David

THE GRAPEVINE

- **'Magic Moments' is the second UK hit written by Burt Bacharach and Hal David, who also penned 'The Story Of My Life' for Marty Robbins.**
- **14-year old Laurie London has become the latest Brit to storm the US chart – with 'He's Got The Whole World In His Hands'.**
- **Jerry Lee Lewis is currently filming *High School Confidential* at MGM's Hollywood studios.**

American success for Laurie London

CONNIE WINS FAME WITH A SONG TWICE HER AGE

Pert and provocative Connie Francis – at 19 the youngest female hit parader for some time – has been trying to make it in show business ever since she was four, when she first appeared on a radio show presenting amateur talent.

Born Concetta Franconero, in Newark, New Jersey, she recently dubbed Tuesday Weld's singing voice in the film *Rock Rock Rock*. But after several vain attempts to find the pop charts, she was ready to give up music and enrolled at New York University.

However, to please her father, she recorded 'Who's Sorry Now' – an oldie written in 1923 – and her singing career promptly took off, landing her in the Top Five on both sides of the Atlantic!

Coincidentally, her only previous chart appearance was a minor US hit called 'The Majesty Of Love', which was a duet with current chart-topper Marvin Rainwater!

THE GRAPEVINE

- 'Breathless', the new chart-stormer from Jerry Lee Lewis, was composed by Otis Blackwell, the man who wrote 'Don't Be Cruel' and 'All Shook Up' for Elvis.
- US rock'n'roller Charlie Gracie has returned to Britain for his second tour.
- Army enlistment has not harmed Elvis Presley's record sales: 'Wear My Ring Around Your Neck' has become his 16th consecutive million seller!

CHARTS

US45 Tequila – *Champs*
USLP My Fair Lady – *Original Cast*
UK45 Magic Moments – *Perry Como*

WEEK 2

US45 He's Got The Whole World In His Hands – *Laurie London*
USLP The Music Man – *Original Cast*
UK45 Magic Moments – *Perry Como*

WEEK 3

US45 He's Got The Whole World In His Hands – *Laurie London*
USLP The Music Man – *Original Cast*
UK45 Magic Moments – *Perry Como*

WEEK 4

US45 Witch Doctor – *David Seville*
USLP The Music Man – *Original Cast*
UK45 Whole Lotta Woman – *Marvin Rainwater*

Hit songwriter Otis Blackwell

ZULU MUSIC COULD END ROCK AGE

When author Wolf Mankowitz returned to London from Africa, after gathering material for his television series *The Killing Stones*, he brought back a record which he thought might be suitable for the soundtrack.

The disc was 'Tom Hark' by Elia & The Zig Zag Jive Flutes – a piece so arresting and unusual that ATV's switchboard was besieged with enquiries about it. EMI learned of the commotion, quickly obtained the rights, and the outcome is that a bunch of six Africans, of Zulu descent, find themselves in the British Top 10!

New though it is to our ears, this type of music – known locally as 'Kwela' – has become so popular in South Africa that it has all but swept rock'n'roll out of the reckoning . . . and some enthusiasts claim that it will do the same thing here.

THE CHAMPS ARE A KNOCK-OUT!

Named after a potent Mexican drink, the rocking 'Tequila' has won overnight acclaim for instrumentalists, The Champs.

The number, written by sax player Chuck Rio, was only recorded to use up left-over time on a session by singer-guitarist Dave Burgess, but the resultant track was so instantly appealing that the owners of the Los Angeles label, Challenge, decided to release it . . . under the name of The Champs.

As the record began its meteoric rise to the very top of the US best sellers, Burgess and Rio roped in three musician friends to replace the session men who had played on the disc and took to the road under their new, prophetically chosen name!

TROUBLE AHEAD FOR FREED?

Alan Freed is not popular with the citizens of New England, who fear that his latest 'Big Beat' package spells nothing but trouble. Other cities look like following the Mayor of New Haven's decision to ban his 17 act tour after a series of stabbings, beatings and robberies at the Boston Arena show.

A sailor was on the danger list at City Hospital, where a dozen others were also taken for treatment. The outbreak of violence came as 6000 poured out of the Arena. Police had refused to let Freed have the house lights turned down during the performance. 'I guess the police here in Boston don't want you kids to have a good time,' he said from the stage.

Custodians of the law have long sought to find a tangible link between rock'n'roll and teen delinquency . . . perhaps this is all the evidence they need.

JERRY LEE DROPS BOMBSHELL!

British fans have long anticipated the arrival of dynamic piano-thumper Jerry Lee Lewis, described as the most frantic and awe-inspiring rock'n'roll artist in America. They expected a 'Whole Lotta Shakin' Goin' On' – but now they're shaking with rage!

Jerry Lee has returned home after the abrupt cancellation of his tour. He played only three nights of his contracted 35.

A media storm blew up when the singer admitted that his third wife, Myra, is only 14. Moreover, she is also his cousin. Indignant parties insisted that Lewis be castigated for his unacceptable behaviour.

The tour will carry on, with The Chas McDevitt Skiffle Group and Terry Wayne filling out the bill.

Jerry Lee with bride Myra

WITCH DOCTOR PRESCRIBES SUCCESS FOR SEVILLE

The son of a California grape farmer, David Seville's first taste of success came in 1951, when he wrote Rosemary Clooney's million-seller, 'Come-On-A My House' – but then he abandoned the music business to become actor.

After landing roles in films like *Rear Window* and *The Proud And The Profane*, however, he returned to records, reaching the US charts with his instrumental, 'Armen's Theme'.

His latest waxing, 'Witch Doctor', is a radical departure – a novelty featuring a speeded-up vocal. In the States, it sold in such quantities that it prevented the new Elvis single from reaching No. 1 . . . unheard of!

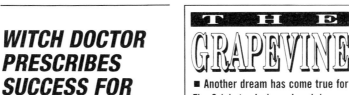

THE GRAPEVINE

- **Another dream has come true for The Crickets: during a break in their touring schedule, all three purchased brand-new imported British motorcycles!**
- **Lonnie Donegan's latest Top Tenner, 'Grand Coolie Dam', is about an American hydro-electric project!**
- **Resting after a mauling he suffered when fans stormed the stage in Dundee, Scotland, Tommy Steele will play a bullfighter in his next film, *Tommy The Toreador!***

CONNIE FRANCIS

'I like speed, yellow convertibles, empty churches, daybreak, sunset, animals, food, occasional parties and dancing. I detest insects, hypocrites, giggly girls, elevators, rigid conformists and men who boast of their innumerable conquests.'

'Witchdoctor' hit man David Seville with proteges for his next project, a trio called . . . The Chipmunks

CHARTS

	Chart	Title	Artist
	US45	Witch Doctor	*David Seville*
	USLP	The Music Man	*Original Cast*
	UK45	Whole Lotta Woman	*Marvin Rainwater*
WEEK 2	US45	All I Have To Do Is Dream	*Everly Brothers*
	USLP	The Music Man	*Original Cast*
	UK45	Whole Lotta Woman	*Marvin Rainwater*
WEEK 3	US45	All I Have To Do Is Dream	*Everly Brothers*
	USLP	The Music Man	*Original Cast*
	UK45	Who's Sorry Now	*Connie Francis*
WEEK 4	US45	All I Have To Do Is Dream	*Everly Brothers*
	USLP	The Music Man	*Original Cast*
	UK45	Who's Sorry Now	*Connie Francis*
WEEK 5	US45	All I Have To Do Is Dream	*Everly Brothers*
	USLP	Johnny's Gratest Hits	*Johnny Mathis*
	UK45	Who's Sorry Now	*Connie Francis*

STEREO – THE COMING THING?

The New York R&B label, Atlantic, have purchased new equipment which will put them in the forefront of recording technology. Their new 8-track console allows eight separate tracks to be recorded independently, thus allowing the instrumentation to be laid down on individual tracks and the vocals to be added and balanced later.

Until now, Atlantic have relied either on live studio takes or on building up a number by dubbing from one tape machine to another.

Though they will still be issuing most of their records in mono, they are building up a library of 'stereophonic' recordings for future release.

RCA have this month begun issuing stereophonic albums – even though relatively few listeners possess players capable of reproducing the three-dimensional sound they deliver. Like Atlantic, the company is convinced that within a few years, all records will be stereo.

The Dallas Boys – resident vocal group for Jack Good's new series

OH BOY! JACK'S BACK!

Positive audience reaction to two pilot programmes has convinced ABC-TV, the British commercial channel, to go ahead with a whole series of *Oh Boy!*, a fast-moving teenage music show devised by Jack Good – the founder-producer of BBC's *Six-Five Special*.

Good's format packs around 17 beat numbers into 35 minutes. Resident performers will include Marty Wilde, The Dallas Boys, Cherry Wainer, and Lord Rockingham's XI – a group sponsored by Good.

CHARTS

US45	Purple People Eater	*Sheb Wooley*
USLP	Johnny's Gratest Hits	*Johnny Mathis*
UK45	Who's Sorry Now	*Connie Francis*
WEEK 2		
US45	Purple People Eater	*Sheb Wooley*
USLP	The Music Man	*Original Cast*
UK45	Who's Sorry Now	*Connie Francis*
WEEK 3		
US45	Purple People Eater	*Sheb Wooley*
USLP	The Music Man	*Original Cast*
UK45	Who's Sorry Now	*Connie Francis*
WEEK 4		
US45	Purple People Eater	*Sheb Wooley*
USLP	Johnny's Greatest Hits	*Johnny Mathis*
UK45	On The Street Where You Live	*Vic Damone*

BERRY LOSES GRIP ON UK FANS

Somewhat surprisingly, British fans have resisted the spell of Chuck Berry's newest American smash, 'Johnny B Goode'. The rags-to-riches story of a locally renowned country boy determined to see his name in lights, it could well be a thinly disguised account of Berry's own rise to fame.

Like the hero of his song, Berry can 'play a guitar just like ringing a bell' – but though he dented the UK charts with both 'School Day' and 'Sweet Little Sixteen', his latest classic has missed the frame altogether.

SECOND GOLD DISC FOR COASTERS

The Coasters, the black vocal group from America's West Coast (hence their name), have secured another massive US seller with their novel rocker, 'Yakety Yak' – now standing at No. 1 on the R&B chart, and No. 2 on the pop list.

Comprising Carl Gardner (tenor), Billy Guy (baritone), Cornell Gunter (tenor) and Will Jones (bass), the group evolved from pioneering Los Angeles unit, The Robins, who worked closely with Johnny Otis.

Now their mentors are the songwriting-producing team of Leiber and Stoller, who were responsible for concocting both 'Yakety Yak' and their last million seller, 'Searchin''.

THE GRAPEVINE

- **Latest hit to employ speeded-up vocals is 'Purple People Eater' by Sheb Wooley, an actor who played a baddy anxious to shoot Gary Cooper in *High Noon*!**
- **New names in the US Top 20 include Bobby Freeman with 'Do You Want To Dance', Jan & Arnie with 'Jennie Lee', Jody Reynolds with 'Endless Sleep', Link Wray with 'Rumble', and Bobby Darin with 'Splish Splash'.**

Will The Coasters (left) be able to repeat their Stateside success here . . . and why is the UK chart proving so elusive for Chuck Berry (right)?

THE EVERLYS REACH THE TOP!

So they've done it! After two very near misses, The Everly Brothers have achieved their first No. 1 in Britain – with 'All I Have To Do Is Dream'.

Raised on country music, the two Kentuckians believe the reason their records have made such an impact is that: 'They are simple, direct and to the point. The kids don't want to have to sit down and decipher a song, or figure it out.'

For their current chart-topper, and their previous hits – 'Bye Bye Love' and 'Wake Up Little Susie' – Don and Phil have to thank the Nashville songwriting team of Felice and Boudleaux Bryant, whose songs are tailor-made for the boys' distinctive style.

It reached the top on both sides of the Atlantic, and has sold well over a million copies, but 'All I Have To Do Is Dream' took only 15 minutes to write! Incidentally, the flip side, 'Claudette', was penned by Texan rockabilly singer Roy Orbison – as a tribute to his wife.

Orbison: Everly 'B' side

THE GIRLS GO WILDE FOR MARTY

If any British artist is going to equal the towering stature of dynamic Tommy Steele, then it's Marty Wilde. His live appearances, which always provoke an intense response from the audience – particularly the girls – have improved immeasurably, and his more recent recordings reveal a degree of confidence quite remarkable for a performer so youthful.

Sales of his fourth release, 'Endless Sleep', have now propelled him into the charts for the first time – much to the glee of his recording manager, Johnny Franz.

'Marty came along on the rock'n'roll wave, but I've always seen more in him than that,' says Franz. 'I believe he's got the kind of lasting talent that can be applied to any sort of song.'

High praise indeed – especially when you consider that this time last year, Marty was still working in a South London timber yard!

THE GRAPEVINE

- Harry Belafonte's next album will be called 'Belafonte Sings The Blues', on which he performs several Ray Charles originals.
- Since his tour eighteen months ago, Bill Haley has been completely absent from the UK charts – though he is currently in the US Top 30 with 'Skinny Minnie'.
- Peggy Lee has waxed the rock'n'roll title which established Little Willie John's career – 'Fever'.

Consistent LP seller Harry Belafonte

DENE SWAPS GUITAR FOR GUN

Following in the footsteps of Elvis, British rock'n'roll star Terry Dene must soon report to Winchester Barracks, where he will join the Kings Royal Rifle Corps for National Service. Originally scheduled for July 7, his call-up has now been deferred until contracted commitments have been completed.

In the meantime, Dene has married singing star Edna Savage, after a whirlwind romance which blossomed during a shared variety tour. When the couple return from their honeymoon in Torremolinos, Spain, agent Hyman Zahl plans to present them as 'Mr and Mrs Music'.

CHARTS

US45	Purple People Eater *Sheb Wooley*
USLP	The Music Man *Original Cast*
UK45	All I Have To Do Is Dream *Everly Brothers*
WEEK 2	
US45	Hard Headed Woman *Elvis Presley*
USLP	Gigi *Soundtrack*
UK45	All I Have To Do Is Dream *Everly Brothers*
WEEK 3	
US45	Hard Headed Woman *Elvis Presley*
USLP	Gigi *Soundtrack*
UK45	All I Have To Do Is Dream *Everly Brothers*
WEEK 4	
US45	Poor Little Fool *Ricky Nelson*
USLP	Gigi *Soundtrack*
UK45	All I Have To Do Is Dream *Everly Brothers*

TEEN-RAVE NELSON TAKES OVER

With Elvis temporarily out of the running, the hottest property in American teenage music right now is young Ricky Nelson.

In just over a year, he has collected golden discs for 'I'm Walkin'', 'Be-Bop Baby', 'Stood Up', 'Believe What You Say' and his current hit, 'Poor Little Fool' – an American No. 1 and his first substantial seller in Britain.

As the long-time child star of US television's *The Adventures of Ozzie and Harriet*, Ricky was virtually 'the boy next door' for every American teenager – and it was on this show that his singing career began.

His growing legion of British fans will shortly be able to see him in a new Western movie, *Rio Bravo* also starring John Wayne and Dean Martin.

OH BOY! NEWCOMER

Cliff Richard – a new British teenage singer whose debut disc, 'Schoolboy Crush', is released at the end of the month – has already been snapped up by producer Jack Good for the first programme of his commercial TV series, *Oh Boy!*

Cliff, who is 17, records with his own group, The Drifters.

reviewer, Keith Fordyce writes: 'Cliff is an expert exponent of rock'n'roll. To a steady beat, he puts over a lyric that has plenty of meaning to the younger listener. The B-side, 'Move It', is an exciting number with a throbbing sound. If you're an addict of the big beat, then this is a must for your collection.'

Oh Boy! which begins its run on September 13 – in the same Saturday time-slot as BBC-TV's *Six-Five Special* – will also feature chart star Marty Wilde.

Cliff: new boy on 'Oh Boy'

CHARTS

US45	Poor Little Fool — *Ricky Nelson*
USLP	Como's Golden Records — *Perry Como*
UK45	All I Have To Do Is Dream — *Everly Brothers*
WEEK 2	
US45	Volare — *Domenico Modugno*
USLP	Tchaikovsky: Piano Concerto No. 1 — *Van Cliburn*
UK45	All I Have To Do Is Dream — *Everly Brothers*
WEEK 3	
US45	Bird Dog — *Everly Brothers*
USLP	Tchaikovsky: Piano Concerto No. 1 — *Van Cliburn*
UK45	All I Have To Do Is Dream — *Everly Brothers*
WEEK 4	
US45	Volare — *Domenico Modugno*
USLP	Tchaikovsky: Piano Concerto No. 1 — *Van Cliburn*
UK45	When — *Kalin Twins*
WEEK 5	
US45	Volare — *Domenico Modugno*
USLP	Tchaikovsky: Piano Concerto No. 1 — *Van Cliburn*
UK45	When — *Kalin Twins*

KALINS PREDICTED SUCCESS – THE ONLY QUESTION WAS WHEN?

There's an old saying that two heads are better than one. Right now, America's Kalin Twins are living proof of this. Both had opportunities to enter show business as 'singles', but they felt they would stand a better chance if they stuck together – and their chart-topping hit, 'When', has certainly vindicated their decision!

As alike as two peas in a pod, Harold and Herbie Kalin were born in Port Jervis, New York, on February 16 1934 – and have shared the same hobbies and interests since childhood. Their singing career got underway when they met songwriter Clint Ballard Jr, who became their manager – but the song he selected for them, 'When', was written not by him, but by another vocalist, Paul Evans.

The Kalins now plan to strike while the iron's hot, and tour Britain within a couple of months.

THE GRAPEVINE

- **Johnny Otis has a US hit with 'Willie And The Hand Jive', inspired by the craze which originated on BBC-TV's *Six-Five Special*.**
- **Sam Phillips, owner of Sun Records, has lost both Carl Perkins and Johnny Cash to Columbia; Cash is currently on US charts with 'Guess Things Happen That Way'.**
- **Buddy Holly has married Maria Elena Santiago – a receptionist at Coral Records' New York office.**

'Willie' hands it to Otis

Cash loss for Sun

SEPTEMBER

DUANE EDDY'S NEW 'TWANG'

With his worldwide hit, 'Rebel Rouser' – an atmospheric instrumental punctuated by whoops and yells – guitarist Duane Eddy brings yet another new sound to the apparently inexhaustible Big Beat.

Duane, a handsome six-footer with a shy smile and a warm 'hello', was born in Corning, New York, on April 26 1938. While still a child, he developed an interest in American frontier history, and the folk music of that period stimulated his interest in the guitar.

When his family decided to trek west and settle in Arizona, 13-year-old Duane began to explore rockabilly and blues material, and within a few years he was in great demand at dances, clubs and shows.

'Rebel Rouser', which he wrote with producer Lee Hazlewood, demonstrates what Duane describes as his 'Twangy Guitar'.

ELVIS POSTED TO EUROPE!

Private Presley obliges a fan

The possibility of Elvis Presley performing in Britain has taken a decided step forward with the announcement that he must report to New York on September 20 for embarkation prior to being posted in Europe.

As a member of the Third American Armored Division, Presley will be stationed near Frankfurt, Germany – a mere hop from the stages of Britain!

Meanwhile, his fans will have to be content with the screen Elvis, currently doing the rounds in *King Creole*, and the vinyl Elvis, singing songs from the soundtrack.

Presley has recently been promoted to Private Second Class – which means a rise in salary to almost 86 dollars a month.

THE GRAPEVINE

■ New artists to the US Top 20 include Jimmy Clanton with 'Just A Dream', Jack Scott with 'My True Love', The Elegants with 'Little Star', Bobby Day with 'Rockin' Robin', The Olympics with 'Western Movies', and Eddie Cochran with 'Summertime Blues'.

■ Pat Boone is writing a book, *Twixt Twelve and Twenty*; it's about the problems of teenagers, according to his own experience and observations.

CHARTS

US45 Volare – *Domenico Modugno*
USLP South Pacific – *Soundtrack*
UK45 When – *Kalin Twins*

— WEEK 2 —

US45 Volare – *Domenico Modugno*
USLP Tchaikovsky: Piano Concerto No. 1 – *Van Cliburn*
UK45 When – *Kalin Twins*

— WEEK 3 —

US45 It's All In The Game – *Tommy Edwards*
USLP Tckaikovsky: Piano Concerto No. 1 – *Van Cliburn*
UK45 When – *Kalin Twins*

— WEEK 4 —

US45 It's All In The Game – *Tommy Edwards*
USLP Sing Along With Mitch – *Mitch Miller*
UK45 Stupid Cupid/Carolina Moon – *Connie Francis*

New to the US chart – Bobby Day

BORN TOO LATE – BUT THEY'LL GET OVER IT!

'I'm so young and you're so old', sang a despairing Paul Anka in Diana – and now a trio of girls are complaining that were also Born Too Late! The three young ladies in question are The Poni-Tails, from Cleveland, Ohio – and they can console themselves with the fact that their song of rejection and dejection has landed them in the best sellers on both sides of the Atlantic!

All 19 years old, Toni Cistone, Patti McCabe and LaVerne Novak teamed up in high school, where there was often friction on the subject of homework coming a poor second to singing.

However, they proved their point when they won a recording contract – and, as fate would have it, the executive who signed them up was ABC Paramount's Don Costa . . . the man who discovered Paul Anka.

Born Too Late – The Poni-Tails

STAR QUOTE

CLIFF RICHARD

'It's wonderful to be going on TV for the first time, but I feel so nervous that I don't know what to do. I shaved my sideburns off last night . . . Jack Good said it would make me look more original.'

CLIFF CELEBRATES BIRTHDAY IN STYLE

Much to the surprise of his record company, Cliff Richard has reached the UK Top 3 . . . with the flip side of his debut disc! Entitled 'Move It', the song was written by Ian 'Sammy' Samwell, lead guitarist with Cliff's backing group, The Drifters – and it was apparently recorded only as an afterthought.

Boosted by appearances on *Oh Boy!*, Cliff has not only rocketed up the chart, but also to the top of the Favourite New Singer section of this year's NME readers' poll. A factory clerk until a few weeks ago, he must truly understand the term 'overnight star'!

Born in Lucknow, India, on October 14 1940, Cliff moved to England with his family and, like so many teenagers, became fascinated by rock'n'roll and skiffle. A promising athlete at Cheshunt Secondary Modern, he spent his evenings playing football or strumming a guitar – and the guitar won.

Soon he had his own group and was performing in London's 2-Is coffee bar and Shepherds Bush Gaumont, where he was spotted by an agent, who alerted Norrie Paramor at Columbia Records. The rest is history.

This month, Cliff celebrates his eighteenth birthday by joining The Kalin Twins, The Vipers and The Most Brothers on a tour of Britain.

Southern drifter Scott

Left: The Kalin Twins

JACK SCOTT – OFF THE SHELF AT LAST

Released way back in May, Jack Scott's recording of 'My True Love' has finally found its way into the NME chart! In the mean time, it has managed to sell a million copies in the States – which must be very gratifying to Scott, who also composed both sides of this, his debut disc for the Carlton label.

A resident of Detroit, Michigan, he was actually born in Windsor, Canada, some 22 years ago and graduated to rock-slanted material after making the rounds of local country and western haunts, leading The Southern Drifters.

While 'My True Love' is a dramatic ballad, the B-side is a fast-moving rockabilly item called 'Leroy' – about a buddy who spends a lot of time in jail!

THE GRAPEVINE

- **His Memphis sweetheart Anita Wood saw Elvis off when he departed for Germany; as he left, he was carrying a book – *Poems that Touch the Heart*.**
- **Making a surprise appearance on Perry Como's TV show was kilted Edinburgh teenager Jackie Dennis, who scaled the NME chart with 'La-Dee-Dah'; said Como: 'You're a kind of Scottish Ricky Nelson.'**
- **Pop impressario Larry Parnes has signed an unknown singer from Liverpool – Billy Fury.**

ELVIS IS STILL NO. 1 . . . THREE TIMES!

Elvis Presley has won three categories in this year's NME readers' poll: World's Outstanding Popular Singer, World's Outstanding Musical Personality and Favourite US Male Singer. Chart-topping Connie Francis was voted Favourite US Female Singer, and The Everly Brothers are the World's Outstanding Vocal Group.

Winners in the British section were Frankie Vaughan, Alma Cogan, and The Mudlarks – with Cliff Richard beating Marty Wilde and Laurie London in the Newcomers list.

Parnes protégé Fury

CHARTS

US45	It's All In The Game – *Tommy Edwards*
USLP	Only The Lonely – *Frank Sinatra*
UK45	Stupid Cupid/Carolina Moon – *Connie Francis*
WEEK 2	
US45	It's All In The Game – *Tommy Edwards*
USLP	Only The Lonely – *Frank Sinatra*
UK45	Stupid Cupid/Carolina Moon – *Connie Francis*
WEEK 3	
US45	It's All In The Game – *Tommy Edwards*
USLP	Only The Lonely – *Frank Sinatra*
UK45	Stupid Cupid/Carolina Moon – *Connie Francis*
WEEK 4	
US45	It's All In The Game – *Tommy Edwards*
USLP	Only The Lonely – *Frank Sinatra*
UK45	Stupid Cupid/Carolina Moon – *Connie Francis*

NOVEMBER

CHARTS

- US45 It's Only Make Believe — *Conway Twitty*
- USLP Only The Lonely — *Frank Sinatra*
- UK45 Stupid Cupid/Carolina Moon — *Connie Francis*
- UKLP South Pacific — *Soundtrack*

WEEK 2

- US45 Tom Dooley — *Kingston Trio*
- USLP South Pacific — *Soundtrack*
- UK45 It's All In The Game — *Tommy Edwards*
- UKLP South Pacific — *Soundtrack*

WEEK 3

- US45 It's Only Make Believe — *Conway Twitty*
- USLP The Kingston Trio — *Kingston Trio*
- UK45 It's All In The Game — *Tommy Edwards*
- UKLP South Pacific — *Soundtrack*

WEEK 4

- US45 To Know Him Is To Love Him — *Teddy Bears*
- USLP Sing Along With Mitch — *Mitch Miller*
- UK45 It's All In The Game — *Tommy Edwards*
- UKLP South Pacific — *Soundtrack*

WEEK 5

- US45 To Know Him Is To Love Him — *Teddy Bears*
- USLP Sing Along With Mitch — *Mitch Miller*
- UK45 Hoots Mon! — *Lord Rockingham's XI*
- UKLP South Pacific — *Soundtrack*

SUMMERTIME BLUES IS WINTERTIME HIT FOR EDDIE!

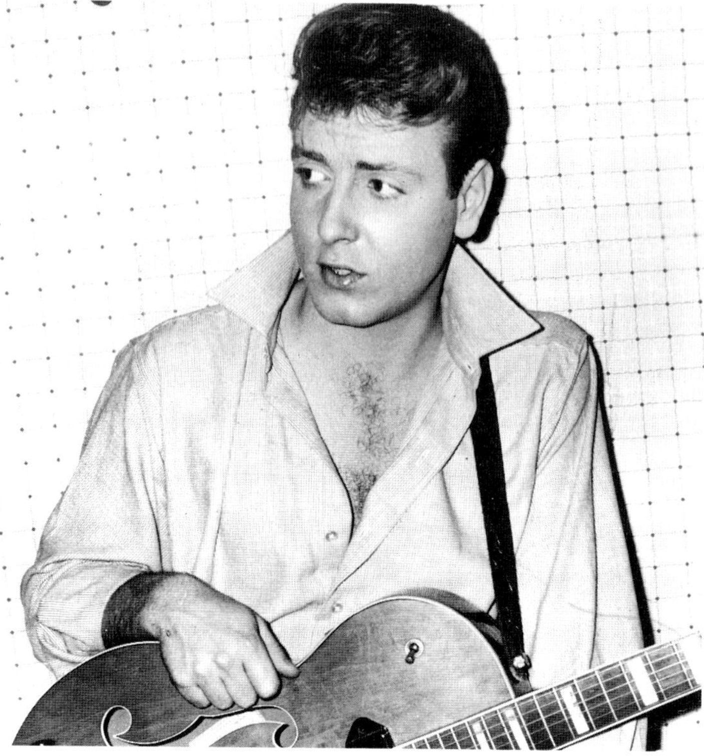

He was first seen last year, singing up a storm in the Jayne Mansfield movie, *The Girl Can't Help It* – and you may have caught him again in the Mamie Van Doren film, *Untamed Youth* . . . but this month marks Eddie Cochran's chart debut in Britain.

His previous releases, 'Twenty Flight Rock' and 'Sittin' In The Balcony', made little impact saleswise, but 'Summertime Blues' is a sure-fire rock'n'roll classic – written, incidentally, by the man himself.

Only five weeks out of his teens, Eddie was born in Oklahoma, but moved to Los Angeles as a schoolboy. A proficient guitarist, he soon attracted the attention of songwriter Jerry Capehart, who became his writing partner and producer.

A contract with Liberty Records followed, and Eddie was on his way . . . even though he still can't find a cure for those 'Summertime Blues'!

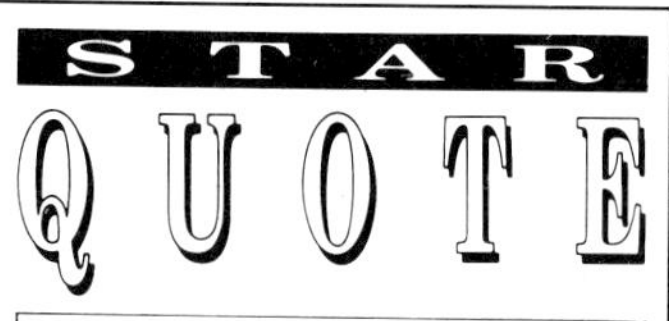

RICKY NELSON

'Anyone who knocks rock'n'roll either doesn't understand it, or is prejudiced against it, or is just plain square!'

TOMMY SELLS A MILLION

Tommy Edwards has been presented with a gold record for 'It's All In The Game' – not surprisingly, since it has topped both the US and UK charts.

Strangely, the song has been mellowing since 1912, when the melody was written by Charles Gates Dawes – a Vice President of the United States, no less.

Lyrics were added by Carl Sigman in 1951, when it was recorded by Nat King Cole, Dinah Shore and . . . Tommy Edwards. Convinced the song had sales potential, Tommy recorded it again this year and his hunch has been proved right – in no uncertain terms!

A gold disc for Tommy Edwards

THE GRAPEVINE

- Cliff Richard has been signed to star alongside Anthony Quayle in U.K. movie *Serious Charge* – in a part turned down by Tommy Steele.
- First release on the new Pye International label is 'Come On, Let's Go' – The US hit by Californian Ritchie Valens.
- Tommy Steele has laid out £2,800 for a silver-grey AC Aceca, capable of 115 mph.

LORD ROCKINGHAM'S XI KNOCKS FANS FOR SIX!

The man who is the personification of the fabulous Lord Rockingham scratched his head in bewilderment. 'I don't know what all the excitement is about,' says Harry Robinson. 'This all started as a gigantic joke and now it's developed into hit-parade proportions!'

Put together by musical director Robinson and TV producer Jack Good, Lord Rockingham's XI was formed to be resident backing band on *Oh Boy!*, but so popular is their recording of 'Hoots Mon' – complete with snatches of exaggerated Scottish doggerel – that it has zoomed all the way to No. 1!

Built around saxophonist Red Price and organist Cherry Wainer, the band comprises seasoned session men, but none has seen anything like this before.

'We always have tremendous fun in the studio,' says Harry. 'In fact, I don't think I've ever been involved in such hilarious sessions!'

CLIFF RICHARD: CRUDE, REVOLTING AND VULGAR

According to NME columnist, The Alley Cat, producer Jack Good must be held responsible for permitting the most crude exhibitionism ever seen on British TV – by Cliff Richard on *Oh Boy!*

'His violent hip-swinging was revolting – hardly the kind of performance any parent could wish their children to see,' writes Alley Cat. 'If we are expected to believe that Cliff was acting naturally, then consideration for medical treatment may be advisable.

'While firmly believing he can become a top star and enjoy a lengthy career, it will only be accomplished by dispensing with short-sighted, vulgar antics.'

TO HEAR THEM IS TO LOVE THEM

From obscurity to the top of the American hit parade with their first recording – that's the amazing success story of the three Los Angeles high-school students known as The Teddy Bears.

'To Know Him Is To Love Him' is the enchanting ballad which has focussed the spotlight on pretty 16-year-old Annette Kleinbard, 19-year-old Marshall Leib, and 18-year-old Phil Spector – who also wrote the song and worked out the vocal harmonies for the trio.

Until October, they had only sung locally, but an appearance on Dick Clark's influential TV show sent their song winging across the nation, straight to No. 1 . . . and now they look like repeating their feat in Britain.

CHARTS

US45	To Know Him Is To Love Him *Teddy Bears*
USLP	Sing Along With Mitch *Mitch Miller*
UK45	Hoots Mon! *Lord Rockingham's XI*
UKLP	South Pacific *Soundtrack*
WEEK 2	
US45	The Chipmunk Song *Chipmunks*
USLP	Sing Along With Mitch *Mitch Miller*
UK45	Hoots Mon! *Lord Rockingham's XI*
UKLP	South Pacific *Soundtrack*
WEEK 3	
US45	The Chipmunk Song *Chipmunks*
USLP	Christmas Sing Along *Mitch Miller*
UK45	It's Only Make Believe *Conway Twitty*
UKLP	South Pacific *Soundtrack*
WEEK 4	
US45	The Chipmunk Song *Chipmunks*
USLP	Christmas Sing Along *Mitch Miller*
UK45	It's Only Make Believe *Conway Twitty*
UKLP	South Pacific *Soundtrack*

TIPPED FOR STARDOM: NEIL SEDAKA

Watch out for Neil Sedaka, whom RCA regard as their hottest new signing, He's 19, a proficient pianist, and together with New York pal, Howard Greenfield, composed his debut single, 'The Diary'.

The songwriting duo have already made their mark on the charts – with the Connie Francis smash, 'Stupid Cupid'.

Connies 'Cupid' a Sedaka song

CONWAY TWITTY'S NAME? IT'S ONLY MAKE BELIEVE!

'When I write songs, I try to anticipate what the trends in pop music will be,' says 23-year-old singer-guitarist Conway Twitty. 'And earlier this year, I thought ballads would be making a comeback. So, back in February, while I was working at the Flamingo Lounge in Hamilton, Ontario, I sat in my dressing room and wrote 'It's Only Make Believe' – in seven minutes!'

Those few minutes of inspiration have provided Twitty with one of the year's biggest selling records . . . but what about that name?

He was born Harold Jenkins, the son of a Mississippi riverboat pilot, but when he embarked on his singing career, he wanted a more memorable name.

According to one source, he stuck pins in a map of the southern States to come up with Conway in Arkansas, and Twitty in Texas!

THE GRAPEVINE

- **Buddy Holly has moved from Texas to New York and is breaking away from The Crickets and manager Norman Petty.**
- **The Playmates have re-recorded their US hit, 'Beep Beep', with new lyrics to avoid a BBC ban on the words Cadillac and Nash Rambler.**
- **J. P. Richardson is the real name of The Big Bopper – currently heading for a Gold Disc with 'Chantilly Lace'.**

1959

FURY SEES WILDE; GETS CONTRACT!

'Maybe Tomorrow' is the first release by Billy Fury, a young Liverpudlian who, last October, gained access to Marty Wilde's dressing room at the Birkenhead Essoldo, hoping to interest him in some songs he'd written.

Marty's manager, Larry Parnes, persuaded Fury to perform his songs on stage that very night – and promptly contracted him!

Billy wins over Vernon's Girls

THE GRAPEVINE

■ It's the end of the line for BBC-TV's *Six-Five Special*, which has been shunted into a siding to make way for new teen show, *Dig This.*

■ Cliff Richard, Lord Rockingham's XI, Cuddly Dudley, The Vernons Girls, Vince Taylor and other stars of the series are now touring as the *Oh Boy!* package show.

■ In America, Jackie Wilson has the number one R&B hit, 'Lonely Teardrops'.

DONEGAN WINS DUEL OVER TOM DOOLEY

In America, The Kingston Trio scored a massive hit with 'Tom Dooley', but in Britain, Lonnie Donegan has made all the running to rack up his ninth Top Tenner.

The song – based on an actual incident which happened almost a century ago – concerns a killer, comdemned to hang for the murder of his true love.

The Trio, three college chums who have become the hottest nightclub attraction in San Francisco, are also high on the US album chart with their collection of folk songs.

Lonnie, meanwhile, has already recorded his follow-up single - his adaptation of an old music-hall song, 'Does Your Chewing Gum Lose Its Flavour On The Bedpost Overnight?'

Champions of American folk music, the Kingston Trio

ALL CHANGE IN CLIFF'S CAMP

Cliff Richard (left) with his new backing group: Bruce Welch, Tony Meehan, Jet Harris and Hank B. Marvin

Since he first found fame last autumn, U.K. star Cliff Richard has seen all his closest colleagues come and go.

First of all, new Drifters arrived in the shape of guitarists Hank Marvin and Bruce Welch – former skifflers from Newcastle who were attracted by the bright lights of the 2-Is coffee bar. Then bass player Jet Harris joined from The Vipers. Now drummer Terry Smart, the sole survivor of Cliff's original group, has gone too – replaced by Jet's friend, Tony Meehan.

Additionally, Cliff has dismissed his manager, Franklyn Boyd, in favour of Tito Burns – and John Foster, who first launched Cliff, has also left his service.

Cliff's former guitarist, Ian Samwell – the man who penned 'Move It' – is now concentrating entirely on songwriting. He provided his old side-kick with both sides of his current hit, 'High Class Baby'/'My Feet Hit The Ground'.

SEVILLE REVELS IN ELECTRONIC TRIO

That 'Witch Doctor' man, David Seville, is back with his speeded-up voices . . . this time three of them, singing in unison as The Chipmunks!

In his clever novelty, 'The Chipmunk Song', Seville is encouraging his creations to make a record – and what a record they've made. In a matter of weeks, over three million copies have been sold.

Two of his Chipmunks are named after executives of his record label, Liberty; Simon after company president Si Waronker and Alvin after vice-chairman Al Bennett. The third, Theodore, is named after Seville's very patient recording engineer, Ted Keep.

CHARTS

US45	The Chipmunk Song *Chipmunks*
USLP	Sing Along With Mitch *Mitch Miller*
UK45	It's Only Make Believe *Conway Twitty*
UKLP	South Pacific *Soundtrack*
WEEK 2	
US45	Smoke Gets In Your Eyes *Platters*
USLP	Sing Along With Mitch *Mitch Miller*
UK45	It's Only Make Believe *Conway Twitty*
UKLP	South Pacific *Soundtrack*
WEEK 3	
US45	Smoke Gets In Your Eyes *Platters*
USLP	Sing Along With Mitch *Mitch Miller*
UK45	It's Only Make Believe *Conway Twitty*
UKLP	South Pacific *Soundtrack*
WEEK 4	
US45	Smoke Gets In Your Eyes *Platters*
USLP	Flower Drum Song *Original Cast*
UK45	The Day The Rains Came *Jane Morgan*
UKLP	South Pacific *Soundtrack*

BUDDY HOLLY DIES IN AIR CRASH HORROR

Buddy Holly and two more of America's top rock 'n' roll stars were killed in a plane crash on their way to a concert in the early hours of the morning of Tuesday February 3.

Earlier Holly, the Big Bopper and Ritchie Valens had entertained over 1,000 teenagers at the Surf Ballroom in Clear Lake, Iowa, then chartered a light aircraft to take them on to their next concert at Moorhead, Minnesota.

Two hours after the dance finished, three of the top names on the show were dead, along with the pilot who was flying them. The others on the bill, Dion and the Belmonts and the Platters, had travelled separately by road.

Word of their death broke on the Tuesday morning when the plane, a four-seater Beechcraft Bonanza – was found in a snow-covered field six miles north of Mason City airport from where it had taken off.

The plane appeared to have come down in a heavy snowstorm, scraping along the ground before bouncing and skidding for 200 yards then coming to a halt, completely demolished. The bodies of the three pop stars were thrown from the aircraft on impact. Guards had to be posted at the scene of the tragedy to keep away a day-long stream of sightseers.

RISING STARS PLUMMET TO DEATH

The two support stars who perished with Buddy Holly were both young performers enjoying the first taste of success.

Born in 1932, Texas DJ J. P. Richardson dubbed himself The Big Bopper on account of his size. A spare-time songwriter, he scored worldwide last year with 'Chantilly Lace', which made No. 6 in the US and just this January got to No. 14 in Great Britain. Ironically he had persuaded bass guitarist Waylon Jennings, who was backing Holly, to give him his seat on the ill-fated plane.

Similarly, the guitarist in the Holly backing group, Tommy Allsup, gave up his seat to the other doomed star, Ritchie Valens. Seventeen-year-old Valens is now posthumously riding the charts with both sides of his second single release – 'La Bamba' which peaked at No. 22 in the US just a few days before the tragedy, and 'Donna' which hit the No. 2 slot a week after his death.

Ritchie Valens, the 17 year old star who died alongside Buddy and The Big Bopper

LAWDY MR LLOYDY!

'Stagger Lee', by 26-year old black singer Lloyd Price, has leapt to No. 1 Stateside.

Born in New Orleans, he grew up surrounded by the city's vibrant music, and forming a band seemed the natural thing to do.

His first success came in 1952, when his recording of 'Lawdy Miss Clawdy' – his own composition – became the year's best selling R&B single . . . in part due to Fats Domino's imaginative piano contribution, which was duplicated on Elvis Presley's subsequent revival.

Military service interrupted his career, but now he's back with a bang! Interestingly, 'Stagger Lee' is Lloyd's rocking update of the old folk song, 'Stack-O-Lee' – which Lonnie Donegan recorded a while back.

CHARTS

US45	Stagger Lee	*Lloyd Price*
USLP	Flower Drum Song	*Original Cast*
UK45	I Got Stung/One Night	*Elvis Presley*
UKLP	South Pacific	*Soundtrack*
WEEK 2		
US45	Stagger Lee	*Lloyd Price*
USLP	Peter Gunn	*Henry Mancini*
UK45	I Got Stung/One Night	*Elvis Presley*
UKLP	South Pacific	*Soundtrack*
WEEK 3		
US45	Stagger Lee	*Lloyd Price*
USLP	Peter Gunn	*Henry Mancini*
UK45	I Got Stung/One Night	*Elvis Presley*
UKLP	South Pacific	*Soundtrack*
WEEK 4		
US45	Venus	*Frankie Avalon*
USLP	Peter Gunn	*Henry Mancini*
UK45	As I Love You	*Shirley Bassey*
UKLP	South Pacific	*Soundtrack*

THE GRAPEVINE

■ Ricky Nelson has been dating 18-year-old songwriter Sharon Sheeley, who composed his hit, 'Poor Little Fool'.

■ Among R&B artists currently storming the US charts are The Crests, LaVern Baker, Clyde McPhatter, Fats Domino, Lloyd Price and Jackie Wilson.

■ Marty Wilde has signed to make his movie debut in *Jet Stream*, a dramatic production set aboard a doomed transatlantic airliner.

Sixteen Candles is a Stateside smash for The Crests

ROCK FESTIVALS

The Rock Festival as a concept has its roots far earlier than one might think. The acclaimed Newport Jazz and Folk Festivals had been going since before rock music's generally accepted birth in the mid-fifties. It was at Newport in 1965 that Bob Dylan was booed because he was backed by Paul Butterfield's Blues Band, and in that same year, Britain's National Jazz Federation Festival was well on the way to becoming an annual occasion.

When the NJF extended its Festival to encompass blues and R&B, the summer rock Festival became a highlight of the canvas of popular music in Britain which has lasted a quarter of a century, but the first really legendary Festival worldwide took place (almost inevitably) in 1967 in California – more precisely at Monterey. There was a mouth-watering array of talent – The Grateful Dead, The Jefferson Airplane, Country Joe & the Fish and others from San Francisco's psychedelic movement, blues bands like Canned Heat and The Electric Flag plus Butterfield's group, LA country rockers The Byrds and Buffalo Springfield, Memphis soul from Booker T & the MGs, UK representatives The Who, plus the Mamas & Papas, whose leader, John Phillips, helped to organise the event. If it looks like a good bill already, what does the addition of Otis Redding, Jimi Hendrix and Janis Joplin, all making their entrance on the world stage turn it into?

Monterey was what every subsequent Rock Festival should have copied, but the major difference was that the idea of Monterey was not to make pots of money – it aspired to provide a benefit to the community and to spread the gospel of peace, love and – maybe – dope. The essence of the good vibes was happily captured in D. A. Pennebaker's 'Monterey Pop' movie, but it's disturbing to note that none of the following star performers at Monterey was alive 25 years later: Redding, Hendrix, Joplin, Keith Moon of The Who, Pigpen of The Dead, Mike Bloomfield of Electric Flag, Paul Butterfield, Al Jackson of the MGs, John Cippolina of Quicksilver, Bob Hite and Al Wilson of Canned Heat and more! Is this disturbing?

Woodstock was probably the most famous rock Festival. It took place in August, 1969. With an audience estimated at 400,000, the Festival boasted a stellar bill, a veritable Who's Who of Rock, including many Monterey stars like Hendrix, the Airplane, the Dead, Butterfield and Canned Heat (plus The Who again), and numerous newer stars like

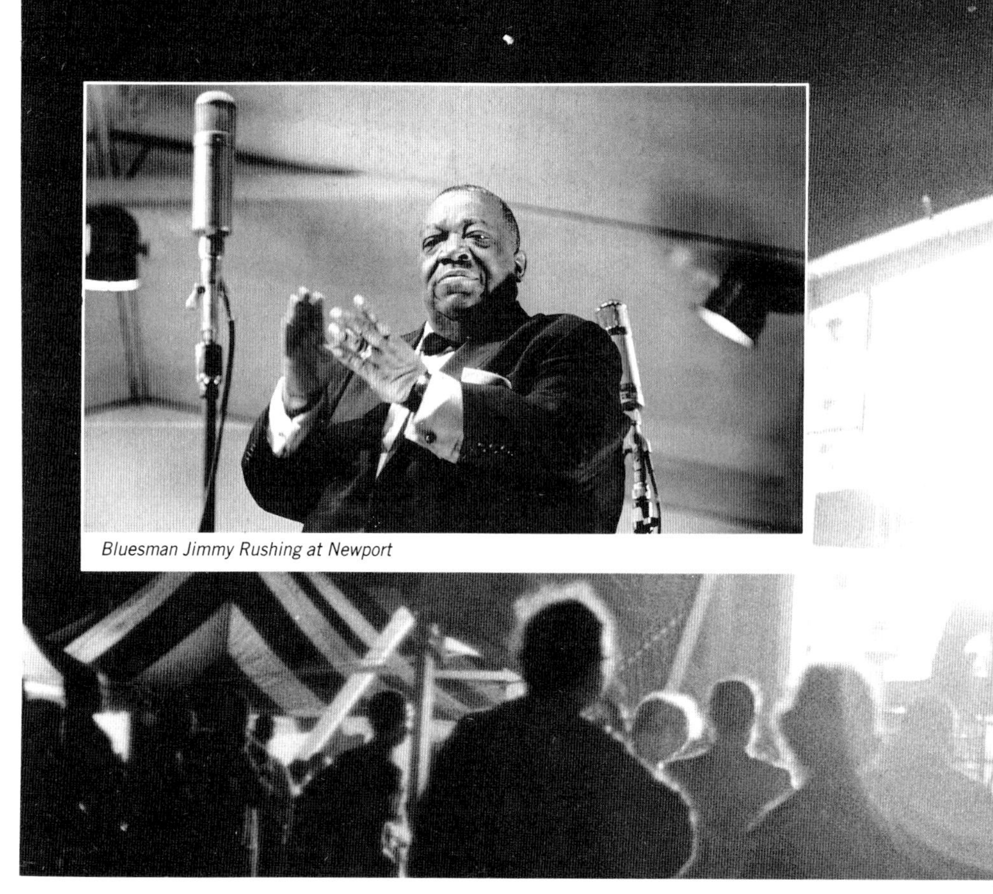

Bluesman Jimmy Rushing at Newport

Reading: rocking through the Eighties

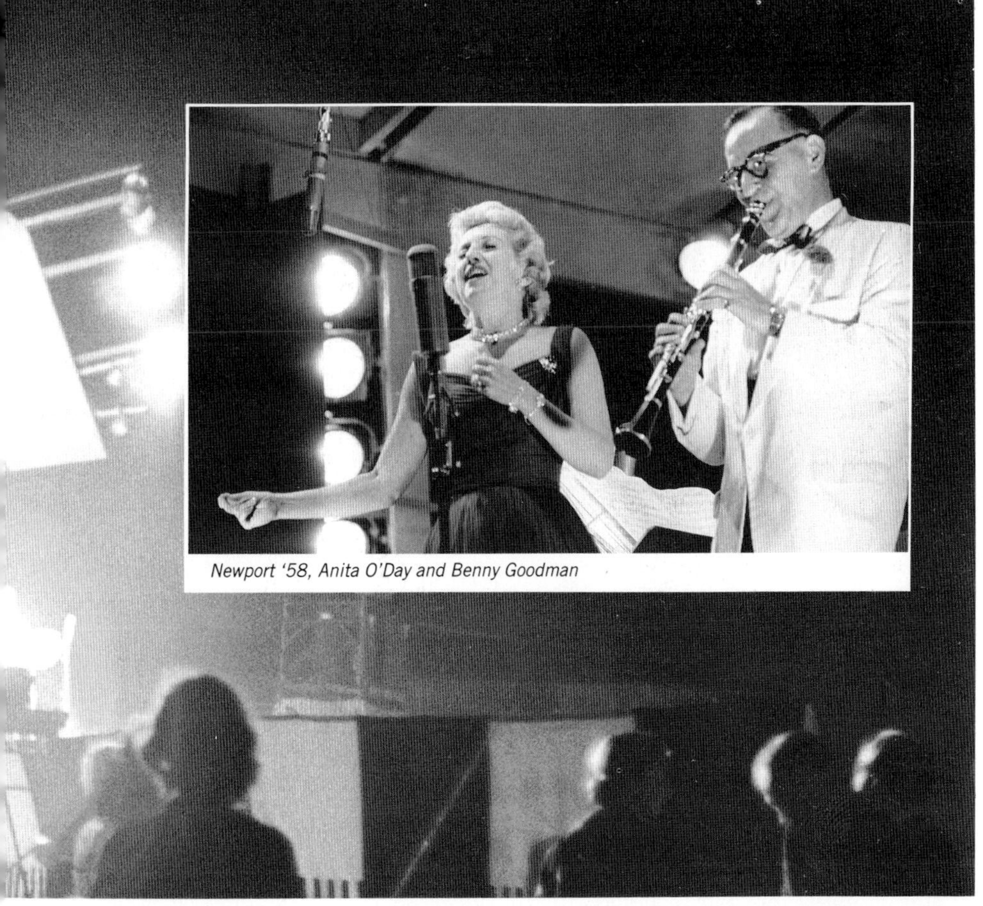
Newport '58, Anita O'Day and Benny Goodman

Monterey Pop 1967

The Who at Monterey

Crosby, Stills, Nash & Young, Joe Cocker, Ten Years After, Santana, Sly & The Family Stone, Creedence Clearwater Revival, The Band, John Sebastian – the list seems impossibly long.

They made 'Woodstock' into a movie too, which features such moments of rock history as Hendrix's alarming version of the American National Anthem, Country Joe McDonald's exhortation to hundreds of thousands of people to shout the ultimate forbidden word in unison and have it recorded in both sound and vision, Joe Cocker, Ten Years After and Santana making an impact similar to those of Hendrix, Joplin and Redding, and John Sebastian unwittingly typecasting himself for life as Mr Tie-Dyed Hippy. After such an artistic success (and commercial nightmare – it became a free Festival when it was swamped by the unexpectedly vast crowd, who were swamped themselves when it rained heavily, turning the site into a quagmire), the idea of the Ultimate Rock Festival became the aim.

The most disastrous Festival was certainly the infamous Altamont, which took place four months after Woodstock. It was going to be a free open-air show by the Rolling Stones, but developed into a whole day concert also featuring the Airplane, CSN&Y and Santana. Someone appointed Hell's Angels as Festival Security – and someone died.

Britain still had the long running National Jazz & Blues Festival with its restricted audience capacity, but you'd be hard pressed to see more than a token jazz act on the bill by 1970, when Britain's most legendary Festival also took place. The Isle Of Wight is a smallish island off England's south coast, easily accessible from the mainland. A perfect site for a major Festival. After a careful small scale start in 1968, the headliner in 1969 was Bob Dylan, and the bill in 1970 was probably the closest to comprehensive of any rock Festival to date. The Doors, Hendrix, Miles Davis, Jethro Tull, The Moody Blues, the unknown Kris Kristofferson, Donovan, Leonard Cohen, John Sebastian, Joni Mitchell and many more.

The swift decline of Rock Festivals occurred soon afterwards. By the middle of the 1970s, the musical styles of the start of the decade were becoming less commercially viable, while newer acts were less suitable for open-air concert exposure, added to which was the fact that the audiences on both sides of the Atlantic were less interested in sitting in fields than their older brothers and sisters.

There have been sporadic Festivals ever since, but of the regular events, only the British NJF Festival has survived.

MARCH

CHARTS

US45	Venus *Frankie Avalon*
USLP	Peter Gunn *Henry Mancini*
UK45	As I Love You *Shirley Bassey*
UKLP	South Pacific *Soundtrack*
WEEK 2	
US45	Venus *Franki Avalon*
USLP	Peter Gunn *Henry Mancini*
UK45	As I Love You *Shirley Bassey*
UKLP	South Pacific *Soundtrack*
WEEK 3	
US45	Venus *Frankie Avalon*
USLP	Peter Gunn *Henry Mancini*
UK45	As I Love You *Shirley Bassey*
UKLP	South Pacific *Soundtrack*
WEEK 4	
US45	Venus *Frankie Avalon*
USLP	Peter Gunn *Henry Mancini*
UK45	Smoke Gets In Your Eyes *Platters*
UKLP	South Pacific *Soundtrack*
WEEK 5	
US45	Come Softly To Me *Fleetwoods*
USLP	Peter Gunn *Henry Mancini*
UK45	Side Saddle *Russ Conway*
UKLP	South Pacific *Soundtrack*

'Bony Moronie' man Larry Williams

GODDESS OF LOVE WHISKS FRANKIE TO NO.1

He hasn't made much impact on British record buyers, but in the States, Frankie Avalon is the latest teenage rage. Having already reached the Top 10 with 'De-De Dinah' and 'Gingerbread', he is now perched on top of the best sellers with his impassioned plea to 'Venus'.

Avalon, a perky 19-year-old, is from the same low-income district of South Philadelphia as Mario Lanza and Eddie Fisher.

'When I was ten, my dad bought me a trumpet,' he explains. 'I'd been running around with a wild crowd, cutting school and getting into all kinds of fights. Dad bought me the trumpet to give me a new interest and stop me from developing into a hardened delinquent.'

The ploy worked. Soon a proficient trumpeter, Frankie appeared on various TV shows, but it was his singing which attracted the attention of songwriters Bob Marcucci and Peter de Angelis, who signed him to become the first star of their newly launched Chancellor label . . . and an appearance in the film *Disc Jockey Jamboree* was his springboard to national fame.

DENE IS NOT AMUSED BY THE ARMY GAME

Terry Dene's U.K. army career is over! Only weeks after reporting to Winchester Barracks for his national service, he has suffered a nervous breakdown and been declared 'unfit for further duties'. He is now convalescing at a civilian hospital in Surrey.

Decca have renewed Dene's contract for another year and his agent, Hyman Zahl, will continue to book him when he returns to the stage. 'I am sure the public still want him,' Zahl maintains.

THE GRAPEVINE

- **Lonnie Donegan found his 'Chewing Gum' hit 'buried within the yellowed pages of a boy scout songbook'!**
- **Frantic rocker Larry Williams was formerly the piano player in Lloyd Price's touring band.**
- **A chart absentee for 18 months, Russ Hamilton is hoping for a comeback with 'The Reprieve Of Tom Dooley'!**
- **Trad-jazz bandleader Chris Barber has won a gold disc for his US chartbuster 'Petite Fleur'.**

THE PLATTERS PUT THEIR FAITH IN OLDIES

Their policy of reviving oldies has paid huge dividends for top vocal group, The Platters. Though they started their chart career with million-selling originals like 'Only You' and 'The Great Pretender' – both written by their manager, Buck Ram – they have enjoyed far greater success in Britain with 'My Prayer', written in 1939, and 'Twilight Time', written in 1944.

Their current hit, and first UK chart-topper, is a sublime version of 'Smoke Gets In Your Eyes' – written by Jerome Kern for the 1933 stage musical, *Roberta*.

There is no doubt that these four boys and a girl have made a lasting impression on the recording scene. It is equally certain that, with their undeniable versatility, they will remain in the forefront of vocal groups for many years to come.

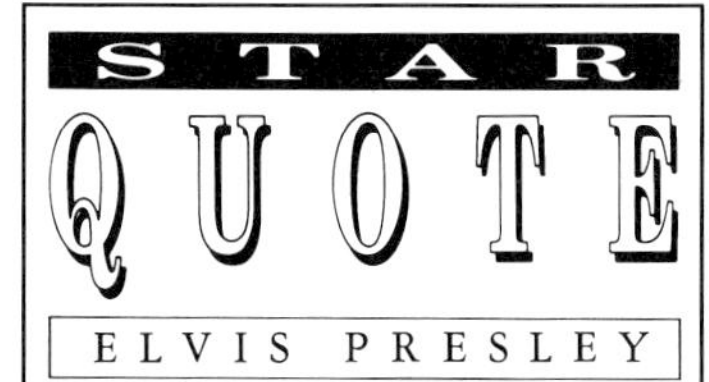

STAR QUOTE

ELVIS PRESLEY

'I'm mighty homesick at times. I wonder if the folks back home have forgotten me . . . it's hard to tell from over here.'

Barber blows a storm

HOLLY'S LEGACY LIVES ON

Recorded only weeks before his death, 'It Doesn't Matter Anymore' has vaulted the late Buddy Holly to No. 1, emphasizing what a truly great artist we have lost. Holly's performance of the Paul Anka song, set in a lush string arrangement, obviously heralded a new chapter in the singer's development.

A tribute disc, dedicated to the stars who died in the tragic plane crash, has appeared in the US Top 20. In 'Three Stars', Tommy Dee discusses all three individually – concluding 'Gee, we're going to miss you; everybody sends their love'.

Meanwhile, The Crickets – from whom Holly split last year – have regrouped. Drummer Jerry Allison and bassist Joe Mauldin have been joined by guitarist Sonny Curtis and vocalist Earl Sinks. Their first release, 'Love's Made A Fool Of You' – written by Holly – is currently climbing the NME Top 30.

STAR QUOTE

CLIFF RICHARD

'When I play variety dates, a lot of the older people in the audience are very disturbed by the continual noise of the kids. I sometimes wish that I could do a show that wasn't swamped with screaming . . . but I do admit, I'd certainly miss it!'

From his screen debut – Eddie Cochran

BERRY SPEAKS FOR TEENS

In the States, Chuck Berry has acquired a solid reputation as the chronicler of the rock'n'roll generation, with his colourful songs about the inconvenience of school, the vexation of parents, the magic of rock music, the excitement of fast cars, the anxieties of dating, and other teen topics.

A consistent US seller, he's been absent from British charts for a year – but his new release, 'Almost Grown', should restore his popularity.

CHARTS

US45	Come Softly To Me – *Fleetwood*
USLP	Peter Gunn – *Henry Mancini*
UK45	Side Saddle – *Russ Conway*
UKLP	South Pacific – *Soundtrack*
WEEK 2	
US45	Come Softly To Me – *Fleetwoods*
USLP	Peter Gunn – *Henry Mancini*
UK45	Side Saddle – *Russ Conway*
UKLP	South Pacific – *Soundtrack*
WEEK 3	
US45	Come Softly To Me – *Fleetwoods*
USLP	Peter Gunn – *Henry Mancini*
UK45	Side Saddle – *Russ Conway*
UKLP	South Pacific – *Soundtrack*
WEEK 4	
US45	Come Softly To Me – *Fleetwoods*
USLP	Gigi – *Soundtrack*
UK45	It Doesn't Matter Anymore – *Buddy Holly*
UKLP	South Pacific – *Soundtrack*

THE GRAPEVINE

- **BBC-TV have cancelled their series, *Dig This*, and are hoping for better results with a new teenage programme, *Drumbeat*.**
- **Marty Wilde has reached the Top 3 with 'Donna' – written by the late Ritchie Valens.**
- **Biggest UK hits to date The Coasters with 'Charlie Brown', Eddie Cochran with 'C'mon Everybody', and Neil Sedaka with 'I Go Ape'.**

FLEETWOODS' DEBUT WINS GLOBAL ACCLAIM

'Come Softly To Me' has brought international recognition to vocal trio, The Fleetwoods – in which handsome Gary Troxell is ably supported by two slim and pretty blue-eyed blondes, Gretchen Christopher and Barbara Ellis. All are senior students at Olympia High School in Washington State.

A mutual interest in songwriting brought them together and they pooled their ideas to create 'Come Softly To Me' – a dreamy, intricately woven ballad which immediately won them a contract with the independent Dolphin label.

The song also fired the imagination of America's vast record-buying public, who took it to their hearts, sending it to No. 1.

Having savoured the sweet smell of success in the States, The Fleetwoods are now keeping a watchful eye on Britain, where they are already in the Top 10.

Fleetwoods Gretchen, Gary and Barbara

CHARTS

US45	The Happy Organ — *Dave 'Baby' Cortez*
USLP	Gigi — *Soundtrack*
UK45	It Doesn't Matter Anymore — *Buddy Holly*
UKLP	South Pacific — *Soundtrack*
WEEK 2	
US45	Kansas City — *Wilbert Harrison*
USLP	Gigi — *Soundtrack*
UK45	It Doesn't Matter Anymore — *Buddy Holly*
UKLP	South Pacific — *Soundtrack*
WEEK 3	
US45	Kansas City — *Wilbert Harrison*
USLP	Gigi — *Soundtrack*
UK45	A Fool Such As I/I Need Your Love Tonight — *Elvis Presley*
UKLP	South Pacific — *Soundtrack*
WEEK 4	
US45	Battle Of New Orleans — *Johnny Horton*
USLP	Gigi — *Soundtrack*
UK45	A Fool Such As I/I Need Your Love Tonight — *Elvis Presley*
UKLP	South Pacific — *Soundtrack*
WEEK 5	
US45	Battle Of New Orleans — *Johnny Horton*
USLP	Gigi — *Soundtrack*
UK45	A Fool Such As I/I Need Your Love Tonight — *Elvis Presley*
UKLP	South Pacific — *Soundtrack*

INTRODUCING THE FABULOUS FABIAN!

Frankie Avalon has a frisky challenger in America's teen-idol stakes . . . his best friend! Known simply by his first name, Fabian is one of the hottest singing fireballs to explode on the music scene for years – in fact, he's stimulated more press coverage than any star since Elvis.

The eldest son of a police officer, 17-year-old Fabian is a lithe and virile six-footer, who believes in putting everything he's got into his vigorous performances.

From the same South Philadelphia neighbourhood as Frankie Avalon, he is also handled by the same management company and records for the same label – but any rivalry is very friendly.

Teenage girls have fainted at his shows, and the young heart throb requires a police escort wherever he appears, but he still intends to complete his education before plunging into show business full time.

Already this year, he has registered two US hits, 'I'm A Man' and 'Turn Me Loose' – both reinforcing the tempestuous personality which has led fans to dub him 'The Tiger'!

JUST FOR A CHANGE, BERT HELPS HIMSELF TO A HIT

After helping out on literally hundreds of other people's discs, Britain's hardest working studio guitarist, Bert Weedon, has a hit of his own – his first, after more than 25 years in the business.

He has put his personal stamp on 'Guitar Boogie Shuffle' – an American hit for The Virtues.

The man who plays the sizzling solos on records by Tommy Steele, Terry Dene and Marty Wilde, admits to having felt a little apprehensive with rock'n'roll first came in.

'After practising so hard to achieve a good, pure tone, it was a bit of a bringdown to play some of the things that were asked of me. However, I always go along with the trend and try to give the public what it wants – and if it wants a clangy guitar, then I'll oblige!'

THE GRAPEVINE

- **Hoping to reinstate himself in our charts, Conway Twitty has arrived in Britain for two appearances on *Oh Boy!*.**
- **As complete unknowns, both Terry Dene and Marty Wilde auditioned for Decca A&R manager, Dick Rowe – who signed Terry but turned Marty down.**
- **'Kookie, Kookie, Lend Me Your Comb' is a Stateside smash for Ed Byrnes, jive-talking star of the TV series, *77 Sunset Strip*.**

STARS HONOURED WITH GRAMMY AWARDS

Comparable in stature to the famous Academy Awards for films, the National Association of Recording Arts and Sciences have introduced a similar ceremony, to present outstanding musical contributors with annual 'Grammy' awards.

Twenty-two categories are devoted to achievements in popular music and jazz – with five nominations in each. Among those winning the first awards, announced this month, were:

Record Of The Year
'Volare' by Domenico Modugno
Album Of The Year
'Peter Gunn' by Henry Mancini
Best Comedy Performance
'The Chipmunk Song' by David Seville
Best C&W Performance
'Tom Dooley' by The Kingston Trio
Best R&B Performance
'Tequila' by The Champs

Twitty tries again

Television heart-throb Ed Byrnes

HIS OWN HIGH STANDARDS LED BOBBY TO STARDOM

Bobby Darin was raised in the tough Bronx tenement district of New York. Amid the poverty and grime of the slums, his early youth was hemmed in by gang wars and theft. He estimates that, out of every ten kids he knew, four wound up in jail sooner or later.

In such surroundings, infamy as a criminal could so easily have been Bobby's destiny. Instead, a rigid set of self-imposed personal standards and his own sound common sense kept him on the right road – and ultimately led him to become one of the brightest new stars on the current scene.

Recently described as 'a young, zestful Frank Sinatra, with a touch of Dean Martin', Bobby has already won gold discs for his international hits, 'Splish Splash' and 'Queen Of The Hop', and he is rapidly heading for a third million seller with his own composition, 'Dream Lover'.

THE GRAPEVINE

- Elvis Presley recorded his current chart-topper last June, when he dashed to Nashville during a weekend's leave, and worked for 24 hours without sleep or food.
- Fabian will make his movie debut in *Hound Dog Man.*
- After 38 weeks, top U.K. teen TV show *Oh Boy!* has ended its run; producer Jack Good has a new series up his sleeve for the autumn.

Film first for Fabian

STAR QUOTE

PAUL ANKA

"It Doesn't Matter Anymore" has a tragic irony about it now, but at least it will help look after Buddy Holly's family. I'm giving my composer's royalty to his widow – it's the least I can do.'

Singer and songwriter Paul Anka

CHARTS

US45	Battle Of New Orleans *Johnny Horton*
USLP	Gigi *Soundtrack*
UK45	A Fool Such As I/I Need Your Love Tonight *Elvis Presley*
UKLP	South Pacific *Soundtrack*
	WEEK 2
US45	Battle Of New Orleans *Johnny Horton*
USLP	Exotica Volume One *Martin Denny*
UK45	A Fool Such As I/I Need Your Love Tonight *Elvis Presley*
UKLP	South Pacific *Soundtrack*
	WEEK 3
US45	Battle Of New Orleans *Johnny Horton*
USLP	Exotica Volume One *Martin Denny*
UK45	Roulette *Russ Conway*
UKLP	South Pacific *Soundtrack*
	WEEK 4
US45	Battle Of New Orleans *Johnny Horton*
USLP	Exotica Volume One *Martin Denny*
UK45	Roulette *Russ Conway*
UKLP	South Pacific *Soundtrack*

GEORGE MARTIN – THE COMEDY SPECIALIST

Off-beat recordings by Britain's top comedy stars – that's the speciality of Parlophone Record's A&R manager, George Martin.

'People used to tell me there was no future in recording comedians,' grinned George. 'And my greatest pleasure has been proving them wrong – with discs like "Splish Splash" by Charlie Drake, "Any Old Iron" by Peter Sellers, and "I'm In Charge" by Bruce Forsyth.'

George's interests cover a wide range, for in addition to pops, he has to cope with EMI's jazz and Scottish catalogues.

Looking to the future, he has great hopes for two newcomers who have recently been launched, Lorne Lesley and Jerry Angelo. Says George: 'It's not so much artistry as individuality which counts today – and it's obvious that the rock influence is here for all time.'

CLIFF RICHARD BUYS HOUSE FOR HIS PARENTS

Cliff Richard is buying a £4,000 ($12,000) house for his parents in Winchmore Hill, North London – and he will be giving up his flat to live with them when they move from their council house in Cheshunt, Hertfordshire.

'This is the realization of an ambition,' said Cliff, who is currently in the Top 10 with 'Mean Streak'. 'When I broke into show business, I promised my parents that if I made good, I would buy them a house. I am so happy it worked out.'

AN ABUNDANCE OF TEENAGERS IN LOVE

While Marty Wilde and Craig Douglas fight for supremacy in the UK chart, the original version of 'A Teenager In Love' is keeping New York vocal group Dion & The Belmonts high in the American Top 10.

Taking their name from Belmont Avenue, which crosses their neighbourhood, the quartet first demonstrated their prowess on 'I Wonder Why', a year ago. Lead singer Dion DiMucci (19) enjoys water sports and skin-diving, while companions Carlo Mastrangelo and Fred Milano are crazy about clothes. Carlo, for instance, boasts no fewer than 100 shirts! Fourth member, Angelo d'Aleo, is currently out of the picture, doing his military service in the Navy. As their names indicate, all the boys have an Italian heritage.

Craig not Wilde for Dion

Dion & the Belmonts

JOHNNY KIDD PATCHES UP HIS ACT!

The label of the debut disc by Johnny Kidd & The Pirates says 'Please Don't Touch' – but fans have clearly ignored this caution, purchasing enough copies to thrust it into the UK Top 30!

This is good news indeed for 18-year-old Fred Heath, from Willesden, North London. The former leader of a comedy skiffle outfit called The Five Nutters, Heath modified his group to embrace a rockier style – and it so happened that, on one of their first dates, an eye infection compelled him to wear a black patch.

This prompted a member of the audience to comment that he resembled a pirate – and it is to this unknown wit that Heath and his pals are indebted for their dashing new name and swashbuckling attire.

Incidentally, Heath also wrote his hot-rocking hit . . . he obviously has a good eye for a song!

CHARTS

US45	Lonely Boy	*Paul Anka*
USLP	Exotica Volume One	*Martin Denny*
UK45	Dream Lover	*Bobby Darin*
UKLP	South Pacific	*Soundtrack*
WEEK 2		
US45	Lonely Boy	*Paul Anka*
USLP	Exotica Volume One	*Martin Denny*
UK45	Dream Lover	*Bobby Darin*
UKLP	South Pacific	*Soundtrack*
WEEK 3		
US45	Lonely Boy	*Paul Anka*
USLP	Film Encores	*Mantovani*
UK45	Dream Lover	*Bobby Darin*
UKLP	South Pacific	*Soundtrack*
WEEK 4		
US45	Lonely Boy	*Paul Anka*
USLP	At Large	*Kingston Trio*
UK45	Dream Lover	*Bobby Darin*
UKLP	South Pacific	*Soundtrack*

THE GRAPEVINE

■ Only recently introduced, *Juke Box Jury* has quickly become the most popular programme on British television.

■ In Britain, C&W star Johnny Horton has conceded defeat in 'The Battle Of New Orleans' – now a Top Three smash for Lonnie Donegan.

■ Cliff Richard has started work on *Expresso Bongo* – in which he plays a singer discovered by Laurence Harvey; meanwhile, 'Living Doll' has become his fastest-selling hit.

EDDY'S ATOMIC GUNN

That Rebel Rouser from Phoenix, Arizona, is back! Twanging away on a chugging opus called 'Peter Gunn', Duane Eddy has crashed into the UK Top 10 – yet his disc is nowhere to be seen on the US chart.

The explanation is simple: the number is the theme from a US TV series – about a private eye called Peter Gunn – and was a colossal hit for Ray Anthony earlier in the year. Additionally, Henry Mancini's soundtrack album was America's top seller for eleven weeks.

In Britain the melody is still very much of a novelty – hence the rush for Duane's timely version.

Guitar virtuoso Duane Eddy on stage with The Rebels

THEY ALL LOVED 'LADY DAY'

Billie Holiday, universally acclaimed as the world's greatest jazz singer, died in the early hours of July 17 at New York's Metropolitan Hotel.

Only 44, she had been critically ill with jaundice and heart trouble for several weeks.

INTRODUCING RAY CHARLES – THE GENIUS

A top R&B star since the start of the decade, Ray Charles has finally broken into Billboard's pop listing with his boisterous recording of 'What'd I Say'.

Born in Georgia 29 years ago, Ray lost his sight at the age of six, and studied music at a school for the blind in Florida. An accomplished pianist by his teens, he first made his name on the West Coast, leading a lounge-jazz trio.

When the Atlantic label signed him, they encouraged Ray to enlarge his band and incorporate a gospel feeling, which has paid increasing dividends.

His most exciting release to date, 'What'd I Say' has hit No. 6 in the U.S., where critics are now describing him as 'The Genius'.

THE GRAPEVINE

■ In America, 'Only Sixteen' is Sam Cooke's biggest hit since 'You Send Me' – but in the UK, radio play has favoured the version by former milkman, Craig Douglas.

■ Cliff Richard's 'Living Doll' was composed by Lionel Bart, who previously supplied Tommy Steele with hits!

■ Disc-jockey Dick Clark will star in the movie *Because They're Young*, along with Tuesday Weld and Duane Eddy.

CHARTS

US45	Lonely Boy *Paul Anka*
USLP	At Large *Kingston Trio*
UK45	Living Doll *Cliff Richard*
UKLP	South Pacific *Soundtrack*
WEEK 2	
US45	Lonely Boy *Paul Anka*
USLP	At Large *Kingston Trio*
UK45	Living Doll *Cliff Richard*
UKLP	South Pacific *Soundtrack*
WEEK 3	
US45	Big Hunk O' Love *Elvis Presley*
USLP	At Large *Kingston Trio*
UK45	Living Doll *Cliff Richard*
UKLP	South Pacific *Soundtrack*
WEEK 4	
US45	Big Hunk O' Love *Elvis Presley*
USLP	At Large *Kingston Trio*
UK45	Living Doll *Cliff Richard*
UKLP	South Pacific *Soundtrack*
WEEK 5	
US45	The Three Bells *Browns*
USLP	At Large *Kingston Trio*
UK45	Living Doll *Cliff Richard*
UKLP	South Pacific *Soundtrack*

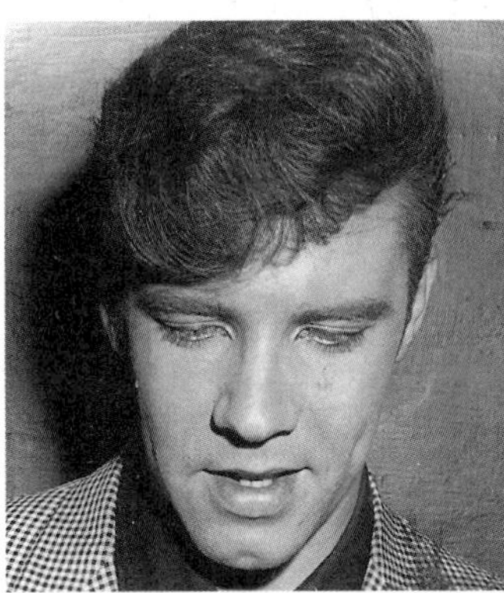

Wilde: big beat bonanza

Sam a smash with 'Sixteen'

GOOD CASTS AN EYE OVER STABLE OF STARS

TV producer Jack Good was at the Southend Odeon for the opening night of 'The Big Beat Show' – the latest package presentation by Larry Parnes.

The most powerful manager in British rock'n'roll, Parnes boasts an ever-expanding 'Stable of Stars', including Marty Wilde, Billy Fury, Terry Dene, Dickie Pride, Johnny Gentle, Duffy Power and Sally Kelly – all of whom appeared on the show.

The only artist missing was Larry's first discovery, Tommy Steele, who has just returned from a successful three-day visit to Moscow.

Wilde is set to star in Good's new series, *Boy Meets Girls*, to be unveiled next month. Also in the cast will be Joe Brown, a hitherto unknown guitarist who was backing the stars at Southend. Apparently, Good thought he was 'quite sensational'.

Pop impresario Larry Parnes

SANTO AND JOHNNY SLEEPWALK TO A HIT

There's an unmistakable Hawaiian flavour about 'Sleep Walk', the US smash hit which is beginning to catch on in Britain. It's a haunting, insistent guitar duet that reflects an atmosphere of swaying palms and swirling grass skirts – yet the fellows who wrote and recorded it, Santo and Johnny, are from Brooklyn!

Santo Farina learned to play the steel guitar at an early age, while his brother Johnny mastered the rhythm guitar. As teenagers, they played at local dances and parties – and 'Sleep Walk' was a melody they penned with their sister, Ann.

Their recording of the number beguiled the owner of the newly set-up Canadian-American label, and he acquired their master tape – little suspecting that the disc's universal success would have his operation working at full capacity for months!

Santo plucks his steel guitar while Johnny plays rhythm

THE GRAPEVINE

- **Buddy Holly's new single is a sequel – 'Peggy Sue Got Married'! Meanwhile, Buddy's old group, The Crickets, provided the backing on 'Til I Kissed You', the latest from The Everly Brothers.**
- **Country star Johnny Cash has arrived in Britain to appear on *Boy Meets Girls.***
- **Director Hal Wallis has been in Europe shooting location scenes for Elvis' first post-army film, *GI Blues.***

CHARTS

US45	The Three Bells *Browns*
USLP	At Large *Kingston Trio*
UK45	Living Doll *Cliff Richard*
UKLP	South Pacific *Soundtrack*
WEEK 2	
US45	The Three Bells *Browns*
USLP	At Large *Kingston Trio*
UK45	Only Sixteen *Craig Douglas*
UKLP	South Pacific *Soundtrack*
WEEK 3	
US45	The Three Bells *Browns*
USLP	At Large *Kingston Trio*
UK45	Only Sixteen *Craig Douglas*
UKLP	South Pacific *Soundtrack*
WEEK 4	
US45	Sleep Walk *Santo & Johnny*
USLP	At Large *Kingston Trio*
UK45	Only Sixteen *Craig Douglas*
UKLP	South Pacific *Soundtrack*

BELLS RING FOR THE BROWNS

The Browns' recording of 'The Three Bells' was first heard in Britain on BBC-TV's *Juke Box Jury*, whose panel were not too impressed – yet the disc has topped the US chart and is already making huge strides here.

Originally written in 1945 by Frenchman Jean Villard, the song was effectively recorded by Edith Piaf and Les Compagnons de la Chanson – and quite how The Browns came across it remains a mystery.

A trio comprising Jim Ed Brown and his sisters, Maxine and Bonnie, they hail from Pine Bluff, Arkansas and have been going strong in C&W circles for several years – but the runaway success of their hit has left them somewhat bewildered!

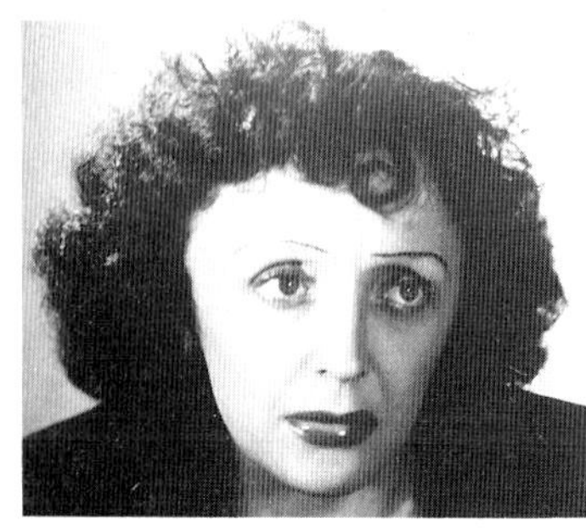

French original . . . Edith Piaf

CBS BANS BRILLIANT BOBBY

Because of a recent wave of teenage violence, America's powerful CBS television and radio network has banned Bobby Darin's latest release, 'Mack The Knife'. Nevertheless, the disc – described by reviewer Keith Fordyce as 'brilliant' – has already become Darin's fastest seller.

TOO MANY DRIFTERS!

Cliff Richard's backing group, though retaining the same personnel, will now be known as The Shadows. This move has been made to avoid confusion with the US group, The Drifters, who have been recording for Atlantic since 1953.

The American Drifters, a black vocal quintet from New York, are currently enjoying their biggest hit to date – with 'There Goes My Baby', an eerie string-backed opus, quite unlike any of their previous offerings.

The song was co-written by lead singer Ben E. King, and produced by the imaginative team of Leiber & Stoller – well known for their work with The Coasters.

The disc, which has already sold a million in the States, is released in Britain this month.

HERE COMES JERRY KELLER

With winter approaching, the optimistic Jerry Keller has rocketed to the very summit of the charts with 'Here Comes Summer'! Also the author of the song, the 20-year-old from Oklahoma will soon be visiting Britain for television appearances.

After singing with a local quartet and working as a disc jockey in Tulsa, Jerry drew out his savings and caught a bus to New York, where he made the rounds of record companies. No one was interested, and he was forced to make ends meet by working as a clerk.

It was through another member of his church, the Church of Christ, that Jerry made his first valuable connection. None other than Pat Boone gave him a list of contacts and soon he found himself on the roster of Kapp Records – cutting 'Here Comes Summer', a song he'd written 18 months earlier . . . and now he's in great demand.

That's showbiz, folks!

DUANE'S LUCKY GUITAR

Since wreaking havoc with 'Rebel Rouser' last year, 'twangy guitar' king Duane Eddy has rarely been out of the NME Top 30.

'Cannonball', 'Peter Gunn', 'Yep', and now 'Forty Miles Of Bad Road' have all contributed to his high placing in this year's Readers' Poll – runner up to Elvis Presley as The World's Outstanding Musical Personality.

He owes it all to the Gretsch guitar he purchased two years ago. 'I had no idea how I was going to make the payments on it,' says Duane. 'But I needn't have worried! It turned out to be real lucky. I've recorded nine hit singles with it, three hit EPs, and two hit albums – so believe me, I really love that guitar!'

ELVIS, CONNIE AND THE EVERLYS ARE STILL FAVOURITES

Elvis Presley, Connie Francis and The Everly Brothers swept to victory in the World sections of this year's NME Readers' Poll – just as they did in 1958.

However, there were changes in the British categories. Cliff Richard was voted top Male Singer, Shirley Bassey was top Female Singer, and Russ Conway was top Instrumental Personality.

Craig Douglas headed the New Singer list, closely followed by Anthony Newley and Billy Fury.

Pollwinning females: Connie Francis (far left) repeats last year's success while Shirley Bassey captures the crown for the first time

■ 'Teen Beat' is a US smash for Sandy Nelson, the Los Angeles drummer who played on The Teddy Bears' hit, 'To Know Him Is To Love Him'.

■ Three Leiber & Stoller compositions grace the American chart: 'Poison Ivy' by The Coasters, 'Dance With Me' by The Drifters, and 'Love Potion Number Nine' by The Clovers.

■ Billy Fury's sexy stage antics have been drawing much press criticism.

Sandy Nelson maintains the Teen Beat

High on the US chart, the Clovers

CHARTS

US45	Sleep Walk	*Santo & Johnny*
USLP	At Large	*Kingston Trio*
UK45	Only Sixteen	*Craig Douglas*
UKLP	South Pacific	*Soundtrack*
WEEK 2		
US45	Mack The Knife	*Bobby Darin*
USLP	At Large	*Kingston Trio*
UK45	Here Comes Summer	*Jerry Keller*
UKLP	South Pacific	*Soundtrack*
WEEK 3		
US45	Mack The Knife	*Bobby Darin*
USLP	At Large	*Kingston Trio*
UK45	Mack The Knife	*Bobby Darin*
UKLP	South Pacific	*Soundtrack*
WEEK 4		
US45	Mack The Knife	*Bobby Darin*
USLP	At Large	*Kingston Trio*
UK45	Mack The Knife	*Bobby Darin*
UKLP	South Pacific	*Soundtrack*

FABIAN

On his audition for Bob Marcucci

'As I'm tone-deaf, I didn't think he'd like it much – but I sang for him. It sounded like a jackass! You could have bowled me over when he said I had possibilities.'

THE GRAPEVINE

- 'At Large' has kept The Kingston Trio on top of the US album chart for 15 weeks – and their latest, 'Here We Go Again', looks set to replace it!
- Cliff Richard has been presented with a gold disc for 'Living Doll'.
- In Washington for National Bible Week, Pat Boone met President Eisenhower, who told him he'd seen Pat's film, *April Love*, twice!

CHARTS

US45	Mack The Knife	*Bobby Darin*
USLP	At Large	*Kingston Trio*
UK45	Travellin' Light	*Cliff Richard*
UKLP	South Pacific	*Soundtrack*
WEEK 2		
US45	Mack The Knife	*Bobby Darin*
USLP	Heavenly	*Johnny Mathis*
UK45	Travellin' Light	*Cliff Richard*
UKLP	South Pacific	*Soundtrack*
WEEK 3		
US45	Mr. Blue	*Fleetwoods*
USLP	Heavenly	*Johnny Mathis*
UK45	Travellin' Light	*Cliff Richard*
UKLP	South Pacific	*Soundtrack*
WEEK 4		
US45	Mack The Knife	*Bobby Darin*
USLP	Heavenly	*Johnny Mathis*
UK45	Travellin' Light	*Cliff Richard*
UKLP	South Pacific	*Soundtrack*
WEEK 5		
US45	Mack The Knife	*Bobby Darin*
USLP	Heavenly	*Johnny Mathis*
UK45	Travellin' Light	*Cliff Richard*
UKLP	South Pacific	*Soundtrack*

DARIN WINS TWO GRAMMY AWARDS

At the second of America's National Academy of Recording Arts and Sciences ceremonies, Bobby Darin's rise to the top echelon of stardom was confirmed when he was presented with two Grammy awards.

The 22-year-old singer was pronounced Best New Artist of 1959, and his single of 'Mack The Knife' won the Record of the Year category. Additionally, Ahmet Ertegun, president of Atlantic Records, received a special award for producing the disc.

Said Darin, who has recently signed with Paramount Pictures: 'Some day I hope to have an Oscar and an Emmy to go along with these Grammies. I'm anxious to prove this isn't a one-shot success.'

Other winners included Dinah Washington, whose 'What A Difference A Day Makes' was declared top R&B Recording; The Kingston Trio, whose 'At Large' album was voted Best Folk Performance; and Johnny Horton, whose 'Battle Of New Orleans' won top C&W honours.

R&B winner Dinah Washington

C&W victor Johnny Horton

US CONGRESS TO PROBE PAYOLA

In the States, a congressional committee intends to investigate the alleged 'payola' racket, in which disc-jockeys have been accepting money to play certain recordings.

The owners of the radio stations involved could also get into trouble for having allowed such practices to go on.

BRITAIN IS SOMETHIN' ELSE, SAYS EDDIE

'My fondest wish is to visit Britain,' says Eddie Cochran, who is currently bobbing around the NME Top 30 with his latest scorcher, 'Somethin' Else'. 'I planned a holiday there last summer, but I was too busy touring. Now it looks like I might be over in the new year.'

Eddie is one of several American stars that Jack Good has contacted with a view to appearing on *Boy Meets Girls*. Others include LaVern Baker, Frankie Avalon, Fabian and Jackie Wilson.

Firm dates have already been fixed for Jerry Keller, Freddy Cannon and Gene Vincent.

SCHOOL PALS TRAVEL TO FAME TOGETHER

An instrumental quintet from Ohio, Johnny & The Hurricanes have duplicated their US success and ripped into the British Top five with their furious revival of 'Red River Valley' – served up as 'Red River Rock'!

The group came together to entertain their friends at high-school hops around Toledo – but now they've turned professional and race all over the States in their own minibus. This not only makes it easier to get some rest, but their instruments can be stored inside with them . . . and their name, brightly painted on the side, is a fine advert too!

LaVern Baker, wooed by Jack Good

ADAM'S STEPPING STONES TO STARDOM

Adam Faith started out on Decca, leading The Worried Men Skiffle Group. He then moved to HMV as a solo artist but, disillusioned by his lack of progress, quit the music business to work in the cutting room at Rank Film Studios.

In April, he was prised out of 'retirement' to become resident rocker on BBC's *Drumbeat*, but a concurrent disc career on Top Rank went nowhere.

A few weeks ago, he signed with his fourth label, Parlophone, and they seem to have found the magic formula! They encouraged Adam to drop his hard-rock style in favour of softer material – and his very first release did the trick.

A beaty ballad, backed by John Barry's distinctive string arrangement, 'What Do You Want?' has catapulted the 19-year-old West Londoner to the top of the chart and to the stardom he fought for so tenaciously.

OVERNIGHT FAME FOR EMILE FORD

A few weeks ago, Emile Ford was completely unknown – but today he has the best-selling record in the country!

Born in St Lucia 22 years ago, he spent the early part of his life in the Caribbean, but moved to London to study engineering.

Distracted by the beat scene, he formed a group and sang in clubs and coffee bars – but it was winning the Soho Fair talent contest in July that led to his Pye recording contract.

His debut disc was 'What Do You Want To Make Those Eyes At Me For?', a vaudeville song dating back to 1916 . . . and Emile's upbeat revival proved popular enough to give him the best Christmas present of his life – a No. 1 hit!

GENE VINCENT MAKES SENSATIONAL UK DEBUT

Gene Vincent – a hit despite the absence of his famous Blue Caps (above)

Wearing a red-and-black sweater and jet-black trousers, Gene Vincent thrilled a capacity audience on his British debut at London's Tooting Granada. He closed the first half of the all-rock show with a sensational performance that put him way above the rest of the artists in stagecraft and showmanship.

In spite of an old leg injury which has left him slightly lame, Vincent performed miracles with the mike stand – hoisting it above his head, twirling it around, and swinging his leg over it. Add a peculiar half-crouching stance, and his act – climaxing with his famous 'Be Bop A-Lula' – was as exciting to watch as it was to hear.

As well as appearing on TV's *Boy Meets Girls*, Gene will be playing at least ten weeks of stage dates around Britain.

CHARTS

Week	Chart	Title	Artist
	US45	Mack The Knife	*Bobby Darin*
	USLP	Heavenly	*Johnny Mathis*
	UK45	What Do You Want	*Adam Faith*
	UKLP	South Pacific	*Soundtrack*
WEEK 2	US45	Heartaches By The Number	*Guy Mitchell*
	USLP	Here We Go Again	*Kingston Trio*
	UK45	What Do You Want	*Adam Faith*
	UKLP	South Pacific	*Soundtrack*
WEEK 3	US45	Heartaches By The Number	*Guy Mitchell*
	USLP	Here We Go Again	*Kingston Trio*
	UK45	What Do You Want	*Adam Faith*
	UKLP	South Pacific	*Soundtrack*
WEEK 4	US45	Why	*Frankie Avalon*
	USLP	Here We Go Again	*Kingston Trio*
	UK45	What D' You Want To Make Eyes At Me For	*Emile Ford*
	UKLP	South Pacific	*Soundtrack*

Perennial hitmaker Guy Mitchell

THE GRAPEVINE

■ **Elvis Presley's former bass player now leads Bill Black's Combo – heading for the US Top 20 with 'Smokie'.**

■ **Marty Wilde has married Joyce Baker, one of The Vernons Girls, whom he first met on *Oh Boy!*, 18 months ago.**

■ **Three years after hitting the top with his version of a country hit, 'Singing The Blues', Guy Mitchell has repeated the process with 'Heartaches By The Number'.**

THE 1960's

Looking back, it's apparent that the 1960s began not with a bang but a whimper. The first three years of what is now regarded as the ultimate decade in popular music produced little more than the Twist, a dance which was more energetic than enjoyable, and the unnerving feeling that the American and British rock icons – Elvis Presley and Cliff Richard – were turning their backs on rock'n'roll. It was grim.

However, there was a burgeoning army of rock and blues bands that had evolved from the 'Fifties schoolboy skiffle groups across Britain. Led by the Beatles, they represented a rock revolution which was to dominate the world.

Liverpool produced the Merseybeat sound, taking the British charts by storm in 1963, while in London the Rolling Stones heralded a boom in UK Rhythm and Blues that included the Animals from Newcastle, Spencer Davis from Birmingham and scores more . . . a truly nationwide phenomen. The conquest of America followed. Between 1964 and 1966, dozens of British groups made fortunes in the 'States, some, like the Dave Clark Five and Herman's Hermits, doing much better there than at home.

Some young American groups, like the Byrds, were even trying to look and sound English, while one trio of unrelated Americans, the Walker Brothers, used Britain as a springboard to international success. Neither would be as enduring as the quintessential Californian group, The Beach Boys, whose more cleancut image would help them to commercial paydirt initially, but whose leading light Brian Wilson was pressured into illness in his efforts to progress, both commercially and artistically.

Phil Spector, part visionary, part eccentric, was producing unique classics with exotic artists like The Ronettes, The Righteous Brothers and finally Ike & Tina Turner. When he went off the boil commercially, The Monkees – a hybrid British/American group – became the teenybop sensation of 1967, not least becuase they were also TV stars.

Black music made as indelible an impression as British Beat, although it had always been around, but without the new focus it enjoyed via Atlantic and Motown, the best known and most successful soul labels ever. Between them, they had all the early soul stars of note, including The Drifters, Aretha Franklin, Otis Redding, The Supremes, The Four Tops, Little Stevie Wonder (who first topped the US charts when he was 13 years old) and Marvin Gaye. They were worshipped by the Beatles and The Stones, which guaranteed their long term success into the 'Eighties.

In 1967, the focus shifted from Swingin' London to San Francisco Bay. Everything was poured into a melting pot and the result was music designed as the perfect soundtrack for hallucination, a state discovered by stars and audiences alike; psychedelia was personified by Jimi Hendrix, a black American who emerged internationally from Britain.

The 'flower power' era embraced extravagant clothes, weird lyrics and music that seemed to have few rules and less form; names like The Grateful Dead, The Jefferson Airplane and The Doors became synonymous with meditation, levitation . . . and drugs. Soon the drugs led to deaths, and a decade which produced more innovation than any other seemed to be slipping into a self-induced oblivion.

1 The Beach Boys
2 The Rolling Stones
3 Diana Ross and the Supremes
4 The Beatles

1

2

3

4

CHARTS

US45 Why
Frankie Avalon
USLP Here We Go Again
Kingston Trio
UK45 What D' You Want To Make Eyes At Me For
Emile Ford
UKLP South Pacific
Soundtrack

WEEK 2

US45 El Paso
Marty Robbins
USLP Here We Go Again
Kingston Trio
UK45 What D' You Want To Make Eyes At Me For
Emile Ford
UKLP South Pacific
Soundtrack

WEEK 3

US45 El Paso
Marty Robbins
USLP Here We Go Again
Kingston Trio
UK45 What D' You Want To Make Eyes At Me For
Emile Ford
UKLP South Pacific
Soundtrack

WEEK 4

US45 Running Bear
Johnny Preston
USLP Here We Go Again
Kingston Trio
UK45 What D' You Want To Make Eyes At Me For
Emile Ford
UKLP South Pacific
Soundtrack

WEEK 5

US45 Running Bear
Johnny Preston
USLP Here We Go Again
Kingston Trio
UK45 Starry Eyed
Michael Holliday
UKLP South Pacific
Soundtrack

ELVIS: 'NO MORE HIGH LIVING!'

In Paris, on a five-day pass, the soon-to-be discharged Sgt Elvis Presley emerged from his £7-a-day suite in the capital's most expensive hotel (Prince of Wales) to offer his thoughts on how he intends to adapt to civilian life.

Said Elvis: 'Being in the Army, I've lost my love of high living. I've learned to relax and take things leisurely during my off-duty Army hours. Before, I was rushin' around 'case I missed somethin'!'

COCHRAN SPILLS THE BEANS

In Britain to promote his latest recording – his version of Ray Charles' 'Hallelujah, I Love Her So' – Eddie Cochran answers a few personal questions.

Who has been the biggest influence on his career? 'Without a doubt, Ray Charles,' Eddie says. 'He's so good – one of the greatest blues singers I've ever heard. But I don't consciously try to copy him. I simply try to generate the same feeling that he produces when he sings.'

As to what has been the most significant break in his young career, Cochran reveals:

'Appearing in the film, *The Girl Can't Help It*. You see, I wasn't even a singer before I made the movie, and hadn't had any vocal discs at all.

'How'd it happen? Well, one day I was playing guitar on a session when up comes a guy, and asks, "How would you like to make a picture?"

'Well, the next day he called and asked if I could sing. I went along with the gag, said I could. Then he asked me to make a demonstration disc of a tune called "20 Flight Rock".

'I still thought it was a joke – let's face it, I didn't know if I could sing. Anyways, I made the record, he liked it, signed me for the film, and that was the start of everything!'

Eddie went on to confirm rumours that on some of his hit records he not only sings but also plays *all* the instruments.

'On the "Summertime Blues" session, for example, I sang the solo voice, the bass voice that comes in now and again, and also wrote the song,' he explains.

'In addition, by using multi-recording techniques, I also played guitar, bass and drums. I also repeated the formula on "C'mon, Everybody".'

'On my latest disc, "Hallelujah, I Love Her So", I play piano, and I sit at the keyboard for quite a few of the tracks on my new album, which should be issued soon.'

Charles: Eddie's inspiration

Bobby socks it to 'em

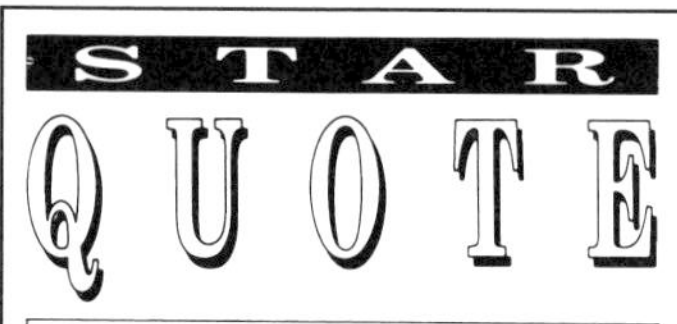

BOBBY DARIN

Shrinking Violet

'If I'm this good now, what will I be like when I'm Sinatra's age?'

THE GRAPEVINE

- **Cliff Richard & The Shadows have been special UK guests on month-long 'Dick Clark's Caravan of Stars' US tour.**
- **Dinah Washington & Brook Benton have been storming US charts with 'Baby (You've Got What It Takes)'; likewise Chuck Berry's 'Let It Rock'.**
- **Adam Faith's new UK single is called 'Poor Me'.**

Brook's got what it takes

GOOD: 'NO CLIFF WITHOUT ELVIS'

Far left: Cliff Richard
Left: erotic Fury

Jack Good, who soared to fame as producer of the pioneering all-live rock'n'roll British TV show *Oh Boy!* (and is currently enjoying success with his latest TV presentation *Boy Meets Girls*) tells it as it is!

Asked if he thinks Cliff Richard would have been more successful or less successful had there never been an Elvis Presley, Good replies: 'I don't think Cliff would have existed at all as a singer without Elvis. He certainly wouldn't be the singer he is today. The initial impetus of Cliff's singing was entirely due to Elvis.'

Asked about public criticism of singer Billy Fury's erotic gyrations on *Boy Meets Girls*, Good stated his position: 'I fully agree that anything suggestive should be avoided – though of course, these things are partially in the minds of individual viewers.

'Frankly, there are one or two things that Billy Fury does that I would rather he didn't. I have, in fact, suggested so to Billy who does tend to get carried away by his performance.'

JESSE BELVIN KILLED – KKK TO BLAME?

West Coast R&B star, Jesse Belvin (27), his wife Jo Anne and driver Charles Shackleford were among the five victims to perish when the rented Cadillac carrying Belvin's party suddenly swerved at great speed across the centre line of US Route 67, near Fairhope, Arkansas, to crash head on into an oncoming car.

Belvin was en route from a Little Rock concert he'd played with Jackie Wilson and Little Willie John to the next evening's appearance in Dallas, Texas.

Conjecture still surrounds the accident: rumours suggest that local Ku Klux Klansmen tampered with the wheel of the vehicle, but the more accepted theory is that Shackleford's abilities as a chauffeur were impaired through his use of heroin, and tiredness from the long journey. Previously, Shackleford had been fired by singer Ray Charles because of erratic driving.

A most influential ballad stylist – earning him the tag of 'Mr Easy' – Belvin proved something of a role model to his closest rival Sam Cooke, whom RCA attempted to style in Jesse's image.

Jesse Belvin will be best remembered as the composer of The Penguin's multi-million selling doo-wop anthem 'Earth Angel', and his own recording of 'Goodnight My Love', which became the signing-off song for dj Alan Freed's radio show.

CHARTS

US45	Running Bear – *Johnny Preston*
USLP	Here We Go Again – *Kingston Trio*
UK45	Why – *Anthony Newley*
UKLP	South Pacific – *Soundtrack*
	WEEK 2
US45	Teen Angel – *Mark Dinning*
USLP	The Sound Of Music – *Original Cast*
UK45	Why – *Anthony Newley*
UKLP	South Pacific – *Soundtrack*
	WEEK 3
US45	Teen Angel – *Mark Dinning*
USLP	The Sound Of Music – *Original Cast*
UK45	Why – *Anthony Newley*
UKLP	South Pacific – *Soundtrack*
	WEEK 4
US45	Theme From 'A Summer Place' – *Percy Faith*
USLP	The Sound Of Music – *Original Cast*
UK45	Why – *Anthony Newley*
UKLP	South Pacific – *Soundtrack*

THE GRAPEVINE

- **The John Barry Seven have released 'Hit and Miss', the theme from BBC-TV's *Juke Box Jury*.**
- **Innovative British producer Joe Meek has launched his own Triumph label with 'Just Too Late' by drummer Peter Jay.**
- **The Everly Brothers have left Cadence for the just-launched Warner Brothers label and debut with 'Cathy's Clown'.**
- **Eddie Cochran and Gene Vincent have begun their mammoth 20-week British tour in Glasgow.**

Peter Jay: a Meek triumph?

ELVIS IS BACK!

Back on civvy street, Elvis faces the press as he says goodbye to US army

CHARTS

US45	Theme From 'A Summer Place' *Percy Faith*
USLP	The Sound Of Music *Original Cast*
UK45	Poor Me *Adam Faith*
UKLP	South Pacific *Soundtrack*
WEEK 2	
US45	Theme from 'A Summer Place' *Percy Faith*
USLP	The Sound Of Music *Original Cast*
UK45	Poor Me *Adam Faith*
UKLP	South Pacific *Soundtrack*
WEEK 3	
US45	Theme From 'A Summer Place' *Percy Faith*
USLP	The Sound Of Music *Original Cast*
UK45	Running Bear *Johnny Preston*
UKLP	South pacific *Soundtrack*
WEEK 4	
US45	Theme From 'A Summer Place' *Percy Faith*
USLP	The Sound Of Music *Original Cast*
UK45	My Old Man's A Dustman *Lonnie Donegan*
UKLP	South Pacific *Soundtrack*

Elvis Presley's demobilization from the US Army has proved to be just as big a media event as his induction.

It commenced at the Friedberg Barracks in West Germany where 'the most publicized soldier since General MacArthur' gave a 'farewell' press conference before leaving Europe. Said Elvis of his immediate future: 'I don't know if I shall manage to get on top again. I only wish I knew. I hear that trends have changed, so it might be pretty difficult for me. But, I'll tell you this . . . I'm sure gonna try hard.

'My attraction to rock'n'roll hasn't changed one bit, and I think it would be a mistake for me to change my style. The public will let me know in due course if they don't like it.'

Asked what he thinks of his new rivals – Fabian and Frankie Avalon – Elvis replies: 'I don't consider them rivals . . . there's room for everyone. And, if other people can make it, good luck to them.'

So, what souvenirs will Elvis be taking back to the USA?

Aside from personal luggage, two tons of fan mail stuffed into 12 large sacks, and a collection of 2,182 records, Elvis reveals: 'Two German guitars, one camera, but no girls!'

What about 16-year-old Priscilla Beaulieu, who has been his steady Army date?

'It's nothing serious,' insists Elvis. 'I can promise you, there's no big romance!'

A howlin' blizzard, singer Nancy Sinatra, 2,000 fans and a press battalion welcomed Elvis back Stateside when, on March 3, the military aircraft carrying his unit back from Germany touched down at McGuire Airbase, New Jersey. Two days later, Elvis was back on civvy street.

On March 20 and 21, he undertook his first post-Army recording date, at the RCA Studios in Nashville. Two of the titles cut, 'Stuck On You'/'Fame and Fortune' (RCA) went on sale in Nashville within 48 hours of having been taped.

The momentum continued: on March 26, Elvis's return to active public life via network television occurred when he appeared as special guest on *The Frank Sinatra Timex Show*. In the show, Elvis performed both sides of his newest single, then duetted with Sinatra.

The King is back.

The Everlys: Cricket match

EVERLY-CRICKETS TOUR

The Everly Brothers have ensured both banner headlines and a box-office stampede when they revealed that Buddy Holly's former band – The Crickets – will do the back-up honours on Don and Phil's UK tour scheduled to open on April 1.

In the meantime, there was standing room only at the opening night of a package show featuring three other hot US chart stars – Bobby Darin, Duane Eddy and Clyde McPhatter – at the Lewisham Odeon, London.

Emile Ford & The Checkmates supplied local interest.

Twang man Duane

THE GRAPEVINE

- **Actor-singer Anthony Newley's latest movie *Jazzboat* has opened at London's New Victoria Cinema**
- **A French singer named Johnny Halliday, of whom much is expected, has released his first single on the Vogue label – 'Laisse Les Filles'.**
- **Soul singer Sam Cooke kicks off a tour of the West Indies.**

EDDIE COCHRAN KILLED, VINCENT INJURED IN TAXI CRASH

Following a concert at the Bristol Hippodrome, Eddie Cochran, Gene Vincent, Sharon Sheeley (Cochran's fiancée) and tour manager Patrick Thompkins set off for London in a Ford Consul taxi driven by a local 19-year old youth.

Cochran was in a hurry, as he was due to fly back to America from Heathrow Airport the next afternoon.

Averaging 70 mph, the taxi reached Chippenham, Wiltshire at midnight. However, the driver had lost his sense of direction and control of the vehicle. As he emerged from beneath a railway viaduct, the car hit the curb, careering 150-yards before crashing into a concrete lampstand.

The impact threw Cochran upwards against the car roof and then through the door and on to the road. Gene Vincent suffered a fractured collar bone and Sheeley back injuries, while Thompkins and the driver escaped unhurt.

At 4 p.m. Easter Sunday, 16 hours after the accident, Eddie Cochran died as a result of severe brain lacerations. He was buried at Forest Lawn Cemetery, Glendate, California, on April 25.

Born on October 30 1938 in Oklahoma City, Cochran was a most accomplished singer and guitarist best remembered for hits such as '20 Flight Rock', 'Summertime Blues', 'C'Mon Everybody', 'Somethin' Else' and 'Hallelujah, I Love Her So'.

He also made guest appearances in such movies as *The Girl Can't Help It*, *Go Johnny Go* and *Untamed Youth*.

A new single, with the sadly prophetic title 'Three Steps To Heaven' is being considered for release by London Records, his British label.

CHARTS

- US45 Theme From 'A Summer Place' — *Percy Faith*
- USLP The Sound Of Music — *Original Cast*
- UK45 My Old Man's A Dustman — *Lonnie Donegan*
- UKLP South Pacific — *Soundtrack*

WEEK 2

- US45 Theme From 'A Summer Place' — *Percy Faith*
- USLP The Sound Of Music — *Original Cast*
- UK45 My Old Man's A Dustman — *Lonnie Donegan*
- UKLP South Pacific — *Soundtrack*

WEEK 3

- US45 Theme From 'A Summer Place' — *Percy Faith*
- USLP The Sound Of Music — *Original Cast*
- UK45 My Old Man's A Dustman — *Lonnie Donegan*
- UKLP South Pacific — *Soundtrack*

WEEK 4

- US45 Theme From 'A Summer Place' — *Percy Faith*
- USLP The Sound Of Music — *Original Cast*
- UK45 Do You Mind — *Anthony Newley*
- UKLP South Pacific — *Soundtrack*

Connie copies the Colonel in pop price stakes

ELVIS: THE PRICE RISES

In an effort to frighten off all but legitimately-interested parties, Colonel Tom Parker has set the non-negotiable price of $150,000 for any future Elvis Presley concert performances.

So far, this has proved even more effective than the Colonel anticipated: there are no takers!

The Colonel's price tag is understandable, given the news that Presley has been named America's best-selling recording artist at the first presentation of the NARM Awards – a new annual prize-giving ceremony instigated by the National Association of Record Merchants.

Connie Francis's manager may follow suit. His client was named top-selling female artist.

THE GRAPEVINE

- **Elvis Presley has gone back in uniform on Paramount Pictures' Hollywood lot, to commence filming *G.I. Blues*.**
- **UK chart newcomer Lance 'Be Mine' Fortune and US singer Jerry 'Here Comes Summer' Keller replaced the late Eddie Cochran on Gene Vincent's current UK tour.**
- **Pye Records have released 'This Is Hancock', a collection of U.K. comedian Tony Hancock's best radio sketches.**

British cult favourite and comic genius Tony Hancock

WHAM UNVEILED

Direct from Manchester, ABC-TV screened the first edition of celebrated producer Jack *Oh Boy!* Good's new weekly rock'n'roll extravaganza, *Wham!* on April 23.

The first show featured Billy Fury, Joe Brown, Jess Conrad, Dickie Pride, Little Tony, Vince Taylor and Johnny Kidd & The Pirates.

Critics' response? A hit!

Fury: Wham! star

MAY 1960

CHARTS

Chart	Title	Artist
US45	Stuck On You	*Elvis Presley*
USLP	The Sound Of Music	*Original Cast*
UK45	Cathy's Clown	*Everly Brothers*
UKLP	South Pacific	*Soundtrack*
WEEK 2		
US45	Stuck On You	*Elvis Presley*
USLP	Sold Out	*Kingston Trio*
UK45	Cathy's Clown	*Everly Brothers*
UKLP	South Pacific	*Soundtrack*
WEEK 3		
US45	Stuck On You	*Elvis Presley*
USLP	Sold Out	*Kingston Trio*
UK45	Cathy's Clown	*Everly Brothers*
UKLP	South Pacific	*Soundtrack*
WEEK 4		
US45	Stuck On You	*Elvis Presley*
USLP	Sold Out	*Kingston Trio*
UK45	Cathy's Clown	*Everly Brothers*
UKLP	South Pacific	*Soundtrack*
WEEK 5		
US45	Cathy's Clown	*Everly Brothers*
USLP	Sold Out	*Kingston Trio*
UK45	Cathy's Clown	*Everly Brothers*
UKLP	South Pacific	*Soundtrack*

CAVERN GOES POP

After three years, Liverpool's popular Cavern Club, in Mathew Street, has moved with the times and finally 'recognized' rock music.

The club's previous jazz-only booking policy has been dropped. The first two local beat groups to benefit – Cass & The Casanovas and Rory Storme & The Hurricanes.

COCHRAN 'NOT DEAD', SAYS SHARON

'Eddie Cochran is not dead!' says his fiancée, Sharon Sheeley, the 20-year-old US songwriter, still recovering in a London hospital from multiple injuries she received in the auto smash that killed Cochran.

'Eddie is away on a long tour and it won't be long before I see him again soon. I don't need to find another lover. My love for Eddie is strong enough to last, and, I thank God for the three years He let me have with him.'

Their relationship began in 1957, when they were introduced by The Everly Brothers. 'It was, on my part, love at first sight, but Eddie paid no attention to me. We did not meet again for about nine months,' recalls Sharon.

'Eddie asked me for a date, but asked if I would first agree to go steady with him – I gladly consented. A month later, we became engaged.

'We planned to marry in America. We were due to fly back last month, and it was on the way to the airport that Eddie was killed. I can tell you that Eddie was singing "California, Here I Come", at the time – and we were both so happy that we were going home to be married.'

Miss Sheeley, who has flatly rejected offers from various US record companies to cut a 'tribute' disc about Eddie, insists that she's sickened by the attempts by certain individuals to make a profit from Cochran's death.

Does she treasure any particular memories of her relationship with Eddie? 'No! our love and the times we had together is the deepest, dearest memory I possess.'

THE GRAPEVINE

- **Stateside, 'The Eddie Cochran Memorial Album' has been rush-released.**
- **Conway Twitty, Freddy Cannon, Johnny Preston are trekking around the UK with locals Wee Willie Harris & Tony Crombie's Rockets.**
- **Safe-As-Milk Elvis surrogate Tommy Sands has commenced a six-month stint with US Air Force.**
- **Liverpool beat group, The Silver Beetles are touring Scotland as Johnny Gentle's backing band.**

Tallahassee, New Orleans, California – it's the UK next for Freddy Cannon

PAYOLA: FREED FOR TRIAL

A Manhattan Grand Jury has indicted eight people – including America's most influential and popular disc jockey, KDAY's Alan Freed – for having received in excess of $30,000 in payola.

This illegal pay-for-play policy has run rampant throughout the US radio industry for many years, but in an effort to improve its poor image, Freed is believed to have been made something of a scapegoat.

Though he has pleaded not guilty as charged, Freed's trial has been set for September 19.

Freed, free for the moment but prison a possibility

STAR QUOTE

RICKY NELSON

'Perhaps the most embarrasing moment in my career was when six girls tried to fling themselves under my car, and shouted to me to run over them. That sort of thing can be very frightening!'

WILLIAMS QUITS PLATTERS

Before Tony Williams abdicated this month from his position as lead singer with vocal group The Platters to embark upon a solo career, the stylish tenor – who sang on such evocative Mercury label hits as 'Only You', 'The Great Pretender' and 'Smoke Gets In Your Eyes' – generously and publicly introduced his replacement, Sammy Turner (21), on stage at the Copa Club, Newport, Kentucky. It was a gesture typical of the man and the group.

Whereas many similar vocal acts have only enjoyed short-lived fame, the secret of The Platters' prolonged success has been their avoidance of gimmicky doo-wop vocal tricks.

Instead, their preference is for straight-ahead beat ballads which, aside from the familiar piano triplets trade mark, are practically acappella.

A major contributory factor in their initial success was the dignity of their appearance in 'Rock Around The Clock' when they were filmed performing their perennial best-sellers, 'Only You' and 'The Great Pretender'.

NEWLEY – NO IDOL ACTOR

Newley-launched musical bound for London opening

Movie actor Anthony Newley – the Artful Dodger to Alec Guinness's memorable Fagin in *Oliver Twist*, who suddenly found himself a bona-fide chart-busting pop star after playing a rock'n'roll singer conscripted into the (British) Army in the hit comedy movie *Idle On Parade*, has adopted an entirely new image.

Stop The World, I Want to Get Off, the avant-garde stage musical he co-wrote with lyricist/composer Leslie Bricusse, and in which he stars, has been hailed an instant hit at its première at Manchester's Palace Theatre.

Plans are now afoot to bring the show, in which Newley plays a confused character called Littlechap, to London, and to record an album of material from the production.

CHARTS

US45	Cathy's Clown *Everly Brothers*
USLP	Sold Out *Kingston Trio*
UK45	Cathy's Clown *Everly Brothers*
UKLP	South Pacific *Soundtrack*
WEEK 2	
US45	Cathy's Clown *Everly Brothers*
USLP	Sold Out *Kingston Trio*
UK45	Cathy's Clown *Everly Brothes*
UKLP	South Pacific *Soundtrack*
WEEK 3	
US45	Cathy's Clown *Everly Brothers*
USLP	Sold Out *Kingston Trio*
UK45	Cathy's Clown *Everly Brothers*
UKLP	South Pacific *Soundtrack*
WEEK 4	
US45	Cathy's Clown *Everly Brothers*
USLP	Sold Out *Kingston Trio*
UK45	Cathy's Clown *Everly Brothers*
UKLP	South Pacific *Soundtrack*

THE GRAPEVINE

- **The Hollywood Argyles' Kim Fowley produced 'Alley-Oop', which is chartbound in the USA.**
- **BBC Radio's weekly celebrity check-list *Desert Island Disc* has celebrated its 500th edition.**
- **Instrumental guitar combo, The Ventures have got their careers off to a quick start with 'Walk Don't Run'.**

EMILE GOES GOLD

Pye recording stars Emile Ford & The Checkmates have joined the exclusive band of British artists to have sold in excess of one million copies of any single in the UK.

They have received a gold disc for 'What Do You Want To Make Those Eyes At Me For'.

PAT BOONE

who married at 19, after a three-year courtship.

'I receive many queries from young people who want to get married. I spend my time discouraging them!'

Nokie Edwards, Don Wilson, Howie Johnson and Bob Bogle make up The Venture

JULY

NO KIDDING JOHNNY THE PIRATE!

Johnny Kidd & The Pirates have 'vibrated' into the UK charts with 'Shakin' All Over' – a record which many insist has come close to wiping away the memory of Cliff Richard's 'Move It' as the greatest-ever British-made rock'n'roll single.

Kidd's self-penned follow-up to his last year hit 'Please Don't Touch' again employs a 'shakin'' theme, but it's quite unlike any other record in the charts.

With an aggressive visual image as unmistakable as his R&B-rooted voice – black patch over his left eye, matching leather waistcoat and thighboots, plus a cutlass – Kidd stands apart from the numerous Elvis imitators who make up the British rock'n'roll scene.

Similarly, his guitarists steer away from Shadows-style 'tremeloing' and Duane Eddy elastic-band 'twang', preferring a hard-edged black blues sound.

For 'Shakin' All Over', top session guitar-picker Joe Moretti was responsible for that hackle-raising guitar lick.

Regarding who influenced Kidd's highly-personalized style, all he had to say was: 'I just open my mouth and sing – that's all there is to it!'

DUANE: 'IT'S HARD WORK!'

Twangy guitar star Duane Eddy, currently enjoying world-wide success with his theme tune for the movie *Because They're Young*, has revealed a few trade secrets:

'A lot of people seem to think it's easy to gather round a studio mike and pluck guitar strings, play tenor sax and make all the other noises that come out on our disc,' he confided.

'How I wish I could make people see how much hard work the boys really put in. From The Rebels to the sound engineer, and from the extra musicians to the guys whose job it is to keep us supplied with coffee and hot dogs, we are all working to one end.'

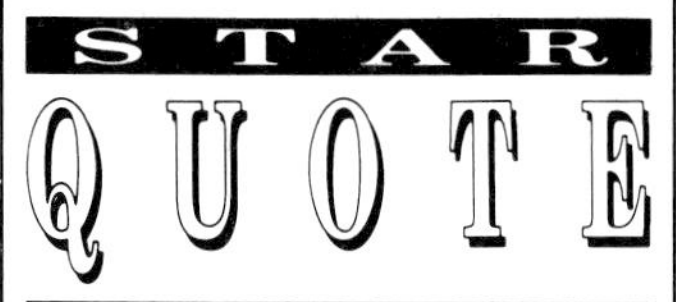

FATS DOMINO

'I don't care if my discs hit the top spot or if they are never seen in the charts, so long as the collectors who appreciate rhythm and blues buy them. When the real collectors lose interest, man, I'll retire.'

Twistin' time with Hank

ROLF'S NEW SOUND

A new decade – a new sound!!!!

The Wobble Board, invention of bearded Australian TV presenter and cartoonist Rolf Harris is the featured instrument on his new record 'Tie Me Kangaroo Down Sport', which has wobbled straight into the UK charts at No. 15.

How To Play The Wobble Board!

Step 1: Locate a piece of hardboard 3ft long by 18in wide.

Step 2: Grasp both ends of the board firmly in your hands.

Step 3: With a flick of the wrists bend the board up and down to produce a rhythmic 'Whoolp' and 'Beloop'.

Step 4: Immediately become rich and famous.

Rolf wobbles into the chart

THE GRAPEVINE

- **Widower Vernon Presley (Elvis' Dad) has married divorcee Dee Elliott.**
- **Hank Ballard & The Midnighters launch 'The Twist'.**
- **Bing Crosby has been presented with a platinum disc to commemorate record sales of 200 million.**
- **Only six months after it commenced, Marty Wilde's two year, £100,000 contract with impresario Harold Fielding is to be terminated in September, by mutual agreement.**

CHARTS

US45	Everybody's Somebody's Fool	*Connie Francis*
USLP	Sold Out	*Kingston Trio*
UK45	Good Timin'	*Jimmy Jones*
UKLP	South Pacific	*Soundtrack*
WEEK 2		
US45	Everybody's Somebody's Fool	*Connie Francis*
USLP	Sold Out	*Kingston Trio*
UK45	Good Timin'	*Jimmy Jones*
UKLP	South Pacific	*Soundtrack*
WEEK 3		
US45	Alley-Oop	*Hollywood Argyles*
USLP	Sold Out	*Kingston Trio*
UK45	Good Timin'	*Jimmy Jones*
UKLP	Elvis Is Back	*Elvis Presley*
WEEK 4		
US45	I'm Sorry	*Brenda Lee*
USLP	The Button-Down Mind Of	*Bob Newhart*
UK45	Please Don't Tease	*Cliff Richard*
UKLP	Elvis Is Back	*Elvis Presley*
WEEK 5		
US45	I'm Sorry	*Brenda Lee*
USLP	The Button-Down Mind Of	*Bobby Newhart*
UK45	Please Don't Tease	*Cliff Richard*
UKLP	Elvis Is Back	*Elvis Presley*

WHICH CAME FIRST – SHADOWS OR BERT?

Cliff 'n' the Shads

Controversy has erupted as Cliff Richard's fancy-footwork backing group The Shadows enjoy chart-topping solo status with their instrumental hit, 'Apache'. The question on BBC disc jockeys lips is: was 'Apache' written for 'Play-Guitar-In-A-Day' personality Bert Weedon (the loser in the singles race), or was it penned for The Shadows?

So what does 'Apache' composer Jerry Lordan have to say?

'I don't write specifically for any artist – I've never really tried. I'm not like Lionel Bart – I wish I was!' he laughs.

'I gave no thought at all who should play it until it was completed,' he says, but lets slip that when 'Apache' was still in manuscript form, Bert Weedon was the first name that sprang to mind.

Nevertheless, while on tour together, The Shadows asked Lordan if he had any material that might be suitable for them.

'As I don't write exclusively for any artist, and I wasn't certain if Bert Weedon was even considering recording the tune, I suggested "Apache" to The Shadows,' Lordan says.

VINCENT CHEWS THE FAT

Gene Vincent takes time out during his hectic UK schedule to chew the fat with the NME in a question-and-answer session:

Q: How does British TV compare with the US in terms of rock'n'roll presentation?

A: 'In Britain, they try to achieve perfection. In the States, they just put you in front of a camera, and tell you to sing!'

Q: How do you think UK rock artists would fare in the US?

A: 'I felt inferior compared to many British singers. Artists over here know all kinds of music – they discuss keys, arrangements and so on. Speaking for myself, somebody just gives me a chord and I sing. That's all I can do!'

Q: Have you thought about branching out into other fields of entertainment?

A: 'I'm a rock singer and I reckon that's the way I'll stay. I don't think that I could alter if I tried!'

DECCA DITHER OVER DEATH DISC

He who hesitates is hitless!

Two British cover versions of American singer Ray Peterson's controversial *death-disc*, 'Tell Laura I Love Her' have been rush-released.

Ricky tells Laura

And, as Ricky Valence and John Leyton competed for attention, Decca Records commenced the first of five high-level boardroom discussions to determine whether or not they should release the 'offending' Peterson original. In doing so, they lost valuable sales – and the No. 1 slot.

CHARTS

US45	I'm Sorry – *Brenda Lee*
USLP	The Button-Down Mind Of – *Bob Newhart*
UK45	Please Don't Tease – *Cliff Richard*
UKLP	Elvis Is Back – *Elvis Presley*
	WEEK 2
US45	Yellow Polka Dot Bikini – *Brian Hyland*
USLP	The Button-Down Mind Of – *Bob Newhart*
UK45	Please Don't Tease – *Cliff Richard*
UKLP	Elvis Is Back – *Elvis Presley*
	WEEK 3
US45	It's Now Or Never – *Elvis Presley*
USLP	The Button-Down Mind Of – *Bob Newhart*
UK45	Apache – *Shadows*
UKLP	Elvis Is Back – *Elvis Presley*
	WEEK 4
US45	It's Now Or Never – *Elvis Presley*
USLP	The Button-Down Mind Of – *Bob Newhart*
UK45	Apache – *Shadows*
UKLP	Elvis Is Back – *Elvis Presley*

THE GRAPEVINE

- **Lonnie Donegan has received a gold disc for one million-plus UK sales of 'My Old Man's A Dustman'.**
- **Stateside, record moguls have insisted that the 45 rpm single is about to be discontinued and soon all records will spin at a uniform 33 1/3 rpm.**
- **Top British dance band leader Ted Heath has celebrated his 15th anniversay as a front man.**

Dustman Donegan cleans up with 'My Old Man's' million-seller

SEPTEMBER

1960

IT'S TRAD, DAD!

Acker Bilk (left) and Ken Colyer (below) both benefitting from the boom in trad jazz

Will Dixieland kill rock? That's the latest topic circulating through the British music scene.

For the first time ever, jazz has become 'pop' music. And, in Britain, locally produced brash revivalist New Orleans-style trad jazz performed by the likes of Acker Bilk, Chris Barber, Kenny Ball, Terry Lightfoot and Ken Colyer, has spread out from the cellar clubs and art college Saturday night 'raves' and into the charts, where it now stands shoulder-to-shoulder with rock'n'roll.

Perhaps employing the theory of embrace one's enemy, or maybe staging a calculated take-the-money-and-run operation, impresario Larry Parnes and TV pop producer Jack Good have packaged together 15 British rock singers including Billy Fury, Joe Brown, Tommy Bruce, Dave Sampson, Dickie Pride, Duffy Power and Georgie Fame, and pushed them in front of a thundering 15-piece band led by show-drummer Jimmy Nicol for an extensive trek around the British Isles under a 'Rock And Trad' banner.

Jack Good commented about the production he has masterminded: 'I want the show to be fast-moving, but with a pronounced Dixieland theme . . . but don't get the idea that we are scrapping rock altogether.'

Does this mean that the package couldn't stand up purely as a rock'n'roll show?

'I can't really answer that!' was Good's final word on the subject.

CHARTS

US45	It's Now Or Never *Elvis Presley*
USLP	The Button-Down Mind Of *Bob Newhart*
UK45	Apache *Shadows*
UKLP	Elvis Is Back *Elvis Presley*
	WEEK 2
US45	It's Now Or Never *Elvis Presley*
USLP	The Button-Down Mind Of *Bob Newhart*
UK45	Apache *Shadows*
UKLP	Down Drury Lane To Memory Lane *101 Strings*
	WEEK 3
US45	It's Now Or Never *Elvis Presley*
USLP	String Along *Kingston Trio*
UK45	Apache *Shadows*
UKLP	Down Drury Lane To Memory Lane *101 Strings*
	WEEK 4
US45	The Twist *Chubby Checker*
USLP	String Along *Kingston Trio*
UK45	Apache *Shadows*
UKLP	Down Drury Lane To Memory Lane *101 Strings*

MORE COCHRAN

The Eddie Cochran memorial industry rolls on.

Liberty Records' President Al Bennett has issued a statement claiming the company is in possession of 40 unreleased studio and demo tapes by the late Eddie Cochran.

Enough, suggests Bennett, for at least four more posthumous singles, plus an album.

BLACK BACK

Elvis Presley's former bassist, Bill Black – now a highly successful instrumental combo leader in his own right – has stormed back into the US charts with a personalized treatment of his ex-boss' hit, 'Don't Be Cruel'.

SHADOWS GO MOVIE

The Shadows have scored another first – starring in the very first 'video-disc': a technicolour promotional film made for use both on television and the specially designed video juke-boxes that have begun appearing in the bars of selected French and Italian coastal holiday resorts.

MOTOWN IN UK

Motivated by the brisk import trade in American soul singles, Oriole Records has acquired the UK release rights to Detroit's Tamla-Motown label, and has celebrated the deal by releasing The Contours' 'Do You Love Me', Mary Wells' 'You Beat Me To The Punch' and The Marvelettes' 'Beechwood 4-5789'.

THE GRAPEVINE

- **Frankie Avalon, having turned 21, has pocketed a $250,000 trust fund.**
- **Lonnie Donegan re-signs with Pye Records for highest-ever UK royalty rate.**
- **In the wake of 'Apache', The Shadows have undertaken their first bill-topping U.K. dates without Cliff Richard.**
- **Meanwhile, Cliff has again asked his loyal fans to select his next single; they chose 'Nine Times Out Of Ten'.**

Contours: UK release

POLL: PRESLEY AND CONNIE TRIUMPHANT

With thousands of votes cast, the NME Annual Reader's Poll shows that Elvis Presley's hold on fans' hearts has not diminished – nor has age dimmed Frank Sinatra's appeal!

On the distaff side, Connie Francis continues to reign supreme, although given a good run by Brenda Lee and Shirley Bassey.

The results in full:

World Section

Male Section
1 Elvis Presley
2 Cliff Richard
3 Frank Sinatra

Female Singer
1 Connie Francis
2 Brenda Lee
3 Shirley Bassey

Vocal Group
1 The Everly Brothers

Musical Personality
1 Duane Eddy

British Section

Male Singer
1 Cliff Richard
2 Adam Faith
3 Anthony Newley

Female Singer
1 Shirley Bassey
2 Alma Cogan
3 Petula Clark

Vocal Group
1 The King Brothers

Vocal Personality
1 Lonnie Donegan

Large Band/Orchestra
1 Ted Heath

Small Group
1 The Shadows

New Disc or TV Singer
1 Emile Ford

Instrumental Personality
1 Russ Conway

Disc-Jockey
1 David Jacobs

British Disc of the Year
1 The Shadows – 'Apache'

Artist For Poll Concert
1 Adam Faith

Shirley shines in Poll

CHARTS

US45	My Heart Has A Mind Of Its Own / *Connie Francis*
USLP	String Along / *Kingston Trio*
UK45	Tell Laura I Love Her / *Ricky Valance*
UKLP	Down Drury Lane To Memory Lane / *101 Strings*
WEEK 2	
US45	Mr. Custer / *Larry Verne*
USLP	String Along / *Kingston Trio*
UK45	Tell Laura I Love Her / *Ricky Valance*
UKLP	Down Drury Lane To Memory Lane / *101 Strings*
WEEK 3	
US45	Mr. Custer / *Larry Verne*
USLP	String Along / *Kingston Trio*
UK45	Only The Lonely / *Roy Orbison*
UKLP	South Pacific / *Soundtrack*
WEEK 4	
US45	Save The Last Dance For Me / *Drifters*
USLP	Nice & Easy / *Frank Sinatra*
UK45	Only The Lonely / *Roy Orbison*
UKLP	South Pacific / *Soundtrack*
WEEK 5	
US45	I Want To Be Wanted / *Brenda Lee*
USLP	The Button-Down Mind Of / *Bob Newhart*
UK45	Only The Lonely / *Roy Orbison*
UKLP	South Pacific / *Soundtrack*

STARS ON FANS

Connie Francis, Cliff Richard and Lonnie Donegan have spoken candidly about fan-power. The results are intriguing:

Connie Francis: 'I estimate that I receive 7,000 fan letters every week from all over the world. I have three offices dealing with them. Of these, I get to read about 250. I always make certain I see any special letters, or correspondence from servicemen.'

Cliff Richard: 'I must confess that I don't enjoy being mobbed, and it's rather a pity the fans don't realize that it's to their disadvantage. You see, if they weren't so fanatic, it would then be possible to stand among them and sign autographs.'

Lonnie Donegan: 'I don't like the idea of being looked up to as an idol – I'd much rather that my supporters were genuinely interested in the music!'

SAM COOKE: NO BIZ, NO SHOW

Words of wisdom from Sam Cooke:

'Show business seems to be inhabited by two types of people - those who merely "show" and those who combine "show" with "business".

'During the past three years, I have devoted as much time as I could to the practical business side of the "show" end. Unemployment offices are full of "one shot" artists – performers who suddenly got "hot" with one recording, then completely faded from the scene.

'Why? Possibly because they had no real talent, and because they did not understand show business *is* a business.'

Soul stylist Sam slams showbiz slackers

THE GRAPEVINE

- **Dion & The Belmonts have split.**
- **Africa is the first stop for the US State Department's newly-inaugurated Jazz Ambassador – Louis Armstrong.**
- **With Frank Sinatra as best man, Sammy Davis Jr. defied racist death threats and has married Swedish blonde actress, Mai Britt.**
- **Youth exploitation flick, *Beat Girl*, starring Adam Faith and featuring a John Barry soundtrack, has opened in London.**

NOVEMBER

JOHNNY HORTON KILLED

Texas-born country music star, Johnny Horton (33), who enjoyed worldwide crossover hit success with 'Battle Of New Orleans' and 'North To Alaska', was killed in an auto smash on November 5 after playing a date at The Skyline, Austin, Texas – the very same venue where Hank Williams gave his last-ever performance.

This wasn't the only bizarre similarity between the singers. Horton had been married to Williams' former wife, Billie Jean.

Discussing her most recent ex-husband, Billie Jean Williams Horton reveals: 'Johnny knew he was going to die – he talked about it constantly. It reached the point where he wouldn't fly any more because he was so certain he'd get killed in a plane crash.'

INSTRUMENTALS RULE UK, OK?

Silk-suited singers were given short-shrift in the NME's UK Top 30, for the week of November 4, as instrumental singles account for no fewer than *nine* positions!

These were:

5 Johnny & The Hurricans: 'Rocking Goose' (London)

11 The John Barry Seven: 'Walk Don't Run' (Columbia)

12 The Piltdown Men: 'Macdonald's Cave' (Capitol)

18 The Ventures: 'Walk Don't Run' (Top Rank)

21 The Shadows: 'Apache' (Columbia)

22 Manuel: 'Never On A Sunday' (Columbia)

23 Don Costa: 'Never On A Sunday' (London)

28 Duane Eddy: 'Because They're Young' (London)

29 Bert Weedon: 'Sorry Robbie' (Top Rank)

Unlike some people in the music business who are spreading alarmist talk to the effect that pop singers are becoming a thing of the past, The Shadows' lead guitarist, Hank B. Marvin gave a realistic personal overview of the situation:

'It seems to me that we are returning to the situation of five or six years ago, when there was a considerable vogue for instrumentals – though of course, in those days it was mostly for big band material.

'Despite this, I don't think there's any slackening of interest in vocals.'

I like Ike says Tina

THE GRAPEVINE

- **Pat Boone's second book, *Betwixt You and Me and the Gatepost* has been published with 75,000 advance orders.**
- **Tina Turner has celebrated her 21st birthday.**
- **The Shirelles have posed the eternal question, 'Will You Love Me Tomorrow'.**
- **One-time Devil's Advocate, Elvis Presley has recorded a Gospel LP, 'His Hand In Mine'.**

CHARTS

US45	Save The Last Dance For Me — *Drifters*
USLP	The Button-Down Mind Of — *Bob Newhart*
UK45	It's Now Or Never — *Elvis Presley*
UKLP	South Pacific — *Soundtrack*
WEEK 2	
US45	Save The Last Dance For Me — *Drifters*
USLP	The Button-Down Mind Of — *Bob Newhart*
UK45	It's Now Or Never — *Elvis Presley*
UKLP	South Pacific — *Soundtrack*
WEEK 3	
US45	Georgia On My Mind — *Ray Charles*
USLP	The Button-Down Mind Of — *Bob Newhart*
UK45	It's Now Or Never — *Elvis Presley*
UKLP	South Pacific — *Soundtrack*
WEEK 4	
US45	Stay — *Maurice Williams & The Zodiacs*
USLP	The Button-Down Mind Of — *Bob Newhart*
UK45	It's Now Or Never — *Elvis Presley*
UKLP	South Pacific — *Soundtrack*

Left: The Shirelles

Hank B. Marvin, of the tremelo guitar sound, defends vocals in the wake of the Shadows' solo success

SUCCESS AT LAST FOR ORBISON

Though Roy Orbison recorded for Sam Phillips' Sun label in Memphis at around the same time as Elvis, Jerry Lee Lewis, Carl Perkins and Johnny Cash, the success enjoyed by those stars has rubbed off belatedly on the introverted Texan.

A move to Monument Records in Nashville, and suddenly The Big 'O' has *three* tunes on the UK charts: there's his angst-ridden former No. 1, 'Only The Lonely' plus 'Blue Angel' (No. 21) and 'Today's Teardrops' (No. 28).

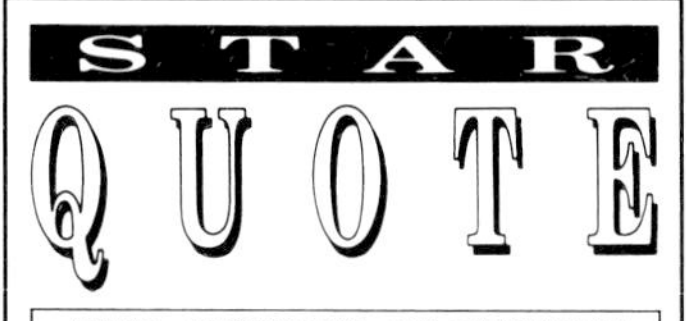

STAR QUOTE

THE EVERLY BROTHERS

'We're not Grand Ole Opry . . . we're obviously not Perry Como . . . we're just pop music. But, you could call us an American skiffle group!'

ELVIS – HIT DISC, HIT MOVIE

Colonel Parker is in seventh heaven – it has taken just six weeks for ex-soldier Elvis Presley's 'It's Now or Never' to sell one million copies in Britain alone, thereby beating the previous 1957 sales record held by RCA-Victor label-mate Harry Belafonte's 'Mary's Boy Child'.

However, prior to its release (Aug 21), this record (a re-write of the Italian standard 'O Solo Mio') was the subject of long-winded UK copyright law entanglement.

At one point, RCA Records (UK) feared that it might take another seven years before the track was cleared for release.

Things are also buzzing for Elvis on the movie front. His *G.I. Blues* film is grossing an incredible $190,000 nightly in 22 prestigious US movie houses.

THE GRAPEVINE

- Station WNTA dj Clay Cole has replaced disgraced Alan Freed following the latter's conviction on payola charges, to host Brooklyn Paramount Theater's 'Christmas Rock'n'Roll Show' which featured Chubby Checker, Bobby Rydell, Dion, Neil Sedaka, Bo Diddley and The Drifters.
- Bobby Darin has married movie actress Sandra Dee.
- Cliff & The Shadows have begun a six-month London Palladium variety season.

CLIFF BUYS BACK MOVIE DEAL

Cliff clinches movie move

In an unprecedented behind-the-scenes deal said to involve a five figure sum, Cliff Richard has bought back the option movie producer Mickey Delamar holds on his future services as a movie actor.

'It's all been settled very amicably,' insists the singer's manager, Tito Burns.

Though it was announced at the end of July that Delamar was about to star Cliff in an adaption of Margery Allingham's novel *Hide My Eyes*, Burns claims that Delamar had chosen to take a rest from a heavy work schedule.

'We had arranged for Cliff to begin work at the end of January on the first of the outstanding films,' Burns reveals. 'We did not want a further postponement because of our plans for next year, Delamar realized that Cliff was being inundated with offers and was anxious not to stand in his way.'

The original Cliff Richard-Mickey Delamar contract was signed soon after the singer's success with 'Move It', and immediately resulted in Cliff winning a major role in the controversial movie 'Serious Charge.'

The contract called for Cliff to make two more movies at the option of Delamar. This option was initially waived, in 1959, to allow Cliff to star with Laurence Harvey in the box office hit *Expresso Bongo*.

CHARTS

	Title	Artist
US45	Are You Lonesome Tonight	*Elvis Presley*
USLP	G.I. Blues	*Elvis Presley*
UK45	It's Now Or Never	*Elvis Presley*
UKLP	South Pacific	*Soundtrack*
WEEK 2		
US45	Are You Lonesome Tonight	*Elvis Presley*
USLP	The Button-Down Mind Of	*Bob Newhart*
UK45	It's Now Or Never	*Elvis Presley*
UKLP	G.I. Blues	*Elvis Presley*
WEEK 3		
US45	Are You Lonesome Tonight	*Elvis Presley*
USLP	G.I. Blues	*Elvis Presley*
UK45	It's Now Or Never	*Elvis Presley*
UKLP	G.I. Blues	*Elvis Presley*
WEEK 4		
US45	Are You Lonesome Tonight	*Elvis Presley*
USLP	G.I. Blues	*Elvis Presley*
UK45	It's Now Or Never	*Elvis Presley*
UKLP	G.I. Blues	*Elvis Presley*

MGM BUY VERVE

MGM Records have purchased impresario/producer Norman Granz's famed Clef/Verve jazz label for $2.5 million.

The extensive catalogue includes numerous sessions by Ella Fitzgerald, Louis Armstrong, Billie Holiday, Charlie Parker, Dizzy Gillespie, Count Basie, Oscar Peterson, Art Tatum, Lester Young, Stan Getz, Buddy Rich and Gene Krupa, plus the entire Jazz At The Philharmonic concert recordings.

Norman grants MGM deal

FAITH TO FACE

In a bid to be taken seriously, singer Adam Faith has appeared on Britain's most controversial interview programme, BBC-TV's *Face To Face*. For 30 minutes, host John Freeman subjected Faith to a relentless and probing cross-examination. Faith came through his trial-by-combat with flying colours.

STAR QUOTE

PETER SELLERS

When asked what he thought the music business would be like in ten years' time!

'Ten years older!'

ADAM KEEPS THE FAITH

For his second shot at stardom, it's taken 20-year-old London-born singer Adam Faith just 12 hectic months and six top five singles (including 'What Do You Want?', 'Poor Me' and 'Someone Else's Baby') to transform himself from a has-been to Cliff Richard's closest rival as Britain's premier teenage idol.

A product of the Soho coffee bar skiffle craze, Adam Faith's initial attempt at stardom proved a dismal failure: a couple of flop 45s and forgettable TV appearances prompted a quick return to his old job as a messenger boy at Rank Screen Services. A year later, an appearance in the teen-flick *Beat Girl* and the offer from songwriter Johnny Worth of his composition, 'What Do You Want?' reversed his luck.

With a John Barry arrangement – stylistically, almost identical to Buddy Holly's 'It Doesn't Matter Anymore' – Faith's flat nasal hiccuping and a tendency to over-emphasize the word 'Bay-Bee', made 'What Do You Want?' the biggest hit of 1960 in the UK.

With advance orders for his next single 'This Is It' guaranteeing him another hit, Faith has been booked to headline the prestigious prime-time TV show, *Sunday Night At The London Palladium* and negotiations are underway for a four-movie deal.

Faith's ambition is to become an all-round entertainer.

THE GRAPEVINE

- The Hollywood Women's Press Club have nominated Elvis 'the Least Co-Operative Actor of 1960.'
- UK Decca Records boss, Edward Lewis, received a knighthood in the Queen's New Year Honours List.
- Barry Mann (half of the successful songwriting team Mann & Weil) has screamed into the US charts with 'Who Put The Bomp (In The Bomp, Bomp, Bomp).

CHARTS

	Title	Artist
US45	Are You Lonesome Tonight	*Elvis Presley*
USLP	G.I. Blues	*Elvis Presley*
UK45	It's Now Or Never	*Elvis Presley*
UKLP	G.I. Blues	*Elvis Presley*
WEEK 2		
US45	Are You Lonesome Tonight	*Elvis Presley*
USLP	G.I. Blues	*Elvis Presley*
UK45	Poetry In Motion	*Johnny Tillotson*
UKLP	G.I. Blues	*Elvis Presley*
WEEK 3		
US45	Wonderland By Night	*Bert Kaempfert*
USLP	The Button-Down Mind Strikes Back	*Bob Newhart*
UK45	Poetry In Motion	*Johnny Tillotson*
UKLP	G.I. Blues	*Elvis Presley*
WEEK 4		
US45	Wonderland By Night	*Bert Kaempfert*
USLP	Wonderland By Night	*Bert Kaempfert*
UK45	Poetry In Motion	*Johnny Tillotson*
UKLP	G.I. Blues	*Elvis Presley*
WEEK 5		
US45	Wonderland By Night	*Bert Kaempfert*
USLP	Wonderland By Night	*Bert Kaempfert*
UK45	Are You Lonesome Tonight	*Elvis Presley*
UKLP	G.I. Blues	*Elvis Presley*

Sartorially splendid Marty Wilde

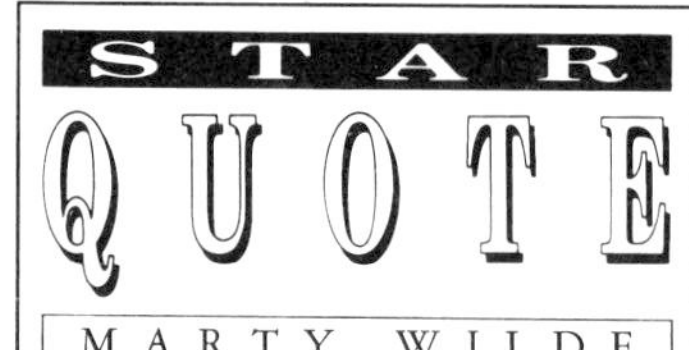

STAR QUOTE

MARTY WILDE

'I'm out to take Lonnie Donegan's crown as Britain's best-dressed pop singer. I doubt if I can do it this year, but I'm having a shot at the title for 1962.'

SINATRA ANNOUNCES OWN LABEL

Following much gossip column speculation, Frank Sinatra has announced the formation of his very own record label – Reprise – which he intends to launch in March with his new album, 'Ring A Ding Ding.'

Sinatra has also intimated that some of his notorious 'Rat-Pack' friends (such as Sammy Davis Jr) might be among the initial signings.

This eagerly-anticipated project is believed to have been partly bankrolled by Sinatra himself, as a result of a rumoured $15-million movie deal the singer has entered into with the United Artists' Studios.

Frank Sinatra – label owner

MITCHELL TO GO SOLO?

Les Chaussettes Noire – the popular French rock group that features the explosive Eddy Mitchell – have just made their eagerly-awaited disc debut on the Paris-based Barclay label, with a four-track EP that contains French-language covers of Gene Vincent's 'Be-Bop-A-Lula' and Presley's 'Dirty Dirty Feeling'.

However, it's the slow 'Daniela' that has become the unexpected hit, prompting Mitchell (who is seen as a rival to Johnny Halliday) to seriously consider a solo career.

JACKIE WILSON SHOT

Jackie Wilson, the 25-year-old R&B hitmaker of 'Reet Petite', 'Lonely Teardrops' and 'Doggin' Around', and on whom it is said that Elvis Presley first modelled both his singing style and extrovert stage antics, has been shot and seriously wounded at his New York apartment. His assailant was a female acquaintance, 28-year-old Juanita Jones.

Wilson, whose in-person appearances trigger off scenes of female mass hysteria, first came to fame by replacing Clyde McPhatter in Billy Ward's Dominoes when still only 17.

At the time of the shooting, Wilson had established his reputation as one of America's most visually exciting performers.

JOHNNY BURNETTE

'My brother Dorsey and I first got to know Elvis Presley when he went to Humes High and we went to the Catholic High . . . Elvis would tote his guitar on his back when he rode past on his motor-cycle on his way to school. He would see us and always wave.'

Rock'n'roller Johnny Burnette

PLATTERS SUE MERCURY

Platters – pictured during happier times

February 14: St Valentine's Day – but there's no love lost between The Platters and their record company, Mercury. Though Tony Williams left the act to go solo back in June of last year, he is at the root of a dispute that has escalated into litigation.

Because Mercury have chosen not to accept and release new Platters' tracks which don't feature ex-lead singer Williams, the group are taking legal action.

Their manager, Buck Ram, claims that The Platter's contract with Mercury doesn't stipulate that Williams has to be the featured solo voice. According to the group themselves, when Williams was a member of the act, it was common for any one of the other four singers to take over the lead.

CHARTS

US45	Will You Love Me Tomorrow *Shirelles*
USLP	Exodus *Soundtrack*
UK45	Are You Lonesome Tonight *Elvis Presley*
UKLP	G.I. Blues *Elvis Presley*
	WEEK 2
US45	Will You Love Me Tomorrow *Shirelles*
USLP	Wonderland By Night *Bert Kaempfert*
UK45	Are You Lonesome Tonight *Elvis Presley*
UKLP	G.I. Blues *Elvis Presley*
	WEEK 3
US45	Calcutta *Lawrence Welk*
USLP	Wonderland By Night *Bert Kaempfert*
UK45	Are You Lonesome Tonight *Elvis Presley*
UKLP	G.I. Blues *Elvis Presley*
	WEEK 4
US45	Calcutta *Lawrence Welk*
USLP	Exodus *Soundtrack*
UK45	Are You Lonesome Tonight *Elvis Presley*
UKLP	G.I. Blues *Elvis Presley*

ELVIS LIVE AGAIN

Elvis Presley has made his first public appearance in four years, playing two 50-minute shows before 10,000 ecstatic fans at the Ellis Auditorium, Memphis, Tennessee.

The receipts of $51,612 were split between 27 local charities.

FRENCH FANS RIOT

The first of three *Festival du Rock* extravaganzas have been staged amid some of the wildest scenes ever experienced in the French capital, at the Palais des Sports de Paris.

Featured artists included Bobby Rydell (USA), Emile Ford & The Checkmates (UK), plus local top rockers Johnny Halliday, Frankie Jordan and Les Chaussettes Noires featuring Eddy Mitchell.

However, it was the concert headlined by Vince Taylor & The Playboys and Dick Rivers & Les Chats Sauvages which turned into a full-scale rock'n'roll riot, to which the local *gendarmerie* were called to give the more excited fans a practical display of modern police tactics!

- **Tamla Records has its first million-selling single with The Miracles' 'Shop Around'.**
- **Frank Sinatra was the main event at President John F. Kennedy's Inaugural Ball in Washington.**
- **The Shadows' new single is 'F.B.I.'**
- **Matt Monro has won ITV's *British Song Contest* with 'My Kind Of Girl'.**
- **Helen Shapiro – a mature-voiced 14-year-old London schoolgirl – has launched a successful disc career with 'Don't Treat Me Like A Child'.**

Contest winner – Matt Monro

Mature of voice – Helen Shapiro

HURRICANES SCORE WITH GOLDEN OLDIES

Johnny & The Hurricanes, with leader Johnny Paris (right)

All-American hot rockin' instrumental combo Johnny & The Hurricanes have just celebrated their sixth UK Top 20 hit in 14 months with 'Ja-Da'.

Firmly established as one of the most consistent transatlantic recording acts, The Hurricanes – led by 19-year-old tenorman Johnny Paris – specialize in 'modernizing' pre-rock era oldies.

Originally from Toledo, Ohio, their widespread appeal commenced when, after the Stateside-only success of 'Crossfire', they transformed the old Army bugle call into 'Reveille Rock', turned the country music weepie 'Red River Valley' into 'Red River Rock', rearranged the traditional folk song 'Blue Tail Fly' as 'Beatnik Fly' and then turned their personal attention to 'Down Yonder' and now the old jazz standard 'Ja-Da'.

However, one of the group's biggest successes has been an original, 'Rockin' Goose' – a novelty number that relied for its gimmick appeal on a shrill squawking goose, made by the shrieking saxophone of Johnny Paris.

Johnny & The Hurricanes have the biggest sound around by having blended Paris's raucous tenor raspings to the piping hot Hammond organ of Paul Tesluk, while Butch Mattice powers the rhythm section with the wall-to-wall rumble produced by his mighty Dan Electro bass.

ELVIS: NO MORE GIGS?

The 4,000-seat Bloch Arena, Pearl Harbor, Honolulu, was the location for what looks like becoming Elvis Presley's last concert appearance for some time.

Staged as a benefit for the USS *Arizona* Memorial Fund, the concert featured Elvis performing 'Heartbreak Hotel', 'All Shook Up', 'A Fool Such As I', 'I Got A Woman', 'Love Me', 'Such A Night', 'Reconsider Baby', 'I Need Your Love Tonight', 'That's All Right (Mama)', 'Don't Be Cruel', 'One Night', 'Are You Lonesome Tonight?', 'It's Now Or Never', 'Swing Down, Sweet Chariot' and 'Hound Dog'.

With film work seeming to take up all of Presley's energy and enthusiasm, concert appearances and tours seem likely to be a low priority in the foreseeable future.

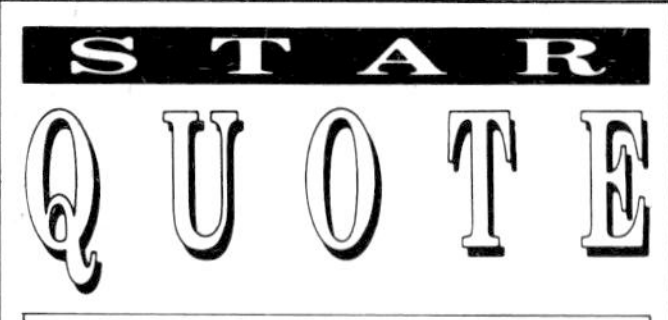

THE EVERLY BROTHERS

'We're often asked whether the fact that we're brothers has ever been a handicap in our careers. The way they figure it is that most brothers quarrel, and in our case if there's no harmony behind the scenes, it's not very likely that there'll be much on stage.'

NME POLL CONCERT

The major British pop event of the year the NME Annual Readers' Poll Winners Concert at Wembley Pool, London was held on March 5.

Among those appearing were The John Barry Seven, Alma Cogan, Russ Conway, Lonnie Donegan, Adam Faith, Emile Ford, Connie Francis, Billy Fury, Ted Heath & His Music, The King Brothers, Jerry Lordan, Bob Millar's Millermen, The Mudlarks, Cliff Richard & The Shadows, Bert Weedon and Mark Wynter.

Skiffle king Lonnie

CHARTS

US45	Pony Time	Chubby Checker
USLP	Exodus	Soundtrack
UK45	Walk Right Back	Everly Brothers
UKLP	G.I. Blues	Elvis Presley
WEEK 2		
US45	Pony Time	Chubby Checker
USLP	Calcutta	Lawrence Welk
UK45	Walk Right Back	Everly Brothers
UKLP	G.I. Blues	Elvis Presley
WEEK 3		
US45	Pony Time	Chubby Checker
USLP	Calcutta	Lawrence Welk
UK45	Walk Right Back	Everly Brothers
UKLP	G.I. Blues	Elvis Presley
WEEK 4		
US45	Surrender	Elvis Presley
USLP	Calcutta	Lawrence Welk
UK45	Wooden Heart	Elvis Presley
UKLP	G.I. Blues	Elvis Presley

THE GRAPEVINE

- **The Allisons' 'Are You Sure' was placed second in the *Song For Europe***
- **Cliff Richard & The Shadows have opened their South African tour in Jo'burg.**
- **Elvis has been recording the soundtrack for his *Blue Hawaii* movie.**
- **Beatles' manager Alan Williams has secured a three month residency at Hamburg's Top Ten Club for the Liverpool group.**

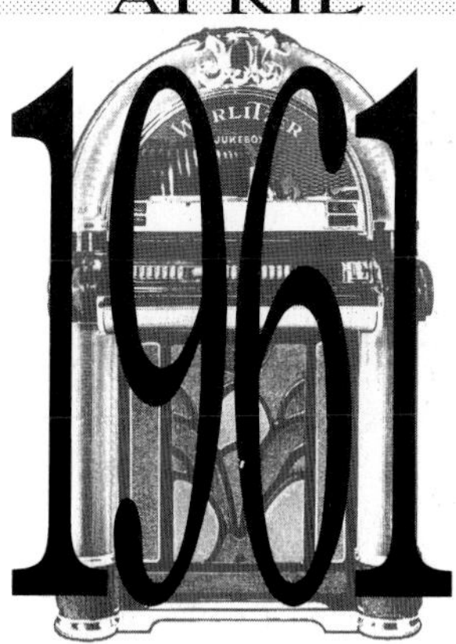

GUITAR ACE SHIVERS DEAD

Wesley Clarence 'Charlie' Shivers, a 27-year-old rockabilly guitarist, died when a methane gas explosion destroyed his farmhouse near Scottsville, Kentucky on April 7.

Shivers was to rockabilly what Buddy Bolden was to jazz – a shadowy, yet influential player who never released any commercial recordings. The son of a wealthy civil engineer-turned-government diplomat, Charlie turned down major label offers from the likes of Norman Petty and Steve Sholes, preferring to work on family engineering projects in Panama's Canal Zone.

His prolific recording activities were confined almost exclusively to sessions he held in the private studio he built at the back of his farmhouse. It was here that many country and bluegrass music stars dropped by to enjoy his hospitality.

It is believed that over 200 privately recorded sides, said to include Johnny Burnette, Tennessee Ernie Ford, Ivory Joe Hunter, Hank Williams and Elvis Presley, perished with Shivers in the fire. The tracks featuring Elvis were thought to have originated from a session held in the studio of a small radio station at which Charlie guided the pre-Sun singer through a selection of recent pop and country jukebox favourites.

Said guitarist Scotty Moore, on hearing of Shivers' death: 'If Charlie had decided to give up building bridges and turn professional, we'd have all had to look for new jobs!'

THE GRAPEVINE

- **Pye Records UK have launched their Piccadilly subsidiary with Joe Brown's 'Crazy Mixed-Up Kid'.**
- **New from Cliff Richard, 'Gee Whiz It's You'.**
- **Shirley Bassey has entered the London Clinic to have her tonsils removed.**
- **Actor/Singer Jess Conrad has released one of the all-time bad singles, 'This Pullover'.**
- **The Drifters' ex-lead singer, Ben E. King, has released 'Stand By Me'.**

Joe Brown as the 'Crazy Mixed-up Kid'

Shirley Bassey – throat problems cured?

CHARTS

US45	Surrender *Elvis Presley*
USLP	Calcutta *Lawrence Welk*
UK45	Wooden Heart *Elvis Presley*
UKLP	G.I. Blues *Elvis Presley*
WEEK 2	
US45	Blue Moon *Marcels*
USLP	G.I. Blues *Elvis Presley*
UK45	Are You Sure *Allisons*
UKLP	G.I. Blues *Elvis Presley*
WEEK 3	
US45	Blue Moon *Marcels*
USLP	Calcutta *Lawrence Welk*
UK45	Wooden Heart *Elvis Presley*
UKLP	G.I. Blues *Elvis Presley*
WEEK 4	
US45	Blue Moon *Marcels*
USLP	Calcutta *Lawrence Welk*
UK45	Are You Sure *Allisons*
UKLP	G.I. Blues *Elvis Presley*
WEEK 5	
US45	Runaway *Del Shannon*
USLP	Calcutta *Lawrence Welk*
UK45	You're Driving Me Crazy *Temperance Seven*
UKLP	G.I. Blues *Elvis Presley*

CMA STAGE COUNTRY FESTIVAL

The first official Country Music Festival has been staged at the Jacksonville Coliseum, Florida by the new Country Music Association.

The all-star line-up included Webb Pierce, Faron Young, Patsy Cline, Porter Wagoner, Flatt & Scruggs, The Louvin Brothers, Mel Tillis, George Hamilton IV plus The Foggy Mountain Boys.

(L to R) Bruce Welch, Cliff Richard, Hank B. Marvin

FILMING STARTS ON NEW CLIFF MOVIE

When they shoot your movies in colour, then you've really hit the big time!

Following the success of *Expresso Bongo*, Cliff Richard & The Shadows have commenced filming a big budget movie, *The Young Ones*. Unlike the former, which was a black and white film, *The Young Ones* will be a full-colour extravaganza.

The basic plot concerns a rumour that the youth club attended by Cliff and his pals is about to be demolished by a big city corporation. £1,500 can save the building from possible destruction, so they decide to stage a show to raise the money. The cast will include Carole Gray as Cliff's love interest, and Robert Morley as his father.

The producers have said that *The Young Ones* will be ready for release in January 1962.

GUITAR GREATS SWAP NOTES

Bert Weedon reflects on fame . . . and make up!

The Twang's The Thang for Duane

When Britain's king-size-guitar man Bert Weedon recently dropped backstage to catch twangy guitar star Duane Eddy's UK tour, the two top players engaged in much mutual back-slapping.

During the course of the conversation, the very outgoing Weedon couldn't help remarking on the American performer's extremely inanimate low-profile before an audience.

Bert: 'Duane, I notice you usually don't use make-up on stage. Any reasons?'

Duane: 'Simply because I don't like it. Frankly, I usually have enough of a sun-tan to get by with.'

Bert: 'May I speak truthfully? I think your stage act with The Rebels is tremendous, but at the same time I'm sure it could do even better with more production. What do you think?'

Duane: 'If you mean movement and choreography, I'm not very keen on the idea. My plan is simply to go on and entertain without too many trimmings. I'd rather it be a spontaneous act than a too-well-planned one.'

CHARTS

US45	Runaway *Del Shannon*
USLP	Calcutta *Lawrence Welk*
UK45	Blue Moon *Marcels*
UKLP	G.I. Blues *Elvis Presley*
WEEK 2	
US45	Runaway *Del Shannon*
USLP	Calcutta *Lawrence Welk*
UK45	Blue Moon *Marcels*
UKLP	G.I. Blues *Elvis Presley*
WEEK 3	
US45	Runaway *Del Shannon*
USLP	G.I. Blues *Elvis Presley*
UK45	Runaway *Del Shannon*
UKLP	G.I. Blues *Elvis Presley*
WEEK 4	
US45	Mother-In-Law *Ernie K-Doe*
USLP	G.I. Blues *Elvis Presley*
UK45	Surrender *Elvis Presley*
UKLP	G.I. Blues *Elvis Presley*

WILDE BIRDIE

Prior to switching to the prestigious Her Majesty's Theatre in London's West-End, the British production of the Elvis-spoof Broadway musical smash, *Bye Bye Birdie* has opened its provincial run at the Manchester Opera House, with pop idol Marty Wilde suitably cast in the title role.

THE GRAPEVINE

■ **Advance sales of 461,500 copies of Elvis's new UK release 'Surrender' qualified it as biggest ever UK pre-sale.**

■ **Lonnie Donegan has adapted traditional cocaine-snorter's anthem 'Have A Whiff On Me' into a cheery bar-room singalong 'Have A Drink On Me'.**

■ **Gene Vincent has become the first US star to feature on the UK ABC-TV's prestigious chart-slanted show, *Thank Your Lucky Stars*.**

STAR QUOTE

ED 'KOOKIE' BYRNES

Actor/Singer

'It's hard for some people to believe, but I only talk like Kookie in 77 Sunset Strip *– never in private. But, I don't live the role 24 hours a day and that disappoints them!'*

Ed Byrnes – not as 'Kookie' in reality

BERRY-GO-ROUND!

Not one to squander his earnings from endlessly touring in support of such definitive rock hits as 'Sweet Little 16', 'Johnny B. Goode', 'Carol', 'Sweet Little Rock And Roller', 'Almost Grown', 'Little Queenie', 'Memphis Tennessee', 'Let It Rock' and a dozen more, Chuck Berry has realized a personal ambition and opened Berry Park – a 30-acre family amusement complex on the outskirts of his St Louis hometown.

Aside from the usual crowd-pulling attractions such as a Ferris Wheel, amusement rides, sideshows and a children's zoo, there's swimming, minature golf, picnic areas and barbecues.

For many, however, the real attraction is the possibility of catching the owner himself performing in the ballroom.

FURY: 'I'M GROWING UP!'

'I recorded "Halfway To Paradise"', confessed Billy Fury, 'because I wanted people to think of me simply as a singer – and not, more specifically, as a rock singer!'

'I'm growing up, and I want to broaden my scope. I shall continue to sing rock songs, but at the same time my stage act isn't going to be as wild in the future,' he says.

And yet, Fury revealed, he was in something of a dilemma over one of the more creative aspects of his young talent. 'Because "Halfway To Paradise" isn't one of my own compositions,' (it was penned by Tony Orlando) 'several people have asked me if I've stopped writing songs. I certainly haven't, but I'm bound to admit that my style of writing has changed radically in recent times.

'The point is I just can't seem to write the rock stuff like I used to. Ideas don't seem to come to me any more.

'My aim now is to write catchy, easy-paced songs after the style of "You Made Me Love You". . . I enjoy that kind of material very much. I'm also writing a lot of rhythm & blues stuff these days, but for the moment I'm having to shelve these, because nobody seems to want to know about them as far as recording is concerned!'

Billy Fury going for the adult audience

THE GRAPEVINE

■ DJ Alan Freed's new American road show features Brenda Lee, The Shirelles, Bobby Vee, Etta James, Gene McDaniels, The Ventures, Clarence 'Frogman' Henry, The Fleetwoods, The Innocents, Kathy Young and Jerry Lee Lewis.

■ Gene Vincent and The Shadows have headlined the latest U.K. to France 'Rock Across The Channel' cruise.

■ Adam Faith celebrated his 21st birthday this month.

BOBBY VEE: 'I'M NO COPY-CAT!'

Bobby Vee – having been plagued by press and fan accusations over the similarity in style between his recent hits, 'Rubber Ball' and 'More Than I Can Say', to material recorded by Buddy Holly – has chosen to publicly rebuff such claims. 'I'm no copycat' has been his defence.

Despite such denials, the truth that his style has been derived from Holly's is further compounded by the fact that, while still an untried amateur, Bobby Vee & The Shadows (no relation to the British group) made their public debut in Minneapolis by filling in for Buddy Holly who (in the company of Richie Valens and The Big Bopper) had perished the previous evening in an air disaster.

Bobby Vee – dreamboat not coypcat!

ELVIS: MORE MOVIE NEWS

20th Century-Fox have released *Wild In The Country* – an implausible melodrama starring Elvis Presley (Glenn Tyler) with both Hope Lange and Tuesday Weld supplying the female interest.

At the same time, Colonel Tom Parker has announced that Elvis is to receive $600,000, plus a hefty percentage of the box office gross, as star of the movie *Pioneer Goes Home*.

The film's title has been changed – to *Follow That Dream*. The money, however, stays the same!

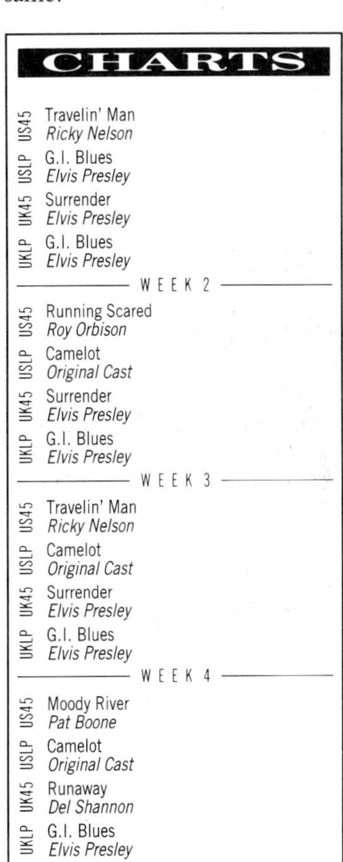

CHARTS

US45	Travelin' Man *Ricky Nelson*
USLP	G.I. Blues *Elvis Presley*
UK45	Surrender *Elvis Presley*
UKLP	G.I. Blues *Elvis Presley*
WEEK 2	
US45	Running Scared *Roy Orbison*
USLP	Camelot *Original Cast*
UK45	Surrender *Elvis Presley*
UKLP	G.I. Blues *Elvis Presley*
WEEK 3	
US45	Travelin' Man *Ricky Nelson*
USLP	Camelot *Original Cast*
UK45	Surrender *Elvis Presley*
UKLP	G.I. Blues *Elvis Presley*
WEEK 4	
US45	Moody River *Pat Boone*
USLP	Camelot *Original Cast*
UK45	Runaway *Del Shannon*
UKLP	G.I. Blues *Elvis Presley*

RICKY – I'M NO TRAVELLIN' MAN

While busy developing the movie acting side of his career, 21-year-old Ricky Nelson has suddenly realized that because he never tours or appears on television outside the States, the progress of his singles is somewhat erratic.

Though both 'Hello Mary Lou' and 'Travellin' Man' have repeated their recent Stateside chart success in the UK, Ricky is confronted by the knowledge that he has yet to build up the kind of fan loyalty he enjoys at home.

'Maybe you've been wondering what has been happening to me during the past 18 months. The fact that my records haven't been doing any too well on your side of the Atlantic came as something of a disappointment to me, I must admit, bearing in mind the luck I had with several of my earlier releases'.

'A lot of people have suggested it was due to the return of Elvis Presley from his period of Army service – and I suppose there might be something in that.

'But you know, I have never really placed myself in the category of Elvis – and I can't honestly imagine that I was regarded as his deputy during his absence. I have no doubt, though, that when Elvis came back from Germany, the competition was rather tough for all young male singers.'

Ricky Nelson – competition for Presley?

CHARTS

US45	Quarter To Three *Gary 'U.S.' Bonds*
USLP	Camelot *Original Cast*
UK45	Runaway *Del Shannon*
UKLP	South Pacific *Soundtrack*
	WEEK 2
US45	Quarter To Three *Gary 'U.S.' Bonds*
USLP	Camelot *Original Cast*
UK45	Runaway *Del Shannon*
UKLP	South Pacific *Soundtrack*
	WEEK 3
US45	Tossin' & Turnin' *Bobby Lewis*
USLP	Camelot *Original Cast*
UK45	Temptation *Everly Brothers*
UKLP	South Pacific *Soundtrack*
	WEEK 4
US45	Tossin' & Turnin' *Bobby Lewis*
USLP	Stars For A Summer Night *Various Artists*
UK45	Well I Ask You *Eden Kane*
UKLP	South Pacific *Soundtrack*
	WEEK 5
US45	Tossin' & Turnin' *Bobby Lewis*
USLP	Stars For A Summer Night *Various Artists*
UK45	Well I Ask You *Eden Kane*
UKLP	Black And White Minstrel Show *TV Cast*

THE GRAPEVINE

- **The Beatles have returned to Liverpool from Germany and were honoured by a 'Welcome Home' night at the Cavern Club.**
- **Self-styled authority Pat Boone has written a 'serious' book on what young people should know about Communism and Democracy.**
- **Memphis soul act, The Mar-Keys have charted with 'Last Night'.**
- **The Twist is reported to be the happening dance craze around Philadelphia.**

HARRY'S MERSEY BEAT

Liverpool live-wire Bill Harry has published the first-ever edition of his alternative pop music paper, *Mersey Beat*.

Devoted almost entirely to the vast local pop scene, the debut edition features the article, 'Being a Short Diversion on the Dubious Origins of Beatles', accompanied by a 'translated from the John Lennon' by-line. Lennon is a member of The Beatles, one of Liverpool's most popular homegrown groups.

Liverpool's Beatles, with (from left) John Lennon, George Harrison & Paul McCartney

TAYLOR'S CADILLAC WINS PRAISE

Vince Taylor & The Playboys' latest recording 'Brand New Cadillac' is receiving instant praise from critics as being the best British-made rock record since Cliff Richard's 'Move It' and Johnny Kidd's more recent 'Shakin' All Over'.

It was at the birthplace of British Rock – Soho's The 2 I's coffee bar in Old Compton Street – that this handsome 21-year-old Anglo-American first attracted sufficient attention to be signed up to launch Palette Records last August – with his single 'I'll Be Your Hero'/'Jet Black Machine'.

Taylor's much-respected Playboys comprise London's finest: Tony Sheridan (guitar), Brian 'Licorice' Locking (bass) and Brian Bennett (drums).

NO BLUES PREDICTED FOR HAWAII

As a front-office exercise intended to erase the recent memory of the much less-than-anticipated box-office business of Elvis Presley's two 20th Century-Fox productions *Flaming Star* and *Wild in the Country*, Paramount Pictures (the makers of last year's more commercially successful *G.I. Blues*) have taken steps to protect the five-year deal they signed with the singer in January, and staged one of their most lavish no-expense-spared 'theme' launches in ages.

For the grand-slam trade preview party for Elvis' upcoming movie, *Blue Hawaii*, Paramount chose 'The Big Easy' – New Orleans. They air-lifted in a large planeload of Hawaiian cooks (and food) to cater for a guest list of one thousand movie-house owners from all over North America.

The guests' verdict? 'More of the same please!' (That goes for the movie – predicted to be a hit – not to mention the food!)

The Supremes, with Diana Ross (right)

MOTOWN A MYSTERY NO MORE

In the two years that have elapsed since Berry Gordy secured an $800 loan to launch his Detroit-based Tamla Record label with 'Come To Me' by Marv Johnson and, more recently, his Motown label, his companies have discovered and developed such local black talent as Eddie Holland, The Miracles, The Supremes, Mary Wells, Mabel John, Marvin Gaye, The Contours, Barrett Strong and, most recently, The Marvelettes.

Previously called The Marvels, this all-girl vocal group has given the label one of its most successful singles to date, with 'Please Mr. Postman'.

Asked about his fabulously successful labels' names, Gordy explains: 'Tamla Records was called after the song "Tammy", and Motown is named after Detroit itself – the Motor City or Motor Town'.

Simple when you know, isn't it?

The first lady of Motown, Mary Wells

Motor City's Marvin Gaye

VINCENT FLIES HOME

Mentally and physically broken by the auto smash in which his friend Eddie Cochran was fatally injured, accident-prone US rocker Gene Vincent has broken off his current UK tour to jet back to the States.

Five days before his departure, Vincent was detained in hospital for 48 hours after collapsing backstage following a Glasgow show.

THE GRAPEVINE

- **Elvis Presley has once again been suggested as the obvious lead in a proposed Hank Williams movie-biography.**
- **New from Ray Charles – 'Hit The Road Jack'.**
- **One-time boy preacher, now rock and soul supremo, Solomon Burke has gone country for his Atlantic debut, 'Just Out Of Reach (Of My Two Empty Arms)'.**

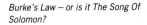

Burke's Law – or is it The Song Of Solomon?

CHARTS

US45	Tossin' & Turnin' *Bobby Lewis*
USLP	Stars For A Summer Night *Various Artists*
UK45	You Don't Know *Helen Shapiro*
UKLP	Black And White Minstrel Show *TV Cast*
	WEEK 2
US45	Tossin' & Turnin' *Bobby Lewis*
USLP	Stars For A Summer Night *Various Artists*
UK45	You Don't Know *Helen Shapiro*
UKLP	Black And White Minstrel Show *TV Cast*
	WEEK 3
US45	Tossin' & Turnin *Bobby Lewis*
USLP	Stars For A Summer Night *Various Artists*
UK45	You Don't Know *Helen Shapiro*
UKLP	Black And White Minstrel Show *TV Cast*
	WEEK 4
US45	Tossin' & Turnin' *Bobby Lewis*
USLP	Something For Everybody *Elvis Presley*
UK45	Johnny Remember Me *John Leyton*
UKLP	Black And White Minstrel Show *TV Cast*

STAR

DUANE EDDY

'Ever since I have been knee-high to a Fender guitar, I've hated photographers. The yearly trip to the local 'snapper' in Phoenix, Arizona, with the rest of the family, was a real ordeal. That hate of having my picture taken has stayed with me through the years.'

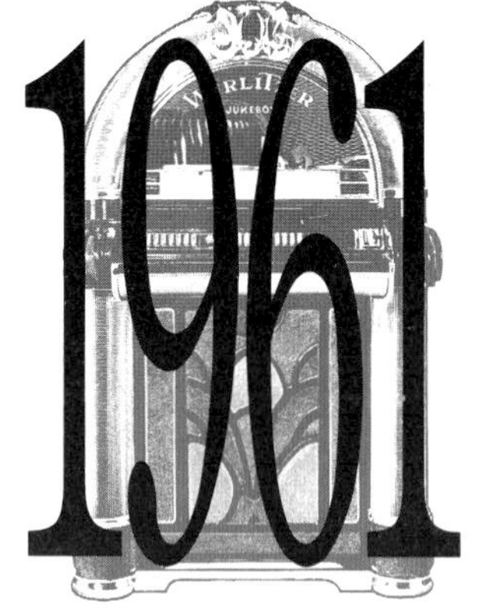

LITTLE RICHARD BACK, BUT NO ROCK

Four years ago, on the fifth date of a two-week Australian tour with Gene Vincent and Eddie Cochran, Little Richard shocked the pop world when he upped and quit rock'n'roll to pursue the infinitely more spiritual lifestyle as a preacher with the Church of God of the Ten Commandments.

The day he left Australia, Richard affirmed his religious convictions by pulling a large expensive diamond ring from his finger and throwing it into the deep waters of Sydney Harbour.

Now, it's reported that Little Richard has been recording again – this time it's gospel material – under the supervision of his long-term friend and collaborator Bumps Blackwell and musical arranger Quincy Jones, for Mercury Records. The album is titled: 'Little Richard, King Of The Gospel Singers'.

This is not the first time that Richard has recorded religious material. However, the Mercury session was a serious attempt by Richard and Mercury to re-establish the singer as a best-selling recording artist.

Little Richard still in retirement from rock'n'roll but attempting a comeback as a gospel singer

MEEHAN LEAVES SHADOWS

Though it comes as no real surprise to insiders, Tony Meehan – whose off-stage lifestyle has frequently been at odds with his fellow group members – suddenly 'quit' The Shadows without warning during their highly successful summer season residency at Brighton's Opera House.

In a flurry of did-he-jump or was-he-pushed press speculation, local drummer Derek Fell proved a more-than-adequate 'dep' until ever-reliable Brian Bennett (formerly with Tony Sheridan and Marty Wilde) arrived from London as permanent replacement.

CHARTS

	US45	Wooden Heart	Joe Dowell
	USLP	Something For Everybody	Elvis Presley
	UK45	Johnny Remember Me	John Leyton
	UKLP	Black And White Minstrel Show	TV Cast
WEEK 2	US45	Michael	Highwaymen
	USLP	Something For Everybody	Elvis Presley
	UK45	Johnny Remember Me	John Leyton
	UKLP	South Pacific	Soundtrack
WEEK 3	US45	Michael	Highwaymen
	USLP	At Carnegie Hall	Judy Garland
	UK45	Johnny Remember Me	John Leyton
	UKLP	South Pacific	Soundtrack
WEEK 4	US45	Take Good Care Of My Baby	Bobby Vee
	USLP	At Carnegie Hall	Judy Garland
	UK45	Wild In The Country	Elvis Presley
	UKLP	The Shadows	Shadows

THE GRAPEVINE

- Mike Berry & The Outlaws have released a most genuine 'Tribute To Buddy Holly'.
- Adam Faith continues his quest for all-round-entertainer respectability and has made his debut in cabaret.
- Pint-sized UK funny man, Charlie Drake, is aiming for the charts with 'My Boomerang Won't Come Back'.
- The Dave Brubeck Quartet have taken modern jazz into the singles chart with 'Take Five'.

Another Hammond production – John Jnr.

HAMMOND SIGNS DYLAN

Having hired young newcomer Bob Dylan to blow harmonica on three tracks ('I'll Fly Away', 'Swing And Turn Jubilee' and 'Come Back, Baby') on a recording date for folk stylist Carolyn Hester, producer John Hammond (who discovered Billie Holiday, Bessie Smith and Count Basie among others) was so impressed by Dylan's raw talent that he immediately signed him to Columbia as a solo artist for the unprecedented royalty rates of four per cent.

Bob Dylan has been signed by John Hammond to record for Columbia

DARIN: 'ROCK PAVED MY WAY'

Back in the charts with the rocked-up oldie 'You Must Have Been A Beautiful Baby', Bobby Darin gives his personal opinion of the current music scene.

'Nowadays, it's extremely difficult for a fan to stay loyal to any one artist for more than a couple of months. I blame the record companies for much of the trouble. The problem is that they try so hard to interest teenagers in new sounds all the time, that many good artists don't have an opportunity to develop their own style,' he says forcefully.

'Immediately after I had a hit with "Mack The Knife", people started to say that I never liked rock'n'roll at all, and that I only sang it to make money. That's not true. I like any sort of music as long as it's good – rock included.

'Of course I wanted the money – well it isn't only a case of wanting – I *needed* the money. But that isn't the only reason I sang rock.

'Three years ago, I was glad to play club dates for $200 a week, and I could only get work for six or seven weeks a year. That's when I wrote "Splish Splash" – that one song put me on the musical map. And, there was also another rock number, "Queen Of The Hop". A year later, "Dream Lover" became a big hit.

'Without those records to pave the way, I'm certain that "Mack The Knife" would never have been the hit it was,' he adds.

CHARTS

US45	Take Good Care Of My Baby *Bobby Vee*
USLP	At Carnegie Hall *Judy Garland*
UK45	Johnny Remember Me *John Leyton*
UKLP	The Shadows *Shadows*
WEEK 2	
US45	Take Good Care Of My Baby *Bobby Vee*
USLP	At Carnegie Hall *Judy Garland*
UK45	Michael *Highwaymen*
UKLP	The Shadows *Shadows*
WEEK 3	
US45	Hit The Road Jack *Ray Charles*
USLP	At Carnegie Hall *Judy Garland*
UK45	Walkin' Back To Happiness *Helen Shapiro*
UKLP	The Shadows *Shadows*
WEEK 4	
US45	Hit The Road Jack *Ray Charles*
USLP	At Carnegie Hall *Judy Garland*
UK45	Walkin' Back To Happiness *Helen Shapiro*
UKLP	The Shadows *Shadows*
WEEK 5	
US45	Runaround Sue *Dion & The Belmonts*
USLP	At Carnegie Hall *Judy Garland*
UK45	Walkin' Back To Happiness *Helen Shapiro*
UKLP	The Shadows *Shadows*

ONE-OFF BEAT-MAKERS

Top Liverpool groups The Beatles and Gerry & The Pacemakers merged to become 'The Beat-Makers' for a one-off performance at the Litherland Town Hall on 19 October. The line-up comprised:

Gerry Marsden (vocal/lead guitar), George Harrison (lead guitar), Paul McCartney (rhythm guitar), John Lennon (vocal/piano), Les Chadwick (bass guitar), Les Maguire (saxophone), Pete Best and Freddy Marsden (drums) plus vocalist Karl Terry from The Cruisers.

Dick James (centre) has a tea-time chat with producer George Martin (left)

FAME AT LAST

Impresario Larry Parnes's latest value-for-money package show, 'Star Spangled Nights', commenced 26 twice-nightly British theatre dates at the Essoldo, Cannock on October 17.

The bill featured such crowd-pullers as Billy Fury, Eden Kane, Joe Brown, Tommy Bruce, The Allisons, The Viscounts, The Karl Denver Trio, Peter Jay & The Jaywalkers, and Terry Hale.

The cast also included a most promising newcomer who, in the best Parnes tradition of renaming his discoveries, is transformed from Clive Powell into Georgie Fame!

Wheeler-dealer Larry Parnes

THE GRAPEVINE

- Booker Little Jr, one of the most promising trumpet stars on the US scene has died, of uraemia, aged 22.
- Big Joe Williams and new prodigy Bob Dylan have appeared as guests on legendary blues artist Victoria Spivey's new album.
- Former UK dance band vocalist Dick James has launched his self-named music publishing house.
- John Barry has visited Hollywood to discuss possibilities of composing for movies.

MOTOWN MOVES ON

Tamla's first chart toppers, The Marvelettes

Tamla Records' boss, Berry Gordy Jr, recently inaugurated a second label which he has called Motown (an abbreviation of Detroit's popular nickname 'The Motor City') with a single by male vocal harmony foursome The Satintones, called 'My Beloved'.

This record was a rush-replacement for The Satintones scheduled disc debut 'Tomorrow And Always' – an 'answer' record to The Shirelles' 'Will You Still Love Me Tomorrow'. At the very last minute, 'Tomorrow And Always' was hastily withdrawn from distribution when Gordy was threatened with a hefty law-suit which claimed copyright infringement of The Shirelles' original international hit.

Undaunted however, Gordy didn't allow this minor set-back to interfere at all with celebrations surrounding Tamla Records' first national No. 1 single, 'Please, Mr Postman' by a local all-girl group, The Marvelettes. This more than compensated for the minor hit status afforded the debut single of another local girl group, first known as The Primettes when recording for Lu-Pine, but renamed The Supremes for their Tamla release 'I Want A Guy'.

With albums from The Miracles ('Hi! We're The Miracles') and Marvin Gaye ('The Soulful Moods Of . . .') accounting for healthy sales figures, Berry Gordy is optimistic of his two labels success in 1962 and is openly enthusing about a new artist soon to debut – Steveland Judkins, the 11-year-old blind son of one of Tamla's regular cleaning ladies.

Gordy has renamed the gifted singer and instrumentalist Little Stevie . . . Little Stevie Wonder.

TEX X 100

Tex Ritter, country music legend and hit recorder of 'High Noon', has set something of a precedent in terms of promotion.

He recently recorded more than *100* different versions of 'Hillbilly Heaven', – his new single for Capitol Records – with each including the names of different peak-listening disc jockeys in the lyric. The records were then mailed out with a personal letter from ol' Tex to the various radio stations concerned!

And Webb Pierce has purchased a $20,000 car which has pistol butts for door handles and gear lever, rifles mounted on the tail-lights and *1000* silver dollar pieces as interior decor.

As the saying goes: if you've got it, flaunt it!

Country singer Jimmie Rodgers

THE GRAPEVINE

- Adam Faith has given a concert for the inmates of Leicester Prison, England.
- The Everly Brothers have enlisted in the US Marine Corps.
- Jimmie Rodgers has been elected the first member of The Country Music Hall Of Fame in Nashville.

Tex – no hick from the sticks

CHARTS

- US45 Runaround Sue – *Dion & The Belmonts*
- USLP At Carnegie Hall – *Judy Garland*
- UK45 Walkin' Back To Happiness – *Helen Shapiro*
- UKLP 21 Today – *Cliff Richard*

WEEK 2

- US45 Big Bad John – *Jimmy Dean*
- USLP At Carnegie Hall – *Judy Garland*
- UK45 His Latest Flame – *Elvis Presley*
- UKLP Another Black And White Minstrel Show – *TV Cast*

WEEK 3

- US45 Big Bad John – *Jimmy Dean*
- USLP At Carnegie Hall – *Judy Garland*
- UK45 His Latest Flame – *Elvis Presley*
- UKLP Another Black And White Minstrel Show – *TV Cast*

WEEK 4

- US45 Big Bad John – *Jimmy Dean*
- USLP At Carnegie Hall – *Judy Garland*
- UK45 His Latest Flame – *Elvis Presley*
- UKLP Another Black And White Minstrel Show – *TV Cast*

Going solo II – Floyd Cramer

STAR QUOTE

FLOYD CRAMER

'Trying to launch myself on a solo career, after being Elvis Presley's pianist for so long, placed me in an unenviable position.

'Some people thought I was trying to cash in. If I had wanted to cash in on my association with Elvis, I would have done it five years ago.'

DECEMBER

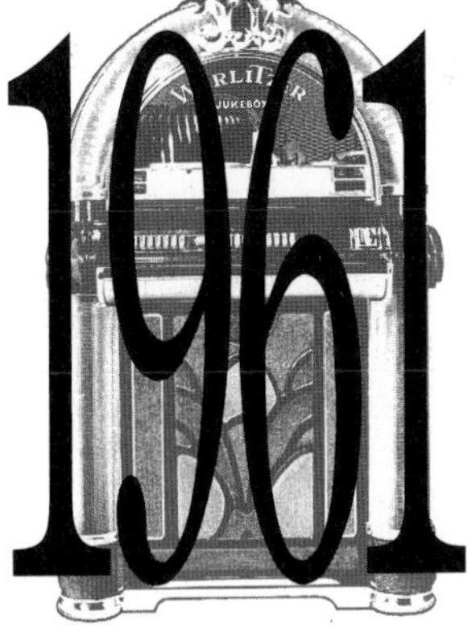

TWISTMANIA HITS US, UK AND FRANCE

Joey Dee and the Starlighters – house-band at the New York temple of twist, the Peppermint Lounge

Over the last few months, The Twist has exploded world-wide as the single biggest popular music phenomenon since 'Rock Around The Clock' and, as a dance craze, even more popular than the cha-cha.

The man who made it all happen, Philadelphia's 20-year-old Chubby Checker, is currently second only to Elvis as the world's best-known singer! As the tubby twister's cover of the Nov '58 Hank Ballard original has now chalked up 23 consecutive weeks on the US charts (making it the longest unbroken chart run to date), Checker – also the star of quickie-producer Sam Katzman's Bill Haley movie remake *Twist Around The Clock* and *Don't Knock The Twist* – has given his account of how he devised the Twist dance:

'One day, my lower half twisted one way and my upper half twisted the other . . . right to the rhythm of the song.' With regard to the dance steps, Checker revealed: 'I pretended I was putting out a cigarette with both feet!'

New York's Peppermint Lounge on West 45th Street has now become the official temple of Twist. The dynamic house-band – Joey Dee & The Starlighters – have released their 'live' at the Lounge LP and have been signed up to star in the movie *Hey, Let's Twist* together with Teddy Randazzo and Jo-Ann Campbell.

More movies are on their way, including *Teenage Millionaire* which features Jimmy Clanton, Jackie Wilson, Dion, The Bill Black Combo and Chubby Checker performing 'Let's Twist Again'.

Outside the US, France has been the first country to capitulate to Twistmania, with two French-language 'Let's Twist Again' covers sharing No. 1. Meanwhile, in London, a double bill of *Twist Around The Clock*and *Gidget Goes Hawaiian* opened on New Year's Eve at the New Victoria where The Lionel Blair Dancers were booked to demonstrate The Twist 'live' on stage, daily at 5.30 and 9.10 pm.

CHARTS

US45	Big Bad John	*Jimmy Dean*
USLP	At Carnegie Hall	*Judy Garland*
UK45	Take Good Care Of My Baby	*Bobby Vee*
UKLP	Another Black And White Minstrel Show	*TV Cast*
WEEK 2		
US45	Big Bad John	*Jimmy Dean*
USLP	At Carnegie hall	*Judy Garland*
UK45	Tower Of Strength	*Frankie Vaughan*
UKLP	Another Black And White Minstrel Show	*TV Cast*
WEEK 3		
US45	Please Mr. Postman	*Marvelettes*
USLP	Blue Hawaii	*Elvis Presley*
UK45	Tower Of Strength	*Frankie Vaughan*
UKLP	Another Black And White Minstrel Show	*TV Cast*
WEEK 4		
US45	The Lion Sleeps Tonight	*Tokens*
USLP	Blue Hawaii	*Elvis Presley*
UK45	Tower Of Strength	*Frankie Vaughan*
UKLP	Blue Hawaii	*Elvis Presley*
WEEK 5		
US45	The Lion Sleeps Tonight	*Tokens*
USLP	Blue Hawaii	*Elvis Presley*
UK45	Moon River	*Danny Williams*
UKLP	Blue Hawaii	*Elvis Presley*

STAR QUOTE

FRANK SINATRA

'I want to avoid having bad rock'n'roll records associated with my new Reprise label and the policy will be, in the main, to concentrate on quality performers. That's why I've signed personalities like Sammy Davis Jr.'

THE GRAPEVINE

- **Johnny Halliday has topped almost every European chart with his French-language version of 'Let's Twist Again'.**
- **Cliff Richard & The Shadows' latest movie has been premiered in London to rave reviews.**
- **Sandy Nelson's 'Let There Be Drums' has gone Top 10 in both the US and UK.**
- **Chubby Checker and Chris Barber's Jazz Band have teamed up to tape a UK-TV Special *Trad With A Twist*.**

Johnny Halliday with Sylvie Vartan

A & R ROLE FOR MEEHAN

Having maintained a low-profile since he suddenly quit The Shadows on September 30, Decca Records have maximized public interest by announcing that the group's former drum star, Tony Meehan, has joined the company in a two-fold capacity.

Apart from pursuing a solo career as a recording artist, Meehan is also a new addition to Decca's A&R department, where his duties will be both to discover and develop potential hit-making artists for the label.

THE COLONEL RAISES THE STAKES

Now that it has been revealed that Frank Sinatra's $250,000 private jet is fitted with a small stage, an electric piano and a fully stocked cocktail bar, Colonel Tom Parker – with an eye for similar basic creature comforts – has informed the world that Elvis' fee for a one-hour TV special has increased to a mere $400,000.

BEATLES FAIL AUDITION, DECCA SIGN POOLE

Liverpudlian group The Beatles undertook an unsuccessful studio audition under the supervision of Decca Records' A&R man Mike Smith, at the company's West Hampstead Studios in London.

Among the 15 songs taped, there were three compositions by the group's John Lennon and Paul McCartney – 'Like Dreamers Do', 'Hello Little Girl' and 'Love Of The Loved'.

The remainder were all cover versions – 'To Know Him Is To Love Him', 'Three Cool Cats', 'Memphis Tennessee', 'The Sheik of Araby', 'Money (That's What I Want)', 'Oh Carol', ''Till There Was You', 'Red Sails In The Sunset', 'Please, Mr. Postman', 'What'd I Say', 'Lend Me Your Comb' and 'I Forgot To Remember To Forget'.

Also auditioned and signed to the label, were a five-piece from Dagenham, England, Brian Poole & The Tremeloes.

TWISTING ROUND TRAD JAZZ

The Twist looks like it has sidelined trad jazz as Britain's latest teenage trend, as Chubby Checker dances into the charts with two singles featuring his biggest Stateside hits, 'Let's Twist Again' and 'The Twist'. Joey Dee & The Starlighters have also clicked with 'The Peppermint Twist'.

While the British public are eager to buy any single with 'Twist' in the title, opinions within the British music business have been mixed. Trad jazz star Mr Acker Bilk has been quoted as saying: 'I don't think the public is going to swallow this one whole! In America, they needed a new craze – something to revive interest in rock'n'roll. The Twist filled the bill, but over here you should remember we've already got one new fad – It's Trad, Dad!'

Cliff Richard is among the more vocal Twist supporters: 'Sure, I dig The Twist. It knocks me out!'

Party-goer Helen Shapiro finds The Twist 'tremendous', adding: 'It's bound to catch on with the girls . . . after all, let's face the facts, the hip swinging movement is almost a natural for us!'

Frankie Vaughan, who has entered the race with 'Don't Stop, Twist', is ecstatic: 'I think that The Twist is the greatest musical thing to hit England since rock'n'roll.'

Ernest Evans, a.k.a. Chubby Checker

THE GRAPEVINE

- **Thailand has banned all Elvis movies following riots prior, during and following the screening of *Blue Hawaii*.**
- **Cliff Richard's 'The Young Ones' 45 has been released with 500,000 advance U.K. sales.**
- **The Marketts' 'Surfer Stomp' making much chart noise Stateside.**
- **Billy Fury has been filming *Play It Cool*.**
- **Folk favourites, Peter, Paul & Mary have been signed to Warner Bros Records.**

Brian Poole & The Tremoloes – preferred by Decca to the Beatles

CHARTS

US45	The Lion Sleeps Tonight	*The Tokens*
USLP	Blue Hawaii	*Elvis Presley*
UK45	Stranger On The Shore	*Acker Bilk*
UKLP	Blue Hawaii	*Elvis Presley*
WEEK 2		
US45	The Twist	*Chubby Checker*
USLP	Blue Hawaii	*Elvis Presley*
UK45	The Young Ones	*Cliff Richard*
UKLP	The Young Ones	*Cliff Richard*
WEEK 3		
US45	The Twist	*Chubby Checker*
USLP	Blue Hawaii	*Elvis Presley*
UK45	The Young Ones	*Cliff Richard*
UKLP	The Young Ones	*Cliff Richard*
WEEK 4		
US45	Peppermint Twist	*Joey Dee & The Starliters*
USLP	Blue Hawaii	*Elvis Presley*
UK45	The Young Ones	*Cliff Richard*
UKLP	The Young Ones	*Cliff Richard*

BEACH BOYS BREAK THROUGH

The Beach Boys' debut single, 'Surfin'', has entered Billboard Magazine's chart at No. 118.

Formerly known as The Pendletons (named after a fashionable wide-stripe shirt), The Beach Boys comprise the three Wilson brothers – Brian (who writes the songs), Carl and Dennis, their cousin Mike Love and a friend, David Marks.

To date, their only appearance was when they received $300 to play a Ritchie Valens New Year's Eve memorial dance at Long Beach Municipal Auditorium.

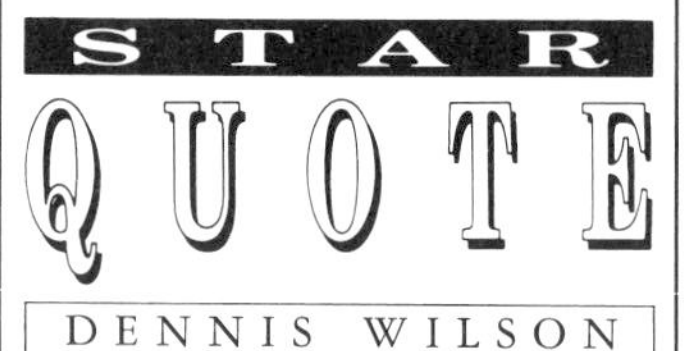

DENNIS WILSON

on the first time The Beach Boys heard 'Surfin' on the radio

'We got so excited hearing our record on the radio that Carl threw up, and I ran down the street screaming!'

BRUBECK: CLOSET HOLLY FAN

Brubeck – Sunday Night with Buddy

Innovative West-Coast 'Cool School' modern jazz pianist/composer Dave Brubeck, who has repeated his 'Take Five' hit status of last year with the equally catchy 'It's A Raggy Waltz', has revealed that one of his closest, yet most unlikely, musical buddies was called Holly – Buddy Holly!

'One of the least-reported of all friendships was mine with the late, great Buddy Holly,' confessed the coolest of cats. 'I had known Buddy for some time before he died, and I always regretted that I did not see him as often as I would have liked.

'Almost the last occasion we met was when he was in London for concerts, and he appeared on *Sunday Night at the London Palladium*. That evening, I called on him in his dressing room, and we chatted about music – Buddy had a great knowledge of this subject. He knew as much about the modern jazz scene as he did about what was happening in rock and blues and country.

'I saw him only twice more for fleeting moments before I was shattered by the news of his death. It's just a pity that we never did get to record something together.'

THE GRAPEVINE

- Duane Eddy has married singer Miriam Johnson.
- Everly Brother Don has married movie starlet Venetia Stevenson.
- Ricky Nelson has officially dropped the 'Y' from his christian name.
- Bobby Vee, Tony Orlando, Clarence 'Frogman' Henry and The Springfields have been touring the UK together.
- New from The Shadows, the haunting 'Wonderful Land'.

The Crickets: Jerry Allison (top), Buddy Holly, Joe B. Mauldin

CHARTS

	US45	Peppermint Twist	*Joey Dee & The Starliters*
	USLP	Blue Hawaii	*Elvis Presley*
	UK45	The Young Ones	*Cliff Richard*
	UKLP	The Young Ones	*Cliff Richard*
WEEK 2	US45	Peppermint Twist	*Joey Dee & The Starliters*
	USLP	Blue Hawaii	*Elvis Presley*
	UK45	The Young Ones	*Cliff Richard*
	UKLP	The Young Ones	*Cliff Richard*
WEEK 3	US45	Duke Of Earl	*Gene Chandler*
	USLP	Blue Hawaii	*Elvis Presley*
	UK45	The Young Ones	*Cliff Richard*
	UKLP	The Young Ones	*Cliff Richard*
WEEK 4	US45	Duke Of Earl	*Gene Chandler*
	USLP	Blue Hawaii	*Elvis Presley*
	UK45	Let's Twist Again	*Chubby Checker*
	UKLP	Blue Hawaii	*Elvis Presley*

STAR QUOTE

SAM KATZMAN

Movie Producer

'Twist Around The Clock' only cost $250,000 to make, but in less than six months it grossed six million – so of course I'm gonna make more Twist movies!'

BROKEN LEG LED DENVER TO HIT

One-time merchant seaman Karl Denver was pretty much a rough diamond before becoming a professional singer.

The tattoo on the back of the left hand of this 26-year-old Glaswegian is a reminder of 30 days spent in an Egyptian jail for hitting an Arab policeman ('I had the tattoo done to pass the time away'), while a broken leg was indirectly responsible for his second U.K. hit, 'Wimoweh'.

Karl confesses: 'About ten years ago, when I'd just turned sixteen, the ship I was serving on docked at a South African port. That evening, I went on one big binge with some pals.

'On the way back to my cabin, I fell down a gangway and broke my leg. I found I had plenty of spare time for convalescence, so I toured the local beauty spots, and came across an African tribe in the middle of a ceremonial dance. They were singing "Wimoweh" in Swahili, and I kept the song in my head ever since.'

TWIST DISCS DOMINATE US CHARTS

Joey Dee & The Starlighters

No less than *four* Twist singles are featured in the US Top 20 as the craze takes a hold.

Chubby Checker's 'The Twist' is at No. 5, while Joey Dee & The Starlighters' 'The Peppermint Twist' holds down the No. 9 slot, Gary US Bonds' 'Dear Lady Twist' is at No. 11 and Billy Joe & The Checkmates' 'Perculator Twist' is at No. 27.

Meanwhile, a spot-check of New York's Temple of Twist – The Peppermint Lounge on West 45th Street – reveals that the Big Apple's most popular Twist albums are: (1) Chubby Checker: 'For Twisters Only', (2) Chubby Checker: 'Let's Twist Again', (3) Chubby Checker: 'Your Twist Party', (4) Ray Charles: 'Do The Twist', (5) Joey Dee: 'Doin' The Twist Live At The Peppermint Lounge' and (6) Louis Prima: 'Doin' The Twist'.

CHUBBY CHECKS INTO UK CHARTS

On the other side of the Atlantic, Chubby Checker is thrilled-to-bustin' with three singles in the UK Top 30: 'Let's Twist Again' (7), 'Slow Twistin'' (20) and a duet with Bobby Rydell, 'Teach Me To Twist' (26).

Despite his worldwide success, Chubby is being cautious with his cash. Seemingly, his one luxury is a Thunderbird Convertible.

Says Chubby, who won't be 21 until October: 'My parents are investing my money in real estate just in case, but I'm allowed *thirty-five dollars* a week spending money!'

Bobby Rydell rides the Twist craze

ELVIS'S DREAM

United Artists' Studios have released *Follow That Dream* with Elvis Presley (Toby Kwimper) at the centre of a strictly-for-laughs conflict between shiftless Florida poor folks and corrupt local authorities.

Elvis as Toby Kwimper

THE GRAPEVINE

- **The Beatles have made their radio debut on the BBC's *Teenager's Turn – Here We Go.***
- **Helen Shapiro has become the first British artist to top the Japanese charts with 'You Don't Know Me'.**
- **The Shadows have become the first British group to headline the prestigious L'Olympia Theatre, Paris.**
- **Chicago blues legend Howlin' Wolf (Chester Burnett) has been touring the UK with Chris Barber's Jazz Band.**

CHARTS

Chart	Title	Artist
US45	Duke Of Earl	*Gene Chandler*
USLP	Blue Hawaii	*Elvis Presley*
UK45	Let's Twist Again	*Chubby Checker*
UKLP	Blue Hawaii	*Elvis Presley*
WEEK 2		
US45	Hey ! Baby !	*Bruce Channel*
USLP	Blue Hawaii	*Elvis Presley*
UK45	March Of The Siamese Children	*Kenny Ball*
UKLP	Blue Hawaii	*Elvis Presley*
WEEK 3		
US45	Hey ! Baby !	*Bruce Channel*
USLP	Blue Hawaii	*Elvis Presley*
UK45	Wonderful Land	*Shadows*
UKLP	Blue Hawaii	*Elvis Presley*
WEEK 4		
US45	Hey ! Baby !	*Bruce Channel*
USLP	Blue Hawaii	*Elvis Presley*
UK45	Wonderful Land	*Shadows*
UKLP	Blue Hawaii	*Elvis Presley*
WEEK 5		
US45	Don't Break The Heart That Loves You	*Connie Francis*
USLP	Blue Hawaii	*Elvis Presley*
UK45	Wonderful Land	*Shadows*
UKLP	Blue Hawaii	*Elvis Presley*

DYLAN DEBUT RELEASED

CBS Records have released a self-titled debut album by Bob Dylan. Of the 22 folk and blues tracks he recorded with just his own guitar accompaniment between November 20 and 22 1961, a total of 13 songs are premiered.

Most of young Dylan's influences are in evidence: 'You're No Good' (Jesse Fuller), 'Talkin' New York' (Dylan), 'In My Time Of Dyin' (Jesus Gonna Make Up My Dyin' Bed)' (Blind Willie Johnson), 'Man Of Constant Sorrow' (trad., arr. Dylan), 'Fixin To Die' (Bukka White), 'Pretty Peggy-O' (trad., arr. Dylan), 'Highway 51' (Curtis Jones), 'Gospel Plow' (trad., arr. Dylan), 'Baby, Let Me Follow You Down' (Eric Von Schmidt), 'House Of The Risin' Sun' (trad.), 'Freight Train Blues' (trad.), 'Song To Woody' (Dylan), 'See That My Grave Is Kept Clean' (Blind Lemon Jefferson).

IT'S ALL GO FOR ACKER!

Trumpeter Kenny Ball woos the Kremlin

A Band of Thieves led by Acker Bilk (left)

Mr Acker Bilk & His Paramount Jazz Band have topped off the most hectic period in their career by commencing the first day's filming on their first full-length movie, *Bank of Thieves*, at Pinewood Studios.

Earlier that week, the popular bowler-hatted jazz clarinettist was an unsuspecting victim of the *This Is Your Life* (BBC-TV) team, and was also awarded a gold disc for a million-plus sales of 'Stranger On The Shore'.

The single, with 21 consecutive weeks on the UK charts, is only five weeks short of Shirley Bassey's all-time best of 26 weeks with 'As Long As He Needs Me'.

In the interim, 'Stranger On The Shore' has repeated the recent Stateside success of fellow-Brit Kenny Ball's 'Midnight In Moscow' million-seller by moving up to No. 4 on *Billboard* magazine's Hot 100.

CHARTS

US45	Johnny Angel *Shelley Fabares*
USLP	Blue Hawaii *Elvis Presley*
UK45	Wonderful Land *Shadows*
UKLP	Blue Hawaii *Elvis Presley*
WEEK 2	
US45	Johnny Angel *Shelley Fabares*
USLP	Blue Hawaii *Elvis Presley*
UK45	Wonderful Land *Shadows*
UKLP	Blue Hawaii *Elvis Presley*
WEEK 3	
US45	Good Luck Charm *Elvis Presley*
USLP	Blue Hawaii *Elvis Presley*
UK45	Wonderful Land *Shadows*
UKLP	Blue Hawaii *Elvis Presley*
WEEK 4	
US45	Good Luck Charm *Elvis Presley*
USLP	Blue Hawaii *Elvis Presley*
UK45	Wonderful Land *Shadows*
UKLP	Blue Hawaii *Elvis Presley*

STAR QUOTE

FRANK SINATRA

'I'm an over-privileged adult who would like to help underprivileged children.'

THE GRAPEVINE

- **Chubby Checker's *Don't Knock The Twist* movie has been premiered in New York.**
- **With 'Apache', The Shadows are the first British instrumental group to sell over a million singles domestically.**
- **Steve Allen Lewis – three year old son of Jerry Lee and Myra – has drowned in the family swimming pool.**

NME NO. 1 – OFFICIAL!

In the *New Musical Express'*, Tin Pan Alley offices in Soho's Denmark Street, London, the staff haven't only been celebrating the paper's 10th anniversary, but the good news that, for the first time ever, the paper's circulation now exceeds 200,000 copies weekly.

The certified circulation figure is not only the biggest in the world for any kind of musical paper, but it is greater than the combined weekly sales of all other British music papers.

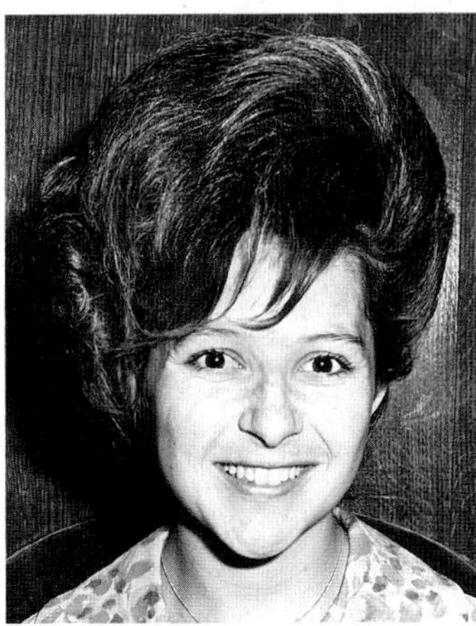

Brenda Lee, unbilled but still dynamite!

The Brooks Brothers

EX-BEATLE SUTCLIFFE DIES

Following a brain haemorrhage the previous day, former Beatles bassist Stuart Sutcliffe died, aged 21, in the arms of his German fiancée, photographer Astrid Kirchherr, in the back of an ambulance carrying him to a Hamburg hospital.

Since leaving The Beatles last year, Sutcliffe had been studying art in his adopted city.

Sutcliffe's untimely death may have been brought about as a result of being savagely kicked in the head outside a Liverpool dance hall, two years earlier.

POLL-WINNERS SHOW

The NME annual Readers' Poll-Winners Concert was again staged at London's Wembley Pool on April 15.

Those who performed included: Cliff Richard & The Shadows, Billy Fury, Adam Faith, American rocker Johnny Burnette, Eden Kane, Joe Brown, Shane Fenton, Mr Acker Bilk, The Karl Denver Trio, Jet Harris, The Brooks Brothers, John Leyton, Bert Weedon, Helen Shapiro, Danny Williams, The Springfields, Red Price, Ted Heath & His Music and Bob Miller & The Millermen.

Also appearing, as unbilled guest star, was America's 'Miss Dynamite', Brenda Lee.

A STING IN THE TALE

British fans have much cause for complaint over the lack of attention given to B. Bumble & The Stingers' 'Nut Rocker' by BBC Radio djs.

Though 'Nut Rocker' (or as one observer commented: 'a diabolical liberty taken with Mr Tchaikovsky's "Nutcracker Suite"') has been featured 'live' by a number of BBC studio performers, the original Kim Fowley-produced Stateside recording has made the UK Top 10 without any BBC airplay!

It wasn't that the record was banned, it was just ignored. Only when 'Nut Rocker' reached the upper reaches of the charts under its own steam did it receive a solitary spin on Alan Freeman's *Top Ten Show* as a matter of course.

The only way British fans could hear the record was by tuning into European based Radio Luxembourg, where it was on the playlist of all the station's EMI Records sponsored shows. It was due entirely to this that The Stingers buzzed into the British bestsellers lists.

Ironically, 'Nut Rocker' has proved to be one of Top Rank Records' biggest-ever selling hits at a time when the label is about to be discontinued, and the catalogue absorbed into other EMI divisions. To complete the bizarre circumstances that have surrounded 'Nut Rocker's' success, heavyweight piano-poundin' B. Bumble is persistently miffed that nobody believes that he's recorded under his *real* name: B (Bill) Bumble!

Kim Fowley tries to retrieve his nutcrackers from a hungry pillar box

CHARTS

- US45 Soldier Boy — *Shirelles*
- USLP West Side Story — *Soundtrack*
- UK45 Wonderful Land — *Shadows*
- UKLP Blue Hawaii — *Elvis Presley*

WEEK 2

- US45 Soldier Boy — *Shirelles*
- USLP West Side Story — *Soundtrack*
- UK45 Nut Rocker — *B. Bumble & The Stingers*
- UKLP Blue Hawaii — *Elvis Presley*

WEEK 3

- US45 Soldier Boy — *Shirelles*
- USLP West Side Story — *Soundtrack*
- UK45 Good Luck Charm — *Elvis Presley*
- UKLP Blue Hawaii — *Elvis Presley*

WEEK 4

- US45 Stranger On The Shore — *Acker Bilk*
- USLP West Side Story — *Soundtrack*
- UK45 Good Luck Charm — *Elvis Presley*
- UKLP Blue Hawaii — *Elvis Presley*

OL' BLUE EYES TWISTS

Frank Sinatra, who was once quoted as saying he didn't want 'bad rock and roll records' on his Reprise record label, has sent his most devoted finger-poppin' fans into shock by jumping aboard Chubby Checker's commercial bandwagon and releasing a single, 'Ev'rybody's Twistin'', an update of an old jazz standard, 'Ev'rybody's Truckin''.

IS THERE A DOCTOR IN THE CHARTS?

The trend for actor-singer continues: Richard Chamberlain – the handsome 26-year-old actor who stars in the title role of hit US-TV hospital drama, *Dr Kildare* – has released his vocal version of the programme's popular theme tune under the title 'Three Stars Shine Tonight'.

Chamberlain, whose daily fan mail is reported to exceed 3,500 letters is, so MGM Studios inform the press, a quiet, studious chap who doesn't drink, rarely goes to nightclubs and doesn't have a steady girlfriend.

However, he takes his new-found fame as a singer as seriously as his acting, and has already named Elvis's 'Love Me Tender' as a likely follow-up.

Chamberlain, the singing doctor

THE GRAPEVINE

- **Don and Phil Everly have been discharged from the US Marines.**
- **Cliff Richard & The Shadows have been filming *Summer Holiday* in Greece.**
- **The two most-played jukebox hits in the US in 1961 were Jimmy Dean's 'Big Bad John' and Chubby Checker's 'The Twist'.**
- **Blues legend John Lee Hooker has made the UK charts for the first time with 'Boom Boom'.**

SINATRA HONOURS UK WRITERS

The main event in London this month has been Frank Sinatra's three days of recording – before invited audiences of fans and friends – at Pye's Marble Arch studios. With Robert Farnon conducting a 40-piece orchestra (and visitor Nelson Riddle occasionally advising from the sidelines), Sinatra recorded a selection of 11 ballads, all from the pens of British composers, to be released on Reprise as 'Great Songs From Great Britain'.

Among those recorded were 'The Very Thought Of You' and 'We'll Meet Again'.

Midway through the first session, Sinatra indicated that he would be returning next year to complete a companion L.P.

CHARTS

US45	I Can't Stop Loving You *Ray Charles*
USLP	West Side Story *Soundtrack*
UK45	Good Luck Charm *Elvis Presley*
UKLP	Blue Hawaii *Elvis Presley*
WEEK 2	
US45	I Can't Stop Loving You *Ray Charles*
USLP	West Side Story *Soundtrack*
UK45	Good Luck Charm *Elvis Presley*
UKLP	Blue Hawaii *Elvis Presley*
WEEK 3	
US45	I Can't Stop Loving You *Ray Charles*
USLP	West Side Story *Soundtrack*
UK45	Good Luck Charm *Elvis Presley*
UKLP	Blue Hawaii *Elvis Presley*
WEEK 4	
US45	I Can't Stop Loving You *Ray Charles*
USLP	Modern Sounds In Country & Western Music *Ray Charles*
UK45	Come Outside *Mike Sarne*
UKLP	West Side Story *Soundtrack*
WEEK 5	
US45	I Can't Stop Loving You *Ray Charles*
USLP	Modern Sounds In Country & Western Music *Ray Charles*
UK45	Come Outside *Mike Sarne*
UKLP	West Side Story *Soundtrack*

CAROLE'S BABY-SITTING BLUES

Summer rain doesn't worry Carole King

Deciding that the end product is so good, songwriter Carole King (of Goffin & King fame) has been persuaded to release her studio demo of 'It Might As Well Rain Until September' on the Dimension label.

Keeping it in the family, Carole King's babysitter, Eva Narcissus Boyd has recorded and released 'The Loco-Motion' under the name of Little Eva to become a summertime chart-topper. The single was written by her erstwhile employers, who were impressed by the ex-babysitter's singing around the house.

Now the only question is: where on earth are they going to find another babysitter?

No babysitting blues for Little Eva

THE GRAPEVINE

- The Beatles have been signed to UK Parlophone Records.
- Owen Gray's 'Twist Baby' is the first release on Chris Blackwell's recently formed Island label.
- Bruce Channel, Delbert McClinton, Frank Ifield and Johnny Kidd & The Pirates have been touring the UK together.
- Swedish guitar combo The Spotnicks have twanged their way into the UK charts with 'Orange Blossom Special' update.

DAVE CLARK BOWS IN

Fronted by their 19-year-old drum-thumping leader, The Dave Clark Five – from the North London area of Tottenham – have made their disc debut with 'That's What I Said'.

The group, apart from Clark, comprises: Mike Smith (vocals and organ), Denny Payton (tenor sax), Lenny Davidson (guitar) and Rick Huxley (bass).

Formed two years ago during the skiffle music craze, they have built up a local following playing at Tottenham's South Grove Youth Club.

CORDET HIT FOR EX-SHADOW MEEHAN

Louise Cordet, daughter of TV-presenter Helen Cordet, has become the newest object of affection for Britain's male youth following the release of her coquettish 'I'm Just A Baby'.

The single was produced by Tony Meehan shortly before he left his A&R post with Decca Records, to rejoin his former colleagues, Cliff Richard & The Shadows (from whom he split last year), as A&R chief of their newly formed Shad-Rich record production company. However, he will not be involved with either Cliff or The Shadows in a performing capacity.

Though no longer on Decca's team of salaried globe-trotting talent scouts, Meehan (19) will continue to record for the label in a solo capacity.

Meehan – a star looking for new talent

JULY 1962

ANKA'S AWAY!

Paul Anka, now 21, has the legal freedom to spend the hundreds of thousands of dollars he has been earning for years as a minor!

Some measure of how much that may be can be gauged from the fact that not only has Anka been awarded 20 gold discs (each in recognition for over one million records sold), but that many of them, like 'Lonely Boy' and 'Puppy Love', were self-penned.

Biggest of all has been 'Diana'. This song is said to have been covered 320 times in 22 countries in the past six years, total sales of such recordings being close to ten million records, while Paul's own sales worldwide stand at more than 30 million. Additionally, his current deal with RCA is said to be worth a minimum of one million dollars over the next five years.

Coupled to this, twangy guitar man Duane Eddy has recently signed to Anka's production company Camay, which is distributed by RCA-Victor. His first disc for Anka/Camay is 'Deep In The Heart Of Texas', and shows a return to his familiar hit formula.

Meanwhile, Anka – whose upcoming single is 'Eso Beso' – has had one of his paintings accepted by the United Nations Art Club. It is to be hung in the General Assembly building in New York prior to being auctioned off by UNICEF.

STAR QUOTE

JOE BROWN

'I have the world's most shocking memory . . . I only manage to remember the words of my songs because they're in rhyme!'

Mr Memory – Joe Brown

STONES ROLL IN

With a line-up comprised of Mick Jagger (vocals), Keith Richards and Elmo Lewis (Brian Jones) on guitars, Ian 'Stu' Stewart (piano), Dick Taylor (bass) and Mick Avery (drums), The Rolling Stones make their London Marquee Club debut deputizing for the club's regular Thursday Night R&B attraction – Alexis Korner's Blues Incorporated who are broadcasting 'live' on the BBC's weekly *Jazz Club* radio programme.

THE GRAPEVINE

- **Connie Francis has slipped behind the Iron Curtain to represent the USA at the Polish Music Festival.**
- **Following their release from the US Marines, The Everly Brothers have engaged in a six-week 'comeback' tour of the States.**
- **British disc jockey Jimmy Savile has made his disc debut with 'Ahab The Arab'.**
- **Buddy Holly clone, Tommy Roe is in the US charts with 'Sheila'.**

Connie – polishing up her act

Tommy Roe – charting with 'Sheila'

CHARTS

US45	The Stripper — *David Rose & His Orchestra*
USLP	Modern Sounds In Country & Western Music — *Ray Charles*
UK45	A Picture Of You — *Joe Brown*
UKLP	Pot Luck — *Elvis Presley*
	WEEK 2
US45	Roses Are Red — *Bobby Vinton*
USLP	Modern Sounds In Country & Western Music — *Ray Charles*
UK45	I Can't Stop Loving You — *Ray Charles*
UKLP	Pot Luck — *Elvis Presley*
	WEEK 3
US45	Roses Are Red — *Bobby Vinton*
USLP	Modern Sounds In Country & Western Music — *Ray Charles*
UK45	I Remember You — *Frank Ifield*
UKLP	Pot Luck — *Elvis Presley*
	WEEK 4
US45	Roses Are Red — *Bobby Vinton*
USLP	Modern Sounds In Country & Western Music — *Ray Charles*
UK45	I Remember You — *Frank Ifield*
UKLP	Pot Luck — *Elvis Presley*

TWIST AND TRAD GAIN GROUND

With both the Twist and trad jazz taking sales away from the previously rock'n'roll dominated singles market, NME's analysis of the paper's weekly charts for the period January 1 – June 30 makes compulsive reading.

Looking at the Top 10 positions, Elvis again is secure at No. 1 followed by Cliff Richard, but with Chubby Checker fast gaining ground at No. 3. There are no other US artists in this top half of the results.

Trad jazz is represented by Mr Acker Bilk at No. 4 and Kenny Ball at No. 7. The remaining best-sellers are: Karl Denver (No. 5), Billy Fury (No. 7), The Shadows (No. 8), Eden Kane (No. 9) and Helen Shapiro who, at No. 10 is a full eleven places ahead of her closest female rival, Brenda Lee!

CHECKER CHAT

It's not so much a case of biting the beat that feeds him, but for all the hysteria that has surrounded The Twist phenomenon, 20-year-old Chubby Checker has still been able to take a realistic and unbiased view of the circumstances that have placed his records on all the world's major charts, and elevated him to the position of being the first major star of the Sixties.

As far as Chubby is concerned, his seemingly overnight success was as much a case of inspired opportunism than any other fancy theory that has been put forward.

'There is absolutely nothing new about The Twist,' Checker admits. 'People have been doing the same sort of thing for centuries – wiggling their hips and their shoulders in time to music, especially people who can't dance properly.

'Now, I've just been smart enough to exploit something which the public failed to recognize was no more than swaying naturally to musical rhythms.

'And, I'm not worried if it doesn't last. Right now, I'm looking for something else that's been done for years, so that I can exploit that in a way the public won't recognize!'

THE GRAPEVINE

- Previously The Four Lovers, Vee-Jay Records' The Four Seasons have hit paydirt first time out with 'Sherry'.
- Memphis-based Booker T & The MGS are charting everywhere with 'Green Onions'.
- Robert Allen Zimmerman has legally changed his name to Bob Dylan.
- Motown vocal group, The Contours, are enjoying heavy action with 'Do You Love Me'.

BEST OUT, STARR JOINS BEATLES

Officially a Beatle, drummer Ringo Starr has made his controversial Cavern Club debut on August 14, during which scuffles broke out inside the venue, guitarist George Harrison received a black eye and manager Brian Epstein's car was vandalized in the street outside the club.

The series of events began five days earlier when Epstein contacted Ringo Starr, then resident at Butlin's Holiday Camp, Skegness, with Rory Storme & The Hurricanes to offer him the soon-to-be-vacant drum stool with The Beatles.

It was too good an offer for Mr Starr to refuse!

The fact that Pete Best was easily the most popular member of the group was – in the opinion of John, Paul and George – quite incidental. The fact remained that EMI's George Martin had expressed concern about Best's potential as a recording drummer. On hearing these remarks, Epstein and The Beatles instantly rectified the problem, which could easily have jeopardized their upcoming recording plans.

On August 16, Epstein – at the behest of John, Paul and George – informed Pete Best that he was no longer The Beatles' drummer. Two days later, Ringo Starr made his public debut with the group at the Hulme Hall, Port Sunlight. Liverpool fans were not happy – hence the Cavern kerfuffle.

CHARTS

US45	Roses Are Red *Bobby Vinton*
USLP	Modern Sounds In Country & Western Music *Ray Charles*
UK45	I Remember You *Frank Ifield*
UKLP	West Side Story *Soundtrack*
WEEK 2	
US45	Breaking Up Is Hard To Do *Neil Sedaka*
USLP	Modern Sounds In Country & Western Music *Ray Charles*
UK45	I Remember You *Frank Ifield*
UKLP	Pot Luck *Elvis Presley*
WEEK 3	
US45	Breaking Up Is Hard To Do *Neil Sedaka*
USLP	Modern Sounds In Country & Western Music *Ray Charles*
UK45	I Remember You *Frank Ifield*
UKLP	Pot Luck *Elvis Presley*
WEEK 4	
US45	The Locomotion *Little Eva*
USLP	Modern Sounds In Country & Western Music *Ray Charles*
UK45	I Remember You *Frank Ifield*
UKLP	West Side Story *Soundtrack*

Pete Best (far right) has been elbowed out of The Beatles' line up and is replaced by Hurricanes' drummer Ringo Starr

THE GRAPEVINE

- Connie Francis' first book, 'For Every Young Heart' has been published.
- The Spotnicks back in the UK charts with 'Rocket Man'.
- Buddy Holly has scored a posthumous hit with 'Reminiscin'.
- This year's novelty disc is US rock-horror recording 'The Monster Mash' by Bobby 'Boris' Pickett & The Crypt-Kickers.

CHARTS

US45	Sheila	*Tommy Roe*
USLP	Modern Sounds In Country & Western Music	*Ray Charles*
UK45	I Remember You	*Frank Ifield*
UKLP	West Side Story	*Soundtrack*
	WEEK 2	
US45	Sheila	*Tommy Roe*
USLP	Modern Sounds In Country & Western Music	*Ray Charles*
UK45	I Remember You	*Frank Ifield*
UKLP	West Side Story	*Soundtrack*
	WEEK 3	
US45	Sherry	*Four Seasons*
USLP	Modern Sounds In Country & Western Music	*Ray Charles*
UK45	She's Not You	*Elvis Presley*
UKLP	West Side Story	*Soundtrack*
	WEEK 4	
US45	Sherry	*Four Seasons*
USLP	Modern Sounds In Country & Western Music	*Ray Charles*
UK45	She's Not You	*Elvis Presley*
UKLP	West Side Story	*Soundtrack*
	WEEK 5	
US45	Sherry	*Four Seasons*
USLP	West Side Story	*Soundtrack*
UK45	She's Not You	*Elvis Presley*
UKLP	West Side Story	*Soundtrack*

HATS OFF TO DEL!

Such was the speed with which former US Army serviceman Del Shannon topped the charts on both sides of the Atlantic last Spring with 'Runaway', it was assumed the 22-year old from Grand Rapids, Michigan was just another in the line of one-hit-wonders.

Shannon quickly silenced those sceptics with a quick-fire succession of self-penned hits which included 'Hats Off To Larry', 'So Long Baby', 'Hey Little Girl', 'Cry Myself To Sleep', 'Swiss Maid' and currently 'Little Town Flirt'.

As to the circumstances surrounding his initial Big Break, Shannon (real name Charles Westover) has revealed that, back in Michigan, it was local entrepreneur Ollie McLaughlin who motivated him to go for the big one.

'He heard me performing in a club and told me to look him up when I had written a song I thought stood some chance of being a hit!' he says. 'Immediately after the gig, I sat up all night trying to think up new words to songs, and, eventually, I had 'Runaway' – something easy to remember, but still sufficiently out of the ordinary.'

ELVIS GETTING BIGGER

Elvis's dresser, Sy Devore has to kit out the singer with a new $9,300 wardrobe for an upcoming movie. Seeing how Elvis earns $10,000-plus a day singing and dancing before the cameras, Devore has to hire a stand-in with identical measurements to Elvis.

There is one problem – sources close to the star have intimated that Elvis is having weight problems!

Big 'Bossa Nova' Charlie Byrd finds Brazilian rhythm his route into the US charts

BYRD'S NEW BEAT

Among the more unusual souvenirs guitarist Charlie Byrd brought back home to Washington DC from his US State Department Tour of South America, was a bag full of Brazilian rhythms.

One in particular – the *bossa nova* (the new beat) – intrigued both him and tenor saxist Stan Getz, with the result that a single plucked from their best-selling 'jazz samba' album, 'Desafinado (Slightly Out Of Tune)', has charted and, in doing so, prompted dozens of artists to ride the bossa nova bandwagon.

Tenor saxist Stan Getz – Charlie Byrd's partner and certainly not 'desafinado' with the US record-buying public

OCTOBER

JB – OUTTA SIGHT

It's reported that prior to The James Brown Revue commencing yet another headlining season at New York's world-famous Apollo Theater, Harlem, Syd Nathan (the head of King Records) argued vigorously against Brown's wish to record his complete act.

'You mean,' said Nathan, 'you want to record your stage show *live*! – you can't keep on recording the same songs over and over . . . nobody's going to buy that!'

When Brown explained that his hits sounded infinitely better when performed against a gale-force blast of his screamin' fans, Nathan thought the idea quite crazy and made no commercial sense. Nathan's final word on the subject was that, if Brown was so obsessed with the project, he should fund it entirely from out of his own pocket.

King Records, insisted Nathan, won't contribute a cent! The bottom line for recording is $5,700, so JB laid his money down and recorded all four of the shows he gave on Wednesday, October 24.

It's a time of historical importance for 'the hardest working man in show business'. Unsatisfied with the Apollo's financial arrangements, JB has set a precedent by insisting that he will cancel his shows unless he's allowed to rent the venue for the duration of his season.

In this way, once all the overhead costs have been covered, JB will earn something nearer his true box-office worth.

CHARTS

US45	Sherry *Four Seasons*
USLP	West Side Story *Soundtrack*
UK45	Telstar *Tornados*
UKLP	West Side Story *Soundtrack*
WEEK 2	
US45	Sherry *Four Seasons*
USLP	West Side Story *Soundtrack*
UK45	Telstar *Tornados*
UKLP	West Side Story *Soundtrack*
WEEK 3	
US45	Monster Mash *Bobby 'Boris' Pickett*
USLP	Peter, Paul & Mary *Peter, Paul & Mary*
UK45	Telstar *Tornados*
UKLP	West Side Story *Soundtrack*
WEEK 4	
US45	Monster Mash *Bobby 'Boris' Pickett*
USLP	Peter, Paul & Mary *Peter, Paul & Mary*
UK45	Telstar *Tornados*
UKLP	Out Of The Shadows *Shadows*

PHIL EVERLY ALONE

Don Everly flew out of London en route for the States on October 15, leaving younger brother Phil with the daunting task of completing a bill-topping Everly Brothers UK tour, solo!

The circumstances behind this bizarre situation took place two days earlier, on Sunday, October 13. During a rehearsal at London's Prince of Wales Theatre, brother Don broke down completely during 'Crying In The Rain' and was immediately rushed to the nearby Charing Cross Hospital before being taken on to the Middlesex Hospital for treatment not unconnected with medicine he has been taking.

IF YOU HAVE TO ASK . . .

Asked Elvis Presley's going rate for inaugurating the lavish New York Americana Hotel, Colonel Tom Parker replied: 'The first ten floors!'

THE GRAPEVINE

- **Parlophone are said to have selected two Lennon & McCartney originals, 'Love Me Do' and 'P.S. I Love You' as the debut single from The Beatles.**
- **Bobby 'Boris' Pickett's 'Monster Mash' has been banned by BBC radio and TV for being 'offensive'.**
- **Cliff Richard, The Shadows and Frank Ifield were the token pop acts on Royal Command Variety Performance.**

Elvis (left) – a fair day's work for a fair day's pay?

Hank Marvin (right) – he and the Shadows are considered suitable viewing for the Royal Family

HOT NEWS FROM NJF

The British National Jazz Federation/Marquee Club 'house' publication *Jazz News* has printed its first weekly 'Rhythm & Blues Column' noting:

'Alexis Korner and Blues Incorporated have been Thursday residents at famous Marquee Club in Oxford Street for some months now . . . audiences now reach almost 700 nearly every session . . . an exciting line-up including Dick Heckstall-Smith, Graham Bond, Peter 'Ginger' Baker, Jack Bruce, and Johnny Parker guarantees the jazz content . . . jiving, twisting, raving, just listening, that's the Marquee on Thursdays.

'Mick Jagger and The Rolling Stones are touring the local clubs to appreciative audiences, with a history of appearances at the first R&B club in London, the Ealing Saturday Club, where Korner used to play.'

Alexis Korner and Blues Incorporated – Marquee residents

The Rolling Stones – one time regulars at the Ealing Club

LITTLE RICHARD ROCKS BACK

When Little Richard agreed to headline a UK tour supported by Sam Cooke and Jet Harris, it was in the belief that it was in his three-year old adopted role of gospel music performer.

On the opening night (8 October) at the Gaumont Theatre, Doncaster, Richard took the stage for the first of two evening shows dressed in the long robes favoured by gospel preachers and, with teenage Billy Preston at the Hammond organ, began to sing such familiar old-time quasi-religious standards as 'Peace In The Valley' and 'I Believe'.

The house-full audience, who had anticipated a full-throttle rock'n'roll assault from the Georgia Peach, went into shock and the promoter into a panic.

At the second show, Sam Cooke, delayed from making the earlier performance, whipped the audience into a frenzy prior to intermission time and left them howling for more. Sensing a serious challenge to his reputation, Richard abandoned his gospel set to rock out in a rough impromptu manner and secure his bill-topping status. And that's how it continued for the remainder of the tour, which culminated in Brian Epstein booking Richard to headline an all-Merseyside 5½-hour/12 group marathon at the Tower Ballroom, New Brighton and, two weeks later, to headline at the Empire Theatre, Liverpool. On both occasions, The Beatles also appeared.

Though he was now singing rock'n'roll, Richard was determined to quash rumours that he was in fact godless and deceitful.

Richard sidekick – Billy Preston

CHARTS

US45	He's A Rebel	*Crystals*
USLP	Peter, Paul & Mary	*Peter, Paul & Mary*
UK45	Telstar	*Tornados*
UKLP	West Side Story	*Soundtrack*
WEEK 2		
US45	He's A Rebel	*Crystals*
USLP	Peter, Paul & Mary	*Peter, Paul & Mary*
UK45	Lovesick Blues	*Frank Ifield*
UKLP	West Side Story	*Soundtrack*
WEEK 3		
US45	Big Girls Don't Cry	*Four Seasons*
USLP	Peter, Paul & Mary	*Peter, Paul & Mary*
UK45	Lovesick Blues	*Frank Ifield*
UKLP	West Side Story	*Soundtrack*
WEEK 4		
US45	Big Girls Don't Cry	*Four Seasons*
USLP	Peter, Paul & Mary	*Peter, Paul & Mary*
UK45	Lovesick Blues	*Frank Ifield*
UKLP	On Stage With	*George Mitchell Minstrels*

THE GRAPEVINE

- **A new disc has just been released this month by The Miracles – 'You Really Got A Hold On Me'.**
- **EMI Parlophone producer George Martin has announced that he's to record The Beatles 'live' at The Cavern Club.**
- **A new release from The Four Seasons: 'Big Girls Don't Cry'.**

HARRIS, MEEHAN JOIN FORCES

The Shadows' former bass player and drummer – Jet Harris and Tony Meehan – have announced that they've chosen to join forces as an instrumental team and promise a spectacular debut early in the New Year.

CHRIS MONTEZ STEPS OUT

Chris Montez – inspired by Presley and Haley and stepping into Valens' shoes

The logical successor to the late lamented Ritchie Valens, is how 17-year old Chicano, Chris Montez is being hailed. 'Let's Dance' with its piping-hot organ, thunderbolt drums and Montez's nasal invitation to hit the floor in style, carries on where Valens' 'C'mon, Let's Go' left off.

Actually, it was only a chance encounter with some old Presley and Haley discs that got this young Los Angelino rockin' 'n' rollin'. 'That stuff really set me off – I was hooked. After that, I used to spend all my pocket money buying second-hand discs in junk shops, trying to build a collection,' Montez admits.

He also reveals how 'Let's Dance' almost didn't get released! 'That's not for me, I told my manager, when I first heard it,' he says. The fact that it was his manager Jim Lee who had penned the tune didn't colour his initial judgement. However, Jim was convinced that Chris should at least record the song and then decide upon its fate.

'I agreed to do so only after realising that Jim had a great deal of faith in his composition,' Chris says. 'It wasn't conceit, it was conviction, and by the time he'd hired musicians and had worked out a good backing, I decided the song was for me after all.

'We tried to achieve a new sound on 'Let's Dance'. I think this had a lot to do with it becoming a success, because frankly I don't have big ideas about my ability as a singer. I should think that most kids bought it just to dance to. After all, that's what it's about – not to listen to me!'

■ **The Tamla-Motown Rock & Roll Show has booked into New York's Apollo Theatre for a 10-day Christmas season; artists appearing: The Supremes, Marvin Gaye, The Miracles, The Contours, Mary Wells.**

■ **D.J. Alan Freed has gone on trial in New York on payola charges.**

■ **'Kinematograph Weekly' has named Cliff Richard as the year's most successful UK box office movie star.**

STAR QUOTE

DUSTY SPRINGFIELD

'Until recently, I didn't take any interest in the charts. I didn't have any dislike of pop music for we (The Springfields) set out to reach the charts, too, but my own interest in R&B meant that I was buying records that weren't regarded as commercial.'

Dusty R&B fan

PRESLEY: LUCKY 13 HITS

'Return To Sender' has given Elvis Presley his 50th entry in the NME singles chart – an unprecedented achievement which is unlikely to be equalled in the forseeable future.

On the subject of Elvis chart statistics: since his first UK No. 1 'All Shook Up', Elvis has occupied the coveted top slot for a total of 52-weeks – in other words, he's been No. 1 on the UK charts for a total of one year, with the longest run of nine consecutive weeks being with 'It's Now Or Never'.

The grand total of 52-weeks at No. 1 was accumulated by 13 separate singles.

CHARTS

US45	Big Girls Don't Cry	*Four Seasons*
USLP	My Son The Folk Singer	*Allan Sherman*
UK45	Lovesick Blues	*Frank Ifield*
UKLP	On Stage With	*George Mitchell Minstrels*
WEEK 2		
US45	Big Girls Don't Cry	*Four Seasons*
USLP	My Son The Folk Singer	*Allan Sherman*
UK45	Lovesick Blues	*Frank Ifield*
UKLP	On Stage With	*George Mitchell Minstrels*
WEEK 3		
US45	Big Girls Don't Cry	*Four Seasons*
USLP	The First Family	*Vaughan Meader*
UK45	Return To Sender	*Elvis Presley*
UKLP	On Stage With	*George Mitchell Minstrels*
WEEK 4		
US45	Telstar	*Tornados*
USLP	The First Family	*Vaughan Meader*
UK45	Return To Sender	*Elvis Presley*
UKLP	On Stage With	*George Mitchell Minstrels*
WEEK 5		
US45	Telstar	*Tornados*
USLP	The First Family	*Vaughan Meader*
UK45	The Next Time	*Cliff Richard*
UKLP	On Stage With	*George Mitchell Minstrels*

Elvis the record breaker

RULE BRITANNIA – BRITISH BEAT INVADES AMERICA

It's interesting to note that each time popular music has gone off the boil in the 35 years covered by this book, history reveals that a return to the roots will usually provide rehabilitation. The first time it occurred was the most significant, back in 1964, when an event known in the US as "The British Invasion" took place.

Rock'n'roll music was hardly ten years old, but already its youthful audience had demonstrated one of its most noticeable characteristics, one which still continues today – a short attention span coupled with an insatiable appetite for something new. Early rock'n'roll's first hero, Bill Haley, seemed too old, Elvis Presley's stint as a GI seemed to have made his music soft, Jerry Lee Lewis was in disgrace for marrying his 13 year old cousin, Little Richard had got religion, Chuck Berry was in prison, Buddy Holly was dead, and the new stars who had risen seemed less exciting and flamboyant.

Very few British records had penetrated the US chart before 1964 – you could almost count them on the fingers of one hand: Laurie London, Lonnie Donegan, The Tornados, maybe one or two more. However, in the wake of Donegan, innumerable semi-professional British groups had sprung up all over Great Britain, most of them playing songs they'd heard on records by Americans, in particular songs with a strong rhythm & blues bias à la Berry or Holly.

Liverpool (the port where many ships from America docked) was one port where American sailors sold their records, London was obviously another, and it was these international cities which became the headquarters of the British beat group phenomenon. In fact, many of the best Liverpool bands had already ventured to Hamburg (the Liverpool of West Germany), where they not only played music in the style of the great rock'n'roll

Overnight success – The Stones

Herman's Hermits

The Dave Clark Five

DJ John Peel made it first in US

The Kinks regularly toured the State

pioneers, but also began writing original (if primitive) material. The Beatles, Gerry & The Pacemakers, The Searchers and others were rocking in Hamburg while the US and UK were pretending that the twist, ersatz rockers like Frankie Avalon and Bobby Rydell, and in Britain, Cliff Richard & The Shadows, were filling the gap caused by the demise of original rock'n'roll.

It initially happened in Britain. The charts for the first three months of 1963 were dominated by Cliff & Co., then Liverpool acts shut out virtually all the competition for the top slot in the UK singles chart. Initially, the United States was unenthusiastic, despite the fact that the rest of the English-speaking world had capitulated, but the appearance of The Beatles on the influential 'Ed Sullivan Show' opened the floodgates for literally dozens of British groups to achieve commercial success in the New World. Some acts, such as Dave Clark, Herman and The Zombies (from St. Albans), found greater success in North America than they would ever achieve in their own country. Ultimately, virtually every British group of any note from the mid-1960s made it in the States, including The Who, The Rolling Stones, The Hollies, The Yardbirds, The Moody Blues, Cream, Traffic, Pink Floyd and The Troggs (although in some cases, success did not occur overnight as it had for The Beatles and The Stones).

For the first time since rock'n'roll was born, America wasn't totally predominant, and American acts like The Walker Brothers and later Jimi Hendrix successfully launched themselves in Britain before returning to reap the bigger rewards provided in their homeland.

America's return to control came via '60s soul music and then psychedelia – both these styles had much in common with R&B and country music, the joint sources of rock'n'roll, and their victory over the marauding Brits came much more gradually than the tidal wave bearing British beat music. What was different – and remains one of the British Invasion's most impressive achievements – was that Britain would henceforth be taken seriously as an inventive and trend-setting source of popular music.

nfred Mann

Original UK export Lonnie Donegan

Bigger in the US – Peter and Gordon

The Beatles – opened the floodgates

1, 2, 3 FOR EX-SHADS, SHADS AND BOSS

An amazing set of circumstances has resulted in a most unique chart hat-trick: Jet Harris and Tony Meehan – once The Shadows' rhythm section – have leap-frogged to No. 1 on the UK charts with their duo debut, 'Diamonds'.

In the process of establishing themselves as a new instrumental chart force to be reckoned with, Jet and Tony pushed their former colleagues' 'Dance On' from the top slot down to No. 2, while front man Cliff Richard's 'Bachelor Boy' has moved up to No. 3 and his 'The Next Time' rests at No. 7.

Other artists with two singles each in this week's UK Top 30: The Tornados ('Globetrotter' at No. 4 and 'Telstar' at No. 22) and Frank Ifield ('The Wayward Wind' at No. 17 while 'Lovesick Blues' is at No. 19).

Tony (left) and Jet – 'Diamonds' takes ex-Shads to the top

BLIND BOY GRUNT

In London, Bob Dylan adopted the unlikely pseudonym 'Blind Boy Grunt' when he dropped by Doug Dobell's Jazz Record Shop at 77, Charing Cross Road to blow harmonica on a Dick Farina and Eric Von Schmidt recording session taking place on the premises.

The reason for Dylan's visit to London was to perform 'Blowin' In The Wind' and 'Swan On The River' in his role as a hobo in BBC-TV's drama 'Mad House On Castle Street'.

ELVIS ACAPULCO-BOUND

With Swedish femme fatale Ursula Andress cast as his leading lady, Elvis Presley has been a little more eager than usual to begin work on a new movie.

This time around, the sun'n' sand scenario has been entitled 'Fun In Acapulco'. In sticking close to a Mexican theme, the soundtrack material will include 'Bossa Nova Baby' and '(There's) No Room To Rhumba In A Sports Car'.

THE GRAPEVINE

- Hollywood's latest rock spot, The Whiskey-A-Go-Go discotheque has opened on Sunset Boulevard.
- A second UK single from The Beatles: 'Please Please Me' backed with 'Ask Me Why'.
- Phil Everly has married Jackie Ertel.
- 'Rhythm Of The Rain' by The Cascades promises to be one of the month's more endurable hits.
- The Beatles have signed to Chicago's Vee-Jay label for the States.

Beatles records to be released Stateside

TORNADOS DOUBLE GOLD

Joe Meek-produced instrumental five-piece and singer Billy Fury's backing group The Tornados, have received a second Gold Disc in recognition of their hit 'Telstar' having sold in excess of two million copies world-wide.

The Tornados are the third British-based act to gain this coveted double-gold award inside twelve months.

Mr Acker Bilk with his lyrically haunting 'Stranger On The Shore' was the first. Similarly, Aussie singer Frank Ifield struck double-gold with his reworked oldie, 'I Remember You'.

CHARTS

US45	Telstar *Tornadoes*
USLP	The First Family *Vaughn Meader*
UK45	Dance On *Shadows*
UKLP	On Stage With *George Mitchell Minstrels*
WEEK 2	
US45	Go Away Little Girl *Steve Lawrence*
USLP	The First Family *Vaughn Meader*
UK45	Dance On *Shadows*
UKLP	West Side Story *Soundtrack*
WEEK 3	
US45	Go Away Little Girl *Steve Lawrence*
USLP	The First Family *Vaughn Meader*
UK45	Dance On *Shadows*
UKLP	West Side Story *Soundtrack*
WEEK 4	
US45	Walk Right In *Rooftop Singers*
USLP	The First Family *Vaughn Meader*
UK45	Diamonds *Jet Harris & Tony Meehan*
UKLP	West Side Story *Soundtrack*

TRAD AT PALACE

It's still Trad, Dad! – the single biggest trad jazz event to be staged in Britain, has taken place in the Great Hall of North London's Alexandra Palace.

Held from 10 pm on Friday until 7 am the following morning, hosts George Melly and Diz Disley introduced the New Orleans-style jazz of such popular British bandleaders as Mr Acker Bilk, Chris Barber, Kenny Ball, Alex Welsh, Ken Colyer, Monty Sunshine, Bob Wallis, Bruce Turner, Mick Mulligan and at least half-a-dozen others.

AUSSIE FRANK CLEANS UP

Ifield's yodelling hat trick

In the space of just 12 months, clean-cut blond Australian singer Frank Ifield has emerged from obscurity to slip in comfortably behind both Elvis Presley and Cliff Richard as the third most popular best-selling recording artist in the UK during 1962.

This has been achieved on the strength of three consecutive country-pop oldies which have all grabbed the No. 1 position: 'I Remember You', 'Lovesick Blues' and 'Wayward Wind' – the first two being million-plus gold record winners in double-quick time.

Ifield (25), a successful recording artist back in Australia, arrived in Britain an unknown and that's how things remained for three years until, after a few false starts, he clicked in a big way – both here and in the US – with 'I Remember You'.

This hitmaker, whose vocal trade mark is a small yodel, confessed: 'When I arrived in Britain, I thought to myself, "Well, one thing that's out of the act now is yodelling!" After I got here, I gave myself five years to get to the top, but I did it in three.'

His worldwide success has made Ifield a much in-demand performer and his 1963 diary is almost filled. A debut album is to be released next month, and it has been announced that he's to be the main attraction during the London Palladium's prestigious 1963 resident Summer Revue. Meanwhile, he's considering offers to star in a full-length semi-autobiographical movie.

CHARTS

US45	Walk Right In *Rooftop Singers*
USLP	The First Family *Vaughn Meader*
UK45	Diamonds *Jet Harris & Tony Meehan*
UKLP	Summer Holiday *Cliff Richard*
WEEK 2	
US45	Hey Paula *Paul & Paula*
USLP	The First Family *Vaughn Meader*
UK45	Diamonds *Jet Harris & Tony Meehan*
UKLP	Summer Holiday *Cliff Richard*
WEEK 3	
US45	Hey Paula *Paul & Paula*
USLP	The First Family *Vaughn Meader*
UK45	Diamonds *Jet Harris & Tony Meehan*
UKLP	Summer Holiday *Cliff Richard*
WEEK 4	
US45	Hey Paula *Paul & Paula*
USLP	The First Family *Vaughn Meader*
UK45	The Wayward Wind *Frank Ifield*
UKLP	Summer Holiday *Cliff Richard*

THE GRAPEVINE

- **Helen Shapiro plus The Beatles have embarked on a twice-nightly 15-city UK tour.**
- **Paul Anka has married Anne De Zogheb – daughter of Comte and Comtess Charles Zogheb – in Paris.**
- **Actor Clint Eastwood has attempted to capitalize on his popular *Rawhide* TV role as cowpoke Rowdy Yates, with a single 'Rowdy'.**
- **Publisher Dick James has started Northern Songs to handle the songs of Lennon and McCartney.**

Clint Eastwood – Rowdy record

ELVIS – NEW RCA DEAL

Elvis Presley, who has sold the equivalent of 100 million singles in eight years, has renewed his contract with RCA-Victor. This new deal, which lasts for ten years, guarantees Elvis a minimum of around two million dollars with scope to earn much more.

From his records and movies alone, Presley's personal income is now reported to be in excess of one-and-a-half million dollars a year. The lucrative long-term contract is viewed within the record industry as RCA's faith in Presley's world-wide staying power as a major recording star.

Aside from movies and records – the former bringing him approximately $10,000-a-day on the set, Elvis is said to receive 2.5% of all souvenir products retailed in the US in his name. These include soft toys, record players, stationery, jewellery and clothes, and sales of these are estimated to reach two million dollars.

PATSY CLINE KILLED IN PLANE CRASH

Country music stars Patsy Cline (30), Lloyd 'Cowboy' Copas (50) and Harold 'Hawkshaw' Hawkins (41) all perished when the light aircraft carrying them home after a benefit concert in Kansas City crashed at Camden, Tennessee, on March 5.

Patsy Cline was best known for a string of hits that included 'Walking After Midnight' and 'I Fall To Pieces'. Cowboy Copas had recently enjoyed a chart comeback with 'Alabam', while Hawkshaw Hawkins had 'Sunny Side Of The Mountain' and 'Lonesome 7-7203' to his credit.

Only two years ago, Patsy Cline narrowly escaped death in a road crash. She was a passenger in her brother's car when it was involved in a collision in which a man in another vehicle was killed. She overcame her serious injuries and fought her way back to the top again, winning Billboard magazine's dj poll last autumn as best female country vocalist.

Early reports suggest that the plane carrying Cline and friends may have been flying upside down when it crashed – it was in the middle of a severe windstorm at the time, which could account for it being flipped over.

CHARTS

US45	Walk Like A Man *Four Seasons*
USLP	The First Family *Vaughn Meader*
UK45	Please Please Me *Beatles*
UKLP	Summer Holiday *Cliff Richard*
WEEK 2	
US45	Walk Like A Man *Four Seasons*
USLP	The First Family *Vaughn Meader*
UK45	Summer Holiday *Cliff Richard*
UKLP	Summer Holiday *Cliff Richard*
WEEK 3	
US45	Walk Like A Man *Four Seasons*
USLP	Songs I Sing On The Jackie Gleason Show *Frank Fontaine*
UK45	Summer Holiday *Cliff Richard*
UKLP	Summer Holiday *Cliff Richard*
WEEK 4	
US45	Our Day Will Come *Ruby & The Romantics*
USLP	Songs I Sing On The Jackie Gleason Show *Frank Fontaine*
UK45	Summer Holiday *Cliff Richard*
UKLP	Summer Holiday *Cliff Richard*
WEEK 5	
US45	He's So Fine *Chiffons*
USLP	Songs I Sing On The Jackie Gleason Show *Frank Fontaine*
UK45	Foot Tapper *Shadows*
UKLP	Summer Holiday *Cliff Richard*

Chart newcomer Otis Redding

Marriott borrows from Buddy?

THE GRAPEVINE

- Otis Redding has made his first chart appearance with 'These Arms Of Mine'.
- Tommy Roe and Chris Montez upstaged by both The Beatles and their fans on their 21-day UK trek.
- Cockney child actor Steve Marriott has made his disc debut with Buddy Holly-inspired 'Give Her My Regards'.
- Merseysiders Gerry & The Pacemakers also on disc for the first time with 'How Do You Do It?'.

TORME: I'M NO ROCKER!'

Mel Torme, currently enjoying crossover chart success with 'Comin' Home Baby', is attempting to distance himself from the rest of the hit parade pack.

'Please, please, don't call it rock and roll,' he says of his single. 'I do not like rock and roll and I do not sing rock and roll.

'Now that I have a hit record – which is a great feeling for both ego and wallet – I still won't sing rock and roll. 'Comin' Home Baby' is a jazz song. To be more specific, it's rhythm'n'blues that started life as a jass instrumental on an album by jazz flute player, Herbie Mann and written by bassist Ben Tucker.

'And, I hope it is sung by jazz singer – Melvin Howard Torme. That's me! The teenage market may be where the big money is today, and they may well be the ones who are buying it. But it's not rock and roll!' he added.

BERRY SUES BRIAN

Brian Wilson was audacious enough to have fitted a brand new set of self-penned lyrics to Chuck Berry's 'Sweet Little Sixteen', retitled it 'Surfin' U.S.A.', and put it out as The Beach Boys' latest single for Capitol.

Natch, Chuck and his music publisher have sued, but a co-composer name-check and a sackful of greenbacks have helped make the injured parties feel less hurt!

Chuck makes up with The Beach Boys

Gerry & The Pacemakers rehearse their action-packed show. How do they do it?

EPSTEIN LAUNCHES BILLY J

Billy J. cuts Beatlesongs

On what appears to be an unstoppable winning streak, Brian Epstein has launched his very latest Liverpudlian protegées, Billy J. Kramer & The Dakotas, and ensured them instant success with their first Parlophone single by pairing two valuable Lennon & McCartney compositions 'Do You Want To Know A Secret' and 'I'll Be On My Way'.

As with other NEMS managed acts such as The Beatles, Gerry & The Pacemakers, The Fourmost and Cilla Black, ballad-singing Billy J. Kramer's records have been produced by George Martin.

So as not to feel outdone, Manchester's answer to NEMS – Kennedy Street Enterprises' local comic-rockers, Freddie & The Dreamers – have also debuted with a cover of James Ray's R&B waltz-time classic, 'If You Gotta Make A Fool Of Somebody'.

Cavern cloakroom attendant Priscilla White, one of the NEMS stars

PYE RELEASE CHESS IN UK

Having acquired the UK rights to the Chicago-based Chess label catalogue, Pye Records have proudly launched their red and yellow label 'Chicago R&B series with albums from Chuck Berry and Bo Diddley, plus inaugural singles from Sonny Boy Williamson, Howlin' Wolf, Bo Diddley and local Marquee Club favourites, harmonica man Cyril Davies & His All-Stars.

Bo Diddley for Pye

OLDHAM, EASTON SIGN STONES

Flamboyant pop publicist, Andrew 'Loog' Oldham and his boss, theatrical manager Eric Easton, have signed London R&B group The Rolling Stones to an exclusive management contract.

At the recommendation of George Harrison, both Oldham and Easton drove out to The Crawdaddy Club, Richmond on April 28, to catch The Rolling Stones in action.

Easton was impressed by the group's energy, but had certain reservations about just how commercial they were. There were no such doubts for Oldham, who admitted gazing at the prancing Mick Jagger the way Sylvester looks at Tweetie Pie.

'I knew what I was looking at,' confessed the pole-axed publicist as The Stones worked the audience up into a frenzy. 'It was SEX. And, I was 48 hours ahead of the pack.'

ROE SOUNDS OFF

In a candid interview, America's Tommy Roe expressed his views on the current crop of UK groups:

'Somebody asked me if I liked British pop music, and I'm afraid I had to tell them the truth: I don't. Not most of it anyway,' he said.

'I don't mean they are of poor quality – I was constantly impressed by the high standard of singing and production. It's just that there is something about the 'feel' of them, the atmosphere, that I feel unable to appreciate.

'Perhaps that's why British vocal discs haven't done so well in the States . . . all the big British hits have been instrumentals like 'Stranger On The Shore', 'Telstar' and 'Midnight In Mosow'.

'There's only one British group I rave over – it's The Beatles. They have a truly fantastic *American* sound. If they went to the States, they couldn't go wrong!'

CHARTS

US45	He's So Fine	*Chiffons*
USLP	Songs I Sing On The Jackie Gleason Show	*Frank Fontaine*
UK45	How Do You Do It	*Gerry & The Pacemakers*
UKLP	Summer Holiday	*Cliff Richard*
WEEK 2		
US45	He's So Fine	*Chiffons*
USLP	Songs I Sing On The Jackie Gleason Show	*Frank Fontaine*
UK45	How Do You Do It	*Gerry & The Pacemakers*
UKLP	Summer Holiday	*Cliff Richard*
WEEK 3		
US45	He's So Fine	*Chiffons*
USLP	West Side Story	*Soundtrack*
UK45	How Do You Do It	*Gerry & The Pacemakers*
UKLP	Summer Holiday	*Cliff Richard*
WEEK 4		
US45	I Will Follow Him	*Little Peggy March*
USLP	West Side Story	*Soundtrack*
UK45	From Me To You	*Beatles*
UKLP	Summer Holiday	*Cliff Richard*

THE GRAPEVINE

- **Bob Dylan has given his first major solo concert, to ecstatic reviews, at New York's Town Hall.**
- **A third Parlophone single has been produced by The Beatles: 'From Me To You'.**
- **Having scored sales of 60-million records, Fats Domino has quit Imperial Records to sign with ABC-Paramount.**
- **This month's dance floor-filler: Ray Barretto's 'El Watusi'.**

MAY

1963

STAR QUOTE

BILLY FURY

'I have often been called the last of the rock and rollers – and quite frankly I take this as a compliment – but I don't agree with this tag line: there are a lot of great rock singers in this country.'

Fury: last of a line?

DYLAN'S DREAM: NO HASSLES

The fact that Bob Dylan's album debut has only sold 5,000 copies has prompted many CBS Records' executives to be less than enthusiastic over the young protest singer's immediate future on the label.

Only producer John Hammond's valuable patronage and the unshakeable support of Johnny Cash, have led to the release of a second LP, 'The Freewheelin' Bob Dylan'.

However, before the record reached the public, a number of behind-the-scenes dramas were enacted. Firstly, Dylan's New York Town Hall Concert of April 12 was taped for release and then promptly shelved.

On May 12, Dylan failed to make his national TV debut on 'The Ed Sullivan Show', when CBS top brass vetoed Dylan's plan to perform his controversial 'Talking John Birch Society Blues' on the programme. The decision prompted him to turn on his boot-heels and walk.

The knock-on effect was that CBS Records scrapped 'Freewheelin's' original track listing and replaced four songs – 'Rocks And Gravel', 'Alabama Woman Blues', 'Let Me Die In My Footsteps', 'Ramblin', Gamblin Willie' and the ultra-sensitive 'Talking John Birch Paranoid Blues' – with four Dylan had recorded on April 24: 'Girl From The North Country', 'Masters Of War', 'Bob Dylan's Dream' and 'Talking World War III Blues'.

Not-quite-folk, not-quite-pop, but a success formula for chart-toppers The Springfields

SPRINGFIELDS MAKE HITS FROM FOLK

Though voted No. 1 British vocal group in NME's 1961 and 1963 readers' poll, things have moved slowly chartwise in the UK for folk-pop trio The Springfields – currently in the top five with 'Say I Won't Be There'.

However, it has been the success of their uptempo rewrite of the traditional French song 'au Clair de Lune', and their previous single 'Island Of Dreams' which has transformed them into one of Britain's major musical exports.

Londoners all, The Springfields comprise brother and sister Tom and Dusty Springfield (Dion and Mary O'Brien), and Mike Hurst (Michael Longhurst-Pickworth).

'Say I Won't Be There' has followed The Springfields' pattern of re-interpreting traditional folk material.

Their disc debut, 'Dear John' was the American Civil War song 'Marching Thro' Georgia' with new lyrics and 'Silver Threads And Golden Needles' yet another country folk standard.

Recalling the group's early days, Tom Springfield revealed: 'Once, when we auditioned for a BBC producer, he told us we had to make a decision. We either had to be a folk group or a pop group if we were going to have any success at all. But, of course, we fell between the two!'

CHARTS

Chart	Title	Artist
US45	I Will Follow Him	*Little Peggy March*
USLP	Days Of Wine And Roses	*Andy Williams*
UK45	From Me To You	*Beatles*
UKLP	Summer Holiday	*Cliff Richard*
WEEK 2		
US45	I Will Follow Him	*Little Peggy March*
USLP	Days Of Wine And Roses	*Andy Williams*
UK45	From Me To You	*Beatles*
UKLP	Please Please Me	*Beatles*
WEEK 3		
US45	If You Wanna Be Happy	*Jimmy Soul*
USLP	Days Of Wine And Roses	*Andy Williams*
UK45	From Me To You	*Beatles*
UKLP	Please Please Me	*Beatles*
WEEK 4		
US45	If You Wanna Be Happy	*Jimmy Soul*
USLP	Days Of Wine And Roses	*Andy Williams*
UK45	From Me To You	*Beatles*
UKLP	Please Please Me	*Beatles*

THE GRAPEVINE

- **Bob Dylan, Joan Baez, Pete Seeger, Peter, Paul & Mary, The Weavers and Mance Lipscomb headlined the first Monterey Folk Festival in California.**
- **Innovative Mississippi-bluesman Elmore James has died, aged 45.**
- **Billy Fury has released his first album of all-new material in three years.**
- **The once outlawed Jerry Lee Lewis has returned for a UK tour with Gene Vincent.**

LENNON LASHES OUT

Though there was much amusement when Paul McCartney was dragged out of Abbey Road Studios two days earlier by John, George and Ringo and publicly bumped to celebrate his 21st birthday, the atmosphere at a party held in Liverpool on June 20 turned violent.

Bob Wooler, the Cavern Club d.j, loudly insinuated to anyone who'd listen, that Brian Epstein and John Lennon were lovers, and was promptly gifted with a black-eye from the latter for his troubles.

Although news of the fracas made an item in the first edition of the next morning's Liverpool Echo, the NEMS PR machine went into overdrive to stop the news spreading further afield. Within days, the fight was no more than an unsubstantiated rumour, with everyone at the party maintaining a wall of secrecy.

Cover up – The Beatles

MARTIN: 'NO LIVERPOOL SOUND'

'There is no such thing as a *Liverpool Sound*,' George Martin, Britain's leading record producer insists. 'I prefer to talk of the Beatles sound – after all, they started it!'

Martin, who has masterminded massive hits for such acts as The Beatles, Gerry & The Pacemakers and Billy J. Kramer & The Dakotas, explains his theory:

'I'm not suggesting that other groups copy The Beatles. Quite the contrary, for their styles are wholly different. That's why you can't lump them together under the heading of a Liverpool Sound.'

Jerry Lee – Bible part?

STAR QUOTE

JERRY LEE LEWIS

'Though it's a little hard to imagine, I wanna get a part in a Bible movie . . . 'bout the only thing I could do is be a slave or somethin' . . . that would really be a good lick!'

CHARTS

US45	It's My Party	*Lesley Gore*
USLP	Days Of Wine And Roses	*Andy Williams*
UK45	Do You Want To Know A Secret	*Billy J Kramer*
UKLP	Please Please Me	*Beatles*
WEEK 2		
US45	It's My Party	*Lesley Gore*
USLP	Days Of Wine And Roses	*Andy Williams*
UK45	Do You Want To Know A Secret	*Billy J Kramer*
UKLP	Please Please Me	*Beatles*
WEEK 3		
US45	Sukiyaki	*Kyu Sakamoto*
USLP	Days Of Wine And Roses	*Andy Williams*
UK45	I Like It	*Gerry & The Pacemakers*
UKLP	Please Please Me	*Beatles*
WEEK 4		
US45	Sukiyaki	*Kyu Sakamoto*
USLP	Days Of Wine And Roses	*Andy Williams*
UK45	I Like It	*Gerry & The Pacemakers*
UKLP	Please Please Me	*Beatles*
WEEK 5		
US45	Sukiyaki	*Kyu Sakamoto*
USLP	Days Of Wine And Roses	*Andy Williams*
UK45	I Like It	*Gerry & The Pacemakers*
UKLP	Please Please Me	*Beatles*

THE GRAPEVINE

- **The BBC have launched a new Radio series: 'Pop Go The Beatles'.**
- **The late Buddy Holly is back in the UK charts for the second time this year with 'Bo Diddley'.**
- **The Rolling Stones have released their reworking of Chuck Berry's 'Come On'.**
- **'Fingertips Part 2' by 12-year old blind singer-instrumentalist Little Stevie Wonder turning into a hot summer hit.**

LOW-KEY STONES DEBUT, SWEETER FOR SEARCHERS

The Rolling Stones' debut single – a cover of Chuck Berry's seldom-heard 'Come On' – has been given a somewhat low-key launch by Decca Records.

Over the last few weeks there has been much more media interest in the first singles from three Manchester groups: The Hollies '(Ain't That) Just Like Me', Wayne Fontana & The Mindbenders 'Roadrunner' and comic rockers Freddie & The Dreamers 'If You Gotta Make A Fool Of Somebody'.

Popular London band Manfred Mann have made it on to vinyl with 'Why Should We Not', while on Merseyside, it's been The Swinging Blue Jeans with 'It's Too Late' and Freddie Starr & The Midnighters who tried their luck with 'Who Told You'.

But the biggest interest has been centred on The Searchers, whose combination of high-pitched nasal vocals and jingly-jangly guitars has made them one of the 'Pool's most popular local groups. They have only just released their first single on Pye, a highly-personalized treatment of The old Drifters' song 'Sweets For My Sweet'.

The Searchers, who all sing, comprise Mike Pender (lead guitar), John McNally (rhythm guitar), Tony Jackson (bass) and Chris Curtis (drums).

Sweets sound of Searchers

CHARLES: 'NO ROOM FOR COMPLACENCY'

Ray Charles's influence on a broad spectrum of contemporary American popular music is immeasurable.

From fashioning soul music through to incorporating elements of blues, jazz, gospel, R&B, pop and country & western into his work, he has scored countless worldwide crossover hits such as 'What'd I Say', 'Georgia On My Mind', 'I Got A Woman', 'Busted', 'Hit The Road Jack', 'One Mint Julep', 'I Can't Stop Loving You' plus such best-selling LPs as 'The Genius Of Ray Charles', 'Genius + Soul = Jazz' and 'Modern Sounds In Country & Western'.

Not for nothing is Ray Charles referred to as 'The Genius Of Soul'. The man and his music are inseparable.

'I try to put on a show . . . a band show that is, not just a band of musicians playing a set pattern of numbers and nothing else. That's why I branched out into what people call pop material, although I reckon some of my early blues singing and playing was popular enough,' he explains.

'But I don't want to get known as a labelled man. I want to work any kind of concert, to fit in anywhere. I used to sing a lot more of the down home blues, but since songs like 'I Can't Stop Loving You', I have really broadened out.

'About the only concrete thing you can say about my singing, as far as I'm concerned, is that I try to instil a little bit of soul into everything. It comes from suffering some sort of depression, some kind of hard times.

'Right now, there's no question of hard times, but these things have a habit of lingering,' he adds. 'You remember them – those early years of struggle. And, you also remember that nobody has it made. I can't afford to slip into a rut, into complacency.'

Miracles, with leader Smokey Robinson

THE GRAPEVINE

- 'Mickey's Monkey' is the latest release from The Miracles.
- Del Shannon has become the first US artist to make Billboard's charts with a Beatles' cover – 'From Me To You'.
- Former Tornadoes' bassist Heinz has released his Joe Meek-produced Cochran tribute, 'Just Like Eddie'.
- Billy J. Kramer is backing another winner with two more unheard Lennon & McCartney songs: 'Bad To Me' and 'I Call Your Name'.

VEE-JAY IN UK

Launched in Britain to meet and fuel the growing demand among young clubgoers for authentic American R&B singles without having to pay inflated import prices, EMI's Stateside label has got it right first time with a trio of singles leased from Chicago's Vee-Jay operation: John Lee Hooker's insistent and commercial 'Boom Boom', Jimmy Reed's 'Shame, Shame, Shame' and Roscoe Gordon's 'Just A Little Bit'.

CHARTS

US45	Easier Said Than Done *The Essex*
USLP	Days Of Wine And Roses *Andy Williams*
UK45	I Like It *Gerry & The Pacemakers*
UKLP	Please Please Me *Beatles*
WEEK 2	
US45	Easier Said Than Done *The Essex*
USLP	Days Of Wine And Roses *Andy Williams*
UK45	Confessin' (That I Love You) *Frank Ifield*
UKLP	Please Please Me *Beatles*
WEEK 3	
US45	Surf City *Jan & Dean*
USLP	Days Of Wine And Roses *Andy Williams*
UK45	Confessin' (That I Love You) *Frank Ifield*
UKLP	Please Please Me *Beatles*
WEEK 4	
US45	Surf City *Jan & Dean*
USLP	Days Of Wine And Roses *Andy Williams*
UK45	Confessin' (That I Love You) *Frank Ifield*
UKLP	Please Please Me *Beatles*

MORE MERSEY BEAT

Liverpool hasn't been completely plundered of talent.

All those Merseyside groups that were not immediately signed up by London recording managers looking for another Beatles have been assembled by producer John Schroeder on to two Oriole LPs entitled 'This Is Mersey Beat'.

Among those featured are such local heroes as Faron's Flamingoes, The Mojos and Rory Storme & The Hurricanes.

More Merseybeat from the Mojos

Blues hero John Lee Hooker

AUGUST

JAN AND DEAN SURF TO THE TOP

Beat from the beach with surf songsters Jan and Dean

Britain might not have the climate in which to emulate Southern California's highly-desirable sun-soaked surfin' lifestyle, but it has a keen ear for the accompanying soundtrack, as supplied by such recent UK chart entries as The Chantays ('Pipeline'), The Surfaris ('Wipeout'), The Beach Boys ('Surfin' USA') and Jan & Dean ('Surf City').

The latter are Los Angelinos Jan Berry (21) and Dean Torrance (22), boyhood friends who were scoring close-harmony hits when still at university.

Following the initial success of local label hits, a switch to Liberty and a nation-wide best-seller – 'Linda' – made the duo turn their attention more towards music-making.

Soon after, a link-up with Brian Wilson (and his songwriting partner Roger Christian) quickly made Jan & Dean an even bigger attraction than The Beach Boys, by virtue of 'Surf City'. A furious Capitol Records threatened to sue The Beach Boys because of Brian Wilson's audible contributions to the record's success.

Jan & Dean's sun-bleached athletic good-looks have come to epitomise the surfin' image ('Surfin' all day – sturdy surf bunnies by night!') especially since it became known that for all The Beach Boys' endeavours to promote this new beach culture, only drummer Dennis Wilson actually surfs!

CHARTS

Chart	Title	Artist
US45	So Much In Love	*Tymes*
USLP	Days Of Wine And Roses	*Andy Williams*
UK45	Sweets For My Sweet	*Searchers*
UKLP	Please Please Me	*Beatles*
	WEEK 2	
US45	Fingertips Part II	*Stevie Wonder*
USLP	Days Of Wine And Roses	*Andy Williams*
UK45	Sweets For My Sweet	*Searchers*
UKLP	Please lease Me	*Beatles*
	WEEK 3	
US45	Fingertips Part II	*Stevie Wonder*
USLP	Days Of Wine And Roses	*Andy Williams*
UK45	Sweets For My Sweet	*Searchers*
UKLP	Please Please Me	*Beatles*
	WEEK 4	
US45	Fingertips Part II	*Stevie Wonder*
USLP	Little Stevie Wonder	*Stevie Wonder*
UK45	Bad To Me	*Billy J Kramer & The Dakotas*
UKLP	Please Please Me	*Beatles*
	WEEK 5	
US45	My Boyfriend's Back	*The Angels*
USLP	My Son, The Nut	*Allan Sherman*
UK45	Bad To Me	*Billy J Kramer & The Dakotas*
UKLP	Please Please Me	*Beatles*

DYLAN: VOICE OF PROTEST

With 'The Freewheelin' Bob Dylan' having sold in excess of 250,000 copies, Dylan has become acknowledged as America's foremost folk singer.

Peter, Paul & Mary have transformed two 'Freewheelin'' tracks – 'Blowin' In The Wind' and 'Don't Think Twice, It's All Right' – into Top 40 hits and protest movement anthems, Joan Baez features many of Dylan's songs in her concert repertoire and is frequently joined onstage by the singer-composer.

As the protest movement gathers momentum across the United States, Bob Dylan makes his position clear, in words and music.

SUTCH FOR PARLIAMENT?

Screamin' Lord Sutch has announced that he will stand as an independent candidate in the forthcoming Stratford-On-Avon by-election.

Should he win, the optimistic Lord David Sutch – a rock horror performer noted for such endearing ballads as 'Jack The Ripper' – insists that he will give up the pop business altogether to concentrate on his political career as a responsible Member of the British parliament. His loyal backing group, The Savages, will carry on their flamboyant act alone.

However, just in case the prized Stratford-On-Avon seat is, by a strange twist of fate, won by a member of one of the established political parties, His Lordship's manager has taken the precaution of booking an October UK tour for Sutch, to be followed by a Paris engagement.

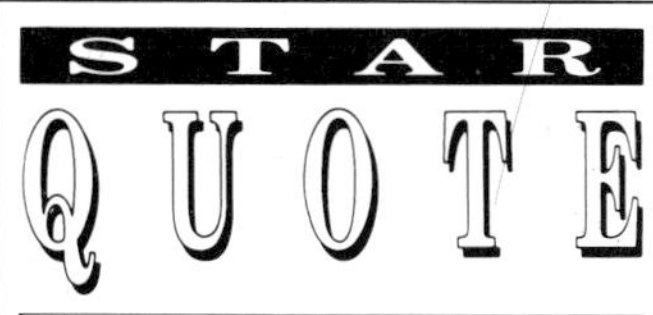

- **The Beatles collected £300 ($900) for their last-ever Cavern Club date, and the first edition of 'The Beatles Monthly' has gone on sale.**
- **Jerry Lee Lewis has announced that he's not resigning from Sun Records: Liberty have guaranteed him $10,000 a year until 1968.**
- **A new movie trend is catching on Stateside with 'Beach Party' starring Frankie Avalon, Annette Funicello and Dick Dale & The Del-Tones.**

STAR QUOTE

GERRY MARSDEN

'The Beatles and ourselves (The Pacemakers) – we let go when we get on-stage. I'm not being detrimental, but in the south, I think the groups have let themselves get a bit too formal. On Merseyside, it's beat, beat, beat all the way. We go on and really have a ball.'

More beach fun: Frankie Avalon

PACEMAKERS – HOW DO THEY DO IT?

In the space of just eight brief months, chirpy Liverpudlians Gerry & The Pacemakers have earned themselves the unprecedented distinction of becoming the first act ever to reach the UK chart top slot with their first three consecutive single releases.

First, there was the breezy 'How Do You Do It?' – the Mitch Murray composition The Beatles had earlier vetoed – followed by an equally carefree Murray ditty 'I Like It'. And, now they have made it a hat-trick with a complete change of mood and an anthemic big beat ballad treatment of Rodgers & Hammerstein's 'You'll Never Walk Alone' from the hit US musical, 'Carousel'.

At the time of preparing both this crucial third single, plus a bunch of their stage show covers for their upcoming LP debut, 'How Do You Like It?' Gerry openly confessed his anxieties as well as his immediate plans.

'I can't begin to tell you how we're worried about our next single: getting the number just right and so on,' he said. 'I don't even know what it's going to be, though the chances are on a certain little ditty I've written myself!'

He wasn't disclosing too much about the mainly R&B material he and The Pacemakers have been recording over the previous weeks, except to enthuse over 'You'll Never Walk Alone', which has long been a popular cornerstone of The Pacemakers' 'live' performances.

'I'm really made up by the way that turned out. Because we play it every night in our set, there wasn't any difficulty recording it,' he confided.

CHARTS

US45	My Boyfriend's Back – *The Angels*
USLP	My Son, The Nut – *Allan Sherman*
UK45	She Loves You – *Beatles*
UKLP	Please Please Me – *Beatles*
WEEK 2	
US45	My Boyfriend's Back – *The Angels*
USLP	My Son, The Nut – *Allan Sherman*
UK45	She Loves You – *Beatles*
UKLP	Please Please Me – *Beatles*
WEEK 3	
US45	Blue Velvet – *Bobby Vinton*
USLP	My Son, The Nut – *Allan Sherman*
UK45	She Loves You – *Beatles*
UKLP	Please Please Me – *Beatles*
WEEK 4	
US45	Blue Velvet – *Bobby Vinton*
USLP	My Son, The Nut – *Allan Sherman*
UK45	She Loves You – *Beatles*
UKLP	Please Please Me – *Beatles*

RICHARD ROCKS TO THE RESCUE!

Little Richard, who'd previously vowed he'd never do another rock tour, is being airlifted into Britain by local promoter Don Arden to take over as headline attraction on The Everly Brothers flagging 30-date UK tour.

Richard, who is regarded by British and European rock fans as the nearest thing to perfect, is to join up with the tour on October 5 hopefully to boost hitherto bad box-office business.

Surprisingly, the support bill of US R&B cult star Bo Diddley and The Rolling Stones, plus Julie Grant and Mickie Most, hasn't been sufficient to create more than half-full halls.

However, before leaving for the UK, Little Richard has the task of informing his family and friends that after years of religious studies – and despite the fact that he's soon to qualify as a Billy Graham-style evangalist preacher – the emergence of the British beat boom, the threat of The Beatles ('I taught them how to rock!') and the continued success of his friend Sam Cooke, has convinced him to leave the Church for what he truly does best – rockin' and rollin' . . .

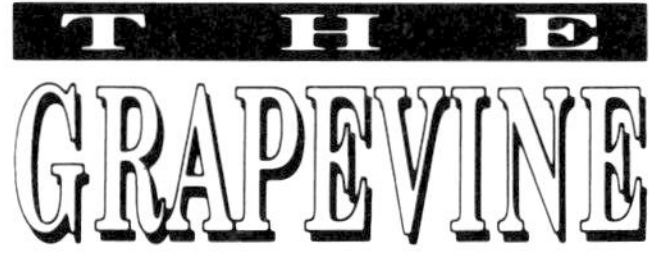

- Buddy Holly has notched up his third posthumous UK hit this year with 'Wishin''.
- 'We Want Billy' – a live LP from Billy Fury & The Tornados has been this month's hot UK long-player.
- Jet Harris and his singer girlfriend Billie Davis have been badly hurt in auto accident.
- Despite insisting that he's to join Elvis at RCA, Jerry Lee Lewis has signed to Smash.

THE SHADOWS

'What's the most distinctive sound of our group? We often wondered what it is ourselves. Really, it is the sound we had when we recorded 'Apache' – that kind of Hawaiian sounding lead guitar . . . plus the beat.'

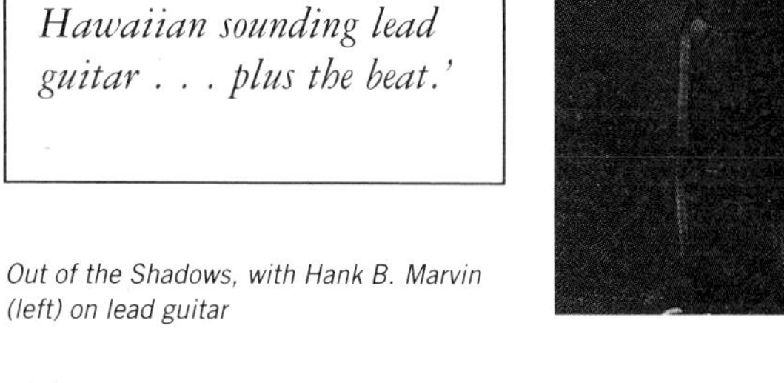

Out of the Shadows, with Hank B. Marvin (left) on lead guitar

Richard to the rescue of the Everly Brothers tour

COLONEL PARKER DISMISSES PRESLEY MOVIE CRITICS

As Elvis Presley records the truly dreadful soundtrack for his equally-dreadful MGM Li'l Abner-style *Kissin' Cousins* movie, Colonel Tom Parker chooses to ignore grumblings from fans concerning the quality and quantity of Elvis's conveyor-belt movie vehicles.

When pressed on why he didn't demand approval, the Colonel insisted: 'We have approval, but only on money. Anyway, what does Elvis need? A couple of songs, a little story and some nice people to go with him!'

According to the Colonel, he actually returned the script of *Kissin' Cousins* to the studio, unread. Attached to it was a personal memo: 'If you want an opinion or evaluation of this script, it will cost you an additional $25,000.'

To the movie's hapless director, Gene Nelson, the Colonel remarked: 'We don't know how to make movies. We have you for that. All we want are songs for an album.'

THE GRAPEVINE

- France's most popular singer, Edith Piaf, has died in Paris, aged 48.
- Voluptuous ex-Mouseketeer and Beach movie star, Annette (Funicello) celebrated her 21st birthday.
- There were incredible airport scenes this month as thousands of fans greeted The Beatles return home from a tour of Sweden.
- A second Searchers' single, 'Sugar and Spice', has been released.

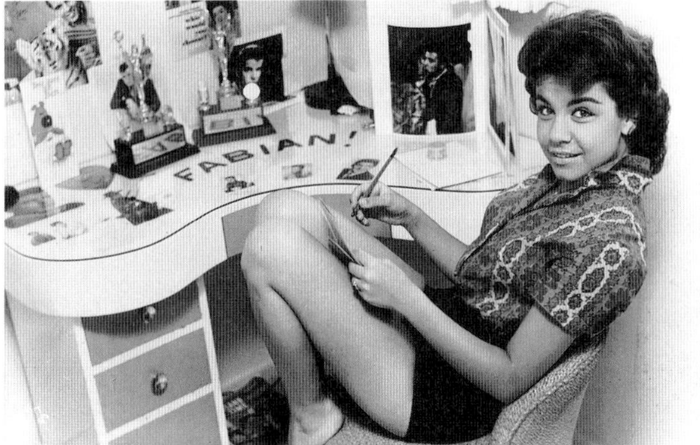

Funicello gets the vote and chooses Fabian

STAR QUOTE

FREDDIE

of The Dreamers

'The Dreamers and I have always been daft. You couldn't call me a sex-idol, could you? Collectively, we're no glamour boys!'

Freddie the Dreamer proves he's daft!

CHARTS

US45	Blue Velvet	*Bobby Vinton*
USLP	My Son, The Nut	*Allan Sherman*
UK45	Do You Love Me	*Brian Poole & The Tremeloes*
UKLP	Please Please Me	*Beatles*
	WEEK 2	
US45	Sugar Shack	*Jimmy Gilmer & The Fireballs*
USLP	My Son, The Nut	*Allan Sherman*
UK45	Do You Love Me	*Brian Poole & The Tremeloes*
UKLP	Please, Please Me	*Beatles*
	WEEK 3	
US45	Sugar Shack	*Jimmy Gilmer & The Fireballs*
USLP	My Son, The Nut	*Allan Sherman*
UK45	Do You Love Me	*Brian Poole & The Tremeloes*
UKLP	Please Please Me	*Beatles*
	WEEK 4	
US45	Sugar Shack	*Jimmy Gilmer & The Fireballs*
USLP	Peter, Paul & Mary	*Peter, Paul & Mary*
UK45	You'll Never Walk Alone	*Gerry & The Pacemakers*
UKLP	Please Please Me	*Beatles*

LOCKING QUITS SHADOWS, WELCH STAYS

Brian 'Licorice' Locking has announced that he's to leave The Shadows, while Bruce Welch has reversed his earlier decision and will stay with the group.

Locking, who replaced bass guitarist Jet Harris 17 months ago, has secretly been thinking of vacating his position for several months. A Jehovah's Witness, Locking believes that he would better further his religious beliefs working in one place, as opposed to constantly touring with The Shadows.

In the case of rhythm guitarist Bruce Welch – who previously had insisted his final appearance with The Shadows would be a bill-topping spot on the September 22 edition of the top-rated *Sunday Night At The London Palladium* TV show – he is now determined to overcome the nervous ailment that he claimed was responsible for him giving notice to quit.

Said Welch: 'I feel much better. After my three week holiday in Barbados with my wife, and filming in The Canary Islands, I should be fine by March, when we are due to tour again.'

On the same day, Dusty Springfield – who announced she was going solo following The Springfields' final performance together on October 6 – revealed that her solo debut, 'I Only Want To Be With You', will be released November 8, to coincide with the start of a UK tour she is making with The Searchers, Brian Poole & The Tremeloes and Freddie & The Dreamers as opening acts.

Dusty – no more Springfields

JFK DEAD – SPECTOR CANCELS CHRISTMAS

As a nation mourned the assassination of President John Kennedy in Dallas on November 22, distraught whizkid record producer Phil Spector immediately withdrew his all-star Philles label seasonal meisterwerk, 'A Christmas Gift To You', from the stores out of personal respect.

'Nobody's going to want happy Christmas songs this year,' Spector was quoted as saying.

During the summer, Spector had devoted considerable time to what he envisaged as a no-expense-spared celebration of his distinctive Wall Of Sound approach to creating, what he fondly termed, 'Little symphonies for the kiddies!'

With arrangements by Jack Nitzsche and performances from Philles' stars The Crystals, The Ronettes, Darlene Love and Bob B. Soxx & The Blue Jeans, here was a collection of familiar Yuletide pop standards as you'd never heard them before. It was a concept album of varied moods, which reached its peak on The Crystals' snowcap-melting romp through 'Santa Claus Is Comin' To Town'.

Finally, Spector's closing salutations over 'Silent Night', in the current circumstances, evoked an atmosphere of eerie sentimentality.

LENNON'S ROYAL QUIP

The Beatles performed before the Queen Mother, Princess Margaret and Lord Snowdon at this year's Royal Variety Command Performance held at London's Prince Of Wales Theatre.

Midway through the group's performance, Lennon rose to the occasion by requesting: 'On the next number, would those in the cheap seats clap their hands? The rest of you rattle your jewellery!'

The House Of Windsor did the latter.

CHARTS

US45	Sugar Shack *Jimmy Gilmer & The Fireballs*
USLP	In The Wind *Peter, Paul & Mary*
UK45	You'll Never Walk Alone *Gerry & The Pacemakers*
UKLP	Please Please Me *Beatles*
WEEK 2	
US45	Sugar Shack *Jimmy Gilmer & The Fireballs*
USLP	In The Wind *Peter, Paul & Mary*
UK45	You'll Never Walk Alone *Gerry & The Pacemakers*
UKLP	Please Please Me *Beatles*
WEEK 3	
US45	Deep Purple *Nino Tempo & April Stevens*
USLP	In The Wind *Peter, Paul & Mary*
UK45	You'll Never Walk Alone *Gerry & The Pacemakers*
UKLP	Please Please Me *Beatles*
WEEK 4	
US45	I'm Leaving It Up To You *Dale & Grace*
USLP	In The Wind *Peter, Paul & Mary*
UK45	She Loves You *Beatles*
UKLP	Please Please Me *Beatles*
WEEK 5	
US45	Sugar Shack *Jimmy Gilmer & The Fireballs*
USLP	In The Wind *Peter, Paul & Mary*
UK45	She Loves You *Beatles*
UKLP	With The Beatles *Beatles*

Dylan – Commie claim claptrap!

RED FOLKIE SCARE

With Peter, Paul & Mary's interpretations of two Bob Dylan songs 'Blowin' In The Wind' and 'Don't Think Twice, It's All Right' chartbound on both sides of the Atlantic, it has been left to UK music writer Derek Johnson to go boldly into print and publicly dismiss as rubbish scare-stories in Britain's more lurid Sunday tabloids which claim the current worldwide folk music trend masks subversive tactics by the Kremlin to 'poison young minds'!

These fantasy stories have implied that folk music is having a 'conditioning, brain-washing effect upon its followers', that the songs have an 'insidious, detrimental effect' upon the younger generation because the majority of folk singers such as Bob Dylan, Peter, Paul & Mary and their ilk are 'communists'.

Johnson jokingly asks whether the sudden leap into the UK charts by this winsome trio's 'Blowin' In The Wind' is all down to the fact that, unbeknown to the public, Russian leader Mr Kruschev has taken a hand in the hit parade!

STAR QUOTE

CHRIS CURTIS

Drummer with The Searchers

'We were terrible before we went to Germany to play at the Star Club. In fact, the first time we went I don't think they were keen on us at all. By our second visit, though, we were going down really well. You can't help but improve when you play in an atmosphere like that.'

Duane – touring with Richard

THE GRAPEVINE

- The Rolling Stones are the latest group to try their chart luck with a Lennon & McCartney song – 'I Wanna Be Your Man'.
- Meanwhile, Billy J. Kramer continues his John & Paul association with 'I'll Keep You Satisfied'.
- Little Richard, Duane Eddy and The Shirelles are touring the UK together.

We'll love The Shirelles tomorrow

QUEEN DINAH FOUND DEAD

It'll be a blue Christmas without her! The 'Queen Of The Blues', Dinah Washington, was found dead from an overdose of sleeping pills in her Detroit home on December 14. She was 39.

Born Ruth Jones, in Tuscaloosa, Alabama, August 29, 1924, this one-time singer with the Lionel Hampton Orchestra scored 36 chart entries between 1949 and 1963. Of these, the most popular were her Mercury label recordings 'What A Difference A Day Makes' and 'September In The Rain'.

Dinah Washington also enjoyed world-wide chart success with her 1960 hit duets with Brook Benton, 'Baby (You've Got What It Takes)' and 'A Rockin' Good Way'.

Her private life was text-case turmoil – just five months prior to her tragic death, Dinah Washington married her *seventh* husband, Detroit Lions' football star, Dick 'Night Train' Lane.

SONNY BOY VS YARDBIRDS

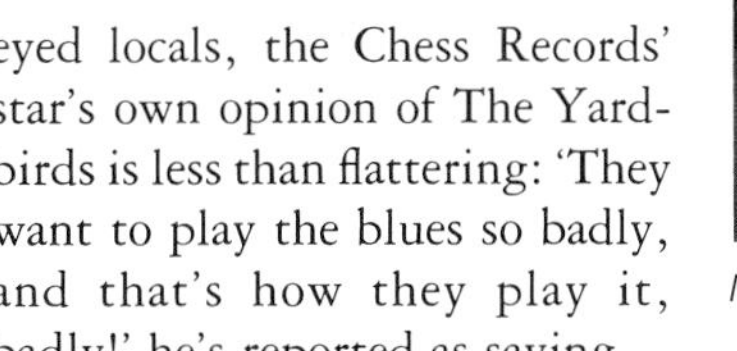

Yardbirds – slagged off by Sonny Boy Williamson

Almost semi-resident in the UK, harmonica bluesman Sonny Boy Williamson's appearance with The Yardbirds at London's R&B Crawdaddy Club has been recorded for a proposed 'Live In London' Fontana Records release.

Sometimes over-critical of even the most enthusiastic wide-eyed locals, the Chess Records' star's own opinion of The Yardbirds is less than flattering: 'They want to play the blues so badly, and that's how they play it, badly!' he's reported as saying.

THE GRAPEVINE

- Cliff Richard & The Shadows have been filming *Wonderful Life* in the Canary Islands.
- *What A Crazy World*, starring Joe Brown and Marty Wilde, has its world premiere in London.
- The Swinging Blue Jeans have covered Chan Romero's riotous 'Hippy Hippy Shake'.
- After countless rejections, Capitol Records have picked up the US rights to The Beatles.

BEATLES XMAS CRACKER

Following one-nighters in Bradford (December 21) and Liverpool (December 22), Brian Epstein's production 'The Beatles' Christmas Show' – a combination of music, laughter and traditional pantomime – began a season at The Finsbury Park Astoria, London on December 24 until January 11.

Apart from the bill-topping Beatles (who also acted in comedy sketches) the show featured Billy J. Kramer & The Dakotas, Cilla Black, The Fourmost and Tommy Quickly, plus light entertainment from Australian Rolf Harris and comedy group The Barron-Knights featuring Duke D'Mond.

With a top ticket price of 75p ($2), all available 100,000 tickets were sold by November 16.

New from NEMS – Tommy Quickly

Crazy! Joe Brown, Sid James & Co.

CHARTS

US45	Dominique *The Singing Nun*
USLP	The Singing Nun *The Singing Nun*
UK45	I Want To Hold Your Hand *Beatles*
UKLP	With The Beatles *Beatles*
WEEK 2	
US45	Dominique *The Singing Nun*
USLP	The Singing Nun *The Singing Nun*
UK45	I Want To Hold Your Hand *Beatles*
UKLP	With The Beatles *Beatles*
WEEK 3	
US45	Dominique *The Singing Nun*
USLP	The Singing Nun *The Singing Nun*
UK45	I Want To Hold Your Hand *Beatles*
UKLP	With The Beatles *Beatles*
WEEK 4	
US45	Dominique *The Singing Nun*
USLP	The Singing Nun *The Singing Nun*
UK45	I Want To Hold Your Hand *Beatles*
UKLP	With The Beatles *Beatles*

JFK – A MEMORIAL

As a shocked America mourns, Premium Records have released 'John Fitzgerald Kennedy – A Memorial Album (The Last Hours)' for just 99 cents.

It sold four million copies in six days, thereby qualifying it as the fastest-ever selling record in history, and assuring it a place in the famous Guinness Book of World Records.

Compiled by producer Eli Oberstein and son Maurice from broadcasts on the day of the assassination, 'The Last Hours' marks a coup for the former RCA A&R man, previously best known for his productions of black and country artists, including Duke Ellington.

The Teddy Bears, Spector on left

The Righteous Brothers

Ike and Tina Turner

Archetypal girl group The Crystals

Spector rehearses for that Wall of Sound

Bruce Lee – Spector's fabled bodyguard

The Ronettes

Spector with session singer Ronee Blakeley

THE TYCOON OF TEEN

One of the several books written about Phil Spector is sub-titled 'The Truth About Rock & Roll's Legendary Madman', and it's certainly true that there are almost as many possibly apocryphal anecdotes about Spector as there are utterly amazing and timeless records which he produced.

Spector's first success came in 1958, when 'To Know Him Is To Love Him', a song written by him topped the 'Billboard' singles chart and sold a million copies, but it wasn't until the end of 1960 that Spector was again responsible for a Top 10 hit ('Corinna Corinna' by Ray Peterson, which he produced). The end of 1961 saw the first release on Spector's own label, Philles Records. That was 'There's No Other (Like My Baby)' by The Crystals, and it reached the US Top 20, as did a follow up, 'Uptown', in spring 1962. In the autumn of that year, a third Crystals single, 'He's A Rebel', topped the US chart. This was swiftly followed by another US Top 10 hit, 'Zip-A-Dee-Doo-Dah', performed by Bob B. Soxx & The Blue Jeans. In 1963, Spector began producing hits for Darlene Love while The Crystals remained successful with Top 10 hits like 'Da Doo Ron Ron' and 'Then He Kissed Me.

Part of the appeal of these records was Spector's so called 'Wall Of Sound'' – where other records were produced by overdubbing a single guitarist as many times as required, Spector preferred to have several guitarists playing in unison together, and the same for each instrument involved in a track. The result was certainly unique, although other producers have called this method, which calls for numerous musicians, expensive and self-indulgent.

By this point, Spector had discovered another female vocal trio who were based in New York, The Ronettes, and was captivated by the voice and the exotic beauty of lead singer Veronica 'Ronnie' Bennett, with whom he instantly fell in love. The first and biggest Ronettes hit was 'Be My Baby', and soon after it peaked in the US chart, Spector's problems can be seen to have begun. The Crystals, Bob B. Soxx and Darlene Love were all effectively forgotten as Spector concentrated his energy and ingenuity on recording masterpieces with The Ronettes, although the other three acts were also represented on what is often critically regarded as Spector's finest work, an album of seasonal songs titled variously 'A Christmas Gift For You' or

'Phil Spector's Christmas Album'. The album was first released only days before the assassination of President John F. Kennedy, and immediately after Kennedy's death, America in general was too stunned to think of buying records of any sort. By the middle of January, 1964, America had discovered The Beatles, and Spector's Christmas Album was forgotten.

But things began to improve at the end of that year, when he started producing Bill Medley and Bobby Hatfield, a white juo known as The Righteous Brothers, whose approach to singing was known as "blue eyed soul". The first hit Spector produced for them was the unforgettable 'You've Lost That Lovin' Feelin'', which topped charts around the world. The Righteous Brothers had several more Spector-produced hits like 'Unchained Melody' and 'Ebb Tide', before they fell out with their Svengali-like producer, who only worked with one other act during 1965, The Ronettes.

In mid-1966, after admiring Tina Turner's vocal ability when they worked together on a TV show, he proposed to her then husband, Ike, that he produce records for Tina. The single which first resulted from these sessions, 'River Deep - Mountain High', was another masterpiece, which reached the Top 3 in Britain, but was an utter failure in the US.

Phil Spector had always been admired by the aristocrats of British pop music, The Beatles and The Rolling Stones. The first album by The Stones included a song titled 'Now I've Got A Witness (Like Uncle Phil & Uncle Gene)', referring to Messrs. Spector and Pitney, who were present at the recording sessions for the album. The Beatles were not quite so close to Spector, but when Allen Klein suggested Spector to remix the recordings made for the group's 'Let It Be' album, the idea was favourably received.

This led to Spector producing George Harrison's classic triple album, 'All Things Must Pass' (which included 'My Sweet Lord') and several albums for John Lennon, among them 'John Lennon/Plastic Ono Band' and 'Imagine' and several hit singles, such as 'Instant Karma' and 'Happy Xmas (War Is Over)', as well as the 'Concert For Bangla Desh' triple album and part of what was eventually released as 'Rock'n'Roll' by John Lennon, an album which Spector had previously licensed without Lennon's approval.

That was in 1975, since when Spector has only occasionally emerged from his Hollywood mansion for shortlived one-off projects like albums with Dion, Leonard Cohen and The Ramones. There are many who think its time he ended this self-imposed exile . . . .

The recluse of rock

TOTP LAUNCHED

'It's No. 1, it's *Top Of The Pops!*'

In Britain, BBC-Television has inaugurated its weekly look at the British record charts.

THE GRAPEVINE

- The Beach Boys have adopted the pseudonym The Survivors for a Brian Wilson-produced one-off single, 'Pamela Jean'.
- Elvis has paid $55,000 for Franklin D. Roosevelt's former presidential yacht, 'Potomac'.
- The Beatles were the UK's top record selling act last year with 18 weeks at No. 1.
- Pye Records have signed North London R&B foursome, The Kinks.

CHARTS

US45	There! I've Said It Again *Bobby Vinton*
USLP	The Singing Nun *The Singing Nun*
UK45	I Want To Hold Your Hand *Beatles*
UKLP	With The Beatles *Beatles*
WEEK 2	
US45	There ! I've Said It Again *Bobby Vinton*
USLP	The Singing Nun *The Singing Nun*
UK45	I Want To Hold Your Hand *Beatles*
UKLP	With The Beatles *Beatles*
WEEK 3	
US45	There ! I've Said it Again *Bobby Vinton*
USLP	The Singing Nun *The Singing Nun*
UK45	Glad All Over *Dave Clark Five*
UKLP	With The Beatles *Beatles*
WEEK 4	
US45	There ! I've Said it Again *Bobby Vinton*
USLP	The Singing Nun *The Singing Nun*
UK45	Glad All Over *Dave Clark Five*
UKLP	With The Beatles *Beatles*

DYLAN: NEW ALBUM, NEW PRODUCER

Although Bob Dylan's SRO New York Carnegie Hall concert of October 26 1963 was recorded for release (and given the catalogue number 77110) it has remained unheard. In the interim Dylan's new manager, Albert Grossman, has unsuccessfully attempted to renegotiate his client's original royalty deal with CBS.

In the course of much unpleasantness, Grossman secured Tom Wilson instead of John Hammond (who discovered and signed Dylan to CBS) to produce Dylan's third studio album, 'The Times They Are A-Changin''.

Recorded in August and October 1963, it comprises ten Dylan originals.

PARIS: NO BEATLEMANIA

The Beatles picked The Cyrano Theatre, Versailles, Paris to warm-up prior to their season at the world-famous L'Olympia Theatre with Trini 'If I Had A Hammer' Lopez and France's most popular 'pop' femme, Sylvie Vartan.

The following evening (16th), Beatlemania was not visible in Paris when Les Fabs attempted to impress unimpressionable L'Olympia patrons on the first night of a three week variety season.

STONES ON THE ROAD

Stones Watts, Jagger and Richards

The Rolling Stones and The Ronettes opened their UK tour at The Granada, Harrow, supported by The Swinging Blue Jeans, Marty Wilde & The Wildcats, Dave Berry & The Cruisers, The Cheynes (with Peter Green and Mick Fleetwood) and Johnny Kidd & The Pirates.

Recordwise, The Stones' first EP has entered the singles chart and the group have acted as unbilled back-up band for their friend Cleo (Sylvester) who debuted with a cover of 'To Know Him Is To Love Him'.

CYRIL DAVIES DIES

British blues father-figure Cyril Davies, with the All Stars, including Long John Baldry (second from right)

January 7 was a black day for British R&B – Cyril 'Squirrel' Davie, pioneering British R&B harmonica star, died of leukeamia, aged 32.

Along with Alexis Korner, Davies co-formed Blues Incorporated which, at one time or another, featured Mick Jagger, Eric Burdon, Charlie Watts, Jack Bruce, Ginger Baker, Graham Bond and Paul Jones as singers and musicians.

Equal in musical status to most of the US blues stars he sought to emulate, Davies quit Blues Inc. in November 1962, to form his own All-Stars (featuring Long John Baldry) and to record his remarkable 'Country Line Special' (Pye).

KINSLEY QUITS MERSEYBEATS

Billy Kinsley, bass-guitarist and vocalist with The Merseybeats, has quit the group – in the UK charts at the moment with 'I Think Of You' – to marry hairdresser Pat Allman.

While most groups who lose a key member gloss over such predicaments, Merseybeats founder Tony Crane admitted: 'We're in trouble. Things are really starting to happen now we're in the charts, but now Billy has walked out on us, we've had to stop everything and return to Liverpool to find a replacement as quickly as possible.

'It's not easy, because Billy has been with me since we were a double act called The Mavericks.'

With drummer John Banks and Aaron Williams on guitar, they became known as The Merseybeats.

Tony continued: 'Don't ask my why Billy should leave just as we're on the verge of getting somewhere. I mean, he played on both 'I Think Of You' and our previous hit 'It's Love That Really Counts' – then out of the blue he told me he doesn't like the life, and that's that!'

For the moment, The Merseybeats are honouring bookings as a trio. 'Surprisingly, we sounded quite reasonable. This could be because we feature quite a few slow numbers. We didn't deliberately start out to be a quiet group – it just happened that way,' said Tony.

'We got a recording contract some time after a lot of other Liverpool groups and we felt we'd just be lost in the crowd if we did wild numbers like the rest.'

It's likely that ex-Big Three bass player and frontman Johnny Gustavson will be Kinsley's replacement.

CHARTS

Week	Chart	Title	Artist
1	US45	I Want To Hold Your Hand	*Beatles*
	USLP	The Singing Nun	*The Singing Nun*
	UK45	Needles And Pins	*Searchers*
	UKLP	With The Beatles	*Beatles*
WEEK 2	US45	I Want To Hold Your Hand	*Beatles*
	USLP	The Singing Nun	*The Singing Nun*
	UK45	Needles And Pins	*Searchers*
	UKLP	With The Beatles	*Beatles*
WEEK 3	US45	I Want To Hold Your Hand	*Beatles*
	USLP	Meet The Beatles	*Beatles*
	UK45	Needles And Pins	*Searchers*
	UKLP	With The Beatles	*Beatles*
WEEK 4	US45	I Want To Hold Your Hand	*Beatles*
	USLP	Meet The Beatles	*Beatles*
	UK45	Anyone Who Had A Heart	*Cilla Black*
	UKLP	With The Beatles	*Beatles*
WEEK 5	US45	I Want To Hold Your Hand	*Beatles*
	USLP	Meet The Beatles	*Beatles*
	UK45	Anyone Who Had A Heart	*Cilla Black*
	UKLP	With The Beatles	*Beatles*

Georgie Fame, here seen on guitar rather than his usual Hammond organ

FAME AT LAST!

Firmly established on London's flourishing club scene as premier exponents of Hammond 'n' horns urban R&B, scenemakers Georgie Fame & The Blue Flames – who skilfully blend the best elements of Jamaican Blue Beat, James Brown funk, Stax soul, Tamla Motown melodies and hard bop into a danceable crowd-pulling mix – packed mohair mods and US servicemen into the Soho basement of 37 Wardour Street. With the tapes rolling, they recorded their debut album, 'Rhythm And Blues At The Flamingo Club', for release on Columbia.

THE GRAPEVINE

- **The Kinks have made their Pye label debut with a cover of Little Richard's 'Long Tall Sally'.**
- **The Dave Clark Five less than impressive on ATV's *Sunday Night at the London Palladium.***
- **Billy Fury has covered 'Hippy Hippy Shake' and 'Glad All Over' exclusively for Scandinavian single.**
- **Vee-Jay have released latest Beatlemania cash-in: 'Jolly What! The Beatles and Frank Ifield On Stage'.**

STAR QUOTE

JUDITH SIMONS

London *Daily Express*

'They look like boys whom any self-respecting mum would lock in the bathroom! But The Rolling Stones – five tough young London-based music makers are not worried what mum thinks! . . . The Stones have taken over as the voice of the teens.'

BLUEBEAT'S OWN LABEL

BlueBeat – the latest variant of Jamaican popular dance music – has also loaned its name to a UK-based record label specializing in the popular club phenomenon.

London's two top-selling BlueBeat singles are 'Madness' by Prince Buster and 'Carolina' by The Folks Brothers.

Brothers Dave and Ray Davies (centre) with bassist Peter Quaife and Mick Avory on drums – The Kinks

CHARTS

- US45 I Want To Hold Your Hand — *Beatles*
- USLP Meet The Beatles — *Beatles*
- UK45 Anyone Who Had A Heart — *Cilla Black*
- UKLP With The Beatles — *Beatles*

WEEK 2

- US45 I Want To Hold Your Hand — *Beatles*
- USLP Meet The Beatles — *Beatles*
- UK45 Anyone Who Had A Heart — *Cilla Black*
- UKLP With The Beatles — *Beatles*

WEEK 3

- US45 She Loves You — *Beatles*
- USLP Meet The Beatles — *Beatles*
- UK45 Little Children — *Billy J Kramer & The Dakotas*
- UKLP With The Beatles — *Beatles*

WEEK 4

- US45 She Loves You — *Beatles*
- USLP Meet The Beatles — *Beatles*
- UK45 Can't Buy Me Love — *Beatles*
- UKLP With The Beatles — *Beatles*

BEATLES – THE DOMINATION CONTINUES

The Beatles have pulled off an unprecedented music industry coup, covering all top *five* slots on *Billboard* magazine's singles chart with 'Can't Buy Me Love' at No. 1, 'Twist And Shout' at No. 2, 'She Loves You' at No. 3, 'I Want To Hold Your Hand' at No. 4 and 'Please Please Me' at fifth spot.

Not content with *just* that, Beatles singles also hold down positions 16, 44, 49, 69, 78, 84 and 88 on the same Hot 100.

The group accounted for 60 per cent of *all* records sold in North America during February, according to industry sources.

Meanwhile, John Lennon's first book, *In His Own Write*, has won the presitigious Foyle's Literary Prize in Britain.

As guest speaker at the celebrated literary luncheon held in his honour in London, Lennon's entire acceptance speech was a mumbled: 'Thank you very much. You've got a lucky face!' after which he immediately fled the banquet!

THE GRAPEVINE

- **Filming has begun on Beatles movie, *A Hard Day's Night*.**
- **Beatles German-language versions of 'I Want To Hold Your Hand (Komm, Gib Mir Deine Hand)' and 'She Loves You (Sie Liebt Dich)' are on sale in the Fatherland.**
- **Stan Getz has headlined the last show at the Marquee Club's Oxford Street premises in London.**

Getz closes Marquee in Oxford Street

BEWARE, ANIMALS AT LARGE!

Newcastle R&B group, The Animals, have made their debut with the Mickie Most-produced 'Baby Let Me Take You Home' – a gung-ho rework of an old blues standard the group discovered on Bob Dylan's first album.

Formerly, The Alan Price Combo, they were renamed The Animals by their Tyneside fans because of their wild appearance and stage act!

The Animals comprise: Eric Burdon (vocals), Alan Price (organ), Hilton Valentine (guitar), Chas Chandler (bass) and John Steel (drums).

ELVIS FANS SEE DOUBLE

Duplicate Elvis with a blond wig – two for the price of one!

Kissin' Cousins is the latest Elvis epic from the MGM Studios. A Li'l Abner-style hillbilly romp, it has Presley playing both a US Army officer (Josh Morgan) and his hick double (Jodie Tatum) – achieved by the application of a tatty blond wig.

The only selling point of this disaster is that fans get two Elvises for the price of one!

SULLIVAN RE-BOOKS DC5

It has been a hectic month for The Dave Clark Five. Hot on the heels of The Beatles, Tottenham's finest made an impressive debut on *The Ed Sullivan Show* on March 8, performing 'Glad All Over'.

Taken with their clean-cut appearance and politeness, Mr Sullivan immediately invited them to return. Having taken the unanimous decision to turn professional on March 14, now that 'Glad All Over' is a chart-topper, The Dave Clark Five cancelled the first night of their week-long season at Liverpool's Empire to make their second appearance on *The Ed Sullivan Show* where they performed 'Do You Love Me', 'Bits And Pieces' and 'Glad All Over'.

HENTOFF SLAMS BEATLES & CLARK, LIKES SEARCHERS

Noted US critic Nat Hentoff's opinion of The Beatles' recent *Ed Sullivan Show* TV debut was decidely lukewarm: 'Musically, this reviewer cannot understand the fervour of Beatles' admirers, or the scorn of their detractors. Except for their visual uniqueness, The Beatles are a run of the mill rock'n'roll attraction.'

Hentoff's views on The Dave Clark Five's' *Sullivan* appearance were equally dismissive: 'Clark leads an ordinary rock'n'roll group with no particular musical direction,' he wrote.

However, Hentoff was more impressed by The Searchers on April 5: 'The Searchers seem to be the most professional British rock group to have appeared in America. To this viewer, the initial impression was more favourable musically than had been the case with The Beatles or The Dave Clark Five.

'They sustained an exuberant mood, punctuated by several unison jumps in the air. They showed a more subtle command of dynamics than the two groups that preceded them.'

CHARTS

US45	Can't Buy Me Love *Beatles*
USLP	Meet The Beatles *Beatles*
UK45	Can't Buy Me Love *Beatles*
UKLP	With The Beatles *Beatles*
WEEK 2	
US45	Can't Buy Me Love *Beatles*
USLP	Meet The Beatles *Beatles*
UK45	Can't Buy Me Love *Beatles*
UKLP	With The Beatles *Beatles*
WEEK 3	
US45	Can't Buy Me Love *Beatles*
USLP	Meet The Beatles *Beatles*
UK45	Can't Buy Me Love *Beatles*
UKLP	With The Beatles *Beatles*
WEEK 4	
US45	Can't Buy Me Love *Beatles*
USLP	Meet The Beatles *Beatles*
UK45	A World Without Love *Peter And Gordon*
UKLP	The Rolling Stones *Rolling Stones*

THE GRAPEVINE

- **The Rolling Stones have broadcast four weekly 15-minute shows for Radio Luxembourg.**
- **Roy Orbison, Tony Sheridan, Freddie & The Dreamers, Wayne Fontana & The Mindbenders and Ezz Rico are touring the U.K.**
- **The Beatles have completed work on their first feature-length movie, *A Hard Day's Night*.**
- **Success by Peter & Gordon with Lennon & McCartney song, 'World Without Love'.**

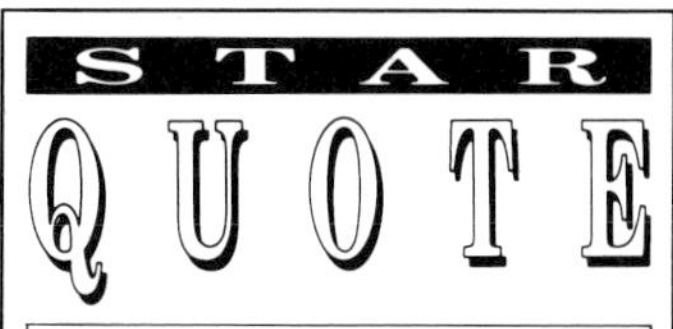

STAR QUOTE

BRIAN BENNETT

The Shadows

'Comparisons between us and The Beatles? No one has said anything to our faces. Occasionally, some of the local press boys ask if we consider ourselves to be slipping, on account of The Beatles' success. Our reply usually varies, depending on our mood!'

ELVIS: VIVA ROMANCE?

MGM have released *Viva Las Vegas* with Elvis Presley as racing driver Lucky Jordan. Not only has this film been judged as slightly superior in terms of script and soundtrack than critics have come to expect from an Elvis musical, but the dynamic presence of the statuesque Ann-Margret (Rusty Martin) has added to the public's interest.

Gossip columnists have picked up on the fact that the romantic involvement between the two stars wasn't just restricted to the movie set.

Ann-Margret has made no secret about the relationship having passed the 'just good friends' stage. However, Elvis's more loyal fans were most displeased when she said she anticipated announcing wedding plans.

Elvis and Ann-Margret – more than friends?

STONES FOR THE CHOP

Stones (l to r) Jones, Watts, Jagger, Richard, Wyman keep names off album and annoy hairdressers – business as usual

Mr Wallace Scowcroft, President of Britain's National Federation of Hairdressers has offered a free haircut to the next No. 1 group or soloist in the pop charts, adding: 'The Rolling Stones are the worst. One of them looks as if he has got a feather duster on his head.'

With The Rolling Stones having defined their rebellious image long before their musical identity, manager Andrew Oldham has taken the unprecedented gamble of exploiting this, by removing all but the Decca logo (including the group's name) from the front of their debut album and selling it on the strength of a highly atmospheric photograph.

The group's rise to the top continues unchecked, with now-obligatory riots accompanying their live appearances.

Security battled with 8,000 Stones fans inside Empire Pool, Wembley during the 'Ready Steady Go Rave Mad Mod Ball'.

Outside, police arrested a battalion of thirty warlike bikers.

CHARTS

US45	Can't Buy Me Love — *Beatles*
USLP	The Beatles' Second Album — *Beatles*
UK45	A World Without Love — *Peter And Gordon*
UKLP	The Rolling Stones — *Rolling Stones*
WEEK 2	
US45	Hello Dolly ! — *Louis Armstrong*
USLP	The Beatles' Second Album — *Beatles*
UK45	Don't Throw Your Love Away — *Searchers*
UKLP	The Rolling Stones — *Rolling Stones*
WEEK 3	
US45	My Guy — *Mary Wells*
USLP	The Beatles' Second Album — *Beatles*
UK45	Juliet — *Four Pennies*
UKLP	The Rolling Stones — *Rolling Stones*
WEEK 4	
US45	Can't Buy Me Love — *Beatles*
USLP	The Beatles' Second Album — *Beatles*
UK45	Juliet — *Four Pennies*
UKLP	The Rolling Stones — *Rolling Stones*
WEEK 5	
US45	Love Me Do — *Beatles*
USLP	The Beatles' Second Album — *Beatles*
UK45	You're My World — *Cilla Black*
UKLP	The Rolling Stones — *Rolling Stones*

THE GRAPEVINE

- **Two pirate radio station ships have begun transmitting off the coast of Britain – Radio Caroline and Radio Atlanta.**
- **Wayne Fontana & The Mindbenders have covered 'Duke Of Earl'.**
- **An exhibition of ex-Beatle Stuart Sutcliffe's paintings has opened at Liverpool's Walker Gallery.**
- **John Mayall's Bluesbreakers have made their debut on disc with 'Crawling Up A Hill'.**

STONES – MORE ROWS, MORE RIOTS

Mirror mocks Stones

The London *Daily Mirror* is the latest paper to lambast The Rolling Stones, in an editorial which said: 'Everything seems to be against them on the surface. They are called the ugliest group in Britain. They are not looked on very kindly by most parents, or by adults in general. They are even used to the type of article that asks big brother if he would let his sister go out with one of them.'

Confronted with this and similar criticism, Mick Jagger replies: 'We know a lot of people don't like us 'cause they say we're scruffy and don't wash.

'So what? They don't have to come and look at us, do they? If they don't like me, they can keep away!'

Determined not to keep away, even if they didn't atually have tickets, were Scottish fans at the Stones' May 19 gig at Chantinghall Hotel, Hamilton.

More than 4,000 people tried to gate-crash the gig and found themselves in the middle of a full-scale battle with local police. Unable to control the crush, officers let the fans in.

As final proof of the Stones' popularity, BBC-TV was deluged with over 8,000 postal applications for studio tickets when they announced the group's scheduled appearance on *Juke Box Jury* on June 27.

THE NIGHT OF THE LIVING LEGENDS

Forget The Beatles and The Stones! London audiences haven't witnessed anything quite as spectacular as when three living legends – Chuck Berry, Gene Vincent and Carl Perkins – headlined a one-nighter at London's Hammersmith Odeon.

In supporting slots: The Animals, The Nashville Teens and Kingsize Taylor & The Dominoes.

Nashville Teens (right) in Tobacco Road? Possibly not . . .

But Gene Vincent (below) probably is

LENNY'S SIDEKICK SHOOTS HIMSELF

Joe Maini (34), the widely respected madcap sax-playing sidekick of comedian Lenny Bruce, was killed in Los Angeles on May 8 during a bizarre shooting incident at a friend's house.

Maini placed the muzzle of a revolver to his head and, laughing, pulled the trigger, shooting himself fatally.

GETZ AND THE GIRL FROM RIO

Having instigated the immensely profitable bossa nova phenomenon with his 1962 Grammy Award-Winning Verve Records album, 'Jazz Samba' and the hit single 'Desafinado' (on which he was partnered by guitarist Charlie Byrd), master of the 'cool' jazz tenor Stan Getz is again chartbound with 'The Girl From Ipanema', which has resulted in instant global stardom for singer Astrud Gilberto, who appears on this record by pure accident.

As part of a series of bossa nova albums with various artists, Stan Getz commenced a two-day recording session in New York in March 1963 with top Brazilian singer-composers, Antonio Carlos Jobim and Joao Gilberto.

One of the eight songs they taped was 'The Girl From Ipanema', a gently sensual sun-kissed samba meant to showcase Getz's tenor sax and the voice of guitarist Joao Gilberto. However, it became clear that Gilberto could only sing in Portuguese and could not perform Normal Gimbel's specially commissioned English lyric.

At the session was Gilberto's 24-year-old Bahia-born wife, Astrud. She spoke English and possessed a voice of sorts. Though she had never sung professionally, she was coaxed into softly crooning the wistful lyrics.

At the time of release, Astrud Gilberto's nonchalant vocal contribution was viewed as being so slight she was not name-checked on the album.

Ironically, public demand for a single version of 'The Girl From Ipanema' resulted in the original LP version being drastically cut for commercial appeal. Joao Gilberto's vocal was edited out, leaving just the magical combination of Stan The Man and The Girl From Rio.

In the face of a mounting bossa nova backlash, both the 'Stan Getz/Joao Gilberto Album' and the appearance of 'The Girl From Ipanema' on the charts have proved a point by succeeding in a spectacular manner for entirely artistic reasons.

Below: 'Desafinado' partners Getz (left) and Byrd and (above) Astrud Gilberto

CHARTS

US45	Chapel Of Love	*Dixie Cups*
USLP	Hello Dolly !	*Original Cast*
UK45	You're My World	*Cilla Black*
UKLP	The Rolling Stones	*Rolling Stones*
WEEK 2		
US45	Chapel Of Love	*Dixie Cups*
USLP	Hello Dolly !	*Louis Armstrong*
UK45	You're My World	*Cilla Black*
UKLP	The Rolling Stones	*Rolling Stones*
WEEK 3		
US45	Chapel Of Love	*Dixie Cups*
USLP	Hello Dolly !	*Louis Armstrong*
UK45	It's Over	*Roy Orbison*
UKLP	The Rolling Stones	*Rolling Stones*
WEEK 4		
US45	A World Without Love	*Peter & Gordon*
USLP	Hello Dolly !	*Louis Armstrong*
UK45	It's Over	*Roy Orbison*
UKLP	The Rolling Stones	*Rolling Stones*

MARTIN MOCKS STONES

For their American debut, The Rolling Stones were set up for ritual slaughter on the network TV show *Hollywood Palace*, where host Dean Martin set them up for a string of cheap laughs.

'Their hair is not long,' quipped Martin. 'It's just smaller foreheads and higher eyebrows.'

Of a trampoline artist also on the show, he said: 'That's the father of The Rolling Stones. He's been trying to kill himself ever since.'

Martin: "Higher eyebrows"

THE GRAPEVINE

- **Sam Cooke has appeared in cabaret at New York's swish Copacabana Club.**
- **Peter & Gordon have charted yet again with a Lennon & McCartney tune, 'Nobody I Know'.**
- **The Beatles have kicked off the European leg of their world tour with Jimmy Nicol depping for a sick Ringo.**
- **Summer film plans for the proposed Clive Donner-directed Rolling Stones have been shelved.**

MEADE LUX DIES

Boogie Woogie piano ace Meade Lux Lewis – best known for his hit 'Honky Tonk Train Blues', plus classic collaborations with fellow Boogie pianomen Albert Ammons and Pete Johnson – has died, aged 58, in a Minneapolis auto accident.

JIM REEVES KILLED IN AIR CRASH

Texas-born country music star Jim Reeves became the object of instant cult hysteria when he was killed, aged 40, in an air crash on July 31.

The light aircraft which was carrying Reeves and his manager Dean Manuel, from Arkansas back to Nashville, flew into heavy rain four miles from Beery Field Airport and plunged into thick foliage.

A prolific recording artist, Reeves' innumerable hits included: 'He'll Have To Go', 'I Love You Because', 'Adios Amigo', 'Welcome To My World' and 'You're The Only Good Thing'.

A year before his death, Reeves starred in the title role of a South African-made feature film, *Kimberly Jim*.

CHARTS

US45	I Get Around *Beach Boys*
USLP	Hello Dolly ! *Louis Armstrong*
UK45	House Of The Rising Sun *Animals*
UKLP	The Rolling Stones *Rolling Stones*

WEEK 2

US45	I Get Around *Beach Boys*
USLP	Hello Dolly ! *Louis Armstrong*
UK45	House Of The Rising Sun *Animals*
UKLP	The Rolling Stones *Rolling Stones*

WEEK 3

US45	Rag Doll *Four Seasons*
USLP	Hello Dolly ! *Original Cast*
UK45	A Hard Day's Night *Beatles*
UKLP	A Hard Day's Night *Beatles*

WEEK 4

US45	Rag Doll *Four Seasons*
USLP	A Hard Day's Night *Beatles*
UK45	A Hard Day's Night *Beatles*
UKLP	A Hard Day's Night *Beatles*

THE GRAPEVINE

- **The Beatles' movie *A Hard Day's Night* received a Royal Premiere in London.**
- **An impromptu song in Adam Faith's dressing room by 17-year-old fan Sandie Shaw has been rewarded with a Pye Records contract.**
- **Big demand in the UK for imported EPs by French 'Yeh! Yeh!' star Francoise Hardy has prompted the WH Smith chain to stock her records nation-wide.**

STONES ESCAPE RIOT, EQUIPMENT DOESN'T

Britain's biggest-ever rock'n'roll riot erupted when The Rolling Stones and The Executives played The Empress Ballroom at The Winter Gardens, Blackpool before a crowd of 9,000 fans, which included many drunken holidaying Scots.

Mid-show, Keith Richards lashed out with his boot at troublemakers who spat at Brian Jones. With a blood-hungry gang of drunks on their heels, the Stones fled the building.

The mob then took out their vengeance on the equipment, reducing a grand piano to matchwood. However, they failed to break into the Winter Gardens theatre, where The Dave Clark Five were heading a summer-season variety show.

Tottenham's finest, the Dave Clark Five, who escaped the rampaging revellers during the Blackpool orgy of destruction

HIGH NUMBERS COUNT ON HIT

The High Numbers, who are fast becoming the most popular West London R&B mod group, have made their Fontana label debut with two songs written by their manager, Peter Meadon – 'I'm The Face' (a rewrite of Slim Harpo's 'Got Love If You Want It') and 'Zoot Suit' (based on The Showmen's 'Country Fool').

Both songs, Meaden has insisted, accurately reflect the teenage lifestyle in such mod strongholds as the Goldhawk Club in London's Shepherd's Bush and Soho's Scene Club.

The High Numbers, who are known to smash up pairs of maracas on stage, comprise: Roger Daltrey (vocals), Pete Townshend (guitar), John Entwistle (bass) and newcomer Keith Moon (drums).

The group who, until recently, were known as The Detours, have been booked for some Sunday concerts with The Beatles.

BEATLES TOUR AMERICA

The Fab Four look set to conquer the U.S. as Beatlemania takes hold

Though The Beatles had previously visited the United States in February for a short promotional expedition, their first full-blown North American concert tour kicked off at San Francisco's Cow Palace before a screaming, jelly-baby-throwing audience of 17,000.

The rest of their previously announced dates are as follows: *August*: (20) The Convention Centre, Las Vegas; (21) The Coliseum, Seattle; (22) Empire Stadium, Vancouver; (23) Hollywood Bowl, Los Angeles; (26) Red Rocks Amphitheatre, Denver; (27) The Gardens, Cincinnati; (28/29) Forest Hills, New York City; (30) The Convention Centre, Atlantic City. *September*: (2) The Convention Hall, Philadelphia; (3) Indiana State Fair Coliseum, Indianapolis; (4) The Arena, Milwaukee; (5) The International Amphitheatre, Chicago; (6) Olympia Stadium, Detroit; (7) Maple Leaf Gardens, Toronto; (8) The Forum, Montreal; (11) The Gator Bowl, Jacksonville; (12) The Garden, Boston; (13) The Civic Centre, Baltimore; (14) The Civic Arena, Pittsburg; (15) The Public Auditorium, Cleveland; (16) City Park Stadium, New Orleans; (17) Municipal Stadium, Kansas City.

DYLAN IS NOT TAKING SIDES

'Another Side Of Bob Dylan', the eagerly-awaited fourth album from America's most influential contemporary performer, has been released to brisk activity at the nation's check-outs.

Though again accompanied by just his own guitar and occasional piano, the 'Side' of the singer for all to hear isn't quite the Voice of Protest most expected.

Recorded in just one day (June 9), the songs are more of a look inward with eight of the eleven tracks concerned with women. Yet there is still an undercurrent of his often-apocalyptic view of life.

The songs are: 'All I Really Want To Do', 'Black Crow Blues', 'Spanish Harlem Incident', 'Chimes Of Freedom', 'I Shall Be Free No. 10', 'To Ramona', 'Motorpsycho Nitemare', 'My Back Pages', 'I Don't Believe You', 'Ballad In Plain D' and 'It Ain't Me Babe'.

Bob Dylan – an album a day?

CHARTS

US45	A Hard Day's Night *Beatles*
USLP	A Hard Day's Night *Beatles*
UK45	A Hard Day's Night *Beatles*
UKLP	A Hard Day's Night *Beatles*
WEEK 2	
US45	A Hard Day's Night *Beatles*
USLP	A Hard Day's Night *Beatles*
UK45	A Hard Day's Night *Beatles*
UKLP	A Hard Day's Night *Beatles*
WEEK 3	
US45	Everybody Loves Somebody *Dean Martin*
USLP	A Hard Day's Night *Beatles*
UK45	Do Wah Diddy Diddy *Manfred Mann*
UKLP	A Hard Day's Night *Beatles*
WEEK 4	
US45	Where Did Our Love Go *Supremes*
USLP	A Hard Day's Night *Beatles*
UK45	Do Wah Diddy Diddy *Manfred Mann*
UKLP	A Hard Day's Night *Beatles*
WEEK 5	
US45	Where Did Our Love Go *Supremes*
USLP	A Hard Day's Night *Beatles*
UK45	Have I The Right *Honeycombs*
UKLP	A Hard Day's Night *Beatles*

THE GRAPEVINE

- **The Dave Clark Five soon to film the John Boorman-directed *Having A Wild Weekend*.**
- **The Rolling Stones are to headline Britain's National Jazz & Blues Festival at Richmond . . . advance orders for their Chicago Chess Sessions EP souvenir 'Five By Five' have topped 250,000.**
- **20-year-old Sheffield gas-fitter Joe Cocker is to cover The Beatles' 'I'll Cry Instead' for his disc debut.**

JOHNNY BURNETTE DROWNED

Johnny Burnette has drowned in a fishing accident, aged 30.

Memphis-born Burnette – whose legendary Rock'n'Roll Trio sides for Decca-Coral (1956/57) rank alongside Elvis's Sun sessions as essential seminal rockabilly classics – really only found international recognition once he'd joined Liberty Records, smoothed out both his style and appearance, and charted with such songs as 'Dreamin'', 'You're Sixteen' and 'Little Boy Sad'.

More British beat: The Animals headline for ten days at the Brooklyn Paramount

NEW YORK ROCKS

CHARTS

US45	House Of The Rising Sun *Animals*
USLP	A Hard Day's Night *Beatles*
UK45	Have I The Right *Honeycombs*
UKLP	A Hard Day's Night *Beatles*
WEEK 2	
US45	House Of The Rising Sun *Animals*
USLP	A Hard Day's Night *Beatles*
UK45	You Really Got Me *Kinks*
UKLP	A Hard Day's Night *Beatles*
WEEK 3	
US45	House Of The Rising Sun *Animals*
USLP	A Hard Day's Night *Beatles*
UK45	I'm Into Something Good *Herman's Hermits*
UKLP	A Hard Day's Night *Beatles*
WEEK 4	
US45	Oh, Pretty Woman *Roy Orbison*
USLP	A Hard Day's Night *Beatles*
UK45	I'm Into Something Good *Herman's Hermits*
UKLP	A Hard Day's Night *Beatles*

New York City hasn't seen so much super league rock'n'roll action since the late fifties with Brooklyn being the epicentre of this current activity.

On September 4, one of the city's great auditoriums – the Brooklyn Paramount Theatre – re-opened its doors after many years of darkness to welcome 'The House Of The Rising Sun' hit-makers The Animals who, along with Chuck Berry, Jan & Dean, Del Shannon, Bobby Rydell, The Dixie Cups and Dee Dee Sharp, held court for the next ten days.

The smart money says that the show that opened a day earlier (Sept. 3) at the Brooklyn Fox Theatre in competition, amounts to one hot two-dollar fifty ticket.

The Searchers are the token Brit group on a bill which features Marvin Gaye, The Supremes, The Miracles, The Temptations, Martha & The Vandellas and The Contours.

THE GRAPEVINE

- **The Beach Boys have made their *Ed Sullivan* debut.**
- **17-year-old folk-singer Marianne Faithfull has made her professional stage debut.**
- **Brian Epstein has vetoed a three-and-one-half million dollar buy-out bid for The Beatles.**
- **Rod Stewart has made his recording debut with 'Good Morning, Little Schoolgirl'.**

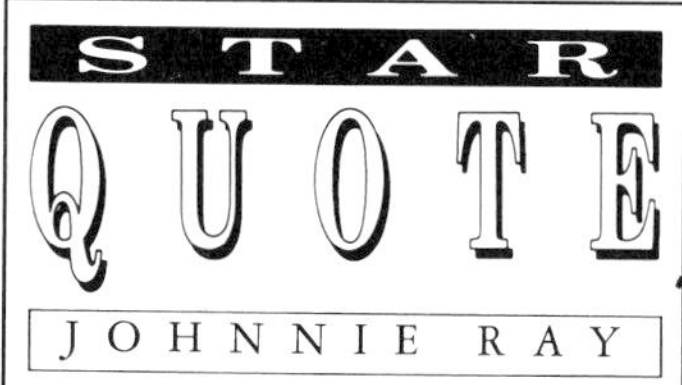

JOHNNIE RAY

I'll tell you one thing: when I had all those teenagers screaming for me, I could control them. If I wanted quiet, I got it. I just told them to be quiet.'

RONETTES – SEXY AND SUCCESSFUL

Not everyone is buying British to the total exclusion of everything else.

US vocal groups still remain a very hot attraction on both sides of the Atlantic, and none more than The Ronettes, whose teen-angst recordings of 'Be My Baby', 'Baby I Love You' and '(The Best Part Of) Breakin' Up' are not only some of the best-ever recordings made in this genre, but have made the group objects of desire.

The group comprisessisters Veronica and Estelle Bennett and their cousin Nedra Talley. They were originally Twist go-go dance demonstrators at New York's famed Temple Of Twist – The Peppermint Lounge. That was until a chance encounter with whizkid Phil Spector led them to be signed to his Philles label and stardom.

With their long hair piled high upon their heads, heavy eye-makeup, pouting bee-stung lips, tight oriental silk dresses slashed to the thigh and stiletto shoes, they have a sexually-dangerous look that is attractive to both girls – who regard them as role models – and boys, who see them as the answer to their prayers, dreams, fantasies . . .

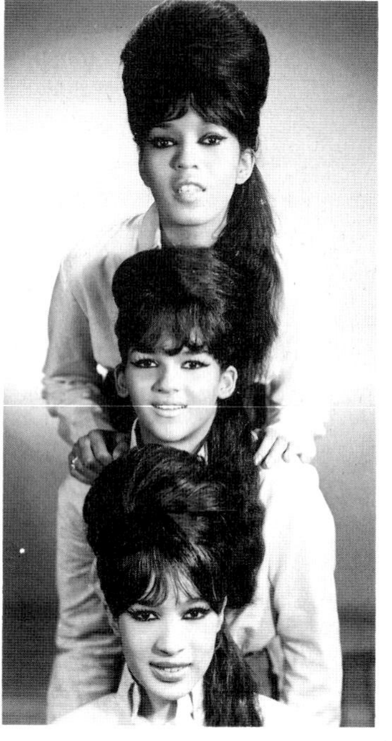

Spector Protégées, The Ronettes

MICKIE – MOST SUCCESSFUL!

Mickie Most, who recently returned to the UK after a three year stay in South Africa where he scored 11 consecutive chart-topping singles, has suddenly emerged as Britain's hottest new record producer.

Having already enjoyed phenomenal success world-wide with The Animals ('The House Of The Rising Sun') and The Nashville Teens ('Tobacco Road'), Most is again at No. 1 as a result of having Manchester group Herman's Hermits re-record Earl Jean's jaunty 'I'm Into Something Good'.

MARIANNE'S TEARS GO BY

'I need to have a boy friend,' admits 17-year-old former convent girl Marianne Faithfull, whose debut single – Jagger & Richard's 'As Tears Go By' – has jumped ten places to No. 13 on the UK best-sellers. 'Often, I get terribly lonely, and it's so nice if there's always someone there.'

Discussing the music business, Marianne doesn't pull her punches: 'People take it all so seriously, it's stupid. Most people are in it for the money, but they just don't admit it.

'I'm not some little girl caught up in the business. I know what I'm doing. I've got two sides. One of them wants money, quick money, and in this business you can make it.

'I thought that I would never be bought. Now I think I have been. Friends of mine say: "Oh Marianne, you're a real mad bird." Yes, that fits me, I'm sure!'

SULLIVAN SLAMS STONES

Immediately following uncontrollable scenes of mass hysteria in the studio during The Rolling Stones' appearance on prime-time 'The Ed Sullivan Show', an irate Mr. Ed told reporters: 'I promise you they'll never be back on our show. If things can't be handled, we'll stop the whole business. We won't book any more rock'n'roll groups, and we'll ban teenagers from the theatre if we have to.

'Frankly, I didn't see the Rolling Stones until the day before the broadcast. They were recommended by my scouts in England. I was shocked when I saw them.

'Now the Dave Clark Five are nice fellows. They are gentlemen, and they perform well. It took me seventeen years to build this show. I'm not going to have it destroyed in a matter of weeks.'

Sullivan – shocked

THE GRAPEVINE

- Mary Wells has been special guest star on The Beatles UK tour.
- The Rolling Stones have cancelled a South African tour following talks with the Musicians' Union, which opposes that country's Apartheid policies.
- CBS have guaranteed Mickie Most £85,000 for the next three years as an independent producer while EMI have signed him to produce new artists for them over the next five years.

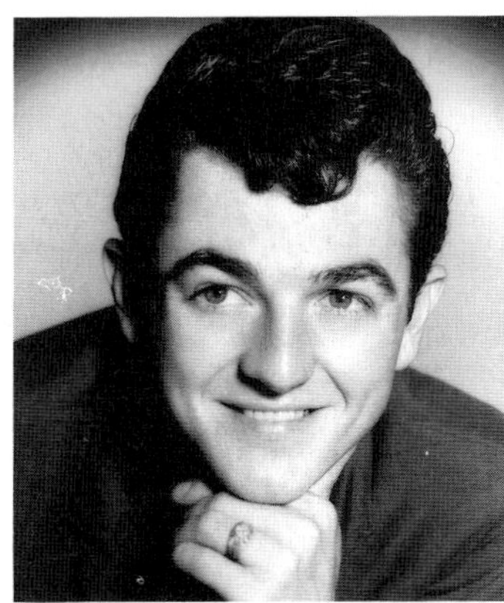

J. Frank Wilson: prophetic disc heralds real-life drama as car crash theme comes true

'LAST KISS' MAN HURT

An automobile carrying 'Last Kiss' car-crash-death-disc hitmaker J. Frank Wilson was involved in an accident near Memphis. The singer was seriously injured, and his 27-year old record producer, Sonley Rouch, was killed.

TAMI TOPS TV

It's already being said of the Steve Binder-directed spectacular, *The TAMI Show* (The Teenage Command Performance), that in terms of production values it will be the yardstick for all future live-in-concert television and cinema presentations.

Filmed a 'live' in Anaheim, California, the non-stop action was supplied by: The Beach Boys, The Barbarians, Chuck Berry, James Brown & The Famous Flames, Marvin Gaye, Gerry & The Pacemakers, Lesley Gore, Jan & Dean, Billy J. Kramer & The Dakotas, Smokey Robinson & The Miracles, The Rolling Stones and The Supremes.

MU BANS SA TOURS

Following the last-minute cancellation of The Rolling Stones' Christmas tour of South Africa, The Swinging Blue Jeans, The Four Pennies, Dave Berry and Freddie & The Dreamers have all called off their scheduled trips. They were told not to go by the British Musicians' Union, which opposes South Africa's apartheid policies. A tour by The Searchers is also threatened. Their agent, Tito Burns, said, 'I haven't cancelled the deal as yet, and I'm hopeful of a M.U. executive meeting next month.'

However, M.U. secretary Harry Francis commented: 'Although South Africa is one of the things our executive committee will discuss, I don't think there's much chance of a change of policy on this issue.'

Mr. Jim Stodel, executive director of African Consolidated Theatres, flew to London from Johannesburg to book artists for South African tours in 1965. But he has already been told by Francis that members of the M.U. will not be permitted to go.

Stodel revealed he would be negotiating with Leslie Grade for Cliff Richard & The Shadows to return to South Africa. Of this, Francis commented: 'We can't speak for Cliff Richard – he is a member of Equity. But as far as we are concerned, The Shadows won't be going.

'The Shadows were not members of the Musicians' Union when they went to South Africa early last year, but they are now. We could never permit our members to work in a country that practises apartheid.'

CHARTS

US45	Oh, Pretty Woman *Roy Orbison*
USLP	A Hard Day's Night *Beatles*
UK45	I'm Into Something Good *Hermin's Hermits*
UKLP	A Hard Day's Night *Beatles*
WEEK 2	
US45	Oh, Pretty Woman *Roy Orbison*
USLP	A Hard Day's Night *Beatles*
UK45	Oh, Pretty Woman *Roy Orbison*
UKLP	A Hard Day's Night *Beatles*
WEEK 3	
US45	Do Wah Diddy Diddy *Manfred Mann*
USLP	A Hard Day's Night *Beatles*
UK45	Oh, Pretty Woman *Roy Orbison*
UKLP	A Hard Day's Night *Beatles*
WEEK 4	
US45	Do Wah Diddy Diddy *Manfred Mann*
USLP	A Hard Day's Night *Beatles*
UK45	Oh, Pretty Woman *Roy Orbison*
UKLP	A Hard Day's Night *Beatles*
WEEK 5	
US45	Baby Love *Supremes*
USLP	People *Barbra Streisand*
UK45	Always Something There To Remind Me *Sandie Shaw*
UKLP	A Hard Day's Night *Beatles*

The Swingin' Blue Jeans, part of the British Musicians Union ban on groups touring South Africa

NOVEMBER

1964

NASHVILLE TEENS TO BUY 2ND ALBUM?

British group The Nashville Teens are back in the charts with 'Google Eye' – a song about a fish(!) from the album 'Twelve Sides Of John D. Loudermilk'.

The Teens' first world-wide hit 'Tobacco Road' also came from the same source. It wasn't intended that way, it's just that country music star Loudermilk is a dab hand with a tune and lyrics.

Ramon Phillips, one of The Teens' two lead singers revealed: 'What do you do when someone comes up and says, "You're making another record next week?" Well, we looked at the LP and found 'Google Eye' was the next track.'

Seems the Loudermilk album is the only one the group own: 'So if you want to know what our next ten records are going to be,' joked Phillips, 'Best buy Loudermilk's LP and work your way through it!'

Currently on tour with The Animals, Carl Perkins and Tommy Tucker, The Teens say their upcoming U.S. tour will give them the chance to investigate new material.

They believe it's the overall sound of any record, rather than the lyrical content, that decides whether or not it's a hit.

'You listen to 'Baby Love' by The Supremes,' fellow frontman Art Sharp argued. 'And you won't hear all the words. People go around singing 'Baby love, my baby love,' because that's all they know – only the hook line.'

ELVIS: THE HONDA THEY FALL

Paramount Pictures have released *Roustabout*. Though Elvis Presley stars and Raquel Welch makes her screen debut, the standard of such formula movies is cause for increasing concern among even die-hard fans.

Elvis' movie double and song choreographer Lance Le Gault offers his thoughts on the subject: 'We shot 'Kissin' Cousins' in seventeen days, and I think that was the turning point. Up until then, certains standards had been maintained. Once they realized they could do a film so quickly, we were on fast pictures.

'The first time I noticed it was in *Roustabout*. Elvis rode a Honda in it. Which is pretty silly, when you think about it, because Elvis rides Harleys. Yet, in the film they put him on a 350 Honda.

'And this is a guy who's playing a drifter whose only mode of transportation is his bike. This is a guy who supposedly goes across country on a machine that's about right for the driveway, a 350 Honda.'

CHARTS

	US45	Baby Love – *Supremes*
	USLP	People – *Barbra Streisand*
	UK45	Always Something There To Remind Me – *Sandie Shaw*
	UKLP	A Hard Day's Night – *Beatles*
WEEK 2	US45	Baby Love – *Supremes*
	USLP	People – *Barbra Streisand*
	UK45	Baby Love – *Supremes*
	UKLP	A Hard Day's Night – *Beatles*
WEEK 3	US45	Baby Love – *Supremes*
	USLP	People – *Barbra Streisand*
	UK45	Little Red Rooster – *Rolling Stones*
	UKLP	A Hard Day's Night – *Beatles*
WEEK 4	US45	Leader Of The Pack – *Shangri-Las*
	USLP	People – *Barbra Streisand*
	UK45	Little Red Rooster – *Rolling Stones*
	UKLP	A Hard Day's Night – *Beatles*

A still from 'Roustabout', latest Elvis quickie to come out of Hollywood

THE GRAPEVINE

- Radio Manx – transmitting from a caravan on the Isle of Man – has become Britain's first land-based commercial radio station.
- The Isley Brothers and Marvin Gaye have appeared on *Ready, Steady, Go!*.
- Rolling Stones have covered 'Little Red Rooster' as their latest single.
- The Beach Boys have been in Europe on a radio/TV promo tour.
- Bluesman Jimmy Reed has been touring UK clubs.

EMI SIGN AUSSIE GROUP

EMI Records have announced the signing, to their Columbia label, of an Australian group (one girl and three boys) who 'sound like The Springfields' and are called The Seekers.

The comparison is not unsurprising considering that Tom Springfield wrote the 'A' side of their debut single, 'I'll Never Find Another You'. EMI are predicting big things for the group.

Also on the EMI schedule is the 'comeback' disc of The Beatles' music publisher Dick James after a 5-year silence. Best known for his hit recording of the 'Robin Hood' TV theme, James is again aiming high with a sing-a-long medley of Beatles' hits.

Vocalist Judith Durham fronts a new folk-based group from Down Under, The Seekers

SOUL PIONEER COOKE KILLED

Soul singer Sam Cooke was shot dead by the manageress of a Los Angeles motel on December 10.

Earlier that evening, Cooke picked up a Eurasian girl named Elisa Boyer in a bar and offered to driver her home. Instead, Cooke drove to a motel on South Figueroa, where he signed the register as 'Mr and Mrs Cooke'.

It's alleged that once inside the motel room, Cooke began to rip the woman's clothes off. Then, when he went to the bathroom, Boyer fled from the room with both her clothes and Cooke's, and hid in a nearby telephone booth, from which she called the police.

Emerging from the motel room dressed in nothing but his sports' coat and shoes, Cooke kicked in the door of the manageress Mrs Bertha Lee Franklin. She testified that Cooke punched her twice and that, in self-defence, she fired at him three times with a .22 revolver.

One shot wounded Cooke in the chest. However, this didn't halt his attack, so Franklin bludgeoned him with a stick. Sam Cooke was already dead by the time the police arrived at the scene of the incident.

Unproven rumours within the U.S. music industry suggest that the Mafia had taken out a contract on the singer, who refused to throw in his lot with some of the criminal elements who control part of the record industry.

Born, 22 January 1931 in Chicago, Sam Cooke is revered as a soul music pioneer who, by way of such songs as 'A Change Is Gonna Come', is said to have heralded the Black Power movement.

The vocal purity of his gospel-derived style on hits such as 'You Send Me', 'Cupid', 'Only Sixteen', 'Wonderful World', 'Another Saturday Night', 'Bring It On Home To Me', 'Twistin' The Night Away' and 'Chain Gang' greatly influenced the current generation of soul singers.

CHARTS

US45	Ringo *Lorne Greene*
USLP	Beach Boys Concert *Beach Boys*
UK45	I Feel Fine *Beatles*
UKLP	A Hard Day's Night *Beatles*
WEEK 2	
US45	Mr. Lonely *Bobby Vinton*
USLP	Beach Boys Concert *Beach Boys*
UK45	I Feel Fine *Beatles*
UKLP	Beatles For Sale *Beatles*
WEEK 3	
US45	Come See About Me *Supremes*
USLP	Beach Boys Concert *Beach Boys*
UK45	I Feel Fine *Beatles*
UKLP	Beatles For Sale *Beatles*
WEEK 4	
US45	I Feel Fine *Beatles*
USLP	Beach Boys Concert *Beach Boys*
UK45	I Feel Fine *Beatles*
UKLP	Beatles For Sale *Beatles*

THE GRAPEVINE

- **The Miracles have made their first visit to Britain to appear on ITV's *Ready, Steady, Go!***
- **The Animals have recorded, as their next single, a song normally associated with Nina Simone – 'Don't Let Me Be Misunderstood'.**
- **New from Gerry & The Pacemakers: 'Ferry 'Cross The Mersey'.**
- **19-year old Kink Ray Davies has married his 18-year old sweetheart.**

BEATLES XMAS SHOW

Vocalist Elkie Brooks is the only girl on the Beatles' bill

A repeat of last year's formula of music, laughter and traditional pantomime is planned for 'Another Beatles Christmas Show'. This year, The Fabs are joined at London's Hammersmith Odeon by a varied bill that includes: The Yardbirds, Freddie & The Dreamers, Elkie Brooks, Jimmy Saville, Michael Haslam, Ray Fell, Sounds Incorporated and The Mike Cotton Sound.

As Brian Wilson (top) quits touring, The Beach Boys go on without him

BRIAN WILSON BOWS OUT

The Beach Boys' main-man Brian Wilson suffered a nervous breakdown on a scheduled flight from Los Angeles to Houston.

As a result, he says he's to quit touring with the group to concentrate on song writing and record production.

AMERICA SHUTS OUT BRITISH GROUPS

Nashville Teens, victims of visa embargo Stateside

Official action by the US Government seems destined to put an end to the tours by British rock groups which proved so popular and lucrative during 1964. The Labor Department in Washington, without stating any clear reasons for the decision, has declared that no UK rock groups will in future be granted H-1 visas – the type necessary for a US tour.

This has already washed out New Year tours by The Zombies, The Nashville Teens and The Hullaballoos, all of whom were working in New York over Christmas on lesser H-2 visas. Existing bookings have already been cancelled.

US journalist Nat Hentoff notes: 'Individual promoters of each concert could apply for a group to work in their town, but setting up a tour this way would be time-consuming and impractical. It is likely, therefore, that British groups will only come to America for TV, radio, or New York stage engagements in future.'

THE GRAPEVINE

■ Freddie Garrity of Freddie & The Dreamers had a narrow escape on January 26 when he was involved in a car accident. Thrown through the windscreen, he was taken to hospital with cuts and bruises, but discharged after five hours.

■ Capitol Records has announced that the LP 'Beatles '65' has sold almost three million copies in the US alone in its first month on release.

CHARTS

US45	I Feel Fine *Beatles*
USLP	Roustabout *Elvis Presley*
UK45	I Feel Fine *Beatles*
UKLP	Beatles For Sale *Beatles*
WEEK 2	
US45	I Feel Fine *Beatles*
USLP	Beatles '65 *Beatles*
UK45	I Feel Fine *Beatles*
UKLP	Beatles For Sale *Beatles*
WEEK 3	
US45	Come See About Me *Supremes*
USLP	Beatles '65 *Beatles*
UK45	Yeh Yeh *Georgie Fame*
UKLP	Beatles For Sale *Beatles*
WEEK 4	
US45	Downtown *Petula Clark*
USLP	Beatles '65 *Beatles*
UK45	Go Now *Moody Blues*
UKLP	The Rolling Stones No.2 *Rolling Stones*
WEEK 5	
US45	Downtown *Petula Clark*
USLP	Beatles '65 *Beatles*
UK45	Go Now *Moody Blues*
UKLP	The Rolling Stones No.2 *Rolling Stones*

ANIMALS QUARANTINED IN HARLEM

Two live shows by The Animals at the Apollo Theatre in Harlem on January 21 and 22 – which were to be recorded live by MGM Records for a spring album – were cancelled by the US immigration department.

Only a last-minute decision by the department allowed the group to fulfil their TV booking on *The Ed Sullivan Show*, on which they performed their new single 'Don't Let Me Be Misunderstood'.

Producer Mickie Most said: 'The Apollo shows were specially set up so I could record a live LP, but as they were preparing to go on stage on Thursday, an official stopped the show.

'Apparently, our American agents had only got permission for the Sullivan show. As a result of our breaking a rule by appearing at the Apollo, The Animals almost lost the TV show too.'

STAR QUOTE

MICK JAGGER

to the New York Daily News

'We get all kinds of kooky requests from the kids. Many mail us sticks of gum to chew and return. Others ask us for locks of our hair. We receive around 1,000 letters a week, and answer as many as we can'.

SPECTOR'S LOVIN' TRIUMPH

Concerned that The Righteous Brothers' 'You've Lost That Lovin' Feeling' hit might be eclipsed in the UK by Cilla Black's George Martin cover version, Rolling Stones' producer Andrew Loog Oldham took the following quarter-page ad in the NME on his own initiative:

'This advertisement is not for commercial gain. It is taken as something must be said about the great new Phil Spector record - The Righteous Brothers singing "You've Lost That Lovin' Feelin'", already in the American Top 10.

'This is Spector's greatest production, the last word in tomorrow's sound today, exposing the overall mediocrity of the music industry, and typifying his greatness.'

Spector's latest, the Righteous Brothers

CHARTS

US45	You've Lost That Lovin' Feelin' *Righteous Brothers*
USLP	Beatles '65 *Beatles*
UK45	You've Lost That Lovin' Feelin' *Righteous Brothers*
UKLP	The Rolling Stones No. 2 *Rolling Stones*
	WEEK 2
US45	You've Lost That Lovin' Feelin' *Righteous Brothers*
USLP	Beatles '65 *Beatles*
UK45	Tired Of Waiting For You *Kinks*
UKLP	The Rolling Stones No.2 *Rolling Stones*
	WEEK 3
US45	This Diamond Ring *Gary Lewis & The Playboys*
USLP	Beatles '65 *Beatles*
UK45	I'll Never Find Another You *Seekers*
UKLP	The Rolling Stones No.2 *Rolling Stones*
	WEEK 4
US45	This Diamond Ring *Gary Lewis & The Playboys*
USLP	Beatles '65 *Beatles*
UK45	I'll Never Find Another You *Seekers*
UKLP	The Rolling Stones No.2 *Rolling Stones*

WESTERN MOVIE FOR THE BEATLES

The Beatles are expected to film a famous western story next year. It will be based on Richard Condon's novel *A Talent For Loving*, which centres on a 1,400-mile horse race which took place in 1871 between the Rio Grande and Mexico City.

Condon, who also wrote *The Manchurian Candidate*, which was filmed by Frank Sinatra, is currently working on the screenplay at his Geneva home.

The movie is to be made by Pickfair Films, a production company formed by Brian Epstein with former United Artists executive Bud Ornstein, and will be shot on location in England and Spain.

However, this is not expected to be the third Beatles film which they will make in the autumn – that is almost certain to be the last of a three-picture deal with United Artists, which began with *A Hard Day's Night*.

Meanwhile, the group fly to the Bahamas on February 22 to begin work on their second film, which will be premiered August and released simultaneously in Britain and the US.

ONLY EIGHT US GOLD SINGLES IN 1964?

The Record Industry Association Of America has announced that eight singles were given gold discs last year for RIAA-certified US sales of over one million.

They were 'Rag Doll' by The Four Seasons, 'I Get Around' by The Beach Boys, Dean Martin's 'Everybody Loves Somebody', Roy Orbison's 'Oh, Pretty Woman', and four by The Beatles: 'I Want To Hold Your Hand' (the year's biggest seller), 'Can't Buy Me Love', 'A Hard Day's Night' and 'I Feel Fine'.

It is believed that several more singles also reached gold status in the US in 1964, but were not applied for by RIAA companies. These include Louis Armstrong's 'Hello Dolly' (on Kapp), The Animals' 'House Of The Rising Sun' (on MGM), Manfred Mann's 'Do Wah Diddy Diddy' (Ascot), and three further Beatles singles: 'She Loves You' (a two million seller for Swan), 'Twist And Shout' and 'Love Me Do' (both on Tollie).

The Tamla-Motown group, America's most successful independent record company, is not an RIAA member, but had a clutch of 1964 million-sellers with Mary Wells' 'My Guy', Martha & The Vandellas' 'Dancing In The Street', and three singles by The Supremes: 'Where Did Our Love Go', 'Baby Love' and 'Come See About Me'.

Manfred 'Diddy' Mann

THE GRAPEVINE

■ **Gene Pitney has recorded an album of duets in Nashville with country star George Jones, Pitney commented: 'George is a real deep-down, bass-y singer, and next to him I sounded like a shrieking witch. But I was really singing country, and I found George was going pop on me, bending words and so on . . . a fantastic experience.'**

The Four Seasons (left) and Beach Boys (above) among last year's US million-sellers

UK TOUR SELL-OUT FOR FOLK FAVOURITE DYLAN

Announcements of a British tour in May by Bob Dylan, acknowledged as the world's leading folk singer, have resulted in a rapid sell-out and the addition of extra dates to the original itinerary – including a second night in London at The Royal Albert Hall. The Beatles are expected to be in the audience for this show, and many other celebrities – including the UK's own new folk star Donovan – have also sought tickets.

Promoter Tito Burns announced: 'Without a single poster having been printed, every ticket was sold for Dylan's concerts in Manchester on May 7 and at The Albert Hall three nights later. His other appearances, at Liverpool, Sheffield, Leicester, Birmingham and Newcastle are also almost sold out already.

'I have to cable this week to tell him that if he wanted to avoid riots in London – and my blood being shed – he must do an extra date at The Albert Hall, which he agreed to.'

While in the UK, Dylan will film his own TV special, and Burns is currently deciding between offers from two of the four major ITV companies for its screening.

CBS Records, meanwhile, has released the title track of Dylan's LP 'The Times They Are A-Changin'' as his first British single, and plans to follow up with his new US 45 'Subterranean Homesick Blues' on the eve of the tour.

CRICKETS – NO MORE CHIRPIN'

The Crickets, the group originally fronted by Buddy Holly, and which in the years since Holly's death has scored particularly strongly in Britain with hits like 'Don't Ever Change', 'My Little Girl' and 'They Call Her La Bamba', have disbanded.

Although leader and drummer Jerry Allison retains ownership of The Crickets' name, and may reform the group at some future date for recording purposes, the hit-making line-up will not be reunited. The recent single 'Now Hear This' was the band's final disc.

Vocalist Jerry Naylor has been ill and is convalescing, while Sonny Curtis is to concentrate on his music publishing business in Los Angeles. As a songwriter Curtis has hits like The Everlys' 'Walk Right Back' under his belt.

Pianist Glenn Hardin has also turned to songwriting, as well as appearing as a session player every week on Jack Good's *Shindig* TV show.

THE GRAPEVINE

- Andrew Oldham recorded Rolling Stones concerts at Liverpool and Manchester on March 6 and 7, in order to extract live tracks for a Stones EP to be titled 'Got Live If You Want It' for Decca release in April.
- Decca is also seeking to record Tom Jones' first major concert date, for an eventual similar live EP.
- Jeff Beck, formerly with the Tridents, has replaced Eric Clapton as lead guitarist with The Yardbirds.

CHARTS

	Chart	Title	Artist
WEEK 1	US45	My Girl	*Temptations*
	USLP	Beatles '65	*Beatles*
	UK45	It's Not Unusual	*Tom Jones*
	UKLP	The Rolling Stones No.2	*Rolling Stones*
WEEK 2	US45	Eight Days A Week	*Beatles*
	USLP	Mary Poppins	*Soundtrack*
	UK45	The Last Time	*Rolling Stones*
	UKLP	The Rolling Stones No.2	*Rolling Stones*
WEEK 3	US45	Eight Days A Week	*Beatles*
	USLP	Goldfinger	*Soundtrack*
	UK45	The Last Time	*Rolling Stones*
	UKLP	The Rolling Stones No.2	*Rolling Stones*
WEEK 4	US45	Stop ! In The Name Of Love	*Supremes*
	USLP	Goldfinger	*Soundtrack*
	UK45	The Last Time	*Rolling Stones*
	UKLP	The Rolling Stones No.2	*Rolling Stones*

Rolling Stones, live on the road if you want it

Jones' concert debut

HELP! COMES TO THE BEATLES

The title of The Beatles' forthcoming film has now been switched to *Help!* after a new song written by John Lennon and Paul McCartney, which the group recorded in a night-time studio session on Tuesday, 13 April.

This will also be their next single, timed for release about a fortnight before the movie is premiered. The previous working title, *Eight Arms To Hold You*, was scrapped before Lennon and McCartney attempted the daunting task of writing a title song around it!

British comedian Frankie Howerd is now slated for a guest role in the film, in the role of an elecution teacher to The Beatles.

STAR QUOTE

JOHN LENNON

filming with the Beatles in the Bahamas

'We still get a kick out of hearing our name on the radio and from working together. There's no chance that we'd ever continue if one of us left the group, and we won't be doing charity shows at 30, combing down our hair for the occasion.'

HERMAN'S HERMITS HITS

Mrs. Brown and daughter herald huge hit for Herman

Herman's Hermits' single 'Mrs Brown You've Got A Lovely Daughter' after massive US airplay as a track on their debut album, has been issued as a single by public demand, despite the group's 'Can't You Hear My Heartbeat' still being in the US Top Five, and the recently released 'Silhouettes' already soaring Top 10-wards.

The day before release, advance orders for the single totalled over 600,000, and it leapt on to the *Billboard* singles chart as No. 12, the highest first-week entry since Sheb Wooley's 'Purple People Eater' debuted in the Top 10 in 1958.

CHARTS

Chart	Title	Artist
US45	Stop ! In The Name Of Love	*Supremes*
USLP	Goldfinger	*Soundtrack*
UK45	The Last Time	*Rolling Stones*
UKLP	The Rolling Stones No.2	*Rolling Stones*
WEEK 2		
US45	I'm Telling You Now	*Freddie & The Dreamers*
USLP	Goldfinger	*Soundtrack*
UK45	The Minute You're Gone	*Cliff Richard*
UKLP	The Rolling Stones No.2	*Rolling Stones*
WEEK 3		
US45	I'm Telling You Now	*Freddie & The Dreamers*
USLP	Goldfinger	*Soundtrack*
UK45	Ticket To Ride	*Beatles*
UKLP	The Rolling Stones No.2	*Rolling Stones*
WEEK 4		
US45	Game Of Love	*Wayne Fontana & The Mindbenders*
USLP	Goldfinger	*Soundtrack*
UK45	Ticket To Ride	*Beatles*
UKLP	Beatles For Sale	*Beatles*

ROULETTE SPONSORS PIRATE RADIO AIRTIME

For the first time, a record company-sponsored show is being broadcast by one of the UK's offshore pirate radio stations, Radio Caroline – despite the British record industry's call to the government to ban the stations.

The sponsor is US label Roulette Records, which is presenting an hour-long show five evenings a week, recorded in the US with DJ Jack Spector. Tapes for the first shows arrived in London on April 10, and were immediately rushed to Caroline's North and South stations, off the Isle of Man and the Essex coast respectively, for first transmission two days later.

A Caroline spokesman said: 'Our contract with Roulette is for two years, and is worth a lot of money to us – it runs into five figures. In addition to the show, Roulette is to take advertising spots.'

The label's UK licensee is EMI, one of the industry's anti-pirate leaders, and none too pleased by the development. An EMI spokesman stated: 'We have written to Roulette Records giving them full details of the attitude of the British record industry - and of the British government – to the pirate stations in general.'

Freddie: dreams come true

THE GRAPEVINE

- **Over a four-day period, Mercury Records received orders for 142,000 copies of its first US album by Freddie & The Dreamers, topping the singles chart with their two-year-old UK hit 'I'm Telling You Now'. The advance sale of this LP so far breaks the all-time advance order record for any LP in the label's 18-year history.**

PRICE LEAVES ANIMALS

Alan Price, The Animals' organist, who originally formed the group in Newcastle as The Alan Price Combo, has quit. His replacement is Dave Rowberry, previously with The Mike Cotton Sound.

Price's decision was forced upon him by an increasing fear of flying, which came to a head just as the group were due to depart for live dates in Sweden.

He announced: 'My nerve broke just a few hours before we were due to fly to Scandinavia,' and added that he was now resting in Newcastle on doctor's orders, with no immediate plans for the future.

Animals' guitarist Hilton Valentine confirms that Price 'said he was sorry, but he just couldn't force himself on to the plane'.

At short notice, the group recruited 19-year-old Mickey Gallagher, of South Shields group Chosen Few, as temporary organist for the nine-day Swedish trek. Rowberry was then recruited as full-time replacement on their return.

Comments vocalist Eric Burdon: 'Alan was a good blues organist, but I think Dave Rowberry's a better musician. We've been working out some arrangements with him on numbers like the Everlys' 'Bye Bye Love'. We believe the group will be even better.'

Flying fear grounds Price

FREDDIE, BY GUM

A major US manufacturer of bubble gum is introducing a new series of Freddie & The Dreamers cards to be given free with packs of gum.

There will be a set of 66 cards in all, which, when they are all placed together, will make a 3ft square picture of the British group.

CHARTS

Week	Chart	Title	Artist
	US45	Mrs. Brown, You've Got A Lovely Daughter	*Herman's Hermits*
	USLP	Goldfinger	*Soundtrack*
	UK45	Ticket To Ride	*Beatles*
	UKLP	Beatles For Sale	*Beatles*
WEEK 2	US45	Mrs. Brown, You've Got A Lovely Daughter	*Herman's Hermits*
	USLP	Goldfinger	*Soundtrack*
	UK45	Ticket To Ride	*Beatles*
	UKLP	Beatles For Sale	*Beatles*
WEEK 3	US45	Mrs. Brown, You've Got A Lovely Daughter	*Herman's Hermits*
	USLP	Goldfinger	*Soundtrack*
	UK45	Ticket To Ride	*Beatles*
	UKLP	The Freewheelin' Bob Dylan	*Bob Dylan*
WEEK 4	US45	Ticket To Ride	*Beatles*
	USLP	Goldfinger	*Soundtrack*
	UK45	Where Are You Now	*Jackie Trent*
	UKLP	Bringing It All Back Home	*Bob Dylan*
WEEK 5	US45	Help Me Rhonda	*Beach Boys*
	USLP	Goldfinger	*Soundtrack*
	UK45	Long Live Love	*Sandie Shaw*
	UKLP	Bringing It All Back Home	*Bob Dylan*

Author Lennon with wife Cynthia

THE GRAPEVINE

- **John Lennon's second book, *A Spaniard In The Works*, is to be published in the UK on June 24 by Jonathan Cape, although Lennon will be out of the country at the time, playing with The Beatles in their debut live appearance in Milan, Italy.**
- **Simon & Schuster are to publish the book in the US, where Lennon's previous volume, *In His Own Write*, sold 175,000 copies.**

POLITICIANS ENTER US VISA ROW

On May 13, as 30 leading American theatrical agents met in New York to formulate a policy in the face of US Government policy apparently aimed at preventing British rock groups from being able to work in America, their cause was joined by a number of US Senators opposed to the current situation.

Meanwhile, on the other side of the Atlantic, Kenneth Lomas, Member of Parliament for Huddersfield West, sought action from the British government.

Having been told that the British government 'cannot accept responsibility for the laws of another country', Lomas told the NME: 'The only other way I could draw attention to this problem was by asking the Minister of Labour to restrict permits to Americans who wish to work in Britain, as a reciprocal measure.'

The Minister, in a written reply, refused to introduce reciprocal action.

WHO'S DALTREY: HE'D RATHER DIE THAN GROW OLD

The Who: explosive

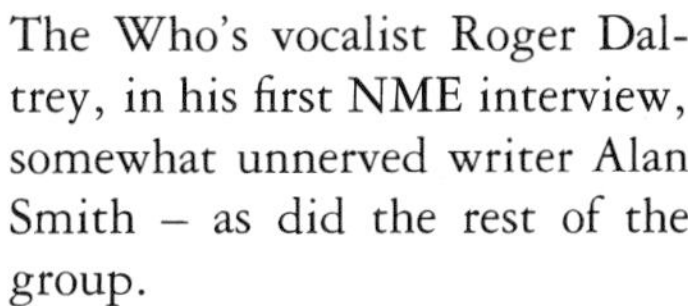

The Who's vocalist Roger Daltrey, in his first NME interview, somewhat unnerved writer Alan Smith – as did the rest of the group.

Assesses Smith: 'There's a sort of vicious strangeness about these four beatsters from Shepherds Bush – and they admit it. They talk quite happily about the way guitarist Pete Townshend smashes his guitar against an amplifier when the mood takes him. Pete says it produces an unusual sound, and I can well believe him.'

Daltrey, after startling his interviewer with the opening observation: 'I never want to grow old – I want to stay young forever,' asserts that The Who were not particularly pleased with their debut hit 'I Can't Explain': 'We just did it to get known. As time goes by, we'll do the kind of thing we really like, really way out.'

'Arguments? Sure, we have 'em all the time. That's why we get on so well; it kind of sharpens us up. We've all got kind of - well, explosive temperaments – and it's like waitin' for a bomb to go off. If it wasn't like this, we'd be nothin'. I mean it: if we were always friendly and matey . . . well, we'd all be a bit soft. We're not mates at all. When we've finished a show and we've got time off, that's it, we go our own ways.'

Daltrey feels that James Brown is going to be the next craze. The Who have been playing his material for some time, and think that it will catch on quicker than people suspect.

Pete Townshend is described by Daltrey as 'very political, a right Bob Dylan', while of himself, he says, with all seriousness: 'If I wasn't with a group, I don't know what I'd do. It means everything to me. I think I'd do myself in.'

THE GRAPEVINE

■ **In an apparent reciprocation against the continued refusal of work visas to UK acts in the US, American singer Bobby Vinton was refused a work permit when he arrived in Britain for two weeks of radio and TV dates. A planned appearance on *Top of the Pops* was an early casualty. Ironically, the single Vinton hopes to plug in Britain is 'Don't Go Away Mad'.**

Visa veto vexes Vinton

CHARTS

US45	Help Me Rhonda *Beach Boys*
USLP	Goldfinger *Soundtrack*
UK45	Long Live Love *Sandie Sahw*
UKLP	Bringing It All Back Home *Bob Dylan*
WEEK 2	
US45	Back In My Arms Again *Supremes*
USLP	Goldfinger *Soundtrack*
UK45	The Price Of Love *Everly Brothers*
UKLP	Bringing It All Back Home *Bob Dylan*
WEEK 3	
US45	I Can't Help Myself *Four Tops*
USLP	Goldfinger *Soundtrack*
UK45	Crying In The Chapel *Elvis Presley*
UKLP	Bringing it All Back Home *Bob Dylan*
WEEK 4	
US45	Mr. Tambourine Man *Byrds*
USLP	Goldfinger *Soundtrack*
UK45	Crying In The Chapel *Elvis Presley*
UKLP	The Sound Of Music *Soundtrack*

JONES BECOMES A HOME-OWNER

Tom Jones has paid £8,000 to buy himself and his family their first home of their own.

His 25th birthday present to himself is a newly built open-plan house of ultra-modern design, in Shepperton, Middlesex, in the comfortable outer London suburbs. He expects to move wife Linda and eight-year-old son Mark in as soon as he returns from a US trip towards the end of June.

Comments Jones: 'This is the first real home of our own we've had since we were married. We used to live with our in-laws in Pontypridd. I can't wait to move in!'

KINKS KAUGHT IN A SONG TUG-OF-WAR

Release of the new Kinks' single has been held up because of a dispute between Larry Page, one of their managers, and Shel Talmy, the producer contracted to record them for Pye. Both men had recorded the group on new Ray Davies compositions, and each barred the other from allowing Pye to release either track.

Talmy, who produced 'See My Friend' with the group before their recent US trip, said: 'I served legal notice on the group while they were in America, restraining them from recording without me.'

Page, who produced a session with The Kinks in Hollywood at the end of the US tour, said: 'I want what is best for the boys – and 'Ring The Bells' is the best record. As publisher of Ray's compositions, I have the final say on any recordings.'

Page also claimed that as publisher/manager he was legally entitled to record the group in Hollywood on one of its own compositions.

A few days after the deadlock was joined, and following The Kinks' return to London from the US, Page resolved the row by agreeing to the release of the Talmy-produced 'See My Friend'.

Kontract krisis for Kinks

CHARTS

US45	I Can't Help Myself — *Four Tops*
USLP	Goldfinger — *Soundtrack*
UK45	I'm Alive — *Hollies*
UKLP	Bringing It All Back Home — *Bob Dylan*
WEEK 2	
US45	(I Can't Get No) Satisfaction — *Rolling Stones*
USLP	Beatles VI — *Beatles*
UK45	I'm Alive — *Hollies*
UKLP	Bringing It All Back Home — *Bob Dylan*
WEEK 3	
US45	(I Can't Get No) Satisfaction — *Rolling Stones*
USLP	Beatles VI — *Beatles*
UK45	Mr. Tambourine Man — *Byrds*
UKLP	Bringing It All Back Home — *Bob Dylan*
WEEK 4	
US45	(I Can't Get No) Satisfaction — *Rolling Stones*
USLP	Beatles VI — *Beatles*
UK45	Mr Tambourine Man — *Byrds*
UKLP	The Sound Of Music — *Soundtrack*

ORBISON SIGNS DUAL RECORD DEAL

Roy Orbison's long-term recording contract with Monument Records, which has brought him almost five years of hits, has expired and not been renewed.

The singer made his last recordings with Monument's owner/producer Fred Foster last month, some of which may yet emerge as singles.

For the future, however, Orbison has taken the unprecedented step of signing parallel deals, each understood to be for 20 years, with different record companies in the US and UK. At home, he will be released on MGM, a company which is also committed to building – via its parent film division – his career in movies.

In Britain, the singer has signed directly to Decca Records for release on its London-American label – the same outlet which previously handled his Monument repertoire in the UK. Orbison is reported to have been so happy with Decca's work (in 1964, he sold more records in the UK than any other US act), that he was keen to see the relationship continue.

The basis of both deals is that Orbison will supervise his own recording sessions at a studio near his Nashville home. From these, master tapes will be delivered to both MGM and Decca for release.

THE GRAPEVINE

- **It has been agreed in the London High Court that The Honeycombs' hit 'Have I The Right' was the work of the group's managers, Ken Howard and Alan Blaikeley. Composer Geoff Goddard agreed to drop allegations that he, not they, had written the song.**
- **Dusty Springfield has recorded an EP titled 'Mademoiselle Dusty', with versions of 'Will You Love Me Tomorrow', 'Summer Is Over', 'Losing You' and 'Stay Awhile' all sung in French.**

Honeycombs men have right to song

BEATLES: MASSIVE SHEA CONCERT AND TV SHOW PLANS

The Beatles played to a massive audience of 56,000 fans at New York's Shea Stadium on August 15, in a concert which was filmed for TV by Ed Sullivan Productions in conjunction with Brian Epstein, who is 'confident that it will be suitable for presentation on British television at Christmas'.

The concert's promoter, Sidney Bernstein, has offered the group a record $350,000 to return to the venue next July or August. Their share from the recent Shea concert was $160,000.

Meanwhile, John Lennon and Paul McCartney will host a 50-minute Granada TV spectacular devoted to their songwriting, to be recorded in the autumn for screening before Christmas. They are unlikely to sing in the show, which is to be produced by John Hamp, but will introduce guests such as Cilla Black, Billy J. Kramer, Peter & Gordon, The Silkie, and other acts singing their hit versions of the duo's songs.

American artists are likely to be featured in film clips, including Ella Fitzgerald, who had a hit with 'Can't Buy Me Love'.

Hamp produced a similar Granada spectacular built around Burt Bacharach, and had discussions with Lennon, McCartney and Brian Epstein concerning the content of the forthcoming show, prior to The Beatles' departure for their US tour.

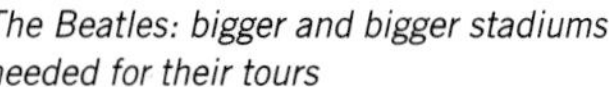

The Beatles: bigger and bigger stadiums needed for their tours

TOP PRODUCERS FORM NEW INDEPENDENT COMPANY

Four of Britain's top record producers – George Martin, Ron Richards and John Burgess from EMI, and Peter Sullivan from Decca - have formed their own production company, to be known as Associated Independent Records (London) Limited, or AIR for short.

Each of the four will continue to work with the acts he has handled on behalf of his previous employer – which amounts to many of EMI's and Decca's top acts, including The Beatles, Tom Jones, Cilla Black, The Hollies, Lulu and P.J. Proby.

George Martin told the NME: 'This will not affect my position as The Beatles' recording manager. Both the group and Brian Epstein stressed that they would like me to continue, and I am happy to do so.'

AIR intends to sign further artists of its own, and there is a possibility that some of those already produced could sign directly with the company after present contracts expire. For the moment, EMI will have first option on AIR's productions, except where the act concerned is currently signed to Decca.

(Below) Five get mobbed in Chicago

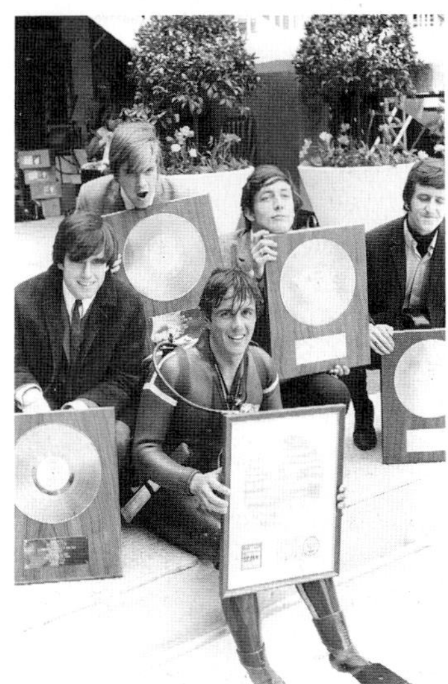

CHARTS

- US45: (I Can't Get No) Satisfaction — *Rolling Stones*
- USLP: Beatles VI — *Beatles*
- UK45: Help! — *Beatles*
- UKLP: The Sound Of Music — *Soundtrack*

WEEK 2

- US45: I'm Henry VIII, I Am — *Herman's Hermits*
- USLP: Beatles VI — *Beatles*
- UK45: Help! — *Beatles*
- UKLP: The Sound Of Music — *Soundtrack*

WEEK 3

- US45: I Got You Babe — *Sonny & Cher*
- USLP: Beatles VI — *Beatles*
- UK45: Help! — *Beatles*
- UKLP: Help! — *Beatles*

WEEK 4

- US45: I Got You Babe — *Sonny & Cher*
- USLP: Out Of Our Heads — *Rolling Stones*
- UK45: Help! — *Beatles*
- UKLP: Help! — *Beatles*

WEEK 5

- US45: I Got You Babe — *Sonny & Cher*
- USLP: Out Of Our Heads — *Rolling Stones*
- UK45: I Got You Babe — *Sonny & Cher*
- UKLP: Help! — *Beatles*

THE GRAPEVINE

- **Dave Clark Five vocalist Mike Smith had two ribs broken when the group was mobbed in Chicago on the first date of its current US tour, while Clark and sax player Dennis Payton lost their jackets and had their shirts torn. After hospital treatment, Smith was allowed to rejoin the group, his chest strapped and in plaster.**

STAR MEETING IN HAWAII – HERMAN QUESTIONS, ELVIS DODGES

Herman's Hermits fulfilled a long-held ambition when they met Elvis Presley on the set of his film, *Paradise Hawaiian Style*, while the group were appearing in Honolulu.

Said Herman's singer Peter Noone: 'I told Sam Katzman, who was producing the film we were in, that I would love to meet El. He was also producing Elvis' picture, and arranged for us to get together when we flew to Hawaii.

'I expected him to be a bit moody, but he was a really nice guy. He told me how much he liked our recordings of 'Mrs Brown' and 'Henry VIII', and Colonel Tom Parker chipped in and said that his wife was always singing 'Henry VIII'!

'Elvis looks *exactly* like he appears on film, and was perfectly natural. He's got a very broad Tennessee accent, and his favourite expressions are "why, sure" and "yessir".

'When I asked him about long hair, and why he didn't grow his, he reminded me that ten years ago, he had long sideburns. It was difficult for me to realize that he was that old!

'We talked for about an hour . . . Elvis said how much he liked British groups, especially The Beatles and The Stones, and said that he was sorry he couldn't meet The Beatles. Every time I mentioned his records to him, though, he seemed to dodge the question.

'I also asked him a few questions about his films, but again he discreetly avoided answering. Colonel Parker protects him all the time. He listens to everything Elvis says, and he won't let him be photographed except by his own photographers.'

Herman and the group (top) meet long-time hero Elvis, chaperoned as usual by the Colonel

THE GRAPEVINE

■ Decca has guaranteed The Animals £100,000 to issue their records outside North America, once the group's contract with producer Mickie Most expires in February 1966. MGM Records, is paying $250,000 for the group's contract for the US and Canada.

■ Husband and wife act Sonny and Cher are reported to be considering the film script of *The Marriage Game*, submitted to them in New York by producer Charles Casher.

CHARTS

- US45 Help! *Beatles*
- USLP Out Of Our Heads *Rolling Stones*
- UK45 (I Can't Get No) Satisfaction *Rolling Stones*
- UKLP Help! *Beatles*

WEEK 2

- US45 Help! *Beatles*
- USLP Help! *Beatles*
- UK45 (I Can't Get No) Satisfaction *Rolling Stones*
- UKLP Help! *Beatles*

WEEK 3

- US45 Help! *Beatles*
- USLP Help! *Beatles*
- UK45 (I Can't Get No) Satisfaction *Rolling Stones*
- UKLP Help! *Beatles*

WEEK 4

- US45 Eve Of Destruction *Barry McGuire*
- USLP Help! *Beatles*
- UK45 Tears *Ken Dodd*
- UKLP Help! *Beatles*

RADIO LONDON IN THRILLER MOVIE

The MV Galaxy, offshore home of UK pirate radio station Radio London, will be one of the locations for the movie *Deadline For Diamonds*, a thriller now going into production at Pinewood Studios, London.

The film will also feature performance cameos by several acts including The Small Faces and Kiki Dee, and some Radio London DJs may also appear.

GERRY TO MARRY

Gerry Marsden of Gerry & The Pacemakers has announced that he will marry his former fan club secretary Pauline Behan in Liverpool on October 11. The couple will then honeymoon for two weeks before Gerry and the group resume UK cabaret dates.

The three Pacemakers – all already married – will be among the guests at the ceremony.

FAITH AND ROULETTES SPLIT

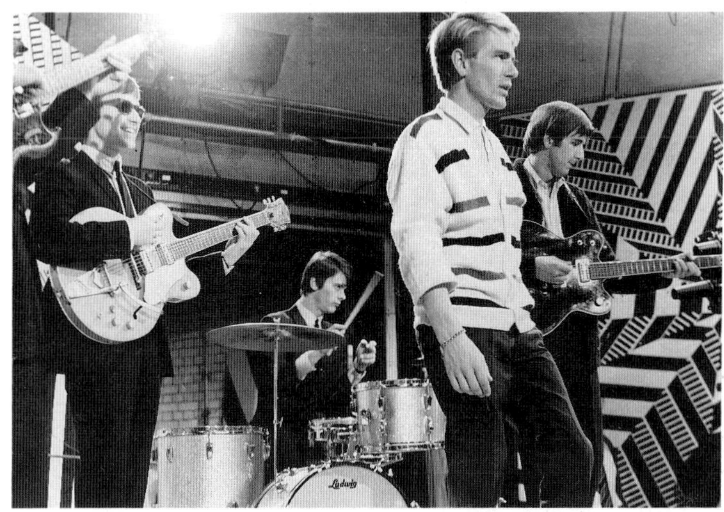

Adam Faith has parted company with his backing group, The Roulettes, after a three-year partnership, and told reporters: 'It's a friendly parting: they've gone to concentrate on their own career.'

Both singer and group will continue to record individually for EMI's Parlophone label, but The Roulettes have also left the Starcast organisation of Evelyn Taylor (who manages Faith), to Unit 4+2's managers John Barker and Anne Niven.

Faith is currently auditioning other groups who could work with him on his few personal appearances, and in their own right at other times.

During the association, The Roulettes backed Faith on several chart singles, beginning with the 1963 UK Top five hit 'The First Time', and including his biggest US success 'It's Alright'. They also released six singles and one album of their own.

CHARTS

US45	Hang On Sloopy *McCoys*
USLP	Help! *Beatles*
UK45	Tears *Ken Dodd*
UKLP	Help! *Beatles*
WEEK 2	
US45	Yesterday *Beatles*
USLP	Help! *Beatles*
UK45	Tears *Ken Dodd*
UKLP	Help! *Beatles*
WEEK 3	
US45	Yesterday *Beatles*
USLP	Help! *Beatles*
UK45	Tears *Ken Dodd*
UKLP	Help! *Beatles*
WEEK 4	
US45	Yesterday *Beatles*
USLP	Help! *Beatles*
UK45	Tears *Ken Dodd*
UKLP	Help! *Beatles*
WEEK 5	
US45	Yesterday *Beatles*
USLP	Help! *Beatles*
UK45	Tears *Ken Dodd*
UKLP	The Sound Of Music *Soundtrack*

ELVIS BASSIST DIES

Bill Black the bass player who appeared on all Elvis Presley's pre-army recordings and live dates, as well as in the films *Loving You* and *Jailhouse Rock*, died on October 21 in Memphis, aged 39. He had been ill for some time, and had undergone surgery at the Baptist Hospital on a brain tumour, from which he did not recover.

After parting from Presley, Black formed his own instrumental outfit, The Bill Black Combo, which scored eight US Top 30 hits between 1959 and 1962, including an instrumental reworking of Elvis' 'Don't Be Cruel'.

Cliff turns to Stones

THE GRAPEVINE

- **UK comedian Lance Percival is to dub the voices of Paul McCartney and Ringo Starr for US TV's Beatles cartoon series.**
- **Cliff Richard plans to record a Mick Jagger/Keith Richards song, 'Blue Turns to Grey'.**
- **Them's lead singer Van Morrison has cut a session at London's Decca Studios which may yield a debut solo single for late October release.**

Van takes a vocal vocation from Them

LUXEMBOURG BOOSTS ITS AIR POWER

The switching on of Radio Luxembourg's new medium wave transmitter means widespread improved reception of the station's 208 metre English language pop music service, which is beamed at the British Isles but listened to across Europe.

A recent survey in the UK by Gallup indicates that the British weekly audience for Luxembourg is nearly three times as great as that for offshore pirate stations Radios London and Caroline combined.

The poll states that Luxembourg's audience in the UK and Ireland exceeds 37 million – compared to 13 million claimed by London and Caroline after their own survey.

Also, several of 208's top-rated shows have more than two million listeners apiece, compared with 500,000 late-night listeners claimed by BBC radio. The station's leading show, *Top 20*, based on the NME singles chart, claims more than three million listeners between 11pm and midnight each Sunday.

P.J. PROBY: DOWN AND NEARLY OUT?

The turbulent career of P.J. Proby has lurched from crisis to crisis even more than usual in recent weeks.

Firstly, he parted company with his manager John Heyman after a 12-month association – 'by mutual consent and on friendly terms', according to both parties. On November 10, a new management pact was signed with the partnership of London club owner Bernie Green and former Bachelors publicist Mel Collins.

However, within days this agreement too was terminated, again 'by mutual agreement', though with no further explanation by either side.

New management offers were being discussed at the end of the month: the next to take on the job would be Proby's fifth since he started to work in the UK in Spring, 1964.

The singer also cancelled previously-booked cabaret dates in London and three provincial cities. A week at Catford's Savoy Club was 'postponed indefinitely' because, according to Proby, 'my new act isn't ready'.

Also imminent is a move from his rented flat in London's Chelsea. 'The neighbours have signed a petition complaining about the noise and parking on the kerb outside,' he told journalists. Proby will move out on December 4 – the same date that his current UK work permit expires.

Proby continued: 'If I haven't got a new manager to straighten out my problems by December 4, I'll probably put on my jeans, borrow the fare home to Hollywood, and get out there and then.

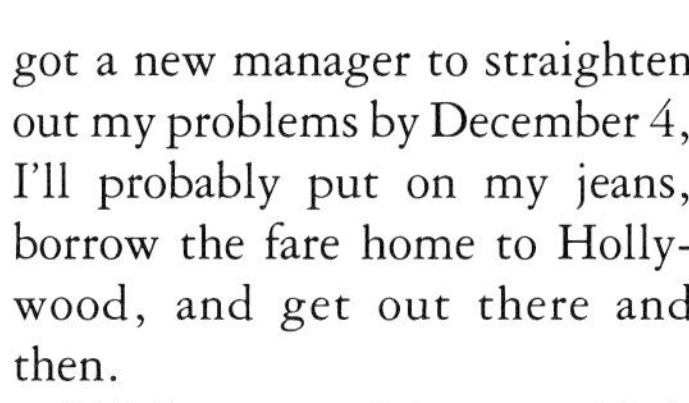

'Right now, things couldn't be much worse – I'm flat broke, penniless, destitute, call it what you like.'

P.J.: Noise annoys neighbours

MARIANNE IS A MUM

Marianne Faithfull and husband John Dunbar found themselves the parents of a son on November 10, somewhat earlier than anticipated.

Marianne fell on the steps of her Chelsea home that morning, went into labour, and gave birth – almost two months prematurely - during the afternoon at a London nursing home. The boy is to be named Nicholas.

BAROQUE BEATLES

Elektra Records, best known as a folk music label, is to release an album of Beatles compositions arranged in baroque style and performed by a small chamber orchestra.

The group reportedly gave their permission for the project, though otherwise have no involvement in it. Title of the LP will be 'Eine Kleine Beatle Musik'.

THE GRAPEVINE

- **The Small Faces, hitmakers in the UK with their debut single 'Whatcha Gonna Do About It', have had a personnel switch. Organist Jimmy Winston has left to form his own group, and has been replaced by 18-year-old Ian McLagan, formerly with The Boz People. McLagan played his debut with the group on a ballroom date at London's Lyceum on November 2.**

McLagan (left), the newest Small Face

CHARTS

- US45 Get Off Of My Cloud *Rolling Stones*
- USLP Help! *Beatles*
- UK45 Get Off Of My Cloud *Rolling Stones*
- UKLP The Sound Of Music *Soundtrack*

WEEK 2

- US45 Get Off My Cloud *Rolling Stones*
- USLP The Sound Of Music *Soundtrack*
- UK45 Get Off Of My Cloud *Rolling Stones*
- UKLP The Sound Of Music *Soundtrack*

WEEK 3

- US45 I Hear A Symphony *Supremes*
- USLP The Sound Of Music *Soundtrack*
- UK45 Get Off Of My Cloud *Rolling Stones*
- UKLP The Sound Of Music *Soundtrack*

WEEK 4

- US45 I Hear A Symphony *Supremes*
- USLP Whipped Cream & Other Delights *Herb Alpert & The Tijuana Brass*
- UK45 1-2-3 *Len Barry*
- UKLP The Sound Of Music *Soundtrack*

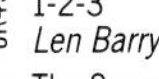

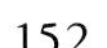

BEATLES DOUBLE-A? – LENNON SAYS NO

On December 19, 16 days after its release, UK sales of The Beatles' double A-side single 'We Can Work It Out'/'Day Tripper' passed one million, qualifying the group for their fifth gold disc from home sales alone. It has been their fastest seller on home ground since 'Can't Buy Me Love', having reached three-quarters of a million after only five days on sale. The single has also reached No. 1 – and gone gold – in the US.

EMI and John Lennon voiced different opinions about the disc's double-A status just prior to its release. The company announced it as 'We Can Work It Out' coupled with 'Day Tripper', but said there was no preferred A-side. Both tracks would be promoted equally, being played in rotation on EMI's sponsored Radio Luxembourg shows, for example.

Lennon insisted to the NME that 'Day Tripper' would be the A-side as far as the group were concerned, and George Martin concurred that, after we gave both titles to EMI, the boys decided they preferred "Day Tripper" – but both are extremely good and deserve a lot of plays.'

Beatles: working it out

1965 POLL FAVOURITES

The NME's annual Readers Poll produced the following results for 1965:

World Section
Male Singer: 1 Elvis Presley; 2 Cliff Richard. Female singer: 1 Dusty Springfield; 2 Brenda Lee. Vocal Group: 1 Beatles; 2 Rolling Stones. Musical Personality: 1 Elvis Presley; 2 John Lennon.

UK Section
Male Singer: 1 Cliff Richard; 2 Paul McCartney. Female Singer: 1 Dusty Springfield; 2 Sandie Shaw. Vocal Group: 1 Beatles; 2 Rolling Stones. Vocal Personality: 1 John Lennon; 2 Cliff Richard. TV/Radio Programme: 1 *Top Of The Pops* 2 *Ready Steady Go!* DJ: 1 Jimmy Savile; 2 David Jacobs. New Singer: 1 Donovan; 2 Chris Andrews. New Group: 1 Seekers; 2 Walker Brothers. UK Single: 1 '(I Can't Get No) Satisfaction' – Rolling Stones; 2 'Help' – Beatles.

This, the 14th NME poll, pulled in more votes than any previously held.

THE GRAPEVINE

■ New fathers: Don Everly has a daughter, and Roger Miller a son.

■ A pair of Paul McCartney's gloves fetched 22 shillings ($3.50) when auctioned for charity in England.

■ Publisher Simon & Schuster has ordered a 13th US printing of John Lennon's book *In His Own Write*, which has now sold 213,000 copies in America; the follow-up *A Spaniard In The Works* has US sales of 95,000 to date.

CHARTS

US45	Turn! Turn! Turn! *Byrds*
USLP	Whipped Cream & Other Delights *Herb Alpert & The Tijuana Brass*
UK45	The Carnival Is Over *Seekers*
UKLP	The Sound Of Music *Soundtrack*
WEEK 2	
US45	Turn! Turn! Turn! *Byrds*
USLP	Whipped Cream & Other Delights *Herb Alpert & The Tijuana Brass*
UK45	We Can Work It Out/Day Tripper *Beatles*
UKLP	Rubber Soul *Beatles*
WEEK 3	
US45	Turn! Turn! Turn! *Byrds*
USLP	Whipped Cream & Other Delights *Herb Alpert & The Tijuana Brass*
UK45	We Can Work It Out/Day Tripper *Beatles*
UKLP	Rubber Soul *Beatles*
WEEK 4	
US45	Over & Over *Dave Clark Five*
USLP	Whipped Cream & Other Dlights *Herb Alpert & The Tijuana Brass*
UK45	We Can Work It Out/Day Tripper *Beatles*
UKLP	Rubber Soul *Beatles*

WILSON TO PRODUCE ANIMALS AFTER DYLAN AND S&G

US Producer Tom Wilson, who produced Bob Dylan's first rock-influenced album 'Bringing It All Back Home' and its hit single 'Subterranean Homesick Blues' earlier this year, and is also responsible for Simon & Garfunkel's current US chart-topper 'The Sound Of Silence', will undertake a UK assignment in the New Year.

Wilson has been engaged as The Animals' producer for their future Decca (UK) and MGM (US) material, following the group's recent split from Mickie Most. He will arrive in London on January 5, to begin work with the Animals on a new single – already set by Decca for an February 11 UK release.

Tom Wilson (above) to produce Animals

. . . as Mickie Most leaves them

The cause of all the trouble – The Animals, with Alan Price (right) leaving the group

GEORGE HARRISON MARRIES

George and Patti embark on honeymoon

Beatle George Harrison became the third married member of the group when he wed Pattie Boyd on January 21, in a quiet Friday morning ceremony near his Epsom home.

The wedding was a surprise not only to press and public, but also to most of the bride and groom's friends and relatives. Although the couple (who had first met in 1964 on the set of *A Hard Day's Night*, in which model/actress Pattie had a bit part) had made their decision some four weeks earlier, they kept the date a secret almost until it arrived.

George's parents had four day's notice to travel from Liverpool. The other Beatles were also told, but Paul McCartney was the only one present since both John and Ringo and their families were on holiday.

Asked at the subsequent press conference how they had managed to keep it a secret, George replied: 'Simple – we didn't tell anyone.'

He told the press: 'Just before Christmas, we were in the car and Pattie was driving, and I said "How about getting married, then?", and she said "Yes, okay" without taking her eyes off the road. What a driver!

'We've had some great wedding presents, you know. Things for the house and that. Paul gave us a fantastic Chinaman's head that you hang on the wall. We also had a smashin' antique table from Brian Epstein.'

STAR QUOTE

PAUL McCARTNEY

'I wouldn't mind being a white-haired old man writing songs, but I'd hate to be a white-haired Beatle at the Empress Stadium playing for people.'

CHARTS

Chart	Title	Artist
US45	Sounds Of Silence	*Simon & Garfunkel*
USLP	Whipped Cream & Other Delights	*Herb Alpert & The Tijuana Brass*
UK45	We Can Work It Out/Day Tripper	*Beatles*
UKLP	Rubber Soul	*Beatles*
WEEK 2		
US45	We Can Work It Out	*Beatles*
USLP	Rubber Soul	*Beatles*
UK45	We Can Work It Out/Day Tripper	*Beatles*
UKLP	Rubber Soul	*Beatles*
WEEK 3		
US45	We Can Work It Out	*Beatles*
USLP	Rubber Soul	*Beatles*
UK45	Keep On Running	*Spencer Davis Group*
UKLP	Rubber Soul	*Beatles*
WEEK 4		
US45	Sounds Of Silence	*Simon & Garfunkel*
USLP	Rubber Soul	*Beatles*
UK45	Keep on Running	*Spencer Davis Group*
UKLP	Rubber Soul	*Beatles*
WEEK 5		
US45	We Can Work It Out	*Beatles*
USLP	Rubber Soul	*Beatles*
UK45	Keep On Running	*Spencer Davis Group*
UKLP	Rubber Soul	*Beatles*

MOTOWN SELLS IN MILLIONS

The Detroit-based Motown Record Corporation outpaced all other companies in the US during 1965 in total sales of singles. The label, which describes itself as 'The Sound Of Young America', took the top-selling tag away from Capitol, which led the field in 1964, thanks to its success with The Beatles.

Through the year, Motown had million-selling singles by The Four Tops ('I Can't Help Myself'), The Temptations ('My Girl'), Jr Walker & The All-Stars ('Shotgun'), and no less than three by The Supremes ('Stop! In The Name Of Love', 'Back In My Arms Again' and 'I Hear A Symphony'), while Marvin Gaye, The Miracles and Martha & The Vandellas also enjoyed Top 10 hits.

Remarkable aspects of this success are that Motown has had no share in the flood of British acts which has found US success in 1965, and that the label is an entirely independently run and distributed black-owned record company, with no ties to any of the corporate major US labels.

THE GRAPEVINE

■ The Merseybeats are now down to two members, Tony Crane and Billy Kinsley, who will continue as vocalists, abbreviating their name to The Merseys. Former group colleagues, John Banks and Aaron Williams, have quit the business.

■ John Carter has left The Ivy League, though he will continue to write songs with Ken Lewis, who remains with the group. The duo are also setting up a production company.

Motown best-sellers The Supremes in action

OLDHAM'S STONES DOCUMENTARY

Manager Andrew Oldham has made an hour-long documentary on the Rolling Stones, entitled *Charlie's My Darling*. It was filmed when the group were touring Ireland in the Autumn, and features both concert footage and backstage interviews.

Brian Jones discusses his fear of marriage, Charlie Watts his limitations as a musician, while Mick Jagger impersonates Elvis Presley! The film is being offered to TV companies.

CHAD AND JEREMY SEEK US CITIZENSHIP

British duo Chad Stuart and Jeremy Clyde have applied for US citizenship, a radical decision following two years of considerable record and TV success in America, unmatched at home.

Most of the duo's immediate commitments require their availability in the US. The main worry in their minds is that, as US citizens, they would become eligible for military service. They have no wish to end up defending their adopted country in Vietnam.

Jeremy Clyde told reporters in Hollywood: 'We really don't know what to do. If we live in Britain, we pay double taxes, and have to go through so much red tape to come over to the US. But if we move here, we may end up in the army!'

It is thought to be impracticable to arrange constant renewal of work permits to film an ongoing TV series. As currently projected, this will feature the duo as English actors stranded in Texas with a trunkful of costumes but no money.

Various episodes will show them trying to work their way across the US to New York, and thence to the UK, making use of the theatrical outfits.

There is only one Them, as far as the record-buying public is concerned, the original group from Belfast fronted by Van Morrison (second from left)

THEM AND THEM AGAIN

The existence of two groups called Them has led to a bitter dispute between two agencies, and could also affect record releases.

The first Them is managed by Dorothy Solomon (also manager of The Bachelors), and includes vocalist Van Morrison and guitarist Alan Henderson, both of whom were on the hits 'Baby Please Don't Go' and 'Here Comes The Night'. The namesake group is managed by Ray Henderson who, in January, registered the band as Them Ltd., in an effort to prevent the Morrison-led group using the name.

In retaliation, Dorothy Solomon's husband Phil registered Fortunes Ltd. and Pinkerton's Assorted Colours Ltd. (both names of acts represented by Henderson's Them agency), giving and assigning the names to two little-known Birmingham groups. Solomon then informed Decca's Sir Edward Lewis that unless all records by groups using those names were withdrawn, he would sue for 'substantial damages'.

Solomon said: 'Our Them have lost worldwide bookings because of confusion caused by this other group. I intend to cause similar confusion by booking out duplicate Fortunes and Pinkerton's Colours – after all, I've registered the names. I shall only give way when I have compensation from King's Agency for all the work we have lost, and a promise that they will drop the name.'

The real Pinkerton's Assorted Colours

THE GRAPEVINE

■ Sonny Bono of Sonny and Cher is reckoned to be the envy of all Hollywood after taking delivery of a unique new 'toy' – one of the first of the new home video tape recorders . . . when he's too busy (which is often) to watch his favourite TV shows, he just has them taped by the machine to view at his leisure later in the week . . . what will they think of next!

CHARTS

US45	My Love *Petula Clark*
USLP	Rubber Soul *Beatles*
UK45	Michelle *Overlanders*
UKLP	Rubber Soul *Beatles*
WEEK 2	
US45	My Love *Petula Clark*
USLP	Rubber Soul *Beatles*
UK45	These Boots Are Made For Walkin' *Nancy Sinatra*
UKLP	Rubber Soul *Beatles*
WEEK 3	
US45	Lightnin' Strikes *Lou Christie*
USLP	Rubber Soul *Beatles*
UK45	19th Nervous Breakdown *Rolling Stones*
UKLP	Rubber Soul *Beatles*
WEEK 4	
US45	These Boots Are Made For Walkin' *Nancy Sinatra*
USLP	Rubber Soul *Beatles*
UK45	19th Nervous Breakdown *Rolling Stones*
UKLP	Rubber Soul *Beatles*

STAR QUOTE

TOM JONES

on his formative years

'In my teens, we were all very aggressive. Our girls were aggressive, too. They wore a lot of make-up and were very tough. That's the kind of thing I grew up with, and it's left its mark.'

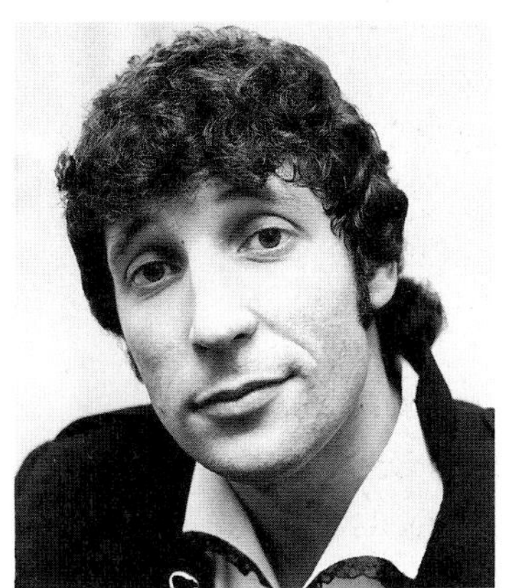

The macho boyo, Tom Jones

WHO SINGLE: A LEGAL MATTER

The Who's single 'Substitute', the first under the group's new deal with the Reaction label via Polydor, was released in the UK on Friday, March 4, and quickly set off a complex chain of events.

Firstly, The Who's previous label Brunswick – marketed by UK Decca – rushed out a Who single of its own, coupling 'A Legal Matter' from their debut LP with 'Instant Party' – a track formerly scheduled as the group's next A-side under the title 'Circles'.

A day later, producer Shel Talmy, responsible for every Who recording prior to their Reaction debut, successfully applied for a temporary injunction to prevent Polydor from marketing 'Substitute'. His complaint was that 'Instant Party' was also on the B-side of the Brunswick single, and his copyright was thus infringed.

Polydor was served with the injunction on March 9, and stopped pressing the record. In the London High Court on the afternoon of the same day, counsel for Polydor told the judge that a sale ban might kill the chances of the record 'which in less than a week has entered the New Musical Express chart (compiled that morning) at No. 19, and is expected to rise to No. 1.'

On Monday 14, Polydor circumvented the injunction by releasing a new pressing of 'Substitute' with a different B-side, an instrumental track titled 'Waltz For A Pig'.

Then on March 18, the injunction on the original pressing was removed by the High Court, and Polydor was able to shift a warehouse stock of 40,000.

Confusion surrounds The Who as rival record companies wrangle over their rights

CHARTS

US45	Ballad Of The Green Berets *Sgt. Barry Sadler*
USLP	Going Places *Herb Alpert & The Tijuana Brass*
UK45	19th Nervous Breakdown *Rolling Stones*
UKLP	The Sound Of Music *Soundtrack*
	WEEK 2
US45	Ballad Of The Green Berets *Sgt. Barry Sadler*
USLP	Ballads Of The Green Berets *Sgt. Barry Sadler*
UK45	I Can't Let Go *Hollies*
UKLP	The Sound Of Music *Soundtrack*
	WEEK 3
US45	Ballad Of The Green Berets *Sgt. Barry Sadler*
USLP	Ballads Of The Green Berets *Sgt. Barry Sadler*
UK45	The Sun Ain't Gonna Shine Anymore *Walker Brothers*
UKLP	The Sound Of Music *Soundtrack*
	WEEK 4
US45	Ballad Of The Green Berets *Sgt. Barry Sadler*
USLP	Ballads Of The Green Berets *Sgt. Barry Sadler*
UK45	The Sun Ain't Gonna Shine Anymore *Walker Brothers*
UKLP	The Sound Of Music *Soundtrack*

LULU LOSES LUVVERS

Lulu and her backing group The Luvvers are to split in mid-March after a tour of Poland.

It has been decided that the former romance between the singer and Luvvers' guitarist Alec Bell is likely to hold back their careers if they continue working together, though a split was not originally planned until May.

The group will henceforth record for Decca in their own right, with Bell as lead singer.

Don't drop her – she shouts!

THE GRAPEVINE

- **According to a New York Times article, CBS is close to developing a disc which can reproduce picures on a TV screen, as well as sound. The price of a disc is likely to be low – around the retail cost of a 45rpm single.**
- **Drummer Barry Jenkins has left The Nashville Teens to join The Animals in place of John Steele.**
- **Paul McCartney has owned up to writing Peter & Gordon's 'Woman' under the pseudonym of 'Bernard Webb'.**

NANCY GETS 'WRONG' GOLD!

Nancy Sinatra was presented with a gold disc to mark over a million US sales of 'These Boots Are Made For Walkin'' in a ceremony at Hollywood's It's Boss Club.

Because the actual gold record of 'Boots' failed to arrive in time from New York, British expatriot dj 'Lord Tim' Hudson actually presented Nancy with the similar award earned by Dean Martin (his prospective father-in-law) for 'Everybody Loves Somebody'.

Nancy's boots made for dancing?

DUSTY DEMANDS NEW US LABEL

Dusty Springfield has announced that she will not record again until her UK record label Philips Records releases her from the American part of her contract, which until now has seen her US releases on the Philips-owned Mercury label.

With 'You Don't Have To Say You Love Me' giving the singer her first UK No. 1, Mercury president Irving Green has flown to London to try to sort out the situation, but Dusty's manager Vic Billings says that she is determined to have a new US label.

It seems likely that Philips will indeed accede to the demand and release her – possibly to Atlantic.

Dusty said: 'I have no real quarrel with the company in Britain, but in the US they have done virtually nothing to promote me or my records. Most of the kids there seem to have no idea when I have a disc on release – in fact, they write telling me how badly I am being promoted in America!

'I've just had an 18-page letter from a fan in Los Angeles about the situation, and it was heartbreaking to read.

Dusty defects

'Anyway, I am totally dissatisfied with the whole set-up in the States, and I'm just not going to record again until something is done. Some people might say this attitude is unfair to my fans in Britain, but the present situation is unfair to the fans in the States, too, and I have to think of them as well.'

BRITISH WALKER BROTHERS!

US hitmaking trio The Walker Brothers, based for a year in Britain and currently topping the UK chart with 'The Sun Ain't Gonna Shine Anymore' are to relinquish their American citizenship and apply for Biritsh nationality.

Manager Maurice King announced that the three individual Walkers – vocalists Scott Engel and John Maus and drummer Gary Leeds – have already begun the complicated procedure of applying for British naturalization, although they will probably have to live in the UK for a further two years to establish the necessary residential qualification.

Scott is quoted as saying: 'It takes a long time for the whole thing to become finalized – but even if we are not still at the top

Walker Bros to become Brits?

in Britain when everything is completed, it will make no difference. We like it here, and we intend to stay for good. Once, being American helped an artist in the UK; now it means nothing at all. We are essentially British stars.'

CHARTS

US45	Ballad Of The Green Berets – *Sgt. Barry Sadler*
USLP	Ballads Of The Green Berets – *Sgt. Barry Sadler*
UK45	The Sun Ain't Gonna Shine Anymore – *Walker Brothers*
UKLP	The Sound Of Music – *Soundtrack*
WEEK 2	
US45	(You're My) Soul & Inspiration – *Righteous Brothers*
USLP	Ballads Of The Green Berets – *Sgt. Barry Sadler*
UK45	The Sun Ain't Gonna Shine Anymore – *Walker Brothers*
UKLP	The Sound Of Music – *Soundtrack*
WEEK 3	
US45	(You're My) Soul & Inspiration – *Righteous Brothers*
USLP	Ballads Of The Green Berets – *Sgt. Barry Sadler*
UK45	Somebody Help Me – *Spencer Davis Group*
UKLP	The Sound Of Music – *Soundtrack*
WEEK 4	
US45	(You're My) Soul & Inspiration – *Righteous Brothers*
USLP	Ballads Of The Green Berets – *Sgt. Barry Sadler*
UK45	You Don't Have To Say You Love Me – *Dusty Springfield*
UKLP	The Sound Of Music – *Soundtrack*
WEEK 5	
US45	Good Lovin' – *Young Rascals*
USLP	Ballads Of The Green Berets – *Sgt. Barry Sadler*
UK45	You Don't Have To Say You Love Me – *Dusty Springfield*
UKLP	Aftermath – *Rolling Stones*

THE GRAPEVINE

■ Drummer Chris Curtis has left The Searchers, following a five-week absence, suffering from 'overstrain'. He has joined Pye Records as a producer, and label boss Louis Benjamin has given him a virtually free hand to record what he likes – including himself as a soloist or with a new group.

The Searchers' new drummer, meanwhile, is John Blunt, Curtis's recent tour stand-in.

CHARTS

US45	Monday Monday *Mamas & Papas*
USLP	Ballads Of The Green Berets *Sgt. Barry Sadler*
UK45	Pretty Flamingo *Manfred Mann*
UKLP	Aftermath *Rolling Stones*
WEEK 2	
US45	Monday Monday *Mamas & Papas*
USLP	Ballads Of The Green Berets *Sgt. Barry Sadler*
UK45	Pretty Flamingo *Manfred Mann*
UKLP	Aftermath *Rolling Stones*
WEEK 3	
US45	Monday Monday *Mamas & Papas*
USLP	If You Can Believe Your Eyes & Ears *Mamas & Papas*
UK45	Pretty Flamingo *Manfred Mann*
UKLP	Aftermath *Rolling Stones*
WEEK 4	
US45	When A Man Loves A Woman *Percy Sledge*
USLP	What Now My Love *Herb Alpert & The Tijuana Brass*
UK45	Paint It Black *Rolling Stones*
UKLP	Aftermath *Rolling Stones*

MOON DOWN, BUT NOT OUT

Who drummer Keith Moon has withdrawn a threat to leave the group and take bass player John Entwistle with him, five days after he announced that he was quitting following an onstage incident which left him injured.

On Friday May 20, the group was playing at the Ricky Tick club in Newbury, UK, when Pete Townshend accidentally struck Moon in the face with his guitar as they went through a 'wild' routine on 'My Generation'. The drummer collapsed on his kit, and ended up with a black eye and a knee injury which required three stitches.

In the aftermath, he told a reporter that he and John Entwistle were both getting out of The Who to work as a duo.

A temporary drummer deputized on the next few days' dates while Moon recovered from his injuries at his London home, but by Wednesday he had relented over quitting, and the group's agent Robert Stigwood said: 'Everything has been sorted out. Keith will probably be back for concerts this weekend in Blackpool and Morecambe.'

Col. Parker looking in appropriately expansive mood

Spector, currently in the studio with Ike and Tina Turner

THE GRAPEVINE

- Colonel Tom Parker's office has categorically denied a report that Elvis Presley has given 22-year old Priscilla Beaulieu – who has been living for some time in Memphis with Presley's grandmother – a diamond engagement ring and a house near Hollywood.
- Worldwide sales of the *West Side Story* film soundtrack album have topped five million.
- Frank Sinatra recorded a cover of 'Downtown' with Petula Clark standing in the studio beside him.

SPECTOR VS RIGHTEOUS BROTHERS

Phil Spector has filed a three and one half million dollar lawsuit against The Righteous Brothers, who have left his Philles label to sign to Verve, a subsidiary of MGM. Spector commented: 'If they can get out of this contract, then no contract in the record business is worth the paper it's written on.'

STONES TO ACT INDIVIDUALLY IN FILM PLAN

A new film project has been announced for The Rolling Stones. This previously-slated *Back, Behind And In Front*, on which the group were originally to have started work in April, has now been scrapped, and instead they have bought the movie rights to *Only Lovers Left Alive*, a British novel written by teacher David Wallis, which details an imaginary conquest of the country by its violent and rebellious youth.

Andrew Oldham says that The Stones will NOT be portrayed as a group in the film, but that Mick, Charlie, Keith, Brian and Bill will all be playing individual character roles. However, there will be several featured songs penned by Jagger and Richard – who are to write the whole score – and the group will record the soundtrack in Los Angeles at the end of their American tour in late July.

Filming is planned to start in Britain in August, as soon as The Stones return from the US.

ROY ORBISON'S WIFE DIES IN CRASH

Claudette Orbison, 26-year-old wife of singer Roy (and inspiration behind 'Claudette', the song he wrote for the Everly Brothers in 1958), died on June 7, two hours after her motorcycle was in collision with a truck on the road between Nashville and the Orbisons' home in Hendersonville, Tenn.

Roy and Claudette were riding together on separate machines when the crash occurred, and he witnessed the tragedy. The couple, reunited a few months ago after an earlier separation, had just begun a holiday at home following a lengthy bout of overseas touring.

Roy himself had a minor motorbike injury while performing in Britain last month, and Claudette had flown to join him for the remainder of the tour (including the all-star NME poll winners concert in London) to ensure that all was well. She died exactly four weeks after accompanying him home for a well-earned rest.

CLIFF'S CLUB CLOSES

Cliff Richard's official fan club, which has been running for nine years and has 42,000 members, is to wind down and close completely in April 1967 – the same month in which Cliff, at the end of a London Palladium season, is expected to semi-retire to undertake a three-year college course in divinity.

Jane Vane (22), who has run the club since its inception, has relinquished her post as secretary, but will oversee the closure.

CHARTS

US45	When A Man Loves A Woman *Percy Sledge*
USLP	What Now My Love *Herb Alpert & The Tijuana Brass*
UK45	Strangers In The Night *Frank Sinatra*
UKLP	Aftermath *Rolling Stones*
	WEEK 2
US45	Paint It Black *Rolling Stones*
USLP	What Now My Love *Herb Alpert & The Tijuana Brass*
UK45	Strangers In The Night *Frank Sinatra*
UKLP	Aftermath *Rolling Stones*
	WEEK 3
US45	Paint It Black *Rolling Stones*
USLP	What Now My Love *Herb Alpert & The Tijuana Brass*
UK45	Strangers In The Night *Frank Sinatra*
UKLP	Aftermath *Rolling Stones*
	WEEK 4
US45	Paperback Writer *Beatles*
USLP	What Now My Love *Herb Alpert & The Tijuana Brass*
UK45	Paperback Writer *Beatles*
UKLP	Aftermath *Rolling Stones*

David 'Screaming Lord' Sutch

MU IN TV MIME BAN

Britain's Musicians' Union has tightened its stranglehold on the country's pop music by successfully ordering an all-out ban on TV shows which allow artists to mime to their records. Both the BBC and Independent Television have given in to the union's 'no miming' demand, and the previously widespread practice will end on July 31.

One immediate effect is that BBC-1's *A Whole Scene Going*, due to return for a new series on September 8 after a summer recess, has been scrapped. *Top Of The Pops*, however, will continue by having artists remake their records in the BBC's studios the day before the show, and mime to the new tapes during transmission.

The union allows this procedure, since accompanying musicians thereby receive additional work, even though it is being recorded.

MU general secretary Hardie Ratcliffe says that the mime ban is something which groups as a whole should welcome, and claims: 'We believe this move will open the door for hundreds of groups who have never had the chance to appear on TV, just because they have not made a record.'

THE GRAPEVINE

■ **The Beatles' LP 'Yesterday And Today' has been delayed in the US because of a last-minute decision by Capitol Records to change the sleeve design. Early reactions to a shot of the group surrounded by chunks of meat and broken dolls convinced the label that controversy might ensue.**

■ **British singer Geneveve has called off her brief engagement to eccentric rocker Screaming Lord Sutch, to concentrate on her singing career.**

CHARTS

US45	Strangers In The Night *Frank Sinatra*
USLP	What Now My Love *Herb Alpert & The Tijuana Brass*
UK45	Paperback Writer *Beatles*
UKLP	The Sound Of Music *Soundtrack*
	WEEK 2
US45	Paperback Writer *Beatles*
USLP	What Now My Love *Herb Alpert & The Tijuana Brass*
UK45	Sunny Afternoon *Kinks*
UKLP	The Sound Of Music *Soundtrack*
	WEEK 3
US45	Hanky Panky *Tommy James & The Shondells*
USLP	Strangers In The Night *Frank Sinatra*
UK45	Sunny Afternoon *Kinks*
UKLP	The Sound Of Music *Soundtrack*
	WEEK 4
US45	Hanky Panky *Tommy James & The Shondells*
USLP	Strangers In The Night *Frank Sinatra*
UK45	Out Of Time *Chris Farlowe*
UKLP	The Sound Of Music *Soundtrack*
	WEEK 5
US45	Wild Thing *Troggs*
USLP	Yesterday & Today *Beatles*
UK45	Out Of Time *Chris Farlowe*
UKLP	The Sound Of Music *Soundtrack*

'Sheila' hitman Tommy Roe

HAYDOCK SACKED FROM HOLLIES

Bass guitarist Eric Haydock has left The Hollies, and despite widespread reports that he disliked touring and wanted to spend more time at home, he was actually sacked from the group.

Hollie Graham Nash explained: 'We gave him a month's notice before we went on holiday – it was joint decision. Musically we had no complaint, but his unreliability got to the point where we didn't know whether we were coming or going.

'We had to get an emergency replacement for Eric immediately before our trip to Sweden, and he was also missing from the session for "Bus Stop". The uncertainty had been getting us down, particularly when we knew we were all as tired and overworked as he was. After all, the bass player does the least work in the group.'

Admitting his sacking, Haydock said: 'It's a raw deal, and I'm consulting my lawyers. I wanted a few days off in November, when my wife is expecting a baby. It's true that I've missed a few dates through illness, but on each occasion I've produced a doctor's certificate.'

The new Hollies bassist is 23-year old Bern Calvert from Nelson, Lancashire, who deputized for Haydock on the group's recent European jaunt.

JONES QUITS MANFREDS TO GO SOLO

Following the announcement of their recording move from EMI's HMV to Philips' Fontana label, Manfred Mann announced at a press conference on July 6 that lead singer Paul Jones would leave the group at the end of the month. His replacement is Michael D'Abo, formerly with A Band Of Angels.

Mike D'Abo, seated centre

Jones makes his final live apperance with the Manfreds at Blackpool South Pier on July 31, and D'Abo will join the group when they fly to Copenhagen for live work a week later. He has aleady taken over on the first recording sessions for the new label, and sings lead on the group's forthcoming single, a cover of Bob Dylan's 'Just Like A Woman', produced by Shel Talmy.

Jones, meanwhile, remains with HMV as a soloist, and will continue to work with producer John Burgess. He has also been signed to co-star with another novice actor – model Jean Shrimpton – in a film for controversial director Peter Watkins (who made *The War Game*), which will go into production on August 1, mostly on location in London and Birmingham, UK.

Titled *Privilege*, it concerns a pop singer who is manipulated into a cultural phenomenon.

Leaving to do his own thing, ex-Manfred vocalist Paul Jones

- **Righteous Brother Bill Medley had an operation on July 12 to remove nodes from his vocal chords. Back home, he explained (via a note): 'I won't be allowed to talk at all for a week, and then I'll be another four weeks gradually getting back to full-time singing'.**
- **Tommy Roe has been screen-tested for the movie *The Cool Ones*, which has a Lee Hazlewood score.**

STAR QUOTE

JOHN LENNON

'There were some I used to have repeatedly. One was about finding lots of money in an old house, as much of the stuff as you could carry. I could never pick up enough. I don't have that old dream any more – so that's solved THAT one, doctor!'

AUGUST

1966

LENNON IN THE WARS

John Lennon is to split from The Beatles for two months – just days after the group return to the UK from their current US tour. He has been offered a part in the Second World War film *How I Won The War*, which is to be made on location in West Germany and Spain during September and October by director Dick Lester, who made The Beatles' *A Hard Day's Night* and *Help!* movies.

Meanwhile, when The Beatles arrived in Chicago at the opening of their 1966 US tour, controversy surrounded them. Remarks made by John Lennon in a UK press interview earlier in the year, to the effect that The Beatles were currently more popular than Jesus, were hardly noticed at home. However, following belated US syndication, the comments have upset many religious-minded Americans, and ignited fury among some who choose to conceal their own bigotry behind religion, notably the Ku Klux Klan, which has leaped in with Beatle record-burning bonfires, denouncing him as the devil's emissary and the group in general as foreign undesirables.

Lennon took the bit between his teeth and, for the sake of good relations on the tour, publicly apologized at a Chicago press conference to those he had offended. He was sorry for having expressed himself poorly, and thus giving mistaken impressions, and added that he would be more guarded in future. He also made clear, however, that he defended his right to hold controversial opinions.

HOLLIES FOR HOLLYWOOD?

Partly as a result of a chewing gum TV ad. made by The Hollies, currently being seen across the US, the group have been offered a Hollywood movie at the end of the year.

It would feature Graham Nash and Allan Clarke playing the lead parts, with the whole group in acting roles, as well as music by The Hollies.

However, the group's agent Colin Hogg commented: 'I must emphasise it's far from definite, and cannot be agreed until I have approved both terms and script.'

THE GRAPEVINE

■ The Lovin' Spoonful have revealed that 'Summer In The City' is proving a pain to perform on stage. Zal Yanovsky says: 'It turns out that while Steve is playing organ, poor John has to play piano, which he can only do by concentrating – and not singing. So Joe sings lead when we do it live.

■ Jeff Beck's contraction of severe tonsillitis has caused The Yardbirds to cancel their appearance at the UK's Windsor Jazz & Blues Festival.

'Summer In The City' during a recent television performance

A long way from home Manchester's Hollies are Hollywood bound

CHARTS

US45	Wild Thing *Troggs*
USLP	Yesterday & Today *Beatles*
UK45	With A Girl Like You *Troggs*
UKLP	The Sound Of Music *Soundtrack*
WEEK 2	
US45	Summer In The City *Lovin' Spoonful*
USLP	Yesterday & Today *Beatles*
UK45	With A Girl Like You *Troggs*
UKLP	Revolver *Beatles*
WEEK 3	
US45	Summer In The City *Lovin' Spoonful*
USLP	Yesterday & Today *Beatles*
UK45	Yellow Submarine/Eleanor Rigby *Beatles*
UKLP	Revolver *Beatles*
WEEK 4	
US45	Summer In The City *Lovin' Spoonful*
USLP	Yesterday & Today *Beatles*
UK45	Yellow Submarine/Eleanor Rigby *Beatles*
UKLP	Revolver *Beatles*

NAPOLEON XIV – WHO IS THAT MASKED MAN?

As well as John Lennon, another hitmaker causing controversy is Napoleon XIV, whose surprise smash 'They're Coming To Take Me Away, Ha-Haaa!' takes a comic look at mental illness. Radio stations on both sides of the Atlantic have banned the disc as offensive, but this has done nothing to halt its sales.

The artist is now revealed to be New York recording engineer Jerry Samuels, who made the disc himself and then had its commercial potential spotted by Warner/Reprise's George Lee.

CHARTS

US45	Sunshine Superman *Donovan*
USLP	Yesterday & Today *Beatles*
UK45	Yellow Submarine/Eleanor Rigby *Beatles*
UKLP	Revolver *Beatles*
WEEK 2	
US45	You Can't Hurry Love *Supremes*
USLP	Revolver *Beatles*
UK45	Yellow Submarine/Eleanor Rigby *Beatles*
UKLP	Revolver *Beatles*
WEEK 3	
US45	You Can't Hurry Love *Supremes*
USLP	Revolver *Beatles*
UK45	All Or Nothing *Small Faces*
UKLP	Revolver *Beatles*
WEEK 4	
US45	Cherish *Association*
USLP	Revolver *Beatles*
UK45	Distant Drums *Jim Reeves*
UKLP	Revolver *Beatles*

KINKS: KONTRACTUAL KOMPLICATIONS, AND QUAIFE KWITS

A deadlock over The Kinks' recordings between the group, its management and Pye Records may mean an indefinite postponement of their next album and single.

The group are currently in the US Top 20 with 'Sunny Afternoon', which was issued in June in the UK and became a No. 1 hit. However, a new single is not expected before late November, and the 16-track LP 'Kinks', originally scheduled for an August UK release, will not now appear at all until business negotiations are concluded between their US business director Allen Klein and Pye managing director Louis Benjamin.

The deadlock is said to be similar to that currently preventing Pye from releasing new Donovan material in the UK – including his US chart-topper 'Sunshine Superman'.

Meanwhile, The Kinks have also lost an original member. After weeks of rumours, manager Robert Wace confirmed that bass guitarist Pete Quaife, who has been unable to play with the group for three months because of injuries sustained in a road accident, has now left permanently. He seems likely to settle in Copenhagen, and is rumoured to be marrying a Danish girl, Annette Paustian.

Wace says: 'I feel that Pete may have made the wrong decision to leave – but it is his decision. It could be at least six months before he would have been well enough to rejoin the group, and he has decided instead to make his career in other fields.'

John Dalton, who has been deputizing for Quaife, has now joined The Kinks as his permanent replacement. One report suggests that Quaife may be joining British European Airways' advertising department as a designer.

Ray Davis (top) and the other Kinks look to unsettled times in the immediate future

The Big 'O' – 'Too Soon' not too soon

ORBISON: 'TOO SOON NOT SICK!'

Roy Orbison is unhappy that people are making the wrong connection between new single 'Too Soon To Know' – a ballad about loss – and the recent death of his wife Claudette.

He told the press: 'After the accident, I didn't care what was released . . . there were several possibilities, but the content of others, like "You'll Never Be Sixteen Again", was, under the circumstances, even worse.

'I didn't want to go into the studio to record something new, so I just said "release whatever you think is best" – and that was "Too Soon To Know".

'Every song I do from now on could be subject to misinterpretation, but anyone who thinks that "Too Soon To Know" was released at this time so that I could make sympathy-money, must have a sick mind!'

THE GRAPEVINE

- **Drummer Barry Jenkins will be the only one of the existing Animals to remain with Eric Burdon in the singer's soon-to-be formed 'new' Animals; Hilton Valentine and Chas Chandler are both moving into production.**
- **Georgie Fame is parting from his long-time backing group the Blue Flames, following a final gig in Amsterdam on October 1.**

Georgie Fame – extinguishing The Flames?

AUSTRALIA AND US CENSOR UK DISCS

Two current UK Top 10 singles are running into difficulties elsewhere in the world. Dozens of US radio stations have banned Dave Dee, Dozy, Beaky, Mick & Tich's 'Bend It' because the lyrics are considreed too suggestive, and the group have responded by recording a new version in London with a different set of words.

The tapes of this have been flown to the US for rush release, while the original single has been withdrawn.

Meanwhile, in Australia, the Commercial Broadcasting Federation is debating whether to approve a total ban on the Troggs' 'I Can't Control Myself' – which, if effected, will mean not only no radio or TV plays, but dealers being prevented from selling it, too.

This would be the first complete state censoring of a pop record in Australia. The Troggs' lead singer Reg Presley commented: 'Naturally we're disappointed, but there's no point in getting angry about it.'

Dave Dee, Dozy, Beaky, Mick and Tich: new version of 'Bend It' to combat suggestive allegations

STAR QUOTE

ERIC CLAPTON

'If I get any more popular, I shall have to have plastic surgery and get myself a Dr Kildare face, but by that time they'll probably have Scott Engel rubber masks for everyone anyway!'

THE GRAPEVINE

■ Lead singer Denny Laine has left The Moody Blues, and the group has 'ceased activities for the present'.

■ Johnny Kidd, UK rocker of 'Shakin' All Over' and 'Please Don't Touch' fame, died in a car crash on October 8, en route to a gig.

■ Memphis' Beale St., immortalized by 'Father of the Blues', W.C. Handy, has been deemed a US national landmark as birthplace of the blues.

CHARTS

	US45	USLP	UK45	UKLP
	Cherish *Association*	Revolver *Beatles*	Distant Drums *Jim Reeves*	The Sound Of Music *Soundtrack*
WEEK 2	Cherish *Association*	Revolver *Beatles*	Distant Drums *Jim Reeves*	The Sound Of Music *Soundtrack*
WEEK 3	Reach Out, I'll Be There *Four Tops*	Revolver *Beatles*	Distant Drums *Jim Reeves*	The Sound Of Music *Soundtrack*
WEEK 4	Reach Out, I'll Be There *Four Tops*	Supremes A GoGo *Supremes*	Distant Drums *Jim Reeves*	The Sound Of Music *Soundtrack*
WEEK 5	96 Tears *? & The Mysterians*	Supremes A GoGo *Supremes*	Reach Out, I'll Be There *Four Tops*	The Sound Of Music *Soundtrack*

Moody Blues – on hold pending change of Laine

WHO RECORDING ROW FINALLY ENDS

The Who have amicably settled their differences with their former producer Shel Talmy, and the group's long-awaited second LP, provisionally titled 'Jigsaw Puzzle', will be released in the UK in December on Track – a new label being launched by Polydor principally for Who recordings.

The Who's next release, the EP 'Ready Steady Who', will appear in the UK on Robert Stigwood's Reaction label (as have their last two singles 'Substitute' and 'I'm A Boy'), and it competes with a same-week release on Brunswick of 'La-La-La Lies', the third single to be extracted from the Talmy-produced 'My Generation' album since The Who left their original label.

McCARTNEY TO SCORE HAYLEY MILLS FILM

Paul McCartney is writing the musical score for *Wedlocked*, a new Boulting Brothers film starring Hayley Mills and Hywel Bennett, which has just been completed at England's Shepperton Studios.

Written by Bill Naughton (of *Alfie* fame), it is based on the West End play *All In Good Time*, and concerns the trials of a newlywed couple forced to spend their honeymoon with parents.

Although neither Boulting Brothers nor the Beatles' office will yet provide official confirmation of McCartney's involvement, manager Brian Epstein had already hinted that Paul would soon be undertaking a solo project on the heels of John Lennon's film work in *How I Won The War*.

This will be the first time that McCartney has written officially without his partner, though the duo's exclusive songwriting contract with Northern Songs will still apply to this music.

NOVEMBER

MYSTERY OF THE MISSING BOB DYLAN

The normally reclusive Bob Dylan has virtually disappeared completely since his mysterious motorcycle smash

A mystery is deepening over the whereabouts and condition of Bob Dylan, who is now three months into a complete disappearance. In August, he reportedly had an accident on his motorbike, sustaining broken neck vertebrae and concussion, and it was said that a couple of months' convalescence would be necessary before he could resume his normal engagements.

However, Dylan did not simply retreat home to nurse his injuries, but dropped out of sight completely. Many of his closest friends do not know where he is, or even how badly he was hurt.

Such a total absence of news, over such a lengthy period, is now leading to widespread speculation that his accident – and the injuries – were far worse than originally suggested, and that his career is over. His manager Albert Grossman dismisses such suggestions as nonsense, but can give no definite news of Dylan, or of when he is likely to re-emerge.

To further fuel these rumours, the publication of Dylan's book *Tarantula*, previously scheduled for this autumn, has been postponed indefintely, while a TV special originally slated for mid-November is now cancelled.

It is believed that only two people have known Dylan's whereabouts since the accident – the determinedly silent Grossman, and the singer's close friend, poet Allen Ginsberg. In mid-October, the World Journal Tribune tracked down a hideaway where Dylan had been staying – a rambling old house miles off the beaten track on the Cape Cod peninsula in Massachusetts.

The paper challenged Ginsberg with this information, and he admitted visiting Dylan there and taking him some reading material. However, when a Tribune reporter called at the house, nobody was prepared to say whether or not Dylan was still in residence.

Until this cloak-and-dagger behaviour ends, just what has happened to Dylan will remain a mystery.

CHARTS

- US45 Last Train To Clarksville — *Monkees*
- USLP Doctor Zhivago — *Soundtrack*
- UK45 Reach Out, I'll Be There — *Four Tops*
- UKLP The Sound Of Music — *Soundtrack*

WEEK 2

- US45 Poor Side Of Town — *Johnny Rivers*
- USLP Doctor Zhivago — *Soundtrack*
- UK45 Reach Out, I'll Be There — *Four Tops*
- UKLP The Sound Of Music — *Soundtrack*

WEEK 3

- US45 You Keep Me Hangin' On — *Supremes*
- USLP The Monkees — *Monkees*
- UK45 Good Vibrations — *Beach Boys*
- UKLP The Sound Of Music — *Soundtrack*

WEEK 4

- US45 You Keep Me Hangin' On — *Supremes*
- USLP The Monkees — *Monkees*
- UK45 Good Vibrations — *Beach Boys*
- UKLP The Sound Of Music — *Soundtrack*

THE GRAPEVINE

■ Pete Quaife has rejoined The Kinks after a five-month absence. John Dalton, whose temporary tenure as bassist was thought permanent, has left. 'Pete thought again, and asked to rejoin' said manager Robert Wace.

■ The Yardbirds are said to be on the verge of splitting as soon as their US tour closes on November 27, with guitarists Jeff Beck (whose health has been suffering) and Jimmy Page likely to leave.

ELVIS FIGHTS FLAB

Elvis Presley is reported to have won an important personal battle on November 7 as shooting on his film *Easy Come, Easy Go* wrapped up. He had been concerned about his weight, and while in Hollywood embarked on a programme to trim himself to 170 pounds – his exact weight on leaving the US Army in 1960.

On his last day at the studio, he hit his target.

During filming, Presley was also presented with two awards for being the public figure setting the highest standard for American youth to follow.

Elvis's weight – "Easy come, easy go"

The Yardbirds, Long plagued by health problems

TOM JONES: GOODBYE DECCA, HELLO MOTOWN?

Tom Jones may leave British Decca to accept an offer from Motown chief Berry Gordy Jr to become his Detroit-based company's first white British artist.

Gordy has long cherished an ambition to sign Jones, and the singer in turn is keen to record at the Motown studios in Detroit. A 'substantial offer' has now been made, and Jones is presently seeking to establish whether he is contractually tied to Decca. His lawyer has already begun discussions with the company.

Jones signed to Decca in July 1964, and has subsequently released nine singles and three albums. A spokesman for the label claimed that his contract does not, in fact, expire until 1970. Meanwhile, his current single, 'Green, Green Grass Of Home', is topping the UK chart and has become the biggest-selling British single of 1966. Domestic sales are close to a million, and Jones is expected to become the first British artist in Decca's history to win a gold disc for sales entirely at home.

In fact, only three previous singles released by or through Decca have ever topped the million sale in the UK alone, and all were by Americans: Bill Haley ('Rock Around The Clock'), Harry Belafonte ('Mary's Boy Child') and Elvis Presley ('It's Now Or Never').

CHARTS

US45	Winchester Cathedral *New Vaudeville Band*
USLP	The Monkees *Monkees*
UK45	Green Green Grass Of Home *Tom Jones*
UKLP	The Sound Of Music *Soundtrack*
WEEK 2	
US45	Good Vibrations *Beach Boys*
USLP	The Monkees *Monkees*
UK45	Green Green Grass Of Home *Tom Jones*
UKLP	The Sound Of Music *Soundtrack*
WEEK 3	
US45	Winchester Cathedral *New Vaudeville Band*
USLP	The Monkees *Monkees*
UK45	Green Green Grass Of Home *Tom Jones*
UKLP	The Sound Of Music *Soundtrack*
WEEK 4	
US45	Winchester Cathedral *New Vaudeville Band*
USLP	The Monkees *Monkees*
UK45	Green Green Grass Of Home *Tom Jones*
UKLP	The Sound Of Music *Soundtrack*
WEEK 5	
US45	I'm A Believer *Monkees*
USLP	The Monkees *Monkees*
UK45	Green Green Grass Of Home *Tom Jones*
UKLP	The Sound Of Music *Soundtrack*

IKE AND TINA IN ROAD CRASH

Soul singer Tina Turner suffered minor head injuries, though husband Ike Turner escaped unhurt, when the tour bus carrying the duo and their backing band crashed outside Topeka, Kansas.

Seven band members were detained in hospital, including bassist Ron Johnson with a broken jaw, and drummer Ed Mosley with a back injury.

All equipment was damaged beyond repair, but thanks to borrowed gear and deputy band members, the Turners managed to avoid missing any tour dates.

THE GRAPEVINE

- **Scott Engel of The Walker Brothers entered a monastery on the Isle Of Wight for ten days' retreat. However, he left after only seven days at the abbot's request as fans had arrived to besiege the monastery gate.**
- **The Supremes have turned down $25,000 and a percentage of the box office of a week at Harlem's Apollo Theatre, because they are too tied up with cabaret dates.**

TOP OF THE POLLS FOR 1966

The results of the annual NME readers' poll for this year produce the following winners in the World Section:

Male singer – Elvis Presley; *Female singer* – Dusty Springfield; *Vocal group* – Beach Boys; *Musical personality* – Elvis Presley.

In the British-only section: *Male singer* – Cliff Richard; *Female singer* – Dusty Springfield; *Vocal group* – Beatles; *Instrumental group* – Shadows; *New singer* – Stevie Winwood; *New group* – Spencer Davis Group; *Single* – 'Eleanor Rigby' – Beatles; *Disc jockey* – Jimmy Savile; *TV or radio show: Top Of The Pops* (BBC TV).

The Beatles were surprisingly defeated by The Beach Boys as the world's top vocal group by just 101 votes. However, their lead over the second-placed Rolling Stones in the UK group category was a very comfortable 3,838 votes.

Beach Boys – beat Beatles

THE ROLLING STONES – PLAYIN' WITH FIRE

Above: Epitome of youth gone wild?

On the night of 12 February 1967, Chief Inspector Gordon Dineley of the West Sussex police and more than a dozen other officers under his command, drove up to the front door of Redlands, a large mansion house set in the heart of a wooded estate a few miles from the English seaside town of Lewes.

Inside, they could hear the sound of music playing loudly. The owner was at home and, from the snatches of conversation and laughter Dineley could make out, he was not alone.

The house was owned by Keith Richards, guitarist of The Rolling Stones – a group which probably most personified every nightmare the establishment had of youth gone wild. And his guests that night included the Stones' lead singer Mick Jagger – arguably one of the most formidable symbols of that youth – and Marianne Faithful, the beautiful ex-convent girl singer who was a flagrant example of how far good girls could fall in the wrong company.

By the end of the raid, Keith and Mick had been arrested and charged with a variety of offences: Keith for possession of hash and allowing his home to be used for the consumption of illegal drugs, and Mick for possession of four pep pills he'd purchased quite legally in Italy for himself and Marianne.

There was little doubt in everyone's minds that The Rolling Stones had been targeted for some perceived greater good. By catching them red-handed, and then making an example of them, the powers that be probably assumed they'd be handing out some great moral lesson – don't play with us, 'cos you're playing with fire. Or words to that effect.

If proof were needed of that theory, the fact that the Stones' other guitarist, Brian Jones, was busted by London police on 10 May – the very same day that Mick and Keith first appeared in court to face their charges – is stretching the law of coincidence way beyond breaking point.

When Mick and Keith finally came to trial on 27 June, few believed they wouldn't have the book thrown at them if they were found guilty. They were, and it was.

Mick was sentenced to three months' jail, despite evidence from his doctor that the pills had been bought legally and that

Bottom Right: Brian Jones
Centre: Mick and Keith leave court
Right: Keith surrenders

he would have prescribed them in any case, had Mick asked for them.

Keith was given a one-year jail sentence and ordered to pay £500 ($1,000) costs. The establishment had won – or so it thought.

Within days, it became clear that it hadn't.

Setting a complete precedent in legal and journalistic terms, *The Times* newspaper (as Establishment as they come) published an editorial comment headed: 'Who Breaks A Butterfly On A Wheel?'.

That editorial, which slammed the severity of Mick and Keith's sentences, was echoed in the next few days by similar articles in other leading British papers. The two Stones were immediately released from prison, pending the result of their appeals.

On 31 July, before the court of the Lord Chief Justice, Mick and Keith were told that their original sentences had been thrown out. Mick's was commuted to a conditional discharge, while Keith was completely acquitted.

That the British establishment should have focussed so much on The Rolling Stones in their search for sacrificial lambs is not surprising when you consider how much a symbol of youth-in-revolt the group were from the very beginning.

They lived with girlfriends, and swapped girlfriends. They wrote songs about sex with no pretence they were talking about true love. They dressed in drag to promote singles. They were a pain in the establishment's butt, no buts about it.

Jagger's obvious intelligence and undoubted articulacy made him especially dangerous, and he gave great copy on the subject of politics. He was The Bad Boy incarnate – and we all know what happens to bad boys, don't we?

The Stones rolled on, however. And although they've caused their fair share of shock-horror headlines in the intervening years, age and time – and a new wave of angry younger men coming up behind – have meant a steady erosion of their importance as figureheads, symbols or bad boys.

Maybe the establishment won, after all.

Left: Mick Jagger being driven to Brixton Prison to begin a three-month sentence

Below: Girl in the centre of it all, Marianne Faithfull

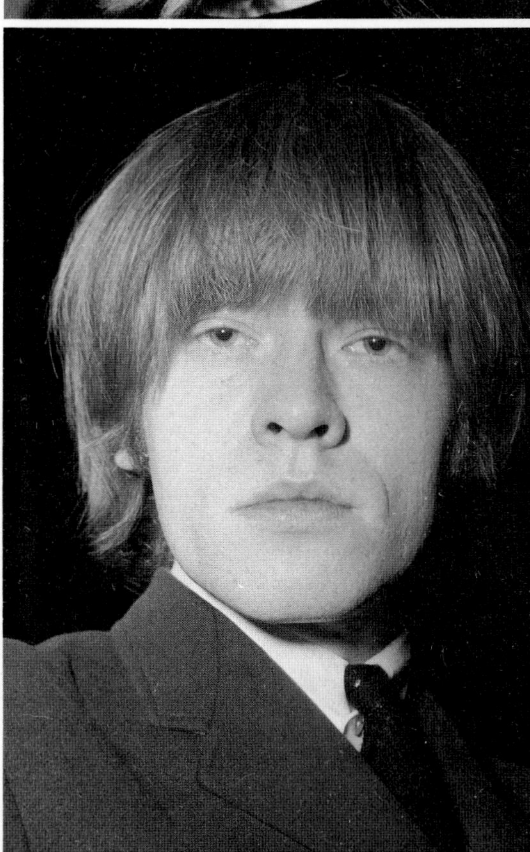

CHARTS

US45	I'm A Believer *Monkees*
USLP	The Monkees *Monkees*
UK45	Green Green Grass Of Home *Tom Jones*
UKLP	The Sound Of Music *Soundtrack*
WEEK 2	
US45	I'm A Believer *Monkees*
USLP	The Monkees *Monkees*
UK45	Green Green Grass Of Home *Tom Jones*
UKLP	The Sound Of Music *Soundtrack*
WEEK 3	
US45	I'm A Believer *Monkees*
USLP	The Monkees *Monkees*
UK45	I'm A Believer *Monkees*
UKLP	The Sound Of Music *Soundtrack*
WEEK 4	
US45	I'm A Believer *Monkees*
USLP	The Monkees *Monkees*
UK45	I'm A Believer *Monkees*
UKLP	The Sound Of Music *Soundtrack*

Fame for The Game – or notoriety? BBC chickens out of drug-taking implications in 'The Addicted Man'

NME: HANG THE JURY!

In a rare venture into serious newspaper editorial, the NME has been prompted into the following statement on the drugs-in-pop-lyrics issue.

Last Saturday, seven minutes were cut from the BBC Juke Box Jury. The show – pre-recorded the previous weekend – had included a lengthy discussion on The Game's recording 'The Addicted Man' which the Corporation decided was unsuitable for transmission.

The Game's disc is concerned with drug-taking, and the panel had criticised it mercilessly. Rightly so! BUT IF THE BBC IS GOING TO TURN A COLD SHOULDER TO ALL DRUG-TAKING IMPLICATIONS IN POP MUSIC, IT MIGHT AS WELL SCRUB JBJ IMMEDIATELY.

Directly or indirectly, drugs are playing an increasingly prominent part in pop lyrics, and in last week's show the BBC had a golden opportunity – in the hands of five acknowledged pop authorities – to dismiss this trend as distasteful rubbish. But they funked the chance. The object of introducing the new resident panel on JBJ was to allow discs to be discussed informatively and authoritatively. How pointless, then, that the BBC should insist upon the panel's chat being sugar-coated and whitewashed – at the expense of the most topical pop controversy of the day.

'The Addicted Man' should never have been released. But the fact that it is now available in the shops – even though EMI is belatedly trying to suppress it – makes it a matter of public concern. For this reason, producer Albert Stevenson was right to include it in the programme. The pity is that the corporation bigwigs thought otherwise.

If the panel of four disc-jockeys is only to be allowed to pronounce upon obvious hits, with a veto on any subject which might be construed as slightly offensive, Juke Box Jury might as well revert to its time-honoured formula of comedians and glamour girls.

GOLDEN 1966: BEATLES MINED THE RICHEST ORE

The RIAA's annual survey reveals that 80 Gold Disc awards were made for US record sales during 1966. 57 of them went to albums (awarded for ½ million sales apiece), and 23 to singles (signifying one million sales). Most-awarded act were The Beatles, who won six golds, while The Beach Boys, The Mamas & The Papas, Bill Cosby and Herb Alpert & The Tijuana Brass all collected four apiece.

Triple winners included The Rolling Stones and new sensation, The Monkees, who have had a 100% gold score with their one LP and two singles to date.

80 Gold Discs – four such for The Beach Boys (pictured) The Mamas & The Papas, Bill Cosby and Herb Alpert & The Tijuana Brass

THE GRAPEVINE

- **Col. Tom Parker is reported to have given Elvis Presley a cup of drinking water for his 32nd birthday. 'Elvis drinks more water than anyone else I know; he figures it keeps him healthy'.**
- **Donovan has been invited to write music for the British National Theatre production of Shakespeare's *As You Like It* at the Old Vic, to star Laurence Olivier.**

EPSTEIN SHOWS THREATENED BY STRIKE

Beatles manager Brian Epstein has run into trouble with the National Association of Theatrical and Kine Employees, following his sacking of London's Saville Theatre house manager Michael Bullock, which in turn led to a strike threat by the rest of the backstage staff. The union has now ordered its members to boycott Epstein's Sunday concerts at the Saville. This could in turn cause the loss of his NEMS Enterprises' Sunday licence for the venue.

The trouble arose at a Sunday night concert by Chuck Berry, during which two fans climbed on to the stage. Bullock, following local safety regulations, lowered the curtain while Berry continued to play – to the intense displeasure of the audience, who proceeded to near-riot.

Epstein, a witness to all from his box seat, said after the show that he sided with the audience, and dismissed Bullock.

The union has subsequently called for a withdrawal of Epstein's 'irresponsible attack on his staff', while the promoter himself has said that, if his licence for the Saville should be withdrawn at any time, he would 'simply move the shows to another theatre'. A follow-up Berry concert the next Sunday was scheduled to go ahead as planned.

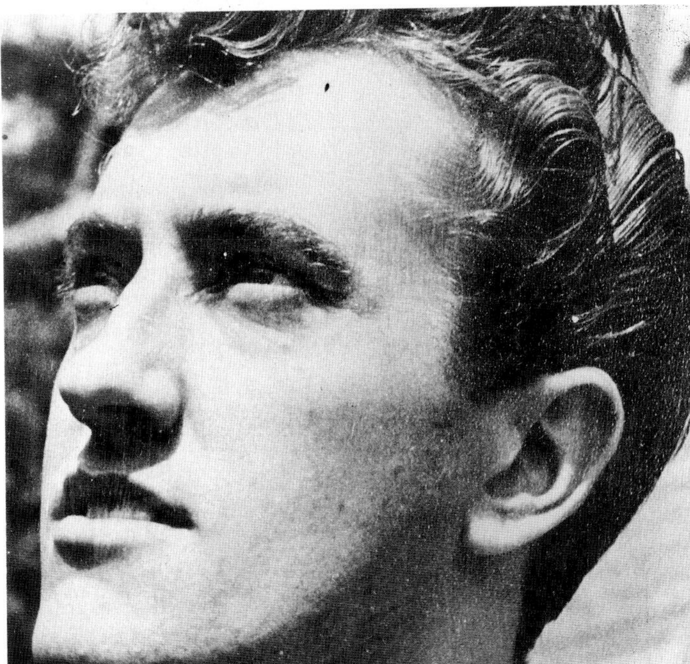

JOE MEEK GUN DEATH TRAGEDY

Joe Meek, the songwriter/producer who created international smashes like 'Telstar' and hits by artists like The Honeycombs, Heinz, John Leyton and Mike Berry from a home-built and equipped studio in his flat (nicknamed 'The Bathroom') in London's Holloway Road, has been found dead from gun wounds to the head on the floor of that same studio.

The evidence suggests suicide, and it was known that Meek had been depressed for some time as he fought to come to terms with the rapidly changing styles that have taken over pop music since his 'Telstar' heyday in 1962. His last major successes were with The Honeycombs in 1964 and 1965.

One of Meek's abiding musical inspirations was Buddy Holly, and it has already been suggested as being no coincidence that February 3 – the day on which he apparently chose to take his own life – was the eighth anniversary of Holly's death.

MOVIE PLANS FOR BEATLES AND MONKEES

The Beatles have approved a basic script by writer Owen Holder for their third – as yet untitled – film, and await a final screenplay before setting a shooting date. The movie will feature the group in comedy character roles, with a minimum of singing. The main musical element will be the incidental score, penned by Lennon and McCartney.

The Monkees are scheduled to make a full-length feature in Hollywood for Columbia Pictures, probably in the spring. It is suggested that the quartet might not necessarily be playing their TV series characters in the movie.

Beatles: *Acting naturally. Their third movie is planned though the title is not yet confirmed and they are awaiting the final screenplay*

CHARTS

US45	I'm A Believer *Monkees*
USLP	The Monkees *Monkees*
UK45	I'm A Believer *Monkees*
UKLP	The Monkees *Monkees*
WEEK 2	
US45	I'm A Believer *Monkees*
USLP	More Of The Monkees *Monkees*
UK45	I'm A Believer *Monkees*
UKLP	The Monkees *Monkees*
WEEK 3	
US45	Kind Of A Drag *Buckinghams*
USLP	More Of The Monkees *Monkees*
UK45	This Is My Song *Petula Clark*
UKLP	The Monkees *Monkees*
WEEK 4	
US45	Kind Of A Drag *Buckinghams*
USLP	More Of The Monkees *Monkees*
UK45	This Is My Song *Petula Clark*
UKLP	The Monkees *Monkees*

THE GRAPEVINE

- **P. J. Proby has filed for bankruptcy in Los Angeles, listing debts of £180,000, including £50,000 to the UK Inland Revenue.**
- **Girl drummer Honey Lantree has left The Honeycombs to work solo, and is planning a cabaret act. The group is seeking a replacement (preferably female) drummer.**
- **The Beatles have been nominated for eight of this year's Grammy Awards.**

MARCH

CHARTS

US45	Ruby Tuesday *Rolling Stones*
USLP	More Of The Monkees *Monkees*
UK45	Release Me *Engelbert Humperdinck*
UKLP	The Monkees *Monkees*
WEEK 2	
US45	Love Is Here & Now You're Gone *Supremes*
USLP	More Of The Monkees *Monkees*
UK45	Release Me *Engelbert Humperdinck*
UKLP	The Monkees *Monkees*
WEEK 3	
US45	Penny Lane *Beatles*
USLP	More Of The Monkees *Monkees*
UK45	Release Me *Engelbert Humperdinck*
UKLP	The Monkees *Monkees*
WEEK 4	
US45	Happy Together *Turtles*
USLP	More Of The Monkees *Monkees*
UK45	Release Me *Engelbert Humperdinck*
UKLP	The Sound Of Music *Soundtrack*

Alpert – Grammy for 'What Now My Love'

HENDRIX TO REPRISE

A deal concluded in Los Angeles on March 14 between Warner-Reprise Records and the Jimi Hendrix Experience's co-manager Mike Jeffrey, will give Reprise the North American release rights to Hendrix's recordings, and guarantee the guitarist a signing fee stated to be 'in excess of $50,000'.

Warner-Reprise president Mo Ostin claims that this is the highest advance the company has ever paid for a new artist.

A major publicity campaign, the details of which were being worked out in further discussions between Jeffrey and Ostin, is to promote Hendrix in his native US as 'the greatest talent since The Rolling Stones'.

Said a record company spokesman: 'We shall introduce a completely new conception in promotion, which should put Jimi right at the top in a very short time.'

GRAMMIES LIST

The National Academy Of Recording Arts And Sciences' Grammy Awards for 1966, just announced in New York, include the following:

Song Of The Year – 'Michelle' by John Lennon and Paul McCartney.

Record Of The Year – Frank Sinatra's 'Strangers In The Night' (also Best Male Vocal Performance, Best Engineered Record, and Best Accompanying Arrangement).

Album Of The Year – Sinatra again, with 'A Man And His Music'.

Best R&B Record – Ray Charles's 'Crying Time' (also Best R&B Solo Vocal).

Best Contemporary Group Performance – The Mamas & The Papas with 'Monday Monday'.

Best Instrumental Performance – Herb Alpert's 'What Now My Love'.

Best Instrumental Theme – 'Batman' by Neal Hefti.

Best Contemporary Recording – New Vaudeville Band's 'Winchester Cathedral'.

Best Contemporary Solo Vocal – Paul McCartney, on The Beatles 'Eleanor Rigby'.

The New Vaudeville Band

VIETNAM INSPIRES CLIFF & SHADOWS MOVIE DRAMA

The war in Vietnam is the inspiration behind a major film drama featuring Cliff Richard and The Shadows.

As yet untitled, this will be the first dramatic cinema project undertaken by singer and group together, although Cliff did have a (supporting) dramatic role in his movie debut *Serious Charge*, eight years ago.

He is already signed for another in the production he's agreed to make for the Billy Graham Organization during the spring and early summer – also, as yet, untitled. Tentatively scheduled to begin shooting in September, a month or so after the Graham film is completed, the new movie is expected to have acting roles for all the group.

Cliff has said: 'I particularly wanted to make this war story. I hope it will be a believable production showing how a group of young people can become easily involved in warfare, even though they do not want to be. The movie will not actually be *about* Vietnam, but it has been inspired by it, and it will project a similar situation.

'The story will be about the moral issues involved. Four songs will be featured, but the movie won't be a musical by any means – and we don't intend to play up the comedy angle as we did with the H-bomb in *Finders Keepers*.'

THE GRAPEVINE

- **Rolling Stone Brian Jones has written the incidental soundtrack music for a short, independently-produced feature film, as yet untitled, starring his girlfriend Anita Pallenberg,**
- **The Dave Clark Five will have acting roles in a thriller to be produced by Clark's own company in the Autumn; no songs will be featured, but the group will record all the incidental music.**

THE WORLD WANTS SANDIE AFTER EUROVISION WIN

Sandie Shaw won the 1967 Eurovision Song Contest, held in Vienna on April 8, with the Bill Martin/Phil Coulter-penned UK entry 'Puppet On A String'.

It collected 147 votes out of a possible 160, more than double the score of the runner-up Irish entry, Sean Dunphy's 'If I Could Choose'.

Manager Eve Taylor told journalists that offers for Sandie flooded in from all over the world as soon as the contest – watched by an estimated 200 million TV viewers via Eurovision – was over. Bookings worth in excess of £250,000 were currently being considered, but taking up all the offers from places as far apart as Argentina and Czechoslovakia would be impossible, partly because of existing UK and European live commitments.

A co-starring role with Peter Noone of Herman's Hermits in the MGM film *Mrs Brown You've Got A Lovely Daughter* had also been rejected.

Sandie: 'Puppet' winner

IF DAVY IS DRAFTED, WILL ROONEY'S SON BE A MONKEE?

Jones: a GI?

Unconfirmed reports have suggested that Monkee Davy Jones, having earlier been passed A-1 by the US Medical Board, has already received his draft papers, and will shortly be leaving the group.

However, Jones' business representative Hal Cone, speaking to journalists during a London visit, said: 'Davy can't be called up until he has undergone further tests – and in any case, he is seeking reclassification or deferment. He still has to undergo various educational and psychological tests, and cannot be drafted until these are completed.

'We think it probable he will be deferred under a hardship case, as his father is a dependent relative. Davy's appeal is certain to take several weeks, and even if it fails, the draft board will probably allow him to complete existing commitments. If the government insists on his drafting, we shall make every effort to ensure it does not take place until 1968.'

Another US report states that 20-year old Tim Rooney, son of actor Mickey and his second wife Betty Jane Rase, is standing by to become Jones' Monkee replacement if he leaves.

The group's UK publicist commented: 'Obviously there is a possibility of Davy being drafted, and they would be foolish not to prepare for this contingency, but we have had no valid confirmation of this story from The Monkees or their management.

'The Monkees would, of course, carry on as a group even if Davy were drafted; the TV series would continue in the same way. There is absolutely no question of them not coming to Britain in June, and we are certain Davy will be with them.'

CHARTS

US45	Happy Together *Turtles*
USLP	More Of The Monkees *Monkees*
UK45	Release Me *Engelbert Humperdinck*
UKLP	The Monkees *Monkees*
WEEK 2	
US45	Happy Together *Turtles*
USLP	More Of The Monkees *Monkees*
UK45	Release Me *Engelbert Humperdinck*
UKLP	The Sound Of Music *Soundtrack*
WEEK 3	
US45	Somethin' Stupid *Frank & Nancy Sinatra*
USLP	More Of The Monkees *Monkees*
UK45	Somethin' Stupid *Frank & Nancy Sinatra*
UKLP	The Sound Of Music *Soundtrack*
WEEK 4	
US45	Somethin' Stupid *Frank & Nancy Sinatra*
USLP	More Of The Monkees *Monkees*
UK45	Puppet On A String *Sandie Shaw*
UKLP	More Of The Monkees *Monkees*
WEEK 5	
US45	Somethin' Stupid *Frank & Nancy Sinatra*
USLP	More Of The Monkees *Monkees*
UK45	Puppet On A String *Sandie Shaw*
UKLP	The Sound Of Music *Soundtrack*

THE GRAPEVINE

- **The Move have offered a £200 reward for the recovery of the master tapes of ten songs intended for the group's June LP. The tapes were stolen from their agent's car when it was parked in London's 'Tin Pan Alley', Denmark Street.**
- **Reports that Monkee Davy Jones is to play the title role in the film version of *Oliver* have been dismissed as 'rubbish' by the producers.**

ELVIS WEDS HIS ARMY SWEETHEART

Elvis Presley married his long-time girlfriend, 23-year old Priscilla Beaulieu, on May 1 in Las Vegas.

The civil ceremony at the Aladdin Hotel, before 100 invited guests, was conducted by Nevada Supreme Court Justice David Zenoff. Elvis' personal assistant Joe Esposito was his best man, while Priscilla's sister Michelle was her maid of honour.

A reception was held at the hotel, after which the couple left for a Palm Springs honeymoon.

The two first met during Elvis' US Army service in West Germany, late in 1959. Priscilla was the 15-year old stepdaughter of a US Air Force officer. Elvis dated her regularly, and was quoted as saying at the time: 'She is very mature and intelligent.'

For some years since Elvis' demob, Priscilla has lived at his Graceland mansion with his grandmother. She completed her schooling in Memphis, and on her 18th birthday was given a scarlet Chevrolet and $3000-worth of clothes by Elvis.

Rumours around Memphis suggested that the couple had been married for some time. Colonel Tom Parker denied the rumours.

WALKER BROTHERS SPLIT TO GO SOLO

Hit-making UK-based American trio The Walker Brothers announced on May 3 – three days after completing a four week tour with a final show at Tooting Granada, London – that they have broken up the team.

Each member is to pursue a solo career. Individual recording contracts are under negotiation, and new backing groups are being formed.

As individuals, Scott Engel, John Maus and Gary Leeds will continue with management company Capable, which – in a joint statement with agent Harold Davidson – said of the split: 'This decision results from an agreed opinion that they have accomplished as much as possible as a group, and that their future progress lies in the freedom to exploit their individual talents. They part on the best of terms, and will continue to work in Britain.'

THE GRAPEVINE

■ **The Bee Gees have signed a $250,000 five-year deal with Atlantic Records for release of their material in the US; the group is signed to Polydor in the UK, and has charted with the self-penned 'New York Mining Disaster 1941', after failing to hit with first UK single 'Spicks And Specks' (which, however, was a No. 1 hit in Australia).**

Carl Wilson still wearing his hat after a late arrival on the Beach Boys current trek of Europe

BEACH BOY PLAYS TOUR ON BAIL

Carl Wilson of The Beach Boys paid $5000 for a private transatlantic jet flight to Dublin, Ireland, to join the rest of the group for the first night of a European tour.

The others had arrived a day earlier, but Wilson had been in custody for five days charged with avoiding the draft and refusing to take the Oath of Allegiance.

At a court hearing in LA, he was released on bail but will face the court again when the group returns to California after the rest of its European dates.

Scott, John and Gary – together for the last time?

CHARTS

US45 Somethin' Stupid – *Frank & Nancy Sinatra*
USLP More Of The Monkees – *Monkees*
UK45 Puppet On A String – *Sandie Shaw*
UKLP The Sound Of Music – *Soundtrack*

WEEK 2

US45 The Happening – *Supremes*
USLP More Of The Monkees – *Monkees*
UK45 Puppet On A String – *Sandie Shaw*
UKLP The Sound Of Music – *Soundtrack*

WEEK 3

US45 Groovin' – *Young Rascals*
USLP More Of The Monkees – *Monkees*
UK45 Silence Is Golden – *Tremeloes*
UKLP The Sound Of Music – *Soundtrack*

WEEK 4

US45 Groovin' – *Young Rascals*
USLP More Of The Monkees – *Monkees*
UK45 Silence Is Golden – *Tremeloes*
UKLP The Sound Of Music – *Soundtrack*

A LOOK AT SERGEANT PEPPER

The Beatles' eagerly-awaited LP 'Sergeant Pepper's Lonely Hearts Club Band' was released simultaneously around the world on June 1st. NME album reviewer Allen Evans (alter ego of editor Andy Gray) made one of his rare breaks from one-paragraph reviews to appraise it more deeply:

'Trust The Beatles to come up with something different! Their latest LP is a sort of concert, starting with 'Sergeant Pepper's Lonely Hearts Club Band' and ending with it, except for a finale piece called 'A Day In The Life'. In between, we get 10 other tunes, all varied and interesting, with George's sitar-and-song startler 'Within You, Without You' the most memorable.

'But I must admit I also liked Paul's amusing 'When I'm 64' and 'Getting Better', his melodrama-in-song 'She's Leaving Home', and Ringo's homely 'With A Little Help From My Friends' very much.

'John Lennon and Paul McCartney have written all the songs, except for 'Within You', which is by George Harrison. Whether the album is their best yet, I wouldn't like to say after one hearing. Whether it was worth the five months it took to make, I would also argue. But it is a very good LP, and will sell like hot cakes.'

MONKEE JONES WILL NOT BE DRAFTED

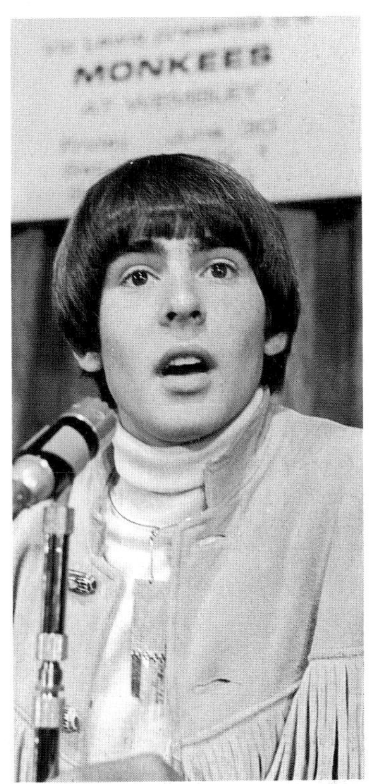

Davy Jones of the Monkees will now definitely not be drafted into the US Army, having just been officially notified of his exemption from service with the Armed Forces. It is understood that the draft board – in a much earlier decision than anticipated – has agreed to Jones' reclassification into the 2A group, which makes him unacceptable for active military service. This ruling has been made on the grounds that he is responsible for supporting his father: a possible alternative plea based on Jones' insufficient height is now no longer necessary. Although he is a British citizen, Jones was liable for US military service in common with all who work and are currently resident in America.

CHARTS

US45	Respect – *Aretha Franklin*
USLP	More Of The Monkees – *Monkees*
UK45	Silence Is Golden – *Tremeloes*
UKLP	Sgt. Pepper's Lonely Hearts Club Band – *Beatles*
WEEK 2	
US45	Respect – *Aretha Franklin*
USLP	More Of The Monkees – *Monkees*
UK45	A Whiter Shade Of Pale – *Procol Harum*
UKLP	Sgt. Pepper's Lonely Hearts Club Band – *Beatles*
WEEK 3	
US45	Respect – *Aretha Franklin*
USLP	Sounds Like – *Herb Alpert & The Tijuana Brass*
UK45	A Whiter Shade Of Pale – *Procol Harum*
UKLP	Sgt. Pepper's Lonely Hearts Club Band – *Beatles*
WEEK 4	
US45	Respect – *Aretha Franklin*
USLP	Headquarters – *Monkees*
UK45	A Whiter Shade Of Pale – *Procol Harum*
UKLP	Sgt. Pepper's Lonely Hearts Club Band – *Beatles*

Who's a lucky girl?

BEACH BOYS CUT MONTEREY, BUT FESTIVAL IS A HUGE SUCCESS

The Beach Boys withdrew from the Monterey pop festival, at which they were to have headlined the Saturday evening programme (the first to be sold out), at almost the last minute. The group cited pressure from Capitol for a new single and album as being overwhelming, while Carl Wilson felt that with his trial regarding the draft being due on June 20, he would not be able to concentrate fully on giving a good performance.

The three-day event, with a stellar line-up (including Simon and Garfunkel, Eric Burdon, Johnny Rivers, Lou Rawls and the Association on Friday, Otis Redding, Jefferson Airplane, the Byrds and Big Brother & The Holding Company on Saturday, and the Who, Jimi Hendrix, Ravi Shankar, Buffalo Springfield and organisers the Mamas & Papas on Sunday) attracted a huge audience. By the Friday opening at 9.15pm. it was estimated that there were at least 10,000 people in the auditorium, a similar number of fans around the grounds and booths, and some 20,000 ticketless milling outside.

- **John Entwistle of the Who married former schoolfriend Alison Wise on June 23.**
- **Steve Winwood has been asked by his local vicar in Birmingham, UK, to write music for two psalms.**
- **Larry Page's bid to retain his former 10% interest in the Kinks has been dismissed by London's high court.**
- **Byrd David Crosby filled in with Buffalo Springfield at Monterey.**

Hendrix holds Monterey

CHARTS

US45	Windy *Association*
USLP	Sgt. Pepper's Lonely Hearts Club Band *Beatles*
UK45	A Whiter Shade Of Pale *Procol Harum*
UKLP	Sgt. Pepper's Lonely Hearts Club Band *Beatles*
WEEK 2	
US45	Windy *Association*
USLP	Sgt. Pepper's Lonely Hearts Club Band *Beatles*
UK45	A Whiter Shade Of Pale *Procol Harum*
UKLP	Sgt. Pepper's Lonely Hearts Club Band *Beatles*
WEEK 3	
US45	Windy *Association*
USLP	Sgt. Pepper's Lonely Hearts Club Band *Beatles*
UK45	All You Need Is Love *Beatles*
UKLP	Sgt. Pepper's Lonely Hearts Club Band *Beatles*
WEEK 4	
US45	Windy *Association*
USLP	Sgt. Pepper's Lonely Hearts Club Band *Beatles*
UK45	All You Need Is Love *Beatles*
UKLP	Sgt. Pepper's Lonely Hearts Club Band *Beatles*
WEEK 5	
US45	Light My Fire *Doors*
USLP	Sgt. Pepper's Lonely Hearts Club Band *Beatles*
UK45	All You Need Is Love *Beatles*
UKLP	Sgt. Pepper's Lonely Hearts Club Band *Beatles*

THE GRAPEVINE

■ In an attempt to lure Elvis Presley back to long-neglected live performance, Gary Singler – responsible for artist bookings at the Statler Hilton Plaza in Miami – has offered a $85,000 fee for Presley to appear in cabaret at the hotel. No response is reported from Col. Parker's office, but should the deal be accepted, it would be Elvis' first stage appearance since early 1961.

THE WHO SALUTE JAGGER AND RICHARDS ON IMPROMPTU SINGLE

Townshend and Co. lend support to jailed Stones, Mick 'n' Keef

With Rolling Stones Mick Jagger and Keith Richards both convicted on drug charges, with appeals to be heard before the Lord Chief Justice and two other judges on July 31, The Who, in a move of solidarity, have recorded two Jagger/Richards songs, and will use their royalties to assist the two Stones with legal costs.

Recorded at a rapidly-convened session on the afternoon of Friday June 30 – the day after The Who held an 'emergency meeting' to discuss the situation – 'The Last Time' and 'Under My Thumb' were available as a UK single within five days, with the label crediting 'The Who in support of Mick and Keith'.

Kit Lambert and Chris Stamp co-produced the session, which was originally booked to cut a follow-up to the group's hit 'Pictures Of Lily'. This project was postponed until a New York session eight days later. Because bassist John Entwistle was out of the country at the time, honeymooning aboard the Queen Elizabeth, the bass guitar part was overdubbed by Pete Townshend.

A statement from the group noted: 'There was no time to consider production or arrangements, and what has emerged is a straightforward and very rough cover version of the two songs. The Who intend to continue recording Jagger/Richard compositions for as long as they are in jail, in order to keep their work before the public.'

YANOVSKY QUITS THE SPOONFUL

Zal Yanovsky, guitarist with The Lovin' Spoonful, has left the group to pursue a solo career. His final live appearance with them was at the Forest Hills Music Festival in New York, on June 24, since when his replacement, 24-year-old Jerry Yester (brother of Jim Yester of The Association), has already stepped into Yanovsky's shoes.

Yanovsky's departure was said to be 'on the most amicable terms', and The Spoonful's John Sebastian was well forewarned, enabling him to recruit Yester with a minimum of disruption. Yanovsky, who has immediate plans for solo recording sessions, said: 'I was getting bored. I want to look around and see what's been happening for the past two years. I feel I've lost touch, and there are so many things I want to do alone.'

Expected to sign a record deal within a couple of weeks, he does not intend to form a group of his own in the forseeable future.

A report that Yanovsky's split had precipitated a complete break-up of The Spoonful is thought to be inaccurate.

Zal: 'Getting bored'

HENDRIX: DID HE GO OR WAS HE PUSHED?

After playing only seven dates as support act on The Monkees' US tour, The Jimi Hendrix Experience have quit the package. Conflicting reports suggest that Hendrix either quit in anger because he resented having to open the shows, or that he was sacked after protests from the conservative women's league, The Daughters Of The American Revolution, that his act was 'too erotic'.

Co-manager/producer Chandler announced that Jimi left 'by mutual agreement with The Monkees', after being asked to tone down his act but refusing to do so.

Said Chandler: 'There had been many protests and a lot of parents were up in arms because the audiences which The Monkees draw are primarily in the 7-12 age group. So they moved Jimi to the opening spot and asked him to cool his act. He felt he could not co-operate, as it was like asking him to play with one hand. He talked it over with The Monkees and decided to quit.'

Hendrix decided to stay on in the US to undertake recordings and play club dates – including an unexpected few days at the Whisky A-Go-Go in New York's Greenwich Village.

'There is no problem about him getting work,' said Chandler. 'He has been offered plenty of dates following his success at the Monterey Festival, and 'The Wind Cries Mary' is now shooting up the US singles chart.'

A total of 42 studio hours in New York produced 'The Burning Of The Midnight Lamp', which Hendrix plans as his new single. 'The Wind Cries Mary', was cut in one take lasting all of six minutes!

Hendrix and the Experience: too wild for teenybop Monkees fans, pull out of tour and opt for club dates

CHARTS

Chart	Title	Artist
US45	Light My Fire	Doors
USLP	Sgt. Pepper's Lonely Hearts Club Band	Beatles
UK45	All You Need Is Love	Beatles
UKLP	Sgt. Pepper's Lonely Hearts Club Band	Beatles
WEEK 2		
US45	Light My Fire	Doors
USLP	Sgt. Pepper's Lonely Hearts Club Band	Beatles
UK45	San Francisco	Scott McKenzie
UKLP	Sgt. Peppers' Lonely Hearts Club Band	Beatles
WEEK 3		
US45	All You Need Is Love	Beatles
USLP	Sgt. Pepper's Lonely Hearts Club Band	Beatles
UK45	San Francisco	Scott McKenzie
UKLP	Sgt. Pepper's Lonely Hearts Club Band	Beatles
WEEK 4		
US45	Ode To Billie Joe	Bobbie Gentry
USLP	Sgt. Pepper's Lonely Hearts Club Band	Beatles
UK45	San Francisco	Scott McKenzie
UKLP	Sgt. Pepper's Lonely Hearts Club Band	Beatles

SCOTT McKENZIE

'I played a 50-year old general in John Loves Mary*, which was a hit on Broadway back in 1949. . . . In the original production, Ronald Reagan played the role I had!'*

Hippy hypster McKenzie recalls re-run of Reagan role

THE SUPREMES: NUNS WITH TARZAN!

The Supremes have been signed for their first dramatic acting roles – not in a feature film, but in a guest appearance on the next season of NBC's *Tarzan* TV series, starring Ron Ely.

The group are cast as three American nuns working in Africa, and will wear the appropriate habit throughout. They will also do some singing – of hymns!

■ Marianne Faithfull has been signed for a starring part opposite French actor Alain Delon in a film to be shot in Europe this Autumn. Titled *Girl On A Motor Cycle*, it is being made by Mid-Atlantic films, whose directors include Radio Caroline boss Ronan O'Rahilly. Last month, Marianne failed a screen test for the new British movie *The Magus*.

RADIO CAROLINE WAVES THE JOLLY ROGER

Good lolly on the pop ship

As the UK government's legislation to ban offshore broadcasting took effect after midnight on August 14, the pirate stations which had ruled the airwaves for three years shut up shop.

The most powerful, Radio London, shut down at 3pm on the 14th. Radios Scotland, 390 and 270 also closed before the law made them illegal, but the original UK pirate, Radio Caroline – broadcasting a northern service from a ship off the Isle Of Man, and a southern service from a vessel off the Essex coast – continued defiantly into illegality. The station has announced that it will defy the UK ban by moving its offices from London to Amsterdam and Paris.

The company would continue to take internationally-based advertising, supplemented, it says, by 'fake adverts, to confuse the police should they consider prosecuting advertisers!'

McCARTNEY: 'NO EPSTEIN REPLACEMENT'

Epstein, architect of the Beatles success and Merseybeat manager supreme

Following the sudden death of Brian Epstein at his London home, The Beatles have decided NOT to appoint another manager. Paul McCartney, speaking for the group, explained: 'No one could possibly replace Brian.'

The group were under a personal management contract to Epstein, but have now decided to manage themselves. Their agency contract with NEMS Enterprises is due to expire in October, but is likely to be renewed.

Epstein's brother Clive has been elected by directors as the NEMS chairman, and Robert Stigwood becomes managing director. The company has announced that it will continue to pursue Brian Epstein's policies and projects.

NEMS ownership remains in doubt, since Epstein owned 70 per cent of the shares, with the rest being split between his brother and The Beatles. In the absence of a will, Epstein's majority holding passes to his widowed mother, who may sell if death duty taxes prove exorbitant.

A spokesman for The Beatles stated: 'They would be willing to put money into NEMS if there was any question of a takeover from an outsider. The Beatles will not withdraw their shares from NEMS. Things will go on just as before.'

Epstein was buried at Long Lane Cemetery, Liverpool. A memorial service is likely to be held in London in the near future.

MAGICAL BEATLES TOUR

The Beatles and a cast of extras have been touring Devon and Cornwall in a 60-seater coach, filming their TV movie *Magical Mystery Tour* at a variety of England's West Country locations.

Three further weeks will be spent in studio editing and soundtrack recording when the two-week jaunt on the road is complete.

CHARTS

US45	Ode To Billie Joe — *Bobbie Gentry*
USLP	Sgt. Pepper's Lonely Hearts Club Band — *Beatles*
UK45	San Francisco — *Scott McKenzie*
UKLP	Sgt. Pepper's Lonely Hearts Club Band — *Beatles*
WEEK 2	
US45	Ode To Billie Joe — *Bobbie Gentry*
USLP	Sgt. Pepper's Lonely Hearts Club Band — *Beatles*
UK45	The Last Waltz — *Engelbert Humperdinck*
UKLP	Sgt. Pepper's Lonely Hearts Club Band — *Beatles*
WEEK 3	
US45	Ode To Billie Joe — *Bobbie Gentry*
USLP	Sgt. Pepper's Lonely Hearts Club Band — *Beatles*
UK45	The Last Waltz — *Engelbert Humperdinck*
UKLP	Sgt. Pepper's Lonely Hearts Club Band — *Beatles*
WEEK 4	
US45	The Letter — *Box Tops*
USLP	Sgt. Pepper's Lonely Hearts Club Band — *Beatles*
UK45	The Last Waltz — *Engelbert Humperdinck*
UKLP	Sgt. Pepper's Lonely Hearts Club Band — *Beatles*
WEEK 5	
US45	The Letter — *Box Tops*
USLP	Sgt. Pepper's Lonely Hearts Club Band — *Beatles*
UK45	The Last Waltz — *Engelbert Humperdinck*
UKLP	Sgt. Pepper's Lonely Hearts Club Band — *Beatles*

THE GRAPEVINE

■ **Herman's Hermits have been invited to play at the Shah of Persia's coronation in Teheran next month. They will fly to Persia on October 23 and stay at the royal palace for five days. Although the group had intended to be on holiday during this period, they are likely to accept the invitation – particularly as it came from the Shah personally.**

MOTHER WOULDN'T LIKE IT

Mothers: 'mind shattering'

NME's assistant editor John Wells witnessed the first-ever UK performance by Frank Zappa and The Mothers Of Invention. These are his comments:

'The 40-year-old flower children in The Royal Albert Hall's half-full audience for the British stage debut of America's Mother Of Invention last Saturday hung on every word of leader Frank Zappa, applauded every mind-shattering sound (even when it was a mistake), and laughed at the crudest of jokes.

'This was the greatest send-up (or down) of pop music, the audience, America and the group themselves I've ever witnessed. As musicians they were fantastically good, and the entire act was unbelievably professionally presented.

'But, frankly, what was the point of it all? An entire concert of biting ridicule, both verbal and musical – however well done – is just a bore.'

MAMAS AND PAPAS: CHANGES IN THE FAMILY?

Their career currently in crisis, Mamas and Papas take a break

With The Mamas & The Papas 'on indefinite leave of absence', in the words of their producer and label boss Lou Adler, speculation is rife concerning their future, after cancelled live dates in London and Paris were followed by John Phillips and his wife Michelle Gilliam moving on to West Germany, and Cass Elliott and Denny Doherty returning unexpectedly to the US.

The group's new album is a compilation of earlier tracks, titled (some would suggest ominously) 'Farewell To The First Golden Era'.

However, they have signed a new long-term deal with Adler's Dunhill Records, while Phillips has also signed to Dunhill as record producer.

Adler announced: 'They were halfway through cutting another album when they decided to take a break for an indefinite period to seek inspiration. They will not record again until they feel more creative, and are able to come up with the right product.'

Current speculation concerns likely changes in the group's personnel, and suggests that Doherty is to be replaced by 'San Francisco' hitmaker Scott McKenzie, who once sang with John Phillips in The Journeymen and is presently produced by him. McKenzie's close association with the group – he travelled to Europe with them – lends plausibility to a tie-up, notwithstanding his current chart success as a soloist.

CHARTS

US45	The Letter *Box Tops*
USLP	Sgt. Pepper's Lonely Hearts Club Band *Beatles*
UK45	The Last Waltz *Engelbert Humperdinck*
UKLP	Sgt. Pepper's Lonely Hearts Club Band *Beatles*
WEEK 2	
US45	The Letter *Box Tops*
USLP	Ode To Billie Joe *Bobby Gentry*
UK45	The Last Waltz *Engelbert Humperdinck*
UKLP	Sgt. Pepper's Lonely Hearts Club Band *Beatles*
WEEK 3	
US45	To Sir With Love *Lulu*
USLP	Ode To Billie Joe *Bobbie Gentry*
UK45	Massachusetts *Bee Gees*
UKLP	The Sound Of Music *Soundtrack*
WEEK 4	
US45	To Sir With Love *Lulu*
USLP	Greatest Hits *Diana Ross & The Supremes*
UK45	Massachusetts *Bee Gees*
UKLP	The Sound Of Music *Soundtrack*

THE GRAPEVINE

■ **Cliff Richard has now decided not to quit show business to become a teacher of religion, and explained: 'I shall continue with my religious studies, but I now realize that I can be an entertainer as well as a Christian. Provided that the public continues to accept me, I am quite prepared to remain in the business for another 20 years. On reflection, it was foolish even to think of quitting.'**

Cliff changes mind on Christian career, opting for pop after all

JONES THE BREAD

Tom Jones will become a millionaire on the strength of a 13-week cabaret booking at the Las Vegas Flamingo. The million-dollar fee, negotiated by Jones' agent and manager Colin Berlin and Gordon Mills and US agent Lloyd Greenfield, is believed to be the highest ever guaranteed to a British singer in the US.

Under the deal, Jones will play three separate Flamingo engagements spread over 18 months, the first being a four-week season opening on March 19, immediately after a month-long stint at the Copacabana in New York.

PROCUL NIX MOVIE

Procul Harum have turned down an offer for the group to star in the film *Seventeen Plus*, to be produced by the makers of Paul Jones' *Privilege*. The main reason for this refusal is that work on the movie would have meant curtailing a vital US promotional visit, regarded as a key part of the campaign to solidly establish Procul Harum in the States.

Following this decision, the group have announced that they are to write their own film, for shooting late next spring. Coincidentally, ex-members Ray Royer and Bobby Harrison have announced that their group Freedom has been signed to appear in the movie *The Attraction*.

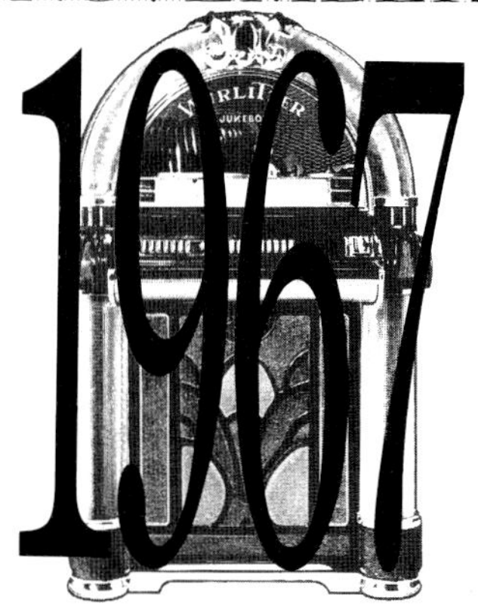

CHARTS

US45	To Sir With Love *Lulu*
USLP	Greatest Hits *Diana Ross & The Supremes*
UK45	Massachusetts *Bee Gees*
UKLP	The Sound Of Music *Soundtrack*
WEEK 2	
US45	To Sir With Love *Lulu*
USLP	Greatest Hits *Diana Ross & The Supremes*
UK45	Baby Now That I've Found You *Foundations*
UKLP	The Sound Of Music *Soundtrack*
WEEK 3	
US45	To Sir With Love *Lulu*
USLP	Greatest Hits *Diana Ross & The Supremes*
UK45	Baby Now That I've Found You *Foundations*
UKLP	The Sound Of Music *Soundtrack*
WEEK 4	
US45	Incense & Peppermints *Strawberry Alarm Clock*
USLP	Greatest Hits *Diana Ross & The Supremes*
UK45	Baby Now That I've Found You *Foundations*
UKLP	The Sound Of Music *Soundtrack*

MARTIN TO SCORE BEATLES CARTOON FILM

The Beatles' producer George Martin has been appointed musical director for the film *Yellow Submarine*, a full-length cartoon based on the group and their music. Produced by King Features and Subafilms, the movie is said to incorporate the most advanced techniques in animation ever used.

The drawings, influenced by pop and psychedelic art, are in a style reflective of the 'mod world of the Beatles'. *Yellow Submarine* is a musical chase and rescue comedy written by Al Brodax, Jack Mendelsohn and Erich Segal, and will feature all The Beatles in animated form – though not with their own speaking voices. These will be dubbed by actors.

George Martin will produce a musical score to complement the Beatles' songs heard on the soundtrack, which – in addition to the title number – will include three new and previously-unreleased Lennon/McCartney numbers, and eight tracks taken from the 'Sergeant Pepper' LP. The group have recently completed recording the new numbers, and a soundtrack album is planned for release in the spring of 1968.

Musical mentor Martin

BAILED STONE AWAITS TRIAL APPEAL RESULT

Rolling Stone Brian Jones has been resting at a friend's home after being released on bail pending his appeal against a sentence of nine months' imprisonment for drug offences. He was released 'in the light of further medical evidence, and on condition that he undertakes to have medical treatment'.

It is likely that Jones' case will take up to six weeks to come before the appeal court. In the meantime, stressed a spokesman for The Rolling Stones, the group WILL continue in any eventuality. Business manager Allan Klein commented: 'There is absolutely no question of bringing in a replacement'.

Klein is currently having discussions in New York with Mick Jagger and Keith Richards regarding the probable late-November release of the recently completed new LP by The Stones.

Asked how Brian Jones' position affects the group's future plans, their publicist Les Perrin said: 'They have not appeared in concert since April, and have not played a British date since October last year, so you will see that they are not very interested in touring.

'There are no tour plans whatsoever. We will meet all other obstacles as they present themselves – but if necessary The Stones can continue for an interim period as a four-man group.'

'Mining Disaster' Bee Gees almost hit by real tragedy

THE GRAPEVINE

■ Robin Gibb of The Bee Gees escaped shaken but unhurt from the rail crash at Hither Green, South London, in which several passengers died.

■ In Argentina, the annual international record festival Mar Del Plata has acclaimed The Troggs as 'the new interpreters of youthful rhythm in international dancing music'; they received gold diplomas, and now plan an in-person visit.

OTIS REDDING DIES IN PLANE CRASH

Soul star Otis Redding, aged 26, died with four members of his backing group, The Bar-Kays, when their plane crashed into Lake Monoma in Wisconsin.

Also killed were the twin-engined light plane's pilot, and Redding's 17-year-old valet Matthew Kelly. The only survivor of the crash was Bar-Kay Ben Cauley, who was found by rescuers in the icy water.

Eddie Floyd, Redding's friend and Stax label-mate, told the NME: 'The last time I spoke to Otis was in the States. I was joking with him about training for his pilot's licence. Now I will never forget that day – he wasn't flying himself, but he died in his own plane.

'I can only say that I've lost my brother. We as soul brothers are as one; he wasn't the only one . . . there was the great Sam Cooke . . . I don't know my own destiny, either.'

CHARTS

US45	Daydream Believer *Monkees*
USLP	Pisces, Aquarius, Capricorn & Jones Ltd. *Monkees*
UK45	Let The Heartaches Begin *Long John Baldry*
UKLP	The Sound Of Music *Soundtrack*
WEEK 2	
US45	Daydream Believer *Monkees*
USLP	Pisces, Aquarius, Capricorn & Jones Ltd. *Monkees*
UK45	Hello Goodbye *Beatles*
UKLP	The Sound Of Music *Soundtrack*
WEEK 3	
US45	Daydream Believer *Monkees*
USLP	Pisces, Aquarius, Capricorn & Jones Ltd. *Monkees*
UK45	Hello Goodbye *Beatles*
UKLP	The Sound Of Music *Soundtrack*
WEEK 4	
US45	Daydream Believer *Monkees*
USLP	Pisces, Aquarius, Capricorn & Jones Ltd. *Monkees*
UK45	Hello Goodbye *Beatles*
UKLP	The Sound Of Music *Soundtrack*
WEEK 5	
US45	Hello Goodbye *Beatles*
USLP	Pisces, Aquarius, Capricorn & Jones Ltd. *Monkees*
UK45	Hello Goodbye *Beatles*
UKLP	The Sound Of Music *Soundtrack*

THE GRAPEVINE

- **Lulu's 'To Sir With Love' has sold over two million copies in the US, making it the biggest-ever American hit by a British female singer.**
- **The Bee Gees have written a Christmas carol titled 'Thank You For Christmas', to be performed by the group in a televised Christmas Eve carol service from Liverpool Cathedral.**

YARDBIRDS BALLET STAGED IN PARIS

An hour-long ballet written by The Yardbirds and with all music played by the group, is premiered at the Paris Olympia on December 13 and 14. Still untitled, it is being presented by French impresario Bruno Coquetrix, and the initial performance will be filmed for subsequent TV screening in France and Sweden.

The ballet will be danced by BBC-TV dance team Pan's People, choreographed by Flick Colby, and the director is Sean Murphy. The Yardbirds will perform the music from a vantage point at the side of the stage.

Discussions are taking place with regard to the group recording an LP of the ballet music, primarily for the French market. There are no present plans for the production to be staged elsewhere, although promoters are being sounded out on the possibility of a UK presentation.

One-time raw blues blowers the Yardbirds branch into ballet

'Pops' prancers Pans People prepare for Paris premier

NME READERS' FAVOURITES OF 1967

The annual NME popularity poll, based on the votes of its readers, included the following results:

World Section

Male singer
1 Elvis Presley; 2 Tom Jones.

Female singer
1 Dusty Springfield; 2 Lulu.

Vocal group
1 Beatles; 2 Beach Boys.

Musical Personality
1 Elvis Presley; 2 John Lennon.

UK Section

Male singer
1 Tom Jones; 2 Cliff Richard.

Female singer
1 Lulu; 2 Dusty Springfield.

Vocal group
1 Beatles; 2 Rolling Stones.

Instrumental group
1 Shadows; 2 Sounds Incorporated.

UK single
1 'A Whiter Shade Of Pale' – Procul Harum; 2 'All You Need Is Love' – Beatles.

TV or radio programme
1 *Top Of The Pops*; 2 *Dee Time*.

DJ
1 Tie between Jimmy Savile and Tony Blackburn.

GROUP CHANGES, TEMPORARY AND OTHERWISE

Shadows drummer Brian Bennett is temporarily out of the group, recuperating after an appendix operation.

His stand-in – who has already deputized for Bennett on an ATV *Showtime* TV slot, and is expected to do so again for the telerecording of a Cliff Richard & The Shadows TV spectacular for Rediffusion in February – is Tony Meehan, the drummer Bennett replaced in 1961.

Meehan back in Shadows

Bassist John Rostill, who suffered a nervous breakdown shortly after Christmas, was declared fit after two weeks and rejoined The Shadows just before Bennett's enforced absence.

Another temporary group absence involves Dave Davies of The Kinks, who is to play his first-ever solo concerts on a tour of Germany, Sweden, Belgium and France, between late February and the end of April.

Auditions have been held to select a band to accompany Dave, but it is stressed by Kinks manager Robert Wace that this is purely a temporary arrangement between Kinks live commitments, and there is no question of Dave actually leaving The Kinks.

Meanwhile, Pink Floyd has grown to a five-piece with the addition of 21-year-old David Gilmour, who has been rehearsing with the group for several weeks, and is currently recording with them. The Floyd are quoted as saying that the augmentation is to 'explore new instruments and add further experimental dimensions to our sound.'

Finally, Freddie & The Dreamers are set to split – but only on new singles to be released shortly. The Freddie-less Dreamers debut will be 'The Maybe Song' at the end of January, while the singer's solo, scheduled for early February, will either be the Reg Presley-penned 'Little Red Donkey' or an Italian song with English lyrics by Mitch Muray.

The group reunites for cabaret work in February, and a tour of Australia in April.

Kink Dave Defects

Gilmour joins Floyd

PRESLEY RETURNS TO TV

Elvis Presley has been signed to make his first TV appearance for nearly eight years. He will star in a one-hour spectacular for NBC, to be filmed in New York in the summer, for probable US screening on the network in December. The producer will be Bob Finkel, who is currently responsible for NBC's *Jerry Lewis Show* series.

Presley last appeared on TV in 1960 soon after leaving the US Army, in a 'welcome home' show hosted by Frank Sinatra, which included duets between the two singers. At present, it is not known whether any guests will be added to the planned NBC show.

CHARTS

Chart	Title	Artist
US45	Hello Goodbye	*Beatles*
USLP	Magical Mystery Tour	*Beatles*
UK45	Hello Goodbye	*Beatles*
UKLP	Sgt. Pepper's Lonely Hearts Club Band	*Beatles*
WEEK 2		
US45	Hello Goodbye	*Beatles*
USLP	Magical Mystery Tour	*Beatles*
UK45	Hello Goodbye	*Beatles*
UKLP	Sgt. Pepper's Lonely Hearts Club Band	*Beatles*
WEEK 3		
US45	Judy In Disguise (With Glasses)	*John Fred & His Playboy Band*
USLP	Magical Mystery Tour	*Beatles*
UK45	The Ballad Of Bonnie And Clyde	*Georgie Fame*
UKLP	Val Doonican Rocks, But Gently	*Val Doonican*
WEEK 4		
US45	Judy In Disguise (With Glasses)	*John Fred & His Playboy Band*
USLP	Magical Mystery Tour	*Beatles*
UK45	Everlasting Love	*Love Affair*
UKLP	The Sound Of Music	*Soundtrack*

THE GRAPEVINE

- **Georgie Fame is to sing the theme song, written by Don Black and Johnny Dankworth, for the Elizabeth Taylor/Richard Burton film *Goforth*.**
- **Cat Stevens has split with producer Mike Hurst, and will produce himself in future.**
- **Former hitmaker Bobby Rydell has signed a long-term contract with Reprise Records.**
- **Johnny Rivers has been taking sitar lessons from Ravi Shankar.**

More fame for Georgie with Burton/Taylor film song

SUPREMES RECORD LIVE IN LONDON

Supremes – the talk of the town

The Supremes' one-hour cabaret act at London's Talk Of The Town nitespot has been recorded for a projected Motown album. It is only the second time the trio have recorded outside Detroit, the earlier occasion being a similar live recording in 1966 at New York's Copacabana.

EMI producer Tony Palmer (who has worked with The Yardbirds, Georgie Fame and The Scaffold), supervised tapings of The Supremes' performances over three nights from 1 to 3 February. They were backed by the resident Burt Rhodes Orchestra, augmented to a 28-piece unit for this season.

Items likely to be included on the LP which will be edited down from the three shows, are show tunes like 'Mame' and 'Thoroughly Modern Millie', a Sam Cooke tribute selection, and a medley of the group's own biggest hit singles.

Diana Ross commented: 'We want to come back to Britain. The response from everybody has been fantastic, though next time we feel we really must try and get closer to the fans. Concert dates would be the ideal thing next time.'

CHARTS

Chart	Title	Artist
US45	Green Tambourine	*Lemon Pipers*
USLP	Magical Mystery Tour	*Beatles*
UK45	Everlasting Love	*Love Affair*
UKLP	The Supremes' Greatest Hits	*Supremes*
WEEK 2		
US45	Love Is Blue	*Paul Mauriat*
USLP	Magical Mystery Tour	*Beatles*
UK45	Everlasting Love	*Love Affair*
UKLP	The Supremes' Greatest Hits	*Supremes*
WEEK 3		
US45	Love Is Blue	*Paul Mauriat*
USLP	Magical Mystery Tour	*Beatles*
UK45	The Mighty Quinn	*Manfred Mann*
UKLP	The Supremes' Greatest Hits	*Supremes*
WEEK 4		
US45	Love Is Blue	*Paul Mauriat*
USLP	Magical Mystery Tour	*Beatles*
UK45	The Mighty Quinn	*Manfred Mann*
UKLP	The Supremes' Greatest Hits	*Supremes*

NON-MONKEE BUSINESS: NESMITH'S ROCK/JAZZ SYMPHONY

Mike Nesmith of The Monkees has written and produced, in collaboration with jazz trumpeter Shorty Rogers, a full-length rock'n'roll symphony, believed to be the first work of its kind. Nesmith and Rogers have recorded the piece, titled 'The Wichita Train Whistle', with over 50 jazz musicians from the Duke Ellington, Woody Herman, Stan Kenton, and other major bands.

Nesmith has worked on the project independently of The Monkees and their label, Colgems. Having sunk $70,000 of his own money into it, he intends to lease the masters of the recording to the record company offering the most favourable deal, and hopes for a rush US release in March, once a label is finalized.

Nesmith has also written 'Tapioca Tundra' for the B-side of the next Monkees single 'Valleri'. The song was inspired by the group's summer 1966 tour.

THE GRAPEVINE

- **Cliff Richard has accepted an invitation to preach three sermons during May at Kensington Temple in Notting Hill, London, as part of a series of special guest speaker sevices at the church. He will talk on the Christian faith and its relationship to the world of show business.**
- **Secretly married Roger Daltrey of The Who is being sued for divorce.**

Soul queen Aretha, poll-winner and Atlantic best-seller

ARETHA'S GOLD

Aretha Franklin's single 'Chain Of Fools' has been certified by the RIAA as having sold a million copies in the US within six weeks of release, which makes it Atlantic Records' fastest million seller of all time.

Aretha has now collected four gold singles (previous ones being for 'I Never Loved A Man', 'Respect' and 'Baby I Love You') and one gold album within one year – an achievement unequalled by any other female singer.

She has also topped five polls as the best female singer of 1967.

Preacherman Cliff

Daltrey – on and off marriage

GRAMMYS: FOUR EACH FOR BEATLES AND 5TH DIMENSION

Four live Beatles take their place on the set for the 'Sergeant Pepper' album cover

The National Academy of Recording Arts and Sciences' Grammy Awards for 1967 saw the Beatles' 'Sergeant Pepper's Lonely Hearts Club Band' album win in four categories: Album of the Year, Best Contemporary Album, Best Engineered Recording, and Best Album Cover Graphic Art.

The Fifth Dimension also collected four Grammys for their first hit 'Up, Up And Away', which was voted Record of The Year, Best Contemporary Single, Best Performance by a Vocal Group up to Six Persons, and Best Contemporary Group Peformance, Vocal or Instrumental.

'Up, Up And Away' then went further still, winning Song of the Year for its writer Jim Webb, and even a Grammy to the Johnny Mann Singers for their cover version of the song: Best Performance by a Chorus of Seven or More Persons.

Other Grammy winners included Bobbie Gentry (Best New Artist, Best Female Vocal Performance for 'Ode To Billy Joe', and Best Performance of a Contemporary Song for the same record), Glen Campbell (Best Male Vocal Performance and Best Country Solo Vocal for 'By The Time I Get To Phoenix').

Lou Rawls won his Grammy Award for Best Male R&B Performance for 'Dead End Street', while Aretha Franklin won hers for the Best Female R&B Performance (for 'Respect'), Elvis Presley winning the Best Sacred Performance Award for 'How Great Thou Art'.

BROTHERS: DIFFERENT BUT STILL RIGHTEOUS

With Bill Medley about to launch a solo recording career, the original Righteous Brothers are no more, but the act continues.

Bobby Hatfield is now being partnered by Jimmy Walker, former singer with The Knickerbockers (of 'Lies' fame), in a similar blue-eyed-soul style.

CHARTS

Chart	Title	Artist
US45	Love Is Blue	*Paul Mauriat*
USLP	Blooming Hits	*Paul Mauriat*
UK45	Cinderella Rockefella	*Esther & Abi Ofarim*
UKLP	The Supremes' Greatest Hits	*Supremes*
WEEK 2		
US45	Love Is Blue	*Paul Mauriat*
USLP	Blooming Hits	*Paul Mauriat*
UK45	Cinderella Rockefella	*Esther & Abi Ofarim*
UKLP	The Supremes' Greatest Hits	*Supremes*
WEEK 3		
US45	(Sittin' On) The Dock Of The Bay	*Otis Redding*
USLP	Blooming Hits	*Paul Mauriat*
UK45	Cinderella Rockefella	*Esther & Abi Ofarim*
UKLP	John Wesley Harding	*Bob Dylan*
WEEK 4		
US45	(Sittin' On) The Dock Of The Bay	*Otis Redding*
USLP	Blooming Hits	*Paul Mauriat*
UK45	Cinderella Rockefella	*Esther & Abi Ofarim*
UKLP	John Wesley Harding	*Bob Dylan*
WEEK 5		
US45	(Sittin' On) The Dock Of The Bay	*Otis Redding*
USLP	Blooming Hits	*Paul Mauriat*
UK45	Lady Madonna	*Beatles*
UKLP	John Wesley Harding	*Bob Dylan*

THE GRAPEVINE

- **Sandie Shaw secretly married fashion designer and boutique owner Jeff Banks on 6 March at Greenwich Register Office, London.**
- **Jimmie Rodgers, found unconscious with a fractured skull in Hollywood in December, is sueing LA City Council for $10 million, accusing police of assault and battery. He claims he is now unable to play the guitar, and has lost his senses of balance, taste and smell.**

Sandie banks on Jeff

Troggs for the troops?

TROGGS TO PLAY IN VIETNAM?

The Troggs may be the first British group to perform in Vietnam. The group has applied through the Australian and New Zealand authorities for permission to entertain their troops in the country after completing a US tour in April.

A previous request had been made to entertain US forces based in Vietnam, but the group's management were told that responsibility could not be accepted by the US authorities for the safety of non-American artists.

Manager Stan Phillips told the NME: 'We are still hopeful that Australia and New Zealand will help us – so far they have been very co-operative.'

The Troggs' vocalist Reg Presley, says that the group's motive in going to Vietnam is 'strictly as entertainers – it must be dreadful out there, and we would just like to provide a few hours' music for the troops.'

PRESLEY AND JONES MEET IN LAS VEGAS

Elvis the Pelvis takes time out to take in Jones the Voice

Tom Jones: standing ovation

On 6 April Elvis Presley, his wife Priscilla and a party of eight friends journeyed 400 miles from LA to Las Vegas to watch Tom Jones's cabaret act at the Flamingo. Presley took a bow when Jones introduced him to the audience, and led a standing ovation at the end of the show as Jones encored with 'Land Of 1000 Dances'.

The Presleys then went backstage, and the two singers chatted for an hour. Jones had previously visited Presley on a film set in 1965, but he is the first UK singer that the American has ever seen performing live.

As they talked over a cigar and a glass of champagne apiece, Presley recalled his own less-than-wonderful memories of performing in Vegas: 'I was at the Frontier Hotel about ten years ago, and I died a terrible death. When I came out with those hip movements (demonstrating) – man, they just weren't ready for me!'

The two also discussed songwriter Jerry Reed, who wrote the most recent Presley hit, 'Guitar Man'. 'Glad you had a hit with that – I publish the song in Britain through my company, Valley Music!' said Jones.

Presley mentioned that he rated Jones's 'Delilah': 'A great record – I see it was a smash in Britain.' To Jones's observation that it was moving less quickly in the US, he countered: 'Man, I want to make a prediction – it'll be a smash here, too.'

On the subject of Jones's 'Green Green Grass Of Home', Presley recalled, 'When it was issued here, the boys and I were on the road, driving in our mobile home. Man, that record meant so much to us boys from Memphis, we just sat there and cried. Then we called the radio station and asked them to play it again - they did, four times! We just sat there and sobbed our hearts out.'

CHARTS

US45	(Sittin' On) The Dock Of The Bay — *Otis Redding*
USLP	The Graduate — *Soundtrack*
UK45	Lady Madonna — *Beatles*
UKLP	John Wesley harding — *Bob Dylan*
WEEK 2	
US45	Honey — *Bobby Goldsboro*
USLP	The Graduate — *Soundtrack*
UK45	Congratulations — *Cliff Richard*
UKLP	John Wesley Harding — *Bob Dylan*
WEEK 3	
US45	Honey — *Bobby Goldsboro*
USLP	The Graduate — *Soundtrack*
UK45	What A Wonderful World — *Louis Armstrong*
UKLP	John Wesley Harding — *Bob Dylan*
WEEK 4	
US45	Honey — *Bobby Goldsboro*
USLP	The Graduate — *Soundtrack*
UK45	What A Wonderful World — *Louis Armstrong*
UKLP	John Wesley Harding — *Bob Dylan*

TOP EURO-SONGS SUED OVER COPYRIGHT

Irish songwriters Shay O'Donoghue and Aiden Magennis of The Debonaires Showband are sueing British writers Bill Martin and Phil Coulter for breach of copyright, claiming that the latter's Cliff Richard-sung 'Congratulations' – the UK's second-placed song in the Eurovision Song Contest – has 'the same chord sequence' as their 'Far Away From You', which was recorded 18 months ago by Doc Carroll & The Royal Blues, and reached No. 8 in the Irish charts.

A writ has also been issued in connection with the winning Eurovision song, Spain's 'La La La', which is alleged to infringe on the copyright of Ray and Dave Davies's 'Death Of A Clown'.

Congratulations Cliff, runner-up in this year's Eurovision Song Contest

THE GRAPEVINE

■ Chris 'Ace' Kefford has, after a period of absence due to illness, now permanently left The Move, who will continue as a four-piece.

■ Zoot Money has disbanded his group Dantalian's Chariot and joined Eric Burdon's Animals, though he will also continue to record as a soloist for CBS; he is likely to have an acting role alongside Burdon in the forthcoming film *The Death of Harry Farmer.*

BEACH BOYS – MAHARISHI TOUR FLOP

An apathetic reaction has greeted the opening of the joint US tour by the Transcendental Meditation guru Maharishi Mahesh Yogi with The Beach Boys, leading to two weeks of dates being cancelled.

Arriving in the US a day late and missing a New York press conference, the Maharishi joined the group for the low-key opening concert at Georgetown University in Washington on 3 May. The next afternoon's show at New York's Singer Bowl was cancelled after The Beach Boys had already set up to play, because only 300 people had turned up. Philadelphia that night attracted a healthier 5,000 – but half of them walked out following the group's set, before the guru's lecture.

After two more moderately successful dates, the Maharishi dropped out, probably displeased by his ultra-lukewarm reception, but ostensibly to honour a movie contract he had signed with Four Star Productions in Hollywood; this project should have been made earlier, but illness had prevented it.

The upset and somewhat angry Beach Boys decided not to press cancellation charges, 'since the tour was all in the cause of love, friendship and peace', and in return the Maharishi has promised to join them again from 17 May, for the final scheduled bookings in Denver, Col. and several venues in California.

Diversifying: Jagger and the Stones pursue movies, solo album, new group LP later

JAGGER ACTING DEBUT (AND STONES FILM?)

Mick Jagger is to make his dramatic acting debut in a film which goes into production in London in July. He will play opposite James Fox in Warner/7 Arts' *Performance*, directed by Donald Cammell and Nicolas Roeg from an original screenplay by Cammell.

The movie tells of a pop musician (Jagger) who is a 'drop-out from the social stream of contemporary life' until he meets a vicious gangster (Fox). Though Jagger's role is dramatic, he will sing one song within the context of the script, and has also written the musical score for the project.

Meanwhile, it is understood that The Rolling Stones as a whole are to start making their own feature film almost immediately, subject to contracts being signed. If, as expected, production on this starts within two or three weeks, it will be completed in time for Jagger to make his solo debut. The group also has a new LP scheduled for June, completed with producer Jimmy Miller.

THE GRAPEVINE

- **Dave Mason, who left Traffic at the end of last year to work as a soloist and producer, has rejoined the group in New York, where he worked on recording sessions for their next album, on which he has several songs.**
- **Resting on Cream's US tour, Eric Clapton went to see The Mothers Of Invention at LA's Shrine Auditorium, and ended up guesting on stage with them.**

CHARTS

US45	Honey *Bobby Goldsboro*
USLP	The Graduate *Soundtrack*
UK45	What A Wonderful World *Louis Armstrong*
UKLP	This Is Soul *Various*
WEEK 2	
US45	Honey *Bobby Goldsboro*
USLP	The Graduate *Soundtrack*
UK45	What A Wonderful World *Louis Armstrong*
UKLP	This Is Soul *Various*
WEEK 3	
US45	Tighten Up *Archie Bell & The Drells*
USLP	The Graduate *Soundtrack*
UK45	Young Girl *Union Gap*
UKLP	This Is Soul *Various*
WEEK 4	
US45	Tighten Up *Archie Bell & The Drells*
USLP	Bookends *Simon & Garfunkel*
UK45	Young Girl *Union Gap*
UKLP	This Is Soul *Various*

Currently Stateside, Clapton, Baker and Bruce

Return of Dave Mason

STONES IN STUDIO BLAZE DRAMA

The Rolling Stones were involved in a fire drama at London's Olympic Sound studios in the early morning of 11 June. At 4.15 am, while the group were filming a sequence for their movie *One By One* with French director Jean Luc Godard, the roof of the building was seen to be ablaze, and the fire brigade were called.

The film crew, ironically, were following the Stones recording a new number called 'Sympathy For The Devil' at the time. Their performance of this song, in gradual development from sketchy beginnings to full studio production, is their key part in the movie, being described as a 'musical embroidery' to the plot's parallel themes of 'construction and destruction'.

Mick Jagger commented: 'The fire brigade was so thorough in extinguishing the blaze that our Hammond organ and all the electronic equipment was completely drenched. The squence will have to be re-taken.'

Stones extinguished

MANFREDS' 'JACK' IS CHANGED TO AVOID RACE PROTEST

Manfred's struggle with a lyrical problem

All first pressings in the UK of the new Manfred Mann single 'My Name Is Jack' have been scrapped after being recalled by the distributor just days before the scheduled release date. Mercury Records in the States had complained about a phrase in the lyric (by US writer John Simon) which might antagonize race relations.

The group returned to the studio on Wednesday, 5 June (only two days before the original scheduled UK release date) to re-record the track with the potentially offending phrase changed.

A spokesman told the NME: 'We were told that the record could not possibly be released in the States in its original form, so rather than re-record the disc specially for the US market, we decided to maintain consistency by changing the lyric for Britain too. It should only hold up UK release by a week.'

HUMPERDINCK TOPS ON US JUKEBOXES

A cross-section survey by *Billboard* magazine of America's 480,000 jukeboxes – covering the 12 months between March 1967 and February 1968 – reveals that Engelbert Humperdinck was the most-played artist, followed by Nancy Sinatra and then The Monkees.

Humperdinck's 'Release Me' was also the most-played individual jukebox record of the period.

Jukebox giant Engelbert

ROSSI TO WRITE FILM MUSIC

Mike Rossi of Status Quo, who wrote the group's 'Pictures Of Matchstick Men' and it's follow-up, has been invited to write the title song and incidental music for *Je*, a French feature film which starts production in August.

Status Quo will be seen in the movie's opening credits, performing the title number.

THE GRAPEVINE

■ Cream have recorded a series of commercials for the Falstaff Brewing Company in California.

■ The Monkees are fighting Screen Gems over ownership of the group name.

■ Glen Campbell has been signed by Paramount to co-star with John Wayne in a Western.

■ The sight of Elvis Presley chatting to Paul Revere (of The Raiders) on a Sunset Boulevard sidewalk brought traffic to a standstill.

CHARTS

Chart	Title	Artist
US45	Mrs. Robinson	*Simon & Garfunkel*
USLP	Bookends	*Simon & Garfunkel*
UK45	Young Girl	*Union Gap*
UKLP	This Is Soul	*Various*
WEEK 2		
US45	Mrs. Robinson	*Simon & Garfunkel*
USLP	Bookends	*Simon & Garfunkel*
UK45	Young Girl	*Union Gap*
UKLP	This Is Soul	*Various*
WEEK 3		
US45	Mrs. Robinson	*Simon & Garfunkel*
USLP	The Graduate	*Soundtrack*
UK45	Young Girl	*Union Gap*
UKLP	This Is Soul	*Various*
WEEK 4		
US45	This Guy's In Love With You	*Herb Alpert*
USLP	The Graduate	*Soundtrack*
UK45	Jumpin' Jack Flash	*Rolling Stones*
UKLP	This Is Soul	*Various*
WEEK 5		
US45	This Guy's In Love With You	*Herb Alpert*
USLP	Bookends	*Simon & Garfunkel*
UK45	Jumpin' Jack Flash	*Rolling Stones*
UKLP	This Is Soul	*Various*

CHARTS

Chart	Title	Artist
US45	This Guy's In Love With You	*Herb Alpert*
USLP	Bookends	*Simon & Garfunkel*
UK45	Baby Come Back	*Equals*
UKLP	Ogdens Nut Gone Flake	*Small Faces*
WEEK 2		
US45	This Guy's In Love With You	*Herb Alpert*
USLP	Bookends	*Simon & Garfunkel*
UK45	Baby Come Back	*Equals*
UKLP	Ogdens Nut Gone Flake	*Small Faces*
WEEK 3		
US45	Grazin' In The Grass	*Hugh Masakela*
USLP	Bookends	*Simon & Garfunkel*
UK45	Baby Come Back	*Equals*
UKLP	Ogdens Nut Gone Flake	*Small Faces*
WEEK 4		
US45	Grazin' In The Grass	*Hugh Masakela*
USLP	The Beat Of The Brass	*Herb Alpert*
UK45	Mony Mony	*Tommy James & The Shondells*
UKLP	Ogdens Nut Gone Flake	*Small Faces*

PRESLEY TALKS TO THE PRESS!

As part of the pre-publicity build-up for his NBC television special, now in production at the company's Burbank studios, Elvis Presley held his first press conference for many years. Asked why he was doing the TV show, he said: 'We figured it was about time. Besides, I thought I had better do it before I got too old!' he chuckled.

Asked about the content of the show, Presley quipped: 'Well, I insisted that the cameras keep on me most of the time! What I do is sing, almost exclusively. And I sing the songs I'm known for.'

'Hell, if he sang the songs he's known for, that would take hours,' butted in Col. Tom Parker. 'NBC only gave us an hour. He is going to sing *some* of the songs he's famous for.'

On fans, Presley thought that his had probably changed a little through the years: 'A lot of them are now young mothers, or girls about to get married.'

Did he ever write songs? 'All I've written is two lines of "Love Me Tender", and that was a while ago.'

Elvis relaxes – TV special soon

NOT NICE AT ALL, CLAIM GROUP

The Nice have asked their label, Andrew Oldham's Immediate Records, to withdraw a controversial poster advertising their single 'America', claiming that bookings and even record sales are suffering as a result of the poster's 'adverse effect' on the public.

It pictures the group members with small boys on their knees, but superimposed on the children's heads are the faces of the assassinated John F. Kennedy, Robert Kennedy and Dr Martin Luther King.

A spokesman for The Nice says: 'Several record stores in the UK have refused to stock our current single, and some promoters will not book the group because of this poster.

'The Nice feel that if the posters are issued in America, they will do considerable harm. The group has been offered a US college and TV tour in September, and has no wish to create ill-will from the outset.'

A poster poser for Immediate trio The Nice as they look to sales across the Atlantic

Blonde Tom: Tommy James of the Shondells and jukebox that doubtless contains their latest hit

THE GRAPEVINE

- **Scott Walker has had to withdraw from a tour of Japan on doctor's orders; he has been certified as suffering from 'psychoneurosis', and is forbidden to travel.**
- **On 12 July, Mickey Dolenz of The Monkees married Samantha Juste – the British girl he met 16 months ago on BBC-TV's *Top of the Pops* – in a secret ceremony performed by his clergyman father, at Dolenz's Hollywood home.**

LIGHTS INSPIRE JAMES

Tommy James has described how he and songwriting partner Richard Cordell found the inspiration for 'Mony Mony', Tommy James & The Shondells' biggest international success to date:

'We were writing one night at my apartment, and we happened to look out of the window. Across the street is a neon sign for "Mutual Of New York", and when it's lit up, it spells out M-O-N-Y. That was just the type of title we wanted!'

AUGUST

RECORD US GOLD DISC TALLY

Sellers supreme in the growing album market, folk-rock duo Simon and Garfunkel

More gold discs were awarded in America during the first six months of this year than for any similar period in the past. The RIAA, certification of 54 awards (21 singles and 33 albums) is eight more than the previous all-time-high six-month tally – a clear sign that record sales continue to climb steadily.

Million-selling singles included Bobby Goldsboro's 'Honey', The Monkees' 'Valleri', The Beatles' 'Lady Madonna', Simon & Garfunkel's 'Mrs Robinson', Otis Redding's '(Sittin' On) The Dock Of The Bay' and The 1910 Fruitgum Company's 'Simon Says'.

The Union Gap scored two in a row with 'Woman, Woman' and 'Young Girl' (and have subsequently made it a hat-trick with 'Lady Willpower').

In the LP field, where discs need to sell half a million within the US to qualify, Dean Martin picked up four golds, while Elvis Presley, Ray Charles, Bob Dylan and Andy Williams collected two apiece.

The biggest album sellers of the period were Simon & Garfunkel's 'Bookends', and the soundtrack from 'The Graduate', which also showcases the duo.

Gold disc Goldsboro

CHARTS

US45	Hello I Love You	*Doors*
USLP	The Beat of The Brass	*Herb Alpert*
UK45	Mony Mony	*Tommy James & The Shondells*
UKLP	Bookends	*Simon And Garfunkel*
WEEK 2		
US45	Hello I Love You	*Doors*
USLP	Wheels Of Fire	*Cream*
UK45	Mony Mony	*Tommy James & The Shondells*
UKLP	Delilah	*Tom Jones*
WEEK 3		
US45	People Got To Be Free	*Rascals*
USLP	Wheels Of Fire	*Cream*
UK45	Mony Mony	*Tommy James & The Shondells*
UKLP	Bookends	*Simon And Garfunkel*
WEEK 4		
US45	People Got To Be Free	*Rascals*
USLP	Wheels Of Fire	*Cream*
UK45	Help Yourself	*Tom Jones*
UKLP	Bookends	*Simon And Garfunkel*
WEEK 5		
US45	People Got To Be Free	*Rascals*
USLP	Wheels Of Fire	*Cream*
UK45	Help Yourself	*Tom Jones*
UKLP	Bookends	*Simon And Garfunkel*

SHADOWS TO LOSE BENNETT – AND WELCH TOO?

Despite wildly exaggerated UK media reports, The Shadows are not breaking up.

However, drummer Brian Bennett intends to leave in December - after the group's London Palladium season with Cliff Ricahrd – and founder-member Bruce Welch is considering quitting at the same time, probably to go into music publishing and management.

Manager Peter Gormley said: 'Bruce has been talking about settling down for some time, and now that Brian is going and the group is having to be reshaped, he feels this might be an opportune time for him to leave, too.

'But nothing will be decided until the boys' return from holiday at the end of the month – and I must stress that Bruce may equally well decide to stay on. Whatever happens, The Shadows will continue – both Hank Marvin and John Rostill are quite determined about that.'

THE GRAPEVINE

- **Fleetwood Mac now have three lead guitarists since adding Danny Kirwen (a protégé of group leader Peter Green and manager Clifford Davis) alongside Green and Jeremy Spencer.**
- **Honeybus lead singer Pete Dello, who wrote the group's hit 'I Can't Let Maggie Go', has left to concentrate on writing and production.**
- **The Beatles have closed down their Apple boutique in London's Baker Street.**

Apple crumbles

STONES' GRAFFITI SLEEVE DISPUTE

The sleeve illustration for the new Rolling Stones album 'Beggars Banquet' is the subject of a dispute between the group and Decca Records, their British label.

It depicts a lavatory wall, inscribed with such slogans as 'John Loves Yoko' and 'Mao Loves Lyndon', and Decca is concerned that these and other scrawlings may cause offence in the US.

Mick Jagger, though, is adamant that nothing will be altered on the LP sleeve despite its controversial photograph.

THE NEW YARDBIRDS

Plant (left) Page (back to camera) and Jones

The Yardbirds have now completed the re-shaping of their personnel, and have formulated their plans for the next four months.

Leader Jimmy Page, in partnership with group manager Peter Grant, has formed a company called Super-Hyp Recording, which will now be responsible for the production of all Yardbirds records, ending their recording link with producer Mickie Most.

It is also likely that the group will no longer appear on their current labels (EMI in the UK, Epic in the US), since it is understood that four major British record companies are currently negotiating for the rights to Super-Hyp's output, while Warner-Reprise is tipped as the likely US licencee.

The new line-up teams Page (lead and steel guitar) with John Paul Jones (bass guitar and organ), John Bonham (drums), and Robert Plant (vocals). A six-week US tour of one-nighters and college dates will begin on November 14.

The group are currently in Scandinavia, fulfilling bookings made on behalf of the previous line-up earlier in the year.

CHARTS

US45	People Got To Be Free *Rascals*
USLP	Waiting For The Sun *Doors*
UK45	I've Gotta Get A Message To You *Bee Gees*
UKLP	Bookends *Simon And Garfunkel*
WEEK 2	
US45	People Got To Be Free *Rascals*
USLP	Waiting For The Sun *Doors*
UK45	Hey Jude *Beatles*
UKLP	Bookends *Simon And Garfunkel*
WEEK 3	
US45	Harper Valley PTA *Jeannie C. Riley*
USLP	Waiting For The Sun *Doors*
UK45	Hey Jude *Beatles*
UKLP	The Hollies' Greatest Hits *Hollies*
WEEK 4	
US45	Hey Jude *Beatles*
USLP	Time Peace *Rascals*
UK45	Hey Jude *Beatles*
UKLP	The Hollies' Greatest Hits *Hollies*

THE GRAPEVINE

- **The Doors' third LP 'Waiting For The Sun' became a gold record on the day of release, with over a million dollars'-worth of advance orders.**
- **Mixed and confused audience reactions to advance screenings of The Monkees' feature film *Head* have prompted Screen Gems to re-edit it and put back the opening.**
- **The Beach Boys lost 300-400,000 dollars touring with the Maharishi.**

DUSTY IN MEMPHIS

Dusty Springfield is in Memphis to make her first recordings for Atlantic Records. Producer Jerry Wexler said prior to the sessions: 'Everybody expected us to go the Aretha Franklin route with Dusty, but we're not: I've lined up the same rhythm and string sections that The Box Tops and Merilee Rush use in Memphis. Tom Dowd and Arif Mardin will also be on the session.

'I've taken Dusty to Memphis because it's important that she gets away from the sound we've been producing in New York. She's tough in the studio – very picky and choosey with material, and highly critical – but I wouldn't have it any other way.

'We're loaded with songs,' he added. 'For the past few weeks we've done nothing but send stuff to London. I just hope she likes them.'

US DISC SALES AT ALL-TIME PEAK

Record sales in America reached an all-time peak in 1967, according to industry figures. Over $1,000 million were spent on records, and for the first time ever, more albums were sold than singles in the US: 192 million against 187 million. In terms of dollar value, LP sales represented 82 per cent of total turnover.

Total annual revenue from US record sales has almost doubled in the last decade – from 511 million dollars in 1958 to 1967's 1,051 million dollars.

There were 7,231 singles released in the US during 1967 (against 7,086 in 1966), and 4,328 albums (3,752 in 1966).

Financial vibes not good as transcendental trek bombs for the Beach Boys

SPENCER'S NEW MEN

Spencer Davis has engaged two new musicians to replace drummer Pete York and organist Eddie Hardin, both of whom quit his group on October 26, due to 'differences over musical policy'.

The newcomers – both formerly in a group named Mirage – are Dave Hynes (drums) and Dee Murray (bass), and both will join Davis for concerts in West Germany before undertaking a five-week tour of the US and Canada from November 1.

Prior to the personnel switch, on October 9, Davis himself collapsed from what was described in the music press as 'exhaustion and hypertension', while in Berlin completing work on a version of the song 'Aquarius' (from the musical *Hair*) which is planned as a Germany-only single. He was ordered to convalesce for two weeks, and his wife flew to join him in Berlin.

Left: Outpacing even 'Pepper, The Sound of Music remains in the album charts after more than three years

Right: Cream to call it a day at London finale

THE GRAPEVINE

- **The last Yardbirds performance was at Liverpool University on October 20: Jimmy Page has now decided to rename the new line-up Led Zeppelin.**
- **Cream will play their farewell concert at London's Royal Albert Hall on 26 November, and the BBC intend to film it as a TV special.**
- **The Beatles' 'Hey Jude' has sold 4,738,000 copies worldwide in eight weeks.**

THE BRITISH HILLS ARE ALIVE WITH THEM

This month, the soundtrack album from the film *The Sound of Music* became the biggest-selling LP in British record history.

Its UK sales hit two million on October 2, and an RCA Records spokesman estimated that one out of every four homes in the country with a record player also own a copy of this disc.

The soundtrack is still in the top ten of the NME album chart after over 180 weeks, and its sales gross is said to have now exceeded £3,225,000.

It has also been estimated that if all the copies of the album so far sold in Britain were stacked up together, they would reach fifteen times the height of the Empire State Building!

CHARTS

US45	Hey Jude *Beatles*
USLP	Waiting For The Sun *Doors*
UK45	Those Were The Days *Mary Hopkin*
UKLP	The Hollies' Greatest Hits *Hollies*
	WEEK 2
US45	Hey Jude *Beatles*
USLP	Cheap Thrills *Big Brother & The Holding Company*
UK45	Those Were The Days *Mary Hopkin*
UKLP	The Hollies' Greatest Hits *Hollies*
	WEEK 3
US45	Hey Jude *Beatles*
USLP	Cheap Thrills *Big Brother & The Holding Company*
UK45	Those Were The Days *Mary Hopkin*
UKLP	The Hollies' Greatest Hits *Hollies*
	WEEK 4
US45	Hey Jude *Beatles*
USLP	Cheap Thrills *Big Brother & The Holding Company*
UK45	Those Were The Days *Mary Hopkin*
UKLP	The Hollies' Greatest Hits *Hollies*

MASON QUITS TRAFFIC AGAIN AFTER ABORTIVE TOUR

Dave Mason has left Traffic for the second time, to concentrate on record production.

He departed after the group's US tour, which was planned to last six weeks, but was called off after only 10 days because 'venues which had been hoped for did not materialize', and because Steve Winwood became plagued by a throat infection.

Traffic returned to the UK to start recording work on another LP, but without Mason, who went to Los Angeles to discuss business deals. A Traffic spokesman said: 'Dave is too individual to be part of a group, and he feels he will be happier working alone, producing records.'

DJs: THE YARD GOES OFF FOREVER!

Richard Harris's new single 'The Yard Went On Forever', written (like his 'MacArthur Park') by Jim Webb, is causing controversy on US radio, where some DJs are refusing to play it.

Though its lyrics are oblique, it is an anti-Vietnam war song, based on a speech by the late Robert Kennedy.

MELOUNEY TO QUIT BEE GEES

Vince Melouney's departure from The Bee Gees has been confirmed by the group's manager Robert Stigwood, who said: 'For some time there has been a musical disagreement between the Gibb brothers and Vince, who wanted to play more blues-based material. We have decided it would be better for him to leave, though we have not yet decided about his future.'

The guitarist's final concert with the group will be on December 1, at the end of the current German tour. He will not then be replaced; instead, Maurice Gibb will move to take over his lead guitar slot.

There will now be a delay in the production of The Bee Gees' film *Lord Kitchener's Little Drummer Boys*, as Melouney has to be written out of the script. Filming originally due to start in December will now take place in February, and the group will complete the recording of the January-scheduled double album 'Masterpiece' before Christmas.

CHARTS

US45 Hey Jude
Beatles
USLP Cheap Thrills
Big Brother & The Holding Company
UK45 Those Were The Days
Mary Hopkin
UKLP The Hollies' Greatest Hits
Hollies

WEEK 2

US45 Hey Jude
Beatles
USLP Cheap Thrills
Big Brother & The Holding Company
UK45 With A Little Help From My Friends
Joe Cocker
UKLP The Hollies' Greatest Hits
Hollies

WEEK 3

US45 Hey Jude
Beatles
USLP Electric Ladyland
Jimi Hendrix Experience
UK45 The Good, The Bad & The Ugly
Hugo Montenegro
UKLP The Hollies' Greatest Hits
Hollies

WEEK 4

US45 Hey Jude
Beatles
USLP Electric Ladyland
Jimi Hendrix Experience
UK45 Eloise
Barry Ryan
UKLP The Hollies' Greatest Hits
Hollies

WEEK 5

US45 Love Child
Diana Ross & The Supremes
USLP Cheap Thrills
Big Brother & The Holding Company
UK45 Eloise
Barry Ryan
UKLP The Beatles
Beatles

MAMA CASS VOCAL UNCERTAINTY

Mama Cass (left) in more carefree days with the Mamas and Papas

Mama Cass Elliott faces grave uncertainty over her future singing career. She collapsed with a throat haemorrhage on the opening night of a six-week season at Las Vegas's Caesar's Palace – an engagement which would have earned her $250,000 – and is now awaiting a major throat operation.

At present, Cass cannot sing at all, and, assuming the operation is successful, it would be many months before she could resume recordings or concerts. More seriously, there is a risk that surgery could adversely affect her vocal chords, and thus place her whole career in jeopardy.

NASH TO LEAVE HOLLIES

Graham Nash is to split from The Hollies following their December 8 appearance in the all-star 'Save Rave' charity concert at the London Palladium – which Nash himself is organizing.

It is understood that Nash is tired of live performance, and is anxious to develop some new ideas he has been formulating for several months, but which group commitments have prevented him from pursuing.

Most of his future career is likely to be in songwriting and record production, though he will also probably record as an artist in the US.

A spokesman for The Hollies told the NME: 'We are in the process of sorting out a replacement for Graham, and have two or three names on our shortlist. Meanwhile, the group are already recording backing tracks for a new album, which will be completed after the newcomer is selected.'

Herman with DJ Stuart Henry

THE GRAPEVINE

- **Peter Noone – Herman of The Hermits – married Mireille Strasser on November 5 (his 21st birthday), at the Church of the Immaculate Conception in Mayfair, London.**
- **Cream's farewell US tour grossed over $700,000.**
- **Aretha Franklin has broken a leg following a fall at a Honolulu hotel; expected to be in plaster for six weeks, she is currently making live appearances in a wheelchair.**

STONES' ROCK'N'ROLL' CIRCUS

The Rolling Stones filmed their *Rock'n'Roll Circus* TV special on 11 December, at Wembley's Intertel TV studios in London, before an invited audience of fans.

One of the highlights of the day was the formation of a one-off 'supergroup' comprising John Lennon, Keith Richard, Eric Clapton (late of Cream), and drummer Mitch Mitchell from The Jimi Hendrix Experience. They performed two numbers, including Lennon's 'Yer Blues', a song from the new Beatles double LP.

As well as the Stones' own show-closing spot, other sections of the special included a solo by Marianne Faithfull, a classical contribution from Julius Katchen, and various circus acts – including Keith Richard and Mick Jagger in a knife-throwing interlude!

Other groups on the bill were Jethro Tull and special guests The Who – the latter replacing the previously scheduled Traffic, who have now split up.

No plans have yet been announced for the screening of the special.

Left to right, Clapton, Lennon, Mitchell and Richards jam in front of the TV cameras

THE GRAPEVINE

- **Dave Edmunds' Love Sculpture have signed a US deal with London Records guaranteeing £250,000.**
- **Mary Hopkin is 'sympathetically considering' a lead acting role in Stanley Baker's forthcoming film *The Rape of the Fair Country*.**
- **Mark Volman of The Turtles has insured his distinctive frizzy hair for $100,0000 against fire, theft(!) or loss due to illness.**

Turtle vocalist Volman

CHARTS

US45	Love Child — *Diana Ross & The Supremes*
USLP	Cheap Thrills — *Big Brother & The Holding Company*
UK45	Lily The Pink — *Scaffold*
UKLP	The Beatles — *Beatles*
WEEK 2	
US45	I Heard It Through The Grapevine — *Marvin Gaye*
USLP	Cheap Thrills — *Big Brother & The Holding Company*
UK45	Lily The Pink — *Scaffold*
UKLP	The Beatles — *Beatles*
WEEK 3	
US45	I Heard It Through The Grapevine — *Marvin Gaye*
USLP	Wichita Lineman — *Glen Campbell*
UK45	Lily The Pink — *Scaffold*
UKLP	The Beatles — *Beatles*
WEEK 4	
US45	I Heard It Through The Grapevine — *Marvin Gaye*
USLP	The Beatles — *Beatles*
UK45	Lily The Pink — *Scaffold*
UKLP	The Beatles — *Beatles*

A TRIO OF MONKEES

Jones, Nesmith and Dolenz

The Monkees are now reduced to a trio, following the departure of Peter Tork to pursue a solo career.

The others have already filmed a Christmas TV appearance on NBC's *Hollywood Squares* as a threesome, and it seems that they will continue this way rather than recruit a replacement for Tork – who is understood to be currently negotiating a recording contract and considering forming a backing group.

PRESLEY TRIUMPHS IN TV SPECIAL

Elvis Presley's return to TV in his own one-hour NBC special (with the unlikely sponsorship of Singer Sewing Machines) was screened on December 3.

It proved to be an artistic and commercial triumph, pulling in big ratings and finding acclaim not only from fans, but also from critics who had written off Presley's ability to generate musical excitement after a string of increasingly minor movies.

NME's New York correspondent June Harris commented: 'Elvis, at 33, with his weight tapered down, and moving his body with all the sex that resulted in waist-upward-only shots on the Ed Sullivan TV show in 1956, is sensational . . . he still sings those Memphis blues like they've just been written, and "Jailhouse Rock", "Hound Dog" and others didn't sound dated at all – they sounded like new rock.

'Elvis's second career, after closing a twelve-year rock gap, starts off from the top. A personal appearance tour now seems like the next logical move to make.'

1969

CHARTS

US45	I Heard It Through The Grapevine *Marvin Gaye*
USLP	The Beatles *Beatles*
UK45	Lily The Pink *Scaffold*
UKLP	The Beatles *Beatles*

WEEK 2

US45	I Heard It Through The Grapevine *Marvin Gaye*
USLP	The Beatles *Beatles*
UK45	Ob-La-Di, Ob-La-Da *Marmalade*
UKLP	The Beatles *Beatles*

WEEK 3

US45	I Heard It Through The Grapevine *Marvin Gaye*
USLP	The Beatles *Beatles*
UK45	Ob-La-Di, Ob-La-Da *Marmalade*
UKLP	The Beatles *Beatles*

WEEK 4

US45	I Heard It Through The Grapevine *Marvin Gaye*
USLP	The Beatles *Beatles*
UK45	Albatross *Fleetwood Mac*
UKLP	The Beatles *Beatles*

Dusty – stitched up cheek, broken nose

ATLANTIC'S BEST-EVER YEAR

Atlantic Records enjoyed the greatest year in its history in 1968, with sales up by 85 per cent over 1967, and a tally of 23 certified gold records – more than any other company has ever achieved in one year.

The label's top-selling artist was Aretha Franklin, who had four million-selling singles and two gold albums. Since joining Atlantic in 1967, Franklin has amassed 10 gold trophies in all, more than any other female singer in pop history.

Rock groups, once not regarded as an Atlantic strength, also scored well for the label, notably its UK signings: Arthur Brown and Cream had US million-selling singles with 'Fire' and 'Sunshine Of Your Love'. Cream also scored three gold albums, including one for their 'Wheels of Fire' double set.

HENDRIX AND DUSTY: BASE OVER APEX

Jimi Hendrix and Dusty Springfield both saw in the New Year with injuries from falls. Hendrix has been resting in New York, obliged to cancel an appearance at the Utrecht Pop Festival in Holland, after he fell very awkwardly in a heavy snowstorm at Christmas, tearing several ligaments in his leg.

Dusty, meanwhile, tripped over a paving stone on the balcony of her parents' home in Richmond, England, where she was spending Christmas. She had to have two stitches in her cheek, and was later discovered to have also broken her nose. She had to cancel her New Year's Eve cabaret date at London's Hilton hotel, though was fit to appear at Atlantic Records' Bahamas convention on 16 January.

Aretha: a solid gold soul star

THE GRAPEVINE

- **Three of The Troggs – Ronnie Bond, Reg Presley and Chris Britten – are to have solo records released by Page One in February or March.**
- **Lead singer Peter Frampton is to leave The Herd for a solo career; the remaining members have already recorded without him for a new single.**
- **120 gold disc awards were made in the US during 1968 – 25 more than the previous record figure in 1967.**

The Herd: Frampton (top) to go solo

NEW-LOOK CREAM HAS WINWOOD IN BRUCE'S PLACE!

The recently-split Cream are to re-form, though under a different name, and with Steve Winwood, former leader of Traffic, replacing Jack Bruce.

The trio have spent early February living and rehearsing together in Winwood's Berkshire (England) cottage, and intended to start recording on the 8th. However, suitable studio time was not available, so the initial sessions were postponed. A suitable name for the group is currently being sought, as well as a permanent bass player to augment them as a quartet.

Clapton said that initial intentions were to get an album together, and that live performances would probably then commence within about a month. The group's attitude to singles would be similar to that of Cream: 'We will not set out with the principal object of making them, but if any track stands out as an obvious single, we'll release it.'

On the rapid reunion with Baker, Clapton adds: 'We haven't really picked each other – we simply floated back together. I don't anticipate any contractual difficulties for the new group, because anyone who stood in the way of a project like this would be mad!'

CHARTS

US45	Crimson & Clover *Tommy James & The Shondells*
USLP	The Beatles *Beatles*
UK45	Albatross *Fleetwood Mac*
UKLP	The Best Of The Seekers *Seekers*
WEEK 2	
US45	Crimson & Clover *Tommy James & The Shondells*
USLP	TCB *Diana Ross & Supremes and Temptations*
UK45	Albatross *Fleetwood Mac*
UKLP	Diana & Supremes Join The Temptations *Diana Ross & Supremes and Temptations*
WEEK 3	
US45	Everyday People *Sly & The Family Stone*
USLP	The Beatles *Beatles*
UK45	Blackberry Way *Move*
UKLP	Diana & Supremes Join The Temptations *Diana Ross & Supremes and Temptations*
WEEK 4	
US45	Everyday People *Sly & The Family Stone*
USLP	The Beatles *Beatles*
UK45	(If Paradise Is) Half As Nice *Amen Corner*
UKLP	Diana & Supremes Join The Temptations *Diana Ross & Supremes and Temptations*

THE GRAPEVINE

- **Jim Morrison of The Doors has had a black suit made from the hide of an unborn pony.**
- **Doubleday books has advance orders for 80,000 hardback copies of Tiny Tim's biography.**
- **Guitarist Trevor Burton has left The Move, to be replaced by Rick Price, previously with Sight & Sound.**
- **Art Garfunkel has taken a straight acting role in the film *Catch 22*, with location shooting in Mexico.**

Mr. & Mrs. Tiny Tim

Garfunkel the movie star

Morrison and the unborn pony (puke!)

BEATLES CALL IN KLEIN; GIVE ROOFTOP PERFORMANCE

The Beatles have called in American business negotiator Allen Klein – who has previously handled the financial affairs of other major UK groups like The Rolling Stones and The Animals – to advise them on the running of their Apple Enterprises.

He flew to London for a preliminary business conference with the group on 3 February, and took over the reins of Apple a week later.

Meanwhile, rehearsals for the much-announced Beatles London concert have now definitely become the basis of a TV documentary film. Several new, specially written songs were heard by startled passers-by in London's Savile Row on the afternoon of Thursday, 30 January, when the group gave a spontaneous performance on the Apple roof, and were filmed and recorded for the programme.

Almost all 12 tracks of the new Beatles album, centred around the documentary, are now complete, with final recordings to take place before the end of February. An April or May release is slated for the LP.

PRESLEY RECORDS IN MEMPHIS

Elvis Presley has recorded in Memphis for the first time since leaving Sun REcords in 1955.

At American Studios, with the resident band, he has cut over 30 new tracks, including a version of the Beatles' 'Hey Jude'.

CHARTS

US45	Everyday People *Sly & The Family Stone*
USLP	The Beatles *Beatles*
UK45	Where Do You Go To My Lovely *Peter Sarstedt*
UKLP	Diana & Supremes Join The Temptations *Diana Ross & Supremes and Temptations*
	WEEK 2
US45	Everyday People *Sly & The Family Stone*
USLP	Wichita Lineman *Glen Campbell*
UK45	Where Do You Go To My Lovely *Peter Sarstedt*
UKLP	Diana & Supremes Join The Temptations *Diana Ross & Supremes and Temptations*
	WEEK 3
US45	Dizzy *Tommy Roe*
USLP	Wichita Lineman *Glen Campbell*
UK45	Where Do You Go To My Lovely *Peter Sarstedt*
UKLP	Diana & Supremes Join The Temptations *Diana Ross & Supremes and Temptations*
	WEEK 4
US45	Dizzy *Tommy Roe*
USLP	Wichita Lineman *Glen Campbell*
UK45	Where Do You Go To My Lovely *Peter Sarstedt*
UKLP	Goodbye *Cream*
	WEEK 5
US45	Dizzy *Tommy Roe*
USLP	Blood, Sweat & Tears *Blood, Sweat & Tears*
UK45	I Heard It Through The Grapevine *Marvin Gaye*
UKLP	Goodbye *Cream*

THE GRAPEVINE

- **Motown vice-president Barney Ales has visited London in a bid to sign The Pretty Things as the US label's first British act.**
- **Ex-Shadow Brian Bennett is to be Tom Jones's drummer on his world tour.**
- **Mason, Capaldi, Wood & Frog, the group formed out of Traffic after Steve Winwood's departure, has split after just 60 days together, without recording.**

MORRISON IN TROUBLE

Jim Morrison of The Doors was arrested on March 1 in Miami on multiple charges, including lewd and lascivious behaviour in public, indecent exposure, and public profanity and drunkenness – which could land him with a total three and a half year jail sentence.

During a concert at Dinner Key Auditorium, Morrison (who has had previous brushes with the law in New York, New Haven and Phoenix) apparently appeared drunk, screamed obscenities, and exposed himself in full view of the sold-out 10,000-strong audience.

Miami and Dade County police did not arrest him on the spot, for fear that it would cause a riot. They sought him immediately after the concert, but he had left the auditorium. The Doors then left for the Caribbean the next morning.

Morrison's felony charge has made him liable to arrest and extradition anywhere within the US. Joe Durant, an assistant to the Florida State Attorney, comments: 'I was extremely shocked at the facts in this case as to what this man did. The State Attorney's office will prosecute, and ask for the maximum sentence on each count to run consecutively.'

Pretties to Motown

With Tom Jones: Shadow Brian Bennett

DYLAN RECORDS WITH CASH

Bob Dylan has completed the sessions for his next album in Nashville, using the same trio (Charlie McCoy, Pete Drake and Kenny Buttrey) who played with him 18 months ago on 'John Wesley Harding', plus three further session men.

An unexpected development at the sessions was a series of duets with country star Johnny Cash – according to reports, the two of them 'just went into the studio and jammed', producing some 15 tracks.

Some of these may make it on to the new LP, but there is speculation that a whole album of Dylan-Cash duets may now follow later.

LENNON AND McCARTNEY BOTH WED

Paul McCartney and John Lennon have married within days of each other. On March 12, McCartney wed American photographer Linda Eastman at Marylebone Registry Office in London, while on March 20, Lennon tied the knot with Japanese avant-garde artist Yoko Ono in Gibraltar.

Mr. & Mrs. Macca

Meanwhile, no date has yet been set for the next Beatles LP because they still have to select the tracks from at least two dozen recent recordings. Among likely candidates are 'Maxwell's Silver Hammer', 'Polythene Pam', 'All I Want Is You', 'Teddy Boy'. 'Jubilee', 'Octopus's Garden' (a Ringo solo), George Harrison's 'Not Guilty' and John's solo 'What's The New Mary Jane'.

ALBUMS OVERTAKE SINGLES IN UK

In 1968, for the first time ever, production of albums in the UK exceeded that of singles. A total of 49,184,000 LPs (an increase of 11 million over 1967) were manufactured during the year, compared with 49,161,000 singles.

UK record sales as a whole also hit a new high peak in 1968, with revenue topping £30 million – over £2 million more than in the previous year.

The grand total of 98,345,000 records produced in 1968 is second only to 1964's all-time peak figure of 101,257,000. However, singles accounted for almost three-quarters of the 1964 total, and the subsequent spectacular growth in LP sales means the revenue from 1968 sales was greater than that of 1964.

Barry Ryan celebrates three million sales

THE GRAPEVINE

- Rolling Stone Bill Wyman and his wife are divorcing.
- Marital breakup is also strongly rumoured for John and Michelle Phillips of The Mamas & The Papas, though the group are recording again, without the now-solo Cass Elliott.
- The Kinks' Ray Davies has produced the next Turtles single.
- Barry Ryan's 'Eloise' has sold over three million worldwide, and topped charts in 17 countries.

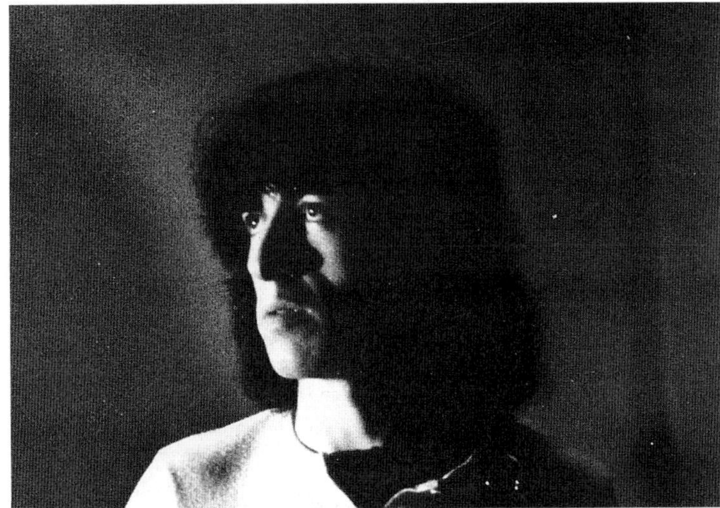

Wyman – divorce

FOUR EUROVISION WINNERS!

The 1969 Eurovision Song Contest, held in Madrid, produced the most amazing result in the competition's history, when four entries tied for first place with (unsurprisingly) the lowest-ever winning totals of 18 points apiece.

The joint winning songs were Holland's 'De Troubadour', sung by Lennie Kuhr, Spain's 'Vivo Cantata', sung by Salome, France's 'Un Jour Un Enfant', sung by Frida Boccara, and the UK's 'Boom Bang-A-Bang', sung by Lulu.

Lulu – first equal

Lulu, who departed soon afterwards for a belated honeymoon in Acapulco with Bee Gee husband Maurice Gibb, as her agent was being inundated with overseas offers on the strength of her win, told the NME: 'I don't mind sharing the prize, as long as I'm one of the firsts. It's better this way, because we're all happy.'

However, a week later, Sweden (whose entry finished ninth) declared 'We have taken part in a mediocre programme long enough,' and announced that it would not participate next year. Yugoslavia (which finished 13th) is also having 'second thoughts' about next year, while Austria and Denmark did not compete this year because of similar feelings about the quality of this supposedly presitigious musical event.

TORK FINDS RELEASE

Former Monkee Peter Tork is now working with his own group, named Release. He told the NME's Hollywood correspondent: 'Three is the quorum for our group. We sometimes have four members, and are thinking of having a rotating fourth – at the moment it's a girl that I'm promoting, named Judy Mayhan.'

The other three are Tork himself on vocals and lead guitar, Ripley Wildflower on bass and vocals, and Tork's girlfriend Reine Stewart on drums.

'I'd rather work with friends,' says Tork, 'because that makes much better music.'

CHARTS

US45	Dizzy / *Tommy Roe*
USLP	Wichita Lineman / *Glenn Campbell*
UK45	I Heard It Through The Grapevine / *Marvin Gaye*
UKLP	Goodbye / *Cream*
WEEK 2	
US45	Aquarius/Let The Sunshine In / *Fifth Dimension*
USLP	Blood, Sweat & Tears / *Blood, Sweat & Tears*
UK45	I Heard It Through The Grapevine / *Marvin Gaye*
UKLP	Goodbye / *Cream*
WEEK 3	
US45	Aquarius/Let The Sunshine In / *Fifth Dimension*
USLP	Blood, Sweat & Tears / *Blood, Sweat & Tears*
UK45	The Israelites / *Desmond Dekker*
UKLP	Goodbye / *Cream*
WEEK 4	
US45	Aquarius/Let The Sunshine In / *Fifth Dimension*
USLP	Hair / *Original Cast*
UK45	The Isrealites / *Desmond Dekker*
UKLP	Goodbye / *Cream*

BLIND FAITH

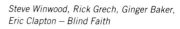

Steve Winwood, Rick Grech, Ginger Baker, Eric Clapton – Blind Faith

It was announced on May 6 that the Eric Clapton-Steve Winwood-Ginger Baker 'supergroup' is to be called Blind Faith.

The fourth member has also now been chosen: on bass (and also possibly electric violin) will be Rick Grech from Family. He joined the others at Winwood's Berkshire cottage on May 3 to begin rehearsals, and has played in the studio sessions which completed the group's debut LP, scheduled for June release.

They are said to have 14 hours of tape in the can, though not all of it is suitable for release.

Blind Faith begin a US tour on July 11, for which manager Robert Stigwood has negotiated them a minimum of $25,000 a concert against a percentage (60-70 per cent) of the gross. One date alone is known to be worth $60,000.

Grech has been replaced in Family by John Weider, formerly with Eric Burdon's Animals.

CHARTS

US45	Aquarius/Let The Sunshine In – *Fifth Dimension*
USLP	Hair – *Original Cast*
UK45	Get Back – *Beatles*
UKLP	Goodbye – *Cream*
WEEK 2	
US45	Aquarius/Let The Sunshine In – *Fifth Dimension*
USLP	Hair – *Original Cast*
UK45	Get Back – *Beatles*
UKLP	On The Threshold Of A Dream – *Moody Blues*
WEEK 3	
US45	Aquarius/Let The Sunshine In – *Fifth Dimension*
USLP	Hair – *Original Cast*
UK45	Get Back – *Beatles*
UKLP	On The Threshold Of A Dream – *Moody Blues*
WEEK 4	
US45	Get Back – *Beatles*
USLP	Hair – *Original Cast*
UK45	Get Back – *Beatles*
UKLP	Nashville Skyline – *Bob Dylan*
WEEK 5	
US45	Get Back – *Beatles*
USLP	Hair – *Original Cast*
UK45	Get Back – *Beatles*
UKLP	Nashville Skyline – *Bob Dylan*

STAR QUOTE

JIMMY PAGE

on Led Zeppelin's instant conquest of the US

'I was anxious to get to America; we came as soon as we could. I didn't have any confidence in English audiences at all. That's because The Yardbirds had their biggest success in the US, and I just assumed it would be the same with us.'

US VISA BAN ON LENNON

John Lennon is no longer able to visit America. An official of the US Embassy in London told the NME that Lennon's 'standing visa' was revoked at the time of his recent drug conviction, and that 'very serious consideration' would have to be given before it could be renewed.

The Embassy also suggested that any immediate application by Lennon would almost certainly be turned down, but he is known to have subsequently (on May 5) reapplied for a visa to visit the US on a business trip.

It is understood that any American visit would be for Lennon to join in talks on The Beatles' bid for Northern Songs, or discussions on Apple's US interests – and not for a tour by the group.

FAIRPORT DRUMMER IS KILLED IN CRASH

Martin Lamble, 19-year old drummer with UK folk-rock group Fairport Convention, was killed in the early hours of Monday, May 12, when the group's van crashed on the M1 motorway as they returned to London from a gig in Birmingham.

Also killed in the crash was American stage clothing designer Jeannie Franklin, while Fairport guitarists Richard Thompson and Simon Nicol, bassist Ashley Hutchings, and road manager Harvey Bramham, were all injured.

The group's lead singer Sandy Denny was travelling separately by car, and was not involved.

Mickie Most: splitting with Lulu

THE GRAPEVINE

- **Lulu has split from producer Mickie Most after a two-year association.**
- **The Rolling Stones may launch their own Pear label, patterned after The Beatles' Apple, when their Decca/London contract runs out next February.**
- **Peter Green and Jeremy Spencer of Fleetwood Mac plan an orchestral-choral LP telling the life story of Christ.**

Fleetwood Mac get religion?

THE BALLAD OF JOHN AND YOKO

John and Yoko Lennon were joined in their hotel room in Toronto, Canada, by more than 40 friends, to record Lennon's anthemic composition 'Give Peace A Chance', which is to be released as a single by Apple, credited to The Plastic Ono Band.

Among the group were Tom Smothers of The Smothers Brothers, and a Montreal Jewish religious leader, Rabbi Feinberg.

Meanwhile, The Beatles' single 'The Ballad Of John And Yoko' has been banned by many US radio stations, and by the Australian Broadcasting Corporation, because of alleged blasphemy.

Lennon sings the phrase, 'Christ, you know it ain't easy' several times on the disc, which has caused no similar upset in the UK. An Apple spokesman commented that the words were 'a natural expression within the context of the song.'

CHARTS

US45	Get Back *Beatles*
USLP	Hair *Original Cast*
UK45	Dizzy *Tommy Roe*
UKLP	Nashville Skyline *Bob Dylan*
WEEK 2	
US45	Get Back *Beatles*
USLP	Hair *Original Cast*
UK45	Dizzy *Tommy Roe*
UKLP	Nashville Skyline *Bob Dylan*
WEEK 3	
US45	Get Back *Beatles*
USLP	Hair *Original Cast*
UK45	The Ballad Of John And Yoko *Beatles*
UKLP	My Way *Frank Sinatra*
WEEK 4	
US45	Love Theme From Romeo & Juliet *Henry Mancini Orchestra*
USLP	Hair *Original Cast*
UK45	The Ballad Of John And Yoko *Beatles*
UKLP	My Way *Frank Sinatra*

KING: ROBBERY AND CURRY VANDALISM

Thieves broke into the unoccupied Marble Arch, London, home of recording artist, producer and TV presenter Jonathan King on the night of 7 June. They stole a collection of albums, a white fur coat, and some tapes of a musical score composed by King.

In an eccentric act of vandalism, the thieves also disposed of a large amount of chicken curry: when King returned home some hours later to discover the burglary, he also found this uneaten meal liberally covering the floor of his house.

STEWART GOES SOLO

Rod the Mod Stewart (second left) leaves The Jeff Beck Group

Rod Stewart, lead singer with The Jeff Beck group, has been signed to a solo recording contract by Mercury – although it is stressed that this will be a parallel independent venture, and that he will not be leaving Beck.

Stewart begins recording for a single and album in mid-June, with producer Lou Reizner. Former Manfred Mann vocalist Mike D'Abo (whose own group announced its split this month) is handling arrangements on some of the tracks.

THE GRAPEVINE

- **Cilla Black has had plastic surgery to remodel her nose; this puts her in a club with Tom Jones, Dave Clark, Connie Francis, Herb Alpert, Paul Anka and many more.**
- **John Sebastian is writing the music for the Peter Sellers/Ringo Starr film *The Magic Christian*.**
- **Davy Jones of The Monkees has revealed a secret 18-month marriage to 24-year old Linda Haines.**

Cilla – a new hooter

TOMMY ROE FILM MUSICAL

Tommy Roe, whose 'Dizzy' has now topped both the US and UK charts and is the biggest-selling single of his seven-year hitmaking career, is to make his starring film debut later this year.

The movie, titled *Tommy Who*, will begin production for Roe's own independent film company in October. Location shooting will take place in Florida and parts of California.

Roe told the NME: 'It will be a musical comedy in colour, and will include about eight songs. It should take about a month to shoot, but we haven't cast it yet. We don't expect it to be shown before mid-1970.'

BRIAN JONES TRAGEDY; STONES TRIUMPH

The Stones In The Park

The Rolling Stones played a highly successful Saturday afternoon outdoor free concert in front of an estimated 250,000 fans in London's Hyde Park on July 5, though the joy of the event was inevitably muted by the death of former group member Brian Jones only two days before.

Jones had left the group to pursue his divergent musical interests (a return to R&B basics) during June; the Stones recruited a replacement, former John Mayall Bluesbreakers guitarist Mick Taylor, in time to prepare for Hyde Park.

Brian died at his home, Cotchford Farm in Hartfield, Sussex, after taking a midnight swim in his pool. He was found floating by house guests who tried to revive him, but was pronounced dead by a doctor at around 3am on July 3.

The Stones dedicated their Hyde Park concert to Jones's memory. Mick Jagger opened the performance with words of tribute and a poem by Shelley, after which a host of butterflies were released into the air.

The Stones' 75-minute act was filmed by Granada TV, which plans a documentary of the event.

REDDING QUITS HENDRIX

Bassist Noel Redding has quit The Jimi Hendrix Experience, following a dispute with Hendrix in the US. Redding flew home to London for discussions about his future with the group's former manager Chas Chandler.

It is understood that Redding's decision was prompted by Hendrix's failure to consult him about future plans. The guitarist is believed to be considering dropping the name 'Experience' in order to augment his group into a 'creative commune', which would include both writers and musicians.

Redding has already been running his own part-time outfit known as Fat Mattress since the beginning of the year, and now intends to devote his full-time energy to this group.

Rumours suggest that the third Experience member, drummer Mitch Mitchell – who also flew home to London a few days after Redding – may also decide to leave Hendrix and form his own band.

Redding: leaving the Experience to devote full-time energy to his Fat Mattress

CHARTS

US45	Love Theme From Romeo & Juliet — *Henry Mancini Orchestra*
USLP	Hair — *Original Cast*
UK45	Something In The Air — *Thunderclap Newman*
UKLP	This is Tom Jones — *Tom Jones*
WEEK 2	
US45	In The Year 2525 — *Zager and Evans*
USLP	Hair — *Original Cast*
UK45	Something In The Air — *Thunderclap Newman*
UKLP	This Is Tom Jones — *Tom Jones*
WEEK 3	
US45	In The Year 2525 — *Zager and Evans*
USLP	Hair — *Original Cast*
UK45	In The Ghetto — *Elvis Presley*
UKLP	This Is Tom Jones — *Tom Jones*
WEEK 4	
US45	In The Year 2525 — *Zager and Evans*
USLP	Blood, Sweat & Tears — *Blood, Sweat & Tears*
UK45	Honky Tonk Women — *Rolling Stones*
UKLP	This Is Tom Jones — *Tom Jones*

Stills, Crosby, Nash & Young

THE GRAPEVINE

- **Crosby, Stills & Nash have recruited Stills's former Buffalo Springfield colleague Neil Young as their fourth member; he will join their first US concert tour in August.**
- **Controversy over the sleeve of Blind Faith's debut LP, which pictures a naked teenage girl, has forced Atlantic Records to design a replacement; many US dealers have cancelled orders, claiming it is 'salacious'.**

ROCK TAKES NEWPORT

The 16th annual Newport Jazz Festival at Rhode Island included heavy rock for the first time, and attracted a record three-day audience of over 80,000.

Bands like Jethro Tull, John Mayall, Ten Years After and Jeff Beck played alongside an extensive jazz line-up, and R&B/blues acts James Brown, Johnny Winter and B.B. King. Led Zeppelin played the final night, despite requests from local authorities that they should not appear, 'in the interest of public safety'!

WOODSTOCK: DISASTROUSLY GREAT

The three-day Woodstock Music and Art Fair, held in rural upstate New York, attracted an enormous audience, estimated at around half a million, to a piece of farmland which stood little chance of catering adequately for such a vast horde – particularly when torrential rain turned the whole area into a quagmire.

However, despite being declared an official disaster area, the festival developed a tribal spirit of its own, focused by an array of some of the world's top rock talent.

Acts who performed (and were filmed and recorded for hoped-for albums and a movie) included Jimi Hendrix, The Who, Creedence Clearwater Revival, Santana, Jefferson Airplane, Crosby, Stills, Nash & Young, Ritchie Havens, Ten Years After, Joan Baez, Sly & The Family Stone, and many more.

THE GRAPEVINE

- **Kiki Dee has become the first British girl singer to be signed by Motown; her five-year contract calls for her to record in Detroit with producer Frank Wilson.**
- **Dave Dee plays a motorbike gang leader in the Marty Feldman film *Every Home Should Have One*, currently shooting in London.**
- **Fairport Convention have named drummer Dave Mattacks to replace the late Martin Lamble, after auditioning 50 possibles.**

GOLD ZEPPELIN

Led Zeppelin, currently on a record-breaking seven-week US tour, have won a gold disc for over a million dollars' worth of sales of their debut album. The award was presented to the group by Atlantic vice-president Jerry Wexler at a special luncheon in New York.

Meanwhile, work on the group's second LP is almost complete, and US advance orders already total over 200,000.

(l to r) Jones, Plant, Page – Zep go gold

Kiki for Motown

CHARTS

US45	In The Year 2525	*Zager and Evans*
USLP	Blood, Sweat & Tears	*Blood, Sweat & Tears*
UK45	Honky Tonk Women	*Rolling Stones*
UKLP	Flaming Star	*Elvis Presley*
WEEK 2		
US45	In The Year 2525	*Zager and Evans*
USLP	Blood, Sweat & Tears	*Blood, Sweat & Tears*
UK45	Honky Tonk Women	*Rolling Stones*
UKLP	Stand Up	*Jethro Tull*
WEEK 3		
US45	In The Year 2525	*Zager and Evans*
USLP	Blood, Sweat & Tears	*Blood, Sweat & Tears*
UK45	Honky Tonk Women	*Rolling Stones*
UKLP	Stand Up	*Jethro Tull*
WEEK 4		
US45	Honky Tonk Women	*Rolling Stones*
USLP	At San Quentin	*Johnny Cash*
UK45	Honky Tonk Women	*Rolling Stones*
UKLP	Stand Up	*Jethro Tull*
WEEK 5		
US45	Honky Tonk Women	*Rolling Stones*
USLP	At San Quentin	*Johnny Cash*
UK45	In The Year 2525	*Zager and Evans*
UKLP	Stand Up	*Jethro Tull*

FRAMPTON AND PIE FREE TO RECORD

A dispute between Peter Frampton and Steve Roland's Double-R Productions, which had forced Frampton's recording career with his new group Humble Pie on to ice, is over.

A statement announced: 'As the result of a substantial settlement from Immediate Records, the courts have lifted the injunction which prevailed on recordings by Peter Frampton.'

Roland had claimed that Frampton was still under contract to Double-R from his Herd days. An ex-parte injunction stopped Immediate from releasing any Humble Pie product until this dispute was revolved.

Frampton – full steam ahead

ELVIS: VIVA LAS VEGAS!

Elvis Presley has made a triumphant return to live work after nearly a decade performing only for the movie cameras.

His four-week cabaret season at Las Vegas's new International Hotel has been critically acclaimed, with all agreeing he had lost little of the stage fire that made him famous. The show mixed Presley classics with rock standards, Beatles covers and new material including his next single 'Suspicious Minds'.

Asked at the pre-opening press conference if he now felt it was a mistake to have done so many film soundtrack LPs, Presley replied: 'I think so. When you do ten songs in a movie, they can't all be good songs. Anyway, I got tired of singing to turtles!'

WOODSTOCK: ROCK MUSIC COMES OF AGE

It wasn't the first of its kind, despite what convenient omissions history may have passed down. But Woodstock reigns supreme in most people's memory as *the* rock festival – the quintessence of that peculiar urge huge numbers of people have to make their way to some fairly remote spot, grab a few square feet of land and sit in various states of discomfort for days on end while a steady line of performers do their best to make the brief time they've been given to perform as memorable as possible.

Woodstock's pre-eminence undoubtedly stems from the fact that – with the recent exceptions of Live Aid and the Nelson Mandela birthday celebrations of 1989 (known as Freedom Fest in the USA), and the Maysles Brothers' excellent *Gimme Shelter* movie of The Rolling Stones' tragic Altamont fiasco – the Woodstock Music and Arts Festival (to give it its correct name) is the most chronicled and quoted example of its genre.

It started, as most music business events do, as a great and relatively simple plan to make a lot of money. Attendance figures from previous festivals suggested there was an almost unlimited audience out there who'd be more than happy to fork out between five and ten dollars for 'Three days of peace and music'.

A site was found – 600 acres of land near Bethel, in upstate New York, owned by farmer Max Yasgur – and a date set: 15-17 August 1969. Work began on assembling the biggest and best list of rock's top names, and of putting together the infrastructure of what would be an ad hoc

township with a population of around 200,000, all of whom would need feeding, watering and washing, and some of whom (for sure) would require medical help after over-indulging on the many and varied substances which would undoubtedly be on sale.

In the event, there were three deaths, two births and four miscarriages – what you'd expect from a town that size.

What you wouldn't expect – and the organizers certainly didn't – was the complete chaos the festival would cause in the surrounding countryside as more than 400,000 people tried to make it to Yasgur's farm. There were traffic jams of 20 or more miles all round, including freeways. On-site security, including ticket booths and official entrances, became swamped so quickly and comprehensively that the gates were simply thrown open and the festival was designated 'free'.

Musically the commitment and passion which comes out of the Michael Wadleigh movie, and from the grooves of the ten album sides Atlantic Records released, more than compensate for the flaws.

Among those who battled through the traffic and rain to fulfil their debt of honour by playing Woodstock were The Band, The Who, Jimi Hendrix (pictured bottom left), Jefferson Airplane, Crosby Stills, Nash & Young, Creedence Clearwater, Tim Hardin, Country Joe & The Fish, The Grateful Dead, Sly & The Family Stone, Joe Cocker (pictured bottom right), Blood Sweat & Tears, Joan Baez, Mountain and Canned Heat.

Johnny Winter was there, too. Alvin Lee became a superstar via his appearance with Ten Years After, Ravi Shankar probably doubled sitar sales in America with his set, and Joni Mitchell (who didn't play) was inspired enough by the instant mythology to write a hit song.

Woodstock was the birthday party to celebrate rock 'n' roll music's coming of age. Nothing would ever be the same.

DYLAN ON ISLE OF WIGHT

Bob Dylan and The Band topped the bill of the UK's 1969 Isle of Wight Festival, drawing an open-air crowd of over 200,000 – including rock celebrities like John Lennon, George Harrison, Ringo Starr, Steve Winwood, Keith Richards and others.

Dylan presented mainly familiar material, all of it well-received, but there was some disappointment in the audience that his act only lasted for an hour. This, it seems, was mainly the fault of poor organization.

As Dylan said afterwards: 'I was here at five-thirty, ready to go on, but I was kept waiting until eleven. I played long enough – I didn't want to go on much later.' Indeed, the NME was told earlier that Dylan would take the stage at 9pm, probably to play until midnight, but organizers' estimates kept changing through the evening.

The Band's own set preceded him, and focussed on their 'Music From Big Pink' LP.

Other acts highlighting the three-day event included The Who, The Moody Blues, The Nice, Joe Cocker, Julie Felix, Richie Havens and Fat Mattress.

Dylan – well received at the concert but inconvenienced by organizers

CHARTS

US45	Honky Tonk Women *Rolling Stones*
USLP	At San Quentin *Johnny Cash*
UK45	In The Year 2525 *Zager and Evans*
UKLP	Stand Up *Jethro Tull*
WEEK 2	
US45	Honky Tonk Women *Rolling Stones*
USLP	At San Quentin *Johnny Cash*
UK45	In The Year 2525 *Zager and Evans*
UKLP	Stand Up *Jethro Tull*
WEEK 3	
US45	Sugar Sugar *Archies*
USLP	Blind Faith *Blind Faith*
UK45	Bad Moon Rising *Creedence Clearwater Revival*
UKLP	Johnny Cash At San Quentin *Johnny Cash*
WEEK 4	
US45	Sugar Sugar *Archies*
USLP	Blind Faith *Blind Faith*
UK45	Bad Moon Rising *Creedence Clearwater Revival*
UKLP	Johnny Cash At San Quentin *Johnny Cash*

BEE GEES SACK THEIR DRUMMER

The Bee Gees with departing drummer Colin Peterson (right)

The Bee Gees, who have already lost original lead guitarist Vince Melouney and currently-soloing Gibb brother Robin over the last year, have now parted company with drummer Colin Petersen.

The official group statement announced: 'Barry and Maurice Gibb have terminated their association with Colin, who will cease to be a member of the Bee Gees.'

Barry Gibb commented that Petersen's departure is 'all part of our natural progression . . . he has been spending an increasing amount of time on his management activities, and we have been aware for some time that he would eventually leave.'

Peterson disagrees, claiming an agreement exists whereby he is an equal partner in the group for five years from July 4, 1967. Alleging breach of obligation, he has served writs asking for the affairs of the partnership to be wound up in court.

As well as claiming damages, Peterson seeks to restrain the Gibb brothers from performing as The Bee Gees without his participation.

Mary Hopkin – for Eurovision

THE GRAPEVINE

- **All five members of The Equals have been injured in Germany, where their car ran off an autobahn in a gale.**
- **James Taylor has broken an arm and a leg in a motorbike crash.**
- **Mary Hopkin is to be the UK's representative in the 1970 Eurovision Song Contest.**
- **Deep Purple guitarist Ritchie Blackmore has married German dancer Barbel Hardie.**

NASH KEEPS QUIET

Graham Nash, who fell ill shortly after his first major shows with Crosby, Stills & Nash, has recovered, but has been ordered to rest his throat or threaten his singing voice.

He whispered to the NME's New York correspondent: 'My doctor told me that if I don't overdo talking, I won't need an operation - so I'm keeping mum.'

Nash's vow of silence

MOODIES ON THE THRESHOLD

Moody Blues: On The Threshold Of A Label

The Moody Blues have launched their own record label, named Threshold Records after their worldwide hit album 'On The Threshold Of A Dream'.

Owned jointly by The Moodies and their producer Tony Clarke, the label's intention is 'to provide a small company atmosphere with major company facilities'. The group has signed a five-year deal with Decca for marketing and distribution of Threshold, leaving the Moodies with 'complete artistic control'.

The label will concentrate on LPs, among the first of which will be by a new Liverpool singer named Timon, whom Justin Hayward is producing, and Wolverhampton group Trapeze, with whom John Lodge has been working.

The Moody Blues will launch Threshold themselves, however, with their LP 'Dedicated To Our Children's Children's Children', in November.

THE GRAPEVINE

- Cliff Richard has signed a three-year deal with Warner Bros. for US releases, starting with current UK hit single 'Throw Down A Line'.
- Tyrannosaurus Rex – Marc Bolan and Steve Took – are to split, though Bolan will retain the name.
- Christine Perfect, singer with Chicken Shack and wife of Fleetwood Mac's John McVie, to form her own group, yet unnamed.

Christine Perfect (centre) to leave the Shack

CLAPTON WITH DELANEY & BONNIE

Despite frequent denials of a Blind Faith split, Eric Clapton is booked to tour Europe as a member of Delaney & Bonnie & Friends, the husband-and-wife-led group he met when they supported Blind Faith's US tour.

'This group is incredible – the best group in the world,' commented Clapton.

BATTERY-POWERED BOWIE

David Bowie has revealed that the electronic astral effects on his hit single 'Space Oddity' were made on a Stylophone. This is a pocket-sized electronic organ, powered by batteries and operated by touching a metal stylus tip to its keyboard – hence the name.

The portable instrument was introduced to UK TV in 1968 by Australian singer Rolf Harris, who made frequent demonstrations of its use.

Bowie now apparently does all his composing on a stylophone, while sales of the instrument are also spreading among teenagers - frequently for use in playing along with groups on disc!

Bowie's stylophone oddity

DIANA TO LEAVE SUPREMES

It has been officially announced that lead singer Diana Ross will leave The Supremes in January 1970. She will spend February rehearsing her new act, and make her solo cabaret debut in Framingham, Massachusetts, on March 8.

Mary Wilson will take over as The Supremes leader, and Ross will be replaced in the group by Jean Terrell, who is the sister of former heavyweight boxer Ernie Terrell, and former vocalist in his sideline vocal group Ernie & The Heavyweights, which broke up when he retired from the ring.

The group are likely to be renamed The New Supremes, and both they and Ross will continue to record separately for Motown.

CHARTS

US45	Sugar Sugar *Archies*
USLP	Green River *Creedence Clearwater Revival*
UK45	Bad Moon Rising *Creedence Clearwater Revival*
UKLP	Abbey Road *Beatles*
WEEK 2	
US45	Sugar Sugar *Archies*
USLP	Green River *Creedence Clearwater Revival*
UK45	I'll Never Fall In Love Again *Bobbie Gentry*
UKLP	Abbey Road *Beatles*
WEEK 3	
US45	I Can't Get Next To You *Temptations*
USLP	Green River *Creedence Clearwater Revival*
UK45	I'll Never Fall In Love Again *Bobbie Gentry*
UKLP	Abbey Road *Beatles*
WEEK 4	
US45	I Can't Get Next To You *Temptations*
USLP	Green River *Creedence Clearwater Revival*
UK45	I'll Never Fall In Love Again *Bobbie Gentry*
UKLP	Abbey Road *Beatles*

ELVIS RETURNS TO CONCERTS; TV WITH RINGO?

Elvis Presley, back atop the US singles chart for the first time since 1962 with 'Suspicious Minds', is to return to the concert arena in the New Year, when he takes his own two-hour package to the Houston Astrodome in Texas (the world's largest indoor arena, with a capacity of 72,000) for three nights from February 27.

Presley's last concert appearance was a charity one-off in Hawaii in 1961, and he last toured regularly in 1956!

The new initiative is seen as a logical step on from his return to the live stage in Las Vegas this summer. He is also booked for a return four-week engagement at the city's International Hotel, which will this time guarantee him one million dollars – 25 per cent more than his first-time fee.

Meanwhile, US press reports suggest that Ringo Starr, along with his *Magic Christian* co-star Raquel Welch, has been invited to join Presley in a second TV spectacular, planned for US screening shortly before Christmas. Apple's press office in the UK, however, could make no comment about such a projected link-up.

Starr and Sellers

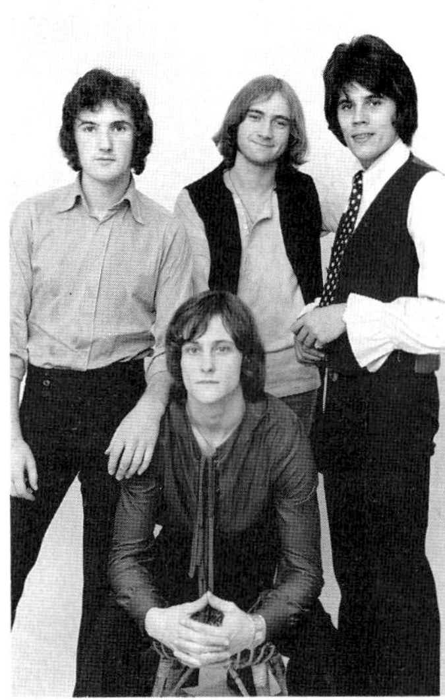
Flaming Youth – Dutch TV Special

CHARTS

US45	Suspicious Minds	*Elvis Presley*
USLP	Abbey Road	*Beatles*
UK45	Sugar Sugar	*Archies*
UKLP	Abbey Road	*Beatles*
	WEEK 2	
US45	Wedding Bell Blues	*Fifth Dimension*
USLP	Abbey Road	*Beatles*
UK45	Sugar Sugar	*Archies*
UKLP	Abbey Road	*Beatles*
	WEEK 3	
US45	Wedding Bell Blues	*Fifth Dimension*
USLP	Abbey Road	*Beatles*
UK45	Oh Well	*Fleetwood Mac*
UKLP	Abbey Road	*Beatles*
	WEEK 4	
US45	Wedding Bell Blues	*Fifth Dimension*
USLP	Abbey Road	*Beatles*
UK45	Sugar Sugar	*Archies*
UKLP	Abbey Road	*Beatles*
	WEEK 5	
US45	Come Together/Something	*Beatles*
USLP	Abbey Road	*Beatles*
UK45	Sugar Sugar	*Archies*
UKLP	Abbey Road	*Beatles*

THE GRAPEVINE

- **World sales of The Bealtes' 'Abbey Road' album have topped four million in its first two months.**
- **Flaming Youth's debut LP, the concept album 'Ark 2', is the subject of an hour-long TV special which the group have filmed in Holland.**
- **Blind Faith's Ginger Baker has been offered a starring role in the Hollywood Western *Zachariah*, and is said to be keen to accept.**

STONES ON THE SCREEN

The film *Michael Kohlhaas*, in which Rolling Stone Keith Richards plays a character role, opens in London on November 13, with a general UK release in December.

Richard's cameo appearance marks his dramatic debut in the cinema, and caused him to have his first haircut for two years! Stars of the film are David Warner, Anna Karina, and Richard's girlfriend Anita Pallenberg.

Meanwhile, the long-awaited film *Performance*, in which fellow Stone Mick Jagger made his starring dramatic debut opposite James Fox (and – again – Anita Pallenberg), has been reprieved by Warner Bros.

It had originally been planned to scrap the movie after studio executive had declared it 'unintelligible', but Warner now says it can be salvaged, and will be a 1970 cinema release.

Jagger as Turner

PURPLE CONCERTO FOR HOLLYWOOD

Deep Purple are to perform their rock/classical work 'Concerto For Group And Orchestra', written by keyboard player Jon Lord, at the Hollywood Bowl in March next year, during the group's more conventional tour of the United States.

Other performances of the work in Vienna and Zurich will similarly be slotted into a European tour in January.

The concerto was first performed at London's Royal Albert Hall on September 24, when the group played with the Royal Philharmonic Orchestra conducted by Malcolm Arnold. This was recorded by EMI, and will be released as a live album in the UK in December.

HENDRIX: NEW GROUP AND FAREWELL TOUR WITH OLD?

Jimi Hendrix is planning what he describes as a 'farewell tour' of the US, Britain and Europe, and has asked the two former members of The Experience, Noel Redding and Mitch Mitchell, to rejoin him for six weeks of concerts in the spring.

Several reports that Fat Mattress – Redding's current group - have broken up may leave him in a position to accept this offer, although the bassist is currently convalescing after a nervous breakdown.

Hendrix is also reported to be putting together a larger group for future work, possibly in a new direction. He has named drummer Buddy Miles as a definite member, but has not selected the other musicians.

Until recently, Hendrix has been unable to travel because he was due to face drugs charges in Canada which could have given him a maximum of seven years in prison. However, a Toronto court has acquitted him, and he is now free to tour abroad.

He has devoted much of the last three months to recording with session musicians, and now has a large stockpile of tracks available for future release.

THE GRAPEVINE

- UK group The Peddlers have been booked for a three-week Las Vegas cabaret season at Caesar's Palace.
- Pink Floyd are writing the score for Antonioni's next movie *Zabriski Point*.
- Rumours (and aural evidence) suggest that the lead singers of The Archies ('Sugar Sugar') and The Cuff Links ('Tracy') are one and the same person.
- George Harrison is another on-stage guest with Delaney & Bonnie.

Floyd: to score Zabriski Point

AND THEN THERE WAS ONE BEE GEE . . .

Barry Gibb has quit The Bee Gees, leaving his brother Maurice (currently holidaying in Australia with wife Lulu) as the sole remaining member of a group which was once a quintet!

Barry gave his reasons for leaving as being that he is 'fed up, miserable and completely disillusioned'. He now intends to embark on a solo career, following in the steps of brother Robin, whose fractious split last year has involved the Gibbs in a legal wrangle which has only just been amicably settled.

Discussions are now necessary between manager Robert Stigwood, Barry and Maurice regarding several projects which may not now take place – including their own Bee Gee record label, and a proposed TV series. Meanwhile, speculation is growing in music business circles that Maurice himself will now drop the Bee Gees name, and concentrate on working with Lulu.

UNHEARD BEATLES TRACK FOR CHARITY

'Across The Universe', a John Lennon song recorded in 1968 by The Beatles but never released, is to be included in an EMI mid-priced all-star charity album to be issued in the New Year. All profits from the release will go to the World Wildlife Fund.

Meanwhile, the proposed Plastic Ono Band single 'You Know My Name', due for release by Apple on December 5, has been cancelled.

CHARTS

US45 Na Na Hey Hey Kiss Him Goodbye *Steam*
USLP Abbey Road *Beatles*
UK45 Yester-Me Yester-You Yesterday *Stevie Wonder*
UKLP Abbey Road *Beatles*

WEEK 2

US45 Na Na Hey Hey Kiss Him Goodbye *Steam*
USLP Abbey Road *Beatles*
UK45 Ruby Don't Take Your Love To Town *Kenny Rogers & The New Edition*
UKLP Abbey Road *Beatles*

WEEK 3

US45 Leaving On A Jet Plane *Peter, Paul & Mary*
USLP Abbey Road *Beatles*
UK45 Two Little Boys *Rolf Harris*
UKLP Abbey Road *Beatles*

WEEK 4

US45 Someday We'll Be Together *Diana Ross & The Supremes*
USLP Led Zeppelin II *Led Zeppelin*
UK45 Two Little Boys *Rolf Harris*
UKLP Abbey Road *Beatles*

THE 1970s

The worst excesses of the end of the 1960s didn't stretch too far into the Seventies, although the decade started with numerous deaths – Hendrix, Morrison, Joplin. The most noticeable trend was the divergence of music on opposite sides of the Atlantic.

America began to worship the hysteria, posturing and volume of what became known as Heavy Metal music, whose first major practitioners were Led Zeppelin, a quartet whose rise neatly dovetailed with the demise of The Beatles. Ever since, metal has remained an international musical force, although its stars tend to remain individually anonymous.

Britain started the 1970s pointing away from metallic pomp and towards a hybrid known as 'glam-rock', which produced Marc Bolan, David Bowie and several groups who further emphasised the sartorial overkill of psychedelia, while strongly de-emphasising the intellectual content of popular music.

Most of the glam-rockers didn't really catch on in the States, because the era of the stadium band was beginning in the wake of metal. Supergroups like Crosby, Stills & Nash attracted huge crowds to concerts, as did The Stones, The Who and Led Zep. Bands spent years making technically perfect but sometimes uninspired albums costing huge sums to produce.

During the last three years of the 1970s, the musical paths of Britain and America became even more widely separated. British youth, many of whom in the cities had become the unemployed victims, of an economic slump, could find little relevance in the sun-kissed utopia in which The Eagles seemed to live. They didn't have much time either for the biggest British stars of the era – Elton John, Fleetwood Mac, Pink Floyd and all the rest – who spent much more time in America, where they were better appreciated and could earn infinitely more than in economically divided Britain.

Neither were they greatly moved by the seamless efficiency and catchy songs of Abba, the Swedish quartet who sold more records than anyone internationally during the decade, and topped the UK charts nine times in all, or the superbly crafted but terminally unhip music of brother and sister duo, The Carpenters.

Rock music has always been the rallying call of rebellious youth, and in 1977 disenchanted Britons like The Sex Pistols, The Clash and The Boomtown Rats thumbed their runny noses at the disco music craze spearheaded by the improbably high voices of The Bee Gees.

Punk rock brought outrage back to annoy older generations, but things weren't as tough in the States, so it didn't catch on as much. The first places in the US which did get the picture were industrial cities like Detroit. Motown had moved out to California and lost its street credibility, and earlier in the decade, the car capital of America had produced louder and louder bands.

But by the end of the decade, New York had become America's most innovative city, spawning punk's godparents Lou Reed, The New York Dolls and Patti Smith, as well as supporting disco and producing punk stars like The Ramones and Blondie.

As the end of the 1970s approached most records were only popular for months rather than years. The public appetite for frequent change was becoming voracious!

1 Pink Floyd
2 David Bowie
3 John Travolta
4 The Sex Pistols

1

2

3

4

SHEP BEATEN TO DEATH

James 'Shep' Sheppard, lead singer with The Heartbeats and Shep & The Limelites, was found dead in his car on the Long Island Expressway on January 24, having been beaten and robbed. Sheppard wrote and recorded 'A Thousand Miles Away', a top 10 single in the American R&B charts during 1956, and one of the best loved doo wop anthems of the decade.

In 1961 he formed The Limelites and immediately scored massively with 'Daddy's Home', a US top 5 single that was an answer record to 'A Thousand Miles Away'. Signed to the Hull label during the early sixties, Shep & The Limelites also had minor hits with 'Ready For Your Love', 'Three Steps To The Altar' and 'Our Anniversary.'

Shep And The Limelites (from the top) Charles Baskerville, Clarence Bassett and James 'Shep' Sheppard, once one of New York's finest doo-wop outfits

THE GRAPEVINE

- **Pentangle are writing the soundtrack score to 'Tam Lin', a movie starring Ava Gardner and Ian McShane.**
- **The Bonzo Dog Band has split in the wake of a London Lyceum gig.**
- **Carl Wayne is to play his final date as lead singer with The Move at Stockport, England on January 31.**

CHARTS

US45	Raindrops Keep Falling On My Head	*B.J. Thomas*
USLP	Abbey Road	*Beatles*
UK45	Two Little Boys	*Rolf Harris*
UKLP	Abbey Road	*Beatles*
WEEK 2		
US45	Raindrops Keep Falling On My Head	*B.J. Thomas*
USLP	Abbey Road	*Beatles*
UK45	Two Little Boys	*Rolf Harris*
UKLP	Abbey Road	*Beatles*
WEEK 3		
US45	Raindrops Keep Falling On My Head	*B.J. Thomas*
USLP	Led Zeppelin II	*Led Zeppelin*
UK45	Two Little Boys	*Rolf Harris*
UKLP	Abbey Road	*Beatles*
WEEK 4		
US45	Raindrops Keep Falling On My Head	*B.J. Thomas*
USLP	Abbey Road	*Beatles*
UK45	Two Little Boys	*Rolf Harris*
UKLP	Abbey Road	*Beatles*
WEEK 5		
US45	I Want You Back	*Jackson Five*
USLP	Led Zeppelin II	*Led Zeppelin*
UK45	Reflections Of My Life	*Marmalade*
UKLP	Abbey Road	*Beatles*

ELVIS AND THE NUN

NBC-Universal International Productions have just released *'Change Of Habit'*, a movie in which Elvis Presley portrays ghetto doctor John Carpenter, while toothsome Mary Tyler Moore is Sister Michelle, a plain-clothes nun who, for moments of drama, reverts to haute couture and carefully applied eye-liner.

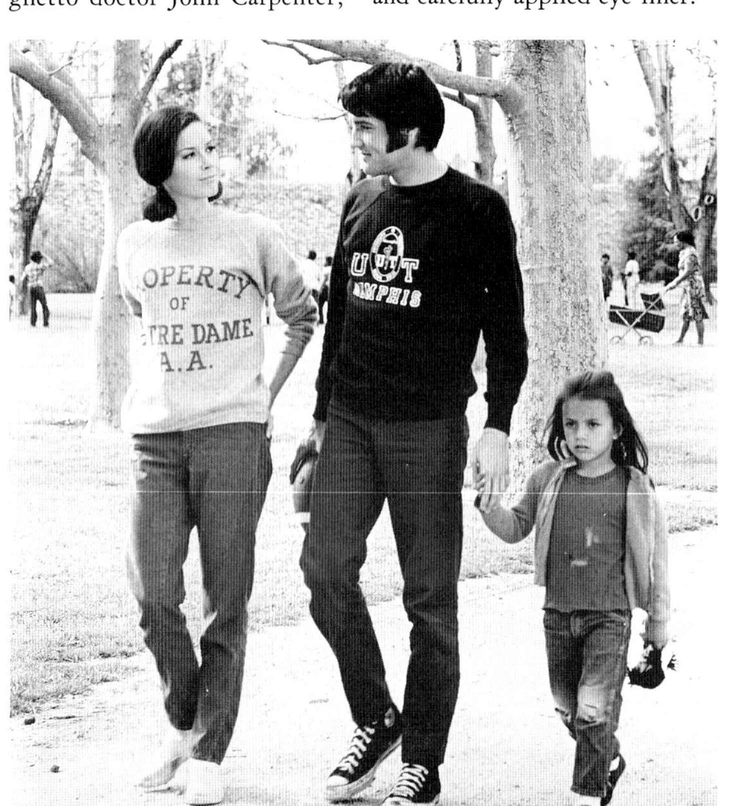

Dr Elvis discusses swapping T-shirts with Sister Mary Tyler Moore in a scene from Universal's Change Of Habit, El's 30th movie since 1956

BILLY STEWART KILLED IN CRASH

Sweet soul, stutter-scat hit-maker Billy Stewart (32) and three members of his band were tragically killed when their car crashed off a bridge and into the River Neuse, in North Carolina. Stewart will best be remembered for such Chess waxings as 'Summertime', 'Secret Love', 'I Do Love You' and 'Sitting In The Park'.

THE ALBERT VETOES LENNON-WHO SHOW

The future of all pop concerts at London's Royal Albert Hall is in doubt because the venue has refused to host a charity event planned for March. The show, involving John Lennon, The Who, The Incredible String Band and King Crimson, was to have benefitted Britain's National Council for Civil Liberties, plus Release, the organisation that aids drug offenders.

But the RAH, who turned down a Rolling Stones concert last December, will not allow the gig to take place, and now the Musicians Union have threatened to blacklist the venue, which normally presents around 40 rock concerts each year.

ELLIS QUITS LOVE AFFAIR

Steve Ellis, often called 'The Last of the Teen Idols', has quit as lead singer with Love Affair to pursue a solo career. Says Ellis: 'We never really made it big anywhere but Britain and I think that if we had started to happen in America, I wouldn't have left.'

PETER TO PART WITH THE GREEN STUFF

Peter Green says he would like to give some of his money away. The Fleetwood Mac guitarist is quoted as saying that he would like to provide financial help to those who are starving or merely lack a good education and opportunities.

Home after a three month tour of America, Green said, as he reversed his £700 white Jaguar out of a Richmond, Surrey, car park: 'Not that I have millions and millions, but there are some big chunks coming in compared to what the average man earns. I would like to go yachting. I would like to buy an A.C.Cobra. But before I do, I would like to know that everyone is getting their bowlful of rice every day. You know, I used to be just as happy when I was a butcher earning five pounds a week.'

LED ZEP BECOME NOBS

Just one of the nobs – Robert Plant

Led Zeppelin have been forced to play Copenhagen under the pseudonym The Nobs because Eva Von Zeppelin has objected to the group using her family name. It's Zep's third setback this month. Earlier, a proposed Singapore concert was cancelled by the local authority because of objections to the length of the group's hair, while at the start of the month singer Robert Plant was involved in a road accident after attending a Spirit concert.

The Tull's award winning 'Stand-Up' sleeve

STARR STARS IN MOVIE

The movie *'The Magic Christian'* premiered in New York City on February 11. Directed by Joseph McGrath and featuring a screenplay by McGrath, novelist Terry Southern and Peter Sellers, with additional material by Monty Python's John Cleese and Graham Chapman, it's a wacky offering about the world's wealthiest man (Sellers) and his protegé (Starr), who wreak havoc on the world at large in an effort to prove that people do anything for money.

Apple have released an album by Liverpool group Badfinger called 'Magic Christian Music' which contains songs from the film plus other items. One of the movie songs is 'Come And Get It', written and produced by Paul McCartney.

CHARTS

US45	Venus *Shocking Blue*
USLP	Led Zeppelin II *Led Zeppelin*
UK45	Love Grows *Edison Lighthouse*
UKLP	Led Zeppelin II *Led Zeppelin*
WEEK 2	
US45	Thank You (Falettinme Be Mice Elf Agin) *Sly & The Family Stone*
USLP	Led Zeppelin II *Led Zeppelin*
UK45	Love Grows *Edison Lighthouse*
UKLP	Led Zeppelin II *Led Zeppelin*
WEEK 3	
US45	Thank You (Falettinme Be Mice Elf Agin) *Sly & The Family Stone*
USLP	Led Zeppelin II *Led Zeppelin*
UK45	Love Grows *Edison Lighthouse*
UKLP	Bridge Over Troubled Water *Simon & Garfunkel*
WEEK 4	
US45	Bridge Over Troubled Water *Simon & Garfunkel*
USLP	Led Zeppelin II *Led Zeppelin*
UK45	I Want You Back *Jackson 5*
UKLP	Bridge Over Troubled Water *Simon & Garfunkel*

THE GRAPEVINE

- **Joni Mitchell has announced her retirement in the wake of her London Royal Albert Hall show.**
- **The Who have taped a Leeds University gig for a live album.**
- **The NME awards for the best sleeve designs of the past year have been awarded to 'Motown Chartbusters' (EMI), Jethro Tull's 'Stand Up' (Chrysalis), Keef Hartley's 'Half Breed' (Decca) and The Who's 'Tommy' (Track).**

STAR

FRANCOISE HARDY

'Elvis – all those tight suits look sexy on him. It's unbelievable to think he's 34. I can't think of anybody but Elvis I'd put myself in trouble for.'

BLUES TRIBUTE AT THE FILLMORE

On February 11, The Butterfield Blues Band played a benefit for legendary bluesman Magic Sam at the Fillmore West in San Francisco. Also on the bill were Mike Bloomfield, Elvin Bishop Group, Charlie Musselwhite and Nick Gravenites.

MARCH

1970

TAMMI TERRELL DEAD

Tamla Motown star Tammi Terrell, best known for her series of duets with Marvin Gaye – 'Ain't No Mountain High Enough', 'Your Precious Love', 'Ain't Nothing Like The Real Thing', 'If This World Were Mine', 'You're All I Need To Get By', 'What You Gave Me' and others – died at Graduate Hospital, Philadelphia on March 16, after undergoing the last of several brain tumour operations she had in the past eighteen months.

A one-time student at the University of Pennsylvania, where she studied psychology and pre-med until she quit to take up singing, Tammi signed to Mowtown in 1965 and had a couple of solo hits before becoming a major star via the Gaye duets.

During 1967 she collapsed in Gaye's arms during a show at Virginia's Hampton-Sydney college, her partner carrying her off into the wings. Initially, her collapse was believed to be due to exhaustion, but doctors later discovered a brain tumour. Tammi, real name Tammy Montgomery, was 24.

STAR QUOTE

GEORGE HARRISON

'I don't want to die as George Harrison, record producer, or George Harrison, lead guitarist, or even just a Beatle.'

THE GRAPEVINE

- **Country Joe McDonald has been charged with obscenity and fined $500 for doing his Fish cheer ('Gimme an F . . .') at a Massachusetts gig.**
- **Andrew Loog Oldham's record label Immediate has gone into liquidation.**
- **Peter Yarrow, of Peter, Paul And Mary, has pleaded guilty to 'taking immoral liberties' with a 14 year-old girl.**

Human windmill Cocker

JOE COCKER GETS FRESH HELP

Joe Cocker has split with The Grease Band, with whom he recorded such hits as 'With A Little Help From My Friends' and 'Delta Lady'. He arrived in LA on March 11 to recuperate from months of strength-sapping road work with The Grease Band, but was informed by entrepreneur Dee Anthony that he had been contracted to commence a seven week tour due to begin on March 19, and that to cancel out would seriously jeopardise his chances of ever working in the USA again.

Singer-pianist-guitarist Leon Russell has assembled a 43-strong circus of singers and musicians (including former Grease Band keyboardist Chris Stainton and singer Rita Coolidge) to embark on the cross-America jaunt which will be known as The Mad Dogs And Englishmen Tour.

BOWIE WEDS

March 20: 'Space Oddity' hit-maker David Bowie, who's currently working with theatrical group The Hype, married Cyprus-born model Angela Barnett at London's Bromley Register Office.

The wedding began an hour and a half late because the twosome had overslept. Bowie's latest single, 'Prettiest Star', featuring Marc Bolan on guitar, was released by Mercury on March 6.

Bowie and spouse

CHARTS

	US45	Bridge Over Troubled Water – *Simon & Garfunkel*
	USLP	Bridge Over Troubled Water – *Simon & Garfunkel*
	UK45	Wanderin' Star – *Lee Marvin*
	UKLP	Bridge Over Troubled Water – *Simon & Garfunkel*
WEEK 2	US45	Bridge Over Troubled Water – *Simon & Garfunkel*
	USLP	Bridge Over Troubled Water – *Simon & Garfunkel*
	UK45	Wanderin' Star – *Lee Marvin*
	UKLP	Bridge Over Troubled Water – *Simon & Garfunkel*
WEEK 3	US45	Bridge Over Troubled Water – *Simon & Garfunkel*
	USLP	Bridge Over Troubled Water – *Simon & Garfunkel*
	UK45	Wanderin' Star – *Lee Marvin*
	UKLP	Bridge Over Troubled Water – *Simon & Garfunkel*
WEEK 4	US45	Bridge Over Troubled Water – *Simon & Garfunkel*
	USLP	Bridge Over Troubled Water – *Simon & Garfunkel*
	UK45	Bridge Over Troubled Water – *Simon & Garfunkel*
	UKLP	Bridge Over Troubled Water – *Simon & Garfunkel*

PAUL McCARTNEY GOES SOLO

Paul McCartney has released 'McCartney', his first solo album. 'I made it because I've got a Studer four track machine at home, practised on it, liked the result and decided to make an album', he's reported as saying. A week earlier, a specially prepared McCartney 'interview', designed to accompany the release of the album, was leaked to the British press, causing 'Beatles Breakup' headlines around the world.

Earlier in the month, on April 3, Ringo released his solo effort 'Sentimental Journey'. But though the Fab Four may be falling apart, Apple Records still seem to be in full flight, and have signed Billy Preston to a solo contract.

THE SCHWARZ CAPER

New band Brinsley Schwarz hired a 707 jet and took 133 British media people to see them play live at New York's Fillmore East. However, the charter plane was delayed and arrived late, causing most of the extremely 'tired and emotional' scribes to miss the group's tepid, bill-opening spot. Managed by Irishman Dave Robinson, Brinsley Schwarz's line-up includes vocalist and bassist Nick Lowe.

SABS 'NOT SATANIC' SAYS IOMMI

Black Sabbath, the group formed by Ozzy Osbourne, Geezer Butler, Tony Iommi and Bill Ward, have denied that their name has anything to do with black magic. Said lead guitarist Iommi: 'Everybody thinks we're a black magic group but we picked the name because we liked it. I agree some of the numbers on our album are about supernatural things, but that's as far as it goes. We're a bit worried about the black magic bit, though. In America, people might take it seriously.'

From left: Bill Ward, Ozzy Osbourne, Geezer Butler and Tony Iommi – the sadly maligned Black Sabbath

TULL – 'NO MORE SINGLES'

Jethro Tull have announced that they are finished with releasing singles. 'Singles didn't really work for us,' said Ian Anderson. 'We sold lots of copies of "Witches Promise" for instance, but not as many as we did with the last album. And we find that most of the singles were going to people who'd already bought the album and not, as we hoped, to Edison Lighthouse fans'.

Tull's new album, 'Benefit', is released this month.

STAR

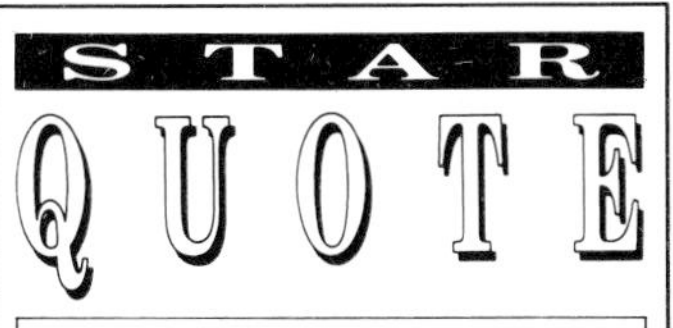

PETE TOWNSHEND

'What I want to do is sophisticate our sound a little. One of the troubles is Moon. He's so deafening.'

CHARTS

	US45	Bridge Over Troubled Water	*Simon & Garfunkel*
	USLP	Bridge Over Troubled Water	*Simon & Garfunkel*
	UK45	Bridge Over Troubled Water	*Simon & Garfunkel*
	UKLP	Bridge Over Troubled Water	*Simon & Garfunkel*
WEEK 2	US45	Let It Be	*Beatles*
	USLP	Bridge Over Troubled Water	*Simon & Garfunkel*
	UK45	Bridge Over Troubled Water	*Simon & Garfunkel*
	UKLP	Bridge Over Troubled Water	*Simon & Garfunkel*
WEEK 3	US45	Let It Be	*Beatles*
	USLP	Bridge Over Troubled Water	*Simon & Garfunkel*
	UK45	Bridge Over Troubled Water	*Simon & Garfunkel*
	UKLP	Bridge Over Troubled Water	*Simon & Garfunkel*
WEEK 4	US45	ABC	*Jackson Five*
	USLP	Bridge Over Troubled Water	*Simon & Garfunkel*
	UK45	Spirit In The Sky	*Norman Greenbaum*
	UKLP	Bridge Over Troubled Water	*Simon & Garfunkel*

THE GRAPEVINE

- **Lord Sutch has released his latest album titled 'Lord Sutch And Heavy Friends', featuring contributions from Jimmy Page, Noel Redding, Jeff Beck, John Bonham and Nicky Hopkins.**
- **Tom Jones commenced his biggest-ever American tour on April 2.**
- **George Goldner, co-founder of the Roulette and Red Bird labels, has died age 52: also gone is bluesman Otis Spann, who has died of cancer, age 40.**

Lord Sutch reprises 'You Need Hands'!

MAY

CHARTS

US45 ABC — *Jackson Five*
USLP Bridge Over Troubled Water — *Simon & Garfunkel*
UK45 Spirit In The Sky — *Norman Greenbaum*
UKLP Bridge Over Troubled Water — *Simon & Garfunkel*

WEEK 2

US45 American Woman — *Guess Who*
USLP Bridge Over Troubled Water — *Simon & Garfunkel*
UK45 Back Home — *England World Cup Squad*
UKLP Bridge Over Troubled Water — *Simon & Garfunkel*

WEEK 3

US45 American Woman — *Guess Who*
USLP Deja Vu — *Crosby, Stills, Nash & Young*
UK45 Back Home — *England World Cup Squad*
UKLP Bridge Over Troubled Water — *Simon & Garfunkel*

WEEK 4

US45 American Woman — *Guess Who*
USLP McCartney — *Paul McCartney*
UK45 Back Home — *England World Cup Squad*
UKLP Bridge Over Troubled Water — *Simon & Garfunkel*

WEEK 5

US45 American Woman — *Guess Who*
USLP McCartney — *Paul McCartney*
UK45 Question — *Moody Blues*
UKLP Bridge Over Troubled Water — *Simon & Garfunkel*

THE GRAPEVINE

- The Doors' Jim Morrison revealed that he's made a film called *'Hitchhiker'* that runs for 50 minutes.
- Tom Jones has pocketed £150,000, reckoned to be the biggest solo fee to date, for a Louisville concert held on the eve of the Kentucky Derby.
- The Beatles' 'Let It Be' has set a new record for advance US sales with a $3.7 million upfront order.

NEW BAND ALBUM TO BE MADE AT WOODSTOCK

The Band's second Capitol album, says Robbie Robertson, was cut 'in luxurious fashion' at the former home of Sammy Davis Jr, and they plan to record the next at a studio in Woodstock – doing the whole thing in one all-night session!

The idea came from listening to tapes made of shows in the States. 'They'd make great bootleg material,' says Robertson. 'We've tried different ways of recording our albums and for this one we're going to learn all the songs as best we can and then we'll go down to a little place, here in Woodstock town, and do it all in a night.

'Our first album, "Music From Big Pink", was written first and then we went in to record it. The new one we wrote as we went along, and it's got a more spontaneous feel. In a way it was a miracle that it worked, because we had gone out with a hair-brained idea and actually pulled it off.'

The Band (l to r) Garth Hudson, Richard Manuel, Levon Helm, Robbie Robertson, Rich Danko

THE POLL WINNERS CONCERT

This year's NME poll-winner's concert proved a pop bonanza, the line-up including Blue Mink, Bob & Marcia, Brotherhood Of Man, Lou Christie, Dana, Edison Lighthouse, Steve Ellis, The Johnny Howard Band, Juicy Lucy, Marmalade, Hank Marvin & The Shadows, Pickettywitch, The Pipkins, Cliff Richard, Clodagh Rodgers, Vanity Fare, White Plains, Love Affair, Rare Bird and Brinsley Schwarz. It was hosted by Tony Blackburn and Jimmy Savile.

GREEN FOR GO

Peter Green has quit Fleetwood Mac, playing his final gig with the band at London's Chalk Farm Roundhouse. The band is looking for a suitable replacement.

Meanwhile, a British tour (due to commence on June 1) has been cancelled. A Mac single featuring Peter Green, 'The Green Mahalishi (With The Two Prong Crown)', was released on Reprise earlier this month.

BEATLES RELEASE 'CHEAPSKATE' ALBUM

The Beatles have released a new album 'Let It Be', which bears three production credits. George Martin (assisted by Glyn Johns) produced the original tracks which – after being pronounced 'worthless' by the Fabs – were salvaged by Phil Spector.

Comments NME's Alan Smith: 'If The Beatles soundtrack album "Let It Be" is to be their last, then it will stand as a cheapskate epitaph, a cardboard tombstone, a sad and tatty end to a musical fusion which wiped clean and drew again the face of pop music.'

A movie, also called *'Let It Be'*, documenting the making of the album, is to be premiered in New York on May 13.

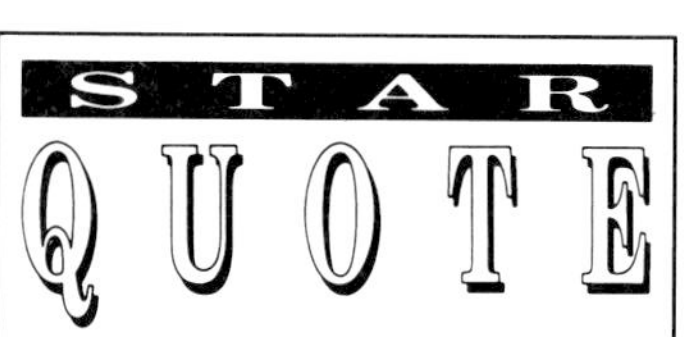

STAR QUOTE

STEVIE WONDER

'You know something about music? I regard it as a colourless colour. I feel the sounds are like paints and I like to paint with sound.'

ELP – THE GROUP MOST LIKELY?

New group Emerson, Lake & Palmer are currently rehearsing for their first tour. Born out of a slice of The Nice, King Crimson and Atomic Rooster respectively, the band came to be out of Emerson and Lake's informal conversations in America last year, where King Crimson and The Nice were on tour.

Bassist Greg Lake has affirmed that contractual hassles have absorbed a great deal of their time, particularly so with drummer Carl Palmer, who only got his release from Atomic Rooster at the beginning of June. Carl thought it highly amusing that his final gig on May 31 had been thought big deal enough to merit the billing 'Atomic Rooster – Last performance with Carl Palmer'.

Among the material they're rehearsing is 'Rondo', plus a delightful composition titled 'Take A Pebble'. 'It's not ready yet though,' said organist Keith Emerson, 'give us two more months to knock it together.'

RAY DAVIES FLIES 6,000 MILES FOR A WORD

Ray Davies of The Kinks made a 6,000 mile round trip from New York to London and back – just to change one word of the Kink's new single 'Lola'.

The original lyric contained a reference to Coca-Cola, which Britain's BBC Radio One – the country's most powerful station – would regard as advertising and slap a broadcasting ban on the disc.

Ray, who came back to change the reference to 'Cherry Cola', thus ensuring airplay, is currently touring the States with The Kinks, where they're fully booked until June 23, when they play Seattle. After this they move on to play dates in Canada before completing their tour at Honolulu Earth Station (June 29-July 1) and LA's Whiskey A Go-Go (July 3-5).

Ray Davies wondering whether the BBC are into soda pop

GRACE SLICK

'Everyone in the band is allowed to be a jerk once in a while without getting thrown out.'

CHARTS

US45	Everything Is Beautiful *Ray Stevens*
USLP	McCartney *Paul McCartney*
UK45	Yellow River *Christie*
UKLP	Let It Be *Beatles*
WEEK 2	
US45	The Long & Winding Road *Beatles*
USLP	Let It Be *Beatles*
UK45	In The Summertime *Mungo Jerry*
UKLP	Let It Be *Beatles*
WEEK 3	
US45	The Long & Winding Road *Beatles*
USLP	Let It Be *Beatles*
UK45	In The Summertime *Mungo Jerry*
UKLP	Let it Be *Beatles*
WEEK 4	
US45	The Love You Save *Jackson Five*
USLP	Let It Be *Beatles*
UK45	In The Summertime *Mungo Jerry*
UKLP	Bridge Over Troubled Water *Simon & Garfunkel*

SYD RE-APPEARS

The enigmatic Syd Barrett selected Extravaganza '70, at London's Olympia Stadium, to make his first public appearance since leaving Pink Floyd two years ago. Assisted by fellow Floydian Dave Gilmour on bass, and Humble Pie drummer Jerry Shirley, Syd played 'Terrapin', 'Gigolo Aunt', 'Effervescing Elephant' and 'Octopus' before beating a hasty retreat.

Syd Barrett – the police can now remove their missing person notices

A twist in fate for Chubby

THE GRAPEVINE

- **Chubby Checker has been arrested at Niagara Falls after police found various forms of drugs in his car.**
- **Janis Joplin unveiled her Full Tilt Boogie Band in Louisville on June 12, but the gig was sparsely attended.**
- **Grand Funk Railroad have spent $100,000 on a New York Times Square billboard to advertise their latest release, 'Closer To Home'.**

'JUST CALL ME MRS McVIE'

Christine Perfect, whose self-titled debut album was released in Britain by Blue Horizon on June 13 has announced that she is to leave the music business. Also, in future, she will be content to be known as plain Mrs John McVie.

The main reason for this, she admitted, was that her solo career was not following its predicted route. 'I was not even making enough money to pay my band,' she confided.

HOW CAT FOUGHT OFF THOUGHTS OF DEATH

Cat Stevens has revealed that he became a split personality a while back. He was ill in hospital with TB and claims: 'Every morning I would see a coffin go by my window and I thought I'd had it. Then in the middle of some deep meditation, I found myself in a rainstorm. But only my outside was getting wet. You know, the real me was still dry inside and I thought: 'I'm not really ill, I just think I am.'

Stevens, whose comeback single, 'Lady D'Arbanville', has just gone Top 20 in Britain, said that his new album, 'Mona Bone Jakon', has a cover painting titled 'The Dustbin Cried The Day The Dustman Died'. 'I did that one to draw attention to dustbins - they're very underprivileged.' Cat is currently writing the music for *'Deep End'*, a movie directed by Jerzy Skolmowski and starring Jane Asher, Paul McCartney's ex.

Sebastian in 'festivals are no daydream' shock!

DIY PAYS OFF FOR HOTLEGS

The growing trend among groups to write their own material and produce their own records is paying off handsomely for Hotlegs, who've entered the UK charts with their 'Neanderthal Man' single. But Hotlegs have taken the process a step further by recording at Stockport's Strawberry Studios, which are part owned by their lead guitarist Eric Stewart, who used to be with The Mindbenders.

Eric's fellow members of Hotlegs are Kevin Godley (drums, percussion, vibes and vocals) and Lol Creme (acoustic guitars, records, piano, bass and vocals). Both Kevin and Lol are basically graphic artists and are currently working on models to go with the Pan Books novel of the film *'Oliver Cromwell'*. The next project Kevin and Lol will be undertaking is the creation of more models, this time to go with the film *'The Railway Children'*.

Hotlegs – Neanderthal men

ATLANTA FESTIVAL – 'A DISASTER ZONE'

The Governor of Georgia, Lester Maddox, is attempting to have rock festivals banned in his state following drug-related problems at the recent Atlanta Festival, which spanned July 3-5.

A crowd of 200,000 attended the show, which featured Jimi Hendrix, John Sebastian, Mountain, Procol Harum, Poco, Jethro Tull, Johnny Winter, B.B. King and others, but the drug-control system quickly deteriorated, causing local medics to attempt to have the area declared an official health disaster zone.

CHARTS

US45	The Love You Save — *Jackson Five*
USLP	Let It Be — *Beatles*
UK45	In The Summertime — *Mungo Jerry*
UKLP	Bridge Over Troubled Water — *Simon & Garfunkel*
WEEK 2	
US45	Mama Told Me Not To Come — *Three Dog Night*
USLP	Woodstock — *Soundtrack*
UK45	All Right Now — *Free*
UKLP	Bridge Over Troubled Water — *Simon & Garfunkel*
WEEK 3	
US45	Mama Told Me Not To Come — *Three Dog Night*
USLP	Woodstock — *Soundtrack*
UK45	All Right Now — *Free*
UKLP	Let It Be — *Beatles*
WEEK 4	
US45	(They Long To Be) Close To You — *Carpenters*
USLP	Woodstock — *Soundtrack*
UK45	All Right Now — *Free*
UKLP	Bridge Over Troubled Water — *Simon & Garfunkel*

THE GRAPEVINE

- **The Everly Brothers now have their own series of one-hour TV shows in the States. The series goes out over the ABC network and runs until September 16.**
- **The Rolling Stones have split from manager Allen Klein and his company, ABKCO.**
- **The FBI is mounting an investigation into counterfeit record rings following a flood of bootleg releases in the States.**

FLOYD IN THE PARK

Pink Floyd are to headline a free concert in London's Hyde Park on July 18. Also booked for the gig are Roy Harper, Edgar Broughton, Kevin Ayers, Robert Wyatt, Lol Coxhill and Formerly Fat Harry.

NO MORE I O W FESTIVALS SAY FOULKS

Even before the third Isle of Wight festival was over, the Foulk brothers of Fiery Creations, the shindig's promoters, announced that there would be no more in the series because their losses totalled some £90,000 ($180,000). As a musical experience, however, the festival, which took place over the August Bank Holiday weekend, was an enormous success, the line-up including Melanie, Procol Harum, Chicago, Taste, Family, Cactus, Emerson Lake & Palmer, The Doors, Joni Mitchell, Ten Years After, The Who, Sly & The Family Stone, Donovan, Leonard Cohen, Moody Blues, Jimi Hendrix, Joan Baez, Voices Of East Harlem, Miles Davis, Tiny Tim, Richie Havens, Free, Arrival, and Jethro Tull.

Joni Mitchell's set was marred when one spectator jumped on stage and began yelling to people on a nearby hill – but she recovered to complete an act that proved worthy of four encores.

There was also a pause in the proceedings on the Sunday night, when one DJ ambled to the mike and casually informed the crowd: 'There's something I have to tell you – the stage is on fire.' This flare-up, caused by a stray firework, proved momentarily spectacular, but was got under control eventually without much hassle.

Peace! Or something ruder

That, though, was the least of the Foulks' problems. They'd laid out nearly £500,000 ($1 million) up front – about half going on talent costs alone – and it seems highly improbable that they will be able to recoup much on movie rights, unlike the Woodstock Festival promoters. Nevertheless, British Rail claims to be happy, reckoning that, during the period of the festival, 600,000 people used their ferries to reach the island.

CHARTS

US45	(They Long To Be) Close To You — *Carpenters*
USLP	3 — *Blood, Sweat & Tears*
UK45	Lola — *Kinks*
UKLP	Let It Be — *Beatles*
WEEK 2	
US45	(They Long To Be) Close To You — *Carpenters*
USLP	3 — *Blood, Sweat & Tears*
UK45	The Wonder Of You — *Elvis Presley*
UKLP	Let It Be — *Beatles*
WEEK 3	
US45	(They Long To Be) Close To You — *Carpenters*
USLP	3 — *Blood, Sweat & Tears*
UK45	The Wonder Of You — *Elvis Presley*
UKLP	Bridge Over Troubled Water — *Simon & Garfunkel*
WEEK 4	
US45	Make It With You — *Bread*
USLP	Cosmo's Factory — *Creedence Clearwater Revival*
UK45	The Wonder Of You — *Elvis Presley*
UKLP	Bridge Over Troubled Water — *Simon & Garfunkel*
WEEK 5	
US45	War — *Edwin Starr*
USLP	Cosmo's Factory — *Creedence Clearwater Revival*
UK45	Tears Of A Clown — *Smokey Robinson & Miracles*
UKLP	Bridge Over Troubled Water — *Simon & Garfunkel*

Dave Clark ready-steady-going with Kathy McGowan (second right)

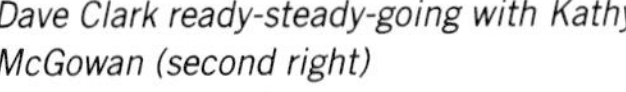

DAVE CLARK CALLS IT A DAY

After selling 35 million records since they turned professional in March 1964, The Dave Clark Five have disbanded. Though Clark says that the group will never again appear in public, he has stockpiled over 60 tracks to be released periodically.

Additionally, another Dave has been involved in a split this week. Stax soulmen Sam and Dave are going their separate ways after a 10-year partnership, which included such modern classics as 'Hold On, I'm Coming', 'You Don't Know Like I Know' and 'Soulman'.

CHRISTINE JOINS THE MAC

Christine McVie has confirmed rumours that she is to join Fleetwood Mac. The band's manager Clifford Davis revealed that she had been invited to join after sitting in with them at their Hampstead hideout and immediately accepted the offer.

THE GRAPEVINE

- **Led Zep have commenced their sixth US tour, a four-week jaunt billed as 'The Greatest Live Event Since The Beatles'.**
- **Mick Jagger has been accidentally shot in the hand during the filming of his movie *'Ned Kelly'*, in Australia.**
- **Elvis Presley opened his second season of the year at Las Vegas' International Hotel on August 10.**

RIGHT SONG SAVES THE CARPENTERS

Singing drummer Karen Carpenter with keyboard-playing relative

The Carpenters are snowed under with requests for in-person concerts and TV appearances and their records are selling by the boatload – all thanks to 'Close To You', a song written six years ago by Burt Bacharach and Hal David for Dionne Warwick.

But only a couple of months ago, the brother/sister act were wondering if they'd still be working together by the end of the year. Now, in the wake of success with 'Close To You', a US No. 1 which is also riding high in the UK charts, the couple look certain to achieve further kudos with 'We've Only Just Begun', their latest US release. All of which causes Richard Carpenter to declare: 'Everything is going according to plan.'

Richard does all the arranging and orchestrations on the Carpenters' albums, on which sister Karen takes lead vocals. In addition, Richard wrote 10 songs on their A&M debut album and four on the second. Herb Alpert signed the group after hearing them sing 'Ticket To Ride' on the radio.

ELVIS ON TOUR

Elvis Presley has begun his first US tour in almost 14 years – and finished it! The tour began in Phoenix, Arizona on September 9 and visited St Louis (10), Detroit (11), Miami (12), Tampa (13) and Mobile (14). In Phoenix a bomb scare delayed the start of the show.

INVICTUS – THE NEW MOTOWN?

The Invictus label has Britain's two top singles – Freda Payne's 'Band Of Gold' holding the pole position while Chairman Of The Board's 'Give Me Just A Little More Time" is at No. 2.

This represents a remarkable achievement for Holland-Dozier-Holland, the songwriting and production team that left Motown to form a rival record company. Now, after just a brief life span, Invictus is already proving a worthy challenger to Berry Gordy's previously all-conquering label.

HENDRIX 'NO JUNKIE' SAYS PATHOLOGIST

A coroner's inquest into the death of Jimi Hendrix, who died at a London, Notting Hill, flat on September 18, has established that the guitarist died of 'suffocation from inhalation of vomit'. Pathologist Professor Donald Teare added that there was no evidence that Hendrix had been a drug addict and had no needle marks anywhere on his body. Jimi was 27.

CANNED HEAT MEMBER FOUND DEAD

Al 'Blind Owl' Wilson, singer and guitarist with Canned Heat, has been found dead in fellow band member Bob Hite's garden in Topanga Canyon, California. Aged 27, he was discovered with an empty bottle of barbiturates at his side.

Wilson's death casts doubt on the continued survival of Canned Heat, who have scored major international hits with 'On The Road Again', 'Going Up The Country' and 'Let's Work Together', although the band have been preparing to record with blues veteran John Lee Hooker.

Al Wilson and hip harp

THE GRAPEVINE

- **Bing Crosby has been awarded a second platinum disc by US Decca for record sales in excess of 300 million.**
- **Fleetwood Mac have released their first post-Peter Green album, 'Kiln House' (Reprise).**
- **Miami authorities have acquitted 'Flasher' Jim Morrison on a charge of lewd behaviour, but have adjudged him guilty of indecent exposure and profanity.**

CHARTS

US45	War — *Edwin Starr*
USLP	Cosmo's Factory — *Creedence Clearwater Revival*
UK45	Tears Of A Clown — *Smokey Robinson & Miracles*
UKLP	A Question Of Balance — *Moody Blues*
WEEK 2	
US45	War — *Edwin Starr*
USLP	Cosmo's Factory — *Creedence Clearwater Revival*
UK45	Tears Of A Clown — *Smokey Robinson & Miracles*
UKLP	A Question Of Balance — *Moody Blues.*
WEEK 3	
US45	Ain't No Mountain High Enough — *Diana Ross*
USLP	Cosmo's Factory — *Creedence Clearwater Revival*
UK45	Tears Of A Clown — *Smokey Robinson & Miracles*
UKLP	A Question Of Balance — *Moody Blues*
WEEK 4	
US45	Ain't No Mountain High Enough — *Diana Ross*
USLP	Cosmo's Factory — *Creedence Clearwater Revival*
UK45	Band Of Gold — *Freda Payne*
UKLP	Bridge Over Troubled Water — *Simon & Garfunkel*

JANIS O.D.s

Janis Joplin was found dead of a drug overdose in a room at Hollywood's Landmark Hotel on October 4. She was discovered laying face down with fresh puncture marks in her arm. The singer had frequently suffered from drink and drugs problems in the past, yet things seemed to be taking an upturn in her career.

She claimed to be extremely happy with her new Full Tilt Band and had just completed work on 'Pearl', a forthcoming CBS album. Additionally, she'd recently become engaged to Seth Morgan, the son of a prestigious New York family and a student at Berkeley.

Earlier in the year, referring to Jimi Hendrix's death, she said: 'I can't go out this year because he was a bigger star.'

STAR NAMES FOR TV

Ray Stevens, Lesley Gore, Jerry Reed and Esther Ofarim are flying to Britain for guest spots on BBC 1's new series hosted by Australian Rolf Harris, beginning on Saturday, October 24. Other guests set to appear include Dusty Springfield, The Hollies, Lulu, Italy's Caterina Valente and Tom Paxton.

Black Sabbath, Julie Felix and Labi Siffre guest in Granada's TV 'Lift-Off' on October 21, while Mott The Hoople and Bridget St John are showcased in BBC 2's 'Disco 2' on October 10.

Nashville picker Jerry Reed

TAYLOR-MADE STAR OF FILM AND TV

James Taylor, in Britain to play a Sunday concert at the London Palladium, has been filming an 'In Concert' programme for BBC Television. Talking about shooting the movie *'Two Lane Blacktop'*, in which he plays the driver of a cross-country dragster, Taylor said: 'That took us all over the Midwest: Macon, Georgia, Little Rock, Arkansas, Boswell, Oklahoma, and everywhere like that. That movie took about two months and involved working 13 hours a day, at least.'

Taylor opened his TV concert with 'With A Little Help From My Friends', and continued with 'Fire And Rain', before indulging in a very funny take-off of Ray Charles's 'Things Go Better With Coca-Cola', which may be edited out of the show before screening. 'Sweet Baby James', 'Carolina On My Mind' and 'Sunny Skies' were also included, along with 'Steamroller', a song written when James was with New York group Flying Machine, in 1966.

MOVE BECOMES 10-PIECE

Roy Wood's ambitious plans to augment The Move into a 10-piece ensemble named The Electric Light Orchestra have, at last, been realised. The project, which was first reported last year, has finally reached fruition this month with the news that the much enlarged outfit is currently rehearsing.

The line-up includes a string quartet, a french horn and two miscellaneous instruments – plus Jeff Lynn on piano and lead guitar, Roy Wood on bass, acoustic guitar and oboe, and Bev Bevan on drums. It is, however, stressed that The Move will still continue to operate as a small group.

CHARTS

US45	Ain't No Mountain High Enough	*Diana Ross*
USLP	Cosmo's Factory	*Creedence Clearwater Revival*
UK45	Band Of Gold	*Freda Payne*
UKLP	Bridge Over Troubled Water	*Simon & Garfunkel*
WEEK 2		
US45	Cracklin' Rosie	*Neil Diamond*
USLP	Cosmo's Factory	*Creedence Clearwater Revival*
UK45	Band Of Gold	*Freda Payne*
UKLP	Bridge Over Troubled Water	*Simon & Garfunkel*
WEEK 3		
US45	I'll Be There	*Jackson Five*
USLP	Cosmo's Factory	*Creedence Clearwater Revival*
UK45	Band Of Gold	*Freda Payne*
UKLP	Paranoid	*Black Sabbath*
WEEK 4		
US45	I'll Be There	*Jackson Five*
USLP	Abraxas	*Santana*
UK45	Band Of Gold	*Freda Payne*
UKLP	Paranoid	*Black Sabbath*
WEEK 5		
US45	I'll Be There	*Jackson Five*
USLP	Led Zeppelin III	*Led Zeppelin*
UK45	Black Night	*Deep Purple*
UKLP	Led Zeppelin III	*Led Zeppelin*

THE GRAPEVINE

- **Four Dawn label acts, Demon Fuzz, Titus Groan, Heron and Comus are due to take part in a series of UK concerts next month - and at all venues the price of admission will be one penny.**
- **In England a Wolverhampton Civic Hall concert by Jack Bruce with Lifetime has been cancelled because the band refused to allow such lines as 'ex-Cream' and 'ex-Miles Davis' in the advertising.**

NOVEMBER

BEE GEES TOGETHER AGAIN

"Maurice only has courgettes" – Barry Gibb in the upcoming Cucumber Castle

The first record by the newly-reunited Bee Gees, 'Two Years On', gains a release at the end of the month. The group have been arguing for ages but, as Robin Gibb explains: 'We actually came together on Friday, August 21. We had been together the night before – but with our lawyers, arguing about the same things that we had been fighting over for months. Next day, we met at Robert Stigwood's office to carry on the argument and suddenly it was all over. We just threw it out the window and decided to go straight into the studio again.'

Maurice Gibb has now returned from Ireland, where he went to attend the premiere of Richard Harris's latest film, *'Bloomfield'*, for which he wrote part of the score.

Other Bee Gee news involves a forthcoming TV spectacular called *'Cucumber Castle'*. Shortly to be screened by the BBC, the show was shot before Robin rejoined the group and includes appearances by Lulu, former Goon Spike Milligan and horror king Vincent Price.

BEACH BOY GENIUS FIGHTS DEAFNESS

Brian Wilson – his return to live work was brief

Brian Wilson is fighting against total deafness. This development has apparently been caused by The Beach Boys, the group he nurtured, playing too loudly! Brian has experienced ear trouble for some years and this was given as the reason he gave up playing regularly with the group to assume a more background role.

However, earlier this month, he decided to sit in with the Beach Boys when they were playing LA's Whiskey A Go-Go – the first time he's played with the group in public for some five years. But, after having to be helped off stage, Brian is now undergoing treatment in LA. It's said that even if he does retain his hearing, Brian will be unlikely ever to risk playing with the group again on a full-time basis.

THE GRAPEVINE

■ The Rolling Stones have turned down the chance of signing chart-topping British group Matthews Southern Comfort to their new label because Mick Jagger reckons that they're 'not funky enough'.

■ George Harrison's long-awaited solo album 'All Things Will Pass' will be released by Apple on November 27.

■ World sales of Mungo Jerry's 'In The Summertime' single are now in excess of six million.

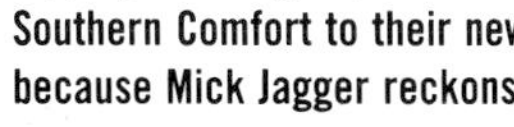

CLAPTON IN NASHVILLE

Eric Clapton is in Nashville recording the TV debut of his new band, The Dominoes, for the Johnny Cash Show. Earlier, he'd been in Miami producing an album for blues giants Junior Wells and Buddy Guy. Asked if he'd played on the sessions, he replied: 'Are you kidding? With cats like that, there's really no reason to play. I just produced it for them.'

Talking about his role as lead vocalist with The Dominoes, Eric said: 'I was hoping Duane Allman would come up and do the Cash show with me. We're doing a couple of songs Duane did with me on the album, and with him playing lead I would have more chance to get into my singing.'

Allman, for his part, claimed: 'Eric Clapton's the only English guitarist I respect. He's a gas to work with and just a totally nice dude.'

STAR QUOTE

JOE JACKSON

(The Jackson 5's father)

'All the boys have to clean their own rooms, wash dishes, mop and wax the floors. We want them to be good boys and respect their mother and father.'

CHARTS

US45	I'll Be There *Jackson Five*
USLP	Led Zeppelin III *Led Zeppelin*
UK45	Woodstock *Matthews' Southern Comfort*
UKLP	Motown Chartbusters, Vol. 4 *Various*
WEEK 2	
US45	I'll Be There *Jackson Five*
USLP	Led Zeppelin III *Led Zeppelin*
UK45	Woodstock *Matthews' Southern Comfort*
UKLP	Led Zeppelin III *Led Zeppelin*
WEEK 3	
US45	I Think I Love You *Partridge Family*
USLP	Led Zeppelin III *Led Zeppelin*
UK45	Woodstock *Matthews' Southern Comfort*
UKLP	Led Zeppelin III *Led Zeppelin*
WEEK 4	
US45	I Think I Love You *Partridge Family*
USLP	Abraxas *Santana*
UK45	Voodoo Chile *Jimi Hendrix*
UKLP	Led Zeppelin III *Led Zeppelin*

PURPLE AND THE FRAULEIN

Ian Gillan gets ready to duck

Deep Purple are the latest band to suffer from the deplorable antics of German 'fans' who want all concerts to be free. At the slightest suggestion of an entrance fee, upwards of 1,000 troublemakers gather at the hall and then provoke everybody in sight into damaging property. 'They had battering rams in Heidelberg and they were trying to get at the band,' claimed Purple's Ian Paice. 'We saw a girl driving round in a car with a loudspeaker on top, organising the riots. She was at Heidelberg and in Hanover too. At Hanover, we were about four floors up and they were throwing lumps of rock up at the windows.'

STAR QUOTE

ROBERT FRIPP

(King Crimson)

'We had a band the other Sunday night and on the Monday we didn't. Our good fairy seems to have deserted us.'

BEATLES – THE FINAL CHAPTER?

Paul McCartney has filed a writ in the London High Court against 'The Beatles Co', seeking the legal dissolution of the Beatles' partnership. Just prior to Christmas, speculation favoured a Beatles reunion, despite the fact that during 1970 the four members of the group all emerged as highly successful solo artists.

CHARTS

US45	I Think I Love You *Partridge Family*
USLP	Abraxas *Santana*
UK45	I Hear You Knocking *Dave Edmunds*
UKLP	Led Zeppelin III *Led Zeppelin*
WEEK 2	
US45	Tears Of A Clown *Smokey Robinson & The Miracles*
USLP	Abraxas *Santana*
UK45	I Hear You Knocking *Dave Edmunds*
UKLP	Led Zeppelin III *Led Zeppelin*
WEEK 3	
US45	Tears Of A Clown *Smokey Robinson & The Miracles*
USLP	Abraxas *Santana*
UK45	I Hear You Knocking *Dave Edmunds*
UKLP	Motown Chartbusters, Vol.4 *Various*
WEEK 4	
US45	My Sweet Lord *George Harrison*
USLP	Abraxas *Santana*
UK45	When I'm Dead And Gone *McGuinness Flint*
UKLP	Led Zeppelin III *Led Zeppelin*

THE GRAPEVINE

- **Both John Lennon and Yoko Ono have released albums titled 'The Plastic Ono Band'.**
- **The Rolling Stones' documentary *'Gimme Shelter'* had its US premiere on December 6, the first anniversary of Altamont.**
- **Beach Boy Dennis Wilson and Rumbo's single 'Sound Of Free' has been given a release in the UK only on Stateside.**

MORRISON RECORDS POEMS

The Doors' Jim Morrison spent several hours of his 27th birthday, December 8, recording poetry at Elektra's LA studio. The Doors have since played two sell-out shows in Dallas (December 10) where they previewed their forthcoming album and received two encores after each set. They also played New Orleans (December 11), but this was reportedly a disaster, Morrison picking up the mike in frustration, smashing it repeatedly into the stage until the wood shattered, after which he threw the stand into the crowd and then slumped down, sitting motionless before a stunned audience.

ROCKFIELD NO BARN SAYS EDMUNDS

Though Dave Edmunds has a massive UK hit in 'I Hear You Knockin', he says that his band, Rockpile, is not yet ready to tour and he intends to complete an album first. Said Edmunds: 'The papers are saying there's a lot of money behind me – but that is complete rubbish. I'm not part of the manufactured pop world, I paid for my own sessions and worked hard to produce the sound I want.

'I would also like to correct a statement put out by my publicist. I do not own Rockfield Studio, where I work – it's owned by two very good friends of mine, Charles and Kingsley Ward. And it is NOT a barn!'

Dave Edmunds who's covered Smiley Lewis' 1955 R&B biggie

BYE BYE BEATLES – THE FAB FOUR FALL APART

The precise date when The Beatles, the most successful and popular group of the rock era, split up is difficult to pinpoint. The process was gradual and probably began in August 1967 when their manager Brian Epstein died, ostensibly of an accidental overdose of sleeping pills.

Epstein had tried, usually with some success, to provide a barrier between the group and the rest of the world. With his absence, the individual Beatles found that they lacked an objective critic who could talk them out of their worst excesses. While the group had provided employment for several old friends from Liverpool like Mal Evans and Neil Aspinall, none of these mates felt sufficiently confident to question the unlikely schemes dreamed up by John, Paul, George and Ringo, who were pleased to have stepped off the touring treadmill, but were also rather bored.

Another significant occurrence came with the romance between John Lennon and Japanese avant-garde artist Yoko Ono, which would result before long in Lennon's divorce from his first wife, Cynthia. This affair coincidentally took place around the same time that Paul McCartney's long-running relationship with actress Jane Asher started to disintegrate, and Paul met Linda Eastman, a photographer from New York, who later became his wife.

The presence of two new close companions forced the Beatles' main songwriting partnership to spend more time away from each other and the rest of the group than had been their habit since coming to fame.

Added to these new attachments was the increased pressure on all The Beatles to keep producing hit records. One of the reasons for the group's deciding to stop touring after 1965 was that it would leave them greater opportunities for writing and recording.

But when Epstein died, the group found itself without a decision-maker. Lennon was too besotted with Yoko Ono to want to spend time thinking about the group's career, yet he was also resentful towards McCartney for undertaking duties which many felt he should have assumed himself. In the wake of Epstein's death, many powerful managers were offering their services to The Beatles, and while Lennon was most interested in a New York accountant named Allen Klein, who had previously worked with The Rolling Stones, his songwriting partner (not surprisingly) favoured the New York law practice of Eastman & Eastman, run by his future father-in-law and brother-in-law.

Ultimately, George and Ringo sided with John Lennon, supposedly after Klein had provoked Lee Eastman into a verbal attack which the group witnessed. Lennon, in particular, was impressed by what he felt he had in common with Klein who thus represented 75 per cent of The Beatles during the early 1970s, while the Eastmans looked after Paul's business. It was hardly an ideal situation, especially as the group was now firmly divided into two camps, each of which seemed to be pulling in different directions much of the time.

Things were not helped by the shelving of what was planned as a filmed documentary about the making of a new Beatle album, to be titled 'Get Back', which eventually emerged as 'Let It Be' after it had finally become evident that The Beatles did not intend to work together again. John Lennon was far more interested in his other group, The Plastic Ono Band, which had enjoyed several hits while Paul, George and Ringo had all become involved in their

JOHN

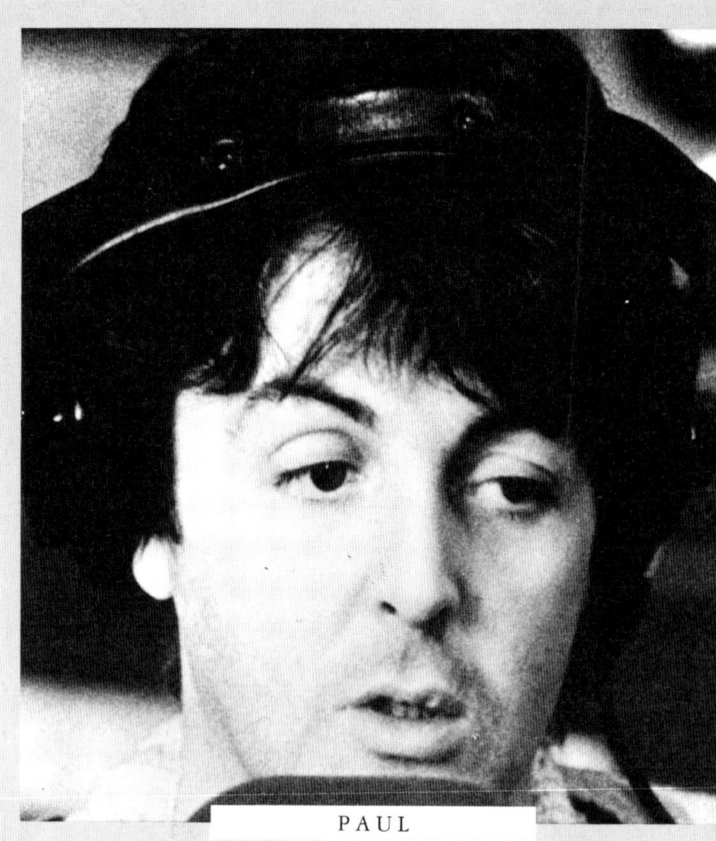

PAUL

The peak? 'Sergeant Pepper'

own recording projects. When Paul announced that he was leaving the group and a week later released his first solo album, The Beatles officially came to an end. By the start of 1974, when McCartney released 'Band On The Run', each of the erstwhile Beatles had proved that there was life and commercial success to be found as an artist in his own right.

Nevertheless, it was only after John Lennon had been murdered in December 1980, that the world finally stopped clamouring for the biggest group in the world to reform for just one more album.

RINGO

GEORGE

End of the road 'Let It Be'

Yoko, Julian and John

Denny Laine, Linda and Paul

CHARTS

US45	My Sweet Lord *George Harrison*
USLP	All Things Must Pass *George Harrison*
UK45	Grandad *Clive Dunn*
UKLP	Andy Williams' Greatest Hits *Andy Williams*
WEEK 2	
US45	My Sweet Lord *George Harrison*
USLP	All Things Must Pass *George Harrison*
UK45	Grandad *Clive Dunn*
UKLP	Any Williams' Greatest Hits *Andy Williams*
WEEK 3	
US45	My Sweet Lord *George Harrison*
USLP	All Things Must Pass *George Harrison*
UK45	Grandad *Clive Dunn*
UKLP	Bridge Over Troubled Water *Simon & Garfunkel*
WEEK 4	
US45	Knock Three Times *Dawn*
USLP	All Things Must Pass *George Harrison*
UK45	Grandad *Clive Dunn*
UKLP	Andy Williams' Greatest Hits *Andy Williams*
WEEK 5	
US45	Knock Three Times *Dawn*
USLP	All Things Must Pass *George Harrison*
UK45	My Sweet Lord *George Harrison*
UKLP	All Things Must Pass *George Harrison*

THE GRAPEVINE

■ Folk-rockers Fotheringay (which features ex-Fairport Convention singer Sandy Denny and her bassist hubby Trevor Lucas) are the first band of the year to announce a split - their London Queen Elizabeth Hall gig on January 30 will now be a farewell performance.

■ Diana Ross marries PR man Robert Silberstein in Las Vegas on January 21. Silberstein is also known as Robert Ellis.

ZAPPA ZAPS PRESSMEN

Frank Zappa. He'll be checking into a motel shortly

Frank Zappa, who has never disguised his low opinion of music press journalists, walked out of a London press conference called to unveil plans for the filming of The Mothers Of Invention's sex, drugs and rock'n'roll fantasy, *200 Motels*, due to begin at Pinewood Studios in February.

A row began when writers complained that much of what was being announced had already appeared in a Sunday newspaper interview Zappa had done. At first he apologized, claiming that he had been duped into doing the interview – but that brought the response: 'Why didn't you check it out with United Artists, your record label?'

The discussion became increasingly heated and acrimonious, with two UK national paper writers pressing Zappa to say whether or not he trusted his PR people.

Eventually tiring of the barrage of awkward questions, Zappa began a dialogue which began: 'There's one sequence in the movie where a girl journalist comes onstage and sits in a chair and begins asking me a series of really banal questions . . .'. After which, he downed his drink and stalked out of the room.

For the record, *200 Motels* is to star Theodore Bikel, and will include acting roles for Ringo Starr, Keith Moon (who plays a nun!), former Turtles singers Mark Volman and Howard Kaylan (now members of The Mothers and re-named Flo & Eddie by Zappa), and Mothers' drummer Aynsley Dunbar. British music critic and film maker Tony Palmer is to direct, and the soundtrack will feature The Mothers Of Invention and The Royal Philharmonic Orchestra, conducted by Elgar Howarth.

DEMOB FOR BAKER'S AIRFORCE

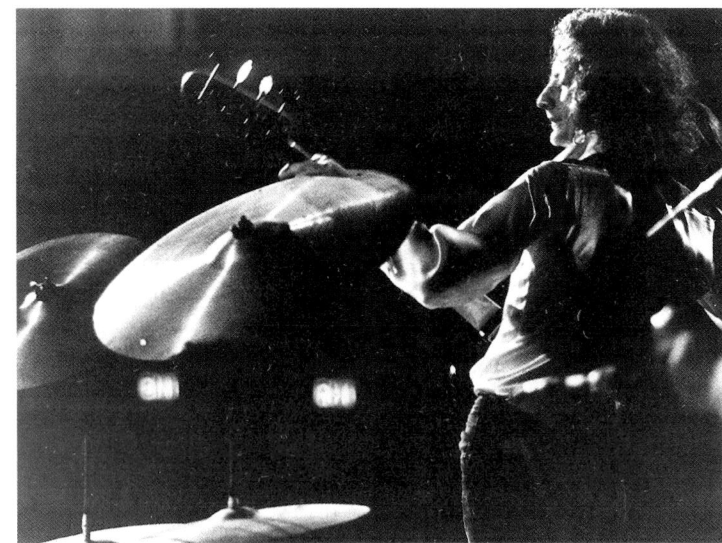

Ginger Baker, showman supreme

Ginger Baker's Airforce, whose second album 'Airforce 2' was recently released, is to disband at the end of the group's current series of British club and concert dates.

The group's lifetime will have spanned just 17 months when the final date is played on February 20. Airforce was originally formed by the former Cream drummer for just one Royal Albert Hall concert, but has since featured such members as Steve Winwood and Chris Wood (ex Traffic), former Family bassist Ric Grech, one-time Moody Blues singer Denny Laine, jazz drummer Phil Seaman and The Plastic Ono Band's Alan White.

STAR QUOTE

GILBERT O'SULLIVAN

'When I'm dressed normally, the girls hang around and talk and maybe ask for autographs. When I get dressed up, the girls run away.'

DYLAN ON TV

Bob Dylan made a rare TV appearancve on *Earl Scruggs: His Family And Friends*, a NET-TV Special aired in the US on January 100, the twosome playing 'East Virginia Rag' and 'Nashville Skyline Rag'. Scruggs, a legendary bluegrass banjoist, is best-known as half of Flatt and Scruggs, who had a 1962 hit with 'The Ballad Of Jed Clampett', theme to *The Beverly Hillbillies* TV show.

FEBRUARY

HARRISON HARASSED

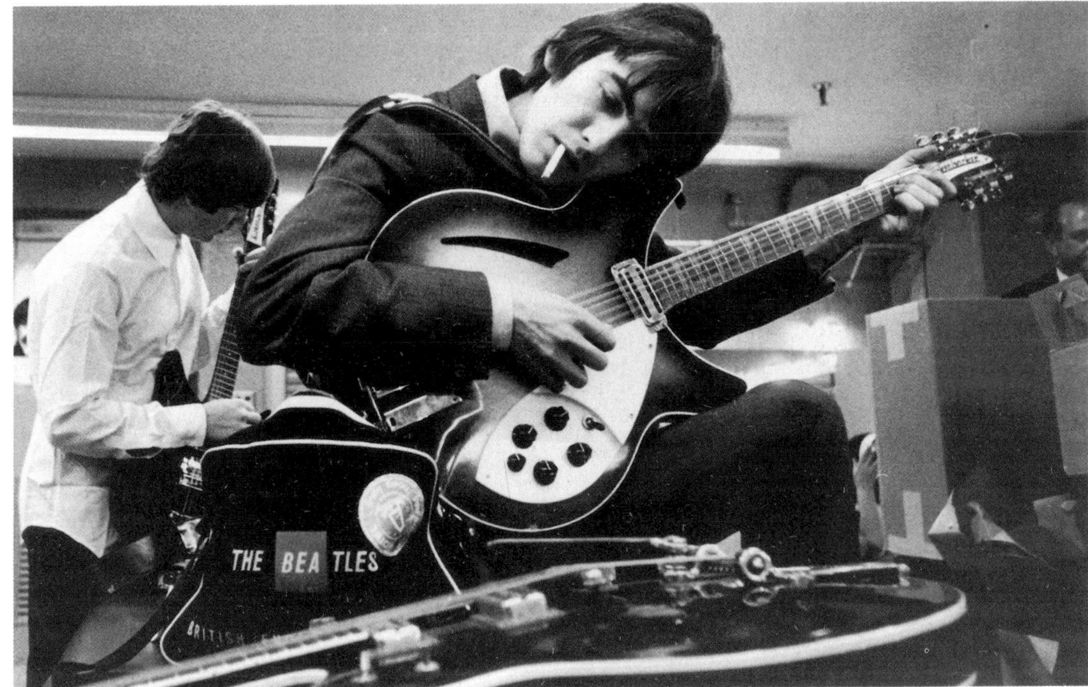

George – the way he was

George Harrison's publishing company and Apple are being sued over his world-wide hit 'My Sweet Lord'.

According to papers filed by American writer/manager Ronald Mack, the ex-Beatle's song infringes the copyright of The Chiffons' 1963 million-seller 'He's So Fine', which Mack wrote while managing the Brooklyn quartet.

Details published in connection with Paul McCartney's action to dissolve The Beatles' partnership indicate that 'My Sweet Lord' will earn Harrison more than a million pounds this year, which makes the Mack lawsuit potentially huge in settlement terms, should Harrison fail to establish his innocence.

WEATHERMEN IS/ ARE KING

British pop prankster Jonathan King has admitted what everyone has suspected for weeks – he is The Weathermen, whose single 'It's The Same Old Song' is currently riding high in the UK charts, and he supplied all three lead vocal voices on the disc, as well as writing and producing it.

King, a graduate of Cambridge University and until recently personal assistant to Sir Edward Lewis, chairman of British Decca Records (The Stones' label), is now looking for three singer-musicians who can go out as The Weathermen for concert appearances.

Initially, however, they'll back King whenever The Weathermen are booked to appear on TV or radio. Explains Jonathan: 'I'm willing to go on TV or radio, but I won't go back on the road again. I turned that in a long time ago.'

Music fans with long memories will recall King first achieving prominence when his 'Everyone's Gone To The Moon' was a huge British and European hit in 1965, while he was still a student. He was also the man behind Hedgehoppers Anonymous' 'It's Good News Week', and host of the ATV series 'Good Evening' in 1966.

NO RETIREMENT SAYS SANDIE

'The Lump' – as Sandie Shaw affectionately called it – has gone, and Sandie is now the proud mother of daughter Grace. But there is no way that motherhood is going to force Sandie into premature retirement, or to settling down to just being plain Mrs Banks (she's married to fashion designer Jeff).

Until a few weeks before Grace's birth, Sandie was hard at work promoting her new single 'Rose Garden', and she will return to recording as soon as she's able, and once she's found the right nanny for Grace.

"These days I can afford shoes. But it's still the park bench at night." Pop mum of the month Sandie Shaw

CHARTS

US45	Knock Three Times *Dawn*
USLP	All Things Must Pass *George Harrison*
UK45	My Sweet Lord *George Harrison*
UKLP	All Things Must Past *George Harrison*
	WEEK 2
US45	One Bad Apple *Osmonds*
USLP	All Things Must Pass *George Harrison*
UK45	My Sweet Lord *George Harrison*
UKLP	All Things Must Pass *George Harrison*
	WEEK 3
US45	One Bad Apple *Osmonds*
USLP	Jesus Christ Superstar *Various Artists*
UK45	My Sweet Lord *George Harrison*
UKLP	All Things Must Pass *George Harrison*
	WEEK 4
US45	One Bad Apple *Osmonds*
USLP	Jesus Christ Superstar *Various Artists*
UK45	My Sweet Lord *George Harrison*
UKLP	All Things Must Pass *George Harrison*

THE GRAPEVINE

- **Eric Burdon's UK tour with War was cancelled when it was discovered the singer had flown back to LA, seemingly suffering from 'sheer exhaustion'.**
- **Balls, the new supergroup which included Denny Laine and Steve Gibbons in its line-up, has split.**
- **Cabaret singer Annie Haslam has joined Renaissance, replacing American vocalist Binky.**

'I WANTED TO BE A VET' SAYS OLIVIA

Ex-Toomorrow singer Olivia Newton-John, whose version of Bob Dylan's 'If Not For You' has gone Top 10 in Britain, says: 'I haven't always thought about going into show business professionally. I originally wanted to be a vet. I got as far as my 'O' level exams, then left school and started singing.

'I formed a duo with a friend from Australia – we were called Pat and Olivia – but we kept forgetting each other was on stage and the mike leads got tangled up!'

She describes life with supergroup Toomorrow as 'frustrating', adding: 'Our film died a death and it was all a bit of a shambles. But it was good experience.'

Olivia has just completed some guest spots on the Cliff Richard BBC TV series in London.

SECOND WOODSTOCK ALBUM – DETAILS

Editing of a second double-album 'Woodstock' compilation has now been completed. The resulting set is to be released in the States shortly, with a British release expected to follow within the next two months.

The albums are dedicated to the late Jimi Hendrix, who's featured throughout one entire side. Also showcased in this latest collection are Crosby, Stills, Nash and Young, Melanie, Joan Baez, Jefferson Airplane, The Butterfield Blues Band, Canned Heat and Mountain.

And there is still enough material left over from the legendary 1969 festival recordings for a third double-album to be issued in the future.

CHARTS

US45	One Bad Apple *Osmonds*
USLP	Pearl *Janis Joplin*
UK45	My Sweet Lord *George Harrison*
UKLP	All Things Must Pass *George Harrison*
	WEEK 2
US45	One Bad Apple *Osmonds*
USLP	Pearl *Janis Joplin*
UK45	Baby Jump *Mungo Jerry*
UKLP	All Things Must Pass *George Harrison*
	WEEK 3
US45	Me & Bobby McGee *Janis Joplin*
USLP	Pearl *Janis Joplin*
UK45	Another Day *Paul McCartney*
UKLP	Bridge Over Troubled Water *Simon & Garfunkel*
	WEEK 4
US45	Me & Bobby McGee *Janis Joplin*
USLP	Pearl *Janis Joplin*
UK45	Hot Love *T.Rex*
UKLP	Bridge Over Troubled Water *Simon & Garfunkel*

SINATRA QUITS

Frank Sinatra has announced that he's quitting what he describes as 'the show biz scene'. The 55 year-old entertainer plans to spend most of his time writing and possibly teaching.

It is not yet clear whether he will make any more records, but the tone of his announcement indicates that he will not. Sinatra is due to play farewell charity concerts in the States in May and June.

FLY AWAY PETER, PAUL AND MARY TOO!

Peter, Paul And Mary – they first got together in Greenwich Village during the early '60s, after Mary had appeared in a flop Broadway musical

Peter, Paul and Mary have broken up with Peter Yarrow, Paul Stookey and Mary Travers all agreeing to go their separate ways. First to announce plans for the future is Mary Travers, whose solo album 'Mary' has just been released in America.

She'll do an American concert tour during April and May with a specially formed quartet before spending time guesting on various TV shows in New York and LA.

Yarrow and Stookey's plans have not yet been revealed.

THE GRAPEVINE

- **Junior Campbell has quit British group Marmalade.**
- **Equals man Eddie Grant has gone home to Guyana following a collapsed lung and heart infection which put him out of action at the beginning of the year.**
- **Singer Sandie Shaw was recently snapped by a *Sunday Mirror* photographer in London, breast-feeding her baby.**

RIC LEE

Ten Years After drummer

'I don't like Ginger Baker, his solos are always far too long. They go on and on.'

DIANA TO PORTRAY LADY DAY

Diana Ross has confirmed that she is to appear in her first movie role. She will portray Billie Holiday in *'Lady Sings The Blues'*, a film based around the life of the famous jazz singer who died in 1969.

Tamla Motown are to finance the movie to the tune of five and a half million dollars with Berry Gordy producing. Motown recently announced that it was widening the scope of its activities and would allocate 15 million dollars this year to film, stage and TV productions. Its first venture was a Diana Ross TV special.

Diana Ross (left) and the late, great Billie Holiday (right). Billie, known as Lady Day, was a one-time prostitute who eventually became acclaimed the greatest of all jazz vocalists

MAMAS AND PAPAS REFORM

The Mamas And Papas are back together four years after they announced their disbandment – and they're already fashioning a new album.

It is not known whether the quartet intend to make any live appearances in the immediate future but if the reunion is permanent, concert dates will certainly follow.

SWEET: PURE POP AND PROUD

The Sweet are the most recent new group to break into the UK Top 30, with their single 'Funny Funny'. Its appeal is strictly to the teen market – a fact the group don't try to hide. Indeed, they are positively proud of it.

'We enjoy playing pop music', guitarist Andy Scott explains. 'We do other numbers onstage which are less obviously commercial than "Funny Funny", but whatever we do is centred around vocal harmonies.'

Record producers Nicky Chinn and Mike Chapman have already written The Sweet's follow-up single, which is called 'Co-Co', Scott revealed, adding: 'We've also got an album coming out soon, for which Nicky and Mike have written four songs.'

All four members of the group, (which was formed in 1968 by drummer Mick Tucker and lead singer Brian Connolly, along with Andy Scott and bassist Steve Priest), seem to accept that people will compare them to bubblegum supergroup The Archies.

'The Archies had a number one, didn't they?', quipped Brian Connolly.

CHARTS

US45	Just My Imagination *Temptations*
USLP	Pearl *Janis Joplin*
UK45	Hot Love *T.Rex*
UKLP	Bridge Over Troubled Water *Simon & Garfunkel*
WEEK 2	
US45	Just My Imagination *Temptations*
USLP	Pearl *Janis Joplin*
UK45	Hot Love *T.Rex*
UKLP	Home Lovin' Man *Andy Williams*
WEEK 3	
US45	Joy To The World *Three Dog Night*
USLP	Pearl *Janis Joplin*
UK45	Hot Love *T.Rex*
UKLP	Bridge Over Troubled Water *Simon & Garfunkel*
WEEK 4	
US45	Joy To The World *Three Dog Night*
USLP	Pearl *Janis Joplin*
UK45	Hot Love *T.Rex*
UKLP	Home Lovin' Man *Andy Williams*

THE GRAPEVINE

- **After a stay of eight years on UK Decca, Billie Davis has now left the label.**
- **Irish singer Clodagh Rodgers, who failed to appear at the opening night of the Tommy Steele show 'Meet Me In London' at London's Adelphi Theatre, says she has been sacked.**
- **Jeremy Spencer's replacement with Fleetwood Mac will be 25 year-old Bob Welch from San Francisco.**

STAR QUOTE

BILL GRAHAM

Impresario

'A couple of years ago, a couple of geniuses put on something called Woodstock Festival. It was a tragedy. Groups recognised that they could go into larger cattle markets, play less time and make more dollars. What they've done is to destroy the rock industry.'

STONES LAUNCH OWN LABEL

The Rolling Stones have signed with the Kinney Group and their recordings will, henceforth, be released on a newly created label called Rolling Stones Records. The group's first album under the new deal will be released in the UK on April 23 and is titled 'Sticky Fingers'.

The album was produced by Jimmy Miller and is to be issued in a special cover designed by Andy Warhol. The first single on Rolling Stones Records will be a maxi-single containing three A-sides – 'Brown Sugar'/'Bitch'/'Let It Rock' – and represents tremendous value for money.

MAY

MANFREDS OUT – KINKS IN DOWNUNDER

The Manfred Mann group have flown back from Australia, cutting short their projected month-long tour by three weeks. This follows an incident in a Melbourne motel where their tour manager Bob Foster was attacked.

A spokesman commented: 'Bob had threats made on his life and was given 24 hours to get out of Australia. Manfred feared for his own safety too and decided to return to Britain as soon as possible.'

No explanation was offered for the threats. But, as The Manfreds headed back, The Kinks announced that they are to pay their first visit down under for four years, commencing a 12 day tour on May 29.

CHARTS

WEEK 1	US45	Joy To The World – *Three Dog Night*
	USLP	Jesus Christ Superstar – *Various Artists*
	UK45	Double Barrel – *Dave And Ansell Collins*
	UKLP	Motown Chartbusters, Vol.5 – *Various*
WEEK 2	US45	Joy To The World – *Three Dog Night*
	USLP	Jesus Christ Superstar – *Various Artists*
	UK45	Double Barrel – *Dave And Ansell Collins*
	UKLP	Sticky Fingers – *Rolling Stones*
WEEK 3	US45	Joy To The World – *Three Dog Night*
	USLP	Four Way Street – *Crosby, Stills, Nash & Young*
	UK45	Brown Sugar – *Rolling Stones*
	UKLP	Sticky Fingers – *Rolling Stones*
WEEK 4	US45	Joy To The World – *Three Dog Night*
	USLP	Sticky Fingers – *Rolling Stones*
	UK45	Knock Three Times – *Dawn*
	UKLP	Sticky Fingers – *Rolling Stones*
WEEK 5	US45	Brown Sugar – *Rolling Stones*
	USLP	Sticky Fingers – *Rolling Stones*
	UK45	Knock Three Times – *Dawn*
	UKLP	Sticky Fingers – *Rolling Stones*

Mick and missus

FREE BECOME THREE!

With their current single 'My Brother Jake' standing high in the UK charts, Free have disbanded! The decision to break up was taken during the group's recent Australian tour and now the various members are planning new bands.

Announcing the split, a spokesman said: 'The boys felt they had achieved as much together as they possibly could within their existing framework. They have now decided to pursue individual careers.' The group had been together for three years.

It is expected that guitarist Paul Kossoff and drummer Simon Kirke will stay together and assemble a new group. Singer Paul Rodgers and bassist Andy Fraser will form their own separate bands.

A farewell live album, recorded at Sheffield and Croydon's Fairfield Hall, is planned for release in June, but there will be no follow-up single to 'My Brother Jake'.

THE GRAPEVINE

- **Mick and Bianca Jagger got married in France on May 12; guests included Paul McCartney, Ringo Starr, Steve Stills and Eric Clapton.**
- **Dickie Valentine was killed on May 6, in a car crash. One-time page-boy at the London Palladium, he won the NME poll as Britain's top singer from 1953 to 1957.**
- **Dionne Warwick has left Scepter Records after a hit-filled 10 years.**

STAR

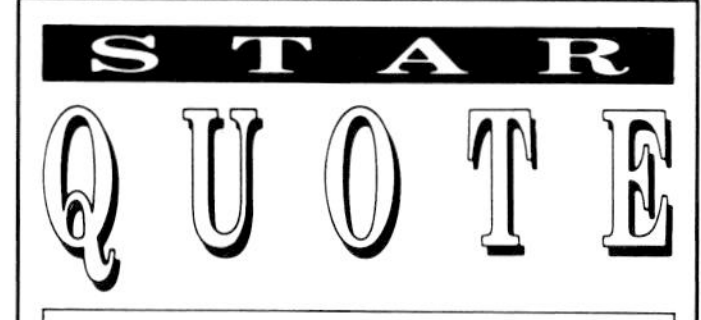

MARC BOLAN

on the eve of his sell-out UK tour

'I am so pleased that people are there, I feel I might just go on stage and burst into tears.'

CLAPTON PIPS HENDRIX AS GREATEST EVER

An NME poll in which Tom Fogerty, Alexis Korner, Dave Davies, Ritchie Blackmore, Ronnie Wood, Eric Clapton, Gary Moore, Dave Edmunds and many more guitarists took part, has resulted in a narrow win for Eric Clapton (16 points) over Jimi Hendrix (15) with B.B.King third (12) and Frank Zappa fourth (11).

Buddy Guy and Robbie Robertson both received nine points, while Peter Green received eight.

STRANGELY STRANGE NO MORE

Dr Strangely Strange are to split after playing a concert with Al Stewart at London's Drury Lane Theatre on May 16. Ivan Pawls has decided that he will only play occasional gigs, Tim Booth has not yet formulated future plans, and Neil Hopwood may give up being a professional musician.

Terry and Gay Woods, who joined the outfit at the beginning of the year, will form a new group in which the emphasis will be on traditional Irish music.

Eric Clapton – who donated his own votes to B.B. King, Freddie King and Duane Allman

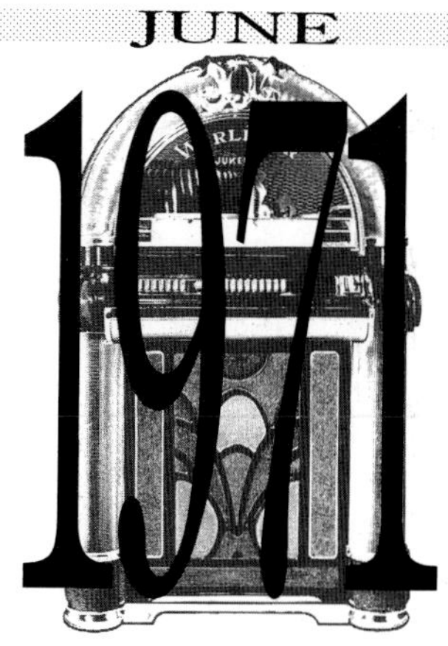

HERD REFORM

The Herd have re-formed. The group – one of Britain's top record acts a year or so back – already has a comeback single released, an album in preparation and a series of gigs planned.

At the moment, the line-up is fluid, but it is understood that The Herd's erstwhile drummer Andrew Steele will be joining the group when it starts undertaking one-nighters.

Though the single, 'You've Got Me Hangin' From Your Loving Tree', only features two original Herd members – Gary Taylor (bass and vocals) and Louis Rich (vocals) – plus session musicians, it is expected that the group will eventually settle down to the same line-up it had at the time of disbandment.

The exception will be guitarist/vocalist Peter Frampton, who is now an integral part of Humble Pie. There are also some contractual problems concerning keyboard player Andy Bown, but these are expected to be resolved shortly.

Gary Taylor: One of the two confirmed members of the new Herd. Their last hit, 'I Don't Want Our Loving To Die", came way back in 1968

THE GRAPEVINE

■ Most prized current bootleg: Eric Burdon & War with Jimi Hendrix, recorded in London the night before Jimi's death.

■ The Celebration Of Life Festival, in Louisiana, has proved a shambles. The event opened on June 21, three and a half days late, and was closed down three days later when the promoters failed to supply food and medical facilities and with only nine of the 27 advertised acts having showed.

CHARTS

Week	Chart	Title	Artist
	US45	Brown Sugar	*Rolling Stones*
	USLP	Sticky Fingers	*Rolling Stones*
	UK45	Knock Three Times	*Dawn*
	UKLP	Sticky Fingers	*Rolling Stones*
WEEK 2	US45	Want Ads	*Honey Cone*
	USLP	Sticky Fingers	*Rolling Stones*
	UK45	My Brother Jake	*Free*
	UKLP	Sticky Fingers	*Rolling Stones*
WEEK 3	US45	It's Too Late	*Carole King*
	USLP	Tapestry	*Carole King*
	UK45	I Did What I Did For Maria	*Tony Christie*
	UKLP	Sticky Fingers	*Rolling Stones*
WEEK 4	US45	It's Too Late	*Carole King*
	USLP	Tapestry	*Carole King*
	UK45	Chirpy Chirpy Cheep Cheep	*Middle Of The Road*
	UKLP	Sticky Fingers	*Rolling Stones*

BEACH BOY IN HOSPITAL

Dennis Wilson, the only surfing Beach Boy, a better drummer than a glazier

Beach Boys' drummer Dennis Wilson has lost the use of his right hand for several months as a result of an accident at his California home. He was fixing a pane of glass into a window frame when the glass shattered and severed nerves in his hand and wrist.

The Beach Boys are due to begin a 10-day tour shortly and, if Wilson is fit enough to take part, he will appear in a singing role only. a deputy drummer is meanwhile being sought.

Wilson also hopes to be fit enough to attend the New York premiere of *Two Lane Blacktop*, the movie in which he co-stars with James Taylor.

CLYDE McPHATTER DIES

Clyde McPhatter, the son of a North Carolina baptist minister, who became one of the world's finest soulmen, has died, aged 40.

Once lead singer with Billy Ward's Dominoes, he went on to form The Drifters in 1953, appearing on such hits as 'Money Honey' and 'Such A Night'. Drafted into the Air Force in 1954, upon his discharge he became a solo performer and recorded such US hits as 'A Lover's Question' and 'Lover Please', along with 'Treasure Of Love', McPhatter's only UK hit as a solo artist.

JULY

1971

ANDY WILLIAMS TV SERIES SCRAPPED

Andy Williams' weekly TV series is being taken off the air. the 1970/71 series, which is currently being screened in the UK by BBC-1, is to be his last.

Andy gave up making weekly shows three years ago in order to concentrate on occasional specials but, within 12 months, was forced back into the weekly format by public demand. But now his show is being dropped because of falling ratings in America.

THE GRAPEVINE

- In the wake of Edgar Broughton's plan to play free concerts in UK seaside towns, the city of Blackpool has slapped a ban on all such free shows for the next 25 years!
- U.K. Pop group Dando Shaft have been booked to appear in the play *You Must Be Joking*, at Coventry's Belgrade Theatre in September.
- Billy Preston has been signed to A&M and is recording an album.

THE END FOR JIM MORRISON

Jim Morrison, who ducked out from leading The Doors in order to concentrate on creative writing, died in Paris on July 3, aged 27.

On the night of July 2, Morrison regurgitated a small amount of blood, but claimed he felt fine and announced his intention of taking a bath. Early next morning, his wife Pamela found him dead in the water-filled bath, apparently from natural causes. Morrison had recently consulted a local doctor concerning a respiratory problem.

The singer-poet is to be buried in the same Paris cemetery as French chanteuse Edith Piaf and playwright Oscar Wilde, as well as a number of illustrious French authors, painters and artists.

LED ZEP: A REAL GAS

Led Zeppelin were involved in a massive riot when, playing to a crowd of over 15,000 in Milan's Vigorelli Stadium, the group's act was disrupted by charging police and soldiers wielding batons and lobbing tear-gas canisters.

Even before the show started, the stadium was ringed by hundreds of police and soldiers, while outside there were trucks full of reinforcements waiting for any sign of crowd trouble. They went into action with scarcely any provocation, and this led to a full-scale riot during which some of the group's equipment was damaged.

Said a group member: 'It'll be refreshing to come home for a bit of sanity.'

THE JAMES GANG RIDE OUT

The James Gang – Dale Peters, Joe Walsh and Jimmy Fox – who are in Britain for a tour, held a press reception at which Walsh, the band's lead guitarist, recalled: 'I did a jam with Eric Clapton and Peter Green at the Boston Tea Party a while back and I didn't know about it until 10 minutes before we did it!

'There was so much respect between those two that they were playing very quiet and I stayed out of the way, but contributed a bit. Usually when you show up for a jam, everybody's ego gets into it and that defeats the whole purpose of jamming.'

The band play the London Lyceum on July 25.

CHARTS

US45	It's Too Late *Carole King*
USLP	Tapestry *Carole King*
UK45	Chirpy Chirpy Cheep Cheep *Middle Of The Road*
UKLP	Bridge Over Troubled Water *Simon & Garfunkel*
WEEK 2	
US45	It's Too Late *Carole King*
USLP	Tapestry *Carole King*
UK45	Chirpy Chirpy Cheep Cheep *Middle Of The Road*
UKLP	Ram *Paul McCartney*
WEEK 3	
US45	It's Too Late *Carole King*
USLP	Tapestry *Carole King*
UK45	Chirpy Chirpy Cheep Cheep *Middle Of The Road*
UKLP	Bridge Over Troubled Water *Simon & Garfunkel*
WEEK 4	
US45	Indian Reservation *Paul Revere & The Raiders*
USLP	Tapestry *Carole King*
UK45	Chirpy Chirpy Cheep Cheep *Middle Of The Road*
UKLP	Bridge Over Troubled Water *Simon & Garfunkel*
WEEK 5	
US45	You've Got A Friend *James Taylor*
USLP	Tapestry *Carole King*
UK45	Get It On *T.Rex*
UKLP	Bridge Over Troubled Water *Simon & Garfunkel*

STAR QUOTE

AL KOOPER

'I'm so pleased to be in Britain, I could just sit and pour tea over my head.'

Anglophile Al Kooper

BIG DEAL AT WEELEY

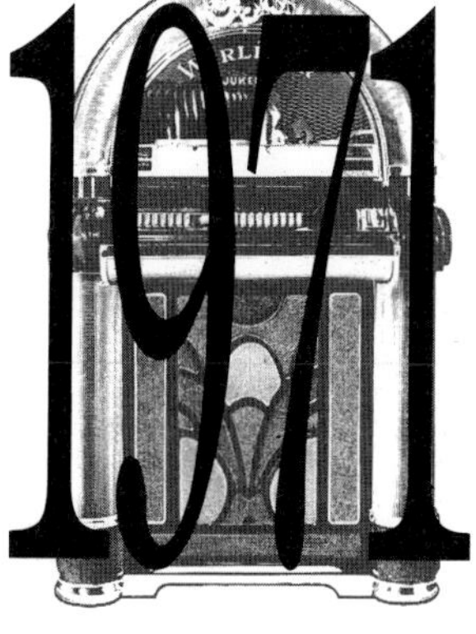

(Far left) Lindisfarne, Newcastle Brown downers and suppliers of Weeley singalongs

(Left) One-time bopping elf Marc Bolan, now a festival favourite

A rampage by gangs of Hells Angels bikers failed to stop The Weeley Festival – held at the south of England resort of Clacton on August 28-9 – from being one of Britain's most successful-ever rock events.

Although the Angels destroyed a concession stand, reaped a deal of other damage, and savagely beat up a girl who got in their way, they were routed by a squad of festival-goers who formed themselves into a vigilante group, mounted a counter-attack and destroyed most of the Angels' prized, hand-built choppers.

But the music went on.

Headliners The Faces turned in a storming set, as did T. Rex and Lindisfarne, all of whom received tumultuous receptions from the massive crowd.

Other acts appearing included Rory Gallagher, folkie Julie Felix, King Crimson, Stone The Crows, Caravan, Colosseum, Barclay James Harvest, Mott The Hoople, The Edgar Broughton Band, Juicy Lucy, Mungo Jerry and Curved Air – a bill which caused one reviewer to describe it as 'DeMille gone mad!'

The Hells Angels were not available for comment.

THE GRAPEVINE

- **Tony Kaye has left Yes, his replacement being The Strawbs' Rick Wakeman.**
- **Mick Jagger has made an unprintable comment regarding UK Decca's decision to release the 'Gimme Shelter' album, which has nothing to do with the movie but contains six old cuts plus extracts from the Albert Hall concert of 1966.**
- **Elton John made his US debut at the LA Troubadour on August 22.**

Bad Jokebook raider Tony Blackburn

UK DJ TONY BLACKBURN

'There is an opinion that I'm a complete idiot and that I've never had sex. That's not true!'

US45	How Can You Mend A Broken Heart *Bee Gees*
USLP	Tapestry *Carole King*
UK45	Get It On *T.Rex*
UKLP	Bridge Over Troubled Water *Simon & Garfunkel*
	WEEK 2
US45	How Can You Mend A Broken Heart *Bee Gees*
USLP	Tapestry *Carole King*
UK45	Get It On *T.Rex*
UKLP	Every Good Boy Deserves Favour *Moody Blues*
	WEEK 3
US45	How Can You Mend A Broken Heart *Bee Gees*
USLP	Tapestry *Carole King*
UK45	Never Ending Song Of Love *New Seekers*
UKLP	Every Good Boy Deserves Favour *Moody Blues*
	WEEK 4
US45	How Can You Mend A Broken Heart *Bee Gees*
USLP	Tapestry *Carole King*
UK45	I'm Still Waiting *Diana Ross*
UKLP	Every Good Boy Deserves Favour *Moody Blues*

ARETHA AND STEVIE AT CURTIS FUNERAL

August 17: Stevie Wonder, Aretha Franklin, Cissy Houston, Brook Benton, Delaney and Bonnie, Duane Allman, Herbie Mann and Arthur Prysock were among those who attended the funeral of soul saxman King Curtis in New York City.

Curtis, who was born Curtis Ousley, was stabbed to death on August 13, following an argument outside his New York apartment. He was 37.

WILL THE REAL P.J. PROBY SIGN HERE?

P.J. Proby's new look nearly landed him in trouble when he opened a new nightspot in Preston, Lancashire. Some members of the audience at the club, The Piper, refused to believe he was P.J. because the singer has lost 49lbs in weight and has grown a beard for a movie he's shooting with Peter Fonda.

Suspicion spread, and the owners of the club threatened to pull out of the £1,500 deal. The police were brought in to collect specimens of Proby's signature to verify his identity.

Eventually, in order to satisfy patrons, the club owners had to offer £1,000 to anyone who could prove that the artist was not the real P.J. Proby.

P.B. Proby – we think!

FRAMPTON CUTS UP THE PIE

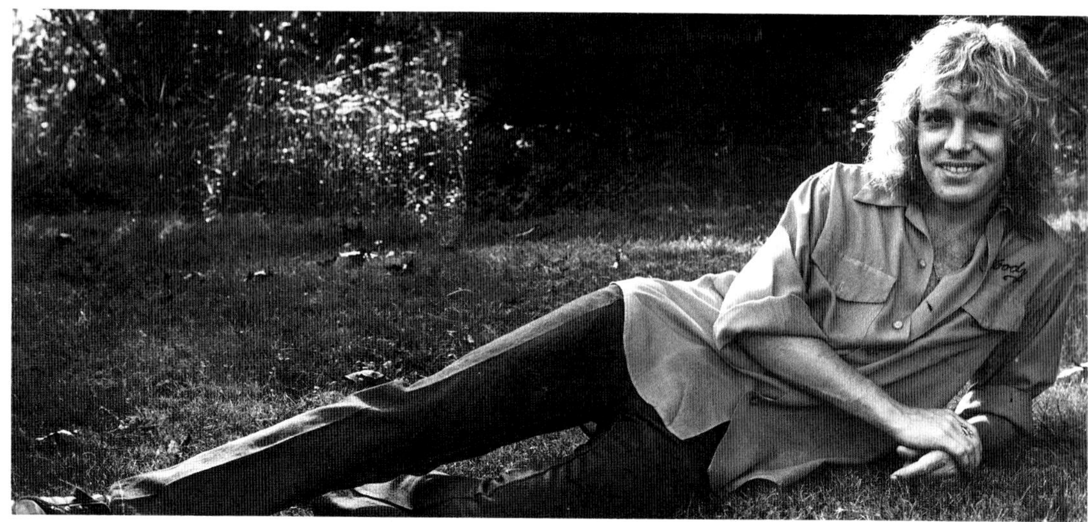

Peter Frampton – no longer humble

Founder member Peter Frampton has quit Humble Pie in order to concentrate on a solo career. The announcement was made by Pie manager Dee Anthony, who is visiting London to finalize plans for the group's forthcoming European tour, which opens in Frankfurt on November 1.

The final album featuring Frampton with Humble Pie will be issued by A&M in October. Titled 'Performance', it's a double set which was recorded live at New York's Fillmore East earlier this year.

Asked for a comment, Peter Frampton replied: 'At last I'm doing something I've always wanted to do. It's time I found out if people are prepared to listen to what I can do myself.'

CHARTS

US45	Uncle Albert/Admiral Halsey *Paul & Linda McCartney*
USLP	Tapestry *Carole King*
UK45	I'm Still Waiting *Diana Ross*
UKLP	Every Good Boy Deserves Favour *Moody Blues*
	WEEK 2
US45	Go Away Little Girl *Donny Osmond*
USLP	Tapestry *Carole King*
UK45	I'm Still Waiting *Diana Ross*
UKLP	Every Good Boy Deserves Favour *Moody Blues*
	WEEK 3
US45	Go Away Little Girl *Donny Osmond*
USLP	Tapestry *Carole King*
UK45	Hey Girl, Don't Bother Me *Tams*
UKLP	Tapestry *Carole King*
	WEEK 4
US45	Go Away Little Girl *Donny Osmond*
USLP	Tapestry *Carole King*
UK45	Hey Girl, Don't Bother Me *Tams*
UKLP	Every Picture Tells A Story *Rod Stewart*

JAMES TAYLOR INJURY CAUSES PANIC

Panic broke out in the New York office of manager Nathan Weiss after a phone call announced that James Taylor had injured his right hand after tinkering with some machinery at his farm on Martha's Vineyard, Mass. Initially it was suggested that James might even lose the hand, but a doctor later confirmed that it was only a severe flesh wound and that all tendons and bones had been left intact.

Even so, New Yorkers will have to wait a while before seeing Taylor in concert again. His three sell-out Carnegie Hall dates for this month have now been rescheduled for November.

The ultra-noisy Sly Stone

15,000 LIMIT FOR BANGLA DESH GIG

Only half the potential capacity of 30,000 will be allowed into the mammoth Who-Faces-Mott The Hoople-Lindisfarne Bangladesh concert at London's Oval stadium on September 18. City authority regulations have been clamped on fans, even though thousands more are allowed into the ground for cricket matches.

Atomic Rooster have now been added to the bill and will be flying in from America, where they've been touring. Also playing at the event will be The Grease Band, Quintessence, America and Eugene Wallace.

CARL WILSON SENTENCED TO SING

Carl Wilson of The Beach Boys will not have to fight in Vietnam after all. He's been opposing military service for nearly four years and, at one time, looked as if he might face a term of imprisonment because of his views.

But, at a final court hearing, he's been put on probation for three years and fined $4,000, one proviso being that, during the next two years, he must sing regularly at prisons, hospitals and orphanages.

Carl Wilson sings on but no Saigon

THE GRAPEVINE

- **Sly Stone's landlord is sueing him for $3 million, because Sly has allegedly filled the building with 'loud, noisy, boisterous persons'.**
- **Elvis Presley has received the Bing Crosby Award from America's NARAS. He's the sixth recipient of the prestigious award, previous winners being Crosby, Frank Sinatra, Duke Ellington, Ella Fitzgerald and Irving Berlin.**

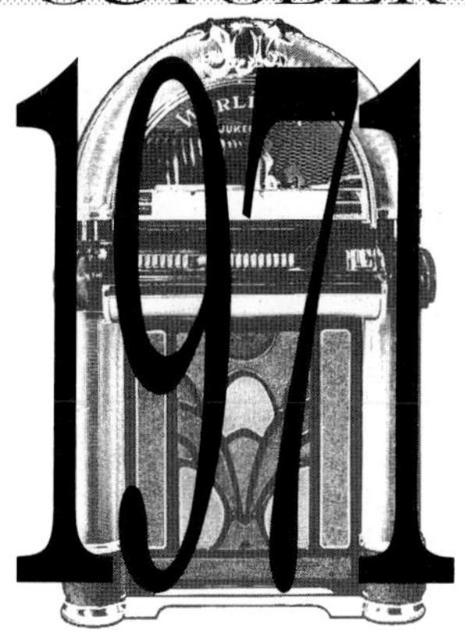

LENNON WANTS CLAPTON FOR BAND

A fully clothed John and Yoko

John Lennon is hoping to persuade Eric Clapton to join the band he is proposing to take on a world tour next year. Lennon has already announced that the bassist will be Klaus Voorman, while pianist Nicky Hopkins will also be in the outfit, which will be completed by Yoko Ono and drummer Jim Keltner.

Lennon also stated, in New York, that he's asked Phil Spector to produce an act for the group which he proposes to call The John & Yoko Mobile Plastic Ono Band Fun Show.

STAR QUOTE

KEITH MOON

'Give me a mandolin and I'll play you rock'n'roll.'

STAR NAMES OVER THE RAINBOW

The Rainbow – London's newest live rock centre – is lining up an impressive list of star names for its first season of concerts. The 3,500-seater, formerly The Finsbury Park Astoria and famed in rock history as the venue for The Beatles' Christmas shows in the sixties, plans to open on November 4 with a three-day engagement by The Who.

Alice Cooper is now confirmed to follow The Who on November 7, while other acts booked for the theatre include Grand Funk, The Grateful Dead, Mountain, The Doors, The Faces, Fairport Convention, Family, Leon Russell, Climax Chicago and Barclay James Harvest.

The cost of converting the cinema to modern rock standards was £150,000 ($300,000), of which nearly £15,000 ($30,000) was spent on a new computerized lighting rig.

Alice in Rainbowland

AL LEAPS – AFTER THREE MONTHS

A record that has been in the stores for three months has suddenly leapt from nowhere into the NME UK singles charts. Titled 'Tired Of Being Alone', it's by American singer Al Green who, last year, was voted fifth most promising R&B singer by US publication *Cashbox*.

Originally from Forrest City, Arkansas, Green began singing spirituals with his four brothers while still at school and, by the age of 16, was part of The Creations. Later Al Green & The Soulmates' 'Back Up Train' notched up sales of 70,000, helping to put his name on the map.

ROD CHART SENSATION

Faces vocalist Rod Stewart has pulled off an amazing feat by having his 'Every Picture Tells A Story' album at No. 1 on both sides of the Atlantic, while his 'Maggie May' single has also gone top of the singles charts both here and in America.

'The single is a freak, a million to one chance,' said Rod. 'But the album has permanence and a lasting value. I still can't see how the single is such a bit hit. It has no melody. Plenty of character and nice chords, but no melody.'

Rod luvs Maggie true

CHARTS

US45	Maggie May – *Rod Stewart*
USLP	Every Picture Tells A Story – *Rod Stewart*
UK45	Maggie May – *Rod Stewart*
UKLP	Every Picture Tells A Story – *Rod Stewart*
WEEK 2	
US45	Maggie May – *Rod Stewart*
USLP	Every Picture Tells A Story – *Rod Stewart*
UK45	Maggie May – *Rod Stewart*
UKLP	Every Picture Tells A Story – *Rod Stewart*
WEEK 3	
US45	Maggie May – *Rod Stewart*
USLP	Every Picture Tells A Story – *Rod Stewart*
UK45	Maggie May – *Rod Stewart*
UKLP	Every Picture Tells A Story – *Rod Stewart*
WEEK 4	
US45	Maggie May – *Rod Stewart*
USLP	Every Picture Tells A Story – *Rod Stewart*
UK45	Maggie May – *Rod Stewart*
UKLP	Every Picture Tells A Story – *Rod Stewart*
WEEK 5	
US45	Maggie May – *Rod Stewart*
USLP	Imagine – *John Lennon*
UK45	Maggie May – *Rod Stewart*
UKLP	Every Picture Tells A Story – *Rod Stewart*

THE GRAPEVINE

- **Gene Vincent died of a bleeding ulcer on October 12. He has lived in severe pain ever since a motorcycle accident back in 1955.**
- **The death is also reported of Duane Allman, who was killed in a motorcycle crash near his Macon, Georgia home on October 29.**
- **Allan Clarke has announced that he'll be leaving The Hollies before the end of the year.**

NOVEMBER

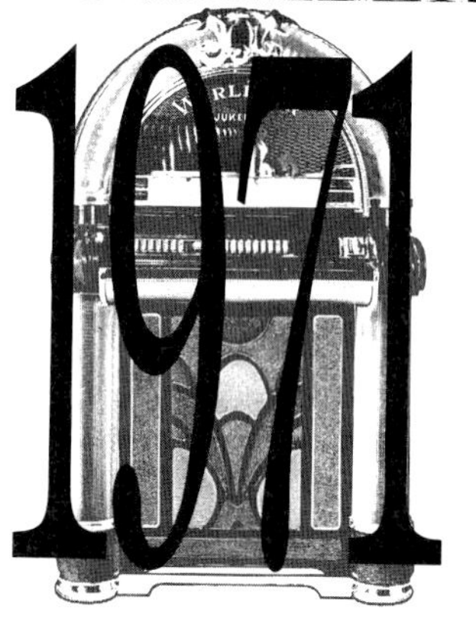

SUPERSTAR OUSTS PEPPER

MCA is claiming a British sales record for its 'Jesus Christ Superstar' album. The previous LP record was established by The Beatles' 'Sgt. Pepper's Lonely Hearts Club Band' which has now sold seven million copies throughout the world. Combined international sales of 'Superstar' have already passed three and a half million, and – since it is a double-album – this represents a total in excess of seven million units.

Composers Tim Rice and Andrew Lloyd Webber are to be presented with a gold disc for sales of the album in Australia. Then they're booked for Israel next year, where location work begins on a film version of the musical, to be directed by Norman Jewison. A stage version of the rock opera – already running on Broadway – is expected to open in Britain during late spring 1972.

SLADE – NO 'NEW BEATLES' LAUNCH

Slade claim to have turned down the opportunity of being launched in America as the next Beatles. The offer would have involved a multi-million dollar campaign, including a TV series shot in the group's native Wolverhampton, plus a full-length film set in locations round the world and a heavily promoted debut tour of the States.

'But,' commented singer Noddy Holder, 'Acceptance would have meant the cancellation of many commitments here – and the last thing we want to do is to mess around the people who have put us where we are.'

Wolverhampton wanderer Noddy Holder

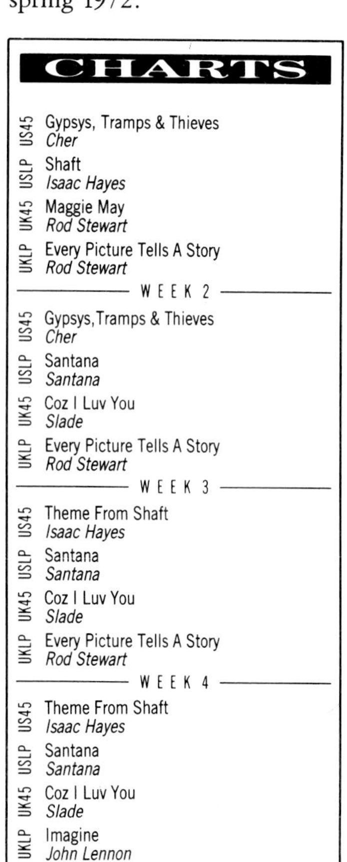

CHARTS

US45	Gypsys, Tramps & Thieves	*Cher*
USLP	Shaft	*Isaac Hayes*
UK45	Maggie May	*Rod Stewart*
UKLP	Every Picture Tells A Story	*Rod Stewart*
WEEK 2		
US45	Gypsys, Tramps & Thieves	*Cher*
USLP	Santana	*Santana*
UK45	Coz I Luv You	*Slade*
UKLP	Every Picture Tells A Story	*Rod Stewart*
WEEK 3		
US45	Theme From Shaft	*Isaac Hayes*
USLP	Santana	*Santana*
UK45	Coz I Luv You	*Slade*
UKLP	Every Picture Tells A Story	*Rod Stewart*
WEEK 4		
US45	Theme From Shaft	*Isaac Hayes*
USLP	Santana	*Santana*
UK45	Coz I Luv You	*Slade*
UKLP	Imagine	*John Lennon*

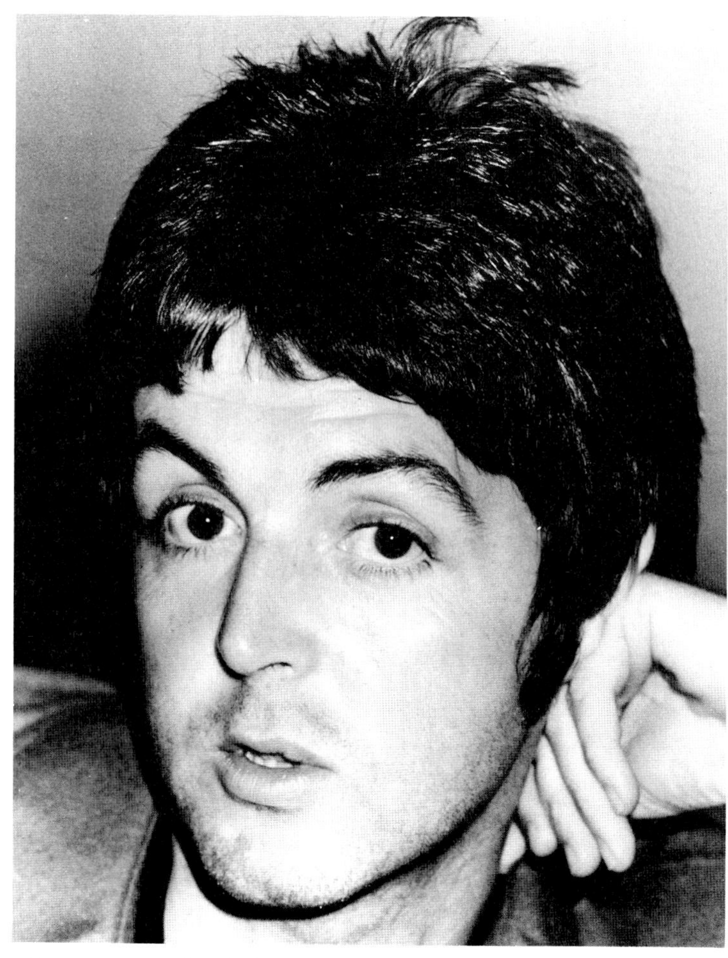

NO LOLLIPOP WANTED, SAYS PAUL

Paul McCartney has said that he's not getting out of Apple, The Beatles' own label. 'I've not got to go down, as Allen Klein said recently,' he added. But he's far from happy with the way the label has been handled.

'Apple isn't a democracy,' he complained. 'It's way out of line with what I thought was going to happen. None of The Beatles have, to this day, seen any of that money. As far as the money off The Beatles' records is concerned, The Beatles still haven't got it.

'I'd like to see the four Beatles split whatever's left of what The Beatles made. George calls it throwing a tantrum whenever I say things like that. But I only want what I earned. I'm not asking for a lollipop.'

Once B.S. & T. now gone A.W.O.L.

THE GRAPEVINE

- **Colosseum, the outfit featuring drummer Jon Hiseman and singer Chris Farlowe, has split.**
- **David Clayton Thomas, lead vocalist with B.S. & T. since the departure of Al Kooper, has gone solo.**
- **Wings' first album, 'Wild Life', released on November 15.**
- **Donovan's current US tour, his first in two years, has proved a failure, one concert drawing only half as many people as expected.**

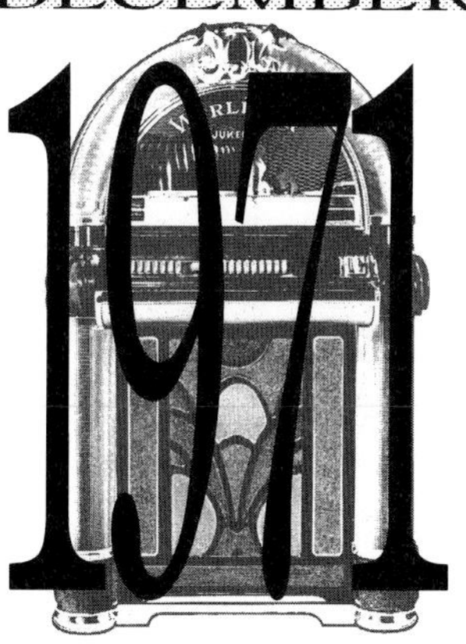

TEN YEARS AFTER SET UK TOUR

Ten Years After, who have just returned from the United States with their first gold disc – awarded for one million sales of the 'A Space In Time' album, – are to start the new year with a tour of selected British universities.

The tour opens at Reading on January 8, then visits campuses in Birmingham, Sheffield, Lancaster, Cardiff, Liverpool, Leeds, Brighton, Nottingham, Salford and Leicester.

'This tour is something we've wanted to do for a long time,' explained guitarist Alvin Lee. 'It was the university audiences, along with London clubs like The Marquee, who picked up on us in the first place.'

Supporting Ten Years After at selected gigs will be Jude, the group formed by ex-Procol Harum guitarist Robin Trower and ex-Jethro Tull drummer Clive Bunker.

GILBERT 'TOO SHY TO TOUR'

An offer of an extensive British tour for songwriter Gilbert O'Sullivan has been turned down because he is 'too shy' to appear in public.

According to manager Gordon Mills, he has also declined two major film roles for his *protégé*. So, instead of expanding his activities, Gilbert (real name Raymond) will spend the early part of 1972 in his Surrey cottage, writing material for his second album, plus new singles.

FACES ALBUM BANNED

The Faces' album, 'A Nod's As Good As A Wink To A Blind Horse', has been banned in America. Over 400,000 copies have been pressed and dispatched, but distributors are refusing to handle it, alleging that the poster included in the sleeve is obscene.

Arrangements are now being made to re-release the album without the offending poster, which is a different one to that released in Britain.

THE GRAPEVINE

- **Traffic are now down to a trio, Rich Grech and Jim Gordon having left.**
- **Marc Bolan is the first artist confirmed for a triple-album set issued as a benefit for last June's UK Glastonbury Festival.**
- **Because the Royal Albert Hall has banned him, Isaac Hayes' forthcoming London appearances on January 27 and 28 have been rescheduled for the Rainbow.**

ZAPPA AND FURY HOSPITALIZED

"Frankly, I've been zapped!"

Mothers Of Invention leader Frank Zappa is currently in a London clinic, nursing a broken leg and his pride after being pushed into the orchestra pit by an audience member during his December 10 show at the Rainbow Theatre. Zappa also suffered concussion in the fall, which the performer claims could have been avoided if the pit had been covered over.

Initially taken to a public hospital nearby, Zappa refused to be treated there, describing it as 'absolutely filthy'. He was then taken to the private clinic, where he is expected to remain for two more months. Litigation is in the air.

Hayes – shafted by the Albert

Another rock star now hospitalized is British veteran Billy Fury, who was admitted to the National Heart Hospital on December 13. He is to undergo an operation for the replacement of two heart valves.

CHARTS

US45	Family Affair *Sly & The Family Stone*
USLP	Santana *Santana*
UK45	Coz I Luv You *Slade*
UKLP	Imagine *John Lennon*
WEEK 2	
US45	Family Affair *Sly & The Family Stone*
USLP	Santana *Santana*
UK45	Ernie (Fastest Milkman In The West) *Benny Hill*
UKLP	Imagine *John Lennon*
WEEK 3	
US45	Family Affair *Sly & The Family Stone*
USLP	There's A Riot Goin' On *Sly & The Family Stone*
UK45	Ernie (Fastest Milkman In The West) *Benny Hill*
UKLP	Four Symbols *Led Zeppelin*
WEEK 4	
US45	Brand New Key *Melanie*
USLP	There's A Riot Goin' On *Sly & The Family Stone*
UK45	Ernie (Fastest Milkman In The West) *Benny Hill*
UKLP	Four Symbols *Led Zeppelin*

IT WAS SINFIELD OR ME, SAYS FRIPP

Crimson's Robert Fripp. The band is now down to a four piece

Pete Sinfield, the founder member of King Crimson who announced his departure from the band this month, has told music journalists: 'Bob Fripp seemed to be unhappy when I complained that I was unable to do my job properly on our recent Stateside trip. The Tuesday before Christmas, he rang me up and said he couldn't continue working with me.'

Talking about the American trip, Sinfield remembered: 'When we got there, Ian (Wallace), Boz and Mel (Collins) went straight into a shop that sold Levi's and cowboy boots and bought themselves lots of American clothes so that they then looked like their audience. I refused to do this and, instead, always wore the green corduroy poet's suit.'

Asked for his comments, Robert Fripp replied: 'It was Sinfield or me, one of us had to quit. He's a very talented guy but there's a lot about Peter that I intensely dislike.'

LENNON'S NEW GROUP

John and Yoko have chosen Elephant's Memory, a New York rock outfit, to be their new band. They have taken this step because the various members of The Plastic Ono Band are now scattered around the world.

So, on the recommendation of Yippie guru Jerry Rubin, Lennon watched Elephant's Memory at a Max's Kansas City gig, then immediately invited them to work with him and Yoko.

Elephant's Memory, who have recorded for Buddah, recently received a gold disc for their contribution to the soundtrack of the movie *Midnight Cowboy*.

DRUMMER'S INJURY DELAYS BECK TOUR

A projected British tour by The Jeff Beck Group has now been postponed. Reason is that drummer Cozy Powell recently sustained a broken hand as a result of a fall while recording in Memphis and the injury has proved more serious than was at first thought.

Powell has been forbidden by a London specialist to work for another five weeks. Consideration was given to using a stand-in drummer for the tour but it has now been decided to postpone the proposed February itinerary until March.

REXMANIA!

T. Rex, on their current UK tour, are turning the musical clock back to the early Sixties. Their Boston Gliderdrome gig saw scenes of hysteria and confusion unparalleled since the days of Beatlemania.

More than 30 people fainted, and one girl had to be taken to hospital after falling from the balcony in the excitement. Extra police were drafted in to cope with a crowd of more than 5,000 who came from all parts of the country.

CHARTS

US45	Brand New Key — *Melanie*
USLP	Music — *Carole King*
UK45	Ernie (Fastest Milkman In The West) — *Benny Hill*
UKLP	Electric Warrior — *T.Rex*
WEEK 2	
US45	Brand New Key — *Melanie*
USLP	Music — *Carole King*
UK45	I'd Like To Teach The World To Sing — *New Seekers*
UKLP	Electric Warrior — *T.Rex*
WEEK 3	
US45	American Pie — *Don McLean*
USLP	Music — *Carole King*
UK45	I'd Like To Teach The World To Sing — *New Seekers*
UKLP	Electric Warrior — *T.Rex*
WEEK 4	
US45	American Pie — *Don McLean*
USLP	American Pie — *Don McLean*
UK45	I'd Like To Teach The World To Sing — *New Seekers*
UKLP	Teaser And The Firecat — *Cat Stevens*
WEEK 5	
US45	American Pie — *Don McLean*
USLP	American Pie — *Don McLean*
UK45	I'd Like To Teach The World To Sing — *New Seekers*
UKLP	Teaser And The Firecat — *Cat Stevens*

THE GRAPEVINE

- **Blues belter Big Maybelle died in Cleveland on January 23 at the age of 47.**
- **Allan Clarke, former lead singer with The Hollies, has signed with RCA as a solo act.**
- **Ian Matthews, who separated from Southern Comfort a year ago, has teamed with Andy Roberts, Dave Richards and Bob Ronga to form Plainsong.**

BEEB BAN MACCA

Macca – a legend in Nottingham's lunchtime

The BBC have banned 'Give Ireland Back To The Irish', the new Paul McCartney single, as being 'politically controversial'.

A spokesman for the Corporation explaining the ban said: 'At a time when we are striving our utmost to remain impartial, this record can only be described as inflammatory.'

Radio Luxembourg have also banned the single, but EMI Records say that they're going ahead with distribution to stores.

Meanwhile, Paul chose to break his five-year absence from live gigs with a surprise lunchtime concert, given by Wings at Nottingham University on 9 February, before an audience of around 700 disbelieving students.

BLACK OAK GO ROCK AND ROLLER-SKATE

Wheeler-dealers Black Oak Arkansas

Black Oak Arkansas have held one of the most unusual press receptions Hollywood has seen for some time.

The party was held at the Hollywood Roller Bowl and everybody spent the evening on roller skates, listening to the band play – 'everybody' included members of LA's professional skating team, The Thunderbirds, through to Phil Spector and a topless female.

The final casualty report read just one broken arm, but countless bruises.

CHARTS

US45	American Pie *Don McLean*
USLP	American Pie *Don McLean*
UK45	A Horse With No Name *America*
UKLP	Teaser And The Firecat *Cat Stevens*
WEEK 2	
US45	Let's Stay Together *Al Green*
USLP	American Pie *Don McLean*
UK45	Telegram Sam *T.Rex*
UKLP	Teaser And The Firecat *Cat Stevens*
WEEK 3	
US45	Without You *Nilsson*
USLP	American Pie *Don McLean*
UK45	Son Of My Father *Chicory Tip*
UKLP	Teaser And The Firecat *Cat Stevens*
WEEK 4	
US45	Without You *Nilsson*
USLP	American Pie *Don McLean*
UK45	Son Of My Father *Chicory Tip*
UKLP	Teaser And The Firecat *Cat Stevens*

THE GRAPEVINE

- **Chris Farlowe, who has been inactive since Colosseum split, has joined Atomic Rooster as vocalist.**
- **Jazz trumpet star Lee Morgan was shot to death in a New York club. He was 33.**
- **Following concentrated recording sessions with Humble Pie, Stevie Marriott has collapsed, suffering from nervous exhaustion.**

Stevie Marriott, diminutive Pie man feeling the strain

POCO IN UK

Poco have arrived in Britain to play a short tour that includes shows at London's Rainbow Theatre on 4 and 5 February.

They've just flown in from Copenhagen, where reporter Nick Logan said: 'Their main strength is as a band but, vocally, Richie Furay, the one remaining ex-member of Buffalo Springfield now that Jim Messina has gone, provides no-nonsense upfronts, finding support from George Grantham, while Paul Cotton has a voice that has a compelling, quivering quality, something reminiscent of Neil Young.'

It's Poco's first time out of the States.

TULL SET POEM TO MUSIC

Jethro Tull's new album 'Thick As A Brick' is scheduled for release on 18 February. The LP is based on a poem by eight-year-old Gerald Bostock of St Cleve, Lancashire. The poem won a national prize before it was withdrawn, following psychiatric reports on Bostock.

Tull have set the poem to music and the work covers both sides of the album. There are no individually titled tracks, just one continuous piece of music lasting 45 minutes.

The group recently returned from a five-week European tour and are now set to play two consecutive nights at London's Royal Albert Hall on 21 and 22 March as part of their biggest-ever British concert tour.

MARCH

BOLAN WOWS WEMBLEY

'It was a religio-sensual experience. He pulled the strings. He had the power. He used it.' So says reviewer Tony Tyler about Marc Bolan's two concerts at London's Wembley Pool on March 18.

The first T. Rex concerts to be held in Britain for six months, they attracted 20,000 fans plus Ringo Starr, who headed a film crew intent on filming the event as an Apple documentary on the Bolan phenomenon.

For Bolan, the shows proved an undoubted triumph and have been heralded as 'the concerts that changed the face of British rock'. For Ringo, it was a return to the place of former triumphs - he stood on the same stage seven years ago at an NME Pollwinners concert.

Meanwhile, in the States, T. Rex's 'Bang A Gong (Get It On)' has become a massive hit, reaching the Top 10. The single's change of name was necessary because Chase had a hit with another song called 'Get It On' during 1971, and it was decided to alter the title of the T. Rex single to avoid confusion.

John and Yoko in the queue to obtain a new US visa. It's believed that all the others in the room are actually members of the CIA!

CHARTS

US45 Without You – *Nilsson*
USLP American Pie – *Don McLean*
UK45 American Pie – *Don McLean*
UKLP Paul Simon – *Paul Simon*

WEEK 2

US45 Without You – *Nilsson*
USLP Harvest – *Neil Young*
UK45 Without You – *Nilsson*
UKLP Paul Simon – *Paul Simon*

WEEK 3

US45 Heart Of Gold – *Neil Young*
USLP Harvest – *Neil Young*
UK45 Without You – *Nilsson*
UKLP Paul Simon – *Paul Simon*

WEEK 4

US45 A Horse With No Name – *America*
USLP America – *America*
UK45 Without You – *Nilsson*
UKLP Paul Simon – *Paul Simon*

JOHN LENNON TO BECOME AN AMERICAN?

John and Yoko Lennon have bid for US citizenship in order to avoid deportation.

Earlier in the month, Lennon's visa extension was cancelled by the New York Office of Immigration, who'd granted the extension just five days earlier. The official explanation is given as John's 1968 pot bust in London, but the Lennons suspect the true reason might have something to do with their performance at Alice Tully Hall in January, given without obtaining American work permits.

There, they performed from their seats, Yoko conducting the band with the aid of an apple.

Gentle Giant have appeared as The Howling Wolves, The Road Runners and Simon Dupree and the Big Sound, and The Moles. Line-up (left to right) Kerry Minnear (keyboards, woodwinds, guitars), John Weathers (drums), Gary Green (guitar, percussion, woodwind), Ray Shulman (bass, violin, trumpet), Derek Shulman (sax, recorder, bass, vocals)

PETE TOWNSHEND

'On the last tour of the States, I smashed guitars because I was really frustrated. I couldn't get into playing all of the old stuff.'

THE GRAPEVINE

- **Gentle Giant are to be co-featured with the Hendrix movie *Jimi At Berkeley* in a forthcoming UK tour.**
- **Bill Haley has been billed as appearing in the forthcoming UK-touring Rock & Roll Revival Show, but he writes to NME: 'I know nothing about this and have signed for no such tour.' Chuck Berry, another supposedly on the tour, also expressed surprise.**

BEACH BOYS ADD TWO

The Beach Boys have become a septet with the addition of two new members. They have been joined by black musicians Blondie Chaplin (guitar) and Ricky Fatarr (drums), both of whom were previously with South African group Flame, an outfit which supported The Beach Boys on their last British dates.

MOTT HEAD ROCK CIRCUS

Ian Hunter leads the Mott in a prayer for the upcoming tour

Mott The Hoople are to head one of the most ambitious and unusual packages ever conceived for a rock group.

It will be billed as The Mott The Hoople Rock 'n' Roll Circus, and will also feature new Island group Hackensack, plus a knife-throwing act called Las Vivas, juggler Frank Paulo and – as special guest star – comedian Max Wall.

The tour plays 16 major UK venues this month, including an appearance at London's Lyceum on April 19.

A spokesman for Island Records said: 'It will be a good, solid rock show, with an element of variety to give it spice. It will be a fast, all-happening show, with the knife-throwing and juggling going on while the groups are actually performing.'

Careful with that axe, Eugene!

CHARTS

US45	A Horse With No Name	*America*
USLP	America	*America*
UK45	Without You	*Nilsson*
UKLP	Paul Simon	*Paul Simon*
	WEEK 2	
US45	A Horse With No Name	*America*
USLP	America	*America*
UK45	Without You	*Nilsson*
UKLP	Fog On The Tyne	*Lindisfarne*
	WEEK 3	
US45	The First Time Ever I Saw Your Face	*Roberta Flack*
USLP	America	*America*
UK45	Without You	*Nilsson*
UKLP	Harvest	*Neil Young*
	WEEK 4	
US45	The First Time Ever I Saw Your Face	*Roberta Flack*
USLP	America	*America*
UK45	Amazing Grace	*Royal Scots Dragoon Guards Band*
UKLP	Harvest	*Neil Young*
	WEEK 5	
US45	The First Time Ever I Saw Your Face	*Roberta Flack*
USLP	First Take	*Roberta Flack*
UK45	Amazing Grace	*Royal Scots Dragoon Guards Band*
UKLP	Harvest	*Neil Young*

NME'S FREEBIE MAXI

NME are to give away a free 12-minute maxi-single with the April 29 issue. The single includes an advance preview of tracks from The Rolling Stones' new album 'Exile On Main Street', plus the title track to the new Curved Air album, 'Phantasmagoria', and 'Blind Alley', a solid rocker from all-girl group Fanny's 'Fanny Hill'.

Also included is a Mick Jagger solo blues that will never be issued elsewhere and which is undoubtedly destined to become a collector's item.

RINGO FILMS FLEET STREET

Ringo Starr is now concentrating almost entirely on his work as a film producer and cameraman. In addition to his film on Marc Bolan and T. Rex, Ringo is simultaneously working on a documentary called *Models And Fleet Street*.

Said a spokesman: 'It's about the lives of the girls who appear in various poses on pages two and three of popular UK dailies, and how they fit into London's Fleet Street scene.'

Ringo is also set to appear in a film called *Count Down* which has a Dracula-style plot.

New Island signings Vinegar Joe

THE GRAPEVINE

- **Vinegar Joe have released their debut Island album this month; the band's line-up now stands as Robert Palmer (rhythm guitar and vocals), Elkie Brooks (vocals), Pete Gage (guitar), John Hawken (piano), Mick Shaw (bass) and John Woods (drums).**
- **Four people died during Puerto Rico's Mar y Sol Festival, which ran 1-3 April and included performances by The Allman Brothers, ELP, Black Sabbath, and The J. Geils Band.**

FAIRPORTS BUNCH UP FOR ROCK

Various Fairport Convention members past and present, plus friends, are to release an island album as The Bunch.

The album, which will be in UK shops on 21 April, is titled 'Rock On' and features 'Nadine', 'The Loco-Motion', 'Willie and The Hand Jive' and other rock classics, performed by such singers and musicians as Richard Thompson, Linda Peters, Trevor Lucas, Sandy Denny, Dave Mattacks, Tyger Hutchings and The Dundee Horns.

Given away free with the album will be a flexi-disc of 'Let There Be Drums' featuring drummer Gerry Conway.

Drummer Dave Mattacks recently quit the Fairports to join The Albion Country Band.

Ex-Fairport Richard Thompson, rocking with the folkies

STAR

MARC BOLAN

'I've written a film about a messiah who visits earth. He expects to find a race of Gods and what he finds is just a mess.'

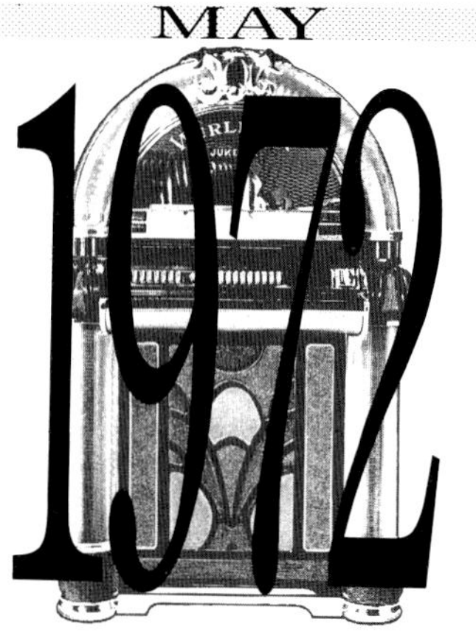

CINDY – A SUPREME NO MORE

After months of conflicting reports, it has been confirmed that Cindy Birdsong has left The Supremes.

She has been replaced in the Tamla group by Lynda Laurence, who has already been recording with the group and is featured on their new single, 'Automatically Sunshine', which gains a UK release on 16 June.

Cindy, who married two years ago, is retiring from show-business and says she wants to 'just settle down as a housewife, and raise a family.' She joined The Supremes in 1967, when she replaced Florence Ballard.

CHARTS

- US45 The First Time Ever I Saw Your Face — *Roberta Flack*
- USLP First Take — *Roberta Flack*
- UK45 Amazing Grace — *Royal Scots Dragoon Guards Band*
- UKLP Machine Head — *Deep Purple*

WEEK 2

- US45 The First Time Ever I Saw Your Face — *Roberta Flack*
- USLP First Take — *Roberta Flack*
- UK45 Amazing Grace — *Royal Scots Dragoon Guards Band*
- UKLP Machine Head — *Deep Purple*

WEEK 3

- US45 The First Time Ever I Saw Your Face — *Roberta Flack*
- USLP First Take — *Roberta Flack*
- UK45 Metal Guru — *T.Rex*
- UKLP Fog On The Tyne — *Lindisfarne*

WEEK 4

- US45 Oh Girl — *Chi-Lites*
- USLP First Take — *Roberta Flack*
- UK45 Metal Guru — *T.Rex*
- UKLP Bolan Boogie — *T.Rex*

LES HARVEY ELECTROCUTED

Stone the Crows in happier days with Les Harvey on Maggie Bell's left

Les Harvey, guitarist and co-founder of Stone The Crows, was electrocuted and killed when he came onstage to announce the first number of the group's May 3 gig at Swansea University's Coming-Out Ball, and touched a faultily connected mike-stand.

Thrown in the air by the shock, Harvey landed with his guitar in contact with the mike-stand, and other members of the group received shocks as they tried to pull him clear.

Somebody eventually managed to kick the guitar clear, but it was too late and mouth-to-mouth respiration failed to resuscitate the young Scot.

Maggie Bell, Stone The Crows vocalist, who helped Harvey found the group two years ago, was taken to a local hospital and placed under heavy sedation.

BLUESMAN DAVIS DIES

Blues, ragtime and gospel performer the Rev. 'Blind' Gary Davis died on May 5, age 76.

An influence on Ry Cooder and Taj Mahal, he began as a street singer, then became a gospel preacher working camp meetings and country churches. He found national fame via a Newport Festival performance in 1964.

South Carolina's 'Blind' Gary Davis

GIANTS OF TOMORROW

NME is to sponsor a Giants of Tomorrow marquee at the massive Great Western Express Lincoln Festival on May 26-9.

Twenty up-and-coming acts will appear in the tent, the current list including: Budgie, Mark Ashton, Rab Noakes, Walrus, Skin Alley, Tea & Sympathy, Capability Brown, Bitch, Byzantium, Akido, Sleaze Band, John Martyn, Patto, Good Habit, Smith Perkins & Smith, Demick & Armstrong, Warhorse, Gnidrolog, Spreadeagle and Morgan.

Noddy, the singer you can swear by

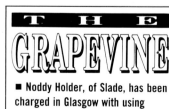

- **Noddy Holder, of Slade, has been charged in Glasgow with using obscene language during the group's set at Green's Playhouse; when cautioned and asked if he had anything to say, Noddy reportedly replied, 'It's a load of old ******'**
- **John Lennon, interviewed on the Dick Cavett show, has claimed that his phone is being tapped by US Security authorities.**

FILLMORE FILM PREMIERED

Fillmore, a documentary about the final days at Bill Graham's Fillmore East, San Francisco, was premiered in New York on May 16. Performers include Santana, Grateful Dead, Quicksilver Messenger Service, Hot Tuna, It's A Beautiful Day, Boz Scaggs, Elvin Bishop Group, and Jefferson Airplane.

Creedence Clearwater Revival don't appear in the film because they failed to approve release of their segment.

BOLAN TO QUIT TOURING?

With T. Rex fan fever reaching unprecedented heights, Marc Bolan has announced that he may be forced to give up gigging in Britain after one more farewell tour of the country.

Speaking after hysterical scenes during T. Rex's Manchester concert, Bolan said: 'It's becoming almost impossible. One more tour, I should think, and that'll be the last.'

During the sell-out show, one fan suffered a broken jaw and dozens of seats were smashed to pieces as members of the audience dashed to reach the front stage. Offstage, Bolan has now been forced to become something of a recluse, stating: 'I haven't been out of my house for two weeks. It's just like living in a goldfish bowl.'

Fans now await the arrival of the new T. Rex album, 'The Slider', in mid-July.

Bolan – if he becomes too exhausted will he seek help from the National Elf Service?

CHARTS

Week	Chart	Title	Artist
	US45	I'll Take You There	*Staple Singers*
	USLP	Thick As A Brick	*Jethro Tull*
	UK45	Metal Guru	*T.Rex*
	UKLP	Bolan Boogie	*T.Rex*
WEEK 2	US45	The Candy Man	*Sammy Davis Jr.*
	USLP	Thick As A Brick	*Jethro Tull*
	UK45	Metal Guru	*T.Rex*
	UKLP	Bolan Boogie	*T.Rex*
WEEK 3	US45	The Candy Man	*Sammy Davis Jr.*
	USLP	Exile On Main Street	*Rolling Stones*
	UK45	Vincent	*Don McLean*
	UKLP	Exile On Main Street	*Rolling Stones*
WEEK 4	US45	The Candy Man	*Sammy Davis Jr.*
	USLP	Exile On Main Street	*Rolling Stones*
	UK45	Vincent	*Don McLean*
	UKLP	Exile On Main Street	*Rolling Stones*

SOLO BELL

Maggie Bell goes into the studio next month to cut her own solo album. She will be supported by members of Stone The Crows plus various well-known guests.

Meanwhile, Stone The Crows have named Les Harvey's replacement. He is 20-year-old Scottish guitarist Jim McCulloch who, until recently, let his own band. The first gig by the new Stone The Crows line-up will be at Birmingham University on June 23.

THE GRAPEVINE

- **Dion & The Belmonts reunited for a Madison Square Garden show on June 2; the event was recorded for a possible forthcoming album.**
- **CBS's John Hammond, who discovered Billie Holiday, Count Basie and Bob Dylan, has signed highly rated New Jersey singer Bruce Springsteen to the label.**
- **The Tallahatchie Bridge, made famous by Bobbie Gentry in her 'Ode To Billy Joe', has collapsed.**

Maggie Bell: "I've always wanted to work on my own album. Not just rock but maybe also using strings"

ELVIS PLAYS NEW YORK – AT LAST!

Elvis Presley played his first-ever concerts in New York at Madison Square Gardens on June 9-11, and drew more than 80,000 people, none of whom received complimentary tickets – not even the mayor!

John Lennon and Bob Dylan found themselves sitting to the rear of the arena, while George Harrison could only obtain a seat in the balcony.

A billboard welcoming the King to New York was hung in Times Square and the Hilton hosted a Presley press conference that lasted just 20 minutes.

RCA recorded the evening show on June 10 for immediate album release.

DOWNPOUR AT THE PALACE

Though 16,000 fans were drenched at London's Crystal Palace Bowl Garden Party on Saturday, June 3, the event was still a musical success. The show, hosted by Keith Moon and opened by Sha Na Na, stayed afloat until Richie Havens' set, when the rain commenced and then never ceased.

A 90-minute change-over between Havens and The Beach Boys failed to help matters and Melanie was adjudged boring, while David Blue pulled out.

But Joe Cocker and The Chris Stainton All-Stars were acclaimed as marvellous – Cocker providing a fine set including 'St James Infirmary', 'The Letter' and 'Feelin' Alright'.

STAR QUOTE

DON McLEAN

'People ask me if I tended to leave my lyrics open to ambiguity – and that bores me because I wanted to say a hundred things with each verse and not just one thing.'

American pieman Don McLean

HAWKWIND MOVE UP

Hawkwind, who have taken a major step towards popular acceptance through the entry of 'Silver Machine' into the UK singles charts, are to put on a six-hour party at the London Rainbow next month.

Long dismissed as a lower division U.K. band, despite a reputation as crowd pleasers, Hawkwind are also being lined-up for their first major UK tour.

CHARTS

Chart	Title	Artist
US45	Song Sung Blue	*Neil Diamond*
USLP	Exile On Main Street	*Rolling Stones*
UK45	Vincent	*Don McLean*
UKLP	American Pie	*Don McLean*
	WEEK 2	
US45	Lean On Me	*Bill Withers*
USLP	Exile On Main Street	*Rolling Stones*
UK45	Take Me Bak Ome	*Slade*
UKLP	American Pie	*Don McLean*
	WEEK 3	
US45	Lean On Me	*Bill Withers*
USLP	Honky Chateau	*Elton John*
UK45	Puppy Love	*Donny Osmond*
UKLP	20 Dynamic Hits	*Various*
	WEEK 4	
US45	Lean On Me	*Bill Withers*
USLP	Honky Chateau	*Elton John*
UK45	Puppy Love	*Donny Osmond*
UKLP	American Pie	*Don McLean*
	WEEK 5	
US45	Alone Again (Naturally)	*Gilbert O'Sullivan*
USLP	Honky Chateau	*Elton John*
UK45	Puppy Love	*Donny Osmond*
UKLP	Greatest Hits	*Simon And Garfunkel*

EVERYBODY QUITS

Roy Wood – moving on

Roy Wood has quit the Electric Light Orchestra, and leadership of the group will be taken over by Jeff Lynne, while Hookfoot bassist and founder member Dave Glover has left the group to be replaced by Fred Gandi, formerly of Bluesology. Additionally, John Wetton is to leave Family because of what are described as 'clashes in musical policy'.

The news also comes that Andy Fraser has walked out on Free and will not be accompanying the band on their Japanese tour, which is due to begin late this month.

Fraser has been replaced in the band by Japanese bassist Tetsu, and Free, at the same time, have been augmented by the inclusion of Texan keyboardsman John Bundrick.

Announcing the changes, a spokesman added: 'Free return to Britain on 1 August, when a decision will be taken as to whether the new members remain with the band'.

Fraser – free at last?

HAIR CLOSES ON BROADWAY

The UK cast of Hair

Hair, the tribal-rock musical, closed on Broadway on 1 July after 1,729 performances. The show first opened at the off-Broadway Public Theatre in October 1967, then moved on to play the Cheetah nightclub before transferring to the Biltmore Theater.

During its run, Diane Keaton and Melba Moore were among its leads, while the tally of hit songs included 'Aquarius', 'Let The Sun Shine In', 'Ain't Got No' and 'Good Morning Sunshine'.

The British edition of the show, at London's Shaftesbury Theatre, which opened in September 1968, continues to pull audiences.

- **Mott The Hoople's 'All The Young Dudes', written and produced by David Bowie, has been released by UK CBS.**
- **Paul McCartney and Wings have embarked on a 26-date European tour aboard a double-decker London bus.**
- **Rolling Stones' Jagger and Richards arrested in Warwick, Rhode Island, on charges of obstructing the police after a fracas with a news photographer.**

THE VANDELLAS DISBAND

Martha Reeves, who has fronted The Vandellas for more than ten years, has disbanded the group and will, henceforth, pursue a solo career.

This follows the departure from the group of Sandra Tilley, who has married and is retiring from the business. Said Martha: 'Over the years, I have had five different girls in the Vandellas, and the thought of finding yet another one, made me decide to go it alone.'

Martha is to make her first solo appearance this month, on Smokey Robinson's farewell tour with The Miracles. The other remaining Vandella, Martha's sister, Lois Reeves, is to join a new group, Quiet Elegance.

Vandellas, going it alone

ROCK 'N' ROLL WEMBLEY

A rock 'n' roll revival extravaganza takes place at London's Wembley Empire Stadium on 5 August, the line-up including Chuck Berry, Little Richard, Jerry Lee Lewis, Bill Haley, Emile Ford, Heinz and Dr Feelgood, Billy Fury, Gary Glitter, Wizzard and Bo Diddley, who was recently in Kansas City, jamming with Elephant's Memory.

The Drifters, Platters and Coasters, who were originally billed, will not now take part because the promoters have been threatened with legal action over the authenticity of these groups.

'But', claimed promoters Ron and Ray Foulk, 'our main problem is that we are obliged to protect the Wembley turf by laying down coconut matting, and we're having difficulty in obtaining sufficient quantities.'

ALICE IN RECORD-LAND

Promoting the UK success of 'Schools Out', Alice poses with models dressed as traditional English schoolgirls

Alice Cooper's hit 'School's Out' – now No. 1 in Britain, with the album in the Top 5 – has become the biggest-selling record in the history of Warner Brothers.

Said a record company spokesman in the States: 'The reaction here is fantastic. Alice has been breaking records all over the country, and the latest was at Dillon Stadium, Connecticut, at which he smashed the Stones' gross for the same venue.'

Alice shortly ends a major tour of the USA and then begins work on a new album, using the band's own 16-track mobile, parked in the grounds of a 40-room Connecticut mansion.

BOWIE'S BIG SELL-OUT

David Bowie's London Rainbow gigs on 19 and 20 August – part of a tour promoting his latest album 'The Rise And Fall Of Ziggy Stardust And The Spiders From Mars' – have completely sold out.

Bowie now plays Bristol Locarno (27) and Bournemouth Starkers (31) before moving on to a string of dates in September, one concert being scheduled for the opening date of the 3,000 seater Manchester Hard Rock, Britain's first purpose-built rock arena.

Bowie – sell-out for Ziggy

CHARTS

Chart	Title	Artist
US45	Alone Again (Naturally)	*Gilbert O'Sullivan*
USLP	Honky Chateau	*Elton John*
UK45	Puppy Love	*Donny Osmond*
UKLP	Greatest Hits	*Simon And Garfunkel*
WEEK 2		
US45	Alone Again (Naturally)	*Gilbert O'Sullivan*
USLP	Honky Chateau	*Elton John*
UK45	School's Out	*Alice Cooper*
UKLP	Greatest Hits	*Simon And Garfunkel*
WEEK 3		
US45	Alone Again (Naturally)	*Gilbert O'Sullivan*
USLP	Chicago V	*Chicago*
UK45	School's Out	*Alice Cooper*
UKLP	Never A Dull Moment	*Rod Stewart*
WEEK 4		
US45	Brandy (You're A Fine Girl)	*Looking Glass*
USLP	Chicago V	*Chicago*
UK45	School's Out	*Alice Cooper*
UKLP	Never A Dull Moment	*Rod Stewart*

IAN MACLAGAN

Faces keyboardist

'The Faces are a rock 'n' roll band but Rod's a bit of a folkie at heart.'

THE GRAPEVINE

- **McCartney Wings trek has been marred by drug arrests of Paul, Linda and drummer Denny Seiwell.**
- **Tear gas and police truncheons floored Grace Slick and Paul Kantner at 'Airplane gig in Akron, Ohio.**
- **U.K. newcomer Gilbert O'Sullivan has a first gold disc for 'Alone Again (Naturally)'.**

WATTSTAX FILMED

Luther Ingram in 'Wattstax'

The Stax Organization have followed in the footsteps of Tamla Motown by making a full-length feature film. In association with producer David Wolper, Stax filmed the all-star 'Wattstax '72' charity concert, which was staged last month at Los Angeles' Memorial Coliseum.

The six-hour show featured gospel, spiritual and soul roots, the very essence of black music and the Stax-Memphis way of things and featured such acts as The Dramatics, Little Milton, Johnny Taylor, Albert King, Frederick Knight, Isaac Hayes, Eddie Floyd, Rufus & Carla Thomas, Kim Weston, The Bar-Kays and others.

A two hour film should be on cinema screens by the end of the year.

LENNON'S THE GREATEST

John Lennon has been voted The World's Greatest Vocalist, ahead of Free's Paul Rodgers, in this year's NME Musicians' poll.

The nominations were diverse – everything from Forties crooner Vera Lynn to blues guitarist Albert King! – but the final results were: 1 John Lennon, 2 Paul Rodgers, 3 Bob Dylan, 4 Maggie Bell/Mick Jagger (equal), 6 Ray Charles/Joni Mitchell (equal), 8 Stevie Wonder, 9 Joe Cocker, 10 Rod Stewart, 11 Steven Stills, 12 Billie Holiday/Aretha Franklin (equal), 14 Elton John, 15 David Bowie/Randy Newman/Paul McCartney/Van Morrison (equal).

Elton John listed Mick Jagger, Aretha Franklin and Dusty Springfield as his choices, while Rod Stewart opted for Maggie Bell, Paul Rodgers and Labi Siffre, and Marc Bolan went for Elton John, John Lennon and Al Green.

Among the many others who voted were Bryan Ferry, Ian Hunter, Rick Nelson, Ozzy Osbourne, Lou Reed, Rick Danko, Brian Wilson, Lulu, Iggy Pop and Robert Plant.

CHARTS

- US45 Brandy (You're A Fine Girl) *Looking Glass*
- USLP Chicago V *Chicago*
- UK45 You Wear It Well *Rod Stewart*
- UKLP Never A Dull Moment *Rod Stewart*

WEEK 2

- US45 Alone Again (Naturally) *Gilbert O'Sullivan*
- USLP Chicago V *Chicago*
- UK45 You Wear It Well *Rod Stewart*
- UKLP Never A Dull Moment *Rod Stewart*

WEEK 3

- US45 Black & White *Three Dog Night*
- USLP Chicago V *Chicago*
- UK45 Mama Weer All Crazee Now *Slade*
- UKLP Never A Dull Moment *Rod Stewart*

WEEK 4

- US45 Baby Don't Get Hooked On Me *Mac Davis*
- USLP Chicago V *Chicago*
- UK45 Mama Weer All Crazee Now *Slade*
- UKLP Greatest Hits *Simon And Garfunkel*

WEEK 5

- US45 Baby Don't Get Hooked On Me *Mac Davis*
- USLP Chicago V *Chicago*
- UK45 Children Of The Revolution *T.Rex*
- UKLP Never A Dull Moment *Rod Stewart*

VINEGAR JOE BECOME SEVEN-PIECE

Vinegar Joe are now a seven-piece unit following two personnel changes and the addition of Jim Mullen from Brian Auger's Oblivion Express.

Steve York rejoins the band from Climax, replacing Nic South. And Mike Deacon, formerly with Juicy Lucy and The Greatest Show On Earth, takes over from John Hawken on piano.

The new line-up has been recording at London's Olympic Studios with a view to a new album release in October.

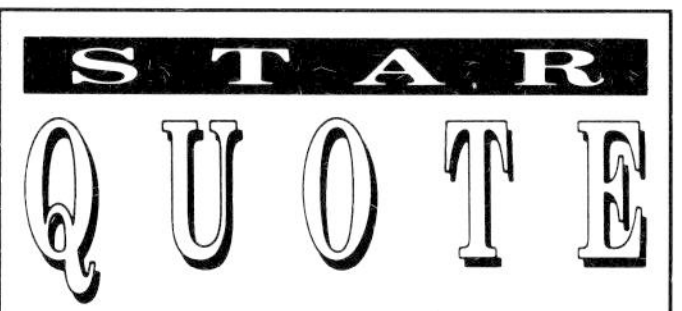

STAR QUOTE

NICK TURNER

of Hawkwind

'We wanted to play the Windsor Sex Olympics but only half the band turned up.'

REGGAE MOVIE OPENS

Jamaica's first major movie, *The Harder They Come*, makes its debut at London's Notting Hill Gaumont on September 1, where it plays for three weeks.

Directed by Perry Henzell, the film stars Jimmy Cliff as a reggae singer who gets involved in music business rip-offs and a fight against authority. Among those heard on the film's soundtrack are Desmond Dekker, The Maytals, The Melodians, The Slickers, and Cliff himself.

A soundtrack album is available through Island Records, who financed the movie.

Movie star Jimmy

The one-time Steven Georgiou

THE GRAPEVINE

- **Pete Townshend's 'Who Came First' album is scheduled for UK release by Track Records on September 29.**
- **The Bee Gees, who were to have made a horror movie called *Castle X* in Yugoslavia, have now shelved the project.**
- **Cat Stevens opens his latest US tour on 29 September at LA's Shrine Auditorium. Supporting act is Ramblin' Jack Elliott.**

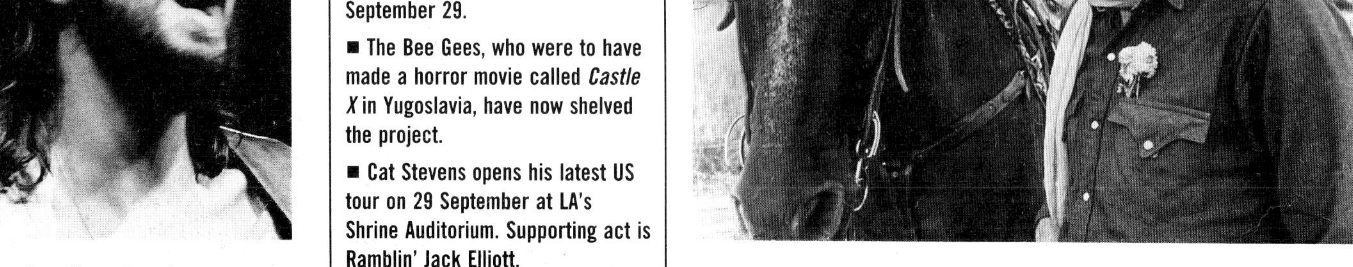

Ramblin' Jack – 'And I'm really Elliott Charles Adnopoz!'

MOODY MANIA IN THE STATES

The Moody Blues have suddenly and unexpectedly been swept to a new peak of acclaim in the States on the strength of their re-promoted 1967 album, 'Days Of Future Passed', and the single, 'Nights In White Satin'.

Both are now in the Top 10 of the respective US charts and are challenging for No. 1 positions.

Meanwhile, the band's opening American tour date, at Hampton Rhodes coliseum, was a double sell-out, as was their double concert at New York's Madison Square Garden. The fastest sale was at Boston Gardens, where 19,000 tickets went in just 90 minutes.

CHARTS

Chart	Title	Artist
US45	Baby Don't Get Hooked On Me	*Mac Davis*
USLP	Chicago V	*Chicago*
UK45	How Can I Be Sure	*David Cassidy*
UKLP	Never A Dull Moment	*Rod Stewart*
WEEK 2		
US45	Ben	*Michael Jackson*
USLP	Chicago V	*Chicago*
UK45	Mouldy Old Dough	*Lieutenant Pigeon*
UKLP	Never A Dull Moment	*Rod Stewart*
WEEK 3		
US45	My Ding-A-Ling	*Chuck Berry*
USLP	Superfly	*Soundtrack/Curtis Mayfield*
UK45	Mouldy Old Dough	*Lieutenant Pigeon*
UKLP	Greatest Hits	*Simon And Garfunkel*
WEEK 4		
US45	My Ding-A-Ling	*Chuck Berry*
USLP	Superfly	*Soundtrack/Curtis Mayfield*
UK45	Mouldy Old Dough	*Lieutenant Pigeon*
UKLP	Greatest Hits	*Simon And Garfunkel*

STAR QUOTE

DAVID CASSIDY

'I'm exploited by people who put me on the back of cereal boxes. I asked my housekeeper to go and buy a certain kind of cereal and when she came home, there was huge picture of me on the back. I can't even eat breakfast without seeing my face.'

Cassidy croons

MICHAEL JACKSON'S RATTY HIT

British songwriter Don Black, who penned the words to Lulu's 'To Sir With Love' – a US No. 1 in 1967 – also provided the lyric to 'Ben', the Michael Jackson single which went to the top of the American charts on October 14.

Black, who wrote the song with composer Walter Scharf for the movie about an ailing boy who befriends a pack of rats, was the man who suggested that Michael Jackson provided the vocal.

'He's quite an animal lover,' claims Black. 'Very sensitive. He enjoys anything that crawls or flies.'

THE GRAPEVINE

- **Jon Mark, leader of Mark-Almond, has been involved in an accident in Hawaii and lost most of his left-hand ring finger.**
- **Phil Seaman, a great jazz drummer, and the man who taught Ginger Baker, has died.**
- **David Essex is leaving the London production of *Godspell* to star in the film *That'll Be The Day*, with Ringo Starr, Billy Fury and Keith Moon.**

McCARTNEY AND WINGS FOR BOND MOVIE

Paul McCartney is writing some – and possibly all – of the music for the next James Bond movie, *Live And Let Die*, which has just gone into production in America, with Roger Moore taking over the 007 role from Sean Connery.

The exact extent of McCartney's contribution to the film hasn't yet been determined, but he has already penned the title theme and recorded it for the movie soundtrack with his group, Wings.

COCKER VICTIMIZED IN OZ

Joe Cocker and The Chris Stainton Band headed back to LA after leaving Australia on October 21, where they had played two Melbourne concerts. But three concerts had to be missed following drugs charges on which Cocker was convicted and which became 'a political issue with the Australian elections close at hand.'

Cocker has now been invited to appeal against the court's decision convicting him of drug offences and will be able to apply for re-entry into Australia on December 2 – after that country's general election.

Cocker – done down-under

CREEDENCE SPLIT

Creedence Clearwater Revival have finally called it a day after a career that's encompassed seven Top 10 US hits.

The band has been falling apart for some time now and guitarist Tom Fogerty left in January 1971, just after the release of CCR's fifth album 'Pendulum'. Since his departure, the group have struggled on as a trio.

Creedence – And once there was four. Tom Fogerty (left) quit the group in 1971. Now his brother John (second right) and the others are moving on

POMPEII FLOYD

A remarkable film of Pink Floyd performing in the ruins of Pompeii, in southern Italy, is to have its official British premiere on November 25.

The movie, a joint French/German/Belgian production, directed by Adrian Maben and titled *Pink Floyd At Pompeii*, was shot in the old Roman open-air amphitheatre, both by day and night.

The music performed includes 'Echoes', 'Careful With That Axe, Eugene', 'A Saucerful Of Secrets', 'One Of These Days I'm Gonna Cut You Into Little Pieces', 'Set The Controls For The Heart Of The Sun', 'Mademoiselle Nobs' and 'Dark Side Of The Moon'.

Previewed at this year's Edinburgh Film Festival, where it was greeted with considerable acclaim, it is now hopefully destined for general release.

Pink Floyd perform pomp rock of their own kind with an extravaganza from the ruins of Pompeii

CHARTS

US45	I Can See Clearly Now / *Johnny Nash*
USLP	Superfly / *Soundtrack/Curtis Mayfield*
UK45	Mouldy Old Dough / *Lieutenant Pigeon*
UKLP	Greatest Hits / *Simon And Garfunkel*
WEEK 2	
US45	I Can See Clearly Now / *Johnny Nash*
USLP	Superfly / *Soundtrack/Curtis Mayfield*
UK45	Clair / *Gilbert O'Sullivan*
UKLP	Greatest Hits / *Simon And Garfunkel*
WEEK 3	
US45	I Can See Clearly Now / *Johnny Nash*
USLP	Catch Bull At Four / *Cat Stevens*
UK45	Clair / *Gilbert O'Sullivan*
UKLP	Greatest Hits / *Simon And Garfunkel*
WEEK 4	
US45	I Can See Clearly Now / *Johnny Nash*
USLP	Catch Bull At Four / *Cat Stevens*
UK45	My Ding-A-Ling / *Chuck Berry*
UKLP	Back To Front / *Gilbert O'Sullivan*

THE GRAPEVINE

- **Andy Fraser and Chris Spedding have formed a new band, Sharks.**
- **Berry Oakley, bassist and vocalist with the Allman Brothers, killed in bike accident.**
- **Slade's Dave Hill has had his left leg put in plaster after his six-inch high heels caused him to fall during a Liverpool Stadium gig, sustaining a broken ankle.**

ALL-STAR TOMMY FOR RAINBOW

Following the refusal of London's Royal Albert Hall to allow an all-star production of *Tommy* to be staged there, co-producer Lou Reizner has announced that he will now be presenting the show at the Rainbow Theatre on December 9.

An impressive list of guest stars has been lined-up for this event, headed by Ringo Starr, Rod Stewart, Richard Harris and Richie Havens. Also taking part are Maggie Bell, Sandy Denny, Steve Winwood and Graham Bell, plus all four members of The Who.

The work is being performed by the London Symphony Orchestra, and the star names are appearing as the LSO's guests. The orchestra initially booked the Albert Hall, only to have the booking rejected when the list of guests was seen!

Jim'n'Carly get wed

CARLY BECOMES MRS TAYLOR

Carly Simon became Mrs James Taylor on November 2, the wedding ceremony being held in Carly's Manhatten apartment.

Taylor announced the splice later in the day at a Radio City Music Hall concert where he claimed: 'I don't know whether to be more nervous about the concert, or the marriage!'

CHUCK IN ROYALTY ROW

A major royalty row has blown up between Chess Records and Coventry's Lanchester Polytechnic College, where Chuck Berry recorded his 'My Ding-A-Ling'.

The track was recorded live at the college's Arts Festival last winter, and the festival committee is now claiming that a percentage of the royalties is due to them from sales of the single, which has sold nearly two million copies throughout the world.

The Festival incurred a £12,000 ($24,000) loss but this would be wiped out by the royalties to which the Polytechnic feels it is entitled. Chess, however, deny ever having made any royalty agreement with Lanchester.

Berry: royalty wrangle

DIANA FILM HONOUR

Diana Ross in her role as Billie Holliday, which despite acclaim, did not meet with universal approval

Diana Ross, tipped for an Academy Award, collected the Actress Of The Year award in the highly respected NAACP Annual Image Awards presentation at the Hollywood Palladium.

The Awards proved a landslide for the Tamla-Motown organisation, with five of their acts winning categories.

These were: Jackson 5 (Male Vocal Group Of The Year), Stevie Wonder (Producer Of The Year for his 'Music Of My Mind' album); The Supremes (Female Vocal Group Of The Year), The Temptations (Album Of The Year with 'All Directions') and Nicholas Ashford and Valerie Simpson (Writers Of The Year).

THE GRAPEVINE

- **James Brown arrested after a Knoxville, Tennessee show and charged with disorderly conduct.**
- **It's been announced that the live double-album by The Rolling Stones and Stevie Wonder, recorded when they toured together in America, is now unlikely to be released due to contractual difficulties.**
- **Roberta Flack, guitarist Cornell Dupree and bassist Jerry Jemon have been slightly injured in a Manhattan car accident.**

Roberta – auto incident

NO BAN ON BERRY, BUT MACC AXED

Self-styled protector of British public morals, Mrs Mary Whitehouse, has lashed out at Chuck Berry's No. 1 hit 'My Ding A Ling'. She is demanding a UK TV and radio ban on the record because, she says, the BBC is using it 'as a vehicle for mass child molestation'.

The BBC say that they will carry on playing the record though, inconsistently, they have slapped a ban on 'Hi Hi Hi', the new single from Paul McCartney's Wings. They insist that the sexual implications of this song are too blatant and so the record has become the second Wings single to be banned this year – the other being 'Give Ireland Back To The Irish'.

Press reports had suggested that 'Hi Hi Hi' was banned because of drug assocations, but a BBC press officer explained that the ban had nothing to do with drugs, but was primarily concerned with the part of the lyric that refers to lying on a bed and getting out 'a body gun'.

Apparently 'My Ding A Ling' escapes any ban because 'it is in the tradition of the music hall.'

MARC MOVIE GETS CRITICS NO-NO

The Marc Bolan film *Born To Boogie*, which premiered at London's Brewer Street Oscar One on December 14, has been described by one *NME* writer as 'bad, atrocious, cheap, pretentious, narcissistic and noisy.'

As a rock'n'roll film it's one of those total-personality efforts – as opposed to the *Mad Dogs And Englishmen* syndrome of boring documentaries.

Bolan claims that this is a film with surrealistic overtones. Which means that it contains some embarrassing episodes which would be Fellini-esque, except that it would be an insult to use the name of that director in the context of this film.

Perhaps the only really good scene in the film is when T. Rex perform 'Tutti Frutti' with Ringo Starr on drums and Elton John playing piano. But mainly it's Marc, Marc and more Marc.

CHARTS

US45	Papa Was A Rolling Stone *Temptations*
USLP	Catch Bull At Four *Cat Stevens*
UK45	My Ding-A-Ling *Chuck Berry*
UKLP	Greatest Hits *Simon And Garfunkel*
WEEK 2	
US45	I Am Woman *Helen Reddy*
USLP	Seventh Sojourn *Moody Blues*
UK45	My Ding-A-Ling *Chuck Berry*
UKLP	Back To Front *Gilbert O'Sullivan*
WEEK 3	
US45	Me & Mrs. Jones *Billy Paul*
USLP	Seventh Sojourn *Moody Blues*
UK45	Gudbuy 'Jane *Slade*
UKLP	Back To Front *Gilbert O'Sullivan*
WEEK 4	
US45	Me & Mrs. Jones *Billy Paul*
USLP	Seventh Sojourn *Moody Blues*
UK45	Long-Haired Lover From Liverpool *Little Jimmy Osmond*
UKLP	Back To Front *Gilbert O'Sullivan*
WEEK 5	
US45	Me & Mrs. Jones *Billy Paul*
USLP	Seventh Sojourn *Moody Blues*
UK45	Long-Haired Lover From Liverpool *Little Jimmy Osmond*
UKLP	Slayed *Slade*

1973

CHARTS

US45	You're So Vain *Carly Simon*
USLP	Seventh Sojourn *Moody Blues*
UK45	Long-Haired Lover From Liverpool *Little Jimmy Osmond*
UKLP	Slayed *Slade*
WEEK 2	
US45	You're So Vain *Carly Simon*
USLP	No Secrets *Carly Simon*
UK45	Long-Haired Lover From Liverpool *Little Jimmy Osmond*
UKLP	Slayed *Slade*
WEEK 3	
US45	You're So Vain *Carly Simon*
USLP	No Secrets *Carly Simon*
UK45	The Jean Genie *David Bowie*
UKLP	Slayed *Slade*
WEEK 4	
US45	Superstition *Stevie Wonder*
USLP	No Secrets *Carly Simon*
UK45	Blockbuster *Sweet*
UKLP	Slayed *Slade*

AUSTRALIA OKAYS THE STONES

Stones to roll down under

The Rolling Stones, who open their Far East tour with concerts in Honolulu this month, will be admitted to Australia after all.

The band's visit was in jeopardy because of an outstanding warrant the French police had issued against Keith Richards on a drugs charge.

However, the Australian Government have announced that they have no objection to the tour, though Japan has banned The Stones.

It had originally been planned for the band to be in Japan for five days, but they'll now bypass that country and resume touring in Hong Kong on February 5.

Prior to leaving for their Far East dates, the Stones managed to arrange a last-minute charity concert at Los Angeles Forum on January 18, to aid victims of the recent Nicaraguan earthquake disaster. The resulting concert raised a reported $200,000.

STAR QUOTE

DAVID BOWIE

'I enjoy being on a tightrope. It gives me the excitement that I need in life.'

JERRY LEE RECORDS IN BRITAIN

An impressive line-up of top-flight British musicians has been assembled to support Jerry Lee Lewis on the album he is recording in London. So far confirmed are Peter Frampton, Rory Gallagher, Albert Lee, Tony Ashton, Gary Wright, Alvin Lee, Chas Hodges and Kenny Jones.

Lewis arrived in London on January 5 for his first-ever UK sessions, which are being produced by Steve Rowland. The fare will consist of mainly old rock classics.

The Killer goes UK

ELTON IN ARGUMENT

Elton John has slammed his own management and recording company, claiming that DJM did not want his new single, 'Daniel', to be released.

The song is a track from his upcoming album 'Don't Shoot Me, I'm Only The Piano Player', as was his last hit single 'Crocodile Rock'.

Commented Elton: 'Dick James said he didn't want another single released to detract from the sales of the next album. So I've more or less forced him to put it out – he has disowned it. I'm having to pay for all the advertising, but he says he'll pay for the ads if the single makes the UK Top 10. Isn't that nice?'

Elton – single disowned

THE GRAPEVINE

- **Neil Young stopped a New York concert and announced 'Peace has come' after learning of the ceasefire in Vietnam.**
- **The live double-album of Elvis Presley's concert in Hawaii on January 14 is to be rush released all over the world. Advance orders of over one million copies have already been received.**
- **The Sutherland Brothers and Quiver have joined forces.**

PAUL AND LINDA'S ZOO GANG

Paul & Linda McCartney have been signed to write the music for an ambitious new British TV series, *Zoo Gang*, which goes into production in March.

The six one-hour shows, which star John Mills, Brian Keith, Lili Palmer and Barry Morse, are based upon the Paul Gallico book of the same name. This will be the McCartneys' first venture into TV theme music.

MIDLER FLIES IN

Bette Midler, whose 'Do You Want To Dance' recently entered the US Top 20, arrived in London to talk about herself and her debut album.

'I'm not worried about my relationship with decadence, simply because I transcend it,' she told reporters. 'I'm at once a part of it and not a part of it. For instance, there are some performers who are right in there, in the centre of it.

'I'm thinking more of Lou Reed in this sphere of decadence. The same would hold true of David Bowie. I've never seen him performing live, but I've heard his albums.'

Miss Midler, who has just appeared on the cover of *Rolling Stone* magazine, made her name performing to audiences at The Continental Baths, a New York club frequented by homosexuals.

CHARTS

US45	Crocodile Rock *Elton John*
USLP	No Secrets *Carly Simon*
UK45	Blockbuster *Sweet*
UKLP	Slayed *Slade*
WEEK 2	
US45	Crocodile Rock *Elton John*
USLP	No Secrets *Carly Simon*
UK45	Blockbuster *Sweet*
UKLP	Don't Shoot Me, I'm Only The Piano Player *Elton John*
WEEK 3	
US45	Crocodile Rock *Elton John*
USLP	The World Is A Ghetto *War*
UK45	Blockbuster *Sweet*
UKLP	Don't Shoot Me, I'm Only The Piano Player *Elton John*
WEEK 4	
US45	Killing Me Softly With His Song *Roberta Flack*
USLP	The World Is A Ghetto *War*
UK45	Part Of The Union *Strawbs*
UKLP	Don't Shoot Me, I'm Only The Piano Player *Elton John*

RICK AND HANK

Rick Wakeman is releasing 'Six Wives Of Henry VIII', a concept album on which the keyboard wizard employed three drummers, three guitarists, four bass players and a six-girl choir.

Wakeman wrote the music for the album after reading *The Private Life Of Henry VIII* on a plane to Chicago. He actually began recording the project back in November 1971 and has since slotted sessions in between US tours with Yes, spending some eight months in the studio.

Asked if he would play concerts to promote the work, Wakeman said: 'I think that would be wrong. I want people to buy the album for the right reasons, not because it's forced upon them.'

Rick previewed the album on BBC TV's *Old Grey Whistle Test* show during January.

Ex-strawb Wakeman

STRAWBS SINGLE 'HARMFUL'

The Strawbs' current UK hit 'Part Of The Union' has been termed generally harmful by Conservative member of Parliament Harold Soref. But Britain's trades union leaders have come out in strong support of the record and have even launched a poster campaign throughout the country urging young people to join a union.

As a result, political controversy seems to be brewing, Soref complaining to the BBC about the record being played on the air.

He claims that it misrepresents the unions and its tone could lead to industrial troubles. However, a Conservative Party headquarters spokesman offered a bland 'no comment'.

The Strawbs – (from left) John Ford, Richard Hudson, Dave Lambert, Blue Weaver and Dave Cousins

THE GRAPEVINE

- Max Yasgur, whose farm housed the 1969 Woodstock Festival, died on 8 February at the age of 53.
- Emerson, Lake & Palmer are to form their own label, Manticore.
- German band Saturnalia have released what is claimed to be the world's first 3D picture disc.
- David Bowie collapsed from exhaustion at the end of a Valentine's Day show in New York.

MARCH

OSMONDS IN LONDON

The Osmonds, in London for a press conference and a *Top of the Pops* TV appearance, say that Donny's voice is changing. Asked if the public had yet heard Donny's new voice, Alan Osmond replied, 'I guess "Puppy Love" is pretty near it.'

Asked why the two eldest Osmonds aren't bopping, Alan explained: 'They're both married now and they have some kids. I should explain that our two older brothers are hard of hearing. That kind of kept them from being in show business.'

Other points included the fact that the Osmonds don't even drink Coca Cola and that, though they played at a Nixon rally, they feel politics should not be brought into music.

Meanwhile, Osmondmania continues. The brothers are currently fashioning an album which Alan Osmond claims will be 'our Sgt Pepper'.

THE GRAPEVINE

■ Ian Matthews – formerly of Fairport Convention, Southern Comfort and, more recently, Plainsong – has left Britain with his wife and child, for Los Angeles, where he intends to work with former Monkee Mike Nesmith.

■ Paul McCartney has pleaded guilty to the charge of growing marijuana near his Scottish farm.

■ Jimi Hendrix's manager, Mike Jeffrey, has died in a plane crash.

STAR QUOTE

JON LORD

of Deep Purple

'We're as valid as anything by Beethoven'.

CHARTS

Chart	Title	Artist
US45	Killing Me Softly With His Song	*Roberta Flack*
USLP	Don't Shoot Me, I'm Only The Piano Player	*Elton John*
UK45	Part Of The Union	*Strawbs*
UKLP	Don't Shoot Me, I'm Only The Piano Player	*Elton John*
WEEK 2		
US45	Killing Me Softly With His Song	*Roberta Flack*
USLP	Don't Shoot Me, I'm Only The Piano Player	*Elton John*
UK45	Cum On Feel The Noize	*Slade*
UKLP	Don't Shoot Me, I'm Only The Piano PLayer	*Elton John*
WEEK 3		
US45	Killing Me Softly With His Song	*Roberta Flack*
USLP	Dueling Banjos	*Eric Weissberg & Steve Mandel*
UK45	Cum On Feel The Noize	*Slade*
UKLP	Don't Shoot Me, I'm Only The Piano Player	*Elton John*
WEEK 4		
US45	Love Train	*O'Jays*
USLP	Dueling Banjos	*Eric Weissberg & Steve Mandel*
UK45	Cum On Feel The Noize	*Slade*
UKLP	Don't Shoot Me, I'm Only The Piano Player	*Elton John*
WEEK 5		
US45	Love Train	*O'Jays*
USLP	Dueling Banjos	*Eric Weissberg & Steve Mandel*
UK45	The Twelfth Of Never	*Donny Osmond*
UKLP	Billion Dollar Babies	*Alice Cooper*

Taking rock presentation to new extremes, so-called 'supergroup' Emerson, Lake & Palmer

DR HOOK 'COVER' VERSION

Dr Hook & The Medicine Show were featured on the cover of the March 29 edition of *Rolling Stone* magazine, thus gaining a massive plug for their current CBS single, 'The Cover Of The Rolling Stone', which recently entered the US Top 10.

The song was penned by Shel Silverstein, the *Playboy* writer and cartoonist, who also wrote Johnny Cash's 'A Boy Named Sue', Loretta Lynn's 'One's On The Way' and Dr Hook's earlier hit 'Sylvia's Mother'.

AIRPLANE ALBUM WINGS ITS WAY

Jefferson Airplane's new album '30 Seconds Over Winterland', due out in the States this month, is a half-live, half-studio affair that includes a Grunt dictionary.

Grace Slick and Paul Kantner are still slaving away at their own album, Jorma Kaukonen is working on an acoustic solo LP, and Grace is also writing songs for an upcoming solo album.

In Singapore the vice squad recently confiscated a shipment of the band's 'Long John Silver' album because it contains a photograph of marijuana.

E.L.P WORLD TREK

Emerson, Lake & Palmer have mobilized a musical caravan for their 1973 world tour, which opens in Germany at the end of this month. Operating under the banner of 'Get Me A Ladder', the production is described as the most ambitious spectacular ever for a rock group.

The presentation will involve the transportation of 50 tour personnel and 20 tons of equipment valued at $750,000. Two 40-foot articulated trucks will carry the specially designed prosecenium, a Roman-style arch and a stage which will be erected at every performance.

Supporting act on the tour will be Stray Dog, who recently signed to ELP's Manticore label.

LINDISFARNERS GO AS THEY GO GOLD

It's officially confirmed that Newcastle folk-rock bank Lindisfarne are splitting into two. Only Alan Hull and Ray Jackson of the current line-up will feature in the completely re-shaped Lindisfarne and they will be bringing in four new musicians Tommy Duffy, Charlie Harcourt, Paul Nichols and Kenny Craddock.

The three departing members of the band – Rod Clements, Simon Cowe and Ray Laidlaw – are forming a breakaway band. This will be a quartet when they are joined by a singer-songwriter whose name is not being revealed yet due to contractual difficulties, but is rumoured to be Billy Mitchell.

The full personnel for both bands will be officially announced on May 2, when members of the old outfit will be presented with gold discs for their hit album 'Fog On The Tyne'.

Ray Jackson of Lindisfarne

NEIL YOUNG'S WEIRD JOURNEY

Journey Through The Past, a documentary about Neil Young, was screened at the US Film Festival, in Dallas, on April 8.

A surrealistic affair that's said to owe something in approach to Italian director Federico Fellini, Young claims it is: 'A film about me – a collection of thoughts. Every scene means something to me – although with some of them, I can't say what.'

THE GRAPEVINE

■ David Clayton-Thomas, now signed to RCA as a solo artist, is sueing Blood, Sweat & Tears for back royalties.

■ It's understood that Bread have cancelled a forthcoming UK tour because the group are on the verge of breaking up.

■ According to *Rolling Stone* magazine, violinist David LaFlamme, a founder-member of It's A Beautiful Day, has been asked to leave the group.

Bread – likely to be sliced?

PENTANGLE FOR FINAL SPLIT

After several months of indecision, Pentangle have decided to split – but not before they have cut another album together.

At the beginning of the year they denied reports that they were breaking up but, now that their various individual projects are gathering momentum, they have finally decided to disband. However, a new-look Pentangle could still emerge.

'Certainly Jacqui McShee and John Renbourn will continue to record together,' claimed co-manager Arthur Lubin. But Bert Jansch, Danny Thompson and Terry Cox are intent on splitting, and Jansch is heading out on a solo tour this month.

RODEN JOINS DOORS

John Densmore, Robbie Krieger and Ray Manzarek of The Doors

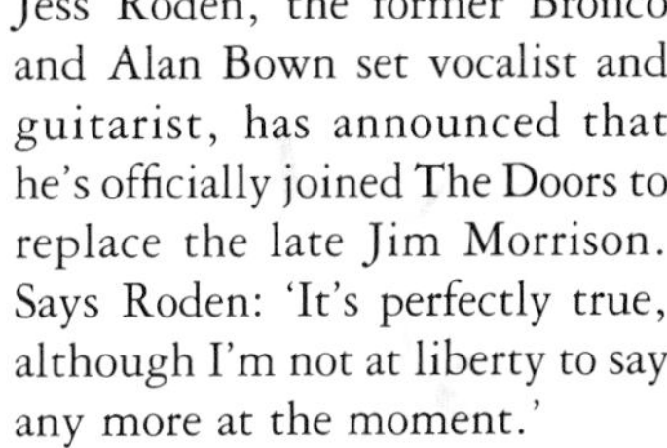

Jess Roden, the former Bronco and Alan Bown set vocalist and guitarist, has announced that he's officially joined The Doors to replace the late Jim Morrison. Says Roden: 'It's perfectly true, although I'm not at liberty to say any more at the moment.'

His statement ends weeks of on-and-off speculation about the British singer becoming part of the US group. It's also understood that keyboard player Ray Manzarek has now left The Doors, who are currently in London for recording sessions.

Roden is already laying down tracks with them.

Former Bronco-buster Jess Roden

CHARTS

US45	The Night The Lights Went Out In Georgia *Vicki Lawrence*
USLP	Lady Sings The Blues *Diana Ross*
UK45	The Twelfth Of Never *Donny Osmond*
UKLP	Dark Side Of The Moon *Pink Floyd*
WEEK 2	
US45	The Night The Lights Went Out In Georgia *Vicki Lawrence*
USLP	Lady Sings The Blues *Diana Ross*
UK45	Get Down *Gilbert O'Sullivan*
UKLP	Don't Shoot Me, I'm Only The Piano Player *Elton John*
WEEK 3	
US45	Tie A Yellow Ribbon *Dawn*
USLP	Billion Dollar Babies *Alice Cooper*
UK45	Tie A Yellow Ribbon *Dawn*
UKLP	Houses Of The Holy *Led Zeppelin*
WEEK 4	
US45	Tie A Yellow Ribbon *Dawn*
USLP	Dark Side Of The Moon *Pink Floyd*
UK45	Tie A Yellow Ribbon *Dawn*
UKLP	Ooh La La *Faces*

ELTON SCRAPS ALBUM TRACKS

Elton John has scrapped most of the tracks he recorded in Jamaica before his recent British tour and has flown to France to work on his new album almost from scratch.

It is understood that Elton was dissatisfied with some of the sounds achieved in the Jamaican studios, and is quoted as saying: 'The piano wasn't good enough.'

Lyricist Bernie Taupin has accompanied him to France to work on the LP, which has the tentative title 'Silent Movies And Talking Pictures'.

Before they left, John and Taupin were presented with three gold records by DJM Records. Two were for 'Honky Chateau' and 'Don't Shoot Me, I'm Only The Piano Player', which have both sold over 100,000 copies in Britain. The third was for one million dollars' worth of US sales for 'Don't Shoot Me'.

CHARTS

US45	Tie A Yellow Ribbon *Dawn*
USLP	Aloha From Hawaii Via Satellite *Elvis Presley*
UK45	Tie A Yellow Ribbon *Dawn*
UKLP	Aladdin Sane *David Bowie*
	WEEK 2
US45	Tie A Yellow Ribbon *Dawn*
USLP	Houses Of The Holy *Led Zeppelin*
UK45	Tie A Yellow Ribbon *Dawn*
UKLP	Aladdin Sane *David Bowie*
	WEEK 3
US45	You Are The Sunshine Of My LIfe *Stevie Wonder*
USLP	Houses Of The Holy *Led Zeppelin*
UK45	Tie A Yellow Ribbon *Dawn*
UKLP	The Beatles, 1967-1970 *Beatles*
	WEEK 4
US45	Frankenstein *Edgar Winter Group*
USLP	The Beatles, 1967-1970 *Beatles*
UK45	See My Baby Jive *Wizzard*
UKLP	Aladdin Sane *David Bowie*

THE GRAPEVINE

- **The new band formed by ex-Lindisfarne members Rod Clements, Ray Laidlaw and Simon Cowe has been named Jack The Lad; as rumoured, the fourth member is Billy Mitchell, a friend of Lindisfarne's for many years.**
- **CBS President Clive Davis has been fired for allegedly mis-using company funds.**
- **Paul Simon has embarked on his first solo tour, playing his initial date at Boston's Music Hall on May 6.**

LANE QUITS FACES

Ronnie Lane has announced his decision to quit The Faces. Lane, who has just returned from the band's seventh American tour, commented: 'It's time to move on – I feel the need for a change.'

The group are currently auditioning for a new bass player and expect to announce Lane's replacement very shortly. In an official statement, drummer Kenny Jones said: 'Ronnie obviously wants to do something on his own and there is no reason why we should stand in his way.'

Meanwhile, Mercury Records are lining up a solo Rod Stewart album for July. Titled 'Play It Again Sam', it's a compilation from his previous four albums.

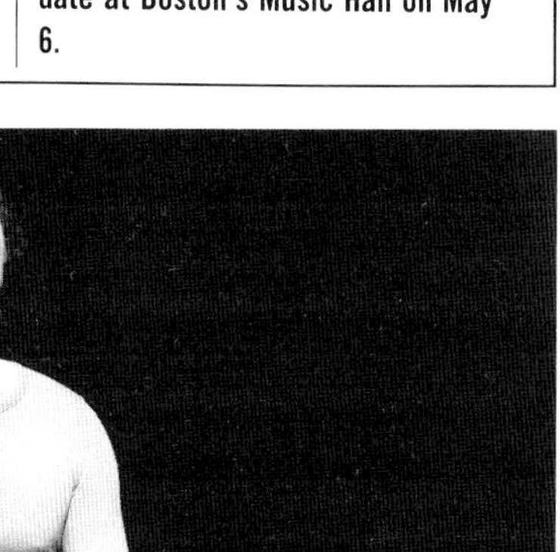

(above) Simon says it solo

SOLO MAGGIE

Maggie Bell has quit Stone The Crows and, as a result, the band's projected British tour – due to start on May 25 – has been cancelled.

Maggie's departure from the band is reportedly down to 'increasing involvement with her solo album'. The album, which is called 'Queen Of The Night', is currently being recorded at New York's Electric Ladyland Studio.

In charge is former Cream producer and Mountain main-man Felix Pappalardi, who has also been playing bass on the sessions. Reports suggest that the project should be finished towards the end of this month, and a late June release is being planned for both sides of the Atlantic.

(below) Maggie Bellts out!

Ronnie Lane in change of Face

HENDRIX FILM OPENS

The late, great Jimi keeps rockin' on film

The film *Jimi Hendrix* is to open at London's Warner Theatre on June 14, a date that coincides with the release of the Warner Bros' double-album soundtrack recording.

The movie, which runs for nearly two hours, includes sequences of Hendrix in action at the Monterey and Isle Of Wight festivals, London's Marquee Club, the Filmore East and at Berkeley, California. There are also extensive filmed interviews with Hendrix, as well as conversations with many of his friends including Mick Jagger, Pete Townshend, Eric Clapton and Lou Reed.

The movie's producer is Joe Boyd, former head of Witchseason and the man responsible for recordings by The Incredible String Band, Fairport Convention and Sandy Denny before he sold the management/production company to Island Records and went to work for Warner Brothers.

PETER, PAUL AND MARY REUNITE FOR ONE-OFF

John Denver and Bill Withers headlined the second annual One To One Benefit at New York's Madison Square Garden in aid of retarded children at the Willowbrook Home.

Also on the bill were Eric Weissberg & Deliverance and Judy Collins, while Kris Kristofferson, Rita Coolidge, Richie Havens and Sly Stone all made unbilled appearances, along with Peter, Paul & Mary, who reunited for the evening.

"Lean On Me" says Bill

NO UNION FOR THE STRAWBS

The Strawbs have split in two. Founder member Dave Cousins and guitarist Dave Lambert retain the Strawbs name, while John Ford, Richard Hudson and Blue Weaver are forming a breakaway group with another, as yet unnamed, guitarist.

The announcement came from America, where the band have just completed a major tour. Ford and Hudson were The Strawbs members responsible for penning the band's recent 'Part Of The Union' hit.

WYATT BADLY INJURED

Robert Wyatt, drummer with Matching Mole and formerly of Soft Machine, is in Stoke Mandeville hospital near London with a broken spine, after falling from a third floor window.

Wyatt had been attending a party in London when – sometime after midnight on June 1 – he decided to leave by climbing down a drainpipe, but fell during the descent.

Doctors now fear that Wyatt will never walk or play again.

Asked if he had been taking drugs before the fall, Wyatt said that he was merely drunk, claiming: 'It was good old alcohol. You know – the legal one.'

Matching Mole's last album, 'Little Red Record', came out in October, last year, and Wyatt was said to be forming a revised version of the band at the time of his accident.

CHARTS

US45 My Love — *Paul McCartney & Wings*
USLP Red Rose Speedway — *Paul McCartney & Wings*
UK45 See My Baby Jive — *Wizzard*
UKLP Aladdin Sane — *David Bowie*

WEEK 2

US45 My Love — *Paul McCartney & Wings*
USLP Red Rose Speedway — *Paul McCartney & Wings*
UK45 Can The Can — *Suzi Quatro*
UKLP The Beatles, 1962-1966 — *Beatles*

WEEK 3

US45 My Love — *Paul McCartney & Wings*
USLP Red Rose Speedway — *Paul McCartney & Wings*
UK45 Can The Can — *Suzi Quatro*
UKLP Aladdin Sane — *David Bowie*

WEEK 4

US45 My Love — *Paul McCartney & Wings*
USLP Living In The Material World — *George Harrison*
UK45 Can The Can — *Suzi Quatro*
UKLP Pure Gold — *Various*

WEEK 5

US45 Give Me Love (Give Me Peace On Earth) — *George Harrison*
USLP Living In The Material World — *George Harrison*
UK45 Rubber Bullets — *10cc*
UKLP Aladdin Sane — *David Bowie*

THE GRAPEVINE

- **Mick Jagger has been named in a paternity suit by Marsha Hunt, who claims he's the father of her daughter Karis.**
- **The Sarstedt Brothers, Peter, Rick (better known as Eden Kane) and Clive, make their first appearance as a group at London's Croydon Fairfield Hall on June 20.**
- **Murry Wilson, father of Beach Boys Brian, Carl and Dennis died on June 4, aged 55.**

BOWIE: 'NO MORE GIGS'

Bowie – no more gigs for Zig

David Bowie's gigs at London's Hammersmith Odeon on July 2 and 3 marked the end of his career as a live entertainer.

Afterwards he announced: 'Those were my final gigs. That's it. Period. I don't want to do any more gigs, and all my forthcoming American dates have been cancelled. From now on, I'll be concentrating on various activities that have very little to do with rock and pop.'

After his hit with 'Space Oddity' in 1969, Bowie retired from rock music and ran an arts lab in Beckenham, South London for 18 months. He only returned to performing at the insistence of Mercury, then his record company, to record 'The Man Who Sold The World'.

A year ago, Bowie told NME: 'I can't envisage stopping gigging for the next year at least, because I'm having such a good time doing it – I've never had such a good time.'

But now, it seems, things have changed.

CHARTS

US45	Will It Go Round In Circles – *Billy Preston*
USLP	Living In The Material World – *George Harrison*
UK45	Skweeze Me Pleeze Me – *Slade*
UKLP	Aladdin Sane – *David Bowie*
WEEK 2	
US45	Will It Go Round In cirlces – *Billy Preston*
USLP	Living In The Material World – *George Harrison*
UK45	Skweeze Me Pleeze Me – *Slade*
UKLP	Aladdin Sane – *David Bowie*
WEEK 3	
US45	Bad Bad Leroy Brown – *Jim Croce*
USLP	Living In The Material World – *George Harrison*
UK45	Welcome Home – *Peters And Lee*
UKLP	We Can Make It – *Peters And Lee*
WEEK 4	
US45	Bad Bad Leroy Brown – *Jim Croce*
USLP	Chicago VI – *Chicago*
UK45	Welcome Home – *Peters And Lee*
UKLP	Aladdin Sane – *David Bowie*

. . . AND RAY DAVIES STOPS TOO!

Emotional stress has been given as the reason behind the shock 'I quit!' announcement made by Ray Davies from the stage at London's White City Festival on July 15.

The Kinks' press secretary explained: 'One has to understand that Ray is in a very emotional and confused stated. Two and a half weeks ago, his wife Rasa left, together with Ray's two children – and he hasn't heard from her since.

'Ray is, naturally, a very worried man. He hasn't been eating since she left. He hasn't slept. It's a miracle he got through the gig. He feels that touring has contributed to the situation.

'And don't forget that Rasa had a nervous breakdown – so Ray knows all about nervous breakdowns. He's a grieving man and he just made an emotional announcement.'

Right: Ray Davies on stage at the White City Festival

VAN MORRISON HARD NOSES THE HIGHWAY

All of Van Morrison's upcoming UK gigs – staged to support his new album 'Hard Nose The Highway' – have been sell-outs.

Morrison recently gave his first press conference in over six years and claimed that he couldn't seriously accept the half legend, half myth persona bestowed on him by many.

'The only reason journalists call me this,' he said, 'is simply because they can't think of anything else to write – it's just a convenient label.'

His gigs include Birmingham Town Hall (July 22), London Rainbow (23-24), Bristol Colston Hall (25), Manchester Free Trade Hall (26) and Newcastle City Hall (27).

THE GRAPEVINE

- **NME has become the biggest selling weekly music publication in the world, the latest official trade audit showing the paper's average weekly sale between January-June this year as 204,512.**
- **Family have announced that they are to disband in the autumn.**
- **It's reckoned that the recent US rock festival held at Watkins Glen raceway was the biggest of all time, the audience totalling 600,000; The Grateful Dead headlined.**

Van Morrison who is, er..half legend, half myth

STAR

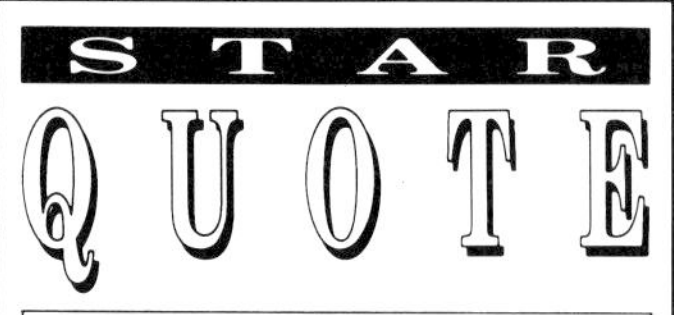

VAN MORRISON

'David Bowie's just doing what Phil May of the Pretty Things used to do. He's just wearing different clothes.'

TOMMY GOES TO THE MOVIES

Pete Townshend's rock opera *Tommy* is to be made into a major feature film, it has been announced. The movie will be directed by Ken Russell and be produced by Track Records in association with the Robert Stigwood Organisation.

The Who will have starring roles in the film, which goes into production next January, on location in England and abroad. And an entirely new soundtrack will be recorded for the film later this year, with additional new material by Townshend.

The Who are currently completing work on their upcoming double-album, 'Quadrophenia', which they expect to complete anytime now, in readiness for autumn worldwide release.

Hear him – see him! Pete goes widescreen

HAWKS' GUERRILLA TACTICS

Hawkwind – IRA bomb scares led to dropping single

Hawkwind's 'Urban Guerrilla' single has been withdrawn from the UK market at the request of the group themselves – despite the fact that Hawkwind are currently undertaking a tour to promote the record, which is likely to be a chart entry.

At the group's suggestion, the B-side of 'Urban Guerrilla' will be the new single. Titled 'Brainbox Pollution', it will be out as soon as possible.

STAR QUOTE

ROD STEWART

'I want to sing a song from "My Fair Lady". You can leave the blues to Muddy Waters.'

'Here's my impression of Rex Harrison'

STEVIE INJURED IN CAR CRASH

Stevie Wonder and his driver are reported as being in a 'satisfactory' condition after an accident on August 6, when their car ploughed into the back of a truck.

Doctors said that Wonder was under intensive care and being hospitalized in Salisbury, North Carolina, before being moved to nearby Winston for specialist treatment.

Both vehicles were completely wrecked in the smash.

THE GRAPEVINE

- **Paul Williams, one of the original Temptations, was found shot dead on August 17. He was 34.**
- **Paul Kossoff has been busted for driving under the influence of drink or drugs; he's been fined £500 and ordered to undertake in-patient treatment at a London Hospital.**
- **David Bowie's 'Pin-Ups' album, which was recently completed in France, is now being mixed in London.**

CHARTS

US45	The Morning After *Maureen McGovern*
USLP	Chicago VI *Chicago*
UK45	I'm The Leader Of The Gang *Gary Glitter*
UKLP	We Can Make It *Peters And Lee*
WEEK 2	
US45	The Morning After *Maureen McGovern*
USLP	Chicago VI *Chicago*
UK45	I'm The Leader Of The Gang *Gary Glitter*
UKLP	We Can Make It *Peters And Lee*
WEEK 3	
US45	Touch Me In The Morning *Diana Ross*
USLP	A Passion Play *Jethro Tull*
UK45	I'm The Leader Of The Gang *Gary Glitter*
UKLP	We Can Make It *Peters And Lee*
WEEK 4	
US45	Brother Louie *Stories*
USLP	Chicago VI *Chicago*
UK45	I'm The Leader of The Gang *Gary Glitter*
UKLP	Now And Then *Carpenters*

ETTA BETTA – YOU BETCHA!

Chess Records have just released Etta James' first album in two years. Titled 'Etta James', it was produced by Gabriel Mekler, former producer of Steppenwolf and others.

At a reception given for her at Mediasound Studios in New York, the singer – dressed in shocking pink – sang over the album's backing tracks and announced: 'I've been a bad girl but I'm better now.'

Etta, a confessed heroin addict for 14 years, has been participating in a methadone treatment course which she commenced last year. She has lost 75 lbs and is now looking back to her best.

A portion of the profits from the album will be donated to the Dr Eugene Silberman Methadone Maintenance Treatment Programme in New York City, and the Centre City 'Kick' Programme, in Los Angeles.

Rehabilitated, Etta James stages a welcome come-back

1973

CHARTS

US45	Brother Louie *Stories*
USLP	Brothers & Sisters *Allman Brothers*
UK45	Young Love *Donny Osmond*
UKLP	Now And Then *Carpenters*
	WEEK 2
US45	Let's Get it On Marvin Gaye
USLP	Brothers & Sisters *Allman Brothers*
UK45	Young Love *Donny Osmond*
UKLP	Sing It Again Rod *Rod Stewart*
	WEEK 3
US45	Delta Dawn *Helen Reddy*
USLP	Brothers & Sisters *Allman Brothers*
UK45	Angel Fingers *Wizzard*
UKLP	Sing It Again Rod *Rod Stewart*
	WEEK 4
US45	Delta Dawn *Helen Reddy*
USLP	Brothers & Sisters *Allman Brothers*
UK45	Rock On *David Essex*
UKLP	Sing It Again Rod *Rod Stewart*
	WEEK 5
US45	We're An American Band *Grand Funk Railroad*
USLP	Brothers & Sisters *Allman Brothers*
UK45	Ballroom Blitz *Sweet*
UKLP	Goat's Head Soup *Rolling Stones*

THE GRAPEVINE

■ **Deep Purple have settled on a new lead singer to replace Ian Gillan – he's 22 year-old David Coverdale, a complete unkown.**

■ **A sequel to the film *That'll Be The Day* will go into production in the new year; the movie has the working title of *Stardust* and will feature David Essex and Ringo Starr, re-creating the roles they played in the original movie.**

LENNON RECORDING

John Lennon is currently in New York's Record Plant recording a song called 'Imagination', which is said to be a traditionally tough yet pretty original composition.

Spooky Tooth are working in the studio next door and came into Studio B when John's work was completed. Actress Julie Christie also came in with record producer Bob Ezrin, the former being greeted by Lennon with a 'Hello, Julie Christie'.

Ezrin appeared to be cut up when Lennon didn't recognise him and snapped: 'How come he says hello to Julie Christie? He probably knows me as the guy who borrowed his car for the night. Anyway, I'll match my last year's sales against his any-day!'

As John left the studio, he glanced at Julie Christie in her floppy T-shirt and jeans and grinned. 'You've changed a bit since Leeds,' he said, before bounding into a waiting limo.

MORE ROCK DEATHS

Gone, gone, gone, Jim Croce (left) and Gram Parsons (right)

Gram Parsons, ex-member of The Byrds and founder of The Flying Burrito Brothers, died in California on September 19. Parsons, 26, collapsed in a motel and was rushed to hospital in Uyya Valley, but was found to be dead on arrival. An initial post-mortem failed to reveal the cause of death and further tests are being made.

Jim Croce and his guitarist Maury Mulheisen were killed the very next day (20) when the small plane in which they were travelling from Louisiana to Texas crashed into a tree while attempting to take off.

The singer-songwriter had recently returned to America after his recent visit to Britain. Highly successful, he logged four Top 10 singles in the US charts before his death, including the recent No. 1 'Bad Bad Leroy Brown'.

MACCA IN AFRICA

Paul McCartney and the remnants of Wings – now down to Denny Laine and Linda McCartney – are soldiering on, recording their new album in Lagos, Nigeria.

Both Denny Seiwell and Henry McCulloch have departed due to reasons of musical policy, but McCartney denies that McCulloch and he had a fight that left the ex-Beatle with a black eye and injured pride.

He adds that, at present, there is no thought of adding new members to Wings to compensate for the resignations. 'Anyway,' says Paul, 'When we're recording, I could play the lot myself!'

The new Deep Purple line-up with David Coverdale (centre)

Macca – now in Lagos

CASSIDY MAKES QUICK GETAWAY

David Cassidy flew into London's Heathrow Airport on October 6 and gave a lightning press conference at the nearby Skyway Hotel.

Asked if he had any vices, Cassidy replied: 'Well I do bite my nails.'

He spoke about his latest album, which includes a version of 'Bali Hai' from *South Pacific*, 'I remember being very young and hearing my father humming that song in the next room' and the Peggy Lee classic 'Fever'.

Cassidy claimed: 'The album's like the story of my life. The songs are like vignettes in a way.' When questioned about drugs, Cassidy said: 'That's a past issue – I stated a long time ago that I took drugs when I was younger and I don't do them any more.'

He admitted that one friend had OD'd but concluded: 'I don't want to talk about that. He was a close friend, but it all happened years ago.'

THE GRAPEVINE

- **Rebop, Traffic's percussionist, has been jailed for a month for attacking two policemen; he was also fined £20($40) for biting a cab driver's ear.**
- **Sopwith Camel, one of San Francisco's most notable bands in the Sixties, have reformed and already cut an album for Reprise.**
- **Crosby, Stills, Nash & Young were re-united onstage during a recent Manassas concert at San Francisco's Winterland.**

GOSPEL AND JAZZ LEGENDS DIE

Gospel singer and guitarist Sister Rosetta Tharpe died in Philadelphia on October 9 at the age of 57. She made her first record in 1938 and pioneered the development of gospel singing into worldwide popularity. Sister Rosetta had a leg amputated in 1970, but continued with her singing career and was planning a new album for Savoy Records at the time of her death.

The death of Gene Krupa has also been reported. The first of the showmen drummers, he was a victim of leukaemia, dying in New York, on October 16, at the age of 64.

STAR QUOTE

RAY DAVIES

of the Kinks

'I'm still only five years old. I know what food I like. I've got two pairs of shoes and, when they wear out, I replace them. I'm reasonably alright.'

CHARTS

US45	Half-Breed *Cher*
USLP	Brothers & Sisters *Allman Brothers*
UK45	Eye Level *Simon Park Orchestra*
UKLP	Goat's Head Soup *Rolling Stones*
WEEK 2	
US45	Half-Breed *Cher*
USLP	Goat's Head Soup *Rolling Stones*
UK45	Eye Level *Simon Park Orchestra*
UKLP	Sladest *Slade*
WEEK 3	
US45	Angie *Rolling Stones*
USLP	Goat's Head Soup *Rolling Stones*
UK45	Eye Level *Simon Park Orchestra*
UKLP	Sladest *Slade*
WEEK 4	
US45	Midnight Train To Georgia *Gladys Knight & The Pips*
USLP	Goat's Head Soup *Rolling Stones*
UK45	Eye Level *Simon Park Orchestra*
UKLP	Hello *Status Quo*

BOWIE AND THE GNOME

The UK success of a rather elderly David Bowie recording called 'The Laughing Gnome' has provided a talking point. Recorded some six years ago for Deram, the single has remained in the catalogue ever since.

Amidst signing autograph books at Lou Reed's recent London Rainbow gig, Angie Bowie commented that she found the record 'gloriously nostalgic – rather like "White Christmas" ', while a flue-ridden Bowie staggered from his bed long enough to opine that he considered it to be 'a charming children's song'.

Bowie remembering Gnome life

ELVIS AND PRISCILLA CALL IT QUITS

Elvis and Priscilla Presley divorced in Santa Monica, California on 9 October. Elvis began proceedings in August on the grounds of irreconcilable differences after it was reported that Priscilla was living with karate instructor Mike Stone.

Elvis' lawyer stated: 'The reason for the divorce is that Elvis has been spending six months a year on the road, which put a tremendous strain on the marriage.'

BOWIE'S MILLIONS

David Bowie has now sold over one million RCA albums since he joined the label just under two years ago – the exact figure up to the beginning of November being 1,056,400. And, during the same period, he also sold over a million singles in Britain (1,024,068), plus a total of 120,000 eight track cartridges and cassettes.

To these must be added the sales of Bowie's 'Laughing Gnome' single, which are now in the region of 200,000.

General practice within the recording industry used for the purposes of gold record qualification calculates an album as being equal to six single units. On this basis Bowie has sold nearly eight and a half million units in Britain alone, in less than two years.

This easily makes him the biggest record seller in the country since the peak period of The Beatles. Meanwhile, British sales of 'Pin-Ups', Bowie's latest album, are fast approaching 200,000.

FORMER SHAD ELECTROCUTED

Former Shadows bassist John Rostill was found dead in his Radlett, Hertfordshire studio on November 26. He had apparently been electrocuted while using his guitar to write new material.

A fine writer, he composed several songs for Olivia Newton-John, including 'Let Me Be There' and 'If You Love Me Let Me Know'.

Olivia Newton-John had hits with Rostill songs

LENNON'S 'MIND GAMES'

At one time I would have said that 'Mind Games' is a terrible album because it in no way reflects Lennon's capabilities. But, after four solo albums, each one lousier than the other, I'm no longer sure that Lennon is capable of anything other than leading a friendly corner-superstar existence, facing nothing more challenging than whether to watch *Sesame Street* on the living room or the bedroom TV set.

In conclusion, this album is not offensive, it is not inoffensive. It is simply nothing at all.

Coming shortly – The Return Of The Living Dead!

TRAGEDY HITS JERRY LEE AGAIN

The ill-fated Jerry Lee

Jerry Lee Lewis' son, Jerry Lee Lewis Jr (19), was killed in a car accident on November 13, while driving near Hernando, Mississippi. Just a few days before, he'd appeared as drummer with his father's band on the *Midnight Special* TV show.

Jerry Lee's brother died in an auto accident while the singer-pianist was still young, and in 1962, Steven Allen – Jerry Lee's other son – drowned in the family swimming pool.

Former Columbia University students Sha Na Na

CHARTS

US45	Midnight Train To Georgia *Gladys Knight & The Pips*
USLP	Goat's Head Soup *Rolling Stones*
UK45	Day Dreamer/The Puppy Song *David Cassidy*
UKLP	Pin-Ups *David Bowie*
WEEK 2	
US45	Keep On Truckin' *Eddie Kendricks*
USLP	Goodbye Yellow Brick Road *Elton John*
UK45	Day Dreamer/The Puppy Song *David Cassidy*
UKLP	Pin-Ups *David Bowie*
WEEK 3	
US45	Keep On Truckin' *Eddie Kendricks*
USLP	Goodbye Yellow Brick Road *Elton John*
UK45	Let Me In *Osmonds*
UKLP	Pin-Ups *David Bowie*
WEEK 4	
US45	Photograph *Ringo Starr*
USLP	Goodbye Yellow Brick Road *Elton John*
UK45	I Love You Love Me Love *Gary Glitter*
UKLP	Pin-Ups *David Bowie*

THE GRAPEVINE

- **A split has caused a major upheaval in Sha Na Na, three members of the group quitting.**
- **For his second album, Bruce Springsteen has reportedly moved his bed into the studio.**
- **Two men have been charged with stealing the coffin containing the body of Gram Parsons; they claimed that they were merely carrying out Parsons' wish to be cremated in the desert.**

DECEMBER

DARIN DEAD AT 37

Bobby Darin, the singer who claimed he would be a legend at 25, died in Los Angeles' Cedars Of Lebanon hospital on December 20, at the age of 37. The end of a life-long battle against heart trouble came after a six-hour operation to replace two valves.

It was his second bout of open heart surgery within a short space of time. Said one friend: 'He was just too weak to recover.'

Perhaps best known for his early rock hits such as 'Splish Splash', 'Dream Lover' and his swinging version of 'Mack The Knife' (which sold two million copies), Darin later sold off all his possessions and moved to Big Sur on the Californian coast, where he lived in a trailer for a lengthy period.

In 1963 he collapsed from exhaustion and overwork and underwent major open-heart surgery in February 1971. In June, this year, he was married to Andrea Yeager, his companion for the past four years. However, the couple were divorced in November.

Darin's first wife was one-time teen-queen Sandra Dee, whom he divorced in 1966. He leaves a son, Dodd, now 12.

'TOMMY' AT THE RAINBOW

Dress-rehearsal for those Rainbow chasers

Lou Reizner is to present another new version of The Who's *Tommy* at the London Rainbow on December 13 & 14. This time the cast features Roy Wood, Elkie Brooks, David Essex, Marsha Hunt, Jon Pertwee, Richie Havens, Graham Bell, Merry Clayton and Viv Stanshall.

The production will be broadcast in full on London's Capital Radio on December 26.

The Who completed their American tour in Washington on December 6, where they played a concert before an audience of 28,000. They suffered a mild setback at Montreal Forum on December 2, when the band and some friends were jailed overnight for wrecking hotel property.

Tammy still stands by her man

SLADE CELEBRATE XMAS

Slade's 'Merry Xmas Everybody', which was released on December 7, has proved to be the band's fastest-selling single to date, registering a quarter of a million sales on the first day of release and providing Noddy Holder and Co with an instant UK No. 1.

The single was recorded at New York's Record Plant during Slade's US summer tour. Jim Lea claims that the tune to the song came to him while he was taking a shower in Memphis.

Slade luv Santa

THE GRAPEVINE

- The Doobie Brothers' Tom Johnston has been arrested in California on a charge of marijuana possession; his case comes up on January 10.
- The Glittermen, Gary Glitter's band, are now touring without the leader of the gang.
- George Jones and Tammy Wynette have denied stories of an impending D-I-V-O-R-C-E.

CHARTS

- US45 Top Of The World — *Carpenters*
- USLP Goodbye Yellow Brick Road — *Elton John*
- UK45 I Love You Love Me Love — *Gary Glitter*
- UKLP Pin-Ups — *David Bowie*

WEEK 2

- US45 Top Of The World — *Carpenters*
- USLP Goodbye Yellow Brick Road — *Elton John*
- UK45 I Love You Love Me Love — *Gary Glitter*
- UKLP Pin-Ups — *David Bowie*

WEEK 3

- US45 The Most Beautiful Girl — *Charlie Rich*
- USLP Goodbye Yellow Brick Road — *Elton John*
- UK45 I Love You Love Me Love — *Gary Glitter*
- UKLP Pin-Ups — *David Bowie*

WEEK 4

- US45 The Most Beautiful Girl — *Charlie Rich*
- USLP Goodbye Yellow Brick Road — *Elton John*
- UK45 Merry Xmas Everybody — *Slade*
- UKLP Stranded — *Roxy Music*

WEEK 5

- US45 Time In A Bottle — *Jim Croce*
- USLP Goodbye Yellow Brick Road — *Elton John*
- UK45 Merry Xmas Everybody — *Slade*
- UKLP Goodbye Yellow Brick Road — *Elton John*

The original supergroup – Cream

Emerson, Lake and Palmer

SUPERGROUPS – AN IMPERFECT CONCEPT?

Maybe the first supergroup was Cream, the British trio of Eric Clapton, guitarist from The Yardbirds and John Mayall's Bluesbreakers, Jack Bruce on bass and vocals, also from one of the innumerable Bluesbreakers line-ups and before that The Graham Bond Organisation, where he had worked with drummer Ginger Baker.

In 1966, the trio of Clapton, Bruce and Baker decided to work together as Cream, and for just over two years, were hugely successful, until they announced their disbandment on the grounds that they had achieved what they set out to do, and wanted to explore fresh avenues.

A few months later, in early 1968, a new supergroup – to be known as Blind Faith – was announced, starring Clapton and Baker again, with the addition of singer/guitarist/keyboard player Steve Winwood, previously of Traffic and, before that, the star of The Spencer Davis Group, and bass and violin player Rick Grech from Leicester group Family.

Blind Faith's debut UK appearance was a mammoth free concert in London's Hyde Park attended by at least a quarter of a million people, preceding their debut album by a few weeks. It turned out to be their only UK gig. After a six week US tour around the release of the eponymous album came an ominous silence, broken less than a year after the group's formation by the announcement of its demise.

At the start of the 1970s, these sentiments were ignored as a plethora of supergroups emerged, particularly in the USA. Around the time Cream disbanded, Al Kooper, who had left Blood, Sweat & Tears – a group he founded from the ashes of The Blues Project – was offered the chance to become a record producer and to collaborate with other musicians with similar track records.

The first result of the latter was

Cream spin-off – Blind Faith

Crosby, Stills, Nash and Young

'Supersession', an excellent album on which he worked with guitarists Mike Bloomfield (ex-Butterfield Blues Band and Electric Flag) and Stephen Stills (ex-Buffalo Springfield). The project led to a double album, 'The Live Adventures of Mike Bloomfield & Al Kooper', released in 1969.

However, Stephen Stills was already making plans to collaborate with David Crosby of The Byrds and – more surprisingly – with Graham Nash of British hitmakers The Hollies. In 1969, perhaps the most famous supergroup of them all, Crosby, Stills & Nash, was launched with a worthy debut album. Before long, the trio had expanded to a quartet with the addition of Stills's ex-Buffalo Springfield comrade, Neil Young.

What CSN had lacked was sufficient instrumental power to match their immense vocal talents, and Young's recruitment not only gave the quartet an additional distinctive vocalist and great songwriter, but also an equally distinctive co-lead guitarist to share instrumental solo duties with Stills.

However, certain elements of CSN&Y were not content only to be members of that group, and wanted other outlets for their talents, via solo projects and even perhaps collaborations with others. Predictably, Neil Young was the first to strike out on his own, followed by Stills, while Crosby & Nash remained as a duo as well as making solo albums. Twenty years later, CSN&Y are an on/off celebration, still congregating (albeit infrequently) to record and tour.

Then there was (Keith) Emerson, (Greg) Lake & (Carl) Palmer, from respectively The Nice, King Crimson and Atomic Rooster. ELP went on to make probably more continuous hit albums than any other supergroup, before the inevitable desire to work outside the confines of the group made itself known. Amusingly enough, when a reunion took place in the 1980s, in which Palmer was not willing to be involved, his two ex-partners recruited drummer Cozy Powell to ensure that the name ELP was still accurate!

There have been innumerable attempts over the years to assemble latter day supergroups, most of them unsuccessful.

CHARTS

US45	Time In A Bottle *Jim Croce*
USLP	The Singles 1969-1973 *Carpenters*
UK45	You Won't Find Another Fool *New Seekers*
UKLP	Goodbye Yellow Brick Road *Elton John*
WEEK 2	
US45	The Joker *Steve Miller*
USLP	You Don't Mess Around With Jim *Jim Croce*
UK45	You Won't Find Another Fool *New Seekers*
UKLP	Goodbye Yellow Brick Road *Elton John*
WEEK 3	
US45	Show & Tell *Al Wilson*
USLP	You Don't Mess Around With Jim *Jim Croce*
UK45	The Show Must Go On *Leo Sayer*
UKLP	Brain Salad Surgery *Emerson, Lake & Palmer*
WEEK 4	
US45	You're Sixteen *Ringo Starr*
USLP	You Don't Mess Around With Jim *Jim Croce*
UK45	Teenage Rampage *Sweet*
UKLP	Brain Salad Surgery *Emerson, Lake & Palmer*

HIGH NOON FOR TEX

Tex Ritter, the singer who had a huge hit with 'High Noon', the theme from the Gary Cooper movie, died in Nashville on January 2.

An actor who originally made his name on radio, he appeared in more than 50 films, usually playing a singing cowboy. Last year he ran for the US senate but lost, incurring heavy debts.

But he'll always be remembered, not only for his music but also for his part in setting up the Country Music Foundation and Hall Of Fame, to which he was elected in 1964.

BOWIE HEADS FOR THE STATES

David Bowie leaves Britain in February to spend several months in New York preparing his stage revue, *The 1980 Floor Show*, the title provisionally chosen for his musical adaptation of George Orwell's *1984*, which he's hoping to premiere in London's West End later this year.

It's understood that the switch in title from 1984 to 1980 is intended to avoid any copyright problems which might arise.

Helping Bowie mount the show will be Rony Ingratsia, co-author with Andy Warhol of *Pork*, which played a season at London's Roundhouse in 1971. Meanwhile, Bowie is currently working at London's Olympic Studios on the album for the *1980 Floor Show* and tracks in production include 'Big Brother' and 'Are You Coming, Are You Coming?'

Bassist Trevor Bolder and keyboardist Mike Garson have been playing on the sessions, and recent visitors have included Pete Townshend, Mick Jagger, Ronnie Wood and Rod Stewart.

ENERGY CRISIS HITS BRITISH ROCK

Victims of the power game – Steely Dan (above) and Chi Coltrane (left)

Because of the UK miners' strike and the ensuing energy crisis, which has resulted in nationwide power cuts, many American acts have withdrawn from British tours claiming that the situation is too risky.

These include The Allman Brothers, Steely Dan, Chi Coltrane and Joe Walsh. Some studios have suffered cancelled bookings as a result of the strike but at Abbey Road, engineers have continued working, thanks to the use of their own generators.

BAD COMPANY FOR FREE

All-star Company

The new-look Free has finally taken shape and, following a lengthy period of rehearsals, the band – to be known as Bad Company – are at present recording an album, to be issued by Atlantic.

The line-up comprises Paul Rodgers (vocals), Simon Kirke (drums), Boz Burrell (bass) and ex-Mott The Hoople guitarist Mick Ralphs.

Meanwhile, two former Free members, Paul Kossoff and Andy Fraser, have reportedly teamed-up with ex-Hendrix drummer Mitch Mitchell and have commenced rehearsals with a view to a spring tour.

THE GRAPEVINE

- **Chicken Shack have disbanded after eight years; leader Stan Webb is joining Savoy Brown.**
- **Dino Martin, son of Dean Martin, and once part of Dino, Desi & Billy, has been arrested after attempting to sell a machine-gun to an undercover government agent.**
- **Bob Dylan, in the middle of his first US tour since 1965, has received a gold record for his 'Planet Waves' album.**

DYLAN-BAND CONCERTS HAILED

Robbie Robertson and The Zim

Bob Dylan's tour with The Band ended in Los Angeles on February 14, when the singer played to a star-studded audience at the city's Forum. Jack Nicholson, Carole King, Neil Young and Ringo Starr were among those who stayed to cheer.

Dylan's recent concerts at New York's Madison Square Garden have been hailed by some as being among the greatest rock'n-'roll concerts of all-time, Dylan opening on acoustic guitar and rendering songs such as 'Most Likely You'll Go Your Way And I'll Go Mine', 'Lay Lady Lay', 'Just Like Tom Thumb's Blues', 'Rainy Day Women Nos 12 and 35', 'It Ain't Me Babe' and 'Ballad Of A Thin Man'.

He accompanied himself on piano for the last-named, returning after a Band set for an electric fling involving 'Like A Rolling Stone' and others.

He was forced back to encore on 'Maggie's Farm' and, finally, 'Blowin' In The Wind'.

The tour encompassed 39 shows in 21 cities.

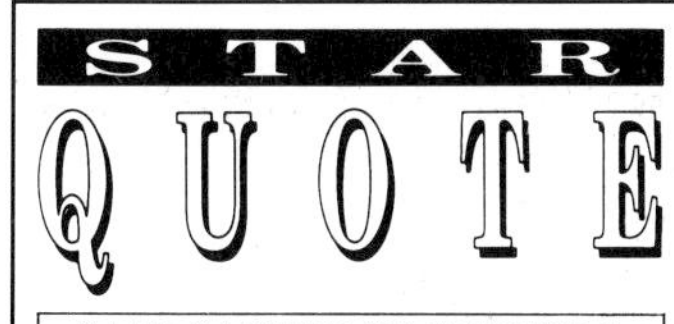

MARIANNE FAITHFULL

'My first move was to get a Rolling Stone as a boyfriend. I slept with three and decided the lead singer was the best.'

Diarist Hunter

BIG MAC ROW

The strange case of the two Fleetwood Macs has turned into a major dispute between the original group and manager Clifford Davis, who recently launched a new band using the same name.

Davis contends that the group currently touring America as Fleetwood Mac is the only authentic Mac, even though none of its members has previously been connected with the group of that name. Their line-up is: Elmer Gantry (vocals), Paul Martinez (bass), David Wilkinson (piano), Craig Collinge (drums) and ex-Curved Air guitarist Kirby.

This outfit recently topped the bill at New York's Academy of Music and, on that particular evening, Gantry was ill with laryngitis, causing the remaining members to play a 43-minute instrumental set which was described by one critic as 'tedious, routine bluesy rock – all right for a street band but decidedly not for a headline act'.

CHARTS

US45	The Way We Were — *Barbra Streisand*
USLP	You Don't Mess Around With Jim — *Jim Croce*
UK45	Tiger Feet — *Mud*
UKLP	The Singles, 1969-1973 — *Carpenters*
WEEK 2	
US45	Love's Theme — *Love Unlimited Orchestra*
USLP	You Don't Mess Around With Jim — *Jim Croce*
UK45	Tiger Feet — *Mud*
UKLP	The Singles, 1969-1973 — *Carpenters*
WEEK 3	
US45	The Way We Were — *Barbra Streisand*
USLP	Planet Waves — *Bob Dylan*
UK45	Tiger Feet — *Mud*
UKLP	The Singles, 1969-1973 — *Carpenters*
WEEK 4	
US45	The Way We Were — *Barbra Streisand*
USLP	Planet Waves — *Bob Dylan*
UK45	Devil Gate Drive — *Suzi Quatro*
UKLP	The Singles, 1969-1973 — *Carpenters*

BOWIE TOPS POLL

In the 1974 NME Reader's Poll, David Bowie has been voted Top Male singer in the World Section, while Diana Ross is the Best Female Singer spot.

Other winners include Yes (Top Group), Alice Cooper (Stage Band), 'Dark Side Of The Moon' by Pink Floyd (Album), 'Radar Love' by Golden Earring (Single), 'Yessongs' by Yes (Best Dressed Album), Golden Earring (Most Promising New Name), Stevie Wonder (Soul Act), Elton John and Bernie Taupin (Songwriters).

The explosive Keith Emerson

THE GRAPEVINE

- **Ian Hunter is shortly to publish *Diary of a Rock and Roll Star*, a tale of Mott The Hoople on the road. It's to be published in the UK by Panther, price 50p.**
- **Bobby Bloom (28) whose 'Montego Bay' was a hit in 1970, has shot himself to death.**
- **Keith Emerson damaged his hands when a rigged piano exploded prematurely at a San Francisco gig on 2 February.**

SPECTOR – STILL ON DANGER LIST

Celebrated record-producer and composer Phil Spector is reportedly still in a serious condition in a Los Angeles hospital after suffering 'near-fatal' injuries in a car accident last month.

Spector was involved in a massive pile-up while driving out of town for a short vacation, and is understood to have sustained serious burns and severe head injuries, though exact details have still not been revealed. Even close friends in London and America have been unable to glean more information.

CHARTS

- US45 Seasons In The Sun – *Terry Jacks*
- USLP Planet Waves – *Bob Dylan*
- UK45 Devil Gate Drive – *Suzi Quatro*
- UKLP The Singles, 1969-1973 – *Carpenters*

WEEK 2

- US45 Seasons In The Sun – *Terry Jacks*
- USLP Planet Waves – *Bob Dylan*
- UK45 Jealous Mind – *Alvin Stardust*
- UKLP The Singles, 1969-1973 – *Carpenters*

WEEK 3

- US45 Seasons In The Sun – *Terry Jacks*
- USLP The Way We Were – *Barbra Streisand*
- UK45 Jealous Mind – *Alvin Stardust*
- UKLP The Singles, 1969-1973 – *Carpenters*

WEEK 4

- US45 Dark Lady – *Cher*
- USLP The Way We Were – *Barbra Streisand*
- UK45 Billy Don't Be A Hero – *Paper Lace*
- UKLP The Singles, 1969-1973 – *Carpenters*

WEEK 5

- US45 Sunshine On My Shoulders – *John Denver*
- USLP Greatest Hits – *John Denver*
- UK45 Billy Don't Be A Hero – *Paper Lace*
- UKLP The Singles, 1969-1973 – *Carpenters*

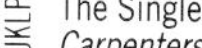

ELKIE GOES SOLO

Elkie Brooks is going solo and, as a result, Vinegar Joe have decided to disband, following their week-long tour of Yugoslavia later this month. Their last British date takes place at Cheltenham St Paul's College on March 9.

Elkie's manager, John Sherry, revealed that her decision to embark on a solo career was, to a large extent, sparked by her appearance in the London production of *Tommy* before Christmas, which aroused great interest. He added that she had since been approached about starring in a London West End musical, and for a leading part in a major TV play.

The male members of Vinegar Joe have not made any firm plans for the future, although it is understood that singer Robert Palmer is going to America to record solo.

CSN&Y TO REFORM

CSN&Y – reunion at last. But rehearsals are needed to loosen the rust

Crosby, Stills, Nash & Young are to tour again. 'The first gig,' says Steve Stills, 'is on July 4, in Tampa, Florida, at a football stadium. We'll do about ten days on tour. I'm really looking forward to it.

'I know we can still sing well together, it's just down to deciding on arrangements and stuff.'

He revealed he's shelved an album called 'Stolen Stills' of which he says: 'It's all out-takes. It's songs that didn't make the two solo albums or the Manassas releases because we had too many songs of the same type. Some were roadies' favourites – things like that.'

THE GRAPEVINE

- **Stevie Wonder, who recently won five Grammy Awards, has announced plans to quit the music business in 1976 and work with handicapped children in Africa.**
- **Sandy Denny is to rejoin Fairport Convention.**
- **Jefferson Airplane are now touring under the name Jefferson Starship.**
- **Nashville's Grand Ole Opry moved to a ritzy new home on March 16, after 33 years at the Ryman Auditorium.**

CHRISSIE ON KISS *BY KISS*

The lyrics are pretty turgid but they've got good taste in rip-offs. 'Everybody says she's looking good – and the lady knows it's understood.' Yeah, John Winston was coming up with some real classics, huh? I dunno – I suppose even after eating a can of beans, every little fart is its own self-contained composition – but perhaps I'm being too kind.

Kiss is an essay in rock mannerisms, and stale ones at that – Chrissie Hynde.

Kiss – kissed off by Chrissie

YES-MEN SOLO ALBUMS

All five Yes members are likely to have solo albums on the market before the end of the year. Rick Wakeman already has two albums of his own on release but the other four – Jon Anderson, Chris Squire, Steve Howe and Alan White – will each be spending three months, this summer, working on individual projects.

A spokesman for the band revealed: 'Steve and Chris already have demo tracks on tape and plan to develop these further. Alan and Jon each have a lot of ideas which they want to put down on tape. And while these four are working, Rick, who has no future solo plans at present, will be busy producing the two bands he has taken under his wing – Warhorse and Wally.

'There is no question of a Yes split, neither is there any question of Rick taking his *Journey To The Centre Of Earth* show on tour. He would like to be able to do this, but it's only a pipedream, uneconomic and impractical.'

Yes – no split yet

Bowie looking unscathed by the fall-out, radiates as usual

BOWIE'S 1980 PROJECT TOUR

David Bowie arrived in New York on Good Friday aboard the SS France and is now preparing for his major concert tour of the North Americas.

The tour opens at The Montreal Forum Concert Bowl on June 14 and runs for two months. The concert concept, described as a 'theatrical extravaganza', is based upon Bowie's RCA album 'Diamond Dogs', which will have a simultaneous release in Britain and America in May.

This forms the basis of what was to have been Bowie's '1980 Floor Show', freely based upon George Orwell's *1984* novel. But the intended London West End revue has now been translated into concert tour terms, replete with an adaptable and packable set provided by noted Broadway lighting man Jules Fisher, whose credits include *Pippin* and *Hair*.

Mike Garson (keyboards), Herbie Flowers (bass) and Tony Newman (drums) will be backing Bowie on the tour, while auditions are taking place for a guitarist.

The theme of the album and the show is the breakdown of society after the holocaust, when men are deformed from the effects of radiation.

CHARTS

US45	Hooked On A Feeling	*Blue Swede*
USLP	Greatest Hits	*John Denver*
UK45	Billy Don't Be A Hero	*Paper Lace*
UKLP	The Singles, 1969-1973	*Carpenters*
WEEK 2		
US45	Bennie & The Jets	*Elton John*
USLP	Band On The Run	*Paul McCartney & Wings*
UK45	Seasons In The Sun	*Terry Jacks*
UKLP	The Singles, 1969-1973	*Carpenters*
WEEK 3		
US45	TSOP (The Sound Of Philadelphia)	*MFSB with The Three Degrees*
USLP	Band On The Run	*Paul McCartney & Wings*
UK45	Seasons In The Sun	*Terry Jacks*
UKLP	The Singles, 1969-1973	*Carpenters*
WEEK 4		
US45	TSOP (The Sound of Philadelphia)	*MFSB with The Three Degrees*
USLP	Chicago VII	*Chicago*
UK45	The Cat Crept In	*Mud*
UKLP	The Singles, 1969-1973	*Carpenters*

Below: Shades of Eric

ERIC'S BACK

Elton John and Pete Townshend were among those who attended a party held at The China Garden, in London's Berwick Street, to celebrate Eric Clapton's return to the fray.

Clapton has now flown to America to commence work on a new album. Carl Radle, who worked with Clapton in Derek & The Dominoes, will be playing with him on the sessions.

THE GRAPEVINE

- **Ex-Family members Roger Chapman and Charlie Whitney have completed their new album 'Streetwalkers'.**
- **Vinnie Taylor, guitarist with Sha Na Na, has died of a drug overdose.**
- **Also gone is Pam Morrison, Jim Morrison's widow; she was found dead in her Hollywood apartment on April 24.**
- **The California Jam Festival on April 6, attracted 200,000 punters to hear ELP, Black Sabbath, Deep Purple and The Eagles.**

Below: Sha Na Na supply the latest rock casualty

FAREWELL TO THE DUKE

Duke Ellington, one of the most influential jazz musicians of all time, died of cancer and pneumonia, in a New York hospital on May 24.

Composer of such classics as 'Mood Indigo', 'Sophisticated Lady', 'Satin Doll' and 'Solitude', he created a big band whose sound was never completely imitated.

In 1969, President Nixon honoured Ellington by inviting him to The White House for a party on the occasion of Duke's 70th birthday.

THE GRAPEVINE

- **Eno has been producing John Cale in London; both Cale and Eno – together with Nico – are to be the special guests of Kevin Ayers when he appears with his new band at the London Rainbow on June 1. The project was originally envisaged as a Velvet Underground reunion but Lou Reed was unable to take part.**
- **Led Zeppelin have launched a new label – Swansong.**

BOGERT SAYS BBA ARE FINISHED

Rumours concerning a split in Beck, Bogert & Appice, have been confirmed by bassist Tim Bogert.

Speaking in New York, he said that he expected to remain together with drummer Carmen Appice in a new band, but it was highly unlikely either of them would play with Jeff Beck again.

Bogert said that he hoped Robin Trower would join them, but Trower did not want to be tied down. No comment was available from Beck or his manager.

The band-less Beck

COCKNEY REBEL DEBUT TOUR

Cockney Rebel are to undertake their first-ever British tour – a six week schedule, starting on May 25 and running into July. Highlight of the itinerary is a Sunday gig at London's Victoria Palace on June 23.

Throughout the tour, Rebel will be promoting their second EMI album, 'The Psychomodo', set for release on June 2. It features nine Steve Harley compositions and is produced by Harley and Alan Parsons, engineer of Pink Floyd's 'Dark Side Of The Moon'.

Rebel will be supported by Bebop DeLuxe, the four-piece fronted by singer-guitarist Bill Nelson. Their debut album, 'Axe Victim', will be released in early July to coincide with tour dates.

Cockney Rebel onstage

GRAHAM BOND KILLED IN FALL

Graham Bond, a leading pioneer in the British R&B movement, died on May 8 when he fell in front of a train at London's Finsbury Park Station. He was identified from his fingerprints.

Bond first gained attention as a jazz saxist with the Don Rendell quintet, later fronting various Sixties bands as a gifted organist, his sidemen including Ginger Baker, Jack Bruce, John McLaughlin and Jon Hiseman. He formed his first band in 1963 and eventually progressed to the renowned Graham Bond Organization.

After its break-up, he concentrated on session work and writing before joining Ginger Baker's Airforce. Later still, he formed a new band with his wife Diana Stewart and Pete Brown and, when his marriage ended, formed yet another new group, called Magus, with singer Carolanne Pegg. Magus played a few gigs, then folded with financial problems.

Bond, who had quit drugs, was recently hospitalized but was planning a major comeback at the time of his death.

CHARTS

US45	The Loco-motion *Grand Funk Railroad*
USLP	The Sting *Soundtrack/Marvin Hamlisch*
UK45	Waterloo *Abba*
UKLP	The Singles, 1969-1973 *Carpenters*
WEEK 2	
US45	The Loco-motion *Grand Funk Railroad*
USLP	The Sting *Soundtrack/Marvin Hamlisch*
UK45	Waterloo *Abba*
UKLP	The Singles, 1969-1973 *Carpenters*
WEEK 3	
US45	The Streak *Ray Stevens*
USLP	The Sting *Soundtrack/Marvin Hamlisch*
UK45	Sugar Baby Love *Rubettes*
UKLP	The Singles, 1969-1973 *Carpenters*
WEEK 4	
US45	The Streak *Ray Stevens*
USLP	The Sting *Soundtrack/Marvin Hamlisch*
UK45	Sugar Baby Love *Rubettes*
UKLP	The Singles, 1969-1973 *Carpenters*

WAKEMAN QUITS YES

Rick Wakeman (centre) journeys to the centre of Crystal Palace next month

Rick Wakeman has quit Yes. Speculation has been rife for some time, and it reached a head in January, when Rick performed a solo concert at London's Royal Festival Hall, at which his current album, 'Journey To The Centre Of The Earth', was recorded.

But, until now, the question of Wakeman parting company from Yes has always been strenuously denied by the band. A few weeks ago, Wakeman criticized Yes' 'Topographic Oceans' double-album and the band's last British tour, adding: 'Yes could last ten years or ten minutes. But if anybody did leave, the band would survive.'

Wakeman plays his first date since quitting Yes when he headlines the first of this year's Garden Parties at London's Crystal Palace on July 27, when he will once more present 'Journey To The Centre Of The Earth', supported by the 102-piece New World Symphony Orchestra.

NME'S TOP ALBUMS

In the UK NME writers have compiled a list of the 99 best rock albums ever made, the Top 20 comprising (1) The Beatles, 'Sgt Pepper'; (2) Bob Dylan, 'Blonde On Blonde'; (3) Beach Boys, 'Pet Sounds'; (4) The Beatles, 'Revolver'; (5) Bob Dylan, 'Highway 61 Revisited'; (6) Jimi Hendrix, 'Electric Ladyland'; (7) Jimi Hendrix, 'Are You Experienced'; (8) The Beatles, 'Abbey Road'; (9) Rolling Stones, 'Sticky Fingers'; (10) The Band, 'Music From Big Pink'; (11) Rolling Stones, 'Let It Bleed'; (12) Derek & The Dominoes, 'Layla and Other Assorted Love Songs'; (13) Velvet Underground, 'The Velvet Underground and Nico'; (14) Chuck Berry, 'Golden Greats'; (15) The Beatles, 'Rubber Soul'; (16) The Who, 'Tommy'; (17) Simon & Garfunkel, 'Bridge Over Troubled Water'; (18) David Bowie, 'Hunky Dory'; (19) Rolling Stones, 'Beggars' Banquet'; (20) Cream, 'Disraeli Gears'.

CHARTS

	Chart	Title	Artist
	US45	The Streak	*Ray Stevens*
	USLP	The Sting	*Soundtrack/Marvin Hamlisch*
	UK45	Sugar Baby Love	*Rubettes*
	UKLP	The Singles, 1969-1973	*Carpenters*
WEEK 2	US45	Band On The Run	*Paul McCartney & Wings*
	USLP	The Sting	*Soundtrack/Marvin Hamlisch*
	UK45	Sugar Baby Love	*Rubettes*
	UKLP	The Singles, 1969-1973	*Carpenters*
WEEK 3	US45	Billy Don't Be A Hero	*Bo Donaldson & The Heywoods*
	USLP	The Sting	*Soundtrack/Marvin Hamlisch*
	UK45	The Streak	*Ray Stevens*
	UKLP	Diamond Dogs	*David Bowie*
WEEK 4	US45	Billy Don't Be A Hero	*Bo Donaldson & The Heywoods*
	USLP	Sundown	*Gordon Lightfoot*
	UK45	The Streak	*Ray Stevens*
	UKLP	Diamond Dogs	*David Bowie*
WEEK 5	US45	Sundown	*Gordon Lightfoot*
	USLP	Sundown	*Gordon Lightfoot*
	UK45	Always Yours	*Gary Glitter*
	UKLP	Diamond Dogs	*David Bowie*

REBEL RE-BOOK AFTER RIOT

Cockney Rebel are to play a return gig at Aylesbury's Friars on June 6, following the near-riot at the venue which greeted the opening night of their current UK tour, two weeks ago.

Over 2,500 people applied for 700 tickets, and a further 400 were turned away at the door.

Ticket demand has forced Rebel to switch to larger venues in Scarborough and Bristol – they now play Bristol Locarno on June 25 instead of Boobs, while a new Scarborough venue for their June 12 date is being finalized.

STEVE HARLEY

'Maybe in six months time, some perceptive journalist will say: "Didn't Steve Harley do this a year ago and didn't we say it was rubbish?"'

THE GRAPEVINE

- **The live album of the London Rainbow concert by Kevin Ayers, Eno, John Cale and Nico, will be released by Island on June 28. Title is '1st June, 1974'.**
- **Blue Mink are splitting after two final appearances in the north of Scotland.**
- **The Who began a four day stint at New York's Madison Square Garden on June 10. All shows were sold out two months ago.**

Cockney Rebel's Steve Harley

Geoff Britton and friend.

WINGS ADD DRUMMER

After several months without a drummer, Paul McCartney's Wings have announced the addition of Geoff Britton, who replaces Denny Seiwell.

Wings' next single 'Band On The Run'/'Zoo Gang' gains a UK release on June 28.

ALAN PRICE BECOMES ALFIE AND DALTREY GETS LISZT

Price as Alfie

Daltrey as Liszt

Alan Price has landed the title role in a new major film, *Alfie Darling*, which goes before the cameras next month. It's planned as the sequel to the original *Alfie*, which starred Michael Caine.

Nat Cohen of EMI said that the film will have a budget of over half a million and will be shot at Elstree Studios and on location in France, the director being Ken Hughes, who also did the screenplay.

A spokesman said: 'We are not sure if it will have any musical content, but whatever music there is, Alan will write it.'

Roger Daltry of The Who has also been offered a title role in a movie, namely Ken Russell's upcoming film biography of composer Franz Liszt, which goes into production in the new year.

Russell, who has already filmed biographies of classical composers Tchaikovsky and Mahler, had originally planned to approach Mick Jagger to play Liszt. But he was so impressed with Daltrey's work in the movie version of *Tommy*, which he is currently directing, that he decided to offer the part to The Who singer.

MAMA CASS ELLIOT DEAD

Cass Elliot, Mama Cass of The Mamas And The Papas, died in the early morning of July 29 in the London flat of Harry Nilsson, where she was living with her friend and road manager George Caldwell during her stay in the UK.

At a coroner's hearing, held the next day, it was established that she had died as a result of choking on a sandwich while in bed, and from inhaling her own vomit. Cass, who went solo in late 1968 but rejoined The Mamas And The Papas for an ill-fated reunion in 1971, had her biggest solo hit with 'Dream A Little Dream Of Me' in 1968.

She linked with Dave Mason for an album and tour during 1970, but in recent times had enjoyed considerable success on the nightclub circuit.

BLUESMAN DIES

Lightnin' Slim, who's been described as 'the king of the blues in Louisiana, a man who influenced everybody', died in Detroit of stomach cancer on July 27.

Born Otis Hicks in St Louis in 1913, he last toured Britain with the American Blues Legends package in 1973 and recorded for Big Bear during his stay.

CHARTS

US45	Rock The Boat *Hues Corporation*
USLP	Sundown *Gordon Lightfoot*
UK45	She *Charles Aznavour*
UKLP	Diamond Dogs *David Bowie*
	WEEK 2
US45	Rock Your Baby *George McCrae*
USLP	Caribou *Elton John*
UK45	She *Charles Aznavour*
UKLP	Band On The Run *Paul McCartney & Wings*
	WEEK 3
US45	Rock Your Baby *George McCrae*
USLP	Caribou *Elton John*
UK45	She *Charles Aznavour*
UKLP	Band On The Run *Paul McCartney & Wings*
	WEEK 4
US45	Annie's Song *John Denver*
USLP	Caribou *Elton John*
UK45	Rock Your Baby *George McCrae*
UKLP	Band On The Run *Paul McCartney & Wings*

THE GRAPEVINE

- **Tir Na Nog are to play their final gig in Dublin on July 27.**
- **Vangelis Papathanassiou is said to be the hottest contender as Rick Wakeman's replacement with Yes.**
- **Silverhead have broken up and singer Michael Des Barres is going ahead with a solo career, cutting an album for Purple Records with producer Gus Dudgeon.**

STAR QUOTE

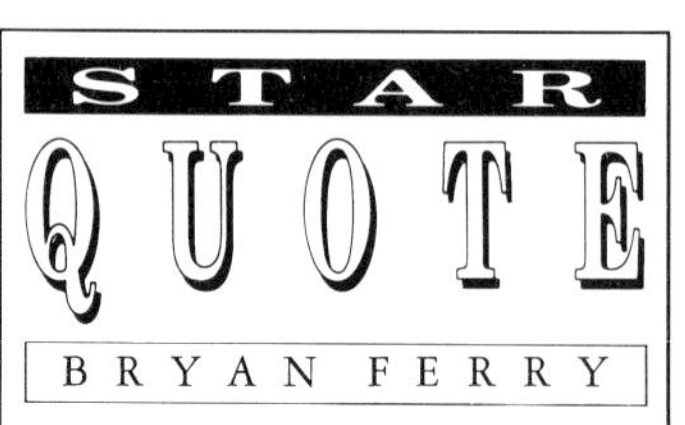

BRYAN FERRY

'Bowie's a nice guy but maybe a little misguided in some ways.'

Despite reputation as fellow guru of glam rock, Ferry distances himself from the more theatrical Bowie

SLADE IN FLAME FLICK

Slade's planned film *Flame* is a comedy drama in which the band play struggling rock musicians battling against the seedy elements of the pop business.

Shooting starts on July 29, with four weeks on location in London, two in the English Midlands and one in Spain. The movie will be directed by Richard Loncraine.

WYATT RETURNS

(l to r) Mike Oldfield, Nick Mason, Julie Tippett (Driscoll) – helping Wyatt

Robert Wyatt, the one-time Soft Machine drummer, makes his first major stage appearance since the accident which paralysed the lower half of his body when he leads a band at London's Theatre Royal on Sunday, September 8. Among the guest stars booked for the event are Mike Oldfield (whose new album 'Hergest Ridge' is released at the end of this month), trumpeter Mongezi Feza, sax-player Gary Windo, Pink Floyd's Nick Mason, ex-Egg keyboardist Dave Stewart, drummer Laurie Allen, and Fred Frith, who played viola on Wyatt's highly acclaimed 'Rock Bottom' solo album.

Julie Tippett, formerly Julie Driscoll, will appear in a solo spot. A Wyatt single gets released on September 1. Titled 'I'm A Believer', it's a reworking of the old Monkees hit.

THE GRAPEVINE

- **ELP's usual dynamic stage show became even more De Mille-like when a tornado hit their gig at New Jersey's Roosevelt Stadium. The equipment is still drying out.**
- **Patrick Moraz has been named as Rick Wakeman's replacement with Yes.**
- **Peter Wolf got spliced to Faye Dunaway on August 5.**
- **John and Michelle Phillips, Sonny Bono and Lou Adler were among those who attended Mama Cass' funeral on August 2.**

Moraz: replacing Rick

DYLAN RE-SIGNS

Bob Dylan has re-signed with CBS Records. The agreement was announced on August 2 at the label's annual convention, in Los Angeles, and is a five-year deal.

Although no figures were given, the contract is reportedly worth a minimum eight million dollars to Dylan. Since his previous deal with CBS expired, he has had two albums released on Island (in Britain) and Asylum (in the States), namely 'Planet Waves' and 'Before The Flood'.

The Zim is now due to start recording a new set for CBS before the month is out.

MAC ARE BACK

Fleetwood Mac have been granted a High Court injunction preventing anyone other than the original group – Mick Fleetwood, John McVie, Bob Welch and Christine McVie – from operating under the name The Fleetwood Mac.

The band now intend to sue their old manager Clifford Davis for damages arising from his formation of a bogus group. The Mac are at present in Los Angeles, where they have just completed an album for Warner Bros and are currently rehearsing in preparation for an American tour which is due to start on October 1 – 'to repair the damage done by the other band'.

BILL CHASE DIES IN CRASH

Trumpeter Bill Chase, 39, plus three other members of his group, Chase, died in a plane crash in Jackson, Minnesota on August 9.

Chase, who worked for the Maynard Ferguson, Stan Kenton and Woody Herman big bands before forming his own jazz-rock outfit, had a US Top 30 hit during 1971 with 'Get It On'. The other Chase members who died in the crash were Wally Yohn (keyboards), John Emma (guitar) and Walter Clark (drums).

The band were touring in support of their current Epic album 'Pure Music' at the time of the disaster.

CHARTS

Chart	Title	Artist
US45	Annie's Song	*John Denver*
USLP	Caribou	*Elton John*
UK45	Rock Your Baby	*George McCrae*
UKLP	Band On The Run	*Paul McCartney & Wings*
WEEK 2		
US45	Feel Like Makin' Love	*Roberta Flack*
USLP	Back Home Again	*John Denver*
UK45	Rock Your Baby	*George McCrae*
UKLP	Band On The Run	*Paul McCartney & Wings*
WEEK 3		
US45	The Night Chicago Died	*Paper Lace*
USLP	461 Ocean Boulevard	*Eric Clapton*
UK45	When Will I See You Again	*Three Degrees*
UKLP	Band On The Run	*Paul McCartney & Wings*
WEEK 4		
US45	(You're) Having My Baby	*Paul Anka*
USLP	461 Ocean Boulevard	*Eric Clapton*
UK45	When Will I See You Again	*Three Degrees*
UKLP	Band On The Run	*Paul McCartney & Wings*
WEEK 5		
US45	(You're) Having My Baby	*Paul Anka*
USLP	461 Ocean Boulevard	*Eric Clapton*
UK45	When Will I See You Again	*Three Degrees*
UKLP	Band On The Run	*Paul McCartney & Wings*

RONSON LINKS WITH MOTT

It has been confirmed that guitarist Mick Ronson is joining Mott The Hoople, replacing Ariel Bender and making his live debut with the band in a European tour that runs from October 10 to November 2. His first UK appearance with Mott will be at London's Hammersmith Odeon on December 6.

Ronson has already recorded with Mott and is on the single 'Saturday Gigs' which CBS are to release in mid-October. Also scheduled for release at the same time is Mott's live album, recorded half at Broadway's Uris Theatre and half at the Hammersmith Odeon, although, of course, Ronson does not figure on this set.

The former Spiders From Mars leader will be performing some of his own material during Mott's stage act. He will also be involved in production and arrangements for the live show.

At the same time, he is also working on a new solo album and single, which RCA hope to issue during November. This indicates that Ronson will continue with his solo career whenever it does not interfere with Mott's commitments.

STAR QUOTE

TODD RUNDGREN

'If I get that one minute of total illumination then I don't care if my whole career goes down the drain. I'd know there was an answer to everything – to existence, to death.'

On his Todd

HEEP'S THAIN BADLY HURT

Uriah Heep's current American tour has been disrupted by an injury to bassist Gary Thain, who was rushed to hospital in Dallas after collapsing onstage during the band's September 15 gig at the Moodie Coliseum. He appeared to have suffered a severe shock and burns.

Said one onlooker: 'Gary leapt about three feet in the air and then collapsed unconscious on the floor.' The remainder of the tour is now in doubt.

THE GRAPEVINE

- All 18 members of Hawkwind's entourage, including the band themselves, were arrested in Indiana for alleged non-payment of US taxes.
- Robert Fripp has disbanded King Crimson – but their new album 'Red' gets an October release.
- The New York Dolls have also reportedly split after a brief two-album career.
- Ringo Starr has announced that he's shortly to launch his own record label, Ring O Records.

Hawkwind blows no good for US taxman

CHARTS

US45	(You're) Having My Baby *Paul Anka*
USLP	461 Ocean Boulevard *Eric Clapton*
UK45	Love Me For A Reason *Osmonds*
UKLP	Band On The Run *Paul McCartney & Wings*
WEEK 2	
US45	I Shot The Sheriff *Eric Clapton*
USLP	Fulfillingness' First Finale *Stevie Wonder*
UK45	Love Me For A Reason *Osmonds*
UKLP	Band On The Run *Paul McCartney & Wings*
WEEK 3	
US45	Can't Get Enough Of Your Love Baby *Barry White*
USLP	Fulfillingness' First Finale *Stevie Wonder*
UK45	Kung Fu Fighting *Carl Douglas*
UKLP	Hergest Ridge *Mike Oldfield*
WEEK 4	
US45	Rock Me Gently *Andy Kim*
USLP	Bad Company *Bad Company*
UK45	Kung Fu Fighting *Carl Douglas*
UKLP	Hergest Ridge *Mike Oldfield*

OLDFIELD SCORES VADIM FILM

Mike Oldfield, whose 'Tubular Bells' was used as the main theme for *The Exorcist*, has been commissioned to write the music for a new film by celebrated French director Roger Vadim. Literally translated, the title of the film is *The Murdered Young Woman*, and shooting is now nearing completion. Oldfield will pen the entire score and has already commenced work on it.

The multi-instrumentalist is now confirmed to play a London Royal Albert Hall gig on December 9. His 'Tubular Bells' and 'Hergest Ridge' works will be featured, both being performed in orchestrated form by the Royal Philharmonic Orchestra, conducted by David Bedford, while Oldfield himself will be featured on guitar.

During the new year he will make his debut UK tour with a band which, he claims, 'Will not consist merely of established superstars but of sympathetic and, quite possibly, unknown musicians whom I think will fit in with my ideas.'

ELVIS ON THE DEFENSIVE

Elvis Presley is the subject of rumours that he is either sick, messed up on drugs, dying or gay. He is currently the undisputed hot number as far as the US show biz scandal sheets are concerned and each week at least two dozen of them are offering hot poop on Elvis' alleged illegitimate kids or terminal cancer.

Not that he's been taking this lying down – during his last season at the Las Vegas Hilton, Presley's act became a marathon of denials and denunciations with songs fitted in between.

He launched into long diatribes against bellhops and head waiters who carried lies to the gutter press and showed the audience the badge and certificate the Federal Bureau of Narcotics gave him when they made Elvis an honorary nark in an attempt to prove that he'd never used drugs.

Priscilla Presley has even been pressed into service to produce a series of syndicated newspaper confessions to prove that Elvis' sexual tastes ran along conventional lines.

THE GRAPEVINE

- **Mary Woodson, a friend of Al Green's, shot herself to death at the singer's Memphis home, after scalding Green with a pot of boiling grits.**
- **Although Gentle Giant have been together for four and a half years, they've just released their first single, 'The Power And The Glory'.**
- **Lulu has recorded the title song for the forthcoming Bond movie, *The Man With The Golden Gun*.**

Lulu: Bond ballad

CHARTS

US45	I Honestly Love You *Olivia Newton-John*
USLP	Endless Summer *Beach Boys*
UK45	Kung Fu Fighting *Carl Douglas*
UKLP	Tubular Bells *Mike Oldfield*
WEEK 2	
US45	I Honestly Love You *Olivia Newton-John*
USLP	If You Love Me, Let Me Know *Olivia Newton-John*
UK45	Kung Fu Fighting *Carl Douglas*
UKLP	Tubular Bells *Mike Oldfield*
WEEK 3	
US45	Nothing From Nothing *Billy Preston*
USLP	Not Fragile *Bachman-Turner Overdrive*
UK45	Gee Baby *Peter Shelley*
UKLP	Back Home Again *John Denver*
WEEK 4	
US45	Then Came You *Dionne Warwick & The Spinners*
USLP	Can't Get Enough *Barry White*
UK45	Everything I Own *Ken Boothe*
UKLP	Smiler *Rod Stewart*

NICK DRAKE FOUND DEAD

Nick Drake, the U.K. singer-songwriter was found dead in bed at his parent's home in Tamworth, near Stratford-on-Avon, on October 25. A very private man who was hardly known even to the people at his record label, he spent a great deal of time in various mental hospitals after the release of 'Pink Moon' in 1972.

At the time of his death, resulting from an overdose of anti-depressants, Drake, 26, was recording tracks for a new album with producer Joe Boyd.

'HAMMY' McCARTNEY

Though 'Junior's Farm' is Wings' 'official' UK single release this month, 'Walking In The Park With Eloise', an EMI release which purports to be by The Country Hams, is also by Wings.

Recorded in Nashville with help from country stars Chet Atkins and Floyd Cramer, the A-side features a song penned over 20 years ago by Paul's father.

INCREDIBLES – IT'S THE END

The Incredible String Band have broken up. They were lining up for a string of concerts in Britain and Ireland but, in the wake of various rumours, the band have announced: 'We realize that we have learned a lot and achieved much in our years as The Incredibles. That stage is over and now is the time for all of us to start a new phase.

'There were no hassles, no big emotional scenes, no financial or legal complications. So, with just a little nostalgia and a great deal of affection for each other and our public, we are all getting our new directions together.'

Incredible announcement

NOVEMBER

BEATLEMANIA YET AGAIN

Beatlemania ruled in New York once more when the show *Sgt Pepper's Lonely Hearts Club Band On The Road* opened at the city's Beacon Theatre. John Lennon was mobbed as he and girlfriend May Pang tried to make their way past the hordes being held back by the police, May Pang getting knocked to the ground.

Also there were Bianca Jagger with Andy Warhol, Ruby Keeler in a fabulous sable coat, Wayne County, Divine, Yoko Ono all in white satin and furs, Robert Stigwood, Elton John's manager John Reid and Atlantic Records' Ahmet Ertegun.

Playing the lead role of Billy Shears in the show is Ted Neely, while the role of his romantic counterpart, Strawberry Fields, is performed by Kay Cole. However, the show is stolen by Alaina Reed, whose costumes and stage presence were highly reminiscent of LaBelle's Nona Hendryx.

Lennon and May Pang were practically the last to leave, going on to a party which Alice Cooper attended with Cindy Lang. The Ronettes also showed up, Wayne County and Divine were photographed together and John Phillips and Genevieve Waite danced together.

But Wayne County proved a party pooper. When asked by Warhol to meet Bianca Jagger, he declined, saying 'My Mama told me not to have anything to do with those kind of people.'

Wright off

THE GRAPEVINE

- **Keef Hartley, who has been largely inactive since his last band broke up in early 1972, has formed a new outfit called Dog Soldier.**
- **Gary Wright has quit Spooky Tooth.**
- **Ivory Joe Hunter, the bluesman, died in Memphis on November 8, aged 63. Hunter, who wrote some 7,000 songs had hits with 'I Almost Lost My Mind' and 'Since I Met You Baby'.**

Mud (above) and Peter 'Herman' Noone (right) among balding bubblegummers pleading they're 'Never Too Young To Rock'

MUD, GLITTERMEN IN ROCK MOVIE

Mud, The Glitter Band and The Rubettes are among the UK chart groups who have major roles in a new film titled *Never Too Young To Rock*, which has just gone into production.

Described as a high speed comedy with music, the cast also includes Peter Noone, Sally James (presenter of London Weekend Television's *Saturday Scene*) and Scott Fitzgerald. Producer is Denis Abey.

MOTT SCRAP TOUR

Mott The Hoople have now scrapped their entire British tour which was originally scheduled to open on November 10 and continue until December 12. The reason for calling off the jaunt is that Ian Hunter – whose collapse from physical exhaustion, while on a brief private trip to America to visit his US manager Fred Heller, caused the initial four dates to be cancelled – has not recovered and has been ordered to rest for two months.

Accordingly, he is staying in America to recuperate and is not expected to return to Britain until Christmas. In the interim, speculation has been growing on both sides of the Atlantic that Hunter's illness may lead to Mott breaking up.

One proffered reason for Hunter being in the States at the time of his collapse was that he was looking for a house in the USA because he has an American wife and is likely to be spending more time there.

CHARTS

US45	You Haven't Done Nothin' — *Stevie Wonder*
USLP	So Far — *Crosby, Stills, Nash & Young*
UK45	Everything I Own — *Ken Boothe*
UKLP	Smiler — *Rod Stewart*
WEEK 2	
US45	You Ain't Seen Nothin' Yet — *Bachman-Turner Overdrive*
USLP	Wrap Around Joy — *Carole King*
UK45	Gonna Make You A Star — *David Essex*
UKLP	Rollin' — *Bay City Rollers*
WEEK 3	
US45	Whatever Gets You Thru The Night — *John Lennon*
USLP	Walls & Bridges — *John Lennon*
UK45	Gonna Make You A Star — *David Essex*
UKLP	Rollin' — *Bay City Rollers*
WEEK 4	
US45	I Can Help — *Billy Swan*
USLP	It's Only Rock'n'Roll — *Rolling Stones*
UK45	Gonna Make You A Star — *David Essex*
UKLP	David Essex — *David Essex*
WEEK 5	
US45	I Can Help — *Billy Swan*
USLP	Greatest Hits — *Elton John*
UK45	Gonna Make You A Star — *David Essex*
UKLP	Elton John's Greatest Hits — *Elton John*

PHIL COLLINS

'It's not as if by having that middle class status Genesis have evaded the hassles that every other band goes through.'

MICK TAYLOR IN NEW BAND

Mick Taylor has left The Rolling Stones to join a new outfit being formed by Jack Bruce. News of Taylor's departure broke when it became apparent that he was not working with The Stones in a Munich studio.

Reports from Germany at first suggested he had been sacked, but Jagger quickly squashed these rumours in a statement saying: 'After five and a half years, Mick wishes a change of scene. While we're all sorry that he is going, we wish him great success and much happiness.'

Also in the new Bruce band are Carla Bley, keyboardist on the 'Escalator Over The Hill' album, and pianist Max Middleton, who was recently part of the Jeff Beck group. A drummer still has to be signed.

Taylor-made move

STAR QUOTE

JIMMY PAGE

'1974 didn't really happen. 1975 will be better.'

THE GRAPEVINE

■ Ravi Shankar was hospitalized in Chicago on December 2 after complaining about chest pains.

■ David Crosby and Graham Nash performed together in San Francisco at a benefit concert for the United Farm Workers and a whale protection project.

■ George Harrison was presented to President Ford at a recent White House shindig after the President's son attended a Harrison gig in Salt Lake City.'

LED ZEP GIGS

Led Zeppelin will definitely be playing spring gigs in the UK, claims Jimmy Page. These will follow the band's extensive US tour which opens on January 18 and continues into March.

Zeppelin have been out of the public eye for the greater part of the year and have been spending the past few months on their new film and album. It was because of these commitments that they were forced to withdraw from the UK Knebworth open-air concert during the summer.

The album, called 'Physical Graffitti', will be Atlantic's first release in January. Reporter Nick Kent, given a preview claims: 'It's 82 minutes and 30 seconds of inimitable heavy metal grandiosity for mass consumption. Whatever you do, set the volume switch to "loud" (on second thoughts make that "VERY loud") because Led Zeppelin are still, absolutely, the best mainstream metal band around.'

The film is a semi-documentary that includes in-concert sequences, shot on the band's last American tour – notably at New York's Madison Square Garden, plus several fantasy sequences filmed at various locations.

Ravi Shankar

HUNTER GOES SOLO

Ian Hunter, back in Britain earlier than expected, has quit Mott The Hoople and is now making a solo album with the aid of Mick Ronson. It's said that he's accepted a lucrative, six-figure deal (rumours suggest $750,000) with CBS that will 'set him up for life.'

It seems that Hunter's plans have come as a shock to the other members of Mott, who claim that they didn't know what was happening, though it seems a rift developed between Hunter and drummer Buffin over the recently released live album, while other sources suggest that some members of the band became unhappy about Ronson's Mott involvement.

Was 1974 just a Page missing from history?

CHARTS

US45	Kung Fu Fighting *Carl Douglas*
USLP	Greatest Hits *Elton John*
UK45	Gonna Make You A Star *David Essex*
UKLP	Elton John's Greatest Hits *Elton John*
WEEK 2	
US45	Kung Fu Fighting *Carl Douglas*
USLP	Greatest Hits *Elton John*
UK45	You're The First, The Last, My Everything *Barry White*
UKLP	Elton John's Greatest Hits *Elton John*
WEEK 3	
US45	Cat's In The Cradle *Harry Chapin*
USLP	Greatest Hits *Elton John*
UK45	Lonely This Christmas *Mud*
UKLP	Elton John's Greatest Hits *Elton John*
WEEK 4	
US45	Angie Baby *Helen Reddy*
USLP	Greatest Hits *Elton John*
UK45	Lonely This Christmas *Mud*
UKLP	Elton John's Greatest Hits *Elton John*

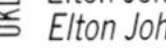

Hunter foxes Mott

ZEP ZAP WINDY CITY

They rioted just to get tickets for Led Zeppelin's latest US onslaught. In New York 60,000 tickets at Madison Square Gardens were snapped up in four hours after the crowd forced the box office to open a day early. In Boston they trashed the foyer and the mayor was so angry he cancelled the show.

It's nearly two years since 'Houses Of The Holy', and the new album, the double 'Physical Graffiti', isn't out in time for the start of their tour. But Led Zeppelin are the band everyone wants to see this time around.

'It's not only that we think we're the best group in the world – it's just that in our minds we're so much better than whoever is No. 2', boasts Robert Plant as he prepares for the first of three shows in Chicago. Not even the wrecked throat that traditionally haunts him at the start of the tour can dampen his spirits. But it's not just Robert's voice; Jimmy Page has a broken finger, sustained during rehearsals, when he trapped it in a door.

'It's the most important finger for a guitarist,' he says. 'It's the one that does all the leverage and most of the work. I'm still not really playing with it but I'm starting to master a three-fingered technique!' Their collective ailments get the better of them on the first night. They are depressed all next day. But on the second night the band turn in a blinder. After the third night everyone goes out partying. And out at Chicago's O'Hare Airport the super Starship, painted red white and blue with white stars and LED ZEPPELIN written along the side, waits patiently . . .

CHARTS

US45	Lucy In The Sky With Diamonds *Elton John*
USLP	Greatest Hits *Elton John*
UK45	Lonely This Christmas *Mud*
UKLP	Elton John's Greatest Hits *Elton John*
	WEEK 2
US45	Lucy In The Sky With Diamonds *Elton John*
USLP	Greatest Hits *Elton John*
UK45	Streets Of London *Ralph McTell*
UKLP	Elton John's Greatest Hits *Elton John*
	WEEK 3
US45	Mandy *Barry Manilow*
USLP	Greatest Hits *Elton John*
UK45	Streets Of London *Ralph McTell*
UKLP	Elton John's Greatest Hits *Elton John*
	WEEK 4
US45	Please Mr. Postman *Carpenters*
USLP	Greatest Hits *Elton John*
UK45	Down Down *Status Quo*
UKLP	Elton John's Greatest Hits *Elton John*

STAR QUOTE

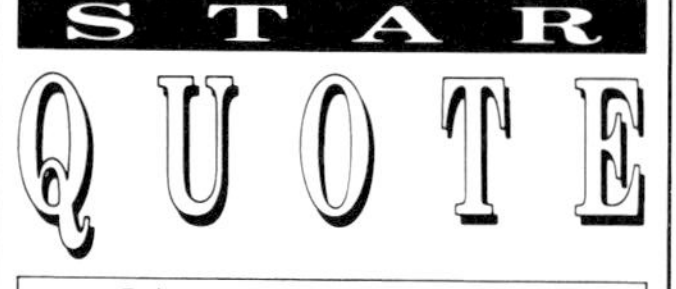

IAN ANDERSON

JETHRO TULL

'I don't think it's very easy to make friends with musicians. We're all a bit paranoid. It soon becomes very heavy.'

THE GRAPEVINE

- **John Lennon has won access to the Department Of Immigration file on his pending deportation case.**
- **Bob Dylan has released 'Blood On The Tracks', his first album back on CBS after his brief encounter with Asylum.**
- **17-year-old Elvis fan Areecia (Honeybee) Benson and her 19-year-old friend wrapped themselves up in brown paper and a packing case and had themselves delivered to Gracelands.**

AVERAGE WHITE BAND PICK UP THE PIECES

The Average White Band are playing a benefit show for the widow of drummer Robbie MacIntosh at London's Marquee Club. Robbie's death was caused by snorting heroin laced with poison. According to bassist Alan Gorrie: 'Somebody gave him a nasty. It's as simple and stupid as that. It's easy to say "Stupid sod for taking it" when you read about it a thousand miles away. You always do that when it's someone you don't know. But when you're in the middle of it you see it as an accident . . . Oh well.'

The Average White Band

JUST A KISS AWAY

Klassic Kiss, all made up and breathing glam-rock fire into heavy metal. From left to right Ace Frehley guitar, Peter Criss drums, Paul Stanley guitar, Gene Simmons bass

The latest glam-rock band to totter out of New York on their stack heels are Kiss, four boys who conceal their identities behind a tray full of war-paint and flame-throwing antics.

The music is heavy metal, the lyrics are juvenile escapism shot through with blatant sexual fantasy. But there are two obvious deviations from the norm: they can actually play and they are deliberately steering away from the traditional glam'n'glitter clichés.

'That thing is dead and the participants are finished too,' growls bassist Gene Simmons. 'But we're getting a bigger response all the time. I don't want to sound malicious, but with people like The New York Dolls . . . well, you can't go on fooling audiences all the time. We can play. Before this came together we were practising for months in a loft to get it right.'

Simmons is getting better at flame-throwing too. The first time he tried it the fire rebounded from his dagger and set his hair alight. 'It wasn't until my roadie smothered me with his jacket that I knew what was happening. The crowd loved it though. They thought it was all part of the act.'

Their 110 dB sound on stage has the audiences bouncing off the walls, but Simmons insists it's a healthy attitude. 'It's not a negative vibe, like smashing seats. They get rid of their frustration with the music. Personally I'd be insulted if people didn't react immediately. Groups have tried that laid-back experimental trip too long.'

THE GRAPEVINE

- **The Who's bassist John Entwistle has started a five week solo tour of the States with his band, Ox.**
- **John Lennon is releasing 'Rock'n'Roll', an LP of oldies produced by Phil Spector.**
- **Bob Marley is producing a new album, 'Natty Dread'.**
- **Lou Reed has three albums on the go at present: 'Rock & Roll Animal II', 'Metal Machine Music' and 'Coney Island Baby'.**

FEATS DON'T FAIL IN UK

Little Feat arrive in Britain for their first visit, headlining over The Doobie Brothers in Manchester and supporting them in London – where the audience makes it clear they should be headlining as well.

'The thing is,' says a Warner Brothers UK person, 'the American side didn't know the extent of Little Feat's following here, although we've tried to tell them often enough. . . . As it happens we've been trying to get them over here for the last two years. It's no surprise to us . . .'

Lowell George, the enigmatic force behind Little Feat's soul strut

BOWIE THE 'CRACKED ACTOR'

'Cracked Actor', a documentary on David Bowie by Alan Yentob screened by BBC Television, does the Thin White Duke no favours. 'Bowie is seen alternating neurotic, speedy exhilaration, irritation and moments of deadpan depression, spouting platitudes and attempts at self-revelation that indicate nothing so much as that he doesn't really have a self to reveal'. But he does have a new single to reveal – 'Young Americans'.

TODD RUNDGREN

'A red polygon is only a red polygon if it knows it's a red polygon . . . I guess'

CHARTS

US45	Laughter In The Rain *Neil Sedaka*
USLP	Greatest Hits *Elton John*
UK45	Ms. Grace *Tymes*
UKLP	Elton John's Greatest Hits *Elton John*
WEEK 2	
US45	Fire *Ohio Players*
USLP	Fire *Ohio Players*
UK45	January *Pilot*
UKLP	Elton John's Greatest Hits *Elton John*
WEEK 3	
US45	You're No Good *Linda Ronstadt*
USLP	Heart Like A Wheel *Linda Ronstadt*
UK45	January *Pilot*
UKLP	Greatest Hits *Engelbert Humperdinck*
WEEK 4	
US45	Pick Up The Pieces *Average White Band*
USLP	Average White Band *Average White Band*
UK45	Please Mr Postman *Carpenters*
UKLP	Greatest Hits *Engelbert Humperdinck*

1975

JOHN LENNON – LONG TIME IN NEW YORK CITY

Lennon faces lawsuits from his ex-Beatle mates, his manager and the US Government

John Lennon still faces deportation from America after three years of legal battles. Officially, a British drug conviction (for marijuana) disbars him from US residency. Unofficially, his political activities have made him a pain in President Richard Nixon's ass.

'It was getting to be a bug (pun intended) because I had to keep going to court and court cases got to be a way of life,' admits Lennon. 'I guess it showed in me work. Whatever happens to you happens in your work. So while on the surface I tried to make it appear as if I was making a game of it, trying not to take it seriously, there were periods of real paranoia.'

Lennon is also facing lawsuits from former manager Allen Klein, the other three Beatles and a photographer who claims he was hit in the Los Angeles Troubadour during Lennon's infamous 'lost weekend'.

But at least his personal life is on an even keel again. 'I just sort of came home, is what happened. I went out to get a newspaper or a coffee somewhere and it took a year . . . like Sinbad. I had a mad trip which I'm glad is over. It was a long year – maybe it was the seven-year crutch!'

GENESIS SAY BAA TO UK CRITICS

Genesis's *'Lamb Lies Down On Broadway'* live extravaganza has been going down better in America and Europe than Britain.

And singer Peter Gabriel believes he knows why: 'I think Europeans like the exaggeration and the sense of festival whereas the English are more reserved. In America I find it much healthier. There's room for different opinions and you don't have to justify yourself when you like a band.'

UK critics remain distrustful of Genesis's pomp rock music and art-rock motives. But Gabriel reckons they just don't understand: 'While it's fun to be pompous and sermonise it's still an illusion, a grand illusion. If you can retain your sense of humour and be cynical, it's better. I go right inside my lyrics and laugh at them at the same time.'

Which is why he can act out his Mick Jagger parody and sing 'It's only knock and knowall but I like it' at the climax of *'The Lamb Lies Down'*.

'Is there a man alive who hasn't performed his Jaggerisms in front of the mirror? I know I have.'

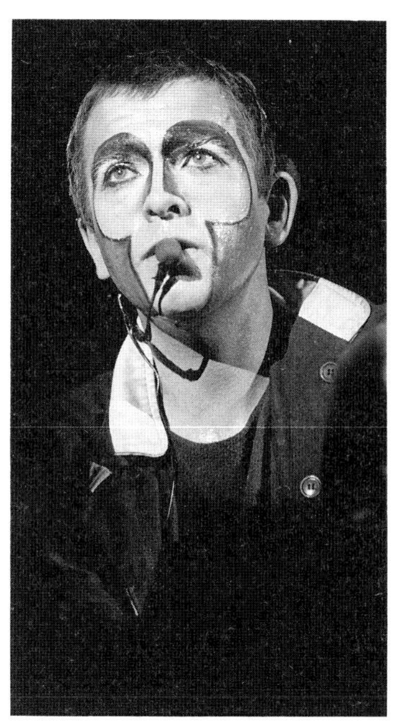

Peter Gabriel as Rael in The Lamb Lies Down On Broadway

CHARTS

US45	Best Of My Love — *Eagles*
USLP	Blood On The Tracks — *Bob Dylan*
UK45	Make Me Smile — *Steve Harley & Cockney Rebel*
UKLP	Elton John's Greatest Hits — *Elton John*
WEEK 2	
US45	Have You Never Been Mellow — *Olivia Newton-John*
USLP	Blood On The Tracks — *Bob Dylan*
UK45	If — *Telly Savalas*
UKLP	On The Level — *Status Quo*
WEEK 3	
US45	Black Water — *Doobie Brothers*
USLP	Have You Never Been Mellow — *Olivia Newton-John*
UK45	If — *Telly Savalas*
UKLP	On The Level — *Status Quo*
WEEK 4	
US45	My Eyes Adored You — *Frankie Valli*
USLP	Physical Graffiti — *Led Zeppelin*
UK45	Bye Bye Baby — *Bay City Rollers*
UKLP	On The Level — *Status Quo*
WEEK 5	
US45	Lady Marmalade — *Labelle*
USLP	Physical Graffiti — *Led Zeppelin*
UK45	Bye Bye Baby — *Bay City Rollers*
UKLP	Physical Graffiti — *Led Zeppelin*

CAN YOU HEAR ME ABOVE THE HYPE?

'Tommy' the movie premiered in New York to unprecedented ballyhoo. A planeload of celebrities flying in from Los Angeles suffered from culture shock when they were decanted into a subway station for the post-premiere party. Co-stars Elton John and Tina Turner joined The Who for celebrations which lasted three days and included two $50,000 parties to stretch the combined publicity resources of the film and rock industry.

Having worked painstakingly on the 'quintaphonic' soundtrack, Pete Townshend was upset by the sound problems on the opening night: 'How are they going to get the sound right in the 40 cinemas across the country equipped for quintaphonic sound if they can't get it right in New York?" He'd spent three hours trying to fix the delay between the front and back speakers.

The next day the caravan trekked back to Los Angeles to repeat the whole shebang.

Elton John the Pinball Wizard

THE GRAPEVINE

- **David Bowie has filed a lawsuit in London against MainMan and Tony Defries to annul his management contract. MainMan responded with a US injunction against Bowie's new album, 'Young Americans', which has been lifted on appeal.**
- **LA police have busted Linda McCartney for 'six to eight' ounces of marijuana. Hubby Paul was not charged.**

STEELY DAN – REINING IN THE YEARS

The brains behind Steely Dan – Walter Becker (left) and Donald Fagen

Walter Becker and Donald Fagen of Steely Dan are rock'n'roll's odd couple – a couple of disrespectful misfits who've stuck to their unconventional guns until it finally paid off.

Which it did when they finally got the chance to record their first album, 'Can't Buy A Thrill'. Since then, they've fallen in and out of favour with each successive album. 'Our music is somehow a little too cheesy at times and turns off the rock intelligentsia for the most part,' admits Fagen.

Their latest album, 'Katy Lied', has taken a while because of various technical hitches. They've also lost a couple of members along the way, which has curtailed their touring activities.

But Becker and Fagen explain that Steely Dan is not your conventional rock band. 'If you think of it more as a concept than a group of specific musicians, there's no way it will break up,' says Fagen. 'We have a bunch of satellite performers who are more or less interchangeable. Usually we pick musicians who we think will fit a particular song. We grew up listening to jazz musicians and they're always playing with different people . . . It makes it much more interesting.'

They're more evasive on defining the Steely Dan 'concept', however. 'All we can do is give clues because we're too close to it,' says Fagen. 'It's all on the record, you know.' 'Even if we could answer the question,' says Becker smiling, 'you know that we would lie. We would deliberately lead you off the scent.'

PATTI SMITH – FIRST TIME IN NEW YORK CITY

'I don't want to do a record unless it's fantastic and will really do something to people. I mean, I could make a few thousand dollars other ways – I'm a good hustler. I haven't done that much, but most of what I've done is real good and I don't ever want to do a lousy thing.'

Patti Smith, variously described as 'the female Jim Morrison' and 'Keith Richards' kid sister', has signed to Clive Davis' Arista label.

Best known in media circles for her poetry and contributions to *Rolling Stone, Creem, Crawdaddy* and the now-defunct *Rock* (where she was fired when her interview with Eric Clapton consisted of asking him to list his five favourite words), her band includes fellow rock journalist Lenny Kaye on guitar.

Her credentials are impeccable, including a period spent living at New York's Chelsea Hotel, the obligatory Paris sojourn and friendship with artist Robert Mapplethorpe.

Patti Smith: born in Chicago and brought up in New Jersey, she moved to New York in 1967 and began writing poetry which she performed to the backing of a rock and roll band

THE GRAPEVINE

- **Bob Dylan, Neil Young, The Grateful Dead, Jefferson Starship, The Doobie Brothers and Santana played a benefit gig for SNACK (Students Need Athletics, Culture and Kicks) in San Francisco.**
- **Al Green says he'll be dedicating more of his act to God after the incident in Miami last year when a girlfriend poured boiling grits over him in the bath and then shot herself.**

CHARTS

US45	Lovin' You – *Minnie Riperton*
USLP	Physical Graffiti – *Led Zeppelin*
UK45	Bye Bye Baby – *Bay City Rollers*
UKLP	Physical Graffiti – *Led Zeppelin*
WEEK 2	
US45	Philadelphia Freedom – *Elton John*
USLP	Physical Graffiti – *Led Zeppelin*
UK45	Bye Bye Baby – *Bay City Rollers*
UKLP	Physical Graffiti – *Led Zeppelin*
WEEK 3	
US45	Philadelphia Freedom – *Elton John*
USLP	Physical Graffiti – *Led Zeppelin*
UK45	Bye Bye Baby – *Bay City Rollers*
UKLP	Young Americans – *David Bowie*
WEEK 4	
US45	Another Somebody Done Somebody Wrong – *B.J. Thomas*
USLP	Physical Graffiti – *Led Zeppelin*
UK45	Bye Bye Baby – *Bay City Rollers*
UKLP	Once Upon A Star – *Bay City Rollers*

MAY

1975

NEIL YOUNG – THE NEEDLE AND THE DAMAGE DONE

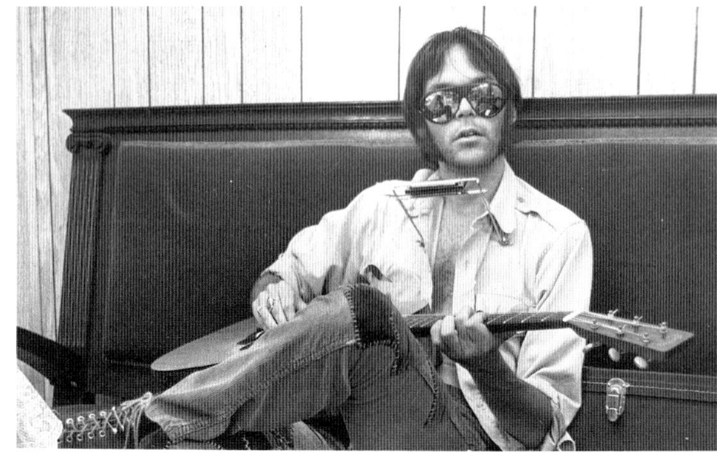
Neil Young tears it down

Three years ago, Neil Young was on the brink of superstardom, with his 'Harvest' album selling in huge quantities. But since then Neil has deliberately refused to play the chords of fame.

'It's odd, I don't know why. It was a subconscious move. I think "Tonight's The Night" is the most grand example of that resistance,' Neil agrees.

'Tonight's The Night' is a harrowing album. The title track is the story of Bruce Berry, Young's guitar roadie, who 'died, out on the mainline'. 'Lookout Joe' is the song they were working on when Crazy Horse rhythm guitarist Danny Whitten OD'd, and 'Tired Eyes' is about a dope-dealing vendetta that ends in bloodshed.

'These two cats had been a close part of our unit – our force and our energy. And they were both gone to junk – both of them OD'd,' sighs Neil. 'I don't think "Tonight's The Night" is a friendly album. It's real, that's all. I'm really proud of it. You've got to listen to it at night, which was when it was done.'

So is that it for Neil Young, Superstar? 'We gotta tear all that down,' he laughs. 'It's gone now. Now we can do whatever. It's open again, there's no illusions that someone can say what I'm going to do before I get there. That's how I have to feel. I don't want to feel like people expect me to be a certain way. If that's the way it is, then I quit.'

STAR QUOTE

MARIA MULDAUR

'People ask me – why do you do these sexist songs? That's bullshit. That's a valid emotion that's a part of us all.'

IGGY ON THE BRINK

'There are basically three kinds of people who "perform". there are those who do it naturally, those who desperately want to possess that ability but don't have that touch, and there are those who want to and don't give a damn either way. I'm part of the last category.'

Iggy Pop is coming up for the third time, and even Iggy knows that he can't afford to sink once more. The kamikaze panache of The Stooges has already claimed two victims. Sax player Steve McKay died from an overdose and bassist Dave Alexander is dead from alcohol poisoning.

'Yeah . . . I just know for a fact that if anyone is going to be next to go, it'll be me. I'm not afraid to die. I know that sounds like a dumb boast or something, but it's a fact. I've proved it enough times, for chrissakes.'

His good buddy David Bowie isn't much help at the moment; the pair were recently reduced to fisticuffs to settle an argument. But he does have the makings of a band. Guitarist and Stooges survivor James Williamson is still on hand, and Hunt and Tony Sales are interested in taking on the rhythm section. 'If a guy walked into this room right now and handed me a cheque for a million dollars, I'd only spend it all on forming a band.'

Iggy Pop: next in line?

THE GRAPEVINE

- **Pete Ham, a founder member of Badfinger, has been found dead, hanging in the garage of his house.**
- **Van Morrison is planning to return to his native Ireland to settle after a six-year sojourn on the American West Coast.**
- **Ten Years After have confirmed their demise after months of speculation.**
- **Stevie Wonder played to 125,000 people at the Washington Monument for Human Kindness Day.**

Van Morrison goes home

CHARTS

US45	He Don't Love You (Like I Love You) *Tony Orlando & Dawn*
USLP	Chicago VIII *Chicago*
UK45	Honey *Bobby Goldsboro*
UKLP	Once Upon A Star *Bay City Rollers*
WEEK 2	
US45	He Don't Love You (Like I Love You) *Tony Orlando & Dawn*
USLP	Chicago VIII *Chicago*
UK45	Loving You *Minnie Riperton*
UKLP	Once Upon A Star *Bay City Rollers*
WEEK 3	
US45	He Don't Love You (Like I Love You) *Tony Orlando & Dawn*
USLP	That's The Way Of The World *Earth, Wind & Fire*
UK45	Stand By Your Man *Tammy Wynette*
UKLP	Once Upon A Star *Bay City Rollers*
WEEK 4	
US45	Shining Star *Earth, Wind & Fire*
USLP	That's The Way Of The World *Earth, Wind & Fire*
UK45	Stand By Your Man *Tammy Wynette*
UKLP	Once Upon A Star *Bay City Rollers*
WEEK 5	
US45	Before The Next Teardrop Falls *Freddy Fender*
USLP	That's The Way Of The World *Earth, Wind & Fire*
UK45	Stand By Your Man *Tammy Wynette*
UKLP	Once Upon A Star *Bay City Rollers*

STONES REV UP WITH RON

The Stones roll out on the road again with two new members: Ron Wood on guitar and Mick Jagger's latest stage prop (not shown here). And they say this could be the last time

The Rolling Stones unveiled their 1975 touring model – featuring Ron Wood – on the back of a truck cruising around Greenwich Village. Officially, Ron's just the guest guitarist for the tour. He's supposed to be touring with The Faces again in August.

But right from the opening show of the Stones' US tour at Louisiana State University, Baton Rouge, Ron looks like a permanent fixture. He's changed the musical shape of the band too. Mick Taylor's guitar solos are a thing of the past, to be replaced by a strong, funky, strutting twin guitar attack from Ron and his lookalike, Keith Richards.

The Stones have gone out with their most elaborate stage show yet. The stage is a six-petalled flower that unfolds at the start of the show to the gladiatorial strains of Aaron Copeland's 'Fanfare For The Common Man'.

Jagger makes full use of the 360 degrees in which to prance, preen and pose. There's even another toy for him during 'Star Star' – a giant hosepipe that rears up from the ground and ejaculates a stream of confetti over the audience. It's only rock'n'roll . . .

'Just sort of funny entertainment,' says Jagger philosophically. 'Mass funny entertainment. There is a certain element in the form which is agreeable, especially performing it in these sports arenas. It's like an un-art event. I prefer that to, say, the Metropolitan Opera House.'

Jagger designed the stage with Charlie Watts. 'There's no obstructed view. The people at the back can see. They get a fantastic view because the sound is all hung from above. And it sounds better too, because it's directional sound.'

How about the rumours that this is the last Stones tour? 'They said it in 1969, and they said it again in 1972. Why do they say it? They don't have anything else to write.'

STAR QUOTE

ALICE COOPER

'I lost my virginity to a pillow. The very first orgasm I ever had was with a pillow. Honest! I wish I still had that pillow case.'

ELTON LIES BLEEDING

Elton John forgot to give his audience what they wanted at Wembley Stadium and introduced them to Captain Fantastic And The Brown Dirt Cowboy. The crowd made their excuses and left

A week before his London Wembley Stadium gig in front of 80,000 people, Elton John was worried. 'I've never had a nervous rash before in my life. I came out in blotches all over the place.'

The blotches knew something Elton didn't, because on the night, he got it all wrong. The crowd didn't want to listen to an hour's worth of new and unfamiliar material. But that's what they got – the whole of the scarcely released and definitely undigested 'Captain Fantastic And The Brown Dirt Cowboy' album.

Elton got it wrong right from the opening 'Love Lies Bleeding', miscalculating the atmosphere in the wake of the heady nostalgia The Beach Boys had created as opening act. Midway through Elton's set, a steady stream of punters was heading for the exit. His grandiose gesture had misfired.

THE GRAPEVINE

■ **Alice Cooper took a tumble during his 'Welcome To My Nightmare' tour in Vancouver and broke six ribs.**

■ **Former Columbia Records head Clive Davis and Philly Soul bosses Kenny Gamble and Leon Huff are among ten record company executives indicted for payola in New Jersey.**

■ **Folksinger Tim Buckley has died of a heroin/morphine overdose in Santa Monica.**

CHARTS

US45	Thank God I'm A Country Boy *John Denver*
USLP	Captain Fantastic & The Brown Dirt Cowboy *Elton John*
UK45	Whispering Grass *Windsor Davies & Don Estelle*
UKLP	Once Upon A Star *Bay City Rollers*
WEEK 2	
US45	Sister Golden Hair *America*
USLP	Captain Fantastic & The Brown Dirt Cowboy *Elton John*
UK45	Three Steps To Heaven *Showaddywaddy*
UKLP	Captain Fantastic & The Brown Dirt Cowboy *Elton John*
WEEK 3	
US45	Love Will Keep Us Together *Captain & Tenille*
USLP	Captain Fantastic & The Brown Dirty Cowbo *Elton John*
UK45	Whispering Grass *Windsor Davies & Don Estelle*
UKLP	Captain Fantastic & The Brown Dirt Cowboy *Elton John*
WEEK 4	
US45	Love Will Keep Us Together *Captain & Tenille*
USLP	Captain Fantastic & The Brown Dirt Cowboy *Elton John*
UK45	I'm Not In Love *10cc*
UKLP	Captain Fantastic & The Brown Dirt Cowboy *Elton John*

JULY 1975

BOB MARLEY – RASTAMAN VIBRATIONS

'Y'call me natty 'ead . . . greyat. Because who care what you think? Me no vex meself while you laugh. Laugh and make the world laugh mon, so me dig it, so me live.'

Bob Marley has come out of the Trenchtown ghetto of Kingston, Jamaica, to give reggae music inspiration and charisma.

London's Lyceum ballroom was the venue where a show by Bob Marley & The Wailers was recorded, and the resulting live album has become the catalyst to launch Marley's career as a superstar.

He's released three albums since Chris Blackwell signed him to Island Records, and each has rolled back the boundaries of reggae. His own stature has grown faster than his dreadlocks, aided by Eric Clapton, who took Marley's song, 'I Shot The Sheriff', to the top of the US charts last year.

Live, Marley is a mesmeric character, driven by the hypnotic force of his music and the commitment to Rastafari that peppers his lyrics and conversation: 'Y'know, Jah appear to me in a vision – and every time he look just a bit older then me. Man, it's so sweet: it's me brother, me father, me mother, me creator, everything . . .'

But The Big Guy didn't tell Bob to be tolerant of everyone: 'Politicians, they are devils; devils who corrupt. They don't smoke 'erb, because when y'smoke, y'think alike, and them don't want that . . .'

But beyond the politics and the rasta, Marley has found a new twist to the oldest inspiration of all – 'No Woman, No Cry'.

CLAPTON TELLS THE TRUTH

'Half way through the second Derek & The Dominoes album, we realised we'd hit our peak. We broke up and it took three years to pluck up enough courage to do "461 Ocean Boulevard."'

During those three years, Eric Clapton developed a heroin habit that threatened to destroy him. Pete Townshend got him cured – 'He gave me faith in myself again. I owe him that.'

And he's back on the road again, touring America. But wherever he goes, day or night, his 'minder', Mick Turner, stays three paces behind. Just in case.

Clapton back on the road again

CHARTS

US45	Love Will Keep Us Together *Captain & Tenille*
USLP	Captain Fantastic & The Brown Dirt Cowboy *Elton John*
UK45	I'm Not In Love *10cc*
UKLP	Venus And Mars *Wings*
WEEK 2	
US45	Love Will Keep Us Together *Captain & Tenille*
USLP	Captain Fantastic & The Brown Dirt Cowboy *Elton John*
UK45	Tears On My Pillow *Johnny Nash*
UKLP	Venus And Mars *Wings*
WEEK 3	
US45	Listen To What The Man Said *Wings*
USLP	Venus & Mars *Wings*
UK45	Tears On My Pillow *Johnny Nash*
UKLP	Venus And Mars *Wings*
WEEK 4	
US45	The Hustle *Van McCoy & The Soul City Symphony*
USLP	One Of These Nights *Eagles*
UK45	Give A Little Love *Bay City Rollers*
UKLP	Venus And Mars *Wings*

THE GRAPEVINE

- **Keith Richards has been charged with reckless driving and carrying a concealed weapon (a hunting knife) in Arkansas.**
- **Three Dog Night's Chuck Negron has been arrested for cocaine possession in Kentucky.**
- **'Miami' Steve Van Zandt has left Southside Johnny to play guitar with Bruce Springsteen & The E Street Band.**
- **US Immigration is backtracking as Lennon starts revealing details of the file against him.**

PINK FLOYD – WELCOME TO THE MACHINE

Dave Gilmour of Pink Floyd who were dwarfed by a barrage of special effects at the Knebworth Festival

Two Spitfires – relics of the fighter plane that stood between Britain and the German Luftwaffe in 1941 – buzzed the 70,000 crowd at the start of Pink Floyd's Knebworth Festival show in the grounds of a stately home 20 miles north of London.

As the roar died away, Floyd took off for a two-hour journey around 'The Dark Side Of The Moon', 'Echoes' and bits of 'Wish You Were Here', the album EMI are anxiously waiting to release as the follow-up to 'Dark Side Of The Moon', which is now two years old.

As ever, the Floyd didn't stint on the special effects: quadrophonic sound, another plane (this time a model) swooping over the crowd and crashing in front of the stage, a 30ft circular screen showing Gerald Scarfe's paranoid animations and a gigantic mirror ball.

THE WORST PART OF BREAKING UP

It's been a bad month for some of Britain's biggest bands. Rod Stewart has released his solo album, 'Atlantic Crossing', and it looks as if The Faces are finished. Ron Wood's looking set in The Rolling Stones and the rest of The Faces are squabbling with each other. Rod admits they're further away from each other than ever.

Peter Gabriel has quit Genesis after months of speculation. Says Gabriel: 'I need to absorb a wide variety of experiences. It's difficult to respond to intuition and impulse within a band.'

Rod Stewart looking for his Faces

The Who aren't looking too healthy either. Pete Townshend has been notably acerbic in the wake of the movie version of 'Tommy', which prompted Roger Daltrey to unload his own grievances. Meanwhile Keith Moon has carried on blowing up hotel rooms, oblivious to it all.

And Led Zeppelin have cancelled their second US tour this year after Robert Plant and his wife were badly injured in a car crash in Greece.

BOWIE LEANING TO THE RIGHT

Out on the set of *The Man Who Fell To Earth*, David Bowie is feeling none too enamoured with the rock'n'roll world he's left behind: 'Rock'n'roll is dead – a toothless old woman. It's embarrassing.'

And his own latest album, 'Young Americans', isn't exempted. 'I tried to do a little stretch of how it feels musically in America, which is sort of . . . relentless plastic soul, really.'

If the present is bad, the future looks even worse. And so does Bowie's solution. 'Dictatorship. There will be a political figure in the not too distant future, who'll sweep this part of the world like early rock'n'roll.'

'The best thing that can happen is for an extreme right-wing government to be elected. It will do something at least to cause commotion in people. They'll either accept the dictatorship or get rid of it.'

STAR QUOTE

ROGER DALTREY

'Pete was being held back by two roadies . . . he was spitting at me and hitting me with his guitar . . . I was forced to lay one on him.'

CHARTS

US45	One Of These Nights	*Eagles*
USLP	One Of These Nights	*Eagles*
UK45	Barbados	*Typically Tropical*
UKLP	Venus And Mars	*Wings*
WEEK 2		
US45	Jive Talkin'	*Bee Gees*
USLP	One Of These Nights	*Eagles*
UK45	Barbados	*Typically Tropical*
UKLP	Venus And Mars	*Wings*
WEEK 3		
US45	Jive Talkin'	*Bee Gees*
USLP	One Of These Nights	*Eagles*
UK45	I Can't Give You Anything	*Stylistics*
UKLP	Best Of The Stylistics	*Stylistics*
WEEK 4		
US45	Fallin' In Love	*Hamilton, Joe Frank & Reynolds*
USLP	One Of These Nights	*Eagles*
UK45	I Can't Give You Anything	*Stylistics*
UKLP	Best Of The Stylistics	*Stylistics*
WEEK 5		
US45	Get Down Tonight	*K.C. & The Sunshine Band*
USLP	One Of These Nights	*Eagles*
UK45	Sailing	*Rod Stewart*
UKLP	Best Of The Stylistics	*Stylistics*

THE GRAPEVINE

■ Alice Cooper is being sued by Warner Brothers, for failing to make enough 'commercially successful' albums.

■ CBS has released Dylan's 'Basement Tapes'; tracks recorded with The Band in 1967 and previously only available on bootleg.

■ Lou Reed has pulled out of a European tour, and Back Street Crawler cancelled a concert when Paul Kossoff was taken 'seriously ill' with kidney failure.

SPRINGSTEEN – READY TO RUN

The rock event of the summer in New York has been ten shows at The Bottom Line by Bruce Springsteen & The E Street Band. Every show was sold out in advance and around 600 people lined up for the 50 standing tickets available each night.

Bruce is the emerging talent of the year, a fact that his new album, 'Born To Run', will confirm. There are comparisons with Dylan and Van Morrison, but Bruce has a presence all his own, performing for two hours with much mumbled 'street style' rapping, whispered introductions and a slick stage image.

He played just two songs from the new album, one of them the awesome title track. And all of it was familiar to the crowd – most of whom seemed to come from Asbury Park to judge from the whoops every time he mentioned New Jersey or 'The Shore'.

Bruce Springsteen: standing room only

CHARTS

US45 Rhinestone Cowboy *Glen Campbell*
USLP Red Octopus *Jefferson Starship*
UK45 Sailing *Rod Stewart*
UKLP Atlantic Crossing *Rod Stewart*

WEEK 2

US45 Rhinestone Cowboy *Glen Campbell*
USLP The Heat Is On *Isley Brothers*
UK45 Sailing *Rod Stewart*
UKLP Atlantic Crossing *Rod Stewart*

WEEK 3

US45 Fame *David Bowie*
USLP Between The Lines *Janis Ian*
UK45 Sailing *Rod Stewart*
UKLP Atlantic Crossing *Rod Stewart*

WEEK 4

US45 I'm Sorry *John Denver*
USLP Between The Lines *Janis Ian*
UK45 Moonlighting *Leo Sayer*
UKLP Atlantic Crossing *Rod Stewart*

STARSHIP BOLDLY GO . . .

Three years ago, Jefferson Airplane played their last concert - typically, it was a free one. Jefferson Starship isn't so much of an institution, it's really more of an evolution.

As the Airplane disintegrated, Grace Slick and Paul Kantner tried to pretend it wasn't happening by making albums together and then helping each other out on their solo albums. After a while they got bored with that, put a band together, called it Jefferson Starship and went out for test flights.

Their first album ('Dragonfly') sold nearly half a million copies. And the song that got them noticed most was 'Caroline', sung by Marty Balin, who'd baled out of Airplane but was lured aboard Starship for a couple of songs.

For their new album, 'Red Octopus', which has just dislodged Elton John's 'Captain Fantastic' from its marathon run at the top of the US album charts, Marty is back on the payroll full-time.

Kantner says the band works on 'anarchistic democracy. There's never total agreement on things.'

'Trouble is, that same reason separated the Airplane,' adds Grace. 'But I think Starship people appreciate the difference . . . or are at least amused by it.'

THE GRAPEVINE

■ Gregg Allman and Cher got married – for four days.

■ Elvis Presley said he's coming to Britain next year; and promptly checked into the Memphis Baptist Memorial Hospital midway through a Las Vegas residency.

■ Members of Black Oak Arkansas, sleeping in their carbon monoxide-filled tour bus, narrowly escaped asphyxiation.

■ Jackie Wilson collapsed on stage in Cherry Hill, New Jersey, and has lapsed into a coma.

BLAND ON THE RUN

Paul McCartney's reputation has been up and down like a yo-yo since he started his solo career. Just when he though he'd got everybody on his side with the genial 'Band On The Run', he scared half of them away again with 'Venus And Mars'.

Multi-millionaire he may be, but he's no tax exile. He's currently taking his two-hour show around the same venues that the Beatles played to screaming hordes in '63.

The difference is that this time you can hear what he's playing. And while the songs tend towards the cloyingly comfortable there's enough rockers like 'Jet', 'Lady Madonna' and "Hi Hi Hi' to remind you of the mercurial talents of his bachelor days.

Paul McCartney, Linda McCartney and Denny Laine. The gold albums roll in though the quality varies. And Wings are playing the same halls as The Beatles

MAN-MACHINE MUSIC

Kraftwerk means 'power plant' and the German band of that name describes its music as *menschmachine* or people-machine. They are four men in sober suits and short-cropped hair whose single, 'Autobahn', has been a major hit across Europe.

In the United States, people say that it won't go beyond the Top 30, but their synthesised, robotic rock is making such a wideranging impact that it's spreading beyond the charts.

'I think the synthesiser is more sensitive than a traditional instrument like a guitar,' explains Ralf Hulter.

Kraftwerk refer to their studio as a laboratory and make their music on banks of synthesisers and computers: 'The whole complex of equipment we use can be regarded as one machine,' adds co-leader Florian Schneider.

They met up at a musical academy in 1970 and have been 'working on the music building equipment' ever since.

WHO'S IN LOVE AGAIN?

After a bout of full, frank and acrimonious exchanges of views via the press, all is sweetness and light in The Who once more. The band are boisterously touring Britain in the wake of their 'Who By Numbers' album.

'There's absolutely no excuses any more,' says Pete Townshend. 'You're there on stage to enjoy yourself and if you don't then you might as well stop because that's how close we were to splitting.'

Roger Daltrey admits he was only able to communicate his feelings through the press. 'Pete read what I'd said and realised that all was far from well. I thought Pete had got thoroughly disillusioned with what he was doing. That's all in the past now. The 'Oo'v have become a challenge again and Pete's guitar playing is unbelievable.'

Keith Moon only ever heard the rumours, but it was enough to make him consider taking a day job to ensure his supply of drinking money. 'Perhaps it's because we hardly see each other socially. I mean, I wouldn't pick 'em as friends . . . but I wouldn't pick any one else as musicians to play with.'

If the new album reveals a more intricate side to Townshend's writing, on stage the band are still the same bundle of intense and unpredictable energy. Their shows seldom run smoothly.

'That doesn't mean we don't give a shit,' says Daltrey. 'We do. But life's too short to worry about missing a beat or forgetting the lyrics. The only thing that really matters is the 'Oo'v.'

CHARTS

US45	Fame *David Bowie*
USLP	Wish You Were Here *Pink Floyd*
UK45	Hold Me Close *David Essex*
UKLP	Atlantic Crossing *Rod Stewart*
WEEK 2	
US45	Bad Blood *Neil Sedaka*
USLP	Wish You Were Here *Pink Floyd*
UK45	Hold Me Close *David Essex*
UKLP	Atlantic Crossing *Rod Stewart*
WEEK 3	
US45	Bad Blood *Neil Sedaka*
USLP	Windsong *John Denver*
UK45	Hold Me Close *David Essex*
UKLP	Atlantic Crossing *Rod Stewart*
WEEK 4	
US45	Bad Blood *Neil Sedaka*
USLP	Windsong *John Denver*
UK45	I Only Have Eyes For You *Art Garfunkel*
UKLP	Wish You Were Here *Pink Floyd*

THE LONG AND SHORT OF BOC

Blue Oyster Cult attribute their music to the "primal paranoia" in the air

The heaviest band in America right now is Blue Oyster Cult. Their live album, 'On Your Feet Or On Your Knees', was widely panned by the critics, but it's their most successful so far. The reasons aren't hard to find.

On stage, Blue Oyster Cult are explosive operators out to dazzle, and by the time they've finished everyone's on their feet; no-one's on their knees.

Their formula works in the heat of the moment, because they don't have hits as such; just a balanced, destructive blitz. BOC are redefining heavy metal.

Offstage it doesn't always look like it. Tough punk Eric Bloom is positively diminutive. 'I often have to apologise to fans for not fulfilling my reputation. But how can we be our size and serious about it?'

STAR QUOTE

ERIC CLAPTON

'When "Layla" was finished we were so chuffed. We couldn't believe it was so good. We knew it was great, but nobody else seemed to. In the end we were right. We were just too far ahead.'

THE GRAPEVINE

- **John Lennon has won his four-year battle to stay in America and Yoko celebrated his 35th birthday by giving birth to son Sean.**
- **Paul Simon has released 'Still Crazy After All These Years' and reunited with Art Garfunkel on 'Saturday Night Live'.**
- **Drummer Al Jackson (who backed Otis Redding, Sam & Dave, and Booker T) has been shot dead in Memphis. His wife has been arrested.**

RHYTHM & BOOZE

Those good ole Southern boys Lynyrd Skynyrd ain't looking so good in the Hamburg dressing room. Singer Ronnie Van Zant has bust his fist and guitarist Gary Rossington has two slashed wrists.

And this is only the first night of their European tour!

As manager Peter Rudge says, 'They didn't have to fight before the opening of the tour. It's stupid.'

Stupid or not, Skynyrd played the gig. And then it was back to the bar . . .

Ronnie Van Zant: Southern comforts

NOVEMBER

CHARTS

US45	Island Girl *Elton John*
USLP	Windsong *John Denver*
UK45	I Only Have Eyes For You *Art Garfunkel*
UKLP	Atlantic Crossing *Rod Stewart*
WEEK 2	
US45	Island Girl *Elton John*
USLP	Rock Of The Westies *Elton John*
UK45	Space Oddity *David Bowie*
UKLP	40 Golden Greats *Jim Reeves*
WEEK 3	
US45	Island Girl *Elton John*
USLP	Rock Of The Westies *Elton John*
UK45	Space Oddity *David Bowie*
UKLP	40 Golden Greats *Jim Reeves*
WEEK 4	
US45	That's The Way (I Like It) *K.C. & The Sunshine Band*
USLP	Rock Of The Westies *Elton John*
UK45	D.I.V.O.R.C.E. *Billy Connolly*
UKLP	40 Golden Greates *Jim Reeves*
WEEK 5	
US45	Fly, Robin, Fly *Silver Convention*
USLP	Rock Of The Westies *Elton John*
UK45	You Sexy Thing *Hot Chocolate*
UKLP	Perry Como's 40 Greatest Hits *Perry Como*

BORN TO SURVIVE THE HYPE

A couple of months ago, Bruce Springsteen was the future of rock'n'roll, his reputation increasing with every gig and his growing army of fans waiting impatiently for his third album, 'Born To Run'.

Suddenly, he's a household name, his picture on the front of *Time* and *Newsweek* in the same week and the hype machine in overdrive. CBS have decided to hurl him into the superstar arena, hailing him as 'the new Dylan'.

Bruce is worried. 'They made the mistake. They came out with the big hype. I mean, how can they expect people to swallow something like that? I was trying to tell these guys at the record company "Wait a second, gimme a break!"

'I was in this big shadow right from the start and I'm just getting over this Dylan thing, then phooweee – "I have seen the future of rock'n'roll and it's name is Bruce Springsteen." John Landau's piece meant a lot to me, but it was like they took it out of context and blew it up. I called up the company and told them to get that quote out.'

But the hype won't let go as easily as that. He's just made his first trip to Britain where he found the theatre billboards proclaiming 'Finally London is ready for Bruce Springsteen'. That was a hype he couldn't live up to, and for the second concert he'd made CBS take the posters down.

Springsteen: running for cover

NEW YORK SUBWAY?

Down in the New York underground scene, something's stirring: a thriving club scene centred around venues like CBGB's, Max's Kansas city and the Bottom Line which present acts like Television, The Heartbreakers (featuring ex-New York Doll Johnny Thunders), Talking Heads, The Ramones, Blondie, The Shirts and Patti Smith, the only one of them with a recording contract so far.

At the moment, the record companies don't know what to make of this outburst of nervous energy; they've been lulled into complacency by their mega-buck superstars. But the noise is getting too loud to be ignored.

STAR QUOTE

RON WOOD

(temporarily back in The Faces)

'If Rod's gonna leave the band, then Rod's gonna leave the band. We wouldn't necessarily know about it.'

Dylan: singing for Hurricane Carter

IS IT ROLLING, BOB?

While 'the new Dylan' is gathering all the publicity with the release of the legendary 'Basement Tapes', the old Dylan is embarking on an idiosyncratic tour with a selection of old and new friends under the title The Rolling Thunder Review.

Among the friends – Joan Baez, Ronnie Blakely, Bobby Neuwirth, Ramblin' Jack Elliott, Allen Ginsberg, Bette Midler, Eric Andersen, Mick Ronson and Patti Smith. Most of this unlikely crowd piled on to a bus and headed to Plymouth, Massachussetts, to begin a series of small-scale shows.

In typical Dylan fashion, they've decided to make a film at the same time to record anything that moves . . . and a lot of things that don't.

Just to give the whole adventure a focus, there's a campaigning Dylan single called 'Hurricane', in defence of boxer Hurricane Carter, imprisoned after allegedly being framed for murder.

THE GRAPEVINE

- **The Who have started their US tour in traditional style: John Entwistle was arrested for disorderly conduct at a party in Houston and spent the night in jail.**
- **Elton John flew 120 of his mates to Los Angeles to admire his sequined Dodgers outfit onstage at his Dodgers Stadium shows.**
- **The Sex Pistols played their first show at London's St Martin's College of Art.**

LITTLE FEAT STILL SHUFFLING

Lowell George isn't a star – he's a musician. A stocky, bearded man in jeans and scuffed suede boots, he fronts Little Feat. Greatly admired by musicians and critics, they just can't seem to crack the commercial market.

Their last album, 'Feats Don't Fail Me Now', was their first to reach the Top 40. They're looking to improve on that with 'The Last Record Album' which has been getting the usual rave reviews.

Trouble is, Lowell George can't seem to be bothered with the glitzy end of it. He's not even impressed with half the big stars who came to see the band recently at a show in Vance, California.

'It cracked me up that these people should be concerned enough about us to go to Vance, California. I was impressed pretty much, despite myself!'

And the business aspect really turns him off. 'I'd rather sit down and try to write a good song. I guess I'm a real negative factor for many of the people who have to deal with the band. But I've realised that none of the people in this business see any reason why you should do it other than to make money.

Little Feat: not starstruck

'I will cancel a show – and have – if we're supposed to be opening for a band I despise. The logic behind why you do it is something that a lot of people forget too early on. I want to try and hold on to it . . .'

CHARTS

US45	That's The Way (I Like It) *K.C. & The Sunshine Band*
USLP	Still Crazy After All These Years *Paul Simon*
UK45	Bohemian Rhapsody *Queen*
UKLP	Perry Como's 40 Greatest Hits *Perry Como*
WEEK 2	
US45	Fly, Robin, Fly *Silver Convention*
USLP	Chicago IX-Greatest Hits *Chicago*
UK45	Bohemian Rhapsody *Queen*
UKLP	Perry Como's 40 Greatest Hits *Perry Como*
WEEK 3	
US45	Fly, Robin, Fly *Silver Convention*
USLP	Chicago IX-Greatest Hits *Chicago*
UK45	Bohemian Rhapsody *Queen*
UKLP	Perry Como's 40 Greatest Hits *Perry Como*
WEEK 4	
US45	Let's Do It Again *Staple Singers*
USLP	Chicago IX-Greatest Hits *Chicago*
UK45	Bohemian Rhapsody *Queen*
UKLP	A Night At The Opera *Queen*

FACES FINALLY SPLIT

Maggie may, Faces won't

The long-running Faces-to-split saga is finally over. Rumours have been circulating for the past 18 months, and when Ron Wood left for the Stones earlier this year, everyone thought that was that.

Rod recorded his own 'Atlantic Crossing' album which has become a big hit, although Faces keyboard player Ian McLagan doesn't think much of it. 'It's sterile and unemotional. "Sailing" is pandering to the crowds. Deep down, Rod hasn't changed at all, but he's into all that Hollywood thing.'

Yet this autumn Rod unfurled himself from Britt Ekland's arms and got back with The Faces for a US tour. But the rumours kept on growing. Finally, just before Christmas, Rod announced that he could 'no longer work in a situation where Ron Wood seems to be permanently on loan to The Rolling Stones'.

He will form his own band while The Faces decide what to do next. There's even talk of a Small Faces reunion. And Ron Wood can always go back to the Stones.

THE GRAPEVINE

- **Middle America was stunned when John Denver confessed that he's smoked marijuana.**
- **Keith Moon, having bought a cop uniform, has taken to frisking Who audiences for illicit substances.**
- **Led Zeppelin played a club gig to 350 people in Jersey, where Robert Plant is recovering from car-crash injuries.**
- **Ex-Uriah Heep bassist Greg Thain (27) has died after being rushed to hospital with respiratory failure.**

THE COST OF ROYALTY

A night at the opera? More like four months. But then Queen had to get the sound of their new album absolutely right.

'We wanted to experiment with sound. Sometimes we used three studios simultaneously,' says singer Freddie Mercury, '"Bohemian Rhapsody" took bloody ages to record but we've had all the freedom we wanted and we've been able to go to greater extremes.'

PAUL SIMON

'Before I perform, I go through my own peculiar brand of anxiety, and part of that is being embarrassed that I'm going out to perform. Your ego is exposed . . .'

CHARTS

Chart	Title	Artist
US45	Saturday Night	Bay City Rollers
USLP	Chicago IX-Greatest Hits	Chicago
UK45	Bohemian Rhapsody	Queen
UKLP	A Night At The Opera	Queen
WEEK 2		
US45	Convoy	C.W. McCall
USLP	Chicago IX-Greatest Hits	Chicago
UK45	Bohemian Rhapsody	Queen
UKLP	A Night At The Opera	Queen
WEEK 3		
US45	I Write The Songs	Barry Manilow
USLP	Gratitude	Earth, Wind & Fire
UK45	Bohemian Rhapsody	Queen
UKLP	A Night At The Opera	Queen
WEEK 4		
US45	Theme From 'Mahogany'	Diana Ross
USLP	Gratitude	Earth, Wind & Fire
UK45	Glass Of Champagne	Sailor
UKLP	A Night At The Opera	Queen
WEEK 5		
US45	Love Rollercoaster	Ohio Players
USLP	Gratitude	Earth, Wind & Fire
UK45	Mamma Mia	Abba
UKLP	A Night At The Opera	Queen

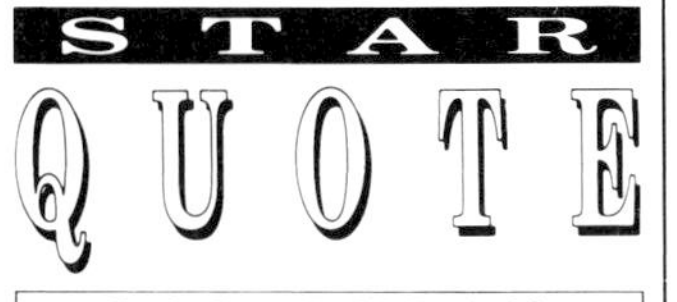

STAR QUOTE

BOB DYLAN

'My name is no big deal. It's meaningless. I tried to get rid of the burden of the Bob Dylan myth for a long time.'

AEROSMITH WALK THIS WAY

After three years on the road, Aerosmith are the second hottest act in America after Springsteen. Singer Steven Tyler reckons he takes a plane virtually every day, and has to moisturise his face three times daily to prevent in-flight skin dryness.

But it does have its compensations, 'I'll tell you what's fun. It's finding the right stewardess and having her take you to the back of the plane . . . It's the greatest . . . Just the thought that you might get caught. That's the extent of our fun on the road. Waiting for it to happen. Waiting for it not to happen.'

So what's the secret of Aerosmith's success? 'I think we're really rocking out and nobody else is doing that. People are getting dressed up for a masquerade, doing this, doing that . . . but nobody's really going on and rocking out.'

And the downside? 'It might be a little more fun if things weren't so hectic. If we had more time to cut albums . . .

'I feel like an old shoe. Sometimes I'll be looking at the audience and I'll just stop dead in the middle of a song. I'll look out at them and think, what is this? There's one thing that keeps me doing it though – I really love it. I believe in it.'

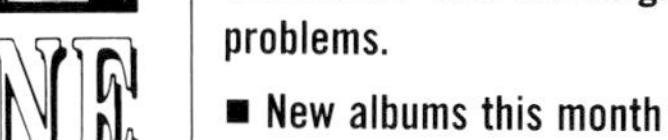

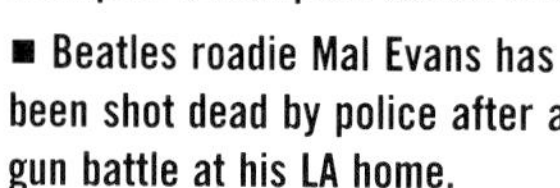

THE GRAPEVINE

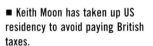

- Keith Moon has taken up US residency to avoid paying British taxes.
- Elvis Presley is reported to be 'distressed' over his weight problems.
- New albums this month from: Bob Dylan ('Desire'), David Bowie ('Station To Station') and Peter Frampton ('Frampton Comes Alive').
- Beatles roadie Mal Evans has been shot dead by police after a gun battle at his LA home.

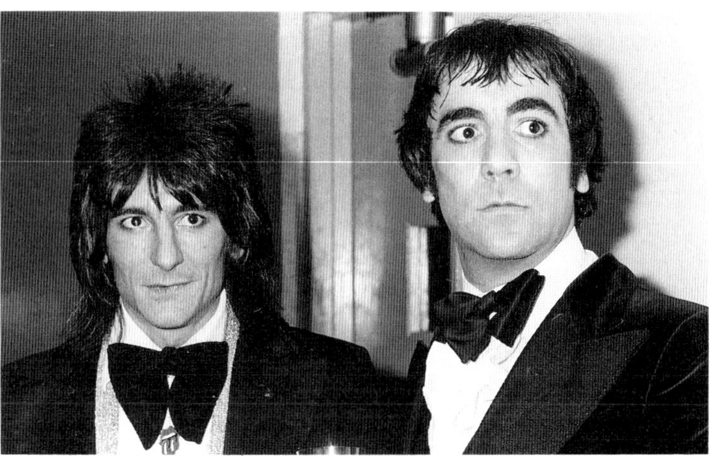

The Who's Keith Moon (left) seen sharing a drink with Ron Wood

TELEVISION IN FOCUS

'There must be 400 bands in New York right now,' says Television's leader/singer/guitarist Tom Verlaine. 'I don't think we're like any of them.'

Television have become the focus of the New York new wave, now that Patti Smith is gaining national prominence with her debut album. But record companies still regard the quartet with suspicion.

Island Records tried to interest Eno in producing the band but Tom would have none of it. 'He's an intellectual and I really don't think we are. I just want a commercial sound.'

This uncompromising stance has already caused bassist Richard Hell to quit. Verlaine wants to get signed so that he can get ahead. 'I don't want to be some little underground sensation. I think there's a big audience out there for us.'

LOU REED DEFIANT

Lou Reed may be churning out vinyl like it's going out of fashion but he's not winning many friends in the process. Last year's 'Metal Machine Music' was greeted with derision and the latest, 'Coney Island Baby', isn't faring much better.

He's defiant about it. 'I was never that interested in the other albums. I mean, they're OK but they weren't Lou Reed albums. Or if they were, I was on automatic pilot. But this one is the way we all wanted it, so if people don't like it they're definitely not liking my kind of album.'

THE LAMB STANDS UP AGAIN

Genesis: spot the missing Gabriel

Genesis haven't bothered to recruit a replacement for Peter Gabriel – they've just brought Phil Collins out from behind the drumkit to handle the vocals on their new album, 'Trick Of The Tail'.

Casual fans might find it difficult to notice the difference. Collins' voice is unnervingly like Gabriel's. But critics have found the new album more accessible than the complex 'Lamb Lies Down On Broadway'.

'I think there was less friction between vocals and instrumentals,' explains Mike Rutherford. 'Peter's going has made us more of a band.'

They've also nailed the misconception that Gabriel wrote all Genesis' material. Rutherford and Tony Banks now have their contributions individually credited instead of being under the group banner. And they've already got a pile of material prepared for another album.

But first they'll be going on the road, adding ex-Yes and King Crimson drummer Bill Bruford, so that Collins can divide his time between drumming and singing.

QUEEN WILL ROCK YOU

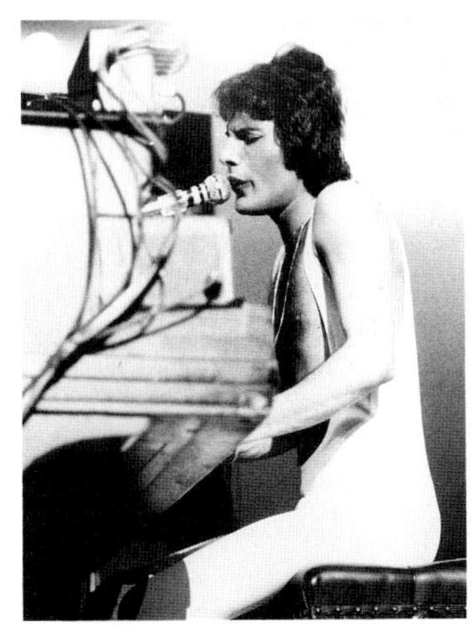
Freddie Mercury tinkles his ivories

Finally, New York is ready for Queen. Four sell-out shows at the Beacon Theatre have created the kind of impact that has already conquered Britain and Europe.

Their spectacular stage show combines the theatrically outrageous with a camp humour which blunts any accusations of pretentiousness.

Freddie Mercury's wardrobe defies description. On stage he opts for a white satin jump suit slashed to the navel . . . until he changes into a similar black number slashed even further down. He saves his flowing satin Zandra Rhodes top for the encore.

But beyond the lights, dry ice, flashpots and stage props, Queen demonstrate a musical ability that outshines the visual excesses.

'We're riding on the crest of a wave and things are opening up for us here,' exclaims a delighted Freddie.

- Donna Summer's 'Love To Love You Baby' has gone gold.
- The Eagles 'Greatest Hits' album has become the first to qualify for newly introduced platinum award to honour one million sales.
- Florence Ballard, founder member of The Supremes, has died of coronary thrombosis, aged 32.
- Rudi Pompilli, sax player on Bill Haley's early rock classics, has died in Philadelphia.

KEVIN GODLEY

10CC

'If I was to pick one track from everything we've done, "I'm Not In Love" would be my favourite. It's got something that none of our other tracks have at all. It's not clever in a conscious way but it says it all so simply in, what, six minutes.'

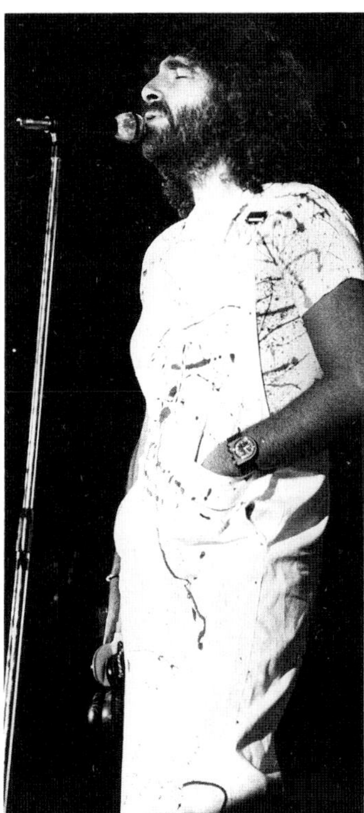
Kevin Godley of 10cc

Florence Ballard, a Supreme alone

CHARTS

US45	Fifty Ways To Leave Your Lover — *Paul Simon*
USLP	Desire — *Bob Dylan*
UK45	Mamma Mia — *Abba*
UKLP	How Dare You — *10cc*
WEEK 2	
US45	Fifty Ways To Leave Your Lover — *Paul Simon*
USLP	Desire — *Bob Dylan*
UK45	Forever And Ever — *Slik*
UKLP	Desire — *Bob Dylan*
WEEK 3	
US45	Fifty Ways To Leave Your Lover — *Paul Simon*
USLP	Desire — *Bob Dylan*
UK45	December '63 (Oh What A Night) — *Four Seasons*
UKLP	Desire — *Bob Dylan*
WEEK 4	
US45	Theme From 'S.W.A.T.' — *Rhythm Heritage*
USLP	Desire — *Bob Dylan*
UK45	December '63 (Oh What A Night) — *Four Seasons*
UKLP	Desire — *Bob Dylan*

LOADED PISTOLS

A chair flies through the air, hitting the PA system with a noise that's indistinguishable from the sound emanating from it.

The chair was thrown by singer Johnny Rotten during The Sex Pistols' London Marquee gig. But it's impossible to tell whether he'd thrown it in anger or excitement.

The Pistols have played less than a dozen gigs so far, but they've already built up a fanatical teenage following.

They play Small Faces numbers, early Kinks B-sides, a couple of Stooges tracks and only a handful of their own songs.

'Actually we're not into music,' says one of the group afterwards. 'We're into chaos.'

BOWIE – STRIPPED DOWN TO BASICS

For the first time in David Bowie's career it's impossible to predict what audience he's going to attract for his latest world tour. The success of 'Fame' has opened him up to both the Top 40 and the disco crowd.

The audience at the 17,000-capacity Vancouver Coliseum for the opening date of the tour have scarcely had time to digest the contents of the just-released 'Station To Station' album. And the 'support act' of non-stop Kraftwerk tapes, plus a screening of the 1927 surrealist film *Un Chien Andalou* are not calculated to put them at ease.

But there are few such complications once the show gets underway. The staging is as stripped-down as the presentation. There are no distracting visuals; not even any coloured lights.

Gone are the props, the costumes and the other theatrics on which Bowie has built his reputation. Instead, he's gone back to basics and for 90 minutes he plays the front man for a hot rock'n'roll band.

THE SPECTRE OVER SPECTOR

'How could they hate me? I made records like 'River Deep Mountain High', 'Da Doo Ron Ron', 'Be My Baby'. How could they hate anybody whose records are overflowing with so much love, and not only love but honesty? . . . and so much pure fuckin' talent!'

It's been ten years since Phil Spector vanished from public view, reportedly emotionally destroyed by the failure of Ike & Tina Turner's 'River Deep Mountain High' to climb above 93 in the US Top Hundred, despite reaching the Top Three in the British charts and being hailed worldwide as a masterpiece.

He returned to salvage The Beatles' ill-fated 'Let It Be' album and has produced George Harrison's 'All Things Must Pass', plus several John Lennon albums. But his genius is hard to work with and most record companies are easily scared off by his eccentric behaviour.

Yet Spector's self-belief remains inviolate: 'There's nobody in the world who can make better records than I can. Anytime I'm ready I'm tomorrow's headlines . . . And I'm ready now!'

Wings' Jimmy McCulloch: fingered

Soul survivor Bobby Womack

THE GRAPEVINE

- Former MC5 guitarist Wayne Karmer is facing five years in prison after pleading guilty to cocaine dealing.
- Gregg Allman has been subpoenad by a Federal Grand Jury in Georgia, investigating a multi-million dollar drug ring.
- The Who's Keith Moon collapsed on stage at the Boston Gardens – two more shows were cancelled.
- Wings' US tour has been delayed three weeks as guitarist Jimmy McCulloch has broken a finger.

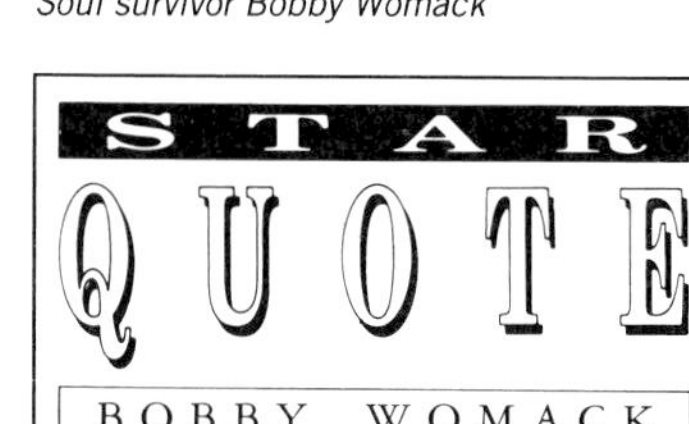

STAR QUOTE

BOBBY WOMACK

'Record industry people don't understand people who create. They'll say, "We've gotta get you a room and a piano and see how many songs you can turn out a day." But it doesn't work like that. You can't put your feelings on a time schedule.'

CHARTS

Chart	Title	Artist
US45	Love Machine (Part One)	*Miracles*
USLP	Desire	*Bob Dylan*
UK45	I Love To Love	*Tina Charles*
UKLP	The Very Best Of	*Slim Whitman*
WEEK 2		
US45	December 1963 (Oh What A Night)	*Four Seasons*
USLP	Greatest Hits 1971-1975	*Eagles*
UK45	I Love To Love	*Tina Charles*
UKLP	The Very Best Of	*Slim Whitman*
WEEK 3		
US45	December 1963 (Oh What A Night)	*Four Seasons*
USLP	Greatest Hits 1971-1975	*Eagles*
UK45	I Love To Love	*Tina Charles*
UKLP	Desire	*Bob Dylan*
WEEK 4		
US45	December 1963 (Oh What A Night)	*Four Seasons*
USLP	Greatest Hits 1971-1975	*Eagles*
UK45	Save Your Kisses For Me	*Brotherhood Of Man*
UKLP	Blue For You	*Status Quo*

ELO FIND ELDORADO

Would you believe 20,000 people clapping along to an unaccompanied cello solo? It's a nightly occurrence in America where Electric Light Orchestra are barnstorming their way across the country.

'People back home in Britain don't realize what's happening,' says ELO leader Jeff Lynne. 'Even my own mum thinks I'm making it up!' Roll over Beethoven and tell Jeff's mum the news!

Jeff cites Lennon & McCartney as his main influence. The hype says they're picking up where 'I Am The Walrus' left off and the stage show is what the Beatles might have produced if they'd taken 'Sgt Pepper' out on the road.

Despite the techno-flash, ELO have resisted the temptations of self-indulgence. The set is action-packed songs jammed together in a steadily mounting crescendo that American audiences find irresistible.

Lynne is still a little overawed by the process that turns his home-written songs into tracks on mega-selling albums.

'The first time I heard an orchestra record one of my songs it was like an orgasm. I got there and there were 30 musicians tuning up. I had to tell them what I wanted them to play. It was a great feeling.'

GIMME GIMME GIMME, MONEY MONEY MONEY

Ever since Abba won the 1974 Eurovision Song Contest with a song called 'Waterloo' they've been dominating the European, American, Australian and Asian charts with a succession of pure pop hits.

Abba are a phenomenon: the first Swedish pop group to achieve international success, they are currently Sweden's second biggest export behind Volvo. Songwriters Bjorn Ulvaeus and Benny Anderson and their partners Agnetha and Amrifrid have come up with a formula that no continent appears able to resist.

Their music is skilfully put together with infinite patience and technology. The lyrics remain banal, but it makes them easy to understand in Hong Kong or the Phillippines.

STAR QUOTE

IAN STEWART

Rolling Stones original member.

'You can squawk about money, but the money The Stones have made hasn't done them much good. It's really gotten them into some trouble. They can't even live in their own country now.'

THE GRAPEVINE

- **Former Free and Back Street Crawler guitarist Paul Kossoff has died of heart failure on a London-New York flight aged 26. He had been suffering heart and drug problems for years.**
- **Folk singer Phil Ochs hanged himself at his sister's house in Queens, New York.**
- **Stevie Wonder has re-signed to Motown for a reported $13 million advance.**

CHARTS

US45	Disco Lady — *Johnnie Taylor*
USLP	Greatest Hits 1971-1975 — *Eagles*
UK45	Save Your Kisses For Me — *Brotherhood Of Man*
UKLP	Blue For You — *Status Quo*
WEEK 2	
US45	Disco Lady — *Johnnie Taylor*
USLP	Frampton Comes Alive! — *Peter Frampton*
UK45	Save Your Kisses For Me — *Brotherhood Of Man*
UKLP	Their Greatest Hits — *Eagles*
WEEK 3	
US45	Disco Lady — *Johnnie Taylor*
USLP	Greatest Hits 1971-1975 — *Eagles*
UK45	Save Your Kisses For Me — *Brotherhood Of Man*
UKLP	Rock Follies — *TV Cast*
WEEK 4	
US45	Disco Lady — *Johnnie Taylor*
USLP	At The Speed Of Sound — *Wings*
UK45	Save Your Kisses For Me — *Brotherhood Of Man*
UKLP	Rock Follies — *TV Cast*

WHITE DOPES ON PUNK

Nobody hires The Tubes as a support band since Led Zeppelin were unable to follow their stunt of throwing giant amphetamine tablets at a 60,000 crowd in San Francisco.

The Tubes specialize in warp-rock theatrics. Singer Fee Waybill splits his persona into a weird and wonderful assortment of characters, climaxing the band's staggering show as the ultimate glamster, Quay Lewd, singing The Tubes' finest anthem, 'White Punks On Dope'.

Despite selling out everywhere, The Tubes lose money. But it hasn't stopped them so far. 'I may grow tits for the next tour,' confides Waybill.

BERNIE TAUPIN: THE WRITE STUFF

Bernie Taupin is 'The One Who Writes The Words For Elton John'. That's the title of his newly published illustrated book of lyrics. He's happy to let Elton take all the glory. Royalties provide their own compensation, particularly when you consider that Elton John albums accounted for 2 per cent of all world record sales last year.

'If we actually sat down together and attempted to write songs in the orthodox manner – sweating out inspiration over ashtrays full of cigarette ends – we'd probably drive each other nuts,' says Taupin.

Instead, he knocks out his lyrics in solitary splendour and passes them on to Elton, who puts them into musical shape.

It's a speedy process but never slapdash. 'Elton and I are very aware of our success and we've tried not to be complacent about it. We both want to retain our popularity and therefore we both work hard at our respective jobs.'

Taupin: lyrics and flares

LOFGREN BOUNCES BACK

Nils Lofgren is one of the few young artists who genuinely understands the true spirit of rock'n' roll. Which is strange considering how straight his upbringing was. Trained as a classical musician, he took no interest in rock music until his mid-teens.

Seeing Hendrix in concert clinched it. Lofgren formed a band called Grin and spent time in Neil Young's Crazy Horse before setting out on his own. His second solo album, 'Cry Tough', has cracked the US and UK charts, and his current UK tour has inspired Nils to his finest playing yet.

'I'm into playing rock'n' roll whenever and wherever I can,' he says, doodling on an acoustic guitar in his hotel room. 'We leave a lot of space in the songs for improvisation, and I don't just mean the guitar solos. I'm up for playing and travelling as far as I can.'

THE GRAPEVINE

- Four Brunswick Records execs have been indicted for payola.
- Arista President Clive Davis has pleaded guilty to failing to declare $8,800 income back in 1972. A further charge has been dropped.
- Keith Richards was arrested after crashing his Bentley during the Stones UK tour. Various substances from the wreckage were confiscated by police.
- Yardbirds singer Keith Relf was fatally electrocuted while playing his guitar at home.

NO PARTICULAR THING TO SAY

Chuck Berry's habit of using unrehearsed pick-up musicians on British tours is frustrating in the extreme. This time around he doesn't even know who he's going to be playing with.

So doesn't he ever feel the urge to get up with a really good band and jam? 'What?' Question repeated. 'It's up to the promoter'.

Is he aware of his influence on rock'n'roll? 'I wouldn't know about that. I just do what I do. Writing, doing my thing.'

Sometimes legends are a letdown.

CHARTS

US45	Let Your Love Flow *Bellamy Brothers*
USLP	Presence *Led Zeppelin*
UK45	Fernando *Abba*
UKLP	Rock Follies *TV Cast*
WEEK 2	
US45	Welcome Back *John Sebastian*
USLP	Presence *Led Zeppelin*
UK45	Fernando *Abba*
UKLP	Rock Follies *TV Cast*
WEEK 3	
US45	Boogie Fever *Sylvers*
USLP	Black & Blue *Rolling Stones*
UK45	Fernando *Abba*
UKLP	Greatest Hits *Abba*
WEEK 4	
US45	Silly Love Songs *Wings*
USLP	Black & Blue *Rolling Stones*
UK45	Fernando *Abba*
UKLP	Greatest Hits *Abba*
WEEK 5	
US45	Love Hangover *Diana Ross*
USLP	At The Speed Of Sound *Wings*
UK45	Fernando *Abba*
UKLP	Greatest Hits *Abba*

STAR

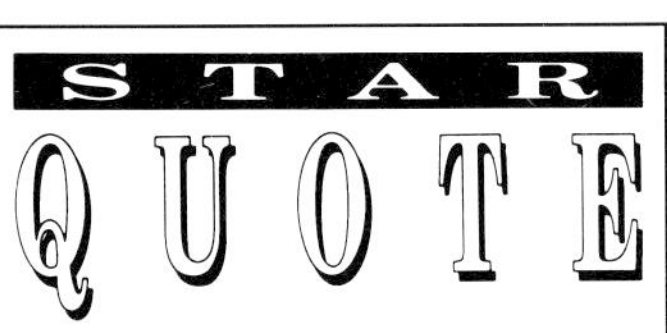

KEITH RICHARDS

'I only really listen to black groups these days. I ain't too interested in white bands who rip off white bands who ripped off black bands.'

Keith Richards lets rip

LISTEN TO THE NEW MUSIC

The Doobie Brothers get down and boogie their way out of adversity

A year ago, Doobie Brothers singer/guitarist Tom Johnston bowed out of the band midway through a US tour. 'He was ill from different things,' says colleague Pat Simmons. 'He had an ulcer. He was run down, spaced out, doped out . . .'

As Johnston had written the best known Doobies songs – 'Listen To The Music', 'China Groove' and 'Long Train Coming' – his collapse could have been a mortal blow for the band.

They reacted by recruiting Steely Dan keyboard player Mike McDonald and carrying on the tour.

Johnston is back for the new album, 'Taking It To The Streets' – but only just. He's written one song and doesn't even make the group shot on the back cover. But the rest of the band have broadened out to take up the slack.

'Audiences are more inclined to listen to us now,' says Simmons, smiling.

ROD – NO REGRETS

'The name of the game is to get people there,' says Rod Stewart, 'but you never know whether you've done it or not. Especially when you've lived with an album for three or four months.'

Rod certainly did it with 'Atlantic Crossing', last year's hit album. And 'A Night On The Town' looks set to go even better. But the recriminations that followed at the end of last year's break up of The Faces have left a bitter taste that Rod still has to overcome.

Rod, – in Britain to form a new band, – remains unrepentant: 'The river dried up with The Faces. I'd heard some things by other people and I suddenly realized I could be doing a lot better if I was to branch out. And then I met my producer Tom Dowd . . .'

Rod Stewart: never look back

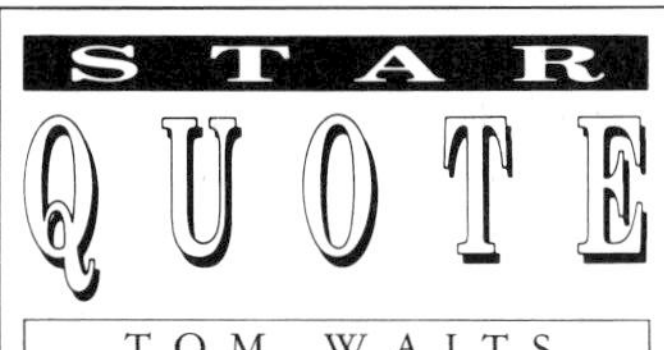

'I once worked in a jewellery store and when I quit I took a gold watch. I figured they weren't gonna give me one 'cause I'd only been with them six months.'

CHARTS

US45	Love Hangover *Diana Ross*
USLP	Black & Blue *Rolling Stones*
UK45	Fernando *Abba*
UKLP	Greatest Hits *Abba*
WEEK 2	
US45	Silly Love Songs *Wings*
USLP	Black & Blue *Rolling Stones*
UK45	No Charge *J.J. Barrie*
UKLP	Greatest Hits *Abba*
WEEK 3	
US45	Silly Love Songs *Wings*
USLP	At The Speed Of Sound *Wings*
UK45	Silly Love Songs *Wings*
UKLP	Greatest Hits *Abba*
WEEK 4	
US45	Silly Love Songs *Wings*
USLP	At The Speed Of Sound *Wings*
UK45	You To Me Are Everything *Real Thing*
UKLP	Greatest Hits *Abba*

WINWOOD PASSES GO

You don't see too much of Steve Winwood these days since Traffic got jammed. Last time he played live was with salsa band The Fania All-Stars. Now he's resurfaced via Japanese percussive genius Stomu Yamashta's 'Go' album, and a series of European dates.

This East-West fusion project also features former Tangerine Dream synthesist Klaus Schulz, ex-Santana drummer Michael Shrieve, nearly ex-Roxy Music guitarist Phil Manzanera and former Return To Forever guitarist Al DiMeola.

Winwood is making slow but steady progress on his own solo album. 'I try not to be narrow-minded, but I don't know whether that's good or not,' he says.

THE GRAPEVINE

- **As Wings tour America, Capitol have released Beatles' 'Rock'n'Roll Music' compilation.**
- **Roxy Music have confirmed a trial separation.**
- **S/M advertisement for Rolling Stones 'Black And Blue' album has caused outrage in America.**
- **Ramones' debut album released.**
- **ZZ Top tour USA with a 2,000lb buffalo, two turkey vultures and four rattlesnakes on a stage shaped like Texas.**

Sharp-dressed ZZ Top

JULY

FRAMPTON SHOWS THE WAY

'Frampton Comes Alive' has sold three million copies since it came out in the spring, so it's not surprising that Peter Frampton is the hottest touring act in America this summer.

This is the third time Frampton has been a 'star', and he's still only 26. He started in the UK with The Herd back in the last Sixties, then formed Humble Pie with Steve Marriott (ex-Small Faces) in the early Seventies. Despite the fame, neither band made any money and by the time he'd disbanded the ill-fated Frampton's Camel, he was a quarter of a million dollars in debt.

These days he can earn nearly that in a weekend, selling out stadiums on his own.

The reasons for his success aren't hard to find; pretty, clean, spacey music, equally pretty looks and an astute management and record company.

Frampton plays guitar with rare melody and fluidity, with very little trace of the blues – something unusual for a rock guitarist. 'Eric Clapton turned me on incredibly but I tried not to listen too much because everyone else was copying him. The guitarists who intrigue me most are the old jazzers like Django Reinhardt.

'People have been saying some ridiculous things – the new Elton John and all this shit. I'm not, but it's quite possible.'

SAYIN' IT LOUD ...

The Ohio Players and War bear little relation to each other musically, but they have enough similarities – both are black and flash with a rare artistic and financial freedom – to make a dynamite package tour that's peeling the scales off European eyes.

The Players are more easily definable, growing up with Sixties soul and taking it a stage further. They're the leaders of the convoy along the highway of modern black music. Any white interest is unsolicited but welcome.

War are camped over in the middle ground, attracting an equal number of blacks and whites and unconcerned about moving off in any particular direction.

Both bands use a barrage of lights and effects to put across their energetic brands of funk, ostentatiously reaching out to pull the audience right in there with them. They can do it because they've never let go of their roots. They understand their audiences as well as they understand their music and they funk with both feet firmly on the ground.

War and a funky piece

CHARTS

US45	Silly Love Songs *Wings*
USLP	At The Speed Of Sound *Wings*
UK45	You To Me Are Everything *Real Thing*
UKLP	Greatest Hits *Abba*
	WEEK 2
US45	Afternoon Delight *Starland Vocal Band*
USLP	At The Speed Of Sound *Wings*
UK45	Young Hearts Run Free *Candi Staton*
UKLP	A Night On The Town *Rod Stewart*
	WEEK 3
US45	Afternoon Delight *Starland Vocal Band*
USLP	At The Speed Of Sound *Wings*
UK45	The Roussos Phenomenon (EP) *Demis Roussos*
UKLP	A Night On The Town *Rod Stewart*
	WEEK 4
US45	Kiss & Say Goodbye *Manhattans*
USLP	Frampton Comes Alive! *Peter Frampton*
UK45	Don't Go Breaking My Heart *Elton John & Kiki Dee*
UKLP	20 Golden Greats *Beach Boys*
	WEEK 5
US45	Kiss & Say Goodbye *Manhattans*
USLP	Breezin' *George Benson*
UK45	Don't Go Breaking My Heart *Elton John & Kiki Dee*
UKLP	20 Golden Greats *Beach Boys*

STAR

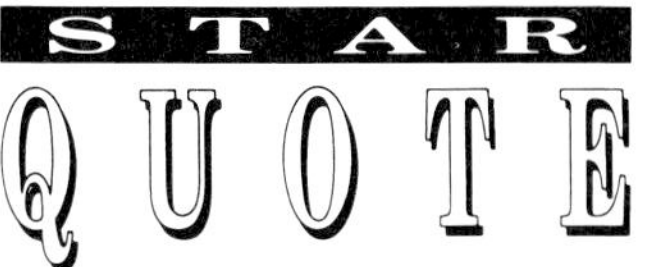

DOLLY PARTON

'There have been times when I've really had to adjust to hearing one of my songs recorded by somebody else. It's like taking one of your kids and doing plastic surgery on its face.'

Dolly Parton: plastic surgery?

THE GRAPEVINE

■ After two platinum and nine gold albums, Deep Purple have disbanded.

■ The Allman Brothers have split up after Gregg 'fingered' roadie Scooter Herring during a police drugs probe.

■ Bruce Springsteen is sueing manager Mike Appel for fraud and breach of trust.

■ Stevie Wonder's still holding back on his new LP but has released a T-shirt proclaiming 'Stevie's Nearly Ready'.

AUGUST 1976

FLEETWOOD MAC'S 'BAD B-MOVIE' WINS AN OSCAR

Stevie Nicks can give up being a waitress now that 'Fleetwood Mac' has sold two million copies

Fleetwood Mac released their eponymous album nearly a year ago. It became their first US Top 10 LP, had a good run and dropped out. Meantime the band went out on the road for five months solid, and for the past three months the album has been back in the Top 5.

It's spawned two hit singles – 'Over My Head' and 'Rhiannon' – and sold two million copies so far. In Britain it's done only five thousand.

But then the Fleetwood Mac Britain knew and loved in the mid-Sixties bears little relation to the current outfit. At the start of the Seventies, guitarist Peter Green went AWOL in New Orleans. The other guitarist, Jeremy Spencer, joined the Children Of God cult. Mick Fleetwood describes the period as 'a bad B-movie'.

The arrival of Lindsey Buckingham and Stevie Nicks just before they started recording 'Fleetwood Mac' proved the turning point.

'It felt right. It was very quick,' says Fleetwood. 'I think it's wrong to start analysing the whys and wherefores. That was it.'

It certainly was. And Stevie Nicks could quit her job as a waitress.

THE GRAPEVINE

- **The Rolling Stones played Britain's Knebworth Festival to 150,000 people with 10cc, Todd Rundgren and Lynryd Skynryd.**
- **The Clash have made their first appearance in London**
- **Cliff Richard has embarked on a 25-date sell-out tour of Russia.**
- **Blues singer Jimmy Reed, whose songs were covered by The Rolling Stones, The Who and The Yardbirds, has died in San Francisco immediately after a three-night club engagement.**

RAMONES LEAVE HOME

'We may not be the brightest guys in the world,' says Dee Dee Ramone. 'But I don't think I'm no mutant weed, either.'

At the band's soundcheck at London's Roundhouse, he's yelling at the English roadcrew about the lack of power emanating from his stack. The Ramones' ideal is to play with their amps juiced to maximum. Their fingers bleed so that your ears can.

Not everyone's a fan. Glasgow politician James Dempsey is trying to get the track, 'Now I Wanna Sniff Some Glue', banned. Twenty Scottish kids have died from glue sniffing in recent years.

But the publicity is guaranteed to have the opposite effect. And as Ramones manager, Danny Fields, says: 'Why should the song be banned? War films aren't banned on the grounds that they advocate violence.'

RON WOOD

'I mean, I suppose most of the time I'm honest. That's not too bad really is it? 'Cause basically it's too easy to be a bastard in this business.'

CHARTS

	Chart	Title	Artist
	US45	Don't Go Breaking My Heart	*Elton John & Kiki Dee*
	USLP	Breezin'	*George Benson*
	UK45	Don't Go Breaking My Heart	*Elton John & Kiki Dee*
	UKLP	20 Golden Greats	*Beach Boys*
WEEK 2	US45	Don't Go Breaking My Heart	*Elton John & Kiki Dee*
	USLP	Frampton Comes Alive!	*Peter Frampton*
	UK45	Don't Go Breaking My Heart	*Elton John & Kiki Dee*
	UKLP	20 Golden Greats	*Beach Boys*
WEEK 3	US45	Don't Go Breaking My Heart	*Elton John & Kiki Dee*
	USLP	Frampton Comes Alive!	*Peter Frampton*
	UK45	Don't Go Breaking My Heart	*Elton John & Kiki Dee*
	UKLP	20 Golden Greats	*Beach Boys*
WEEK 4	US45	Don't Go Breaking My Heart	*Elton John & Kiki Dee*
	USLP	Frampton Comes Alive!	*Peter Frampton*
	UK45	Don't Go Breaking My Heart	*Elton John & Kiki Dee*
	UKLP	20 Golden Greats	*Beach Boys*

TED NUGENT'S STRANGLEHOLD

'Wasn't I great? Wasn't that the best show you ever saw?' enthuses modest Ted Nugent backstage in Amarillo, Texas.

Nugent hails from Detroit, where he saw off the likes of Wayne Kramer (MC5) and Mike Pinero (Iron Butterfly) in a series of guitar duels.

He's scathing about drugs and alcohol, only eats what he shoots, and preserves his energy for playing his guitar at ear-splitting volume – and sex. 'Some chicks think I'm crazy when I'm on top of them, I don't want to hurt them. I just do everything like that.'

Nugent: ear-splitting meat eater

SEPTEMBER

THE GRAPEVINE

- Boston's first album has become the fastest selling debut of all time.
- Queen's free gig in London's Hyde Park attracted 60,000 people.
- Eric Clapton has been accused of making 'racist' remarks on stage during his UK tour.
- Jerry Lee Lewis has been arrested after shooting a soda bottle, missing and hitting his bassist in the chest.

No silver lining for Jeff

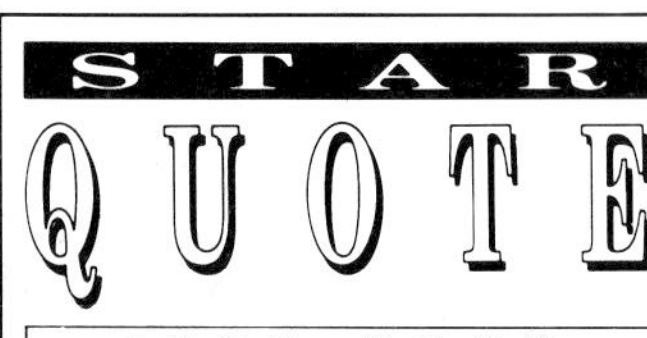

STAR QUOTE

JEFF BECK

'Everyone thinks of the Sixties as something they really weren't. It was the frustration period of my life. The electronic equipment just wasn't up to the sounds I had in my head.'

CALIFORNIA DREAMING

The Runaways cheek to cheek. They just wanna be your Cherry Bomb

If you're looking for the ultimate image of Southern California then look no further than The Runaways – five 16-year-old honeys epitomising the wacked-out nuttiness of Hollywood rock 'n' roll.

But wait a minute. These chicks are blasting out the kind of raucous rock you'd find in a South London pub any night of the week. That's because they are the creation of two of Hollywood's most notorious Anglophiles.

Rodney Bingenheimer and Kim Fowley are the Hollywood hustlers who've put The Runaways together. The girls cut their (baby) teeth in Rodney's English disco, and producer Kim Fowley directed the girls' career to a recording contract with Phonogram and takes a composer's credit on seven of the ten tracks on their first album.

Naturally, the girls have their own influences. Lead guitarist Lita Ford (actually she's 17 but she won't tell if you won't) goes all the way back to Led Zeppelin and Black Sabbath's first albums. Bassist Jackie Fox passionately believes in Kiss and Aerosmith. And you just have to glance at guitarist Joan Jett's Suzi Quatro cut and singer Cherie Currie's Ziggy quiff to know where they're coming from.

The Runaways bring a new vehemence to the generation gap. 'We're putting our feelings into music in a way that no 30-year-old man could. They can sing about teenagers and sneaking out at night. But they don't really know,' says Cherie.

'I mean, 30-year-old guys don't have to sneak past their mothers to go out at night,' adds Joan Jett helpfully.

WHO ARE YOU CALLING PUNK, PUNK?

Patti Smith may be a punk. The Ramones may be punk, even Springsteen might sometimes be a punk. But they ain't punk rock; not the punk rock that's alive and kicking in the UK.

At the Screen on the Green cinema in North London – because no regular rock venue would have them – The Sex Pistols, The Clash and The Buzzcocks play nasty music for nasty kids.

For a while, record company execs might flash on a déjà-vu of the sixties as mutant misfits dance under freaky lights while films are projected onscreen. But the atmosphere is fuelled by amyl-nitrate, not hallucinogenics. This is definitely not the summer of love.

The Clash are exceedingly rough and scarcely ready musically. But singer/guitarist Joe Strummer has a vehemence that rises above their deficiencies.

In comparison, The Sex Pistols have the clean, tight sound of punk veterans. Within 30 seconds they've wiped out all the mock decadence that preceeded them with a sneering dose of realism. They are energetic, charismatic, arrogant and uncouth. Any minute now, record companies are going to have to deal with them.

The Clash: exceedingly rough and scarcely ready but very willing

CHARTS

US45	You Should Be Dancing *Bee Gees*
USLP	Fleetwood Mac *Fleetwood Mac*
UK45	Don't Go Breaking My Heart *Elton John & Kiki Dee*
UKLP	20 Golden Greats *Beach Boys*
WEEK 2	
US45	(Shake, Shake, Shake) Shake Your Booty *K.C. & The Sunshine Band*
USLP	Frampton Comes Alive! *Peter Frampton*
UK45	Dancing Queen *Abba*
UKLP	20 Golden Greats *Beach Boys*
WEEK 3	
US45	Play That Funky Music *Wild Cherry*
USLP	Frampton Comes Alive! *Peter Frampton*
UK45	Dancing Queen *Abba*
UKLP	20 Golden Greats *Beach Boys*
WEEK 4	
US45	Play That Funky Music *Wild Cherry*
USLP	Frampton Comes Alive! *Peter Frampton*
UK45	Dancing Queen *Abba*
UKLP	A Night On The Town *Rod Stewart*

OCTOBER

1976

SONGS IN THE KEY OF MONEY

Stevie Wonder's 'Songs In The Key Of Life' is finally out after the longest sell-in in the history of the record industry.

Pre-sold to dealers four times already this year, it's been a double-album, a triple album and now it's back down to a double with a 'free' EP of four extra songs

Its tortuous history is inextricably linked with Wonder's re-signing to Motown (after ostentatiously being seen in the company of other record label executives) for $13 million – the largest advance ever secured by an artist.

Motown needed Wonder's signature: they've recently lost the services of The Four Tops, Gladys Knight, Martha Reeves, Ashford & Simpson, The Detroit Spinners, four of The Jackson Five and songwriters Holland, Dozier & Holland.

And the word is that Motown were determined to exploit every trick in the book to recoup as much of their advance as possible. It seems to be working – 'Songs In The Key Of Life' has worldwide advance orders of more than one million.

But what about the album itself? Like any double album it's self-indulgent, and there's scarcely a track that couldn't have been prudently edited. But Wonder's music has expanded enormously and his stylistic range pays full dividends.

CHARTS

US45	Play That Funky Music *Wild Cherry*
USLP	Frampton Comes Alive! *Peter Frampton*
UK45	Dancing Queen *Abba*
UKLP	Greatest Hits *Abba*
	WEEK 2
US45	A Fifth Of Beethoven *Walter Murphy & The Big Apple Band*
USLP	Frampton Comes Alive! *Peter Frampton*
UK45	Dancing Queen *Abba*
UKLP	Greatest Hits *Abba*
	WEEK 3
US45	Disco Duck (Part One) *Rick Dees & His Cast Of Idiots*
USLP	Songs In The Key Of Life *Stevie Wonder*
UK45	Mississippi *Pussycat*
UKLP	A Night On The Town *Rod Stewart*
	WEEK 4
US45	If You Leave Me Now *Chicago*
USLP	Songs In The Key Of Life *Stevie Wonder*
UK45	Mississippi *Pussycat*
UKLP	A Night On The Town *Rod Stewart*
	WEEK 5
US45	If You Leave Me Now *Chicago*
USLP	Songs In The Key Of Life *Stevie Wonder*
UK45	Mississippi *Pussycat*
UKLP	The Story Of The Who *Who*

George Harrison gets those subconscious sue me sue you blues

THE GRAPEVINE

- **The Sex Pistols have signed to EMI Records. 'Here at last is a group with a bit of guts for younger people to identify with,' says a spokesman.**
- **George Harrison has been found guilty of 'subconsciously' plagiarising The Chiffons' 'He's So Fine' for 'My Sweet Lord'.**
- **Ike & Tina Turner have split up after 19 years.**
- **Victoria Spivey, blues singer, has died, aged 70.**

Pass the sick bag Patti

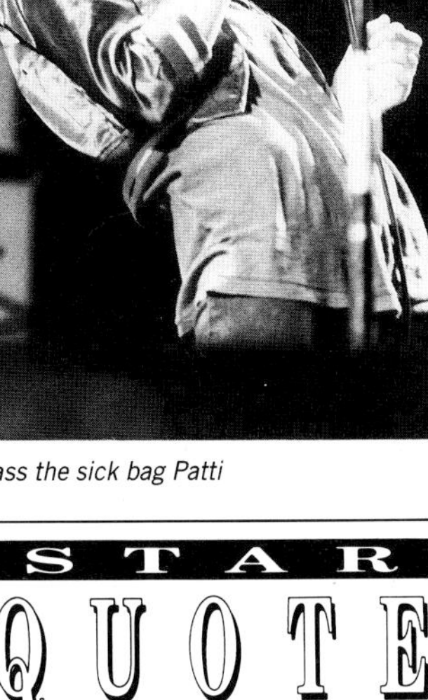

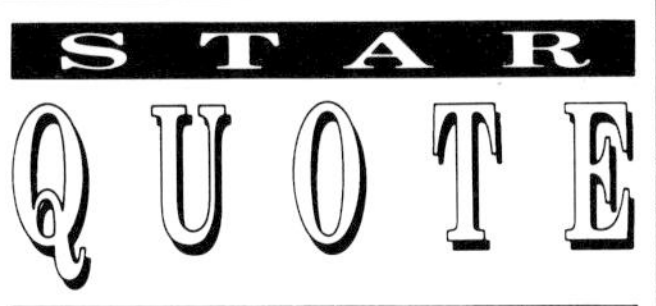

STAR QUOTE

PATTI SMITH

'Every man I've ever screwed has thrown up on me at least once.'

CLINTON'S GAININ' ON YA!

'There's a lot of chocolate cities around. We got Newark. We got Gary. Somebody told me we got LA. And we're working on Atlanta. But you're the capital and I love ya. God bless Chocolate City and its vanilla suburbs!'

That's how George Clinton tells it to his audience in Washington DC, where 80 per cent of the population is black. 'They still call it the White House but that's a temporary condition too. Gainin' on ya!' he cackles.

George Clinton raps and sometimes sings. He's got a band called Parliament. He's also got a band of equal freaky funkiness known as Funkadelic. George mainly writes and raps and whips it all together. He's the producer.

Let him explain. 'Parliament is more vocal, more disco with horns, and a bit more conservative. Funkadelic is more guitars, no horns, more free-form feelings and more wild. Sometimes there's a criss-cross but generally Funkadelic gets more pussy than Parliament.'

Then there's Bootsy's Rubber Band, put together by Bootsy Collins who used to be James Brown's guitarist, which is the root of where this whole Parliafunkedelicbootsyment thang got started. Except that was then and this is now. And George and Bootsy are playing all kinds of games that are turning white folks' perception of black music on its head. And some black folks too.

George Clinton: funk bench spokesman

NOVEMBER

LED ZEPPELIN'S COMMUNICATION BREAKDOWN

Robert Plant and Jimmy Page climbing the stairway to self-indulgence

Led Zeppelin manager Peter Grant has described *The Song Remains The Same* as 'the most expensive home movie ever made'. Maybe it should have stayed that way.

What seemed like a good idea at the time – capturing Zeppelin's live show on film – has been ruined by turning it into an orgy of self-indulgence.

The live material is slickly filmed, but Zeppelin have never been the most visual of rock bands. You have to be there.

The film falls most flat on its expensive face in the fantasy sequences. They are so banal and infantile one has to wonder why nobody dared to point out the folly of it all.

They don't even leave the music alone. The soundtrack sounds heavily doctored, and the best performance of the film, 'Since I've Been Loving You', is inexplicably absent from the double album.

Even Jimmy Page is not rushing to the film's defence. 'It's not a great film. Just a reasonably honest statement of where we were at that particular time.'

CHARTS

US45	Rock'n Me *Steve Miller Band*
USLP	Songs In The Key Of Life *Stevie Wonder*
UK45	If You Leave Me Now *Chicago*
UKLP	Songs In The Key Of Life *Stevie Wonder*
WEEK 2	
US45	Tonight's The Night *Rod Stewart*
USLP	Songs In The Key Of Life *Stevie Wonder*
UK45	If You Leave Me Now *Chicago*
UKLP	Songs In The Key Of Life *Stevie Wonder*
WEEK 3	
US45	Tonight's The Night *Rod Stewart*
USLP	Songs In The Key Of Life *Stevie Wonder*
UK45	If You Leave Me Now *Chicago*
UKLP	Songs In The Key Of Life *Stevie Wonder*
WEEK 4	
US45	Tonight's The Night *Rod Stewart*
USLP	Songs In The Key Of Life *Stevie Wonder*
UK45	If You Leave Me Now *Chicago*
UKLP	20 Golden Greats *Glen Campbell*

THE DAMNED SAY IT WITH FLOWERS

Other British punk bands may be grabbing the limelight, but The Damned are the first to get a record out.

'New Rose', released by the newly formed independent Stiff Records ('Today's Sound Today') opens with singer Dave Vanian asking coyly 'Is she really going out with him?' before the thunder of Rat Scabies' drumkit paves the way for guitarist Brian James' power chords and Captain Sensible's heavy bass line.

Captain Sensible is so called because he's 'so bleedin' stoopid', according to Scabies, whose own name comes from his constant itching. The rat hanging down the front of his drumkit is, alas, only plastic.

Brian James does his best to look like former New York Doll Johnny Thunders and Dave Vanian, who resembles a runaway from the Adams Family, used to be a gravedigger.

What else do you wanna know?

STAR QUOTE

MALCOLM McLAREN

Sex Pistols' manager

'Rock is fundamentally a young people's music, right? And a lot of kids feel cheated. They feel that the music's been taken away from them by that whole over-25 audience.'

Sex Pistols manager Malcolm McLaren trying hard to feel cheated

MARVIN GETS IT ON

'I Want You' is Marvin Gaye's first album for more than two years and seems trapped in the shadow of the superb 'Let's Get It On' which established his reputation for being more than just a Motown stooge with a flair for interpreting ready-made hits.

He hasn't visited Britain since the mid Sixties, but any doubts that he might have lost his following there have been laid to rest by the audience acclaim at his concert at London's Royal Albert Hall.

From the moment an admirer leapt on stage during 'Trouble Man' and ran off with Marvin's bow-tie, the show was constantly interrupted by adoring fans invading the stage to grab a piece of the star, or an item of clothing.

Those who preferred to listen were enthralled by his Seventies material. He remains a truly great singer, if a somewhat vulnerable artist.

THE

- **George Harrison has switched his Dark Horse label from A&M to Warners.**
- **Lol Creme and Kevin Godley have left 10cc to pursue their own projects; Eric Stewart and Graham Gouldman are to carry on as 10cc with new members.**
- **Jerry Lee Lewis has been arrested (again) after causing a disturbance outside Elvis Presley's Graceland home.**
- **Bread have re-formed with their original line-up.**

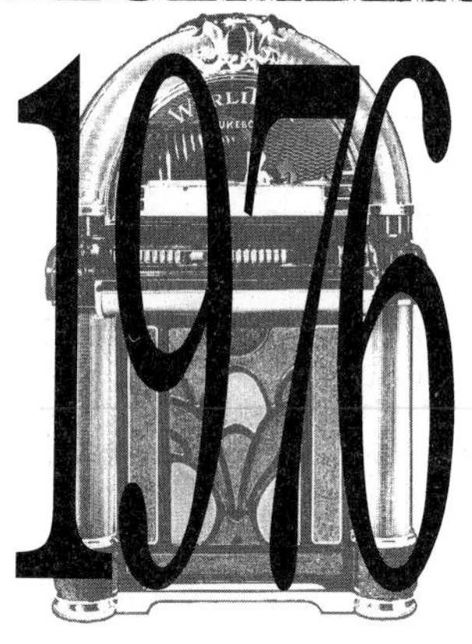

FROM ANARCHY TO CHAOS

Catapulted into the eye of a media hurricane after their infamous two-minute television interview, The Sex Pistols' debut UK tour has collapsed in ruins around them.

Within days, 12 out of 16 halls cancelled. In the town of Derby, town councillors insisted that The Pistols perform a private show so they could evaluate the band's threat to the nation's moral fibre. The group refused and another gig bit the dust.

At one of the few remaining dates (Leeds University), students were outnumbered by journalists eagerly awaiting another outrage to report. Sadly for them – and the punks who'd turned up – the gig was a dumb, castrated apology of a show that even Johnny Rotten's sneers couldn't enliven.

EMI Records are still considering their position. A statement from Chairman Sir John Read talks of making 'value judgements' within the 'contemporary limits of decency and good taste'. Meanwhile, EMI continue to press, distribute and collect the proceeds of 'Anarchy In The UK'.

Joe Strummer letting them know

STAR

JOE STRUMMER

The Clash

'I think people ought to know that we're anti-fascist, we're anti-violence, we're anti-racist and we're procreative. We're against ignorance.'

THE GRAPEVINE

■ **Rick Wakeman has rejoined Yes.**

■ **An inflatable pig being photographed for the cover of the Pink Floyd's 'Animals' broke loose and floated into the London Airport flightpath.**

■ **Bob Marley, his wife and manager were shot and wounded at the singer's Kingston, Jamaica, home during the country's general election campaign.**

■ **Former Deep Purple guitarist Tommy Bolin has died of a drug overdose in Miami.**

Flying pig over Battersea

CHARTS

US45	Tonight's The Night — *Rod Stewart*
USLP	Songs In The Key Of Life — *Stevie Wonder*
UK45	Under The Moon Of Love — *Showaddywaddy*
UKLP	20 Golden Greats — *Glen Campbell*
WEEK 2	
US45	Tonight's The Night — *Rod Stewart*
USLP	Songs In The Key Of Life — *Stevie Wonder*
UK45	Under The Moon Of Love — *Showaddywaddy*
UKLP	20 Golden Greats — *Glen Campbell*
WEEK 3	
US45	Tonight's The Night — *Rod Stewart*
USLP	Songs In The Key Of Life — *Stevie Wonder*
UK45	Under The Moon Of Love — *Showaddywaddy*
UKLP	20 Golden Greats — *Glen Campbell*
WEEK 4	
US45	Tonight's The Night — *Rod Stewart*
USLP	Songs In The Key Of Life — *Stevie Wonder*
UK45	When A Child Is Born — *Johnny Mathis*
UKLP	Arrival — *Abba*

JACKSON BROWNE'S GREAT PRETENDER

Nobody epitomizes the Seventies singer/songwriter better than Jackson Browne. He writes songs about the fundamental themes with a perception that puts him on a different level from his contemporaries.

Browne started work on his latest album, 'The Pretender', at the beginning of March. On March 25 his wife, to whom he'd been married less than six months, committed suicide. He stopped work on the album, starting again in May. In September he worked every waking hour to complete it, apart from one brief spell when he took his son on a camping holiday.

'"The Pretender" is just about being totally lost,' says Browne. 'He's a character in a story, and the poor fucker's so confused he thinks that maybe if he got a job the world would fall into place, and he might be actually happy watching the *Tonight* show.'

THE BAND'S LAST WALTZ

The Band have bowed out after 16 years on the road with a star-studded spectacular that left scarcely a dry eye at The Winterland, San Francisco.

Lead guitarist Robbie Robertson wanted 'a party with our friends . . . like a New Orleans funeral.' He got it.

Ronnie Hawkins, Dr John, Paul Butterfield, Muddy Waters, Eric Clapton, Neil Young, Joni Mitchell, Van Morrison and Bob Dylan joined The Band for a song or two each.

Five thousand people paid $25 to be wined, dined and entertained in the hall, which has been festooned with decorations. Promoter Bill Graham cheerfully lost $40,000 on the evening.

And to make sure it was all preserved for posterity, six camera crews, under the direction of Martin Scorsese, filmed 'The Last Waltz', as the evening was called.

Dylan's farewell to The Band

1977

PISTOLS FIRED ONCE

After nearly a month of pious procrastination, EMI have terminated their contract with The Sex Pistols. The straw that broke the camel's back was the group's widely publicized 'drunken and abusive' behaviour at London Airport en route for Holland for gigs in Amsterdam.

But the Pistols can console themselves with a £50,000 pay-off, and if the hysterical publicity surrounding them has made it impossible for them to play any concerts in the UK, there's no shortage of offers from Europe where they will be playing a 24-date tour throughout February.

It's not just record companies who are having trouble coming to terms with punk. The Who's Pete Townshend was involved in a 'tired and emotional' altercation with The Sex Pistols at London's Speakeasy Club. The man who wrote 'Hope I die before I get old' told drummer Paul Cook: 'I don't need to know what you're about' after lunging at a photographer who tried to take a picture of the pair of them.

'He thinks he's past it,' said Cook later. 'But he ain't. He's still great.' Guitarist Steve Jones agreed. 'He was really a great geezer even though he was, like, paralytic.'

Apocalyptic looking Stranglers

STAR QUOTE

JEAN-JACQUES BURNEL

The Stranglers

'We're due for tyranny. You may laugh but it's going to happen.'

PIGS ON THE WHINGE

The phenomenal success of Pink Floyd's 'Dark Side Of The Moon' – still in the charts four years after its release – hasn't made them a happier band.

As they prepare to release their new 'Animals' LP, drummer Nick Mason admits that the pressure of recording 'Wish You Were Here', the follow-up to 'Dark Side Of The Moon', nearly caused the band to split up. 'I really did find the time in the studio extremely horrible,' he says.

And bassist Roger Waters found the last tour 'very unpleasant, un-nerving and upsetting . . . The quality of life is full of stress and pain in most of the people I meet and in myself.'

Pink Floyd's Roger Waters showing the stress and pain of mega-stardom

The Bay City Rollers riding the wave of tartan teen hysteria

AMERICA LOVES THE ROLLERS

Bay City Roller-mania has come to America. The cute Scottish pop quintet, who've caused teenybopper hysteria wherever they appeared in the UK last year, have been greeted with the same reaction on their first US tour.

At New York's Palladium more than 30 teen and pre-teen girls fainted at their show. The banner-carrying fans were mostly dressed in tartan, displaying a visual identification which other teenybopper bands have never been able to achieve. 'What could the girls do to identify with the Osmonds?' asked one teen magazine. 'Dress up like Mormons?'

The Bay City Rollers' first two albums have already gone gold and the latest, 'Dedication', has sold 350,000 in four months.

Singer Les McKeown is feeling the strain: 'Psychologically it can be a real drag, all the travelling, never getting out of the hotel. But I think it'll mature eventually and they'll just scream at the end of numbers instead of all the way through.'

CHARTS

US45	Tonight's The Night *Rod Stewart*
USLP	Songs In The Key of Life *Stevie Wonder*
UK45	When A Child Is Born *Johnny Mathis*
UKLP	Arrival *Abba*
WEEK 2	
US45	You Don't Have To Be A Star *Marilyn McCoo & Billy Davis Jr.*
USLP	Songs In The Key Of Life *Stevie Wonder*
UK45	Don't Give Up On Us *David Soul*
UKLP	Arrival *Abba*
WEEK 3	
US45	You Make Me Feel Like Dancing *Leo Sayer*
USLP	Hotel California *Eagles*
UK45	Don't Give Up On Us *David Soul*
UKLP	Arrival *Abba*
WEEK 4	
US45	I Wish *Stevie Wonder*
USLP	Wings Over America *Wings*
UK45	Don't Give Up On Us *David Soul*
UKLP	Red River Valley *Slim Whitman*
WEEK 5	
US45	Car Wash *Rose Royce*
USLP	Hotel California *Eagles*
UK45	Don't Cry For Me Argentina *Julie Covington*
UKLP	Red River Valley *Slim Whitman*

THE GRAPEVINE

- **Keith Richards has been fined £750 for possession of cocaine found in his car during the Stones' UK tour last May.**
- **Original Fleetwood Mac guitarist Peter Green has been admitted to a mental hospital after trying to shoot a messenger delivering a royalty cheque.**
- **Patti Smith fell off stage in Florida and has broken her neck.**
- **Blues guitarist Freddie King, has died of heart failure in Dallas, Texas, aged 42.**

MORE THAN A FEELING

From out of Boston – Boston. Their album, released last September, is the fastest-selling debut in history. It went platinum within three months and is now heading for two and a half million US sales.

Tom Scholz – a Massachussetts Institute of Technology graduate who has applied his scientific expertise to the art of rock 'n' roll – is the brains behind this five-piece band. The result is an album of technical perfection influenced by 'a lotta English groups' from The Yardbirds to Queen.

The band were signed to Epic on the strength of a set of demos that were not dissimilar from the finished album, such was Scholz's sophisticated studio technique.

Radio leapt all over their first single, 'More Than A Feeling', and the rest was simply a matter of getting the records into the shops fast enough.

The studious, self-assured Scholz denies accusations that he's a depersonalized rock star. 'Technology had nothing to do with it. "More Than A Feeling" hasn't sold just because it's a good production. I get off playing rock!'

HALL & OATES SWING INTO STYLE

Hall & Oates: blue-eyed soul

Sweet soul musicians and brainiac hard rockers Daryl Hall & John Oates have cracked it with their fifth album, 'Bigger Than Both Of Us', which has yielded their first No. 1 single, 'Rich Girl'.

Nobody's ever doubted the potential of the New York duo who learnt their craft at Gamble & Huff's Sigma Studio, the Philly Sound factory. But packaging their white soul has been more of a problem.

Three albums on Atlantic in the early Seventies with producers as diverse as Arif Mardin and Todd Rundgren achieved nothing but one minor hit with 'She's Gone'.

But a switch to RCA and a more straightforward blend of rock and R&B has been more productive, starting with 'Sara Smile' which reached No. 4.

But there's an ostentation about Hall & Oates that sits uneasily with their music. The latest album has the casually bare-chested duo writing a song together at a table whose designer gets a sleeve credit.

You can rock my soul but you can't ruffle my hairdo . . .

CHARTS

Chart	Title	Artist
US45	Torn Between Two Lovers	*Mary MacGregor*
USLP	Hotel California	*Eagles*
UK45	Don't Give Up On Us	*David Soul*
UKLP	Red River Valley	*Slim Whitman*
WEEK 2		
US45	Torn Between Two Lovers	*Mary MacGregor*
USLP	A Star Is Born	*Barbra Streisand/Kris Kristofferson*
UK45	Don't Cry For Me Argentina	*Julie Covington*
UKLP	Red River Valley	*Slim Whitman*
WEEK 3		
US45	Blinded By The Light	*Manfred Mann's Earth Band*
USLP	A Star Is Born	*Barbra Streisand/Kris Kristofferson*
UK45	Don't Cry For Me Argentina	*Julie Covington*
UKLP	Evita	*Various*
WEEK 4		
US45	New Kid In Town	*Eagles*
USLP	A Star is Born	*Barbra Streisand/Kris Kristofferson*
UK45	When I Need You	*Leo Sayer*
UKLP	20 Golden Greats	*Shadows*

THE GRAPEVINE

- **Led Zeppelin's eagerly awaited US tour – their first since Robert Plant's serious car crash – has been postponed at the last minute after he went down with tonsillitis.**
- **Sex Pistols bassist Glen Matlock leaves – his replacement is Sid Vicious.**
- **Fleetwood Mac have released their new album 'Rumours'.**
- **Debut albums have been released by Blondie, The Damned, Television and Peter Gabriel.**

STAR QUOTE

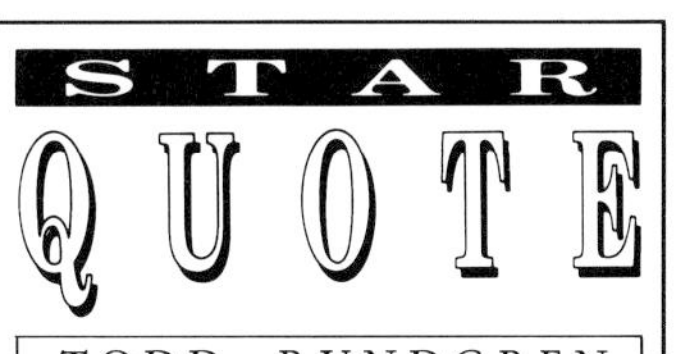

TODD RUNDGREN

'I was driving along in my car one day and this deep voice boomed out of the radio: "Rundgren, your next album will be called Ra. So now we're on this neo-Egyptian trip, a false Sphinx with smoke coming out of it, the works."'

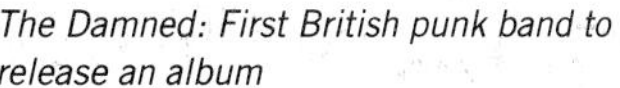

The Damned: First British punk band to release an album

KEITH RICHARDS' TORONTO BUST

Keith Richards' rock 'n' roll lifestyle is catching up with him – in the courts. Just a month after being fined £750 in the UK for possessing cocaine, the Royal Canadian Mounted Police raided his Toronto hotel room and seized 22 grams of heroin and 5 grams of cocaine.

Richards had arrived in Toronto to join the rest of The Stones completing their upcoming live album.

He's been charged with 'intent to traffic', which carries a life sentence. And although he's out on bail, the odds are mounting up against his chances of staying free and The Stones' chances of being able to tour America again.

PISTOLS FIRED TWICE

The Sex Pistols' first contract with EMI lasted three months. Their second with A&M lasted a week.

In one of the most extraordinary turnabouts by any record company, A&M – who signed the group in a blaze of publicity outside Buckingham Palace – reneged on the deal almost before the ink had dried.

A&M would give no reason for their change of heart, but speculation has centred on reports of the group going on a drunken rampage through A&M's offices, complaints from other A&M acts, and a scuffle at London's Speakeasy Club.

Whatever the reasons, 25,000 copies of the band's eagerly-awaited debut single, 'God Save The Queen', have been scrapped. And The Pistols have received another pay-off – this time £75,000, making £125,000 in all this year for very little work indeed.

'But it's not very satisfying to us,' moans manager Malcolm McLaren. 'We want to get back into action.'

STAR

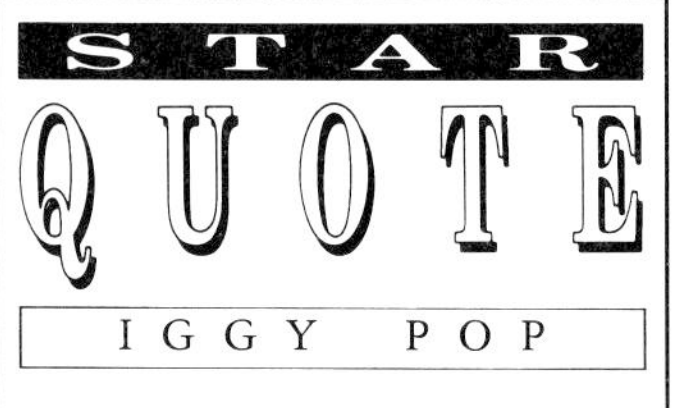

QUOTE

IGGY POP

'I had a mirror last night and I looked at it and it seemed to say . . . I just said: Wow this is just like . . . you know?'

Mirror mirror on the wall . . .

THE GRAPEVINE

- **Sara Lowndes Dylan is sueing Bob for divorce.**
- **The Ramones' 'Carbona Not Glue' track from 'Leave Home' has been cut from the UK version.**
- **Margaret Trudeau, wife of Canadian Prime Minister Pierre, attended The Rolling Stones' Toronto club shows.**
- **The Clash have signed to CBS and released their first single, 'White Riot'.**
- **Fleetwood Mac's 'Rumours' has gone platinum after a month.**

GRAHAM PARKER'S HEAT TREATMENT

Graham Parker: a mod, a hippy and now surrounded by Rumours

Graham Parker ain't no punk. In fact he used to be a hippy, 'but a sneering one'.

But he has all the energy of punk and his second album, 'Heat Treatment', recorded in two tight weeks, is a superb example of his sweat 'n' sneakers rock 'n' roll that typifies the London pub and club scene.

'I saw The Damned once and I didn't like them,' Parker admits. 'They were the kind of band I used to watch when I was eating brown rice. They had this huge rush of energy but no tenderness. I prefer Gladys Knight & The Pips, because they move me.'

Before he was a hippy, Graham Parker was an Otis Redding-fixated mod which explains some of the aggression in his music and lyrics.

As the title track of the new album puts it: 'Out in the jungle there's a war going down/You wind up eating all the friends you've found.'

And as he himself says: 'I know what it's like to be woken up by a copper at two in the morning.'

THE WHO SEE THE LIGHT

John 'Wiggy' Wolff, the man behind The Who's spectacular lights and laser show, had his own exhibition at London's Royal Academy this month.

Regarded as one of the world's foremost innovators of laser-beam technology, Wolff demonstrated his £250,000 ($500,000) worth of equipment, all paid for by The Who – which makes them the UK's biggest laser owners.

'They're as dangerous as a truck – it depends what you do with them,' says Wolff, who explains that his lasers are very different from the metal-cutting variety. He also takes elaborate precautions to prevent the beam getting anywhere near the eyes of a Who audience.

But that doesn't stop petty bureaucrats giving him a hard time. They tried to stop him at London's Wembley Arena, claiming reflections off the girders would blind the crowd.

'I had to point out to them that the girders hadn't been cleaned in forty years, and nothing was going to reflect off that gunge!' laughs Wolff.

CHARTS

US45	Evergreen *Barbra Streisand*
USLP	A Star Is Born *Barbra Streisand/Kris Kristofferson*
UK45	When I Need You *Leo Sayer*
UKLP	20 Golden Greats *Shadows*
WEEK 2	
US45	Evergreen *Barbra Streisand*
USLP	A Star Is Born *Barbra Streisand/Kris Kristofferson*
UK45	Chanson D'Amour *Manhattan Transfer*
UKLP	20 Golden Greats *Shadows*
WEEK 3	
US45	Evergreen *Barbra Streisand*
USLP	A Star Is Born *Barbra Streisand/Kris Kristofferson*
UK45	Chanson D'Amour *Manhattan Transfer*
UKLP	20 Golden Greats *Shadows*
WEEK 4	
US45	Rich Girl *Daryl Hall & John Oates*
USLP	Hotel California *Eagles*
UK45	Knowing Me, Knowing You *Abba*
UKLP	20 Golden Greats *Shadows*

APRIL

1977

TOWER BLOCK ROCK

No compromise, just commitment – live hostilities from the Clash

'It ain't punk. It ain't new wave. It's the next step, and the logical progression for groups to move. Call it what you want – all the terms stink. Just call it rock 'n' roll' – Mick Jones, guitarist.

'I ain't gonna fuck myself up like I seen those other guys fuck themselves up. Keeping all their money for themselves and getting into their heads, and thinking they're the greatest. I've planned what I'm gonna do with my money if it happens. Secret plans' – Joe Strummer, vocals/guitar.

The Clash are not just a band. They are a commitment. Bassist and former South London skinhead Paul Simenon knew what he was doing when he named them. One of the first bands he saw was The Sex Pistols. He is a pure Seventies child.

Their no-compromise attitude has got them an uncompromising deal with CBS and an equally uncompromising debut album.

But it's also cost them a drummer, and finding the right replacement – musically and personally – is proving a problem. Particularly when there's gigs to be played. Or, as Mick Jones calls them, 'the hostilities'.

'I don't believe in guitar heroes,' he says. 'If I walk out to the front of the stage it's because I wanna reach the audience. I don't want them to suck my guitar off.'

CHARTS

US45	Rich Girl *Daryl Hall & John Oates*
USLP	Rumours *Fleetwood Mac*
UK45	Knowing Me, Knowing You *Abba*
UKLP	20 Golden Greats *Shadows*
WEEK 2	
US45	Dancing Queen *Abba*
USLP	Rumours *Fleetwood Mac*
UK45	Knowing Me, Knowing You *Abba*
UKLP	Portrait Of Sinatra *Frank Sinatra*
WEEK 3	
US45	Don't Give Up On Us *David Soul*
USLP	Hotel California *Eagles*
UK45	Knowing Me, Knowing You *Abba*
UKLP	Arrival *Abba*
WEEK 4	
US45	Don't Leave Me This Way *Thelma Houston*
USLP	Hotel California *Eagles*
UK45	Knowing Me, Knowing You *Abba*
UKLP	Arrival *Abba*
WEEK 5	
US45	Southern Nights *Glen Campbell*
USLP	Hotel California *Eagles*
UK45	Knowing Me, Knowing You *Abba*
UKLP	Arrival *Abba*

THE GRAPEVINE

- **Bruce Springsteen's ex-manager Mike Appel has won an injunction against The Boss's recording, pending the outcome of their dispute.**
- **Studio 54, an exclusive disco, has opened in New York.**
- **The Damned have become the first British punk band to play New York.**
- **New albums: Iggy Pop ('The Idiot'), The Beach Boys ('Love You'), The Stranglers ('Rattus Norvegicus') and ELP ('Works').**

Muddy's mojo working

MUDDY WATERS – HARD AGAIN

Muddy Waters was nearly 50 when The Rolling Stones started picking up on his records. He's just turned 62, and has come up with an album that can still teach his students a thing or two.

The aptly titled 'Hard Again' finds Muddy getting back to the Fifties style he perfected in the tough Chicago clubs. And the man responsible for getting that sound out of him again is Johnny Winter.

Muddy's respect for Winter knows no bounds. 'I figured this was my greatest chance, man, of all my days, to get with somebody who's still got it, got that early Fifties sound. This is one of the best records I've made in a long time.'

THE SPLITS THAT BIND FLEETWOOD MAC

'Being in Fleetwood Mac is more like being in group therapy!'

So says drummer and leader Mick Fleetwood, and he should know. Just as the band achieved breakthrough with their 'Fleetwood Mac' album, they went into an emotional tailspin.

Long-standing singer/pianist Christine McVie split from bassist/husband John mid-way through an American tour.

Lindsey Buckingham and Stevie Nicks stopped sharing a room soon after. And then Mick Fleetwood's own marriage broke up, although he has since salvaged it.

Scarcely the right atmosphere in which to record 'Rumours', the follow-up to their four-million selling album.

'It turned out to be the reverse,' says Mick. 'Because it all came out in the music. Things never got bitchy. Sure, the atmosphere was confused – to say the least – but it wasn't destructive. We could all relate to each other's desperation.'

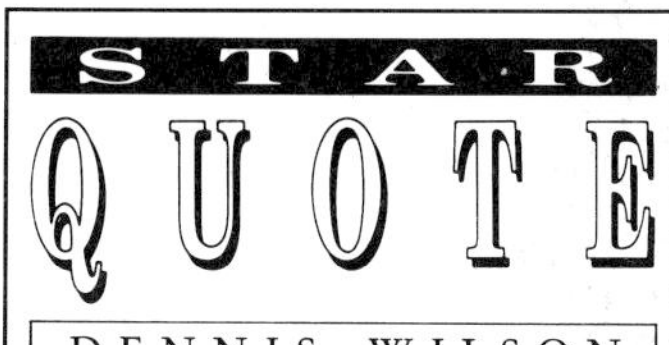

DENNIS WILSON

'There'd be many times when I'd look at my brother and think to myself, maybe he won't ever pull it together again. Brian went through a lot of bad times. Drugs didn't help.'

VIRGIN SAVES THE SEX PISTOLS

After weeks of speculation, The Sex Pistols have signed their third record deal in less than six months. Virgin are the brave label to take them on, and their new single, 'God Save The Queen' is out at the end of the month – just in time for the Queen's Silver Jubilee celebrations across the UK.

Advance orders are described as 'massive', but Virgin's marketing campaign has already been restricted by TV's refusal to run an ad for the record. And the chances of daytime radio play look slim.

Live gigs are a problem too, thanks to squeamish promoters. And other bands such as The Stranglers are being deemed 'unsuitable' at several provincial venues around the UK.

Not without some cause either. A Clash/Jam show at London's Rainbow Theatre resulted in 200 trashed seats, although there was little other damage. In fact, as riots go, it was an orderly one.

STEVE MILLER TAKES THE MONEY AND RUNS

When you finally get a hit after six years of trying, leaving a two-and-a-half year gap before you release another album scarcely makes sense – unless you're Steve Miller.

Exhausted by touring, Miller came off the road, took up farming and secured a better record deal before going back into the studio.

The next album, 'Fly Like an Eagle', spawned three hit singles – 'Take The Money And Run', 'Fly Like An Eagle' and 'Rock 'n' Me' – and is approaching four million sales. Miller has stripped his late Sixties San Francisco psychedelia down to a pure pop R&B sound that's a natural for the charts.

Not surprisingly his new album, 'Book Of Dreams', sticks closely to the formula. 'I feel I have a pretty good understanding of what a lot of people will like,' he says. 'I know how to make records, produce records, sing lots of parts and make this little thing that's music. I'm a craftsman.'

CHARTS

US45	Hotel California – *Eagles*
USLP	Hotel California – *Eagles*
UK45	Free – *Deniece Williams*
UKLP	Arrival – *Abba*
WEEK 2	
US45	When I Need You – *Leo Sayer*
USLP	Hotel California – *Eagles*
UK45	Free – *Deniece Williams*
UKLP	Arrival – *Abba*
WEEK 3	
US45	Sir Duke – *Stevie Wonder*
USLP	Rumours – *Fleetwood Mac*
UK45	Free – *Deniece Williams*
UKLP	Arrival – *Abba*
WEEK 4	
US45	Sir Duke – *Stevie Wonder*
USLP	Rumours – *Fleetwood Mac*
UK45	I Don't Want To Talk About It – *Rod Stewart*
UKLP	Hotel California – *Eagles*

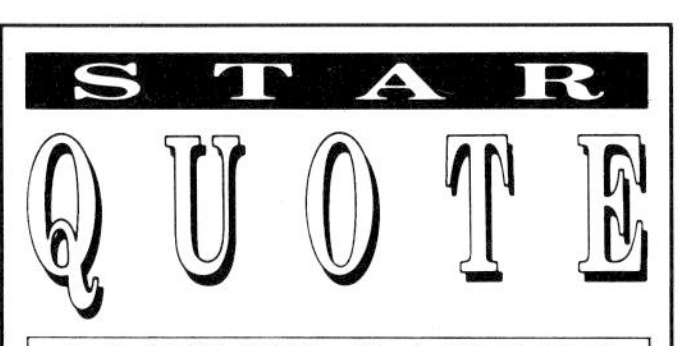

JOHNNY RAMONE

The Ramones

'We usually wear out our audience before we wear out ourselves. And we're getting faster every day. Our first album sounds real slow now.'

Linda keeps her clothes on

SHARP DRESSED PUNKS

The Jam fly the flag just like the Who did back in the '60s

'We're the black sheep of the new wave,' asserts Paul Weller, singer and guitarist with The Jam.

For a start, their mohair suits and tight playing owe more to the Sixties beat groups than the new wave. They're not afraid of their influences either. Otis Redding is Weller's favourite singer. Bassist Bruce Foxton admits to listening to Bad Company and Thin Lizzy, while drummer Rick Buckler even confesses to owning a couple of Genesis albums.

The Jam have been together a couple of years, starting off covering Chuck Berry and progressing to Mersey Beat and soul. Even now they include 'Midnight Hour', 'Sweet Soul Music' and The Who's 'So Sad About Us' in their set.

'I didn't want to work,' says Weller. 'I didn't want to become Mister Normal.

'For the first time in years I realized that there was a younger audience there, young bands playing to young people. It was something we'd been looking for in a long time.'

Their first single, 'In The City', is the perfect response: a genuine late Seventies teen anthem.

THE GRAPEVINE

- **Led Zeppelin have broken their own world record for the largest audience at a single-act gig – 76,000 at Michigan's Pontiac Silverdome.**
- **Bruce Springsteen has settled out of court with former manager Mike Appel who gets a million dollars. Springsteen gets his freedom.**
- **ELP have started a US tour with a 72-piece orchestra.**
- **Linda Ronstadt has turned down a nude modelling offer from *Hustler*.**

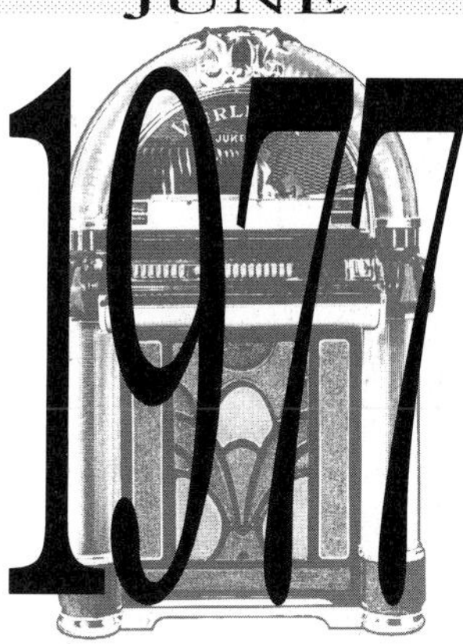

VAN MORRISON – EXPECT THE UNEXPECTED

Van Morrison's first album for three years is rightly called 'A Period Of Transition'. After nearly a decade's exile in California, Van the Man is resident in his native Ireland once more.

The album too is back to his R&B roots; he sounds more like a singer with a club band than a singer/songwriter with a backing band. It's unpredictable, which is not what a lot of his fans want.

But the normally reclusive Van is unrepentant: 'People begin to get a preconceived idea about a particular artist and that can work against you . . . most definitely. I think I need to break a lot of that expectancy down.

'Quite recently I dug out all my old blues records, and there's something about that music that still turns me on. But you see, I was in that singer/songwriter phase . . . progression . . . what have you . . . I ain't knockin' it, but I realized I was missing out on all the many other things I can do and, more important, enjoy doing.

'The moment you start to think you're one thing, you're not.'

'BANNED' SEX PISTOLS SINGLE IN THE CHARTS

Despite a blanket airplay ban across the UK, The Sex Pistols' 'God Save The Queen' single has reached No. 1, even though several chain stores are refusing to stock the record.

Chart shows are mentioning the single without playing it, although one station is pretending it doesn't exist.

The Pistols attempted to get round their concert ban by hiring a boat and sailing down the River Thames, playing at their own private party. But when they arrived back, the police were waiting for them. Eleven people were arrested, several more beaten up.

Within a week The Pistols became everybody's whipping boys – literally. Johnny Rotten was slashed by a razor outside a North London pub and needed stitches. And Paul Cook was attacked at a tube station by a gang who identified him as a Sex Pistol. He too needed stitches in hospital.

Boomtown Rats looking for No 1

CHARTS

US45	Sir Duke	*Stevie Wonder*
USLP	Rumours	*Fleetwood Mac*
UK45	I Don't Want To Talk About it	*Rod Stewart*
UKLP	Hotel California	*Eagles*
WEEK 2		
US45	I'm Your Boogie Man	*K.C. & The Sunshine Band*
USLP	Rumours	*Fleetwood Mac*
UK45	I Don't Want To Talk About It	*Rod Stewart*
UKLP	Arrival	*Abba*
WEEK 3		
US45	Dreams	*Fleetwood Mac*
USLP	Rumours	*Fleetwood Mac*
UK45	God Save The Queen	*Sex Pistols*
UKLP	Arrival	*Abba*
WEEK 4		
US45	Got To Give It Up, Part One	*Marvin Gaye*
USLP	Rumours	*Fleetwood Mac*
UK45	Show You The Way To Go	*Jacksons*
UKLP	Live At The Hollywood Bowl	*Beatles*

DODGING THE RAT TRAP

Irish punks – some kind of joke? No, The Boomtown Rats actually.

Led by Bob Geldof, who's been described as 'a Jagger for the New Depression', they've broken out of Ireland by being abnormal – giving away raw liver as prizes at their gigs, letting live rats out into the audience, showing blue movies at their gigs and, when promoters got scared, hiring a truck and playing in the streets.

'We've definitely come from the R&B thing, but we've swung off it,' declares Geldof. Their demo was good enough to secure a deal and they've already recorded an album. But they're waiting until they're better known before releasing it.

'We want a credibility that definitely comes from people who see the band,' says Geldof. 'If people come to see you because you've been hyped and you're not what they expected, they get disappointed.'

STAR QUOTE

FREDDIE MERCURY

'People want art. They want showbiz. They want to see you rush off in your limousine.'

THE GRAPEVINE

- **The UK's punk gig ban is spreading, with The Damned, The Stranglers and The Jam all having dates cancelled.**
- **Two members of The Clash were arrested after painting their names on a London wall.**
- **Alice Cooper's boa constrictor died when it was bitten by its rat dinner.**
- **Stevie Wonder has played his first show for a year and a half - to students at UCLA.**

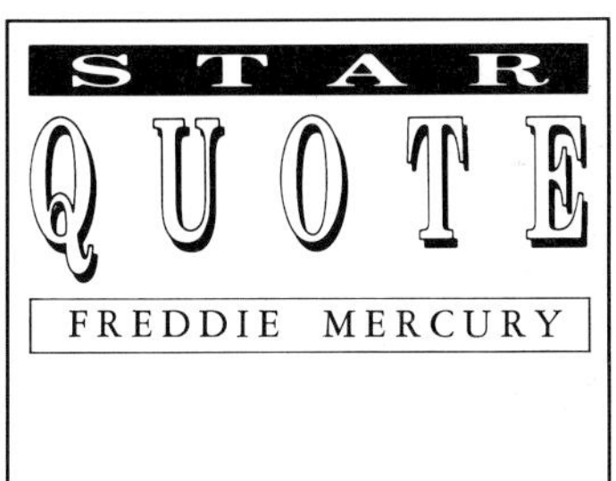

Alice looking for rat poison

WAITING FOR WINWOOD

At 15, Steve Winwood was a precocious pop star with The Spencer Davis Group. Since then he's been a rock star in Traffic and a superstar in Blind Faith. But it's taken him a while to summon up the confidence to record his first solo album.

'I had a lot of material ready and waiting, but I couldn't force myself any further. I couldn't see any reason, any real justification for doing it,' says Winwood.

He brought in his Traffic buddy and lyricist Jim Capaldi on four of the six tracks. Which makes you wonder why he broke up Traffic in the first place?

'There wasn't the cohesion to keep it together, and there were various personal problems which are best forgotten. I wasn't committed any more, and I felt that we'd achieved as much as we could with that version of the group.'

Winwood's impetus has slowed since he moved into the country. Even he admits that he's lost that sense of desperation that 'makes strong music'. Some of it also comes from rejecting the rock-star-making machinery.

'There was a time when I was ambitious in that sense, but not now. It can mess you up. I somehow doubt it did anyone any good in the long run.'

LED ZEPPELIN JINXED

Led Zeppelin's ill-fated US tour has collapsed in tragedy and violence.

The tragedy happened in England where Robert Plant's five-year-old son Karac died suddenly, while being treated for a stomach ailment. Plant immediately flew home from New Orleans, and the rest of the tour was cancelled.

The violence happened backstage at the group's previous show at the Oakland Coliseum. John Bonham, manager Peter Grant and two other Zeppelin employees were involved in a fight with two of promoter Bill Graham's security staff, one of whom was seriously beaten.

Police have charged all four with assault and Graham, America's top promoter, says he 'can never in all conscience book the band again.'

The tour – the first following Robert Plant's recovery from injuries received in a car accident nearly two years ago – was postponed when Plant went down with 'flu just before the first date. Chicago concerts were also postponed when Jimmy Page became ill.

With Bonham and Grant facing arrest if they return to America, and Plant grieving for his son, it's uncertain when or whether Zeppelin will return to complete the tour.

CHARTS

US45	Gonna Fly Now (Theme From Rocky) *Bill Conti*
USLP	Rumours *Fleetwood Mac*
UK45	Show You The Way To Go *Jacksons*
UKLP	The Muppet Show *Muppets*
WEEK 2	
US45	Undercover Angel *Alan O'Day*
USLP	Rumours *Fleetwood Mac*
UK45	So You Win Again *Hot Chocolate*
UKLP	A Star Is Born *Soundtrack*
WEEK 3	
US45	Da Doo Ron Ron *Shaun Cassidy*
USLP	Live *Barry Manilow*
UK45	Ma Baker *Boney M*
UKLP	A Star Is Born *Soundtrack*
WEEK 4	
US45	Looks Like We Made it *Barry Manilow*
USLP	Rumours *Fleetwood Mac*
UK45	I Feel Love *Donna Summer*
UKLP	The Johnny Mathis Collection *Johnny Mathis*
WEEK 5	
US45	I Just Want To Be Your Everything *Andy Gibb*
USLP	Rumours *Fleetwood Mac*
UK45	I Feel Love *Donna Summer*
UKLP	A Star Is Born *Soundtrack*

THE GRAPEVINE

- **The Sex Pistols have rush-released their new single, 'Pretty Vacant', but despite the assistance of airplay and TV it's failed to emulate 'God Save The Queen'.**
- **19-year-old Patrick Coultry has been stabbed to death at a Dublin punk gig.**
- **Local councils are continuing to ban many punk gigs around the UK in response to random outbreaks of violence.**
- **The Who have bought Shepperton Film Studios.**

STAR QUOTE

STEVE HARLEY

'I set out to be a winner. I don't want to lose. I spent four years in a hospital but I never expected favours from anyone. I don't give sympathy because I don't expect it. Nice guys don't make it.'

Steve Harley looking for favours

Manchester's Buzzcocks, part of the Roxy scene immortalized in vital vinyl

A DIFFERENT ROXY MUSIC

The birthplace of the London punk scene was the seedy Roxy Club, and its birth pangs have been captured for posterity on a live album called 'The Roxy London WC2 (Jan-Apr 77)' which was recorded documentary-style over four days in early April. Hi fi it ain't, but enough nostalgic punks(!) have bought it to push it into the UK Top 20.

The club still books punk acts, but most of the 'elite' bands have shunned it, or grown out of it.

AUGUST

ELVIS IS DEAD . . .

Elvis Aaron Presley. Born January 8, 1935. Died August 16, 1977

The King of Rock 'n' Roll is dead.

Elvis Presley was found lying on his bathroom floor at his Memphis home in the early hours of August 16 and, despite efforts to resuscitate him, was pronounced dead at Memphis Baptist Memorial Hospital.

Within hours, thousands of people gathered outside the gates of Graceland and the scene was set for the biggest media event of the decade. 75,000 people were present for his funeral two days later, when he was laid to rest in a white marble mausoleum near his mother.

Speculation over the cause of Presley's heart-attack is rife. His health had been deteriorating for the past four years. He was hospitalized five times for intestinal problems, eye trouble, recurrent 'flu and fatigue. No amount of skilful tailoring could disguise the fact that he was overweight, and there were incessant rumours of drug abuse.

But none of this matters to his millions of fans. Within a week, the second biggest selling artist of all time was back in the singles and album charts around the world as fans rushed out to buy whatever they could.

However, it is believed that RCA will not be releasing an 'instant' memorial album.

As President Jimmy Carter says, 'Elvis Presley's death deprives our country of a part of itself.'

THE GRAPEVINE

- Runaways bassist Jackie Fox has quit after an alleged suicide bid.
- Singer Cherie Currie followed two weeks later after a clash of egos with guitarist Joan Jett.
- Bachman Turner Overdrive have disbanded.
- 'Self confessed homosexual' and committed political singer/songwriter Tom Robinson has signed to EMI.
- Sid Vicious has been fined £125 ($250) for possessing a flick-knife at a punk gig.

CHARTS

US45	I Just Want To Be Your Everything *Andy Gibb*
USLP	Rumours *Fleetwood Mac*
UK45	I Feel Love *Donna Summer*
UKLP	The Johnny Mathis Collection *Johnny Mathis*
WEEK 2	
US45	I Just Want To Be Your Everything *Andy Gibb*
USLP	Rumours *Fleetwood Mac*
UK45	I Feel Love *Donna Summer*
UKLP	The Johnny Mathis Collection *Johnny Mathis*
WEEK 3	
US45	Best Of My Love *Emotions*
USLP	Rumours *Fleetwood Mac*
UK45	I Feel Love *Donna Summer*
UKLP	Going For The One *Yes*
WEEK 4	
US45	Best Of My Love *Emotions*
USLP	Rumours *Fleetwood Mac*
UK45	Angelo *Brotherhood Of Man*
UKLP	Going For The One *Yes*

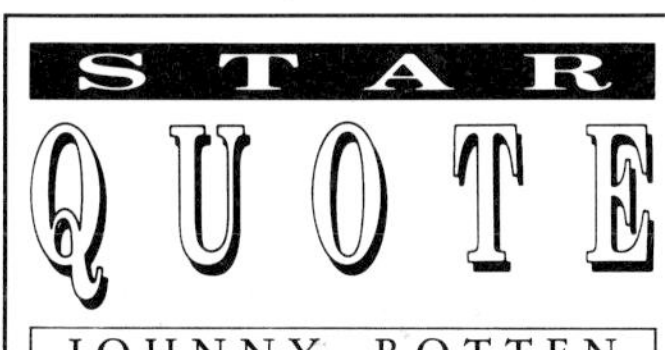

JOHNNY ROTTEN

'Turn the other cheek too often and you get a razor through it.'

. . . LONG LIVE ELVIS!

Most singer/songwriters write about love and romance. Not Elvis Costello.

'The only two things that matter to me, the only motivation points for me writing all these songs, are revenge and guilt,' he claims. 'Those are the only two emotions I know about. Love? I dunno what it means really, and it doesn't exist in my songs.'

Elvis Costello has just released his debut album, 'My Aim Is True', on the bubbling UK indie label Stiff Records. But that doesn't mean he's feeling talkative. He refuses to give any details about his background (Liverpool) or his past career as a member of country/rock combo Flip City and as a folk singer.

His demo was the first that Stiff bosses Dave Robinson and Jake Riviera listened to when they set up shop. They were so impressed they had to listen to a week's worth of dross before they could believe they weren't dreaming.

Elvis hates trendies, won't allow other guitar players on stage with him, keeps a 'black book' of enemies and scrutinizes guest lists to cross off 'undesirables'.

Despite his motivation, his musical passion is country music - particularly George Jones and Gram Parsons.

'Parsons had it all sussed – he did his best work and then he died. I'm never going to stick around long enough to churn out a bunch of mediocre crap like all those guys from the Sixties. I don't intend to be around to watch my artistic decline.'

Elvis Costello takes aim

CHARTS

US45	Best Of My Love *Emotions*
USLP	Rumours *Fleetwood Mac*
UK45	Way Down *Elvis Presley*
UKLP	Moody Blue *Elvis Presley*
WEEK 2	
US45	Best Of My Love *Emotions*
USLP	Rumours *Fleetwood Mac*
UK45	Magic Fly *Space*
UKLP	Oxygene *Jean Michel Jarre*
WEEK 3	
US45	Best Of My Love *Emotions*
USLP	Rumours *Fleetwood Mac*
UK45	Magic Fly *Space*
UKLP	Oxygene *Jean Michel Jarre*
WEEK 4	
US45	Best Of My Love *Emotions*
USLP	Rumours *Fleetwood Mac*
UK45	Magic Fly *Space*
UKLP	20 Golden Greats *Diana Ross & The Supremes*

THE BOYS ARE BACK IN TOWN

Phil Lynott (left) of Thin Lizzy: all the ego a rock star needs

A black Irishman, a Roman Catholic with a decidedly irreligious lifestyle, a bass-playing poet in a rock 'n' roll band called Thin Lizzy – that's Phil Lynott.

A couple of years ago, Thin Lizzy were considered hapless losers. But with the new wave sweeping aside the old guard, Thin Lizzy have come into their own. Their image may be slightly *passé*, but they possess that vital chemistry that marks all great bands.

Their 'Jailbreak' album and hard-assed rockin' stage show have cracked it for them in the UK. And they'd be doing better in America right now if Lynott hadn't gone down with hepatitis mid-way through a tour that was successfully breaking the album there too.

The songs Phil's written for the new album, 'Bad Reputation', were composed while he was recuperating. They are 'more mellow', but his vanity remains undaunted.

'The main thing that pushes me to write songs is to share my personal experiences. Plus the sheer ego of thinking my life is so important it should be shared!' he grins.

RANDY NEWMAN – GUNNING FOR SHORT PEOPLE

Randy Newman is a master of black comedy. Such a master that he frequently gets misunderstood. His last album, 'Good Ole Boys', was labelled 'racialist' in *Rolling Stone* magazine.

While his songs have successfully been covered by a wide variety of artists, his own records have been less successful. Despite praise from the likes of Dylan and McCartney, Newman remains a cult hero – not least because of his prolonged bouts of inactivity.

He's currently putting the vocals on his new album, 'Little Criminals'.

'There's one about a child murderer,' Newman deadpans. 'That's fairly optimistic. Maybe. There's one called "Jolly Coppers On Parade" which isn't an absolutely anti-police song. Maybe it's even a fascist song. I didn't notice at the time.

'There's also this one about me as a cowboy called "Rider In The Rain". I think it's ridiculous. The Eagles are on there. That's what's good about it. There's also this song "Short People". It's purely a joke. I like other ones on the album better but the audiences go for that one.'

Wonder if short people will get the joke?

MARC BOLAN KILLED IN CAR CRASH

Marc Bolan, the pixie in T. Rex who spanned psychedelia and glam rock and was on the verge of a solo comeback, has been killed in a car accident.

He was a passenger in the yellow Mini being driven by his girlfriend, singer Gloria Jones, when the car spun off a wet road on Barnes Common, south-west London, and crashed into a tree. Bolan was killed instantly, and Gloria was rushed to hospital with a broken jaw.

Bolan scored a string of UK hits in the early Seventies with such songs as 'Hot Love', and 'Get It On', but failed to repeat the success in America where he became a tax exile.

He'd just started his British comeback, touring with The Damned and filming a TV series.

- **Bob Marley had part of his right big toe removed in a 'routine' operation in Miami. The toe had failed to heal after a football accident.**
- **Guitarist Jimmy McCulloch has left Wings.**
- **110,000 hippies fought back against the new wave, attending a Grateful Dead/New Riders Of The Purple Sage/Marshall Tucker Band concert at Old Bridge, New Jersey.**

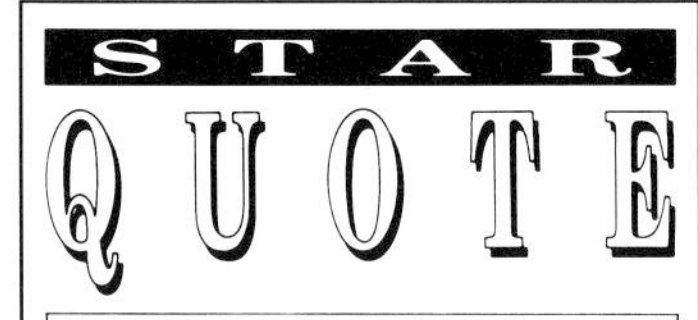

SOUTHSIDE JOHNNY

'Rock 'n' roll should be made by truck drivers from Tupelo, Mississippi, not studio musicians with an album commitment to fulfil.'

Song titles on Randy Newman's 'Little Criminals' album include 'Sigmund Freud's Impersonation of Albert Einstein in America', 'Texas Girl at the Funeral Of Her Father' and 'Kathleen (Catholicism Made Easy)'. Rock and roll huh?

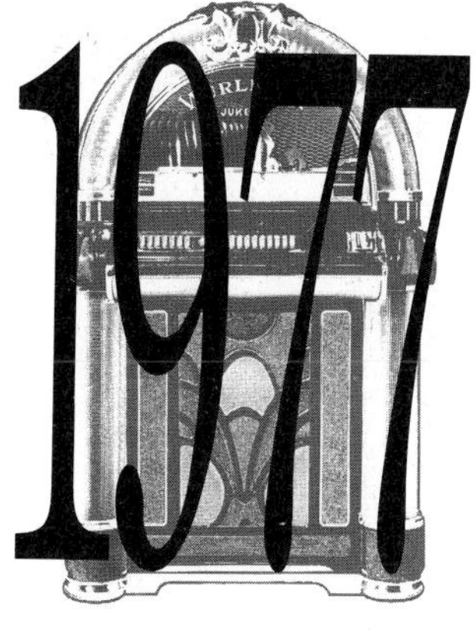

PETER GABRIEL'S RE-GENESIS

'I was going to take a bet that I wouldn't be back on the road within a couple of years of leaving Genesis,' smiles Peter Gabriel. 'I kept on with the songwriting, but I wasn't interested in performing.

'Then once the songs came out, I got back into recording and started enjoying it. And here I am on the road again!'

Gabriel is playing his first solo shows since quitting Genesis, who were on the brink of major success after nearly a decade of hard graft. Speculation continues to surround his departure, but in essence he simply wanted to make his music in a different way.

His debut solo album has yielded a hit single, 'Solsbury Hill'. And now he's touring the UK with a show that's essentially musical rather than visual.

'It would have been quite easy for me to develop a visual show, but I felt I needed to try and base it on my music and my performance.'

Which is why his show doesn't include any Genesis numbers but does feature covers of The Kinks' 'All Day And All Of The Night' and Marvin Gaye's 'I Heard It Through The Grapevine' and 'Ain't That Peculiar'.

'I'm not that interested in being a mythical superstar,' he explains. 'I would like to be a successful one, but the opportunity to live out that image doesn't appeal to me.'

Peter Gabriel has climbed Solsbury Hill leaving Genesis far behind him

NO MORE HEROES?

'In 1977, rock has become very much a gladiatorial sport,' avers Jean-Jacques Burnel, bass player of The Stranglers, the most successful chart band of the British new wave.

And yet The Stranglers' punk credentials are shaky to say the least. It's not just their ages which are closer to the old wave than the new. There's a strain of chauvinism and macho bravado about songs like 'Bring On The Nubiles' that sits uncomfortably with what the new wave is supposed to be about.

And then there's their private army of minders and hangers on, the Finchley Boys, whose gang mentality is definitely suspect.

The Stranglers are the perfect band for supplying reassurance to the nightmare of adolescent insecurity. Which goes a long way to explaining their huge popularity in Britain.

'We're up there singing "No More Heroes" and in front of us thousands of kids are going crazy,' muses singer Hugh Cornwell. 'It's almost as if we're perpetuating the very myth we set out to destroy.'

ROCK 'N' ROLL WITH THE MODERN LOVERS

Jonathan Richman certainly has the rock critics in a spin. Three of them are pacing the back of London's Hammersmith Odeon earnestly debating his status as a new wave messiah. Meanwhile, the object of their attention is crawling round the stage on all fours singing 'I'm A Little Dinosaur'!

The first 'Modern Lovers' album contained two Seventies rock classics – 'Roadrunner' and 'Pablo Picasso'. But subsequent albums have revealed a twee, naïve charm that's harder to take seriously.

At the Hammersmith Odeon, the boy from Boston sings 'Ice Cream Man', repeating the last verse five times to increasingly rapturous applause.

STAR QUOTE

MICK JAGGER

'I couldn't make a total Rolling Stones album without Keith. I could make another kind of album of course . . .'

Lynyrd Skynyrd RIP

CHARTS

US45	Star Wars Theme/Cantina Band	*Meco*
USLP	Rumours	*Fleetwood Mac*
UK45	Way Down	*Elvis Presley*
UKLP	20 Golden Greats	*Diana Ross & The Supremes*
WEEK 2		
US45	Star Wars Theme/Cantina Band	*Meco*
USLP	Rumours	*Fleetwood Mac*
UK45	Way Down	*Elvis Presley*
UKLP	20 Golden Greats	*Diana Ross & The Supremes*
WEEK 3		
US45	You Light Up My Life	*Debby Boone*
USLP	Rumours	*Fleetwood Mac*
UK45	Silver Lady	*David Soul*
UKLP	20 Golden Greats	*Diana Ross & The Supremes*
WEEK 4		
US45	You Light Up My Life	*Debby Boone*
USLP	Rumours	*Fleetwood Mac*
UK45	Yes Sir I Can Boogie	*Baccara*
UKLP	20 Golden Greats	*Diana Ross & The Supremes*
WEEK 5		
US45	You Light Up My Life	*Debby Boone*
USLP	Rumours	*Fleetwood Mac*
UK45	You're In My Heart	*Rod Stewart*
UKLP	20 Golden Greats	*Diana Ross & The Supremes*

- **Lynyrd Skynyrd have been wiped out by an air-crash in Mississippi which killed singer Ronnie Van Zant, guitarist Steve Gaines and his sister, backing singer Cassie and critically injured three others.**
- **Guitarist Steve Hackett has quit Genesis on the eve of their live double 'Seconds Out'. The remaining three pledge to continue.**
- **Damned drummer Rat Scabies has quit the band.**

NOVEMBER

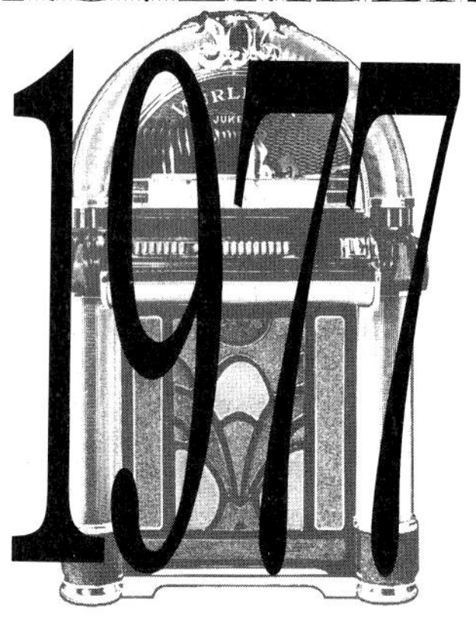

BOWIE IST EIN BERLINER

David Bowie has retreated from the excesses of his 'Station To Station' tour and *The Man Who Fell To Earth* movie to Berlin – scarcely an auspicious choice for someone whose recent utterances have shown a disturbing flirtation with fascism.

But he went to Berlin to experience the claustrophobic isolation of a city surrounded by barbed wire. And at the Hansa Studio – 20 yards from the Berlin Wall – he has recorded two albums that signal a dramatic shift in his musical style: 'Low' and 'Heroes'.

'The initial period of living in Berlin produced "Low",' explains Bowie. 'The first side of "Low" was all about me. "Always Crashing In The Same Car" and all that self-pitying crap. But side two was more of a musical observation – my reaction to seeing the Eastern bloc, how West Berlin survives in the middle of it, which is something I couldn't express in words. It required textures instead.

'It's also a reaction to that dull greeny-grey limelight of American rock and its repercussions; pulling myself out of it and getting to Europe and saying: "For God's sake re-evaluate why you wanted to get into this in the first place. Did you really want to clown around in LA?

'"Find some people you don't understand and a place you don't want to be and just put yourself into it. Force yourself to buy some groceries . . .".'

BOB SEGER – GETTING OUT OF DETROIT

Bob Seger is the greatest local success story in the history of rock 'n' roll. He is massive in Michigan, his home state. In Detroit he plays to audiences of 90,000 and his albums outsell The Stones, Zeppelin, anyone you care to mention.

Outside Michigan his progress has been slower, mainly because record companies have found it difficult to market his albums of steaming rockers and gritty ballads about the pangs of life on the road.

But his 'Live Bullet' double album, recorded in front of a partisan Detroit crowd finally caught Seger's power and energy. And one of his finest rockers, the breakneck 'Get Out Of Denver', has been adopted by more than one British new wave band.

STAR QUOTE

BRIAN ENO

ex-keyboard player with Roxy Music

'I could understand exactly how Bryan Ferry felt. He'd be singing the beautiful, quiet song and some pranny at the back of the hall would bellow "Eno!" Obviously Bryan got progressively more pissed off.'

CHARTS

US45	You Light Up My Life *Debby Boone*
USLP	Rumours *Fleetwood Mac*
UK45	Yes Sir I Can Boogie *Baccara*
UKLP	20 Golden Greats *Diana Ross & The Supremes*
	WEEK 2
US45	You Light Up My LIfe *Debby Boone*
USLP	Rumours *Fleetwood Mac*
UK45	Name Of The Game *Abba*
UKLP	The Sound Of Bread *Bread*
	WEEK 3
US45	You Light Up My Life *Debby Boone*
USLP	Rumours *Fleetwood Mac*
UK45	Name Of The Game *Abba*
UKLP	The Sound Of Bread *Bread*
	WEEK 4
US45	You Light Up My Life *Debby Boone*
USLP	Rumours *Fleetwood Mac*
UK45	Rockin' All Over The World *Status Quo*
UKLP	The Sound Of Bread *Bread*

THE GRAPEVINE

- **Ozzy Osbourne has quit Black Sabbath, who have decided to carry on without him.**
- **Elton John announced his 'retirement' during a concert.**
- **Veteran Scottish rocker Alex Harvey has also retired.**
- ***The Last Waltz*, Martin Scorsese's film of The Band's farewell concert, has been premiered in New York.**
- **The Sex Pistols have released their debut album, 'Never Mind The Bollocks, Here's The Sex Pistols'.**

WEATHER OUTLOOK FINE

Joe Zawinul and Wayne Shorter, both in their mid-forties are the leaders of the most successful jazz group of the Seventies. Weather Report sell enough albums to get into the charts these days, but they're still willing to take chances.

They were both in Miles Davis' epoch-making band of the late Sixties that produced 'In A Silent Way' and 'Bitches Brew' and pulled jazz into the new decade.

'Jazz had become so boring,' says Zawinul. 'Sly Stone and Jimi Hendrix had this other quality, an attitude that jazz unfortunately didn't have. Now we're reaching the people on the streets. Not the critics but the people. And we don't play down to the people, ever.'

Jazz-rock giants Weather Report

JOHNNY WINTER'S WOES

The world's whitest blues player is finally getting it together – after eight years of heavy rock, drug addiction and suicidal depression.

Johnny Winter is a Texas albino who played the blues as sweet as any black guitarist. But just as he was starting to make it in New York, he began to be compared with Cream and Hendrix instead of Muddy Waters and Otis Rush. He got waylaid into heavy metal and heavy drugs, but never stopped playing the blues. In fact, he played them better because he was in such mental anguish.

'I thought of myself as the best white blues player around. In my own mind I was sure of that. But I never thought of myself as Jimi Hendrix or Cream. I loved them both but I wasn't trying to compete,' he says.

It took nine months to get the monkey off his back, and what completed his cure was producing and playing on Muddy Waters' 'Hard Again' album.

He's also toured with Muddy, although he has to keep a wary eye on the road these days. 'I won't stay out there more than six weeks at a time. I couldn't handle it.'

HOLIDAYS IN THE UK

The Sex Pistols have ended 1977 in the same way they ended 1976 – in a blaze of controversy.

London's Capital Radio got the ball rolling by banning the group's 'Holidays In The Sun' single because the lyrics likened Belsen to a holiday camp. EMI then got in on the act, suggesting a track on the 'Never Mind The Bollocks' album might be an infringement of copyright.

Nottingham police had a go at taking a local shop to court for displaying the album, claiming that the word 'bollocks' was indecent. Two expensive attorneys and a few star witnesses later, the case was dismissed.

A week later, Sid Vicious and his American girlfriend Nancy Spungen were arrested following the discovery of 'certain substances' in their London hotel room. Police were called after complaints of a 'disturbance'.

But at least the band have been able to get round the unofficial ban that prevents them from playing in the UK. They lined up a series of 'secret' gigs over the Christmas period – including one on Christmas day – that passed off without incident.

But they've now got problems in the States. They were denied a visa to visit New York for a TV show two days before they were due to fly.

Ian Dury salutes the perverse

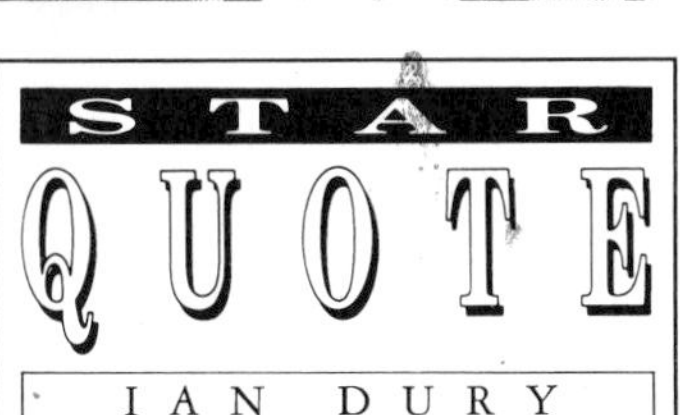

STAR QUOTE

IAN DURY

'Every Englishman's perversion is to be the wrong way round all the time.'

CHARTS

US45	You Light Up My Life	*Debby Boone*
USLP	Rumours	*Fleetwood Mac*
UK45	Mull Of Kintyre	*Wings*
UKLP	The Sound Of Bread	*Bread*
	WEEK 2	
US45	You Light Up My Life	*Debby Boone*
USLP	Simple Dreams	*Linda Ronstadt*
UK45	Mull Of Kintyre	*Wings*
UKLP	The Sound Of Bread	*Bread*
	WEEK 3	
US45	You Light Up My Life	*Debby Boone*
USLP	Simple Dreams	*Linda Ronstadt*
UK45	Mull Of Kintyre	*Wings*
UKLP	Disco Fever	*Various*
	WEEK 4	
US45	How Deep Is Your Love	*Bee Gees*
USLP	Simple Dreams	*Linda Ronstadt*
UK45	Mull Of Kintyre	*Wings*
UKLP	Disco Fever	*Various*
	WEEK 5	
US45	How Deep Is Your Love	*Bee Gees*
USLP	Simple Dreams	*Linda Ronstadt*
UK45	Mull Of Kintyre	*Wings*
UKLP	Disco Fever	*Various*

Macca mulling in Kintyre

THE GRAPEVINE

- **The Who have played a 'secret' gig in London for their *Kids Are Alright* film rockumentary.**
- **Elvis Costello, banned from singing 'Radio Radio' on *Saturday Night Live* in the US because of its caustic comments on the radio industry, sang it anyway.**
- **Wings' 'Mull Of Kintyre' has topped the UK Xmas charts to become the biggest selling British single in history.**
- **Jazz instrumentalist Rahsaan Roland Kirk has died, aged 41.**

BUZZCOCKS – POP PUNKS

The Buzzcocks played their first gig supporting The Sex Pistols, a month after they'd formed in June '76. But it's taken them a lot longer to get signed.

'If we'd come from London, we'd have been signed a year ago, and we wouldn't be in the position we are now,' asserts Pete Shelley who, like the rest of the band, hails from Manchester.

Their first single, 'Orgasm Addict', wasn't so much banned as simply never played on the radio. And their London gigs have been few and far between. Even so, they were included in the legendary 'Roxy' compilation.

The Buzzcocks play love songs. The love may be bitter, vitriolic and vengeful, but it's still love.

'There's bitterness in our songs, yeah,' concedes Shelley. 'But there's hope in them too.'

Buzzcocks: no radio orgasms

DISCO FEVER WITH THE BEE GEES

As rock music has grown older, its audience has become more attuned to the occasional renaissance – a once big act, which had fallen on difficult times commercially, rising from its shallow unmarked grave for a further jouste at the fickle public. It happens, and more often than might be imagined, but one of the greatest Lazarus acts in the modern history of popular music involved The Bee Gees, the trio of brothers born in the Isle of Man who first came to fame in Australia before returning to Britain to become major stars of the late 1960s.

Big brother Barry Gibb and his twin younger siblings, Maurice and Robin, had discovered at an early age the unique vocal harmonic similarities enjoyed by close relatives and, coupled with a desire to entertain inherited from their bandleader father, had performed in local talent contests in the North of England even before the family emigrated to Australia in 1958.

Having arrived in their new surroundings, the trio became known as the Bee Gees (short for 'brothers Gibb') and appeared on television, becoming local celebrities during the first half of the 1960s before deciding to return to Britain and try their luck in a major market.

The First Coming

Soon after they arrived in England in early 1967, the group were signed for management by Australian born showbiz mogul Robert Stigwood, and before the year was out, had scored four hits in both Britain and America including 'Massachusetts', which topped the UK chart. They were almost instantly

The brothers Gibb

Stigwood and Travolta at 'Grease' launch

The Bee Gees in 'Sergeant Pepper'

international pop stars as several more hits in 1968, including another UK No. 1, 'I've Gotta Get A Message To You', emphasized. However, after releasing their first US chart topper, 'How Can You Mend A Broken Heart', in 1971, things began to go wrong and by 1972, the group, rocked by personnel changes and fraternal disagreements, seemed to have run out of steam, before Stigwood, a steadying influence, restored stability.

Return to the Charts

By 1975, the trio's talents had brought them back to prominence with another big international hit, 'Jive Talkin'', which became their second US No. 1 and also reached the UK top five. It seemed a short term revival in Britain, although in America – where it was followed by another big hit, 'Nights On Broadway – The Bee Gees appeared to have successfully reinvented themselves as hotshot songwriters and performers of disco music, which was newly established as a major force.

Hit Film

In 1976 Robert Stigwood purchased the rights to a yet unnamed movie to be scripted by British writer Nik Cohn after reading an article by Cohn in a New York magazine entitled 'Tribal Right of the New Saturday Night', about the lives of discothéque afficionados in New York. The movie was eventually to become one of the most successful ever made centred around popular music and was sensationally to revive the career of the Bee Gees.

Record Album

Two key elements in *Saturday Night Fever's* triumph were the casting of John Travolta in the starring role, and the use of The Bee Gees as the main contributors to the film's soundtrack. The group actually performed six self-composed

Travolta and Finola Hughes, 'Stayin' Alive'

Kool And The Gang

K.C. of the Sunshine Band

songs used in the movie, one of which was also additionally performed by another group, Tavares, and they also wrote another song, 'If I Can't Have You', which was performed for the film by another artist signed to Stigwood's RSO label, Yvonne Elliman.

Both choices proved to be inspired – Travolta became a superstar and The Bee Gees topped the charts with all six of the songs which they had performed in the movie, five of them in succession 'Jive Talkin', 'You Should Be Dancing', 'How Deep Is Your Love' and 'Stayin' Alive'.

Stayin' on top

When 'Stayin' Alive' fell off the peak, its place was taken by '(Love Is) Thicker Than Water' by Andy Gibb, (youngest brother of the Bee Gees family), before 'Night Fever' became the sixth chart-topper in the film. That was replaced by Yvonne Elliman's 'If I Can't Have You', which made seven No. 1s on one soundtrack, a record which is hard to believe.

Four more singles from the movie entered the chart and the *Saturday Night Fever* album became the biggest selling soundtrack disc of all time, topping the US album chart for 24 weeks and its British equivalent for a mere 18, and selling considerably more than one million units.

They win again

The Bee Gees remained on the crest of the 'SNF' wave until 1980, but then – pop fashion being ultimately unpredictable – once more fell from favour for much of the 1980s, especially in Britain. Just when everyone had more or less forgotten them, out of the blue came another UK chart-topper, 'You Win Again', in 1987.

Subsequently, they seem to have disappeared again, but on the strength of their past achievements, it would take a gambler to predict that their absence will be permanent.

'Saturday Night Fever'

PIANO MAN GROWS UP

Billy Joel's latest press release calls him a '28-year-old former punk'. Previous descriptions include a 'poor man's Elton John', but he's neither.

Billy Joel played on the Shangri Las' 'Leader Of The Pack' and became a songwriter. He grafted and got his first hit in 1973 with 'Piano Man'. That made him a singer-songwriter and he's still grafting, on the road and in the studio.

His songs have developed a cool, cosmopolitan, urban feel, although he's not afraid to bite the hand that buys him on his latest album, 'Turnstiles', mocking hip radicalism, the decadence of modern luxury and nostalgia.

'Nostalgia's unhealthy. I don't remember the young days to be all that great. Yeah, we had fun but we live now.'

SEX PISTOLS SPLIT

At the beginning of the month, The Sex Pistols started their first US tour. At the end of the month the group are in tatters – Johnny Rotten back home in disgust having been fired, Sid Vicious rushed to hospital in Los Angeles having been carried unconscious off a plane, and Steve Jones and Paul Cook down in Brazil making a video with train robber and celebrated British fugitive Ronnie Biggs.

The Pistols' US tour quickly turned into a fiasco with the media looking for any excuse, and the FBI just looking. Sid Vicious's behaviour became increasingly unpredictable. They were banned by American Airlines and the Holiday Inn chain. And they'd stopped talking to each other.

The final break-up occurred over manager Malcolm McLaren's plan to fly the band to Brazil and hook up with Ronnie Biggs – which was one publicity stunt too many for Rotten. At a showdown in San Francisco, McLaren accused Rotten of 'behaving like a constructive cissy rather than a destructive lunatic'.

Rotten stormed out and flew back to England via New York, Vicious flew back via an OD, and Cook and Jones went with the stunt. The only sure thing is that this may be the end of The Sex Pistols, but it isn't the end of the story.

STAR QUOTE

JOHNNY ROTTEN

'Love is 2 minutes and 50 seconds of squelching noises.'

BANSHEES HOLD OUT

Siouxsie & The Banshees are the last great unsigned UK punk band. They were in the audience at the earliest Sex Pistols' gigs and formed their band soon after. They even had Sid Vicious as a drummer to start with.

But while their contemporaries have taken the first reasonable record company bait that was offered, Siouxsie & The Banshees have held out, preferring to sell out gigs rather than their souls.

Their Teutonic style and occasional flirtations with Nazi regalia have stirred up strong feelings – which are perhaps calculated, because they themselves give away no feelings of exhilaration, exhaustion or even frustration on stage.

They play sound rather than music. 'We go out of our way not to be musicians. We don't rehearse til our fingers bleed. We can play rock'n'roll but we ignore it. We're out on a limb. It's dangerous but it excites us, makes it worth while.'

THE GRAPEVINE

- **EMI have censored The Buzzcocks 'Oh Shit', the B-side of 'What Do I Get' single, but they OK'd Tom Robinsons's'Glad To Be Gay'.**
- **Thin Lizzy guitarist Brian Robertson, who damaged his left hand in a brawl a year ago has split open his right hand on a flick knife in a pub.**
- **Original Fleetwood Mac guitarist Peter Green has played his first gig since quitting a decade ago.**

Brian Robertson (left) with Scott Gorham

CHARTS

US45	How Deep Is Your Love *Bee Gees*
USLP	Rumours *Fleetwood Mac*
UK45	Mull Of Kintyre *Wings*
UKLP	Disco Fever *Various*
WEEK 2	
US45	Baby Come Back *Player*
USLP	Saturday Night Fever *Soundtrack*
UK45	Mull Of Kintyre *Wings*
UKLP	Disco Fever *Various*
WEEK 3	
US45	Baby Come Back *Player*
USLP	Saturday Night Fever *Soundtrack*
UK45	Mull Of Kintyre *Wings*
UKLP	Rumours *Fleetwood Mac*
WEEK 4	
US45	Baby Come Back *Player*
USLP	Saturday Night Fever *Soundtrack*
UK45	Mull Of Kintyre *Wings*
UKLP	Rumours *Fleetwood Mac*

HEAD CASES!

'The name of this band is Talking Heads.' And the name of the singer who always introduces the band that way on stage is David Byrne.

Talking Heads are without precedent. They take the basic rock ingredients – guitar, bass, keyboards and drums – and come up with a crackling new syntax.

'There are certain things I feel need to be done in terms of music and performance,' declares Byrne. 'and what these things amount to is that what the world doesn't need is another posturing clown yammering away about his baby.

'Our premise is that we are trying to present something that's convincing; music that we believe in. It can get a little complicated that way . . .'

Their first single, 'Love Goes To A Building On Fire', sounds like a cross between a Cossack dance and a child's riddle, - but try getting it out of your head – and their debut album reveals more of the same.

As keyboard player Jerry Harrison puts it: 'We're not trying to be bigger than life, we're trying to be about life.'

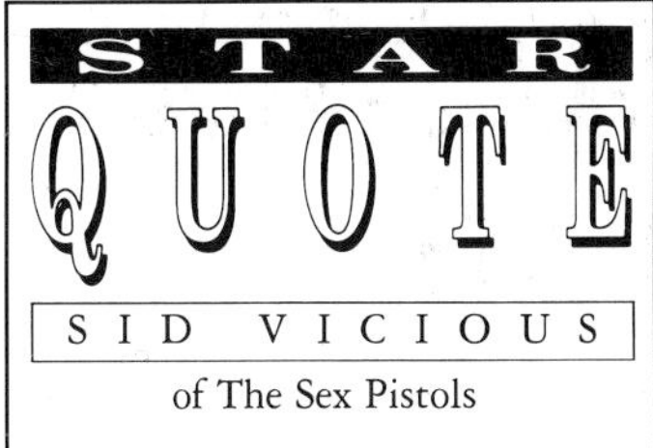

SID VICIOUS

of The Sex Pistols

'I think fresh air might kill me.'

- The Damned have broken up and announced a farewell UK tour.
- UK punk fanzine *Sniffing Glue* has given up in sympathy.
- Bob Dylan has released his documentary film of the Rolling Thunder tour called *Renaldo and Clara* and set off on a world tour.
- Sid Vicious and girlfriend Nancy Spungen have been arrested on drug charges at New York's Chelsea Hotel.

CHARTS

US45	Stayin' Alive *Bee Gees*
USLP	Saturday Night Fever *Soundtrack*
UK45	Uptown Top Ranking *Althia & Donna*
UKLP	Rumours *Fleetwood Mac*
WEEK 2	
US45	Stayin' Alive *Bee Gees*
USLP	Saturday Night Fever *Soundtrack*
UK45	Uptown Top Ranking *Althia & Donna*
UKLP	Abba: The Album *Abba*
WEEK 3	
US45	Stayin' Alive *Bee Gees*
USLP	Saturday Night Fever *Soundtrack*
UK45	Take A Chance On Me *Abba*
UKLP	Abba: The Album *Abba*
WEEK 4	
US45	Stayin' Alive *Bee Gees*
USLP	Saturday Night Fever *Soundtrack*
UK45	Take A Chance On Me *Abba*
UKLP	Abba: The Album *Abba*

BOB MARLEY – EASY SKANKING

Bob Marley is an exile twice over: from his native Jamaica where he faces death threats because of the tense political situation there, and from his spiritual home in Ethiopia which is racked by an even more violent civil war.

So he's been recording the follow-up to his hugely successful 'Exodus' album in England. Several of the songs on 'Kaya' were recorded around the same time as 'Exodus', and some of them date back still further.

So what does 'Kaya' mean? 'Erb. Man sometimes seh Kaya because he sell 'erb in the yard and people seh him can't come in because he sell 'erb so he seh kaya.

'This album is about slowin' down and takin' it e-e-easy. Easy skanking y'know? So this is like a rest . . . for some kaya.'

Exodus for Marley

X-OFFENDERS

Just when you thought the new wave was wiping out that male chauvinist mentality, along come Blondie. Lead singer Debbie Harry, the blonde bombshell who fronts the band, has become an instant sex object for punks in Britain, where this New York band have made their initial impact. But then what do you expect with a single called 'Rip Her To Shreds'?

'The attitude to women in rock is totally sexist,' affirms Debbie. 'I might not like it when a crowd shouts at me, but I certainly thrive on it.'

Debbie has a past: she escaped from her silver-spoon New Jersey college education to hang out with the avant-garde jazz crowd in Greenwich Village, dropped acid and joined a band called Wind In The Willows at the end of the Sixties, became a heroin addict and a groupie, recovered from both and got together with Chris Stein, the guitarist in Blondie.

So she's inured to anything the sexists have to throw at her and, as the first track on the second Blondie album, 'Plastic Letters', puts it: 'I sold my vision for a piece of the cake/I haven't ate in days.'

'I'd sooner have hecklers than no reaction at all,' she smiles.

MARCH

WUTHERING KATE BUSH

Kate Bush is staring doe-eyed and sensuous out of the back of hundreds of London buses at the moment, advertising her first album, 'The Kick Inside' and the single that's taken Kate's extraordinary voice to the top of the charts – 'Wuthering Heights'.

Those high swooping vocals are just one facet of a voice that sounds different on virtually every track of the album. And Kate sings with a self-assurance remarkable for a teenager.

More remarkable still is that Kate signed to EMI three years ago when she was 16, and they've been prepared to wait and let her record in her own time. It helps that she arrived with a personal recommendation from Pink Floyd guitarist Dave Gilmour, who'd sponsored her demo tapes.

After she'd signed, she enrolled at Lindsey Kemp's Mime School. 'He taught me that you can express with your body – and when your body is awake so is your mind.'

She applies the same principle to her voice. 'I always enjoy reaching notes that I can't quite reach. A week later you'll be on top of that one and trying to reach the one above it.

'The reason I sang "Wuthering Heights" so high is that I felt it called for it. The book has a mood of mystery and I wanted to reflect that.'

THIS YEAR'S COSTELLO

Elvis Costello bounded on to the scene last year with a well-defined cynicism that hasn't mellowed with the success of his 'My Aim Is True' album and acclaim for his live shows. He still bears the same grudges on his second album, 'This Year's Model'.

'This job isn't designed to make you nicer or even more mature. People can say, "Oh, he's just immature, he'll soften up" but I f-in' won't. People don't realize that I may not be mature because I don't want to be. I don't know what being grown-up is, see.

'The first album was politics and revenge. This one is politics and fashion. And the songs were written before I became a "fashion". I never wanted that, mind you. I could never imagine a lot of people wanting this ugly geek in glasses ramming his songs down their throats. And that's exactly what I'm in it for. I'm in it to disrupt people's lives.'

STAR QUOTE

NICK LOWE

'When you're younger you get influenced by people. Nowadays I just steal the stuff. If I hear a good lick I'll just pinch it.'

DE-EVOLUTION

Evolving backwards at speed out of Akron, Ohio, Devo have brought an automaton touch to the new wave. Their robotic cover of the Stones' 'Satisfaction' has been one of the most original singles of the past year – the essentials were stripped bare, becoming naggingly insistent in the process.

On stage, they strut mechanically, clad in industrial cleaning outfits, and they maintain the pose offstage as well.

'We were all basically aliens – alienated aliens – who happened to be in Akron through accidents of birth,' explains architect of the Devo ideology Jerry Casale, who also plays bass.

Akron All Stars Devo

THE GRAPEVINE

- **Paul Simonon and Topper Headon of The Clash have been arrested in London for shooting pigeons from the roof of their rehearsal studio.**
- **UK punk movie *Jubilee* premieres in London**
- **America responds with *American Hot Wax.***
- **250,000 show up for California Jam II featuring Santana, Dave Mason, Ted Nugent and Aerosmith.**

CHARTS

US45	(Love Is) Thicker Than Water – *Andy Gibb*
USLP	Saturday Night Fever – *Soundtrack*
UK45	Take A Chance On Me – *Abba*
UKLP	Abba: The Album – *Abba*

WEEK 2

US45	(Love Is) Thicker Than Water – *Andy Gibb*
USLP	Saturday Night Fever – *Soundtrack*
UK45	Wuthering Heights – *Kate Bush*
UKLP	Abba: The Album – *Abba*

WEEK 3

US45	Night Fever – *Bee Gees*
USLP	Saturday Night Fever – *Soundtrack*
UK45	Wuthering Heights – *Kate Bush*
UKLP	Abba: The Album – *Abba*

WEEK 4

US45	Night Fever – *Bee Gees*
USLP	Saturday Night Fever – *Soundtrack*
UK45	Wuthering Heights – *Kate Bush*
UKLP	Abba: The Album – *Abba*

PATTI PUTS HER NECK BACK ON THE BLOCK

Patti struggles back

'Rock'n'roll is the hardest work any of us in the band has ever done. The physical toil, the mental toil, the 24 hours a day that it has to be lived. Going out on stage is almost the only time that you relax.'

Lenny Kaye is a respected rock journalist and expert of the new wave. He is also guitarist in The Patti Smith Group.

A year ago, Patti Smith fell off stage and broke her neck. She has struggled to regain her fitness, and the band are back on the road, merging rock'n'roll and improvisation into one crucial but speculative performance, night after night.

'Every night something greater happens, we take another risk,' says Patti. 'We go through another membrane, we've been through that one so we're gonna push and push and penetrate another one.'

This is no rock'n'roll band looking for money or fame. They are into exploring instead. 'And when the time comes that we're just going through the motions, there won't be a Patti Smith Group any more,' says Kaye. 'Patti will be the first to cast it into the ocean and move on to something else.'

THE GRAPEVINE

- Over forty rock performers have petitioned US President Carter to end U.S. commitment to nuclear power, including Bruce Springsteen, Jackson Browne and Tom Petty.
- The Clash have headlined a massive Rock Against Racism rally in London.
- The Damned have played their farewell gig.
- Sandy Denny, singer with Fairport Convention, has died of a cerebral haemorrhage after falling down stairs at her home.

ONE LOVE IN JAMAICA

The gang warfare, murder and violence that characterizes Jamaican politics came to an uneasy truce long enough for Bob Marley & The Wailers and the cream of reggae music to play the One Love Peace concert at the Kingston National Arena.

Youth leaders of the two feuding political parties organized the concert which climaxed with Bob Marley – making a return to his country after an assassination attempt – clasping hands with rival politicians Michael Manley and Edward Seaga in a gesture of solidarity.

Former Wailer Peter Tosh took the opportunity to lecture government officials about marijuana laws while smoking a spliff.

GENERATION X – HONEST PUNKS

The difference between Generation X and every other punk band is that they want to be stars. And maybe they're too honest about it for their own good.

Each of their singles so far – 'Your Generation', 'Wild Youth' and 'Ready Steady Go' – has made the Top 50.

'And they'd have done more if Chrysalis had made us an instant big act by buying us into the Top 30. We asked them to, of course, but they refused,' says guitarist Tony James.

They've taken flak for the lack of punk credibility – bleached blond singer Billy Idol studying English Literature at Sussex University for example – but James reckons: 'There isn't a name punk musician who doesn't have a skeleton in his cupboard.'

Billy Idol is now addicted to the rock'n'roll lifestyle. 'No wonder people in straight jobs can't take rock'n'roll. It must be so-o-o painful to see people enjoying themselves and making a loud noise, and then they've gotta get up and got to work in the morning.'

Hoping to live up to his name, Idol (left) and Generation X

PAUL McCARTNEY

'At the moment I've got a punk song, but I daren't do it. People will only slag me off. It's called "Boil Crisis" – "One night in the life of a kid named Sid He scored with a broad in a pyramid".

CHARTS

Week	Chart	Title	Artist
	US45	Night Fever	Bee Gees
	USLP	Saturday Night Fever	Soundtrack
	UK45	Denis	Blondie
	UKLP	The Kick Inside	Kate Bush
WEEK 2	US45	Night Fever	Bee Gees
	USLP	Saturday Night Fever	Soundtrack
	UK45	Denis	Blondie
	UKLP	The Kick Inside	Kate Bush
WEEK 3	US45	Night Fever	Bee Gees
	USLP	Saturday Night Fever	Soundtrack
	UK45	I Wonder Why	Showaddywaddy
	UKLP	20 Golden Greats	Nat 'King' Cole
WEEK 4	US45	Night Fever	Bee Gees
	USLP	Saturday Night Fever	Soundtrack
	UK45	Night Fever	Bee Gees
	UKLP	20 Golden Greats	Nat 'King' Cole
WEEK 5	US45	Night Fever	Bee Gees
	USLP	Saturday Night Fever	Soundtrack
	UK45	Night Fever	Bee Gees
	UKLP	Saturday Night Fever	Soundtrack

MEAT LOAF LIES DOWN ALL OVER BROADWAY

Meat Loaf is a man who's always known how to go over the top. He's been known as Meat Loaf since he was a kid because of his eating habits. He aims big too.

He played Eddie in *The Rocky Horror Show* movie and soon after ran into songwriter Jim Sheinman, who shared his vision of the outrageous with heavy metal knobs on.

The final piece of the equation is Todd Rundgren, the multi-faceted rock star who never seems to know which of his facets to use next. He produced the 'Bat Out Of Hell' album, a glorious monument to heavy metal theatrics that nobody believed in but them.

'Record company people kept telling me I wasn't rock'n'roll,' says Meat. 'They said: "We don't wanna hear it, it's Broadway music." That's bullshit, I've done ten shows on Broadway so I know what I'm talking about.'

Epic eventually took the bait, but the record snoozed until they made a video for the title track. Suddenly they have a monster on their hands.

CHARTS

US45	Night Fever – *Bee Gees*
USLP	Saturday Night Fever – *Soundtrack*
UK45	Night Fever – *Bee Gees*
UKLP	Saturday Night Fever – *Soundtrack*
WEEK 2	
US45	If I Can't Have You – *Yvonne Elliman*
USLP	Saturday Night Fever – *Soundtrack*
UK45	Night Fever – *Bee Gees*
UKLP	Saturday Night Fever – *Soundtrack*
WEEK 3	
US45	With A Little Luck – *Paul McCartney & Wings*
USLP	Saturday Night Fever – *Soundtrack*
UK45	Rivers Of Babylon – *Boney M*
UKLP	Saturday Night Fever – *Soundtrack*
WEEK 4	
US45	With A Little Luck – *Paul McCartney & Wings*
USLP	Saturday Night Fever – *Soundtrack*
UK45	Rivers Of Babylon – *Boney M*
UKLP	Saturday Night Fever – *Soundtrack*

RICH ROCK FROM CHEAP TRICK

The guy with the home-made T-shirt at the Newcastle Empire Ballroom says it all – 'Cheap Trick. Rocks like nuts.'

Newcastle is four thousand miles from Cheap Trick's hometown of Chicago, but the message travels easy. It's based on good rock'n'roll and good songs, and it works on new wave, heavy metal and rock audiences alike.

Cheap Trick may look wacky and behave wacky, but they work hard – 300 gigs a year for the past three years and three albums inside the last 14 months.

The band, led by Rick Neilsen (who owns 60 guitars and is reputed never to have taken off his baseball cap) play short songs. 'Playing long songs is a waste,' says bassist Petersson. 'Who wants to hear tedious instrumental passages? Most people who aren't musicians don't care, and we know we could do it so we don't care either.'

STAR QUOTE

BOB DYLAN

'That particular song, "Sara", well . . . some songs you figure you're better off not to have written. There's a few of them lyin' around.'

LOWIE BOWIE

Another tour, another personality change; nobody can accuse David Bowie of playing safe these days.

The first hour of his latest tour is taken up with a low-key homage to his 'Low' and 'Heroes' albums, his avowedly conscious rejection of the commercial avenues he opened up with 'Young Americans' and 'Station To Station'. But the crowd at New York's Madison Square Gardens have come for former glories, and they remain restless for all but the title track of 'Heroes'.

'Five Years', 'Soul Love', 'Ziggy Stardust' and 'Suffragette City' are performed slickly, but without any exaggeration. Bowie then takes a left-field turn for the Brecht-Weill Anthem, 'Moon Of Alabama' ('Show me the way to the next whiskey bar').

The tension of his last tour is gone, and so is some of the vital edge.

THE GRAPEVINE

- **Ramones drummer Tommy Ramone has quit to become a producer called Tommy Erdelyi.**
- **The Tubes have cancelled their British tour after singer Fee Waybill fell off stage, breaking a leg and ripping tendons.**
- **John Lydon, previously known as Johnny Rotten, has unveiled his new combo, Public Image Limited.**
- **Led Zeppelin are back in the studio.**

GABRIEL – DOING IT HIMSELF

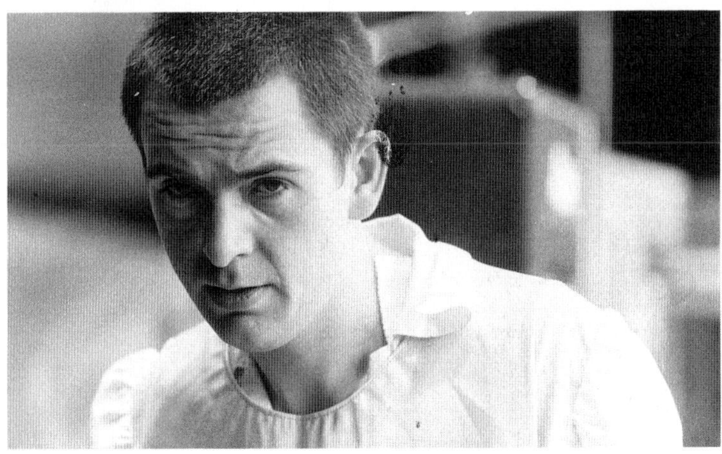

Peter Gabriel's second solo album is causing problems. Atlantic can't see a "commercial, immediate single". And in Britain, 'DIY', the likeliest single, has foundered three weeks after release.

The problem is compounded because although 'Solsbury Hill' from the first album was a big British hit, it failed to take off in the US.

So there's no tour being lined up, although Gabriel claims he's got a band ready. Instead, he's being sent out on a tour of American radio stations in the hope that they'll give the album some airplay.

Gabriel admits he refused to listen to nudging whispers from record company executives who wanted 'another album full of "Solsbury Hills".' And he reckons his bank balance is mostly made up of royalties from his former band, Genesis, who have turned into a successful stadium band since he left.

'If I consider my current position realistically, I would say I'd be able to survive in this cottage with my wife and children for another five years. Therefore I am concerned about selling records and being a success. Right now I'm just not compromising, that's all.'

CHARTS

US45	Too Much, Too Little, Too Late *Johnny Mathis & Deniece Williams*
USLP	Saturday Night Fever *Soundtrack*
UK45	Rivers Of Babylon *Boney M*
UKLP	Saturday Night Fever *Soundtrack*
	WEEK 2
US45	You're The One That I Want *John Travolta & Olivia Newton-John*
USLP	Saturday Night Fever *Soundtrack*
UK45	Rivers Of Babylon *Boney M*
UKLP	Saturday Night Fever *Soundtrack*
	WEEK 3
US45	Shadow Dancing *Andy Gibb*
USLP	Saturday Night Fever *Soundtrack*
UK45	You're The One That I Want *John Travolta & Olivia Newton-John*
UKLP	Black And White *Stranglers*
	WEEK 4
US45	Shadow Dancing *Andy Gibb*
USLP	Saturday Night Fever *Soundtrack*
UK45	You're The One That I Want *John Travolta & Olivia Newton-John*
UKLP	Saturday Night Fever *Soundtrack*

BRUCE IS BACK

Finally, the record industry is ready for Bruce Springsteen again. Two and a half years after 'Born To Run', he's back with the follow-up, 'Darkness On The Edge Of Town'.

Most of the time in between has been taken up with legal wrangles to free himself from his former managers. Prevented by court injunctions from recording, Springsteen took to the road, giving bootleggers a field day. He's also written songs for Patti Smith, Southside Johnny and Robert Gordon while waiting to start work on his own album.

On 'Darkness On The Edge Of Town', the blockbuster production techniques and incurably romantic visions of 'Born To Run' have been avoided, although 'Badlands' and 'The Promised Land' are as epic as anything he's written.

Most important of all, however, there's remarkably little hype surrounding 'Darkness On The Edge Of Town'. That is the way Bruce wants it.

THE GRAPEVINE

- Bob Dylan's world tour has reached the UK for his first British gigs in nine years.
- The Rolling Stones have released their 'Some Girls' album and started another US tour.
- The Sex Pistols have released 'The Biggest Blow' EP, featuring train robber Ronnie Biggs and Sid Vicious' inimitable version of 'My Way'.
- Peter Frampton has been injured in a car crash in the Bahamas.

GRACE BOTTLES OUT OF STARSHIP

Jefferson Starship do not travel well. Their first trip out of America to Europe for a series of festival appearances has ended in chaos and near disaster with singer Grace Slick literally bottling out of the band.

The trouble started at the Lorelei Festival in Germany when Grace, a reformed alcoholic, hit the bottle again. In the ensuing fracas she stormed out and back to the States. The rest of the band cancelled the show but the 60,000 crowd were already waiting for them and trashed the group's equipment.

Starship fulfilled the final date of their tour – at Britain's Knebworth Festival with Genesis – without Grace, before slinking home to nurse their wounds.

Ray Davies

STAR QUOTE

RAY DAVIES

of The Kinks

'I write songs because I get angry, and now I'm at the stage where it's not good enough to brush it off with humour.'

JULY

FOREVER DYLAN

They traipsed across the fields in their tens of thousands, just like they had nine years earlier on the Isle Of Wight. That time it was to see Bob Dylan resurrected from his motorbike smash - or whatever it was that had turned him into a recluse for four years.

This time it's to see Dylan coming to terms with his heritage at Blackbushe Aerodrome, 40 miles west of London. His audience are nine years older now, and many of them have brought their children along.

Word of his triumphant London concerts last month has got around, and there are 50,000 people in front of the stage by 11 am when the first band appears. Nine hours later, after Graham Parker, Joan Armatrading and Eric Clapton, Dylan strolls on to a gigantic howl of applause and spends the next two and a half hours running through the last 15 years.

He reworks old favourites like 'Masters Of War' and 'Ballad Of A Thin Man' into powerful rockers, disco riffing through 'Maggie's Farm', lacing 'One More Cup Of Coffee' with large dollops of gospel and getting everyone to sing 'Forever Young' as a farewell anthem.

STAR QUOTE

TOM WAITS

'People who get morally offended by all that should talk to some of those girls, check out what goes into being a good stripper. It's not just taking yer clothes off, it's goddam art to them. Plus, that's what I happen to consider real performing.'

CHARTS

US45	Shadow Dancing — *Andy Gibb*
USLP	Saturday Night Fever — *Soundtrack*
UK45	You're The One That I Want — *John Travolta & Olivia Newton-John*
UKLP	Saturday Night Fever — *Soundtrack*
WEEK 2	
US45	Shadow Dancing — *Andy Gibb*
USLP	City To City — *Gerry Rafferty*
UK45	You're The One That I Want — *John Travolta & Olivia Newton-John*
UKLP	Saturday Night Fever — *Soundtrack*
WEEK 3	
US45	Shadow Dancing — *Andy Gibb*
USLP	Some Girls — *Rolling Stones*
UK45	You're The One That I Want — *John Travolta & Olivia Newton-John*
UKLP	Saturday Night Fever — *Soundtrack*
WEEK 4	
US45	Shadow Dancing — *Andy Gibb*
USLP	Some Girls — *Rolling Stones*
UK45	You're The One That I Want — *John Travolta & Olivia Newton-John*
UKLP	Saturday Night Fever — *Soundtrack*
WEEK 5	
US45	Shadow Dancing — *Andy Gibb*
USLP	Grease — *Soundtrack*
UK45	You're The One That I Want — *John Travolta & Olivia Newton-John*
UKLP	Saturday Night Fever — *Soundtrack*

Lucille Ball: objection

SOUNDTRACK FEVER

Bee Gees in 'Sergeant Pepper' movie

With one bound, The Bee Gees have leapt off the Saturday Night dance floor and into Sergeant Pepper uniforms to become surrogate Beatles for the soundtrack of the *Sergeant Pepper's Lonely Hearts Club Band* movie.

What's that? Yes, that's right, there are only three Bee Gees but there were four Beatles. That's why Peter Frampton has been roped in as the fourth Beatle.

True, they don't look like The Beatles or sound like The Beatles, but neither does Aerosmith's version of 'Come Together'. Which means that the whole soundtrack is a turkey. As is the movie.

Trouble is, the movie industry is obsessed with The Bee Gees. That's why the *Grease* people have drafted in Barry Gibb to write one song for their new film and given him a blockbusting credit for it.

SULTANS OF NEW-WAVE SWING

This is scarcely the time to start parading your J.J. Cale, Bob Dylan and Ry Cooder influences around the London pub circuit. But somehow Dire Straits have made the anachronisms work for them, and prospered amid the new wave.

A demo tape played on BBC Radio London alerted A&R men who finally heard something they could understand. And so did a growing number of punters who started showing up at their gigs.

Singer/songwriter/guitarist Mark Knopfler doesn't subscribe to image or self-analysis. 'We're not on a music-by-mind-and-body trip – getting a synthesizer and playing a few notes just because you've read a book by Herman Hesse.

'Things tend to go wrong when the perspective's directed more towards the artist than what he's doing. What counts is your two per cent: what you're doing!'

THE GRAPEVINE

- **The Russians have cancelled a planned concert/film by The Beach Boys and Santana at short notice.**
- **The Rolling Stones have experienced problems with their 'Some Girls' album sleeve when Lucille Ball objected to her 'celebrity appearance'.**
- **The Clash's Joe Strummer and Paul Simonon have been arrested in Glasgow for drunk and disorderly behaviour.**
- **Prince has entered the US soul charts with 'Soft And Wet'.**

VAN HALEN SAY IT LOUDER

'This is the maximum escape trip, because it's so loud you cannot think of anything else but what's in front of you. You can't think about work, you can't think about the wife, the bills, the kids, nothing. Just that music being pounded into your skull.'

Dave Lee Roth is the singer with Van Halen, the 'maximum' heavy-metal band whose self-titled debut album has been firmly lodged in the US Top 30 for weeks.

Roth, guitarist Eddie Van Halen, drummer Alex Van Halen and bassist Mike Anthony, got bored with doing Zeppelin and Sabbath covers in Hollywood bars and took the plunge with their own gigs – renting halls and PAs, printing posters. When they started attracting 3,000 people, Warner Brothers signed them up.

Roth sees it all quite simply. 'We all work for a living, we all fall in love, we all make love, we all feel happy, we all feel sad, pretty much the same ways. Those are the needs that Van Halen caters to.'

Their trick is catering for them extravagantly. 'I like to make spectacles, y'know. We're gonna hire some elephants for our Long Beach Arena show when we get back from Japan. I want Van Halen beach balls!'

CHARTS

US45	Miss You *Rolling Stones*
USLP	Grease *Soundtrack*
UK45	You're The One That I Want *John Travolta & Olivia Newton-John*
UKLP	Saturday Night Fever *Soundtrack*
WEEK 2	
US45	Three Times A Lady *Commodores*
USLP	Grease *Soundtrack*
UK45	You're The One That I Want *John Travolta & Olivia Newton-John*
UKLP	Saturday Night Fever *Soundtrack*
WEEK 3	
US45	Three Times A Lady *Commodores*
USLP	Grease *Soundtrack*
UK45	You're The One That I Want *John Travolta & Olivia Newton-John*
UKLP	Saturday Night Fever *Soundtrack*
WEEK 4	
US45	Grease *Soundtrack*
USLP	Grease *Soundtrack*
UK45	Three Times A Laldy *Commodores*
UKLP	Saturday Night Fever *Soundtrack*

THE GRAPEVINE

- **Muddy Waters played at Jimmy Carter's White House Picnic.**
- **Roxy Music are reported to be together again.**
- **Temptation Melvin Franklin has been shot and mugged in Los Angeles.**
- **Bebop Deluxe have split.**
- **New York's chic-est disco, Studio 54, has been busted by members of the narc squad posing as cocaine dealers.**

STAR QUOTE

PETE TOWNSHEND

'When the new wave came along it was a great affirmation for me. I thought "Aye aye, we're not dead yet!" It was part of what had been nagging me. It didn't seem that the music business was ever going to get back to rock again.'

KEEF CLEANS UP

'What can I tell you about it? I can't tell you how it works because they don't even know for sure. All they know is that it works. It's a little metal box with leads that clip on to your ears, and in two or three days – which is the worst period for kickin' junk – it leaves your system.'

Keith Richard has taken the cure. His Toronto bust and the consequences left no alternative. He's used the method that's already worked for Eric Clapton and Pete Townshend, perfected by London doctor Meg Patterson.

And after three days? 'It's up to you.'

Keith hasn't found it a problem, and he confesses that he doesn't even feel that different. But then as he says: 'I've never had a problem with drugs. Only with policemen.'

Keith also has an unresolved problem with the Toronto Justice Department, where he faces heroin charges. But the fact that he's finally cleaned himself up should help his case.

TELEVISION'S MEDIA BURN

Television have switched off, just weeks after playing six sell-out shows at New York's Bottom Line. The band's four-year career has been punctuated by ego clashes, management problems and general temperamental instability.

Leader Tom Verlaine forced Richard Hell out of the band before they even landed a record contract, and guitarist Richard Lloyd left twice, only to return each time within a week.

Their debut album, 'Marquee Moon', was hailed as a new-wave masterpiece, but the recent follow-up, 'Adventure', got the full force of a critical backlash.

Lloyd says that after the Bottom Line gigs, 'It was clear none of the band wanted to continue together.' Verlaine says: 'There was a full moon that night. Moby Grape broke up on a full moon. So we decided to do the same.'

Townshend: not dead yet

SEPTEMBER

THE GRAPEVINE

- Public Image Ltd – formed by John Lydon (aka Rotten) – have released their first single, 'Public Image'.
- Sid Vicious has played a gig at Max's Kansas City in New York with ex-New York Dolls drummer Jerry Nolan and The Clash's Mick Jones.
- Bob Dylan's world tour has reached America for a 65-date leg.
- Teddy Pendergrass has played a 'For Women Only' gig in New York.

CHARTS

US45	Grease *Soundtrack*
USLP	Grease *Soundtrack*
UK45	Three Times A Lady *Commodores*
UKLP	Saturday Night Fever *Soundtrack*
WEEK 2	
US45	Boogie Oogie Oogie *Taste Of Honey*
USLP	Grease *Soundtrack*
UK45	Three Times A Lady *Commodores*
UKLP	Night Flight To Venus *Boney M*
WEEK 3	
US45	Boogie Oogie Oogie *Taste Of Honey*
USLP	Grease *Soundtrack*
UK45	Three Times A Lady *Commodores*
UKLP	Night Flight To Venus *Boney M*
WEEK 4	
US45	Boogie Oogie Oogie *Taste Of Honey*
USLP	Grease *Soundtrack*
UK45	Dreadlock Holiday *10cc*
UKLP	Night Flight To Venus *Boney M*
WEEK 5	
US45	Kiss You All Over *Exile*
USLP	Grease *Soundtrack*
UK45	Dreadlock Holiday *10cc*
UKLP	Grease *Soundtrack*

KEITH MOON TAKEN AWAY

On the cover of The Who's new album, Keith Moon is sitting on a chair inscribed 'Not to be taken away'. But the seemingly indestructible drummer has died – from the drug he was taking to get him off the drug that was most likely to kill him: booze.

After an evening with his girlfriend Annette Walter-Lax at the premiere, of *The Buddy Holly Story* movie, and a party with Paul McCartney, Keith went home to his Mayfair flat. Annette found him dead the next morning. A post-mortem revealed an overdose of Heminevrin.

Pete Townshend's reaction was immediate: 'No-one could ever take Keith's place and we're not even going to try to replace him. But we're more determined than ever to carry on.'

The Who have just finished making a film documentary of their career called *The Kids Are Alright*, and Moon's last gig for the band earlier in the summer was filmed for the movie.

According to Keith: 'People often say to me, "Keith, you're crazy." Well, maybe I am, but I live my life and I live out my fantasies, thereby getting them all out of my system.'

STAR QUOTE

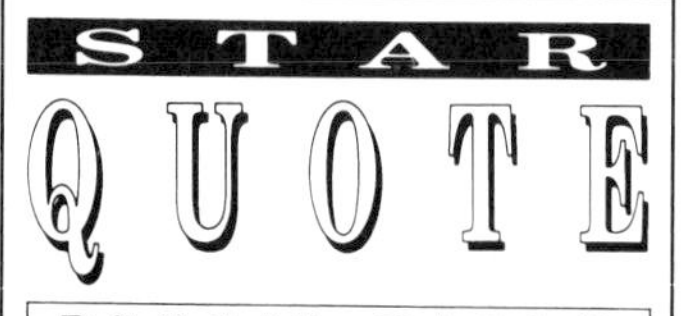

DEBBIE HARRY

'If I read anything cruel I have to have a couple of days to get over it or else I'd freak out. If it came at me all the time, I'd go around throwing acid in people's faces or become a sniper.'

THE DEAD'S PYRAMID PRANK

Grateful Dead and the pyramid – American rock and bedouin wailing

When The Grateful Dead discovered last March that it was possible to stage a gig at the Egyptian pyramids, their vibes were tickled. When they discovered that there would be an eclipse of the moon there on the evening of September 16, they nearly blew their cosmic minds.

They've landed up playing three nights to 3,000 people on the stone Apron theatre of the Giza Son Et Lumière Theatre in front of the Pyramid. And on the third night, three hundred San Franciscans flew in to see the show. As the moon began to darken, the wind rose, blowing sand from the desert and the noise of bedouin tribesmen wailing in their caravans across the theatre, mingling with the Dead's supremely self-indulgent American rock music.

'This is The Grateful Dead's annual Pyramid prank. It's great, I love it,' says Jerry Garcia.

FEELS LIKE FOREIGNER

Latest band to clean upon the American melodic heavy rock circuit are Foreigner, whose two albums have sold over 7½ million 'units' (that's industry-speak for copies sold).

The relentlessly old-wave band have had minimal press coverage during their sudden rise. In the mid-Sixties British-born guitarist Mick Jones wrote and recorded hits for French heart-throb Johnny Halliday. After spending ten years on the fringes of the US scene with Gary Wright, a reformed Spooky Tooth and Leslie West, he wrote the first Foreigner album before recruiting the band.

He picked an unknown singer, American-born Lou Gramm, ex-Ian Hunter drummer Dennis Elliott and original King Crimson keyboard player Ian McDonald.

'What we've got is not just a blend of Britain and America,' says Mick Jones. 'But a blend of relative experience and relative inexperience. I think that's important.'

Not to mention successful.

SID VICIOUS ON MURDER CHARGE

The Sex Pistols saga is turning from hype to horror. On October 13 Sid Vicious's girlfriend Nancy Spungen was found dead from abdominal stab wounds in their room at the New York Chelsea Hotel.

Sid, suffering from the effects of heroin, barbiturates and alcohol, was charged with second degree murder and taken to the hospital wing of Riker's Island Prison.

Nobody knows what really happened in their hotel room, including Sid. The pair, who had been together since the spring of 1977, were a volatile but inseparable couple, fuelled by a shared and growing heroin habit.

When The Sex Pistols broke up, they returned to London and became registered addicts, adding a severe methadone habit to their problems. Just before they left for New York, where Sid was planning to get a band together with former New York Doll and fellow dope fiend Johnny Thunders, 19-year-old John Shipcott OD'd at their flat and died.

While Sid was waiting to be released from Rikers Island on bail, he tried to commit suicide.

CHARTS

US45	Kiss You All Over *Exile*
USLP	Grease *Soundtrack*
UK45	Summer Nights *John Travolta/Olivia Newton-John*
UKLP	Grease *Soundtrack*

WEEK 2

US45	Kiss You All Over *Exile*
USLP	Grease *Soundtrack*
UK45	Summer Nights *John Travolta/Olivia Newton-John*
UKLP	Grease *Soundtrack*

WEEK 3

US45	Kiss You All Over *Exile*
USLP	Grease *Soundtrack*
UK45	Summer Nights *John Travolta/Olivia Newton-John*
UKLP	Grease *Soundtrack*

WEEK 4

US45	Hot Child In The City *Nick Gilder*
USLP	Grease *Soundtrack*
UK45	Summer Nights *John Travolta/Olivia Newton-John*
UKLP	Grease *Soundtrack*

STAR QUOTE

JOHN LYDON

'It's power that runs any country; you can't change things overnight with a hit record. Rock singers getting into politics is rather stupid . . .'

THE GRAPEVINE

- **Peter Tosh acquired a broken arm and head wounds needing 20 stitches while being detained overnight by Jamaican police on marijuana charges.**
- **Aerosmith's Steve Tyler and Joe Perry were injured by a cherry bomb thrown on stage at Philadelphia.**
- **The Clash have fired their manager Bernie Rhodes.**

Peter Tosh

KEITH OFF THE HOOK

Keith Richards has been given one year's probation by a Toronto court for heroin possession. An earlier charge of trafficking was dropped after he entered a guilty plea to possessing 22 grams of heroin. Richards has also agreed to play a benefit concert for the blind in Toronto.

Meanwhile, The Stones have run into charges of racism from the Rev. Jesse Jackson over their 'Some Girls' single. The Stones reply: 'It never occurred to us that our parody of certain stereotypical attitudes would be taken seriously by anyone who has heard the entire lyrics of the song. We sincerely apologize.'

SPRINGSTEEN'S ON FIRE

Bruce Springsteen is slumped in the dressing room of the New York Palladium after a four-hour show. He seldom does less these days, and often spends a couple of hours soundchecking beforehand.

It's the last of three nights in front of a partisan crowd. During the summer he did three Madison Square Gardens and in between he's been pummelling the road promoting his 'Darkness On The Edge Of Town' album.

Night after night he drives himself beyond the brink of exhaustion. His shows have become almost a religious celebration of the spirit of rock'n'roll.

'Yeah, there's a lotta morality in the show,' he says. 'And it's a very strict morality. Anybody that works for me has gotta understand that. I know how I'd feel if I'd paid money to see a show and what I wanted wasn't delivered.'

The managerial trials and tribulations that have blighted his career for the past two years have left him stronger than ever. And it's reflected in his songs.

'I couldn't do an innocent album like "Born To Run", because things ain't like that for me anymore. The characters on the new album ain't kids, they're older – you been beat, you been hurt – but there's still hope. There's always hope.'

DRIVE, SHE SAID

The Cars are a tight piece of machinery, a pop-driven new-wave model that's found favour with radio programmers. In the past six months the Boston quartet have scored a Top 20 hit with 'Just What I Needed', a platinum debut album and a second hit single with 'My Best Friend's Girl'.

Fortunately, singer/songwriter/guitarist Ric Ocasek has no illusions. 'All written words are fiction,' he declares.

The Cars deliberately aimed for the charts by getting Roy Thomas Baker, the doyen of 'clean' producers, to produce them. 'We figured he knew how to mix for radio – more than us,' says Ric.

Drummer Dave Robinson, formerly of The Modern Lovers, gave the band their name. Ric approves: 'Cars are great; they go through all the changes that musicians do, too. They all wear out, they get broken parts, some are better than others and some go in the junkyard . . .'

THE JAM'S MOD CONS

'I feel that the mod scene was very close to the punk thing; wholly youth – like going out with green hair. It changed you, made you something. It's something every kid goes through. You just want to be noticed, to be recognized.'

Paul Weller sits on the edge of the bed in his hotel room, chain-smoking, anxious to be understood. On stage with The Jam it's the same nervous need to communicate to legions of fans.

Like the mods, the Jam are a very British phenomenon. 'I wrote a load of songs when we were in America, but they were all crap. We went through Harlem, which is really inspiring, but that has nothing to do with me. I've got no right to write about it. We've got Harlems of our own – go up to Glasgow.'

But doesn't he worry about becoming too complex and introverted for his audiences to relate to?

'Sometimes yes, but I don't think that should necessarily stop you. I mean, I'd be too embarrassed to write something like "We're all going down the pub" (from 'Hurry Up Harry', current UK hit for punk rabble rousers Sham 69) 'even though that is probably very real to thousands of kids. I just feel that I should reach for something higher.'

The Jam: (l to r) Rick Buckler, Paul Weller, Bruce Foxton

POLICE GIVE EVIDENCE

'This band have had a really hard time from the press. We've been accused of "bandwagon punk" and now we're accused of "bandwagon reggae"'.

Police guitarist Andy Summers may complain but as an ex-guitarist with Zoot Money's Big Roll Band, Eric Burdon, Kevin Ayers and Kevin Coyne, he's nobody's idea of a punk, despite his bleached hair.

Neither is singer/bassist Sting, previously with Newcastle jazz-rock big band Last Exit. Or drummer Stewart Copeland, ex-Curved Air.

But their attitude is new-wave and Sting who wrote their hit singles 'Roxanne' and 'Can't Stand Losing You', admits the reggae influence. 'They're not reggae all the way though. Both of them go into straight rock'n'roll. You can't expect us to play old Led Zeppelin riffs now . . .'

'Stone cold sober? I don't believe in that.'

THE GRAPEVINE

- **Chic have their second gold record of the year with 'Le Freak'.**
- **The disco boom has reached out to pull in hits from 'legendary' soul/R&B names like Jerry Butler (from The Impressions), Gene Chandler, Gladys Knight, Joe Simon and The Temptations.**
- **The Jam's Paul Weller has been arrested for assault while staying at the same hotel as the Australian rugby league team.**

CHARTS

US45	You Needed Me – *Anne Murray*
USLP	Living In The USA – *Linda Ronstadt*
UK45	Summer Nights – *John Travolta/Olivia Newton-John*
UKLP	Grease – *Soundtrack*
WEEK 2	
US45	MacArthur Park – *Donna Summer*
USLP	Live & More – *Donna Summer*
UK45	Summer Nights – *John Travolta/Olivia Newton-John*
UKLP	Grease – *Soundtrack*
WEEK 3	
US45	MacArthur Park – *Donna Summer*
USLP	52nd Street – *Billy Joel*
UK45	Rat Trap – *Boomtown Rats*
UKLP	Grease – *Soundtrack*
WEEK 4	
US45	MacArthur Park – *Donna Summer*
USLP	52nd Street – *Billy Joel*
UK45	Rat Trap – *Boomtown Rats*
UKLP	Grease – *Soundtrack*

THE CLASH SORT IT OUT

Most of '78 has been a battleground for The Clash. Their UK tours became prey to all kinds of random violence from the audience and band alike; they've been in constant conflict with CBS over the recording of the second album, 'Give 'Em Enough Rope'; and they were constantly made to feel 'second best' to The Sex Pistols as their respective managers bitched over the title of 'Svengali Of Punk'.

But the T-shirts for the band's year-end tour display a new attitude. The message reads 'The Clash – The Sort It Out Tour', and the band appear to be doing just that.

On stage, the band are channelling their energies into their music, although the behaviour of their fans still manages to keep many gigs on a knife-edge. The UK chart success of 'Give 'Em Enough Rope' has resulted in a truce with their record company. And they've parted company with manager Bernie Rhodes.

Guitarist Mick Jones, who recalls 'breaking down in tears all the time' during the band's bleakest hours, admits that the band fell into a time-honoured rock'n'roll trap.

'Two years ago I did the band's first major TV interview and I was all young and naive. I blamed bands taking too many drugs for the great mid-Seventies drought in rock. I remember saying it really well. And a year or so later I found myself taking as many drugs as them.'

THE (DE) HUMAN FACE OF DISCO

'The disco sound is not art, or anything so serious. Disco is music for dancing and I know that people will always want to dance.'

Giorgio Moroder is the man responsible for the synthetic wizardry behind Donna Summer's 'Love To Love You Baby', 'I Feel Love' and 'MacArthur Park', and is fast becoming the hottest name in disco.

Italian-born Moroder fashions his records at Munich's Music machine in Germany, adding the gloss in Los Angeles or London. He acknowledges the influence of The Philly Sound and, like Gamble & Huff, maintains a house band.

He's not worried about accusations of dehumanizing disco. 'Disco is the soul and R&B sound of today,' he declares.

Donna Summer

THE GRAPEVINE

■ The Who have recruited ex-Faces drummer Kenny Jones to replace Keith Moon.

■ Public Image Limited, formed by John Lydon (Rotten) have played their first gig in London and released their debut LP.

■ San Francisco's Winterland auditorium has been closed by promoter Bill Graham after a farewell gig by The Grateful Dead and The Blues Brothers.

■ Big Star founding member Chris Bell has been killed in a car crash.

CHARTS

	US45	USLP	UK45	UKLP
Week 1	You Don't Bring Me Flowers – *Barbra Streisand & Neil Diamond*	52nd Street – *Billy Joel*	Rat Trap – *Boomtown Rats*	Grease – *Soundtrack*
Week 2	Le Freak – *Chic*	52nd Street – *Billy Joel*	Do Ya Think I'm Sexy – *Rod Stewart*	20 Golden Greats – *Neil Diamond*
Week 3	Le Freak – *Chic*	52nd Street – *Billy Joel*	Mary's Boy Child – *Boney M*	20 Golden Greats – *Neil Diamond*
Week 4	Le Freak – *Chic*	52nd Street – *Billy Joel*	Mary's Boy Child – *Boney M*	Grease – *Soundtrack*
Week 5	Le Freak – *Chic*	52nd Street – *Billy Joel*	Mary's Boy Child – *Boney M*	Grease – *Soundtrack*

Kenny Jones: replacing Moon

STILL LOOKING FOR NUMBER ONE

A year ago, Bob Geldof was bragging that The Boomtown Rats would be a No. 1 band in a year's time. They'd already had UK chart success by then, but the difference between a Top Ten hit and a chart topper is bigger than they knew – and 'Rat Trap' stalled at No. 6.

But that hasn't stopped Geldof being a star. He was a rock journalist before he formed the Rats, and knows not to bullshit the media. Or his audiences. Which is why The Boomtown Rats are drawing huge crowds as they tour the UK on their wittily titled 'Seasonal Turkey Tour'.

'The Rats are the band I sing with,' he says. 'It's a job. I don't consider myself to be a big deal. But rock'n'roll, along with TV and the movies, is a great twentieth-century art form.'

SEX AND DRUGS AND ROCK'N'ROLL

'Sex and drugs and rock and roll/Is all my brain and body needs/Sex and drugs and rock and roll/Is very good indeed.'

Last year's rock'n'roll anthem across Britain and Europe never made the charts. But 'Sex And Drugs And Rock And Roll' by Ian Dury & The Blockheads sums up the perennial fantasy of the rock generation – and the gruesome reality for a select few.

Ian Dury, the ex-art-school lecturer who rasps the song in a half-spoken hoarse Cockney accent, is a Great British Eccentric. Known to The Blockheads as Raspberry – Cockney rhyming slang: raspberry ripple = cripple – he wears his affliction, caused by polio, like a badge. He limps round the stage and clutches the mike stand with his withered hand while throwing knotted handkerchiefs around with his other.

And all the while The Blockheads are pumping out sandpaper-textured funky riffs written by keyboard player Chas Jankel, whose ear for a catchy hook has hit paydirt.

Their latest single, 'Hit Me With Your Rhythm Stick', barrelled its way through the UK Top 40 during December and up the Top 10 this month to hit No. 1 after two weeks at No. 2.

Ian Dury and the Blockheads

BEDROOM FEVER

America's latest fad for the nouveau riche is the disco bedroom. Affluent Travolta types are forking out up to $20,000 to instal a full disco and light show to bolster their egos in the boudoir.

Jack Ransom, head of MGM Stage Equipment, a leading disco supply company, reckons it's a new twist on the age-old art of seduction, and says the playboy types 'are willing to pay top dollar to indulge their whims'.

Even the oil-rich Arabs are succumbing to Saturday Night Fever, converting sections of their palaces into discos.

STAR QUOTE

ELVIS COSTELLO

'If two days go by without an idea for a song, I become obsessive about writing. That's what taking it up as a career does, as opposed to it merely being a hobby.'

CHARTS

	Week 1
US45	Too Much Heaven – *Bee Gees*
USLP	Greatest Hits Volume 2 – *Barbra Streisand*
UK45	Y.M.C.A. – *Village People*
UKLP	Greatest Hits 1976-1978 – *Showaddywaddy*

	WEEK 2
US45	Too Much Heaven – *Bee Gees*
USLP	Greatest Hits Volume 2 – *Barbra Streisand*
UK45	Y.M.C.A. – *Village People*
UKLP	Greatest Hits 1976-1978 – *Showaddywaddy*

	WEEK 3
US45	Le Freak – *Chic*
USLP	Greatest Hits Volume 2 – *Barbra Streisand*
UK45	Y.M.C.A. – *Village People*
UKLP	Greatest Hits 1976-1978 – *Showaddywaddy*

	WEEK 4
US45	Le Freak – *Chic*
USLP	52nd Street – *Billy Joel*
UK45	Hit Me With Your Rhythm Stick – *Ian Dury*
UKLP	Don't Walk, Boogie – *Various*

Elvis giving up his hobby

THE GRAPEVINE

- **Sid Vicious has been sent for trial for murdering his girlfriend Nancy Spungen.**
- **The Clash have released their first US single, 'I Fought The Law'.**
- **Jazz giant Charlie Mingus has died of a heart attack, aged 56.**
- **Singer Donny Hathaway died after falling from the 15th floor of his New York hotel.**

Marvin Gaye: loser in love

MARVIN GAYE'S ALIMONY ALBUM

All proceeds from Marvin Gaye's new album will go to his ex-wife Anna Gordy, daughter of Tamla Motown founder Berry Gordy. The album is on Tamla Motown. It's called, not without irony, 'Here, My Dear'.

The divorce has left Marvin bankrupt. And the songs on the album are a loser's guide to love and marriage. Even Marvin's staunchest fans aren't arguing that it's his best to date, but it's remarkably candid about his own reality – admittedly different from most people's reality.

'I think this is man's last-ditch effort to maintain whatever supremacy we have,' Gaye declares, although he maintains that he bears his ex-wife no personal ill-will.

'Although there is some bitterness on the album, there are also respectful cuts that tell of a wonderful love,' he says. 'It was just lack of compatibility . . . in a marriage compatibility is everything.'

SID DID IT HIS WAY

The predictable death of Sid Vicious came early on February 2 – from a heroin overdose.

He was at a party given by his current girlfriend Michelle Robinson and his mother Ann Beverley, to celebrate his release from jail pending a hearing of his murder trial.

While in prison, Sid was put on a detoxification course and, as a result, his tolerance to heroin was lowered. Sid collapsed after being given the drug, but recovered before the party broke up and went to bed around 3 am. Ann Beverley found him dead in his bed the following morning. A syringe and spoon were found near the body.

Sid would have been 22 in May.

Just to prove that The Sex Pistols are also dead, John Lydon has forced Malcolm McLaren's Glitterbest management company into liquidation. A receiver is being appointed to sort out the group's financial affairs, with authority to release *The Great Rock and Roll Swindle* film and album, into which most of Glitterbest's money has been invested. The judge said the film represented 'the only realistic hope of any substantial funds being rescued for anyone'.

Anyone except Sid, that is.

THE

■ A US Grand Jury has been investigating alleged links between Chicago (the band) and the mafia.

■ One hit wonder Sgt Barry ('Ballad Of The Green Berets') Sadler also facing a Grand Jury investigation after shooting songwriter Lee Bellamy dead; Sadler claims he aimed to miss.

■ 10cc's Eric Stewart has suffered serious head injuries in a car crash.

■ The Clash start their first US tour.

Chicago – under investigation

JOE JACKSON LOOKS SHARP

'Look Sharp' is the title of Joe Jackson's debut album and the tall, thin man with a truculent baby face looks just that.

His songs have energy, wit and melody. His first single, 'Is She Really Going Out With Him', proves the point perfectly and has alerted enough people to mark him down as one to watch this year.

His lyrics are defiant, idealistic and ironic. 'I want to get away from all that macho shit, but at the same time I don't want to do the Elvis Costello god-I've-been-hurt-in-love thing either,' he explains.

He's pitched his album quite deliberately. 'I didn't want your typical '77/'78 new wave band sound. I wanted more of a reggae mix, where you have a very upfront bass and drums and a thin sounding guitar that goes in and out. The idea is to leave a lot of gaps to let the song really come through.'

STAR QUOTE

GRAHAM PARKER

'All I want to do is send a shiver up people's spines.'

CHARTS

US45	Le Freak *Chic*
USLP	Briefcase Full Of Blues *Blues Brothers*
UK45	Hit Me With Your Rhythm Stick *Ian Dury*
UKLP	Don't Walk, Boogie *Various*
WEEK 2	
US45	Da Ya Think I'm Sexy? *Rod Stewart*
USLP	Blondes Have More Fun *Rod Stewart*
UK45	Heart Of Glass *Blondie*
UKLP	Parallel Lines *Blondie*
WEEK 3	
US45	Da Ya Think I'm Sexy? *Rod Stewart*
USLP	Blondes Have More Fun *Rod Stewart*
UK45	Chiquitita *Abba*
UKLP	Parallel Lines *Blondie*
WEEK 4	
US45	Da Ya Think I'm Sexy? *Rod Stewart*
USLP	Blondes Have More Fun *Rod Stewart*
UK45	Heart Of Glass *Blondie*
UKLP	Parallel Lines *Blondie*

VILLAGE PEOPLE'S COTTAGE INDUSTRY

The Indian, the cowboy, the labourer, the cop, the army bloke, the leather man – all of them treading the line between what is deft and what is daft with a visual onslaught that cannot fail to leave you uncommitted one way or the other.

Village People are the brainchild of French-born New York producer Jaques Morali, and their 'YMCA' disco blast has been tucked in at No. 2 in the US charts for three weeks. In the UK it's No. 1.

The boys in Village People may complain that people are only interested in whether or not they're gay, but they should have thought about that before they started putting on such butch costumes and started singing songs like 'Macho Man', 'YMCA', and 'I Am What I Am', with lyrics that are so camp they have to be held down with tent pegs.

Village People: cottage industry

MARCH

1979

CHARTS

US45 Da Ya Think I'm Sexy? *Rod Stewart*
USLP Spirits Having Flown *Bee Gees*
UK45 Heart Of Glass *Blondie*
UKLP Parallel Lines *Blondie*

WEEK 2

US45 I Will Survive *Gloria Gaynor*
USLP Spirits Having Flown *Bee Gees*
UK45 Tragedy *Bee Gees*
UKLP Parallel Lines *Blondie*

WEEK 3

US45 I Will Survive *Gloria Gaynor*
USLP Spirits Having Flown *Bee Gees*
UK45 Oliver's Army *Elvis Costello*
UKLP Parallel Lines *Blondie*

WEEK 4

US45 Tragedy *Bee Gees*
USLP Spirits Having Flown *Bee Gees*
UK45 I Will Survive *Gloria Gaynor*
UKLP Spirits Having Flown *Bee Gees*

WEEK 5

US45 Tragedy *Bee Gees*
USLP Spirits Having Flown *Bee Gees*
UK45 I Will Survive *Gloria Gaynor*
UKLP C'Est Chic *Chic*

THE JACKSONS – ON THE WALL

Jackson 5 heading for destiny

Ten years after bounding into the charts with 'ABC' and 'I Want You Back', Michael Jackson still refuses to grow up. He's no longer the youngest of the Jackson 5 – Randy is three years younger – but he remains the Peter Pan of the group.

He's totally dedicated to his profession because he knows no other way of life. From the age of five, when he started singing and dancing with the group, he has grown in an environment so completely cloistered that he can only regard the imaginary as reality.

On stage, the band create real magic, from the infectious 'Let Me Show You The Way' to the up-market soul of 'Destiny'. They even get away with a hurried medley of their old hits.

Off-stage, Michael is closely guarded to prevent unnecessary contact with the real world. Far from turning him precocious and arrogant, he gets off on the simple things of life, like swimming in the hotel pool after dark. And his biggest thrill right now is holding the record attendance at the Houston Astrodome. There's even a commemorative plaque to prove it.

'It makes me feel really good when other bands who've played there meet us and tell us they've seen our plaque,' he says.

THE GRAPEVINE

- **David Bowie has finished filming *Just A Gigolo* and has set out on a US tour.**
- **Twisted Sister sold out the 3,000-capacity New York Palladium without a record deal or radio play.**
- **Punk riots have come to the US when Los Angeles police broke up a Zeros gig at Elks Hall.**
- **Elvis Costello was punched by Bonnie Bramlett in a Columbus, Ohio, hotel bar after allegedly making racist remarks.**

Twisted Sister: selling out

TOTO AIM FOR THE MEGA BUCKS

Toto are the latest American radio rock stars. Their debut single, 'Hold The Line', was a monster hit and their debut album has cleaned up a million copies in four months.

The six-piece band are all seasoned West Coast session musicians, and their approach is practical to say the least. 'The way the rock field is set up right now, you either don't make a nickel or you make over two million dollars,' says drummer Jeff Porcaro.

'There's no making half a million dollars. It's just not worth it. It's too much trouble. You either make a lotof money or get out of the business.'

He's scathing about punk too: 'All new wave music and punk music is bullshit. The music's ugly and the people are ugly.'

JOAN ARMATRADING'S ENIGMATIC EMOTIONS

Joan Armatrading has become Britain's most successful singer/songwriter over the last couple of years, yet she remains an enigma.

After a critically acclaimed but poor-selling debut album in the early Seventies, she signed to A&M where she continued to gather plaudits for her 'Back To The Night' and 'Joan Armatrading' albums and finally landed a UK Top 10 single with the powerful and emotive 'Love And Affection' at the end of 1976.

Since then her 'Show Some Emotion' and 'To The Limit' albums have consolidated her reputation as a perceptive writer experimenting with reggae, gospel and blues styles.

But she reveals little of herself in her songs, preferring to write from personal observation rather than personal experience.

'Although they're not personal, I do get very involved in the songs,' this self-confessed loner contends. 'It's not just a bunch of words. They have to mean something to me.'

STAR QUOTE

NEIL YOUNG

'I'm lucky. Somehow, by doing what I want to do, I manage to give people what they don't want to hear and they still come back for more. I haven't been able to figure that out yet . . . '

THE POLICE – BORN IN THE FIFTIES

The Police: too young for Woodstock and too old for punk

Still ignored in the UK where they've been accused of bandwagon jumping, The Police are making inroads in America where their 'Roxanne' single and 'Outlandos D'Amour' album have just cracked the Top 30.

Significantly, they are doing better than The Clash, The Sex Pistols, The Stranglers, The Boomtown Rats and all the other British new-wave bands. They've achieved the breakthrough by playing a shoestring tour of the East Coast, where college radio took 'Roxanne' to its airplay bosom.

They've just completed a second tour climaxing with a series of gigs at New York's Bottom Line, where their reggaefied new-wave sound has lured the likes of Robert Fripp, Return To Forever drummer Lenny White, and Mick Jagger.

The word is out: the Police can actually play.

'We're too young to have been into Woodstock and all that, and we're too old to be punks,' explains Sting. 'We're stuck with being wise in one way and naive in another.

'We didn't elect the dinosaurs of rock. They've been put up there by people older than us. Our generation has to establish itself and we're not going to vanish just because we're over 23. What do people expect us to do?'

CHARTS

US45	I Will Survive	*Gloria Gaynor*
USLP	Minute By Minute	*Doobie Brothers*
UK45	In The Navy	*Village People*
UKLP	Greatest Hits Vol.2	*Barbra Streisand*
WEEK 2		
US45	What A Fool Believes	*Doobie Brothers*
USLP	Minute By Minute	*Doobie Brothers*
UK45	Bright Eyes	*Art Garfunkel*
UKLP	Greatest Hits Vol.2	*Barbra Streisand*
WEEK 3		
US45	Knock On Wood	*Amii Stewart*
USLP	Spirits Having Flown	*Bee Gees*
UK45	Bright Eyes	*Art Garfunkel*
UKLP	Greatest Hits Vol.2	*Barbra Streisand*
WEEK 4		
US45	Heart Of Glass	*Blondie*
USLP	Minute By Minute	*Doobie Brothers*
UK45	Bright Eyes	*Art Garfunkel*
UKLP	The Very Best Of Leo Sayer	*Leo Sayer*

Mike Oldfield works out another definite sequence of behaviour

STAR

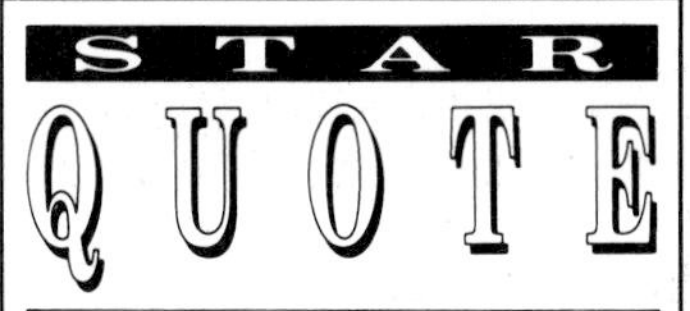

MIKE OLDFIELD

'People are very complicated machines – to get them to do what you want, you have to be very careful. You have to behave towards them in a very definite sequence.'

SQUEEZING OUT HITS

Squeeze freely admit they rode the new wave to get a record deal although they were never really a part of it. Their latest and biggest UK hit to date, 'Cool For Cats' is a jokey, lightweight song with some rude lyrics which have somehow escaped the censorious minds that control UK radio.

'A lot of people find it hard to categorize us,' says Chris Difford, one of the band's singers, 'and that puts them off.'

Squeeze are a six-piece quirky pop band from Catford, south London who now have two singles and a confessedly 'patchy' debut album to their credit. They are more pleased with their second album, also called 'Cool For Cats'.

'It's one of the best I've heard,' says Glenn Tilbrook, who co-writes most of the songs with Difford. 'It's intelligent, both musically and lyrically, and the playing is great. It's just that the general public don't happen to realize it at the moment.'

THE GRAPEVINE

- **Rod Stewart has married Alana Hamilton, ex-wife of film star George Hamilton, in Beverley Hills.**
- **Keith Richards played his benefit for the blind in Ottowa, debuting his New Barbarians band featuring Ron Wood and Stanley Clarke.**
- **Mickey Thomas has joined Jefferson Starship to replace Marty Balin.**
- **Iggy Pop has been banned from some venues on his UK tour because his backing band features former Sex Pistol Glenn Matlock (!)**

LOU REED CAN'T DANCE

Lou Reed should be an idol for the punk generation, but instead he's rubbing them up the wrong way. His new LP, 'The Bells', has been panned as 'a delusion disguised as an album', and the London show on his European tour was dismissed as 'a crushing, oppressive, indulgent thrash'.

His behaviour became increasingly unpredictable during the German leg of the tour. In Berlin he enthralled the audience with a three-hour show. But in Frankfurt he stormed off after less than an hour, demanding that a GI be removed from the hall. When he returned 40 minutes later, he knocked down and kicked a girl who'd climbed on stage before beating a hasty retreat.

Lou spent the night in police custody on an assault charge.

Lou Reed not fearing for whom the bell tolls, it's for him

MAY

J GEILS BAND SEEK SANCTUARY

For nearly a decade The J Geils Band have been touted as America's answer to The Rolling Stones. In fact, they came closest on their debut album back in 1970, but nobody's ever forgotten the connection, which ultimately hasn't done the band many favours.

They've had more than a few of the right connections too: managed by Dee Anthony before he came alive with Peter Frampton, road managed by Fred Lewis until he drove off with The Cars, and produced by Bill Szymczyk until he flew off with The Eagles.

Everybody around them made it big except The J Geils Band. But they've kept their integrity, and nobody was ever able to tell them what to do.

'We made it a rule to care about ticket prices, the sound, the comfort, the security,' says singer Peter Wolf. 'If a guy brings his girl to a show, we want to know there won't be some goons around to spoil their fun.

'And that goes for recording, the pressing, the cover. And each other. See, we've only got one career, we have to be protective of it.'

Maybe they've been over-protective. There have been albums when they've pandered to their fans. But their latest album, 'Sanctuary', puts a tougher resolve into their adventurous music and sets them back on the right road.

WHO'S NEXT?

The Who are back – as defiant as ever – with a film documentary of their illustrious career so far, a movie version of their 'Quadrophenia' rock opera, and gigs with their new drummer.

Kenny Jones faces the unenviable task of replacing Keith Moon for the first time at London's Rainbow Theatre – a gig announced with two days' notice. He succeeded by avoiding comparison and playing in his own style.

A few days later at the Roman amphitheatre in Frejus, in the South of France, Kenny was even more confident, stamping his own identity on the band who in turn responded with rejuvenated energy.

After all, they've nothing to lose now. Their past is behind them, neatly encapsulated on celluloid. *The Kids Are Alright* is the story of The Who from TV and film clips dating back to 1964. It never tries to put a gloss on the band, so the result is a perceptive documentary that's as much about the era of The Who as The Who themselves.

The Who hang on

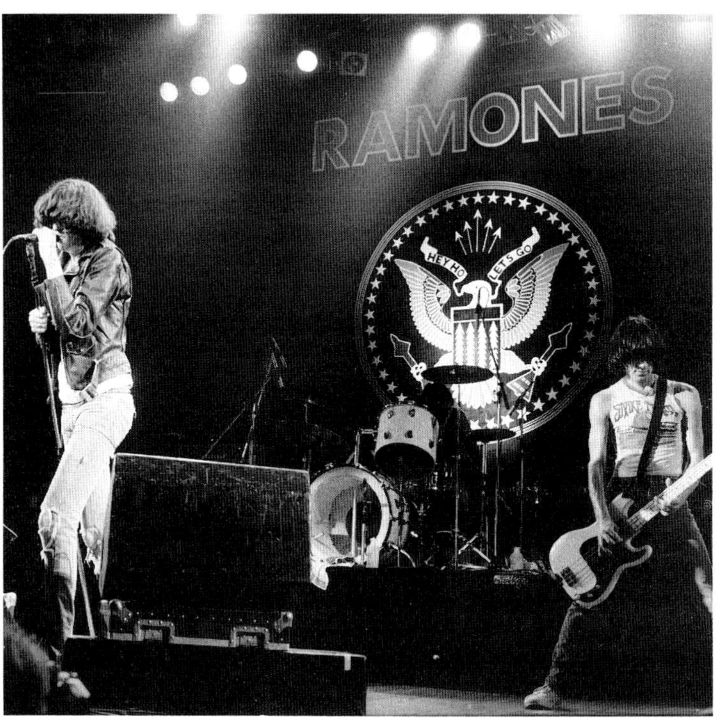

Da brudders: preppy punks

THE RAMONES GRADUATE

Rock 'n' Roll High School, featuring The Ramones, is bidding to become the cult film of American punkhood and bring da brudders the fame which has so far eluded them in the U.S.

The movie was shot in three weeks by Roger Corman, undisputed master of the B-movie – including *Attack Of The Crab Monsters, The Day The World Ended, The Wild Angels* and nearly 200 others.

A tale of teen romance and adolescent anarchy, *Rock 'n' Roll High School* is a perfect celebration of The Ramones and all they stand for.

DEBBIE HARRY

Blondie

'I wouldn't mind being a mom. I already am a housewife. I guess I vacuum once in a while.'

US45	Reunited *Peaches & Herb*
USLP	Minute By Minute *Doobie Brothers*
UK45	Bright Eyes *Art Garfunkel*
UKLP	The Very Best Of Leo Sayer *Leo Sayer*
WEEK 2	
US45	Reunited *Peaches & Herb*
USLP	Minute By Minute *Doobie Brothers*
UK45	Bright Eyes *Art Garfunkel*
UKLP	The Very Best Of Leo Sayer *Leo Sayer*
WEEK 3	
US45	Reunited *Peaches & Herb*
USLP	Breakfast In America *Supertramp*
UK45	Pop Muzik *M*
UKLP	The Very Best of Leo Sayer *Leo Sayer*
WEEK 4	
US45	Reunited *Peaches & Herb*
USLP	Breakfast In America *Supertramp*
UK45	Bright Eyes *Art Garfunkel*
UKLP	Voulez Vous *Abba*

THE GRAPEVINE

- **Led Zeppelin have announced their first gig for nearly two years – at the Knebworth Festival in August.**
- **Falling LP sales have forced record companies to cut back on the quantity of releases.**
- **Jefferson Starship begin to pick up the pieces with a free gig in San Francisco and new vocalist, Mickey Thomas.**
- **Elton John has played gigs in Israel and Russia.**

JUNE
1979

DIRE STRAITS – THAT'S THE WAY YOU DO IT!

In a business that can cheerfully blow £50,000 'repackaging' a disco artist you never heard first time round, Dire Straits have achieved the biggest-selling debut album in the US by any British band for a £15,000 production bill and a miniscule promotional budget.

The promotional budget would have been bigger, but by the time Warner Brothers had analysed the radio station feedback, the album was already the most-played on radio, coast-to-coast.

Rhythm guitarist David Knopfler says he once jumped stations to hear three different tracks being played simultaneously. The album literally sold itself into the charts, peaking at No. 2, just behind the Bee Gees.

At least America released the album. Some countries, like Canada and Germany, didn't want to know. But every country that did reported the same reaction.

Dire Straits left their record company standing with the fastest selling debut album in America

Unconcerned, Dire Straits set about their follow-up: a more expensive affair at Nassau, with Jerry Wexler and Barry Beckett supervising. By the time their debut was turning several shades of platinum in America, they'd finished the follow-up.

But Warners wanted to delay the second album to give them more time to milk the first. 'No deal,' said Dire Straits, aware of the danger of over-exposure. They set a June release date in Europe, leaving Warners to catch up or face massive imports.

Warners caught up. Undeterred, they are already making promotional plans for the third single from the album.

NO STOPPIN' McFADDEN & WHITEHEAD

'Look, soul music is only some guy singing his songs. I know you folks believe it's some cat with all gravel in his voice and stuff singing about hard times, but that ain't soul music. Most of those guys are singing someone else's songs so how in hell can they be feeling soul? No – soul music is any cat who feels enough to sing what he wrote himself.'

John Whitehead is busy putting the media right about soul. Together with Gene McFadden he's just scored a massive hit with the monumental 'Ain't No Stoppin' Us Now'.

It's a real break for them. They've been an integral part of the Philly sound, writing for the O'Jays and Harold Melvin & The Blue Notes. Now it's their turn, and the success is all the sweeter after they tried and failed to go it alone before. They've fulfilled their own definition of soul.

STAR QUOTE

IAN DURY

'If somebody's looking at me with rapture all over their face I want to throw a bucket of water over them.'

HEADBANGING BABES

Headbanging can start earlier than you think.

Respected UK medical journal *The Practitioner* reveals that headbanging can afflict children from six months to four years, and is started by the child trying to rock itself to sleep.

Doctors call it rhythmic motor habits, but they were surprised to find that Ted Nugent fans at a recent London concert were exhibiting the same symptoms: 'Most headbangers, as with head rollers, adopt an "on all fours" position when banging. A few, however, sit bolt upright.'

Ain't that a real mutha for ya?

Ted Nugent reverts to childhood

CHARTS

US45	Hot Stuff *Donna Summer*
USLP	Breakfast In America *Supertramp*
UK45	Sunday Girl *Blondie*
UKLP	Voulez Vous *Abba*
WEEK 2	
US45	Love You Inside Out *Bee Gees*
USLP	Breakfast In America *Supertramp*
UK45	Dance Away *Roxy Music*
UKLP	Voulez Vous *Abba*
WEEK 3	
US45	Hot Stuff *Donna Summer*
USLP	Bad Girls *Donna Summer*
UK45	Ring My Bell *Anita Ward*
UKLP	Voulez Vous *Abba*
WEEK 4	
US45	Hot Stuff *Donna Summer*
USLP	Breakfast In America *Supertramp*
UK45	Ring My Bell *Anita Ward*
UKLP	Discovery *Electric Light Orchestra*
WEEK 5	
US45	Ring My Bell *Anita Ward*
USLP	Breakfast In America *Supertramp*
UK45	Ring My Bell *Anita Ward*
UKLP	Discovery *Electric Light Orchestra*

THE GRAPEVINE

- **Chuck Berry is facing prison after pleading guilty to evading $200,000 in taxes, one week after performing at The White House.**
- **Jefferson Starship have lured Grace Slick back into their ranks.**
- **Little Feat have broken up after ten years . . . two weeks later, mainman Lowell George is dead of a heart attack caused by obesity and drug problems.**

JULY 1979

THE PRETENDERS TURN THE DIAL

They've played less than 50 gigs and only had a couple of singles so far, but already The Pretenders are being swamped with media praise.

They are an odd matching of Chrissie Hynde, a precious, Iggy Pop-fixated tomboy from Akron, Ohio, who came over to Britain just before punk struck, and three boys from Hereford, a market town near the Welsh border.

'There was nothing to do there but get wasted,' says guitarist James Honeyman-Scott, who admits the band has saved him from becoming a rabid speed freak.

Their first single was a jangly cover of The Kinks' 'Stop Your Sobbing', which failed to break into the UK Top 30, while the second, 'Kid', has scarcely done better. It's a major leap forward for the band however, as Chrissie wrote it.

She's been accused of leaning on the Sixties but says her only influence was the radio. 'I was in a very advantageous position living where I did. I could lay down at night and just . . . with my hand on the radio . . . with the slightest flick of the wrist . . . get another station; Nashville, Chicago, New York, Cleveland.'

Chrissie Hynde tunes in

CHARTS

US45	Ring My Bell *Anita Ward*
USLP	Bad Girls *Donna Summer*
UK45	Ring My Bell *Anita Ward*
UKLP	Discovery *Electric Light Orchestra*
WEEK 2	
US45	Bad Girls *Donna Summer*
USLP	Bad Girls *Donna Summer*
UK45	Are Friends Electric *Tubeway Army*
UKLP	Parallel Lines *Blondie*
WEEK 3	
US45	Bad Girls *Donna Summer*
USLP	Bad Girls *Donna Summer*
UK45	Silly Games *Janet Kay*
UKLP	Replicas *Tubeway Army*
WEEK 4	
US45	Bad Girls *Donna Summer*
USLP	Bad Girls *Donna Summer*
UK45	Are Friends Electric *Tubeway Army*
UKLP	Replicas *Tubeway Army*

GOING DIGITAL

Fleetwood Mac, Giorgio Moroder, Stephen Stills, Ry Cooder, Randy Newman and Bonnie Pointer are the first artists to discover the benefits of a new breakthrough that's being hailed as the biggest advance since stereo-digital recording.

Instead of simply storing sound on tape, the digital recorder samples the noise – 40-50,000 times per second – and stores the information in an electronic shorthand of binary numbers. So what you get back is exactly what you played.

It ain't cheap though, as Fleetwood Mac have discovered. You have to go through an expensive production system which costs around $100,000.

VAN HALEN'S ENERGY DRIVE

Dave Lee Roth is a fireball of energy, onstage and off. Onstage, his frenzied antics have propelled Van Halen into the heavy-metal mega-league with 'Van Halen II' a top ten album and 'Dance the Night Away' a top 20 single. Off-stage, his mouth works just as hard promoting the band to anyone in earshot.

The fact that Van Halen play the kind of hard rock that makes Led Zeppelin sound sluggish helps give his extravagant claims some substance.

'We're out to establish Van Halen as the most energized band on the planet. And I'm talking about a constant output of natural high energy, not coked-out high energy,' he proclaims.

'Sure, I've been up two or three nights at a time, but when the time comes to move on I just throw back a load of vitamins and like, OK, show me to the next gig. I tell ya, there's none that can keep up with us. Groupies, dealers – you name it, they hang around for a couple of days and then it hits 'em. They're flaked out and we're awake, heading for the next gig!'

Vitamin time for Van Halen

STAR QUOTE

DAVID BYRNE

of Talking Heads

'Anyone who tries to be naive these days is a fool. I know that most of this business is just merchandise.'

THE GRAPEVINE

- **Chicago DJ Steve Dahl burned a pile of disco records during a White Sox double header, and the ensuing riot caused the second game to be cancelled.**
- **Van McCoy has died of a heart attack, aged 38; Minnie Riperton is also dead of cancer, aged 31.**
- **Scott Cantrell, a 17 year old staying with Keith Richards' girlfriend Anita Pallenberg, shot himself dead in her bedroom.**

Minnie Ripperton: still lovin' you

AUGUST

RY COODER – BOPPING TIL HE DROPS

There are four great reasons for getting into Ry Cooder's music: unbeatable artistry, funky humour, warmth and a genuine introduction to America's most vital genre of popular music. And you'll find them all on his new album, 'Bop Til You Drop'.

Cooder's music draws on the American blues experience – country, gospel, uptown R&B and the folk styles of Texas, Mexico, Hawaii and the Bahamas.

He neither plagiarizes nor bastardizes other people's work. He keeps the music alive and undiminished, and he's lucky enough to have a major label – Warner Brothers – that's prepared to support him in his efforts.

'If I did it on a little label, no one would pay a bit of attention,' he admits. 'But I've been lucky to grease by with some stuff that normally wouldn't be a part of anyone's roster.

'I don't want to be thought of as unmarketable – y'know, weird and eccentric. Because then you're in a bad position, you're unable to work.'

So far, his seven albums haven't produced the return that Warners might have liked. But 'Bop Til You Drop' is his most accessible and commercial offering yet. And so far neither Cooder nor Warner's patience has run out.

WHALES FOR MINGUS

Joni Mitchell was the last person to record with Charlie Mingus. He wrote six songs which feature on her new album, 'Mingus'. The album has given Joni jazz kudos which she finds remarkable, but not as remarkable as Mingus himself.

'He died aged 56 in Mexico,' she says. 'And on the day he was cremated, 56 whales beached themselves on the Mexican coast. The locals didn't know what to do, so they burned them too. There was a lot of mojo in his life.'

Mitchell meets Mingus: the last album of the jazz bass pioneer

THE GRAPEVINE

- **Led Zeppelin packed the Knebworth Festival two weeks running for their first UK gigs in four years.**
- **The Cars played to half a million people in New York's Central Park.**
- **British rocker Nick Lowe has married Johnny Cash's daughter Carlene.**
- **The surviving members of Little Feat and friends staged a benefit for Lowell George in Los Angeles.**
- **Stan Kenton, modern jazz band leader, has died, aged 67.**

Zeppelin still pack 'em in

JOY DIVISION's DREAM WORLD

The themes of Joy Division's music are sorrowful, painful and sad, with sometimes harrowing glimpses of confusion and alienation.

Not that this Manchester band are giving any clues. They refuse to put a lyric sheet with their debut album, 'Unknown Pleasures', even though it's obvious that they've got something to say.

'Haven't you ever been listening to a record where you've been singing a certain line, and when you find out what it really is you feel let down?' asks bassist Peter Hook.

Joy Division are insular and possessive about their music. Signed to the Manchester independent label Factory, they recorded their album for £8,500, mistrusted the rave reviews and now wait dispassionately for the backlash.

'I used to work in a factory, and I was really happy because I could daydream all day,' says shy singer Ian Curtis. 'All I had to do was push this wagon with cotton things in it up and down. I didn't have to think. I could dream about the weekend, imagine what I was going to spend my money on, which LP I was going to buy . . . You can live in your own little world.'

Taj – for the old cats

CHARTS

Week	Chart	Title	Artist
	US45	Bad Girls	*Donna Summer*
	USLP	Bad Girls	*Donna Summer*
	UK45	I Don't Like Mondays	*Boomtown Rats*
	UKLP	The Best Disco Album In The World	*Various*
WEEK 2	US45	Bad Girls	*Donna Summer*
	USLP	Get The Knack	*The Knack*
	UK45	I Don't Like Mondays	*Boomtown Rats*
	UKLP	The Best Disco Album In The World	*Various*
WEEK 3	US45	Good Times	*Chic*
	USLP	Get The Knack	*The Knack*
	UK45	I Don't Like Mondays	*Boomtown Rats*
	UKLP	The Best Disco Album In The World	*Various*
WEEK 4	US45	My Sharona	*The Knack*
	USLP	Get The Knack	*The Knack*
	UK45	I Don't Like Mondays	*Boomtown Rats*
	UKLP	Discovery	*Electric Light Orchestra*

STAR QUOTE

TAJ MAHAL

'You get off-days when you think: "I've been banging this out for 20 years and what does it amount to?" But the quality of life is where it's at. That's why I enjoy covering old blues tunes – hoping to send those old cats six or eight thousand dollars.'

CHARTS

Chart	Title	Artist
US45	My Sharona	*The Knack*
USLP	Get The Knack	*The Knack*
UK45	We Don't Talk Anymore	*Cliff Richard*
UKLP	The Best Disco Album In The World	*Various*
WEEK 2		
US45	My Sharona	*The Knack*
USLP	Get The Knack	*The Knack*
UK45	We Don't Talk Anymore	*Cliff Richard*
UKLP	Discovery	*Electric Light Orchestra*
WEEK 3		
US45	My Sharona	*The Knack*
USLP	In Through The Out Door	*Led Zeppelin*
UK45	We Don't Talk Anymore	*Cliff Richard*
UKLP	Discovery	*Electric Light Orchestra*
WEEK 4		
US45	My Sharona	*The Knack*
USLP	In Through The Out Door	*Led Zeppelin*
UK45	Cars	*Gary Numan*
UKLP	Discovery	*Electric Light Orchestra*
WEEK 5		
US45	My Sharona	*The Knack*
USLP	In Through The Out Door	*Led Zeppelin*
UK45	Cars	*Gary Numan*
UKLP	Rock'n'Roll Juvenile	*Cliff Richard*

VAN MORRISON

'I reckon that anything that anybody wants to know about Van Morrison they'll find out in my records.'

THE SPECIALS – 2-TONE RUDE BOYS

Rude boys out of Coventry, England, The Specials are a curious mixture of old and new. Their musical inspiration comes originally from the Jamaican ska and rock-steady styles of the Sixties and they include covers of Prince Buster, The Skatalites, The Maytals and The Pioneers in their set.

But there's also a bunch of songs written by keyboard player Jerry Dammers with a contemporary intelligence all of their own. Like 'Gangsters', the biggest-selling independent single of the year on their own 2-Tone label, 'It's Up To You', 'Stupid Marriage', and the new single, 'Too Much Too Young'.

The Specials look smart

'Ska is just somewhere to start,' says Dammers. 'It's dead simple, but there's so many variations you can make out of it.'

But it's not just the music. 'The clothes are almost as important,' states singer Terry Hall. 'We're not a mod band or a skinhead band. The rude boy thing is a real mixture.'

Rude boy? 'He's a rebel that don't go around causing unnecessary trouble,' says co-singer Neville 'Judge Roughneck' Staples. 'He enjoys himself and dresses nice. And he's cool. If he goes around kicking people, then he's no rudie.'

THE GRAPEVINE

- **Bruce Springsteen, Jackson Browne, The Doobie Brothers, Bonnie Raitt, James Taylor and Carly Simon have played a five-night series of 'No Nukes' shows at Madison Square Gardens.**
- **The Clash, Country Joe, Peter Tosh, Robert Fripp and Canned Heat play the Second Annual Tribal Stomp at Monterey.**
- **Jimmy McCulloch, guitarist with Thunderclap Newman and Wings, has died in London from 'undetermined causes' aged 26.**

REGATTA DE BLANC

Brought to you by the same team that made 'Outlandos D'Amour', The Police have realized the potential of their second album in contrast to the first which nobody really understood.

As a result, the trio's distinctive style – Sting's reggae voice, Stewart Copeland's dub rhythms and Andy Summers' stripped down guitar – are reinforced as an investment for the future.

Their brilliance is too erratic to survive over an album's worth of songs but it confirms The Police as a great pop singles band as 'Message In A Bottle' and 'Walking On The Moon' clearly demonstrate. For this The Police are dependent on Sting's singer/songwriter/hitmaker image, his charismatic dry, strained voice and his skill in concocting 'original' melodies and hooklines – 'original' because the origins are buried too deeply in people's subconscious to identify.

DISCO CRUSADERS

Currently topping the US disco and jazz charts with their 'Street Life' single and album, The Crusaders are veterans of thirty albums and eight solo efforts. They were The Jazz Crusaders until the beginning of the Seventies, when they grew out of their Texan jazz roots and into the growing funk movement.

They've had an awesome studio reputation for years and have worked with The Rolling Stones, Steely Dan, Joni Mitchell, Marvin Gaye, Diana Ross, The Jackson Five, Barry White, Sarah Vaughan and Buddy Miles.

But their own progress has been hampered by the lack of a permanent singer. Which is by choice, not by accident.

Instead, they pick and choose, and the girl who's been lucky enough to be at the microphone as they suddenly tap into the disco market is Randy Crawford. The combination is the classiest thing you can dance to.

Randy Crawford stirs up disco fever, courtesy of the Crusaders

THE CLASH TAKE THE FIFTH

After a short dip in the spring, The Clash are back for their first major tour of America. Called the Take The Fifth Tour, it's as much of a crusade as a tour.

'I want to reach the kid in high school,' says Joe Strummer. 'The one with the Kansas and Kiss albums in his bedroom. I feel he should have a dose of us.'

Paradoxically, it's a quest that The Clash can never fulfil without destroying the purpose of the crusade. 'If all we achieve is someone wanting my autograph, then we've gone wrong,' admits Strummer.

Commercial success would be another problem. 'If we were just going to be another Stones or a Who, it would be a bit of a bore. That's why we're going to try and turn left where we should have turned right.'

The confusion that surrounds The Clash is certainly helping them make a few left turns. There is confusion over management, which means that conflicting advice is being given to each member of the band. And their record company is being cautious. Tour subsidies are hard to come by.

The uncertainties and distractions are causing frustrations, but the positive aspect is that the essence of The Clash is not set and sealed. There is nothing certain about The Clash. Nothing comfortable.

And that includes the reaction of the American public they've come to find.

THE GRAPEVINE

- ***The Rose*, starring Bette Midler as a James Joplin-like rock singer, has opened, in Los Angeles.**
- **Madison Square Gardens has had an eventful month: Jethro Tull's Ian Anderson was hit in the eye by a rose thrown by a fan, 15 people were arrested for mugging at an Earth Wind & Fire concert, but Elton John played eight nights without incident.**

BLONDIE EAT THE BEAT

Blondie rode in on the crest of the new wave, and now they're riding the crest of the discowave, courtesy of their 'Parallel Lines' album and the monstrously successful 'Heart Of Glass' single – a perfect merger of pop and the disco beat.

And to judge from Debbie Harry's comments, it seems the new wave has learnt nothing from the old when it comes to avoiding the perils of the rock'n 'roll business. The band are still counting the cost of extricating themselves from less than satisfactory label and management deals.

'People playing stupid little games . . . Yuck! It really disturbs me. It's horrible when you actually see it happen. For me, the only good thing about all of this is going into the studio, because you're isolated and surrounded by all this electricity and all you have to think about is what you're doing.

'The next best thing is the hour or so you're on stage in front of an audience. Take it from me, the rest of it sucks,' says Debbie vehemently.

She's not over-enamoured at her sex-symbol image either: 'In America they put girls in two categories. Either you're a sweet clean-cut girl or a real nasty bitch. And I know which one they've figured me out to be.'

Blondie's new album is 'Eat To The Beat', and although guitarist Chris Stein admits that there isn't another 'Heart Of Glass' to send the disco crowd crazy, he's convinced that it's their best album to date.

STAR QUOTE

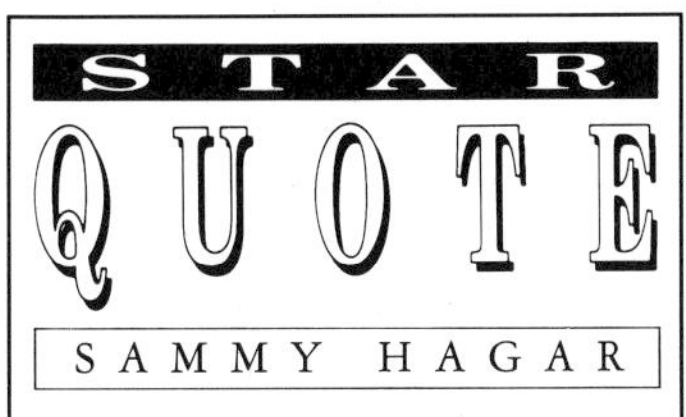

SAMMY HAGAR

'I don't want to be a fake star y'know. I wanna legitimately be the baddest mother up there.'

CHARTS

US45	Sad Eyes *Robert John*
USLP	In Through The Out Door *Led Zeppelin*
UK45	Message In A Bottle *Police*
UKLP	The Pleasure Principle *Gary Numan*
WEEK 2	
US45	Don't Stop 'til You Get Enough *Michael Jackson*
USLP	In Through The Out Door *Led Zeppelin*
UK45	Message In A Bottle *Police*
UKLP	The Pleasure Principle *Gary Numan*
WEEK 3	
US45	Rise *Herb Alpert*
USLP	In Through The Out Door *Led Zeppelin*
UK45	Video Killed The Radio Star *Buggles*
UKLP	Regatta De Blanc *Police*
WEEK 4	
US45	Rise *Herb Alpert*
USLP	In Through The Out Door *Led Zeppelin*
UK45	Video Killed The Radio Star *Buggles*
UKLP	Regatta De Blanc *Police*

Big bad Sammy Hagar

NOVEMBER

FROM BABYLON TO HARLEM

'Tell me Bob, why are you playing the Apollo Theater in Harlem? Is there any significance in that?' asks the elegant black lady from the TV station.

'Well, Marcus Garvey was there,' begins Bob Marley before launching into an unintelligible diatribe that ends with an abrupt 'Rastafari!' at the camera crew. The lady looks baffled.

Later, one of The Wailers' entourage explains it more simply: 'The Apollo is an important part of our black heritage. There isn't a single major black star who hasn't played there at one point – from Bessie Smith and Billy Holiday to all the soul stars. Bob had to play there, to put him in that tradition for people to understand.'

Bob Marley is carrying the message of reggae to the soul of black America. The slower, more considered pace of his latest album, 'Survival', allows him to concentrate on the lyrics and connect with his audience.

He uses three stage backdrops to reinforce the message: the Ethiopian flag, a portrait of Emperor Selassie, and a collage of Marcus Garvey and other black freedom fighters.

Harlem gets the message.

Bob Marley carrying his heritage

CHARTS

US45	Pop Muzik *M*
USLP	In Through The Out Door *Led Zeppelin*
UK45	One Day At A Time *Lena Martell*
UKLP	Regatta De Blanc *Police*
WEEK 2	
US45	Heartache Tonight *Eagles*
USLP	The Long Run *Eagles*
UK45	You're In Love With A Beautiful Woman *Dr Hook*
UKLP	Regatta De Blanc *Police*
WEEK 3	
US45	Still *Commodores*
USLP	The Long Run *Eagles*
UK45	You're In Love With A Beautiful Woman *Dr Hook*
UKLP	Regatta De Blanc *Police*
WEEK 4	
US45	No More Tears (Enough Is Enough) *Barbra Streisand & Donna Summer*
USLP	The Long Run *Eagles*
UK45	You're In Love With A Beautiful Woman *Dr Hook*
UKLP	Greatest Hits *Rod Stewart*

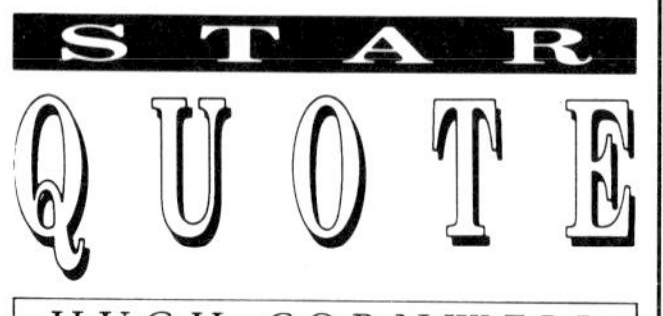

HUGH CORNWELL

of The Stranglers

'We're never going to use a producer again. They are just shitty little parasites. All they're good for is telling jokes. And we know better jokes than any of 'em.'

Shalamar crack the Solar system

DISCO BUSINESS

Solar stands for Sound Of Los Angeles Records, an independent disco label set up by writers/producers Dick Griffey and Leon Sylvers, who sell their product with hefty dollops of Californian 'sincerity' and business acumen.

'You gotta understand that disco is a positive music, it's not gloomy. You won't hear a sad disco song. People want positive music,' they say.

They may be selling it like soap powder, but Solar has some of the best disco music of the moment coming from acts like Shalamar, Carrie Lucas, Dynasty and The Whispers.

Most of the young acts have an almost religious attitude to the music business. 'I want to become one of those all-round entertainers known for giving his all to show business,' gushes Jeffrey Daniel of Shalamar.

But Scotty of The Whispers believes that marketing is sometimes winning out over the music. 'Blacks in this business are running scared. I hear the young blacks saying that you've gotta bend to the companies, and it's deplorable.

'But it's gonna come, ain't no getting away from that.'

THE LAST BRICK?

Is 'The Wall' the last brick in Pink Floyd's own towering edifice? Having constructed their own wall around themselves, this double album finds them rather shocked by the realization of this fact – that rock and roll is not the autonomous wonderland they had assumed it to be.

It's a seemingly fatalistic piece of work, a monument of self-centred pessimism. Its 'point' is everywhere and nowhere. Roger Waters' lyrics, set in stark relief against their targets, sink into dogged depths of self-expression and social concern – 'Hey teacher, leave those kids alone'.

'The Wall' is the rock musician's equivalent of the tired executive's toy, a gleaming, frivolous gadget that serves to occupy midspace. It's misplaced boredom with graphics by Gerald Scarfe.

THE GRAPEVINE

- **Bob Dylan was booed by San Francisco fans at the start of his 'Slow Train Coming' Tour.**
- **Chuck Berry released from prison after two months of his four-month sentence.**
- **Marianne Faithful has been arrested for possession of marijuana in Norway.**
- **Anita Pallenberg has been cleared of murder charges over the death of Scott Cantrell at her house.**

WALKING ON THE CHARTS

Suddenly The Police are the latest teenybop sensation in the UK. After a lengthy struggle for any kind of recognition, the band have hit paydirt with two singles from their 'Regatta De Blanc' album.

'Message In A Bottle' made No. 2 in August, and its successor, 'Walking On The Moon', has stormed to No. 1 to coincide with the band's 10th tour of the year – a dozen-date shindig that's produced mass hysteria at every stop.

'I never thought we'd get that kind of teenage audience,' grins guitarist Andy Summers. 'But we haven't compromised at all. Some of our music is definitely not teenage-oriented, but I don't mind. You get a tremendous amount of enthusiasm with kids of that age.'

Sting: original moonwalker

Sting is the object of most of this pubescent adulation. 'To a lot of people, teenyboppers are a sub-species not even to be entertained. I don't agree. If you can transcend the screaming, you can take a generation with you into something else. It's a real challenge.'

The tour climaxed with two shows in London on the same night – the seated Hammersmith Odeon and the standing-only Hammersmith Palais – with the band travelling between the two in an armoured personnel carrier.

And they still had enough energy to slot in a charity show afterwards.

THE GRAPEVINE

■ The Who, Paul McCartney, Elvis Costello, The Clash, The Pretenders and The Specials have played benefit gigs for the people of Kampuchea.

■ The Eagles, Linda Ronstadt and Chicago have staged a benefit for the presidential campaign of Linda's boyfriend, Governor Jerry Brown.

■ The Clash have won their battle with CBS to sell their album, 'London Calling,' at a reduced price, by taking lower royalties.

Talking Heads: if the cap fits

HEADS DOWN NO NONSENSE FEAR OF MUSIC

Talking Heads' 'Fear Of Music' is not an easy listening album. It has a disquieting tonal quality, some bizarre conceits and unappealing song titles like 'Life During Wartime', 'Animals', 'Air', 'Paper' and 'Mind'.

But the album has been nestling in the lower reaches of the US Top 30 and provided the band with the bridgehead they need to reach a mass audience.

'The first two albums used up all the songs I had, so I had to compose a whole new set,' says David Byrne.

Musically, Talking Heads are reaping the fruits of their collaboration with Eno on their second album. Not surprisingly, he's co-produced the new one, too.

Lyrically, Byrne is honing his stark, conversational style. 'It's not so much what is said as how it's put across. I can't stand all those unnecessary embellishments, the idea of lyrics as poetry that demands reams of verses, all of them superfluous or just pointless.'

ELEVEN FANS KILLED AT WHO GIG

The Who's comeback tour of America has been struck by tragedy in Cincinatti.

Thousands of fans arrived early for their Riverfront Coliseum gig to grab the best seats. But only two doors were opened to let them in, and in the ensuing crush 11 fans were trampled to death and 20 more taken to hospital.

The Who played unaware of the disaster, because police feared a riot if the show was cancelled. But afterwards they were in a state of emotional turmoil.

Roger Daltrey: 'If it had happened on stage – if just one person had been killed because of us – I would have been on the first plane back home and never played another gig in my life.

CHARTS

US45	No More Tears (Enough Is Enough) *Barbra Streisand & Donna Summer*
USLP	The Long Run *Eagles*
UK45	You're In Love With A Beautiful Woman *Dr Hook*
UKLP	Greatest Hits, Vol.2 *Abba*
	WEEK 2
US45	Babe *Styx*
USLP	The Long Run *Eagles*
UK45	Walking On The Moon *Police*
UKLP	Greatest Hits, Vol.2 *Abba*
	WEEK 3
US45	Babe *Styx*
USLP	The Long Run *Eagles*
UK45	Another Brick In The Wall *Pink Floyd*
UKLP	Greatest Hits, Vol.2 *Abba*
	WEEK 4
US45	Escape *Rupert Holmes*
USLP	The Long Run *Eagles*
UK45	Another Brick In The Wall *Pink Floyd*
UKLP	Greatest Hits, Vol.2 *Abba*
	WEEK 5
US45	Escape *Rupert Holmes*
USLP	The Long Run *Eagles*
UK45	Another Brick In The Wall *Pink Floyd*
UKLP	Greatest Hits, Vol.2 *Abba*

STAR QUOTE

JOE JACKSON

'You know, I looked at myself in the mirror this morning and I just laughed.'

Joe 'Pretty Boy' Jackson

The DAMNED

the PiSTols' JohNny Rotten

PUNK PISTOLS PULVERISE POP

By 1975, a new generation of British teenagers began to reject the current chart fodder, preferring the uninhibited attitudes of people like Patti Smith, The New York Dolls and Iggy Pop to the seamless success of groups like The Eagles.

Malcolm McLaren, who ran a shop in London's trendy Kings Road, recognized this trend and decided to try to manage a group which involved a kid who worked in the shop on Saturdays and some regular customers who were always hanging around the place. McLaren had got the music biz bug from managing the New York Dolls in that group's death throes, and after noting that the most interesting band from New York at the time was Television, led by two kids who had renamed themselves Tom Verlaine and Richard Hell, and played with little regard for the state-of-the-art perfection of Boston, Pink Floyd or the other "dinosaurs".

Into this self-satisfied status quo charged The Sex Pistols, (a name guaranteed to annoy), a quartet fronted by a surly youth who clearly was neither able to sing nor interested in learning; Johnny Rotten was well-named – a sinister figure screaming abuse at an audience of his own contemporaries, who were lapping it up!

It wasn't long before British record labels sensed potential profits, and eventually McLaren signed them to Britain's oldest company EMI. Their first single, 'Anarchy In The UK', crashed into the Top 50 of the UK chart at the end of 1976.

It all started to go wrong (or maybe right?) when the group appeared on an early evening TV show and were interviewed by a reporter who made little secret of how repugnant he found the Pistols and encouraged them to swear at him. British newspapers continued to report on every move the group made, and EMI, under pressure from its establishment shareholders, paid them off and withdrew the hit from the nation's stores.

By mid-March, 1977, the Pistols – now featuring a new bass player known as Sid Vicious – had signed a new recording contract with A&M Records on tables set up outside Buckingham Palace to draw attention to the fact that their first A&M single would be 'God Save The Queen'.

Before the single was properly released, A&M had paid off McLaren, who was again free to milk the record industry and the media for all he could. Finally, Richard Branson's Virgin label released the single in the same week as Britain celebrated its monarch's Silver Jubilee. The NME listed it as being number one, but other charts – including the one used by BBC Radio One, the national pop network – did not grant it the chart-topping accolade.

In November, 1977, came the album, 'Never Mind The Bollocks', which topped all the UK LP charts.

The Pistols' next moves were a shambolic US tour, during which Rotten left the group, and production of a feature movie which was threatened by his departure. In an act of apparent desperation, McLaren contrived to involve an escaped English convict named Ronnie Biggs, who was exiled in Brazil, and 'The Great Rock & Roll Swindle' finally limped out.

A decade later, Rotten has reverted to his real name, John Lydon, and leads an idiosyncratic combo known as Public Image Limited (PIL), while Sid Vicious died of a heroin overdose while out on parole, accused of murdering his girl friend, Nancy Spungen.

Not all the punks faded away, however. Some, like The Clash, belatedly convinced the US that there was something in their music, while The Damned split up and reformed regularly.

The most successful punk acts were the Americans Blondie, fronted by the eye-catching Deborah Harry, The Ramones and Talking Heads. In exactly the same way as The Stones had reminded America of its own music by refining it and sending it back, so the USA eventually profited more from punk than the UK.

UK Punks 1977

the Clash

the Sex Pistols

Blondie's Debbie Harry

Sid'n'Nancy

THE 1980's

Twenty five years old as the 1980s began, but still wonderfully immature, rock music would spend much of the decade ahead celebrating its past rather than building for its future.

A series of crazes enjoyed brief acclaim – 2 Tone, with racially integrated groups like The Specials, the commercial finale of punk with The Jam, polished post-punk as purveyed by The Police, New Romanticism (aka dressing up and dancing the night away) which spawned Duran Duran, Spandau Ballet and Culture Club, Antmania (as in Adam & The Ants).

They all came from Britain, and for several months during the second quarter of the decade, these acts and others like The Human League and Wham!, helped Britannia rule the waves of the Atlantic, although with less domination than 20 years earlier.

The first major tragedy came just before the end of 1980 when John Lennon, always the ex-Beatle with the most progressive outlook, was murdered only weeks after ending a self-imposed five year exile from the action. It may not be totally coincidental that survivors among rock's royalty not only took self-protective measures, but also started to become far less egotistical and introverted.

Bob Geldof will forever be admired for his charitable work in organising Band Aid, which consisted of dozens of British stars who recorded a charity single in an attempt to save lives in drought-stricken Africa. And later, when he organised Live Aid – which also involved numerous American stars – popular music's controlling force (the major record labels) briefly relaxed its iron grip on the destiny of the artists in whom it had invested millions.

Geldof's major achievement was to convince the music industry that it could make charitable gestures without risking financial ruin. When huge international stars like Michael Jackson, Bruce Springsteen, Paul McCartney, Mick Jagger and David Bowie lent their support, even lawyers and accountants could see the advantages – not just in allowing their stars to take part, but more importantly, in making sure those clients *weren't* excluded, lest it should adversely reflect on their commercial future.

Phil Collins, erstwhile drummer with Genesis, became a huge star and his appearances at Live Aid on both sides of the Atlantic on the same day certainly did his profile no harm.

Charity events starring heroes from the previous 20 years – like Eric Clapton playing alongside contemporary giants Dire Straits – benefitted causes like The Prince's Trust, mobile events aimed at raising political and ecological awareness (like the Nelson Mandela concert) were huge attractions, and many waning careers were revived.

Perhaps these events served to divert media attention from potential new discoveries for, as the 1990s dawned, the world's biggest stars – Dire Straits, Prince, Madonna, Michael Jackson, Bruce Springsteen, Paul McCartney, The Rolling Stones and all the rest – were not eager kids with something to prove, but multi-millionaires whose fervent wish might be that public taste should remain precisely where it was until the end of the century.

1 New Kids On The Block
2 Madonna
3 Michael Jackson
4 Bono of U2

1

2

3

4

JAM STICK IT TO THE CRITICS

The Jam swept the board in the *New Musical Express* readers' poll, indicating they are clearly the band Most Likely To in the Eighties. With wins in the Group, Guitarist, Bassist, Drummer, not to mention Best Writer (Paul Weller) and Best Album ('Setting Sons') sections, they are clearly on the crest of the new wave.

'I'm really pleased,' confessed an unusually ebullient Weller. 'But let's hope that now we've swept out those bands like Led Zeppelin, that the poll winners keep on changing. It's good if they keep on changing every year, as long as they're being replaced by something better – or at least equally good.'

Despite these suitably humble sentiments, the group's achievement is certainly notable. 'Best Drummer' Rick Buckler and 'Best Bassist' Bruce Foxton are looking forward to The Jam's next attempt to break America (their fourth U.S. tour in three years), starting next month.

But Weller is adamant it's no sell-out on their UK fans: 'There's no way I'd sacrifice our following over here. I think we've been accepted over there, but it's like we're just another good rock band from England. We want to be more than that.'

As to the future: 'There's a lot more we can do, but it's obviously a question of time. I think we've achieved a lot more than the bands who romanticize about their aims and aspirations. I just get on with it.'

One look at these unprecedented poll results shows the effect of doing just that.

THE LAST ELVIS INTERVIEW?

It's over two years since The King died – yet one of the most revealing interviews ever has only just been released.

The interview included the information that Colonel Tom Parker used to employ professional screamers . . . including a girl to put her hand down his trousers!

PRETENDERS FIND BRASS IN POCKET

With their third single, 'Brass In Pocket', at the top of the UK charts and their first, eponymous album in at No. 3 with a bullet, there's every reason for Ohio-born Pretenders singer Chrissie Hynde to crack a smile. Yet the one-time NME writer only sees it as the onset of responsibility.

'I didn't want to be a responsible adult,' she complains. 'There's always something to do: TV interviews, photos, rehearsals, recording! We're always busy . . .'

The bad news is that things are going to get even busier for the four piece, completed by James Honeyman-Scott (guitar), Pete Farndon (bass) and Martin Chambers (drums), all of whom were scrabbling to make any kind of musical living just months ago.

Honeyman-Scott in particular is grateful for their new star status. 'Staying in nice hotels makes it a lot easier when you're 25 dates into a tour and you're edgy and very tired.'

Chrissie Hynde: not responsible

CHARTS

- US45 Please Don't Go – *K.C. & The Sunshine Band*
- USLP On The Radio (Greatest Hits) – *Donna Summer*
- UK45 Another Brick In The Wall – *Pink Floyd*
- UKLP Greatest Hits, Vol.2 – *Abba*

WEEK 2

- US45 Rock With You – *Michael Jackson*
- USLP Greatest – *Bee Gees*
- UK45 Another Brick In The Wall – *Pink Floyd*
- UKLP Greatest Hits – *Rod Stewart*

WEEK 3

- US45 Rock With You – *Michael Jackson*
- USLP The Wall – *Pink Floyd*
- UK45 Brass In Pocket – *Pretenders*
- UKLP Greatest Hits, Vol.2 – *Abba*

WEEK 4

- US45 Rock With You – *Michael Jackson*
- USLP The Wall – *Pink Floyd*
- UK45 Brass In Pocket – *Pretenders*
- UKLP Regatta De Blanc – *Police*

STAR QUOTE

JIM KERR

of Simple Minds

'Our main aim must be to take off live so that we can make enough money to be totally independent and self-supporting, so that when it comes to being dropped (by their record label) we should have a good following and some money.'

THE GRAPEVINE

- **U2 played a half-empty London's Moonlight Club, where NME's reviewer could see their 'obvious commercial potential'.**
- **British soul stylists Dexy's Midnight Runners have released their first single, 'Dance Stance'.**
- **Elvis Costello has returned on a new label, his own F-Beat.**
- **The Clash are using the other Elvis to advertise their new LP, 'London Calling', with a cover suspiciously similar to Presley's first long-player.**

U2

RUDE BOYS MEET UNCLE SAM

'This is our first gig in America,' deadpans The Specials singer Terry Hall. 'And we just can't say how pleased you must be to have us here . . .'

New York's first taste of the ska revival that's taken The Specials to the top of the UK pop world was decidedly strange. With their 'Too Much Too Young' EP at No. 1 in the chart at home, the band are playing to a new audience which, for the most part, hasn't heard of them. 'Will The Specials break America or will America break The Specials?' muses guitarist Roddy Radiation.

He needn't have worried. Once the seven-man group hit New Orleans, jet lag long-gone, the joint was rocking.

PRIEST HELD HOSTAGE!

Judas Priest's hopes of having a new album in the shops to coincide with next month's British tour have almost disappeared . . . with the record's master tapes!

The band spent all January recording in the South of France – but the heist happened when the tapes were flown to New York for mixing.

A ransom note was received demanding $100,000 – and although the New York City police department advised them not to pay, the tapes have since been retrieved after an undisclosed sum changed hands.

CHARTS

US45	Rock With You – *Michael Jackson*
USLP	The Wall – *Pink Floyd*
UK45	My Girl – *Madness*
UKLP	Pretenders – *Pretenders*
WEEK 2	
US45	Rock With You – *Michael Jackson*
USLP	The Wall – *Pink Floyd*
UK45	The Special AKA Live (EP) – *Specials*
UKLP	Pretenders – *Pretenders*
WEEK 3	
US45	Do That To Me One More Time – *Captain & Tennille*
USLP	The Wall – *Pink Floyd*
UK45	Coward Of The County – *Kenny Rogers*
UKLP	Pretenders – *Pretenders*
WEEK 4	
US45	Crazy Little Thing Called Love – *Queen*
USLP	The Wall – *Pink Floyd*
UK45	Coward Of The County – *Kenny Rogers*
UKLP	The Last Dance – *Various*

FAB MACCA COMES HOME

Paul McCartney returned from an unexpected ten-day spell in a Japanese jail for possession of marijuana, still unrepentant about his 'crime'. 'The older generation make marijuana out to be some kind of terrible thing,' he declared, adding 'We're all on drugs – cigarettes, whisky and wild women!'

McCartney's brother Mike isn't surprised 'our Paul' has survived the experience unscathed. 'Paul is a very resilient person, and I would imagine that he stood up to the ordeal pretty well,' he said.

Someone seemingly less well-disposed towards the man who unwittingly caused the Wings tour cancellation is right-hand man Denny Laine. He's opted to resume his solo career, his first releases on single and LP pointedly entitled 'Japanese Tears'.

AC/DC TRAGEDY AS SCOTT DIES

Fans of Australia's top rockers AC/DC have been stunned by the news of lead singer Bon Scott's death. Reports suggest that Scott, 33, had been drinking with a friend who left him in the back seat of a car parked in South London to sober up.

His friend returned later on the morning of February 20 and found him still unconscious, but he was dead on arrival at hospital. Though shocked, AC/DC have already vowed to continue.

THE GRAPEVINE

- **Ginger Baker's latest attempt at a comeback has been damned by critics; the former Cream drummer returned with new band Energy, but his London Marquee date has been greeted with the headline 'Ginger Dead?'**
- **Progressive trio Emerson Lake & Palmer have finally disbanded after an 11-year career in which they sold over 25 million LPs and won 25 gold and five platinum albums.**

Emerson, Lake and Palmer

BREAKING BIG: HEAVY METAL'S NEW WAVE

Saxon, new wave northmen brandishing their heavy metal

With the tax-exile status of supergroups like Led Zeppelin and Deep Purple making live gigs a rarity, a new grass-roots movement known as the New Wave of British Heavy Metal (or NWOBHM to abbreviationists) has brought the fans flocking back to the clubs.

Most of the action stems from the north of England, with groups like Saxon and Def Leppard flying the flag.

'We weren't going to play new wave just to get on the bandwagon,' says singer Joe Elliott – and Leppard's rise from supporting AC/DC to headline status and a contract with Phonogram proves he's got a point: 'Heavy metal's back – with a vengeance, and in London, Samson and Iron Maiden are leading the pack.'

CHARTS

US45	Crazy Little Thing Called Love *Queen*
USLP	The Wall *Pink Floyd*
UK45	Atomic *Blondie*
UKLP	The Last Dance *Various*
WEEK 2	
US45	Crazy Little Thing Called Love *Queen*
USLP	The Wall *Pink Floyd*
UK45	Atomic *Blondie*
UKLP	The Last Dance *Various*
WEEK 3	
US45	Crazy Little Thing Called Love *Queen*
USLP	The Wall *Pink Floyd*
UK45	Atomic *Blondie*
UKLP	String Of Hits *Shadows*
WEEK 4	
US45	Another Brick In The Wall Part Two *Pink Floyd*
USLP	The Wall *Pink Floyd*
UK45	Together We Are Beautiful *Fern Kinney*
UKLP	Tears And Laughter *Johnny Mathis*
WEEK 5	
US45	Another Brick In The Wall Part Two *Pink Floyd*
USLP	The Wall *Pink Floyd*
UK45	Going Underground *Jam*
UKLP	Tears And Laughter *Johnny Mathis*

CLAMPDOWN CLOSES ERIC'S

Eric's, the successor to The Cavern and breeding ground for Liverpool groups like The Teardrop Explodes, Echo & The Bunnymen and Orchestral Manoeuvres, has closed.

A drug squad raid at a recent Psychedelic Furs gig has persuaded owners Roger Eagle and Pete Fulwell to shut up shop.

Despite two demonstrations in its favour, it looks as if Liverpool's second most famous venue has gone the way of the first.

THE GRAPEVINE

■ The Boomtown Rats were frustrated in their attempts to play two hometown concerts when Dublin authorities required £2 million insurance cover.

■ Fresh from creating The Sex Pistols and managing Adam & The Ants, Malcolm McLaren now plans to become a singer.

■ Accepting a Grammy for best male rock vocalist, born-again Bob Dylan stated: 'The first person I want to thank is the Lord.'

POLICE RISE IN THE EAST

March 26: Bombay, India, is a long way off the rock'n'roll map . . . the last concert there was Hawkwind, ten years ago. For three-man supergroup The Police, it's a welcome change from London, New York, Los Angeles – and with a film crew along to record the historic visit.

'We are doing this for a charity,' explains Sting. 'And we're actually promoting a few rupees for the people. We can sort of salve our conscience with that.'

Fans at the open air concert didn't care – they danced to all the favourites, the only problem being the people in the front row who objected to their view being obscured.

'It's rock'n'roll, you've got to let it happen,' explained manager Miles Copeland.

'That's cool,' laughed Sting. 'They'll know next time . . . yeah, there'll be a next time.'

PETTY CASH! TOM ROCKS BACK

After a big splash with his 1976 debut album, Tom Petty found himself in deep water when, after a successful follow-up, his record company Shelter was sold to giant MCA.

Petty believed his contract said he could leave; MCA said he couldn't.

'Being kinda stubborn, I agreed to deliver an album, but spent my own money making it,' he explained. 'Then, in the middle of recording, MCA sued me, Shelter sued me, my publishing company sued me and so did a few other people.

'It reached the stage where it was almost funny. If I sing a song do I own it?'

Half a million dollars and a whole lot of hassle later, Petty's titled his third album 'Damn The Torpedoes'!

Tom Petty: lawsuit city

STRANGLERS BEAT THE RAP

Stranglers as they normally appear, with Hugh Cornwell (front centre)

The Stranglers pulled that little bit extra out of the bag at a concert to celebrate the 50th anniversary of London's Rainbow Theatre – as they had to, with guitarist/vocalist Hugh Cornwell absent in prison on drugs charges.

The show must go on, however, and – with the help of Ian Dury, Billy Idol, Toyah, Hazel O'Connor and a cast of thousands to help them out – they emerged triumphant.

'I can think of worse places to be, like in Pentonville (prison)!' growled Dury as he tore 'Peaches' to shreds, to the evident approval of a capacity crowd.

Rock'n'roll pulled together to get the men in black out of a mess – and Cornwell would surely approve.

THE GRAPEVINE

- Humble Pie have reformed, with original members Steve Marriott and Jerry Shirley joined by ex-Jeff Beck singer Bob Tench and US bassist Anthony Jones.
- Highly rated young Merseysiders Echo & The Bunnymen have released their first single, 'Rescue'.
- Sham 69 have had to scrap plans for a London climax to their current tour, with no hall willing to accommodate their rabble-rousing fans!

Sham 69: no place to play to their aroused rabble

ON THE BEACH WITH BRIAN

Brian Wilson, the reclusive Beach Boys genius, emerged from an extended period of hibernation at his Los Angeles hideaway to face New Musical Express writer Nick Kent.

Wilson's story is a sad indictment of the all-American star-making machinery. After some time away from the group with personal problems, he was reunited with brothers Dennis and Carl when 'Endless Summer' – a compilation of Sixties material – became a surprise chart-topper in 1976. The results of the reunion ('15 Big Ones', 'The MIU Album') were unsatisfactory – but in contrast, the just-released 'Keeping The Summer Alive' is their best for ten years.

Kent travelled more in hope than expectation, finding Wilson in consultation with his personal psychiatrist when he arrived to interview him. Wilson's relationship with Dr Eugene Landy is at the heart of the mystery . . . and even Wilson himself seems unable to reconcile his current reclusive state with the need of a pop star to promote his music.

This is a sample of his reflections: 'Ego can be dangerous. It can destroy you, that drive. It almost killed me – almost drove me insane . . . I don't want to make a solo record. I don't see myself making music as strong as the old stuff ever again . . . The group is all I've got.'

'Brian's back!' insisted the record company hype. Well, almost . . .

STAR QUOTE

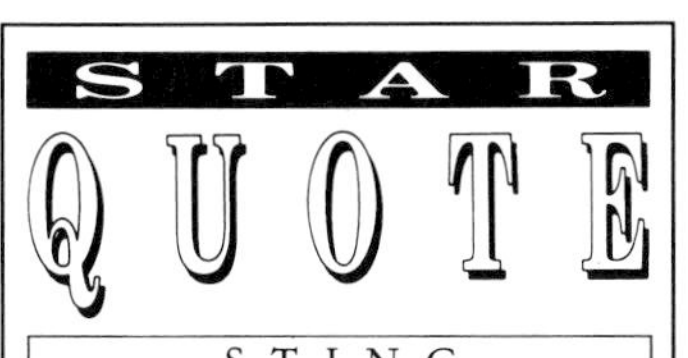

STING

'The constant challenge is, "What next?" In the space of two albums we've sold more records than people do in ten . . . that is a kind of Elvis Presley dream . . . we shouldn't be able to make this amount of money.'

CHARTS

US45	Another Brick In The Wall Part Two / *Pink Floyd*
USLP	The Wall / *Pink Floyd*
UK45	Going Underground / *Jam*
UKLP	Greatest Hits / *Rose Royce*
WEEK 2	
US45	Another Brick In The Wall Part Two / *Pink Floyd*
USLP	The Wall / *Pink Floyd*
UK45	Dance Yourself Dizzy / *Liquid Gold*
UKLP	Duke / *Genesis*
WEEK 3	
US45	Call Me / *Blondie*
USLP	The Wall / *Pink Floyd*
UK45	Dance Yourself Dizzy / *Liquid Gold*
UKLP	Greatest Hits / *Rose Royce*
WEEK 4	
US45	Call Me / *Blondie*
USLP	The Wall / *Pink Floyd*
UK45	Call Me / *Blondie*
UKLP	Greatest Hits / *Rose Royce*

CRASH! ROSE ROYCE HIT TROUBLE . . .

With their 'Greatest Hits' album at the top of the NME charts, US soul band Rose Royce have had to cancel their proposed British tour due to the departure of 'Rose' herself – singer Gwen Dickey.

'I'd made my decision some time before the tour was scheduled,' she revealed amidst the confusion. 'Because of my disagreement over the handling of the group's business. Not participating was a hard decision but under the circumstances – lack of rehearsal time and inadequate tour management – I feel the tour would have had a damaging effect on my solo career.'

YES – IT'S BUGGLES!

Horn (left) and Downes – new Yes men arrive to revitalize the band

Progressive pioneers Yes have reshaped their line-up out of all recognition with the departure of founder member Jon Anderson (vocals) and Rick Wakeman (keyboards).

Their replacements are Trevor Horn and Geoff Downes, better known as pop one-hit wonders Buggles, who topped the UK chart late last year with 'Video Killed The Radio Star'.

The newcomers are already working with Chris Squire, Alan White and Steve Howe on a new album, 'Drama', to be released later this year. Squire claims their recruitment makes Yes 'a revitalized and regenerated band'. The departing Wakeman and Anderson already have solo projects in hand.

THE GRAPEVINE

- The Pirates, Sixties rockers with Johnny Kidd at the helm, have finally disbanded. After reforming as a three-piece in 1977, they became darlings of the new-wave crowd but lost their record deal after two albums.
- Ultravox have signed with Chrysalis, having replaced original lead singer John Foxx with Midge Ure.

(l to r) Cross, Currie, Ure, Cann – Ultravox

BLONDES HAVE MOR(ODER) HITS!

Blondie monopolized the top spot in America for the entire month of May, thanks to a collaboration with German disco wizard Giorgio Moroder, the man behind Donna Summer's success.

'Call Me' has the extra boost of appearing in the film *American Gigolo* and is the band's second US No. 1 single after 1979's 'Heart Of Glass'.

JOY DIVISION GRIEF AT SINGER SUICIDE

Ian Curtis, the lead singer with Manchester quartet Joy Division, committed suicide today on the eve of their first US tour. He was 23.

Ian's lyrics for such songs as 'Love Will Tear Us Apart' helped the band to sign for Factory Records and become confirmed independent label favourites.

Though devastated, it seems likely the band will continue under another name.

Joy Division – tour off after tragedy but band likely to continue under new name

ELVIS DRIVES ON

Elvis Costello intends to fulfil a European tour booked for this month despite the absence of keyboard player Steve Nieve, recently involved in a Los Angeles car crash in which a female passenger was killed.

The Rumour's Martin Belmont has been recruited to fill the gap – a move that is sure to change the group's sound since Belmont is a guitarist!

A pre-crash Nieve contributed vocals to a solo Attractions 45, 'Single Girl', which may or may not foretell a parting of the ways between Costello and band.

Official line: 'There's no question of a break.'

CHARTS

US45	Call Me	*Blondie*
USLP	Against The Wind	*Bob Seger & The Silver Bullet Band*
UK45	Call Me	*Blondie*
UKLP	Greatest Hits	*Rose Royce*
WEEK 2		
US45	Call Me	*Blondie*
USLP	Against The Wind	*Bob Seger & The Silver Bullet Band*
UK45	Geno	*Dexy's Midnight Runners*
UKLP	The Magic Of Boney M	*Boney M*
WEEK 3		
US45	Call Me	*Blondie*
USLP	Against The Wind	*Bob Seger & The Silver Bullet Band*
UK45	What's Another Year	*Johnny Logan*
UKLP	The Magic Of Boney M	*Boney M*
WEEK 4		
US45	Call Me	*Blondie*
USLP	Against The Wind	*Bob Seger & The Silver Bullet Band*
UK45	What's Another Year	*Johnny Logan*
UKLP	The Magic Of Boney M	*Boney M*
WEEK 5		
US45	Funkytown	*Lipps Inc.*
USLP	Against The Wind	*Bob Seger & The Silver Bullet Band*
UK45	No Doubt About it	*Hot Chocolate*
UKLP	The Magic Of Boney M	*Boney M*

STRANGLERS IN TROUBLE AGAIN!

(l to r) Jean-Jacques Burnel, Dave Greenfield, Jet Black, Hugh Cornwell – Stranglers back inside (some of them)

A mere 12 weeks since guitarist Hugh Cornwell was released from a British jail, he and fellow Stranglers Jean Jacques Burnel and Jet Black find themselves languishing in a French one.

Their show at Nice University fell victim to a series of power cuts, after the third of which the group walked off stage. A student's tape of the concert was claimed to contain the words 'You will not be reimbursed . . . and if you don't like it you can smash everything' – a charge the band emphatically denies.

Taciturn keyboard player Dave Greenfield seemingly remains free only because he did not speak on stage.

CHARTS

US45	Funkytown *Lipps Inc.*
USLP	Against The Wind *Bob Seger & The Silver Bullet Band*
UK45	Theme From M.A.S.H. *Mash*
UKLP	McCartney 2 *Paul McCartney*
WEEK 2	
US45	Funkytown *Lipps Inc.*
USLP	Glass Houses *Billy Joel*
UK45	Theme From M.A.S.H. *Mash*
UKLP	McCartney 2 *Paul McCartney*
WEEK 3	
US45	Funkytown *Lipps Inc.*
USLP	Glass Houses *Billy Joel*
UK45	Funkytown *Lipps Inc.*
UKLP	Flesh And Blood *Roxy Music*
WEEK 4	
US45	Coming Up (Live At Glasgow) *Paul McCartney & Wings*
USLP	Glass Houses *Billy Joel*
UK45	Crying *Don McLean*
UKLP	Peter Gabriel (3) *Peter Gabriel*

THE GRAPEVINE

- **The Beach Boys' Brian Wilson took the stage in Britain for the first time in 15 years at London's Wembley Arena on 6 June. The verdict – he made out OK.**
- **The Marshall Tucker Band is to continue despite the death of bassist Tommy Caldwell after a car accident. Franklin Wilkie is replacing him on a temporary basis while the band fulfil engagements.**

Brian's really back!

SWINDLE HITS THE CINEMA

Even more finally than Sid Vicious's demise, the cinema release of *The Great Rock'n'Roll Swindle* brings to a close the Sex Pistols saga. The credits betray an unlikely set of characters – McLaren is the Embezzler, Steve Jones the Crook, Paul Cook the Tea Maker, Johnny Rotten the Collaborator and Sid Vicious the Gimmick.

The perspective is not so much the music but the swindle, McLaren in his own words turning 'chaos into cash'. Ian Penman sees it as McLaren's attempt to 'bring back under his sway all those things that are in fact different from him by virtue of their difference in reality from the way they should be to suit his world-view.'

Things have certainly changed . . . John Lydon is no longer Rotten, Sid is dead and Cook and Jones are languishing in semi-obscurity. If the Sex Pistols represented a musical revolution, you'd hardly know it. With a Top Five comprising the TV theme from MASH, disco from Lipps Inc and Hot Chocolate, folky Don McLean and old wavers Roxy Music, it seems a fitting time for the film to appear . . . if it had to appear at all.

McLean – Top Five

MICK JAGGER

'What I can't believe is that rock'n'roll still exists in the form that it does; even with all its permutations, its entertainment value is very limited. Everything going on I've seen at least twice before.'

BAN THE BAND! SOUTH AFRICA FOIL FLOYD

Pink Floyd's 'Another Brick In The Wall Pt.2', and 'The Wall' LP from which it is taken, have been declared 'prejudicial to South Africa' and banned.

Since its February release, the song has become an anthem for black children boycotting school as part of an organized protest against the apartheid regime. The single has already sold 30,000 copies – an almost unheard of number in the South African market.

Among albums to receive the same treatment are Marianne Faithfull's 'Broken English' and Frank Zappa's 'New York'.

THE GREAT HOME TAPING SWINDLE?

Malcolm McLaren is at it again! The Sex Pistols' svengali has pulled off a scoop by signing his new group Bow Wow Wow to EMI, the self-same company that sacked The Pistols!

They're fronted by a 14-year-old Burmese schoolgirl; they feature three-quarters of the old Adam & The Ants line-up; and their first single 'C-30, C-60, C-90 Go' is already causing a storm with lyrics that encourage the (illegal) act of home taping.

An EMI spokesman said only that 'The song is an everyday story of 1980s folk – as members of the BPI [British Phonographic Industry] we endorse their attitude to home taping.' Since that attitude includes legal action against companies whose ads seem to encourage it (e.g. tape recorder manufacturers), a BPI *vs* EMI suit isn't beyond the bounds of possibility.

Bow Wow Wow: advocating home taping? Whatever, it sounds like another McLaren scam to embarrass the music biz establishment, and make a packet in the process

THE GRAPEVINE

- **Rumour is that Police bassist/vocalist/heart-throb Sting is in line to play a baddie in the next James Bond film, *For Your Eyes Only*.**
- **Keith Godchaux, Grateful Dead keyboard player, died on July 22 in a Californian car crash.**
- **Debbie Harry is filming an episode of *The Muppet Show* in London while the rest of Blondie consider their future.**

ALL CHANGE ON THE ROCK JOB MARKET

In an amazing month for personnel changes, ex-Sex Pistols Steve Jones and Paul Cook announced the formation of The Professionals, while old wavers Jethro Tull said farewell to John Evan, Barrie Barlow and David Palmer.

Meanwhile, Siouxsie & The Banshees continued to hunt for a new guitarist to replace John McKay. Latest betting favours Magazine's John McGeoch.

DEXY'S BLANK THE PRESS

Dexy's: speak no evil? That seems to be the message as they bring in their own brand of press censorship

'From now on, Dexy's Midnight Runners will not take part in any interviews with the *New Musical Express, Melody Maker, Sounds, Record Mirror* or any other music papers . . .'

With full-page ads in the publications they profess to detest, Dexy's Midnight Runners announced an embargo on any publicity other than their own. 'We won't compromise by talking to the dishonest, hippy press,' they claim, adding that they will use advertising space to 'accommodate our own essays, which will state our point of view'.

CHARTS

US45	Coming Up (Live At Glasgow) *Paul McCartney & Wings*
USLP	Glass Houses *Billy Joel*
UK45	Crying *Don McLean*
UKLP	Flesh And Blood *Roxy Music*
WEEK 2	
US45	Coming Up (Live At Glasgow) *Paul McCartney & Wings*
USLP	Glass Houses *Billy Joel*
UK45	Xanadu *Olivia Newton John & ELO*
UKLP	Flesh And Blood *Roxy Music*
WEEK 3	
US45	It's Still Rock & Roll To Me *Billy Joel*
USLP	Glass Houses *Billy Joel*
UK45	Xanadu *Olivia Newton-John & ELO*
UKLP	Emotional Rescue *Rolling Stones*
WEEK 4	
US45	It's Still Rock & Roll To Me *Billy Joel*
USLP	Emotional Rescue *Rolling Stones*
UK45	Xanadu *Olivia Newton-John & ELO*
UKLP	The Game *Queen*

LENNON LIVES!

After five years of very private parenthood, John Lennon has re-emerged in the public eye in the tax haven of Bermuda, where he's holidaying with wife Yoko Ono.

Asked his opinion of Paul McCartney's recent recordings, he showed little enthusiasm, adding 'I like his new one though', gaily chorusing a line or two of 'Coming Up'. As for his own plans, he added only, 'You can't do it if it's not there.'

Back in England, fellow Fab One George Harrison unveiled his latest book, entitled *I Me Mine*, selling at the exorbitant price of £148. NME verdict – 'Curiously empty – don't bother waiting for the paperback.'

PETER GABRIEL

'I wanted to sit at the piano for hours and hours and just scream or whatever it was, just a release of emotions, which was one of the main attractions of rock music for me . . .'

AUGUST

1980

BEAT BAN THE BOMB

The Beat are Britain's brightest, breeziest survivors from the 2-Tone ska explosion that brought us The Specials, The Selecter and Madness. Yet they've chosen to link their lighthearted music with a serious cause by donating all the profits from their new single 'Best Friend/Stand Down Margaret' to the Campaign for Nuclear Disarmament.

Singer Dave Wakeling explains: 'I don't think doing a single for CND is going to stop nuclear reactors poisoning everybody, but in a way we feel spiteful – alright, f*** the world up, but we are going to let you know that we know you're doing it.'

The Birmingham sextet believe their single, already on the way by becoming a Number 22 hit, will bring the anti-nuclear cause the sum of £25,000 – 'Enough to get an office and pay three people's wages'.

According to Wakeling's singing partner Ranking Roger, 'You've got to think of the future. It's important, it's our life, it's our children and grandchildren.' Who said pop groups were here today and gone tomorrow?

PINK FLOYD – CEMENTING A SUCCESS

(l to r) Waters, Wright, Gilmour, Mason

Pink Floyd built their Wall at London's Earls Court in front of a 15,000 crowd. Previously seen at the Los Angeles Arena and New York's Nassau Coliseum, the show was presented by Messrs Waters, Wright, Mason and Gilmour with each having an instrumental double.

The wall, built by an army of roadies, was the real star of the show, along with a crashing aeroplane, a flying pig, fireworks and dry ice.

Stray Cats (l to r) Phantom, Setzer, Rockers

HEAVY METAL RULES OK

August 16: The Monsters of Rock festival is to be held at the Castle Donington racetrack in Derbyshire, England, featuring Deep Purple spin-off group Ritchie Blackmore's Rainbow.

Less than a week later comes the Reading Festival, an annual event once known as the National Jazz and Blues Festival. This year it is to be dominated by the heavy rock of UFO, Def Leppard, Iron Maiden, Whitesnake and Wishbone Ash.

Leppard: for Donington

YANKEE CATS ROCK THE JOINT

Rockabilly is back in the shape of The Stray Cats, three young New Yorkers who've brought the music of Elvis, Eddie Cochran and Buddy Knox back to the dancehalls of Britain.

With no following in their native America, Brain Setzer, Lee Rocker and Slim Jim Phantom came to London to find fame and fortune, bringing their minimal stage gear as luggage.

They've Dave Edmunds as one of their biggest fans, and he's to produce them for an as yet unnamed record company.

One verdict on their knockout performance at London's Thomas A'Becket pub? 'Cool for cats . . . really gone!'

CHARTS

US45	Magic *Olivia Newton-John*
USLP	Emotional Rescue *Rolling Stones*
UK45	Use It Up And Wear It Out *Odyssey*
UKLP	Xanadu *Soundtrack*
WEEK 2	
US45	Magic *Olivia Newton-John*
USLP	Emotional Rescue *Rolling Stones*
UK45	Upside Down *Diana Ross*
UKLP	Xanadu *Soundtrack*
WEEK 3	
US45	Magic *Olivia Newton-John*
USLP	Emotional Rescue *Rolling STones*
UK45	The Winner Takes It All *Abba*
UKLP	Flesh And Blood *Roxy Music*
WEEK 4	
US45	Magic *Olivia Newton-John*
USLP	Emotional Rescue *Rolling Stones*
UK45	The Winner Takes It All *Abba*
UKLP	Flesh And Blood *Roxy Music*
WEEK 5	
US45	Sailing *Christopher Cross*
USLP	Emotional Rescue *Rolling Stones*
UK45	Ashes To Ashes *David Bowie*
UKLP	Give Me The Night *George Benson*

THE GRAPEVINE

- **Things are buzzing for the Q-Tips, a soul revival outfit fronted by singer Paul Young. The group's eponymous debut Lp appeared this month.**
- **A one-off Move reunion is to take place this month when Roy Wood and Carl Wayne of the hitmaking Sixties group play together at the English resort of Margate in a charity performance.**

SEPTEMBER

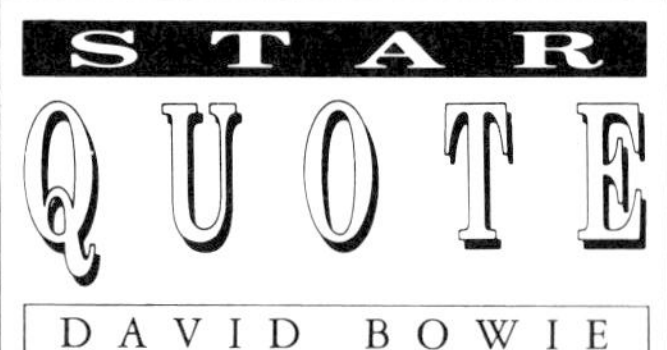

DAVID BOWIE

'What I write is so inadequate . . . the worst joke God can play is to make you an artist, but only a mediocre artist.'

BONZO'S LAST BASH THE END FOR ZEP?

The sudden death of drummer John Bonham on September 25 has cancelled Led Zeppelin's US tour, scheduled to open on October 16, and thrown the whole future of the group into jeopardy.

The drummer was in residence at Jimmy Page's Windsor mansion, where the group were rehearsing for the tour. The cause of death was thought to be Bonham's choking on his own vomit, but this could not be confirmed by the post-mortem.

John 'Bonzo' Bonham

GELDOF RATS ON LABEL

The Boomtown Rats are involved in a financial dispute with Phonogram, their record label – and leader Bob Geldof is refusing to hand over the tapes of their latest album until it's settled!

'We own the tapes,' he growled, 'And they won't get them until we're happy.' A spokesman for The Rats said, 'There are problems over royalties and accounting which could lead to litigation if they're not resolved. It's no Mickey Mouse stuff.'

The album, the fourth the band have recorded, will be known as 'Mondo Bongo'.

TOOTS' REGGAE RECORD-BREAKER

What's the fastest album ever made? Ask Toots Hibbert of reggae group Toots & The Maytals, whose concert at London's Hammersmith Palais on September 29 was available to the man (and woman) in the street less than 24 hours later!

With a mobile recording studio parked outside, producer Alex Adkin mixed the tapes in three hours, ready for cutting at The Sound Clinic. 'Lacquers' were rushed to the Midlands for processing and pressing to be in the shops in Coventry (the Maytals' next port of call) on the afternoon of the 30th.

THE GRAPEVINE

■ Dire Straits plan to augment their line-up with several musicians after the departure of Mark Knopfler's brother David for a writing/production career.

■ The British chart system seems likely to be revamped after *World In Action's* allegation of chart hyping led to the resignation of British Phonographic Industry chairman John Fruin, whose own WEA company stands accused of malpractice.

DANCIN' DI GETS CHIC-Y

Chic's reputation as dance floor darlings took another giant step this month when Diana Ross, the once and future queen of Motown, announced the recruitment of Bernard Edwards and Nile Rodgers to produce and play on her new album, 'Diana'.

But rumour has it that Ross has edited the tapes to their disadvantage – a charge she admits with a cheery, 'I proceeded to make the record more Diana Ross-ish and far less Chic-ish.'

Nevertheless, she added, 'I loved working with Nile, and I'd love to work with him again.'

With her single 'Upside Down' holding firm at the top of the US charts, any talk of a crisis is clearly premature, to say the least.

CHARTS

US45	Upside Down *Diana Ross*
USLP	Emotional Rescue *Rolling Stones*
UK45	Ashes To Ashes *David Bowie*
UKLP	Give Me The Night *George Benson*
WEEK 2	
US45	Upside Down *Diana Ross*
USLP	Hold Out *Jackson Browne*
UK45	Start *Jam*
UKLP	Flesh And Blood *Roxy Music*
WEEK 3	
US45	Upside Down *Diana Ross*
USLP	The Game *Queen*
UK45	One Day I'll Fly Away *Randy Crawford*
UKLP	Signing Off *UB40*
WEEK 4	
US45	Upside Down *Diana Ross*
USLP	The Game *Queen*
UK45	One Day I'll Fly Away *Randy Crawford*
UKLP	Telekon *Gary Numan*

BOWIE ON BROADWAY

David Bowie's packing them in on Broadway with his portrayal of John Merrick, the so-called 'Elephant Man'. Crowds round the stage door have been so great that theatre officials, in shades of Elvis Presley, have taken to announcing that 'Mr Bowie has left the theatre'.

Co-star Patricia Elliot pronounces Bowie 'real dynamite . . . Heaven . . . and so good in the role', but confessed she'd missed her opposite number's 'rock music trip' due to nine years' studying yoga!

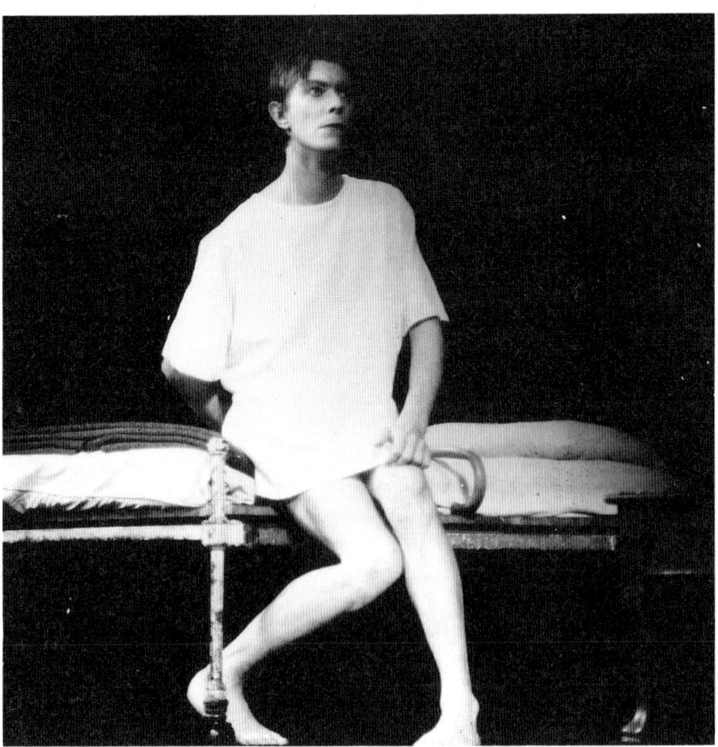

Bowie as Merrick: "Dynamite"

SURF PUNKS HIT LONDON

The Dead Kennedys hit London's Music Machine with the alternative side of the California Dream. By the time they played 'Holiday In Cambodia', they were sharing the stage with at least 20 whirling invaders, but when two microphones were ripped from their sockets, the music had to stop.

As NME commented, 'They've provided punk with a breath of fresh air.'

The Dead Kennedys with singer Jello Biafra (in headlock)

I FOUGHT THE LAW . . .

One-time punk rockers John Lydon and Joe Strummer have both fallen foul of the law – just when you thought they'd both grown up.

The former Mr Rotten finds himself on bail facing three months' jail after being convicted of assaulting two men in Dublin. And he'd only come along for the ride with little brother Jimmy's group, The 4″ Be 2″s. . .

Meanwhile Joe Strummer 'clash'ed with police outside London's King's Cross Railway Station. A handgun and 'certain substances' were allegedly found in his possession.

Also back in England, The Specials' Jerry Dammers has been charged with a breach of the peace after a concert in Cambridge.

CHARTS

Chart	Title	Artist
US45	Another One Bites The Dust	*Queen*
USLP	The Game	*Queen*
UK45	Don't Stand So Close To Me	*Police*
UKLP	Never For Ever	*Kate Bush*
WEEK 2		
US45	Another One Bites The Dust	*Queen*
USLP	The Game	*Queen*
UK45	Don't Stand So Close To Me	*Police*
UKLP	Scary Monsters	*David Bowie*
WEEK 3		
US45	Another One Bites The Dust	*Queen*
USLP	The Game	*Queen*
UK45	Don't Stand so Close To Me	*Police*
UKLP	Zenyatta Mondatta	*Police*
WEEK 4		
US45	Woman In Love	*Barbra Streisand*
USLP	Guilty	*Barbra Streisand*
UK45	Don't Stand so Close To Me	*Police*
UKLP	Zenyatta Mondatta	*Police*

KINKY BUSINESS FOR RAY

Ray Davies, leader of The Kinks, was arrested in Portland, Oregon – the latest stop in the legendary rockers' US tour.

During several unpleasant hours of questioning, he gathered he was being accused of hiring limousines, borrowing money and checking in and out of hotels . . . all without paying!

It transpired this dirty work perpetrated by a lookalike, living it up in San Francisco under Ray's name.

THE GRAPEVINE

- **John Lennon's long-awaited comeback took a step closer when Geffen Records announced his signing, along with Elton John (the latter for the US only).**
- **Elvis Costello appeared on a tribute to Joe Loss, the bandleader who employed his father Ross McManus. 'I used to sit there with my lemonade . . . that's where I stole all the things I'm doing now!' he jokingly confessed.**

TYRANNOSAURUS TOOK DIES

Steve Peregrine Took, the percussionist who, with Marc Bolan, made up the original Tyrannosaurus Rex, was found dead in his West London flat on October 27, aged just 31.

Took – real name Steve Porter – played on the group's first three albums before being replaced by Mickey Finn. His subsequent career produced no vinyl, though he formed many bands in the Ladbroke Grove area of London.

A friend's verdict: 'He just never made a serious attempt to get himself together.'

TALKING THREADS – GREET THE NEW ROMANTICS

Dressing up for money – Spandau Ballet

They wear kilts and velvet breeches; they're into dance music, exclusive nightclubs and parties; they want to make statements with the clothes they wear; oh, and they play music too.

They're Spandau Ballet, first of the New Romantics. The look, they admit, is everything – but they deny accusations of elitism. 'We were on the dole for six months and we still had style,' protests bass player Martin Kemp – with brother Gary the instrumental core of Spandau.

No less a style master than Bryan Ferry has called their first single 'To Cut A Long Story Short', 'very uplifting'. Is this the future of post-punk pop? Watch this space . . .

THE GRAPEVINE

- Ex-King Crimson leader Robert Fripp has been playing the clubs and colleges with his League of Gentlemen, an old-meets-new-wave ensemble featuring ex-XTC keyboardsman Barry Andrews.
- Kinks guitarist Dave Davies releases his first solo album – 13 years after charting with the solo 'Death Of A Clown'. His excuse? 'I'm a lazy bastard,' he explained.

HEADS THEY WIN – BYRNE'S BIG BAND IN TOWN

Last time Talking Heads appeared in London eleven months ago, they were all but played out. They'd been touring eight months a year for the previous four years and were in desperate need of a break.

During their layoff, chief Head David Byrne went walkabout with group producer Brian Eno, Chris Frantz and Tina Weymouth went to Jamaica, Jerry Harrison played with The Escalators and produced demos for Nona Hendryx. Now they've reformed, bringing other musicians with them to form an extended band.

Byrne's experiences in Africa are very much a part of the new sound of the album 'Remain In Light' – though others are quick to emphasize the group effort. 'It was the collective influences that created the result. No-one could put an individual claim on it,' explains Tina Weymouth.

Byrne elaborates: 'The music, when it comes together right, has a feeling like a trance of some sort. That's exactly what happens in traditional African and other Third World music. It's something that isn't sought-after in most pop music – we're aiming at something different.'

The result is spectacular – and, with the assistance of P-Funk keyboardist Bernie Worrell, vocalist Dollette McDonald and bassist Busta Cherry Jones, is set to make the Heads' long-awaited commercial breakthrough.

Head globetrotter David Byrne, assimilating Worldwide influences

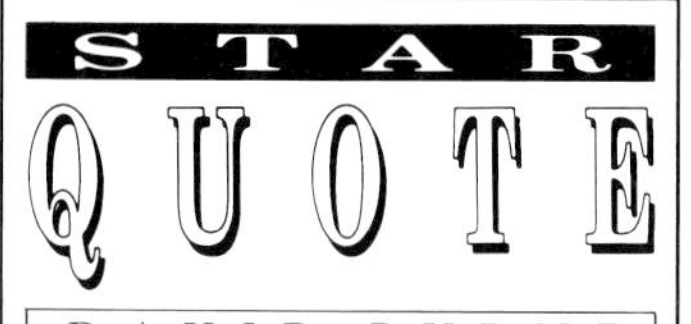

STAR QUOTE

DAVID BYRNE

'This music, when it really comes together right, has a transcendent feeling like a trance of some sort. That's exactly what happens in traditional African music and other Third World music . . . it isn't sought after in most pop.'

CHARTS

	US45	USLP	UK45	UKLP
	Woman In Love *Barbra Streisand*	Guilty *Barbra Streisand*	Woman In Love *Barbra Streisand*	Zenyatta Mondatta *Police*
WEEK 2	Woman In Love *Barbra Streisand*	The River *Bruce Springsteen*	Woman In Love *Barbra Streisand*	Zenyatta Mondatta *Police*
WEEK 3	Lady *Kenny Rogers*	The River *Bruce Springsteen*	Woman In Love *Barbra Streisand*	Hotter Than July *Stevie Wonder*
WEEK 4	Lady *Kenny Rogers*	The River *Bruce Springsteen*	The Tide Is High *Blondie*	Hotter Than July *Stevie Wonder*
WEEK 5	Lady *Kenny Rogers*	The River *Bruce Springsteen*	The Tide Is High *Blondie*	Super Trouper *Abba*

DECEMBER

LENNON MURDERED – WORLD MOURNS

John Lennon pictured recently in New York with his wife, Yoko Ono. They had just finished his first record in five years, subsequently released just days before his death

December 8: John Lennon, ex-Beatle and working class hero to millions, gave his last autograph today – to the man who killed him.

Lennon signed the proffered copy of 'Double Fantasy', his acclaimed comeback LP of 1980 and Mark David Chapman, a 25-year-old Hawaiian, repaid the compliment with five .38 calibre bullets to John's upper body, severing a major artery. His victim was dead on arrival at New York's Roosevelt Hospital.

Crowds gathered to pay their respects, both outside the Dakota apartment building on New York's Upper West Side, and in Lennon's native Liverpool. His wife Yoko Ono, who was at his side at the time of the shooting, requested a ten-minute silent vigil be held on December 14, in which millions more fans could participate and mourn the untimely death of a major rock talent.

STAR QUOTE

ADAM ANT

'Rock is very squalid, impersonal and degrading; an egocentric circus full of people who aren't really human beings . . . there's a new generation of groups who won't take part in it and we're all basing ourselves on something very early . . . more realistic.'

IDOL GOSSIP . . . IT'S GEN X!

Billy Idol and Tony James have reactivated their group Generation X, replacing Derwood Andrews (guitar) and Mark Laff (drums) with James Stevenson (ex-Chelsea) and former Clash man Terry Chimes.

They've also thrown out half their name, and will henceforth be known simply as Gen X. But one man reportedly left in the cold is ex-Pistol Steve Jones, now of The Professionals, who, says James, 'just wasn't right. He can only play one style really.'

Generation game changes

CHARTS

US45	Lady – *Kenny Rogers*
USLP	Guilty – *Barbra Streisand*
UK45	Super Trouper – *Abba*
UKLP	Super Trouper – *Abba*
WEEK 2	
US45	Lady – *Kenny Rogers*
USLP	Greatest Hits – *Kenny Rogers*
UK45	Super Trouper – *Abba*
UKLP	Super Trouper – *Abba*
WEEK 3	
US45	Lady – *Kenny Rogers*
USLP	Greatest Hits – *Kenny Rogers*
UK45	Stop The Cavalry – *Jona Lewie*
UKLP	Super Trouper – *Abba*
WEEK 4	
US45	(Just Like) Starting Over – *John Lennon*
USLP	Double Fantasy – *John Lennon & Yoko Ono*
UK45	Stop The Cavalry – *Jona Lewie*
UKLP	Super Trouper – *Appa*

THE GRAPEVINE

- **U2 played support to Talking Heads in London's Hammersmith Palais – a step up from their London debut a couple of years ago, witnessed by half a dozen onlookers!**
- **In a surprise move, electro-pop pioneers The Human League have split into two, with musical brains Ian Marsh and Martyn Ware quitting to form a production and writing group called the British Electric Foundation.**

JONA SCORES – WITH A STIFF!

Abba's stranglehold at the top of the British charts has been ended by that most seasonal of novelties – the Christmas hit. But compared with the Scandinavian supergroup, little is known about Jona Lewie, the man behind the 'Stop The Cavalry' single on Stiff Records.

Real name John Lewis, he was the brains behind the obscure Brett Marvin & The Thunderbolts and one-hit wonders Terry Dactyl & The Dinosaurs (a UK No. 2 hit in 1972 with 'Seaside Shuffle').

KENNY ROGERS DISCOUNTS THE ZEROES

'Greatest Hits' albums often mark a turning point in an artist's career when they change musical tack. But despite his own collection topping the US album chart (and a single, 'Lady', heading the singles listings), country superstar Kenny Rogers has had an even greater change of mind.

After a year in which he earned a reported 10 million dollars, making him the world's highest-earning musician, Kenny feels like taking it easy in 1981. 'It's worth taking a drop in pay to have some time to myself,' he says.

LENNON – A CONSPIRACY?

Yoko and John, photographed not long before the ex-Beatle's assassination

John Lennon was murdered because US service chiefs were 'worried he would use his powerful influence in the cause of peace'. So claims an organization calling itself the Alternative Information Service, in a three-page communiqué.

The AIS even go so far as to claim Chapman worked for 'a top secret intelligence unit' which has a department in Hawaii associated with the Pearl Harbor military complex.

However much is truth, and however much is fantasy, the fact remains that 80 per cent of the US population believe the deaths of the Kennedy brothers and Martin Luther King are part of the same conspiracy.

As the man said, 'Imagine . . .'

A SPECIAL KIND OF JUSTICE

The Specials in action, but not the legal kind!

Justice of a kind for The Specials and mercy for The Stranglers, both in court this month for alleged misdemeanours committed in 1980. The Specials' singer Terry Hall and organist Jerry Dammers were upset to leave Cambridge Magistrates Court with a £1,000 fine for inciting audience violence during a Midsummer Common concert last October.

'The evidence just didn't stand up,' claimed Dammers. 'The 3,000 people at the concert will see the injustice of this. We detest violence at our concerts.'

The Stranglers emerge a lot happier after *their* clash with the law in Nice, France, last spring when all except keyboard player Dave Greenfield were locked up for allegedly inciting a riot. They have been informed that no further action will be taken, although drummer Jet Black promises his version in a book sardonically titled *Much Ado About Nothing*, due for publication next month.

BRUCE BLASTS BOOTLEGGER!

Bruce Springsteen, probably the most bootlegged rock star of all time, was awarded over two million dollars in damages this month in a LA court.

Andrea Ellen Waters, also known as Vickie Vinyl, was found guilty of infringing 43 separate copyrights, each of which were deemed to be worth 50,000 dollars, by trading in unauthorized concert recordings.

26,000 copies of the Springsteen boots 'Fire', 'Piece De Resistance', 'E-Ticket' and 'Winterland '78' were among the tons of bootleg albums found and later destroyed at her warehouse by the FBI.

Finding the money is the least of the worries for Waters/Vinyl, whose stock included nine different Stones albums, plus everything from Presley to The Sex Pistols, The Beatles to Jimi Hendrix. She faces another case alleging 17 more copyright counts.

Court order – Springsteen

STEVE WINWOOD

'It's quite true rock'n'roll could become redundant at any time. In lots of ways it is meaningless, but there'll always be a music that over-rides fashion. R&R may be dead, but the enjoyment of a certain arrangement of sounds isn't going to go away.'

CHARTS

US45 (Just Like) Starting Over – *John Lennon*
USLP Double Fantasy – *John Lennon & Yoko Ono*
UK45 (Just Like) Starting Over – *John Lennon*
UKLP Super Trouper – *Abba*

WEEK 2

US45 (Just Like) Starting Over – *John Lennon*
USLP Double Fantasy – *John Lennon & Yoko Ono*
UK45 Imagine – *John Lennon*
UKLP Double Fantasy – *John Lennon & Yoko Ono*

WEEK 3

US45 (Just Like) Starting Over – *John Lennon*
USLP Double Fantasy – *John Lennon & Yoko Ono*
UK45 Imagine – *John Lennon*
UKLP Super Trouper – *Abba*

WEEK 4

US45 (Just Like) Starting Over – *John Lennon*
USLP Double Fantasy – *John Lennon & Yoko Ono*
UK45 Imagine – *John Lennon*
UKLP Double Fantasy – *John Lennon & Yoko Ono*

WEEK 5

US45 The Tide Is High – *Blondie*
USLP Double Fantasy – *John Lennon & Yoko Ono*
UK45 Imagine – *John Lennon*
UKLP Kings Of The Wild Frontier – *Adam & The Ants*

THE GRAPEVINE

- **Has that arresting personality Grace Jones joined The Police? Not *quite* – but she has got to sing with Sting with her latest release, the single 'Demolition Man' written especially for her.**
- **Elvis Costello is to produce the next Squeeze album, 'East Side Story', now that the two share a manager in Jake Riviera.**

THE OTHER ELVIS CHARMS US

Two years after hitting a backlash for his 'racist' dismissal of Ray Charles in a drunken argument, Elvis Costello returned to charm America with a series of gigs and interviews.

TV host Tom Snyder was just one of the interviewers exploring the McManus psyche. 'I'm not in the business of maturing,' Elvis protested. 'That makes you sound like cheese or something.' He confessed an antagonism born of the fact that 'When we first came here, we might as well have landed on Mars the way people looked at us. So we were trying to put it over forcefully, that was the way we felt at the time. We're trying to present a wider picture now.'

And he regards his American audience with a lot less suspicion. Playing songs from the most recent 'Get Happy' album, he threw in a few surprises – Bob Marley's jamming in the middle of the encore, 'Watching the Detectives' – and left everybody wanting more.

CLOCK RUNS OUT FOR HALEY

Bill Haley, who died in Texas on 9 February age 55, ensured his place in rock'n'roll history on just one day back in 1954. On April 12 that year, he cut 'Shake Rattle And Roll' and 'Rock Around The Clock', two tracks which will always be remembered as launching rock'n'roll on an unsuspecting world.

The latter is currently still the third best-selling single of all time with sales of 16 million, a total boosted to nearer 25 million by over 140 cover versions. Haley's death, of a heart attack, comes just over a quarter of a century since 'Rock Around The Clock' first hit the top of the charts.

His 1957 British tour saw him swamped by fans on his arrival, almost ignored when he left, a result of fans switching to Elvis and younger teen idols that flourished in Haley's wake. He remained a quiet, unassuming idol. 'I'm just an ordinary guy, making a living the only way I know how,' he said of himself.

Another death in February – Mike Bloomfield, one-time Electric Flag guitarist and the man who played lead on Bob Dylan's 'Like A Rolling Stone'.

YOKO SKATES BACK

Yoko Ono has released 'Walking On Thin Ice', the track she and John Lennon had been mixing before their return to the Dakota Building that fateful evening last year.

An open letter to the *NME* explained her feelings: 'Getting this together after what happened was hard, but I knew John would not rest his mind if I hadn't. I hope you like it John. I did my best.'

BLANK TAPE WIND-UP BY ISLAND

Island Records have caused a home taping furore by introducing their new 1+1 concept – a pre-recorded cassette with a blank B-side to be used for recording and re-recording 'in the usual way'.

Other labels see this as an incitement to tape from forbidden sources. Island, however, insist the blank tape manufacturers will be the only ones to suffer: indeed, chairman Martin Davis believes the new format will benefit the industry as a whole.

'Our attitude,' he said, 'Is that the person who is buying blanks and recording music on them is very much entrenched in that habit. It is these people we are hoping to attract.' The series starts with Steve Winwood's just released 'Arc Of A Diver'.

CHARTS

US45	Celebration *Kool & The Gang*
USLP	Double Fantasy *John Lennon & Yoko Ono*
UK45	In The Air Tonight *Phil Collins*
UKLP	Kings Of The Wild Frontier *Adam & The Ants*
WEEK 2	
US45	Celebration *Kool & The Gang*
USLP	Double Fantasy *John Lennon & Yoko Ono*
UK45	In The Air Tonight *Phil Collins*
UKLP	Double Fantasy *John Lennon & Yoko Ono*
WEEK 3	
US45	9 To 5 *Dolly Parton*
USLP	Hi Infidelity *REO Speedwagon*
UK45	Vienna *Ultravox*
UKLP	Kings Of The Wild Frontier *Adam & The Ants*
WEEK 4	
US45	I Love A Rainy Night *Eddie Rabbitt*
USLP	Hi Infidelity *REO Speedwagon*
UK45	Shaddup Your Face *Joe Dolce*
UKLP	Double Fantasy *John Lennon & Yoko Ono*

THE GRAPEVINE

■ ***Motorhead*** **and** ***Girlschool*** **have joined forces to record 'The St Valentine's Day Massacre' EP, including a cover of Johnny Kidd and The Pirates' 'Please Don't Touch' and renditions of each others' stage favourites.**

■ **Secret gigs by The Jam in their home town of Woking, Surrey ended in tears with fans unconscious and one group member, Bruce Foxton, observed in an altercation with bar staff at The Cricketers pub.**

Girlschool – let their hair down after leaving the convent

Motorhead – enjoying mixed education?

VOODOO CHILE – SLIGHT RETURN?

Lizzy's Lynott (left) and Robin Trower, set to recreate the Hendrix experience on celluloid

Thin Lizzy singer Phil Lynott has been slated to play Jimi Hendrix in a Hollywood motion picture. And, according to the black Irishman, the guitar-playing of Robin Trower will be featured in the on-stage sequences.

'At the moment the script seems a bit corny – they're definitely playing up the wine women and song. However, Hendrix is one of the few musicians who's a real god to me, so if I can rewrite it and capture his subtleties and spirit a bit better I think I'll give it a go,' he said.

Lynott's band have just completed a 14-month world tour. He now plans to record new group and solo albums. He is still upset by reaction to the band's last single, 'Killer On The Loose'.

'There's no way I was trying to glorify rape,' he explains. 'The other day, I was watching Prince Andrew on the TV, and *twice* they said he's a bit of a ladykiller. Does that mean he goes around killing ladies?

'The whole idea of the song was a warning: in every town there's some nut. I thought that in the song *I'd* be the character, to get it across . . .'

CHARTS

US45	I Love A Rainy Night — *Eddie Rabbitt*
USLP	Hi Infidelity — *REO Speedwagon*
UK45	Shaddup Your Face — *Joe Dolce*
UKLP	Kings Of The Wild Frontier — *Adam & The Ants*
WEEK 2	
US45	9 To 5 — *Dolly Parton*
USLP	Hi Infidelity — *REO Speedwagon*
UK45	Jealous Guy — *Roxy Music*
UKLP	Kings Of The Wild Frontier — *Adam & The Ants*
WEEK 3	
US45	Keep On Loving You — *REO Speedwagon*
USLP	Hi Infidelity — *REO Speedwagon*
UK45	Jealous Guy — *Roxy Music*
UKLP	Kings Of The Wild Frontier — *Adam & The Ants*
WEEK 4	
US45	Rapture — *Blondie*
USLP	Hi Infidelity — *REO Speedwagon*
UK45	This Ole House — *Shakin' Stevens*
UKLP	Kings Of The Wild Frontier — *Adam & The Ants*

THE GRAPEVINE

■ **Big-name split of the month – The Buzzcocks, with twomembers already planning new projects; singer Peter Shelley will be going solo, while drummer John Maher is joining The Invisible Girls.**

■ **Comeback of the month – Led Zeppelin singer Robert Plant, who played a 90-minute blues and rock'n'roll set with backing group The Honeysuckers at Keele University in the Midlands to a select crowd of 150.**

STAR QUOTE

PHIL COLLINS

'The divorce was . . . very traumatic, but it terminated with me being able to give my songs a lyrical perspective, an emotional force that they wouldn't have possessed . . . The big difference between 'Face Value' and Genesis is the . . . autobiographical factor . . . a large personal investment.'

NUMAN DELETES HIMSELF!

Like David Bowie before him, whey-faced synthesizer wizard Gary Numan is retiring from the live music scene – and just so people get the message, he's releasing two live albums destined to become rock's quickest collectors items.

'Living Ornaments '79' was recorded during Numan's Touring Principle tour and 'Living Ornaments '80' is taken from his last outing. Neither set duplicates a song. Available separately or together in a box with a free single, they will be released and deleted after exactly one month.

Buy, buy Gary?

Looking a Numan with his blonded hair, Gary contemplates life off the road

HEADPHONE HEAVEN FOR WALKMEN

The Sony Walkman has taken the world by storm – but Human League spinoffs Heaven 17 are the first group to produce music *specifically* for it. 'Music For Stowaways' owes it title to the original name for the device – 'mixed so the sound is surrounding you instead of coming just from two directions,' they explain.

They have released the tape under their *alter ego*, The British Electric Foundation; meanwhile, their first Heaven 17 product with singer Glenn Gregory – the single 'We Don't Need This Fascist Groove Thang' – is currently causing controversy.

Lyrics like 'Reagan fascist guard' are being modified to 'Stateside cowboy guard' to get radio play, the BBC having deemed them unacceptable.

THANKS A MILLION, ELVIS!

Inspired rock archaeology has brought to light the rock'n'roll equivalent of the Holy Grail – the album by the so-called Million Dollar quartet of Elvis Presley, Carl Perkins, Johnny Cash and Jerry Lee Lewis.

Recorded in the afternoon of Tuesday, 4 December 1956, it featured the foursome – reckoned to add up to a cool million dollars' worth of talent – speeding through a selection of gospel songs and current rock'n'roll hits. Inevitably, the music's a little frayed at the edges in places, but it's fascinating listening nonetheless.

It's still unclear how these tapes got out. Carl Perkins, who was recording 'Matchbox' at the time of the session, paid for the studio time. Highlights include duets from Elvis and Jerry Lee on 'Just A Little Walk With Jesus', and 'Peace In The Valley', while Elvis himself imitates country crooners Hank Snow and Bill Monroe before claiming Pat Boone's 'Don't Forbid Me' was, in fact written for him.

Jerry Lee's 'I Walk the Lonesome Valley' and Perkins' 'I Shall Not Be Moved' wrap up a set that may live up to its title if a record company picks it up.

DEXYS DO ANOTHER RUNNER

Kevin Rowland fronts the Runners, back in a pub setting for good?

Dexys Midnight Runners, 1980 UK chart-toppers with 'Geno', have scrapped a comeback UK tour and apparently left their record company EMI, which means they can no longer count on the subsidy necessary to make touring a viable proposition.

Though manager Paul Burton told NME: 'We didn't want our last single, "Plan B", released. They went ahead against our wishes.' EMI responded by claiming it was released 'with the full knowledge, cooperation and active support of the band and their management.'

Burton claims that EMI's failure to take up a contractual option leaves Dexys free agents, and they have already recorded tracks independently with Tony Visconti with a new label in mind.

WHO MAN DEAD

Kit Lambert died from head injuries after falling down the stairs at his mother's home; he was 45. He first produced The Who on 1966's 'Substitute', producing further hits in 'Pinball Wizard', 'I Can See For Miles', 'I'm A Boy' and 'Pictures of Lily'.

He also worked with Pete Townshend on the rock opera 'Tommy', of which its composer said: 'Kit's real contribution will never be known: it wasn't production, it was far deeper.'

CHARTS

Chart	Title	Artist
US45	Rapture	*Blondie*
USLP	Paradise Theatre	*Styx*
UK45	This Ole House	*Shakin' Stevens*
UKLP	Kings Of The Wild Frontier	*Adam & The Ants*
	WEEK 2	
US45	Kiss On My List	*Daryl Hall & John Oates*
USLP	Paradise Theatre	*Styx*
UK45	This Ole House	*Shakin' Stevens*
UKLP	Kings Of The Wild Frontier	*Adams & The Ants*
	WEEK 3	
US45	Kiss On My List	*Daryl Hall & John Oates*
USLP	Hi Infidelity	*REO Speedwagon*
UK45	Making Your Mind Up	*Bucks Fizz*
UKLP	Kings Of The Wild Frontier	*Adam & The Ants*
	WEEK 4	
US45	Kiss On My List	*Daryl Hall & John Oates*
USLP	Hi Infidelity	*REO Speedwagon*
UK45	Making Your Mind Up	*Bucks Fizz*
UKLP	Kings Of The Wild Frontier	*Adam & The Ants*

THE GRAPEVINE

- **NME's April Fool's Joke of reporting that ex-Cream drummer Ginger Baker was joining John Lydon's Public Image Limited, was widely reported as fact in the UK national press.**
- **Johnny Wilder Jr, ex-leader of disco stars Heatwave, has given way to J.D. Nicholas on stage: though paralysed from a car crash, Wilder still sings, produces and writes for the group in the studio.**

Lydon – a rotten trick

Heatwave's Johnny Wilder, now leading the group from the wings

THE LION SLEEPS – REGGAE KING MARLEY DIES

Bob Marley, the man who popularized reggae worldwide, has died after a long illness. Thousands witnessed his official lying in state in Kingston, Jamaica

Seven months after being diagnosed as having cancer, Bob Marley succumbed to the disease on 11 May in Miami's Cedars of Lebanon Hospital. Record company boss Chris Blackwell, a close friend, commented: 'I can say nothing other than that it's a terrible, awful loss. Bob's career was always much larger than music – and there was much more to come.'

Unknown to many, Marley had a toe removed in the same hospital in 1977 while in exile from Jamaica after an attempt on his life. It was described then as a football accident, but the tumour was malignant. Marley played his last live dates at Madison Square Garden on 20-21 September, supporting The Commodores. A tour with Stevie Wonder had to be cancelled due to his state of health.

In a last attempt to beat the disease, he flew to Germany for radical clinic treatment, including abstinence from smoking marijuana and shaving off his dreadlocks – both anathema to a man of the Rastafarian faith.

Marley was the biggest international star reggae had ever known, popularizing the style in Britain with his breakthrough 'Live' album and 1975 hit single 'No Woman No Cry'. Other hits included 'Jamming', 'Could You Be Loved' and 'Exodus'.

1973's 'Catch A Fire' was the first reggae album made with the benefit of a 24-track studio and, with Chris Blackwell's help, Marley took the music to Europe without compromising his beliefs and principles.

His lying in state at Kingston's National Arena drew many thousands of mourners, while Jamaica issued a commemorative stamp with the legend 'The Lion Sleeps'. Marley was buried on 22 May amid spectacular and unprecedented scenes of public mourning . . . legendary to the last.

CHARTS

- US45 Morning Train (Nine To Five) – *Sheena Easton*
- USLP Hi Infidelity – *REO Speedwagon*
- UK45 Chi Mai – *Ennio Morricone*
- UKLP Kings Of The Wild Frontier – *Adam & The Ants*

WEEK 2

- US45 Morning Train (Nine To Five) – *Sheena Easton*
- USLP Paradise Theatre – *Styx*
- UK45 Stars On 45 – *Star Sound*
- UKLP Kings Of The Wild Frontier – *Adam & The Ants*

WEEK 3

- US45 Bette Davis Eyes – *Kim Carnes*
- USLP Hi Infidelity – *REO Speedwagon*
- UK45 Stand And Deliver – *Adam & The Ants*
- UKLP Kings Of The Wild Frontier – *Adam & The Ants*

WEEK 4

- US45 Bette Davis Eyes – *Kim Carnes*
- USLP Hi Infidelity – *REO Speedwagon*
- UK45 Stand And Deliver – *Adam & The Ants*
- UKLP Kings Of The Wild Frontier – *Adam & The Ants*

WEEK 5

- US45 Bette Davis Eyes – *Kim Carnes*
- USLP Hi Infidelity – *REO Speedwagon*
- UK45 Stand And Deliver – *Adam & The Ants*
- UKLP Kings Of The Wild Frontier – *Adam & The Ants*

THE GRAPEVINE

- **Linda Ronstadt presently playing Mabel in the Broadway production of Gilbert & Sullivan's opera 'Pirates Of Penzance'; a move to jazz is rumoured next.**
- **Diana Ross has finally left Motown after two decades and signed with RCA (for the US) and Capitol elsewhere; formation of her own label had been strongly rumoured.**

Diana Ross – signed with RCA

FROM PUNK TO POMP – THE CURE SELL OUT?

The three young men who comprise The Cure are poised on the threshold of breaking out from a sizeable cult to become one of Britain's top bands.

The trio, who forsook odd ditties like 'Killing an Arab' and 'Boys Don't Cry' from their first album 'Three Imaginary Boys', scored a hit single with 'A Forest', a track from their second LP '17 Seconds', and now play venues so big they hire Pink Floyd's PA.

Cure – three 'imaginary' boys

JUNE

PRINCE – HIGH PRIEST OR PERVERT?

He's American music's hottest new sex symbol. He writes songs about incest, troilism and oral sex. His latest album is called 'Dirty Mind', its half-million sales largely through word of mouth. He's Prince . . . and when he speaks the ladies listen.

His secret? He's a one-man band. 'It's easy for me to work in the studio because I have no worries or doubts about what the other musician's going to play because the other musician's almost always *me*.'

Prince (real name Prince Rogers Nelson) sees his childhood musical influences as his father, an Italian Filipino jazz-band leader, and his black mother, whom his father left when he was seven. 'That's when I first started playing music. He left the piano behind when he left us behind.' From the age of nine, his mother's porn collection held an equal fascination. 'She had a lotta interesting stuff that affected my attitude towards my sexuality.'

The state of Minnesota has only ever given the rock world Bob Dylan – until now. Behold your royal ruler . . .

CHARTS

US45	Bette Davis Eyes *Kim Carnes*
USLP	Hi Infidelity *REO Speedwagon*
UK45	Stand And Deliver *Adam & The Ants*
UKLP	Stars On 45 on 33 *Star Sound*
WEEK 2	
US45	Bette Davis Eyes *Kim Carnes*
USLP	Hi Infidelity *REO Speedwagon*
UK45	Being With You *Smokey Robinson*
UKLP	Anthem *Toyah*
WEEK 3	
US45	Stars On 45 *Starsound*
USLP	Hi Infidelity *REO Speedwagon*
UK45	Being With You *Smokey Robinson*
UKLP	Present Arms *UB40*
WEEK 4	
US45	Stars On 45 *Starsound*
USLP	Mistaken Identity *Kim Carnes*
UK45	One Day In Your Life *Michael Jackson*
UKLP	Stars On 45 On 33 *Star Sound*

THE GRAPEVINE

- **Ian Dury & The Blockheads are to celebrate next month's Royal Wedding of Prince Charles and Lady Diana Spencer with a special concert at London's Hammersmith Odeon – one of many to coincide with the event.**
- **Kirsty MacColl, daughter of folk legend Ewan, has started her own recording career with the quaintly titled 'There's A Guy Works Down The Chip Shop Swears He's Elvis'.**

Clash – fire hazards or just hard on the hearing?

DAVE MEETS THE BOSS

Bruce Springsteen's British performances this month drew more than their fair share of famous fans along with the paying punters. One was Dave Edmunds, who was introduced to the Boss backstage at London's Wembley Arena.

'I've written a song for you,' quoth the New Jersey devil to the Welsh wizard, whipping an acoustic guitar from behind his back. 'Sorry it's a bit Chuck Berryish.'

The song's called 'From Small Things Big Things Come' – watch out for it on Edmunds' next album as he prepares for life without Rockpile, who split in February.

NEW YORK FIRE FOUL-UP FOR CLASH

The Clash's assault on New York, with an eight-day residency at Times Square's Bonds International Casino, went disastrously wrong.

After the first night, the New York Fire Brigade slapped a restriction of 1,750 on the club, effectively halving their earlier capacity. The venue moved swiftly, cancelling their new week's shows to allow The Clash to fulfil commitments.

On Saturday, however, the club was closed indefinitely. A quarter of a million dollars in ticket money hung in mid air until the New York's Building Commissioner finally gave the go-ahead for the shows to continue with increased security and improved fire escape procedures.

JULY

KILLER CLOSE TO DEATH

Memphis rock'n'roll pioneer turned country superstar Jerry Lee Lewis was today said to have a 50/50 chance of survival after his second bout of abdominal surgery in the last ten days.

The 45-year-old singer was hospitalized complaining of stomach pains, and an operation for a suspected ulcer was carried out on June 30. His condition then deteriorated and another operation to remove abscesses was carried out.

A spokesman for the Memphis Methodist Hospital would say only that Jerry Lee was still 'extremely critical' three days later. Lewis's hellraising lifestyle has marked him out as the only original Sun rock'n'roller who refused to knuckle down to the music business establishment. But the deaths of two children, divorce, tax and drug problems have clearly taken their toll.

CHARTS

US45	Stars On 45	*Starsound*
USLP	Mistaken Identity	*Kim Carnes*
UK45	One Day In Your Life	*Michael Jackson*
UKLP	Present Arms	*UB40*
WEEK 2		
US45	Stars On 45	*Starsound*
USLP	Mistaken identity	*Kim Carnes*
UK45	One Day In Your Life	*Michael Jackson*
UKLP	No Sleep 'Til Hammersmith	*Motorhead*
WEEK 3		
US45	Stars On 45	*Starsound*
USLP	Mistaken Identity	*Kim Carnes*
UK45	Ghost Town	*Specials*
UKLP	No Sleep 'Til Hammersmith	*Motorhead*
WEEK 4		
US45	The One That You Love	*Air Supply*
USLP	Long Distance Voyager	*Moody Blues*
UK45	Ghost Town	*Specials*
UKLP	Love Songs	*Cliff Richard*

ROAD RUNS OUT FOR SONGSMITH CHAPIN

Harry: solo with Chic

Harry Chapin, America's foremost story-songsmith, has died in a car accident.

Chapin, 38, had built his reputation on a gruelling concert schedule, often appearing in benefit concerts for free – as he was due to when the accident happened. He enjoyed a few hits – 'Taxi', 'WOLD' (the tale of an ageing disc jockey) and 'Cat's In The Cradle', which was his sole US No. 1.

He had just signed to the Boardwalk label and recorded the well-received 'Sequel' album.

DEBS'N'STEVIE . . . SET FAIR FOR SUCCESS

July's been the month for blonde ladies of rock to go solo, with first albums outside a group environment from Blondie singer Debbie Harry and Fleetwood Mac's Stevie Nicks.

And both have recruited special friends to guest on the discs; Harry has used Chic to play and produce, while Nicks duets with Tom Petty on his 'Stop Draggin' My Heart Around' and Don Henley on 'The Highwayman'.

Nicks – solo album

LONDON'S BURNING!

A London rock venue was set ablaze on July 3 when skinhead group The 4 Skins were booked to appear in the heart of a predominantly Asian community.

Trouble flared between the right-wing skinheads and the local population, resulting in a paraffin-bomb attack destroying the Hambrough Tavern in the suburb of Southall.

THE GRAPEVINE

- **Original Police guitarist, Corsican Henri Padovani, has re-emerged at the front of a three-piece outfit, The Flying Padovanis, playing London's Moonlight Club.**
- **Ronnie Lane, once of The Faces, linked with Pirates guitarist Mick Green for a concert at London's Bridge House.**
- **The Jacksons have kicked off a 36-day American tour.**

STONES TO SPLINTER?

Rumour has it that Busta Cherry Jones, American bass player with Sharks, Talking Heads and most recently Dave Allen's replacement in The Gang Of Four, will be replacing Bill Wyman in the touring version of The Rolling Stones when they promote their best-selling 'Emotional Rescue' LP later this year.

The speculation is compounded by Wyman's current solo success in Britain and Europe with the very un-Stones-ish electro-pop single 'Je Suis Un Rockstar'.

Stones: Wyman off tour?

BELL CHIMES SOUR FOR MIKE

Mike Oldfield, the man whose 'Tubular Bells' was the first release on Virgin Records and which made Richard Branson a fortune, is sueing the label.

He claims his contract under Branson's guidance was to his detriment, and is claiming extra profits on the seven million records he's sold worldwide so far.

'We're all rather sad,' commented Branson. 'It's rather bad form issuing press releases before you issue writs . . .'

SSSH! COSTELLO GOES COUNTRY

The secret is out . . . Elvis Costello has embraced country music!

The news emerged when his entourage took over Aberdeen's Hotel Metro to film live performances of songs recorded in Nashville last month with legendary C&W producer Billy Sherrill. The venue was far from full, reflecting the secrecy surrounding this step into the unknown, though those who *were* there toted the obligatory Stetsons, fancy shirts and boots.

Costello himself dressed the part. Resplendant in red cowboy boots, lace tie and shades, he led The Attractions plus ex-Clover guitarist John McFee (who played on Costello's own LP debut, released back in 1977) on steel through a mixture of orignals and cover versions of songs by Loretta Lynn, Charlie Rich and George Jones.

The next single was announced as a cover version of Jones's 'Good Year For The Roses' – and even though his second set featured a fair sprinkling of repeats the audience warmed to him like a brother. So far, so good: now the record buying public awaits . . .

STEVIE'S BIRTHDAY WISH

Stevie Wonder's infectious 'Happy Birthday' is deservedly showing well in singles charts on both sides of the Atlantic, and seems set fair to be a much requested radio record for years to come.

But the Motown hitmaker has a message behind the melody – to make assassinated civil-rights leader Martin Luther King's birthday a public holiday in the United States. Its concert performance is always accompanied by an explanation of Wonder's wish . . . and signs are that the catchy campaign song may well help him achieve his aim.

STAR QUOTE

BOB DYLAN

'What I do is more of an immediate thing, to stand up on the stage and sing – you get it back immediately. It's not like writing a book or even making a record. No-one else does this show, not Bruce Springsteen or anyone.'

CHARTS

US45	Jessie's Girl	*Rick Springfield*
USLP	Long Distance Voyager	*Moody Blues*
UK45	Chant No.1	*Spandau Ballet*
UKLP	Love Songs	*Cliff Richard*

WEEK 2

US45	Jessie's Girl	*Rick Springfield*
USLP	Long Distance Voyager	*Moody Blues*
UK45	Green Door	*Shakin' Stevens*
UKLP	Love Songs	*Cliff Richard*

WEEK 3

US45	Endless Love	*Diana Ross & Lionel Richie*
USLP	Precious Time	*Pat Benatar*
UK45	Happy Birthday	*Stevie Wonder*
UKLP	Love Songs	*Cliff Richard*

WEEK 4

US45	Endless Love	*Diana Ross & Lionel Richie*
USLP	4	*Foreigner*
UK45	Green Door	*Shakin' Stevens*
UKLP	Time	*Electric Light Orchestra*

WEEK 5

US45	Endless Love	*Diana Ross & Lionel Richie*
USLP	4	*Foreigner*
UK45	Green Door	*Shakin' Stevens*
UKLP	Time	*Electric Light Orchestra*

Bananarama: singing to a backing tape

THE GRAPEVINE

- **Three-girl group Bananarama have made their NME debut, talking about their first single 'Aie A Mwana'; they currently perform the song live to a backing tape – the extent of their performance to date.**
- **Despite the UK No. 1 success of their eighth studio album 'Time', The Electric Light Orchestra are reportedly having trouble selling tickets for their late-year US tour.**

The Electric Light Orchestra, the Jeff Lynne project which reveals his many influences, particularly the Beatles

MEATLOAF – WORTH THE WEIGHT!

Meat makes his point

It's taken a long long time . . . but he's back! Meatloaf, the heavyweight talent from Cleveland (born Marvin Lee Aday), weighs in with his second album, 'Dead Ringer' – a mere four years since 'Bat Out Of Hell' hit the racks, sold five million worldwide and threatened to become a chart fixture.

The wait was punctuated by a solo album from songsmith/ arranger Jim Steinman, rumoured to have originated as the follow-up which Meatloaf was unable to complete, due to voice problems.

NME verdict on 'Dead Ringer': 'The record's excess is its very charm . . . perhaps'. The British public's verdict? A No. 1 chart position!

FACING THE FUTURE – YOUNG GUNS AT THE ICA

The London ICA Rock Week is traditionally the showcase for next year's chart-toppers. This year's pick of the crop couldn't have been more different.

Depeche Mode 'danceable, electric, earnest and endearing, with more poise than pose and proud to appeal to all'; Dead or Alive's Pete Burns 'looks like he's escaped from a nightmare, a shock of black hair framing a face in which glass black eyes smoulder with a manic evil'; Pigbag, who opened proceedings, 'play an hour-long set instrumental set and still retain a refreshing vitality and lots of variety while losing none of their continuity.'

Who says Inventive rock is dead?

A total of 16 bands, with The People, Black Roots, and Kaballa giving a multi-racial feel to the usually white rock-dominated bills. Place your bets now on the faces of '82 . . .

SELLING SOUL: SOFT CELL CLEAN UP

Soft Cell – singer Marc Almond and keyboardist Dave Ball – have taken their electronic soul to the top of the UK charts with their fist single, a cover version of Gloria Jones's soul classic 'Tainted Love', backed with a remaking of the Motown classic 'Where Did Our Love Go?'

First showcased on the 'Some Bizzare' (*sic*) album, along with the likes of Depeche Mode and Blancmange, they've become the first to make it to the top.

FOREVER YOUNG: NEIL ON SCREEN

After a two-year wait, Neil Young fans have acclaimed his movie *Rust Never Sleeps*. Coincidentally, Dennis Hopper's *Out of the Blue* – based on Young's song of the same name from the album that titles his film (confused? You will be!) – has also been released.

Hopper's film has been described as 'a far better celluloid realization of Young's vision of punk'. But there's no doubt that the concert-based *Rust Never Sleeps*, which is accompanied by the excellent live double LP 'Live Rust', will outgross its friendly 'rival'.

This is not Rusty Young!

CHARTS

US45	Endless Love – *Diana Ross & Lionel Richie*
USLP	Bella Donna – *Stevie Nicks*
UK45	Japanese Boy – *Aneka*
UKLP	Time – *Electric Light Orchestra*
	WEEK 2
US45	Endless Love – *Diana Ross & Lionel Richie*
USLP	Escape – *Journey*
UK45	Tainted Love – *Soft Cell*
UKLP	Time – *Electric Light Orchestra*
	WEEK 3
US45	Endless Love – *Diana Ross & Lionel Richie*
USLP	Tattoo You – *Rolling Stones*
UK45	Prince Charming – *Adam & The Ants*
UKLP	Dead Ringer – *Meat Loaf*
	WEEK 4
US45	Endless Love – *Diana Ross & Lionel Richie*
USLP	Tattoo You – *Rolling Stones*
UK45	Prince Charming – *Adam & The Ants*
UKLP	Dead Ringer – *Meat Loaf*

THE GRAPEVINE

- **David Bowie, fresh from his Broadway triumph in *The Elephant Man*, has appeared – in a beard – in a TV play in which he plays Baal, the eighteenth-century mystic.**
- **Bob Geldof of The Boomtown Rats has been signed up to play Pink in the film version of Pink Floyd's 'The Wall'.**
- **Album by Prince, 'Controvsy', enters US soul charts**

Geldof: Pink in 'The Wall'

VIDEO VIOLENCE HALTS POLICE

Police: Belfast vid banned despite the trio's insistence they were impartial

Police have returned with a new album – 'Ghost in the Machine' - and straight into a controversy with the video for their new single, 'Invisible Sun'.

The film, shot in strife-torn Belfast, was carefully edited to remain non-partisan – but Britain's BBC television has refused to screen it.

'The video . . . could be misinterpreted, and said to convey meanings which are not present in the lyrics,' they say.

Manager Miles Copeland has also turned down the band's involvement in a CND (anti-nuclear) compilation album.

STAR QUOTE

KEITH RICHARDS

'We are established now musically because we've been around so long. But I don't think anybody would consider us part of "the Establishment" in its full meaning because up until the late Seventies the Establishment was still doing their best to do us in completely.'

TWO'S COMPANY FOR DAVE AND BABS

The Lesley Gore classic and US chart topper from 1967, 'It's My Party', has hit the top again – this time in Britain, performed by little-known instrumental/vocal duo Dave Stewart and Barbara Gaskin.

Keyboardist Stewart has done time in avant-garde jazz-rock outfits Egg, Arzachel, Hatfield & The North and The Tourists, while Gaskin sang backups for the latter outfit.

They licensed the self-made recording to Stiff Records and watched it climb the charts. It just goes to show you can't keep a good song down . . .

CHARTS

US45	Endless Love *Diana Ross & LionelRichie*
USLP	Tattoo You *Rolling Stones*
UK45	Prince Charming *Adam & The Ants*
UKLP	Abacab *Genesis*
	WEEK 2
US45	Endless Love *Diana Ross & Lionel Richie*
USLP	Tattoo You *Rolling Stones*
UK45	Prince Charming *Adam & The Ants*
UKLP	Dead Ringer *Meat Loaf*
	WEEK 3
US45	Arthur's Theme (Best That You Can Do) *Christopher Cross*
USLP	Tattoo You *Rolling Stones*
UK45	Prince Charming *Adam & The Ants*
UKLP	Ghost In The Machine *Police*
	WEEK 4
US45	Arthur's Theme (Best That You Can Do) *Christopher Cross*
USLP	Tattoo You *Rolling Stones*
UK45	It's My Party *Dave Stewart & Barbara Gaskin*
UKLP	Ghost In The Machine *Police*
	WEEK 5
US45	Arthur's Theme (Best That You Can Do) *Christopher Cross*
USLP	Tattoo You *Rolling Stones*
UK45	It's My Party *Dave Stewart & Barbara Gaskin*
UKLP	Ghost In The Machine *Police*

THE GRAPEVINE

■ The *New York Post* has reported that Lennon killer Mark Chapman asked for the copy of 'Double Fantasy' that Lennon autographed just prior to the shooting, to auction for an organization lobbying for hand-gun control.

■ Among new albums this month is 'In The Garden', the debut of a male/female duo called The Eurythmics (previously members of The Tourists); a tour is being set up involving 'a new concept in stage presentation'.

SKA'D FOR LIFE – THE SPECIALS SPLIT

It's finally been confirmed, after weeks of press speculation, that The Specials have split.

The seven-piece multi-racial ska band, whose 2-Tone label provided the first worthwhile post-punk musical movement, have been left by no fewer than four of their number – and since Lynval Golding, Neville Staples and Terry Hall (the three main vocalists) are among them, it's inevitably been suggested that this may be the end of the line for the Coventry band.

The vocal trio have already announced their plans to remain and record together under the banner of the Fun Boy Three. Their first self-penned release, 'The Lunatics Have Taken Over The Asylum', will appear on the Chrysalis label later in the month.

The fourth member to flee is guitarist Roddy Byers, better known as Roddy Radiation, who seems set to turn his sideline rockabilly group The Tearjerkers into a full-time outfit. Meanwhile, drummer Brad Bradbury, bassist Sir Horace Gentleman and leader/keyboardist Jerry Dammers, are currently touring Germany backing 2-Tone artist Ricc.

Dammers commented 'I'm disappointed – but I'm glad they stayed long enough to record "Ghost Town".'

IRON MAN BRUCE JOINS MAIDEN

Iron Maiden made their British debut with their new line-up, including singer Bruce Dickenson.

Previously with second division HM outfit Samson – with whom he was known as Bruce Bruce – he replaced Paul Di'anno at London's Rainbow Theatre.

Iron Maiden's new line-up

NOVEMBER

HIGHWAY ROBBERY FROM ADAM

1981 has been the year of the Ant – Adam Ant, to be precise. Having come from nowhere to register five chart singles in ten months, the former Stuart Goddard tops off the year with 'Prince Charming', the follow-up to 'Kings Of The Wild Frontier' and his second chart-topping LP of the year.

But even the ferociously war-painted Adam couldn't bargain for the theft of a specially commissioned stage set worth £10,000 - stolen, police believe, in error for a lorryload of drink.

Seems Adam's latest album's highwayman theme has already worn a little thin . . .

Adam Ant as Prince Charming with ex-Banshees guitarist Marco Pirroni, in a year that culminated in the Royal Variety Performance before HM the Queen

KOOL FOR OAKLAND

Kool And The Gang, steppin' out at Oakland

When The Oakland A's scored a successful season in the North American baseball league, the first person they thanked was a man from Jersey City – Robert 'Kool' Bell, leader and bass player with ace dance act Kool & The Gang.

The reason? 'Celebration', last year's mega-hit adopted as that – and many other – teams' anthem. Now with a new album 'Steppin' Out', their Concord Pavilion stadium performance in Oakland gave the local fans something else to celebrate.

ROCK'N'ROYAL – BUT NO BEATLES!

The Royal Variety Show is probably the biggest event in the British television calendar – but it will go ahead this year with Adam & The Ants the only contemporary act in a 'History of British Pop' section that includes such golden oldies as veteran skiffle king Lonnie Donegan, Merseybeat survivors The Searchers and wrinkly rocker Alvin Stardust.

This laughable state of affairs is believed to result from the refusal of Paul McCartney, George Harrison and Ringo Starr – the three surviving Beatles – to appear in the show on 23 November at London's Drury Lane Theatre.

In their absence, it's left to cool classicist Andrew Lloyd Webber to take the honours with a selection of material from his hit musicals. But Beatles or not, it seems unjust that Britain's brightest pop hopes are being kept from this showcase 'shop window'. Does Her Majesty know about this?

VERLAINE SWITCHES CHANNELS

Once US new-wavers Television's leading light, guitarist Tom Verlaine steps back into the New York spotlight three years after their split, with a solo band featuring fellow TV player Fred Smith on bass, Patti Smith man Jay Dee Daugherty on drums and Jimmy Ripp on second guitar.

NME verdict: 'The warmest performance I've seen him give . . . He remains a fascinating figure, well worth watching.'

THE GRAPEVINE

- **The demise of progressive supergroup Yes has been confirmed by the partnership of Alan White and Chris Squire with their single 'Run With The Fox' and a final compilation from the band, 'Classic Yes'.**
- **Jam frontman Paul Weller has been booked to read in this month's London Poetry Olympics.**

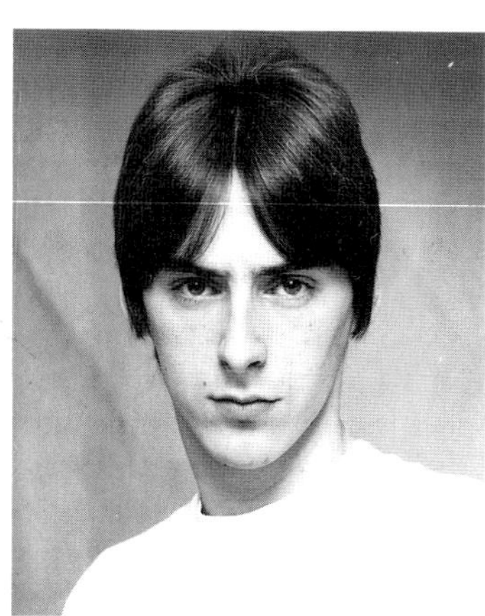

Pop poet Paul Weller

CHARTS

US45	Private Eyes – *Daryl Hall & John Oates*
USLP	Tattoo You – *Rolling Stones*
UK45	Happy Birthday – *Altered Images*
UKLP	Dare – *Human League*
WEEK 2	
US45	Private Eyes – *Daryl Hall & John Oates*
USLP	Tattoo You – *Rolling Stones*
UK45	Every Little Thing She Does Is Magic – *Police*
UKLP	Dare – *Human League*
WEEK 3	
US45	Physical – *Olivia Newton-John*
USLP	4 – *Foreigner*
UK45	Every Little Thing She Does Is Magic – *Police*
UKLP	Prince Charming – *Adam & The Ants*
WEEK 4	
US45	Physical – *Olivia Newton-John*
USLP	4 – *Foreigner*
UK45	Under Pressure – *Queen & David Bowie*
UKLP	Prince Charming – *Adam & The Ants*

STAR QUOTE

ROBERT SMITH

'When we started ,it was just for me to accomplish not ever having to work. That was it. When I was at school, I never wanted to work because I never wanted anyone to tell me when I had to get up.'

STEWART'S SATELLITE FIRST

Rod Stewart has outsmarted The Rolling Stones by stealing the only satellite available to let his British fans in on his 19 December Los Angeles Forum concert. Though boxing matches have previously been shown in Britain by satellite, Stewart's the first rock star to get the silver screen simulcast treatment.

Those fans would be well advised to bring a thermos or two of coffee, not to mention a blanket, since due to time differences the show is scheduled to start at 4.30 in the morning! Australian viewers also taking the concert live are luckier – they can watch it after their Sunday lunch.

All this means that The Rolling Stones have abandoned their plans for a global telecast the previous evening.

THE GRAPEVINE

■ **Tex-Mex star Joe 'King' Carrasco gatecrashed the Go-Gos' sellout Christmas party in New York . . . in nothing but his birthday suit; 'They put me up to it,' he complained bitterly (cold).**

■ **Inspired political slogan of the year from the British Labour Party: 'The Tories have a worse record than Bucks Fizz'; needless to say, both group and record company RCA are less than amused.**

Nothing on Joe Carrasco

THE KING IS DEAD . . .

'*Elvis*. At last the full, terrible story.'

That's how the press ads ran for the latest rock read – but one with a difference. Albert Goldman's biography of Elvis Presley has proved the year's most talked-about music book.

Most critics agree that Elvis Presley's brilliance was dimmed first by Hollywood movies and then by his own weakness for junk food and drugs. Goldman prefers to believe that, in the words of NME reviewer Charles Shaar Murray: 'Presley did not become a worthless shit: he always was one.'

Reaction has been predictable and savage: Greil Marcus whose *Mystery Train* included perhaps the definitive essay on the man, has published an open letter rebutting Goldman's theories.

And at street level, Presley fans have been visting bookshops in the United States, defacing copies of the book and calmly walking out again.

Advance warning to those of a weak disposition: Goldman has promised his next victim will be John Lennon.

CHARTS

Chart	Title	Artist
US45	Physical	*Olivia Newton-John*
USLP	4	*Foreigner*
UK45	Under Pressure	*Queen & David Bowie*
UKLP	Queen's Greatest Hits	*Queen*
WEEK 2		
US45	Physical	*Olivial Newton-John*
USLP	4	*Foreigner*
UK45	Begin The Beguine	*Julio Iglesias*
UKLP	Chart Hits '81	*Various*
WEEK 3		
US45	Physical	*Olivia Newton-John*
USLP	4	*Foreigner*
UK45	Don't You Want Me	*Human League*
UKLP	Dare	*Human League*
WEEK 4		
US45	Physical	*Olivia Newton-John*
USLP	For Those About To Rock, We Salute You	*AC/DC*
UK45	Don't You Want Me	*Human League*
UKLP	Dare	*Human League*

CLIFF: THE COMPLETE ROCK STAR

Cliff Richard, Britain's oldest teenager and self-confessed Rock'n'roll Juvenile, packed out London's Hammersmith Odeon for his traditional Christmas concerts. The show was cleverly split into sections to satisfy all sections of an audience which now spans at least two generations, possibly more.

Cutting across age and class, Cliff Richard is truly the all-purpose pop star – and though he keeps his religious songs for separate gospel tours these days there's little doubt in his inter-song chat that the timing of these concerts is no coincidence. Cliff Richard: the complete rock star.

JANUARY

1982

BUY NO MORE RECORDS?

Renting records could be the thing of the future if a new Japanese scheme catches on.

In Tokyo, the owner of a major chain of record stores has already changed his retail outlets into musical lending libraries. And in New York, there was a near-riot when one record store decided to rent out its stock.

The scheme works in a similar way to video hire, but whereas the retailer would make more money by renting than selling albums, the manufacturer only makes money on the first sale.

With blank cassette sales increasing yearly, it is easy to see how such a method could tie in with home taping. And with record prices going through the roof, it's possible that such a scheme could shake the record industry to its foundations. Whether the industry is ready for that remains to be seen.

NO FUN: RACE ATTACK HOSPITALIZES GOLDING

Fun Boy Three singer Lynval Golding was almost killed – and possibly scarred for life – when he was attacked and knifed in a Coventry, England, disco. The assault, by both white and black youths, was apparently racially-motivated.

Golding was rushed to hospital with two others, where after twelve hours in intensive care and 29 stitches in his face and neck, he was said to be 'quite comfortable'.

Remarkably, Golding holds no malice for this, the second such incident in which he's been the innocent victim. 'My music is about peace,' he said, 'and I'm sure the guys will feel sorry for what they did.'

The attack took place on January 7 when the Fun Boy Three, the spin-off group from The Specials to which Golding belongs, returned to their home town for live interviews on local radio.

Three Coventry men have since been charged with wounding Golding in this incident.

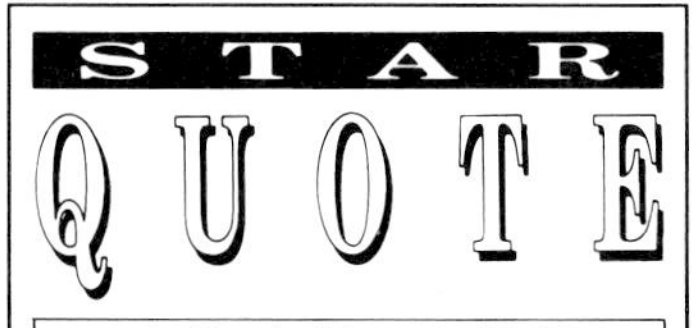

STAR QUOTE

ADAM ANT

'You can do what Sinatra did. I think you can do what Bowie did. I think if you're good enough, if you show that you're going to make more effort than anyone else around, you don't have to lose your fans. I'm not going to stand still.'

FELA IN THE FRAY

Fela Anikulapo Kuti, Nigeria's leading rock musician, has been released on bail following his arrest in Lagos in early December. He was charged with robbing a 7-Up bottling plant, stealing a car, cultivating cannabis and possessing Indian hemp, along with numerous other offences.

It seems the charges owe much to political motives, for Kuti - who attempted to form a party to oppose the Nigerian ruling junta in 1979 – has claimed that he will once more stand in opposition during the 1983 elections.

The recent charge is seen as an attempt to jail him until the elections are safely over. Despite a damaged leg, a legacy of a police beating, Kuti still hopes to embark on an American tour in May.

CHARTS

US45	Physical *Olivia Newton-John*
USLP	For Those About To Rock, We Salute You *AC/DC*
UK45	One Of us *Abba*
UKLP	The Visitors *Abba*
	WEEK 2
US45	Physical *Olivia Newton-John*
USLP	For Those About To Rock, We Salute You *AC/DC*
UK45	Don't You Want Me *Human League*
UKLP	Dare *Human League*
	WEEK 3
US45	Physical *Olivia Newton-John*
USLP	4 *Foreigner*
UK45	The Land Of Make Believe *Bucks Fizz*
UKLP	Dare *Human League*
	WEEK 4
US45	Physical *Olivia Newton-John*
USLP	4 *Foreigner*
UK45	The Land Of Make Believe *Bucks Fizz*
UKLP	Dare *Human League*
	WEEK 5
US45	I Can't Go For That (No Can Do) *Daryl Hall & John Oates*
USLP	4 *Foreigner*
UK45	The Model *Kraftwerk*
UKLP	Dare *Human League*

THE GRAPEVINE

- **Thin Lizzy's Phil Lynott has been the victim of a confidence trickster running up large bills at various London night clubs. The imposter has a tattoo on his left arm, while Lynott has not.**
- **Level 42 have taken their first steps to fame at London's Barracuda Club. One verdict: 'It would have been better to turn your back and use the music as sound track.'**

Lizzy's Lynott: drinks aren't on him . . .

Level 42 liven up their stage act for television

U2 IN THE USA

Irish rock group U2 have more than proved their popularity both in their own country and in Britain, where a poll has just voted them fifth best group and their album 'October' fourth best album.

But this means nothing in the United States, where they start their campaign in New Orleans. Singer Bono believes the atmosphere favours new bands from across the Atlantic, even though the FM radio network seems biased against change.

'In every state, College radio covers groups like U2, Scritti Politti and Teardrop Explodes'.

The band is building on their first tour where they supported everyone who is anyone. 'Celebration' is their latest single, and chart success would see U2 climb several more rungs up the ladder.

The band's gig at the Opry House at Austin, Texas, was followed by an impromptu personal appearance at the West Lake Bible Church. Guitarist The Edge, Bono and drummer Larry are all professing Christians, and their appearance at the church resulted in an avalanche of young admirers.

If they can continue to manage this when on the concert stage, America should soon be eating out of their hands.

CHARTS

US45	Centerfold *J. Geils Band*
USLP	Freeze Frame *J. Geils Band*
UK45	The Model *Kraftwerk*
UKLP	Love Songs *Barbra Streisand*
	WEEK 2
US45	Centerfold *J. Geils Band*
USLP	Freeze Frame *J. Geils Band*
UK45	The Model *Kraftwerk*
UKLP	Dare *Human League*
	WEEK 3
US45	Centerfold *J. Geils Band*
USLP	Freeze Frame *J. Geils Band*
UK45	A Town Called Malice *Jam*
UKLP	Dare *Human League*
	WEEK 4
US45	Centerfold *J. Geils Band*
USLP	Freeze Frame *J. Geils Band*
UK45	A Town Called Malice *Jam*
UKLP	Love Songs *Barbra Streisand*

GOODBYE FAITH HEALER

Alex Harvey, affectionately known as 'Britain's oldest punk', died on the eve of his 47th birthday on February 5.

Glasgow born Harvey's influence on British rock music dated from the late Fifties, but it was his work with The Sensational Alex Harvey Band group for which he will be best remembered.

Harvey's death in Belgium, while waiting for a Channel ferry at the end of a four week tour, follows his younger brother Les' onstage demise when leading Stone The Crows in 1972.

NME writer Charles Shaar Murray dubbed Harvey and his band, 'one of the craziest, most honest, most creative and most courageous bands of their time . . . I never met anyone quite like him and I never will again.'

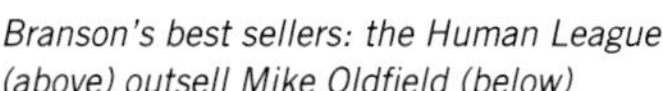

Branson's best sellers: the Human League (above) outsell Mike Oldfield (below)

WHO DARES . . . WINS!

The Human League single 'Don't You Want Me' has become the first platinum selling record in Britain for four years. According to chart statisticians, the last such big seller was Paul McCartney's 1977 Christmas hit 'Mull of Kintyre'.

The League album from which it came, 'Dare', is now Virgin's biggest selling LP since their very first – 'Tubular Bells' by Mike Oldfield – having sold over 750,000 copies and being well on its way to becoming a million-seller.

The B-52's await their new producer

THE GRAPEVINE

- The strangest combination of the month; dance group The B-52's and their record producer, Talking Head David Byrne. Their 'Mesopotamia' album is due to be released this month.
- The most unexpected hit of the month is Kraftwerks 'The Model'. A track that was originally released in the late Seventies, it is now sitting on top of the UK charts.

MARCH

ROAD RUNS OUT FOR RANDY

Randy Rhoads, the flamboyant heavy metal lead guitarist in Ozzy Osbourne's band, has died in a bizarre air accident. Taking advantage of a rest day on Osbourne's US tour, he was given a joy ride in a light aircraft, with the band's wardrobe mistress and tour bus driver.

The plane 'buzzed' the band's Florida hotel before crashing and killing the guitarist.

Rhoads' death coincides with a narrow escape for soul star Teddy Pendergrass, who is currently hospitalized after a car accident. A serious neck injury makes it unlikely that he will be able to perform in the near future – if ever again.

Dead: guitarist Randy Rhoads (with Ozzy)

Disabled: soul singer Teddy Pendergrass

YESTERDAY ONCE MORE

The British Electric Foundation Ian Craig Marsh and Martyn Ware – left The Human League on the verge of multi-million pound stardom. Now they're going for it themselves with 'Music Of Quality And Distinction', an album featuring many of their favourite stars of yesteryear, singing their own versions of other peoples' classics.

Tina Turner, for instance, covers the old Motown track 'Ball Of Confusion'.

'James Brown was going to do it,' explained Ware, 'But we just couldn't agree terms.' Marsh continues: 'Tina's name was thrown in out of the blue . . . a ludicrous suggestion. In the end, following it up paid off.'

Other artists benefitting from the BEF treatment include Sandie Shaw, Gary Glitter, Manfred Mann's Paul Jones and Bob Geldof's girlfriend Paula Yates.

Yet it could have been still more star-studded: Scott Walker and Paul McCartney were among those who declined.

THE GRAPEVINE

- **Seventies glam rockers Slade are facing trouble with their new album 'Till Deaf Us Do Part', with dealers refusing to stock it because of an 'offensive' picture of a nail piercing an ear drum.**
- **Queen's proposed stadium tour of Britain this summer appears in jeopardy; all the arenas they want to play are being held in readiness for an even bigger draw – Pope John Paul II.**

CHARTS

Chart	Title	Artist
US45	Centerfold	*J. Geils Band*
USLP	Beauty & The Beast	*Go-Go's*
UK45	A Town Called Malice	*Jam*
UKLP	Love Songs	*Barbra Streisand*
WEEK 2		
US45	Centerfold	*J. Geils Band*
USLP	Beauty & The Beast	*Go-Go's*
UK45	The Lion Sleeps Tonight	*Tight Fit*
UKLP	Love Songs	*Barbra Streisand*
WEEK 3		
US45	I Love Rock'n'Roll	*Joan Jett & The Blackhearts*
USLP	Beauty & The Beast	*Go-Go's*
UK45	The Lion Sleeps Tonight	*Tight Fit*
UKLP	Pelican West	*Haircut 100*
WEEK 4		
US45	I Love Rock'n'Roll	*Joan Jett & The Blackhearts*
USLP	Beauty & The Beast	*Go-Go's*
UK45	The Lion Sleeps Tonight	*Tight Fit*
UKLP	The Gift	*Jam*

CALL ME BAAL!

David Bowie's new TV venture sees him taking the part of Herbert Beerbolm Baal, the central character of Bertolt Brecht's first play.

Publicity stills show a gap-toothed David clutching a banjo - and it is rumoured an EP of songs will be released if the TV play is a success.

BRIDGE OVER TROUBLED WATER

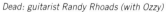

Friends again: Paul (left) and Art

STAR QUOTE

BOB GELDOF

'I want to write a song people will remember, that people will some day hear and be reminded of something they did years ago. Maybe "I Don't Like Mondays", will be the one, but, it's just another minor thing really, once you've achieved the ambition.'

Simon and Garfunkel are back together again, ten years after their acrimonious split. They joined forces for a one-off reunion three years ago, and again last autumn for a concert in New York's Central Park. This is now being released as a live double album to celebrate the resumption of one of pop's most successful partnerships ever.

Simon explained: 'We sat down and talked at length about working together – and, you know, that's something we'd never really done before. Now Art and I have ironed out all our difficulties, and we're back in business as a viable proposition.'

ASIA – WHAT'S IN A NAME?

Four British musicians calling themselves after the continent of Asia seem to have found the success they've all been looking for – in America!

Not that the individuals concerned have exactly been unknowns in their past life: guitarist Steve Howe found superstardom with Yes, where he was joined by Geoff Downes, the former Buggles keyboardist.

John Wetton has played with King Crimson, Family, and Roxy Music, while Carl Palmer was the P in ELP.

Their debut album, simply called 'Asia', is heading to the top of the US charts, as is the single 'Only Time Will Tell'. No wonder their US tour is a complete sell out.

As we said, what's in a name?

Asia drummer Carl Palmer ups sticks

Joan Jett (left) and her aptly-named Blackhearts glower darkly from the top of the US charts

BLACK IS THE COLOUR

23-year old Joan Jett is on top of the world. One minute rhythm guitarist in the all-girl gimmick group The Runaways, she went it alone with her group The Blackhearts. Today she is top of the US single and album charts with the anthem 'I Love Rock And Roll'.

'I'm tired of hearing that girls can't play rock'n'roll,' snarls Jett. 'It's bullshit and it's untrue. It's still really exciting to me. I don't want to grow up.'

She acknowledges that The Runaways were 'tagged with a sex image', but claims to have 'fond memories . . . I learned a lot and it made me wary of the music business and how cut-throat it is.'

Things must look better from where she is now . . .

CUT AND DRIED

Haircut 100 are unquestionably the most successful new band of the year – and after selling out their recent UK tour which climaxed at the Hammersmith Odeon in London on April 1, they have slotted in a new tour at venues where there is no age limit, enabling their youngest fans to see them in action. Their first album, 'Pelican West', has only just been knocked off the top of the NME chart.

But critics who put the band down as merely this month's teen idols get short shrift from the group themselves. According to percussionist Mark Fox: 'The front three are like young kids who picked up guitars but aren't really guitarists, and the rest of us are strong musicians, and then you've got a brass section who are like ex-National Jazz Youth Orchestra.

'We're playing a pop music that's very sophisticated. I mean, I wouldn't have given up an £8,000 a year job just to play in a little no-future pop group.'

CHARTS

US45	I Love Rock'n'Roll	*Joan Jett & The Blackhearts*
USLP	Beauty & The Beast	*Go-Go's*
UK45	Seven Tears	*Goombay Dance Band*
UKLP	The Gift	*Jam*
	WEEK 2	
US45	I Love Rock'n'Roll	*Joan Jett & The Blackhearts*
USLP	Beauty & The Beast	*Go-Gos*
UK45	Seven Tears	*Goombay Dance Band*
UKLP	Pelican West	*Haircut 100*
	WEEK 3	
US45	I Love Rock'n'Roll	*Joan Jett & The Blackhearts*
USLP	Chariots Of Fire	*Vangelis*
UK45	My Camera Never Lies	*Bucks Fizz*
UKLP	Number Of The Beast	*Iron Maiden*
	WEEK 4	
US45	I Love Rock'n'Roll	*Joan Jett & The Blackhearts*
USLP	Chariots Of Fire	*Vangelis*
UK45	My Camera Never Lies	*Bucks Fizz*
UKLP	Love Songs	*Barbra Streisand*

Haircut 100, with heart-throb Nick Heyward well to the fore. Their 'sophisticated' music has proved no barrier to teen stardom

THE GRAPEVINE

- Rod Stewart's anthem 'Sailing' has been re-released and is being used as theme music for a British television programme about life aboard a Royal Navy aircraft carrier.
- Bill Nelson, former BeBop De Luxe and Red Noise front man, has returned to action with a new album, 'The Love That Whirls' – it's his first for three years.

MAY

CHARTS

US45	I Love Rock'n'Roll *Joan Jett & The Blackhearts*
USLP	Chariots Of Fire *Vangelis*
UK45	Ebony And Ivory *Paul McCartney & Stevie Wonder*
UKLP	Pelican West *Haircut 100*
	WEEK 2
US45	Chariots Of Fire *Vangelis*
USLP	Chariots Of Fire *Vangelis*
UK45	Ebony And Ivory *Paul McCartney & Stevie Wonder*
UKLP	Live In Britain *Barry Manilow*
	WEEK 3
US45	Ebony & Ivory *Paul McCartney & Stevie Wonder*
USLP	Asia *Asia*
UK45	I Won't Let You Down *Phd*
UKLP	Tug Of War *Paul McCartney*
	WEEK 4
US45	Ebony & Ivory *Paul McCartney & Stevie Wonder*
USLP	Asia *Asia*
UK45	A Little Peace *Nicole*
UKLP	Complete Madness *Madness*
	WEEK 5
US45	Ebony & Ivory *Paul McCartney & Stevie Wonder*
USLP	Tug Of War *Paul McCartney*
UK45	Goody Two Shoes *Adam Ant*
UKLP	Complete Madness *Madness*

THE GRAPEVINE

- **When is a new single not a new single? When it's The Beatles' 'Movie Medley', excerpts from seven of their film songs on one 45rpm single.**
- **When is a press conference standing room only? When it's Mick Jagger at Le Beat Route club in London, announcing news of The Rolling Stones' forthcoming European tour.**

A TOUCH OF CULTURE

'Obviously I'm into myself, but I'm not walking around just saying, "Oh everybody look at me, look at me!" I wear make-up and dress this way because it makes me look better. I'm not doing it to get people to stare at me. If I wanted to do that I could just put a pot on my head, wear a wedding dress and scream down the high street.'

So says Boy George, this year's most unusual pop star in the making. A first single, 'White Boy', is already causing a stir. After being discovered by Sex Pistols svengali Malcolm McLaren and considered for Bow Wow Wow, he decided to start his own group when the band dropped him.

'I just wanted revenge, and to be exactly like them but better . . . then I decided to do something of my own because I'm a good singer!' His braided hair, outrageous dress and trademark hat have already made him a household name on the circuit – and more is sure to follow.

JOE DON'T GO!

Punk survivors The Clash were forced to postpone a month of dates in their 'Know Your Rights' UK tour when lead vocalist Joe Strummer disappeared. Manager Bernard Rhodes said: 'I feel he's probably gone away for a serious re-think . . .'

Journalist Steve Taylor claimed he had shared a compartment with Strummer on a train from London to Paris – and sure enough it was in Paris that the singer was located at the end of the month. Ironically, after they had fulfilled their headline spot at Holland's Lochem Festival, the band was further rocked when drummer Topper Headon announced that *he* was leaving . . . for good!

Strummer's explanation for his own behaviour: 'It's very much like being a robot, being in a group . . . rather than go barmy, it's better to do what I did . . . I just got up and went to Paris.'

Clash strummer Strummer

SACK THE SYNTH

Musicians' Union Central London Branch has called for the synthesizer to be banned, reckoning that the living of trumpet players, violinists and others is being threatened by this versatile new musical instrument.

'Music is being threatened as a living art form,' claimed MU member Neil Lancaster. A saxophone player who once backed The Beach Boys, he continued by berating 'the terrible essence of amateurism' evident in pop music, and 'all this doodling with drum machines'.

Latest news is that synth players are fighting back by forming The Union of Sound Synthesists, a collective of people who support the instrument.

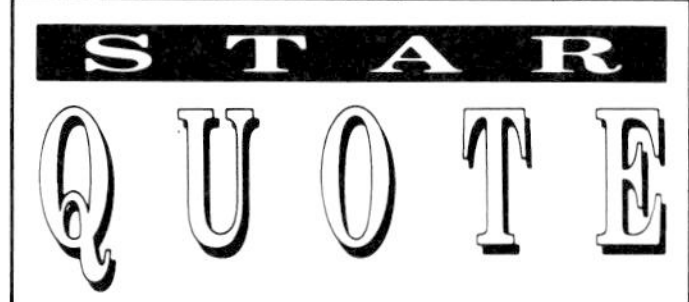

STAR QUOTE

BRUCE DICKINSON

'Fans want to see people who can play: they respect certain values like professionalism, and they don't want to be treated like shit. They pay good money and they look forward to seeing some good music being played by decent musicians who really put their soul into it.'

Maiden's Dickinson

SILENCE IS GOLDEN – THE ONE SIDED SINGLE

Latest McLaren protégés Bow Wow Wow in action with vocalist Annabel Lwin

The latest music biz gimmick is the one-sided single – first of which is Bow Wow Wow's 'I Want Candy'.

The intention is to cut the price of a single, but the purchase price is, in fact, rather more than 50 per cent of the two-sided version. The sleeve simply bears the message 'Special Edition – Special Price' and there is, as yet, no information as to how many buyers have returned the single in disgust at this tactic.

Surprisingly enough, the idea originated from RCA's marketing department and not Bow Wow Wow manager Malcolm McLaren, who's insisted it be repressed with a proper B-side. Meanwhile, the single has sold 50,000 in the week prior to release in advance orders.

Lees, Pritchard and Holroyd

OVER THE WALL

Barclay James Harvest, still only a cult attraction in their native Britain, have always been big in Europe. And to prove it, their new live album, 'A Concert For The People', was recorded on the steps of Berlin's Reichstag before a vast audience of 175,000.

Their recent tour of Germany played to over 400,000 people, and grossed £2,500,000, while their new studio album will be recorded in Frankfurt.

Their concert which took place on the border between East and West Berlin brought them many fans from behind the Iron Curtain, and future plans include concerts behind the wall in the Communist zone.

PRETENDERS DRUG DEATH

The Pretenders entered the Eighties with a No. 1 single – two years later they are devastated by the sacking of Pete Farndon and the death of guitarist James Honeyman-Scott just 24 hours later.

Despite the latter's reputation for a wild lifestyle, his recent marriage was expected to have moderated his behaviour. His death on June 16 leaves the band line-up as vocalist Chrissie Hynde and drummer Martin Chambers.

American Hynde flew to New York 'just to get away from it all', but was expected to return for the funeral. The band's future is as yet unknown.

SIOUX SILENCED

Siouxsie Sioux learnt this month that throat problems mean she must stop singing for the rest of the year. A leading throat specialist has now decided that Siouxsie's vocal chords have swollen to twice the average size, and that every time she has laryngitis they never heal properly.

'I think she's a bit worried,' said group member Steve Severin. 'But as of now nothing is cancelled . . . until it's absolutely certain she's in danger of losing her voice completely. We're just hoping it isn't anywhere near that bad.'

Siouxsie Sioux – under doctor's orders to rest her voice for the next six months

THE GRAPEVINE

- **In hot water – leather-clad UK futurist duo Soft Cell, whose video for their controversial track 'Sex Dwarf' caused a riot when shown in preview form at a nightclub.**
- **Supporting former Television guitar star Tom Verlaine at London's Venue – Liverpool hopefuls China Crisis, playing an early capital city gig.**

CHARTS

US45	Ebony & Ivory *Paul McCartney & Stevie Wonder*
USLP	Tug Of War *Paul McCartney*
UK45	House Of Fun *Madness*
UKLP	Complete Madness *Madness*
WEEK 2	
US45	Ebony & Ivory *Paul McCartney & Stevie Wonder*
USLP	Tug Of War *Paul McCartney*
UK45	House Of Fun *Madness*
UKLP	Complete Madness *Madness*
WEEK 3	
US45	Ebony & Ivory *Paul McCartney & Stevie Wonder*
USLP	Asia *Asia*
UK45	Goody Two Shoes *Adam Ant*
UKLP	Avalon *Roxy Music*
WEEK 4	
US45	Ebony & Ivory *Paul McCartney & Stevie Wonder*
USLP	Asia *Asia*
UK45	Goody Two Shoes *Adam Ant*
UKLP	Avalon *Roxy Music*

ALL CHANGE FOR BRITISH BANDS

Heavy Metal trio Motorhead have announced the recruitment of Brian Robertson, the former Thin Lizzy guitarist, as a permanent member following the departure of 'Fast' Eddie Clarke in the middle of a US tour. Robertson has been helping the band out on a part-time basis, and has now been confirmed.

Meanwhile, R&B stalwarts Dr. Feelgood have lost the services of their rhythm section, the Big Figure and John B Sparks. Both have finally tired of the touring that took the band to No. 1 in 1976 with 'Stupidity', and are replaced by Buzz Barwell (ex-Lew Lewis) on drums and Pat McMullan (ex-Count Bishops) on bass.

Farewell Feelgoods Figure (second left) and Sparko (right)

CHARTS

US45	Don't You Want Me — *Human League*
USLP	Asia — *Asia*
UK45	I've Never Been To Me — *Charlene*
UKLP	Avalon — *Roxy Music*
WEEK 2	
US45	Don't You Want Me — *Human League*
USLP	Asia — *Asia*
UK45	Happy Talk — *Captain Sensible*
UKLP	Avalon — *Roxy Music*
WEEK 3	
US45	Don't You Want Me — *Human League*
USLP	Asia — *Asia*
UK45	Abracadabra — *Steve Miller Band*
UKLP	Lexicon Of Love — *ABC*
WEEK 4	
US45	Eye Of The Tiger — *Survivor*
USLP	Asia — *Asia*
UK45	Fame — *Irene Cara*
UKLP	Lexicon Of Love — *ABC*
WEEK 5	
US45	Eye Of The Tiger — *Survivor*
USLP	Asia — *Asia*
UK45	Fame — *Irene Cara*
UKLP	Lexicon Of Love — *ABC*

THE GRAPEVINE

- **Surprise chart-topper of the month – Captain Sensible with his loopy version of the show tune 'Happy Talk' from *South Pacific*.**
- **The combined effect of a British rail strike and heavy thunderstorms has forced the WOMAD (World of Music and Dance) Festival into liquidation after a disastrous attendance of less than 10,000. Rock star Peter Gabriel was among the Festival's backers.**

STAR QUOTE

KEVIN ROWLAND
of Dexys Midnight Runners

'I did loads of stupid things, like the way I used to argue with EMI Records. I just look back to the time now and wonder how I would have reacted to some prick coming into my office shouting and kicking things.'

PLAY IT AGAIN, CS & N

David Crosby, Steve Stills and Graham Nash have their first new album for five years released this month. Entitled 'Daylight Again', it features eleven new songs including the single 'Wasted On The Way'.

Though they were unable to persuade guitarist Neil Young to return to the fold, the supergroup have attracted such talents as Art Garfunkel and the Eagles' Tim Schmidt to assist them.

EASY AS ABC!

Released this month – 'The Lexicon Of Love', first long-player by acclaimed quartet ABC, produced by ex-Buggles star Trevor Horn.

It's arguably the biggest, brightest, brashest pop record to emerge from Sheffield, England – or *anywhere* – since the Human League's 'Dare'.

A journalist believes they've 'followed two unimpeachably perfect singles with one of the greatest albums ever made . . . people don't make albums like this any more.'

Horn himself sees the group as: 'Great, because they understand, they'll take the obvious and add the vital final twist . . . They said they wanted a record of great quality, a record of complete professionalism, and so I said OK!'

The result has shot to the top of the chart, and looks set to establish ABC and frontman Martin Fry as the heirs to Bryan Ferry's throne.

Perfect pop from Sheffield: with matinee idol looks and voice to match, Martin Fry is leading ABC to fame

UK SUBS PLAY POLAND

The UK Subs this month became the first western band to perform in Poland since the imposition of martial law and the suppression of the trade union, Solidarity.

Though the band have a large fan following in Poland, they were nevertheless surprised to find the government issuing them visas and work permits in just two weeks – and even more surprised that support group Brygadakryzys, until now banned for playing Solidarity benefit concerts, were permitted to play with them.

Their schedule includes a headline appearance at a new wave festival outside Gdansk, the birthplace of Solidarity.

TWO FOR THE TOP

They found pop stardom with The Tourists . . . now duo Annie Lennox and Dave Stewart – The Eurythmics – are set to make it on their own terms.

'This time we want everything to be as *we* want it to be,' confirms Stewart, the guitarist who provides the music to Lennox's lyrics.

Their independence is indeed impressive: they have a home-built recording studio, enlisting friends to help fill out the sound for live performance. The two even manage themselves and both have the power of veto over their output. 'There's no excuses then, you're responsible for what's released,' says Lennox.

CHARTS

US45	Eye Of The Tiger	*Survivor*
USLP	Mirage	*Fleetwood Mac*
UK45	Come On Eileen	*Dexy's Midnight Runners*
UKLP	The Kids From Fame	*TV Cast*
	WEEK 2	
US45	Eye Of The Tiger	*Survivor*
USLP	Mirage	*Fleetwood Mac*
UK45	Come On Eileen	*Dexy's Midnight Runners*
UKLP	The Kids From Fame	*TV Cast*
	WEEK 3	
US45	Eye Of The Tiger	*Survivor*
USLP	Mirage	*Fleetwood Mac*
UK45	Come On Eileen	*Dexy's Midnight Runners*
UKLP	Too-Rye-Ay	*Dexy's Midnight Runners*
	WEEK 4	
US45	Eye Of The Tiger	*Survivor*
USLP	Mirage	*Fleetwood Mac*
UK45	Come On Eileen	*Dexy's Midnight Runners*
UKLP	Too-Rye-Ay	*Dexy's Midnight Runners*

BLONDIE OR BUST?

Blondie's tour of the UK and Europe, scheduled to start in Glasgow on September 1, has been cancelled. 'Ticket sales have not been as good as we hoped,' confessed the tour promoter – and Blondie's future now looks uncertain.

Their new album, 'The Hunter', failed to sell as well as expected, while Debbie Harry's solo LP 'Koo Koo' also bombed. Organist Jimmy Destri has left the band, while guitarist Frank Infante has gone to court to stop the band performing without him.

With reports coming in of disagreements on stage between Harry and her sound men, the future for Blondie looks bleak.

BRANSON STUNG?

After an out of court settlement which both sides claimed as a victory, Virgin Record boss Richard Branson accused Police manager Miles Copeland of arranging 'very questionable' contracts, and Copeland responded by claiming to be 'horrified' at the way Virgin did business.

The subject of the discussion was Sting, whose publishing deal with Virgin was the object of the dispute. During the court case, Sting's diaries were used as evidence. When Branson criticized Copeland's own publishing dealings, the response was typically forthright.

'It's absolute horse shit to say I was hypocritical,' said Copeland. 'Virgin never helped Sting's career, so their returns were unfair. Branson was never at risk himself, whereas I was at risk in every way . . . there's got to be some honour in this business.'

Miles Copeland: "Equine excrement, m'Lud"

WHO'S LAST?

Roger Daltrey's announcement that The Who's current US tour is to be their last sparked huge demand for tickets – the band's Shea Stadium concert selling out within three hours.

'We're going out with a mega blast on this tour, with no intention of limping down memory lane,' he told the US media.

These latest dates have the advantage of a hot support act in The Clash, whose recent album 'Combat Rock' is selling particularly well. A September concert at Birmingham's NEC may well be The Who's farewell British date.

THE GRAPEVINE

- **Cutting a dash in London's clubland: Pride, a jazzy ensemble which features velvety-voiced singer Sade Adu.**
- **Severely panned: this month – 'Vacation', the latest album by The Go Gos featuring lead singer Belinda Carlisle. An unkind and distinctly unimpressed reviewer ran with the headline: 'Uncool Jerkoffs'.**

The Go-Go's onstage with lead singer Belinda Carlisle on the left

SEPTEMBER 1982

CHARTS

US45	Abracadabra *Steve Miller Band*
USLP	Mirage *Fleetwood Mac*
UK45	Eye Of The Tiger *Survivor*
UKLP	Too-Rye-Ay *Dexy's Midnight Runners*
WEEK 2	
US45	Hard To Say I'm Sorry *Chicago*
USLP	American Fool *John Cougar*
UK45	Eye Of The Tiger *Survivor*
UKLP	Upstairs At Eric's *Yazoo*
WEEK 3	
US45	Hard To Say I'm Sorry *Chicago*
USLP	American Fool *John Cougar*
UK45	Eye Of The Tiger *Survivor*
UKLP	The Kids From Fame *TV Cast*
WEEK 4	
US45	Abracadabra *Steve Miller Band*
USLP	American Fool *John Cougar*
UK45	Private Investigations *Dire Straits*
UKLP	The Kids From Fame *TV Cast*

FLOYD'S FINAL CUT

Sixties supergroup Pink Floyd seem to have reached the end of the road, according to bassist Roger Waters and guitarist Dave Gilmour.

According to the latter, keyboardist Rick Wright has left the group. 'None of us have ever been the best of friends,' Gilmour revealed. 'We don't not get along, but we're working partners.'

Waters went even further: 'Now we don't pretend we're a group any more. I could work with another drummer and keyboard player very easily, and it's likely that at some point I will.'

Asked about the group's future, Waters remarked: 'Depends very much on me.'

YAZOO GO FOR GOLD

You must have something special for your first album to enter the charts at No. 1 – especially if you record for an independent label! Both facts are true with Yazoo, the British double act formed by Vince Clarke (ex-Depeche Mode) and bluesey singer Alison Moyet.

And while most bands would be milking their success with a headlining tour, the duo are warming up with some locally-advertised gigs in an attempt to perfect their stage show before subjecting it to full scale scrutiny.

'Rather than just use backing tapes, we are using a programmed computer to play a lot of the music,' explained Clarke. Alison, known to friends as 'Alf', finds the concerts 'completely nerve-wracking'.

Vince and Alf go gold

THE GRAPEVINE

- **Bath-based teen duo Tears For Fears, reviewed playing a small scale concert in Hastings, England, have been described as having 'a vaguely superior attitude of indifference . . . an unwillingness to compromise'.**
- **Making his debut in San Francisco as a solo performer, Billy Idol has been described as 'an all-American glam rock fantasy'.**

ORBISON SUES FOR $50 MILLION

Orbison's punitive fifty million dollars sets a new precedent in music business litigation

Legendary Sixties singer Roy Orbison is suing his manager Wesley Rose for $50 million, half of which is apparently 'punitive damages'. Rose is one of the most respected business men in Nashville and operates the publishing company Acuff-Rose.

Orbison claims one contract he signed was obtained when the singer was 'severely depressed' – possibly referring to a period when his first wife Claudette died in a road accident and two of his children in a fire.

ZAPPA – 'USA IS BEST'

With a hit single recorded with daughter Moon – 'Valley Girl' - and a Top 30 album 'Ship Arriving Too Late To Save A Drowning Witch', Frank Zappa is having his most successful year for some time.

Now he states that he intends to stay in the US for the foreseeable future. 'Europe's too expensive to play, too expensive to travel around and with the anti-American sentiment around, it is hard to go onstage and do what you do.

'I think three people got killed during our last show in Palermo, Italy. For some unknown reason, the cops started firing teargas . . . some of the kids started shooting back.'

Idol: all-American glam rock fantasy

Unlikely hitmakers Zappa and daughter

MADCAP SYD SPEAKS

One-time Pink Floyd main man Syd Barrett has been discovered living the life of a recluse in Cambridge, England. The man who wrote such psychedelic classics as 'Arnold Layne' and 'See Emily Play' has reverted to his given name of Roger Barrett and, at 36, seems to have overcome the worst of the mental illness, probably schizophrenia, that saw him confined to hospital for a spell after leaving the group.

Barrett, who lives with his mother, seemed ill at ease with his questioners, two French journalists who knocked at his door, ostensibly to return a parcel of clothes.

Among his more lucid comments was the statement that he doesn't want to play music any more because: 'I don't have time to do very much.'

He claimed to want to get back to London, 'but I've got to wait . . . there's a train strike on.' (The strike had ended some weeks previously).

When told of the meeting, Dave Gilmour – the man who replaced Barrett in the Floyd ranks – commented: 'Your article must be the last one on him. It's not romantic. It's a sad story. Now it's over.'

JAM FEEL THE SQUEEZE

British rock has been shaken to its foundations by the decision of two of the new wave's most enduring talents to call it a day.

Squeeze have decided to disband 'the band as a horse has run its course and the jockeys are now considering new mounts'.

The Jam are going their separate ways because songwriter Paul Weller is anxious to expand his activities outside a three-piece format. A farewell tour of eight dates will take place before Christmas.

Weller's statement announcing the split stated that: 'The longer a group continues, the more frightening the thought of ever ending it becomes – that is why so many of them carry on until they become meaningless.'

Jam: Weller looking to expand into a larger line-up

Squeeze: horse runs out of course

GABRIEL GOES HOME

The reunion of singer Peter Gabriel and Genesis at Milton Keynes Bowl, England, announced this month has already caused a great deal of interest, but the singer himself is not looking forward to the event.

'The motivation is to pay off the WOMAD (The World of Music and Dance) debts . . . having tried for seven years to get away from the image of being ex-Genesis, there's obviously a certain amount of stepping back. I don't think they would choose at this point to work with me or I with them, but as they've offered, it's very generous, I'm very grateful and I'm intending to enjoy myself.'

NEIL YOUNG

'I'm like a dinosaur with a large tail – I'm so big I have to keep eating all the time. I look around, there's not many dinosaurs left, just a lot of small animals moving very fast. And it's their vibrant energy that I need to stay alive.'

Dexy's Kevin Rowland at the top

CHARTS

- US45 Jack & Diane – *John Cougar*
- USLP American Fool – *John Cougar*
- UK45 The Bitterest Pill (I Ever Had To Swallow) – *Jam*
- UKLP The Kids From Fame – *TV Cast*

WEEK 2

- US45 Jack & Diane – *John Cougar*
- USLP American Fool – *John Cougar*
- UK45 Pass The Dutchie – *Musical Youth*
- UKLP Love Over Gold – *Dire Straits*

WEEK 3

- US45 Jack & Diane – *John Cougar*
- USLP American Fool – *John Cougar*
- UK45 Pass The Dutchie – *Musical Youth*
- UKLP Love Over Gold – *Dire Straits*

WEEK 4

- US45 Jack & Diane – *John Cougar*
- USLP American Fool – *John Cougar*
- UK45 Do You Really Want To Hurt Me – *Culture Club*
- UKLP Love Over Gold – *Dire Straits*

WEEK 5

- US45 Who Can It Be Now? – *Men At Work*
- USLP American Fool – *John Cougar*
- UK45 Do You REaly Want To Hurt Me – *Culture Club*
- UKLP The Kids From Fame Again – *TV Cast*

THE GRAPEVINE

- **Dexys Midnight Runners' hit with Van Morrison's 'Jackie Wilson Said' has a particular irony as the singer referred to in the song remains in a coma after collapsing on stage in 1975.**
- **Steely Dan singer/keyboardist Donald Fagen has launched his solo career this month with 'The Nightfly'. One verdict on the record: 'a mandatory purchase . . . he's still almost too cool.'**

NOVEMBER

STOP THAT VAN!

The Banshees, latest on-the-road casualties to fall by the wayside on the British gig circuit

Touring can be dangerous to your health – and that's official! Ian Gillan, formerly of Deep Purple, has been told by his management that he must retire from the road.

After seeing a specialist, vocalist Gillan learned he must stop singing for nine months, as his recent toll of two hundred gigs per year (not counting recording sessions) has been far too heavy.

And just to prove road fatigue is no respecter of age or reputation, Siouxsie & The Banshees' guitarist John McGeogh has collapsed and was admitted to hospital on the eve of their British tour.

While he is recovering from nervous exhaustion, Cure frontman Robert Smith has taken over as temporary lead guitarist.

WAH – TOO MUCH TOO SOON?

Wah, the latest Merseyside group to follow The Teardrops and Bunnymen on the road to fame, came unstuck with their show at New York's Danceteria.

'Some day I'll sing that in tune and I'll be okay,' admitted Pete Wylie after a flat version of the promising new 'Hope'. And while the admirable 'Seven Minutes To Midnight' woke the patrons up, it was too little too late.

STAR QUOTE

DARRYL HALL

'We try and take chances. Our new single "Maneater" isn't something that sounds like anything else on the radio. The idea is to make things better.'

FAME BRINGS ITS REWARD

Following the blockbusting movie *Fame* from Allan Parker, the UK charts have been deluged by singles and albums from actors and actresses related to the film and its spin-off TV show.

Firstly, Irene Cara notched a UK No. 1 with the film theme – now The Kids from Fame have scored a No. 1 album of the same name. Word is they will even be playing concerts in the near future. Six actors from the TV series, together with ten dancers, will be making their world debut appearances in London, Brighton and Birmingham in what seems the most carefully calculated bid for pop stardom since The Monkees.

The Kids From Fame (above) burst onto the chart scene while the Teardrops (below) have their final explosion

THE GRAPEVINE

- Pentangle, Seventies folk rock supergroup, have reformed to play a one-off Christmas show at London's Barbican Centre.
- Musical Youth, who recently topped the UK chart with their single 'Pass The Dutchie', have pulled out of the Kid Creole Tour, because education authorities said it would interfere with their schooling!

JAPANESE TEARS

New wave survivors Japan and The Teardrop Explodes have both announced their disbandment. Japan will be concentrating on individual pursuits while The Teardrop Explodes have split due to singer Julian Cope choosing a solo career.

Japan's demise has long been on the cards – their current winter tour being announced in the Spring to quell rumours – but the Liverpool-based Teardrop Explodes were regarded as one of the Eighties' brightest hopes.

With the demise of Blondie finally confirmed earlier this month, 1983 may well turn out to be the year of the solo artist.

CHARTS

US45	Up Where We Belong *Joe Cocker & Jennifer Warnes*
USLP	American Fool *John Cougar*
UK45	Do You Really Want To Hurt Me *Culture Club*
UKLP	Love Over Gold *Dire Straits*
WEEK 2	
US45	Up Where We Belong *Joe Cocker & Jennifer Warnes*
USLP	Business As Usual *Men At Work*
UK45	I Don't Want To Dance *Eddie Grant*
UKLP	The Kids From Fame *TV Cast*
WEEK 3	
US45	Up Where We Belong *Joe Cocker & Jennifer Warnes*
USLP	Business As Usual *Men At Work*
UK45	I Don't Want To Dance *Eddy Grant*
UKLP	The Kids From Fame *TV Cast*
WEEK 4	
US45	Truly *Lionel Richie*
USLP	Business As Usual *Men At Work*
UK45	Heartbreaker *Dionne Warwick*
UKLP	Heartbreaker *Dionne Warwick*

JACKSON IN SPACE?

As the blockbusting sci-fi film *ET* prepares to open in London, all eyes are on New York, where CBS are sueing MCA over an album called 'The ET Storybook'.

Featuring Michael Jackson as narrator and singer, it has now been withdrawn in the States as CBS (to whom Jackson is signed) claim that MCA have interfered with their 'contractual relationship' with the singer and are seeking millions of dollars in damages.

Critics believe that CBS are attempting to protect sales of Jackson's new album 'Thriller'; anyone with a copy of the album or single ('Someone in the Dark') has a potential goldmine on their hands.

CHARTS

US45	Truly	*Lionel Richie*
USLP	Business As Usual	*Men At Work*
UK45	Mirror Man	*Human League*
UKLP	The Singles: The First Ten Years	*Abba*
WEEK 2		
US45	Mickey	*Toni Basil*
USLP	Business As Usual	*Men At Work*
UK45	Beat Surrender	*Jam*
UKLP	The Singles: The First Ten Years	*Abba*
WEEK 3		
US45	Maneater	*Daryl hall & John Oates*
USLP	Business As Usual	*Men At Work*
UK45	Beat Surrender	*Jam*
UKLP	The Singles: The First Ten Years	*Abba*
WEEK 4		
US45	Maneater	*Daryl Hall & John Oates*
USLP	Business As Usual	*Men At Work*
UK45	Time (Clock Of The Heart)	*Culture Club*
UKLP	The John Lennon Collection	*John Lennon*

OH BROTHER! EVERLYS TO REFORM

The Everly Brothers are reforming after Christmas and will be back in full time action in 1983 with a new album and a world tour.

With 20 smash hits to their credit in the UK between 1957 and 1965, they are one of rock'n-'roll's major acts – even though they reportedly haven't spoken to each other for the past decade.

A LINDISFARNE XMAS

Newcastle, England, folk rockers Lindisfarne, a major chart act of the Seventies with hits like 'Fog On The Tyne' and 'Lady Eleanor', have added an unprecedented eleventh show to their traditional string of Christmas concerts at their home town's City Hall.

They have, however, announced that this will be the last season of these shows, and with 50 played so far, the final 11 will bring up 61 such concerts.

WELLER MUSES

At the end of The Jam's final fling, singer/songwriter Paul Weller still has no regrets.

'I'm not ungrateful for what I've had,' he said the day before the neo-Mods' final concert, appropriately in Brighton, England 'because I think it's good. I really believed in what we've done and I still do . . . I think I always will. But as a person I need more challenges.'

STAR QUOTE

MARVIN GAYE

'I don't make records for pleasure. I did when I was a younger artist, but I don't today. I record so that I can feed people what they need, what they feel. Hopefully, I record so that I can help someone overcome a bad time.'

Gaye: feeding the people

THE GRAPEVINE

- **Britain's No. 1 album this Christmas is 'The John Lennon Collection', a greatest hits compilation from the ex-Beatle, who was murdered exactly two years ago.**
- **Punk Godfather Iggy Pop sprained his ankle in Canada and had to cancel four shows. A trouper to the last, he appeared in San Francisco complete with gaffer tape bound around his ankle.**

So its come to this; Crass and their followers occupy former venue the Rainbow, which was originally the kitsch cathedral of British cinemas, the Finsbury Park Astoria

CRASS OVER THE RAINBOW

Anarchist band Crass occupied London's deserted Rainbow Theatre on December 10 frustrated at not being permitted to play the London club circuit after adverse newspaper reaction to their controversial anti-Falklands war single 'How Does It Feel'.

'We simply haven't been able to get any club work in London,' said spokesman Andy, 'so, as a last resort, we decided to squat in The Rainbow to give our followers the opportunity of seeing us perform.' Squatters were removed from the venue on the next day, but no charges were brought.

Duran Duran

Bowie – mega UK export

Culture Club's Boy George

Police on the beat

Phil Collins

Dexy's Kevin Rowland

New Romantics Spandau Ballet

Single success – Sheena Easton

Human League

Mercury and May of Queen

Bonnie Tyler

Jagger – regular invader

George Michael

IT HAPPENED BEFORE, IT'LL HAPPEN AGAIN

The first 'British Invasion' occurred in the mid-1960s, when numerous British acts dominated the US chart for a couple of years.

In 1964, American kids were bored by cleancut stars like Bobby Vinton, Lesley Gore, Paul & Paula, Dale & Grace, Neil Sedaka and the rest, and the emergence of free-thinkers like The Beatles with anti-establishment looks and philosophies was of far greater interest than further helpings of uninspiring dross which seemed to be parentally approved.

In 1983, things were a little less domestically dominated – British acts like Queen, Pink Floyd, Paul McCartney, Olivia Newton-John and Sheena Easton had released singles which had topped the *Billboard* chart earlier in the decade, although none of those names could be called standard bearers for a new direction in popular music.

The hangover of disco music from the late 1970s could still be detected in much of the chart, as America had turned its nose up at British punk rock, and seemed less than enthused about 2 Tone acts like Madness and The Specials.

British audiences, whose loyalty and attention span seemed extremely limited, had already started to consign most of their newer heroes to the out-tray by the end of 1982. A new breed of stars began to emerge with a fresh approach to fashion – the so-called New Romantics.

Probably the first of these acts to make a significant chart dent in the US were Duran Duran, a quintet fronted by the photogenic Simon Le Bon. It took a couple of years before the celebrity they had achieved in Britain was equalled on the other side of the Atlantic, but in 1983 and early 1984, the group was virtually resident in the US singles chart.

However, the first British group of this new breed to top the US chart was The Human League from Sheffield whose 'Don't You Want Me' topped the US chart in mid-1982, six months after doing the same in Britain.

A similar time gap occurred for Dexy's Midnight Runners's 'Come On Eileen'. Where The Human League had looked comparatively normal, Dexy's (named after the drug dexedrine, which removes the desire to sleep) appeared to be a band of Irish gypsies.

It was a similar story with Culture Club, a quartet fronted by George O'Dowd (aka Boy George) who outraged the establishment by wearing women's clothing. Hits like 'Do You Really Want To Hurt Me' in 1983 and the irresistible 'Karma Chameleon' in 1984 dominated the British chart. The latter hit also topped the US chart, but as with the vast majority of the acts involved in this second 'British Invasion', Culture Club's appeal waned after two years, especially after Boy George was said to have become a heroin addict. Happily, he recovered and by 1987 had returned to the top of the British chart as a solo artist.

This approval of anything British on the part of American record buyers was not restricted to brand new acts; The Police, Bonnie Tyler, David Bowie, The Eurythmics, Phil Collins and George Michael (in his earlier incarnation as half of Wham!) all found new (or renewed) success during the second British wave. Ever since, America has appeared to regard Britain once more as a major source of new musical ideas and new talent.

1983

FRANK GOES STRAIGHT

Frank Zappa and London have not always got along: in 1971 he was barred from the Albert Hall for obscenity. This month he's in London again to conduct 100 musicians at the Barbican Centre playing orchestral versions of his greatest hits.

Zappa, who 'wrote music for orchestras long before I ever wrote for rock groups' has financed the whole operation himself – and after the concert intends to record orchestral music with the London Symphony Orchestra for three days in the studio.

Formerly far-out Frank in rehearsal with the London Symphony Orchestra

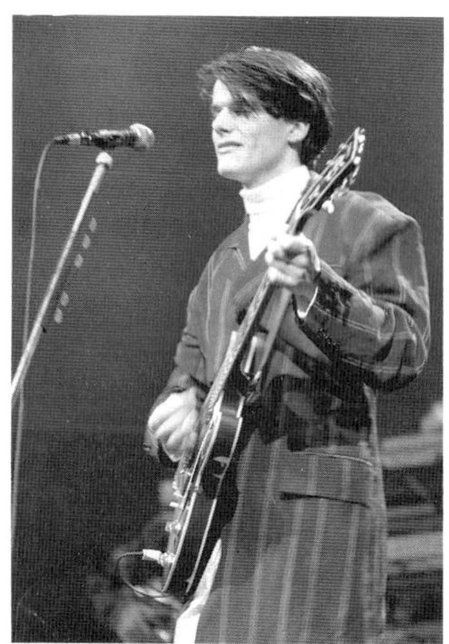

Blow Monkeys moonlighting

CHARTS

	Week 1
US45	Maneater – *Daryl hall & John Oates*
USLP	Business As Usual – *Men At Work*
UK45	Save Your Love – *Rene And Renato*
UKLP	The John Lennon Collection – *John Lennon*

	Week 2
US45	Maneater – *Daryl hall & John Oates*
USLP	Business As Usual – *Men At Work*
UK45	Save Your Love – *Rene And Renato*
UKLP	The John Lennon Collection – *John Lennon*

	Week 3
US45	Down Under – *Men At Work*
USLP	Business As Usual – *Men At Work*
UK45	You Can't Hurry Love – *Phil Collins*
UKLP	The John Lennon Collection – *John Lennon*

	Week 4
US45	Down Under – *Men At Work*
USLP	Business As Usual – *Men At Work*
UK45	You Can't Hurry Love – *Phil Collins*
UKLP	The John Lennon Collection – *John Lennon*

	Week 5
US45	Down Under – *Men At Work*
USLP	Business As Usual – *Men At Work*
UK45	Down Under – *Men At Work*
UKLP	Business As Usual – *Men At Work*

THE GRAPEVINE

■ **What do you do when you stop being a Monkee? Micky Dolenz has just been unearthed at London Weekend Television, where he produces and directs such highbrow material as *Metal Micky* and *No Problem*.**

■ **Starting their live career down the bill at the Moonlight Club in London this month – Dr Robert and The Blow Monkeys.**

ANIMALS FIGHT BACK

Artists For Animals, an offshoot of the British Union for the Abolition of Vivisection, is to form a record label and promote rock gigs in an effort to obtain funds for various animal aid projects. Among the artists and groups putting their name to the project are Kevin Coyne, Paul Gray of The Damned and The Sound, while other groups like Orange Juice, The Thompson Twins and The Raincoats have expressed an interest.

'Even Paul McCartney sent us a really nice book to sell or raffle in order to raise some funds,' claims organizer Viv Smith. 'But we don't really know what to do with it – you see, it's bound in real leather!'

SPLITTING HAIRS

Two notable splits at the start of the year include Haircut 100, last year's teen-idol chart-toppers, and veteran heavy-metal group Thin Lizzy. Both have been torn apart due to their leaders' departures – Haircut singer Nick Hayward and Thin Lizzy frontman Phil Lynott.

Both Lynott and Hayward have plans for solo careers.

Nick leaves, crew cut

BILLY FURY: HALFWAY TO PARADISE?

Billy Fury, one of Britain's foremost rock stars of the late Fifties and early Sixties, died on February 28 after a long history of heart trouble. He had undergone three major operations, including open-heart surgery. He collapsed at his London flat and was found to be dead on arrival. He was 41. Although Fury had nineteen Top 20 hits during the period 1959 to 1965, he never quite made the top spot.

His most successful single was 'Halfway To Paradise', which made No. 2 in 1961. He starred on many top-of-the-bill tours, and was a regular on the TV shows of the time, including *Oh Boy! 6-5 Special* and *Ready Steady Go!* Despite retiring through ill health, he had planned a comeback and recently completed recording an album which was scheduled for release in April. Before The Beatles, Billy Fury (real name Ronald Wycherley) was the nearest thing to Elvis Britain had. His death marks the end of an era.

STAR QUOTE

DONALD FAGEN

Ex-Steely Dan

'You always have to be careful not to repeat yourself. I can't see myself making a spin-off of what I have just done, a standard pop music trick. But everyone only has one idea and it's a matter of finding different ways to couch it.'

KAREN CARPENTER DEAD AT 32

The brother and sister duo of Karen and Richard Carpenter swept all before them in the Seventies, selling over 60 million albums of high-gloss American pop. But the dream ended on February 4 when Karen was found by her parents on the floor of her bedroom in the family's Downey, California, home.

Karen had recently moved to her own apartment in LA following the dissolution of her 1980 marriage to businessman Tom Burris, but was staying with her family. Her mother believes it was her daughter's inability to overcome anorexia nervosa, the so-called 'slimmers' disease', that caused her death. Back in 1975, it caused the cancellation of a British tour by the duo, after which she was confined to bed for two months.

Karen Carpenter at the drum kit with brother Richard in the background, the darling of middle-of-the-road audiences

CHARTS

US45	Africa *Toto*
USLP	Business As Usual *Men At Work*
UK45	Down Under *Men At Work*
UKLP	Business As Usual *Men At Work*
WEEK 2	
US45	Down Under *Men At Work*
USLP	Business As usual *Men At Work*
UK45	Down Under *Men At Work*
UKLP	Business As usual *Men At Work*
WEEK 3	
US45	Baby, Come To Me *Patti Austin*
USLP	Business As Usual *Men At Work*
UK45	Too Shy *Kajagoogoo*
UKLP	Business As Usual *Men At Work*
WEEK 4	
US45	Baby, Come To Me *Patti Austin*
USLP	Thriller *Michael Jackson*
UK45	Too Shy *Kajagoogoo*
UKLP	Business As Usual *Men At Work*

WHAT'S THAT SOUND?

Meet Einsturzende Neubauten. Their names means Collapsing New Buildings, and that gives some idea of the German quintet's obsession with destruction. They use road drills, sledgehammers and axes in their shows to create sounds like you've *never* heard before.

Recently, Neubauten leader Blixa Bargeld recorded the 12-inch single 'Thirsty Animal' with the Birthday Party's Rowland Howard and American anarcho-punk Lydia Lunch. Bargeld miked up his chest to pick up the eerie sound of another group member crushing his bones . . . and if you think that's off the wall, they *had* intended to include the recording of a side of meat being sawn up!

A COMPACT FUTURE?

Hot on the heels of their video disc, Philips are about to follow up with something just as exciting – the compact disc. The player costs between £400 and £500 ($800-$1000) – don't panic, it will plug into your existing hi-fi – thankfully the discs should cost little more than a plastic album.

First commercial development of the CD was by Sony in Japan, where 2,000 were snapped up in a matter of days. In spite of such sales figures, the largest British record company, EMI, has decided to stay on the sidelines for a few years ('We'll wait and see what happens') leaving it to Welsh independent Nimbus Records to start building the first British factory.

Typically adventurous, Virgin Records are quickly into the fray, offering five of their biggest selling albums – 'Tubular Bells' (Mike Oldfield), 'Dare' (Human League), 'Kissing To Be Clever' (Culture Club), 'Face Value' (Phil Collins) and 'Architecture and Morality' (OMD). Virgin expect them to sell for less than £10 ($20) each.

Jackson – busy in London

THE GRAPEVINE

- **Michael Jackson has been in London this month, writing songs with Paul McCartney, producing Gladys Knight and sitting backstage at a Gap Band Concert.**
- **New and old wavers jamming in Los Angeles – The Doors' Robbie Krieger with Adam Ant, and ex-Velvet Underground bassman John Cale with The Psychedelic Furs.**

MARCH 1983

STAR QUOTE

MICK JAGGER

'I don't want to be doing the same thing with no other interest for the rest of my life. I wouldn't mind singing old Rolling Stones' songs when I'm forty-five, but I don't want to do it three hundred and sixty-five days a year.'

DODGY MARC-ETING

Soft Cell's relationship with Phonogram Records seems to have reached the end this month, with singer Marc Almond and his manager Stevo trashing the company offices. The reason for their displeasure was the coupling of their two-year-old chart-topper 'Tainted Love' with the new single 'Numbers' in an attempt to increase the latter's sales potential.

When the singer heard of this, he and his manager confronted the company, setting off a fire extinguisher in a lawyer's office and smashing gold discs on the wall.

Stevo commented that the strategy marked the company's lack of confidence in the record, claiming it was 'degrading to give away a two-year-old record with it without anybody's knowledge or consent.'

Since Almond is contracted to Phonogram through Stevo's own label, Some Bizzare, a parting of the ways seems likely.

CHARTS

US45	Billie Jean *Michael Jackson*
USLP	Thriller *Michael Jackson*
UK45	Billie Jean *Michael Jackson*
UKLP	Thriller *Michael Jackson*
WEEK 2	
US45	Billie Jean *Michael Jackson*
USLP	Thriller *Michael Jackson*
UK45	Billie Jean *Michael Jackson*
UKLP	Thriller *Michael Jackson*
WEEK 3	
US45	Billie Jean *Michael Jackson*
USLP	Thriller *Michael Jackson*
UK45	Total Eclipse Of The Heart *Bonnie Tyler*
UKLP	Thriller *Michael Jackson*
WEEK 4	
US45	Billie Jean *Michael Jackson*
USLP	Thriller *Michael Jackson*
UK45	Total Eclipse Of The Heart *Bonnie Tyler*
UKLP	Thriller *Michael Jackson*

Jagger: not 365 days a year

Wrestling women: Toyah as Trafford Tanzi . . . and Debbie Harry as Teaneck Tanzi

FIGHTING TALK FROM TOYAH, DEBBIE

Toyah Wilcox is to take on the starring role in the hit play *Trafford Tanzi* at London's Mermaid Theatre this month – and Debbie Harry opens on Broadway in the same part in April! The comedy is currently set to play in no fewer than seventeen different countries – and Debbie Harry's run, expected to be limited to three or four months, is just one of these.

Both she and Toyah have been training for the part, which requires them to battle with all manner of opponents in a wrestling ring. The object of the play is to highlight the battle of the sexes – and, no matter what else it does, it's likely to leave the two with muscles where they never knew they had them before. . .

THE UFO HAS LANDED

UFO, one of the hardest working heavy rock bands around, will be splitting after their current British tour, following the collapse last week of lead singer Phil Mogg. The singer is now reportedly in hospital recovering from a nervous breakdown. His onstage problems in Athens provoked a near riot among the 5,000-strong audience.

His co-writer Neil Carter commented, 'The band has been in existence for thirteen years, and I think the pressures of keeping it together through so many changes have been too much for Phil. I don't know what will happen after the UK tour.'

Mogg later confirmed: 'After a long look at UFO, we all feel the time has come to call a halt.'

THE GRAPEVINE

- **On the comeback trail this month – David Bowie, with a new record label, EMI America, an album, 'Let's Dance', upcoming, and a world tour. His new five-year recording contract is said to be worth a cool $10 million.**
- **On the way up – Welsh group The Alarm, releasing their second single 'Marching On'.**

The Alarm march on

TAKE FIVE BOYS . . .

New Edition – their 'Candy Girl' sweetner to be followed by 'Popcorn Love'

New Edition, the five-piece singing sensation currently storming up the US charts, may well have put you in mind of another singing group – The Jacksons, to be precise. Their hit song, 'Candy Girl', even sounds very much like the J5's 'ABC' – and with Michael Jackson topping the charts worldwide, success was surely more than just coincidence.

All five group members grew up within blocks of each other in Boston's Roxbury area, and formed the group two years ago. Bobby Brown and his four companions were spotted at a talent show . . . and the rest is history.

CHARTS

US45	Billie Jean *Michael jackson*
USLP	Thriller *Michael Jackson*
UK45	Is There Something I Should Know *Duran Duran*
UKLP	Sweet Dreams (Are Made Of This) *Eurythmics*
	WEEK 2
US45	Billie Jean *Michael Jackson*
USLP	Thriller *Michael Jackson*
UK45	Is There Something I Should Know *Duran Duran*
UKLP	The Final Cut *Pink Floyd*
	WEEK 3
US45	Billie Jean *Michael Jackson*
USLP	Thriller *Michael Jackson*
UK45	Let's Dance *David Bowie*
UKLP	The Final Cut Pink Floyd
	WEEK 4
US45	Come On Eileen *Dexy's Midnight Runners*
USLP	Thriller *Michael Jackson*
UK45	Let's Dance *David Bowie*
UKLP	Thriller *Michael Jackson*
	WEEK 5
US45	Beat it *Michael Jackson*
USLP	Thriller *Michael Jackson*
UK45	Let's Dance *David Bowie*
UKLP	Let's Dance *David Bowie*

WATERS RUNS OUT

Muddy Waters, godfather of Chicago blues and – along with Chuck Berry – the main inspiration of The Rolling Stones (who took their name from one of his songs) died on 30 April after a heart attack. He was 68.

Like many music legends, Waters actually made some of his greatest music in his latter years – his last two albums, 'Hard Again' and 'I'm Ready', recorded with the help of Johnny Winter, one of his greatest disciples – are among his finest ever recordings.

AMERICA THE BEAUTIFUL?

Once upon a time, black music was the face of protest . . . from The Temptations ('Stop The War') through Sly Stone ('There's A Riot Goin' On') and the cutting social commentary of Curtis Mayfield. Now, a not-so-subtle change of mood has come to light with The Dazz Band, surprise winners of this years' R&B Grammy Award, giving widely publicized pre-vote statements about their 'American image . . . something the youth can look up to and feel proud to be American.'

Strangely enough, The Gap Band's Ronnie Wilson – The Dazz Band's rivals in the Grammy stakes – was quoted spouting in similar jingoistic fasion about 'the greatest country on earth'.

Coupled with The Temptations turning coat with 'Made In America' and Philippe Wynne's 'America, We're Still Number One', it seems there's either been an outbreak of patriotic pride in the black community, or winning a Grammy might be about more than just making music . . .

PRETENDERS – ANOTHER DEATH

Pete Farndon, founder member and bassist with The Pretenders until he was sacked last year, was found dead in the bath at his London flat on Friday, 15 April. A post mortem revealed that he had drowned, which is likely to be the official cause of death.

This is the second tragedy to hit the group: only a week after Farndon left The Pretenders last June, guitarist James Honeyman-Scott was found dead of a cocaine overdose.

Pete Frandon (left) with fellow Pretender Martin Chambers

THE GRAPEVINE

- **A Michael Jackson impersonator managed to fool reporters from the *Village Voice* in New York as well as the management of the Peppermint Lounge disco by signing autographs accompanied by two bodyguards. He also mimed two Jackson songs before being told to 'beat it'.**
- **U2's British No. 1 with 'War' is their record label Island's first No. 1 LP since 'Rock Follies' in 1978.**

U2's Bono: Island's second No. 1 album

MAY 1983

DISCO INFERNO

Disco is making a comeback at the Fun House, a New York warehouse where 3,500 kids all manage to enjoy themselves . . . all night. The dancing starts at 10pm and doesn't stop till 8.30 the next morning.

The man behind the music is one John 'Jellybean' Benitez, who remarks: 'It's something the kids *have* to do. Their whole life revolves around being there on Saturday.'

Dance music producers like Arthur Baker visit the Fun House 'to see what people are getting off on. "Planet Rock", "Walking On Sunshine", those records were consciously made to get over at the Fun House. . . a lot of producers test out records there.'

New stars are being made at the Fun House every weekend: DJ Mark Kamins has already broken a young singer called Madonna, whose 'Everybody' became a New York hit and is now about to go national.

IMPOSTOR IN THE HOUSE

Elvis: politico pop from post-punk craftsman

Elvis Costello's new single 'Pills And Soap' was rush released by Demon Records this month in a limited edition of 15,000. F-Beat, his usual label, are currently negotiating a new licensing deal – and Costello typically took action. 'I wanted it out quickly and the record company lawyers are still arguing.'

He referred to legal complications which have already delayed the release of his latest LP and postponed a UK tour planned for July.

Costello delivered the single to the NME offices himself, commenting: 'It's a new song that will appear on the new album, although that will be a different version. I wanted the song to be heard at this particular time. It couldn't wait the month or two that it will take to finalize legal matters.'

It's certainly no coincidence that the song, painting a bleak picture of life in Britain under the Conservative Party, has been released on the eve of a General Election.

CHARTS

US45	Beat It — *Michael Jackson*
USLP	Thriller — *Michael Jackson*
UK45	True — *Spandau Ballet*
UKLP	Let's Dance — *David Bowie*
WEEK 2	
US45	Beat It — *Michael Jackson*
USLP	Thriller — *Michael Jackson*
UK45	True — *Spandau Ballet*
UKLP	Let's Dance — *David Bowie*
WEEK 3	
US45	Let's Dance — *David Bowie*
USLP	Thriller — *Michael Jackson*
UK45	True — *Spandau Ballet*
UKLP	True — *Spandau Ballet*
WEEK 4	
US45	Flashdance — *Irene Cara*
USLP	Thriller — *Michael Jackson*
UK45	True — *Spandau Ballet*
UKLP	The Luxury Gap — *Heaven 17*

THE GRAPEVINE

- **Over 40,000 turned up to see Paul Weller's new Style Council play a Nuclear Disarmament benefit in London's Brockwell Park; they played just two numbers: 'Speak Like A Child' and 'Money Go Round'.**
- **Yazoo, the partnership of Alison Moyet and Vince Clarke, will be splitting after their forthcoming album, 'You And Me Both' after 15 months and four hit singles.**

Cliff: a quarter of a century, not out

SILVER CLIFF!

Veteran British rock'n'roller Cliff Richard celebrates his 25th anniversary this year – and he's celebrating as only he can.

His new album out this month, 'Dressed For The Occasion', was recorded last year during a charity concert with the London Philharmonic Orchestra at London's Royal Albert Hall, while the single from the album 'True Love Ways', pays tribute to one of his own early influences, Buddy Holly.

He'll also be topping the bill at the Christian Greenbelt Festival, while a nationwide tour includes 27-nights at London's Victoria Apollo Theatre.

Clarke (left) and Moyet: Yazoo to split

JUNE 1983

IT'S GREAT TO BE YOUNG

Wham!: George Michael (left) and Andrew Ridgeley

Wham!, two teenagers from Hertfordshire, England, have just scored their third hit single, 'Bad Boys'. They've shot from unemployment to stardom in a mere 18 months, but even now they're not satisfied.

Wham! guitarist, Andrew Ridgeley reveals that their second single, 'Young Guns', could have been a bigger smash. 'The best illustration of the job CBS can do is that when we were at No. 24, they ran out of records. They hadn't printed enough to meet the demand!'

George Michael, the group's singer and songwriter, has already got a solo career in mind. He plans to release a soul ballad that wouldn't suit Wham! in their present format. 'It's probably going to be bigger than anything we've done before,' he says. 'I just love the idea of being able to keep the identity of the band consistent.'

THE MARQUEE: 25 GLORIOUS YEARS

London's famous Marquee Club, which gave a start to such groups as The Who and The Rolling Stones, celebrates it's silver anniversary this month.

Many of its old friends are coming back for the occasion, including re-unions of John Mayall's Bluesbreakers (featuring Mick Taylor (ex-Stones) on guitar); The Yardbirds (including original members Jim McCarty, Chris Dreja and Paul Samwell-Smith); Manfred Mann, Ten Years After and Man.

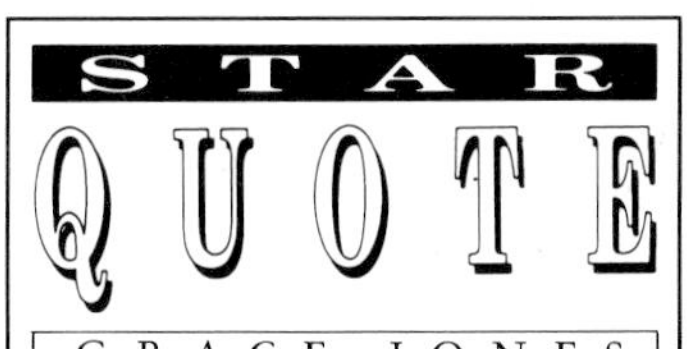

'I was always really determined to look the way I wanted to look, and I wanted to cut my hair. I wanted to look different because I was used to looking different. Because of my religious background I'd always been encouraged to look different.'

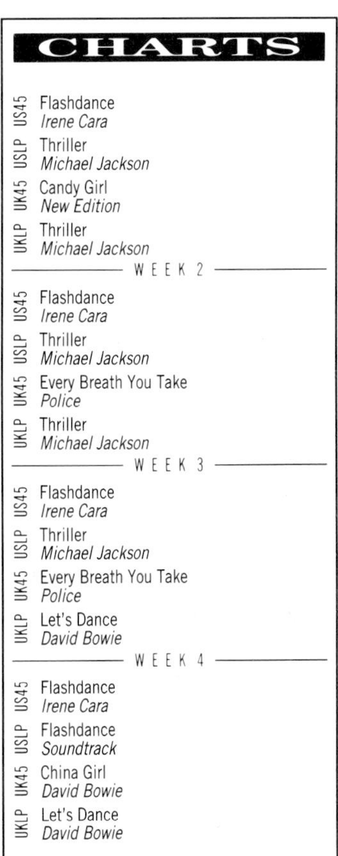

CHARTS

US45	Flashdance	*Irene Cara*
USLP	Thriller	*Michael Jackson*
UK45	Candy Girl	*New Edition*
UKLP	Thriller	*Michael Jackson*
WEEK 2		
US45	Flashdance	*Irene Cara*
USLP	Thriller	*Michael Jackson*
UK45	Every Breath You Take	*Police*
UKLP	Thriller	*Michael Jackson*
WEEK 3		
US45	Flashdance	*Irene Cara*
USLP	Thriller	*Michael Jackson*
UK45	Every Breath You Take	*Police*
UKLP	Let's Dance	*David Bowie*
WEEK 4		
US45	Flashdance	*Irene Cara*
USLP	Flashdance	*Soundtrack*
UK45	China Girl	*David Bowie*
UKLP	Let's Dance	*David Bowie*

COME BACK GARY . . . COME BACK PAUL?

Two and a half years after playing his farewell concert at Wembley Arena, reclusive synthesizer wizard Gary Numan returns with a mega tour. Backed by original members of his group, he opens his tour at Glasgow Apollo – the same venue where he played his very first solo date four years before.

Meanwhile, having finished his movie – *Give My Regards To Broad Street* – it's likely that Paul McCartney will be returning to the stage, very possibly with Beatle colleague Ringo Starr on drums.

Numan: back in black

THE GRAPEVINE

- **Playing a four-week residency in London's Venue this month - up and coming Australian band Midnight Oil.**
- **Said to be going their separate ways are Belfast band The Undertones. They were the first major new wave band to emerge from Northern Ireland. Their lead singer Feargal Sharkey is planning a solo career.**

Grace: religious reasons

AFRICAN BAND BANNED

Juluka, the multi-racial South African group who made the acclaimed 'Scatterlings Of Africa' album, arrived in England this month to find themselves banned by the Musicians Union.

The Union's opinion was that 'Since it would not be possible for us to approve one of our bands working in South Africa, there is no possibility of an exchange.'

The ban was eventually lifted, with the group donating their fees to charity. But unless they decide to become political refugees – something the group claim would defeat the whole object of their existence – they are unlikely to work in Britain again in the near future.

PSYCHO KILLERS!

Punk survivors The Ramones have the 'honour' of making the first video to be banned by America's all music-cable channel MTV. Although their manager and Warner Bros. President Mo Ostin 'defended the film to the last frame', MTV refused to show it. With a hospital patient hallucinating while the doctors are disecting skeletons, perhaps it's not surprising. . .

Meanwhile, The Ramones' record was slipping down the charts. Only when the LP had dropped out completely would MTV relent and show a cut version 'about twice a day'.

YOUNG AT HEART

Paul Young's new album sees some adventurous songs, notably Joy Division's 'Love Will Tear Us Apart'. 'We're expecting some flak for that', he admits of his switch from Sixties Motown to Seventies Manchester. 'A lot of people take Joy Division *very* seriously . . .'

After the classy chart-topping success of his soulful reworking of Marvin Gaye's 'Wherever I Lay My Hat' the same could be said of Paul Young.

STAR QUOTE

GEORGE BENSON

'I think music will change to the point where I am no longer compatible with it. A lot of the electronic things I don't like, you know – WHEEEEE! I don't think that's important at all. Things like that let me know that maybe I'm getting a little senile or something!'

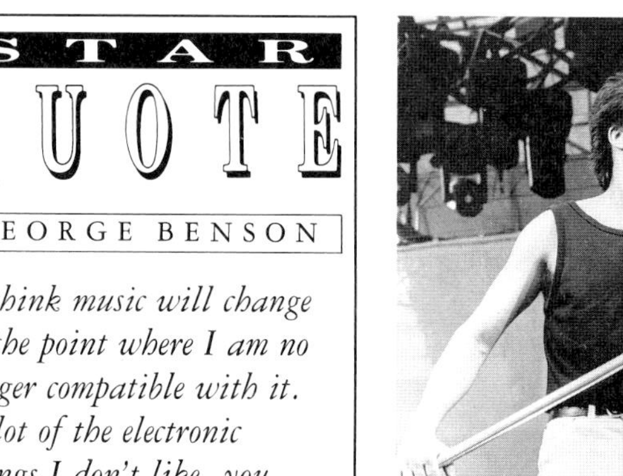

Paul Young: Joy Divison cover

TOWNSHEND – BACK TO BOOKS

Having recently wound up his own publishing company, Eel Pie Books, Pete Townshend this month announced his association with top highbrow publishers Faber & Faber. The Who guitarist will be commissioning not only written work but music, films and videos connected with such books.

Though he won't be dealing solely with music, Townshend did promise 'a guide to rock journalists – so's you can avoid them'.

One of Townshend's first projects will be about heroin and its effect on Britain's youth; Townshend has personal experience of the drug, having been cured by electro-acupuncture.

PARIS IN STYLE

The Style Council are releasing the first of a series of four-track EPs which are to be recorded in different parts of the world, with a view to exchanging cultures and ideas.

The first is 'The Style Council à Paris', featuring 'Long Hot Summer', 'Party Chambers', 'The Paris Match' and 'Le Depart'. Paul Weller commented in typically enigmatic style: 'French boys are the most beautiful in the world. I think there's an undercurrent of tension in Paris that, say, Singapore just doesn't have.'

CHARTS

US45	Flashdance *Irene Cara*
USLP	Flashdance *Soundtrack*
UK45	Every Breath You Take *Police*
UKLP	Synchronicity *Police*
	WEEK 2
US45	Every Breath You Take *Police*
USLP	Thriller *Michael Jackson*
UK45	Baby Jane *Rod Stewart*
UKLP	Synchronicity *Police*
	WEEK 3
US45	Every Breath You Take *Police*
USLP	Thriller *Michael Jackson*
UK45	Wherever I Lay My Hat *Paul Young*
UKLP	Fantastic *Wham!*
	WEEK 4
US45	Every Breath You Take *Police*
USLP	Synchronicity *Police*
UK45	Wherever I Lay My Hat *Paul Young*
UKLP	Fantastic *Wham!*
	WEEK 5
US45	Every Breath You Take *Police*
USLP	Synchronicity *Police*
UK45	Wherever I Lay My Hat *Paul Young*
UKLP	Fantastic *Wham!*

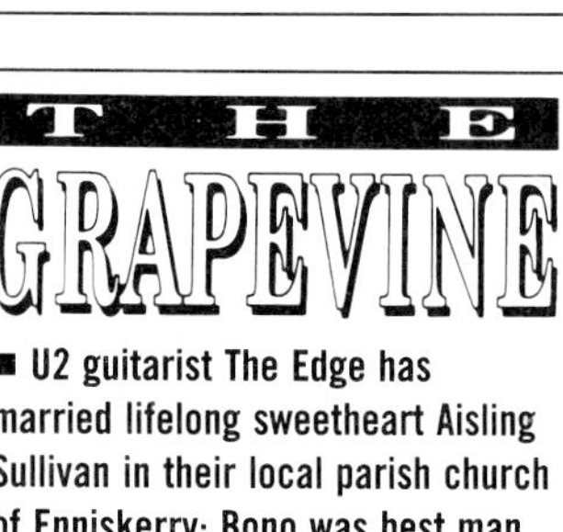

- **U2 guitarist The Edge has married lifelong sweetheart Aisling Sullivan in their local parish church of Enniskerry; Bono was best man.**
- **Splitting up: two groups sired directly or indirectly by The 2-Tones ska explosion – Birmingham's The Beat and Specials spin-offs – Fun Boy Three.**
- **Little Red Rooster, Mick Jagger, turned 40 on the 26th.**

Farewell Fun Boys . . .

. . . and bye bye Beat

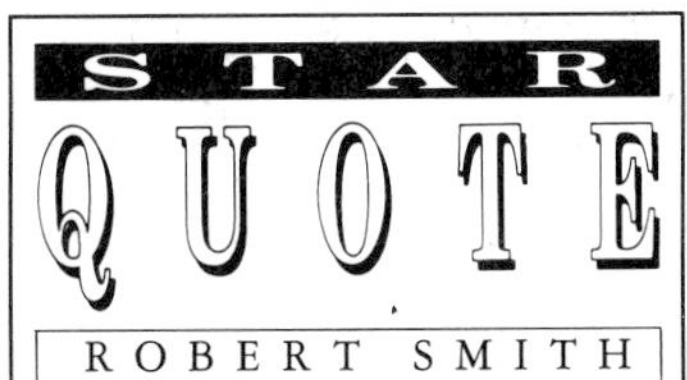

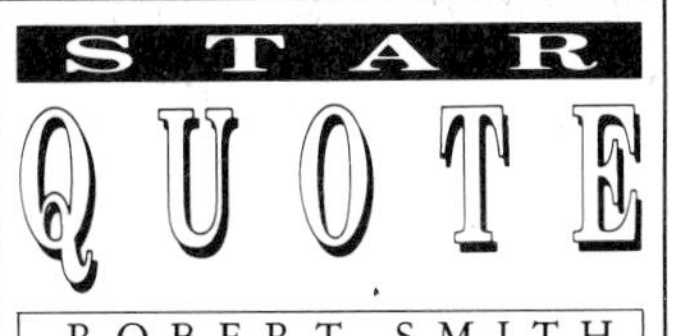

A SINGLE LIFE FOR MICHAEL

With only two-thirds of the year gone, Michael Jackson's 'Thriller' is already destined to be the album of 1983. Since entering the chart in December 1982, just a week after release, it's remained a high flyer, spawning no fewer than four Top 10 singles, namely 'The Girl Is Mine', 'Billie Jean', 'Beat It' and 'Wanna Be Startin' Somethin''.

Riding on its coat-tails is Motown's TV-advertised 'Greatest Hits', a combination of pre-1976 material from Michael and his brothers. What's more, 'Beat It' is returning to the singles chart as part of a medley by Eurodisco act Clubhouse, while the title track of Jackson's album is likely to be the next single.

His previous album 'Off The Wall', boasted five hit singles – and 'Thriller' looks like topping even that.

CHARTS

US45	Every Breath You Take	*Police*
USLP	Synchronicity	*Police*
UK45	Wherever I Lay My Hat	*Paul Young*
UKLP	No Parlez	*Paul Young*
WEEK 2		
US45	Every Breath You Take	*Police*
USLP	Synchronicity	*Police*
UK45	Wherever I Lay My Hat	*Paul Young*
UKLP	No Parlez	*Paul Young*
WEEK 3		
US45	Every Breath You Take	*Police*
USLP	Synchronicity	*Police*
UK45	Give It Up	*KC & The Sunshine Band*
UKLP	Punch The Clock	*Elvis Costello*
WEEK 4		
US45	Every Breath You Take	*Police*
USLP	Synchronicity	*Police*
UK45	Gold	*Spandau Ballet*
UKLP	Fantastic	*Wham!*

COP THAT, AMERICA!

There aren't many honours The Police haven't achieved in their short but illustrious career – yet the British three-piece supergroup have made history in more ways than one this month.

The single 'Every Breath You Take' from the band's fifth album, 'Synchronicity', currently tops the US singles chart at the same time as the album tops the LP chart – thus ensuring immortality as the first-ever act on the A & M label to manage this simultaneous feat.

STAR QUOTE

ROBERT SMITH

of The Cure

'I'm probably even less aware of what's going on now than I was two years ago. . . I'm not a consumer at all. I don't seem to find it interesting. As I do more myself, I get less interested in what other people are doing.'

Police: double top

War – if you can do it we can do it to U2!

MARC WAVES GOODBYE

A 'confused and unhappy' Marc Almond suddenly quit the music business this week via an emotional open letter to the press.

His announcement follows two bizarre incidents, in one of which he threatened a *Record Mirror* journalist with a whip! In the other, he was assaulted outside his home by a passerby when chasing two zealous fans who kept ringing his doorbell and running away.

'I no longer wish to sing on records, in fact I no longer wish to sing,' claimed Almond. 'If there are any future recordings they will be extremely few (if any), which will come as a great relief to those who find my singing a pain to the ears.'

Later reports, however, suggest that Marc may already be regretting his decision. His record label report he is feeling much better and has decided to go ahead with the recording of Soft Cell's next single and third LP next month. Plans of a rumoured collaboration with Nick Cave remain in doubt, however.

THE GRAPEVINE

- **In answer to U2's new album 'War', US soul group War have recorded a three-part track called . . . 'U2'!**
- **Hottest unsigned band of the month – Irish folk-meets-Irish punk sextet Pogue Mahone (Gaelic for 'kiss my ass!'); sample song title: 'Repeal The Licensing Laws'.**
- **Joey Ramone has undergone emergency brain surgery after a street brawl.**

LABOUR OF LOVE

UB40: YTS on video cost band a bomb in bonus beer

UB40, the multi-racial Birmingham reggae group, took their name from a British Unemployment Benefit document – now they're a music legend. And they're confident enough to release an album of cover versions that celebrates their childhood influences. The title? 'Labour Of Love'.

Surprisingly, this was nearly their first album. 'We actually set out to popularize reggae in the first place,' explains guitarist Robin Campbell. 'We felt like we were the only people in the world listening to reggae. Of course it wasn't true, but we felt like nobody else was . . . we saw ourselves as ambassadors.'

The first single from the album is 'Red Red Wine': the band know it as a Tony Tribe song, but the original was written by Neil Diamond. The stars of the video are unemployed local lads on the Youth Training Scheme, whom the band invited down to a local pub to have a drink on the house. The bar bill was 'astronomical'.

Drummer Jim White comments: 'If people are going to accuse us of selling out, then we've sold out on the day we started.'

CLASH! BAND SACKS JONES

Mick Jones has been sacked by The Clash. An official statement read: 'Joe Strummer and Paul Simonon have decided that Mick Jones should leave the group. It is felt that Jones has drifted apart from the original idea of The Clash. In future, it will allow Joe and Paul to get on with the job that Joe and Paul set out to do from the beginning.'

The songwriting duo of Strummer and Jones have had several ups and downs, including one in 1981 when Jones emigrated to the States and last year when Strummer went missing for a month. The first was settled by what Strummer termed 'a simple or garden punch up', while his re-appearance in 1982 co-incided with drummer Topper Headon's departure.

Jones' comment: 'I'll be carrying on in the same direction as in the beginning,' indicates a deep divide between himself and the other two members of Britain's longest-running punk group, and reconciliation this time seems unlikely.

THE GRAPEVINE

- New chart band The JoBoxers have risked life and limb shooting a video in the ring with British boxing champ Frank Bruno.
- Knocked out of Bow Wow Wow this month – Burmese teenage singer Anabella Lewin; a solo career seems likely.
- In the red – Abba, whose Swedish company lost money last year instead of a projected £4 million ($8 m) profit.

Bow Wow Wow's Annabella to go it alone

GLENN TILBROOK

Ex-Squeeze

'The Lennon-McCartney comparison was frequently made and that was an image that critics could relate to. But it wasn't something people in the street could pick up on the way they'll pick up on someone who's really good-looking.'

CHARTS

US45	Sweet Dreams	*Eurythmics*
USLP	Synchronicity	*Police*
UK45	Gold	*Spandau Ballet*
UKLP	Fantastic	*Wham!*
WEEK 2		
US45	Maniac	*Michael Sembello*
USLP	Thriller	*Michael Jackson*
UK45	Red Red Wine	*UB40*
UKLP	Flick Of The Switch	*AC/DC*
WEEK 3		
US45	Maniac	*Michael Sembello*
USLP	Synchronicity	*Police*
UK45	Red Red Wine	*UB40*
UKLP	Construction Time Again	*Depeche Mode*
WEEK 4		
US45	Tell Her About It	*Billy Joel*
USLP	Synchronicity	*Police*
UK45	Red Red Wine	*UB40*
UKLP	No Parlez	*Paul Young*

COPS SAY YES TO LEAGUE

The Anti-Nowhere League's album 'Live In Yugoslavia' finally re-appears three months after the original pressing was seized by the police. Only 1500 copies had reached distributors at that time, and several thousand more were impounded at a police warehouse because of audible obscenities.

The re-cut released album has five offending words bleeped out, although dedicated fans can obtain the record in Europe without bleeps.

Anti-Nowheres back after bleeps

WAR STORIES

Lindisfarne singer Alan Hull has attracted great controversy with his new solo single 'Malvinas Melody'. The song attacks the waste of life occasioned by the Falklands War – and the British press haven't been slow in picking up the story.

Hull's record company, Black Crow, hit back at obvious, 'sick, and cynical' quotes from government politicians, and accused radio stations of censorship.

As for Hull, he believes: 'That two nations could waste young lives fighting over a bit of land and six million sheep is beyond my comprehension.'

CULTURE CRASH

Culture Club, currently top of the British singles chart with 'Karma Chameleon', have had to re-schedule their British tour because of an injury to drummer Jon Moss's hand.

After playing their opening concerts at Brighton, Birmingham and Oxford, the band arrived at Sheffield for their fourth show, only for Moss to sustain his injury in a fall outside the venue.

He tried to play on inside the City Hall to avoid disappointing the full house, but soon had to admit defeat. A specialist has ordered him to rest for two weeks, but he should be fit enough to join the group – featuring flamboyant lead singer Boy George – for their forthcoming European tour.

Joe Moss: hand injury hampers Club outing as tour dates are put back

BLUE IS THE COLOUR

New Order's 'Blue Monday' (no relation to the Fats Domino song of the same name) first appeared in the UK Indie charts in March. It took a week to reach No. 1 there, and remained so for nine weeks.

It reached No. 12 in the major singles chart, surviving a challenge from the follow-up 'Confusion', produced by Arthur Baker, and selling over 400,000 copies to become the highest-selling 12-inch single of all time.

Unfortunately because Factory Records are not members of the body that commissions Gallup's official UK chart, the band will not receive a silver disc for selling over 250,000 records. Not that they'll be worried – the single is on its way back to No. 9.

CHARTS

Week	Chart	Title	Artist
	US45	Total Eclipse Of The Heart	*Bonnie Tyler*
	USLP	Synchronicity	*Police*
	UK45	Karma Chameleon	*Culture Club*
	UKLP	Labour Of Love	*UB40*
WEEK 2	US45	Total Eclipse Of The Heart	*Bonnie Tyler*
	USLP	Synchronicity	*Police*
	UK45	Karma Chameleon	*Culture Club*
	UKLP	Labour Of Love	*UB40*
WEEK 3	US45	Total Eclipse Of The Heart	*Bonnie Tyler*
	USLP	Synchronicity	*Police*
	UK45	Karma Chameleon	*Culture Club*
	UKLP	Labour Of Love	*UB40*
WEEK 4	US45	Total Eclipse Of The Heart	*Bonnie Tyler*
	USLP	Synchronicity	*Police*
	UK45	Karma Chameleon	*Culture Club*
	UKLP	Genesis	*Genesis*
WEEK 5	US45	Islands In The Stream	*Kenny Rogers & Dolly Parton*
	USLP	Synchronicity	*Police*
	UK45	Karma Chameleon	*Culture Club*
	UKLP	Colour By Numbers	*Culture Club*

THE GRAPEVINE

- **Unmasked on American TV – heavy rockers Kiss, 18 albums in make-up before revealing (nearly) all this month.**
- **Temporarily going solo this month – Queen guitarist Brian May, with his first single 'Starfleet'; an album of the same name features fellow guitarist Eddie Van Halen.**
- **Influential country star Merle Travis has died in Nashville, aged 65.**

HAPPY BIRTHDAY MLK

Stevie Wonder's campaign to have Dr Martin Luther King's birthday declared a national holiday in the United States has finally borne fruit.

This month saw President Reagan announce the new national holiday, the bill being passed by 78 votes to 22. And Wonder's campaign, the anthem of which was 'Happy Birthday' from his 'Hotter Than July' album, has clearly been a major factor in achieving this.

Right: Stevie wins campaign for King memorial day

NOVEMBER

THE BRITISH ARE COMING – AGAIN!

Asia: two in the US chart as UK invasion hots up

In a situation unknown since the British Invasion and Beatlemania, almost a third of this month's *Billboard's* Hot 100 are from UK acts.

There are two apiece from Asia, The Eurythmics and The Police, while the old and new waves are equally well represented.

In the veteran category are The Animals, Cliff Richard, David Bowie, Elton John, The Kinks, The Moody Blues, Robert Plant and Rod Stewart. Making up the quota come Bonnie Tyler, Culture Club, Def Leppard, Elvis Costello, The Fixx, Genesis, Human League, JoBoxers, Madness, Naked Eyes, Paul Young, Roman Holiday, Sheena Easton, Spandau Ballet and Wham!

Eurythmics Annie and Dave

Britain can also claim half of the fastest-climbing entry since John Lennon's 'Imagine' leapt in at No. 20 in October 1971 - and fittingly it's his former colleague Paul McCartney, whose duet with Michael Jackson 'Say, Say, Say' is the record in question.

FRANKLY . . . IT'S FRANKIE!

Tipped for the top in 1984 – that's Frankie Goes To Hollywood, a Liverpool band rejoicing in the tag of 'post-punk S & M gay cabaret act' recently signed to the new Zang Tumb Tuum label.

With two outrageous front men, Holly Johnson and Paul Rutherford, they seem to have twice the fun and 'Relax', their first ever release, is clearly bound for the top.

Holly: 'It's like these untamed creatures meet (producer) Trevor Horn and his stamp is all over it. Because it was our first single and there's no ready market we just had to have as much fun as we could when we were making it. We just thought – "buzz" – and then we'll know when it's right.'

Frankie: relaxing to the top

BETTER BY DESIGN

Barney Bubbles, who sadly took his own life this month, was just as influential as the groups whose record sleeves he designed. Working with a style so personal it was as recognizable as a signature, he rose to fame designing for the likes of Ian Dury and Elvis

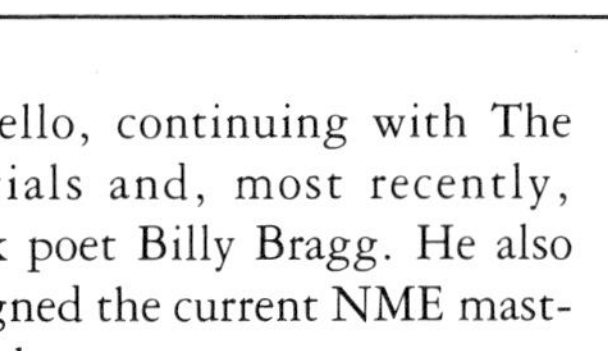

Costello, continuing with The Specials and, most recently, punk poet Billy Bragg. He also designed the current NME masthead logo.

Real name Colin Fulcher, this modest artist also directed videos for the likes of Costello and The Specials, and will probably best be remembered for his work with the pioneering independent 'Stiff' label. Arguably, no one man has had a greater and more influential effect on record sleeve design than the late lamented Bubbles. He will be sadly missed.

CHARTS

US45	Islands In The Stream — *Kenny Rogers & Dolly Parton*
USLP	Synchronicity — *Police*
UK45	Karma Chameleon — *Culture Club*
UKLP	Colour By Numbers — *Culture Club*
WEEK 2	
US45	All Night Long (All Night) — *Lionel Richie*
USLP	Synchronicity — *Police*
UK45	Uptown Girl — *Billy Joel*
UKLP	Colour By Numbers — *Culture Club*
WEEK 3	
US45	All Night Long (All Night) — *Lionel Richie*
USLP	Synchronicity — *Police*
UK45	Uptown Girl — *Billy Joel*
UKLP	Can't Slow Down — *Lionel Richie*
WEEK 4	
US45	All Night Long (All Night) — *Lionel Richie*
USLP	Metal Health — *Quiet Riot*
UK45	Uptown Girl — *Billy Joel*
UKLP	Colour By Numbers — *Culture Club*

STAR QUOTE

OZZY OSBOURNE

'There's no originality in heavy metal any more. When Black Sabbath started, we had a message to give out, we were very politically oriented, but it's got to the point that nobody gives a shit any more. It's just let's get down and bang, bang your heads and all this shit.'

Ozzy: deep and meaningful

THE GRAPEVINE

- **The Pretenders return this month with new additions Robbie McIntosh and Malcolm Foster, both from The Foster Brothers.**
- **Out of a job after sixteen years – J. Geils, banned singer Peter Wolf, has been fired due to 'creative differences'.**
- **Lydia Murdock's 'Superstar' answer to Michael Jackson's 'Billie Jean' the latest in a long line of replies destined to be forgotten.**

KINGS OF AMERICA

If you're American, there's no way you can escape The Police. 'Synchronicity', the album, has notched up 17 weeks at the top of the US album charts, while their videos are an MTV staple.

A current arena tour plays to 17,000-plus fans per night, a far cry from the early days when they carried their gear in a single van and once played to half a dozen people. Fans at the Omni Arena, Atlanta, are typical in their appreciation of two hours of the best of British music.

Guitarist Andy Summers is down to earth about the prospect. 'I prefer to think our audience isn't a lot of beer-swilling numbskulls and I don't think they are. I'm just glad we've got an audience at all. And surprised,' he adds.

Drummer Stewart Copeland doesn't miss the early days. 'Our cycle of work is a lot slower than it was because we don't have to tour the radio stations any more. All we worry about is being on stage.'

But vocalist Sting is the man in charge. 'I'm always aware of how dangerous the whole business is . . . you get 20 or 60,000 in a stadium and exhort them to enjoy themselves and sing or whatever. The audience should be informed, subtly, that they are being manipulated.'

WELL SUNG PICKETS

Their average age is thirty-eight. They are all actors. And they are going to have the Christmas Nº. 1 in Britain!

They are The Flying Pickets, a six-piece acappella group from London, whose unaccompanied version of Yazoo's 'Only You' is being bought by the barrow load.

Theirs is success born from failure; they started singing after the 7:84 Theatre Company – a politically motivated co-operative – closed a production, while even as the single hit the Top 10, lead singer Brian Hibbard and fellow Picket Red Stripe received notice to quit their London flat.

Their live show combines a collection of Sixties pop hits (Phil Spector, Motown and Rolling Stones) with a few originals. 'The past two years have been spent working constantly around the world – we've only had a total of four or five days in the recording studio,' reveals Red Stripe.

'When we do covers we tend not to do obvious harmony songs; we don't do Beach Boys songs for instance. We look for something more than a reasonable facsimile'.

Acappella aces the Flying Pickets, straight off the 'alternative' circuit and into the charts

From political plays to pop stardom – The Flying Pickets have yet to come down.

Fine Young Cannibals looking hungry for stardom

CHARTS

- US45 All Night Long (All Night) *Lionel Richie*
- USLP Can't Slow Down *Lionel Richie*
- UK45 Never Never *Assembly*
- UKLP Colour By Numbers *Culture Club*

WEEK 2

- US45 Say Say Say *Paul McCartney & Michael Jackson*
- USLP Can't Slow Down *Lionel Richie*
- UK45 Love Of The Common People *Paul Young*
- UKLP Under A Blood-Red Sky *U2*

WEEK 3

- US45 Say Say Say *Paul McCartney & Michael Jackson*
- USLP Can't Slow Down *Lionel Richie*
- UK45 Only You *Flying Pickets*
- UKLP Thriller *Michael Jackson*

WEEK 4

- US45 Say Say Say *Paul McCartney & Michael Jackson*
- USLP Thriller *Michael Jackson*
- UK45 Only You *Flying Pickets*
- UKLP Thriller *Michael Jackson*

WEEK 5

- US45 Say Say Say *Paul McCartney & MIchael Jackson*
- USLP Thriller *Michael Jackson*
- UK45 Only You *Flying Pickets*
- UKLP Thriller *Michael Jackson*

THE GRAPEVINE

- **On the comeback trail this month – Janie Jones, sixties British hitmaker jailed for brothel keeping and immortalized in The Clash's 1977 song of the same name.**
- **Wishing they were on the comeback trail – former Beat members David Steel and Andy Cox, who have been looking for a vocalist to complete their 'Fine Young Cannibals' group.**

CHARTS

- US45 Say Say Say — *Paul McCartney & Michael Jackson*
- USLP Thriller — *Michael Jackson*
- UK45 Only You — *Flying Pickets*
- UKLP No Parlez — *Paul Young*

WEEK 2

- US45 Say Say Say — *Paul McCartney & MIchael Jacskon*
- USLP Thriller — *Michael Jackson*
- UK45 Only You — *Flying Pickets*
- UKLP Thriller — *Michael Jackson*

WEEK 3

- US45 Owner Of A Lonely Heart — *Yes*
- USLP Thriller — *Michael Jackson*
- UK45 Pipes Of Peace — *Paul McCartney*
- UKLP Thriller — *Michael Jackson*

WEEK 4

- US45 Owner Of A Lonely Heart — *Yes*
- USLP Thriller — *Michael Jackson*
- UK45 Relax — *Frankie Goes To Hollywood*
- UKLP Thriller — *Michael Jackson*

BYE BYE BLUES – KORNER DIES AT 55

Alexis Korner, the founding father of British rhythm and blues, died on January 1 following a short illness. A member of Chris Barber's jazz band in the Fifties, Korner quit to join harmonica player Cyril Davies and together they opened the London Blues and Barrel House Club. When Barber adopted the Chicago Blues idiom, he re-hired Korner and Davies to provide a finale to his live shows.

In 1961 they left to form Blues Incorporated, one of the first ever white electric blues bands and, on March 17 1962, opened the legendary Ealing R&B Club. It was here that Mick Jagger and Keith Richards first met Charlie Watts (then drummer with Blues Incorporated) and Brian Jones (who occasionally guested).

The list of British singers and instrumentalists Korner worked with is immense – Paul Jones, Long John Baldry, Eric Burdon, Jack Bruce, Graham Bond, Ginger Baker . . . these were just some of the legendary names he brought under his wing.

Unlike his students, Alexis never found commercial success on a large scale, yet continued to work steadily until his death with various combinations of musicians. His chart career was brief, and led to hits under the name of CCS such as 'Whole Lot Of Love' and 'Tap Turns On The Water'.

Latterly, he turned his rich, distinctive voice to TV commercial work, the income from which ensured he never had to compromise his blues ideals.

At the time of his death, Korner was working on a television series covering the history of rock.

Gravel-voiced Korner, a seminal figure in British rock as pioneer of the 1960s R&B boom

Van Morrison – tribute to Wilson, now dead

FAREWELL TO JACKIE

Soul star Jackie Wilson died on January 22 at the age of 49. He had been in a coma since a heart attack eight years ago.

Born in Detroit in 1934, he began his singing career in the early Fifties with Billy Ward's Dominoes. Going solo in 1957, he scored with 'Reet Petite', the first hit record written by future Motown boss Berry Gordy. Wilson graced the US Top 20 more than a dozen times with songs like 'Lonely Teardrops', 'Night', 'Higher and Higher' and 'I Get The Sweetest Feeling'.

And even when the hits dried up his all action performances – rivalled only by James Brown – ensured he could work wherever and whenever he pleased.

His name is best known to British music fans as the subject of Van Morrison's tribute song, 'Jackie Wilson Says'.

THE GRAPEVINE

- Shalamar singer Jeffrey Daniel and Sixties soul star P. P. Arnold are both to feature in Andrew Lloyd Webber's latest London musical, roller-skating opus *Starlight Express*.
- Celebrating 500 weeks on the *Billboard* Chart this month – Pink Floyd's 1973 classic 'Dark Side Of The Moon'.

QUO – THE END OF THE ROAD?

Francis Rossi (centre) balding leader of Quo, considered something of an institution in British rock

After twenty-two years of constant touring, veteran rockers Status Quo have decided to call it a day – but not before they've undertaken a massive thirty-five date farewell tour, including seven nights at London's Hammersmith Odeon.

'We feel that everything has to come to an end some time,' explained guitarist Francis Rossi, 'And this seems to us like it's the right time. No one could accuse us of making a hasty decision, and we all wanted to go out on a high.'

With twelve consecutive Top 5 albums, plus chart singles every year since 1973, the band are unlikely to give up recording completely . . . and a live album from the farewell tour is a possiblity.

THE GRAPEVINE

- Following in Vincent 'Thriller' Price's footsteps – Michael Caine, who has a speaking role in Madness's Top 10 hit titled after him.
- What a drag for Stranglers Jean Jacques Burnel and Dave Greenfield, whose single 'Rain And Dole And Tea' finds them in skirts and high heels for p.r. purposes.

SMITHS PLAY NAME GAME – AND WIN!

The Smiths boast probably the most forgettable name of any new group this year – but it's stuck in the minds of NME readers who remembered, and voted them Best New Group in the annual Readers' Poll.

They recently collaborated with archetypal Sixties singer Sandie Shaw, who recorded a version of their 'I Don't Owe You Anything', as well as scoring hit singles with 'This Charming Man' and 'What Difference Does It Make'.

Lead singer Steven Morrissey – he prefers to be known by his last name alone – is already proving something of an unlikely idol. A self-confessed recluse, his downright miserable lyrics contrast strongly with the uplifting music from the group, composed by guitarist Johnny Marr.

Smiths: memorable

CYNDI'S SO UNUSUAL

A transatlantic Top 3 record with your first solo single is quite an achievement – and Cyndi Lauper is quite some girl!

'Girls Just Want To Have Fun' is her first solo single and she is sure to be around for years and years. Her unique, whooping, high flying sky rocket of a voice is her fortune – 'When I get excited I sound like Minnie Mouse.'

Her single is a plea for women's rights, presented in a fun way. 'The media always isolate women as singers, and that's unfortunate because you fight against that your whole life! There are so many talented women who are not just singers . . . I'd like not to have to make this statement.'

'The actual feeling of singing is such a fabulous feeling, the actual physical thing. It's different from playing an instrument. The sound of my voice gives me strength . . . I want to communicate! I feel as I have something to say and I want to speak my piece.'

CHARTS

US45	Karma Chameleon *Culture Club*
USLP	Thriller *Michael Jackson*
UK45	Relax *Frankie Goes To Hollywood*
UKLP	Thriller *Michael Jackson*
WEEK 2	
US45	Karma Chameleon *Culture Club*
USLP	Thriller *Michael Jackson*
UK45	Relax *Frankie Goes To Hollywood*
UKLP	Milk And Honey *John Lennon & Yoko Ono*
WEEK 3	
US45	Karma Chameleon *Culture Club*
USLP	Thriller *Michael Jackson*
UK45	Radio Ga-Ga *Queen*
UKLP	Touch *Eurythmics*
WEEK 4	
US45	Jump *Van Halen*
USLP	Thriller *Michael Jackson*
UK45	Relax *Frankie Goes To Hollywood*
UKLP	Sparkle In The Rain *Simple Minds*

Cyndi – a touch of flash

MARCH

1984

CHARTS

US45	Jump *Van Halen*
USLP	Thriller *Michael Jackson*
UK45	99 Red Balloons *Nena*
UKLP	Into The Gap *Thompson Twins*
WEEK 2	
US45	Jump *Van Halen*
USLP	Thriller *Michael Jackson*
UK45	99 Red Balloons *Nena*
UKLP	Into The Gap *Thompson Twins*
WEEK 3	
US45	Jump *Van Halen*
USLP	Thriller *Michael Jackson*
UK45	99 Red Balloons *Nena*
UKLP	Into The Gap *Thompson Twins*
WEEK 4	
US45	Jump *Van Halen*
USLP	Thriller *Michael Jackson*
UK45	99 Red Balloons *Nena*
UKLP	Human's Lib *Howard Jones*
WEEK 5	
US45	Footloose *Kenny Loggins*
USLP	Thriller *Michael Jackson*
UK45	Hello *Lionel Richie*
UKLP	Human's Lib *Howard Jones*

THE GRAPEVINE

- Actress/singer Tracey Ullman's new video for the single 'My Guy's Mad At Me' has an unusual co-star – British Labour Party leader Neil Kinnock! He also appears on the picture disc.
- Michael Jackson's 'Thriller' album has now passed 25 million sales world-wide.
- Nena's '99 Red Balloons' hit a plea for reunion of East and West Germany.

FREE NELSON MANDELA!

Ex-Special Dammers gives musical support to Mandela campaign

Specials leader Jerry Dammers launched his band's new single 'Nelson Mandela' by presenting a copy to the African National Congress Publicity Director Thabo Mbeki outside the House of Commons in London. It began an afternoon of protest meetings and lobbying organized by the Anti-Apartheid movement and other groups including the ANC.

Mandela was a leader of the ANC before being arrested in 1962, and the movement to obtain his release is gathering momentum.

Dammers explained his motivation for writing the single: 'I just hope it will make people think about who Nelson Mandela is.' He'd first thought of writing a song at the 1983 African Music Festival in London, which coincided with Mandela's sixty-fifth birthday.

'I hadn't really heard about him until then,' he admitted. 'I read his biography after that, and now I'm reading a collection of his speeches and pamphlets, "The Struggle Is My Life".'

Produced by Elvis Costello, the record sees the re-emergence of The Specials – now known as The Special AKA, their original name – after a two-year silence and many personnel changes, and seems likely to serve as an anthem for those who seek the release of the African leader.

PUNKS JAILED IN HUNGARY

'Anarchy and nihilism are attitudes which cannot be allowed. These young people in certain situations could be dangerous for society.' Not Margaret Thatcher speaking, but a Hungarian judge sentencing the members of Common Punk Group to two years' imprisonment apiece.

CPG, as they are known, have been playing together for two years. In coming to Budapest from their home town of Szeged, they stood out from the crowd. Leader Zoltan Benko is apparently 'an elegant skinhead adopting a hunter's look with a whip in his hand'. Not surprisingly, the authorities objected – and took ten songs into consideration in reaching their verdict of guilty.

The band, who object to such customs as workers' Saturday pay being donated to the State, have been charged and convicted of 'using insulting or derogatory expressions with respect to the Hungarian nation, the constitutional order of the Hungarian People's Republic, or to particular groups of persons for their nationality, race or socialist convictions'.

Coverdale: bragging again?

Nena and band hope for reunited Germany

STAR QUOTE

DAVID COVERDALE
of Whitesnake

'All it is is a group playing music. I'm not saying all take your pants off and play a game of brag. None of that shit. It's just get out of it what you can: if it moves your ass then dance; if it inspires you to something else, fine.'

WHAT'S GOING ON? MARVIN GAYE SHOT

Marvin Gaye, the soul music legend, was shot dead on April 1, the eve of his forty-fifth birthday. His sixty-nine-year old father, a retired minister, has been charged with his murder.

Father and son allegedly argued over 'an insurance matter' and 'a letter', the contents of which are unknown. The argument continued overnight and, when his father refused to leave his room, Gaye Jr. shoved him into the hallway. His father apparently returned with a gun and shot his son twice in the chest.

Gaye had recently left Motown, and had rejuvenated his career at CBS, with his album 'Midnight Love' and single 'Sexual Healing' proving among his best work; the single won him a Grammy in 1983. He had already started work on a follow-up album which may never be released. Gaye's contribution to Motown's 25th Anniversary Celebration in 1983 confirmed that he had made his peace with the label.

In his 32-year career, which started as a session drummer at Motown, Gaye was instrumental in bringing black music to a new and prosperous white audience with albums like 'What's Going On', his 1971 masterpiece which mixed soul with social comment, and 'Let's Get It On', an LP dedicated totally to the sexual act. Of the artists from the Motown stable, his all-round talent was matched perhaps only by Stevie Wonder.

STAR QUOTE

CHER

'My relationships usually last a few years. When I'm involved with a man, other men are fascinated with me, but the minute I'm single again, half of those men disappear because they don't have the balls to really want me.'

Cher: "men disappear"

George: one's enough?

THE GRAPEVINE

■ Culture Club's Boy George caused an ice hockey match in Canada to come to a standstill . . . or rather a lookalike did! 'Boy George Arrives', trumpeted a local paper: just wait till they get the real thing!

■ Heavy metal heroes Van Halen, currently touring the US, insist on a bowl of M & Ms (chocolate sweets) with all the brown ones removed backstage at every concert . . . Whew, rock'n'roll!

FISH OUT OF WATER

Marillion have often been accused of being 'Genesis copyists' - a simplistic judgement to make on a band who've successfully swum against the musical current.

'We started in March 1981,' explains singer Fish. 'That was when we started gigging – and by October we had rejection slips from every single record company in Britain, including EMI (their current label). Everyone told us this style of music is dead, ten-minute songs are out of the window. We did 185 gigs before we got signed. Now we are the most unfashionable band in Britain.'

Despite this becoming modesty, the band's second album 'Fugazi' has sold over 60,000 copies. But the critics are still unconvinced. 'I get really fed up reading another character assassination in a live review which completely ignores the music we played or the atmosphere of the show, that just dishes out the same old prejudice,' says Fish. 'A lot of people who hate Genesis think, well then I hate Marillion. It causes a lot of problems.'

CHARTS

	US45	Footloose	*Kenny Loggins*
	USLP	Thriller	*Michael Jackson*
	UK45	Hello	*Lionel Richie*
	UKLP	Can't Slow Down	*Lionel Richie*
WEEK 2	US45	Footloose	*Kenny Loggins*
	USLP	Thriller	*Michael Jackson*
	UK45	Hello	*Lionel Richie*
	UKLP	Can't Slow Down	*Lionel Richie*
WEEK 3	US45	Against All Odds (Take A Look At Me Now)	*Phil Collins*
	USLP	Footloose	*Soundtrack*
	UK45	Hello	*Lionel Richie*
	UKLP	Can't Slow Down	*Lionel Richie*
WEEK 4	US45	Against All Odds (Take A Look At Me Now)	*Phil Collins*
	USLP	Footloose	*Soundtrack*
	UK45	Hello	*Lionel Richie*
	UKLP	Now That's What I Call Music	*Various*

Marillion, trendy cult band to those really in the know?

CHARTS

US45	Against All Odds (Take A Look At Me Now) *Phil Collins*
USLP	Footloose *Soundtrack*
UK45	Against All Odds *Phil Collins*
UKLP	Legend *Bob Marley & The Wailers*
	WEEK 2
US45	Hello *Lionel Richie*
USLP	Footloose *Soundtrack*
UK45	The Reflex *Duran Duran*
UKLP	
	WEEK 3
US45	Hello *Lionel Richie*
USLP	Footloose *Soundtrack*
UK45	The Reflex *Duran Duran*
UKLP	Legend *Bob Marley & The Wailers*
	WEEK 4
US45	Let's Heart It For The Boy *Deniece Williams*
USLP	Footloose *Soundtrack*
UK45	Automatic *Pointer Sisters*
UKLP	Legend *Bob Marley & The Wailers*

MAD . . . BUT NOT STIFF

Madness made May an eventful month when, after playing a festival in Montreux, Switzerland, they returned to London to find the press claiming (erroneously) that they had smashed up a hotel with the help of UB40.

Rather more authentic news tells of their parting from Stiff Records, with whom they signed in 1979. Plans for their own label include a single with ex-Undertone Feargal Sharkey, and it is possible they will seek a licensing deal with a major record company.

Said Stiff boss Dave Robinson: 'It is sad that they are leaving, but we are a record company and not a registered charity.'

PURPLE TO REFORM – HONESTLY!

The longest running rumour in heavy rock came true this month when Deep Purple announced their re-formation. What's more, the line-up is their classic of Ian Gillan (vocals), Ritchie Blackmore (guitar), Jon Lord (keyboards), Roger Glover (bass) and Ian Paice (drums) – the fivesome that created a rock legend in the early Seventies.

The resurrected Purple will be based in America, and will be recording a comeback album in June and July.

LEAGUE CONTENDERS

The Human League are back after a two-year absence – and they're clearly as popular as ever, if the turnout for a video shoot for their new single 'The Lebanon' is anything to go by. About 400 aspiring stars lined up at London's Theatre Royal to take part.

And if disco dancing to a song about the Middle East seems strange, singer Phil Oakey explains, 'We couldn't do anything else for the song because it means a lot. A dramatization would be insulting to the people.'

NO BUNNY BUSINESS . . .

Day-trippers on the Mersey – Echo And The Bunnymen

Echo & The Bunnymen have frequently gone about things the unconventional way. The Liverpool quartet have been known to send coachloads of fans to mysterious mountain venues, tour Scotland's Outer Hebrides and other distinctly non-rockist manoeuvres.

To promote their fourth album 'Ocean Rain', they decided on an all-day extravaganza in their home town of Liverpool, including a boat trip on the river Mersey (as popularized by another famous group, Gerry & The Pacemakers).

The Crystal Day, as it was known, included a cycle ride around Liverpool, an organ recital at Liverpool Cathedral and drama from the local Chinese Community Centre.

Thankfully, most fans had the energy left for the concert in the evening at the St George's Hall, where the last rock band to play was . . . The Beatles.

Relaxing after their first million-seller, Frankie Goes to Hollywood

■ **Frankie Goes To Hollywood's new single, 'Two Tribes', is described 'as the first genuine protest song for eight years, picking holes in the Official Secrets Act.'**

■ **Tina Turner has continued her comeback this month by guesting on Lionel Ritchie's US Tour: a new album 'Private Dancer', is upcoming.**

WHAM! WE'RE NO.1

Michael, Ridgeley – Wham!

'Everything we do is tongue in cheek,' claims Wham! guitarist Andrew Ridgeley. 'I think people should see immediately that it's all a bit of a joke to us. We just act at being pop stars for one and a half hours a day.'

What *is* deadly serious is that Ridgeley and co-star George Michael have scored their first No. 1 single with 'Wake Me Up Before You Go-Go', an energetic Motown-style stomper.

And with a tour of China on the horizon, the world could soon be eating out of their hand.

HUEY LEWIS? THAT'S NEWS!

Huey Lewis, good News at last

'It couldn't happen to a nicer guy.' That's the opinion of the pop world as Huey Lewis (real name Hugh Cregg) & The News celebrate their first US No. 1 album, 'Sports'.

Asked why he was now toast of the nation when he couldn't give his music away for nearly 13 years, he shrugged and explained 'We've learned how to make records better.'

VIRGIN ON THE RIDICULOUS

Virgin Records boss Richard Branson has just about done it all – his UK chain of record shops is making enormous profits, his first album (Mike Oldfield's 'Tubular Bells') sold ten million and his subsidiary label Ten had a No. 1 single with its first release (The Flying Pickets' 'Only You').

And talking of flying, he's done it again – but the only rock stars to be found on his latest venture were drinking champagne in the first-class seats when Virgin Atlantic's Boeing 747 jumbo jet took off from London on June 22 bound for New Jersey's Newark Airport.

Jersey resident Bruce Springsteen wasn't aboard, but he was about the only notable face not present as 'Wing Commander' Branson, complete with flying cap and goggles, passed round the complimentary drinks.

In line with his shops' policy, the ticket price is bargain-basement – a mere £99 ($200).

MARLEY – THE LEGEND LIVES ON

Three years after his death, a hits compilation of reggae superstar Bob Marley adds yet more lustre to his legend. Aptly entitled 'Legend', the 14-track album celebrates his recordings for the Island label that started with 'Catch A Fire' in 1973 and ended with 1980's 'Uprising'.

The album spent the whole of June and July at the top of the UK chart, while the accompanying video collection displaced Michael Jackson's blockbusting 'The Making Of Thriller' as the UK's best-selling music video.

CHARTS

	Chart	Title	Artist
	US45	Let's Hear It For The Boy	Deniece Williams
	USLP	Footloose	Soundtrack
	UK45	Automatic	Pointer Sisters
	UKLP	Legend	Bob Marley & The Wailers
WEEK 2	US45	Time After Time	Cyndi Lauper
	USLP	Footloose	Soundtrack
	UK45	Wake Me Up Before You Go-Go	Wham!
	UKLP	Legend	Bob Marley & The Wailers
WEEK 3	US45	Time After Time	Cyndi Lauper
	USLP	Footloose	Soundtrack
	UK45	Wake Me Up Before You Go-Go	Wham!
	UKLP	Legend	Bob Marley & The Wailers
WEEK 4	US45	The Reflex	Duran Duran
	USLP	Footloose	Soundtrack
	UK45	Two Tribes	Frankie Goes To Hollywood
	UKLP	Legend	Bob Marley & The Wailers
WEEK 5	US45	The Reflex	Duran Duran
	USLP	Sports	Huey Lewis & The News
	UK45	Two Tribes	Frankie Goes To Hollywood
	UKLP	Legend	Bob Marley & The Wailers

THE GRAPEVINE

- **On the way up – keyboardist Howard Jones, who once hired The Marquee Club in London and invited record companies to come and see him – as his debut LP, 'Human's Lib', reaches the UK top ten.**
- **Going solo – Japan front man David Sylvian, whose debut album 'Brilliant Trees' has made the UK top twenty.**

JULY

1984

CHARTS

US45	When Doves Cry — *Prince*
USLP	Born In The USA — *Bruce Springsteen*
UK45	Two Tribes — *Frankie Goes To Hollywood*
UKLP	Legend — *Bob Marley & The Wailers*
WEEK 2	
US45	When Doves Cry — *Prince*
USLP	Born In The USA — *Bruce Springsteen*
UK45	Two Tribes — *Frankie Goes To Hollywood*
UKLP	Legend — *Bob Marley & The Wailers*
WEEK 3	
US45	When Doves Cry — *Prince*
USLP	Born In The USA — *Bruce Springsteen*
UK45	Two Tribes — *Frankie Goes To Hollywood*
UKLP	Legend — *Bob Marley & The Wailers*
WEEK 4	
US45	When Doves Cry — *Prince*
USLP	Born In The USA — *Bruce Springsteen*
UK45	Two Tribes — *Frankie Goes To Hollywood*
UKLP	Victory — *Jacksons*

FRANKIES REIGN SUPREME

When Frankie Goes To Hollywood's 'Two Tribes' entered the UK charts at No. 1 in June, following the massively successful 'Relax', no one could really have been surprised.

This month, however, saw 'Relax' climb back to No. 2, to give the Merseysiders the top two chart places, and overtake The Human League's 'Don't You Want Me' and Culture Club's 'Karma Chameleon' as the decade's best-selling single so far.

'Frankie Say' T-shirts designed by Katherine Hamnett are selling like hot cakes. All they need now to sweep the board is an album.

MADONNA MAKES HER MARK

For 25-year-old Detroit-born Madonna Louise Ciccone – better known simply as Madonna – this month saw the fulfilment of a dream as her first album, titled 'Madonna', completed three weeks in the US top twenty.

A former dancer, her brand of infectious disco set her up with Nena, Cyndi Lauper and others in the new wave of dance-orientated street kids. But for record company boss Seymour Stein, she was one of a kind.

'I was in hospital when I heard about Madonna,' he says. 'From what I heard, I wanted to sign her immediately. You know you don't care normally what you look like when you're in hospital. But I shaved, I combed my hair and I got a new dressing gown.'

That first meeting only confirmed his feelings: 'It hit me right away. I could tell she had the drive to match her talent.' This month saw Stein's hunch pay off.

Jeff Lynne (centre), fronting ELO for the last time?

WYNNE LOSES FIGHT FOR LIFE

Phillipe Wynne, former lead singer of The Spinners and from 1977 a solo artist, died on stage at a California nightclub on July 14. He was 43.

Wynne joined the five-man vocal group in 1972 (when he replaced G.C. Cameron), and was the major reason why their move from Motown to Atlantic brought them success rather than the expected failure.

They became chart regulars with Wynne supplying the lead voice on hits like 'I'll Be Around' (a US No. 3), 'Could It Be I'm Falling In Love' (No. 4), 'The Rubberband Man' (No. 2) and the 1974 US chart-topping duet with Dionne Warwick, 'Then Came You'.

The Spinners were known as The Detroit Spinners in the UK to avoid confusion with the folk group of the same name.

Quo – finally quit

THE GRAPEVINE

- **Heads were shaken and tears shed at Milton Keynes Bowl on 21 July when Status Quo finally said goodbye to live performance - or did they?**
- **Could The Electric Light Orchestra's long and hit-studded career be over at last? The world wonders as leader Jeff Lynne starts a solo career with his single 'Doing That Crazy Thing'.**

JACKSONS HIT NEW JERSEY

Michael Jackson and his five brothers are without doubt 1984's biggest live act. And if proof were needed, their 'Victory Tour' which hit New Jersey's Meadowlands Stadium this month, provided it.

Home of The Giants baseball team, it was packed with fans buying every kind of memento, including a programme that retailed at $10, dolls, gloves, battery-operated geese and the like.

With a stage set reminiscent of *Close Encounters*, with planes and helicopters buzzing overhead for a free look, the Jacksons managed to achieve the impossible and live up to expectations.

And after the show was over, the spilt cola and squashed frankfurters were witness to the fact that apart from being a major piece of music theatre, the tour is odds-on to become the biggest grossing rock venture of all time.

CHARTS

US45	When Doves Cry *Prince*
USLP	Purple Rain *Prince*
UK45	Two Tribes *Frankie Goes To Hollywood*
UKLP	Legend *Bob Marley & The Wailers*
	WEEK 2
US45	Ghostbusters *Ray Parker Jr.*
USLP	Purple Rain *Prince*
UK45	Two Tribes *Frankie Goes To Hollywood*
UKLP	Diamond Life *Sade*
	WEEK 3
US45	Ghostbusters *Ray Parker Jr.*
USLP	Purple Rain *Prince*
UK45	Careless Whisper *George Michael*
UKLP	Now That's What I Call Music, 3 *Various*
	WEEK 4
US45	Ghostbusters *Ray Parker Jr.*
USLP	Purple Rain *Prince*
UK45	Careless Whisper *George Michael*
UKLP	Now That's What I Call Music, 3 *Various*

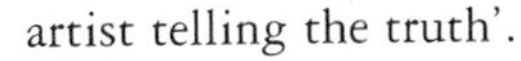

THE GRAPEVINE

- **Daryl Hall has been singing with a new partner – Elvis Costello, whose 'The Only Flame In Town' is a duet.**
- **American music legends The Band have been touring again after their 1976 retirement, with The Cate Brothers replacing original guitarist Robbie Robertson.**
- **The 24th National Rock Festival, due to be held at Reading, was cancelled after a proposed move to Lilford, Northamptonshire, fell through.**

Alf – 'death warmed up'

STAR QUOTE

ALISON MOYET

'It's only in the last few years I've been aware of sexism . . . I come back off some promotional trip, get off the plane looking like death warmed up – and you get this record company executive coming up saying, Dahling! you look gorgeous!" It's like – what's the f ing matter with you?'

THREE FOR 84

Three major artists release long-awaited albums this month: Bruce Springsteen's 'Born In The USA' has 'the boss' getting down to post-Vietnam realities. Reviewer Charles Shaar Murray considers it 'far more real than the power of Springsteen's early work; this is the power of an artist telling the truth'.

The Special AKA'S 'In The Studio', (over two years in the making), is considered 'very special', while reviewer Gavin Martin considers Prince & The Revolution's 'Purple Rain' 'unsatisfying . . . with youth, talent, and the world at his feet (Prince) can find nothing more to sing about than himself and the many marvellous chicks that undoubtedly come his way'.

With their last UK hit single 'Nelson Mandela' over a year ago, the Special AKA contemplate the future

BODY MUSIC FROM BOBBY

Vocal virtuoso McFerrin

On July 11 1977, Bobby McFerrin was walking down a hill in Salt Lake City when a voice inside his head told him to become a singer. The following night saw his first gig, and since then he's been singing for his supper – most recently totally solo with nothing but a microphone and a stool.

His style is totally unique, imitating hecklers, inviting people on to the stage and using his amazing voice to imitate almost anything – a motor car, a jazz quartet or Curtis Mayfield coming equally easily.

With jazz, funk, blues, pop and even opera in his repertoire, we haven't heard the last of this unique talent. Altogether now: 'Dah baba bada dooba dah doo dah dum.'

1984

NO FANGS, MICHAEL

Michael Jackson is frequently to be seen in disguise on the streets, knocking door to door as a Jehovah's Witness. But, according to some fellow witnesses, he has been threatened with expulsion from the Church – the reason being his 'Thriller' video.

A recent issue of *Awake*, a Witness publication, quotes him as saying 'I realize now it was not a good idea . . . I'll never do a video like that again.' It may be significant that the song 'Thriller' was omitted from The Jacksons' set in their current tour. The video itself, now on general release, also has a disclaimer that it does not imply a belief in the occult.

Another problem faced by the Witness's leadership is the development of a Michael Jackson cult within the Church, which believes that the superstar is the Archangel prophesied in the Book of Daniel: 'And at that time shall Michael stand up, the great Prince which standeth for the children of thy people.'

CHARTS

- US45 What's Love Got To Do With It – *Tina Turner*
- USLP Purple Rain – *Prince*
- UK45 Careless Whisper – *George Michael*
- UKLP Now That's What I Call Music, 3 – *Various*

WEEK 2

- US45 What's Love Got To Do With It – *Tina Turner*
- USLP Purple Rain – *Prince*
- UK45 I Just Called To Say I Love You – *Stevie Wonder*
- UKLP Now That's What I Call Music, 3 – *Various*

WEEK 3

- US45 What's Love Got To Do With It – *Tina Turner*
- USLP Purple Rain – *Prince*
- UK45 I Just Called To Say I Love You – *Stevie Wonder*
- UKLP Now That's What I Call Music, 3 – *Various*

WEEK 4

- US45 Missing You – *John Waite*
- USLP Purple Rain – *Prince*
- UK45 I Just Called To Say I Love You – *Stevie Wonder*
- UKLP Now That's What I Call Music, 3 – *Various*

WEEK 5

- US45 Let's Go Crazy – *Prince*
- USLP Purple Rain – *Prince*
- UK45 I Just Called To Say I Love You – *Stevie Wonder*
- UKLP The Woman In Red – *Stevie Wonder*

THE GRAPEVINE

- **Starting her singing career with oddball band Float Up CP is jazz trumpeter Don Cherry's daughter Neneh Cherry – a powerfully exciting singer.**
- **Stevie Wonder has made No. 1 on his own for the first time in the UK with the film theme 'I Just Called To Say I Love You' from *The Woman In Red*.**

Sheffield supergroup Def Leppard – changing spots for America

GOING DEF FOR A LIVING

Sheffield's heavy metal heroes Def Leppard may be popular in their native land – but they're even bigger in the States.

The Gallup Youth Poll, a nationwide gauge of opinion, recently revealed that they are the most popular group in America, finishing higher than The Rolling Stones, The Jacksons and Culture Club. What's more, their 'Pyromania' album has sold nearly seven million copies and rising in the States alone.

The band are currently in Holland recording the follow-up – and it can be revealed that the producer they are working with is none other than Meatloaf Svengali Jim Steinman.

Neneh Cherry – hip, daddy

Number One Wonder

VIDEO A GO GO

After Michael Jackson's 'Thriller' directed by John Landis and The Stones' 'Undercover' by Julien Temple comes the video to top them all – 'Screaming Lord Byron' a 22-minute promo based around David Bowie's 'Blue Jean' single. Its release prompts the question: where do videos go from here?

The answer is the cinema, where the video will be shown as support feature to *The Company of Wolves* from September 14. Its drug scenes are unlikely to endear it to television, which makes its *raison d'être* somewhat unclear.

Directed by Julien Temple, the video sees Bowie playing two distinct roles – the rock idol of the title and a fan who tries to attract a girl with the promise of meeting Lord Byron himself.

BREAKING HEARTS – AND HANDS!

Tom Petty, leader of The Hearbreakers, may never play guitar again after slamming his left hand into a studio wall 'in a fit of unthinking pique'.

The accident happened on October 27 while Petty listened to the final mix of his album 'Southern Accents'. Having damaged several bones in his hand, 'The probability is that things will heal: he's had it set and re-set,' said a spokesman. 'But it will be three or four weeks before anyone knows if he can regain full playing dexterity.'

- **Released this month – U2's 'The Unforgettable Fire' album, which is, according to reviewers: 'music worth getting to know'.**
- **Heading for the top in the UK this month – Glaswegian Jim Diamond, formerly one half of PhD, with his debut solo single 'I Should Have Known Better'.**
- **Frankie Goes to Hollywood have released a 'Two Tribes' video this month.**

Jim Diamond

HENDRIX LIVES!

The late Jimi Hendrix, sharing his Experience with bass player Noel Redding

Great music never dies – and to prove it, Britain's first Jimi Hendrix convention was held this month in Retford, Nottinghamshire. Attracting fans from Sweden, Holland, France, Belgium, Germany, Hungary, Norway and the USA, it featured Hendrix's father Al, whose question and answer session was the high point of the occasion.

Music came from a Hungarian group known as 'Remember Jimi Hendrix', whose lead vocalist was a 6ft 3in leather-jacketed singer with only one leg. This contrasted somewhat with Hendrix bass player Noel Redding, who performed a solo set of rock standards and attempted to auction the 1964 Fender Jazz Bass he played in his Hendrix days for a sum exceeding £4,000.

Though he failed to interest the impecunious punters, his old stage clothes were purchased by a bearded fan – one of many who went home happy.

ELVIS GOES SOLO

The UK faces Costello overkill this winter – for having toured Britain with his backing group The Attractions, he intends to play a second tour as a one-man act. He tried this out in America this summer, and will now be bringing his solo set to British audiences for the first time.

He intends to accompany himself on piano, electric piano, electric and acoustic guitars, returning to play a short encore set with support act T-Bone Burnett. The two of them have recorded a single as The Coward Brothers entitled 'The People's Limousine'.

One man band Costello

CHARTS

US45	Let's Go Crazy *Prince*
USLP	Purple Rain *Prince*
UK45	I Just Called To Say I Love You *Stevie Wonder*
UKLP	The Woman In Red *Stevie Wonder*
WEEK 2	
US45	I Just Called To Say I Love You *Stevie Wonder*
USLP	Purple Rain *Prince*
UK45	I Just Called To Say I Love You *Stevie Wonder*
UKLP	Tonight *David Bowie*
WEEK 3	
US45	I Just Called To Say I Love You *Stevie Wonder*
USLP	Purple Rain *Prince*
UK45	The War Song *Culture Club*
UKLP	The Unforgettable Fire *U2*
WEEK 4	
US45	I Just Called To Say I Love You *Stevie Wonder*
USLP	Purple Rain *Prince*
UK45	Freedom *Wham!*
UKLP	The Unforgettable Fire *U2*

SOUNDTRACK – WHAT SOUNDTRACK?

Eurythmics latest album is the soundtrack from Richard Burton's last film, *1984* – or is it?

The problem has arisen because Virgin Films commissioned two separate soundtracks, one from Dominic Muldowney and one from The Eurythmics. The first had already been dubbed on to the picture when record company boss Richard Branson insisted The Eurythmics version be substituted. A solution has now been reached, involving a joint score by The Eurythmics and Muldowney.

NOVEMBER

CULTURE BALLET – WHO?

Britain's two hottest pop acts, Culture Club and Spandau Ballet, are engaged in a private battle for the championship of Wembley Arena – both groups trying to top each other in the number of concerts they can play at the giant London venue.

When Spandau confirmed their fifth night, they proudly proclaimed themselves to be performing more Christmas shows than any other band at that venue. A week later, Culture Club levelled the score and have just confirmed a sixth – pointing out that they now hold the self-promoted record!

Latest news, however, is that Spandau have now equalized and the score is currently six concerts apiece.

Lining up for concert contest with Culture Club, one-time New Romantics Spandau Ballet

LIVE IN NOVEMBER

This month has seen a plethora of concert recordings hit the charts from groups old, new and in between.

In the former category are The Who, whose 'Who's Last' live double seems likely to be their final chart appearance. Another veteran performer is Bob Dylan with his 'Real Live', while the younger generation are represented by Duran Duran's 'Arena' and The Cure's 'Concert' – no marks for imagination for either of *those* two album titles.

Meanwhile pomp rockers Marillion weigh in with 'Real To Reel', a somewhat more imaginative label for a concert recording.

CHARTS

US45	Caribbean Queen *Billy Ocean*
USLP	Purple Rain *Prince*
UK45	Freedom *Wham!*
UKLP	Steel Town *Big Country*
WEEK 2	
US45	Caribbean Queen *Billy Ocean*
USLP	Purple Rain *Prince*
UK45	I Feel For You *Chaka Khan*
UKLP	Welcome To The Pleasuredome *Frankie Goes To Hollywood*
WEEK 3	
US45	Wake Me Up Before You Go-Go *Wham!*
USLP	Born In The USA *Bruce Springsteen*
UK45	I Feel For You *Chaka Khan*
UKLP	Welcome To The Pleasuredome *Frankie Goes To Hollywood*
WEEK 4	
US45	Wake Me Up Before You Go-Go *Wham!*
USLP	Born In The USA *Bruce Springsteen*
UK45	I Feel For You *Chaka Khan*
UKLP	Make It Big *Wham!*

ZZ – DRIVING TO THE TOP

ZZ Top are a trio from Texas. Two have beards, while one (with a moustache) is *called* Beard. Their current album 'Eliminator' hit the UK Top 10 in September after being out for a whole year. The reason? The hit single 'Gimme All Your Lovin'' and its video featuring a 1932 vintage coupe and some glamorous ladies.

'Hot cars and rock'n'roll have always been synonymous,' comments bass player Dusty Hill. 'We've always been car freaks,' adds guitarist Billy Gibbons. Their music isn't bad either, with more hits in store in 'Legs' and 'Sharp Dressed Man'.

There's no doubt, though, they're going to keep their winning formula simple. Dusty: 'Once you've learnt the fourth chord, you're outa the blues.'

Top beards from Texas

THE GRAPEVINE

- **Noddy Holder and Don Powell of Slade were seen in London assisting Ozzy Osbourne, – who was dressed in sequined ball gown - to a Hammersmith Odeon encore appearance with Waysted.**
- **An old name in the charts again – J. Lennon: Julian this time, with his debut single 'Too Late For Goodbyes'.**
- **Madonna's second album 'Like A Virgin' has been released in Britain this month to indifferent reviews.**

Chart debut for Lennon

Madonna – Like A Virgin?

RICHIE COINS IT

Though he's laboured in Michael Jackson's shadow this year, Lionel Richie would, in any other twelve-month period, have gained huge acclaim for the sales performance of his second solo album, 'Can't Slow Down'. It's still a Top 10 album in the States, after 52 weeks in the charts, while the current single 'Penny Lover' is the fifth from an album with only eight tracks.

ANNIE LENNOX

Eurythmics

'When I was younger I thought, I wanna be artistic. I thought I could make myself artistic somehow. But I discovered it doesn't happen like that. It just develops.'

FEED THE WORLD!

For once, egos didn't intrude as Band Aid gather for the camera

In an unusual and heartwarming display, the denizens of the British charts forgot their differences for a day to assemble at London's Sarm West Studio to record this Christmas's UK No. 1 single. Entitled 'Do They Know It's Christmas' and written by Boomtown Rat Bob Geldof and Ultravox's Midge Ure, the song is intended to raise money for those starving in the Ethiopian famine.

The studio was pretty packed, for, along with seven TV crews from both sides of the Atlantic, were members of Culture Club, Wham!, Spandau Ballet, Duran Duran, U2, Bananarama, Kool & The Gang, The Style Council, Heaven 17, Status Quo, Paul Young and Sting.

According to reports, everything went very smoothly indeed. 'It was unbelievable,' remarked a studio spy. 'The whole thing was like being at school. Sting was the head boy, Geldof and Ure the prefects and Spandau and Duran the lads mucking about at the back of the class. I still can't believe they got all those egos into one room without any rows.'

The single chalked up record advance orders to become the pop success story of 1984. And there is already talk of an all-star famine relief concert next year.

Chaka: "rather carry a gun"

STAR QUOTE

CHAKA KHAN

'I'm almost afraid of (fame). At least I can walk to the grocery store unmolested, or take my children to the doctors. At the moment, Michael Jackson and Diana Ross can't show their faces. I would never have bodyguards – I would rather carry a gun myself.'

TV TIMES

As Christmas approaches, the British charts become a battle ground for television-promoted albums. Mega-labels CBS and WEA alone are promoting ten albums between them this year, while television specialists Telstar pitch in with heavyweights Stevie Wonder, John Denver and Chris de Burgh.

Most controversial, however, are the compilations 'Now That's What I Call Music 4' from EMI and Virgin and 'The Hits Album' from WEA and CBS.

These collections of singles are the highest climbing albums of the month and seem likely to be symptomatic of a trend where compilations will monopolize the top places in Christmases to come – not to mention the possible adverse effect on singles sales.

BYE BYE NEIL . . .

A short and successful career ended in London on December 22 with 'the only farewell gig' from Neil, 1984's token hippy. The flare-wearing, shoulder-length locked, macrobiotic superstar was created by actor Nigel Planer from the British TV series, *The Young Ones*, who had a surprise hit single with a cover of Traffic's psychedelic classic 'Hole In My Shoe', produced and played by keyboardist Dave Stewart (no relation to The Eurythmics man).

After recording an LP, 'The Heavy Concept Album', Neil/Nigel ventured on to the stage of London's Hammersmith Odeon for his first (and last) exposure to public ridicule.

Heavy . . . . Neil splits (man)

CHARTS

US45	Wake Me Up Before You Go-Go *Wham!*
USLP	Born In the USA *Bruce Springsteen*
UK45	I Feel For You *Chaka Khan*
UKLP	Make It Big *Wham!*
WEEK 2	
US45	Out Of Touch *Daryl Hall & John Oates*
USLP	Born In The USA *Bruce Springsteen*
UK45	I Should Have Known Better *Jim Diamond*
UKLP	Make It Big *Wham!*
WEEK 3	
US45	Out Of Touch *Daryl Hall & John Oates*
USLP	Born In The USA *Bruce Springsteen*
UK45	Do They Know It's Christmas? *Band Aid*
UKLP	The Hits Album *Various*
WEEK 4	
US45	Like A Virgin *Madonna*
USLP	Born In The USA *Bruce Springsteen*
UK45	Do They Know It's Christmas? *Band Aid*
UKLP	The Hits Album *Various*
WEEK 5	
US45	Like A Virgin *Madonna*
USLP	Born In The USA *Bruce Springsteen*
UK45	Do They Know It's Christmas? *Band Aid*
UKLP	The Hits Album *Various*

THE GRAPEVINE

- **New in the chart – 'The Waking Hour', first album by Mick Karn and Peter Murphy, ex of Japan and Bauhaus respectively, now known as Dali's Car.**
- **Going solo – temporarily, at least – Bunnymen lead singer Ian McCulloch, with the Kurt Weill standard 'September Song', vintage 1938.**

PRINCE SETS NEW RECORDS

The soundtrack album to Prince's 'Purple Rain' feature movie logged its 24th week at the top of the US album chart to equal the record set by 'Saturday Night Fever' as the longest running No. 1 soundtrack album of the last 20 years. It also beats all-comers as the longest consecutive run at the top since 1965.

'The Purple One' was also nominated in a record ten categories at the American Music Awards and took the trophies for Album of the Year in both the Rock/Pop and Black Music categories. He also won the Top Black Single of the Year award for 'When Doves Cry'.

Prince – six months 'Rain' in US

NOW IT'S VIDEO AID

Band Aid founder-member Bob Geldof has announced his latest fund raising venture: a 22 track compilation video which he describes with typical modesty as 'simply the best collection of pop videos there has ever been'. Over half the proceeds will go to the Ethiopian Famine Relief Appeal.

Lasting more than 90 minutes, featured clips include the award winning 'You Can't Hurry Love' by Phil Collins, and 'Save A Prayer' by Duran Duran, together with recent hits 'Wake Me Up Before You Go Go' by Wham!, Elton John's 'Passengers', 'War Song' by Culture Club, a special US remix of Paul McCartney's 'No More Lonely Nights', plus a bonus of Frankie Goes To Hollywood's performance of 'Relax' on *'The Tube'* TV show.

The compilation, released by Virgin Video, also features special introductions and linked messages from Geldof, David Bowie, Mick Jagger, Bananarama, Boy George, Elton John and others.

THE GRAPEVINE

- ZZ Top's Dusty Hill is reported as having accidentally shot himself in the stomach.
- Def Leppard's drummer Rick Allen has had to have his arm amputated after his bad car crash (the group has re-designed his drum kit so that he can continue to play).
- Crass's 'Penis Envy' has been dubbed obscene by a judge.

Phil Collins – Band Aid video star

CHARTS

US45	Like A Virgin *Madonna*
USLP	Born In The USA *Bruce Springsteen*
UK45	Do They Know It's Christmas? *Band Aid*
UKLP	The Hits Album *Various*
WEEK 2	
US45	Like A Virgin *Madonna*
USLP	Born In The USA *Bruce Springsteen*
UK45	Do They Know It's Christmas? *Band Aid*
UKLP	The Hits Album *Various*
WEEK 3	
US45	Like A Virgin *Madonna*
USLP	Born In The USA *Bruce Springsteen*
UK45	Everything She Wants/Last Christmas *Wham!*
UKLP	The Hits Album *Various*
WEEK 4	
US45	Like A Virgin *Madonna*
USLP	Born In The USA *Bruce Springsteen*
UK45	I Want To Know What Love Is *Foreigner*
UKLP	Alf *Alison Moyet*

FRANKIE GO TO EUROPE

Frankie Goes to Hollywood are to perform their first ever live European concerts, as one of the headline acts on the huge pan-European *'Europe A Go-Go'* TV rock show. Tyne Tees TV's *'The Tube'* will be providing the UK's contribution to the show – shown in 13 continental countries to an estimated 200 million audience – when The Frankies take the live stage at the company's Newcastle studios.

The group have also finally announced plans for their first tour since the massive success of their controversial debut single 'Relax'. It will take in 13 UK dates, with the possibility of more being added where schedules permit. Some European dates and a new single are also being planned.

Frankies Go To Europe in TV special and announce plans to go on tour

BAND AID – GOING LIVE!

Following the huge success of Band Aid's 'Do They Know It's Christmas' single, incredible plans are now afoot for the world's biggest ever rock concert – once again masterminded by Bob Geldof – in aid of the Ethiopian famine appeal.

The concert, featuring some of the greatest names in rock music, is to be televised live to the world, with a target of around $80 million (£50 million). The event will be staged simultaneously at London's Wembley Stadium and at the Shea Stadium in New York, employing two giant TV screens.

Explains Geldof, 'You might have Duran Duran doing three songs at Wembley, then crossing to Bruce Springsteen in New York as we change over – followed by Culture Club here, then you cut to Michael Jackson, and so on.'

The event is being co-ordinated at the US end by Lionel Richie. It is understood that Richie, together with Michael Jackson and Stevie Wonder, are writing songs for a spin-off album project which is rumoured to feature such names as Bruce Springsteen, Prince and Barbara Streisand.

STAR QUOTE

ALISON MOYET

'If it looks as though I've tarted myself up then that's a natural progression for me as a person, not something that CBS have been dictating.'

Alf says CBS not behind her new face

ROCK FOR THE MINERS

Following a recent benefit concert for Britain's striking coal miners at London's Brixton Academy, which featured Orange Juice, The Woodentops, Everything But The Girl and Aztec Camera, the latest rock personalities to lend their support to the striking miners include Frankie Goes To Hollywood, Sting and Mari Wilson.

They have joined luminaries from the sporting, political and theatrical worlds, together with fellow rock stars Paul Weller, UB40 and Aswad, in putting their names to a large fund-raising campaign known as 'Don't Desert Them Now'. A similar appeal just before Christmas raised some £400,000 ($640,000).

Lionel two times a winner

THE GRAPEVINE

- **Winners of 'BRITS' awards include Paul Young (Best Male), Alison Moyet (Best Female), Wham! (Best Group) and Prince (Best International Act). Grammy winners include Tina Turner (with 4), Prince (3), Lionel Richie, Phil Collins and Billy Ocean.**
- **Bronski Beat's Jimmy Somerville has been fined for indecency in London's Hyde Park.**
- **'Go Go Music' from Washington has been tipped as the next big thing in the UK.**

CHARTS

US45	I Want To Know What Love Is *Foreigner*
USLP	Born in The USA *Bruce Springsteen*
UK45	I Want To Know What Love Is *Foreigner*
UKLP	Agent Provocateur *Foreigner*
WEEK 2	
US45	I Want To Know What Love Is *Foreigner*
USLP	Like A Virgin *Madonna*
UK45	I Know Him So Well *Elaine Page/Barbara Dickson*
UKLP	Agent Provocateur *Foreigner*
WEEK 3	
US45	Careless Whisper *Wham!*
USLP	Like A Virgin *Madonna*
UK45	Love And Pride *King*
UKLP	Agent Provocateur *Foreigner*
WEEK 4	
US45	Careless Whisper *Wham!*
USLP	Like A Virgin *Madonna*
UK45	I Know Him So Well *Elaine Page/Barbara Dickson*
UKLP	Born In The USA *Bruce Springsteen*

SPANDAU SUE

Spandau Ballet have issued a writ against Chrysalis Records, alleging negligence on the part of the label. The group have also stated their desire to be released from their current contract, which has over a year to run.

Spandau's lawyer claims: 'The recent writ served against Chrysalis is a direct result of the group's dissatisfaction over their company's failure to honour its contract to support and promote the group as agreed. Overall, they feel they have not enjoyed the support to which a band of their proven stature and success is entitled'.

He added pointedly: 'They are estimated to be currently responsible for 25 per cent of Chrysalis sales alone. They recently broke all box-office records prior to Christmas by selling out six successive Wembley dates and a UK tour.'

WHAM! – BREAK IN CHINA?

Wham! go where no pop group has gone before – George and Andrew break through Chinese bureaucracy to play gigs in Canton and Peking

Hot on the heels of recent visits by Margaret Thatcher and Richard Nixon to the most populous country on earth, Wham! look all set to visit China, where George Michael and Andrew Ridgeley will play a 15,000-seater hall in Peking and the slightly smaller old opera hall in Canton.

This remarkable coup was achieved largely through tireless wheeling and dealing on the part of the group's manager, Simon Napier-Bell. Negotiations were conducted between Napier-Bell and his contacts in Hong Kong and involved cutting through the blanket bureaucracy of twelve Chinese embassy officials, including the cultural attaché. At one point, the representatives even had to attend a Wham! gig at Tokyo before official approval was sanctioned.

Although Wham! records are as yet still unavailable in China, Napier-Bell notes the awesome possibilities of that market: 'There are 200 million potential record buyers in China. The people have been told to be ready to face the rest of the world. They know there's a change coming and the record shops are full of kids waiting for the foreign records they've been told to expect. Wham! can be the first to fill that need.'

AID FROM AMERICA

'We Are The World', the first single emanating from the USA For Africa project, the American equivalent of the UK's Band Aid, will be released in the UK by CBS.

USA For Africa – USA in this instance standing for United Support of Artists – is made up of a galaxy of top US recording stars. The full line up of stars to add vocals to the Quincy Jones-produced backing track was, alphabetically: Dan Ackroyd, Lindsey Buckingham, Kim Carnes, Ray Charles, Bob Dylan, Sheila E, Daryl Hall and John Oates, James Ingram, The Jacksons, Al Jarreau, Waylon Jennings, Billy Joel, Cyndi Lauper, Huey Lewis & The News, Kenny Loggins, Bette Midler, Willie Nelson, Jeffrey Osborne, Steve Perry, The Pointer Sisters, Lionel Richie, Smokey Robinson, Kenny Rogers, Diana Ross, Paul Simon, Bruce Springsteen, Tina Turner, Dionne Warwick and Stevie Wonder.

The song was written by Lionel Richie and Michael Jackson, and recorded after the American Music Awards telecast on January 28. A video of the session will soon be available with profits going to relieve emergency needs in Africa.

USA for Africa – Spot the Stars at the USA for Africa session

CHARTS

US45 Careless Whisper — *Wham!*
USLP Make It Big — *Wham!*
UK45 I Know Him So Well — *Elaine Page/Barbara Dickson*
UKLP Meat Is Murder — *Smiths*

WEEK 2

US45 Can't Fight This Feeling — *REO Speedwagon*
USLP Make It Big — *Wham!*
UK45 You Spin Me Round — *Dead Or Alive*
UKLP No Jacket Required — *Phil Collins*

WEEK 3

US45 Can't Fight This Feeling — *REO Speedwagon*
USLP Make It Big — *Wham!*
UK45 You Spin Me Round — *Dead Or Alive*
UKLP No Jacket Required — *Phil Collins*

WEEK 4

US45 Can't Fight This Feeling — *REO Speedwagon*
USLP Centerfield — *John Fogerty*
UK45 Easy Lover — *Philip Bailey & Phil Collins*
UKLP No Jacket Required — *Phil Collins*

WEEK 5

US45 One More Night — *Phil Collins*
USLP No Jacket Required — *Phil Collins*
UK45 Easy Lover — *Philip Bailey & Phil Collins*
UKLP No Jacket Required — *Phil Collins*

THE GRAPEVINE

- **George Michael has won the Ivor Novello Award for British Song Writer of the Year.**
- **The first shipment of 'Band aid' food has gone to Ethipia.**
- **It's alleged that, for a while, Wembley Stadium refused to stage *'Live Aid'* and certain chain stores refused to stock the 'We Are The World' single as there was no profit in it for them.**

BEATLES NOT FOR SALE

A Beatles album of unreleased tracks and out-takes drawn from Abbey Road archives has been axed at the last minute by EMI following a thumbs down from the three surviving members of the group.

The album, entitled 'Sessions', covered the group's recorded output from 1963 to 1969, and was even thought to have been allotted a catalogue number.

Consisting mostly of Lennon and McCartney or George Harrison compositions, there were also some covers, including a reworking of Little Willie John's 1959 r&b hit 'Leave My Kitten Alone' (a rumoured possible single a couple of years ago along with another of the album's tracks, the Carl Perkins song 'Lend Me Your Comb', as a B-side) and the standard 'Besame Mucho', a relic from The Beatles' Hamburg repertoire.

Other non-Beatles songs included their interpretation of 'How Do You Do It', a number one for Gerry & The Pacemakers, which was offered to the Beatles by writer Mitch Murray, but rejected by them as the follow-up to 'Love Me Do' in favour of 'Please Please Me'.

'Come And Get It' and 'That Means A Lot', (60s hits for Badfinger and P.J. Proby respectively) were to be included, as were alternative takes of 'I'm Looking Through You', 'One After 909', and George Harrison's 'While My Guitar Gently Weeps'.

Harrison's other contribution was 'Not Guilty', with the remaining cuts being 'What's The New Mary Jane' (credited to The Plastic Ono Band), 'If You've Got Trouble' (rejected from the 'Rubber Soul' session) and two Beatles Fan Club Christmas offerings, 'Mailman Blues' and 'Christmas Time (Is Here Again)'.

Speculation has it that despite the group's apparent rejection of this particular compilation, a similar project involving unreleased Beatles material is still a possibility.

Beatles – no entry on Abbey Road archives for Fab Four sessions LP

Beatles say "No" to out-takes and unreleased tracks

THE GRAPEVINE

- **Wham! have become the first Western Pop group to have a record released in China.**
- **Jimi Somerville has left Bronski Beat due to exhaustion.**
- **Police are denying press stories that they have split up.**
- **Following his announcment that he would never perform again in Britain, Prince has announced that he is retiring from all live performances.**

CHARTS

Week	Chart	Title	Artist
	US45	One More Night	*Phil Collins*
	USLP	No Jacket Required	*Phil Collins*
	UK45	Easy Lover	*Philip Bailey & Phil Collins*
	UKLP	No Jacket Required	*Phil Collins*
WEEK 2	US45	We Are The World	*USA For Africa*
	USLP	No Jacket Required	*Phil Collins*
	UK45	Welcome To The Pleasuredome	*Frankie Goes To Hollywood*
	UKLP	The Secret Of Association	*Paul Young*
WEEK 3	US45	We Are The World	*USA For Africa*
	USLP	No Jacket Required	*Phil Collins*
	UK45	Everybody Wants To Rule The World	*Tears For Fears*
	UKLP	The Secret Of Association	*Paul Young*
WEEK 4	US45	We Are The World	*USA For Africa*
	USLP	We Are The World	*USA For Africa*
	UK45	Everybody Wants To Rule The World	*Tears For Fears*
	UKLP	The Hits Album 2	*Various*

AFRICAN WONDER BAN

The South African Broadcasting Corporation has announced an airtime ban on all Stevie Wonder records. This follows the superstar's gesture at last week's Oscar ceremony of dedicating his award for Best Song to Nelson Mandela and his public declaration of support for the imprisoned African National Congress leader.

Observers have noted that the ban will probably have a reverse effect, recalling the enormous surge in popularity of Beatles records twenty years ago when SABC imposed a similar ban after John Lennon's comments claiming they were more popular than Jesus.

Indeed, the morning after SABC's announcement, independent radio stations reported intensive airplay on Stevie Wonder tracks, with record stores showing heavily increased sales.

Stevie's Oscar dedicated to Nelson

MAY 1985

CHARTS

US45	We Are The World *USA For Africa*
USLP	We Are The World *USA For Africa*
UK45	Everybody Wants To Rule The World *Tears For Fears*
UKLP	The Hits Album 2 *Various*
	WEEK 2
US45	Crazy For You *Madonna*
USLP	We Are The World *USA For Africa*
UK45	Move Closer *Phyllis Nelson*
UKLP	The Hits Album 2 *Various*
	WEEK 3
US45	Don't You (Forget About Me) *Simple Minds*
USLP	No Jacket Required *Phil Collins*
UK45	19 *Paul Hardcastle*
UKLP	The Hits Album 2 *Various*
	WEEK 4
US45	Everything She Wants *Wham!*
USLP	No Jacket Required *Phil Collins*
UK45	19 *Paul Hardcastle*
UKLP	Songs From The Big Chair *Tears For Fears*

THE GRAPEVINE

- **Despite having no UK hits, US funk band Maze sold out eight nights at Hammersmith Odeon. Also touring in the UK are Bryan Adams, The Fat Boys and Millie Jackson.**
- **Belinda Carlisle and Jane Wiedlin are embarking on solo careers.**
- **The first royalties from the USA For Africa record have come in at ($6.5 million), following the first shipments of food and other items to Africa.**

BRUCE TO BRITAIN

Born in the USA, Bruce Springsteen takes the E-Street Band to England this summer

After lengthy speculation, it has been announced that Bruce Springsteen & The E-Street Band will play five open air shows in June and July; two in Newcastle, two at Wembley and one in Leeds. Over quarter of a million people are expected to see him in action, despite the exceptionally high ticket prices of £15 ($30).

These will be Springsteen's first British shows since 1981, and he plans to be onstage throughout the performance, which would be around three hours if his recent Australian shows are a yardstick.

Bruce toured Down Under during March and April and played to his largest-ever audiences of 50,000 per show in Melbourne. In the last 12 months he has been elevated from cult figure to pop star-sex symbol there, and during this triumphant tour was hardly off the front pages. Some even went so far as to describe his tour as a 'second coming'.

STRUMMER-TIME BLUES

Skiffle-style Clash go acoustic

After a quiet year The Clash are busking around the north of England – they recently started playing short acoustic sets using three guitars and a pair of drumsticks. They say they are doing it for enjoyment and for something different (although Joe Strummer said 'just say we've gone absolutely raving mad!'). And they plan to keep on doing it until too many people catch on.

The 'tour' started in a low-key fashion in Nottingham where they supported themselves in true busking style by post-show collections. They then descended on Leeds, where the 'men in blue' turned up . . . not to move them on however, but to make a request! The climax of the Leeds visit was a set to 700 fans queueing for tickets to an Alarm gig.

JESUS & MARY BANNED

Jesus & Mary Chain's new single 'You Trip Me Up' has been held up because WEA's pressing plant staff refuse to handle it, apparently offended by the B-side title 'Jesus Suck'.

Other pressing plants turned it down unanimously, claiming it to be 'obscene', 'blasphemous' or 'too controversial'. The group have been forced to record a new track and the single's release has been delayed.

The band stated: 'This is completely typical of the state of the stale-minded music business. Jesus & Mary Chain continually try to break the music business stereotype, but this time the cliché has affected even us.'

LIVE AID FIXED

Geldof, more Aid for Ethiopia

Two massive Live Aid benefit concerts are to be staged simultaneously in London and Philadelphia in July. They will be viewed by a television audience of over two billion in Britain, Europe, USA and the Far East.

The plans are that the 72,000 people at Wembley, and UK/ Eurovision TV viewers, will see the 15-hour show start at 12 noon. From 5p.m. this will also include live coverage from the States. What organiser Bob Geldof calls a 'global jukebox' will go on till 3a.m. UK time and will broadcast the final stages of the US performances in full. Due to the time difference between America and Europe, the US show will start five hours after the Wembley event.

Since the show has been finalised, criticism has been aimed at Geldof for not including reggae, African and Third World groups in the line-up. He claims to have only included acts known on a world-wide basis simply because that way more money is likely to be donated.

SPUTNIK LAUNCHED!

Most talked-about band of the month, Sigue Sigue Sputnik, masterminded by former Generation X bassist Tony James, looks set to pocket a million pound contract in the near future. British A&R men are being spurred on like never before, whetted by a video the Sputniks have created featuring the explosions and screeching of 'Love Missile F1 – 11'.

Tony James set out a few years back with the sole aim of creating a band with an extremely outrageous visual image. He claims he looked only for people with totally individual images, regardless of their lack of musical talent – learning to play and sing would be a breeze. His first find was vocalist Martin Degville, complete with hair extensions, raccoon tails and no eyebrows, who couldn't sing to begin with.

The band call their music 'fifth generation rock'n'roll', and aim for a sound that 'feels' like movies such as *'Terminator', 'Blade Runner' and* 'Clockwork Orange', *while sounding like a sci-fi Eddie Cochran.*

THE GRAPEVINE

- U2 topped the festival at Milton Keynes Bowl, and Deep Purple headlined at Knebworth.
- The new London Docklands Arena has been opened.
- Jimi Somerville has launched The Communards.
- Elton John is suing Dick James over the rights to his earlier material.
- A fund-raising album for 'Greenpeace' is to be issued, with tracks from Tears For Fears, The Eurythmics and Nik Kershaw.

CHARTS

US45	Everything She Wants *Wham!*
USLP	Around The World In A Day *Prince*
UK45	19 *Paul Hardcastle*
UKLP	Brothers In Arms *Dire Straits*
	WEEK 2
US45	Everybody Wants To Rule The World *Tears For Fears*
USLP	Around The World In A Day *Prince*
UK45	19 *Paul Hardcastle*
UKLP	Brothers In Arms *Dire Straits*
	WEEK 3
US45	Everybody Wants To Rule The World *Tears For Fears*
USLP	Around The World In A Day *Prince*
UK45	19 *Paul Hardcastle*
UKLP	Brothers In Arms *Dire Straits*
	WEEK 4
US45	Heaven *Bryan Adams*
USLP	Beverly Hills Cop *Soundtrack*
UK45	You'll Never Walk Alone *Crowd*
UKLP	Boys And Girls *Bryan Ferry*
	WEEK 5
US45	Heaven *Bryan Adams*
USLP	Beverly Hills Cop *Soundtrack*
UK45	Crazy For You *Madonna*
UKLP	Born In The USA *Bruce Springsteen*

CROWD SUPPORT BRADFORD

A group of artists calling themselves The Crowd has recorded 'You'll Never Walk Alone' in aid of the Bradford (Football Club) Disaster Fund. Over 50 people died in a recent fire at the club's ground. Featured on the record are Pacemakers' leader Gerry Marsden, Scotland's Jim Diamond, and MOR stars Tony Christie, The Nolans and Joe Fagin.

Chas, Di, Bowie, Bob, et al

Hall and Oates, Tina, Madonna and Dylan join the Stones

Finale of the US concert

Paul peeps over the piano at close of the London gig

Another donation via Boomtown Bob

LIVE AID – THE GLOBAL JUKEBOX

One night in November 1984, a young Irish rock singer sat at home with his wife and half-watched BBC Television's Nine O-Clock News. An item from Ethiopia came on, and the screen was filled for five minutes with the most terrible and heart-breaking scenes of starvation and deprivation. At the end of the news, the singer's wife broke into tears and ran upstairs to check on their baby.

Bob Geldof was shattered by what he'd seen. Only too aware that The Boomtown Rats' next single was unlikely to generate anything worth passing on, he hit on the idea of cutting a record specifically for charity, and recruiting more heavyweight friends to lend it cred. They decided to call the project Band Aid.

With help from Ultravox's Midge Ure, Geldof put a song together. With further help from above and his natural gift of the gab, he persuaded a Who's Who of British rock to help record it, got free time out of one of the country's best studios, and talked every major record company and distributor into pressing and shifting the disc for nothing. Record stores took no dealer share either. Every penny the record made would go to charity.

"Do They Know It's Christmas" made No. 1 in Britain over Christmas 1984, became the biggest-ever single in the history of UK charts, and also raced up the US charts with over 1,500,000 sales. It made more than £8 million.

In America, Harry Belafonte was one of those who saw Geldof on TV when he visited the States to plug the Band Aid single and with help from Ken Kragen, pulled an American version of Band Aid together. They called it USA For Africa and, like the British original, boasted a galaxy of America's biggest names. Their single was called 'We Are The World', and it made No. 1 in just about every country in the world with electricity.

Geldof, in the mean time, had been to Africa to see for himself the awful reality behind the headlines. If he'd still nurtured any real thoughts of picking up his own career at this stage, they evaporated there and then. There was a far more important job for him, as leader and spokesman for the organisation which the one-off Band Aid project had become.

The decision to mount an international TV-linked rock and pop marathon was taken some time in March 1985. As soon as Geldof's thoughts clarified, he threw them at some of the people he knew had to be involved if the idea was to become reality. As before, the response was immediate and unconditional. Everyone wanted to help. Live Aid was born.

To produce a 12-hour mini-festival with 28 of the world's biggest superstars is something no normal, well-adjusted promoter would dream of staging without a couple of years' notice and a large tub of valium at his disposal. To stage two of them in tandem, link them via satellite to the entire world, where they would run in conjunction with local similar-sized events – and to get it all together in five months?

From all sides came offers of help. British promoters Harvey Goldsmith and Maurice Jones shouldered the nitty-gritty vital organizational details of the Wembley Stadium show. Bill Graham and Larry Magid did the same in America where the US For Africa event was to be staged at The JFK Stadium, in Philadelphia. Behind them were thousands of rock 'n' roll backstage people prepared to work until they dropped to make it happen.

Megastars, who normally wouldn't leave their dressing room if the Dom Perignon was half a degree warmer than their contract stated, lined up with session players to change in a cramped trailer with a ten-minutes-only transformation period allowed. Superstars got to play with other superstars who were their heroes and heroines from school days. Previous unknowns did fill-in spots and went away famous. A couple of legends showed their feet of clay, but survived because they'd done so in pursuit of a great cause.

Live Aid was, sadly, unique. Sadly, because although the millions of dollars raised by the event were used efficiently to help diminish and decrease the immense suffering of African victims of famine and war, they did little more than provide temporary respite for most.

Wars go on, famine continues. It would take a Live Aid every year for the next twenty to solve the worst problems. It would take an outbreak of real peace to ensure these problems never returned.

But Bob Geldof achieved his dream: to change the world, for one day at least, into a global jukebox.

Co-founder Midge Ure

Phil Collins

Sade

SIMPLY RED – FIRST SHOWCASE

It comes as a surprise to find that what is reputedly Simply Red's greatest asset is in fact the proverbial black card playing against them – Red's (Mick Hucknall) voice. It's a confident voice, it has obvious sincerity and it lacks nothing in technical expertise. But where it fails is in its tone – the group doesn't gel – and there is a mismatch of sounds.

They opened with four or five of their most boring songs, which showed an obsession with white boy funk, and only began to make sense when they performed 'Sad Ole Red', which showed they have learned the value of layering but not cluttering songs. Their songs are not special, but they resonate with individuality and clarity and showed a potential marred by a voice that sings at odds.

This is not saying 'can a white boy sing the blues?' but a thought that Red would be better suited elsewhere – perhaps as an Eighties Gene Pitney?

Mick simply an 80s Gene Pitney?

CHARTS

US45	Sussudio *Phil Collins*
USLP	Beverly Hills Cop *Soundtrack*
UK45	Frankie *Sister Sledge*
UKLP	Misplaced Childhood *Marillion*
WEEK 2	
US45	A View To A Kill *Duran Duran*
USLP	Songs From The Big Chair *Tears For Fears*
UK45	Frankie *Sister Sledge*
UKLP	Born In The USA *Bruce Springsteen*
WEEK 3	
US45	A View To A Kill *Duran Duran*
USLP	Songs From The Big Chair *Tears For Fears*
UK45	Frankie *Sister Sledge*
UKLP	Born In The USA *Bruce Springsteen*
WEEK 4	
US45	Everytime You Go Away *Paul Young*
USLP	Songs From The Big Chair *Tears For Fears*
UK45	There Must Be An Angel *Eurythmics*
UKLP	Born In The USA *Bruce Springsteen*

- **Dire Straits have played ten sold out nights at Wembley Arena.**
- **Echo & The Bunnymen headlined at Glastonbury Festival, but the Reading Festival has had to be cancelled at the last minute.**
- **David Lee Roth is rumoured to be leaving Van Halen.**
- **The Thompson Twins have rescheduled their world tour, postponed by the collapse of Tom Bailey earlier this year.**

Thompson Twin Tom is tip top and thankfully touring again

ALTERNATIVE TOTP

The first alternative *Top Of The Pops*, staged recently at Camden Palace by clubland commando Nick Trulocke, was an adventurous showcase for ten up-and-coming bands.

The show recalled the spirit of early punk and post-punk gigs and while it was occasionally chaotic, the assembled pop-pickers were afforded a couple of hours worth of pretty invigorating entertainment.

The bands all performed one song each, with live vocals to pre-recorded backing tracks in true TOTP style. There was considerable variety in both musical character and artistic merit, and performances ranged from short intense bursts of Steel City Metal Funk and Northern Soul through to 'tipped-for-the-top' Curiosity Killed The Cat and show closers Pet Shop Boys.

Curiosity – the best alternative

MICHAEL JACKSON LICKED

Michael Jackson has won the superstar's race to get his winsome features on a postage stamp. Aptly, it's The Virgin Islands who have given the Indiana wonder boy with the chaste loins his big break.

Apparently, the issue was delayed when Michael had second thoughts about his initial submission featuring portraits of himself in a clown's outfit. Luckily he returned to his senses, donning a scarlet and navy military uniform complete with heavy gold epaulettes, reportedly bought from an Earth Wind & Fire end-of-season sale.

Michael has asked that The Virgin Islands donate the revenue (the stamps are priced between 60c and $1.50) to welfare and education.

BOB GELDOF

'I never wanted Band Aid to go on for a long time, then it would become an institution like ICI or the NME.'

STARS AGAINST 'SUN CITY'

Steve Van Zandt, Bruce Springsteen's former guitarist, is launching an Anti-Apartheid campaign with a rock'n'rap record entitled 'Sun City'. The track features a cast of stars including Jackson Browne, Lou Reed, Bobby Womack, Jimmy Cliff, George Clinton, David Ruffin, Melle Mel, Afrika Bambaataa, Kurtis Blow, Pat Benatar, Bono, Eddie Kendricks, Clarence Clemons, Bonnie Raitt, Linton Kwesi Johnson, Run DMC and Miles Davis, all of whom are opposed to the South African regime/policy.

Van Zandt says of the project: 'It's an effort to alleviate a famine. Unlike Band Aid or USA For Africa, it is a direct political confrontation.'

The record was inspired by South Africa's Las Vegas-like gambling and multi-entertainment resort Sun City, which Steve sees as a symbol of the oppression there. 'It's like an oasis of decadence right in the middle of all this starvation', he says.

Little Steven has united a lot of top rockers and rappers to make a stand against apartheid by drawing people's attention to the decadent Sun City entertainment complex

DOES ZAENTZ DANZ?

Fantasy Records boss Saul Zaentz, who's not without a buck or two, is currently trying to put another 144 million dollars into his piggy-bank by sueing former Creedence Clearwater Revival hero John Fogerty and his new label, Warner Brothers.

Zaentz claim his reputation and business image have been damaged by two tracks on 'Centrefold', Fogerty's debut album for Warner Brothers – 'Zanz Kant Danz' and 'Mr. Greed'. He claims Fogerty's lyrics portray him as 'a thief, a robber, an adulterer and murderer', and that in interviews Fogerty depicted him as a man who so pressurized performers that they lost creativity. Zaentz contends that due to these tracks Fantasy has now become something of a turn-off to both artists and punters.

John has problems with 'Mr. Greed'

THE GRAPEVINE

- **ZZ Top, Metallica and Marillion appeared at the Castle Donnington Monsters of Rock Festival.**
- **The search is on for an actor to play Sid Vicious in the '*Sid and Nancy*' movie.**
- **Simon Le Bon was nearly drowned when his boat 'Drum' overturned during an offshore race.**
- **Madonna's '*Desperately Seeking Susan*' movie has been released to acclaim on both sides of the Atlantic.**

CHARTS

US45	Shout *Tears For Fears*
USLP	Songs From The Big Chair *Tears For Fears*
UK45	There Must Be An Angel *Eurythmics*
UKLP	Born In The USA *Bruce Springsteen*
WEEK 2	
US45	Shout *Tears For Fears*
USLP	Reckless *Bryan Adams*
UK45	Into The Groove *Madonna*
UKLP	Brothers In Arms *Dire Straits*
WEEK 3	
US45	Shout *Tears For Fears*
USLP	Reckless *Bryan Adams*
UK45	Into The Groove *Madonna*
UKLP	Brothers In Arms *Dire Straits*
WEEK 4	
US45	The Power Of Love *Huey Lewis & The News*
USLP	Songs From The Big Chair *Tears For Fears*
UK45	Into The Groove *Madonna*
UKLP	Now That's What I Call Music, 5 *Various*
WEEK 5	
US45	The Power Of Love *Huey Lewis & The News*
USLP	Brothers In Arms *Dire Straits*
UK45	Into The Groove *Madonna*
UKLP	Now That's What I Call Music, 5 *Various*

JACKO BUYS MACCA

After more than a year of speculation, Michael Jackson has bought the British music publishing company ATV Music for a reputed £34 million ($50 million). The company owns some 40,000 songs, including the very lucrative Northern Songs catalogue which contains all The Beatles songs up to their Apple days.

Jacko outbid Coca-Cola, EMI, CBS (who will probably be looking after the catalogue for Jackson) and a very disappointed Paul McCartney, who had originally tried to buy Northern Songs for £21 million ($35 million) in 1981 and then later – again unsuccessfully – in conjunction with Yoko Ono.

Jacko's got Paul's 'Silly Love Songs'

CORN IN THE USA

An impressive line-up of country and rock music luminaries descended on the small town of Champaign, Illinois for a 12-hour benefit concert called Farm Aid. The project was organized to alleviate some of the massive problems currently being faced by the farmers of America.

The crisis – likened by some to the Great Depression – has seen bad harvests, bank closures, bad debts and mortgage foreclosures. The resultant hardships have led to dependence upon food banks and handouts, while official abuse of farm families and suicides have been reported.

The project has so far raised approximately $10 million in ticket sales, merchandising and pledges which, according to organizer Willie Nelson, is still only one-fifth of the expected overall total when mail-in pledges are fulfilled and retail sales of Farm Aid merchandising are finally tallied.

Joining country stars like Nelson, Loretta Lynn, Alabama, Waylon Jennings, Kenny Rogers and Merle Haggard were rock giants such as Bob Dylan, Tom Petty, Billy Joel and Neil Young, among others.

BRAIN POLICE?

Arguments in the current controversy over the lyric content of certain pop and rock songs appear to be polarizing with the creation of pro- and anti- censorship groups.

The right wing PMRC (Parents Music Resource Center) has been formed and, in coalition with the Parents/Teachers Association, has urged the record industry to display consumer 'R' (restricted) warning labels on recordings of material deemed sexually explicit, profane, violent, occult or glorifying drugs or alcohol.

Opposing such vetting, the music industry has formed a committee dubbed the Musical Majority, which is supported by American Civil Liberties Union.

A Senate Commerce Committee hearing on rock lyrics included Dee Snyder of Twisted Sister and Frank Zappa, long the victim of censorship.

Commented Zappa after the hearings: 'The whole thing was generated by a group of bored Washington housewives.' He added: 'You now have a nation of kids who don't read. The bulk of the information which enters their brains thus comes from television and records. So, control over one of those sources of information is rather attractive to an authoritarian mentality.'

So far, the rating system has found few supporters outside the US. In Britain, the industry viewpoint is that self-regulation has worked perfectly well in the past and will continue to do so in future.

Willie & Waylon – ol' outlaws raising money for farmers

Zappa – trouble with bored housewives

Who could object to Twisted Sister Dee?

THE GRAPEVINE

- Arcadia has been launched by Simon Le Bon, Roger Taylor and Nick Rhodes from Duran Duran.
- For the first time, singles in the UK Top 75 are available on 12″
- Most UK pirate radio stations have come off the air while awaiting the government's decision regarding their future.
- Mick Jones has reportedly sued The Clash over the use of their name.

Arcadia – What a line-up!

CHARTS

US45	St. Elmo's Fire (Man In Motion) — *John Parr*
USLP	Brothers In Arms — *Dire Straits*
UK45	I Got You Babe — *UB40 With Chrissie Hynde*
UKLP	Now That's What I Call Music, 5 — *Various*
	WEEK 2
US45	St. Elmo's Fire (Man In Motion) — *John Parr*
USLP	Brothers In Arms — *Dire Straits*
UK45	Dancing In The Street — *Mick Jagger/David Bowie*
UKLP	Brothers In Arms — *Dire Straits*
	WEEK 3
US45	Money For Nothing — *Dire Straits*
USLP	Brothers In Arms — *Dire Straits*
UK45	Dancing In The Street — *Mick Jagger/David Bowie*
UKLP	Now That's What I Call Music, 5 — *Various*
	WEEK 4
US45	Money For Nothing — *Dire Straits*
USLP	Brothers In Arms — *Dire Straits*
UK45	Dancing In The Street — *Mick Jagger/David Bowie*
UKLP	Like A Virgin — *Maddona*

NEW MUSIC EXPRESSED

The sixth annual New Music Seminar (NMS) was held in New York. Traditionally seen as a forum for independent labels and alternative music, it was remarkable for the higher-than-usual participation of major labels.

The usual mix of discussion panels and live music was again in evidence. This year the producers' panel, despite comprising such notables as Jellybean Benitez, Mike Thorne and Arif Mardin, was considered a disappointment, as was the artists' panel, which featured Yoko Ono, Herbie Hancock, Jimmy Cliff, Deborah Harry, Adam Clayton and Martin Fry.

Yoko (seen with son Sean) was a disappointment at the seminar

On a more political note, Solar Records' Dick Grissey announced that any profits from his label's record sales in South Africa would be donated to anti-apartheid organisations, while The Specials' Jerry Dammers accused the industry of inherent racism over chart-compiling practices and Frank Zappa spoke vociferously against the proposed introduction of a movie-style ratings system on records.

Musically, there were afternoon sets by The Beastie Boys and John Sex, and rap showdowns between Roxanne Shanté and LL Cool J. In conjunction with NMS, over 80 acts were playing in clubs around town.

BLACK LISTED?

The rumour that BBC's Radio One hierarchy has circulated a memo discouraging DJs from playing black music on daytime shows has gained further currency after presenter Richard Skinner appeared to endorse anti-soul sentiments during a recent programme.

During a chart rundown, he tacitly alluded to the directive and spoke disapprovingly of Cameo's 'Single Life' and René & Angela's 'I'll Be Good', both of which emanated from the club scene, and appeared to suggest that radio jocks should stop playing these records.

Adding to the controversy, BBC Radio London DJ Tony Blackburn allegedly paraphrased the mystery memo on his morning soul show and promptly insituted a phone-in on the 'incompetence' of Radio One producers and DJs.

Radio One has forcefully denied the existence of the document, claiming it to be 'something concocted by the press', and adding that it did not operate positive or negative discrimination against black music.

Cameo – a black band banned by Beeb?

CHARTS

US45	Money For Nothing	*Dire Straits*
USLP	Brothers In Arms	*Dire Straits*
UK45	If I Was	*Midge Ure*
UKLP	Hounds Of Love	*Kate Bush*
WEEK 2		
US45	Oh Sheila	*Ready For The World*
USLP	Brothers In Arms	*Dire Straits*
UK45	The Power Of Love	*Jennifer Rush*
UKLP	Hounds Of Love	*Kate Bush*
WEEK 3		
US45	Take On Me	*A-Ha*
USLP	Brothers In Arms	*Dire Straits*
UK45	The Power Of Love	*Jennifer Rush*
UKLP	Hounds Of Love	*Kate Bush*
WEEK 4		
US45	Saving All My Love For You	*Whitney Houston*
USLP	Brothers In Arms	*Dire Straits*
UK45	The Power Of Love	*Jennifer Rush*
UKLP	Hounds Of Love	*Kate Bush*

THE GRAPEVINE

■ **Motley Crue's Vince Neil has been jailed following a fatal car crash in which he was involved.**

■ **Fine Young Cannibals have embarked on their first UK tour.**

■ **Mick Jones has denied he was trying to stop Clash performing and has announced the formation of Big Audio Dynamite (BAD) . . . Bronksi Beat has added John Foster in place of Jimmy Somerville.**

■ **Badfinger have won an 11-year battle over royalties with The Beatles' Apple company.**

FIZZY POP

Tracks by Dire Straits, Queen, Bryan Ferry, Thompson Twins, Ultravox and Spandau Ballet are to be found on a new budget-priced compilation entitled 'Pepsi Band Aid Hits'. According to Pepsi, the material consists of studio versions of material performed at Wembley and Philadelphia Live Aid shows. The cassettes will cost £2 ($3.20), and 50p (80c) will go from each sale to Band Aid.

Bryan – one of the Pepsi generation

NOVEMBER

1985

CHARTS

US45	Part-Time Lover *Stevie Wonder*
USLP	Miami Vice *TV Soundtrack*
UK45	Take On Me *A-ha*
UKLP	Live After Death *Iron Maiden*
WEEK 2	
US45	Miami Vice Theme *Jan Hammer*
USLP	Miami Vice *TV Soundtrack*
UK45	The Power Of Love *Jennifer Rush*
UKLP	Once Upon A Time *Simple Minds*
WEEK 3	
US45	We Built This City *Starship*
USLP	Miami Vice *TV Soundtrack*
UK45	Nikita *Elton John*
UKLP	Once Upon A Time *Simple Minds*
WEEK 4	
US45	We Build This City *Starship*
USLP	Miami Vice *TV Soundtrack*
UK45	A Good Heart *Feargal Sharkey*
UKLP	The Promise *Sade*
WEEK 5	
US45	Separate Lives *Phil Collins & Marilyn Martin*
USLP	Miami Vice *TV Soundtrack*
UK45	A Good Heart *Feargal Sharkey*
UKLP	The Promise *Sade*

NMA – NO MERIT ARTISTICALLY?

New Model Army appear to be the first victims of a tough new policy inaugurated by the American Immigration Department. With a major US tour already lined up, the British band have been refused work permits on the grounds that their work is of 'no artistic merit'.

The decision – believed to have been made in the climate of the current pressure being applied to the US government by the censorship lobby – has left the band's label, EMI, somewhat perplexed and stressing the strong moral tone the band's lyrics often take.

Nigel Morton, NMA's manager, said: 'If it's all down to the band's politics, it's a bit strange because Billy Bragg and Poison Girls, whose politics are exactly the same as New Model Army's, have all been allowed entry into the States recently. We've already appealed against the decision.'

In New York, the band's attorney Sandra Levich claimed that she was 'pretty certain' that the US immigration authorities would change their minds.

Meanwhile, the band have just released a single – ironically title 'Brave New World'!

NMA can't march into USA

EVERYTHING'S GONE GREEN

Green on Screen, an ambitious fund-raising project combining pop music and film with the politics of ecology and development, is being planned by Don Coutts of RPM Productions, the resulting documentary to be screened by Channel 4.

Seen as an extension to Band Aid, the film will hope to draw music fans' attention to such current ecological issues as the Botswana Swamplands, urban deprivation in Mexico City, the erosion of the Barrier Reef, natural disasters in Kenya and other ecological *causes célèbres*.

Artists so far shortlisted included Fine Young Cannibals, Depeche Mode, Alison Moyet and Echo & The Bunnymen. There is also the rumoured participation of Stevie Wonder, who has already involved himself with ecological matters on his 'Secret Life Of Plants' album.

Jerry Lee Lewis – critically ill

THE GRAPEVINE

- Figures show that for the first time cassettes outsold vinyl LPs in the UK.
- Rocker Jerry Lee Lewis is in hospital on the critical list.
- Spandau Ballet have tried to stop Chrysalis TV-advertising their Greatest Hits album.
- U2 have launched their Mother Records label.
- Pink Floyd's 'Dark Side of the Moon' has spent its 600th week on the US LP chart.

STARS RALLY TO MORE GOOD CAUSES

Paul McCartney, Elvis Costello, Holly Johnson and Bonnie Tyler are among artists contributing to a 30-track double album, 'The Live-In World Anti-Heroin Album', to be released by EMI, with all profits intended to benefit the British anti-drug abuse foundation, The Phoenix House Charity.

The album also includes donated songs from Eurythmics, Dire Straits and Wham!, together with material written by the album's producer and co-ordinator, Charles Foskett.

Another compilation album – 'Conspiracy Of Peace' – has been announced, with all proceeds going to Amnesty International. Artists featured on the album include Steve Winwood, Peter Gabriel, Paul McCartney, Dire Straits and Elton John.

Spandau Ballet – the New Romantics who have no love for their record company Chrysalis

Jesus & Mary Chain – the controversial duo swept the board in the annual Critics Poll with three of the top six singles and the top album

VINYL FINALS

Scotland's Jesus & Mary Chain have triumphed in the annual NME critics poll. Of the band's three 1985 singles, 'Never Understood' was at No. 1, 'Just Like Honey' was one rung lower (and No. 4 on the best video lists!), while 'You Trip Me Up' was ranked sixth. Coming in third was Kate Bush's 'Running Up That Hill', while the Smiths were fourth with 'How Soon Is Now' and Nick Cave & The Bad Seeds were one place lower with 'Tupelo'.

The album results have also confirmed this to be the year of The Jesus & Mary Chain, who shared the pinnacle position with Tom Waits' 'Rain Dogs', a non-runner in 1984. Despite being released comparatively late in the year, Jim and William Reid's 'Psychocandy' turned out to be an irresistible favourite among NME pundits. In contention for album top spot were 'VU' by The Velvet Underground at No. 3, 'Steve McQueen' by Prefab Sprout at No. 4, one slot above Madness' 'Mad Not Mad'.

Surprise of the year was the total non-appearance of Elvis Costello, who has been consistently represented on both the single and album listings since 1974.

No significant trends were perceived, although black music made a significant contribution to the Top 50 singles and albums, while jazz held well, thanks to some fine re-issues. The much-heralded advent of the American guitar band failed to materialise, country music failed significantly and reggae seemed still to be in post-Bob Marley doldrums. Furthermore, two of the top seven albums were re-issues from the sixties!

CHARTS

US45	Broken Wings *Mr. Mister*
USLP	Miami Vice *TV Soundtrack*
UK45	I'm Your Man *Wham!*
UKLP	Brothers In Arms *Dire Straits*
WEEK 2	
US45	Broken Wings *Mr. Mister*
USLP	Miami Vice *TV Soundtrack*
UK45	I'm Your Man *Wham!*
UKLP	Now That's What I Call Music, 6 *Various*
WEEK 3	
US45	Say You, Say Me *Lionel Richie*
USLP	Heart *Heart*
UK45	Saving All My Love For You *Whitney Houston*
UKLP	Now That's What I Call Music, 6 *Various*
WEEK 4	
US45	Say You, Say Me *Lionel Richie*
USLP	Miami Vice *TV Soundtrack*
UK45	Saving All My Love For You *Whitney Houston*
UKLP	Now That's What I Call Music, 6 *Various*

QUEEN SHUN SUN CITY

Following a statement by Sun City's entertainment director, that 'a return appearance by Queen should not be ruled out', the band have issued the following denial:

'Queen categorically state that they have no plans, at present, to return to Sun City and wish to make it plain that they have a total abhorrence of apartheid.'

THE GRAPEVINE

- There are nine different Sex Pistols bootlegs on sale in the UK.
- Grandfather of rock'n'roll Joe Turner ('Shake, Rattle & Roll', etc.) has died, as have Fifties superstar Rick(y) Nelson and Ian Stewart (known as the 6th Rolling Stone).
- Dire Straits claim that they have released the world's first CD single 'Brothers In Arms'.
- 'Carol Aid' was held in London, with Cliff Richard, Chris De Burgh and Alvin Stardust appearing.

STEELY DAN – DO IT AGAIN

Steely Dan have reformed. After delivering their seventh album, 'Gaucho', to MCA in 1980, the band joined Warner Brothers but never provided their new label with any material, although original member Donald Fagen subsequently released a solo album 'The Nightfly' for the company.

Latterly, co-founder Walter Becker has been working as a producer, but following the huge international success of a Steely Dan compilation album, the duo have decided to reform the band and will undertake to tour for the first time in over ten years.

OZZY'S 'SUICIDE SOLUTION' BLAMED

Ozzy Osbourne – listening to "Suicide Solution" cannot seriously damage your health says adamant Ozzy Osbourne as he's charged by a 19 year old U.S. student's parents

The suicide of a Los Angeles youth was alleged to be a direct result of listening to an Ozzy Osbourne composition entitled 'Suicide Solution'.

This claim has been made by the parents of the boy who maintain that the 19-year-old student shot himself to death with his father's .22 revolver after hearing the track from Osbourne's 1980 solo album 'Blizzard of Ozz'.

The suicide, which took place a year ago, came to light again recently when the boy's parents threatened to sue the artist and his record company for damages. Osbourne, whose latest single is by an ironic twist of fate, entitled 'Shot In The Dark', is reported to be extremely angry over the allegation, maintaining that the lyric was actually about AC/DC's Bon Scott who 'drank himself to a slow painful death'. Ozzy adds that it was 'absolutely ridiculous to suggest that I am responsible for their son's death – he was obviously deranged.'

THE GRAPEVINE

- In the NME Survey of 1985, US acts topped all charts, with Madonna the No. 1 single act followed by Bruce Springsteen, whose LP 'Born In The USA' was Top Album. Top single was Jennifer Rush's 'The Power Of Love'.
- The Royal Air Force admit they may have accidentally killed Glenn Miller during the war by shooting down his plane over the English channel.

GREAT ROCK'N'ROLL SWINDLE

The British High Court case begun by John Lydon in 1979 in an attempt to extricate himself and the other Sex Pistols from a management agreement with pop svengali Malcolm McLaren, finally came to court last week. Ruling against the former Pistols' manager, Mr. Justice Mervyn Davies decreed that the name Sex Pistols belonged jointly to Lydon, Paul Cook, Steve Jones and Sid Vicious's mother, Mrs. Anne Beverley.

He awarded the group the £1 million which is thought to be held in receivership by the court, plus all rights to the Pistols' film 'The Great Rock'n'Roll Swindle' and the assets of McLaren's two companies, Glitterbest and Matrixbest.

Lydon, in Britain to shoot a video for his new single 'Rise', made no comment on the outcome of the case. Untypically, Malcolm McLaren was also staying quiet.

LUTHER VANDROSS IN DEATH CRASH

Luther Vandross was taken to LA's Cedars of Sinai hospital with three broken ribs, lacerations to his scalp and face, and a hairline crack of the hip following a crash which killed the passenger of the car he was driving.

Manslaughter charges originally filed against the Epic Records star – recently nominated for a Grammy award for his 'The Night I Fell In Love' album – have been dropped after it was established there was no evidence that the singer was driving under the influence of drugs or drink, and that the car had simply spun out of control.

A spokesman later described Vandross as being in a 'fair and stable condition.'

STAR QUOTE

JOHNNY (ROTTEN)

'I'd love to have been born in a very wealthy family. I might have ended up even more marvellous than I am now.'

Luther Vandross – the injured soul superstar nevertheless thinks he's got off lightly with no drink and drive charges to face

CHARTS

US45	Say You, Say Me – *Lionel Richie*
USLP	Miami Vice – *TV Soundtrack*
UK45	Saving All My Love For You – *Whitney Houston*
UKLP	Now That's What I Call Music, 6 – *Various*
WEEK 2	
US45	Say You, Say Me – *Lionel Richie*
USLP	Miami Vice – *TV Soundtrack*
UK45	West End Girls – *Pet Shop Boys*
UKLP	Brothers In Arms – *Dire Straits*
WEEK 3	
US45	That's What Friends Are For – *Dionne Warwick & Friends*
USLP	Miami Vice – *TV Soundtrack*
UK45	West End Girls – *Pet Shop Boys*
UKLP	Brothers In Arms – *Dire Straits*
WEEK 4	
US45	That's What Friends Are For – *Dionne Warwick & Friends*
USLP	The Broadway Album – *Barbra Streisand*
UK45	The Sun Always Shines On TV – *A-ha*
UKLP	Brothers In Arms – *Dire Straits*

ALBERTS ALL

A combination of Colombian and UK musicians – some old rockers and newer artists – were on stage at London's Royal Albert Hall on Sunday February 9 for a benefit gig in support of those affected by last year's devastating Colombian earthquake, which left 25,000 inhabitants of the town of Armero dead and double that figure homeless.

Any evidence of post-Live Aid 'compassion fatigue' the audience may have felt disappeared completely as footage of the terrible earthquake aftermath was shown.

Among those appearing were Working Week, Anglo-Colombian band Sonido De Londres, pop-soul artist Jaki Graham, Mike Oldfield, traditionalist Joan Shenton with The Communards and Dave Gilmour and friends representing the AOR side. Alternative comic Harry Enfield provided lighter moments in a show which was headlined by Billy Bragg, Annie Lennox and Chrissie Hynde.

Organized by Colombian jazz artist Chucho Merchan, the event sold out in four days, with video royalties expected to raise over £200,000.

Harry Enfield – joined star-studded line-up at Royal Albert Hall, hoping to raise 'loadsamoney' for Columbian earthquake victims

THE GRAPEVINE

- **BRITS award winners included Tears For Fears, Bruce Springsteen and Phil Collins.**
- **Chart topping Billy Ocean's video of 'When The Going Gets Tough' has been banned by the BBC due to non-union members (including Michael Douglas and Danny De Vito) miming to backing vocals.**
- **A London show starring Squeeze and John Parr has been beamed live to 300 US colleges.**

CHARTS

US45	That's What Friends Are For *Dionne Warwick & Friends*
USLP	The Broadway Album *Barbra Streisand*
UK45	The Sun Always Shines On TV *A-ha*
UKLP	Brothers In Arms *Dire Straits*
WEEK 2	
US45	That's What Friends Are For *Dionne Warwick & Friends*
USLP	The Broadway Album *Barbra Streisand*
UK45	The Sun Always Shines On TV *A-ha*
UKLP	Brothers In Arms *Dire Straits*
WEEK 3	
US45	How Will I Know *Whitney Houston*
USLP	Promise *Sade*
UK45	When The Going Gets Tough *Billy Ocean*
UKLP	Brothers In Arms *Dire Straits*
WEEK 4	
US45	How Will I Know *Whitney Houston*
USLP	Promise *Sade*
UK45	When The Going Gets Tough *Billy Ocean*
UKLP	Brothers In Arms *Dire Straits*

MARLEY MUSEUM TO OPEN

On May 11, exactly five years after the death of Bob Marley, a museum commemorating the reggae artist is being opened in Kingston, Jamaica.

The museum, on the site of his home and headquarters of Tuff Gong Records, will feature Marley memorabilia, including guitars and clothes owned by the late artist, a library and exhibition centre and an audio visual room.

A separate merchandising section will offer T-shirts, badges, rare records and 18 in. miniature Bob Marley statues to the thousands of followers expected to visit the museum.

SUE GEORGE

George Benson's name is the latest in the ever-continuing saga of 'Who's Suing Who'.

Although the singing guitar-picker has been with Warner Brothers for nearly eleven years now, his former label CTI have just got around to claiming that Benson owes them 3 albums. Benson's career has flourished since he left them; his debut Warner album 'Breezin' has alone sold 3 million copies, so CTI are doubtless narked that they have been deprived of considerable income and are now putting the legal kibosh on the Warner-Benson liaison.

GRAB A GRAMMY NIGHT

As expected, 'We Are The World' was the big winner on 'Grammy' night, taking four awards including Record and Song of the Year and Best Performance by a Group. Phil Collins grabbed three Grammys for Album Of The Year, Producer of the Year and Top Male Performance. Other winners included Sade, Whitney Houston, Tina Turner, Don Henley and Dire Straits.

Sade – a British based Grammy winner

MARCH

1986

CHARTS

US45	Kyrie *Mr. Mister*
USLP	Welcome To The Real World *Mr. Mister*
UK45	When The Going Gets Tough *Billy Ocean*
UKLP	Brothers In Arms *Dire Straits*

WEEK 2

US45	Kyrie *Mr. Mister*
USLP	Whitney Houston *Whitney Houston*
UK45	When The Going Gets Tough *Billy Ocean*
UKLP	Brothers In Arms *Dire Straits*

WEEK 3

US45	Sara *Starship*
USLP	Whitney Houston *Whitney Houston*
UK45	Chain Reaction *Diana Ross*
UKLP	Brothers In Arms *Dire Straits*

WEEK 4

US45	These Dreams *Heart*
USLP	Whitney Houston *Whitney Houston*
UK45	Chain Reaction *Diana Ross*
UKLP	Brothers In Arms *Dire Straits*

WEEK 5

US45	Rock Me Amadeus *Falco*
USLP	Whitney Houston *Whitney Houston*
UK45	Absolute Beginners *David Bowie*
UKLP	Brothers In Arms *Dire Straits*

WHAM! SPLIT DENIED

To a background of persistent British tabloid press rumours that Wham! are splitting, the future of the group continues to be uncertain.

Despite the group's management confirming that George Michael and Andrew Ridgely will be pursuing separate careers, a spokesperson for Epic Records explained: 'The popular press has put two and two together and come up with their own answer. The facts are that Epic will issue a new George Michael single 'A Different Cover' on March 24, but there'll be a new Wham! single in early summer, and an album by the group in early autumn. A George Michael solo album is also on the cards for early 1987.'

Whether the Wham! concert, being planned for London's Wembley Stadium in June, will be the group's farewell show or not, remains to be seen.

George go-going?

THE GRAPEVINE

- Sixties superstars The Monkees have reformed and seventies superstar Gary Glitter almost O.D'd on sleeping pills.
- Two other faces from the past have died – O'Kelly Isley of the Isley Brothers, and Richard Manuel of The Band, who committed suicide in the midst of a comeback tour.
- Agreements have been made for sessions from John Peel's BBC radio show to be released.

SUGGS AGAINST THE SUN

Madness singer Suggs has reacted angrily to a *Sun* newspaper front page story that he has close connections with notorious racist punk band Skrewdriver.

The newspaper claims that Suggs is a close friend of band member Ian Stewart, that he helped Skrewdriver with their recordings and also acted as the band's road manager.

Denouncing the story, Suggs maintains that, despite knowing Stewart in the past, he severed all connections with him after learning of his association with The National Front, Britain's leading Nazi-style party. Insisting that he had never held right-wing views, Suggs strongly suggested that it was an attempt by the *Sun* to discredit the socialist Red Wedge organisation to which he belongs, and that he was considering legal action.

HEAR'N'AID FOR METAL LOVERS

Not to be outdone by the many other artists who are doing their bit for the starving people of Ethiopia, a collection of the world's top heavy metal artists has got together to make its contribution to the USA For Africa project.

Under the umbrella name of Hear'n'Aid, forty leading metal artists gathered in a Los Angeles studio to record the single 'Stars', written by two members of the band Dio.

Among those in attendance was Ted Nugent, together with members of Iron Maiden, Motley Crue, Judas Priest, Quiet Riot, Y&T, Twisted Sister, Blue Oyster Cult, W.A.S.P. plus many, many more.

With all proceeds going to famine relief and agricultural aid, the project is being launched at a reception in London next Monday, attended by Dio and others.

Ronny Dio – metal man with a heart of gold who organised the World's heaviest musicians to help Africa

ARTISTS UNITE AGAINST SOUTH AFRICA

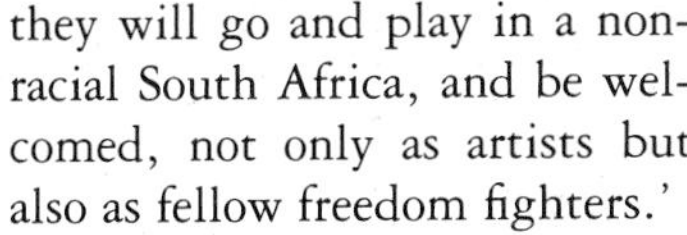

Artists Against Apartheid, the organisation formed by The Specials' Jerry Dammers and Dali Tambo, son of African National Congress leader Oliver Tambo, has held its first press conference in London.

Tambo said, 'Members of AAA will not play Sun City, but they will go and play in a non-racial South Africa, and be welcomed, not only as artists but also as fellow freedom fighters.'

Speaking at the launch, Harry Belafonte – best known for his pop-calypso hits of the 1950s, but in reality an active civil-rights campaigner – spoke passionately in defence of the ANC, calling it 'the legitimate voice of the South African people'. Referring to the American Constitution he stated: 'In the US, racists *break* the law. In South Africa, racists *make* the law.'

Jerry Dammers told the assembled artists: 'In white South Africa, kids are wearing your T-shirts and listening to your music. We must make them realise that we don't condone their system.'

AAA's aims will principally be to raise money for various anti-apartheid causes through concerts and records and to put pressure on the British government to impose sanctions against South Africa.

Artists who have so far expressed their support include Billy Ocean, Simon Le Bon, Junior, Imagination, Hugh Masekela, The Pogues and The Fall.

Jerry Dammers – leading the fight against apartheid

Harry Belafonte – staunch ANC supporter

THE GRAPEVINE

- The Beatles lost their latest case against EMI Records for alleged unpaid royalties.
- Two influential TV shows made their UK debut: *The Chart Show* (UK's first all-video show) and *Solid Soul.*
- Roger Taylor has said he is having a year off from Duran Duran.
- Top songwriter Linda Creed (age 37) has died of cancer – ironically, is song 'The Greatest Love Of All' was climbing to the top on both sides of the Atlantic.

EIRE AID

Self Aid looks set to become the largest ever live event staged in Ireland. U2, Van Morrison, Elvis Costello, Clannad, The Pogues, The Boomtown Rats, Rory Gallagher, and many others will be performing in the main arena of the RDS showgrounds, Dublin.

Masterminded by the co-ordinators of the Irish end of the Live Aid appeal, the idea is for the public to ring in on the day of the concert and pledge either a job or cash for the work-creation fund. The organisers aim to 'provide encouragement and spark off ideas in people's minds'.

CHARTS

US45	Rock Me Amadeus	*Falco*
USLP	Whitney Houston	*Whitney Houston*
UK45	Living Doll	*Cliff Richard & The Young Ones*
UKLP	Brothers In Arms	*Dire Straits*
WEEK 2		
US45	Rock Me Amadeus	*Falco*
USLP	Whitney Houston	*Whitney Houston*
UK45	Living Doll	*Cliff Richard & The Young Ones*
UKLP	The Hits Album, 4	*Various*
WEEK 3		
US45	Kiss	*Prince & The Revolution*
USLP	Whitney Houston	*Whitney Houston*
UK45	Living Doll	*Cliff Richard & The Young Ones*
UKLP	The Hits Album, 4	*Various*
WEEK 4		
US45	Kiss	*Prince & The Revolution*
USLP	5150	*Van Halen*
UK45	A Different Corner	*George Michael*
UKLP	The Hits Album, 4	*Various*

CHARITY FIRST

The record 'Living Doll', which is currently holding the No. 1 position in the UK, brings together Cliff Richard and the cast of the anarchic British TV show *The Young Ones*, who named their show after Cliff's 1962 chart-topper.

All proceeds from this new version will go to Oxfam and Save The Children for their work in Sudan and Ethiopia. It was produced by Stuart Colman, noted for his production work with Shakin' Stevens, and features Hank Marvin of The Shadows on guitar, as did the original version 27 years ago.

Cliff & Young Ones – this unlikely quintet working together to help young ones

MAY

STAR QUOTE

ELVIS COSTELLO

'The virulent anti-American racism in this country (Britain) makes me sick. The idea that they are all stupid and have too much money is all crap.'

CHARTS

US45	Addicted To Love *Robert Palmer*
USLP	5150 *Van Halen*
UK45	A Different Corner *George Michael*
UKLP	Street Life *Bryan Ferry & Roxy Music*
WEEK 2	
US45	West End Girls *Pet Shop Boys*
USLP	5150 *Van Halen*
UK45	A Different Corner *George Michael*
UKLP	Street Life *Bryan Ferry & Roxy Music*
WEEK 3	
US45	The Greatest Love Of All *Whitney Houston*
USLP	Whitney Houston *Whitney Houston*
UK45	Rock Me Amadeus *Falco*
UKLP	Street Life *Bryan Ferry & Roxy Music*
WEEK 4	
US45	The Greatest Love Of All *Whitney Houston*
USLP	Whitney Houston *Whitney Houston*
UK45	The Chicken Song *Spitting Image*
UKLP	Street Life *Bryan Ferry & Roxy Music*
WEEK 5	
US45	The Greatest Love Of All *Whitney Houston*
USLP	Whitney Houston *Whitney Houston*
UK45	The Chicken Song *Spitting Image*
UKLP	Street Life *Bryan Ferry & Roxy Music*

CHARITABLE GREETINGS FROM ASBURY PARK

Bruce Springsteen is involved in the latest rock-for-charity project, Jersey Artists For Mankind '86, with proceeds from records and concerts going to various charities dedicated to the fight against worldwide hunger.

Springsteen, together with members of the E Street Band (including Nils Lofgren and Clarence Clemons), Southside Johnny & The Asbury Jukes, Carolyn Mas and some other 450 musicians and singers, recorded the first single and video for the project, 'We Got The Love'. They also plan to tour the US and Europe with the money going to this good cause.

JACKO BREAKS ANOTHER RECORD

Back in 1984, The Jacksons signed up with Pepsi-Cola to promote their product in TV commercials that tied in with the group's famous 'Victory' tour and netted a cool $5.5 (£3.5) million. Now Jacko has made that figure look small with a deal he has just concluded with Pepsi which will give him at least twice that figure!

Michael and Pepsi bosses are keeping the exact figure quiet, but guesses range from $10 million to a staggering $50 million. A Pepsi spokesman said: 'This new relationship will be the most comprehensive, the most signficant, the most far-reaching ever between a corporation and a performing artist.'

Janet Jackson – dropped a bombshell when she told Europe she would rather do it on the phone

STARS STAY HOME

Fearing retaliatory action by Libya in the wake of the recent US bombing mission against Colonel Gaddafi, scores of US rock artists scheduled to appear in the UK, such as Prince and Lionel Richie, have followed Sylvester Stallone's example and made spur-of-the-moment decisions to stay home.

Carefully sidestepping the Libyan issue, reasons for eleventh-hour pull-outs have shown an enormously imaginative streak.

Patti LaBelle, for example, is not coming because the club that was blown up in Berlin was called The LaBelle – she felt that this might be an omen. (It was the destruction of the club, and the deaths of a number of US servicemen, which led to the US air strike from British bases.)

Janet Jackson has decided that she 'can do all the interviews on the phone' and Husker Dü have stated that their Glastonbury cancellation is due to 'personal problems of mental and physical exhaustion'.

On the other hand, Neil Young has conveniently injured his shoulder in a car crash, and so will not now be playing Britain.

British press reaction – both national and music – has been scathing, with open charges of cowardice being levelled at US performers who have contributed to the mass 'no-show'.

Neil Young – staying at home till he's fighting fit

THE GRAPEVINE

- The UK has staged its first Hip Hop Festival, 'UK Fresh 86' at Wembley Arena.
- In the US, Willie Nelson has announced that Farm Aid II will take place.
- Joe Leeway has left The Thompson Twins and successful UK duo Blancmange have split up.
- Bob Geldof's autobiography, *Is That It?*, has been published.
- Elvis Costello has married ex-Pogue Cait O'Riordan.

JUNE

LIVE SHOWS DEAD?

Leading British concert promoters have issued strenuous denials that there is a crisis facing the tour business. Statements were issued against a backdrop of alarmingly poor turnouts for recent gigs.

The Asgard agency believes there is little connection between chart success and gig attendances. 'We sold out eight nights of Tom Waits in London and we could have sold 16,' a spokesman said. 'Maze did nine nights at Hammersmith, and Robert Cray sold out all his London dates. They don't need singles.'

Another promoter, John Curd, agrees. 'Just because some record companies hype certain bands into the chart, it doesn't follow that the whole world wants to see them.'

Nevertheless, major acts such as The Thompson Twins, Julian Lennon, Bronski Beat, The Communards and Blancmange have all recently cancelled low-gate gigs or simply played to half empty halls.

Although the present difficult economic climate may account for some of the recent mediocre attendances, there is no one clear reason why tours have taken a downturn. It can only be a cause of great concern for the entire industry.

Julian Lennon – not pulling the crowds like his dad did

WHAM! SCAM?

George Michael – Wham!'s last single the double priced (£2.75) 'Edge of Heaven' is flying up the charts but not out of the shops say the dealers!

There has been much industry talk of hype over the new Wham! single 'Edge Of Heaven'. The accusations have been made in the light of extremely poor reported sales and suspiciously high chart placing of the record.

One suggested reason for the single's poor sales has been that since it is deemed a 'double single' it has attracted a £2.75 price tag. Quotes from UK record dealers included: 'It went to No. 2, yet sales have been minimal' and also 'We feel really sorry for the punters being asked to pay the increased price, and as far as we're concerned Wham! are attempting one last rip-off before they go-go.'

UK chart compilers Gallup said: 'The record had sales of around 60,000 in that first week, which was enough to take it to No. 2, and if it repeats those sales this week it should be yet another number one for Wham!'

THE OTHER PRINCE'S SHOW

An all-star benefit concert on behalf of the Prince's (Prince of Wales) Trust is being organised for London's Wembley Arena. Among those shortlisted are Phil Collins, Tina Turner, Eric Clapton, Elton John, Pete Townshend, Level 42, Midge Ure, Joan Armatrading, Suzanne Vega, Alison Moyet, Paul Young, Big Country, Mark Knopfler and Status Quo, with other acts still under negotiation.

Tina Turner – the Acid Queen will be performing for the Prince of Wales at the all star Prince's Trust benefit concert at Wembley

CHARTS

US45	Live To Tell	*Madonna*
USLP	Whitney Houston	*Whitney Houston*
UK45	Spirit In The Sky	*Doctor & The Medics*
UKLP	So	*Peter Gabriel*
WEEK 2		
US45	On My Own	*Patti LaBelle & Michael McDonald*
USLP	Whitney Houston	*Whitney Houston*
UK45	Spirit In The Sky	*Doctor & The Medics*
UKLP	So	*Peter Gabriel*
WEEK 3		
US45	On My Own	*Patti LaBelle & Michael McDonald*
USLP	Whitney Houston	*Whitney Houston*
UK45	Spirit In The Sky	*Doctor & The Medics*
UKLP	So	*Peter Gabriel*
WEEK 4		
US45	On My Own	*Patti LaBelle & Michael McDonald*
USLP	Whitney Houston	*Whitney Houston*
UK45	Spirit In The Sky	*Doctor & The Medics*
UKLP	Invisible Touch	*Genesis*

THE GRAPEVINE

- **The international 'Race Against Time' took place, with everybody wanting to Run the World and help Ethiopia. Belatedly, Bob Geldof has received an honorary knighthood.**
- **After Wham! held their farewell concert, it was announced that they had sold 38 million records in their 5 years together.**
- **Sigue Sigue Sputnik are selling advertising space in the gaps between tracks on their debut LP.**

CHARTS

US45	There'll Be Sad Songs (To Make You Cry) *Billy Ocean*
USLP	Control *Janet Jackson*
UK45	The Edge Of Heaven (EP) *Wham!*
UKLP	Invisible Touch *Genesis*
	WEEK 2
US45	Holding Back The Years *Simply Red*
USLP	Control *Janet Jackson*
UK45	Papa Don't Preach *Madonna*
UKLP	Invisible Touch *Genesis*
	WEEK 3
US45	Invisible Touch *Genesis*
USLP	Winner In You *Patti LaBelle*
UK45	Papa Don't Preach *Madonna*
UKLP	True Blue *Madonna*
	WEEK 4
US45	Sledgehammer *Peter Gabriel*
USLP	Top Gun *Soundtrack*
UK45	Papa Don't Preach *Madonna*
UKLP	True Blue *Madonna*

WHAM! GO-GO

The much discussed final Wham! concert went ahead at Wembley Stadium, London, in front of an ecstatic, predominantly female crowd of some 80,000 young fans.

Andrew Ridgely and George Michael's swansong performance was overtured by lengthy film footage of the duo's recent visit to China, as well as live support from rock veteran Gary Glitter and Nick Heyward.

To a tumultuous reception, the duo eventually took to the stage against a backdrop of a large black curtain reading 'The Final' (a jokey reference to the sports stadium venue where soccer's F.A. Cup Final takes place).

Screaming that at times resembled massive guitar feedback accompanied the set, which included all of Wham!'s hit singles, together with numerous album tracks.

At an emotional close of set, the pair hugged one another and fought back tears as they were joined on stage by many top names for an encore of 'I'm Your Man' and an emotional duet between Michael and Elton John of the latter's 'Candle In The Wind'.

RAP PACKAGE

An impressive line-up of L.L.Cool J, Run DMC, Whodini and The Beastie Boys took the stage before an 18,000 strong audience at Philadelphia's Spectrum Stadium for an all-rap spectacular.

New York's Beastie Boys were on hand to warm proceedings up, while L.L.Cool J – rap's first really convincing sex symbol – hotted up the ladies. A laid-back Whodini paved the way for Run DMC, currently the most popular and devastating rap group in the World. Jam Master Jay on the scratchers' podium mixed out Run DMC's history right up to their current hit 'My Adidas' for the appreciative rap-clapping sneaker-waving audience.

THE QUEEN LIVES ON

The tabloids press politician to ban The Smiths' 'The Queen Is Dead'

A British politican has denied that he tried to ban the new Smith's album 'The Queen Is Dead'. In a telephone call to NME, he explained that in fact he had no powers to impose such a ban, but said that having read the lyrics of the new album, he hoped that radio stations would not programme it.

It's widely believed that the controversy arose from the practice frequently used by British tabloid newspapers – *The Sun* in particular – of finding a controversial title or lyric and phoning an appropriate well-known figure for comment.

A spokesperson for Rough Trade, The Smiths' label, said: 'if anyone goes to the Home Office and tries to ban our record, we will take legal advice. We would regard it as a restriction of trade.'

THE GRAPEVINE

- **A bootleg has appeared, apparently containing The Beatles singing a racist spoof of 'Get Back'.**
- **Sigue Sigue Sputnik have cancelled their UK tour.**
- **A festival was held in Manchester to celebrate ten years of punk. It starred The Smiths, OMD, New Order, The Fall and newcomers Happy Mondays.**
- **The BBC have agreed to pay record companies £150,000 ($240,000) a year for use of promo videos.**

PRINCE: KING OF WEMBLEY

Prince may pledge allegiance to the Almighty, but his recent London shows – his first in the UK for five years – revolved around pleasures of the flesh and private fantasy made public property, with the audience becoming part of his world of excitement and intrigue.

The show opened as it meant to go on – teasing and provocative. His ten-piece group set the mood from behind a drawn curtain before a stripped-to-the-waist Prince cavorted through a repertoire of stunningly-choreographed and dynamic stage moves.

He took his audience on a kaleidoscopic glide through the sleazy and fêted stereotypes of American culture – a dazzling tour de force of rhythmic and melodic inspiration and invention. Sonic funk changed to big-band jazz, then over to a series of monster-stomping Sly-scorched crescendos, before climaxing with a 'Purple Rain' finale.

Prince's versatility, and his sensitivity to his musical heritage, has been used to fuel his lust for an ongoing orgy of stardom. By balancing and blurring sexual roles and musical styles, he has kept one jump ahead of his peers.

The show was both a lavish celebration and tribute to black culture, to those who dare to break barriers, to explicit beauty and sensuality – and to Prince's own career, which has used all those traits.

To celebrate his British return, Prince threw a party at Busby's in London, which attracted a predictable mixture of celebrities, including The Pet Shop Boys, Sigue Sigue Sputnik and Hollywood Beyond.

As the party progressed, the questions most asked were: 'Where is he?' and 'Will he play?'

At around two am, Prince materialized on the club's stage, with Ron Wood in tow. In front of a disbelieving crowd, he turned in an hour-long set which was, if anything, funkier than the show with which he'd just stunned Wembley.

Then, in keeping with his skilfully-contrived mystique, he vanished.

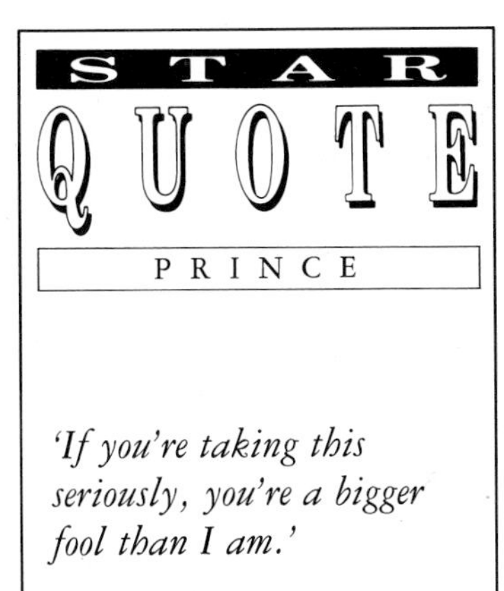

STAR QUOTE

PRINCE

'If you're taking this seriously, you're a bigger fool than I am.'

CHARTS

US45	Glory Of Love – *Peter Cetera*
USLP	Top Gun – *Soundtrack*
UK45	The Lady In Red – *Chris De Burgh*
UKLP	True Blue – *Madonna*
WEEK 2	
US45	Glory Of Love – *Peter Cetera*
USLP	Top Gun – *Soundtrack*
UK45	The Lady In Red – *Chris De Burgh*
UKLP	True Blue – *Madonna*
WEEK 3	
US45	Papa Don't Preach – *Madonna*
USLP	True Blue – *Madonna*
UK45	The Lady In Red – *Chris De Burgh*
UKLP	True Blue – *Madonna*
WEEK 4	
US45	Papa Don't Preach – *Madonna*
USLP	True Blue – *Madonna*
UK45	I Want To Wake Up With You – *Boris Gardiner*
UKLP	Into The Night – *Chris De Burgh*
WEEK 5	
US45	Higher Love – *Steve Winwood*
USLP	True Blue – *Madonna*
UK45	I Want To Wake Up With You – *Boris Gardiner*
UKLP	Now That's What I Call Music, 7 – *Various*

Yoakam plays in the old country

THE GRAPEVINE

- **The case accusing Ozzy Osbourne's music of causing a fan's suicide has been thrown out of a US court. Meanwhile, Ozzy played at the annual Donnington Monsters Of Rock festival.**
- **Top US jazz musicians have recorded an album 'Jazz To End Hunger'.**
- **New country star Dwight Yoakam has made his UK debut.**
- **American keyboard player Michael Rudetsky was found dead at Boy George's London home.**

CROSBY PAROLED

David Crosby, of Crosby, Stills, Nash and Young fame, who was serving a five-year sentence for possession of cocaine and a firearm, has been granted parole.

The singer has spent the last six months in a Texan jail, but has now been released to a half-way house. From there he's likely to return to California and presumably will be fitting in gigs between the random urine tests he will now have to undergo to satisfy the authorities that he is staying drug-free.

Ex-Byrd jail bird Dave out on parole

1986

FIVE STAR SNUB DISCO CHARITY RECORD?

The latest UK music-business related charity to be announced is Disco Aid, organised by Radio London DJ Steve Walsh. A galaxy of British soul talent including Paul Hardcastle, Junior, Jaki Graham and Aswad, gathered in a North London studio to cut the first single, 'Give Give Give', with proceeds going to Band Aid and domestic charities.

One sour note was struck over the apparent refusal by Five Star to participate. The group's father-manager Buster Pearson claimed that Five Star would have been happy to participate, but that rehearsals for their new tour made this impossible. Disco Aid sources claimed that Pearson had categorically vetoed the RCA act's involvement.

INDIE SMITHS SIGN TO EMI

The Smiths have signed a long term deal with EMI, for an advance rumoured to be close to the £1 million ($2.5 million) mark.

However, a spokesman for their former label, Rough Trade, claims that Morrisey and his men still have to deliver at least two more singles and albums to them, and described the EMI signing as 'ridiculous'.

'They could have quite a long wait before they can release any records,' he added.

Differences of opinion between The Smiths and Rough Trade have been well documented; including Morrisey's reluctance to make videos and the numerous wrangles which delayed the release of 'The Queen Is Dead' for months.

The Smiths – darlings of the Independent record scene have signed with EMI, Britains biggest major label

NEW ACTS CHANGING COUNTRY MUSIC

After a long period of decline, country record sales in the US are enjoying a huge upturn, thanks in no small measure to the influx of a new generation of young performers.

At the recent Country Music Association awards in Nashville, newcomers George Strait, Randy Travis and Dwight Yoakam swept the board.

Country music's best-selling act, Alabama, achieve platinum status with every album, while mother-daughter duo The Judds have sold two million albums in less than three years. Randy Travis' first album was No. 1 on Billboard's country album charts for four consecutive weeks and has gone straight into the 80s on the rock charts. Meanwhile, his WEA labelmate Dwight Yoakam has registered sales of 300,000 with his 'Guitars, Cadillacs, Etc. Etc.' album.

Acts like Ricky Skaggs, Kathy Mattea, Restless Heart, Forester Sisters and many others are part of a new wave of country performers who are enjoying bouyant record sales while bringing a freshness and excitement to the industry not seen since the heady days of the 'Urban Cowboy' fad of the early eighties.

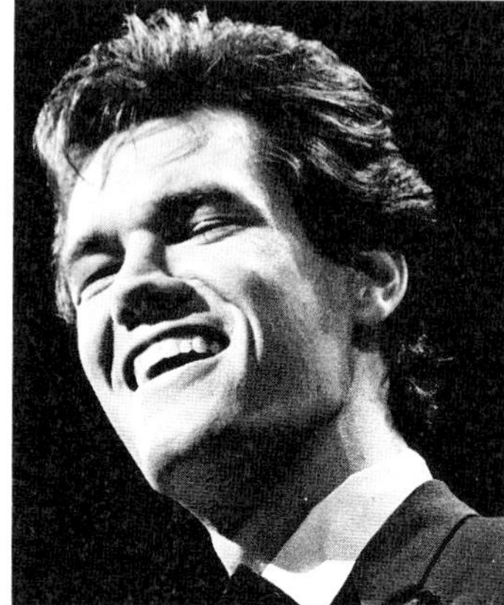

New Country – platinum act Alabama (top) together with George Strait (below left) and Randy Travis (below right) are among the top new faces of the New Country movement in the US

THE GRAPEVINE

- After 22 hits as a septet, Madness have decided to become a quartet with just Suggs, Carl, Chris & Lee.
- ZTT records have brought up Stiff records and RCA has been bought by German company BMG.
- Cliff Burton has died in a crash in Sweden.
- An Anti-Smack record has been released – acts on in it include Cliff Richard, Nik Kershaw, Howard Jones and Alarm.

CHARTS

Chart	Title	Artist
US45	Venus	Bananarama
USLP	True Blue	Madonna
UK45	I Want To Wake Up With You	Boris Gardiner
UKLP	Now That's What I Call Music, 7	Various
WEEK 2		
US45	Take My Breath Away	Berlin
USLP	True Blue	Madonna
UK45	Don't Leave Me This Way	Communards
UKLP	Now That's What I Call Music, 7	Various
WEEK 3		
US45	Stuck With You	Huey Lewis & The News
USLP	Top Gun	Soundtrack
UK45	Don't Leave Me This Way	Communards
UKLP	Now That's What I Call Music, 7	Various
WEEK 4		
US45	Stuck With You	Huey Lewis & The News
USLP	Dancing On The Ceiling	Lionel Richie
UK45	Don't Leave Me This Way	Communards
UKLP	Break Every Rule	Tina Turner

WARNERS AND THE BROTHERS

The black-owned and operated Solar Records label has filed a $200 million, 19-count, 56-page action against the Warner Brothers corporation accusing it of racism and alleging that it reneged on their distribution deal with them.

Solar claim that Warners did not give the same level of promotion to their artists as they did to white acts, and quoted an anonymous Warner Brothers executive as having said: 'When you are black in America, you have to expect to get the short end of the stick, and you have to keep your mouth shut.'

The recording giant is in even more hot water over the race issue as the Rev Jesse Jackson has chosen Warners as his first target in his fight against discriminatory practices in the American music industry. In an open letter to WEA he alleges discrimination against black employees and black music marketing departments and simultaneously sideswipes the corporation over its South African dealings.

Top politician Jackson sees red over Warners treatment of Black employees

CHARTS

Week	Chart	Title	Artist
	US45	Stuck With You	*Huey Lewis & The News*
	USLP	Dancing On The Ceiling	*Lionel Richie*
	UK45	Don't Leave Me This Way	*Communards*
	UKLP	Graceland	*Paul Simon*
WEEK 2	US45	When I Think Of You	*Janet Jackson*
	USLP	Top Gun	*Soundtrack*
	UK45	Don't Leave Me This Way	*Communards*
	UKLP	Graceland	*Paul Simon*
WEEK 3	US45	When I Think Of You	*Janet Jackson*
	USLP	Fore!	*Huey Lewis & The News*
	UK45	True Blue	*Madonna*
	UKLP	Graceland	*Paul Simon*
WEEK 4	US45	True Colors	*Cyndi Lauper*
	USLP	Slippery When Wet	*Bon Jovi*
	UK45	Every Loser Wins	*Nick Berry*
	UKLP	Graceland	*Paul Simon*

ALMOND 'TOO CAMP' VID SHOCKER!

Marc Almond and Some Bizzare Records boss Stevo have clashed with Virgin Records over the promotional video for Almond's new single 'Ruby Red'.

Virgin, who distribute Almond's output for Some Bizarre, have decided that certain parts of the video – which contains scenes of nudity and satanism – are offensive, and have re-edited it for TV. A Virgin spokesman said he personally enjoyed the video, but considered it 'too camp' for television, adding that it was 'not the sort of thing that Saturday morning children's BBC TV show, *Saturday Superstore*, would show'.

In response, Stevo commented: 'Who are Virgin to make moral statements? They have a large roster of transient garbage they can manipulate without trying it on with Marc.'

CHOCS AWAY

Cadbury's Chocolate have taken exception to Demon Records' cassette packaging of Elvis Costello's 'Blood And Chocolate', which imitates a bar of the company's Bourneville chocolate and imitates the famous Cadbury logo.

The chocolate giant called on Demon Records to withdraw all stocks of the offending cassette from the shelves. Demon have subsequently acceded to Cadbury's wishes, so making initial copies of the cassette an instant collectors' item.

A spokesman for Cadbury's marketing department said: 'We took exception to our design being used without permission. We have nothing against pop music, in fact, we're about to launch a massive advertising campaign with Elton John.'

Elvis Costello – his album sleeve has been attacked by a chocolate giant

THE GRAPEVINE

- UB40 have started the biggest Russian Pop tour yet.
- Police have briefly re-united and re-recorded 'Don't Stand So Close To Me'.
- Previously unreleased John Lennon tracks are included on his new 'Menlove Avenue' album.
- The Dead Kennedys have said they will be sueing US Shriners for $45 million.
- Packing them in at London's Wembley venue have been Whitney Houston, ZZ Top and Chris De Burgh.

USSR loves UB40's 'Red Red Wine' and they get the biggest Russian tour yet

NOVEMBER

MTV – ROCK AGAINST DRUGS

A multi-million dollar campaign called Rock Against Drugs has been launched with public service spots on MTV by seven top rock acts.

Musicians appearing in the first broadcasts are Ronnie Dio, Steve Jones (formerly of The Sex Pistols), Jon Bon Jovi, Motley Crue's Vince Neil, Mr Mister's Richard Page, Gene Simmons of Kiss and Andy Taylor.

Each artist brings a different style and message to the anti-drug theme. A swaggering Vince Neil says: 'I still party, but I do it without drugs', while a laid-back Richard Page offers: 'Drugs have nothing to do with making music'.

Executive producer of the spots, Danny Goldberg, says: 'A lot of us in the rock industry have been scared by drug problems, and because of the closeness of the situation we're probably more anti-drug than most people.' He adds: 'We want to keep rock at the vanguard of the anti-drug movement.'

The spots were funded by California's Attorney General with $3 million advertising time donated by MTV. Additional contributions were made by Pepsi and numerous music and video companies. They are available to all cable and TV channels in the US.

The next phase of the campaign will feature The Bangles, Belinda Carlisle, Genesis and Bob Seger amongst others.

'RAND AID' SLAMMED BY DAMMERS

The South African government has organised a Band Aid-style record and video aimed at 'promoting racial harmony' in the country, and Jerry Dammers – leader of Artists Against Apartheid - has urged Bob Geldof to make a statement to the South African media against the Botha regime's latest propaganda stunt.

The record (called 'Together We'll Build A Brighter Future') features 51 black and white musicians singing such lines as: 'Now's the time to join our hands together, prepare ourselves for the days ahead'.

South African anti-apartheid organizations have greeted the song with anger and derision and many of the country's most popular black artists have refused to take part in this Band Aid cash-in.

Dammers said angrily, 'It's blatant perversion of the spirit of Band Aid,' and added, 'It's totally the opposite of the South African government's intentions to continue a process of separate racial development.'

Geldof, doing promotion work in Europe, has been unavailable for comment.

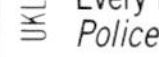

African Aid angers A.A.A.'s Dammers

CHARTS

US45	True Colors *Cyndi Lauper*
USLP	Third Stage *Boston*
UK45	Every Loser Wins *Nick Berry*
UKLP	Graceland *Paul Simon*
WEEK 2	
US45	Amanda *Boston*
USLP	Third Stage *Boston*
UK45	Every Loser Wins *Nick Berry*
UKLP	Graceland *Paul Simon*
WEEK 3	
US45	Amanda *Boston*
USLP	Third Stage *Boston*
UK45	Take My Breath Away *Berlin*
UKLP	Every Breath You Take: The Singles *Police*
WEEK 4	
US45	Human *Human League*
USLP	Third Stage *Boston*
UK45	Take My Breath Away *Berlin*
UKLP	Every Breath You Take: The Singles *Police*
WEEK 5	
US45	You Give Love A Bad Name *Bon Jovi*
USLP	Live 1975-1985 *Bruce Springsteen & The E Street Band*
UK45	Take My Breath Away *Berlin*
UKLP	Every Breath You Take: The Singles *Police*

THE GRAPEVINE

- **The UK re-issue of The Cars 'Drive' has raised £160,000 ($250,000) for 'Live Aid' & the Anti-Sun City records have raised £250,000 ($400,000).**
- **The Anti-Apartheid Association lost £25,000 ($40,000) on their free festival.**
- **King have split up and Prince has ended the Revolution and will now record solo.**
- **Billy Bragg was arrested cutting wires at a US air force base.**

Cars – thanks to video in 'Live Aid' the Cars help Ethiopian money drive

Bragg – the cutting edge of rock

BOSS SALES FOR BRUCE'S XMAS BOX

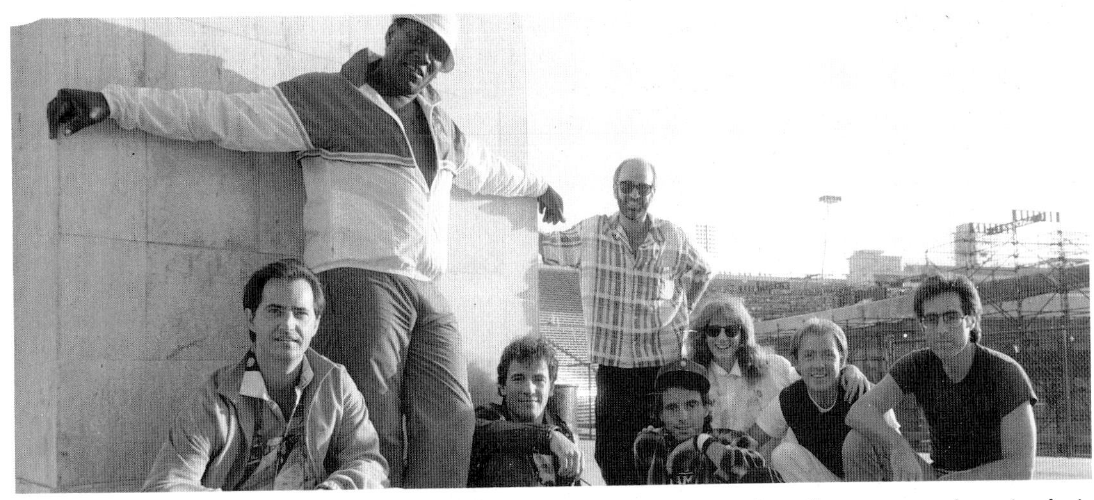

Springsteen – the Boss and the E Street Band relax after hearing about the record breaking sales of their five album box set which entered the US chart in the No. 1 position

'Bruce Springsteen & The E-Street Band Live 1975-85' has leaped straight to the No. 1 spot in the US after astounding sales there. It's the first album to do this in more than 10 years, and the previous three to achieve this feat were normal single albums.

First day sales of the 40-song box set far outstrip any other record in memory, report ecstatic US dealers. Most stores sold out on the first day and it's believed that approximately 1.5 million sets were distributed.

Virtually every dealer reported sales far beyond projections – the head of one large record chain happily commented on the day's sales: 'It's the wildest I've seen in 25 years in the business.'

Tower Records confirmed it was their largest-ever order and a mega-store in California which had ordered 22,000 sets re-ordered 15,000 more by the end of the first day!

CHARTS

US45	The Next Time I Fall *Peter Cetera With Amy Grant*
USLP	Live 1975-1985 *Bruce Springsteen & The E Street Band*
UK45	The Final Countdown *Europe*
UKLP	The Hits Album, 5 *Various*
WEEK 2	
US45	The Way It Is *Bruce Hornsby & The Range*
USLP	Live 1975-1985 *Bruce Springsteen & The E Street Band*
UK45	The Final Countdown *Europe*
UKLP	Now That's What I Call Music, 8 *Various*
WEEK 3	
US45	Walk Like an Egyptian *Bangles*
USLP	Live 1975-1985 *Bruce Springsteen & The E Street Band*
UK45	Caravan Of Love *Housemartins*
UKLP	Now That's What I Call Music, 8 *Various*
WEEK 4	
US45	Walk Like An Egyptian *Bangles*
USLP	Live 1975-1985 *Bruce Springsteen & The E Street Band*
UK45	Caravan Of Love *Housemartins*
UKLP	Now That's What I Call Music, 8 *Various*

CANNIBALS FOR CHILDREN'S SOCIETY

Fine Young Cannibals urge Johnny to go home from un-groovy London

Fine Young Cannibals are at the forefront of a new campaign by The Children's Society organisation to persuade young runaways to go back home.

The group's first hit 'Johnny Come Home' was played over the loudspeakers at London's Euston train station, where the campaign was launched. Roland Gift, lead singer of Fine Young Cannibals, was there to explain why he wrote 'Johnny Come Home'. He said 'It's a myth that London is groovy – you need money, friends and a place to stay'.

The Children's Society run a refuge centre in London for runaways, and there are plans to set up similar projects in other large cities where young people migrate in the hope of finding work.

'TOP OF THE POPS' REACHES THE US

The British chart show *Top Of The Pops* is to be shown on American syndicated TV soon in a modified format. The half-hour pop programme will be combined with a US version taped in Hollywood, and will also feature 'retrospective sections' from its 23-year-old archives.

Drew Savitch Levin, president of The Entertainment Network (TEN) who secured the rights, reports more than 100 calls from interested affiliates despite not making an official pitch yet. 'British rock and those who follow it have been the taste-setters for the world,' he asserts.

TEN, wh co-produce the Montreux Festival TV shows, have also reached an agreement to syndicate a series of *The Tube*, produced by British Tyne-Tees Television.

THE GRAPEVINE

- **A US survey shows that cassettes outsell vinyl two to one there and industry people say the seven inch single is on the way out.**
- **New Model Army have finally gotten the OK to tour in the US.**
- **Cliff Richard has refused to appear on a 'Comic Relief' video due to the company he would keep.**
- **MTV has been launched in Britain.**

Cliff worried who he's seen with!

JANUARY 1987

CHARTS

Chart	Title	Artist
US45	Walk Like An Egyptian	Bangles
USLP	Live 1975-1985	Bruce Springsteen & The E Street Band
UK45	Caravan of Love	Housemartins
UKLP	Now That's What I Call Music, 8	Various
WEEK 2		
US45	Walk Like an Egyptian	Bangles
USLP	Live 1975-1985	Bruce Springsteen & the E Street Band
UK45	Reet Petite	Jackie Wilson
UKLP	Now That's What I Call Music, 8	Various
WEEK 3		
US45	Shake You Down	Gregory Abbott
USLP	Slippery When Wet	Bon Jovi
UK45	Reet Petite	Jackie Wilson
UKLP	Graceland	Paul Simon
WEEK 4		
US45	At This Moment	Billy Vera & The Beaters
USLP	Slippery When Wet	Bon Jovi
UK45	Reet Petite	Jackie Wilson
UKLP	Graceland	Paul Simon
WEEK 5		
US45	At This Moment	Billy Vera & The Beaters
USLP	Slippery When Wet	Bon Jovi
UK45	C'est La Vie	Robbie Nevil
UKLP	Graceland	Paul Simon

THE GRAPEVINE

- **Michael Jackson has denied that he plans to buy Motown records.**
- **The Archibishop of Canterbury's envoy Terry Waite is trying to reform the remaining Beatles for a big 'One World' show at Wembley.**
- **The Dead Kennedys have split up.**
- **It has been announced that DAT and CDVs will be launched shortly.**

ARTISTS AGAINST AIDS

Elton aiding Wembley AIDS show

In the wake of the AIDS crisis, the rock world has met the challenge with a series of concerts intended to raise public money and consciousness of the disease.

The most prestigious show will feature Elton John, Boy George, George Michael, Womack & Womack, Tom Robinson, The Communards and Holly Johnson, who are scheduled to play Wembley Arena on April 5, designated International AIDS Day. The show will also represent the first appearances of George Michael without Wham! and Holly Johnson without Frankie Goes To Hollywood.

In separate developments, The Communards' Jimmy Somerville and Richard Coles are involved in a UK public information film warning of the dangers of AIDS and encouraging the use of condoms, while Kool Moe Dee's single 'Go See The Doctor' has been adopted by the West German government in its campaign against the disease.

The record is being played during official announcements on the radio, and the song title is being reprinted on the packaging of the country's best-selling condoms.

Womacks adding a little soul

Communards commending condoms

BEATLES FOR SALE – ON CD

For the first time ever, Beatles' albums will be available on compact disc, EMI has announced. The four titles are, 'Please Please Me', 'With The Beatles', 'A Hard Day's Night' and 'Beatles For Sale'.

Hitherto, any legitimate Beatles CD product was only available as part of a series of Japanese samplers which launched the format in 1983. According to an EMI spokesman, only manufacturing capacity has caused the delay in introducing Beatles on CD.

He stressed that the company decided to wait until the product was fully store-ready rather than put the titles in the catalogue and then not be able to meet orders.

THE CURE STAND WITH ARABS

Claims have been made by Robert Smith of The Cure that the group's 1979 indie hit 'Killing an Arab' is being played by certain right wing American DJs as a racist incitement against Arabs.

Outraged by the misinterpretation – or deliberate misuse – of the song's ironic intention and its anti-racist and anti-violence message. The Cure have announced, by way of redress, a major concert in the USA in support of Lebanese and Palestinian war orphans.

Furthermore, Smith has requested that the song be withdrawn from all radio play and that their record company, Elektra, fix a disclaimer sticker to the 'Standing On The Beach' album from which the single comes saying that The Cure condemn its use in furthering anti-Arab feeling.

Kill! or Cure misunderstood?

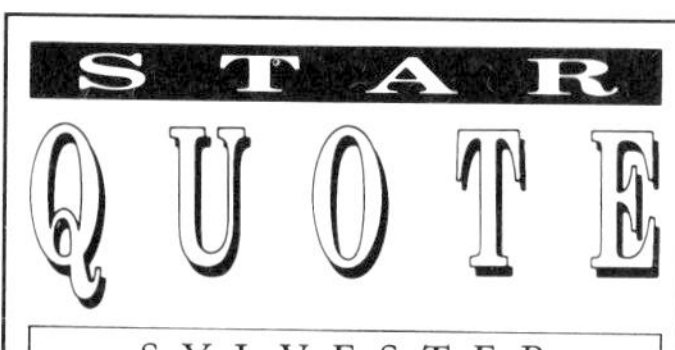

STAR QUOTE

SYLVESTER

Disco Star

'I don't believe that AIDS is the wrath of God. People have a tendency to blame everything on God.'

SIMON SAYS: 'I'M NO SA EXPERT'

The release of Paul Simon's 'Graceland' album – recorded in South Africa and New York using largely South African musicians – has sparked controversy. Its detractors claim that Simon has flouted the UN cultural boycott of South Africa and that the album's sleevenotes make no mention of apartheid, fuelling the rumour that Simon had signed an agreement with the South African government preventing him criticizing the Botha regime.

A stinging attack on the artist, made in a telex by the African National Congress in Lusaka to their Swedish office, has urged a boycott against a Paul Simon European and American tour.

As a result of the furore, a hastily-convened press conference was held in London by Simon and his record company, Warner Brothers, to try and clarify the artist's position.

At the conference – flanked by exiled South African musicians Miriam Makeba and Hugh Masekela – Simon began by reading a letter he had written to the UN Committee Against Apartheid. In it he stated that in his own field he was working to achieve 'the end of apartheid system', and explained that the absence of criticism of apartheid in the sleevenotes was due to the fact that he had approached the project from a cultural point of view, and that he was 'no expert on South African politics'.

In support of the artist, both Masekela and Makeba spoke out against a cultural boycott, saying that it would deprive indigenous black musicians from being heard outside their own country.

Simon said in conclusion that he felt the album should not be withdrawn from the South African market, adding: 'It was made by South African musicians, why should it not be available to them?'

BRITS BUMP UP SALES

Following the huge demand for British Record Industry Awards ('Brits') winners' product last year, record dealers are determined not to be caught on the hop again. Up and down the country they are busily stocking up current and catalogue product by this year's winners, who include: Best British Male Artist – Peter Gabriel; Best British Female Artist – Kate Bush; Best British Group – Five Star; Best British Producer – David A. Stewart; Best British Single – 'West End Girls' by The Pet Shop Boys; Best British LP – 'Brothers In Arms' by Dire Straits; Best International Solo Artist – Paul Simon; Best International Group – The Bangles.

BRITS winners including Paul Simon, Five Star, Peter Gabriel, Eric Clapton, Kate Bush and The Bangles get together at the awards show

Bangles overjoyed at receiving BRITS award for Best International Group

CHARTS

	Chart	Title	Artist
	US45	Open Your Heart	*Madonna*
	USLP	Slippery When Wet	*Bon Jovi*
	UK45	I Knew You Were Waiting (For Me)	*Aretha Franklin & George Michael*
	UKLP	Graceland	*Paul Simon*
WEEK 2	US45	Livin' On A Prayer	*Bon Jovi*
	USLP	Slippery When Wet	*Bon Jovi*
	UK45	I Knew You Were Waiting (For Me)	*Aretha Franklin & George Michael*
	UKLP	Graceland	*Paul Simon*
WEEK 3	US45	Livin' On A Prayer	*Bon Jovi*
	USLP	Slippery When Wet	*Bon Jovi*
	UK45	I Knew You Were Waiting (For Me)	*Aretha Franklin & George Michael*
	UKLP	Graceland	*Paul Simon*
WEEK 4	US45	Livin' On A Prayer	*Bon Jovi*
	USLP	Slippery When Wet	*Bon Jovi*
	UK45	Stand By Me	*Ben E King*
	UKLP	The Phantom Of The Opera	*Original Cast*

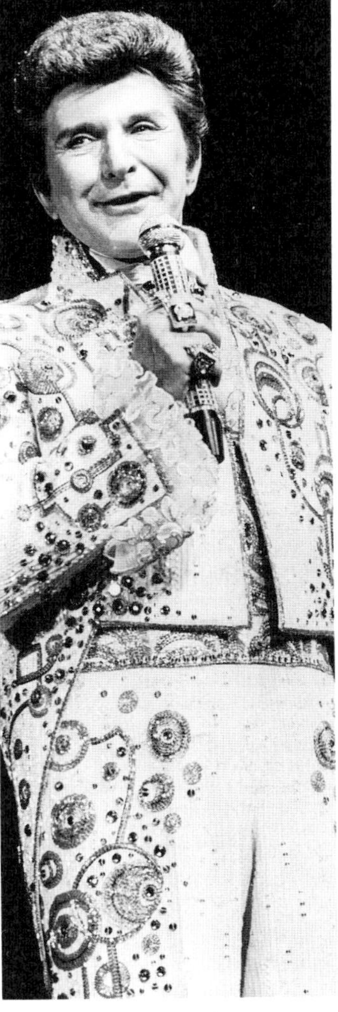

Liberace – The glitter man has gone

THE GRAPEVINE

- **Paul Simon has won top single and album awards at the GRAMMYS.**
- **Led Zeppelin have settled out of court with R&B/Blues writer Willie Dixon who claims that 'Whole Lotta Love' was based on his song 'You Need Love'.**
- **Sly Stone has been jailed on drugs-related charges.**
- **Showman Liberace has died aged 67.**

U2 RETURN WITH 'THE JOSHUA TREE'

U2's 'Joshua Tree' Best LP of 1987?

U2 have rooted themselves in rock history with their new album 'The Joshua Tree', produced by Brian Eno. Their success has made them nationless despite their Irish roots, but the band have a continuing fascination with the States – its vastness and its culture – and once again they have concentrated on portraying American images.

'The Joshua Tree' opens with Bono's despairingly beautiful 'Where The Streets Have No Name', followed by the lyrically simple 'I Still Haven't Found What I'm Looking For', giving the feeling that U2 *care*.

'Bullet The Blue Sky' unleashes a vista of a destructive and hellish America and reverberates with U2's anger at what they perceive as US corruption and gun-craziness. 'Running To Stand Still' looks backwards while forewarning of what will come, and it's this feeling of integration that makes the record so complete.

'Red Hill Mining Town', while still evoking America, is about Britain's coal strike and is the group's response to a heartless state and how people and families draw together to survive. From here on Bono seems on the verge of some visionary breakdown, and yet always there is the underlying feeling of strength which helps U2 turn despair into a positive force.

'Mothers Of The Disappeared', which closes the album, is a bleakly supportive message to those whose sons and daughters get taken away in the night. The last line printed on the sleeve is not sung: Join Amnesty International.

'The Joshua Tree' is the sound of people still trying, still looking and 'still running', and should prove a better and braver record than anything else that's likely to appear this year.

CHARTS

Chart	Title	Artist
US45	Livin' On A Prayer	*Bon Jovi*
USLP	Licensed To Ill	*Beastie Boys*
UK45	Stand By Me	*Ben E King*
UKLP	The Phantom Of The Opera	*Original Cast*
WEEK 2		
US45	Jacob's Ladder	*Huey Lewis & The News*
USLP	Licensed To Ill	*Beastie Boys*
UK45	Stand By Me	*Ben E King*
UKLP	The Phantom Of The Opera	*Original Cast*
WEEK 3		
US45	Lean On Me	*Club Nouveau*
USLP	Licensed To Ill	*Beastie Boys*
UK45	Everything I Own	*Boy George*
UKLP	The Joshua Tree	*U2*
WEEK 4		
US45	Lean On Me	*Club Nouveau*
USLP	Licensed To Ill	*Beastie Boys*
UK45	Respectable	*Mel And Kim*
UKLP	The Joshua Tree	*U2*

THE GRAPEVINE

- **Rumours have been circulating that Quincy Jones told Jacko he must re-write some of the tracks on his forthcoming 'Bad' LP before it can be released.**
- **Raids on UK pirate radio stations have increased**
- **Many top Chicago acts, including Marshall Jefferson and Frankie Knuckles, are in the UK for the first 'house' music tour.**
- **Frankie Goes To Hollywood have announced a temporary split.**

Frankies go separate ways

TRENDY-BASHING SOVIET STYLE

Soviet trendy-bashers – known as Lubers – are out 'to defend the Soviet youth's moral purity from advancing mass culture', and come into the cities in the evenings to hassle heavy-metal fans, punks, breakdancers, rockers and the like as part of an intimidation campaign.

Moscow youth-group leaders, who claim that the Moscow militia have made no effort to combat the Luber bullies, have now met with officials of the Ministry of the Interior criminal department to try and get the vigilantes curbed.

The proposals include holding meetings organized by the Young Communist League to try to bridge the gap created by 'older peoplès intolerance of many adolescents' manners, tastes and clothes'.

Quincy tells Jacko some songs are Bad?

BOWIE'S TOUR NEWS AND VIDEO BAN

David Bowie's 'Glass Spider' tour, billed as his most theatrical in years, has just been announced. It will take in more than 100 cities on 5 continents.

At a recent press conference, the hyper-charming Bowie – one of rock's most elusive figures – elaborated about his tour which is named after one of the tracks on his new LP, 'Never Let Me Down'.

'It's the pivotal song on the album,' he said. 'I see Glass Spider as some kind of mother figure. It's the idea of children who eventually realize their parents are not really someone they can depend upon for everything. They are on their own. It's that kind of feeling I want to put across in the show.'

At the accompanying sneak preview, Bowie and his band – which includes old school chum Peter Frampton – blasted out '87 And Cry' and his new single 'Day In, Day Out' to an elite press posse of what must have been their smallest-ever audience since school days!

However, following the subsequent release of the video for 'Day In, Day Out', Bowie's triumphant return suffered a setback when BBC Television bosses banned it for its 'explicit sexual and violent content'.

The video shows a woman being sexually assaulted and therefore 'was considered unsuitable for screening'.

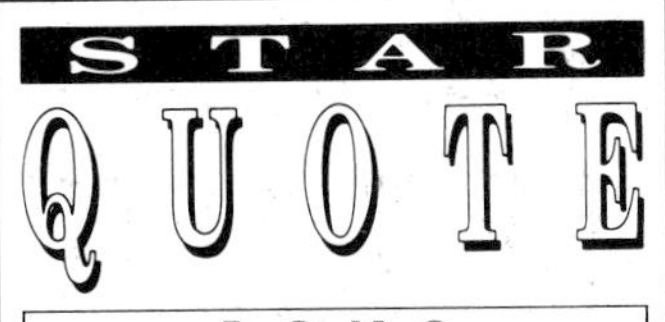

BONO

'Then we heard about this thing called the song, and we thought it would be nice to have a few of them.'

CHARTS

US45	Nothing's Gonna Stop Us Now *Starship*
USLP	Licensed To Ill *Beastie Boys*
UK45	Respectable *Mel And Kim*
UKLP	The Joshua Tree *U2*
WEEK 2	
US45	Nothing's Gonna Stop Us Now *Starship*
USLP	Licensed To Ill *Beastie Boys*
UK45	Let It Be *Ferry Aid*
UKLP	The Joshua Tree *U2*
WEEK 3	
US45	I Knew You Were Waiting *Aretha Franklin & George Michael*
USLP	Licensed To Ill *Beastie Boys*
UK45	Let It Be *Ferry Aid*
UKLP	The Joshua Tree *U2*
WEEK 4	
US45	I Knew You Were Waiting *Aretha Franklin & George Michael*
USLP	The Joshua Tree *U2*
UK45	La Isla Bonita *Madonna*
UKLP	The Joshua Tree *U2*

U2'S US ADVENTURES

Thousands of U2 fans brought Los Angeles traffic to a standstill when a local radio station gave out the location of a video shoot by the band.

Their rooftop performance kept on going, to become a greatest-hits show when the band saw the streets filling with people in a scene similar to The Beatles' infamous impromptu last gig at the Apple building in London in 1969. Festivities came to an abrupt end after 20 minutes when police turned off the generator.

THE GRAPEVINE

■ Topping the UK chart is a version of 'Let It Be' by a collection of stars under the name Ferry Aid, the proceeds of which will go to a fund for victims of the recent Zeebrugge Ferry disaster.

■ Boy George, George Michael, The Communards, Elton John, Kim Wilde, Holly Johnson and Bobby Womack appeared at London's Wembley Arena in an Aids Fund-raiser.

U2 ignored Stevie's plea and play

During this latest US visit, U2 have become embroiled in Stevie Wonder's campaign against Arizona state officials' refusal to introduce the Martin Luther King Remembrance Day like the majority of other US states.

Wonder urged U2 to cancel their gigs there in protest. However, the band have previously paid tribute to the assassinated civil rights leader in songs like 'Pride (In The Name Of Love)' and Bono told reporters that they went ahead with the concerts to draw attention to the issue.

BEASTIES INVADE EUROPE

Beastie Boys – darlings of the British Tabloid press deny crippling allegations

Prior to The Beastie Boys' British tour this month, the UK tabloid press has been running shock-horror stories about Beastie hooliganism, spitting matches on stage, and the inclusion of a 21-foot hydraulic penis in their stage show.

While The Beasties were at the Montreux Festival in Switzerland, reports appeared in *The Daily Mirror* accusing them of screaming 'go away you *!*!*!* cripples' to leukaemia victims. This was dismissed as 'complete fabrication' by their management and several music journalists at the event.

It's this kind of report which is spurring the likes of British politician Peter Bruinvals into action by denouncing them in media interviews. He says: 'They attack common decency, they are violent, they undermine family values, and they encourage anti-social activities, like glue-sniffing.' Joining in the anti-Beastie hysteria are BBC DJs Tony Blackburn and Bruno Brookes, while Capital Radio's John Sachs smashed one of their records on air.

After the first chaotic shows in the UK, hostility reached fever pitch with the 'gruesome threesome' receiving death-threat phone calls.

CHARTS

US45	(I Just) Died In Your Arms *Cutting Crew*
USLP	The Joshua Tree *U2*
UK45	La Isla Bonita *Madonna*
UKLP	Raindancing *Alison Moyet*
WEEK 2	
US45	(I Just) Died In Your Arms *Cutting Crew*
USLP	The Joshua Tree *U2*
UK45	La Isla Bonita *Madonna*
UKLP	The Joshua Tree *U2*
WEEK 3	
US45	With Or Without You *U2*
USLP	The Joshua Tree *U2*
UK45	Nothing's Gonna Stop Us Now *Starship*
UKLP	Keep Your Distance *Curiosity Killed The Cat*
WEEK 4	
US45	With Or Without You *U2*
USLP	The Joshua Tree *U2*
UK45	Nothing's Gonna Stop Us Now *Starship*
UKLP	Solitude Standing *Suzanne Vega*
WEEK 5	
US45	With Or Without You U2
USLP	The Joshua Tree *U2*
UK45	Nothing's Gonna Stop Us Now *Starship*
UKLP	It's Better To Travel *Swing Out Sister*

ROXY MUSIC

Britain's new network TV chart show *'The Roxy'* is to be shown every Tuesday evening from 7.30 to 8.00 p.m. from June 9 and the producers claim the direct clash with BBC's No. 1 rated *'Eastenders'* soap opera won't be a problem.

'The Roxy' is ITV's rival to BBC's *'Top of the Pops'* and will be fronted by Capital Radio's Canadian-born David Jensen. The aim is to have five live acts in the studio every week. There will also be two video clips (one will be a first-time screening) plus a pop gossip slot, news items from around the world, and a video vote segment for 'breakers'.

SIMPLE MINDS GET AMNESTY PRAISE

Simple Minds have been credited this month by Amnesty International for winning the release of a political prisoner.

The group distributed Amnesty postcards calling for the release of P. Udayarahan, who had spent three years in a Sri Lankan jail, to every member of the audience at their San Diego concert last April. They urged everyone to send the card to the Sri Lankan government as part of a campaign to free Udayarahan, imprisoned without trial because he was part of a religious minority group at odds with the authorities.

The band used the same campaign at every US concert, and also donated the entire proceeds of one American and one British show to Amnesty.

Jim Kerr and Simple Minds were highly praised by Amnesty International for their postcard campaign that helped free a political prisoner in Sri Lanka

THE GRAPEVINE

- In a survey of the top singles acts for the first quarter of the year, sixties soul acts Ben E. King, Jackie Wilson and Percy Sledge were Nos. 1, 2 and 7.
- Blow Monkeys' political 'Celebrate' banned by the BBC until after the UK general election.
- Bill Wyman has started 'AIMS', the aim of which is to offer studio time to good acts with little money.
- Matt Johnson, mastermind of THE THE, has announced he is retiring 'for three years.'

MICHELLE SHOCKS GLASTONBURY

Armed only with a battered acoustic guitar, a plaintive voice and a handful of songs which owe more to the folk tradition of the early sixties than the strident rock sounds of the late eighties, Michelle Shocked stole the honours at this year's Glastonbury Festival, when a 60,000 rain-soaked crowd gave her a standing ovation.

The festival – an annual blend of mysticism, music and mild mayhem which is held every summer solstice on 500 acres of farmland near the historic West Country town of Glastonbury – was also a triumph for the Campaign for Nuclear Disarmament, recipient of its profits. This year they topped £100,000, not bad for an event which cost more than £1 million to mount.

Acts who braved the mud included Van Morrison, Elvis Costello, Ben E. King, Los Lobos, Julian Cope, The Communards, New Order, The Proclaimers and Billy Bragg. But it was 'The Campfire Tapes' girl who scored the biggest hit with audience and critics alike.

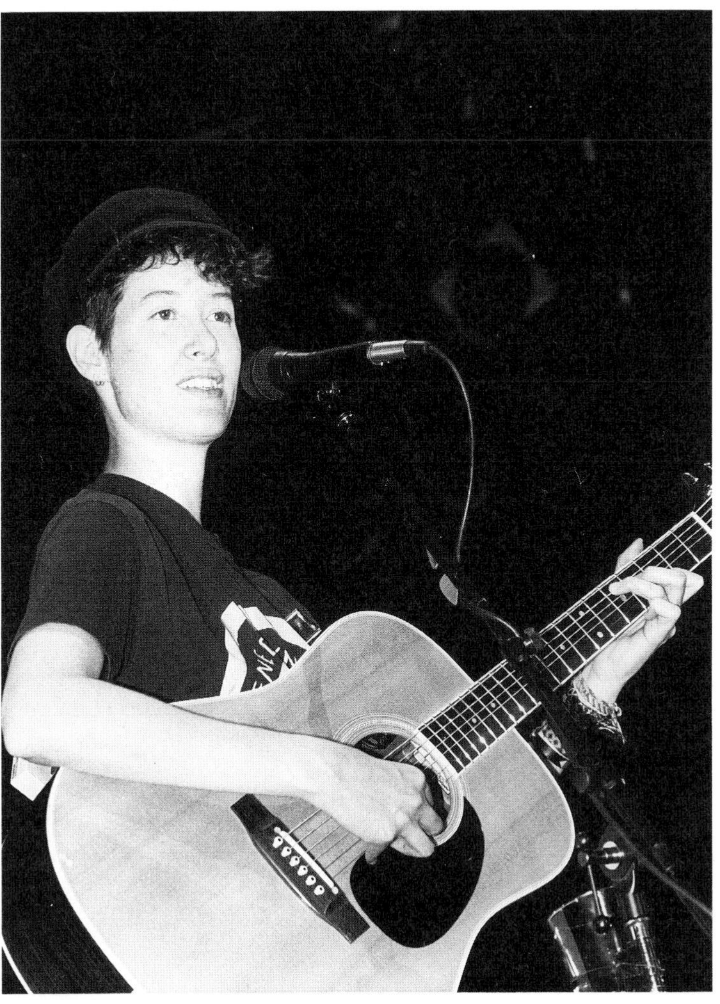

Michelle Shocked – 'The Campfire Tapes' girl was brightest spark at Glastonbury Festival

THE GRAPEVINE

- **The Beastie Boys' Liverpool show has resulted in several crowd injuries and in Ad Rock (Adam Horowitz) being arrested on a charge of causing grievous bodily harm to a member of the audience.**
- **East German fans nearly rioted at the Berlin Wall, trying to hear David Bowie on the other side.**
- **The '*Roxy*' TV show is already in trouble from fans, critics and ratings.**

CHARTS

US45	You Keep Me Hanging On *Kim Wilde*
USLP	The Joshua Tree *U2*
UK45	I Wanna Dance With Somebody *Whitney Houston*
UKLP	Solitude Standing *Suzanne Vega*
WEEK 2	
US45	Always *Atlantic Starr*
USLP	The Joshua Tree *U2*
UK45	I Wanna Dance With Somebody *Whitney Houston*
UKLP	Live In The City Of Light *Simple Minds*
WEEK 3	
US45	Head To Toe *Lisa Lisa & Cult Jam*
USLP	The Joshua Tree *U2*
UK45	I Wanna Dance With Somebody *Whitney Houston*
UKLP	Whitney *Whitney Houston*
WEEK 4	
US45	I Wanna Dance With Somebody *Whitney Houston*
USLP	Whitney *Whitney Houston*
UK45	Star Trekkin' *Firm*
UKLP	Whitney *Whitney Houston*

JACKO TOLD: BEAT IT!

'Wacko' Michael Jackson, who is believed to be creating a 'chamber of horrors' at his home in Los Angeles, has been thwarted in his $1 million bid to buy the remains of the Victorian '*Elephant Man*', John Meyrick.

The London Medical College has said that he wouldn't be allowed to buy it however much he offered.

The increasingly-weird 28-year-old singer is reported to be fascinated by the 'ethical, medical and historical significance' of Meyrick's remains. His collection so far contains deformed skulls and rare medical textbooks with graphic descriptions of lethal diseases!

BEEB TELL GEORGE: NO SEX BEFORE 9!

George Michael has told his record company Epic not to send any copies of his new single 'I Want Your Sex' to BBC's Radio One after they put a daytime ban on it.

The network station has refused to play it before 9p.m. because of what they call its 'sexually explicit' nature. And it won't be getting any play on BBC-TV's '*Top of the Pops*' either, for the same reason.

In the song, Michael advocates a healthy sex life, which the Beeb feel is too risqué for a younger audience. Radio One controller Johnny Beerling said: 'George's following includes many impressionable young girls, and many of their parents would take exception to this record being on Radio One – we feel this one goes too far for daytime radio'.

JULY

1987

MADONNA 'NOT WANTED' AT WEMBLEY

Madonna's three sell-out concerts at Wembley next month could be called off if the local Brent Council gives in to mounting opposition from residents living near the stadium.

More than 1000 protest letters have so far been sent, with a mass petition planned, because angry residents feel enough is enough. So far this year they have been upset by U2, blasted by Bowie and jarred by Genesis. But the complaints extend beyond the subject of noise pollution (although environmental health officers say it is at acceptable levels). Quoted annoyances include drunken and vomiting fans, blocked roads and verbal abuse.

A Wembley Stadium boss said: 'Last week we had 500,000 for the Genesis shows, and only received 20 complaints'. The Madonna concert promoters reassured the 200,000 Madonna ticket holders that they 'don't expect any problems getting the permit', but anxious fans will have to wait a few more days for the final decision.

Wembley residents mad over Madonna

'BAD' NEWS FROM JACKO

Michael Jackson has ended months of speculation by announcing that his long awaited new single will be 'I Just Can't Stop Loving You' – a duet with Siedah Garrett.

The Quincy Jones-produced track is taken from his much-delayed new album 'Bad' (due to be released in August) and is Jacko's first new material since the 'Thriller' LP in 1982.

With a release schedule finally arranged, it is obvious Jacko and Quincy are finally happy with the album – the pair returned to the studio several times to patch up the set, fuelling rumours that the album was well below the usual standard.

His world tour commences in Japan in September with UK dates being next summer at the earliest.

Michael's first 'Bad' single

MOTHERS KNOW BEST?

The American-based moral watchdog group, the Washington Wives, officially known as the Parents Music Resource Center (PMRC), has announced that it will escalate its campaign against sexual and violent lyrics in pop music.

At the top of its Top 10 hit list is The Beastie Boys' 'Licensed to Ill', while other acts it wants censored include The Thrashing Doves, Simply Red, Anthrax, Ozzy Osbourne, Skinny Puppy, Motley Crue, Cinderella and Poison.

Two acts which have already felt the sting of the Washington Wives are W.A.S.P. and the Dead Kennedys. W.A.S.P. claim the campaign has resulted in them being banned in many cities because of their mock-violent stage show. The Dead Kennedys are currently being prosecuted for the inclusion of an 'obscene' poster with their 'Frankenchrist' LP.

Washington Wives think Motley's crude

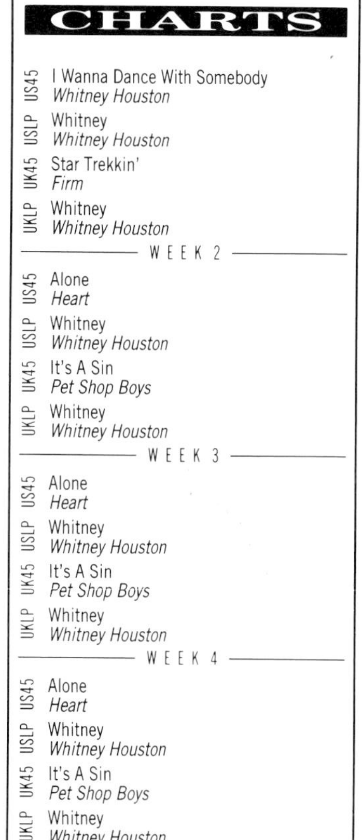

CHARTS

US45	I Wanna Dance With Somebody *Whitney Houston*
USLP	Whitney *Whitney Houston*
UK45	Star Trekkin' *Firm*
UKLP	Whitney *Whitney Houston*
WEEK 2	
US45	Alone *Heart*
USLP	Whitney *Whitney Houston*
UK45	It's A Sin *Pet Shop Boys*
UKLP	Whitney *Whitney Houston*
WEEK 3	
US45	Alone *Heart*
USLP	Whitney *Whitney Houston*
UK45	It's A Sin *Pet Shop Boys*
UKLP	Whitney *Whitney Houston*
WEEK 4	
US45	Alone *Heart*
USLP	Whitney *Whitney Houston*
UK45	It's A Sin *Pet Shop Boys*
UKLP	Whitney *Whitney Houston*

THE GRAPEVINE

- Prince's London shows at Earl's Court have had to be cancelled at the last moment due to problems with the local council.
- '*Top Of The Pops*' has finally launched in the US (it was not successful).
- The first singles and albums charts are introduced in Russia.
- Guns'n'Roses have fulfilled a dream in playing London's Marquee Club, original launch-pad for The Who, The Rolling Stones and The Yardbirds.

SUING SEASON FOR THE BEATLES

Yoko Ono and the three surviving Beatles have recently become embroiled in no less than three separate law actions.

In New York, Harrison, Starr and Ono have filed a $40 million (£25 million) lawsuit against Capitol Records, claiming that a delay in releasing Beatles material on compact disc has cost them millions in lost royalties.

Acting for the three, lawyer Leonard Marks claimed the hold up was Capitol's way of punishing them for an eight year legal battle over disputed income from the 'Abbey Road' album, and an attempt by Capitol to force the group to drop the action.

Paul McCartney, George Harrison and Ringo Starr have also filed a $15 million lawsuit against the sports shoe firm Nike for allegedly debasing their song 'Revolution' through commercial exploitation.

The group told the court they did not 'endorse or peddle sneakers or pantyhose.' The problem appears to have emanated from Michael Jackson, who now owns The Beatles' copyrights and gave Nike permission to use 'Revolution' without consulting the former Beatles.

Meanwhile Yoko, McCartney, Harrison and Starr are taking action against Sixties star Dave Clark, alleging that Clark is selling video compilations of Beatles material – taken from vintage footage of the seminal *Ready Steady Go!* TV show – without permission.

Yoko searching for a few dollars more

THE GRAPEVINE

- **US acts playing to sold out UK crowds have included Madonna, Stevie Wonder and Bon Jovi.**
- **In the US, The Monkees and Donny Osmond have started on the comeback trail.**
- **Janet Jackson headlining American radio unwanted teenage pregnancy campaign.**
- **Dave Stewart (Eurythmics) weds Siobhan Fahey (Bananarama).**
- **Thanks to The Beastie Boys, thousands of Volkswagen car badges have disappeared!**

It's Monkee business as usual for the ageing Davy, Micky and Peter

CHARTS

US45	Shakedown *Bob Seger*
USLP	Whitney *Whitney Houston*
UK45	Who's That Girl *Madonna*
UKLP	Introducing The Hardline *Terence Trent D'Arby*
	WEEK 2
US45	I Still Haven't Found What I'm Looking For *U2*
USLP	Whitney *Whitney Houston*
UK45	La Bamba *Los Lobos*
UKLP	Introducing The Hardline *Terence Trent D'Arby*
	WEEK 3
US45	I Still Haven't Found What I'm Looking For *U2*
USLP	Whitney *Whitney Houston*
UK45	La Bamba *Los Lobos*
UKLP	The Hits Album, 6 *Various*
	WEEK 4
US45	Who's That Girl *Madonna*
USLP	Whitney *Whitney Houston*
UK45	I Just Can't Stop Loving You *Michael Jackson*
UKLP	The Hits Album, 6 *Various*
	WEEK 5
US45	La Bamba *Los Lobos*
USLP	Whitney *Whitney Houston*
UK45	I Just Can't Stop Loving You *Michael Jackson*
UKLP	The Hits Album, 6 *Various*

SMITHS TO SPLIT

In an atmosphere of ill wind and acrimony, the long rumoured breakup of The Smiths has finally been announced. Most inside sources have blamed a personality clash between Morrissey and guitarist Johnny Marr – the nucleus and songwriting partnership of the group – for the split.

Over recent months, Marr has privately related to friends that he no longer regards Morrissey as a friend and is sick of the singer acting the self-centred star.

For his part, Morrisey is rumoured to be displeased with Marr acting as guitar hero and being involved with projects outside The Smiths. Latterly, Marr has played guitar on albums by Keith Richards, Bobby Womack and Bryan Ferry.

The final straw is said to have been when Marr interrupted a Smiths session to fly to the States to record with Talking Heads, using Rough Trade money to finance the trip.

Morrisey reportedly blew his top, declared it was the end of The Smiths and said he never wanted to work with Marr again.

Whether Marr and Morrisey will ever be reconciled is a matter for speculation, although it is generally agreed throughout the rock world that the demise of Britain's premier indie band is a matter of considerable regret.

Will The Smiths be this close again?

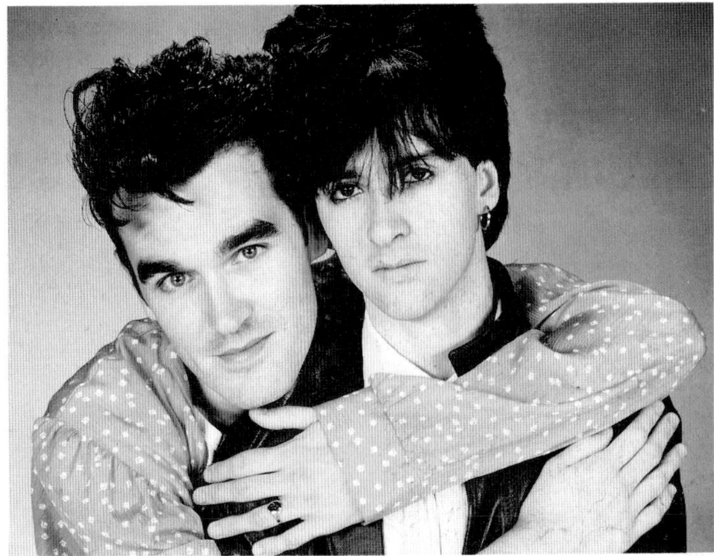

CHARTS

- US45 La Bamba *Los Lobos*
- USLP Whitney *Whitney Houston*
- UK45 Never Gonna Give You Up *Rick Astley*
- UKLP Hysteria *Def Leppard*

WEEK 2

- US45 La Bamba *Los Lobos*
- USLP La Bamba *Los Lobos*
- UK45 Never Gonna Give You Up *Rick Astley*
- UKLP Hysteria *Def Leppard*

WEEK 3

- US45 I Just Can't Stop Loving You *Michael Jackson*
- USLP La Bamba *Los Lobos*
- UK45 Never Gonna Give You Up *Rick Astley*
- UKLP Bad *Michael Jackson*

WEEK 4

- US45 Didn't We Almost Have It All *Whitney Houston*
- USLP Bad *Michael Jackson*
- UK45 Never Gonna Give You Up *Rick Astley*
- UKLP Bad *Michael Jackson*

Paula Abdul dancing for joy

BAD NEWS FROM JACKSON

Over five years in the making, Michael Jackson's much-anticipated follow up album to 'Thriller' – 'Bad' – is finally out and breaking all kinds of sales records.

Retaining the services of producer Quincy Jones, the album finds Jackson in the company of Stevie Wonder on 'Just Good Friends' while gospel group The Winans lend support to another track, 'Man In The Mirror'.

The first single taken from the album – the duet with Siedah Garrett 'I Just Can't Stop Loving You' – is to be followed by the title track.

Incredible statistics are emerging as the album goes double platinum in its first week of release. 'Bad' accounted for one in four of all albums sold in the UK where it has sold nearly as many copies as the rest of the Top 30 combined.

In the US, a ship-out order of two and a quarter million has made it CBS's fastest selling album ever. With the CBS production presses working flat out, it has even delayed the release of the latest Bruce Springsteen album, 'Tunnel Of Love'.

Meanwhile, Jackson has lent his support to the National Association of Colored People in the movement's challenge to widespread discrimination against black artists.

Emerging from a meeting with Jackson to discuss possible strategies to combat racism, a NACP's spokesman said: 'I think he understands our concern. He's sensitive to the obligation black superstars have to help other blacks in the industry.'

THE GRAPEVINE

- Peter Gabriel's *Sledgehammer* video has won a record ten MTV awards; another winner was Paula Abdul, for her choreography on Janet Jackson's *Nasty* video.
- Michael Jackson has started his year-long world tour in Japan.
- M/A/R/R/S/ have announced that they will not follow up their million selling transatlantic smash 'Pump Up The Volume'.
- John Cougar Mellencamp is suing his old label Riva Records for £3 million ($4.8 million).

Where there's a hit there's a writ – John sues Riva label for millions

WORKERS UNITE AGAINST THE BOSS

Bruce underpaying his workers?

A fascinating insight into the workings of the Bruce Springsteen machine has come as a result of a civil action by Mike Batlan and Doug Sutphin, Springsteen's long-serving instrument technicians, against their former 'Boss'.

Under New Jersey law, Springsteen will actually be required to make a courtroom appearance, something many see as a potential embarrassment to the superstar.

Batlan and Sutphin allege that despite Springsteen's assurances that they had 'nothing to worry about', their settlement cheques showed large deductions to the agreed amounts.

Also involved are fines Springsteen levied against Batlan and Sutphin during their time with him and, more seriously, Batlan alleges his signature was forged on a cheque.

A statement issued by the Springsteen office stated: 'Bruce is very generous. He gave them around $120,000 (£75,000) each when they left their jobs. His honour is at stake. The case is going to be quite a scrap.'

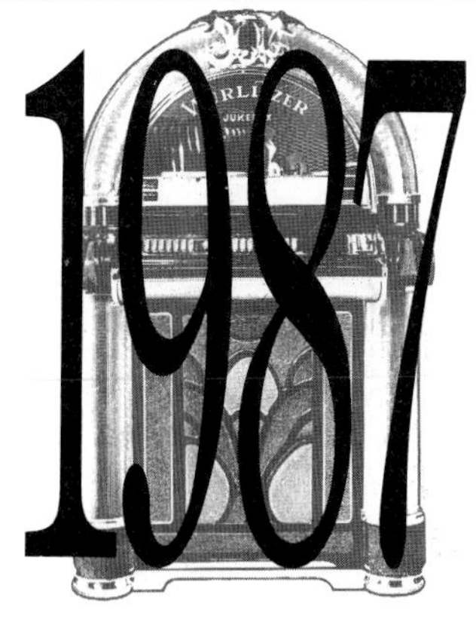

BEASTIES & PWL SAMPLE PROBLEMS

The Beastie Boys are at the centre of a crucial test case over sampling – and the future of rap music may depend on the result. They are being sued by The Jimmy Caster Bunch, who claim that the multi-million selling LP track 'Hold It, Now Hit It' steals from their 1967 hit 'The Return Of Leroy (Part One)'.

If The Beasties lose, rap groups could be afraid to carry on sampling and rap may be forced out of business.

Meanwhile, in the UK, hit producer Pete Waterman has called for controls on sampling, saying anyone sampling other people's music should seek permission first, or piracy will escalate. 'It's obviously time to call a stop and make it clear there are copyright laws,' he says.

Ironically, since speaking out, Waterman has clashed for a second time with Blue Mountain Music, who claim he lifted part of their No. 1 M/A/R/R/S/ hit 'Pump Up The Volume', for a Sybil B-side.

Previously, Waterman had settled out of court after admitting sampling part of the Wally Badarou hit 'Chief Inspector'. A Blue Mountain spokesman said: 'Waterman can't be allowed to get away with this sort of wholesale plundering forever'.

Do the Beasties look like boys who would steal anything?

Stock, Aitken & Waterman setting a good ex-sample?

THE GRAPEVINE

- **Elvis Costello has signed to WEA worldwide.**
- **The UK government has dropped plans to put a levy on blank tapes.**
- **Then Jerico's Mark Shaw has been arrested in Spain for knocking off a police chief's hat.**
- **Willie Nelson has quit Farm Aid because not enough of the money raised has reached the farmers.**
- **Bruce Springsteen joined U2 on stage in Philadelphia.**

SCREAM! VS. MEAT

Meat is murder – Morrissey told us so two years ago, and now he's being supported by Paul Weller, Jim Kerr, Chrissie Hynde, Peter Gabriel, Kate Bush and Annie Lennox.

Those stars and more have endorsed SCREAM! – the School Campaign for Reaction Against Meat – the first Vegetarian Society campaign aimed specifically at young people. Its aim is to publicize the horrors of factory farming and animal abuse to an age group they claim has been bombarded by advertising for meat and dairy products.

DAVE DORRELL

M/A/R/R/S

'Everybody does it man! Sampling is everywhere. It's like AIDS. It's in the blood.'

LL COOL J WROTE OWN SONGS

LL Cool J, currently in the UK Top 10 with 'I Need Love', emerged victorious from court following allegations that he had stolen songs for his 'Radio' album from Lawrence Humphrey, who also claimed to be the original LL Cool J.

The 19-year old rap superstar recently had legal trouble of a different sort. After a Columbus (Georgia) show he was arrested for 'lewdness' and fined.

LL Cool J reckons it's The Beastie Boys' fault: 'They run round the country with this big penis and f . . . it up for everybody – when I go in and play behind them, I get a lot of flack because of the stuff they did.'

But he added: 'I ain't changing the show – it's been getting iller .

LL Cool J – it's official, he's Cool!

CHARTS

US45	Didn't We Almost Have It All	*Whitney Houston*
USLP	Bad	*Michael Jackson*
UK45	Pump Up The Volume	*M/A/R/R/S*
UKLP	Bad	*Michael Jackson*
WEEK 2		
US45	Here I Go Again	*Whitesnake*
USLP	Bad	*Michael Jackson*
UK45	Pump Up The Volume	*M/A/R/R/S*
UKLP	Bad	*Michael Jackson*
WEEK 3		
US45	Lost In Emotion	*Lisa Lisa & Cult Jam*
USLP	Bad	*Michael Jackson*
UK45	Full Metal Jacket	*Abigail Mead/Nigel Goulding*
UKLP	Bad	*Michael Jackson*
WEEK 4		
US45	Bad	*Michael Jackson*
USLP	Bad	*Michael Jackson*
UK45	You Win Again	*Bee Gees*
UKLP	Tunnel Of Love	*Bruce Springsteen*
WEEK 5		
US45	Bad	*Michael Jackson*
USLP	Bad	*Michael Jackson*
UK45	You Win Again	*Bee Gees*
UKLP	Tunnel Of Love	*Bruce Springsteen*

NOVEMBER

JESUS & MARY'S CHAIN OF PROBLEMS

The infamous Jesus & Mary Chain were thrown off the British TV chart show *The Roxy* after refusing to either mime or pretend to play their instruments to their latest record 'Darklands'.

The show's producer said: 'They did not give any performance at all. On a scale of one to ten they didn't register.' A spokesman for the group said: 'The TV people did not understand that it's a slow song, and that the band perform it in a certain way.'

Incidentally, the group prerecorded a spot for rival show Top of the Pops, who were satisfied with their performance. In America however, *Top of the Pops* refused to have the group on because the band's name.

Adding to the group's troubles, vocalist Jim Reid was arrested in Canada for assaulting members of the audience with his microphone stand. He was jailed overnight and must appear in court there early next year.

STATUS QUO ATTACKED

Status Quo are facing a barrage of criticism from fellow musicians for playing at the notorious South African complex Sun City.

Terence Trent D'Arby said: 'I find it ironically repulsive that rock'n'roll, an art form that almost singlehandedly merged the cultures of both black and white, is now being used to maintain the status quo.'

Paul Heaton from The Housemartins added: 'In playing Sun City, an artist is fully embracing the South African apartheid system.'

Status Quo, who donated money earned at Sun City to various children's charities, were unrepentant about playing there.

Terence objecting to the Status Quo

GEORGE, BEST

George Michael's long awaited solo album, 'Faith', has finally been released, and it combines some truly beautiful ballads with some routine uptempo tracks.

As we know, George can write not only from personal experience but also often from imagination, and it's not easy to tell which source the songs here come from.

'Hand To Mouth' is perhaps a little too close to 'Careless Whisper', and lyric-wise there are some thought-provoking lines on 'Father Figure', 'Hard Day' and 'Monkey' – and some of the worst ever on 'I Want Your Sex'.

George handles almost all of the chores on the album including speeded-up backing vocals, and he is not afraid to go for unusual arrangements and heavy doses of sentimentality. Perhaps the two strongest tracks on the set are the ballads 'One More Try' and 'Kissing A Fool', on which his voice has an angelic quality.

Wet Wet Wet allegations of plagiarism have been made

CHARTS

US45	I Think We're Alone Now *Tiffany*
USLP	Tunnel Of Love *Bruce Springsteen*
UK45	Faith *George Michael*
UKLP	Nothing Like The Sun *Sting*
WEEK 2	
US45	I Think We're Alone Now *Tiffany*
USLP	Dirty Dancing *Soundtrack*
UK45	You Win Again *Bee Gees*
UKLP	Tango In The Night *Fleetwood Mac*
WEEK 3	
US45	Mony Mony *Billy Idol*
USLP	Dirty Dancing *Soundtrack*
UK45	China In Your Hand *T'Pau*
UKLP	Faith *George Michael*
WEEK 4	
US45	I've Had The Time Of My LIfe *Bill Medley & Jennifer Warnes*
USLP	Dirty Dancing *Soundtrack*
UK45	China In Your Hand *T'Pau*
UKLP	Bridge Of Sighs *T'Pau*

THE GRAPEVINE

- **Dire Straits' 'Brothers in Arms' album has now sold a record 3 million copies in Britain alone.**
- **The Japanese Sony company has bought CBS Records.**
- **Wet Wet Wet are in trouble for a second time over lyric plagiarism – firstly it was over 'Sweet Little Mystery' (similar lines to a Van Morrison song) and now over 'Angel Eyes' (similar lines to Squeeze's 'Heartbreaking World').**

McCARTNEY ON ELVIS

'Back On My Feet', the flip side of Paul McCartney's new single, is the first offering from his new songwriting partnership with Elvis Costello. It still bears the strong mark of McCartney, but has a Costello-like lyrical twist.

McCartney told NME 'One of the nice things about working with Elvis is that he'll tell me straight "that's gonna come out corny" – he doesn't mince his words, and I like that.'

Responding to the point that the two songwriters were opposites in many ways, Paul said: 'So were me and John. Working with him is very similar. We wrote one song and thought "God, this is just like The Beatles." He was actually taking John's role. At first we were a bit worried by that, but then thought: "Well if it's gonna happen, let it."'

McCartney confessed that he missed having a good collaborator because it was always a big help with Lennon – 'We were able to regulate and edit each other.' But he wouldn't confirm that the liaison with Costello would be on-going, merely saying that, 'It could be,' adding, 'It might not last, but it's certainly worked so far.'

Madonna – the Vatican object to plans to get her stoned in Italy

Astley – 1987's top singles seller

THE GRAPEVINE

- Top-selling singles act for the year in the UK has been Rick Astley.
- The BBC have decided The Tams' 'There Ain't Nothing Like Shaggin'' (about the US dance, of course) should not be played before 9 pm and have temporarily banned Bros's 'When Will I Be Famous' for alleged chart hyping.
- Agnetha and Bjorn from Abba have been prosecuted in Sweden for tax evasion.

MADONNA'S STATUE

Madonna is at the centre of a furious public row between the Catholic Church and residents of the sleepy Italian town of Pacentro. Vatican officials are outraged at plans to immortalize the pop queen by erecting a life-size statue of her in basque and fishnet tights. A spokesman said it would be 'too sexy' and might 'corrupt the morals of Italy's fine young people'.

Pacentro residents want to honour Ms Ciccone because her grandparents lived there before emigrating to America in the early 1900s, and they are determined to push ahead with plans.

USA FOR NEW YORK

Bruce Springsteen and Billy Joel were among surprise guests at a Madison Square Garden charity concert organized by Paul Simon which raised £300,000 ($440,000) for New York's homeless children.

Taking part were Grace Jones, Lou Reed, Chaka Khan, Debbie Harry, James Taylor, Dion, Ladysmith Black Mambazo (the South African choir), Nile Rodgers and Laurie Anderson.

The Boss played a solo acoustic version of 'Born To Run' and then, with Simon on guitar and Joel on piano, performed 'Glory Days'. All 57 stars came on stage for a mass rendition of 'Rock'n 'Roll Music' as a grand finale.

CHARTS

US45	Heaven Is A Place On Earth *Belinda Carlisle*
USLP	Dirty Dancing *Soundtrack*
UK45	China I Your Hand *T'Pau*
UKLP	Whenever You Need Somebody *Rick Astley*
WEEK 2	
US45	Faith *George Michael*
USLP	Dirty Dancing *Soundtrack*
UK45	China In Your Hand *T'Pau*
UKLP	Now That's What I Call Music, 10 *Various*
WEEK 3	
US45	Faith *George Michael*
USLP	Dirty Dancing *Soundtrack*
UK45	When I Fall In Love *Rick Astley*
UKLP	Now That's What I Call Music, 10 *Various*
WEEK 4	
US45	Faith *George Michael*
USLP	Dirty Dancing *Soundtrack*
UK45	Always On My MInd *Pet Shop Boys*
UKLP	Now That's What I Call Music, 10 *Various*

FRANKIE GOING?

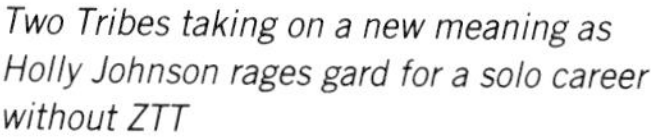

Two Tribes taking on a new meaning as Holly Johnson rages gard for a solo career without ZTT

Frankie Goes To Hollywood did not play on their Number 1 hits! This shock revelation stunned the music world this month.

During the Holly Johnson vs. ZTT label court case in London, it was revealed that session musicians and the studio wizardry of ZTT boss Trevor Horn were responsible for the success of 'Relax' and 'Two Tribes'.

Johnson is fighting a High Court injunction which prevents him from having a solo career under the terms of his ZTT contract. He also claims royalties for earlier recordings.

If Johnson wins, he will become the fifth act to leave the label for contractual reasons in the last two years.

THE GRAPEVINE

- An NME readers poll for the top albums of all time showed The Smith's 'The Queen is Dead' as No. 1 and Jesus & Mary Chain's 'Psychocandy' as runner up.
- Whitney Houston has become the first act to sell 5 million of her first two album releases.
- Inducted into the 'Rock'n'Roll Hall of Fame' were The Beatles, Bob Dylan, The Beach Boys, The Drifters and The Supremes.

PIRATES – PAYOLA OR SPONSORSHIP?

Last year, NME reported that UK pirate radio stations were asking record companies for 'fees' of up to £500 ($800) to play records that the big stations were ignoring. The system known as 'Powerplay' was not payola but 'sponsorship', claimed the pirates, who said they could not guarantee plays.

Now a British TV show has lifted the lid further by interviewing the manager of dance act Krush, who said he had paid £400 ($640) to ensure blanket airplay over 6 weeks for 'House Arrest' which is now a UK Top 5 hit.

The programme exposed how some popular pirate stations have accepted money, with one station claiming to make £3,000 ($4,800) a week.

The big stations' aversion to playing 'club' music means many groups seemingly have no option other than the payola system, so the practice looks set to grow even more.

CHARTS

US45	Faith *George Michael*
USLP	Dirty Dancing *Soundtrack*
UK45	Always On My Mind *Pet Shop Boys*
UKLP	Now That's What I Call Music, 10 *Various*
WEEK 2	
US45	So Emotional *Whitney Houston*
USLP	Dirty Dancing *Soundtrack*
UK45	Always On My Mind *Pet Shop Boys*
UKLP	Now That's What I Call Music, 10 *Various*
WEEK 3	
US45	Got My Mind Set On You *George Harrison*
USLP	Faith *George Michael*
UK45	Always On My Mind *Pet Shop Boys*
UKLP	Now That's What I Call Music, 10 *Various*
WEEK 4	
US45	The Way You Make Me Feel *Michael Jackson*
USLP	Tiffany *Tiffany*
UK45	Heaven Is A Place On Earth *Belinda Carlisle*
UKLP	Popped In, Souled Out *Wet Wet Wet*
WEEK 5	
US45	Need You Tonight *Inxs*
USLP	Tiffany *Tiffany*
UK45	Heaven Is A Place On Earth *Belinda Carlisle*
UKLP	Turn Back The Clock *Johnny Hates Jazz*

BLACK PRINCE MYSTERY

Prince's unreleased 'Black' album may never see the light of day and the Purple One's new set is rapidly becoming one of the great mysteries of modern pop.

The eight-track follow-up to 'Sign O' The Times' was due to be released in the US on December 15, but production was stopped after several hundred copies had been pressed. Rumour has it that the album may now never be released, as Prince is reported to have told Warner Brothers that if the album didn't come out before Christmas – and with minimum publicity – then he wouldn't sanction its release at all.

The record was also due for release this month in Britain, but a Warner spokesman said that 'nobody here really knows what's happening'.

RUN DMC STAY PUT

Run DMC have lost their six-month legal battle with Profile Records and have now agreed to stay with the label – and deliver ten albums!

The group's manager Russell Simmons sued Profile over alleged unpaid royalties of $7 million from the trio's mega-successful 'Raisin' Hell' album, but Profile responded with a countersuit claiming Run DMC had broken their contract by stopping work on the new album 'Tougher Than Leather'.

Russell Simmons, who is the brother of lead singer Run Simmons, is believed to have instigated the lawsuit in an attempt to extricate the group from their contract (which he negotiated personally), so that they could then sign to his Def Jam label.

Plans for tours, the release of the album and the film also entitled *Tougher Than Leather*, which were all shelved pending the outcome of the court case, will now be finalized.

It's tricky – Run DMC in the courts and on the streets

ROCK'N'ROLL HALL OF FAME GALA

Among the rock stars at the third 'Rock'n'Roll Hall of Fame' dinner and gala were Mick Jagger, Bruce Springsteen, Billy Joel, Little Richard, Elton John, Bob Dylan and The Beach Boys.

A hoped-for Beatles re-union failed when Paul McCartney did not join George Harrison and Ringo Star at the gala, due to 'business differences'.

Yoko Ono said: 'I am sure that if John were alive, he would have been there.' Whereas Arlo Guthrie assured the audience that if his late father Woody (newly elected to the Hall of Fame) were alive, 'this is one place he wouldn't be'!

CHARTS

US45	Could've Been — *Tiffany*
USLP	Faith — *George Michael*
UK45	I Think We're Alone Now — *Tiffany*
UKLP	Introducing The Hardline — *Terence Trent D'Arby*
WEEK 2	
US45	Could've Been — *Tiffany*
USLP	Faith — *George Michael*
UK45	I Think We're Alone Now — *Tiffany*
UKLP	Introducing The Hardline — *Terence Trent D'Arby*
WEEK 3	
US45	Seasons Change — *Expose*
USLP	Faith — *George Michael*
UK45	I Should Be So Lucky — *Kylie Minogue*
UKLP	'Blow Up Your Video — *AC/DC*
WEEK 4	
US45	Father Figure — *George Michael*
USLP	Faith — *George Michael*
UK45	I Should Be So Lucky — *Kylie Minogue*
UKLP	Introducing The Hardline — *Terence Trent D'Arby*

SAMPLE DIS

Rhythm King Records have angrily denied claims made by Cybertron (an original member of the Rhythm King Rap trio Three Wise Men) that they stole a sample idea from his track 'Right on Time' to use in their big British hit 'Beat Dis' by Bomb The Bass.

The sample in question is the distinctive 'Get down to the funky beat' which comes from The Funky Four Plus One's 'Everybody in The Street'.

The label denied there was any truth in the allegation, and pointed out that this same sample had also been used recently on 'Rock The House' by Special K and 'Who Is It?' by Mantronix.

The irony is that neither party involved own the sample concerned, which was on Sugarhill records, and in law there is no copyright on mere ideas.

THE GRAPEVINE

- **Frankie goes to MCA – as Holly Johnson has won his court case against ZTT records.**
- **The NME has released an album of Beatles songs performed by Eighties acts entitled 'Sgt Pepper Knew My Father', with proceeds going to the 'Childline' charity.**
- **The Who re-united for a one-off performance at the Brits awards.**
- **Expose has signed with Coke and Cyndi Lauper with a Japanese beer company.**

Who: joining together for The Brits

GRIPES AT GRAMMYS

America's premier music awards, the Grammy's, have come under fire from rock critics, musicians and record companies.

'How can a record win the "Record of the Year" award two years running?' was a question asked by many people when Paul Simon's 'Graceland' did just that.

Perhaps even more disturbing is the fact that there are still no specific awards for rap music, or for hard rock and heavy metal, despite the huge success this year of acts like Run DMC, The Beastie Boys, LL Cool J, Bon Jovi, Aerosmith, and Def Leppard.

To cap it all, the category for Best Female Rock Singer was eliminated altogether this year, with the ladies being grouped together with the males for one single rock vocalist award, even though every other category of music has separate male and female categories.

The National Academy of Recording Arts and Sciences, who organize the awards, stated the reason for this was that their 6,000 members could not come up with the required ten different female rock artist nominations which would entitle them to á separate category.

CHARTS

US45 Father Figure *George Michael*
USLP Faith *George Michael*
UK45 Beat Dis *Bomb The Bass*
UKLP Introducing The Hardline *Terence Trent D'Arby*

WEEK 2

US45 Never Gonna Give You Up *Rick Astley*
USLP Dirty Dancing *Soundtrack*
UK45 Beat Dis *Bomb The Bass*
UKLP Introducing The Hardline *Terence Trent D'Arby*

WEEK 3

US45 Never Gonna Give You Up *Rick Astley*
USLP Dirty Dancing *Soundtrack*
UK45 Together Forever *Rick Astley*
UKLP Introducing The Hardline *Terence Trent D'Arby*

WEEK 4

US45 The Man In TheMirror *Michael Jackson*
USLP Dirty Dancing *Soundtrack*
UK45 Don't Turn Around *Aswad*
UKLP The Best Of *Ochestral Manoeuvres In The Dark*

Bananarama: Jacquie joins the bunch as Siobhan slips away

THE GRAPEVINE

- **Madonna has made her Broadway debut in the play *Speed The Plow.***
- **Jacquie O'Sullivan has replaced Siobhan Stewart in Bananarama.**
- **Mick Jagger has started his first solo tour in Japan.**
- **Japanese sales of Beatles CD's are already over 1.5 million.**
- **Kid Chaos has left The Cult, who plan to relocate to Los Angeles.**
- **Sadly, Andy Gibb and Divine have died.**

BRITAIN'S RICHEST ROCK STARS

Most people would think that Britain's richest rock music man must be Paul McCartney, but that's not so, according to this month's issue of the investment magazine 'Money', which shows our mate at Virgin, Richard Branson, to be numero uno.

Branson, it states, has a fortune of £130 million ($200 million), while Macca trails behind with a mere £79 million ($125 million).

In third place is Elton John with £42 million ($65 million), and the top five is completed by Andrew Lloyd Webber (£25/$40 million) and Phil Collins (£22/$35 million). Also listed in the Top 200 richest people in Britain were Mick Jagger, George Harrison, David Bowie and Dave Clark.

PLAYS FOR PAY (& COKE)

The Eurythmics, Janet Jackson and Duran Duran are among the acts who got airplay on American radio thanks to a massive cash and cocaine racket, it has been alleged.

Two record promoters, the wife of one of them and a radio station executive, have been charged in LA with paying over $260,000 (£160,000) in cash and coke to get airplay. Another nine stations in eight cities were alleged to have received payola between 1980 and 1986.

Individual records named in the trial included Duran Duran's 'Wild Boys' and Robert Plant's 'Principle Of Moments'.

Right by your side: will Eurythmics Dave & Annie survive drug payola allegation?

His secret finally revealed: part-time bar work helps Branson's rise to the top

JAMES BROWN'S RAP IS MURDER

'The Godfather of Funk', James Brown, has been charged with the attempted murder of Adrienne, his wife of eight years.

She claims that Brown fired shots at her while she was in a car, and that when she returned to their house he beat her up with an iron pipe, resulting in her fleeing to a local hospital for emergency treatment.

Brown denies all the charges saying: 'She is just mad because I won't take her on my South American tour', and adding: 'I can tell you now it's all over. She's not coming back to my house.'

A week after the event, Adrienne was arrested at Georgia airport for carrying the drug PCP (angel dust). She claimed she was the victim of a set-up, aimed at 'paying her back' for her case against her husband.

I THINK I'M ALL GROWN NOW

16-year old Tiffany, who has recently topped charts on both sides of the Atlantic, has applied to a US court for legal adult status to restrain her mother Janie Williams from interfering with her business affairs.

Tiffany wishes her affairs to be left in the hands of her manager/producer George Tobin, who is contractually entitled to half her royalties and the exclusive rights to her records and videos, not to mention having the final say on things like musical direction, photographs and tours.

While the court is deciding, Tiffany has left the house she shared with her mother and two sisters, and is living with her aunt Julie Abbas, who has been appointed her guardian.

THE GRAPEVINE

- **Status Quo have apologized to the United Nations for appearing at Sun City.**
- **Randy Travis is heading the UK Route 88 (Country) marketing campaign.**
- **The projected Madonna statue in Italy has been scrapped.**
- **Whitney Houston has started a sell-out UK tour while her 'Whitney' album has passed the ten million sales mark.**
- **Sonny Bono has been elected Mayor of Palm Springs.**

CHARTS

US45	The Man In The Mirror *Michael Jackson*
USLP	Dirty Dancing *Soundtrack*
UK45	Don't Turn Around *Aswad*
UKLP	Viva Hate *Morrissey*
WEEK 2	
US45	Get Outta My Dreams, Get Into My Car *Billy Ocean*
USLP	Dirty Dancing *Soundtrack*
UK45	Don't Turn Around *Aswad*
UKLP	Now That's What I Call Music, 11 *Various*
WEEK 3	
US45	Get Outta My Dreams, Get Into My Car *Billy Ocean*
USLP	Dirty Dancing *Soundtrack*
UK45	Heart *pet Shop Boys*
UKLP	Now That's What I Call Music, 11 *Various*
WEEK 4	
US45	Where Do Broken Hearts Go *Whitney Houston*
USLP	Dirty Dancing *Soundtrack*
UK45	Heart *Pet Shop Boys*
UKLP	Push *Bros*
WEEK 5	
US45	Where do Broken Hearts Go *Whitney Houston*
USLP	Dirty Dancing *Soundtrack*
UK45	Theme From S'Express *S'Express*
UKLP	Seventh Son Of A Seventh Son *Iron Maiden*

Sonny Bono: Palm Springs Mayor!

SAW LOSE THE MIDAS TOUCH?

This month the mega-successful producing/writing trio Mike Stock, Matt Aitken and Pete Waterman walked off with the Ivor Novello award as top British songwriters, and have a record four productions in the Australian Top 10. However, it seems that even they can't please all of the people all of the time, as two of their recent projects have been shelved (at least for the time being) by the record companies concerned.

An estimated £60,000 ($95,000) had been spent on sessions for four tracks at Pete Waterman's PWL studios by top metal band Judas Priest, the results of which appalled the group who allegedly 'haven't stopped laughing since they heard them'.

The other act said to be involved is the controversial Sigue Sigue Sputnik, whose front man Tony James it seems could not get on with the SAW team and their dictatorial stance over the recordings.

STARS GET AIDS SHOW BLAME

The International AIDS day concert at London's Wembley Arena has had to be cancelled due to lack of support from big name artists.

With only 1,000 of the 9,000 seats sold, the Action Against AIDS organizers were hoping that a big draw artist would agree to appear, as Elton John and George Michael did last year.

The bill for the show would have included The Communards, Aztec Camera, Everything But The Girl, Holly Johnson and Roger Daltrey. The Stranglers, who were also due to appear, pulled out just a few days before the announcement of the cancellation.

It appears that many top acts refused to appear on the show because they were playing on either the Nelson Mandela 70th Birthday Concert, The Artists Against Apartheid or the Amnesty International Festival Of Youth events.

A very disappointed spokesman for the AAA stated: 'It seems that AIDS is no longer fashionable'.

CHARTS

US45	Wishing Well	*Terence Trent D'Arby*
USLP	Dirty Dancing	*Soundtrack*
UK45	Theme From S'Express	*S'Express*
UKLP	The Innocents	*Erasure*
WEEK 2		
US45	Anything For You	*Gloria Estefan & Miami Sound Machine*
USLP	Faith	*George Michael*
UK45	Perfect	*Fairground Attraction*
UKLP	Tango In The Night	*Fleetwood Mac*
WEEK 3		
US45	Anything For You	*Gloria Estefan & Miami Sound Machine*
USLP	Faith	*George Michael*
UK45	With A Little Help From My Friends	*Wet Wet Wet*
UKLP	Tango In The Night	*Fleetwood Mac*
WEEK 4		
US45	One More Try	*George Michael*
USLP	Faith	*George Michael*
UK45	With A Little Help From My Friends	*Wet Wet Wet*
UKLP	Lovesexy	*Prince*

Whitney: record seven in a row

THE GRAPEVINE

- **Whitney Houston has achieved a record breaking seventh No.1 US hit in a row.**
- **Run DMC and Public Enemy have been having problems finding London venues due to anticipated crowd problems.**
- **James Brown has been arrested on drug charges after allegedly beating his wife again.**
- **The charity single released by NME featuring Wet Wet Wet and Billy Bragg has topped the UK chart.**

BROS TOUR – A NATIONAL EMERGENCY!

The British government may have to declare a national state of emergency during Bros' first tour next month.

Police will be working overtime around the country, and elaborate preparations have been made to protect the trio from their hordes of fans.

Police forces are preparing themselves for 'probable mayhem, chaos and pandemonium'.

Bros in state of emergency

PRINCE & JAGGER SONG STEALERS?

Prince won the first-round battle against his half-sister Lorna Nelson, who claims that he had ripped off one of her songs. She says that he used part of her song, 'What's Cooking In This Book', in his composition 'U Got The Look', which was a hit for him and Scotland's Sheena Easton.

Meanwhile, Mick Jagger was cleared in a New York court of stealing his song 'Just Another Night' from Bronx-based reggae musician Patrick Alley, who had sued Mick for $6 million (£4 million). The song concerned appears on the 'She's The Boss' album.

MACCA ROCKS FOR REDS ONLY

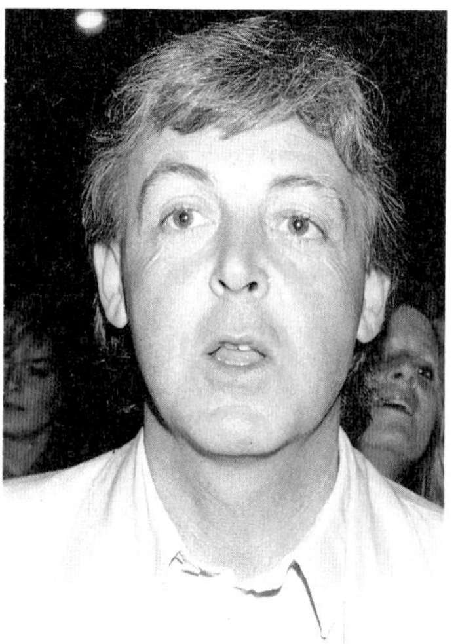

Paul McCartney is releasing a 13 track album of old rock'n'roll favourites, nine of which have never been released before. But it will only be on sale in Russia.

The tracks are 'Kansas City', 'Lawdy Miss Clawdy', '20 Flight Rock', 'Bring It On Home', 'Lucille', 'Don't Get Around Much Anymore', 'I'm Gonna Be A Wheel Someday', 'That's Alright Mama', 'Summertime', 'Ain't That A Shame', 'Cracking Up', 'Just Because' and 'Midnight Special'.

Paul says: 'The new spirit of friendship opening in Russia has enabled me to make this gesture to my Russian fans and let them hear one of my records first for a change.'

Jagger: innocent

INXS KNOCK BRITONS

Hutchence: shoelace colours

Michael Hutchence, lead singer of the internationally successful Australian group INXS, had some controversial things to say about British record buyers, when interviewed in the midst of the group's American tour.

Michael stated: 'The English are a law unto themselves, they're so f . . . ing cool. In England, it seems to me, there is an unhealthy obsession with form rather than function in music, and bands seem desperately concerned about things like the colour of their shoelaces.

'If you close your eyes when watching MTV, all the bands are indistinguishable, but visually it's obvious who the British acts are.'

He bemoaned that in Britain, 'You can only be good if under 500 people have heard of you, otherwise you're uncool. This means that the chart is full of shit, 'cos the good bands feel it's beneath them to go for that market. There's a feeling that it's wrong to be successful – the British are just too cool for their own good.'

- **George Michael's 'Faith' has topped the US black music album charts.**
- **James Brown's murder charge has been dropped.**
- **This year's Prince Charles Trust Gala featured Phil Collins, Rick Astley, Elton John, The Bee Gees, Four Tops and Wet Wet Wet.**
- **Hall & Oates have re-united and have hit the road in the US.**

Charles's Charity brings out the stars as the rock establishment asserts itself. A long way from the music of rebellious youth?

CHARTS

US45	One More Try – *George Michael*
USLP	Faith – *George Michael*
UK45	With A Little Help From My Friends – *Wet Wet Wet*
UKLP	Tango In The Night – *Fleetwood Mac*
WEEK 2	
US45	One More Try – *George Michael*
USLP	Faith – *George Michael*
UK45	With A Little Help From My Friends – *Wet Wet Wet*
UKLP	Tango In The Night – *Fleetwood Mac*
WEEK 3	
US45	Together Forever – *Rick Astley*
USLP	Faith – *George Michael*
UK45	Doctorin' The Tardis – *Timelords*
UKLP	Niteflite – *Various*
WEEK 4	
US45	Foolish Beat – *Debbie Gibson*
USLP	OU812 – *Van Halen*
UK45	I Owe You Nothing – *Bros*
UKLP	Niteflite – *Various*

AMNESTY HIT BY MANDELA SHOW

Amnesty International's world tour started badly, with the poorly-attended *Festival of Youth* at Britain's Milton Keynes Bowl losing as much as £150,000 ($240,000). It was thought that the low attendance figures were due to the festival coming so soon after the Nelson Mandela birthday concert at Wembley.

The first day of the festival featured acts like Howard Jones, The Stranglers, Runrig, Sam Brown, Joe Strummer and Aswad – the last two being the day's highlights.

Sunday's performers included Michelle Shocked, Aztec Camera, New Model Army, B.A.D. and a re-united Damned, with guest vocals from Joey Ramone.

CRY FREEDOM – OF SPEECH?

The Nelson Mandela birthday party at London's Wembley stadium was 'hijacked by extremists', according to a British politician, after many acts – including Mark Knopfler (Dire Straits), Annie Lennox (Eurythmics) and Jim Kerr (Simple Minds) – managed to make political statements from the stage, despite a supposed ban.

Along with the British TV audience, most of the billion-plus viewers around the world saw the top pop acts condemn apartheid live on their TV screens.

However, in the US, the show – which was billed as 'Freedom Fest, A Concert For The Freedom Of The World' – was screened six hours later with the vast majority of references to South Africa, the anti-apartheid movement and even Mandela himself edited out, possibly due to pressures from advertisers like Coca Cola.

Mandela Birthday Party – Miami Steve (left) and Jim Kerr (centre) mix politics with music

ROCK'S CONSCIENCE SPOTLIGHTS MANDELA

Back in 1984, British multi-racial group The Special AKA had reached the UK top ten with a single produced by Elvis Costello and simply titled 'Nelson Mandela'. It had reminded the world that Mandela, a leader of the African National Congress, an organization banned in South Africa, had been in a South African jail since 1962 because of his opposition to apartheid.

Nelson Mandela had been imprisoned when he was in his early forties, more than a quarter of a century before, and he was still in prison on 11 June 1988 when a number of prominent pop and rock stars assembled to celebrate his 70th birthday.

Special AKA leader Jerry Dammers had not only written the song about Mandela, he had launched an organization called Artists Against Apartheid. In 1986, Dammers had helped to organize a free AAA concert, 'Freedom Beat', on London's Clapham Common and now planned to present a whole day show at Wembley Stadium, which could then be sold to worldwide television à la Live Aid. Jim Kerr of Simple Minds added his band's support, as did Bishop Trevor Huddlestone, President of the Anti-Apartheid Movement. With much assistance from Wendy Laister of PR specialists Laister Dickson, a bill began to be assembled which, apart from Simple Minds, also included Mark Knopfler of Dire Straits, undoubtedly one of the biggest acts in the world.

With Knopfler committed, filling the bill became much easier – George Michael agreed to appear before playing another London venue on the same day, and The Eurythmics actually called to offer their services. Whitney Houston, who had in the past refused to work as a model for companies with South

Simple Minds' Jim Kerr

Chapman – encore

Boy George

Miriam Makeba

African connections, was recruited by her concert promoter/agent Barry Marshall of Marshall Arts, and then BBC Television were approached.

When the Corporation agreed to televise the show live, the credibility battle was virtually over.

Among the artists who eventually did appear were Dire Straits (with Eric Clapton as special guest), Sting, George Michael, The Eurythmics, Al Green, Joe Cocker, Natalie Cole, movie star Darryl Hannah, and a segment featuring Paul Young, Bryan Adams, Fish, The Bee Gees and Wet Wet Wet backed by a specially assembled supergroup led by Midge Ure, which included Phil Collins, Paul Carrack, Johnny Marr of The Smiths and Curt Smith from Tears For Fears.

In addition, UB40 (with guest Chrissie Hynde of The Pretenders), South Africa stars Hugh Masakela and Miriam Makeba, Whitney Houston (who had rescheduled a planned concert in Italy to perform at Wembley), Peter Gabriel, Little Steven (aka 'Miami' Steve Van Zandt, ex-Springsteen's E Street Band), Jerry Dammers & Friends, Stevie Wonder and opera star Jessye Norman (who ended the concert with a moving 'Amazing Grace'). Hosts Harry Belafonte, movie star Whoopi Goldberg, British comedians Michael Palin, Billy Connolly and Harry Enfield also gave time and talent to the cause. Quite a galaxy of stars.

Ultimately, a good deal of money was raised for the Anti-Apartheid Movement and Jerry Dammers must have felt a lot better. But another artist, Tracy Chapman, also derived considerable benefit from the Mandela concert. Stevie Wonder's appearance was delayed for some hours because his carefully-prepared backing tapes could not be found, and Chapman volunteered to return to the stage for a further set while Wonder's search continued.

Chapman's debut album had already reached the Top 20 of the US LP chart, but had hardly registered in Britain. After the huge TV exposure she received from playing before an estimated worldwide audience of one billion viewers, her album deservedly topped the British LP chart, seemingly an instance of instant karma.

More to the point, 18 months after the Nelson Mandela 70th Birthday Concert, the man in whose honour it was staged was freed from imprisonment.

Midge Ure – supergroup

Dammers – 'Freedom Beat'

Paul Young

Whitney – modelling boycott

JULY 1988

JACKO SLAYS UK FANS

On this supposedly first and last solo world tour, it's breathtaking to see how Michael Jackson really comes alive with the music, as if suddenly plugged into some mega-watt electric current.

It's as if this pipe-cleaner-thin recluse, subject of more hype and horror stories than any other pop star, finds his only release on stage. As a dancer he's beyond compare – eerie puppet motions during 'Human Nature', the trademark moonwalking for 'Billie Jean' and extravagant crotch-thrusting for 'Bad'.

Jacko is by no means the greatest singer in black pop, but the sheer versatility of his music and the impossibility of separating the sound from the whole show-business package of special effects and costume changes, ensures that the legend grows and grows.

Jackson: moonwalking, crotch-thrusting – beyond compare!

CHARTS

1	US45	Dirty Diana	*Michael Jackson*
	USLP	OU812	*Van Halen*
	UK45	I Owe You Nothing	*Bros*
	UKLP	Tracy Chapman	*Tracy Chapman*
WEEK 2	US45	The Flame	*Cheap Trick*
	USLP	OU812	*Van Halen*
	UK45	I Owe You Nothing	*Bros*
	UKLP	Tracy Chapman	*Tracy Chapman*
WEEK 3	US45	The Flame	*Cheap Trick*
	USLP	OU812	*Van Halen*
	UK45	Nothing's Gonna Change My Love For You	*Glenn Medeiros*
	UKLP	Tracy Chapman	*Tracy Chapman*
WEEK 4	US45	Hold On To The Nights	*Richard Marx*
	USLP	Hysteria	*Def Leppard*
	UK45	Nothing's Gonna Change My Love For You	*Glenn Medeiros*
	UKLP	Now That's What I Call Music, 12	*Various*
WEEK 5	US45	Roll With It	*Steve Winwood*
	USLP	Hysteria	*Def Leppard*
	UK45	Nothing's Gonna Change My Love For You	*Glenn Medeiros*
	UKLP	Now That's What I Call Music, 12	*Various*

THE GRAPEVINE

- The 'Rock Against The Rich' tour has hit the road in the UK.
- The Fat Boys have sued Miller Lite for $5 million.
- Motown records has been sold to MCA.
- Michael Jackson has been seen by a record 500,000 people during his seven day stand at Wembley stadium.
- Kenny Rogers and John Denver have been named as the most popular US acts in China.

ACID HOUSE WITH ~~BALEARIC~~ BEAT

Acid House music has taken the UK club scene into a new Summer of Love with its hypnotic beat, new age drugs and the vibes they induce turning clubland on its head.

Nobody is quite sure as to the true origins of the title Acid House. Many believe it came from Phuture's 'Acid Trax' single. Others, like in-demand producer Todd Terry, think it derives from the slang 'burning' which means to steal from someone else's record.

But whatever its roots, Acid House – characterized by off-beat sounds and a relentlessly driving rhythm – began in Chicago as a natural progression from the other House forms (Deep House, Washing Machine, or Jackin' House), and thrives on a patent weirdness and disregard for conventional structure or form.

It's popularity in clubs stems from its incessant freakbeat to which DJs add the now mandatory strobes and dry ice, and Acid house one-nighters are springing up all over the country.

Balearic Beats were named after the Mediterranean island group, and British DJs vacationing there last year were taken aback by the way local jocks were mixing the usual dancebeats with *the* most unexpected tracks, to massive popular response.

It was a response they also received when they played Balearic Beats to London club-goers on their return. The success of the new sound quickly led to more venues playing Balearic Beats.

The yellow Smiley logo is the most recurrent symbol, while T-shirts with old slogans such as Tune In, Turn On, Drop Out, plus baggy old jeans and long hair are one image aimed for. Another requirement is dance-stamina – the ability to dance for six or seven hours without a break.

Left: Denver: big in China as MOR grips the nation

Far left: Fat Boys: Lite they ain't

MONSTERS OF ROCK DISASTERS

Two fans died and another 450 people were injured, (one critically) during the 'Monsters of Rock' Festival, which was held in front of the biggest-ever Castle Donnington crowd. The deaths were blamed on slam-dancing, which broke out during the set by Guns'n'Roses.

The 100,000 crowd at Britain's biggest regular rock festival saw a strong line up of acts including top US metal acts Megadeth, David Lee Roth, Kiss and the British bill-toppers, Iron Maiden.

Meanwhile, in the US, the 'Monsters of Rock' tour featuring Van Halen, Dokken, Metallica, The Scorpions and Kingdom Come failed to attract the expected audiences, and it is reported that the first three acts were talking about paying a partial refund of concert fees to the promoters who lost a lot of money on the tour.

PINK FLOYD LIVE?

'Enormous aerial pigs floated over the packed Wembley Stadium during "Echoes", and the ticking of loud clocks and the sound of alarms boomed out time to the 50,000-plus people gathered to see and hear Pink Floyd,' an NME critic reports.

'The faceless group played note for note versions of the highlights from their 20-year career in the rock business. The show is spectacular, but it doesn't hide the fact that what you are watching is very up-market hi-fi – you are listening to the largest and most expensive record player in the world.

'Pink Floyd are musically tedium incarnate, and if live music means spontaneous music then you can pronounce Pink Floyd dead.

'These characterless empty vessels certainly made a loud noise, but isn't it time they changed their tune?'

Floyd's Mason, Gilmour & Wright: empty vessels?

- **The Grateful Dead have played nine days at New York's Madison Square Gardens, breaking Neil Diamond's house record there.**
- **Virgin Records are furious that they've been linked in the daily press with a Mafia payola scandal in the US.**
- **Freddie Jackson has attacked George Michael in the *LA Times* over his black music chart success.**
- **Status Quo have released 'Running All Over The World', with proceeds going to 'Sports Aid 88'.**

Dead but won't lie down

CHARTS

US45	Roll With It *Steve Winwood*
USLP	Appetite For Destruction *Guns 'N Roses*
UK45	Nothing's Gonna Change My Love For You *Glenn Medeiros*
UKLP	Now That's What I Call Music, 12 *Various*
	WEEK 2
US45	Roll With It *Steve Winwood*
USLP	Hysteria *Def Leppard*
UK45	The Only Way Is Up *Yazz & Plastic Population*
UKLP	Now That's What I Call Music, 12 *Various*
	WEEK 3
US45	Roll With It *Steve Winwood*
USLP	Roll With It *Steve Winwood*
UK45	The Only Way Is Up *Yazz & Plastic Population*
UKLP	Now That's What I Call Music, 12 *Various*
	WEEK 4
US45	Monkey *George Michael*
USLP	Tracy Chapman *Tracy Chapman*
UK45	The Only Way Is Up *Yazz & Plastic Population*
UKLP	Now That's What I Call Music, 12 *Various*

MACCA KNOCKS LENNON BOOK

Paul McCartney is urging people to boycott Albert Goldman's new book *The Lives of John Lennon*, which he dismisses as 'a piece of trash'.

Reacting to Goldman's claims that Lennon was a homosexual heroin-addicted hermit during his last years, Paul said: 'It's disgusting that he can make up lies and publish them without fear of repudiation.'

Paul denies that John ever had any homosexual inclinations, as alleged by Goldman, who claims John slept with The Beatles' manager, Brian Epstein.

'As for heroin,' Macca added, 'John was completely free of all drugs by the time Sean was born.'

Goldman, whose lurid exposé of Elvis Presley in a 1980 book attracted a similar amount of controversy, has also been attacked by John's first wife Cynthia and the Beatles' producer George Martin.

LIVE ACTS NEED HELP!

This year's Reading Festival included US acts Starship, The Smithereens, Iggy Pop and The Ramones. Making up the British contingent were The Quireboys, Wonder Stuff, Fields Of The Nephilim, Hothouse Flowers, Uriah Heep and Sunday's bill toppers, Squeeze.

There were some acts who probably wished they hadn't bothered to make the trip at all.

Bottles of urine greeted the entrance of Bonnie Tyler – one hit her in the face, but she finished her show like a good 'un. A similar fate met Meatloaf and Deacon Blue, who only sang one song.

Meanwhile, on the other side of Europe, the 'Greek Free Festival' degenerated into the most destructive pop riot ever seen on the continent, with estimated damages of over £1.5 million ($2.4 million) and scores of people hospitalized.

The festival, which was held in an Athens park, ran for only one of the planned three days. Trouble started during The Triffids set, but really erupted when it was announced that PIL had postponed (for security reasons) their appearance for 24 hours. The pandemonium lasted over an hour, with crowds burning the stage, the PA and even vehicles parked back-stage.

LIVE ACTS GIVE HELP

Sport Aid's 'Race Against Time' was the largest mass participation event in history, with over 20 million people running in 117 countries to help the world's starving people.

The major British music event for 'Sport Aid 88' was held in Sheffield, and the audience was reminded from the start: 'Every minute we spend here today, 29 kids will die in Africa.'

Appearing were The Hollies, The Primitives, Spear of Destiny, Mica Paris, Big Country, The Proclaimers, Climie Fisher, Heaven 17, Womack & Womack, Squeeze and Eddy Grant.

The all-star 'Amnesty International Concert' at Wembley stadium was something of a disappointment. Sting's voice seemed shot, but his set still met with a great response. During Peter Gabriels' over-long set, it became clear that all was not well with the sound system. Tracy Chapman's excellent voice could hardly be heard over the p.a., but she managed to steal the show.

Bruce Springsteen headlined, but he seemed to be merely going through the motions in his drastically foreshortened segment of the show.

The whole gang reappeared for a finale version of Bob Dylan's 'Chimes of Freedom'. In all, there were more downs than ups, and the captive audience seemed glad to be free at the end.

CHARTS

US45	Monkey	*George Michael*
USLP	Tracy Chapman	*Tracy Chapman*
UK45	The Only Way Is Up	*Yazz & Plastic Population*
UKLP	First Of A Million Kisses	*Fairground Attraction*
WEEK 2		
US45	Sweet Child O' Mind	*Guns N' Roses*
USLP	Tracy Chapman	*Tracy Chapman*
UK45	The Only Way Is Up	*Yazz & Plastic Population*
UKLP	Kylie	*Kylie Minogue*
WEEK 3		
US45	Sweet Child O' MIne	*Guns N' Roses*
USLP	Tracy Chapman	*Tracy Chapman*
UK45	He Ain't Heavy, He's My Brother	*Hollies*
UKLP	Rank	*Smiths*
WEEK 4		
US45	Don't Worry, Be Happy	*Bobby McFerrin*
USLP	Tracy Chapman	*Tracy Chapman*
UK45	He Ain't Heavy, He's My Brother	*Hollies*
UKLP	Kylie	*Kylie Minogue*

The Boss and Sting sharing a Wembley mike for good cause at Amnesty International bash, high in purpose but low in excitement

THE GRAPEVINE

- **Michael Jackson has played to Britain's biggest crowd for years – 125,000 at Liverpool. Jacko is officially the world's top earning entertainer, with assets of £60 million.**
- **Midge Ure has quit Ultravox, Fish has left Marillion and Clark Datchler has left Johnny Hates Jazz.**
- **Inxs have won five MTV awards.**

Midge Ure (right) leaving Ultravox

Womack & Womack: Sheffield Sport Aid

JEAN-MICHEL JARRE DOCKLANDS CONCERT

It was impossible not to be impressed by the skills which pulled this show together in the face of hassles which continued right up to a few hours before the event.

But as Jarre's sonorous synth thundered out of the giant speakers mounted on dockside cranes, searchlights swept the clouds and lasers stabbed upwards, the sense of awe was shortlived.

Despite the sheer scale of the event – the enormous expanse of London's Royal Victoria Dock, the floating multi-level stage, the looming warehouses painted with coloured light, the vast 100,000 crowd, the fireworks overhead – it was all strangely unmoving.

It was partly the fault of Jarre's music, which only occasionally attains a tinkly-bonk catchiness, and partly because of the staggeringly banal projected images and 'seen-it-all-before' lasers.

Jarre's ambition to get away from the usual rock concert format is a valid one. But this was a cold wet night in Docklands, and it was just a meaningless *son et lumiere*.

Judging by the crowd's reaction however, it was obvious many of them felt they'd had their £30 ($48) worth.

NO POP ON RUN DMC AND PUBLIC ENEMY TOUR

The 'Run House' tour, featuring Public Enemy and Run DMC as headliners, has run into problems with fans.

The show's openers, Britain's Pop Will Eat Itself, have been booted off the tour after facing bigoted and violent audiences in London, Belgium and Holland. Promoters said the group were pulled off for their own safety, as they faced booing, spitting, fireworks, burning balls of newspaper, glass and coin-throwing.

The reason for the hostility from the nearly all-white crowds was said to be because PWEI's music 'is not black enough'.

Their manager said: 'PWEI are on the cutting edge of rock, but obviously the rap audience isn't willing to accept any crossover . . .'

A VISION SHARED

Bruce Springsteen, Bob Dylan, U2, Little Richard and Brian Wilson are among the superstars singing songs of legendary American folk performers Woody Guthrie and Leadbelly on a new tribute album.

The album, 'A Vision Shared', is also a tribute to the Folkway label which recorded both artists.

The label, founded in the Forties, has an important collection of American folk and R&B, and last year the Smithsonian Institute in Washington acquired the entire archive of over 2,200 albums.

Proceeds from the compilation LP and accompanying TV special will help fund the staffing and operations of the institute.

Wilson: vision unimpaired

Leadbelly: tribute

CHARTS

	Week 1	Week 2	Week 3	Week 4	Week 5
US45	Don't Worry, Be Happy *Bobby McFerrin*	Love Bites *Def Leppard*	Red Red Wine *UB40*	Groovy Kind Of Love *Phil Collins*	Groovy Kind Of Love *Phil Collins*
USLP	Tracy Chapman *Tracy Chapman*	Hysteria *Def Leppard*	New Jersey *Bon Jovi*	New Jersey *Bon Jovi*	New Jersey *Bon Jovi*
UK45	He Ain't Heavy, He's My Brother *Hollies*	Desire *U2*	Desire *U2*	One Moment In Time *Whitney Houston*	We Call It Acieed *D.Mob feat. Gary Haisman*
UKLP	Kylie *Kylie Minogue*	New Jersey *Bon Jovi*	New Jersey *Bon Jovi*	Rattle And Hum *U2*	Rattle And Hum *U2*

THE GRAPEVINE

- **Lennon and McCartney's 'Yesterday' has become the most programmed song on US radio, with over five million plays.**
- **This year, ten years after his death, Elvis Presley has reportedly earned $15 million.**
- **James Brown has been arrested again after a high speed car chase.**
- **UB40 top the US chart with their five-year old UK No. 1 'Red Red Wine'.**

CHARTS

US45	Kokomo *Beach Boy*
USLP	New Jersey *Bon Jovi*
UK45	Orinoco Flow *Enya*
UKLP	Money For Nothing *Dire Straits*
WEEK 2	
US45	Wild Wild West *Escape Club*
USLP	Rattle And Hum *U2*
UK45	Orinoco Flow *Enya*
UKLP	Money For Nothing *Dire Straits*
WEEK 3	
US45	Bad Medicine *Bon Jovi*
USLP	Rattle And Hum *U2*
UK45	First Time *Robin Beck*
UKLP	Money For Nothing *Dire Straits*
WEEK 4	
US45	Bad Medicine *Bon Jovi*
USLP	Rattle And Hum *U2*
UK45	First Time *Robin Beck*
UKLP	Kylie *Kylie Minogue*

MORE PROBLEMS FOR U2-BONO ON HIT LIST?

Bono (left) and Adam Clayton: problems busking at London premier

U2 continue to hit the headlines over their film *Rattle and Hum*, with some papers claiming singer Bono has been added to the IRA hit-list.

The reason for this is that a speech he made on the day of the Enniskillen bombing in Ulster is used as an introduction to 'Sunday Bloody Sunday' in the film.

In this speech, Bono says: 'I'm sick and tired of Irish Americans, who haven't been back to their country in years, coming up to me and talking about the glory of the revolution. Where's the glory in taking a man out in front of his wife and kids and shooting him? F . . . the revolution!'

More than 2,000 fans gathered outside the London cinema when the film was premiered. U2 tried to put on a live show, but were told by the police that they would be arrested if they tried to play.

Despite this setback, U2 still intend to play live outside theatres showing the movie in Dublin, Rome, Los Angeles and New York.

ACID HOUSE PARTIES ATTACKED

The British tabloid press – especially the best selling *Sun* – have got their knives into Acid House parties.

Over the last few weeks, the *Sun*, which has incidentally been selling its own Acid House T-shirts(!), ran the following stories:-

October 19 – 'Evil of Ecstasy'. Written by a doctor who had previously claimed 'heterosexuals have nothing to fear from AIDS'.

October 25 – 'The Acid House Horror'. About a young man attacked after an Acid House disco.

October 26 – In a piece about *Top Of The Pops* banning Acid House music, they mentioned 'drug-crazed fans of the drug-linked Acid House craze'.

October 31 – 'Girl 21, drops dead at Acid disco party'.

November 5 – 'Hell of Acid Kids'.

New Scotland Yard police chiefs poured cold water on campaigns to ban Acid House and reported at a special press conference that, 'there is little evidence of drugs being taken at Acid House parties, and there have been relatively very few drug-related arrests at such parties.'

US NO.1 BANNED

Escape Club: "sexist and offensive"

The video for the US No. 1 single 'Wild Wild West' by British group The Escape Club has been banned in their homeland for being 'sexist and offensive'.

The promo shows various limbs, including suspender clad legs, dancing about. The group say the video: 'is making fun of sexist videos'.

THE GRAPEVINE

- **Stevie Wonder, The Rolling Stones, Dion, Otis Reading and The Temptations have been inducted into the 'Rock'n'Roll Hall of Fame'.**
- **Sigue Sigue Sputnik's single 'Success', which was produced by Stock, Aitken & Waterman, has been released to the sound of raspberries all round.**
- **The Pogues' 'Birmingham Six' has been banned on political grounds.**
- **Bros have been mobbed by 6,000 fans on their arrival in Australia.**

Stones in Hall of Fame

. . . and Dion

VIOLENCE RAPPED ON KNUCKLES

Many of America's top rappers and record industry figures have formed 'Stop The Violence', a movement whose aim is to try and turn young people away from self destruction.

Acts including Kool Moe Dee, Public Enemy, KRS-1, MC Lyte and Stetsasonic have come together and recorded a single 'Stop The Violence', to be released on Martin Luther King's birthday, proceeds going to charities which deal with illiteracy, such as the National Urban League.

Rap music has often been linked directly with violence, both in the press and in movies like *Colours* and *Tougher Than Leather*. A spokesman for STV said: 'We want to point out the real causes of violence and the social cost. We want to show that rap is a viable tool for stimulating reading and writing skills.

'Rap music provides a whole pantheon of positive role models, most of whom explicitly promote anti-drug, anti-gang and pro-education messages.'

Kool Moe Dee; stopping the violence

CHARTS

US45	Baby I Love Your Way/Freebird Medley	*Will To Power*
USLP	Rattle And Hum	*U2*
UK45	First Time	*Robin Beck*
UKLP	Now That's What I Call Music, 12	*Various*
WEEK 2		
US45	Look Away	*Chicago*
USLP	Rattle And Hum	*U2*
UK45	Mistletoe And Wine	*Cliff Richard*
UKLP	Now That's What I Call Music, 12	*Various*
WEEK 3		
US45	Look Away	*Chicago*
USLP	Rattle And Hum	*U2*
UK45	Mistletoe And Wine	*Cliff Richard*
UKLP	Now That's What I Call Music, 12	*Various*
WEEK 4		
US45	Every Rose Has Its Thorns	*Poison*
USLP	Giving You The Best That I Got	*Anita Baker*
UK45	Mistletoe And Wine	*Cliff Richard*
UKLP	Private Collection, 1979-88	*Cliff Richard*
WEEK 5		
US45	Every Rose Has Its Thorns	*Poison*
USLP	Giving You The Best That I Got	*Anita Baker*
UK45	Mistletoe And Wine	*Cliff Richard*
UKLP	Private Collection, 1979-88	*Cliff Richard*

Roy Orbison (seated left) with the Travelin' Wilburys, the final success in a 30 year career

IT'S OVER FOR ROY ORBISON

'Roy Orbison was the finest singer on the planet' claimed Bono on hearing of the Big O's death following a heart attack.

Orbison, who was greatly admired by many other artists, including Bruce Springsteen and Elvis Costello, was that rare phenonemon – a first generation rock'n'roller who never degenerated into self-parody or tarnished his credibility.

Unlike others of his generation, he had no gimmicks. He simply stood on stage and relied on the sheer quality of his voice to captivate an audience.

He will be remembered not only for Sixties hits like 'Only The Lonely', 'It's Over', 'Oh Pretty Woman', 'Dream Baby' and 'Running Scared', but also for his new recordings like 'You Got It' and for his part in the million-selling 'Traveling Wilburys'.

Guns N'Roses – Washington wives pin-ups

CRITICS' CHOICE FOR 88

The NME writing team have come up with their annual choices for the album and singles of the year. The Top Five albums:

1 'It Takes A Nation Of Millions To Hold Us Back' – Public Enemy
2 'Irish Heartbeart' – Van Morrison & The Chieftains
3 'Green' – REM
4 'Viva Hate' – Morrissey
5 'To The Batmobile Let's Go' – The Todd Terry Project

The Top five singles are:

1 'The Mercy Seat' – Nick Cave
2 'Everyday Is Like Sunday' – Morrissey
3 'Alphabet Street' – Prince
4 'Suedehead' – Morrissey
5 'Destroy The Heart' – The House Of Love

Choice of Top Country Album was k.d. lang's 'Shadowland', and the Walt Disney collection 'Stay Awake' was named Top Compilation Album of 1988.

THE GRAPEVINE

- **Guns N' Roses are the latest act to come under attack from the Washington Wives.**
- **James Brown has been jailed for six years.**
- **Rod Stewart is stated to be 'upset' that the CIA are using his records to relay messages behind the Iron Curtain.**
- **George Michael is to get £5 million ($8 million) for promoting Diet Coke.**

PRINCE – A PAUPER?

Persistent rumours of serious financial difficulties accompanied Prince's arrival in the UK last week.

Many of these problems are said to have arisen over the costs of the singer's stage shows, which despite regularly selling-out have – with the crippling costs of shipping lavish sets – lost the artist thousands of pounds per week. To compound the situation, Prince's most recent album 'Lovesexy' has yielded very disappointing sales.

Reports in the UK national press say he is paying up to $300,000 a week to keep his various companies afloat.

Speculation also has it that while he is in Britain, Prince will be recording the musical soundtrack for the upcoming 'Batman' movie, which stars Jack Nicholson, Michael Keaton and Kim Basinger.

Prince in action

CHARTS

US45	Every Rose Has Its Thorns *Poison*
USLP	Giving You The Best That I Got *Anita Baker*
UK45	Especially For You *Kylie Minogue/Jason Donovan*
UKLP	Kylie *Kylie Minogue*
WEEK 2	
US45	My Prerogative *Bobby Brown*
USLP	Giving You The Best That I Got *Anita Baker*
UK45	Especially For You *Kylie Minogue/Jason Donovan*
UKLP	Kylie *Kylie Minogue*
WEEK 3	
US45	Two Hearts *Phil Collins*
USLP	Don't Be Cruel *Bobby Brown*
UK45	Especially For You *Kylie Minogue/Jason Donovan*
UKLP	The Innocents *Erasure*
WEEK 4	
US45	Two Hearts *Phil Collins*
USLP	Don't Be Cruel *Bobby Brown*
UK45	The Living Years *Mike & The Mechanics*
UKLP	The Legendary Roy Orbison *Roy Orbison*

YAY OR NAY?

Squabbles have arisen among various members of the original Yes as to which has the legal right to the name.

Chris Squire and Alan White, together with guitarist Trevor Rabin, will shortly be releasing an album on Atlantic as Yes, while Jon Anderson, Rick Wakeman, Bill Bruford and Steve Howe – provisionally known as Anderson, Wakeman, Bruford & Howe – will debut their new album on Arista.

However, many feel that the Arista band, handled by original Yes manager Brian Lane, has a more legitimate claim.

Lane claims that Anderson, Wakeman, and Co will be producing music very much from the classic Yes period of the early seventies. He explains: 'Jon left the Atlantic-signed Yes because he felt they were too much of a pop group.'

THE GRAPEVINE

- **Morrissey was mobbed as 2000 fans tried to get into a packed free concert.**
- **London's famous Marquee club has celebrated its 30th birthday and TV show *Top of the Pops* its 25th.**
- **Indie supergroup of the eighties The Fall has signed to Phonogam.**
- **Disco singer Sylvester has died.**
- **The qualifications for gold singles have been dropped so that more records can earn them.**

Smiths' Morrissey

Sylvester

Island supremo Blackwell

THE GHOST OF MARLEY

Outrage has greeted the news that the Jamaican government has sold Bob Marley's estate to Island Records boss Chris Blackwell at a knock-down price.

The deal, which involves two recording studios, the Bob Marley Museum and the rights to the singer's entire recorded output – valued at a figure of a least £20 million ($32 million) – was concluded last week for only £5 million ($8 million).

Among those who felt a valid claim to the Marley estate and were therefore aggrieved by Blackwell's acquisition, were his mother Cedella Booker – whose bid was rejected despite being higher than Blackwell's – and members of Marley's band, The Wailers.

Public pressure is building for the Ministry of Culture (which unfortunately cannot match the bids) to block the sale of this Jamaican heritage to Blackwell.

MAC IN THE USSR

Linda and Paul, soon to be rockin' in Russia?

'Nearly everyone who plays Russia sings "Back In The USSR" and I think it's about time I went over and did it.' That was the promise made by Paul McCartney during a 55 minute phone-in interview with the Russian people organized by the BBC's Russian Service this month.

McCartney told his estimated 18 million listeners that he hoped his first tour in 13 years could include the USSR.

Tracks from a special album 'Choba B CCCP' ('Back In the USSR'), a set of rock'n'roll classics only available in the Soviet Union, were played during the programme, during which Paul was asked about his family, and his new album and whether the remaining Beatles would reform.

More than 1000 telephone calls were received by the Russian Service during the programme – more than Mrs Thatcher received during a similar phone-in last year.

MORALISTS BROWNED OFF

Brown – explicit?

Bobby Brown was unceremoniously hauled off stage midway through his performance in the small southern town of Columbus, Georgia, last week, by a local moral majority group who claimed that Brown's act was sexually explicit.

After being detained by police for about an hour, he was allowed to resume his performance on the understanding that it would be 'toned down'.

Brown is the latest artist to incur the wrath of the town's watchdog group. Previously, LL Cool J and The Beastie Boys encountered similar problems.

STAR QUOTE

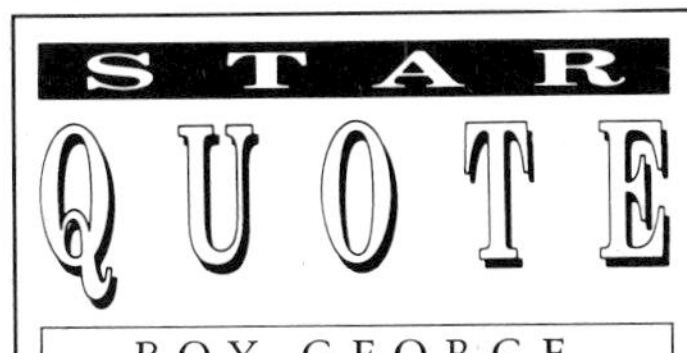

BOY GEORGE

'Best kept secret in the music business? That George Michael is a heterosexual.'

THE DAY THE MUSIC DIED

CBS Records' UK chief executive Paul Russell, director of the BRITS Award Committee, has staunchly defended last week's televised ceremony, co-hosted by Samantha Fox and Mick Fleetwood, which has been almost universally described in the media as 'a shambles'.

Russell claimed the annual event's problems did not lie in the choice of hosts, but in seating difficulties and traffic jams outside the Royal Albert Hall which delayed many people, including guest celebrities. Consequently, autocues and prompt boards had to be repeatedly changed at the last minue. 'Sam Fox and Mick held up particularly well at the end of the day', he asserted.

Other record company executives were less charitable. One commented: 'If you really think that Sam Fox and Mick Fleetwood represent the spirit of UK pop in 1989, you deserve everything you get. It was a fiasco.'

Russell on the other hand claimed: 'It was the first year we actually sold the show to the States and they loved it. It had the spontaneity they love.'

CHARTS

US45	When I'm With You / *Sheriff*
USLP	Don't Be Cruel / *Bobby Brown*
UK45	Something's Gotten Hold Of My Heart / *Marc Almond with Gene Pitney*
UKLP	The Legendary Roy Orbison / *Roy Orbison*
WEEK 2	
US45	Straight Up / *Paula Abdul*
USLP	Appetite For Destruction / *Guns N' Roses*
UK45	Something's Gotten Hold Of My Heart / *Marc Almond With Gene Pitney*
UKLP	Technique / *New Order*
WEEK 3	
US45	Straight Up / *Paula Abdul*
USLP	Don't Be Cruel / *Bobby Brown*
UK45	Something's Gotton Hold Of My Heart / *Marc Almond with Gene Pitney*
UKLP	The Raw And The Cooked / *Fine Young Cannibals*
WEEK 4	
US45	Straight Up / *Paula Abdul*
USLP	Don't Be Cruel / *Bobby Brown*
UK45	Belfast Child (EP) / *Simple Minds*
UKLP	A New Flame / *Simply Red*

Grammy-winner Chapman

THE GRAPEVINE

- **Grammy winners include George Michael, Bobby McFerrin, U2, Robert Palmer and Tracy Chapman.**
- **U2's 'The Joshua Tree' has become the first million selling CD.**
- **Producers L.A. & Babyface have 5 records in the US Top 40.**
- **Michael Jackson has announced that he will do no more live gigs.**
- **Billy Idol has sued a tabloid for saying he urinated on handicapped children at a show.**

Idol gossip

'EVIL' MADONNA DUMPED BY PEPSI

Pepsi Cola, anxious to avoid a boycott of their product, have bowed to pressure from Christian fundamentalist groups and dropped their controversial £5 million ($8 million) Madonna TV commercial.

The ad, which uses scenes from the video for Madonna's new single, 'Like A Prayer', shows a black Christ crying tears of blood after having been kissed by the singer, and depicts Madonna falling into the arms of a black woman in Episcopalian robes.

Despite the video's finale showing the healing power of Christianity with a rape victim, her skinhead attackers and Jesus joining police for a closing redemptive dance, the right-wing American Family Association denounced the ad as evil saying: 'Madonna is ridiculing Christianity while Pepsi Cola is putting the woman up as a clean and wholesome role model.'

Madonna's record company, Sire, has not yet chosen to comment, fearing any religious criticism might provoke a serious backlash against their artist.

GREEN ON RED

Annie Lennox, Peter Gabriel, U2's Edge and Chrissie Hynde were in Moscow this month to publicize the launching of a Greenpeace charity in Russia, and the promotion of a special compilation album, 'The Breakthrough', proceeds of which go to the ecological movement.

Material on the album is by a virtual Who's Who of Eighties rock, with names like Sting, INXS, Sade, Bryan Ferry, Dire Straits, Belinda Carlisle and Terence Trent D'Arby included.

'The scenes at the signing sessions at the state-run Melodiya shops were amazing,' said Neil Storey, publicist for the project.

Commenting on the reaction of pop-starved young Russians, he added: 'You can imagine the excitement at seeing so many pop stars in the flesh. The country is definitely opening up. I can envisage that within the next two years, cities like Leningrad and Kiev will be regular fixtures on world rock tours.'

Green star Chrissie Hynde

RUSHDIE: STEVENS BACKS DEATH THREAT

Music business colleagues of Seventies pop superstar Cat Stevens have been dismayed and angered by the former singer's support of Ayatolla Khomeini's execution order of *Satanic Verses* author, Salman Rushdie.

Addressing a meeting of the Islamic society of Kingston Polytechnic, near London, Stevens (who changed his name to Yusuf Islam after he became a Muslim 12 years ago) told students: 'The Koran makes it clear – if someone defames the Prophet, he must die.'

One music industry figure who worked closely with Stevens during his hit-making days said: 'What on earth is he playing at? Whatever happened to "Morning Has Broken"? His comments are going to alienate a lot of his old fans.'

Many radio stations in the US have started to ban Cat Stevens records in retaliation.

THE GRAPEVINE

- **Guns N' Roses have been kicked off an Aids benefit in New York due to their so-called anti-gay lyrics.**
- **McDonald's hamburgers pressed 45 million records of their menu set to music.**
- **Jethro Tull winning the first Hard Rock/Metal Grammy has got Metal musicians up in arms.**
- **Michael Jackson's 'Moon Walker' has become the all-time top selling music video.**

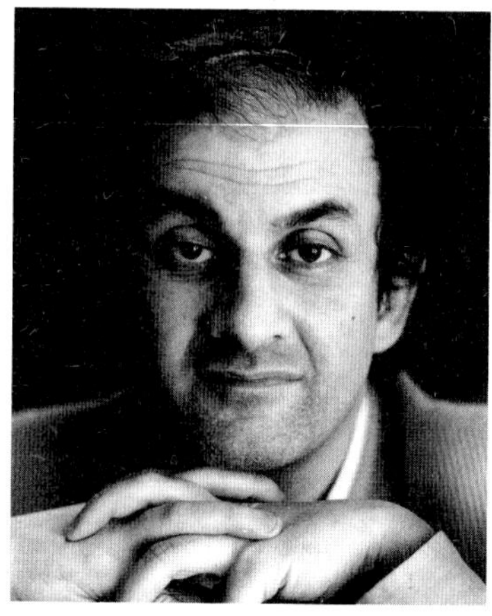

Author Rushdie

CHARTS

US45	Lost In Your Eyes *Debbie Gibson*
USLP	Don't Be Cruel *Bobby Brown*
UK45	Belfast Child (EP) *Simple Minds*
UKLP	A New Flame *Simple Red*
WEEK 2	
US45	Lost In Your Eyes *Debbie Gibson*
USLP	Electric Youth *Debbie Gibson*
UK45	Leave Me Alone *Michael Jackson*
UKLP	A New Flame *Simply Red*
WEEK 3	
US45	Lost In Your Eyes *Debbie Gibson*
USLP	Electric Youth *Debbie Gibson*
UK45	Too Many Broken Hearts *Jason Donovan*
UKLP	A New Flame *Simply Red*
WEEK 4	
US45	The Living Years *Mike & The Mechanics*
USLP	Electric Youth *Debbie Gibson*
UK45	Like A Prayer *Madonna*
UKLP	A New Flame *Simply Red*

HILLSBOROUGH: ROCK RALLIES ROUND

More and more rock artists are donating time and money to the Hillsborough Disaster Fund, set up after scores of Liverpool soccer fans were crushed to death at a recent FA Cup semi-final soccer match in Sheffield, England.

A new version of 'Ferry Across The Mersey' is being recorded by Gerry Marsden, who sang on the original 1964 hit version, together with fellow Liverpudlians Paul McCartney, Holly Johnson and The Christians.

Although producer Pete Waterman's attempt to reunite the three remaining Beatles was in vain, McCartney willingly agreed, delaying his own single for the special project. Many artists, including Cliff Richard, offered their services, but Waterman – who lives just outside Liverpool – incredibly turned them down, saying: 'The gesture has to come from the people who know the city. So I just asked them to make a donation.'

Following her Sheffield show, Yazz gave all the proceeds from her merchandising stall to the Fund and Liverpool-based China Crisis will play the opening night of their forthcoming tour at Sheffield University as a Hillsborough benefit.

Top: Merseyside mourns
Above: Gerry – new 'Ferry'
Left: Yazz – donation

MERLIN TAKES THE RAP

British rapper MC Merlin, who worked with Bomb The Bass, has been given four months youth custody on burglary charges and possession of marijuana, despite character references in court from Martin Heath, boss of Rhythm King Records.

The rapper is featured on the current Beatmasters single, unfortunately entitled 'Who's In The House', while an earlier Merlin single ironically bore the title 'Born Free'.

STRAIGHT OFFA MTV

A video by LA's controversial rap group NWA (Niggers With Attitude) has been banned in the USA by MTV.

The video for 'Straight Outta Compton', the title track from their album, shows Los Angeles police rounding up members of inner city gangs. The group, who hail from the Compton area of the city, are among those being arrested in the documentary-style video.

Bryan Turner, spokesman for NWA's Priority records, said: 'MTV evidently feels that the video may be sympathetic to gangs, but in no way is it pro-gang. It's purpose is to bring about an awareness of the problems facing inner city LA.'

Meanwhile, the European division of MTV is not only regularly showing the video, but is planning two half-hour specials on the group.

A spokesman said: 'I understand why it was banned in America. They felt that kids might see the gang scenes and copy them, but in Europe we don't have the same kind of problems.'

THE GRAPEVINE

- **Bruce Springsteen has lost his 18-month case against two E Street Band members and will have a multi million dollar payout.**
- **Bobby Brown has left his manager (as have Prince and Michael Jackson already this year).**
- **Stevie Wonder has announced he still plans to run for Mayor of Detroit.**
- **Craig Logan has left Bros.**
- **EMI has bought half of Chrysalis Records.**

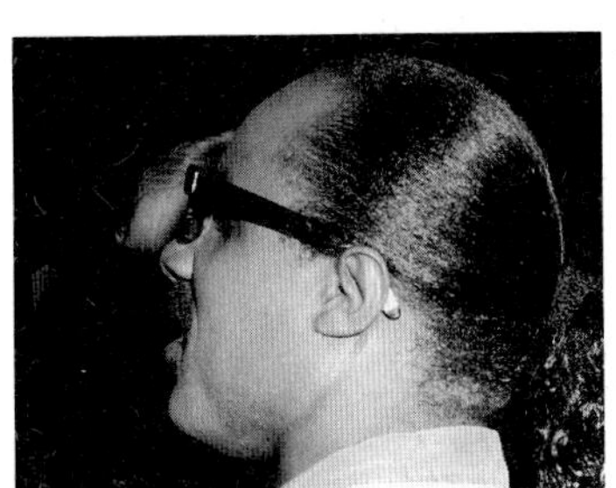

Politics for Stevie?

CHARTS

US45	Eternal Flame	*Bangles*
USLP	Electric Youth	*Debbie Gibson*
UK45	Like A Prayer	*Madonna*
UKLP	Like A Prayer	*Madonna*
WEEK 2		
US45	The Look	*Roxette*
USLP	Electric Youth	*Debbie Gibson*
UK45	Like A Prayer	*Madonna*
UKLP	Like A Prayer	*Madonna*
WEEK 3		
US45	She Drives Me Crazy	*Fine Young Cannibals*
USLP	Loc-Ed After Dark	*Tone Loc*
UK45	Like A Prayer	*Madonna*
UKLP	Now That's What I Call Music, 14	*Various*
WEEK 4		
US45	Like A Prayer	*Madonna*
USLP	Like A Prayer	*Madonna*
UK45	If You Don't Know Me By Now	*Simply Red*
UKLP	When The World Knows Your Name	*Deacon Blue*
WEEK 5		
US45	Like A Prayer	*Madonna*
USLP	Like A Prayer	*Madonna*
UK45	Eternal Flame	*Bangles*
UKLP	A New Flame	*Simply Red*

TABLOIDS SETTLE WITH STARS

Pet Shop Boys are vindicated

Simple Minds' Jim Kerr

Both The Pet Shop Boys and Simple Minds have been awarded substantial damages from British tabloid newspapers following recent libel action cases.

Jim Kerr of Simple Minds agreed to an out-of-court settlement after taking libel action against Tory MP Sir Nicholas Fairbairn and the Glasgow-based *Daily Record*.

In a front page article published by the *Record*, Fairbairn had alleged that Simple Minds and other Scottish bands had only participated in the Nelson Mandela birthday concert at Wembley 'to line their own pockets'. Kerr raised a defamation action in the Scottish Court of Session. Details of the settlement have not been made public.

Meanwhile, The Pet Shop Boys have been awarded 'substantial damages' in a libel action against the *Sun* and Jonathan King, record producer/impresario turned newspaper columnist.

Writing in his *Bizarre* column, King twice alleged that The Pet Shop Boys had infringed the copyright of Cat Stevens' 'Wild World' with their hit 'It's A Sin'.

At the request of the band, the *Sun* and King have agreed to pay the damages to The Jeffries Research Trust, an AIDS-related charity.

TAYLOR-MADE AWARDS

Newcomer Taylor Dayne picked up five awards at the annual New York Music Awards, including that for best debut artist of the year.

Other awards went to Debbie Gibson and Living Colour who each picked up three, while Public Enemy were judged Group of the Year.

Other winners were, 10,000 Maniacs (songwriter), They Might Be Giants (rock indie band), Full Force (r&b group), White Lion (metal band), Vanessa Williams (rising star), David Sanborn (jazz instrumentalist), Sa-Fire (new r&b artist), and Al B Sure (male pop vocalist), while The Smithereens' 'Green Thoughts' was voted Best Rock Album.

LADIES AND GENTLEMAN . . . THE BANK-ROLLING STONES

The Rolling Stones, who are predicted to make nearly $70 million from their new tour of the USA and Canada, are reported to have struck a deal in Toronto with Michael Cohl, who allegedly outbid rival promoter Bill Graham over the deal.

The tour will probably start in September, taking in 60 projected dates. Guns N' Roses, INXS and Living Colour have all been approached as support acts.

Meanwhile, The Who have been forced to add further dates at New Jersey's Giants Stadium, after tickets to their Radio City benefit performance of 'Tommy' sold out in less than four hours. Similarly, all 46,000 tickets to their July 9 25th Anniversary concert sold out in two hours, and a second concert was added for the following day.

Who – more dates

THE GRAPEVINE

- Madonna's video for 'Express Yourself' has cost a record $4 million.
- Ringo Starr has announced a US tour.
- Top Country act Keith Whitley has died of alcohol abuse at 33.
- Hall & Oates played some US dates as The Secret Chiefs.
- Bono joined Bob Dylan on stage during his UK tour.
- Cliff Richard has released his 100th single 'The Best Of Me'.

CHARTS

US45	Like A Prayer – *Madonna*
USLP	Like A Prayer – *Madonna*
UK45	Eternal Flame – *Bangles*
UKLP	Blast – *Holly Johnston*
WEEK 2	
US45	I'll Be There For You – *Bon Jovi*
USLP	Like A Prayer – *Madonna*
UK45	Hand On Your Heart – *Kylie Minogue*
UKLP	Street Fighting Years – *Simple Minds*
WEEK 3	
US45	Forever Your Girl – *Paula Abdul*
USLP	Like A Prayer – *Madonna*
UK45	Hand On Your Heart – *Kylie Minogue*
UKLP	Ten Good Reasons – *Jason Donovan*
WEEK 4	
US45	Forever Your Girl – *Paula Abdul*
USLP	Like A Prayer – *Madonna*
UK45	Ferry Cross The Mersey – *Gerry Marsden, Etc.*
UKLP	Ten Good Reasons – *Jason Donovan*

GREEN MACHINE IN FULL EFFECT

A benefit single, 'Spirit Of The Forest', featuring more than 60 artists, is being released by Virgin Records as part of the movement to focus world attention on the plight of Amazonian rain forests. All proceeds will go to the Earth Love Fund.

The single will be a double A-side, with different artists singing on each version.

Among those featured are Kate Bush, LL Cool J, Iggy Pop, Debbie Harry, Donna Summer, The Ramones, Little Steven, The B52s, Ringo Starr, Brother Beyond, Sam Brown, Fish, Pink Floyd, XTC, Big Country, Kim Wildes, Chris Rea, Was (Not Was), Fleetwood Mac, Thomas Dolby, Brian Wilson, Belinda Carlisle, Bonnie Raitt, Joni Mitchell and Olivia Newton-John.

GLASTONBURY 89: WHAT A SCORCHER!

Elvis, on his own

Simply Red Hucknall

The three-day NME-sponsored Glastonbury CND rock extravaganza took place amid blazing summer sunshine over the long weekend of June 17, 18 and 19 to a crowd estimated up to 100,000.

With people still arriving, the festival got under way with The Pixies and Throwing Muses, who preceded All About Eve and The Wonder Stuff. The Friday evening concluded with US writer/performer Suzanne Vega, who appeared despite two death threat phone calls.

Kicking off with The Bhundu Boys, the early part of Saturday's proceedings were dominated by Van Morrison, with Georgie Fame guesting on keyboards and harmony vocals. Recent BRITS award winners Fairground Attraction and Scotland's Proclaimers preceded Hothouse Flowers before top of the bill act, Elvis Costello, performed a solo acoustic set.

Sunday's bill consisted of Martin Stephenson, reggae band Black Uhuru, African superstars Youssou N'Dour and Fela Kuti, and Donovan acoustically replaying some of his Sixties hits. The Waterboys topped the bill with their folk rock and Gaelic-influenced material.

There were a few arrests, but local police described the event as 'a great success considering the numbers involved'.

CHARTS

US45	Rock On *Michael Damian*
USLP	The Raw And The Cooked *Fine Young Cannibals*
UK45	Ferry Cross The Mersey *Gerry Marsden, Etc.*
UKLP	The Miracle *Queen*
	WEEK 2
US45	Rock On *Michael Damian*
USLP	The Raw And The Cooked *Fine Young Cannibals*
UK45	Ferry Cross The Mersey *Gerry Marsden, Etc.*
UKLP	The Miracle *Queen*
	WEEK 3
US45	I'll Be Loving You (Forever) *New Kids On The Block*
USLP	The Raw And The Cooked *Fine Young Cannibals*
UK45	Sealed With A Kiss *Jason Donovan*
UKLP	The Hits Album, 10 *Various*
	WEEK 4
US45	Satisfied *Richard Marx*
USLP	The Raw And The Cooked *Fine Young Cannibals*
UK45	Sealed With A Kiss *Jason Donovan*
UKLP	The Hits Album, 10 *Various*

STAR QUOTE

MICK HUCKNALL

of Simply Red

'I think a lot of white bands miss the point of rock'n'roll. But when you hear Public Enemy it suddenly comes back to life.'

THE GRAPEVINE

- **The Stray Cats are back on the road and The Pet Shop Boys have announced that their first tour will open in Japan.**
- **Jefferson Airplane have re-united.**
- **100 fans have been hurt at a Pogues/UB 40 gig.**
- **A lot of unseen film footage of *Woodstock* has come to light 20 years after the event.**

GEORGE MICHAEL, DYLAN, ELVIS, STEVIE IN PARIS BASH

Elvis Costello, Stevie Wonder, George Michael and Bob Dylan were among the line up for 'The Liberty Show', a 12-hour extravaganza in Paris on June 25.

The gig, which marks part of the French Revolution bicentenary celebrations, took place at the Hippodrome De Vincennes. It also featured Rod Stewart, Tracy Chapman, Edie Brickell & The New Bohemians, Cyndi Lauper, The Gipsy Kings, Boris Grebenshikov and Deon Estus.

The midday to midnight concert was the largest ever rock gig to take place in France and was transmitted to 50 countries.

Michael in Paris match

Pogues' gallery

PUBLIC ENEMY TO CHUCK IT IN?

Radical rap stars Public Enemy, revolutionary chic or reactionary shock?

CBS Records have gone to great pains to assure record dealers throughout the USA that their rap group Public Enemy are not anti-Semitic. The assurances have been made following controversial remarks made by former group member, Professor Griff, in a *Washington Times* interview.

In the interview, Griff – who is a Muslim and strong supporter of Louis Farrakhan, well-known for his anti-Semitic views – accused Jews of 'the majority of wickedness that goes on across the globe'. He also said that Jews and other white groups had perpetrated genocide and conducted AIDS experiments on black groups in South Africa.

Griff was immediately dismissed from Public Enemy, and they issued a statement disassociating themselves from his remarks. This was circulated to every major record chain-store throughout the country in an attempt to avoid any backlash.

STONES TOUR ANGERS PROMOTERS

The Rolling Stones have angered promoters on their US tour by offering them a flat fee at gigs, rather than the more traditional arrangement of a percentage of ticket sales.

Concert Productions International – who are staging the tour – have proposed a basic $25,000 (£15,600) per concert to promoters. This has angered many, several of whom have threatened to withdraw their services, claiming that the normal gate percentage would yield at least twice as much.

It has been suggested that the deal has been arrived at in the light of CPI's failure to find a second commercial sponsor for the tour, MTV already having been signed.

UK renown for Bobby Brown

SOUL II SOUL IN TOTP WALKOUT

After a five-hour row with *Top of the Pops* producer Paul Ciani, Soul II Soul have pulled out of this top-rated UK TV show.

Ciani objected to two bars of the live vocal which he claimed didn't sound like the seven inch version of the group's No. 1 hit 'Back To Life'. He gave the trio an ultimatum – either mime or scrap their appearance.

Following the group's refusal to comply with Ciani's demand, the video was subsequently shown for the third time. A disappointed Jazzie B. said afterwards for the group: 'It was the principle of the matter. We wanted to perform the song live, as an appreciation to all the people who had bought the record and supported us. Being on *Top of the Pops*, was something we'd waited for all our lives.'

Soul's Jazzie B.

THE GRAPEVINE

- **Band Aid has ceased business after five years having raised £90 million ($140 million).**
- **A Japanese company has bought 25 per cent of Virgin.**
- **Bobby Brown has sold out Wembley for eight nights.**
- **Neil Diamond equalled the crowd record for indoor shows when he played ten nights at the LA Forum.**
- **The Glastonbury festival was the biggest of its kind in the UK since the Sixties.**

CHARTS

US45	Baby Don't Forget My Number – *Milli Vanilli*
USLP	The Raw And The Cooked – *Fine Young Cannibals*
UK45	Back To Life – *Soul II Soul*
UKLP	Batman – *Prince*
WEEK 2	
US45	Good Thing – *Fine Young Cannibals*
USLP	The Raw And The Cooked – *Fine Young Cannibals*
UK45	Back To Life – *Soul II Soul*
UKLP	Batman – *Prince*
WEEK 3	
US45	If You Don't Know Me By Now – *Simply Red*
USLP	The Raw And The Cooked – *Fine Young Cannibals*
UK45	Back To Life – *Soul II Soul*
UKLP	Club Classics Vol.1 – *Soul II Soul*
WEEK 4	
US45	Toy Soldiers – *Martika*
USLP	Batman – *Prince/Soundtrack*
UK45	You'll Never Stop Me From Loving You – *Sonia*
UKLP	Club Classics Vol.1 – *Soul II Soul*
WEEK 5	
US45	Toy Soldiers – *Martika*
USLP	Batman – *Prince/Soundtrack*
UK45	You'll Never Stop Me From Loving You – *Sonia*
UKLP	A New Flame – *Simply Red*

SHERIFF OF NOTTINGHAM STRIKES AGAIN

Controversial rap group Niggers With Attitude and electro band Depeche Mode have run into trouble over their respective British promotional campaigns.

Teaser advertising posters erected in Nottingham as part of a British promotional campaign for Niggers With Attitude have been taken down by the group's label following complaints by the Nottingham police, who learned of NWA's reputation. Tracks on the group's current album include 'Fuck The Police' and 'Gangsta Gangsta'.

Meanwhile, the city's local newspaper, *The Nottingham Evening Post*, along with other provincial papers, has rejected classified ads placed by Depeche Mode which simply read 'Your own personal Jesus' – the title of the group's latest single – together with a telephone number, which, when dialled, played the new release.

Depeche Mode in a recent Los Angeles press conference

The newspapers decided to veto the ads on the grounds that they may cause offence.

MAC THE RIFE

Paul McCartney will play live dates for the first time in 13 years when he starts a world tour in Oslo on September 26. Following a series of shows in Europe, he will embark upon the British leg in January 1990.

At a press conference, McCartney unveiled his new band and played an exclusive set for press and fan club members. He also told journalists that he intends taking along members of Friends of the Earth to each concert, where they will have a booth to spread their ecological message – something McCartney supports strongly.

In North America, box office records were smashed when tickets for 13 shows in four cities – New York, Chicago, Los Angeles and Montreal – sold out in less than an hour.

CHARTS

US45	Batdance *Prince*
USLP	Batman *Prince/Soundtrack*
UK45	Swing The Mood *Jive Bunny & The Mastermixers*
UKLP	Cuts Both Ways *Gloria Estefan*
WEEK 2	
US45	Right Here Waiting *Richard Marx*
USLP	Batman *Prince/Soundtrack*
UK45	Swing The Mood *Jive Bunny & The Mastermixers*
UKLP	Cuts Both Ways *Gloria Estefan*
WEEK 3	
US45	Right Here Waiting *Richard Marx*
USLP	Batman *Prince/Soundtrack*
UK45	Swing The Mood *Jive Bunny & The Mastermixers*
UKLP	Cuts Both Ways *Gloria Estefan*
WEEK 4	
US45	Right Here Waiting *Richard Marx*
USLP	Batman *Prince/Soundtrack*
UK45	Swing The Mood *Jive Bunny & The Mastermixers*
UKLP	Cuts Both Ways *Gloria Estefan*

De La Soul sampling?

MATT & LUKE WARM

With fears growing that many tickets for Bros' London Wembley concert with Debbie Gibson would be unsold, organizers drastically dropped the ticket price.

Outside the stadium, touts were left with their hands full of unwanted tickets. £15 ($24) tickets were desperately being offered for as little as £1 ($1.60).

Wembley officials put on a brave face, saying: 'Things could have been a lot worse. If you believed everything written in the papers, you would have been expecting a half-full stadium. Admittedly, it wasn't sold out, but it was still a successful day from our point of view.'

Bros were similarly upbeat over the gig, brother Matt shouting from the stage: 'We proved the world wrong about Bros. We've played the stadium and we're here to stay.'

THE GRAPEVINE

- **Island records have been sold to Dutch conglomerate Polygram for £300 million ($480 million); Island act (& shareholders) U2 have made £30 million ($48 million) from this.**
- **De La Soul have been sued by Sixties group The Turtles over alleged sampling.**
- **Poco have re-united.**
- **Gloria Estafan has turned down a multi-million deal to advertise Diet Coke.**
- **Public Enemy are back together.**

Gloria – thumbs down diet

CHARTS

US45	Cold Hearted *Paula Abdul*
USLP	Repeat Offender *Richard Marx*
UK45	Swing The Mood *Jive Bunny & The Mastermixers*
UKLP	Now That's What I Call Music, 15 *Various*
	WEEK 2
US45	Hangin' Tough *New Kids On The Block*
USLP	Hangin' Tough *New Kids On The Block*
UK45	Ride On Time *Black Box*
UKLP	Now That's What I Call Music, 15 *Various*
	WEEK 3
US45	Don't Wanna Lose You *Gloria Estefan*
USLP	Hangin' Tough *New Kids On The Block*
UK45	Ride On Time *Black Box*
UKLP	Now That's What I Call Music, 15 *Various*
	WEEK 4
US45	Girl I'm Gonna Miss You *Milli Vanilli*
USLP	Girl You Know It's True *Milli Vanilli*
UK45	Ride On Time *Black Box*
UKLP	Aspects of Love *Original Cast*
	WEEK 5
US45	Girl I'm Gonna Miss You *Milli Vanilli*
USLP	Girl You Know It's True *Milli Vanilli*
UK45	Ride On Time *Black Box*
UKLP	We Two Are One *Eurythmics*

THE GRAPEVINE

- **A UK MP has called for a ban on Guns N' Roses T-Shirts depicting a woman raped by a robot.**
- **Ex-member Roger Waters has sued Pink Floyd over their continued use of his inflatable pig.**
- **The Stones are reportedly not getting on too well together on their US tour.**

MORE PROBLEMS IN IRELAND

For a handful of Irish acts, the last few weeks have been beset by a whole series of troubles and controversy.

Firstly U2's Adam Clayton was found guilty of possession of cannabis after police discovered the substance wrapped in cellophane in the back of his car.

He was ordered to pay £21,000 ($33,000) to the Women's Aid and Refuge Centre in Dublin. His troubles were compounded a week later when police charged him with drink-driving following a farewell celebration party for The Edge's sister, who was emigrating to Australia.

Shortly after, The Pogues' Shane Macgowan was fined £150 ($240) for possession of cannabis after being arrested on suspicion of being drunk and disorderly.

Meanwhile, Sinead O'Connor has attracted press hostility after taking part in a Troops Out rally in Dublin against the presence of British soldiers in Northern Ireland. O'Connor was reportedly annoyed when photographers attempted to take photos of her on stage, and responded with expletives.

Still in Dublin, U2 have also come in for criticism over ticket prices for their five Irish dates. The tickets, priced at £17 and £21 ($27 & $34) are the most expensive ever for rock concerts in Ireland, and have provoked claims that they are 'excessive' and 'exploitative' from community leaders, politicians and representatives from the Union of Students in Ireland.

Sinead (top) runs into Irish troubles, not quite like those besetting Shane (below).

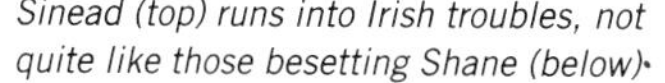

MOTLEY CRUE SUED BY 'STAND IN'

Matthew Trippe, who claims he was asked to masquerade as Nickie Sixx of Motley Crewe for two years, takes the group to court next month over unpaid royalties.

The deception started after Sixx was recovering from a car crash in 1983, at which point Trippe was asked by the group to step in anonymously. He stayed with the band until 1985, during which time he claims he contributed song material under Sixx's name.

After magazine allegations of black magic and satanism, Motley Crue were forced to tone down this aspect of their act. Since Sixx's involvement in this was greatest of all, his car crash was seen as a convenience and the substitution by Trippe encouraged by management.

The bizarre story has been strenuously denied by Motley Crue's label, Elektra.

Nickie Sixx – was Trippe necessary?

NEW KIDS GET OLD BEATLES REACTIONS!

The teenage Boston band New Kids On The Block, who first charted back in 1986, are now the hottest act in America. They have the number one single and LP with another three singles and one album also charting.

The band are brain child of black producer/songwriter Maurice Starr – the man behind New Edition and Bobby Brown. They are evoking the same mania as George Michael or Duran Duran, and many liken the reaction to Beatlemania in the mid 60s.

New Kids On The Block, new name for the 'Nineties

ACID HOUSE – UK GOVERNMENT STRIKES BACK

The British Government are urgently reviewing local authority powers in an effort to control the growing number of Acid House raves, and police have set up special squads to combat the threat of drugs and violence.

Sixteen officers were injured recently at Britain's largest ever Acid House party at Reigate, Surrey, while dozens of drug-related arrests were made at a Santa Pod racetrack rave in Northamptonshire in the East Midlands.

Party-planners are having to think of new ways to bypass the clampdown, and one organiser – Cutmaster J – found a loophole.

'I am making a film and inviting 40,000 people to pay £25 to be extras', he said. But his event was postponed when it transpired the police has 2,000 riot squad officers and 300 plain clothes cops on standby. 'If we had gone ahead it would have been war', Cutmaster J said.

Government and police obviously hope the first prosecution of an Acid House party organiser will be a major deterrent – as the man in question received an unbelievable ten-year sentence for permitting premises to be used for the supply of drugs.

A National Council for Civil Liberties spokesman said: 'It certainly seems excessive and specifically designed to deter Acid House parties. It plays along with the general feeling that Acid House parties are illegal, which of course they're not'.

CHARTS

US45	Miss You Much *Janet Jackson*
USLP	Forever Your Girl *Paula Abdul*
UK45	Ride On Time *Black Box*
UKLP	The Seeds Of Love *Tears For Fears*
WEEK 2	
US45	Miss You Much *Janet Jackson*
USLP	Dr. Feelgood *Motley Crue*
UK45	Ride On Time *Black Box*
UKLP	The Seeds Of Love *Tears For Fears*
WEEK 3	
US45	Miss You Much *Janet Jackson*
USLP	Dr. Feelgood *Motley Crue*
UK45	That's What I Like *Jive Bunny & Mastermixers*
UKLP	Enjoy Yourself *Kylie Minogue*
WEEK 4	
US45	Miss You Much *Janet Jackson*
USLP	Janet Jackson's Rhythm Nation 1814 *Janet Jackson*
UK45	That's What I Like *Jive Bunny & Mastermixers*
UKLP	Wild! *Erasure*

- **After protests, U2 have cut ticket costs for their Irish tour.**
- **Currently suing their ex-managers are Billy Joel, for $90 million, and Gloria Estafan, while Beach Boy Brian Wilson is suing his dad for $100 million.**
- **Top earners for 88/89 were Jacko with $125 million (£78 million), Pink Floyd $56 million (£35 million), The Stones $55 million (£34 million) and George Michael with a paltry $47 million (£29 million).**

Billy Joel sues

Top wack Jacko

BLACK BOXING MATCH

Loleatta Holloway, the singer whose voice has been sampled extensively on Black Box's six-week British No. 1 hit 'Ride On Time', has bitterly attacked the Italian group. She claims she is receiving no money or credit for the half-million-seller, which uses large parts of her vocal from the Seventies Disco hit 'Love Sensation'.

Loleatta, currently in the UK, said: 'What hurts me is that it's being played now, and somebody else is getting the credit for my voice. I say Katrina is a phoney and she knows it'.

In response, Black Box's UK label boss has stated: 'The original owners Salsoul will certainly be paid compensation for the sample; also we have insisted that, as part of any deal, Loleatta is paid'.

'The most important point here is not whether Black Box sampled Loleatta, but the whole issue of sampling itself. Until a ruling is made one way or another, this will continue. You can't de-invent the sampling machine'.

Katrina of Black Box: their sampling of Seventies smash has Holloway hopping mad

NOVEMBER

STONES & ROSES

Guns N' Roses joined the ultra successful Rolling Stones tour for their LA shows – and stole the headlines from the bill toppers!

The reason was the much publicized lyrics of the Guns N' Roses song 'One In a Million', in which they refer to 'faggots' and 'niggers'. There was much speculation about what would happen when they appeared after black rock group Living Colour, who opened the show.

On the first night, Living Colour said nothing and Guns N' Rose's leader Axl Rose tried to defend his controversial lyric on stage before accusing members of his band of drug abuse, saying he would never play with them again. He then fell off stage!

On the second night, Living Colour's leader Vernon Reid announced before their show: 'If you don't have a problem with gay people or black people, don't call them 'faggots' or 'niggers'.'

This met with a wildly enthusiastic reaction from the huge crowd and may have been the reason that Axl Rose on the remaining three shows (yes he did play with them again!) was incredibly subdued and uncharacteristically polite.

As for the Stones – they stole the show, of course, but with carefully planned performances that lacked spontaneity.

AXL ROSE

of Guns n' Roses

'Now I'm a rich successful asshole'.

Guns N'Roses (above) steal the limelight from the Rolling Stones, only to be upstaged eventually by bottom-of-the-bill Living Colour (right)

NEW KIDS ON THE ROAD

The most in-demand tickets in many US towns is not one for the Stones but for the New Kids On The Block's shows.

The tour hit Buffalo, New York and the Kids' energy-packed 90 minute set gave their 16,000 screaming fans many highspots to remember.

Apart from singing all the hits from their five million selling 'Hangin' Tough' album they also did a few Christmas oldies and even the Jackson Five's 'I'll Be There'.

The Kids undoubtedly have the talent to be one of the 90s biggest acts.

DECADE'S BEST ALBUMS, SAYS ROLLING STONE

Rolling Stone magazine editors have announced their top five albums of the eighties. They are: 1 'London Calling' – The Clash 2 'Purple Rain' – Prince 3 'The Joshua Tree' – U2 4 'Remain In Light' – Talking Heads 5 'Graceland' – Paul Simon

CHARTS

US45	Listen To Your Heart *Roxette*
USLP	Janet Jackson's Rhythm Nation 1814 *Janet Jackson*
UK45	That's What I Like *Jive Bunny & Mastermixers*
UKLP	Wild! *Erasure*
WEEK 2	
US45	When I See You Smile *Bad English*
USLP	Janet Jackson's Rythm Nation 1814 *Janet Jackson*
UK45	All Around The World *Lisa Stansfield*
UKLP	Wild! *Erasure*
WEEK 3	
US45	When I See You Smile *Bad English*
USLP	Janet Jackson's Rhythm Nation 1814 *Janet Jackson*
UK45	All Around The World *Lisa Stansfield*
UKLP	The Road To Hell *Chris Rea*
WEEK 4	
US45	Blame It On The Rain *Milli Vanilli*
USLP	Girl You Know It's True *Milli Vanilli*
UK45	All Around The World *Lisa Stansfield*
UKLP	The Road To Hell *Chris Rea*

THE GRAPEVINE

- **Elton John has played Madison Square Garden for a record 30th time.**
- **Five tracks on the new Tracy Chapman album have been banned in South Africa.**
- **Top US production team LA & Babyface have formed their own label.**
- **The Wailers are now claiming 50% of Bob Marley's estate.**
- **New to the 'Rock'n'Roll Hall of Fame': The Who, Four Tops, Kinks and Simon & Garfunkel.**

Premier producers LA & Babyface

ARTISTS STILL HAVE FAITH AND HOPE IN CHARITY

There seems no end to the eighties phenomenon – 'the charity record' – as we enter the nine-

Topping the charts now is Band Aid II with the song that started it all in 1984: 'Do They Know It's Christmas'. This version is a Stock, Aitken, Waterman production featuring 30 current squeaky clean stars, including Kylie Minogue, Jason Donovan, Cliff Richard, Bros, Sonia and Wet Wet Wet.

Also released or coming soon are 'Now That We've Found Love' with Soul II Soul, Curiosity and S'Express (in aid of the 51 people who died in the recent Thames riverboat disaster), the Rock Aid Armenia single 'Smoke On The Water' (starring members of Deep Purple, Black Sabbath, Pink Floyd, Queen, Yes, Iron Maiden and Bryan Adams) and the Make A Difference Foundation's album to help combat drug and alcohol abuse, which includes Bon Jovi, Ozzy Osbourne and Motley Crue.

A galaxy of stars are also involved in Rock Against Repatriation, to help the Vietnamese boat people.

Last (but not least!) NME is releasing its second charity album 'The Last Temptation of Elvis', featuring Presley songs performed by Bruce Springsteen, Paul McCartney, Jesus & Mary Chain, Hall & Oates and others. Money from this project will help handicapped children.

Kylie – squeaky?

Sabbath –our men for Armenia

NME 1989 POLL RESULTS

Winners of the NME Critics and Readers Polls for 1989 were:

Critics' Best Albums

1 'Three Feet High and Rising' – De La Soul
2 'The Stone Roses' – The Stone Roses
3 'New York' – Lou Reed
4 'Doolittle' – Pixies
5 'Technique' – New Order

Critics' Best Singles

1 'She Bangs The Drum' – Stone Roses
2 'Fool's Gold' – Stone Roses
3 'Can't Be Sure' – Sundays
4 'Made of Stone' – Stone Roses
5 'Pacific State' – 808 State

Stone Roses had an almost clear sweep of the NME Readers Poll as well, winning 'Band of the Year', 'LP of the Year', 'Single of the Year' ('Fool's Gold') and 'Best New Artist of the Year'. Morrissey was voted 'Top Solo Artist'.

Comin' up – Roses

STAR

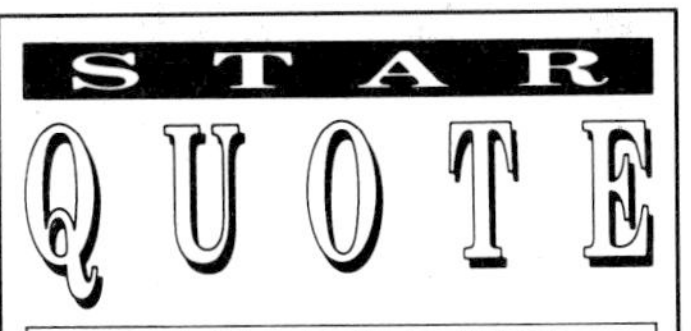

IAN BROWN

of Stone Roses

'We're the most important group in the world, because we've got the best songs and we haven't even begun to show our potential yet'.

1990, '91, '92 . . .?

Over the years, NME writers have had a great track record picking the stars of tomorrow. Their tips for stardom in the nineties are well worth checking out. In alphabetical order they are:

Biting Tongues, Carter The Unstoppable Sex Machine, The Charlatans, The Charlottes, Cranes, Fury Things, Hollow Men, Katydids, Love's Young Nightmare, MC Buzz B, Milltown Brothers, The Mock Turtles, New Fast Automatic Daffodils, The Popinjays, Power of Dreams, Ride, Social Kaos, Vanilla Sound Corps and Where's The Beach.

THE GRAPEVINE

- **US figures show that vinyl record sales account for only 20% of singles and 5% of albums, with cassette singles sales up 500% this year.**
- **In the UK, sales of No. 1 singles are staggeringly low, although cassette singles sales are up 700% and album sales are up 12%.**
- **Personics, the successful US 'tape what you like in the store' system, is to be launched in the UK in 1990.**

CHARTS

Week	Chart	Title	Artist
	US45	Blame It On The Rain	*Milli Vanilli*
	USLP	Girl You Know It's True	*Milli Vanilli*
	UK45	You Got It	*New Kids On The Block*
	UKLP	But Seriously	*Phil Collins*
WEEK 2	US45	We Didn't Start The Fire	*Billy Joel*
	USLP	Girl You Know It's True	*Milli Vanilla*
	UK45	You Got It	*New Kids On The Block*
	UKLP	But Seriously	*Phil Collins*
WEEK 3	US45	We Didn't Start The Fire	*Billy Joel*
	USLP	Storm Front	*Billy Joel*
	UK45	The Eve Of The War	*Jeff Wayne/Ben Liebrand*
	UKLP	But Seriously	*Phil Collins*
WEEK 4	US45	Another Day In paradise	*Phil Collins*
	USLP	Girl You Know It's True	*Milli Vanilli*
	UK45	Do They Know It's Christmas?	*Band Aid 2*
	UKLP	But Seriously	*Phil Collins*
WEEK 5	US45	No Chart Published	
	USLP	No Chart Published	
	UK45	Do They Know Its Christmas	*Band Aid 2*
	UKLP	. . . But Seriously	*Phil Collins*

THE 1990s

Every era in rock history has produced something lasting, and the 1990s saw the arrival of several artists who have made a solid (and commercial) start to the decade.

They come from many musical areas. There is the stadium rock of Extreme and the more raucous Nirvana, the rap of Hammer (who dropped his 'M.C.' epithet in 1991, the year he won three Grammy Awards and a Hammer doll was sold as one of Barbie's 'celebrity friends'), country singer Garth Brooks, who became the biggest selling artist in America with three multi-platinum albums, but meant little elsewhere, Paula Abdul, the Queen of the dance floor, REM (active in the later 1980s, but slow developers), who discovered their destiny as the leading singles act in Britain with six Top 40 hits in 1991, and two young British-based women, the multi-talented black-sounding Lisa Stansfield and Beverley Craven (in the Carole King mould), who proved that it was perfectly feasible to be female and promise a long career, which only a handful of females had achieved in the previous 35 years. The names above were the relatively mainstream newcomers, together with soul/R&B acts like Bobby Brown (ex-New Edition), gospel singer Amy Grant (five platinum albums by 1992, when she was nominated for four Grammies), Robert Clivilles and David Cole (better known as songwriter/producers C&C Music Factory) and such retro-rock acts as The Stone Roses and James. Then there were The KLF and EMF; the former duo, Scotsmen Bill Drummond and Jimmy Cauty, scored three UK Top 3 singles in 1991, even involving country legend Tammy Wynette in 'Justified & Ancient', while the latter, a quintet from the West of England, became perhaps the very first indie band with real teenybop appeal. Among the others who may retain their popularity are Wilson Phillips, the daughters of Beach Boy Brian Wilson and (Mama &) Papa John Phillips, Mariah Carey (whose first five singles reached Number One, a first), doo-wop hip-hop acts Color Me Badd (sic) and Boyz II Men, and Seal, whose music crosses many barriers. While none of these acts are yet in the Madonna/Prince/Michael Jackson/Dire Straits etc. league, several of them could be by mid-decade.

As a new generation of independent labels grows up (including Mute, Factory and Creation), all their role models have been absorbed by the six major corporations: Polygram bought Island and A&M, EMI Chrysalis and Virgin, and with RCA owned by the German conglomerate BMG, and both CBS/Columbia and MCA in Japanese hands, WEA (itself the result of a marriage/merger between three major indies of the 1960s) is the only American major label of the moment. This is probably a natural course of events, and part of the rejuvenation process, just as the mortality rate among stars of the past is bound to increase as original rock immortals of the 1950s and 1960s grow older: Gene Clark, vocalist with The Byrds, erstwhile 'mod' hero Steve Marriott, Freddie Mercury of Queen (the biggest rock celebrity victim of AIDS thus far) plus jazz trumpet star Miles Davis and bluesman Willie Dixon (who had at least reached retirement age), were some of the big names who joined the rock music roll of honour.

The early years of the 1990s have produced no obvious new direction for popular music, but a future sensation is already starting to blossom – rock music will live to fight many more days . . .

1 Happy Mondays
2 Deee - Lite
3 Janet Jackson
4 Vanilla Ice

1

2

3

4

OLD FOLKS ROAM

The Rolling Stones look set to play indoor London shows in April or May. But the band are delaying a final decision until the end of their American commitments.

One rumour is that they will do a string of dates at Wembley Arena, though some sources say the band may opt for the new Docklands Arena.

There is no development on the rumour that the 'Stones may be added to the bill for the Knebworth festival which takes place in June and already features ageing rockers Phil Collins, Paul McCartney and Status Quo.

Still rolling – Wood, Watts, Wyman, Jagger and Richards

CHARTS

Week	Chart	Title	Artist
	US45	No Chart Published	
	USLP	No Chart Published	
	UK45	Do They Know Its Christmas	*Band Aid 2*
	UKLP	. . . But Seriously	*Phil Collins*
WEEK 2	US45	Another Day In Paradise	*Phil Collins*
	USLP	Girl You Know Its True	*Milli Vanilli*
	UK45	Hangin' Tough	*New Kids On The Block*
	UKLP	. . . But Seriously	*Phil Collins*
WEEK 3	US45	How Am I Supposed to Live Without You	*Michael Bolton*
	USLP	. . . But Seriously	*Phil Collins*
	UK45	Tears On My Pillow	*Kylie Minogue*
	UKLP	Colour	*The Christians*
WEEK 4	US45	How Am I Supposed To Live Without You	*Michael Bolton*
	USLP	. . . But Seriously	*Phil Collins*
	UK45	Nothing Compares 2 U	*Sinead O'Connor*
	UKLP	Colour	*The Christians*

DON LETS GO OF MICK

Big Audio Dynamite, pictured here at the European launch of the MTV music channel, may have played their last together after Jones reveals Clash of interests.

Big Audio Dynamite are believed to have split, with Don Letts leaving to form a new group with the core of BAD's musicians. Reports during the bands last tour suggested that despite the success of their last LP 'Megatop Phoenix', Mick Jones was becoming distanced from his colleagues.

If Jones has left the group, it lends credence to rumours that The Clash will reform to play London dates this summer.

Seminal punks, The Clash are still held in high regard by fans worldwide – particularly in the 'States where critics on Rolling Stone magazine recently voted 'London Calling' LP of the 'Eighties.

U2's DAYS NUMBERED?

Sensational reports that U2 were on the verge of splitting have flooded the Irish media after comments made by singer Bono during their four dates in Dublin.

The singer's outburst took place during the second show of U2's residency in the city's dockland venue Point Depot. In front of a 50,000 crowd he explained: "We've been around for ten years and we've enjoyed it . . . we say thank you to those who believed in us from the beginning. But we've got to go away for a little while"

THE GRAPEVINE

- **Neil Young is in a legal wrangle over a TV jeans ad which uses one of his songs without permission.**
- **Fresh from his US tour, Terence Trent D'arby starts the new decade with a "secret" gig at London's Marquee club.**
- **A has offered over £30,000 ($78,000) for the Sex Pistols to reform, but without John (Rotten) Lydon.**
- **Billboard magazine confirm Kids On The Block as biggest selling pop artists of 1989.**

Megastars for the Nineties? New Kids On The Block

NEW SKID IN THE DOCK

Skid Row singer Sebastian Bach is on bail in America after being arrested following a bottle-throwing indident on the band's current tour.

Details are sketchy, but it's thought Bach was detained after throwing a bottle into the audience which struck a young woman causing facial injuries.

Trouble allegedly flared at the gig in Springfield, Massachusetts when Bach was hit by a bottle thrown from the audience – most of whom were waiting for headliners Aerosmith.

CULT GET THEIR ASTBURY KICKED

Ian Astbury, lead singer with The Cult, was badly beaten up during a show on the band's American tour.

The Cult's show in Daytona, Ohio turned ugly when the venue's security was seen to rough-up members of the 8,000 strong audience.

Astbury claimed: "This one guy was beating several people. I jumped down into the pit and this guy turned round and beat me to the ground"

'When I was lying there, these five security guys surrounded me and gestured to me to get up – I knew they just wanted to beat the shit out of me'

Astbury however clambered back to the stage and continued the gig.

Cult rocker Astbury

PHONE DAVE FOR YOUR FAVE

David Bowie is setting up his own global jukebox by inviting fans to choose the songs they want to hear on his 'farewell' world tour.

The 'Dial A Dave Fave' plan gives callers the chance to vote for anything from Bowie's back catalogue, with the most requested songs in each country forming the basis of the live set.

At a London press conference, Bowie said that the tour, which starts in Canada on March 4th, will be the last chance fans will get to hear his biggest hits on the live stage.

'I'm not retiring, it's not going to be my last tour, but I'm afraid it will probably be the last time I play those songs' he said.

Bowie: 'not retiring'

THE GRAPEVINE

- **Ike Turner has been convicted in Santa Monica, on charges of illegal possession of a gun and driving under the influence of cocaine.**
- **Bob Dylan has been awarded one of France's highest honours, the Commander Of The Order Of Arts And Letters. He received the order from the Culture Minister whilst in Paris on his European tour.**
- **Adam Ant makes a comeback after five years, with a single 'Room At The Top'; he has been pursuing acting in the 'States.**

BROKEN BONE IDOL

Billy Idol has been seriously injured and held in intensve care at the famous Cedars-Sinai Medical Centre in America following a motor cycle accident.

Idol's Harley-Davidson collided with another vehicle when he was on his way home from recording his new album, 'Charmed Life', at a Hollywood studio. He sustained a fractured leg and arm in the collision and had to undergo over seven hours of surgery.

It is not known how these injuries will affect Idol's appearance in Oliver Stone's forthcoming Jim Morrison biopic, which is scheduled to start filming soon . . . The release of his new album, his upcoming tour and all other projects have, not surprisingly, been put on hold until his condition can be fully assessed.

Biker Billy Idol on his Harley Davidson during a benefit event for muscular dystrophy charities in Glendale, California, not long before his accident on the same motorcycle

CHARTS

US45	How Am I Supposed To Live Without You *Michael Bolton*
USLP	. . . But Seriously *Phil Collins*
UK45	Nothing Compares 2 U *Sinead O'Connor*
UKLP	. . . But Seriously *Phil Collins*
WEEK 2	
US45	How Am I Supposed To Live Without You *Michael Bolton*
USLP	Forever Your Girl *Paula Abdul*
UK45	Nothing Compares 2 U *Sinead O'Connor*
UKLP	. . . But Seriously *Phil Collins*
WEEK 3	
US45	Opposites Attract *Paula Abdul*
USLP	Forever Your Girl *Paula Abdul*
UK45	Nothing Compares 2 U *Sinead O'Connor*
UKLP	. . . But Seriously *Phil Collins*
WEEK 4	
US45	Opposites Attract *Paula Abdul*
USLP	Forever Your Girl *Paula Abdul*
UK45	Nothing Compares 2 U *Sinead O'Connor*
UKLP	. . . But Seriously *Phil Collins*

MANDELA RELEASE BASH FOR WEMBLEY

A massive concert to celebrate the release from jail after 27 years of South African anti-apartheid leader Nelson Mandela is set for

London's Wembley Stadium on Easter Monday, April 16th. Among those who have agreed to appear are Peter Gabriel, Tracy Chapman, Simple Minds, the Neville Brothers, Neil Young, Hugh Masakela and the Eurythmics. Nelson Mandela himself and his wife Winnie will appear in person at the concert, which is also rumoured to be including Madonna and Bruce Springsteen in the final line-up.

Long-time South African exile, trumpet star Hugh Masakela

CHARTS

US45	Opposites Attract *Paula Abdul*
USLP	Forever Your Girl *Paula Abdul*
UK45	Nothing Compares 2 U *Sinead O'Connor*
UKLP	. . . But Seriously *Phil Collins*
WEEK 2	
US45	Escapade *Janet Jackson*
USLP	Forever Your Girl *Paula Abdul*
UK45	Dub Be Good To Me *Beats International*
UKLP	. . . But Seriously *Phil Collins*
WEEK 3	
US45	Escapade *Janet Jackson*
USLP	Forever Your Girl *Paula Abdul*
UK45	Dub Be Good To Me *Beats International*
UKLP	. . . But Seriously *Phil Collins*
WEEK 4	
US45	Escapade *Janet Jackson*
USLP	Forever Your Girl *Paula Abdul*
UK45	Dub Be Good To Me *Beats International*
UKLP	I Do Not Want What I Havn't Got *Sinead O'Connor*
WEEK 5	
US45	Black Velvet *Alannah Myles*
USLP	Forever Your Girl *Paula Abdul*
UK45	Love Shack *The B 52s*
UKLP	I Do Not Want What I Havn't Got *Sinead O'Connor*

THE GRAPEVINE

- **Madonna to release a single 'Vogue', to preview her new movie 'Dick Tracy'.**
- **Michael Jackson honoured by CBS as 'top selling act of the 'Eighties'.**
- **New York band Ultra Vivid Scene play first UK dates in April.**
- **Mark Knopfler has formed the Notting Hillbillies, named after the location of studios in London's Notting Hill.**

IRON FILLING

Iron Maiden have recruited a replacement following the departure of guitarist Adrian Smith.

The new axeman is Janick Gers, who previously played with Gillan and White Spirit and has also co-written some of the tracks on the solo LP by Maiden vocalist Bruce Dickinson.

Said Maiden's Steve Harris: "We've all known Janick for a number of years and all get on great with the guy. We didn't audition anyone else but just asked him to learn a couple of songs and come to rehearsal"

He added: "We'll probably release an album before the end of the year and then can't wait to get back on tour"

MODE MANIA

Depeche Mode caused a riot at a Los Angeles record store after an estimated 5,000 fans turned up to see the group make an in-person appearance.

More than 130 riot police were called to the Wherehouse record shop where the band were signing copies of their new album. Seven people were injured as the crowd crushed against the glass windows.

In a statement, Depeche Mode said: "No autograph is worth an injury. We apologise for having to leave after an hour, but we wanted to make sure none of our fans were seriously hurt"

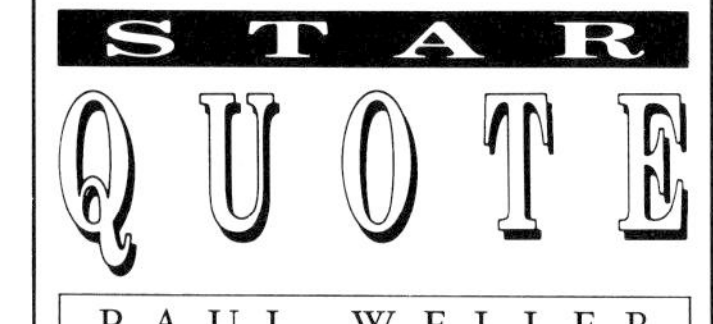

PAUL WELLER

(On Style Council split)

". . . it's something we should have done two or three years ago. We created some great music in our time, the effects of which won't be appreciated for some time'

COUNCIL ADJOURNED

The Style Council have split after eight years together – but chairman Paul Weller looks set to tour later this year.

The group, which Weller formed with Mick Talbot after splitting the Jam, have been quiet for over a year. Their last proper studio LP 'Confessions Of A Pop Group' was released back in 1988, followed last year by a compilation album of their hits, 'The Singular Advantures Of The Style Council', featuring the likes of 'Walls Come Tumbling Down' and 'Long Hot Summer'

There are rumours that Polydor rejected a new Style Council LP which would have been a follow-up to 'Confessions Of A Pop Group'. But the label maintained this week: "As far as we're concerned, The Style Council have split up, there is therefore no Style Council record. We believe that Paul Weller will release a new album when he has finalised his plans for the future"

LENNON LIVERPOOL TRIBUTE

A gigantic festival has been organised to take place on the Liverpool waterfront on May 5th, as a tribute to John Lennon. Fully sanctioned by the Lennon Estate, it will be screened worldwide before an expected crowd of 45,000. Among artists already confirmed are BB King, Terence Trent D'Arby, Lou Reed, Al Green, Roberta Flack, Randy Travis and Kylie Minogue; also set are Cyndi Lauper, Joe Cocker, Herbie Hancock, Wet Wet Wet, Deacon Blue and the Liverpool Philharmonic Orchestra.

Glasgow group Wet Wet Wet in the Liverpool Lennon line-up

AIDS AID

Annie Lennox – pitfalls for Porter project

Under the banner of Red Hot And Blue, an AIDS fundraising project is being planned. Artists including Sinead O'Connor, U2 and Annie Lennox will be performing interpretations of classic Cole Porter songs to be screened in a 90 minute international spectacular on December 1 by America's ABC network. A tie-in double album produced by Steve Lillywhite is also anticipated.

Annie Lennox will perform 'Ev'ry Time We Say Goodbye', the Pogues and Kirsty McColl duet with 'Miss Otis Regrets' while Fine Young Cannibals have chosen 'Love For Sale'. Top film names, including Derek Jarman and Jim Jarmusch, have been recruited to supervise accompanying videos.

The brainchild of New York lawyer John Carlin and American film-maker Leigh Blake, Porter's material was chosen as he himself was thought to have died from an AIDS-related disease. The project's major problem is cashflow and sponsorship; business corporations are wary of AIDS stigmatisation, with even a condom company declining support.

LUKE SKYWALKERS IN STARS WARS

Live Crew's Luke bugs Lucas in rap row

The Star Wars film company has filed a $300 million lawsuit against Luke Skywalker, a member of America's most controversial rap group 2 Live Crew, and their record company president. The lawsuit claims that Skywalker, whose real name is Luther Campbell, is guilty of trademark infringement and unjust enrichment. Lucasfilm Inc say they have received complaints about 2 Live Crew's music and are concerned that people may think that there is a connection between the 'wholesome and clean cut' Star Wars character Luke Skywalker and the rap group.

THE GRAPEVINE

- Bruce Springsteen's 'Born In The USA' album has passed the 12 million sales mark in the US.
- Britain's Soul II Soul have picked up three US 'Soul Train' awards, and so has Janet Jackson.
- Paula Abdul has spent a record 60 consecutive weeks in the Top 40 US singles chart, and producers Stock, Aitken & Waterman have completed a record 156 weeks in the UK Top 40.

RAP AND ROCK AGAINST THE POLL TAX

As part of a growing movement opposing the Government's much-hated Community Charge, Artists Against The Poll Tax has been formed with artists Rebel MC, Beats International and the Wee Papa Girl Rappers playing a mostly dance and rap Anti-Poll Benefit at Brixton. Despite a lukewarm critical reception, the night was deemed a success by the organisers. Neneh Cherry and Jimmy Somerville have also added their support to AATP, together with Labour MP Dave Nellist and the All Britain Anti-Poll Tax League.

Meanwhile an anti-Poll Tax album of 1970's songs is planned by a dozen bands, including The Wedding Present and Lush. Entitled 'Alvin Lives (In Leeds)', revivals such as 'Chirpy Chirpy Cheep Cheep' 'Wanderin' Star' and 'Bohemian Rhapsody' are being considered. The Wedding Present will headline a concert at London's Brixton Fridge venue to tie in with the album's release.

Rebel rap as MC joins Poll Tax protest benefit in Brixton

THE RAITT STUFF!

Bonnie Raitt, for years one of the world's most unfairly neglected artists, has finally topped the US album chart with her Grammy-winning 'Nick Of Time' album on the first anniversary of its initial appearance in the Top 200. The delectable Bonnie, daughter of Hollywood/Broadway star John Raitt, released her debut album back in 1973, and looks younger on the 'Nick Of Time' sleeve than she did 18 years earlier.

CHARTS

US45	Love Will Lead You Back – *Taylor Dayne*
USLP	Nick Of Time – *Bonnie Raitt*
UK45	The Power – *Snap*
UKLP	Only Yesterday – *Carpenters*
	WEEK 2
US45	I'll Be Your Everything – *Tommy Page*
USLP	Nick Of Time – *Bonnie Raitt*
UK45	Vogue – *Madonna*
UKLP	Only Yesterday – *Carpenters*
	WEEK 3
US45	Nothing Compares 2U – *Sinead O'Connor*
USLP	Nick Of Time – *Bonnie Raitt*
UK45	Vogue – *Madonna*
UKLP	Behind The Mask – *Fleetwood Mac*
	WEEK 4
US45	Nothing Compares 2U – *Sinead O'Connor*
USLP	I Do Not Want What I Haven't Got – *Sinead O'Connor*
UK45	Vogue – *Madonna*
UKLP	Only Yesterday – *Carpenters*

MADONNA'S ALBUM BREATHLESSLY AWAITED

Coinciding with her current 'Blond Ambition' tour, Madonna's latest album, 'I'm Breathless', has hit the shops. Including the artist's recent single 'Vogue', the package also includes material included in, or inspired by, the forthcoming movie, **Dick Tracy**, in which she co-stars with Warren Beatty.

In a surprise departure, the album contains three songs from the film which have been especially written for her by showtune supremo Stephen Sondheim, including 'Hanky Panky' which is expected to be the follow-up single to 'Vogue'.

Although Madonna's controversial anti-Catholic posture has been largely eschewed, the album, with showbiz, jazz and cocktail influences, has confounded the critics. However, it is generally agreed that it has been targeted towards an older demographic and in doing so, the star has finally left her 'wannabe' and teenage audience behind.

QUINCY JONES

'I'm so honoured that New Order picked my label to go on in the US – it really flattered me. They're beautiful people.'

ZEALOUS GUYS

A John Lennon charity concert drew over thirty world superstars to Liverpool's Pier Head to perform Lennon material.

Three generations of artists were on hand, with such diverse acts as R&B legend Ray Charles singing "Let It Be", to teenybopper idol Kylie Minogue's "Help" – complete with rap and dance routine – through to country superstar Randy Travis performing "Nowhere Man'.

Despite the stellar lineup, the show was not an unqualified success. Tickets sales were low, there had been some alleged bickering over billing, and the glaring omission of any of the remaining Beatles was palpably noticeable, although Paul McCartney and Ringo Starr were beamed in via satellite from Los Angeles. Furthermore, others felt the inclusion of just one Liverpool act was unsatisfactory.

However, Lennon's 14-year old son Sean provided one of the event's surprise high spots and Yoko Ono, long regarded as the architect of the Beatles' demise, was nevertheless enthusiastically greeted as she led the assembled artists performing 'Give Peace A Chance' at the evening's finale.

SINEAD WON'T PLAY DICE

Sinead O'Connor pulled out of a recent appearance on American comedy series *Saturday Night Live* after discovering the show's host would be controversial comedian Andrew Dice Clay, who has built up a huge following by twisting nursery rhymes into obscene anti-women polemics.

O'Connor, currently topping the US albums and singles charts, said 'I feel it shows disrespect – it would be nonsensical to expect a woman to perform songs about a woman's experiences after a monologue by Clay.'

Producer Lorne Michaels voiced his disappointment at O'Connor's decision. 'We weren't asking her to embrace Andrew Dice Clay. We were asking her to sing two songs'.

Cyndi Lauper (top) was one of the better items in the mixed bag 'tribute' concert to John Lennon, which ended in the inevitable sing-alonga-Yoko (above)

CHARTS

US45	Nothing Compares 2U *Sinead O'Connor*
USLP	I Do Not Want What I Haven't Got *Sinead O'Connor*
UK45	Vogue *Madonna*
UKLP	Only Yesterday *Carpenters*
WEEK 2	
US45	Nothing Compares 2U *Sinead O'Connor*
USLP	I Do Not Want What I Haven't Got *Sinead O'Connor*
UK45	Killer *Adamski*
UKLP	Only Yesterday *Carpenters*
WEEK 3	
US45	Vogue *Madonna*
USLP	I Do Not Want What I Haven't Got *Sinead O'Connor*
UK45	Killer *Adamski*
UKLP	Only Yesterday *Carpenters*
WEEK 4	
US45	Vogue *Madonna*
USLP	I Do Not Want What I Haven't Got *Sinead O'Connor*
UK45	Killer *Adamski*
UKLP	Only Yesterday *Carpenters*

THE GRAPEVINE

- **Alannah Myles is suing Bryan Adams' manager for remarks he made about how she advanced her career.**
- **A CD box of 50 year old recordings by blues man Robert Johnson has made the US album chart.**
- **Led Zeppelin re-united briefly at Jason Bonham's wedding; Jason is the son of their late drummer, John Bonham.**

Alannah – litigation looms

1990

GLASTONBURY 1990

The 1990 Glastonbury three day rock event was held with all its usual attendant problems of drug busts, muddy, quagmire-like fields, and crush-related injuries.

The number attending the festival was put at 75,000, but seasoned observers claimed this figure to be extremely conservative.

An ever-broadening variety of music styles was on offer; everything from Dixieland jazz, Aeolian Harps and Tex-Mex accordian stars.

Friday's main artists included New Orleans soul veterans The Neville Brothers, dancefloor crowd pleaser Adamski, Jesus Jones and 1960s throwback revivalists Happy Mondays.

The Cure's performance on Saturday of their 1980s hits was considered one of the event's highlights, with superstar Sinead O'Connor – now international property – completing a very strong bill. Also present were currently popular acts De La Soul, Del Amitri and James.

Sunday saw reggae from Aswad, more mainstream rock from Hothouse Flowers and Deacon Blue, with African celebrities Ladysmith Black Mambazo rounding off the evening with tribal rhythms and chanting.

U2 MAN SLAMS BEER & CREDIT CARD STARS

Bono and the boys blast booze and bank backing

Macca's millions – 'that'll do nicely'

Both Paul McCartney and The Who came under scathing attacks by U2 manager Paul McGuinness.

The ex-Beatle was described as 'greedy' for accepting millions of dollars in sponsorship from the Visa credit card company. McGuinness commented: 'I know the economics of touring at that level, and it's bullshit to claim that the tour would not be profitable without sponsorship.'

McGuinness also rounded upon The Who for allowing their tour to be sponsored by a brewery. The band's Pete Townshend is a recovering alcoholic.

U2 are renowned for their anti-capitalist stance; they once ordered the removal of all advertisements at a Japanese stadium before they would perform.

NO LOVE LOST

Stan Love, brother of Beach Boy Mike Love, has filed a petition in LA seeking control of his cousin Brian Wilson's personal and financial affairs. Love claims Wilson is 'unable to properly provide for his personal needs' and charges that he has been 'extensively brainwashed' by his former therapist and current creative partner, Dr. Eugene Landy, adding that Wilson is now a 'virtual hostage' of Landy.

In a scathing reply to the same court, Wilson depicts Love as a 'violent thug' motivated by 'insatiable greed' and claims he has been 'drug free and a controlled social drinker for seven years, and makes his own life and career decisions'. As proof of Love's violent character, Wilson details restraining orders made by the late Dennis Wilson, the Beach Boys drummer, and by Mike Love. Wilson also says Love was fired as his bodyguard in 1979 after he physically assaulted him.

Beach Boy Wilson in legal Love affair

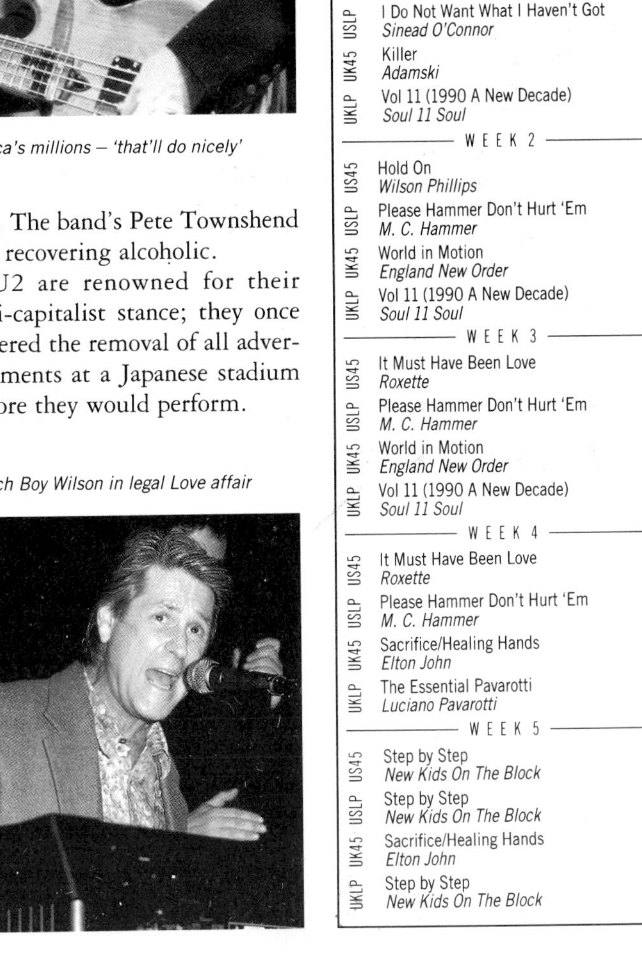

THE GRAPEVINE

- World Cup fever has gripped most of the World, with U2 being involved with the Republic of Ireland's song and New Order singing England's chart topper.
- In Japan, sales of vinyl records are now only 1% of the record market.
- The all star Wembley show for Nelson Mandela had all political references edited out for its American television showing.

CHARTS

US45	Vogue	*Madonna*
USLP	I Do Not Want What I Haven't Got	*Sinead O'Connor*
UK45	Killer	*Adamski*
UKLP	Vol 11 (1990 A New Decade)	*Soul 11 Soul*
WEEK 2		
US45	Hold On	*Wilson Phillips*
USLP	Please Hammer Don't Hurt 'Em	*M. C. Hammer*
UK45	World in Motion	*England New Order*
UKLP	Vol 11 (1990 A New Decade)	*Soul 11 Soul*
WEEK 3		
US45	It Must Have Been Love	*Roxette*
USLP	Please Hammer Don't Hurt 'Em	*M. C. Hammer*
UK45	World in Motion	*England New Order*
UKLP	Vol 11 (1990 A New Decade)	*Soul 11 Soul*
WEEK 4		
US45	It Must Have Been Love	*Roxette*
USLP	Please Hammer Don't Hurt 'Em	*M. C. Hammer*
UK45	Sacrifice/Healing Hands	*Elton John*
UKLP	The Essential Pavarotti	*Luciano Pavarotti*
WEEK 5		
US45	Step by Step	*New Kids On The Block*
USLP	Step by Step	*New Kids On The Block*
UK45	Sacrifice/Healing Hands	*Elton John*
UKLP	Step by Step	*New Kids On The Block*

JULY

1990

KNEBWORTH – SILVER CLEF AWARD WINNERS

Knebworth appeared not to be an exercise to celebrate what's new and fresh in pop, but a rounding up instead of everyone who is Old And In The Way. Everyone on the bill has sold at least 20 million records, they're all drinking chums of one Royal or another, and today they were polite as f . . .

Cliff Richard was a real trooper – he crammed almost his entire career into 45 minutes and went down a storm, unlike smouldering 'bratpack' heart-throb Rob Lowe, who followed Britain's elder statesman of pop.

The day's high point was Robert Plant, who quivered and wriggled and shook his long golden hair. Ironically, he was a late addition to the bill, being the winner of this year's Silver Clef award (bestowed annually on someone Old And In The Way for services to the industry).

Phil Collins did his best 'I'm-just-a-normal-bloke-like-you' party piece, sitting on the edge of the stage for 'In The Air Tonight', following later with an embarassing Blues Brothers revue singalong with Genesis.

Knebworth wouldn't be Knebworth without an Old And In The Way Supergroup, so Eric Clapton was joined by Mark Knopfler and revitalised Elton John. They were followed with gusto by Paul 'value-for-money' McCartney and a headlining Pink Floyd light show.

Ultimately, Knebworth is an incredibly corporate affair. The major labels have their hospitality marquees and as a charity show, it's a pretty good tax-deductible day out. It will raise a lot of money, but it also reeks of all the bloated excesses of the industry at its worst.

Cliff Richard – grand old man of the rock wrinklies

Collins – punters had their Phil?

STAR QUOTE

MARTIN GORE
Depeche Mode

'I think in a way we've been at the forefront of new music, sort of chipping away at the standard rock format stations'

LIVE AIDS

A row is brewing Stateside over the numbers of acts who either mime (lip-synch) on live shows, or who use taped tracks to augment (and sometimes to replace) the sound of the musicians and/or backing singers on the stage.

Acts who have been cited included Madonna, New Kids On The Block, Depeche Mode, New Order, Kylie Minogue, Bobby Brown, Bananarama and Milli Vanilli.

As part of the current consumer protection crusade in various states, laws are being proposed to outlaw miming, which in these days of sampling, computerised technology and elaborately choreographed shows has become common place when a big act is touring.

A spokesman for the instigators of the legislation said: 'The purpose of the bill is to ensure the public know what to expect. If they are expecting live music, they should get it'. Most of the acts mentioned admit to using some backing tapes, but say this is to enable them to give the best performance possible.

THE GRAPEVINE

■ Three of America's top four singles are by artists discovered by producer/writer Maurice Starr. They are New Kids On The Block, Bobby Brown and Bell Biv Devoe.

■ Stone Roses have refused to perform on Terry Wogan's top rated UK chat show because he would not interview them.

■ New Kids on the Block, who have just concluded a record breaking £10 million sponsorship deal with McDonalds, hold three of the Top 4 spots on the US music video chart.

CHARTS

US45	Step by Step	*New Kids On The Block*
USLP	Please Hammer Don't Hurt 'Em	*M. C. Hammer*
UK45	Sacrifice/Healing Hands	*Elton John*
UKLP	The Essential Pavarotti	*Luciano Pavarotti*
WEEK 2		
US45	Step by Step	*New Kids On The Block*
USLP	Please Hammer Don't Hurt 'Em	*M. C. Hammer*
UK45	Sacrifice/Healing Hands	*Elton John*
UKLP	The Essential Pavarotti	*Luciano Pavarotti*
WEEK 3		
US45	She Ain't Worth It	*Glen Medeiros Feat. Bobby Brown*
USLP	Please Hammer Don't Hurt 'Em	*M. C. Hammer*
UK45	Sacrifice/Healing Hands	*Elton John*
UKLP	The Essential Pavarotti	*Luciano Pavarotti*
WEEK 4		
US45	She Ain't Worth It	*Glen Medeiros Feat. Bobby Brown*
USLP	Please Hammer Don't Hurt 'Em	*M. C. Hammer*
UK45	Turtle Power	*Partners In Kryme*
UKLP	Sleeping With The Past	*Elton John*

MADONNA AT WEMBLEY

The current Madonna show is an overblown parody of her past – a dazzling extended disco dance projection of pure will-power, 'f . . . you' determination and sore-core titilation.

It's all attitude in gold lame corsets and working out on stage and says very little beyond 'Don't take any shit' and 'Sexuality is power, girls'.

Maybe it's just because she doesn't have a new album of boppy grooves to show off, so pantomime seemed to be the sole point of the exercise. She cast herself as Barbarella in a brothel for 'Like A Virgin', switched to black mass cassock-gear for a frenzied gospel-rave through 'Like A Prayer', while the songs from her 'Dick Tracy' movie had her stretched out atop a grand piano doing the sequin'n'sleaze nightclub chanteuse bit.

Only the trio of end songs 'Into The Groove', 'Vogue' and 'Holiday' – all of which soared away from the film star charades level of the night – reminded us that Madonna can do much more than just strike a pose. If only she would try something a little less 'easy illusion' and a little more 'real'

PRIEST DENIES SATANIC MESSAGES

Birmingham hard rockers Judas Priest have been in the dock in Reno, Nevada, this month facing charges that alleged subliminal messages on their 12-year old 'Stained Glass' album drove two American teenagers to a suicide-pact.

The parents of the two boys, who shot themselves in 1985, claim they were influenced by the lyrics of the songs 'Beyond The Realms Of Death' and 'Heroes End'. They have brought in an 'expert' who claims backwards Satanic messages are included in the lyrics, including the words 'Do it, do it' and 'F . . . The Lord'.

The band's spokesperson said: 'The band are outraged, worried and upset. There has not been one subliminal message or devil worshipping suggestion on any Judas Priest record ever. They may wear studs and leather on stage but that's just an image, it's just entertainment.'

BOWIE BACKS RAPPED RAPPERS

David Bowie has come out in support of controversial rap outfit 2 Live Crew, who have been panned across America for their sexually explicit lyrics. The group's million selling album, 'As Nasty As We Wanna Be', has been ordered by several state judges to be removed from record shops.

Bowie has joined the Crew's anti-censorship supporters, who include Bruce Springsteen among their number, and spoke out during his Philadelphia show against the ban: 'Freedom of thought, freedom of speech – it's one of the most important things we have'.

Atlantic Records have just announced that advance orders for 2 Live Crew's 'Banned In The USA' have passed the half million mark – a record for the label.

CHARTS

	US45	Vision of Love	*Mariah Carey*
	USLP	Please Hammer Don't Hurt 'Em	*M. C. Hammer*
	UK45	Turtle Power	*Partners In Kryme*
	UKLP	Sleeping With The Past	*Elton John*
WEEK 2	US45	Vision of Love	*Mariah Carey*
	USLP	Please Hammer Don't Hurt 'Em	*M. C. Hammer*
	UK45	Turtle Power	*Partners In Kryme*
	UKLP	Sleeping With The Past	*Elton John*
WEEK 3	US45	Vision of Love	*Mariah Carey*
	USLP	Please Hammer Don't Hurt 'Em	*M. C. Hammer*
	UK45	Turtle Power	*Partners In Kryme*
	UKLP	Sleeping With The Past	*Elton John*
WEEK 4	US45	Vision of Love	*Mariah Carey*
	USLP	Please Hammer Don't Hurt 'Em	*M. C. Hammer*
	UK45	Teeny Weeny Yellow Polka Dot Bikini	*Bombalurina*
	UKLP	Sleeping With The Past	*Elton John*

THE GRAPEVINE

- **Despite a lack of major names, Roger Waters' 'The Wall' concert in Berlin was watched by over 300,000 and was seen on TV in 32 countries.**
- **Turbo Harris, leader of Snap, has run into a lot of trouble in the US after making alleged anti-gay remarks in a gay club.**
- **Soul star Curtis Mayfield is paralysed from the waist down after being hit on stage by a falling light rack.**

As one Wall disappears, along come the Floyd with another

First rap chart toppers Run DMC

LL Cool J

PLEASE RAP DON'T HURT 'EM

Rap is, without doubt, the most successful new musical form of the past decade, and like the majority of 'new' music over the years, its roots are in black music. It evolved from soul and disco music with its musical influences coming from such varied sources as gospel, jazz, blues, salsa, electro, rock, pop and African and Caribbean music. Also, it has been clearly influenced by such things as children's playground rhymes and the jive talk of top US radio DJs.

Rapping was not uncommon on R&B and soul records in the 1960s and 1970s, when artists like Joe Tex, Isaac Hayes, Barry White and Millie Jackson achieved considerable commercial success by relying heavily on the spoken word, rather than by singing. Early rappers didn't just talk about love – serious spokesmen like Gil Scott-Heron, Gary Byrd and The Last Poets paved the way for the many socially-committed black rappers a decade later.

The first exponents of rap as we know it today were young blacks from New York. The first record to sell in significant quantities was 1979's 'Rapper's Delight', a 15 minute epic by The Sugarhill Gang which hit the top in many parts of the world.

Rap was not an instant success beyond the streets where it was a living and growing art. Most of the record industry and record buyers saw 'Rapper's Delight' as a one-off rather than the flag ship for a new generation's musical preference. As so often happens with black music, it took a white performer to bring it to the attention of an international audience, when Blondie scored with the somewhat sanitised 'Rapture' in 1981.

At first, the lyrics of many raps dealt with the MC's prowess, but the genre also became a medium for social messages thanks to records like Grandmaster Flash's 'The Message' in 1982 and 'White Lines' in 1984, which were both UK Top 10 pop hits, even though they failed to make much impression on the US pop chart.

Getting US radio acceptance was (and to some extent, remains) a problem for rap and it was 1986 before the first rap record made the US Top 20, Run DMC's 'Walk This Way'. Since then, rappers who have achieved big US pop hits include

Rapping pioneer Grandmaster Flash

Superstar of rap MC Hammer

White rappers with bad reputation, The Beastie Boys

LL Cool J, Salt-N-Pepa, D.J. Jazzy Jeff & The Fresh Prince, Tone Loc, Partners In Kryme, 2 Live Crew, Candyman, Digital Underground, plus Spanish language rappers Mellow Man Ace and Gerardo.

In Britain, rap has met with a better reception on radio and charts and it is now an essential part of many records with the identi-kit hit act containing at least one (token) black rapper.

The music business is famous for cashing-in on musical trends, exploiting them and then replacing them with the next 'in' thing. This will happen to rap, as it has happened to every other musical trend, but in 1991, the music is still heading towards its peak. Live rap shows have created the kind of reaction unequalled since the early days of punk rock, with shows being banned or attracting heavy police presence, and with many acts being arrested for simply performing their songs. Rappers, who often cloak their lyrics in street slang in order to be understood only by the élite few, can reach more young people with their messages than politicians will ever do.

It took another white act, the notorious Beastie Boys, to first crack the US and UK album Top 10 and to top the US album chart, which they did with their four million selling 'Licensed To Ill', which topped the US chart for seven weeks in 1987. In 1989, the first GRAMMY was awarded for rap and the first official US rap chart was introduced. It was also the year that Tone Loc released rap's first two million selling single, 'Wild Thing'. Since then, massive album sales have been notched up by artists like LL Cool J, Run DMC, Public Enemy and 1990s giants of rap, MC Hammer and Vanilla Ice.

GRAMMY & BRITS winner MC Hammer's 'Please Hammer Don't Hurt 'Em' topped the US album chart for 21 weeks, selling over nine million copies in the process. Vanilla Ice's 'To The Extreme' spent a record (for a debut album) 16 weeks on top of the US charts and sold over five million units in just 12 weeks and from it came the first US No. 1 rap single, 'Ice Ice Baby'. Despite this amazing start to his career, the photogenic Vanilla Ice (born Robert Van Winkle) has been criticized by the rap fraternity for not really being authentic and living the life style he raps about. He has been dubbed by some 'The Elvis Of Rap', which highlights the fact that, unfair as it may be, the formula of a good looking white boy performing his own brand of black music sells records in great quantities, and works as well in rap as it has always done in rock.

American chart stars 2 Live Crew

SINEAD DROPS A STAR-SPANGLED CLANGER

By simply asking for the American national anthem, 'The Star Spangled Banner', not to be played before one of her US shows, the controversial Irish performer Sinead O'Connor recently landed herself in a whole lot of trouble Stateside.

The US media leapt on the story of her banning the 'Star-Spangled Banner' at the Garden Arts Centre in New Jersey and made her public enemy No. 1 overnight. Her shows across the US since have attracted a large number share of protesters and pickets, while some radio stations have urged listeners to burn

her records and others have smashed her records on air. A Pennsylvanian picket summed it up by saying: 'If she takes the American Dollar, she should learn to respect our national anthem'.

O'Connor stressed 'I sincerely harbour no disrespect for America or Americans, but I have a policy of not having any national anthems played before my concerts in any country, not even my own'. She dismissed as probably untrue a comment Frank Sinatra is supposed to have made about the affair saying that he would like to 'kick her ass'.

CHARTS

US45	If Wishes Came True – *Sweet Sensation*
USLP	Please Hammer Don't Hurt 'Em – *M. C. Hammer*
UK45	Teeny Weeny Yellow Polka Dot Bikini – *Bombalurina*
UKLP	Graffiti Bridge – *Prince*
	WEEK 2
US45	Blaze Of Glory – *Jon Bon Jovi*
USLP	Please Hammer Don't Hurt 'Em – *M. C. Hammer*
UK45	Teeny Weeny Yellow Polka Dot Bikini – *Bombalurina*
UKLP	In Concert – *Luciano Pavarotti/Placido Domingo*
	WEEK 3
US45	Release Me – *Wilson Phillips*
USLP	Please Hammer Don't Hurt 'Em – *M. C. Hammer*
UK45	The Joker – *Steve Miller Band*
UKLP	Listen Without Prejudice Vol 1 – *George Michael*
	WEEK 4
US45	Release Me – *Wilson Phillips*
USLP	Please Hammer Don't Hurt 'Em – *M. C. Hammer*
UK45	The Joker – *Steve Miller Band*
UKLP	In Concert – *Luciano Pavarotti/Placido Domingo*
	WEEK 5
US45	Can't Live Without Your Love – *Nelson*
USLP	Please Hammer Don't Hurt 'Em – *M. C. Hammer*
UK45	Show Me Heaven – *Maria McKee*
UKLP	In Concert – *Luciano Pavarotti/Placido Domingo*

GULF CRISIS – US DISC JOCKEYS HAVE THEIR SAY

The current crisis in the Middle East has inspired some American radio DJs to change the lyrics of certain hit records to make their own comments on the situation.

Among the songs being parodied are Milli Vanilli's 'Blame It On The Rain', which has become 'Blame It On Hussein', Simon & Garfunkel's 'I Am A Rock, I Am An Island', which has become "I Am Iraq, I Am A Tyrant', while the Fine Young Cannibals smash, 'She Drives Me Crazy' has become 'Hussein Is Crazy'. A spokesman for the latter group says 'They don't think it's funny. It's not the kind of thing they would wish to be associated with'. BBC's Radio One has denied that any of it's presenters are planning to copy the craze.

NEIL TENNANT

Pet Shop Boys

'Rock music has become the most safe and polite institution of all. Bono inducting The Who into the Rock And Roll Hall Of Fame all in their wing collars and bowties. Talk about bloody irony!'

STARS MOURN VAUGHAN

Stevie Wonder, Bonnie Raitt and Jackson Browne sang 'Amazing Grace' at the graveside of blues guitarist Stevie Ray Vaughan. The funeral attracted over 1,000 people to Dallas including Ringo Starr, ZZ Top, Nile Rodgers and Delbert McClinton.

Vaughan, 35, was killed in a helicoper crash in East Troy, Wisconsin, along with four members of Eric Clapton's touring party. He first came to the public's attention as the guitarist on David Bowie's 'Let's Dance' album in 1983, and was building a very large following which looked set to lead to superstardom.

His recently completed album, 'Family Style', recorded with his brother Jimmy, a member of The Fabulous Thunderbirds, is planned for release next month.

- **Sinead O'Connor has won the Best Video Award at the MTV awards. Other winners include M.C. Hammer, Don Henley, Billy Idol and the B-52's.**
- **Judas Priest have been cleared of all charges in the double suicide case.**
- **Producer's Stock, Aitken & Waterman have scored their 100th UK Top 75 hit.**

Cannibals – want to make joke jocks eat their words

STONE ROSES – FINED FOR PAINTING THE TOWN

Revolver action loaded against the 'Roses as they go to war with ex-label

The four members of Stone Roses were each fined £3000 in a court case for damage they did to their former record label's offices earlier this year.

They had been incensed by a new 'utterly third-rate' video produced by Revolver/FM to promote the re-issue of an old single. After arguing with label boss Paul Birch, the Roses poured paint over him and his girlfriend and liberally covered the surrounding room. They also 're-decorated' Birch's Mercedes and two other cars. The band's lawyer said: 'There are people within the music industry prepared to cash in with second-rate product – that is not the band's style and it was their feelings of outrage which led to this incident'.

Birch has threatened to sue them for £3 million for breach of contract if they do not settle the alleged £22,000 worth of damage, claiming they did not completely fulfil their Revolver/FM deal before signing to Silverstone in 1988.

Stone Roses, currently worth over 10 million per year, were tightlipped, but member John Squire admitted 'I'm just glad to stay out of the nick'.

CHARTS

US45	Close To You	*Maxi Priest*
USLP	Please Hammer Don't Hurt 'Em	*M. C. Hammer*
UK45	Show Me Heaven	*Maria McKee*
UKLP	In Concert	*Luciano Pavarotti/Placido Domingo*
WEEK 2		
US45	Praying For Time	*George Michael*
USLP	Please Hammer Don't Hurt 'Em	*M. C. Hammer*
UK45	Show Me Heaven	*Maria McKee*
UKLP	In Concert	*Luciano Pavarotti/Placido Domingo*
WEEK 3		
US45	I Don't Have The Heart	*James Ingram*
USLP	Please Hammer Don't Hurt 'Em	*M. C. Hammer*
UK45	Show Me Heaven	*Maria McKee*
UKLP	Some Friendly	*Charlatans*
WEEK 4		
US45	Black Cat	*Janet Jackson*
USLP	Please Hammer Don't Hurt 'Em	*M. C. Hammer*
UK45	A Little Time	*Beautiful South*
UKLP	The Rhythm Of The Saints	*Paul Simon*

THE GRAPEVINE

- **Morrissey has announced that his first live shows since 1988 will be in 1991 in the US.**
- **MC Hammer has completed 21 weeks at the top of the US album chart.**
- **In the Skywalker Vs. Skywalker case, Luke the rapper has been ordered to pay $300,000 to Luke the spaceman.**

The Nelson brothers, currently topping US chart column

BAD NEWS ON THE RADIO

The British government recently announced that one new FM and two new MW nation-wide commercial radio stations would be launched in 1991. They say that one of the three stations must feature 'spoken word' output, one will be open to all-comers, and one will be for 'music other than pop'. Unfortunately, the aged Radio Authority Committee, set up by the government, cannot distinguish between pop and rock, saying that 'pop music includes rock music and other types of modern popular music which are characterised by a strong rhythmical element and which rely on electrical amplification for their performance'.

This is bad news for the thousands of rock fans lobbying for the launch of the proposed ROCK-FM radio station, which would have been Britain's first adult-orientated rock (aor) station.

FAMILY AFFAIR

US pop/rock group Nelson, whose single '(Can't Live Without Your) Love And Affection' tops the US chart, are fronted by photogenic brothers Gunnar & Matthew Nelson. The Nelson boys are sons of 1950s superstar Rick(y) Nelson, who topped the chart with 'Poor Little Fool' in 1958 and 'Travelin' Man' in 1961. Ricky, in turn, was the son of Ozzie Nelson who, with his Orchestra, had a US No. 1 with 'And Then Some' in 1935.

Surprisingly, this is not the first time there have been three generations of US chart toppers, as this unusual feat was previously achieved by Debby Boone, her father Pat Boone, and her grand father Red Foley between the years 1950 and 1977.

NOVEMBER

1990

CHARTS

US45	Ice Ice Baby – *Vanilla Ice*
USLP	Please Hammer Don't Hurt 'Em – *M. C. Hammer*
UK45	Unchained Melody – *Righteous Brothers*
UKLP	The Rhythm Of The Saints – *Paul Simon*
WEEK 2	
US45	Love Takes Time – *Mariah Carey*
USLP	To The Extreme – *Vanilla Ice*
UK45	Unchained Melody – *Righteous Brothers*
UKLP	The Very Best Of Elton John – *Elton John*
WEEK 3	
US45	Love Takes Time – *Mariah Carey*
USLP	To The Extreme – *Vanilla Ice*
UK45	Unchained Melody – *Righteous Brothers*
UKLP	The Very Best Of Elton John – *Elton John*
WEEK 4	
US45	Love Takes Time – *Mariah Carey*
USLP	To The Extreme – *Vanilla Ice*
UK45	Unchained Melody – *Righteous Brothers*
UKLP	The Immaculate Collection – *Madonna*
WEEK 5	
US45	Love Takes Time – *Mariah Carey*
USLP	To The Extreme – *Vanilla Ice*
UK45	Unchained Melody – *Righteous Brothers*
UKLP	The Immaculate Collection – *Madonna*

THE GRAPEVINE

■ A record seven of the Top 10 US Dance singles are British. While 1970s teenybop stars Donny Osmond and David Cassidy are both back in the Top 40 of the US singles chart the New Kids On The Block have missed the US Top 40 for the first time.

■ It has been announced that Madonna's total world sales to date are 54 million albums and 26 million singles.

'COME CLEAN' SAYS WASH

Italian-based dance music act Black Box are involved in more legal problems. The group, who had trouble last year when they sampled Loleatta Holloway's 'Love Sensation' in their UK No. 1 hit, 'Ride On Time', have run into similar problems again. This time, session singer Martha Wash is claiming to have sung on their US hit, 'Everybody, Everybody', and on every track bar one on their 'Dreamworld' album. Wash, best known as half of the large singing duo, The Weather Girls, who had a Top 10 hit in 1984 with 'It's Raining Men', is accusing the group of false advertising and claims that Katrin Quinol, who does not speak English, impersonates her in videos and on stage. Wash is currently involved in recording an album with the C&C Music Factory, another project for which she may not get label credits, and therefore another one which may end up with legal problems.

Black Box – more sampling sagas after 'Dreamworld' dubbing charge

PUBLIC ENEMY NO. 1

American rap stars Public Enemy, EPMD and the Intelligent Hoodlum played to a two-thirds full house at London's large new Docklands venue.

The Intelligent Hoodlum has got one half of his name drastically wrong as his act consists of simply shuffling around the stage humourlessly moaning about white oppression.

The much awaited EPMD seemed content to get the young audience swearing at them with their cries of 'Say F . . . You' and the like, whilst strutting around the stage like overgrown playground bullies.

Public Enemy saved the day. The group combines Chuck D's intelligent and humorous lyrics and his deadpan delivery with attention junkie Flavor Flav's outrageous stage antics and extended raps. Live, their energy and passion is undisputable and the racially mixed audience loved them.

P.E. – deadpan delivery in Docklands

THE JACKSON BROWN SHOW

Bobby Brown, the ex-New Edition singer, and would-be love man, treated the Wembley Arena audience to a display of groin grabbing and gave them the opportunity to admire his vocal chords. He slipped from one samey song to another, all showcasing his masterful voice. After an act that seemed to be all climaxes and no foreplay, he left the stage soaked in love sweat.

The powerful voiced bill topper Janet Jackson, together with her large entourage of dancers, worked her way through tracks from her 'Control' album (in the same order as the record!) and then did the same for numbers from her multi-platinum 'Rhythm Nation 1814' album. Despite a large helping of questionable and gushing sincerity, the British audience could not get enough of the lip-synching American superstar.

Janet – mime-time megastar

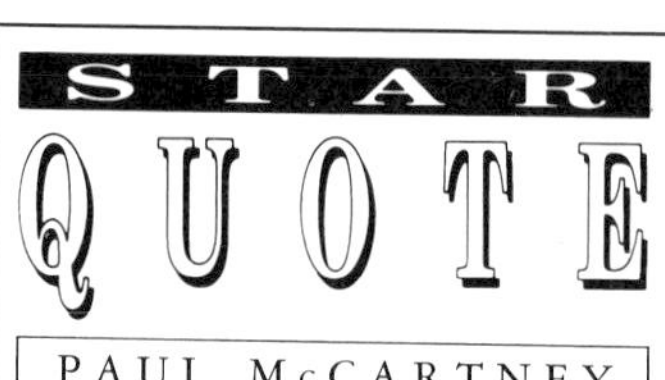

STAR QUOTE

PAUL McCARTNEY

'I saw the Happy Mondays on TV, and they reminded me of the Beatles in their 'Strawberry Fields' phase'

MILLI VANILLI STRIPPED

Milli Vanilli, one of the most successful acts of 1989/90, have been stripped of their GRAMMY award for 'Best New Artist'. This unprecedented event happened after the announcement that Rob Pilatus and Fabrice Morvan, who have been fronting the group on both videos and live work, did not sing on any of their records.

The group's debut album, 'Girl You Know It's True' (UK title 'All Or Nothing'), has sold over seven million copies in the US, and three singles from it, Baby Don't Forget My Number', 'Girl I'm Gonna Miss You' and 'Blame It On The Rain', topped the US chart.

It was said that the singing on the German produced album was actually done by session singers Johnny Davis and Brad Howell and rapper Charles Shaw. The long running scam finally came to light when producer Frank Farian refused to let the duo sing

on Milli Vanilli's follow-up album. Farian, who was also the man behind a string of hits in the 1970s by Boney M, said he would rather scrap the group than have Pilatus and Morvan sing on Milli Vanilli records.

The news of the fraud made headlines on both sides of the Atlantic, not because it was such an unusual occurrence, but because of the success of the act and the length of time the truth took coming out.

The three session singers are working on a new album, as are the disgraced duo, with neither act planning to use the name Milli Vanilli.

THE GRAPEVINE

- **Madonna's video for 'Justify My Love' has been banned by most US and UK TV stations, forcing her to re-edit it and to release the unedited version on video.**
- **Milli Vanilli have been sued for $50 million by an American fan for fraud.**
- **Happy Monday's leader Shaun Ryder has been hospitalised for treatment of his drug problem.**

CRITICS CHOICE FOR 1990

The NME writers favourite records of 1990 were:

Best Albums

1 'Pills 'N' Thrills And Bellyaches'
Happy Mondays

2 'I Do Not Want What I Haven't Got'
Sinead O'Connor

3 'Fear of A Black Planet'
Public Enemy

4 'Ragged Glory'
Neil Young & Crazy Horse

5 'Gold Mother'
James

Best Singles

1 'Groove is In The Heart'
Deee-Lite

2 'Step On'
Happy Mondays

3 'Nothing Compares 2 U'
Sinead O'Connor

4 'Where Are you Baby?'
Betty Boo

5 'Loaded'
Primal Scream

CHARTS

US45	I'm Your Baby Tonight *Whitney Houston*
USLP	To The Extreme *Vanilla Ice*
UK45	Ice, Ice Baby *Vanilla Ice*
UKLP	The Immaculate Collection *Madonna*
WEEK 2	
US45	Because I Love You *Stevie B*
USLP	To The Extreme *Vanilla Ice*
UK45	Ice, Ice Baby *Vanilla Ice*
UKLP	The Immaculate Collection *Madonna*
WEEK 3	
US45	Because I Love You *Stevie B*
USLP	To The Extreme *Vanilla Ice*
UK45	Ice, Ice Baby *Vanilla Ice*
UKLP	The Immaculate Collection *Madonna*
WEEK 4	
US45	Because I Love You *Stevie B*
USLP	To The Extreme *Vanilla Ice*
UK45	Ice, Ice Baby *Vanilla Ice*
UKLP	The Immaculate Collection *Madonna*
WEEK 5	
US45	Because I Love You *Stevie B*
USLP	To The Extreme *Vanilla Ice*
UK45	Saviours Day *Cliff Richard*
UKLP	The Immaculate Collection *Madonna*

Happy 'days here again?

QUEEN & BOWIE WANT A SLICE OF ICE

Queen and David Bowie are wrapped up in a legal wrangle with new American superstar rapper Vanilla Ice. Ice has used, without permission, a sample of a distinctive riff from Queen and Bowie's 1981 UK chart topper 'Under Pressure' on his current US No. 1 hit, 'Ice Ice Baby'. Naturally the British stars feel they should be earning from this usage, which, if Ice's album sells as well as expected, could earn them a queen's ransom.

Queen claim right to royalty

VANILLA – NOT FLAVOUR OF THE MONTH?

The thoughts of most serious rap connoisseurs about Vanilla Ice are unprintable, even though few of them may have heard his American chart topping album, 'To The Extreme'.

They object to Rap Van Winkle for the following reasons. Firstly, he allegedly exaggerated the toughness of his background, as surely did LL Cool J, Public Enemy and no doubt many other black rappers too. The same can also be said for the charges of sexism and arrogance, two vital ingredients, it would seem, for most rappers.

He is also charged with emasculating black music and packaging it for white audiences. If this is a crime, then rappers like De La Soul, Dream Warriors, Monie Love and Technotronic could be similarly accused for incorporating pop into their music.

Yes, Ice's songs are very commercial and contrived but so are those of Madonna, Betty Boo and many other highly rated artists.

'To The Extreme' is a highly competent debut album from a major new pop talent. There is little filler amongst the 15 tracks. Listen without prejudice.

CHARTS

- US45 Justify My Love — *Madonna*
- USLP To The Extreme — *Vanilla Ice*
- UK45 Bring Your Daughter To The Slaughter — *Iron Maiden*
- UKLP The Immaculate Collection — *Madonna*

WEEK 2

- US45 Justify My Love — *Madonna*
- USLP To The Extreme — *Vanilla Ice*
- UK45 Bring Your Daughter To The Slaughter — *Iron Maiden*
- UKLP The Immaculate Collection — *Madonna*

WEEK 3

- US45 Love Will Never Do (Without You) — *Janet Jackson*
- USLP To The Extreme — *Vanilla Ice*
- UK45 Sadness Part 1 — *Enigma*
- UKLP The Immaculate Collection — *Madonna*

WEEK 4

- US45 The First Time — *Surface*
- USLP To The Extreme — *Vanilla Ice*
- UK45 Innuendo — *Queen*
- UKLP MCMXC A.D. — *Enigma*

MORE AGGRO FOR MILLI VANILLI

Those great pretenders who didn't sing on their own album, Milli Vanilli, have now had to hand back their Canadian JUNO award. As well as that indignity, they're also being sued by David Clayton-Thomas, pipe-smoking front man with Blood, Sweat & Tears, who claims that the Milli hit, 'All or Nothing', was based on 'Spinning Wheel', the 1969 hit by B,S & T on which he sang lead. Nothing seems more likely than All . . .

STAR QUOTE

BRUCE DICKINSON

'We tread a fine line between taking ourselves seriously and being Spinal Tap'

MADONNA JUSTIFIES HER MIX

Madonna is in a controversy over a remix of 'Justify My Love' that has upset both American Jews and Arabs. With the 'impending war in the Middle East' in mind, she named it 'The Beast Within' mix after Saddam Hussein. It also contains an anti-semitic quote taken from the biblical Book Of Revelations that speaks of 'the slanders of those who say they are Jews but they are not, they are a synagogue of Satan'. Madonna defended the mix by saying 'I had no anti-semitic intent and the message, if any, is pro-tolerance. The song is, after all, about love'.

LEPPARD DEATH

Def Leppard look certain to continue despite the death of guitarist Steve Clark. Clark, who had studied classical guitar before helping form the multi-platinum group in 1978, was found dead at his home on January 8th.

The group, known as front runners in the New Wave of British Heavy Metal, sold seven million of their 'Pyromania' album Stateside and over 12 million world-wide of their last album, 'Hysteria'.

Singer Joe Elliott said 'He was a really quiet, shy, humble, nice sort of bloke' and added 'He was a master of riffs and wrote some of the best we've done. We'll definitely miss his creative input'.

Leppard – spot the changes

THE GRAPEVINE

- **Janet Jackson has scored a record seven US Top 5 singles from her 'Rhythm Nation 1814' album.**
- **Three fans died at an AC/DC concert in Salt Lake City.**
- **James Brown has performed his first show after two years in jail.**
- **Soul II Soul's Jazzie B has signed his new Funki Dredd label to Motown.**

BRITS 91 –

Elton John was voted Best Male Singer and Status Quo also went away with an award at this years BRITS – as usual, watching the show was like stepping into a time-warp.

We were promised a showcase for the best new British talent, and we did get two seconds of Ride, one second of Billy Bragg and a mimed song from Best Newcomer Betty Boo.

Sinead O'Connor, perhaps wisely, had decided she did not want to appear on the show. However producer Jonathan King, gave her a severe figurative slap across the shaven head, by showing Whitney Houston singing 'Star-Spangled Banner'.

INXS picked up the award for Top International Group and the Australian group's vocalist, Michael Hutchence, collected the prize as Top International Male, suprising thousands of solo International Male singers.

Highspot of the back-patting bonanza was the show by the Best Group the Cure. Chart regulars for 11 years, they seemed young and out of place.

Other winners on this Manchester-free evening included Lisa Stansfield (Best Female), Beautiful South (Best Video) and MC Hammer (Best International Newcomer).

To avoid upsetting viewers all remarks considered controversial by ex-Tory candidate King were chopped out. However, we were allowed to glimpse the after-show eating extravaganza, heart-warming in this year of unprecedented world starvation.

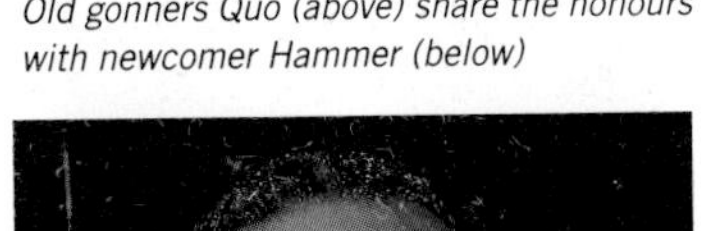

Old gonners Quo (above) share the honours with newcomer Hammer (below)

Whitney pulls out of tour

CHARTS

US45	The First Time *Surface*
USLP	To The Extreme *Vanilla Ice*
UK45	3 a,m. Eternal *KLF*
UKLP	The Soul Cages *Sting*
	WEEK 2
US45	Gonna Make You Sweat *C&C Music Factory*
USLP	To The Extreme *Vanilla Ice*
UK45	3 a.m. Eternal *KLF*
UKLP	Doubt *Jesus Jones*
	WEEK 3
US45	Gonna Make You Sweat *C&C Music Factory*
USLP	To The Extreme *Vanilla Ice*
UK45	Do The Bartman *Simpsons*
UKLP	Innuendo *Queen*
	WEEK 4
US45	All The Man That I Need *Whitney Houston*
USLP	To The Extreme *Vanilla Ice*
UK45	Do The Bartman *Simpsons*
UKLP	Innuendo *Queen*

BRAZIL NUTS ABOUT GEORGE – BUT THEY DON'T LIKE MONDAYS

In the exotic setting of Rio de Janeiro, Brazil, George Michael triumphed at the city's Maracano Stadium. With a set consisting of a surprisingly high count of soul and pop standards like 'Papa Was A Rolling Stone' and 'Fame', he was ecstatically received by the Latin American audience. At an earlier performance, Michael had been joined on stage for a three song encore by erstwhile partner Andrew Ridgely. Sarcastically dubbed 'AND-Aid' by industry cynics and tabloid press alike, it was rumoured to have greatly swelled the coffers of the luckless Ridgely.

On an impressive bill, Michael was supported by Deee-Lite, who won the audience over with their hard dance groove augmented by Lady Miss Kier's distinctive vocals. With much of their material unfamiliar to the punters, Happy Mondays fared less well and were the target of much missile-hurling from a restless audience.

Dance sounds Deee-Lite audience

GULF WAR – LATEST AMERICAN CASUALTIES

It is feared that many US stars will pull out of tours scheduled in Europe, following terrorist threats to transatlantic airlines since the outbreak of war in the Gulf.

However, record labels and agents were keen to confirm that most bands are still scheduled to play. Confirmed as still arriving include Bob Dylan, David Lee Roth, Lenny Kravitz, Dream Warriors, Throwing Musses and Jane's Addiction, but Vanilla Ice has pulled out of his European trip, cancelling a performance at MIDEM, the music business seminar in Cannes, while Whitney Houston has re-scheduled her sell-out tour of Europe from March to late August. US rock band Cinderella, currently on tour in Europe, have postponed the remainder of their shows, and fellow Americans, A Tribe Called Quest, who were set to make a promotional trip to Britain, have pulled out despite the success of their current single, 'Can I Kick It'. Former teen idol Donny Osmond has also decided not to come and cancelled his London shows.

THE GRAPEVINE

- **Iron Maiden's 'Bring Your Daughter To The Slaughter' entered the UK single chart at No. 1 and had dropped out of the Top 75 just four weeks later.**
- **Tom Jones is in the studio working with Van Morrison.**
- **Electric Light Orchestra have reformed without Jeff Lynne, and are now called ELO Part 2.**
- **Whitney Houston has scored her ninth US No. 1 single, equalling the female record held by Madonna.**

GRAMMY AWARDS – SINEAD DOES NOT WANT WHAT SHE HAS NOT GOT

The 33rd annual Grammy awards held in New York were dominated by veteran maestro, Quincy Jones, who took home six statuettes, including those for Best Album Of The Year and Top Producer.

Rapper M.C. Hammer meanwhile fared almost as well with three, including Best R&B Single and Best Music Video.

The event was slightly soured by Sinead O'Connor's much publicised refusal to collect her Grammy for Best Alternative Music Album. The 24 year old Dubliner had previously stayed home for both the MTV and Billboard awards ceremonies, where she had been feted.

More problems for the organizers came with claims of racism, and further absenteeism, with Public Enemy's failure to appear, protesting against their decision by the National Academy of Recording Artists and Songwriters not to air the rap section on TV. Similarly, blues artists Ruth Brown and Charles Brown boycotted the affair because of NARAS's decision not to televise the blues category.

Amongst those who did decide to attend, Phil Collins picked up Best Single for 'Another Day In Paradise', and Mariah Carey mantle-pieced the Best New Talent Award.

Lifetime Achievement Awards were won by John Lennon and Bob Dylan and posthumous awards went to Roy Orbison and Stevie Ray Vaughan.

Quincey has his hands full

THE GRAPEVINE

■ Janet Jackson has signed a deal with Virgin Records that will give her $16 million for three albums. Meanwhile, her brother Michael has agreed to a deal with Sony (previously Columbia) which gives him his own label, Nation Records, and could earn him around $500 million.

■ After spending his whole (30 plus years) career at Motown, Smokey Robinson is finally changing label.

CHARTS

US45	All The Man That I Need *Whitney Houston*
USLP	Mariah Carey *Mariah Carey*
UK45	Do The Bartman *Simpsons*
UKLP	Circle of One *Oleta Adams*
WEEK 2	
US45	Someday *Mariah Carey*
USLP	Mariah Carey *Mariah Carey*
UK45	Should I Stay Or Should I Go? *Clash*
UKLP	Auberge *Chris Rea*
WEEK 3	
US45	Someday *Mariah Carey*
USLP	Mariah Carey *Mariah Carey*
UK45	Should I Stay Or Should I Go? *Clash*
UKLP	Spartacus *Farm*
WEEK 4	
US45	One More Try *Timmy T*
USLP	Mariah Carey *Mariah Carey*
UK45	The Stonk *Hale and Pace*
UKLP	Out Of Time *R.E.M.*
WEEK 5	
US45	Coming Out Of The Dark *Gloria Estefan*
USLP	Mariah Carey *Mariah Carey*
UK45	The One And Only *Chesney Hawkes*
UKLP	Greatest Hits *Eurythmics*

CLASH RE-HASH SMASH – LABEL CASH-IN

Should they stay or should they go poser after post-punk pop success?

The legendary and much missed 70s band the Clash have shot to the top of the UK singles chart with their classic 'Should I Stay Or Should I Go'. The group, whose first album was released 14 years ago this month, have had 19 chart singles previously, but until now, had not hit the UK Top 10.

The reason that the single, which originally peaked at No. 17 in 1982, has taken these heroes of the punk generation back into the pop spotlight is that it is being used in the latest TV advert for Levi jeans.

Columbia Records is to release another of the group's 1982 hits, 'Rock The Casbah', as the follow-up. 'The Story Of Clash' album is also being re-issued and a video, 'This Is Video Clash', has been rushed out.

STAR QUOTE

SINEAD O'CONNOR

'I don't do anything in order to cause trouble. It just so happens that what I do naturally causes trouble. I'm proud to be a troublemaker'

INDIE SUMMERTIME

Many of Britain's foremost idie acts will be appearing at The Great Indie Festival – A Midsummer's Day Dream at the Milton Keynes Bowl in June.

A crowd of over 65,000 are expected to attend to see such media favourites as 808 State, Northside, Flowered Up and Gary Clail. Amongst the other acts expected to play are New Fast Automatic Daffodils, The Shamen, Paris Angels and the Shades of Rhythm.

MICHAEL JACKSON THRILLED

Mega-star Michael Jackson has recently signed an unprecedented, multi-media entertainment partnership contract with Sony that makes him the highest paid entertainer in the world. It has been estimated that in the long-term the deal could be worth more than $1 billion in sales to Sony who would be paying Jackson roughly twice the normal artist royalty.

The contract is believed to be the first made by an entertainer with one company that encompasses music, films, television, home video and electronic software. It gives Jackson his own record label called Nation Records, an entertainment complex in Hollywood and a production/development deal for films and television.

His first release under the new deal will be the album, 'Dangerous' which looks set to continue the block-buster traditions of 'Thriller' and 'Bad' whose combined total worldwide sales have now reached over 65 million.

APOLLO GOT THE BLUES

Harlem's legendary Apollo Theatre may be forced to close due to financial difficulties. Managers of the venue, whose amateur night launched stars such as Michael Jackson, Ella Fitzgerald and Luther Vandross, have persuaded US television's most popular comedian, Bill Cosby, to perform gratis for three nights to raise funds for the stricken theatre. James Brown, Quincy Jones and Dionne Warwick are also reportedly helping the Afro-American institution, which has lost nearly $5 million in the last two years.

Bill Cosby, helping to save Harlem's mecca of soul music

STEVE MARRIOTT DIES

Steve Marriott, the best known Face in the successful sixties group the Small Faces, has died tragically at his home, in a fire believed to have been started by a cigarette.

Marriott was a reluctant star, a chart regular in his teens when the Small Faces had a string of hits including 'All Or Nothing' and 'Sha La La La Lee'. The group adjusted easily to psychedelia in the late 1960s with 'Itchycoo Park' and the classic album 'Ogden's Nut Gone Flake', before Marriott quit to form the 'supergroup' Humble Pie with Peter Frampton.

Marriott spent the best part of the 70s leading Humble Pie after Frampton's 1971 departure and in 1977/78 was involved in the abortive Small Faces reunion. Just days before his death he had been working with Frampton in America.

The well loved R&B star with the big voice will be sorely missed.

Diminutive Face Steve Marriott

THE GRAPEVINE

- **Carter USM have signed to Chrysalis and the highly touted Manic Street Preachers are the subject of many major label record company bids.**
- **New Kid Donnie Wahlberg was charged with starting a fire in a Kentucky hotel – his punishment was to record public service announcements on fire safety, drug abuse and drink driving.**
- **Jesus Jones' US tour reportedly sold out before the UK group's arrival there.**

CHARTS

US45	Coming Out Of The Dark *Gloria Estefan*
USLP	Mariah Carey *Mariah Carey*
UK45	The One And Only *Chesney Hawkes*
UKLP	Greatest Hits *Eurythmics*
	WEEK 2
US45	I've Been Thinking About You *Londonbeat*
USLP	Mariah Carey *Mariah Carey*
UK45	The One And Only *Chesney Hawkes*
UKLP	Greatest Hits *Eurythmics*
	WEEK 3
US45	You're In Love *Wilson Phillips*
USLP	Mariah Carey *Mariah Carey*
UK45	The One And Only *Chesney Hawkes*
UKLP	Greatest Hits *Eurythmics*
	WEEK 4
US45	Baby Baby *Amy Grant*
USLP	Mariah Carey *Mariah Carey*
UK45	The One And Only *Chesney Hawkes*
UKLP	Greatest Hits *Eurythmics*

DEATH KNELL SOUNDS FOR RECORD PAPERS

Well-respected British music papers, 'Sounds' and 'Record Mirror' have folded.

'Sounds' was launched in 1970 in the progressive rock boom with sales peaking during the punk era. Launched in the 1950s, 'RM' was a pioneer in the soul and dance music fields.

Jesus Jones, big in America

MAY

1991

SATELLITE STARS HELP SAVE THE KURDS

Charity campaigners hailed the massive 'Save The Kurds' benefit concert at London's Wembley arena as "an organisational triumph that managed to cut across the bureaucratic red tape that can hamper these events". The show, known as 'The Simple Truth' (after the Chris De Burgh single), was broadcast to 27 countries worldwide and has raised an estimated £10 million.

Given only two weeks to stage the event, the Red Cross, promoter Harvey Goldsmith, BBC TV, author/politician Jeffrey Archer and MC Hammer's live production crew all teamed up and worked against the clock to get the three hour gig off the ground.

The line-up at Wembley included MC Hammer, Chris De Burgh, Gipsy Kings, Snap, Alison Moyet and Lisa Stansfield. By using satellite feeds from around the world for the first time it was possible to also feature live and recorded performances from top acts like Peter Gabriel, Sting, Sinead O'Connor, Gloria Estefan, New Kids On The Block, Paul Simon, Hall & Oates, Rod Stewart and INXS.

Proceeds will go to the Red Cross and other charities including Save The Children, Oxfam and Christian Aid. However, media reports about how the money raised will be distributed to the Kurds has caused concern since the event.

Lisa Stansfield snapped at pre-Grammy Awards party in Beverly Hills

GEFFEN GRAB FREED ROSES

Roses' thorny problem solved

Manchester's critically acclaimed Stone Roses celebrated their court victory over their former record company, Silvertone, by signing a long-term deal with US label Geffen estimated to be worth around £20 million to the group.

The British label claimed the band were in breach of contract in seeking another deal and wanted a court ruling obliging the Roses to record for them. The High Court judge declared their recording and publishing contracts with Silvertone 'entirely one-sided and unfair'.

Their first Geffen release is expected shortly despite the fact that Silvertone/Zomba have appealed against the decision and expect to haul the group through the High Courts again next year.

Country music superstar Garth Brooks

CHARTS

	US45	USLP	UK45	UKLP
	Baby Baby *Amy Grant*	Mariah Carey *Mariah Carey*	The Shoop Shoop Song *Cher*	Greatest Hits *Eurythmics*
WEEK 2	Joyride *Roxette*	Mariah Carey *Mariah Carey*	The Shoop Shoop Song *Cher*	Greatest Hits *Eurythmics*
WEEK 3	I Like The Way *Hi-Five*	Out Of Time *R.E.M.*	The Shoop Shoop Song *Cher*	Greatest Hits *Eurythmics*
WEEK 4	I Don't Wanna Cry *Mariah Carey*	Time, Love And Tenderness *Michael Bolton*	The Shoop Shoop Song *Cher*	Greatest Hits *Eurythmics*

INDIE CHART ATTACK

The British independent chart may soon be scrapped and replaced by an 'alternative' chart based on musical direction.

The indie scene has recently been in turmoil following the collapse of distributor Rough Trade, whose marketing system had been the springboard for many of today's prominent indie acts from The Stone Roses and Happy Mondays to Ned's Atomic Dustbin and The KLF.

However, major labels have long been grumbling because their indie-styled acts like The Housemartins, The Wonder Stuff, Jesus Jones and Blur are excluded from the chart. Many feel that the term 'indie' is redundant now that bands like James and Carter USM are on major labels while ironically Jason and Kylie remain independent.

THE GRAPEVINE

- **The Happy Mondays US tour has proved less successful than expected, with the group returning home early due to 'illness' and 'technical difficulties'.**
- **Johnny Thunders of the New York Dolls and the Heartbreakers has died aged 38.**
- **Garth Brooks has won an unprecedented six Academy Of Country Music Awards.**
- **'Out Of Time' by REM is the first LP by a rock band to top the US chart for eighteen months.**

PMRC FAIL TO JAIL OZZY

US judges have finally cleared Ozzy Osbourne of causing the death of an American fan. The boy's parents alleged that Ozzy's 'Suicide Solution' record contained subliminal messages and that their teenage son committed suicide in 1986 after listening to it repeatedly.

This has been another blow for American pro-censorship campaigners, the influential Parents Music Resource Center (PMRC), following their unsuccessful case against fellow UK metallers Judas Priest, who, they claim, also attempt to drive their audience to suicide through the use of backwards masked messages.

Osbourne: jail threat removed

However, the PMRC has intensified its efforts to prove rock threatens the mental and physical health of young listeners. Their recent reports, produced in conjunction with medical organisations and Parent-Teachers Associations, have stressed the alleged 'racist' and 'sexist' content of the lyrics of Guns N' Roses and several rap acts.

CHARTS

	US45	I Don't Wanna Cry	*Mariah Carey*
	USLP	Out Of Time	*R.E.M.*
	UK45	The Shoop Shoop Song	*Cher*
	UKLP	Seal	*Seal*
WEEK 2	US45	More Than Words	*Extreme*
	USLP	Spellbound	*Paula Abdul*
	UK45	I Wanna Sex You Up	*Color Me Badd*
	UKLP	Seal	*Seal*
WEEK 3	US45	Rush Rush	*Paula Abdul*
	USLP	Spellbound	*Paula Abdul*
	UK45	I Wanna Sex You Up	*Color Me Badd*
	UKLP	Seal	*Seal*
WEEK 4	US45	Rush Rush	*Paula Abdul*
	USLP	Efil4zaggin	*NWA*
	UK45	I Wanna Sex You Up	*Color Me Badd*
	UKLP	Seal	*Seal*
WEEK 5	US45	Rush Rush	*Paula Abdul*
	USLP	Slave To The Grind	*Skid Row*
	UK45	Any Dream Will Do	*Jason Donovan*
	UKLP	Love Hurts	*Cher*

- **Will Sinnott, frontman of the Shamen, drowned in a freak accident in the Canary Islands.**
- **Billy Joel sued his accountant and former manager for $90 million.**
- **Gene Clark of the Byrds died on Bob Dylan's 50th birthday.**
- **In Britain the police impounded 13,000 of NWA's 'Efil4zaggin' album.**

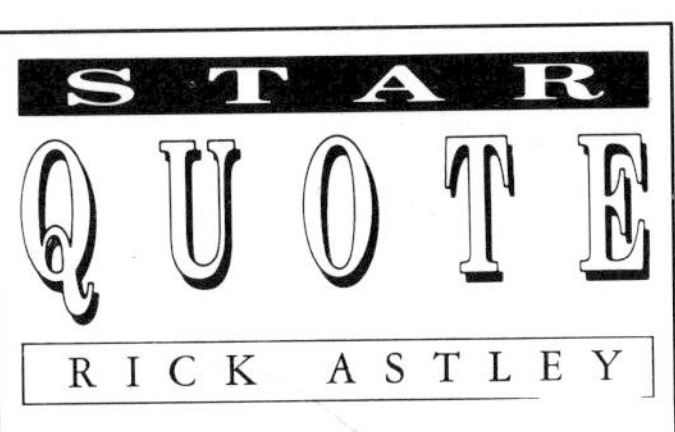

'I'm not your classically handsome devil, and I haven't got animal magnetism. I'm a bit of a git really'

10 YEARS OF INDIE CHARTS

NME celebrated the tenth anniversary of its Indie chart by listing the period's top records. These included:–

Top singles
'Blue Monday' *New Order*
'She Sells Sanctuary' *The Cult*

Top singles artists
New Order
The Smiths
Depeche Mode

Top singles labels
Factory
Rough Trade
Mute

Top albums
'The Stone Roses' *The Stone Roses*
'Pillows And Prayers' *Various Artists*

Top album artists
The Smiths
New Order
Stone Roses/Cocteau Twins

Top album labels
Rough Trade
4AD
Factory

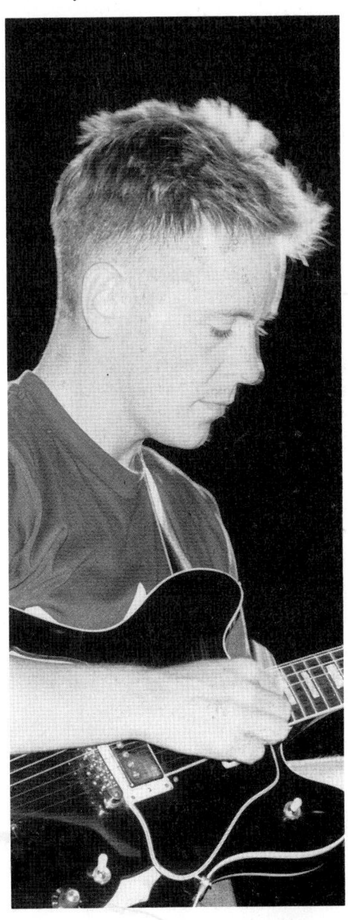
Bernard Sumner of Top Album and Singles band New Order

US BANS BRIT BANDS

Tough new US Immigration regulations to be tabled this autumn look set to jeopardise British bands' chances of breaking into the world's most lucrative record-buying market. The proposed new laws would limit foreign entertainers admitted to the US to 25,000 – just one-third the number currently admitted each year.

The bill could put an end to young British acts emulating the success of Cathy Dennis, Jesus Jones and EMF, in making a major US impact. A spokesman for top US booking agents Triad, whose clients include Brit Bands Happy Mondays and The Wonder Stuff, said 'It's a very dangerous and limiting bill – everybody is up in arms about it.'

TEMPTATION REMOVED

50 year old David Ruffin, a founder member of soul supergroup The Temptations, has died in Los Angeles following a reaction to cocaine.

Lead vocalist on the Motown group's first US No. 1 'My Girl', Ruffin quit the group in 1968. His subsequent career included big mid 70s hits with 'Walk Away With Love' and 'My Whole World Ended'.

The funeral, paid for by Michael Jackson and attended by a galaxy of stars including Stevie Wonder, Aretha Franklin and Diana Ross, was disrupted when fellow Temptation Eddie Kendricks was arrested for non-payment of child support.

G N' R GET THE ST. LOUIS BLUES

Guns N' Roses could face charges of inciting a riot after 60 people were injured in a brawl involving some 2,500 fans at a St. Louis concert whose promoters have charged them with 'evil motive and reckless indifference'.

Ninety minutes into the show, trouble flared after Axl Rose tried to confiscate a concert-goer's unauthorised camera. An eyewitness reported 'Axl got mad, jumped into the audience and started beating the guy up'.

Rose blamed 'inexperienced security staff' for the trouble and claims fans were allowed to retain knives and bottles and to take photos. Following the fracas, the band stormed off the stage in protest.

Reports differ about what happened next. Some say the audience rioted because the band refused to return, others support G N' R's claim that they tried to return but were not allowed to by the police and promoter. Either way, fans ran wild, fighting and destroying seats and stampeding the stage, destroying video screens and the band's drums and amplifiers.

Rose said he hopes that rock fans don't see the event as a signal that the band condones rowdy behaviour . . .

The Guns were out in old St Louis as the local cops tried in vain to control the rioting Roses fans – or more accurately, ex-fans, who took it out on the stadium seats after Axl attacked an audience cameraman.

MONDAYS HAPPY WITH BOOTLEG

Happy Mondays have revealed details of a 14-track 'official bootleg' live album, 'Baby Big Head', recorded directly from the mixing desk at their recent stadium date in Leeds.

Shaun Ryder said, 'The people who've done the bootleg assure me that all profits are going to sick animals and poor children. Unlike most bootlegs, the sound quality is brilliant and so is the cover design'.

Factory Records are planning an official release worldwide later this year.

Mondays live at Leeds

BRITISH INVASION '91

The American music business is again reeling under a 'British Invasion'.

The 'unbelievable' EMF's sell-out tour has been ecstatically received and has been compared to the legendary Beatles shows. Their 'Schubert Dip' has shot into the album Top 20, while their single 'Unbelievable' has become the first Stateside No. 1 from the new wave of British bands.

Also doing brisk business are Jesus Jones who have recently returned from a major US tour, where their single 'Right Here, Right Now' reached the Top 3.

Another UK success story is that of Morrissey who, despite a lack of hit singles, sold out a US indoor stadia tour. His show has been the scene of hysterical fan reaction, record-breaking merchandise sales and ludicrous black market ticket prices.

Other UK acts starting to make their mark Stateside are Ned's Atomic Dustbin, KLF, Seal, The La's and Electronic.

EMF, leading yet another Brit invasion of the good ol' USA

THE GRAPEVINE

- After 10 years with hit act Alarm, leader Mike Peters has gone solo.
- Doors' fans caused considerable damage when they gathered at Jim Morrison's graveside on the 20th anniversary of his death.
- Van Halen have scored their third successive US No. 1 album with 'For Unlawful Carnal Knowledge'.

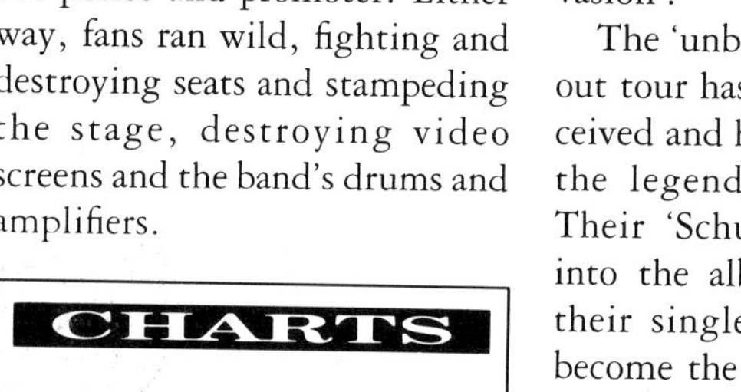

CHARTS

US45	Rush Rush – *Paula Abdul*
USLP	For Unlawful Carnal Knowledge – *Van Halen*
UK45	Any Dream Will Do – *Jason Donovan*
UKLP	Love Hurts – *Cher*
WEEK 2	
US45	Rush Rush – *Paula Abdul*
USLP	For Unlawful Carnal Knowledge – *Van Halen*
UK45	(Everything I Do) I Do It For You – *Bryan Adams*
UKLP	Love Hurts – *Cher*
WEEK 3	
US45	Unbelievable – *EMF*
USLP	For Unlawful Carnal Knowledge – *Van Halen*
UK45	(Everything I Do) I Do It For You – *Bryan Adams*
UKLP	Love Hurts – *Cher*
WEEK 4	
US45	(Everything I Do) I Do It For You – *Bryan Adams*
USLP	Unforgettable – *Natalie Cole*
UK45	(Everything I Do) I Do It For You – *Bryan Adams*
UKLP	Love Hurts – *Cher*

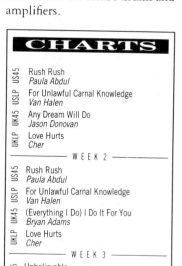

UNBELIEVABLE – EMF GET STATESIDE SET-UP

EMF slammed US authorities after being arrested for criminal damage in Louisiana during their recent sell-out tour.

The band were taken into custody after a club promotion turned sour. Guitarist Ian Dench said 'Without prior warning, we were told to mime to a CD which started 'jumping', for fun we passed a couple of guitars into the audience – they turned out to belong to the deputy sherriff, who also just happened to be the club owner.' Bassist Zak Foley said 'It was a set-up. They wanted $40,000 for the guitars or we would be jailed for 26 days. But they took $20,000, dropped the charges and then just shared it out. It looked so f...ing corrupt.'

CHARTS

US45	(Everything I Do) I Do It For You	Bryan Adams
USLP	Unforgettable	Natalie Cole
UK45	(Everything I Do) I Do It For You	Bryan Adams
UKLP	Love Hurts	Cher
WEEK 2		
US45	(Everything I Do) I Do It For You	Bryan Adams
USLP	Unforgettable	Natalie Cole
UK45	(Everything I Do) I Do It For You	Bryan Adams
UKLP	Essential Pavarotti II	Luciano Pavarotti
WEEK 3		
US45	(Everything I Do) I Do It For You	Bryan Adams
USLP	Unforgettable	Natalie Cole
UK45	(Everything I Do) I Do It For You	Bryan Adams
UKLP	Essential Pavarotti II	Luciano Pavarotti
WEEK 4		
US45	(Everything I Do) I Do It For You	Bryan Adams
USLP	Unforgettable	Natalie Cole
UK45	(Everything I Do) I Do It For You	Bryan Adams
UKLP	Metallica	Metallica
WEEK 5		
US45	(Everything I Do) I Do It For You	Bryan Adams
USLP	Metallica	Metallica
UK45	(Everything I Do) I Do It For You	Bryan Adams
UKLP	Joseph And The Technicolor Dreamcoat	Jason Donovan/Cast

BONO ON AIDS & BOOTLEGGERS

As producers Daniel Lanois & Brian Eno try to finish the long awaited new U2 album, vocalist Bono haa hit out at the 'absurdity' of the Irish Catholic Church's attitude to AIDS and condoms, accusing it on a radio station of 'dark, medieval thinking' in condemning all forms of birth control. U2 recently paid a £500 fine on behalf of the Dublin Virgin Megastore, imposed for selling condoms in protest at 'an absurd law' making it illegal for condoms to be sold anywhere other than pharmacies and doctor's surgeries. A spokesman for the church retorted that it was 'extremely concerned' at the spread of AIDS, and has always taught that the abuse of sex or drugs is morally wrong.

Meanwhile, U2's label and management have declared war on bootleggers dealing in poor quality recordings of rehearsals and out-takes. Commented manager Paul McGuinness: 'I don't like to see people being ripped off'.

SUPERFREAK, CRACK AND ORAL SEX

The end of the line for fallen star Rick James

Ex-Motown star Rick James, who was recently dropped by Warner Bros., and his 21 year old girl friend, Tanya Ann Hijazi, face life imprisonment if they are convicted on charges of imprisonment, torture and sexual assault at their Hollywood home.

It is claimed that they met a 24 year old woman at a party and invited her back to their house, where she was threatened with a gun, tied up and burned with a hot crack/cocaine pipe. James is then said to have forced her to indulge in oral sex with his girl friend and to smoke crack, finally releasing her after three days. A doctor at the hospital into which she was admitted notified the police of her claims.

With bail set at $1 million initially, and with James still in custody, his house has been robbed – an unhappy hat-trick by any standards.

Prince snubs audience at Palace

THE GRAPEVINE

- In an effort to acquire unpaid royalties, The Smiths put in a petition to wind up Rough Trade Distribution.
- At the eleventh hour Prince cancelled an eagerly anticipated show at Blenheim Palace.
- Vaughn Toulouse, vocalist and founder of Department S (of 'Is Vic There?' fame) has died after an AIDS related illness.

LAWSUIT CHUCKED AT LIQUOR CO.

Public Enemy's Chuck D has filed a $5 million lawsuit against the company responsible for marketing St. Ides malt liquor.

The rapper alleges a sample of his voice exclaiming 'The Incredible Number One!' lifted from 'Bring The Noise' has been used in a radio commercial without his permission. Previous commercials have featured rap stars like Ice Cube and EMPD.

His lawyer stated 'Chuck has frequently spoken out against the practice of malt liquor companies targeting black youth. Because people know he's a friend of Ice Cube, they assume he's endorsed the product.'

Chuck chokes on booze backing

MTV, REM, EMF, ETC.

True Brits Jesus Jones, the only UK winners in the annual MTV awards where they collected the Best New Artist trophy

The eighth annual MTV Awards were dominated by REM, who won six categories for their 'Losing My Religion' video, including Best Group and Best Video Of The Year. However, plans for worldwide screening of the award ceremony had to be changed when EMF, who topped the US charts with 'Unbelievable' this summer, liberally used the F-word during a live show in London which was being filmed by an MTV crew. A spokesperson for EMF commented 'The band don't think they went particularly over the top'.

The only British winners were Jesus Jones, who took the Best New Artist category. Other award winners included Chris Isaak, whose 'Wicked Game' clip won Best Male Video and Best Video From A Film, and C&C Music Factory's 'Gonna Make You Sweat'. The award of the Video Vanguard title (for advancing the art of music video) to Bon Jovi was not popular among critics – past winners include Peter Gabriel, Michael Jackson and Madonna.

CHARTS

US45	(Everything I Do) I Do It For You *Bryan Adams*
USLP	Metallica *Metallica*
UK45	(Everything I Do) I Do It For You *Bryan Adams*
UKLP	Joseph And The Technicolor Dreamcoat *Jason Donovan/Cast*
	WEEK 2
US45	The Promise Of A New Day *Paula Abdul*
USLP	Metallica *Metallica*
UK45	(Everything I Do) I Do It For You *Bryan Adams*
UKLP	From Time To Time – The Singles *Paul Young*
	WEEK 3
US45	I Ador Mi Amor *Color Me Badd*
USLP	Metallica *Metallica*
UK45	(Everything I Do) I Do It For You *Bryan Adams*
UKLP	On Every Street *Dire Straits*
	WEEK 4
US45	I Ador Mi Amor *Color Me Badd*
USLP	Ropin' The Wind *Garth Brooks*
UK45	(Everything I Do) I Do It For You *Bryan Adams*
UKLP	Use Your Illusion II *Guns n' Roses*

THE GRAPEVINE

- Clash were offered a reported $10 million to reform for a US tour.
- KLF have teamed on record with country superstar Tammy Wynette to record 'Justified And Ancient'.
- Metallica's self-titled album entered the US chart at No. 1 – a rare feat.
- Joe Strummer replaced Shane MacGowan in the Pogues on the eve of an American tour.
- MC5 vocalist Rob Tyner died of a heart attack.

STAR QUOTE

DAVID BOWIE

'My interest in music dissipated during the '80s as I realised that it was less important than I am'

METAL MAYHEM

Guns N' Roses are involved in controversy again. Frontman Axl Rose turned down a challenge from Motley Crue vocalist Vince Neil to a boxing match.

Neil told NME 'I've listened to him badmouth me and my band for too long. Last year, he challenged me to a fight – now's the time, Axl, unless you're all talk'. A spokesman for Rose noted: 'Axl has got better things to do'.

Rose halted G N' R's Copenhagen show for 15 minutes when a firecracker was thrown at him. The group may be banned from Wembley Stadium after Rose defied instructions from the local council to minimise the use of swear words. He screamed to the audience 'You're all f . . . ers', described the music press as 'motherf . . . ers', and called the Wembley date 'the end of our motherf . . . ing tour'. All this after a poster campaign proclaiming 'Guns N' F . . . ing Roses, Wembley F . . . ing Stadium, Sold F . . . ing Out'.

Crue's Vince calls Axl's bluff

BLACKLISTED BRYAN

Bryan Adams, who has dominated the No. 1 spot on the UK singles charts, has finally surrendered his crown after a record-breaking 16-week run with his single 'Everything I Do (I Do It For You)' smashing Slim Whitman's 11 week record set in 1955 with 'Rose Marie'.

Ironically, Adam's offering was almost shelved by the producers of the movie *Robin Hood: Prince Of Thieves* as being 'too weak'.

Surprisingly, Adams has just been virtually blacklisted in his native Canada. His new LP 'Waking Up The Neighbours' has been declared 'un-Canadian' by the country's Radio And Television Commission, who have restricted airing of the LP tracks to a maximum 19 plays per week on any Canadian FM station.

Adams, previously honoured with The Order Of Canada and The Order Of British Columbia for his work, is 'shocked' about the restrictions, imposed simply because the songs were co-written with British producer Mutt Lange.

Broadcast ban on Bryan

CHARTS

US45	Good Vibrations *Marky Mark & The Funky Bunch*
USLP	Use Your Illusion II *Guns n' Roses*
UK45	(Everything I Do) I Do It For You *Bryan Adams*
UKLP	Waking Up The Neighbours *Bryan Adams*
WEEK 2	
US45	Emotions *Mariah Carey*
USLP	Use Your Illusion II *Guns n' Roses*
UK45	(Everything I Do) I Do It For You *Bryan Adams*
UKLP	Stars *Simply Red*
WEEK 3	
US45	Emotions *Mariah Carey*
USLP	Ropin' The Wind *Garth Brooks*
UK45	(Everything I Do) I Do It For You *Bryan Adams*
UKLP	Stars *Simply Red*
WEEK 4	
US45	Emotions *Mariah Carey*
USLP	Ropin' The Wind *Garth Brooks*
UK45	(Everything I Do) I Do It For You *Bryan Adams*
UKLP	Chorus *Erasure*

TOP 10 WOMEN – NOT WORLD'S BEST DRESSED

'Cher not chic' fashion claim

Cher has just topped an American list of the worst-dressed women of the past 30 years, while Madonna, Sinead O'Connor, Barbra Streisand and Dolly Parton made the Top Ten.

The list's compiler, fashion expert Mr.Blackwell, says Cher is a 'bona fide fashion fiasco – from nose to toes she's the tacky tattooed terror' and calls Sinead 'a monastic monstrosity in baggy rags and combat boots – a creepy cross between Joan of Arc and Kojak'.

BOWIE IN BALLOT BALONEY

David Bowie, who could be nominated for January induction to the US Rock And Roll Hall Of Fame, wants his name removed from the list for consideration. He told a TV interviewer, 'I think the whole thing is bullshit. I know my own worth. I don't need a medal.'

A Hall of Fame spokesperson said the ballot paper, with Bowie's name included, has already been sent to delegates.

(RED) CROSS KURDS – THE SIMPLE TRUTH?

Sinead O'Connor, Peter Gabriel and MC Hammer have now become embroiled in a political row over possible bureaucratic mismanagement of the funds they helped raise for the starving Kurdish refugees with their Simple Truth concerts, which were broadcast worldwide by satellite four months ago.

A controversial report in a national Sunday newspaper has suggested that British writer/politician Jeffrey Archer organiser of the Simple Truth campaign, cancelled a trip to Iraq, dismaying Kurdish leaders who reportedly haven't seen any of the £57 million raised.

Archer insists that the campaign proceeds went directly to Red Cross and United Nations charities, while the Red Cross say money has already been spent in helping the Kurds.

Sinead: Simple Truth support suspect

THE GRAPEVINE

- **Guns N' Roses albums 'Use Your Illusion I & II' (which are stickered 'The album contains language some listeners may find objectionable. They can f..k off and buy something from the New Age section') entered both the UK and US charts in the top two positions.**
- **After a four year legal battle, Bruce Springsteen reportedly had to pay two of his roadies $350,000 compensation.**

QUICKSILVER FREDDIE LOSES AIDS BATTLE

Superstar Queen vocalist Freddie Mercury's death from AIDS has prompted industry rumours that the group's 1975 Number One hit, 'Bohemian Rhapsody', is to be re-released, and will be followed by a marketing blitz of Queen material over Christmas.

Years of speculation over whether Mercury was suffering from the debilitating virus ended with a statement to the press by the star, and within 24 hours another statement announced that he had died of bronchio-pneumonia brought on by AIDS.

EMI Records, Queen's label, would not comment on rumours that the group have recorded between three and eight albums worth of material ready to be released, and that several accompanying videos have already been shot to promote them.

One of the many faces of arch showman Freddie Mercury

CHARTS

	US45	Romantic	Karyn White
	USLP	Ropin' The Wind	Garth Brooks
	UK45	The Fly	U2
	UKLP	Stars	Simply Red
WEEK 2	US45	Cream	Prince & The N.P.G.
	USLP	Ropin' The Wind	Garth Brooks
	UK45	Dizzy	Vic Reeves & The Wonderstuff
	UKLP	Queen's Greatest Hits II	Queen
WEEK 3	US45	Cream	Prince & The N.P.G.
	USLP	Ropin' The Wind	Garth Brooks
	UK45	Dizzy	Vic Reeves & The Wonderstuff
	UKLP	Shepherd Moons	Enya
WEEK 4	US45	When A Man Loves A Woman	Michael Bolton
	USLP	Ropin' The Wind	Garth Brooks
	UK45	Black Or White	Michael Jackson
	UKLP	We Can't Dance	Genesis
WEEK 5	US45	Set Adrift On A Memory Bliss	PM Dawn
	USLP	Ropin' The Wind	Garth Brooks
	UK45	Black Or White	Michael Jackson
	UKLP	Dangerous	Michael Jackson

Michael Bolton tops US chart

MONEY TALKS

The Rolling Stones have signed to Virgin Records in a three album deal worth £25 million, which also involves the rights to all the group's back catalogue post-1971. Polygram are rumoured to have ended negotiations with the veteran superstars because the group would not guarantee that the last ever Stones album would appear on a Polygram label.

Madonna is reportedly close to signing a $20-30 million extension of her current Sire/Warner Bros. contract. It's the latest in a flurry of immense record deals, starting last March with Janet Jackson signing with Virgin for $40 million, a few days before her brother, Michael, completed a $65 million agreement with Sony Inc. involving records, films and videos, while Aerosmith have moved from Geffen to Sony for $37 million and Motley Crue have re-signed with Elektra for $37 million. Madonna's lower advance is balanced by a guaranteed 2% rise in her royalty rate (to 20%!), a $5 million advance per album and $1 million to set up offices for her new company, Home.

THE GRAPEVINE

- **After much transatlantic negative feedback Michael Jackson's controversial video for 'Black And White' had its four minute dance sequence deleted – it contained shots thought to encourage violence and said to simulate masturbation.**
- **Legendary US concert promoter Bill Graham and top songwriter Mort Shuman have both died.**
- **Vanilla Ice's film debut, 'Cold As Ice', met with a very cool reception.**

Madonna re-signs to Sire

. . .while Michael pens Sony deal

RUGBY SONGS BY NWA

Charges relating to Niggers With Attitude's 'Efil4zaggin' album, which was seized by the Obscene Publications Squad in June, have been dismissed. The whole LP, including such titles as 'Findum, F . . . 'em And Flee', 'I'd Rather F . . . You' and 'To Kill A Hooker' was played on a tape machine to Redbridge magistrates. Defending QC Geoffrey Robertson called the album 'the black equivalent to our rugby songs', adding that its lyrics were 'vivid, disturbing and shocking, but a million miles from pornography'. Following their legal triumph, NWA have distributed posters citing Article 19 of the Universal Declaration of Human Rights in a gesture of defiance towards censorship campaigners.

CHARTS

US45	Black Or White *Michael Jackson*
USLP	Achtung Baby *U2*
UK45	Don't Let The Sun Go Down On Me *George Michael/Elton John*
UKLP	Queen's Greatest Hits II *Queen*
	WEEK 2
US45	Black Or White *Michael Jackson*
USLP	Dangerous *Michael Jackson*
UK45	Don't Let The Sun Go Down On Me *George Michael/Elton John*
UKLP	Queen's Greatest Hits II *Queen*
	WEEK 3
US45	Black Or White *Michael Jackson*
USLP	Dangerous *Michael Jackson*
UK45	Bohemian Rhapsody *Queen*
UKLP	Queen's Greatest Hits II *Queen*
	WEEK 4
US45	Black Or White *Michael Jackson*
USLP	Dangerous *Michael Jackson*
UK45	Bohemian Rhapsody *Queen*
UKLP	Queen's Greatest Hits II *Queen*

THE GRAPEVINE

- **Beach Boy Brian Wilson avoided a lengthy legal feud with his family by severing all ties with his therapist and business adviser Dr. Eugene Landy, who it is said 'brainwashed him'.**
- **Kiss' drummer Eric Carr and Jacques Morali, the mentor of the Village People, both died.**
- **Fifties R&R great Little Richard was the preacher at Cyndi Lauper's wedding in New York.**

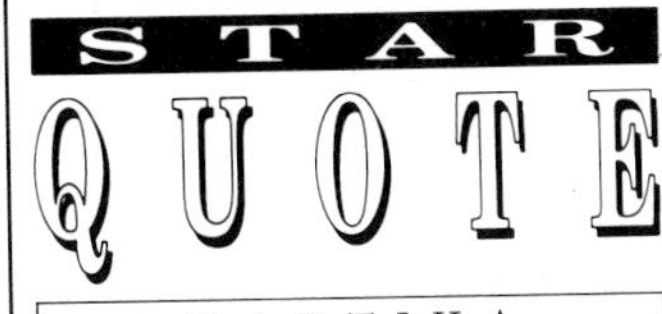

MARTIKA

'Nothing on Earth really exists. It's all an illusion. When human beings manage to connect with each other that is heaven'

THIS IS FOR THE CHILDREN – KIDS LOVE THE KIDS

New Kids – current titleholders in teenybopper sob stakes wham Wembley crowd

Recalling a long tradition of teen hysteria dating from the Beatles and Stones, through the Osmonds and the Bay City Rollers to Wham!, the New Kids On The Block played to a hysterical, overwhelmingly female, Wembley Arena audience. An estimated 13,000 young fans came to see the New York quintet and all the usual manifestations of concert hysteria were present: screaming, sobbing, fainting and the continual flashing of camera bulbs – not to mention some very sexually suggestive banners.

The music – virtually relegated to secondary importance at the event and almost indiscernible behind the screams – was a safe blend of dance songs, AOR ballads and light rap aided visually by breakdancing and fireworks. Vocals were shared, with Donnie Wahlberg mostly handling the rap style numbers, Jordan Knight and Joey McIntyre taking care of the slower songs with Jon Knight and Danny Wood adding harmony.

The audience loved them, yet one couldn't shake the feeling that NKOTB have peaked and, like their predecessors, will soon be replaced in teenage fantasies by some even newer kids.

NME BEST OF 91

Creation Records collected over half the Top 5 honours in the NME 'Best Records Of 1991' as selected by NME critics.

REM lead singer and mainman Michael Stipe

Top 5 LPs

1. 'Nevermind' *Nirvana* (DGC)
2. 'Bandwagonesque' *Teenage Fanclub* (Creation)
3. 'Screamadelica' *Primal Scream* (Creation)
4. 'Weld' *Neil Young and Crazy Horse* (Reprise)
5. 'Out Of Time' *REM* (Warner Bros.)

Top 5 Singles

1. 'Higher Than The Sun' *Primal Scream* (Creation)
2. 'Justified And Ancient' *The KLF* (KLF Communications)
3. 'Losing My Religion' *REM* (Warner Bros.)
4. 'Starsign' *Teenage Fanclub* (Creation)
5. 'The Concept' *Teenage Fanclub* (Creation)

JUSTICE FOR ZIGGY AND MARLEY FAMILY

Bob Marley's family have been given control of the late superstar's estate, after more than a decade of controversial legal wrangles.

The Supreme Court of Jamaica rejected a $15.2 million offer by MCA Music Publishing in favour of a joint bid – almost $4 million less – by Marley's immediate family (widow Rita, children Ziggy, Cedella and Stevie) in tandem with Chris Blackwell's Island Logic company.

The legal minefield over Marley's estate began in 1981 when the singer died intestate – a document purporting to be his will was later declared a forgery – since when numerous million dollar claims and counter-claims from record companies have been made.

As the decision finally was announced, Ziggy Marley's wife was giving birth to their first daughter, who was instantly given the name Justice.

Bob Marley: reggae legacy

SIMON SAYS YES – ENEMY FOLLOW HIM TO S.A.?

Paul Simon, despite success of 'Graceland', still dogged by South African controversy

Paul Simon's upcoming South African tour has hit severe difficulties. Thousands of seats are still unsold at Johannesburg's 70,000 capacity Ellis Park Stadium and continuing threats from black nationalist groups have culminated in a grenade attack by the Azanian National Liberation Army on the offices of the company providing the tour's sound equipment. Nevertheless Simon has vowed to go ahead with the five dates, claiming support from the ANC, Foreign Minister Pik Botha and Inkatha.

No such problems are predicted for Public Enemy's proposed tour of the country. PE with their avowed black consciousness and their firm anti-apartheid stance have consistently been popular in the nation's townships. A local promoter said 'The eyes of many Afro-American artists will be fixed on the tour'.

Meanwhile PE's Hank Shocklee has remixed the Manic Street Preachers' 'Repeat' but the groups are unlikely to work closely together. Preacher Nicky Wire stated 'I'm glad they wouldn't work with us. I wouldn't want them to be wasting time on a poxy white band like us. They're way above anything we could do.'

THAT'S SHOW, BIZ!

Biz Markie and '70s UK pop star Gilbert O'Sullivan have agreed a settlement to resolve a copyright infringement lawsuit over Markie's unauthorised sampling of O'Sullivan's 1972 hit 'Alone Again (Naturally)'.

Following the court ruling in O'Sullivan's favour, Markie's label Warner Brothers ran an unprecedented advertisement in US music magazine 'Billboard' asking retailers not to sell Markie's album 'I Need A Haircut'.

O'Sullivan's lawyers predicted that this case will have a dramatic effect on the future of sampling saying 'This represents the first judicial pronouncement that this practice is theft'.

CHARTS

US45	Black Or White – *Michael Jackson*
USLP	Dangerous – *Michael Jackson*
UK45	Bohemian Rhapsody – *Queen*
UKLP	Stars – *Simply Red*
WEEK 2	
US45	Black Or White – *Michael Jackson*
USLP	Nevermind – *Nirvana*
UK45	Bohemian Rhapsody – *Queen*
UKLP	Stars – *Simply Red*
WEEK 3	
US45	Black Or White – *Michael Jackson*
USLP	Ropin' The Wind – *Garth Brooks*
UK45	Bohemian Rhapsody – *Queen*
UKLP	Stars – *Simply Red*
WEEK 4	
US45	All 4 Love – *Color Me Badd*
USLP	Ropin' The Wind – *Garth Brooks*
UK45	Goodnight Girl – *Wet Wet Wet*
UKLP	Stars – *Simply Red*

THE GRAPEVINE

- A front page article in the UK press claimed that on stage EMF encouraged their fans to take the drug Ecstasy.
- NME readers voted REM top band, Nirvana's 'Smells Like Teen Spirit' top single and Primal Screams 'Screamadelica' top album.
- It was announced that both Elvis Presley and Buddy Holly would be appearing on US postage stamps.

NIRVANA REPLACE U2 IN IRISH HEARTS

Ireland's national radio station 2FM has reported an upset in their end-of-year listeners poll, the Fanning Fab 50. The station's Dave Fanning announced that Nirvana's 'Smells Like Teen Spirit' has dislodged U2 from the top spot, ending the Irish group's six year poll dominance. 'It wasn't expected,' he explained, 'they'd only played Ireland once, supporting Sonic Youth, but it was one of those songs that only comes along once in a while.'

Nonetheless U2 registered with five singles, Bad (Number 2), One (8), The Fly (13), One Tree Hill (17), Sunday Bloody Sunday (43) and Pride (45).

Other bands to score included the Pixies and REM and newcomers included The Frank And Walters, Curve, Carter USM and Ned's Atomic Dustbin.

Bono: U2 losing their touch

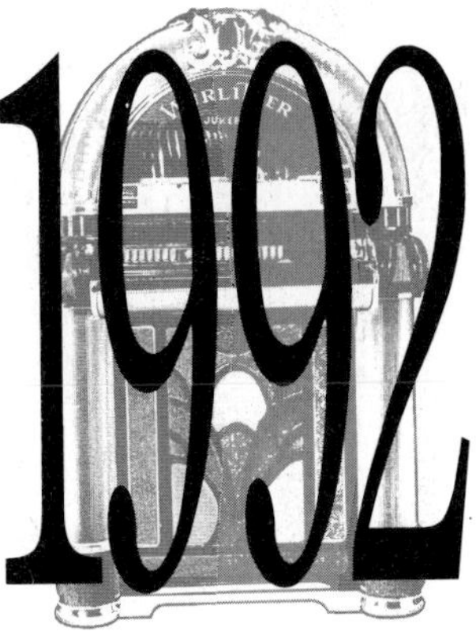

KLF BRIGHTEN UP BRITS

The bizarre antics of KLF brought chaos to the BRITS awards resulting in heavy BBC censorship and almost prompting a walkout by classical winner Sir Georg Solti.

They opened with a thrash version of '3am Eternal' which climaxed when Bill Drummond – dressed in a kilt and propped up by a crutch fired blanks from a machine gun at the black tie audience declaring: 'this is television freedom'. Drummond exited, stating 'KLF have left the music industry.'

BBC lawyers had earlier scrutinised the group's rehearsal after rumours that KLF planned to disembowel a dead sheep and throw buckets of blood at the audience.

The band then left unaware that they had jointly won the Best British Group Award. On hearing the news they sent a motor-cycle courier – who was refused admission – to collect the statuette.

In an event-filled evening Mick Hucknall declined Simply Red's Best British Group Award, donating it to second placed Queen while REM's Michael Stipe, in collecting the Best International Group award, sported a baseball hat declaring 'White House Stop AIDS', and Seal virtually swept the board in the British section.

In other awards, Prince won Best International Solo Artist, Lisa Stansfield Best British Female Artist and Beverley Craven Best British Newcomer.

New Brits superstar Seal

HATS OFF TO GARTH

Current country phenomenon and mega-seller Garth Brooks

America's No. 1 album comes from last year's top selling album artist, country singer/songwriter, Garth Brooks, whose first three albums (with combined sales exceeding 15 million) currently hold the Top 3 positions on the US country chart and are all in the Pop Top 20. Brooks has the two best selling country albums of all time and his 'Ropin' The Wind', which entered the pop chart at No. 1, shipped 2.6 million in a week to become the first album ever to go quadruple platinum in its first month – not bad for an act who has yet to enter the US Pop singles chart.

END OF ERA – BAND AID DISBANDED

Band Aid, the charity organisation formed by Bob Geldof in 1984, has finally closed its accounts, having raised a staggering £110 million for famine relief in Africa.

The movement, which revolutionised charity work through its innovative staging of international events like Live Aid, has distributed the money equally between direct relief work and long term development. Only 2% of the total was spent on administration.

Geldof admitted 'It was only meant to last seven weeks, but I hadn't counted on the fact that hundreds of millions of people would respond.'

THE GRAPEVINE

- **Sinead O'Connor stormed the Irish parliament and made sure the Prime Minister was aware of her views on the current Abortion crisis there.**
- **Influential R&B/Blues writer/performer Willie Dixon has died.**
- **Michael Jackson has signed the biggest sponsorship deal yet with Pepsi Cola.**
- **Record breaking US hit maker Mariah Carey has been sued by her step-father for not sharing her earnings with him.**

CHARTS

Chart	Week 1	Week 2	Week 3	Week 4	Week 5
US45	Don't Let The Sun Go Down On Me *George Michael/Elton John*	I'm Too Sexy *Right Said Fred*	I'm Too Sexy *Right Said Fred*	I'm Too Sexy *Right Said Fred*	To Be With You *Mr. Big*
USLP	Nevermind *Nirvana*	Ropin' The Wind *Garth Brooks*	Ropin' The Wind *Garth Brooks*	Ropin' The Wind *Garth Brooks*	Ropin' The Wind *Garth Brooks*
UK45	Goodnight Girl *Wet Wet Wet*	Goodnight Girl *Wet Wet Wet*	Goodnight Girl *Wet Wet Wet*	Stay *Shakespears Sister*	Stay *Shakespears Sister*
UKLP	Stars *Simply Red*	High On The Happy Side *Wet Wet Wet*	High On The Happy Side *Wet Wet Wet*	Stars *Simply Red*	Stars *Simply Red*

Mariah: step-father sues

QUEEN COLE'S UNFORGETTABLE EVENING

Natalie Cole's 'Unforgettable' album won an astonishing seven Grammys including the Album, Song and Record Of The Year awards and the studio-created duet 'Unforgettable', with her father Nat 'King' Cole, was named Best Single and Best Traditional Pop Performance.

The evening was seen as a triumph for tradition with many more progressive acts being overlooked. The critically acclaimed REM, for example, were beaten by Cole in each of the seven categories in which both acts were nominated, although they did win three awards – for Pop Group Vocal, Alternative Music Album and Shortform Video.

Other victories went to Marc Cohn (New Artist), Patti Labelle and Lisa Fischer (joint R&B Female), LL Cool J (Rap Soloist), Boyz II Men (R&B Vocal Group), Madonna (Long Form Video), Bryan Adams (Best Song From A Motion Picture), Bonnie Raitt (Rock Vocal Solo, Female Pop Vocal).

Easy listening triumph for Natalie

THE GRAPEVINE

- After 11 years as their lead vocalist Joey Belladonna has left Anthrax, who have recently signed a £10 million deal with Elektra.
- Johnny Rogan's biography of Morrissey 'Morrissey & Marr' has apparently made the star very angry.
- Producers Jam & Lewis will receive a record $3 million to produce Janet Jackson's first album for Virgin.

CHARTS

US45	To Be With You *Mr. Big*
USLP	Ropin' The Wind *Garth Brooks*
UK45	Stay *Shakespears Sister*
UKLP	Stars *Simply Red*
WEEK 2	
US45	To Be With You *Mr. Big*
USLP	Ropin' The Wind *Garth Brooks*
UK45	Stay *Shakespears Sister*
UKLP	Divine Madness *Madness*
WEEK 3	
US45	Save The Best For Last *Vanessa Williams*
USLP	Ropin' The Wind *Garth Brooks*
UK45	Stay *Shakespears Sister*
UKLP	Divine Madness *Madness*
WEEK 4	
US45	Save The Best For Last *Vanessa Williams*
USLP	Ropin' The Wind *Garth Brooks*
UK45	Stay *Shakespears Sister*
UKLP	Divine Madness *Madness*

CRUE MAN JUMPS SHIP

Motley Crue and vocalist Vince Neil have split, only six months into a $35 million deal with Elektra.

Elektra Records said, 'Motor racing has become a priority in Neil's life – his colleagues felt he didn't share their determination and passion for music. Neil was the only Crue member who didn't regularly participate in the songwriting process'.

Bassist Nikki Sixx said 'After 11 years together, we've parted ways. I hope it can be as friendly and peaceful as possible.'

However, Neil retorted 'I did not leave the band. I was fired. I wasn't fired for my interest in motor racing, I was fired because I didn't like the direction Nikki (Sixx) was taking on the new album.'

Neil plans to start work on a solo album for Elektra whilst the Crue are currently looking for a new vocalist.

Mutiny in the air as Neil abandons the rest of the Crue

FREDDIE'S FAREWELL

Metallica, seen here in an attractive dressing room pose, were among the host of acts paying a final homage to Queen superstar Freddie Mercury in the year's biggest Wembley bash so far.

Guns N' Roses, Extreme, Metallica, Seal, Spinal Tap, Annie Lennox, David Bowie, Elton John, George Michael, Paul Young, Robert Plant, Def Leppard and U2 (via satellite from California) are among the galaxy of stars set to appear with Queen's remaining members at a Freddie Mercury tribute show at London's Wembley Stadium.

The giant AIDS awareness benefit event will be broadcast to an estimated half-billion people in 70 countries.

The re-issue of Queen's 1975 classic, 'Bohemian Rhapsody', which recently returned to No. 1 in Britain, has given the group their first US Top 10 hit for twelve years thanks partly to its inclusion in the smash hit movie, 'Wayne's World'.

INDEX

PHOTOGRAPHIC ACKNOWLEDGEMENTS

The Publishers gracefully acknowledge the tremendous assistance of London Features International in providing the majority of photographs for this book:

London Features International; 9 TL&BR, 10 L&R, 11 B, 12 L,C&R, 13 T&BR, 14 B, 15 BL, 16 B, 17 CR&B, 18 T, 19 T&BL&BR, 20 BL, 21 L, 22 T&B, 23 T&C, 24 T, 25 TR, 26 T,C&B, 27 TL&B, 28 L&R, 32 T, 33 C, 36 L, 37 TR&BR, 42 B, 44 R, 46 B, 47 CL&B, 48 T&BL&BR, 49 T&C, 53 T, 54 T&B, 5G T, 57 T&BR, 58 CL, 62 T&BL, 63 T, 66 BR, 68T, 70 T, 71 C, 73 TR, 75 T, 77 TR&BL, 78 TR, 79 TL, TR&B, 80 BL&BR, 81 BL&BR, 83 L, 84 C, 85 T,C&B, 86 TL,TR, 87 L, 88 C, 89 L&TR, 90 T,C&B, 91 T,BC&BR, 92 R, 93 L,C&R. 94 TL,TR&BL, 95 T, 96 B, 102 B, 103 L, 105 TL,TR,C&B, 107 B, 108 T&C, 109 T, 111 BL&BR, 112 TL&B, 113 C, 114 TL,TR,BL&BR, 114-5 C, 115 TL,TR&BL, 116 T,C&B, 117 T&B, 118 TL, TR&BR, 119 TL,TR&B, 120 T&B, 121 TL&B, 122 C&R, 124 L&R, 125 R, 126 TR, 127 T, 128 ACL,BCR&BR, 130 T&B, I31 T&B, 132 T, 133 L, 134 T&BR, 136 B, 137 BL, 138 T, 139 B, 140 B, 142 T. 143 TL&BL, 144 BL&BR, 145 L,C&R, 146 T&B, 147 T&B, 148 T&B, 149 B, 150 T, 151 T,BL&BR, 152 T&B, 153 T,BC&B, 154 B, 155 T,C&B, 156 T&BL&BR, 157 T&B, 159 L&R, 160 T&BL&BR, 161 TR&B, 162 T&BL&BR, 163 T&B, 164 BL&BR, 165 L&R, 166, 167 TR&BR, 168 T&B, 169 T&B, 170 T&BL&BR, 171 B, 172 T&B, 173 R, 174 T&B, 175 TL,TR &B, 176 T&B, 177 T&B, 178 L&R, 179 B, 180 TL,TR,C&B, 181 T,BL.BC& BR, 182 T&BR, 183 TR&B, 184 T&BR, 185 T&BL&BR, 186 T,C&B, 187 T, C&B, 188 T,C&B, 189 TR&B, 190 B, 191 TR, 192 T&BL&BR, 193 L&R, 194 TL,R&BL, 195 TL,TR&B, 196 T&BL&BR, 197 TL,TR&B, 198 C, 199 T,BL&BR, 200 BC, 201 BL, 202 T.C,BL&BR, 203 T,C&B, 204 C, 205 T&B, 207 TL,TR&BR, 209 T, 210 BL, 211 T&BR, 212 T,C&B, 213 CL,CR&B, 214 T&B, 215 B, 216 T, 217 T,C&B, 218 T&B, 219 T, 220 L,TR&BR, 221 TL,TR&BL, 224 C, 225 TL&B, 226 T&BL&BR, 227 T&BL, 228 C&CR, 229 BL&BR, 230 T,BL&BR, 231 T&B, 232 T&BR, 233 B, 234 T, 235 T&B, 236 T&B, 237 T,BL&BR, 238 T&B, 239 T&C, 240 TL,TR&BL, 241 TL&B, 242 BL, 243 T,BL&BR, 244 T&BR, 245 B, 246 T, C&B, 247 BL&BR, 248 T, 249 BL, 250 T,C,BL&BR, 251 T, 252 TL&B, 253 T, 254 BL&BR, 255 T&B, 256 TL, 257 T&B, 258 B, 259 T, 260 T,C&B, 261 T&B, 262 L,R&C, 263 T,CR&B, 264, C&B, 265 T&BR,. 266 TL,TR&BR, 267 TC,TR&BR, 268 T&B, 269 BL, 270 T,C&B, 271 T&BL, 272 T, 273 B, 274 T&B, 277 T&B, 278 T&BL, 279 T&B, 280 T&B, 282 T&C,. 283 T,C&B, 284 T&C, 285 CL&CR, 286 T,BL&BR, 788 T&BL, 289 B. 292 T,C&B, 293 T&C, 294 T, 295 BL&BR, 296 T&C, 297 B, 298 L&R, 300 B, 301 T, 304 B, 305 T&B, 306 T&C, 307 T,C&B, 308 T,C&B, 309 BL, 312 C&B, 314 T&B, 315 BL&BR, 316T, 317 B, 318 T&LB, 319 R, 322 BR, 323 R, 324 T&B, 325 T, 326 B, 327 T, 328 T&R, 329 TR&B, 331 T&B, 333 C,335 L&TR, 337 BR, 338 BL, 339 B, 343 B, 344 T, 345 TR, 346 TR&B, 347 L, 348 B,. 349 T, 350 T, 351 T&BL, 352 TR&B, 356 TR&BR, 357 T,C&B, 358 BR, 359 T, 362 T&BL, 363 TR&B, 364 TL&TR, 365 T,C&B, 366 T,BL&BR, 370 T,C&BL, 372 C, 373 T, 374 TL,TC,TR,AC,ACR,BCL,BCR,BL,BC&BR, 376 T, 377 L, 378 TL&BL, 379 BR, 380 T&BR, 381 BR, 382 BL, 385 T,BL&BR, 386 T,CL,CR&B, 388 T, 389 T&BL, 390 B, 391 TR&BR, 397 T&C, 394 B, 395 TL,TR &B, 396 T, 397 T,BL&BR, 398 T&B, 399 T&C, 400 TL,TR&B, 402 T. 403 T&C, 404 T&B, 406 AC, 406-7, 407 L, 410 TR&BR, 411 B, 412 B, 413 B, 416 T, 418 TL, 419 TL, 420 T&B, 423 T, 424 T, 425 B, 426 T,C,BL&BR, 427 TR, 430 B, 432 BL, 433 BR, 436 TL, 439 B, 440 BL, 443 T, 449 BR, 45l T, 453 TR, 455 CL, 456 B, 457 B, 458 T, BL&BR, 459 BR, 462 TL&TR, 463 T&B, 483 BL,BR, 484 TL,TR,B, 485 T, 486 T,C&B, 487 L&R, 488 T, BL&BR, 489 BR, 490 T,C,BL&BR, 491 T&BL, 492 T, 493 T,BL&BR, 494 T,C&B, /Waring Abbott; 244 B, /Julian Barton; 466 B, /Peter Bosari; Il7 C, /Adrian Boot; 225 T, 251 C, 302 T&BR, 303 B, 318 TR, 321 C&B, 330 T, .335 C, 346 C, 349 B, 363 TC, 376 B, 382 BR, /Elaine Bryant; 182 BL, 223 B, 253 C,. 289 T, 290 BL, 299 T, 300 T, 301 C, 302 BL, 304 T, 332 B, 338 R, 342 T&C, 343 C, 382 B, /Kristine Callahan; 469 BL, /Paul Canry; 193 C, 221 BR, 228 T, 231 C, 232 BL, 247 T, 256 TR, 273 T, 276 BR, 278 BR, 281 B, 285 T, 287 T, 289 C, 290 T, 296 B, 299 B, 305 C, 306 B, 310 B, 311 T, 312 T, 315 T, 317 T, 321 R, 328 C, 350 BL, 353 T&BR, 356 L, 360 T&C, 361 R&B, 368T,/R T Capak; 412 C, 418 B, 421 B, 450 BR, 452 BC&BR, 456 C, /Andrew Catlin, 369 C, 423 BR, 424 BR, 441 T, 445 CL, 452 BL, 456 TR, 457 TL, /Angie Coqueran; 436 BL, /Paul Cox; 198 T, 229 TL, 275 B, 281 T&C, 290 BR, 291 B, 309 CL, 311 C, 313 B, 319 L, 322 T&BL, 325 C, 326 T, 333 T&B, 335 B, 339 T, 340 T, 34 3 T, 344 T, 346 TL, 351 BR, 354 BR, 367 T, 368 B, 371 TL, 374 ACL&BC, 387 B, 392 T, 414 T, 436 BR, Kevin Cummins; 479 C, /George de Sora; 470 B, 478 R, /George Dubose; 398 CR, /Scott Downie; 398 CL, 417 C, 422 T, 428 BR, 446 BR, 453 BR, 455 B, /Nick Elgar; 337 TL, 389 BR, 444 LC, 471 TR, 476 C, /David Fisher; 473 R, 481 T, /Simon Fowler; 219B, 264 T, 279 C, 287 B, 320 T, 325 B, 327 B, 329 C, 339 C, 340 B, 341 B, 344 B, 348 T, 359 B, 361 L, 362 BR, 372 B, 374 BR, 383 T&B, 384 T, 392 B, 401 TL, 408 T&B, 417 T&B, 450 BL, 479 B, /Jill Furmanowsky; 294 B, 295 T, 311 B, 334 B, 341 T, 342 B, /Steve Granitz; 392 B, 401 TR, 403 B, 418 TR, 429 L, 450 T, /Frank Griffin; 345 B, 364 B, 375, 394 C, 405 B, 406 BC, 407 R&C, 409 BL, 442 C, 443 C, 463 C, /Goedfroit; 448 BR, /Janet Gough; 396 BR, 409 T, 434 T, 442 BR, 454 T, /Greg de Guire; 370 BR, 419 TR, 451 B, 459 T, 460 CB, /Curt Gunther; 115 BR, 137 T, 223, /Darlene Hammond; 316 B, /Harry Hammond; 15 BR, 21 R, 30 BR. 44 L, 52 BR, 55 T, /David Hill; 222 T, 229 TR, 261 C, 267 TL. 297 T, 323 L, 329 TL, 352 TL, /NeilJones; 249 T, 252 TR, 253 BL, 256 B, 265 BL, 268 C, 269 BR, /Robin Kaplan; 378 TR&BR, 461 L, /Gie Knaeps; 476 T. /David Koppel; 353 BL, 396 BL, 437 T, 453 TL, 468 TL, /Laura Levine; 427 B, /Phil Loftus; 198 B, 377 R, 387 T, 406 B, 414 T, 415 T, 419 B, 427 TL, 440 BR, 448 BL, 454 BL, 462 B, 466 C, 469 BR, /Victor Malafronte; 442 TR, /Ross Marino; 413 T, 416 B, 422 B, 435 T, 436 TR, 447 T, /Peter Mazel; 314 T, /Kevin Mazur; 337 TR&BL, 432 T, 434 BL, 437 B, 442 L, 446 T, 459 C, 465 BL, 470 T&C, 481 CL, 482 T, 483 T, 489 T, /Allen Olivio; 471 B, /Philip Ollerenshaw; 472 L, /Anastasias Pantsios; 224 B, 271 BR, 301 B, 310 C, 354 BL, 379 BL, 422 CR, 433 BL, /John Paschal; 158 T, 429 T, 441 B, 419 BL, 457 C, 460 B, 461 C, 465 BR, /Neal Preston; 233 TL, 248 B, 263 C, 275 T, 276 TL&BL, 284 B, 291 T, 320 C, 321 L, 345 TL, 350 BR, 372 T, 381 T, 391 TL, 425 T, 434 BL, 443 B, 4 4 L&R, 444-445, 445 L,RC&R, 451 C, 453 BL, 471 TL, /Mike Prior; 468 B, /Ronnie Randall; 463 R, 461 R, 478 TL, /Steve Rapport; 358 T, 373 C, 384 BL&BR, 399 B. 411 C, 425 C, 428 BL, 438 T, 476 B, /David Redfern; 179 T, /Ken Regan; Title page, 58 T, 80 T, 161 TL, 200 BR, 200-201, 201 BC, 394 T, 448 T. 450 BC, 466 T, /Derek Ridgers; 401 B, 440 T, 481 CR, /Ebet Roberts; 259 B, 288 BR, 301 T, 354 T, 355 T, 367 B, 369 T, 379 T, 382 T, 406 C, 410 TL&BL, 414 B, 424 BL, 428 T, 431 T&B, 432 B&R, 433 T, 435 B, 438 B, 439 T, 446 BL, 459 BL, 467 BL, 485 B, 491 BR, 492 B, /Werner Roelen; 367 C, 480 B, /Tom Sheehan; 465 TL&TR, 477 L. /Ann Summa; 347 R, 355 B, 369 B, 408 C, 409 BR, 421 C, /Geoff Swaine; 376 C, 381 BL, 415 B, 421 T, 444 RC, 449 T, 455 CR, 456 TL, 489 BL, /Michael Uhll; 412 T, 417 B, /A Vereecke; 402 B, /Kristiin Vraa; 390 C, 476T, /Arnold Williams; 233 TL, 330 B, 363 TL, 371 BL&R, 373 B, /Ron Wolfson; 332 T, 380 BL. 391 BL, 430 T, 441 C, 457 TR, 477 R, 481 B, /Charlyn Zlontnik; 358 TL, 388 B,

Michael Ochs Archive/LFI; Half-title, 9 TR&BL, 11 T, 13 BL&BR, 14 T, 16 T, 17 T&CL, 19 T, 70 BR, 23 B, 24 CL&CR, 25 TL,BL&BR, 27 TR, 29 BL, 30 T&C, 31 B, 33 TL,TR&B, 37 BL, 38 L, 40 TL,TR&B, 41 TL,TC,TR&B, 42 T, 43 T&B, 45 T,C&B, 47 T&CR, 49 B, 52 T,BL&BC, 53 C&B, 55 BL&BR, 56 C&B, 57 BL, 58 CR&B, 59 T&C, 60 T&B, 61 T&B, 62 BR, 63 B, 64 T, 64-5 T, 65 T, 66 T&B, 67 T,BL&BR, 68 BL&BR, 69 TL,TR&B, 70 C,BL&BR, 71 T&BL, 72 T,C&B, 73 TL,BL&BR, 74 T,C,BL&BR, 75 BL&BR, 77 TL, 78 TL,BL&BR, 82 L&R, 83 R,.84 T&B,.86 B,.87 T, 88 T&B, 89 BR, 91 BL, 92 L, 94 BR, 95 B, 96 T, 97 T,C,BL&BR, 98 T.L&BR, 99 T, 100 TL,TR,C&B, 101 T&B, 102 T, 103 R, 104 T&C, 106 TL.TR&B, 107 T&C, 108 BL&BR, 110 T&B, 111 T, 112 TR, 113 T&B, 118 BL, 121 TR, 122 L, 123 T&B, 125 TL&BL, 126 TL&B, 127 C, 128 TL,BC,TR&TCR, 129, 130 C, 132 C, 133 R, 134 BL, 135 T,BL&BR, 136 T, 137 BR, 138 B, 139 T&C, I41 T&BR, 142 B, 143 R, 144 T, 149 T, 150 B, 153 AC, 158 B, 164 T, 171 T, 184 BL, 190 T, 191 C&B, 208 T, 210 T, 222 B, 225 TR, 227 BR, 228 B, 234 B, 235 C, 237 BR, 238 C, 239 BL&BR, 240 BR, 241 TR, 242 T&BR, 249 C&BR, 253 B, 254 TL&TR, 255 C, 257 C, 258 T, 266 BL, 269 T, 271 C, 282 B, 313 T, 338 TL, 422 CL.

The Publishers would like to thank the following organisations for their kind permission to reproduce additional photographs in this book;

Barratt's; 216 B,

Camera Press; 423 BL, 452 T, 454 BR, 455 T, 462 T, /Mark Anderson; 462 CT, /PR Francis; 215 T, /Terry O'Neill; 210 BR,

Central Television Plc; 405 T,

Chrysalis Records Plc; 209 B,

Deram Records (The Decca Record Co. Ltd); 169 C,

Ronald Grant Archive; 31 T, 34 TL&BR, 35 BR, 140 T, 201 BR, 204 B,

The Hulton Picture Company; 30 BR, 32 BL, 37 TL, 39 TR, 59 B,71 BR, 81 T, 99 B, 109 B, 167 TL, 173 L, 335 TC&AC,

Jimi Hendrix Information Management Institute/Allan Kosss; 200 BL,

The Kobal Collection; 15 T, 22 C, 34 TR&BL, 35 TL, TR&BL, 38 R, 77 BR, 104 B, 127 B, 132 B, 183 TL, 189 TL, 204 T, 207 BL, 208 B, 221 CR, 245 T, 274 C, 309 TL&R,

Popperfoto; 50 T&B, 51 T&B, 64-5 B, 141 BL, 167 BL&BC,

Rex Features; 6-7, 20 T, 29 T, 32 BR, 36 R, 39 L, 65 C&B, 128 BL, 154 T, 173 C, 406 T, /Philippe Hamon; 64 B, /Dezo Hoffman; 29 BR, 46 T&C, 99 C, /George Konig; 30 BL, /Sipa; 39 BR,

Eathan A Russell; 191 TL.